AA TOURING GUIDE TO ENGLAND

And green lane traverse heedless where it goes
Naught guessing till some sudden turn espies
Rude battered finger post that stooping shows
Where the snug mystery lies
And then a mossy spire with ivy crown
Clears up the short supprise
And shows the peeping town

from Summer Images by John Clare 1793–1864

Summer Is A-cumin In!
Customs and traditions, bright reflections from a distant and unsophisticated past

It is reassuring to know that even now, in an age dominated by machinery and a preoccupation with day-to-day existence, some aspects of English traditionalism are still maintained. Towns and villages throughout the country consider the perpetuation of ancient ceremonies a matter of local pride, and will staunchly defend their right to flaunt tradition in the face of progress. Features of the English way of life common in medieval and even earlier times are thus preserved by a country-wide scattering of communities who faithfully act out the superstitions and beliefs of their long-dead predecessors. Cynics claim that the Good Old Days were really nothing of the sort. This is an assumption which cannot be proved one way or another, but the romantic in every modern man will stir to echoes of a simpler, less complicated way of life. These echoes are caught and amplified by the enacting of ancient and often blatantly pagan ceremonies – bright splashes of raw colour to relieve the potential drabness of modern living.

The present century's mania for categorization groups these often unique occasions under three main titles – Customs, Festivals and Traditions. There is little point in such terms as they mean much the same thing; by definition many customs are traditionally based and are often revived to form integral parts of festivals. Their number is legion and their variety borders on the infinite. It is probably accurate to say that every English county preserves at least one survival from a past culture, a survival which may have been changed and formalized but which still reflects the age in which it is rooted. The better-known are usually on an ambitious, even extravagant scale, with lots of colour and noise; smaller affairs retain the quiet atmosphere of intimate village life. No matter how these traditions are maintained, they all provide a valuable insight into the past – a welcome break in an era where more faith is placed in the functioning of a motor car than the annual fertility cycle of the revolving seasons.

Each of the occasions described here can be matched by numerous examples of equal interest. The subject is vast and cannot be thoroughly covered in this limited space, but the examples have been chosen to provide an appreciation of customs and traditions which survive in very different parts of the country. The selected areas lie along a zig-zag course which starts in the remotest and most foreign of the English counties, Cornwall, then runs east into Kent and tacks west and east up into the northern counties. Many of the traditions are rooted in the Christian and pagan religions. Some bear the marks of sacrificial and fertility rites and others are ceremonies of thanksgiving. Almost all include exercising charity towards poorer members of the community. This charity is usually symbolic, a reminder of some past good deed, but collecting boxes for contemporary causes are nearly always circulated among spectators. Far from being mere picturesque survivals from the past, these performances continue to fulfil a vital service to society – the collection of alms and maintenance of the under privileged.

A Welcome for Summer

Cornwall is rich in early tradition and folk lore, and the inhabitants of Padstow still celebrate summer's annual victory over winter. Midnight of April 30 is the time that the town's merry-makers have been waiting for, when from the first moment of May morning they break into song and chant
Unite and unite,
Let us unite,
For Summer is a-cumin in!
Excitement grows with the waning of the night and continues to swell throughout the morning, increasing as the celebrations approach their focal point. This is the Hobby Horse, a wildly gyrating figure with a head-dress similar to an aborigine's painted mask, and the centre of the tornado that grips Padstow every May Day. When he and his retinue of equally strange followers are led through the narrow packed streets by the Teaser all inhibitions are forgotten – as many a startled visitor has discovered. Any personable woman may suddenly find herself whipped beneath the great hooped skirt of the Hobby Horse, to re-emerge with her face blackened with soot – a reminder that these celebrations derive from an ancient pagan fertility cult.
The Hobby Horse continues through the town and the local band plays with frenzied enthusiasm; the citizens dance with increasing abandon; collecting boxes circulate. Then, at high noon when music and motion alike have quickened to a crescendo of activity, a thousand throats roar out the triumphant news that *Summer is a-cum today*. This living tradition exists in perfect surroundings; Padstow is one of the most picturesque Cornish ports and the boats are charmingly decorated for the occasion.

Hobby Horse, Padstow

SUMMER IS A-CUMIN IN!

Sacrifice at Kingsteignton

Devon also has its fair share of tradition, including Honiton's Lammas Fair, Bideford's beating-the-Clock Race, Barnstaple's St Giles' Fair, and Shebbear's strange Turning of the Devil's Boulder. Kingsteignton has a Whit Monday Ram Fair, an interesting tradition which derives from the ancient custom of sacrifice. On the appropriate day the beribboned and flower-adorned carcass of a young ram is ceremonially conveyed through the streets – veritably a ram to the sacrifice – and then carried off to a barbecue and cooked to a turn. When ready the meat is carved by an expert to produce a succulent slice for every spectator. The traditional cost per slice was one penny and the proceeds were given to a deserving charity, as they still are today. The origin of this public ram-roasting is rather obscure. All stories agree that it is a thank-offering for water that suddenly flowed during an exceptional local drought, although the cause of the flow is a subject for dispute. Churchmen claim that all other wells and springs in the area ran dry, but this one remained full as a direct result of God's beneficence to those who worshipped Him. Other sources place the origin of the ceremony far back in pagan times and say that a single, miraculous flow of water resulted directly from live sacrifice. Whatever the story it appears that the miracle did occur and was the salvation of this Teign-bank community. The spring is clearly marked on the OS one-inch map as Well Head and has never been known to fail.

Ram Fair, Kingsteington

Flowers for the Boats

Some traditions are not as localized as the previous examples and enjoy a nation-wide following. Maypole dancing is one of these, but equally popular is the making and carrying of wreaths and garlands. This distribution is conducted in many different ways; cattle may be festooned with them and led through villages, they may be worn in various forms by mock kings and queens, or they may be thrown into the sea. Garland Day in Castleton (Derbyshire) is a remarkable example and dates back at least 300 years. It may, in a more emphatic guise, have existed in pagan times. Many fishing communities still favour the idea that garlands thrown onto open water will be a guarantee of good catches to come, and have preserved this tradition as persistently as any. Garland Day at Abbotsbury in Dorset originated from this need to ensure a livelihood but has latterly been changed to perform a less pagan function. It is a charming custom in which garlands and wreaths are made by the village children and carried through a narrow street between picturesque thatched cottages. When fishing was a full-time local occupation garlands or wreaths were made – one for every boat – placed on board and taken to open water to be cast into the sea to float until they disintegrated. Nowadays they are laid at the foot of the war memorial and blessed. Few who witness this simple ceremony realize that it is again another survival of the ancient sacrificial tradition.

Garland Day, Abbotsbury

SUMMER IS A-CUMIN IN!

A Lady Who Died For Her Poor

Distribution of wealth in the form of doles is also very common. The tradition is widespread through Lincolnshire, Hertfordshire, Kent, London and even further afield, but the oldest is probably the one held in Tichborne in Hampshire. This is said to date back some 800 years and takes place annually on March 25. It originally comprised 1,400 26oz loaves plus two pence; its modern equivalent is 30cwt flour which is blessed by a priest and distributed to about 200 villagers. This is no pagan rite, but a picturesque form of thanksgiving to the saintly Lady Marbella who died for the village poor. The story is that Lady Marbella was deeply concerned by the poverty she saw all about her and begged her callous husband to do something about it. Mockingly he agreed to set aside a portion of his estate to provide corn for the poor 'in perpetuity', but that it would be only as much land as she could crawl round while one torch burned. She was a sick woman but managed to encompass 23 acres on her knees before the flame – and her life – expired. This piece of land is still known as The Crawls, and her supreme self-sacrifice is remembered with every annual distribution of the hard-won dole.

The Dole, Tichborne

Marbles for a Wife

Many traditions involve sport which is of a strenuous and often violent nature. An example of this is the Shrovetide football which is played at Ashbourne in Derbyshire, Alnwick in Northumberland, and both St Ives and St Columb Major in Cornwall. A more peaceable contest, calling for delicacy of touch rather than sheer brawn, is the Tinsley Green Marbles Championship. This is held in front of the Greyhound public house and according to legend originated from the rivalry between two Sussex men who wanted to marry the same girl. The two suitors challenged each other to running, jumping, wrestling, single-stick, and other vigorous activities but were judged of equal merit. They eventually resorted to playing marbles, a schoolchildrens' game dating from Roman times. The game lasted for a day and a night, and the victor won the girl. Today the game is played by teams of six, some of whom come from overseas. Each competitor is armed with a three-quarter inch glass marble known as a tolley and is restricted by rules governing a variety of moves which include shooting, flicking, and above all fudging. The highest scorer from each team challenges the others in a form of knock-out competition. Although played in complete silence, this evokes a passionate response from both players and audience.

Marbles Championship, Tinsley Green

SUMMER IS A-CUMIN IN!

Bread and Cheese Land

Kent is a county which has Tilting the Quintain at Offham; Blessing the Cherry Orchards at Newington; the Guy Fawkes Celebrations of Edenbridge; Blessing the sea at Whitstable, Margate and Folkestone; the Biddenden Dole. The latter is a counterpart of the Tichborne Dole in Hampshire, but without the same tragic associations. The Biddenden Maids, Mary and Eliza Chulkhurst, were allegedly the first Siamese twins born in this country. Their brief life was devoted to good works among the neighbouring poor, and they died within six hours of each other at the age of thirty-four. Their will provided a 20 acre field – almost the same area as the land won by Lady Marbella Tichborne – the rent from which was to provide an annual dole of bread and cheese. This used to comprise two 4lb loaves, 1lb of cheese and a small purse of money. The modern ceremony has been formalized. Loaves and cheese are still blessed and given away on Easter Monday, but quantities of small hard biscuits decorated with an effigy of the Maids are also distributed to all and sundry from the window of one of the former 'Work House' cottages. These biscuits are known as Biddenden Cakes, and the cottages stand on the edge of an area locally referred to as Bread and Cheese Land – bequeathed by the twins some 600 years ago.

Biddenden Maid's Dole, Biddenden

The Royal Dole

London itself is the seat of so many ceremonies that it is difficult to know which to select. Particularly famous examples include the Lord Mayor's Show, Westminster School's Pancake Greaze, The Easter Parade, Blessing the Throats, Trooping the Colour, Beating the Bounds, the Changing of the Guard, and many more. The most famous of all the many dole ceremonies is the London-based Royal Maundy, a distribution attended by the reigning monarch. The term Maundy derives from the Latin *mandatum,* meaning an edict. It refers to Christ's instruction to His disciples to care for those in need, delivered while He washed their feet. For several centuries the monarch actually did wash the feet of a few chosen poor before distributing food and garments, but this ceased and the gifts in kind were replaced by money. The dole is offered from one of London's churches on Maundy Thursday and comprises small silver coins known as Maundy Money. The number of recipients tallies with the monarch's age. Yeomen of the Guard are in attendance, one of whom carries a gold dish bearing red and white drawstring purses. A purse of each colour is given to the recipients in turn in the presence of the monarch, and the members of the procession carry posies of flowers – a reminder of the time when it was thought that such precautions were necessary to avoid the risk of infection. The money is legal tender but it is rare for a recipient to dispose of the dole, even for the high prices offered by collectors.

Royal Maundy Dole, London

SUMMER IS A-CUMIN IN!

Locking the Tower

The Ceremony of the Keys is enacted at the Tower of London and is possibly the most ancient military ceremony still existing anywhere in the world. It is very short, taking only a matter of minutes, and has been conducted in the same way for at least 700 years. Its solemnity, sense of sheer antiquity, and military precision more than make up for its brevity. At seven minutes to ten every night the Escort of the Keys arrives at each of the four named towers, presents arms and is challenged as to his identity by the command *Halt! who comes there?* The Chief Warder receives the reply *Queen Elizabeth's Keys*, and calls out *Pass, Queen Elizabeth's Keys. All's Well.* The Escort intones *Amen* and on the first stroke of ten o'clock the Tower Bugler sounds the last post; the Chief Warder then conveys the keys to the Tower's Resident Governor in the Queen's House.

Ceremony of the Keys, London

A Game of Swans Apiece

The Thames is London's river, and for centuries the swan has been regarded as a royal bird. Elizabeth I permitted two exceptions and ruled that the Vintners' and Dyers' Guilds might also regard themselves as the owners of a game of 'swans apiece'. This is the origin of Swan Upping, a ceremony that takes place on the Thames between Henley and London Bridge during the latter half of July. The object is to find all the young birds born in the last year and mark them in such a way that the respective owners can immediately be identified. The number of birds varies from year to year so the length of the ceremony is rarely the same, but the components of this tradition remain unchanged. A small fleet of gaily painted skiffs, the first two flying the personal standards of the reigning monarch and the others representing the Guilds, carry the monarch's Swan Keeper or Master and are propelled by soberly attired oarsmen. The Swan Keeper himself is resplendent in scarlet livery and wears a peaked cap bearing a single feather. Every cygnet has to be traced and numbered; those assigned to the Guilds are distinctively marked by having their beaks nicked on one side or the other; the royal birds remain unmarked

Swan-Upping, London

SUMMER IS A-CUMIN IN!

Kisses and Coins

Hock-tide is the second Tuesday after Easter and is linked with St Michaelmas Day as one of the year's chief rent-collecting days. Hungerford in Berkshire makes an occasion out of this and sends out the Hock-tide or Tutti-men as rent or tithe collectors. The day starts with a blast on the Town Crier's 17th-c horn, a replica of one believed to have been presented by John of Gaunt, and the election of the Officers-for-the-Year at the Court Leet follows. Among these are the two newly appointed Tutti-men, each of whom is ceremonially attired in morning coat and top hat and bears a staff of office comprising a beribboned rod topped by a bouquet and an orange. These two then start their rounds of the town, demanding a coin from every male and a kiss from every female. Accompanying them is the Scrambler or Orange-Man, who presents an orange to every woman who has been kissed – often as the result of 'forcible entry' by ladder through an upper window. Festivities continue with Shoeing the Colt (pretending to shoe the heel of a visitor taken at random), and the distribution of more oranges. Small coins are scattered among the children and a holiday atmosphere persists throughout the day.

Hock-Tide Tutti-Men, Hungerford

Midsummer Druids

One of the most ancient and spectacular settings for the enacting of tradition is the prehistoric circle of Stonehenge, where bronze-age peoples conducted mysterious ceremonies some 4,000 years ago. The English Druids of today still come here to celebrate traditional Druid Rites which culminate when the midsummer sun rises above the Hele Stone, beyond the mis-named Altar Stone. Each participant is dressed in a hooded white robe, and the assembly carries banners bearing mystic symbols as it moves in procession beneath the massive lintels that unite the great megaliths. This picture of unfathomable antiquity haunts the memories of the thousands who assemble here every midsummer evening to await the coming of dawn. Hymns are sung, strange incantations chanted, and magical sprigs of holly and mistletoe carried. In the few short hours between midnight and sunrise the present becomes inextricably linked with pagan sun-worship.

Druid Ceremonies, Stonehenge

A Punky and a Song

Another ancient ceremony connected with the sun is Somerset's Punky Night. Enacted every Hallowe'en – the start of the old New Year and the beginning of true winter according to the Celtic calendar – this tradition is aimed at encouraging the near-dead sun to revive and fulfil its promise of new life. Bonfires, vigorous dancing and chanting, and the making and carrying of Punkies are all essential parts of the ceremony. Punkies are lanterns made from hollowed-out mangold-wurzels. The children of Hinton St George carry these lanterns from door to door, singing their simple songs and knocking in the hope of a coin or at least a new candle. People taking part in such traditional rites probably know little or nothing of the custom's origins, but it is sufficient that they maintain them. The same custom can be found in northern counties under names such as Nut-Crack Night, Dookie-Apple Night, or Apple-and-Candle Night; the ceremonies are similar and may all have resulted from once-widespread pagan festivals. During the medieval period the Church attempted to give the singing a recognisably Christian character by referring to it as 'souling' – singing for the souls of villagers who had died in the preceding year.

Hallowe'en Punky Night, Hinton St George

Hymns and Puppy-Dog Pie

Gloucestershire offers a wide variety of customs and traditions, including the Cranham Feast, the Marshfield Boxing Day Mummers, Bristol's St Anne's Well Pilgrimage, and Chipping Camden's Scuttlebrook Wake. These are all picturesque or impressive in their own ways, but none is more memorable than the Painswick Clipping Ceremony. This takes place among the hundred magnificent yew trees that grow in the churchyard of St Mary's, some more than 200 years old, but the word 'clipping' has nothing to do with the trees. It is a very old term which describes an act of piety which annually takes place here and in other churchyards in Derbyshire, Sussex, Yorkshire and elsewhere. The origin of the ceremony is almost certainly pre-Christian. In medieval times it was characterized by rowdy behaviour and the shouting of the odd slogan *'High Gates'*, the meaning of which has never been satisfactorily explained. Revellers would shout and bawl this slogan while rampaging around and devouring anything they could lay their hands on. Nowadays the ceremony is quieter. A procession of children and adults, decked and garlanded with flowers, halts at the church and sings the traditional clipping song. The vicar delivers his clipping sermon from the steps outside the tower and the day is then declared free. Housewives bake the traditional cake, topped with almond paste and containing a china dog. This is known as Puppy-Dog Pie and is a domestic survival of what was once an act of sacrifice intended to placate an unpredictable god.

Clipping, Painswick

SUMMER IS A-CUMIN IN!

Singing for the Sun

Among the many traditions preserved in Oxfordshire are Bampton's famous Whit Monday Morris Dancing and Oxford's May Morning Service. The latter is held at the top of the beautiful Magdalen College tower, overlooking a bridge spanning the River Cherwell. This tower is one of the glories of the university city and dates back to the year 1501; it is possible that the singing of hymns by the college choristers dates back to an original service held to celebrate the completion of this masterpiece. Although the service is essentially Christian in character, with surpliced choristers singing the *Té Deum Patrem Collimus* as composed by a Fellow of Magdalen some 300 years ago, the fact that it is held at the top of a tower hints at even earlier beginnings. The tower summit is closer to the sun than ground level, and the service starts at sunrise – very similar to Christianized forms of sun worship to be found all over the world.

Morris Dancing

Mayoral Weigh-In

High Wycombe in Buckinghamshire is a smallish town which is well-known for its traditional 'state occasions'. These include the mid-May Mayoral Weigh-In which started in 1893 with the weighing of a mayor who topped 19 stone. The purpose of the ceremony is to ascertain whether the mayor has gained or lost weight during his period of office. If he is heavier than when he started then it is assumed that he cannot have fulfilled his duties properly; if he has lost weight then it has been in the service of his people. No matter what the result, the facts have to be made public. The ceremony is elaborate and begins with a Beadle ringing his handbell and shouting the old cry *Oyez* to command attention. An Inspector of Weights and Measures officiates, and the old-style weighing machine consists of an ornate tripod from which a large pan is suspended beneath a figured dial set out in stones and pounds. The mayoral mace and other official insignia are borne by the various functionaries in attendance. There are no prizes, but there is a penalty. If the outgoing mayor is found to have gained in weight, then the loud cry *and Some More* echoes out over the town. For a sensitive individual this can be humiliating, but it is an accepted occupational hazard.

Mayoral Weigh-In, High Wycombe

SUMMER IS A-CUMIN IN!

Maypoles and Moggies

Some people consider Bedfordshire a rather colourless county, but its traditions certainly have all the warmth that exists in other parts of England. These include the Crowning of the May Queen at Elstow, Orange Rolling on the high Dunstable Downs, and the faithful maintenance of the Maypole tradition. Maypole dancing can be found in counties from Yorkshire and Westmorland in the north, down through the Midland towns of Warwickshire and Gloucestershire, and as far south as Devon. Some villages mainain a permanent maypole, but the decoration and dancing only takes place in the month from which the name is derived. A superb example of the custom can be seen at Ickwell Green, about three miles from Biggleswade. The 70ft, spirally-painted pole stands on the village green like a monumental copy of a barber's trade sign. At the appropriate time it is bedecked with a score or so of coloured streamers, the ends of which are held by children selected to perform the traditional circuit of complicated steps and twistings required to weave the maypole pattern. An additional attraction is the inclusion of medieval Moggies, two weirdly garbed figures with blackened faces. They each wield besom brooms to persuade onlookers to empty their pockets into collecting boxes while the dancing is under way. Another famous feature is the crowning of Ickwell's May Queen.

Maypole Dancing, Ickwell Green

Bottle Kicking at Hallaton

Leicestershire boasts a much more strenuous and certainly less picturesque tradition in Hallaton's Easter-Monday Bottle-Kicking. This ranks with the free-for-alls that constitute the Shrovetide football matches in other counties, and is a contest between the male populations of Hallaton and nearby Melbourne. The two communities are separated by a stream and two miles of countryside, and the object is to manhandle a small cask across the water and into the opponents' territory to score a goal. Rugby football is tame in comparison! There are no rules, and every time a goal is scored the cask is broached and its contents swigged before the battle recommences with a new 'bottle'. A halt is called at the end of several hours and the final score is tallied beside the cross on the village green. A much bigger cask is then broached for the satisfaction of a great many well-earned thirsts.

Bottle Kicking, Hallaton

SUMMER IS A-CUMIN IN!

Boggins-v-the Hood Throwers

Throwing the Hood, Haxey

The Midlands seem to specialize in these strenuous customs, and the Hallaton tradition has a parallel in Haxey's Hood Throwing. This is played out near the village on Plough Monday (January 6) and eventually involves every able-bodied man in the village. It also entails rough and-tumbles and large quantities of ale, but has a little more ceremony attached to it than bottle kicking. The increased sense of occasion is imparted by the King Boggin, his eleven Boggin attendants, and the black-faced Fool. This strangely garbed crew assemble to hear the traditional recounting of Lady de Mowbray's legend – a woman who lived some 700 years ago – then at the cry *Hoose agin Hoose; Toone agin Toone* a number of heavy rolls or hoods of leather are thrown into the crowd of onlookers. From here on it is every man's objective to carry a roll to one or other of the village inns. If he is intercepted by a Boggin the roll is pronounced dead. The Sway follows in due course, and as most of the male population and a number of pubs are involved this unassuming term soon takes on an appropriate significance. Finally, when the last of the leather hoods has been triumphantly placed in the desired goal, strong ale flows freely and the rest of the day is taken up with unrestrained merry-making. Each hood remains in its goal until the next Plough Monday comes round.

Floral Thank-offerings

Well Dressing

Several Midlands customs are performed in a much quieter manner and with a far greater degree of delicacy. Among these is the fairly widespread ceremony of Blessing the Wells, or Well-Dressing as it is more generally known. This is an annual occasion which takes place in a number of Derbyshire villages, notably Tideswell, Youlgreave, Barlow, Wirksworth, and Tissington. It is a charming and well-ordered ceremony which probably dates from medieval times when the terrible Black Death was the scourge of the country. An alternative though less well-established theory is that Derbyshire springs continued to produce water while the rest of England was gripped by the great drought of 1615. No matter what the origin it is certain that it is an act of thanksgiving. Well-springs are elaborately dressed with flowers, petals, moss, feathers, berries and other small natural objects set in clay-filled frames, usually arranged to depict biblical scenes. The custom is enacted on Ascension day and the villagers progress to each well in turn. After the last well has been blessed by a priest the devout and deeply-pious ceremony finishes with a church service. Although mains water has probably been piped to the villages concerned, the descendants of those who were miraculously saved from either the Black Death or thirst still offer these tokens of worship and thanksgiving to the deity who cared for them.

The Twenty-Mile Dance

Horn Dancing, Morris Dancing, and Sword Dancing are widespread traditions that can be found in a number of different counties. A few of the more notable examples of these customs can be seen in Yorkshire's North Skelton and Grenoside, Oxfordshire's Bampton, Berkshire's Abingdon, and Essex's Thaxted. One of the most spectacular of such occasions is the Horn Dancing held at Abbots Bromley in Staffordshire during the early part of September. As usual the participants are men, but these particular dancers need to possess an unusual amount of stamina as each carries a set of reindeer antlers with a span of several feet and weighing over 25lbs. At 8.30 in the morning they collect these relics from the church, where they are stored during the year, then carry them in a dance through the parish which can last for anything up to twelve hours and cover some 20 miles. They are accompanied by such traditional characters as Robin Hood, Maid Marian, the Accordionist, and the Hobby-Horse Man. The entire assembly is curiously dressed, with a predominant hunting motif which is a reminder that the area was once medieval deer-hunting territory. The tradition is thus portrayed as well as maintained, and the participants unwittingly re-enact the pre-Christian rite of ensuring prosperity by active, aggressive movement representing the pursuit of prey.

Horn Dancing, Abbot's Bromley

Pageantry at Knutsford

London is not the only place to witness a Lord Mayor's Show. A miniature version takes place in the little Cheshire township of Knutsford where it is known as the Royal May Day Festival. The Royal prefix is a reminder that it was once patronized by the Prince of Wales, later to become King Edward VII. The occasion takes place on the Saturday nearest May Day and starts with the formation of a procession outside the town hall. This is led by the Town Crier and the Marshall and comprises troupes of Royal Jesters, country dancers, prize bands, legendary characters including Robin Hood and his Merry Men, and the newly elected May Queen riding in a state coach specially loaned by the Lord Mayor of Liverpool. Another interesting feature is the inclusion of characters from Mrs Gaskell's book *Cranford*. The title of the book was the authoress's pseudonym for Knutsford. The May Queen must be a native of the town and no more than fourteen years old, and her entourage is also made up of local children. The cortège includes ladies riding in Broughams and landaus, escorted by Beefeaters and Guardsmen. The entire assembly progresses to an open area on the outskirts of town, where obeisance is made to the May Queen before the commencement of other activities. Although an occasion in miniature, this Knutsford tradition encompasses a wealth of imagination and pageantry.

Royal May Day Festival, Knutsford

SUMMER IS A-CUMIN IN!

Resurrection of Spring

Pace Egg Rolling, Preston

Easter, the New Year, May Day, and Midsummer Eve are the times when traditional festivals and elaborate customs are most widely practised. Easter, with its fundamental associations with the resurrection of life, is particularly popular and includes Pace Egg Rolling among its numerous activities. Pace does not refer to speed, but is a corruption of the term *Paschal* – more popularly known as the Passover. One of the best examples of this ceremony can be seen at Avenham Park, Preston. Hardboiled eggs are brightly painted, then rolled down turfed slopes by hotly competitive children. The origin of this custom is said to be Christian and symbolic of the stone rolling away from the tomb mouth – the first move in the resurrection story. An alternative story is that the egg, itself symbolic of rebirth, may symbolize the passing of winter into spring, the prospect of the first green shoots of crops which will sustain the life of a community. Thus pace egg rolling is yet another custom which could have been born of pagan or Christian beginnings, or a mixture of both.

The Evening Horn Blower

Yorkshire and Westmorland are rich in traditions and offer such examples as Midgley's Pace-egging and Mummers, West Witton's Burning of the Bartle, Barwick-in-Elmet's Maypole Dancing, and Pickering's Waits-on-the-Moors. Less spectacular but interesting because it is a ceremony that occurs each day is the Ripon Horn Blower or Wakeman. This character, wearing his traditional livery of three-quarter-length buttoned tunic, white gloves, and tricorne, has been a familiar figure in the town every day for the last 500 years. It is thought that he may have originated during the reign of King Alfred, although it cannot be proved that the custom has been enacted every day since then. At nine o'clock every evening the Wakeman treads a measured step around the market square, pausing at each corner to sound a blast on the great semicircular, silver-mounted buffalo horn which he carries slung across his chest. The final blast is sounded outside the town hall, in front of the city's motto *Except Ye Lord Keep Ye Cittie Ye Wakeman Waketh In Vain*.
The nightly enactment of this custom is a survival from medieval times, when the civic authorities appointed a watch party to patrol the street on the look-out for fire among the timber and thatch dwellings. The watch also served as a warning to felons bent on crime during the hours of darkness.

Wakeman, Ripon

Rushes for the Church Floor

Rush Bearing ceremonies have a distinctive charm and still exist in many parts of the country. Bristol's example is notable in that the ceremony is attended by the Lord Mayor and city dignitaries Westmorland's ceremonies are less spectacular but in many ways are memorable, and can be enjoyed at places including Musgrave, Warcop, Grasmere, and particularly Ambleside. The latter's custom is enacted at the end of July, on the traditional feast of St Anne. Rushes were used to cover the cold stone floors of medieval buildings; those gathered for domestic use were collected without any fuss, but the delivery of the church rushes was and is accompanied by great ceremony. Traditionally they were borne by white-garbed maidens and presented to the priest for inspection before being laid inside the building. Although this type of flooring is no longer used, the tradition is faithfully maintained. Instead of being brought in bundles, the rushes are fixed in wooden frames and made up into patterns that reveal great imagination and skill. These are carried to the parish church of St Mary for display. After this, as is usual with such occasions, the day is declared free for all to enjoy.

These are just a few examples of the countless traditions and customs that can be found all over England. The diligent searcher will be able to uncover many more, and will find the pursuit of such survivals from an earlier age both interesting and rewarding.

Our Architectural Heritage

A regional guide to the buildings of England – the history of a culture in brick and stone

Fine building in what is now England began about 3,500 years ago with the establishment of secure townships on open hills and the erection of great monuments like Stonehenge. Only the most durable structures survive from this remarkable age, and although the massive earth ramparts of the towns still exist from the South Downs to the Cheviots we can only guess at the appearance of the dwellings that stood inside. It is probable that these were made from timber, earth-walling, or rubble-stone – depending on the area.

Two completely different types of architecture existed over 3,000 years ago, and have not been added to since. One is represented by the trilithons – two posts and a lintel – of Stonehenge and has been consciously designed to be significant; the other embraces peoples' need for accommodation, shelter, and security. The first embodies and symbolizes the values and beliefs of a society, not the least of these being belief in its own corporate existence, and the other provides for the needs of everyday life. They are respectively termed monumental and folk (or vernacular) architecture, but there is no hard and fast division between the two and the emphasis shifts towards one or the other at different times in our history.

Monumental architecture usually takes a form which is influenced by various forces existing outside the community. A good example of this is again Stonehenge, which represents a way of designing with large stones also practised on a grand scale in Brittany and as far away as Mycenae in Greece. Folk architecture is naturally more localized, but although it depends to a large extent upon available materials and climate it is as much a part of a people's culture as their language, clothes, and music.

The Romans brought a foreign architecture into Britain, and remains of their work are preserved in many parts of the country. It is significant, however, that nothing comparable to some of our prehistoric structures has survived from this occupation. Hadrian's wall and its associated garrison towns are of fascinating interest to the student of Roman frontiers, but even this impressive complex pales beside the stupendous achievements of Stonehenge and prehistoric Maiden Castle. It was not until long after the Roman forces had evacuated the country that their influence began to make an impression on English culture, and even then it did not come from within but spread from the mainland of Europe.

True English architecture really begins in the 7thc, when Christianity had begun to return after the Anglo-Saxon conquest. Domestic architecture at this time took the form of simple, mainly timber-built structures. This lack of domestic ostentation suited the simple life-style of the times and persisted throughout the middle ages, with finer architecture reserved as a mainly religious art. Many castles were built during this period, but although they appear to fall into a different category they were always purely functional and impressive mainly because of their size.

Styles and Periods
English medieval architecture is commonly divided into five styles: Anglo-Saxon; Norman; early English; decorated; perpendicular. The first two form part of 'romanesque', and the other three are individual styles of gothic. These terms were invented by the English architect Thomas Rickman in 1817, and the people that had actually employed the styles were quite unaware of such names. Old-fashioned architects often continued to design in ways which had been handed down from teacher to student for years, while medieval architects frequently executed their work in an earlier manner in order to remain in harmony with existing building. This is why we find examples like Brinkburn, where pointed arches can be seen below a round-arched triforium, and Beverley, where 13th-c triforium arcading exists in a part of the church which was built in the 14thc – with decorated architecture above and below it. Likewise after Inigo Jones introduced Palladian design in the Stuart period, Tudor-style architecture was continued. Even in the 18thc William Kent extended Hampton Court Palace in keeping with work done by Wolsey in the 16thc. The names of styles and periods are useful to describe a kind of architecture but cannot be relied upon for dating.

Each of the following sections considers the architecture of an English region in such a way as to emphasize regional characteristics. In addition to this the sections are sequential and use each area to exemplify one of the many periods of English architectural history. Taken in order the next few pages thus provide a brief history of English architecture.

OUR ARCHITECTURAL HERITAGE

THE NORTHERN BORDERLANDS
Cumberland, Durham, Northumberland and Westmorland

The north was a border region for much of our history, and although naturally fertile was not agriculturally developed until the mid 18thc. This is why most of the farms and villages in the area are of Georgian or later date. Solid and well-proportioned folk architecture includes farm buildings such as large byres and barns. The Northumbrian gingans – round houses for a type of horse-driven threshing engine – are especially notable. Building stone is abundant and varies from the green slate of the Lake District to the red sandstone found around Carlisle, but the most widely used is a fine yellow sandstone which may be seen at its architectural best in Newcastle upon Tyne (Grey Street) and Durham Cathedral. South Northumberland and County Durham were once rich in minerals but have been heavily exploited. Both areas are now rapidly changing from extractive to manufacturing industries.

Georgian farm, Dukesfield

Hadrian's Wall was a military zone and stop-line rather than a frontier; the best-preserved stretch lies east and west of Housesteads. Supporting garrison towns of Chesters and *Corstopitum* (Corbridge) are notable, and the Museum of Antiquities at Newcastle University contains a reconstructed Mithraeum. The medieval period has bequeathed a scattering of castles guarding a potentially easy invasion route in the east, leaving the mountainous country south of Carlisle to protect the rest of the region. Defended tower-houses or peles are common and tell their own story of danger and insecurity. Some survive in their original form but many are incorporated in substantial Georgian country houses. Examples of this marriage can be seen at Fowberry, Callaly, Hesleyside, and Elsdon. Church towers sometimes fulfilled much the same purpose and provided both a residence for the vicar and a refuge for the villagers in times of trouble.

15th-c parsonage built on to 14th-c pele tower, Elsdon

The acropolis of Durham, with its castle (now University College) and cathedral, is considered one of the major architectural sights in Europe. Specially interesting is the fact that ribbed vaulting, the invention which made Gothic architecture possible, was first used on a major scale at Durham Cathedral – a structure designed and begun in 1093. As well as being the culminating triumph of Norman architecture, this cathedral has the noble 13th-c Chapel of the Nine Altars and the late 14th-c Neville Screen by Henry Yevele, who was one of the greatest of England's master masons. Monasteries outside the citadel of Durham tended to be small and secluded as can be seen from the examples at Shap, Blanchland, and the beautiful little priory at Brinkburn. Carlisle Cathedral is a very fine fragment of the original building.

Norman doorway, 12th-c Brinkburn Priory

Several country houses in the region are converted and extended castles; Alnwick and Raby are specially notable as products of the romantic movement. Although famous architects did work in the North, notably Vanbrugh at Seaton Delaval and landscaper Capability Brown in his home county of Northumberland, much of the building was done by local men who created a regional tradition. Outstanding among these were David Stephenson, William Newton (architect of the Assembly Rooms in Newcastle), Richard Grainger, and John Dobson. Dobson is often referred to as the North's greatest architect.

18th-c Assembly Rooms, Newcastle upon Tyne

OUR ARCHITECTURAL HERITAGE

Berwick is a unique, essentially 18th-c walled town forming an outpost of England on the far bank of the Tweed. Access across the river is by a series of noble bridges. The southern parts of Durham and Westmorland have a softer and more peaceful character which links them with the mid-north, and abundant local limestone lends a brighter colouring to village buildings.

The Lake District has a beautiful folk architecture based upon dry-walling in slate and shale. Roofs are also slate and everything, including chimney finishes, is made with local materials. Sometimes the walls are stuccoed or roughcast as can be seen at Levens Hall. This house stands in a mature Elizabethan garden which includes a fully-developed yew topiary and displays a marvellous relationship between house and grounds.

Elizabethan mansion built on to 14th-c pele tower, Levens

18th-c corn mill, Netherwitton

Some of the major architectural experiences of the region include the perfect motte-and-bailey of Elsdon Castle; Hexham Abbey; Warkworth Castle; Brinkburn Priory; Grey Street in Newcastle; Escomb Church; Levens Hall; Alnwick and Raby castles; the 'Arts and Crafts' church of St Andrew at Roker in Sunderland. Industrial archaeology enthusiasts will find Neathead and the Beamish Museum in Co Durham of particular interest.

Northumbria was a leading cultural centre in Europe during the 7th and 8thc. King Edwin was baptised by Paulinus from Canterbury in 627, but the main Christian influence came with St Aidan from Celtic Iona in 635 and his establishment at Lindisfarne. St Wilfrid built the greatest church north of the Alps at Hexham *c* 674; missionaries, scholars and statesmen included Wilfrid, Willibrord, Bede the historian, and Alcuin the confidential adviser of Charlemagne. Through the efforts of such men Northumbria became the shining light of civilization. Its architecture survives principally in the Tyne and Wear valleys and is characterized by very fine masonry with tall thin walls which were built with great skill and strengthened at the corners with quoins (long and short work). Arched lintels such as can be seen at Bywell St Peter echo Roman work at *Corstopitum* and elsewhere. Decoration, seen at its best in crosses which include the Acca and Rothbury examples, has affinities with Celtic manuscripts. Notably among these is the Lindisfarne Gospel, which dates from this period and is now in the British Museum. Round arches are common and the pointed arch made of two inclined stones is occasionally found. Escomb, situated on the Wear near Bishop Auckland, is almost completely Anglo-Saxon but was small for its time and needs to be compared with the altered but larger churches at Bywell, Hexham, Jarrow, Wearmouth, and elsewhere. Continental romanesque architecture brought to England by the Normans was grand, massive and crude in comparison to the native Northumbrian romanesque from which it was in some respects derived. This derivation occurred through Northumbrian influence upon France and Germany in the Carolingian period (8th–9thc).

Saxon church, Escomb

OUR ARCHITECTURAL HERITAGE

SHIRES OF THE MID-NORTH
Cheshire, Derbyshire, Lancashire, part of Staffordshire and Yorkshire

Typical upland farm

The rivalry between Lancashire and Yorkshire, as associated with the Wars of the Roses, goes far back into the past. The climatic pattern is divided by the Pennines and the west has a high rainfall while Yorkshire remains relatively dry. Folk architecture of Lancashire and Cheshire is largely based upon timber-framing and comprises the black-and-white houses typical of a once predominantly forested region. On the other side of the watershed in Yorkshire timber is more sparse, moorlands and meadows predominate, and stone is the characteristic building material. An exception is the plain of York, where local clays have been made into a pleasant pinkish brick. Derbyshire has a rugged sandstone character towards Sheffield, but looks to the south with picturesque limestone dales descending to fertile undulating farmlands.

17th c Foster Beck flax mill, Pateley Bridge

The uplands have been inhabited from prehistoric times as the stone circle of Arbor Low, marvellously sited above the sheep-grazing uplands which spread along the spine of England, testifies. Wool sustained the manufacturing towns, but the hill shepherds were poor and their farmsteads ruggedly simple, exposed, and cherishing shelter from wind-bent plantations. More prosperous farms and villages in the dales were famous for cheese, difficult to reach, and as persistent in local traditions of architecture as in their peculiarities of dialect. No region is more rich in folk architecture, and it is fascinating to move from one valley to another and notice the difference of detail in gables, corbels, chimneys and other features. A history of building for the textile industry, first with water and then with steam power, is also connected with the area.

12th- to 15th-c Fountains Abbey, Studley Royal

The typical manor house was very simple – a hall and kitchen with two or three more rooms usually arranged in line. Haddon Hall is one of the thousands of manors in the mid-north, and the oldest part of the house still has antiquated kitchen equipment which is eloquent of the low domestic-convenience standards which our ancestors accepted up to the 19thc.
Like the mills, the homes of the nobility and squires proclaim the abundance of cheap labour. Until the 17thc furniture was rare and very simple – the work of carpenters. In many places the 19thc expansion of industry overwhelmed a rural economy, but traces of the old folk architecture can still be seen in the smaller towns – and to a lesser degree even in the middle of Manchester.

Furness, Fountains, Rievaulx, and Whitby abbeys are among the finest in England. People often say that the monks chose idyllic situations, but in fact they usually settled in a wilderness and made it into a paradise. Each was centred upon the monastery church and formed a self-supporting community often extending over many miles of farm, grazing, and forest land. A good water-supply was required for fishponds, to drive the mill, and to flush the drains. The monks' occupations included scholarship, education, hospitality, medical services, and the improvement of forestry and agriculture. Most of the progress in these things during the middle ages was achieved by monastic foundations before Henry VIII started dissolving them in 1536.

OUR ARCHITECTURAL HERITAGE

Being naturally rich in both agriculture and mineral wealth, the mid-north became a land of great houses and parks. Temple Newsam (Leeds), Bolsover Castle, Hardwick Hall, and timber-built Moreton Old Hall belong to the first age of building after the dissolution of the monasteries, when such residences formed the administrative centres of vast estates. They all owed much to the medieval tradition, which in England seemed to be evolving into a new and beautiful secular version of gothic architecture. Foreign renaissance influence became decisive in the early 17thc. Castle Howard and Chatsworth mark the beginning of an era when palatial country houses were built in the classical style and complemented by extensive landscaping. These beautifully designed parks, although often inspired by vanity and financed by greed, have greatly enriched the English scene.

16th-c hall, Little Moreton

York and Chester were both Roman legionary headquarters and preserve a wealth of historic architecture from the middle-ages onwards. Of particular note are the walls of both cities, the 'rows' of Chester, the Georgian houses of York, and the cathedrals. Manchester was a small market town with a fine collegiate church, and Liverpool a seaport founded by King John. Both grew vastly in the 19thc along with Leeds, Bradford and Sheffield. Notable buildings include the town halls at Leeds (by Broderick), Manchester (by Waterhouse), Halifax (by Barry) and St George's Hall in Liverpool (by Elmes and Cockerell). The latter can be considered the finest thing of its kind in Europe. Throughout the industrial areas there are fine buildings which have been tragically marred by environmental squalor.

The Rows, Chester

Gothic Architecture

The invention of ribbed vaulting at the end of the 11thc led to the development of a way of using stone whereby the structure could be conceived as separate from the walls. Along with this came the pointed arch which has the advantage that it can be varied in width without necessarily making it higher. The old round arch was limited because it could only be made half as high as its diameter. Thinking of stone architecture as a structural frame – almost as if it were timber – made it possible to build walls of coloured glass supported by stone and metal tracery. By the 13thc philosophers and architects were at one in conceiving the interior of the house of God as an enclosure of space in the likeness of heaven, transfused with coloured light.

The minster churches of Beverley and York exemplify the best of the gothic achievement. Beverley's severe 13th-c choir reflects the intellectual theology of such men as St Thomas Aquinas; the 14th-c nave displays more comfortable proportions and humanistic sculptures, and the series culminates in the chancel with the intricate Percy Shrine portraying God receiving a soul into heaven. York shows the best of later 14th- and 15th-c work; a particularly good example is the east window which shows the rectilinear tracery which gives the 'perpendicular' style its name.

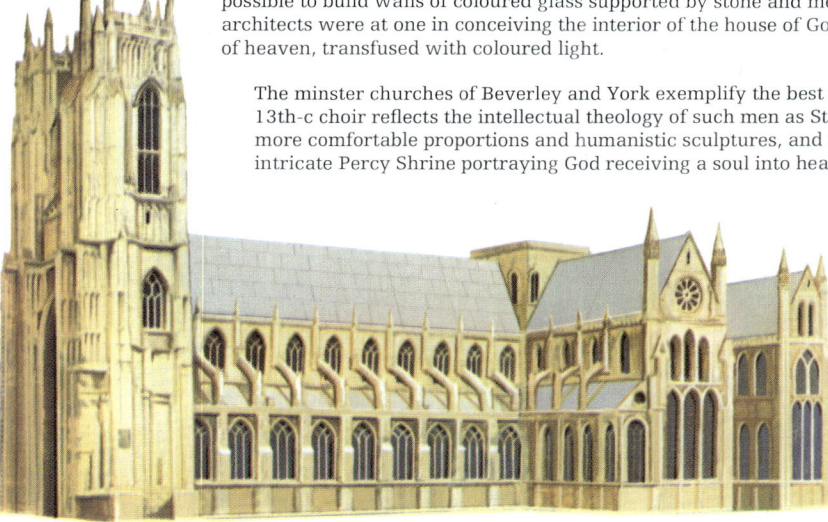
13th-c minster, Beverley

OUR ARCHITECTURAL HERITAGE

THE CENTRAL WILDERNESS
The Midlands, Severn and Thames Valleys

Much of central England was forested and waterlogged in early times and was consequently late in developing. This is indicated by the situation of the old cathedral cities in a ring round the wilderness, and meant that folk architecture tended to have been influenced from the edges of the region towards the centre. The Welsh border counties are rich in castles and characterized by timber-framed houses similar to those seen in Cheshire. An arc from Gloucester and through Northampton to Rutland shows the use of an abundant creamy stone in the creation of beautiful local styles. The heavily polluted industrial belt based upon iron and coal forms a shorter arc in the north-west of the region.

18th-c guildhall, Worcester

Saxon church, Bradford-on-Avon

The ancient prosperity of an attractive and fertile district is reflected in superb cathedrals at Hereford, Gloucester, and Worcester; the abbey church of Tewkesbury; and fine parish churches such as the one at Stratford-upon-Avon. Handsome woollen mills in such places as Bradford-on-Avon lost their business to Yorkshire in the steam age, but this is more than compensated for by the retention of a quality of environment and way of life related to the fertility of nature – upon biology rather than upon chemistry and mechanics. Apart from some modern indiscretions there is an overall harmony of scale and consistency in the use of naturally-beautiful local materials.

Among the most notable early buildings are the tower of Earl's Barton church, parts of Deerhurst church including rare triangular headed windows, the complete Saxon church at Bradford-on-Avon, and our most impressive pre-conquest church – All Saints' at Brixworth. Southwell minster is notable for its Norman front and nave, and for the decorated capitals in its chapter house. Lichfield is among the most beautiful of English cathedrals and the only one with three spires. One of the best early manor houses can be seen at Stokesley.

Kenilworth and the border castles of Ludlow and Chepstow show full castle development up to the time when the invention of gunpowder made this type of defence obsolete. The controlling factor in castle design – right from the early motte-and-bailey type – was defence and it should be noted that English castle building was controlled by the crown as part of the system of government and defence. The constable's dwelling was often a strong gatehouse and had to be secure from within as well as without! A few castles, like Warwick, were turned into great houses with romantic gardens. The gothic revival also led to the building of sham castles like Eastnor and Belvoir, and fancified manor houses such as Blithfield.

Gothicized hall, Blithfield

OUR ARCHITECTURAL HERITAGE

Belton is one of the most pleasant of many classical houses and illustrates the great architectural importance of the building material – in this case a golden-yellow stone. The design is not particularly distinguished and the plan is simple and symmetrical, but the house has a presence without being ostentatious and the gardens are beautifully related to it. The greatest house of all is Blenheim Palace, the nation's gift to John Churchill, first Duke of Marlborough. This was designed by England's most theatrical architect and is untypical in emulating the baroque palace of Europe.

17th- to 18th-c mansion, Belton

The English popular motor-car industry was born from an Oxford bicycle shop, but in spite of this the city is still one of the most beautiful in the world. Like Cambridge, it demonstrated the advantages of closed precincts as compared with outward-looking architectural developments. Except in recent years the colleges never patronised *avant-garde* architects, and the buildings reflect the properly cautious attitudes of the scholarly mind. A reasonable way to trace the sequence of architecture is through New College chapel; Worcester, lower side of quad; St John's quad; Radcliffe Camera; Ashmolean museum; Oxford museum; Keble College; Examination Schools; Law Library.

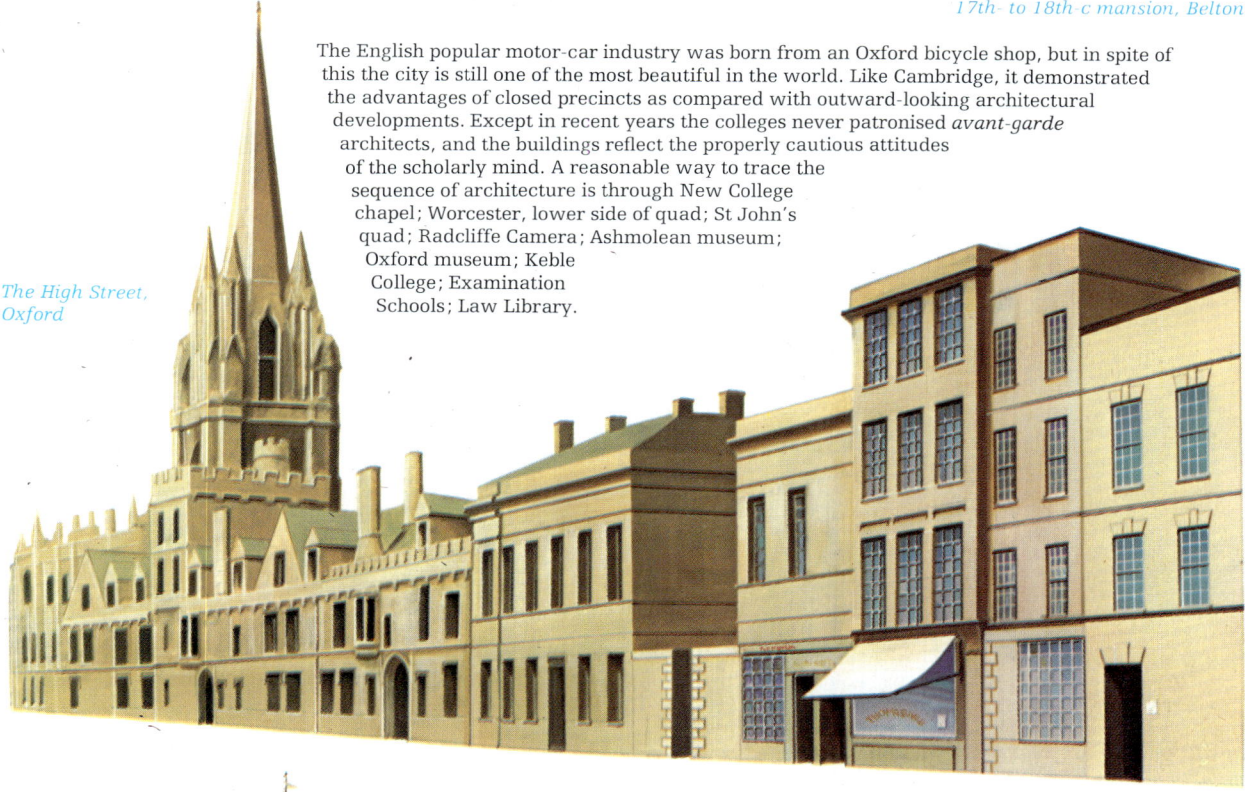

The High Street, Oxford

Tudor and Jacobean Architecture

The gothic way of design was by no means decadent at the end of the middle-ages and England, isolated from Catholic Europe by Henry VIII and the dissolution of the monasteries, began to develop an extension of gothic as a secular way of design. Its principal characteristics were large mullioned windows and a sophistication of internal planning superior to anything in Europe at the time – especially in the sequential relationship of spaces and the development of the internal grand staircase as a linking element between floors. The manorial hall was retained but became essentially a dining room. The solar became the drawing room and the principal festive room was the long gallery. Kitchens were rudimentary in equipment and relied upon cheap domestic service. Stable accommodation was generally lavish. Dressage in England was first developed at the riding school of Bolsover castle in Derbyshire, which was built during this period. Burleigh House, Aston Hall, Hatfield House, and Abingdon town hall are examples of design based upon traditional techniques and awareness of the need to adapt to new conditions. This 'modern movement' of the 16thc was frustrated by the introduction of Italian ideas in the 17thc.

17th-c County Hall, Abingdon

OUR ARCHITECTURAL HERITAGE

EASTERN HEATHS AND FENS
Cambridgeshire, East Anglia, Essex, Fens and Lincolnshire

A great deal of this region is low-lying, and such hills as there are tend to be heaths. The agricultural patterns contrast sharply from the fertile reclaimed lands of the fens to the chalk, sands, and gravels which predominate elsewhere. Up until the 17thc the Fens were a wilderness, and folk architecture was mostly in the form of reed huts. Flint was mined for tools in the stone age and eventually became a characteristic building material, especially around Norwich where very fine knapped flints were used for churches and civic buildings. Good clays for brick and tilemaking were also available, and a sandy, bright-red hand-made brick was used throughout the region.

Flint infilling shown by the church at Long Melford

Water transport is a key to understanding the distribution of materials and the siting of towns and villages in this region. Fine limestone from the western edge and the east midlands was widely used and can be seen in the magnificent cathedral of Ely – built on a low island in the fen. Much of Cambridge is built from materials brought by barge. Timber was extensively used for cottages and windmills which were sometimes half-timbered and sometimes, especially in Essex, weather-boarded. English weather-boarding was the origin of the clap-boarded style of American colonial architecture. Carpentry skills of the region are consummated in the octagonal lantern of Ely cathedral. This brilliant conception probably suggested the design of the central space in St Paul's Cathedral to Wren.

A Lincolnshire windmill

Manufacture of woollen cloth – including the immortal Lincoln Green of Robin Hood – and an export trade through east coast ports contributed to the prosperity of the region in the later middle-ages. This new wealth provided money for a great number of splendid churches in the perpendicular style. Among the finest is St Botolphs at Boston. The church's lofty tower or 'stump' is a landmark for many miles around and is constructed in a form which indicates close links with Flanders. The spacious hall type of church is also common in Holland. The cathedrals of Peterborough, Ely and Norwich all show the evolutionary character of medieval architecture. The intricate Norman arcading on the secure isle of Ely contrasts significantly with the rugged splendour of Durham on the frontier of Norman England.

11th- to 15th-c Lincoln Cathedral rising from a typically varied composition of town buildings

Boston Stump, tower of mainly 15th-c St Botolph's Church, Boston

Lincoln cathedral, though part of the west front survives from the destruction of the Norman cathedral by an earthquake in 1185, is one of the best examples of 13th-c architecture extant. It reflects the intellectualism of which Robert Grosseteste (Bishop of Lincoln 1235, d 1253), a Platonist and one of the earliest commentators upon Aristotle, was an eminent exponent. He also pioneered the establishment of vicarages instead of 'paide chaplaincies' in England, a move which had a profound effect on the social character of village life. This effect is manifest throughout the region, and the numerous tightly-knit communities usually include a village green or market place, dominant parish church, vicarage, often a manor house, and sometimes a castle or great house.

OUR ARCHITECTURAL HERITAGE

The Tudor and Jacobean periods are best represented by the great house of Audley End and collegiate buildings at Cambridge. King's College chapel shows that gothic architecture was certainly not decadent in the early 16thc. Whereas the monastic plan emphasizes the church, its derived collegiate form gives emphasis to the cloister. The cloister later became the 'quad' and the focus of a studious attitude to life furthered in England by Grosseteste and Roger Bacon. Oxford, Cambridge and later Durham Universities grew out of the Church and their rôle was to extend the benefits of scholarship and philosophy into the laity. The community was based upon a quadrangle – a sheltered arcade around a grass lawn – and signified a coming together of minds which seek unity in the common pursuit of truth by way of study and informal discussion. The chapel and the library serve the cloister.

Following the restoration of the Stuart monarchy in 1660 this region shared in the enthusiasm for a robust classical-style influence of baroque architecture from Europe, and the growing achievement of Sir Christopher Wren. East Anglia in particular absorbed ideas of design from the low countries at a time when the fens were being drained and people were coming in from Holland. Henry Bell of King's Lynn was a distinguished regional architect who built the Customs House in his home town. The period also saw many old houses re-styled with brick façades.

Great St Mary's Street, Cambridge

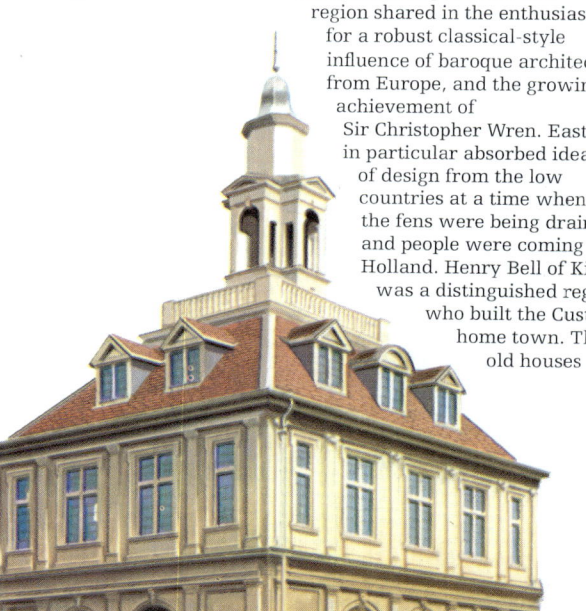

17th-c Custom House, King's Lynn

Palladian Architecture

Although vague Italian influences came to England in the 16thc, the full force of renaissance design was not felt until introduced by Inigo Jones in the early 17thc. Inigo Jones was a disciple of the Venetian architect Palladio, author of *The Four Books of Architecture* (1570). Palladio was out of phase with his own period in Italy and expounded 15th-c rules of classical design. His creed was favoured by the invention of printing and the development of a fairly accurate method for publishing representations of the five classical orders of architecture *ie* types of columns with their related cornices, etc. The orders are variously named Tuscan, Doric, Ionic, Corinthian, and Composite, and all derive from ancient Rome.

The first English Palladian building was the Queen's House at Greenwich by Inigo Jones in 1616. This was followed by the Banqueting Hall in Whitehall in 1619, but the Puritan period did not favour architecture and the style went out of fashion at the Restoration. Early in the 18thc Palladianism was restored, mainly by Lord Burlington who set himself up as an arbiter of taste and favoured the classicism which was out of fashion elsewhere in Europe. This was the beginning of aristocratic patronage for antique art which was to prove disastrous for progressive art in England. Two of the best examples of Palladianism are Haughton Hall by Campbell and Holkham Hall by Kent, both in Norfolk. Palladio's rules were the basis for the simple and dignified Georgian style of architecture.

Palladian mansion, Holkham

CONTRASTS OF THE SOUTH-WEST
Hampshire, The West Country and Wiltshire

Cornwall is basically Celtic. Tintagel and Glastonbury evoke memories of Roman-British struggles against the Saxons, but Winchester was the late-Saxon capital of England and Wessex which under Alfred preserved the essence of England against the Danes. Devon gave birth to the legendary Sir Francis Drake in the 16thc, and the south-west has remained the home base of the navy ever since. Europe's major pre-classical monument is Stonehenge, a circular trilithonic temple in Wiltshire. Maiden Castle was constructed about 4,000 years ago and is a citadel comparable with the Myceanean fortresses of ancient Greece.

Prehistoric Stonehenge, Salisbury Plain

Geologically the region ages to the west, graduating from the chalk downs of Wiltshire, through the limestones of Somerset and Dorset, and finally to the rugged tors of Dartmoor and silver granite of Cornwall. Many of the best buildings in London, including St Paul's, are built of the region's Portland stone. The architectural pattern is similar throughout the area, with simple non-classical forms predominating in the west. Nearer London is Wilton House, which has a south front considered one of the best examples of Palladianism. Palladian Stourhead includes landscaped gardens decorated with classical temples. Folk architecture varies with the availability of materials and the character of the people who, throughout history and despite a relatively gentle climate, have proved themselves as sturdily independent of London as the men of the north.

Cornish harbour buildings at Mousehole, Penzance

Granite and slate are the main materials of Cornish folk architecture and there is an intricate intimacy in the planning of the county's villages. These are often sited in tight valleys and have usually grown by the accretion of small units and adjustments to the needs of people; they are the antithesis of modern housing which has been planned on the drawing board. The difficult materials do not lend themselves to much architectural ornamentation, but miniature gardens, window boxes, hanging baskets, and climbing plants more than compensate for this. The moors of Cornwall are punctuated by the towers of old tin mines which are by no means without beauty. Moorland farms are built low with small windows and strong slate roofs.

14th c slate roofed Old Post Office, Tintagel

Gothic pub – the George, Glastonbury

Hampshire's Romsey abbey indicates close connections with the Normandy that supplied a new English ruling class after the conquest of 1066. Winchester cathedral had a Saxon prototype which has recently been excavated, and displays horseshoe arches which suggest Islamic influence. These can be compared with Fountains Abbey. Salisbury cathedral dates from the 13thc and, like those in Lincoln and Lichfield, is of great beauty but was designed to appeal to the cultivated intellect more than the emotions. Exeter cathedral is in the more sensuous decorated style, and the nearby guildhall is specially notable. Glastonbury was one of the noblest of all medieval monasteries and still retains its abbot's kitchen and abbey barn (c1420) intact. A gothic-style pub in Glastonbury is also of interest.

OUR ARCHITECTURAL HERITAGE

Devon and Somerset cottages are very different from their Cornish counterparts. The walls are commonly thick, sometimes built of compacted earth, and often colour-washed. Thatch is the traditional roofing material and shows a high degree of craftsmanship. In striking contrast to the cosy villages of the south-west is the Roman spa town of Bath, developed with sophisticated classical architecture for the 18th-c gentry. Social distinction is evident throughout the region, but towards the close of the Georgian period a fashion for the romantic led to the building of ornamental 'folksy' cottages as well as the picturesque gothic-revival house.

Country cottage typical of Dorset, Devon and Cornwall

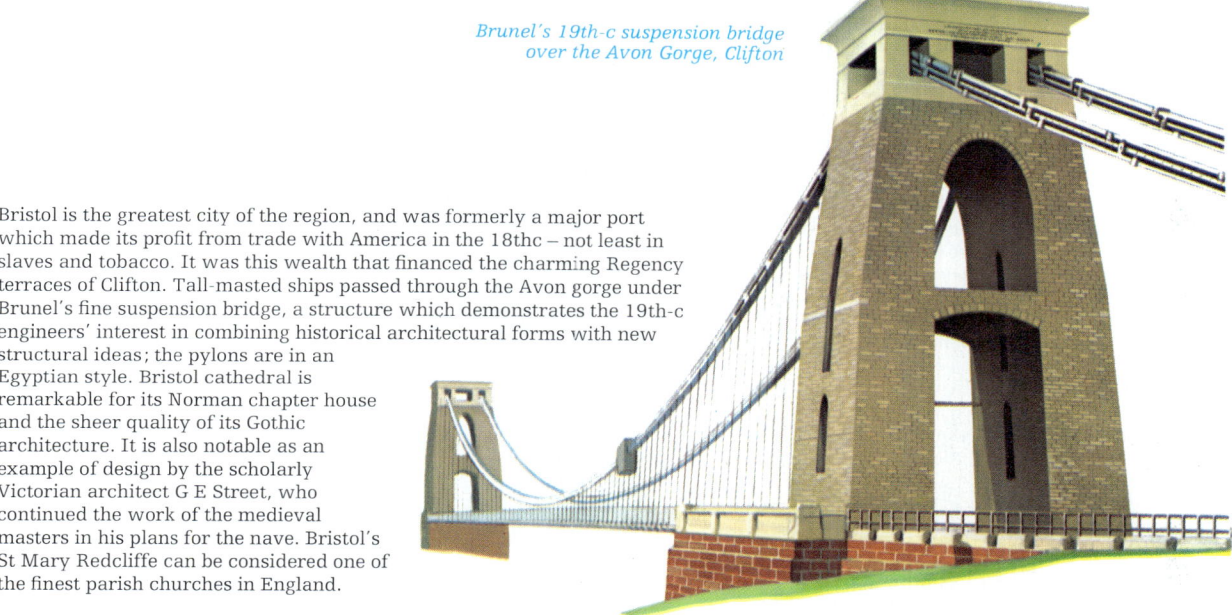

Brunel's 19th-c suspension bridge over the Avon Gorge, Clifton

Bristol is the greatest city of the region, and was formerly a major port which made its profit from trade with America in the 18thc – not least in slaves and tobacco. It was this wealth that financed the charming Regency terraces of Clifton. Tall-masted ships passed through the Avon gorge under Brunel's fine suspension bridge, a structure which demonstrates the 19th-c engineers' interest in combining historical architectural forms with new structural ideas; the pylons are in an Egyptian style. Bristol cathedral is remarkable for its Norman chapter house and the sheer quality of its Gothic architecture. It is also notable as an example of design by the scholarly Victorian architect G E Street, who continued the work of the medieval masters in his plans for the nave. Bristol's St Mary Redcliffe can be considered one of the finest parish churches in England.

Restoration Architecture

From 1660 to 1714, *ie* the Restoration to the death of Queen Anne, English architecture flourished in a robust and sumptuous style which was mainly initiated by Sir Christopher Wren. Nicholas Hawksmore and Sir John Vanbrugh developed the style. Vanbrugh's Kings Western, near Bristol, is a noble mansion which shows the talent for grandeur possessed by the architect of Blenheim and Castle Howard – though on a relatively modest scale. Architects of the period, in particular Sir Christopher Wren, drew inspiration from many sources in Italy, France and the Low Countries in developing the classical formula which had been established by Inigo Jones and John Webb. Avoiding the extravagances of European baroque, restoration architects delighted in rich ornamentation and created an essentially English way of design which was meant to be enjoyed. It was sometimes theatrical, even in the doorway of a simple house of the kind often called 'Queen Anne' – though the style was not limited to her reign – but was rarely if ever dull. Though considered vulgar and unintellectual by the standards of the Georgians, it did, in fact, rest upon firm classical principles of proportion and decorum. Exeter's Customs House is notable.

17th-c Custom House, Exeter

OUR ARCHITECTURAL HERITAGE

SUBURBIA AND THE SOUTH-EAST
Essex, Kent, Surrey and Sussex

The South East was a Saxon Kingdom and geographically open to influence from Europe, as can be seen by the Germanic helm tower of Sompting church – a feature now unique in England. St Augustine brought Italian ideas about church building into the country, and Worth is one of the churches with an eastern apse in the Roman tradition. The geography of the region is mostly chalk hills and rolling wooded lowlands. Good building stone is scarce and was generally imported by sea, but flints, timber, lime, sand, and good clay for bricks and tiles were and are plentiful. Wood-fired kilns were used to burn the clay-formed materials. Agriculturally the south-east is not rich, and larger buildings have often been financed from London rather than from the region's own wealth. The Cinque Ports were once vital to the defence of England. The basic culture is predominantly Saxon with a Norman aristocracy which was imposed in the 11thc – a pattern which has persisted, but with considerable variation in the composition of the aristocracy.

14th- to 20th-c castle, Bodiam

Away from London-overspill areas or coastal resort developments, south-east England remains very rural with feudal traditions and a deep folk culture. Fine buildings of all periods include numerous examples ranging from castles like Bodiam and Arundel to mansions by Sir Edwin Lutyens. It is also a land of small villages and market towns, with many ancient and usually small churches. Folk architecture is mainly the work of carpenter-builders rather than masons, and common flint walling reaches considerable sophistication in building with knapped flints. Knapping is the art of splitting a flint with a special hammer on the workman's knee, then squaring it with a blunt axe on a steel stake set in a block of wood. Tile-hanging is an ancient way of cladding timber-framed structures, and the bonnet-hipped roof is a specially characteristic feature. Weather-boarding is common and a fair number of thatched cottages are still to be seen.

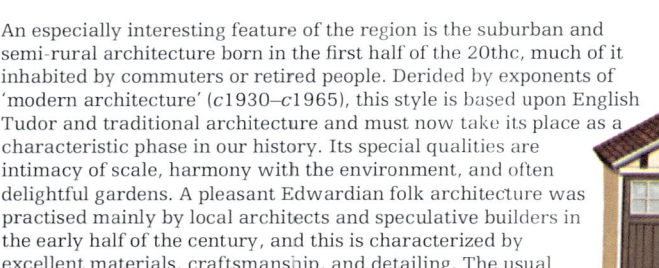
Hypothetical composition of folk architectural styles

Regency Royal Crescent, Brighton

The character of the region's folk architecture, and sometimes its architect-designed buildings, is a smallness of scale and warmth of colour which gives a comely and comfortable quality to the villages and market towns. Folk building techniques are very varied and use local materials with strong local craft traditions. Abundant chalk encouraged the use of slurried or stuccoed finishes to give a fair appearance to quite rough construction.

Cement stucco became a highly developed branch of the plasterer's craft during the 18th and 19thc, and was particularly suited to the south-east as a substitute for stone. All the features of classical architecture could be executed relatively cheaply by this means. It is the predominant facing material in most of the coastal resorts and became the characteristic medium of design for Regency architecture. At Brighton it was used in an oriental style for the Pavilion.

An especially interesting feature of the region is the suburban and semi-rural architecture born in the first half of the 20thc, much of it inhabited by commuters or retired people. Derided by exponents of 'modern architecture' (c1930–c1965), this style is based upon English Tudor and traditional architecture and must now take its place as a characteristic phase in our history. Its special qualities are intimacy of scale, harmony with the environment, and often delightful gardens. A pleasant Edwardian folk architecture was practised mainly by local architects and speculative builders in the early half of the century, and this is characterized by excellent materials, craftsmanship, and detailing. The usual materials are red brick and tile with a great deal of ornamental woodwork; the style derives from the arts and crafts movement.

Early 20th-c 'folksy' suburban architecture

OUR ARCHITECTURAL HERITAGE

Regency work on the Pantiles, Tunbridge Wells

Outstanding architectural experiences of the region are Canterbury and Chichester cathedrals. Canterbury has a splendid crypt and a choir which is one of the earliest buildings we know to have been by master mason William of Sens. Early stained glass, one of the principal glories of gothic cathedrals, is exceptional here. The nave is the principal work of the famous master mason Henry Yevele (c1325–c1400), who also designed Westminster Hall, and has been described as *'of all the English naves . . . the most satisfactory in its proportions'*. Chichester cathedral was founded when the see was transferred from Selsey in 1075, and is considered one of the most beautiful of the earlier English cathedrals. It is built partly of Caen stone and has columns of Purbeck marble. The separate bell tower is unique for an English cathedral.

18th-c rococo Brighton Pavilion

Regency Architecture

The name 'Regency', like all names of period styles, can be misleading. It is customarily applied to an English version of rococo design which flourished from c1795 to c1830 (the actual Regency was 1811 to 1820). English Regency was a mixture of neo-classical design, Greek revival, and Palladianism which had become traditional in England during the Georgian period. These elements were all brought together with a sense of elegance and a deliberate seeking for charm rather than impressiveness. The south-east is very rich in Regency architecture – especially at Tunbridge Wells, Brighton, Lewes, and Hastings – though in all the coastal resorts the charm of a consistent environment has been diminished by modern development of a totally alien character.

This architectural style was practised to a large extent by commercial developers who appreciated the value of good design; the outstanding examples are at Hove and Brighton. The most famous architect involved was John Nash, whose Brighton Pavilion for the Prince Regent can be considered the finest rococo building in England. It is the 'Regency' building *par excellence* and illustrates the important point that a period's character may be expressed in a variety of styles. Major buildings apart, the success of Regency designers arose from the grouping of dwellings in such a way that each individual home took its place in a fully-designed environment which included roads, gateways, and communal gardens.

Classical portico of the Greek-revival style

Interiors of Regency houses are entirely consistent with their smiling facades. They show a version of the style invented by Robert Adam, developed to satisfy equally the demands of a very simple home and a great mansion. Elegance was the keynote of English Regency, and as compared with continental rococo the style is given a special quality by the influence of the academic Greek Revival with which it coincided. Regency forms an architectural and furnishing counterpart to the novels of Jane Austen, and received its commercial impetus from the development of new holiday places which grew as Bath declined. The most famous furniture designer of the period was Thomas Sheraton, a man who contributed much to this age of elegance.

OUR ARCHITECTURAL HERITAGE

THE WEALTH OF LONDON

Like an ellipse the London region has two foci – the cities of London and Westminster. In the east the Tower stands astride the old wall, half in and half out of the community as a reflection of the insecurity felt by royal power inside the City. The west walls began at the mouth of the River Fleet and enclosed Blackfriars. The road to Westminster ran from Ludgate Hill and passed Whitefriars, the Temple, and succession of houses which were owned by great nobles and stood in grounds sweeping down to the river. Whitehall Palace began beyond Northumberland House with Great Scotland Yard. Inigo Jones, who designed the Banqueting Hall in 1619, lived there. The Civil Service grew from the 17thc and took over Whitehall, then royalty eventually moved to Buckingham Palace. Expanding London engulfed many towns and villages, but many of these have retained their identity as organic communities in spite of artificially imposed divisions and boundaries.

Regency Woburn Terrace

The Tower of London is a fascinating example of a castle which has been constantly adapted to remain in use, but its White Tower is still the best example of a Norman Keep extant. Much of medieval London perished in the fire of 1666, and though medieval churches such as St Bartholomew the Great remain, there is better gothic architecture elsewhere. Excellent examples include Westminster Abbey and Westminster Hall. Secular architecture which survived the fire and German bombing displays a richness beloved of prosperous merchants and tradesmen. The great age of London architecture begins with Wren's rebuilding of the city churches, the extension of Hampton Court, and the masterpiece of St Paul's Cathedral.

Inwood's St Pancras Church

The 18thc is remarkable for the building of residential squares on the model of Inigo Jones's Covent Garden. Much of the calm beauty of these places has recently been destroyed by developers, but the architecture was basically a Palladian style which underwent a gradual change – especially under the influence of Robert Adam – towards the more elegant forms of the Regency period. Fine houses of the square were complemented by decent terraces of smaller houses, mews, shopping centres, and service areas. Squares, crescents and terraces in formal order became the pattern of expanding London on both sides of the Thames.

Nowhere in Europe is the Greek revival better exemplified than in London. The lost doric entrance to Euston was the symbolic gateway to northern cities which quickly followed the Grecian ideas of Sir John Soane, who built the Bank of England (extended upwards in the present century), and Sir Robert Smirke who built the British Museum. St Pancras Church was by Inwood and is one of the best examples. The first third of the 19thc saw Greek and Italian influences merged with native tradition in the great contribution of John Nash's development from Carlton House Terrace to Regent's Park. Other architects, notably Decimus Burton, the designer of the Athenaeum, continued the work with the building of Belgravia and the terraces of South Kensington.

Victorian Architecture

The climax of London's development came in the reign of Queen Victoria, when it was the capital of a world-wide political and commercial empire backed by the rising productivity of industrial towns in the midlands and north. The roots of Victorian architecture lie in the 18thc, when Horace Walpole chose a pretty version of gothic for his house at Strawberry Hill and Sir William Chambers designed oriental-style buildings at Kew. It was recognized that instead of one classical rule, there were many possible ways of design out of which various 'styles' had developed; one could choose the most appropriate style for a given project. This *eclecticism*, as it was called, was later extended to permit the selection of appropriate elements from different styles and blending them in one building with modern ideas. This can be seen in St Pancras and Paddington stations, the Natural History and Victoria and Albert Museums, and the Prudential building in Holborn. Londoners saw themselves as being at the centre of an empire which had trading links and governmental responsibilities in lands with widely differing traditions. This bringing together of all that was best in the architecture of the world thus seemed both sensible and pleasing.

Victoria and Albert Museum

Day Drives

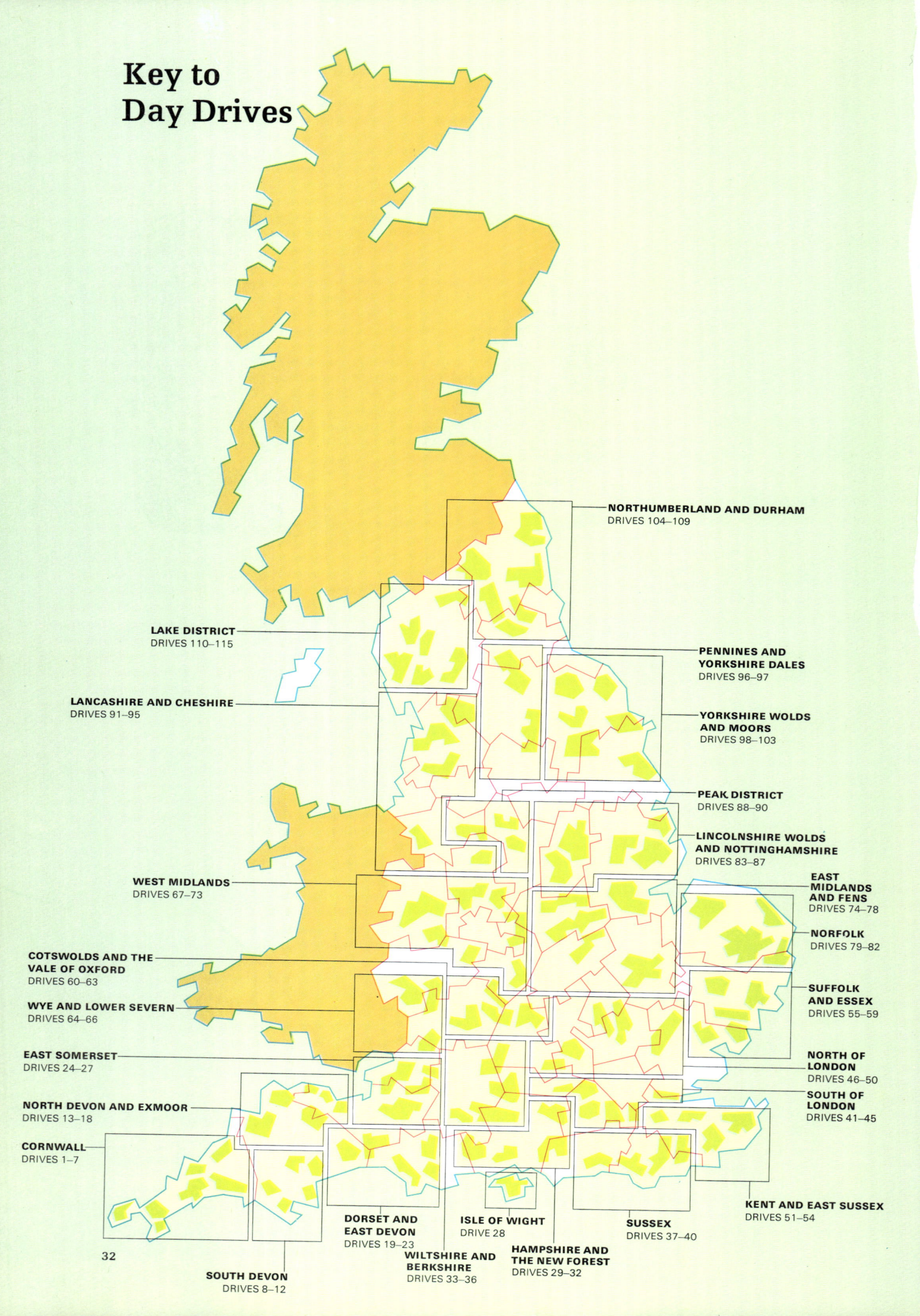

Country of Contrasts

The England of the romantics is a place of wide green fields and little tangled copses, of small clear brooks and timeless summer afternoons on village cricket fields. It is all this and much more, a country of startling variety where high open downs rise suddenly from the gentle undulations of wooded lowland; where wind-torn heaths flow and break into the jagged ruggedness of ancient mountain chains. And this variety begets even greater regional differences – buildings constructed from local materials for local purposes. The windmills of the east are as indicative of their region as Kentish oast houses, and the mellow limestone villages that grow from the Cotswolds as much a part of the English scene as the flint-knapped walls of Sussex.

English people once had a much better appreciation of their country than now. Cheap foreign travel has made the exotic as available as the time-honoured domestic holiday, and the latter has suffered. But it is not necessary to holiday in England to enjoy the contrasts that the country offers – a short drive is usually sufficient for a complete change of scenery.

Each of the tours in the following section of day drives has been specially selected to provide comprehensive coverage of a particular area. The areas have been chosen for their historic or scenic interest; all routes are circular and start from an easily accessible place, and every drive includes a map supported by concise route instructions. Places in *italic* type are listed and described in the gazetteer that follows this section. Features and places of interest used as route landmarks in the text can also be found in the gazetteer, either under their own names or as part of the entry for their nearest town or village.

Most of the drives include several stretches of unclassified road. This has been necessary to ensure maximum coverage of the areas concerned, but it must be remembered that many of these may be very narrow. It is unwise to follow a drive with a caravan or trailer. Maximum gradients are given where necessary, and the very arduous road conditions encountered in the Lake District are detailed at the beginning of this particular series of tours. Various road number changes have been made in recent years, but have not always been brought up to date on local signposts. Where this is the case the text and maps show the new number followed by the old in parentheses, *eg* A4146 (B486). Placenames also differ on direction indicators and may appear in a shortened form, *eg* Bradford-on-Avon as Bradford. The text uses the form that appears on the signposts.

DAY DRIVE SYMBOLS

AA Viewpoint	Marshland
Abbey	Motorway
Airport	Motorway Service Station
Battle Site	Other Roads
Boating Centre	Places off main route
Bridge	Places of Interest
Castle	Places on Route
Church	Racecourse
Crags	Rivers and Lakes
Drive Route	Sandy Beaches
Heights in Feet	Station
Hill Fort	Tower
Houses Open to the Public	TV or Radio Mast
Industrial Building	Waterfall
Inn	Windmill
Lighthouse	Woodland

Cornwall

Granite Cliffs of the Lizard

From Helston

Drive 1   45 miles

Leave *Helston* by the A3083 *Lizard* road, and after passing the Culdrose Royal Naval Air Station turn left on to the B3293 *St Keverne* road. Continue to Mawgan Cross War Memorial, branch left over the crossroads on to an unclassified road for Mawgan. Bear right with signposts marked Maracan and *Helford*, and continue through St Martin's Green to Newtown. Keep left, and in 250yds turn left again. In 1½m go straight over crossroads and in ¾m turn left and descend to Helford. Return for ¾m and turn left to the hamlet of St Anthony. Continue through the village, following the road alongside Gillan Creek, and after 1m turn left following signposts indicating St Keverne. Ascend, and at the edge of Gillan keep right on to a byroad, following signposts to St Keverne. Leave by the B3293 Helston and *Coverack* road, and in 1¼m turn left on to an unclassified road before joining the B3294. Descend to Coverack and return along the B3294 and B3293 Helston road for 4m; approach crossroads and turn left on to an unclassified road signposted *Cadgwith*. Cross the Goonhilly Downs with views of the Satellite Communications station to the right. In 3m turn right at the T-junction, and in ¾m approach crossroads and turn left for Ruan Manor. Turn right and descend a 1 in 4 hill to Cadgwith. Continue along the unclassified road by following Lizard signposts, and ascend. Within ⅜m turn right and in another ¾m turn left on to the A3083

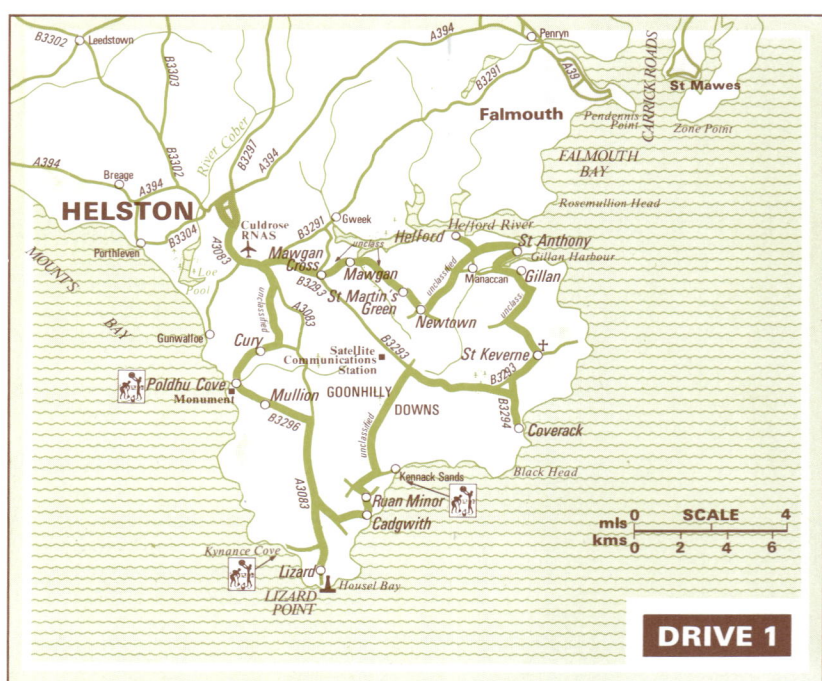

for *Lizard*. Return along this road, following Helston signposts. In 4m turn left on to the B3296 for *Mullion*. Keep left (one-way), then turn right on to an unclassified road signposted Poldhu Cove. Reach the coast at Poldhu Cove. Cross the bridge and bear right, then ascend a 1 in 6 hill and continue through the village of Cury. In ½m turn left, following signs to Helston, and in 1¾m turn left again to rejoin the A3083 to return to Helston.

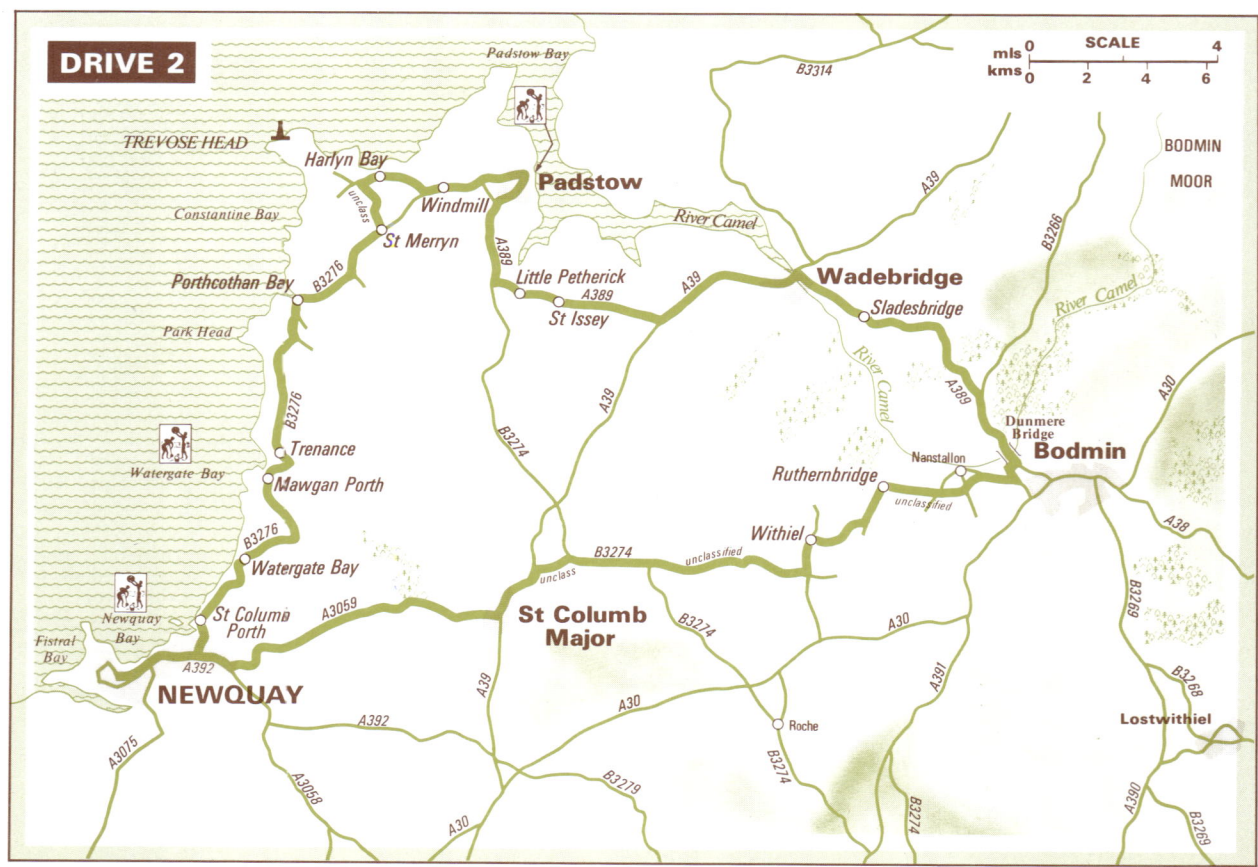

CORNWALL

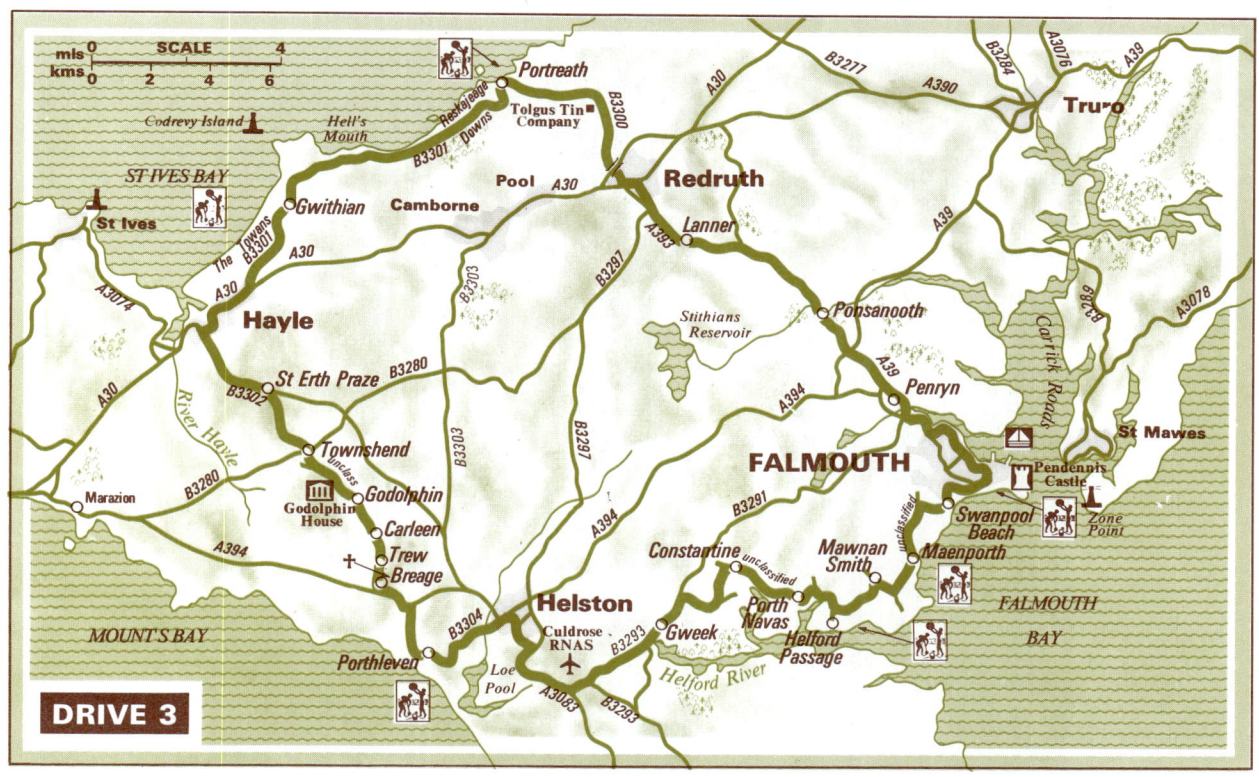

Coves of the South West
From Falmouth
Drive 3   52 miles

From *Falmouth* follow 'Beaches' and 'Helford Passage' signposts to leave by the Swanpool Hill unclassified road. Pass Swanpool Beach and ascend a 1 in 8 hill before continuing for ½m and turning left at the T-junction, signposted Maenporth. Pass through Maenporth, and in 1½m turn right for Mawnan Smith. Approach the Red Lion Inn and turn left with Porth Navas signposts; in 1¼m turn right and continue beyond the Budock Vean Hotel. After 1m turn left across a bridge, then ascend and descend to Porth Navas. Continue to Constantine and ascend through the village. Turn left, following the sign to *Gweek*, and after 1m turn right. After ½m join the B3291 to reach Gweek. Take the *Helston* road from here and proceed for 1¾m. Approach a T-junction and turn right on to the B3293, then after ½m turn right again to join the A3083. Pass the Culdrose Royal Naval Air Station, then within another 1¾m turn left, signposted *Penzance*; continue through Helston on the Penzance road and follow signs to *Porthleven* to leave by the B3304. Continue to Porthleven harbour and turn right then right again, following Penzance signposts. Within 1¼m turn left on to the A394 and after 1m turn right on to an unclassified road signposted Carleen and Godolphin. Enter *Breage*, approach a T-junction and turn left, then continue through Trew and Carleen to Godolphin. Meet crossroads and continue for ¾m before passing Godolphin Manor on the left. After ½m bear right over a bridge, and at Townshend cross the main road with *Hayle* signposts. Within 1¾m turn left on to the B3302, pass through St Erth Praze, and continue to Hayle. Turn right on to the A30 and in 1½m approach traffic signals and turn left on to the B3301, signposted *Portreath*. Continue through grass-covered sand dunes known as The Towans, and proceed to Gwithian. Drive parallel to the coast before descending into Portreath, then leave the latter on the B3300 Redruth road. After 2m pass the Tolgus Tin Company on the right. Continue through *Redruth* with Falmouth signposts, and leave by the A393. Continue through Lanner and Ponsanooth, then join the A39 and pass through *Penryn* on the return to Falmouth.

North Coast and the Moor Edge
From Newquay
Drive 2   43 miles

Take the A392 *Bodmin* road out of *Newquay*, and within ¾m approach traffic signals and turn left on to the B3276, signposted *Padstow*. Continue through St Columb Porth and ascend; after 1m descend through a hairpin bend to Watergate Bay. Keep forward and ascend, then in 1m bear left. Descend through another hairpin bend to *Mawgan Porth*, then ascend steeply to Trenance. Within 2¼m approach a T-junction and turn left. In ½m turn left again, then descend to Porthcothan Bay. After 1m turn left and continue to St Merryn, then drive on to the Farmers Arms public house and turn left on to an unclassified road signposted *Harlyn*. After a further 1m turn right for Harlyn Bay, and in another 1m turn left to rejoin the B3276 for Windmill. After ¾m descend into Padstow; leave by the A389 *Wadebridge* road, and within 2¼m turn left for Little Petherick. Continue through St Issey, approach a T-junction within 2m, and turn left on to the A39 for Wadebridge. Cross the Camel River bridge and turn right on to the A389, signposted Bodmin. Follow the road through Sladesbridge, recrossing the Camel River at Dunmere Bridge, and proceed to the outskirts of Bodmin. Ascend 1 in 8 gradients with *Redruth* and *St Austell* signposts, then in ¼m turn right again on to an unclassified road signposted Nanstallon. Within ¾m bear left, signposted Ruthern, and on meeting crossroads drive straight on to reach Ruthernbridge. Turn left with Withiel signposts and after ¾m turn right before proceeding to Withiel. Drive to the church and turn left with Roche signposts. Ascend, then after ½m approach crossroads and turn right. Follow St Columb signposts, and within 3m join the B3274, signposted Padstow. After 1¼m turn left on to an unclassified road signposted St Columb. On reaching the main road turn left on to the A39 for *St Columb Major*; continue beyond the latter and turn right on to the A3059, signposted Newquay. Within 5½m turn right on to the A392 and return to Newquay.

Placenames in *italic* type are worth stopping at; each is listed and described in the main gazetteer section of the book

CORNWALL

South Coast Bays

From Truro

Drive 4 79 miles

Leave *Truro* by the A39, following *Bodmin* signposts. Continue to Tresillian Creek and after 1m branch left to continue through Ladock and New Mills. Within 3½m turn right on to the A30 and enter Fraddon. Drive beyond Indian Queens and cross open country to reach Bodmin. Follow Lostwithiel signposts to leave Bodmin by the B3268, and after 2m pass the entrance to Lanhydrock Park on the left. Continue to Sweetshouse and turn right on to the B3269, signposted *St Austell*. After 1¾m turn right on to the A390 and continue to *St Blazey*. Go over a level crossing, then while still in the village turn left on to the A3082, signposted *Fowey*. Continue through an industrial area and skirt *Par* before proceeding with St Austell signposts. Within 2m approach a T-junction and turn left on to the A390. After 1½m meet a roundabout and take the second exit to skirt St Austell. Continue to the next roundabout and turn left on to the B3273, signposted *Mevagissey*. Continue through Pentewan to Mevagissey, then return along the B3273 for 1m before turning left on to an unclassified road signposted Gorran. Within 1¼m turn left again and continue to Gorran; in a further ¼m keep left, then turn right and take the next turning right to *Gorran Haven*. Return for 1m, approach a T-junction, then turn left with *Caerhays* signposts. Within 250yds turn left again to follow a byroad to Caerhays Beach. Ascend 1 in 5 gradients to reach St Michael's Caerhays Church, then in ¾m take the second turning left, signposted *St Mawes* and *Veryan*. Take the next left turn on to another byroad, then after 1¼m keep left. In ¾m approach a T-junction and turn right, signposted Truro. Approach the main road and turn left on to the A3078 St Mawes road, passing through Ruan High Lanes to Trewithian. Continue to *St Just in Roseland* and in 1m turn right into Upper Castle Road, signposted 'St Mawes via Castle'. Descend past the castle and enter St Mawes. Follow the road round the harbour and return to St Just in Roseland. Branch left on to the B3289 and take the ferry across the River Fal. Ascend a 1 in 5 hill and after 1m approach crossroads and turn right. Within 1¼m approach a T-junction and turn right again on to the A39. Return to Truro.

DRIVE 4

CORNWALL

Bude Bay and Bodmin Moor

From Wadebridge

Drive 5   81 miles

Follow *Bude* signposts to leave *Wadebridge* on the A39, and in ½m turn left on to the B3314, signposted *Port Isaac*. Within 3m turn left on to an unclassified road signposted *Rock*, and in another 1½m meet a T-junction and turn left. In ¼m turn right to reach Trebetherick and *Polzeath*. From Polzeath ascend a 1 in 7 hill and in 2m branch left, signposted Port Isaac. Within ½m turn left on to the B3314 for *St Endellion*. After a further 1m turn left on to the B3267 and proceed to Port Isaac. Continue with the unclassified road and descend to Port Gaverne. Follow the road inland and after 2m turn left to rejoin the B3314. Proceed to *Delabole*, and after 1¾m turn left on to an unclassified road signposted *Tintagel*. Within ½m keep forward to join the B3263 and drive into Tintagel. Approach the Wharncliffe Hotel and take the *Boscastle* road through Trethevy. Within 1¾m turn left and follow Bude signposts. Descend through a hairpin bend to Boscastle, then cross the river bridge and ascend a 1 in 6 hill. Within 2¾m join the A39 and turn immediately left on to an unclassified road signposted *Crackington Haven*. Descend steeply into Crackington Haven, then continue for 3m to Wainhouse Corner. Turn left here on to the A39. Continue, and in 1¼m past Treskinnick Cross turn left on to an unclassified road signposted Widemouth. After another ¾m follow the sweep of Widemouth Bay and enter Bude. Turn inland and follow *Bideford* signposts on to the A3072. Continue for about 1¼m and turn left on to the A39. Within another ¼m turn right to rejoin the A3072, signposted Holsworthy, and enter *Stratton*. After another 2½m approach crossroads and turn right on to the B3254, signposted *Launceston*. Continue to Whitstone and after ½m turn right on to an unclassified road signposted Week St Mary. Within 1¼m drive over crossroads and follow Canworthy Water signposts. Continue along a narrow byroad for 2m before turning right and continuing to Canworthy Water. Keep forward and within 1m ascend to Warbstow. Drive on to Hallworthy, turn right on to the A395, and in another 2¾m turn left on to the A39 with Wadebridge signposts. Return to Wadebridge via *Camelford*, *Helstone*, and *St Kew Highway*.

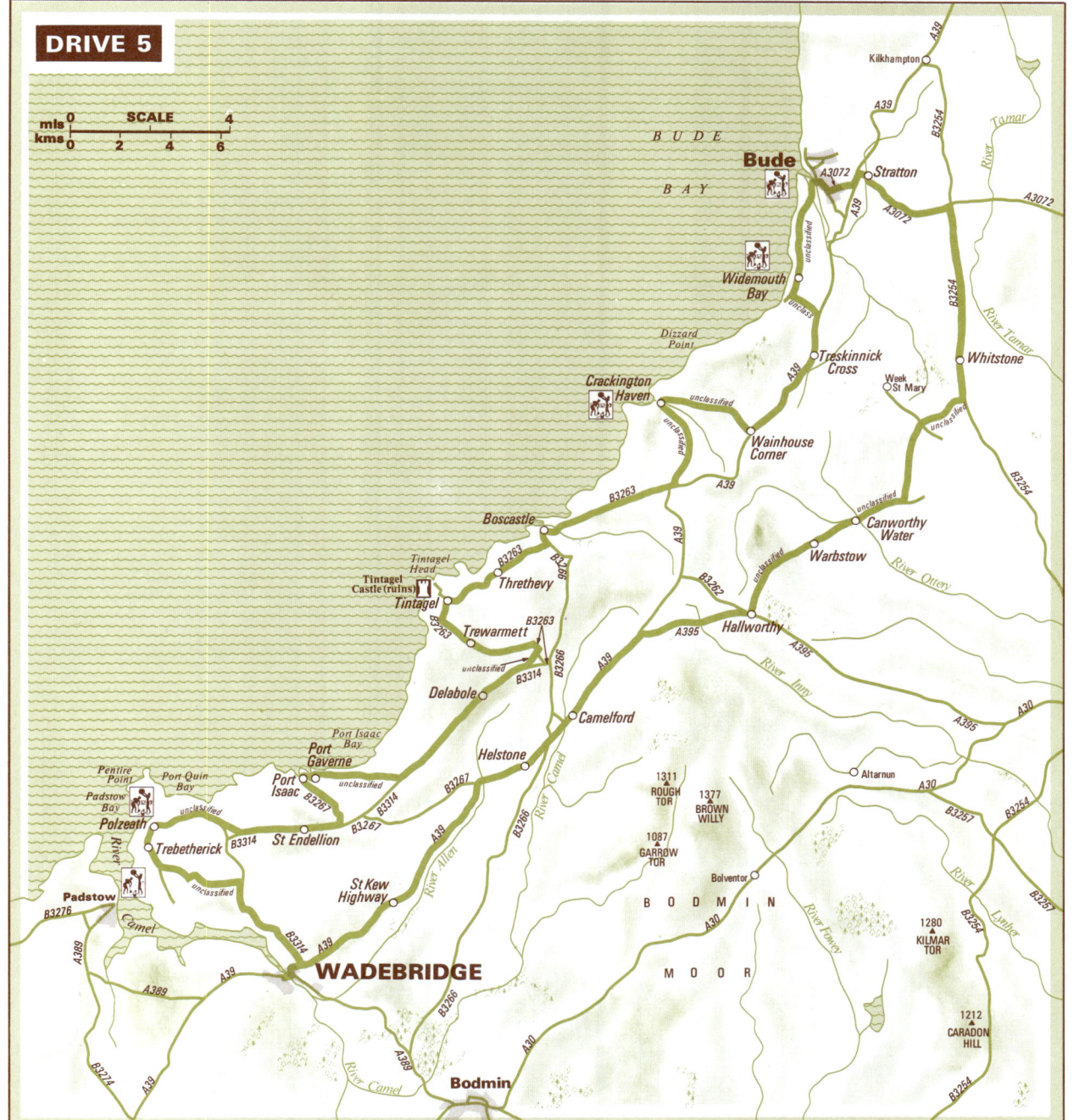

Placenames in *italic* type are worth stopping at; each is listed and described in the main gazetteer section of the book

CORNWALL

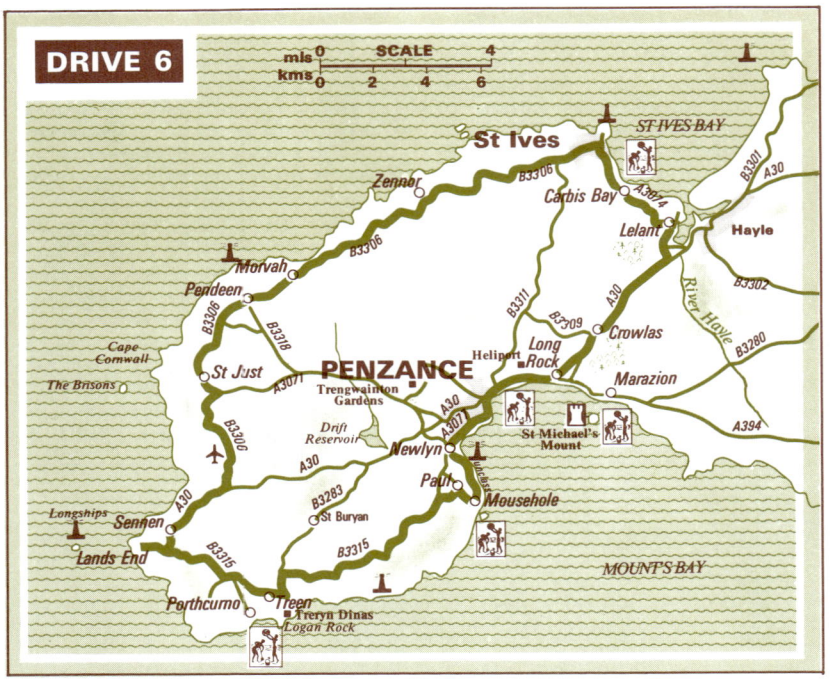

Round Mount's Bay and Land's End
From Penzance
Drive 6 43 miles

From *Penzance* follow *Newlyn* and *Mousehole* signposts to leave by the A3077. Drive alongside the harbour and proceed to Newlyn. Cross a bridge and turn left on to an unclassified road which follows the coast to Mousehole; turn left, and at the harbour turn right and right again, signposted *Paul*. Ascend to the village, pass the church, and turn left. Within ½m meet a T-junction and turn left on to the B3315. After 5m turn left and descend round a hairpin bend before ascending to reach the edge of *Treen*. Remain on the B3315 and after ¾m pass the turning for *Porthcurno*. Continue with the *Land's End* road and in ½m turn right. Within 2¼m turn left on to the A30 to reach Land's End. Return along this road and continue to *Sennen*, then after 1¾m turn left on to the B3306, signposted *St Just*. Within 3m turn left again on to the A3071, then enter St Just. Leave this town on the B3306 and proceed to *Pendeen*. Continue through Morvah and skirt *Zennor* before reaching *St Ives*. Follow *Hayle* signposts to leave St Ives on the A3074. Continue to *Lelant*, turn right, and in ½m keep forward with Penzance signposts. On reaching the A30 turn right to Crowlas. Return to Penzance by way of Long Rock, passing Penzance Heliport on the right.

Woods and Villages of the South
From Bodmin
Drive 7 84 miles

Follow Lostwithiel signposts to leave *Bodmin* by the B3268. After 2m pass the entrance to Lanhydrock Park on the left. Continue to Sweetshouse and keep left for Lostwithiel. Leave the latter by the A390 *St Austell* road, and ascend. Within 1½m turn left on to the B3269, signposted *Fowey*, and after 4½m join the A3082 for the descent into Fowey. Take the car ferry across the River Fowey to *Bodinnick*, then on leaving the ferry turn left and ascend along an unclassified road. Turn inland to pass through Lanteglos Highway, then after 3¾m turn right on to the B3359 to Pelynt. Within 1½m turn right, signposted *Polperro*, then right again on to the A387 to reach Polperro. Return along the A387 to Looe; cross the Looe River bridge and turn left, following *Plymouth* signposts. Within ½m ascend, and on reaching the top of the climb branch right on to the B3253. Within 3¾m rejoin the A387 and continue to the outskirts of Hessenford. Turn right on to the B3247 to *Seaton*, then cross a bridge and continue to Downderry. Drive to the end of the village and ascend (hairpin bend); after 1¾m turn right, following Crafthole signposts. Keep forward at the latter and follow Millbrook signposts. Within 1¼m turn left for Antony, then turn right on to the A374 and continue for 1¾m before passing the entrance to Antony House (NT). Proceed to *Torpoint* and take the car ferry across the River Tamar to *Devonport*. Follow 'City Centre' signposts to enter Plymouth, then leave Plymouth on the A388 by following *Saltash* signposts. Join the A38 to cross the Tamar Bridge (toll), and re-enter Cornwall at Saltash. Approach a roundabout and follow *Liskeard* signposts. Continue through Landrake to Tideford. Beyond this village turn left on to the B3249 for *St Germans*. Pass under the railway bridge and remain on the B3249 to Polbathic. Turn right on to the A374, and at the Trerule Foot Roundabout join the A38 Bodmin road. Remain on the A38 through Liskeard and Dobwalls, and continue through the Fowey Valley before returning to Bodmin.

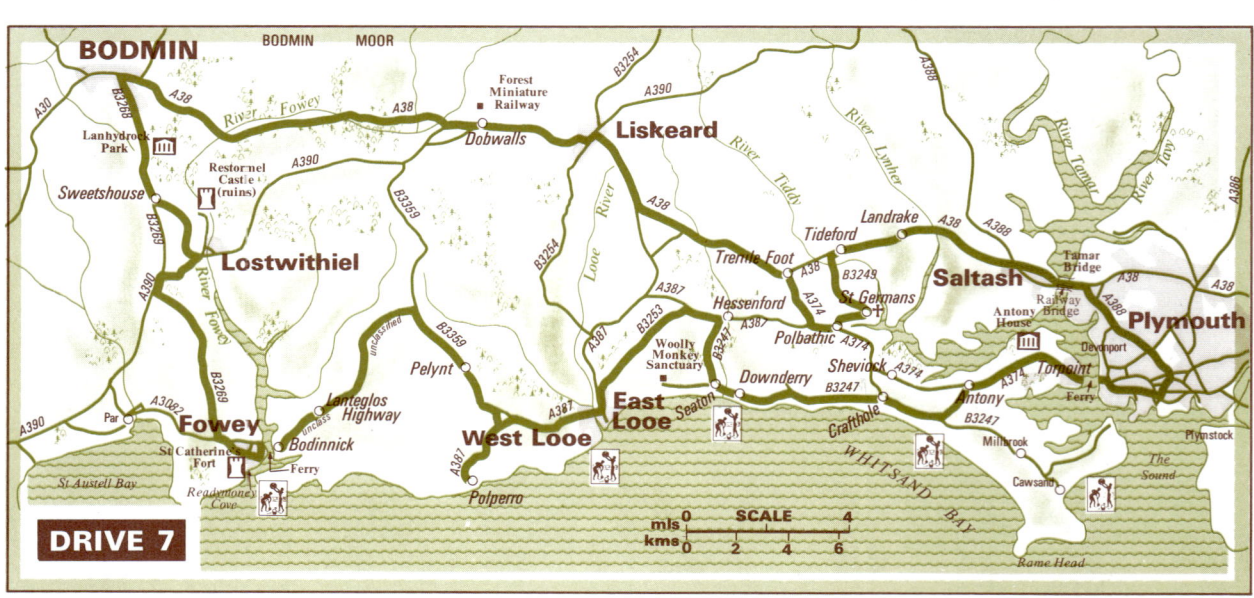

38

South Devon

Torbay and Castles

From Torquay

Drive 8   40 miles

Leave *Torquay* on the A379 and follow the shoreline. Enter *Paignton* and turn left into a one-way street to follow *Dartmouth* signposts along the sea front. Continue to the end of Paignton Sands and turn inland away from Roundham Head. Turn left to cross the railway and then left again on to the A379. Pass Goodrington Sands to the left before skirting Goodrington; continue through Churston and keep forward on the A3022 for *Brixham*. Leave the latter by the B3205 Dartmouth/Kingswear road, and make a long gradual ascent to the A379. Turn left and keep left on to the B3205, signposted 'Dartmouth via Kingswear', and pass Kingswear station on the right. Take the car ferry to Dartmouth and follow Higher Ferry signposts along the quay. Turn left on to the A379 *Totnes* road and climb steeply. At the top of the ascent continue forward on to the B3207, and within 2½m reach crossroads by the Sportsman's Arms public house and bear left. After 3½m continue forward with a signpost marked 'Light Traffic'. Descend to Halwell, turn right on to the A381, and proceed through Harbertonford. Descend in 3¼m and turn right on to the A385 *Torbay* road. Drive into Totnes and turn left with the town centre to the right. Cross the River Dart for the ascent out of town, and in 1m turn left on to the unclassified Berry Pomeroy road. Keep forward with signposts indicating Berry Castle, and within ½m beyond the village bear left for the entrance to *Berry Pomeroy Castle*. Within ¼m turn sharp right with Collaton/Paignton signposts, and at the next crossroads turn left on to the Marldon road. Continue for about 1¾m and drive through Marldon before turning left on to the A3022; turn immediately left again on to an unclassified road signposted Compton Castle. Proceed forward through Compton for Compton Castle, then return to the A3022 and turn sharp left on to the ring road. After a while descend through Shiphay and continue to Torre. Turn right here on to the A380 and return to Torquay.

Plym Forest and the Tors

From Plymouth

Drive 9   47 miles

Follow *Exeter* signposts to *Plympton* roundabout from *Plymouth* city centre (or the A38 Tamar Bridge road). Take the Plympton exit along an unclassified road, and within ½m pass an entrance to Saltram House on the right. Within another ½m turn left on to the Exeter road. Continue forward with Cornwood signposts and in ½m turn left under a railway bridge. Stay with this road through Sparkwell and Lutton to the Yealm-Valley village of Cornwood. Approach crossroads and turn left on to the *Tavistock* road, then make the gentle ascent on to Lee Moor at the edge of *Dartmoor*. Follow the long descent, cross the River Plym at Cadover Bridge, then ascend and turn right for *Meavy*. Drive to the edge of the village and go forward with *Princetown* signposts; within ½m turn right for Burrator reservoir, lying between 1,312ft Sharpitor and 1,150ft Sheeps Tor. Within ½m bear left, signposted Princetown, and in ¾m approach crossroads and turn right on to the B3212. Climb over wild moorland and enter Princetown, then turn left on to the B3357 Tavistock road. Pass the prison on the right and in 1½m turn left on to the A384. Descend from the moor and pass Merrivale quarry in the Walkham Valley before continuing into Tavistock. From Tavistock follow signposts marked Plymouth A386, and after 3½m cross the River Walkham before passing Horrabridge. Approach *Yelverton* roundabout and take the second major exit; within 100yds turn right on to the unclassified Buckland Abbey road. Continue to Crapstone and go forward for about 1m to crossroads. Turn left with Plymouth signposts, then right for the entrance to Buckland Abbey. In ¾m bear right on an ascent and cross Roborough Down. Turn right on to the A386 for the return to Plymouth.

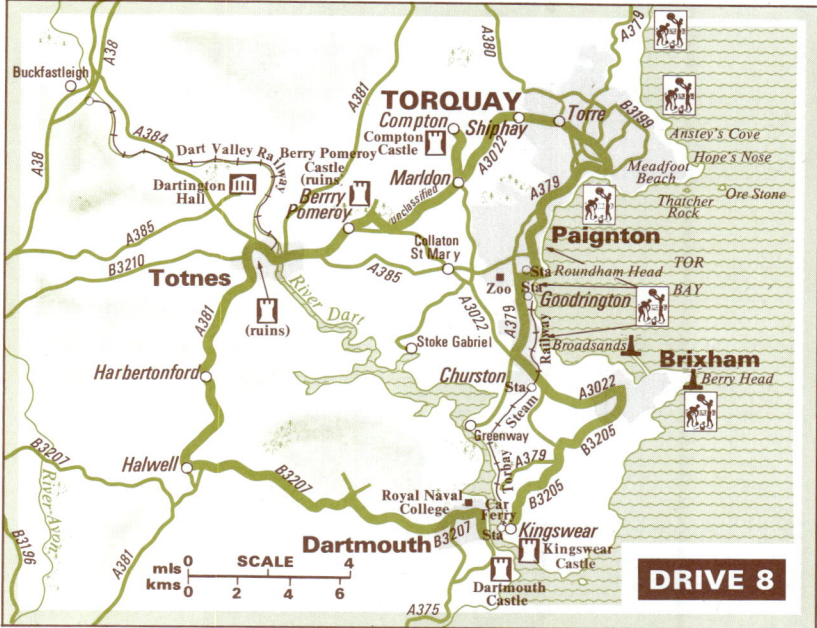

Placenames in *italic* type are worth stopping at; each is listed and described in the main gazetteer section of the book

SOUTH DEVON

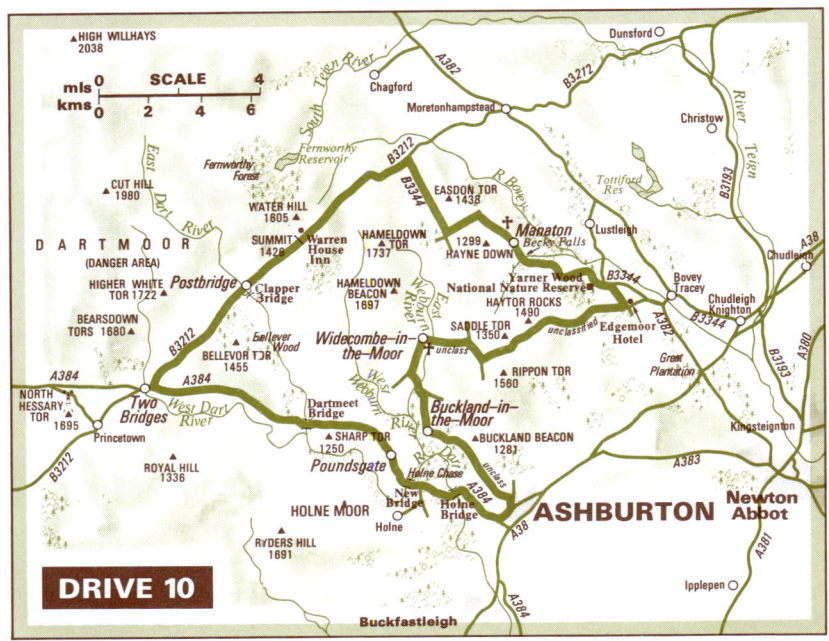

South Eastern Dartmoor
From Ashburton
Drive 10   42 miles

Follow the unclassified Buckland road from *Ashburton* town centre and pass below the slopes of 1,282ft Buckland Beacon. Continue to Buckland-in-the-Moor and follow the Webburn Valley for Widecombe. Approach *Widecombe-in-the-Moor* along narrow and sometimes steep roads, brushing the edge of *Dartmoor*. Leave by the *Bovey Tracey* road and ascend steeply on to open moorland. Pass 1,560ft Ripon Tor on the right, and 1,350ft Saddle Tor and 1,490ft Haytor Rocks on the left. Descend to the Bovey Valley and after 3m approach crossroads by the Edgemoor Hotel. Turn left with Becka Falls/*Manaton* signposts, and in ½m keep straight on for the B3344. Pass the Yarner Wood national nature reserve on the left, and climb the open slopes of Trendlebere Down. Proceed through woodland and past Becky Falls, then continue on the *Moretonhampstead* road to pass through Manaton. Turn left ¾m beyond the church and in 1m turn right. Within 1¾m pass the road from *North Bovey* and after ¾m turn left on to the B3212 *Princetown/Tavistock* road. Ascend to open moorland with high ground leading to 1,737ft Hameldown Tor to the left. Continue to the road's highest point (1,426ft near Warren House Inn) and pass through *Postbridge* before crossing the East Dart River. Drive to the edge of *Two Bridges* and turn left on to the A384 Ashburton road. Follow the line of the West Dart River and descend steeply into Dartmeet Bridge, where the two rivers join. Climb a long winding ascent (1 in 5) to the vicinity of 1,250ft Sharp Tor and continue to Poundsgate. Follow a winding descent from here and cross the River Dart at New Bridge before continuing through the woods of *Holne* Chase. Recross the Dart by Holne Bridge and re-enter Ashburton.

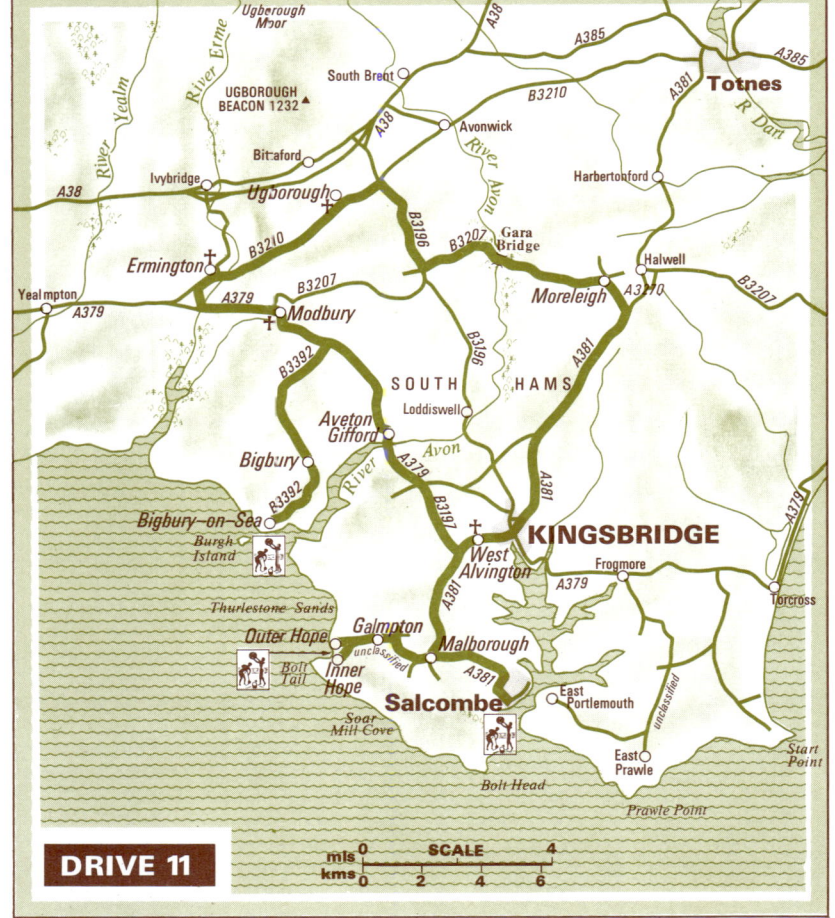

The Hills of South Hams
From Kingsbridge
Drive 11   56 miles

Follow the A381 *Salcombe* road from *Kingsbridge*, and pass through West Alvington and Malborough to Salcombe. On entering the latter bear left to take the town centre road and avoid the quayside one-way system. Return along the A381 to Malborough; approach crossroads and drive forward on to the unclassified *Hope Cove* road. Pass a church and bear right through Galmpton to Hope Cove. Return to Malborough and turn left on to the A381 Kingsbridge road. After 2¼m turn left on to the B3197 *Modbury/Plymouth* road, and in another 1¾m approach crossroads and go forward on to the A379. Descend sharply and cross the River Avon at Aveton Gifford. Within 2½m turn left on to the B3392 Bigbury road, and continue through Bigbury to the modern resort of *Bigbury-on-Sea*. Go back to the A379 and turn left for Modbury. Proceed for 1½m beyond the town and cross the little River Erme before turning right, then right again, on to the B3210 *Totnes* road. Follow the Erme Valley past the edge of Ermington, and in 3m keep forward with the massive tower of Ugborough church to the left. After a further 1m approach crossroads and turn right on to the B3196 Kingsbridge road. Continue through hilly country for 2½m and turn left on to the B3207 *Dartmouth* road. Within 1¾m descend and cross the River Avon at Gara Bridge. Drive on to Moreleigh, bear right, and within ¾m turn right on to the A381 for the return to Kingsbridge.

SOUTH DEVON

Dunes and the Haldon Hills

From Exeter

Drive 12   53 miles

Leave *Exeter* city centre by following signposts marked *'Exmouth* A377', and within 2m approach the Countess Wear roundabout and take the third exit on to the A38 ring road. Cross the Exe and Exeter Canal and continue to the next roundabout; take the first exit on to the A379, signposted *Dawlish.* Pass through Exminster and within 3m enter *Kenton.* Drive to the far end of the village and pass the entrance to Powderham Castle on the left before continuing forward to the shores of the Exe estuary. Drive through Starcross and follow the railway for ½m to crossroads. Turn left on to the unclassified Dawlish Warren road, then left again and proceed through the village of the same name. Within ¾m turn left to rejoin the A379 for Dawlish. Ascend from Dawlish and enter *Teignmouth.* Continue along the *Torquay* road, and on reaching traffic signals at the end of the town cross the long river bridge into *Shaldon.* Climb to the cliff tops and within 2½m pass a left turning leading to Maidencombe Cove. After a further 2½m turn left into Westhill road (B3198 signposted *Babbacombe*), and within another ½m approach traffic signals and turn left into Manor Road for Babbacombe. Leave by driving towards Torquay along the B3199 Babbacombe road, and within 1m pass a left turning leading to Anstey's Cove and Redgate Beach. In another ½m reach Wellswood church and turn sharp left into unclassified Ilsham Road, signposted Kent's Cavern. Pass the entrance to Kent's Cavern and in ¼m pass a left turn leading from Anstey's Cove. Continue beyond this and bear left into Ilsham Marine Drive for a coastal run past Hope's Nose Point. Descend and turn left with signposts marked The Town, and pass Meadfoot Beach before ascending again. Approach crossroads at the top of a short rise after ¾m and turn left into Park Hill road. Descend, then keep forward down Beacon Hill and continue to Torquay Harbour. First follow 'Town Centre', then 'Newton Abbot A380' signposts out of Torquay, negotiating extensive one-way systems. Pass through Kingskerwell, and on entering Newton Abbot turn right with Exeter signposts. Drive into *Kingsteignton* and turn left on to the B3193 Chudleigh road to pass through a clay-extraction area. After 3m cross the A38 and River Teign. Approach a T-junction and turn right, and within another ½m bear right for Chudleigh. Continue to the war memorial and branch left on to an unclassified and unsignposted road, then keep right into Old Exeter Street. In 1m approach crossroads and drive forward with Whiteway/Exeter signposts. Climb through woodland to the summit of the Great Haldon Hills, and at the crossroads turn left with signposts marked *Dunchideock/Ide.* Follow a high ridge and after 1m pass the Lawrence Castle folly tower. After another ½m bear right and descend to Ide, then continue to the war memorial and bear left. Cross a narrow bridge and bear right then left on the ascent. Approach crossroads and turn right on to the A30 for Exeter.

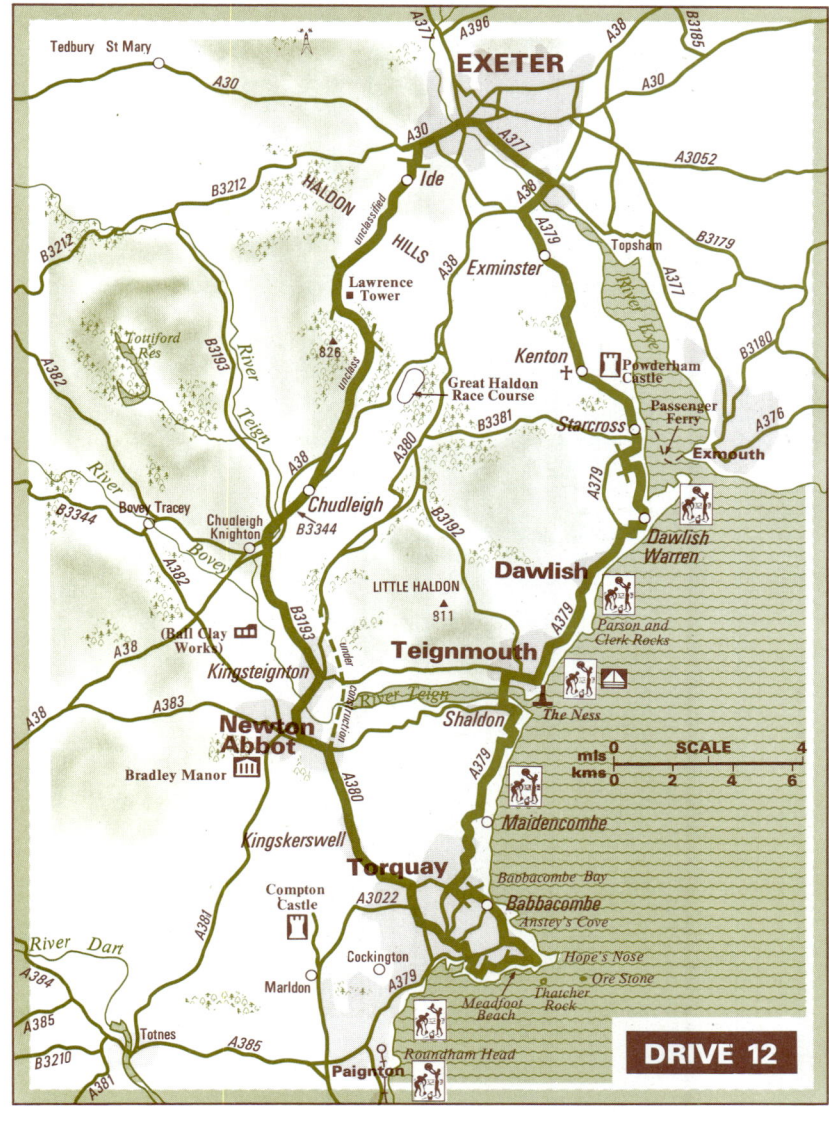

Placenames in *italic* type are worth stopping at; each is listed and described in the main gazetteer section of the book

North Devon and Exmoor

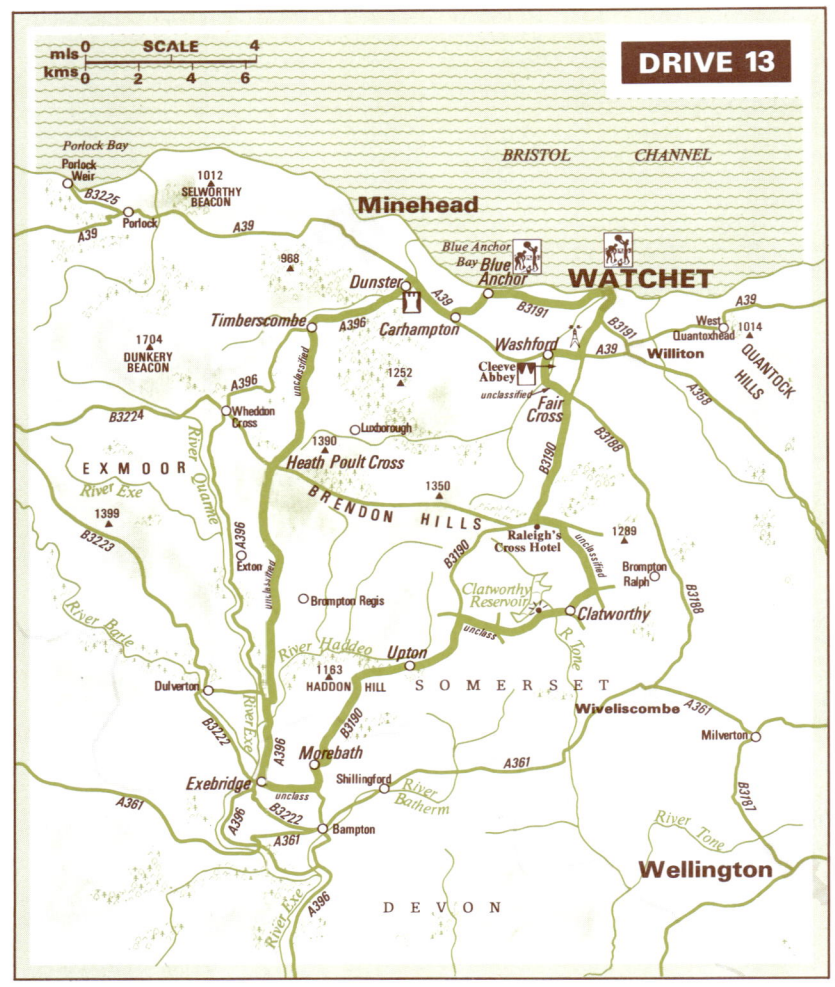

Through the Brendon Hills
From Watchet
Drive 13 44 miles

Take the B3191 from *Watchet* and drive to Blue Anchor. Continue to *Carhampton*, then turn right on to the A39 *Minehead* road and proceed for 1½m before turning left on to the A396, signposted *Tiverton*. Enter *Dunster* and continue along the main road to *Timberscombe*. Approach the Lion Inn and turn left on to an unclassified road following Luxborough and Brompton Regis signposts. Ascend with the Brendon Hills to the left and *Exmoor* to the right. Continue to Heath Poult Cross, approach crossroads, then drive straight across on to the *Dulverton* road. Proceed for 6m with the valley of the River Exe to the right. After descending into the valley turn left on to the A396, signposted *Tiverton*. Proceed to Exbridge and turn left on to an unclassified road signposted Morebath. Approach a T-junction after 1½m and turn left on to the B3190 *Watchet* road. Continue through Morebath to Upton, then within 3m reach crossroads and turn right on to an unclassified road signposted Wiveliscombe. After 1m branch left and approach crossroads; drive straight on with Clatworthy signposts and skirt Clatworthy Reservoir before passing the entrance to the viewing area and car park. Continue to Clatworthy, follow Brompton Ralph signposts through the village, then approach crossroads 1m beyond the latter and turn left with Raleighs Cross signposts. After a further 2m approach a T-junction and turn left. Continue to Raleighs Cross Hotel and turn right on to the B3190, signposted Watchet. Cross high ground, then descend steeply and continue for 3½m before meeting more crossroads and turning left.

continued on page 43

The Doone Country
From Lynmouth
Drive 14 31 miles

Follow the A39 *Barnstaple* road to leave *Lynmouth*, then pass through Watersmeet. After ½m turn left on to the B3223 and follow *Simonsbath* signposts before crossing Hillsford Bridge. Within ¾m negotiate a hairpin bend, then drive forward on to an unclassified road signposted Brendon Valley. Pass *Brendon* church on the left and descend to Brendon; drive on through Malmsmead and cross a river bridge. Proceed to *Oare* church; continue with this road, signposted Oareford, and in 1½m cross the river at Robbers Bridge. Climb steeply and bear right to join the A39. Descend 1 in 4 Porlock Hill into *Porlock*, then return along the Lynmouth road. Immediately branch right on to an unclassified road signposted 'Alternative Route Via Toll Road'. Climb gradually through woods to open moorland and on approaching a main road turn right on to the A39. Pass County Gate on the county border. After 2½m begin the long drive down Countisbury Hill, then continue into Lynmouth.

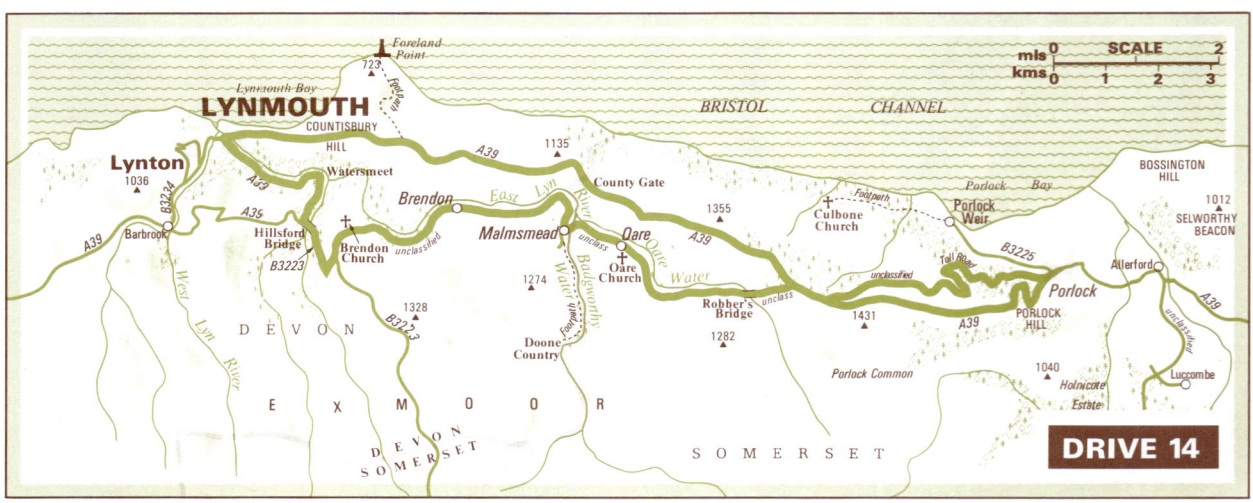

NORTH DEVON AND EXMOOR

Drive 13 continued

Proceed along the unclassified road signposted Washford, and after 1m pass the entrance to *Cleeve Abbey*. Continue into Washford and turn right on to the A39. Drive on for ¾m before turning left on to the B3190 and returning to Watchet.

Dunkery Hill and the Upper Exe

From Minehead

Drive 15 45 miles

Leave *Minehead* on the A39 *Porlock* road and enter the *Exmoor* National Park area. After a further 2½m turn right on to an unclassified road to reach *Selworthy*; return along this road and turn right on to the A39, skirt *Allerford*, and after ½m turn left on to the unclassified road signposted West Luccombe. Continue through the village, passing a pack horse bridge on the right. After 1m turn right at a crossroads and ascend Dunkery Hill. Descend for 2½m and at the main road turn right on to the B3224. After 3½m turn sharp left on to the unclassified *Winsford* road and continue alongside the River Exe on the approach to Winsford. Enter the village and turn right on to the Tarr Steps road before ascending Winsford Hill. Continue to the main road and turn left on to the B3223, signposted *Dulverton*. Descend through a wooded valley to Dulverton, then leave the village on the B3222, signposted Minehead. After 1m cross the River Exe. Meet the main road and turn left on to the A396. Proceed through the valleys of the Exe and Quarme, then cross high ground at Wheddon Cross before descending to *Timberscombe* and *Dunster*. Continue beyond the latter village to a T-junction; turn left on to the A39 and return to Minehead.

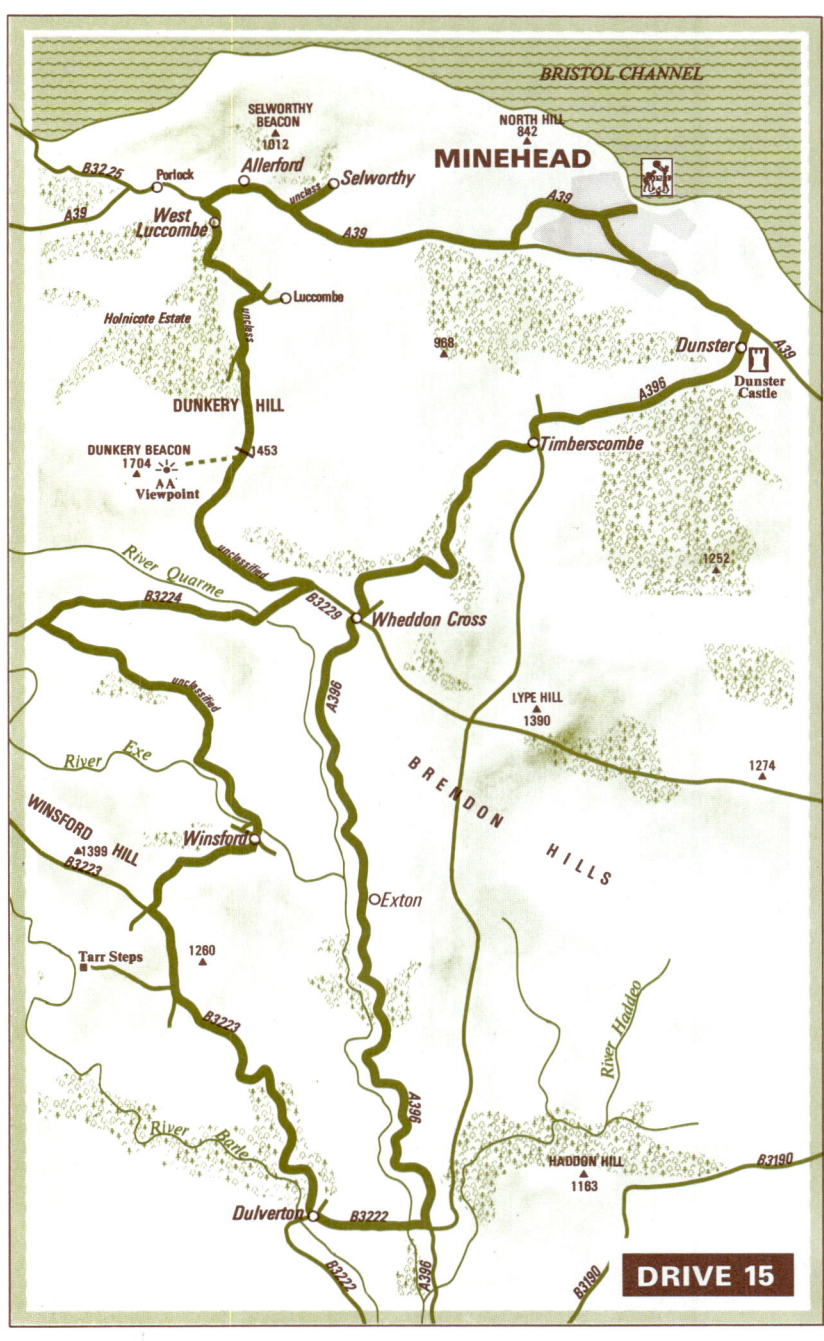

Placenames in *italic* type are worth stopping at; each is listed and described in the main gazetteer section of the book

NORTH DEVON AND EXMOOR

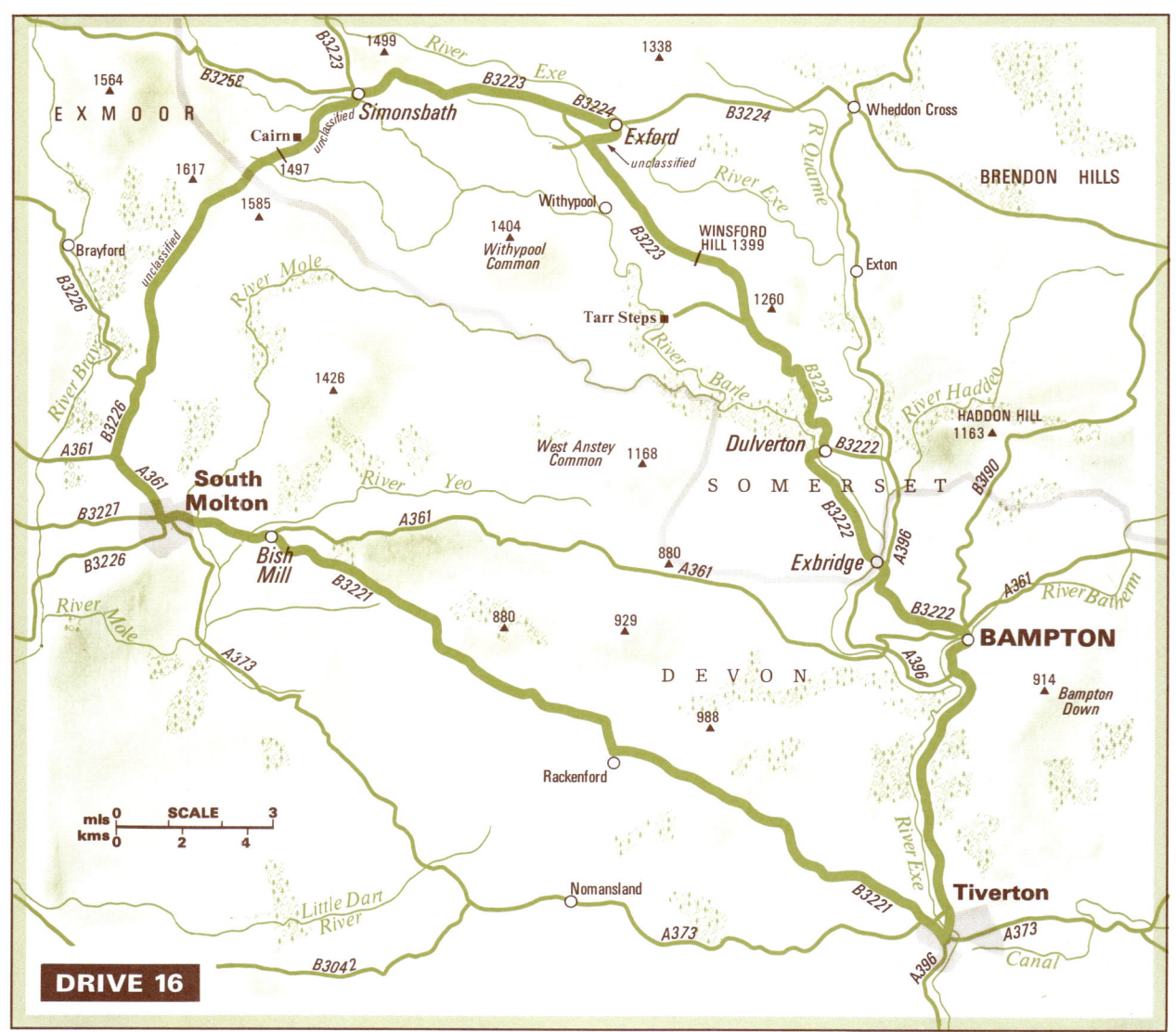

Central Exmoor and the Exe Valley

From Bampton

Drive 16   56 miles

Take the B3222 out of *Bampton,* signposted *Dulverton,* and cross high ground into Exbridge before joining the A396. Immediately turn left to rejoin the B3222, cross the River Exe, and proceed to Dulverton. Turn left on to the B3223 *Lynton* road and drive to the summit of *Winsford* Hill. Continue for 3½m then approach crossroads and turn right on to an unclassified road. Descend to *Exford,* then follow the B3224 Lynton road for 1m before rejoining the B3223. Proceed to *Simonsbath,* turn left on to an unclassified road, and follow *South Molton* signposts. Climb to nearly 1,500ft before continuing forward and joining the B3226. After another 1½m join the A361 and proceed to South Molton. Leave South Molton on the A361 Bampton/*Taunton* road, and after 1½m enter Bish Mill. Branch right on to the B3221 and drive to *Tiverton.* From here turn on to the A396 Bampton road and drive through the Exe Valley before reaching Bampton.

NORTH DEVON AND EXMOOR

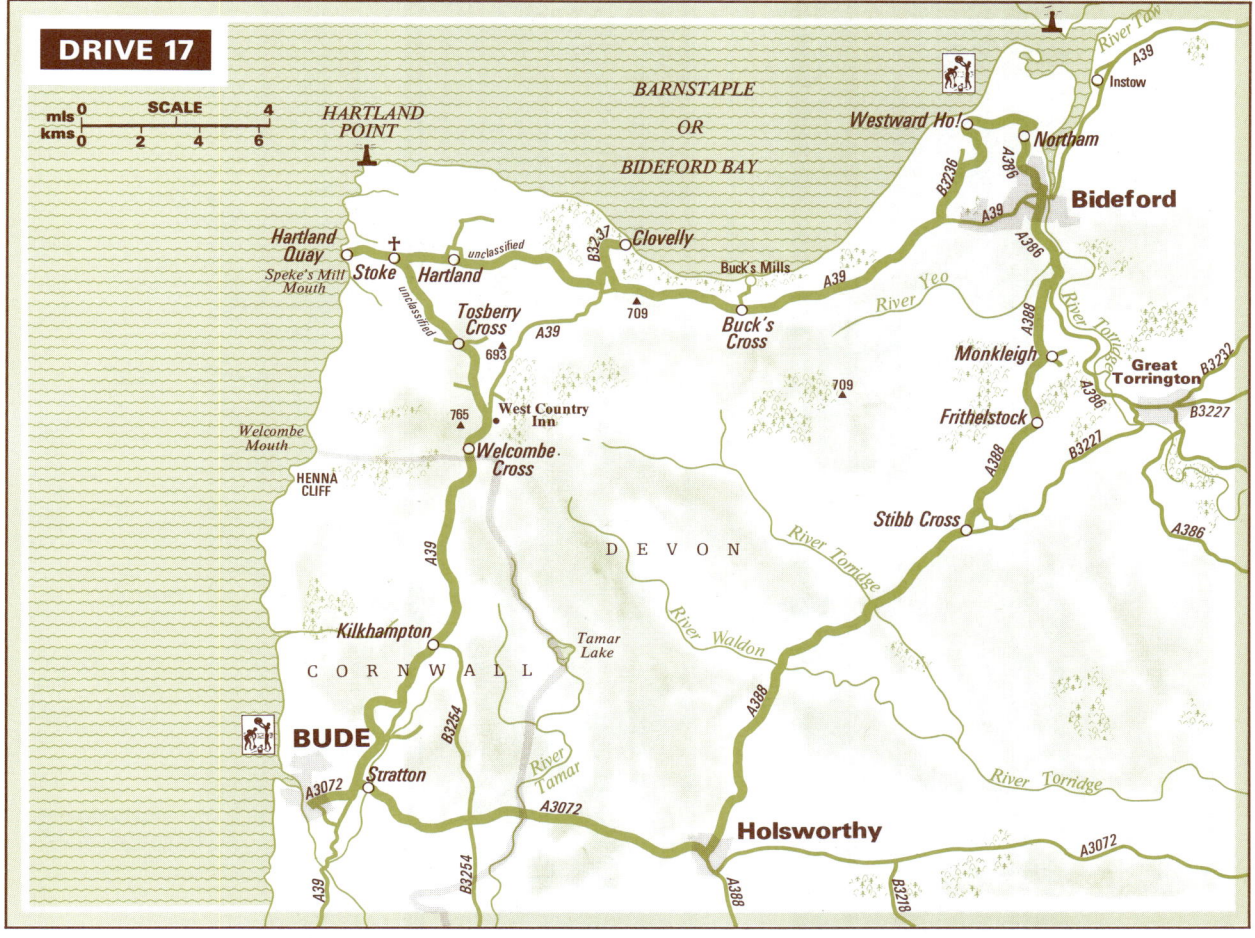

Devon's Atlantic Shore

From Bude

Drive 17   68 miles

Leave *Bude* by the A3072 *Bideford* road. After 1¼m turn left on to the A39 and skirt Stratton. Continue to *Kilkhampton* and after 5m pass over the border into Devon. Proceed to *Welcombe* Cross; 1m north of the cross pass the West Country Inn and branch left on to the unclassified road signposted Stoke. Cross a short stretch of moorland and continue to Tosberry Cross. Bear left then right and proceed to Stoke village. After ½m descend to *Hartland* Quay. Return to Stoke, follow the road signposted Hartland and Bideford, and proceed to the village of Hartland. Leave the latter on the Bideford/*Clovelly* road and continue for 3m. Turn left, then after ½m turn left again on to the B3237 to reach the car park for Clovelly. Return along the B3237 and within 1¼m turn left on to the A39 Bideford road. Stay with the A39 for 5m, then turn left on to the B3236 and continue to *Westward Ho!* Proceed to Northam and follow the A386 into Bideford. Continue alongside the River Torridge with *Torrington*/signposts, then after 2m turn right on to the A388, signposted Holsworthy. Drive to Holsworthy and follow Bude signposts along the A3072 to Bude.

Placenames in *italic* type are worth stopping at; each is listed and described in the main gazetteer section of the book

NORTH DEVON AND EXMOOR

Braunton Burrows and the Yeo Valley

From Barnstaple

Drive 18   40 miles

Leave *Barnstaple* along the A361 *Ilfracombe* road, and continue alongside the Taw estuary to *Braunton*. Approach traffic signals and follow the B3231 Croyde road to *Saunton*. Drive round the headland of Saunton Down to reach Croyde Bay, then continue to Georgeham. After 1½m turn left on to an unclassified road signposted 'Woolacombe/Steep Hill' and descend to *Woolacombe*. Proceed along the Esplanade and coast road to *Mortehoe* before turning inland, then after 1¾m join the B3343 before bearing left. Turn left into the B3231 Lee road and continue into Ilfracombe. Leave Ilfracombe by the A399 *Combe Martin* road and pass Watermouth Castle on the right before reaching Combe Martin. Continue on the A399 road, signposted *Lynton* and after 2m ascend to the top of a long climb. Branch right on to the B3229, signposted Kentisbury Ford. After 1¼m join the A39, signposted Barnstaple, and 1m farther pass a left turn to *Arlington* Court. Continue along the A39 for the return to Barnstaple.

Dorset and East Devon

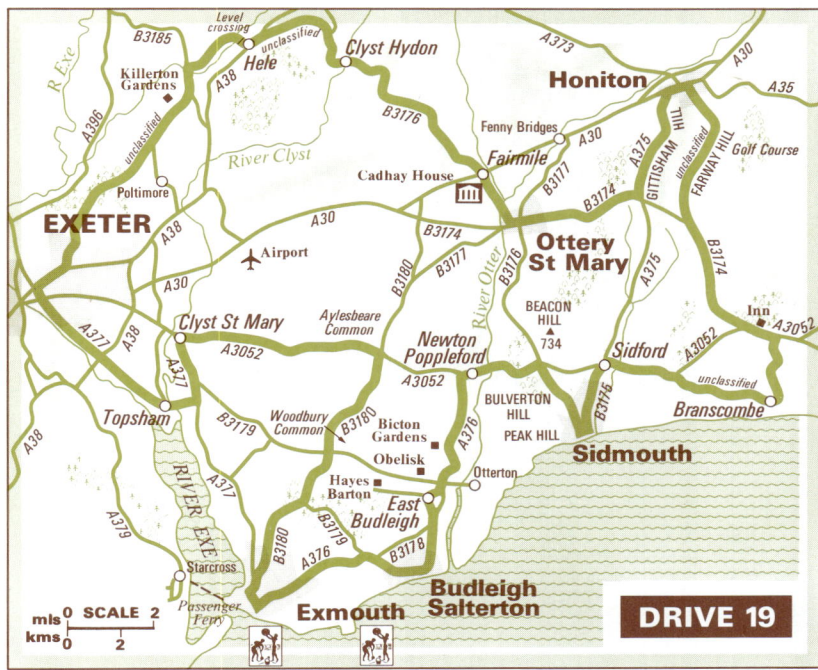

The Hills of East Devon
From Exmouth
Drive 19 73 miles

Leave *Exmouth* on the A376 for *Budleigh Salterton*. Continue with *East Budleigh* signposts for 2m, then turn left on to an unclassified road for East Budleigh. Turn right at the village church and after a short distance rejoin the A376. Continue and pass the entrance to Bicton Gardens and later turn right on to the A3052 into Newton Poppleford. Cross the Otter and ascend alongside Harpford Wood. Drive to the peak of the ascent and turn right on to the B3176, then proceed to *Sidmouth*. Drive to the sea-front and turn left, then turn left again into Fore Street to leave by the B3175. Continue to *Sidford* and turn right on to the A3052 before climbing Orleigh Hill. Cross the summit and continue for ½m before turning right on to an unclassified road for *Branscombe*. Follow signposts indicating *Beer*, and at the top of an ascent turn left, signposted *Honiton*. Within 1m turn left on to the A3052. In another ¾m pass the Three Horseshoes Inn before turning right on to the B3174, then within 3½m take the unclassified Farway road to branch right along wooded Farway Hill. In ¾m drive forward on the Honiton road, and at the golf-course turn left to descend into *Honiton*. Turn left into the High Street (the *Exeter* road), and in ¾m turn left onto the A375. Ascend *Gittisham* Hill and approach the Hare and Hounds Inn before turning right on to the B3174. Descend to *Ottery St Mary*, then leave this village on the B3176 (Hind Street) and head north-west to cross the river. Pass Cadhay House, and cross the A30 at Fairmile; continue with *Cullompton* signposts. Proceed to Clyst Hydon and drive to the end of the village before turning right. Within 1m turn left on to an unclassified road, and after 2m cross the main road into Hele. Go over a level crossing and the River Culm and turn left, then in 1½m keep forward on the B3185. Re-cross the Culm near paper mills, and in ¾m turn right on to the unclassified Killerton road. Passing Killerton Gardens and continue south-west with Poltimore signposts for 1½m. Follow signposts to Exeter, then leave by the A377 Exmouth road. Continue alongside the Exe and the Exeter Canal to *Topsham*, then cross the River Clyst; in 1m approach the St George and Dragon Hotel and turn left for Clyst St Mary. Continue by following the A3052 *Lyme Regis* road to Aylesbeare Common. At the Halfway Inn turn right on to the B3180 for the return to Exmouth.

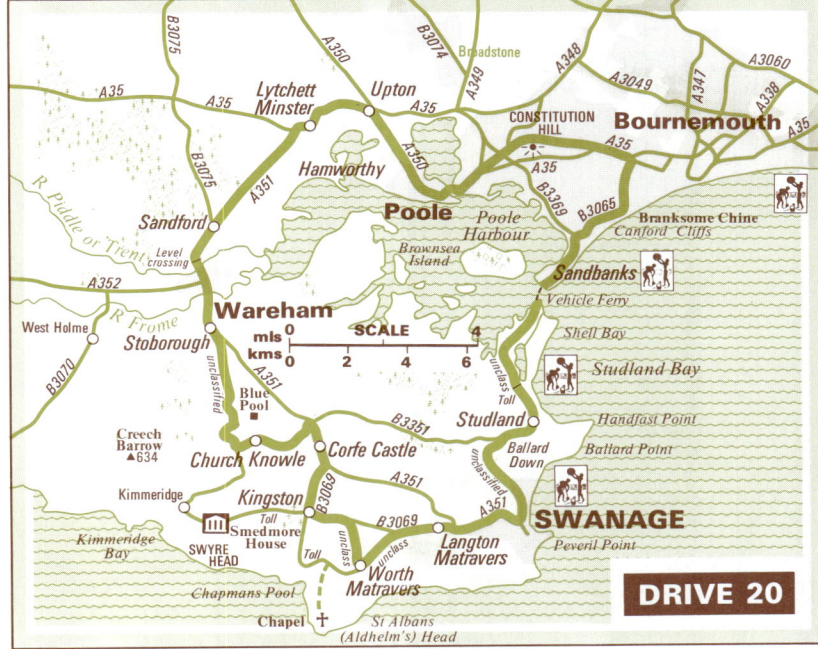

Poole Harbour and the Purbeck Hills
From Swanage
Drive 20 40 miles

Leave *Swanage* on the A351 *Wareham* road and after a short distance turn left on to the B3069 for Langton Matravers. Ascend to 400ft and turn left on to an unclassified road to *Worth Matravers*. Leave the latter on the *Kingston* road and turn left to rejoin the B3069. Continue through Kingston and descend before turning left on to the A351 into the village of *Corfe Castle*. Proceed along the Wareham road, then after a short distance turn left on to an unclassified road and skirt the castle mound to Church Knowle. Pass through Church Knowle, approach crossroads, then turn right to cross the Purbeck Hills. Rejoin the A351 at Stoborough and proceed to Wareham. Stay with the A351 *Bournemouth* road and pass through Lytchett Minster before turning right at Upton to join the A350. Continue through Hamworthy, then cross a bridge into Poole Old Town. Leave Poole town centre by the A348 *Ringwood* road. In 1m approach a roundabout and drive forward into Constitution Hill Road. Proceed through a built-up area to Bournemouth, then return along the A35 Poole road and pass through Westbourne. Turn left along Avenue Rd and continue to *Branksome* Chine. Turn inland through *Canford Cliffs*, then drive along Haven Road for the descent to Poole Harbour and *Sandbanks*. Take a short ferry trip to Shell Bay (the ticket includes a toll charge to *Studland*) and cross heathland on the unclassified road to Studland. Turn inland with the B3351, and in 1m turn left on to an unclassified road. Descend from Ballard Down to Swanage.

Placenames in *italic* type are worth stopping at; each is listed and described in the main gazetteer section of the book

DORSET AND EAST DEVON

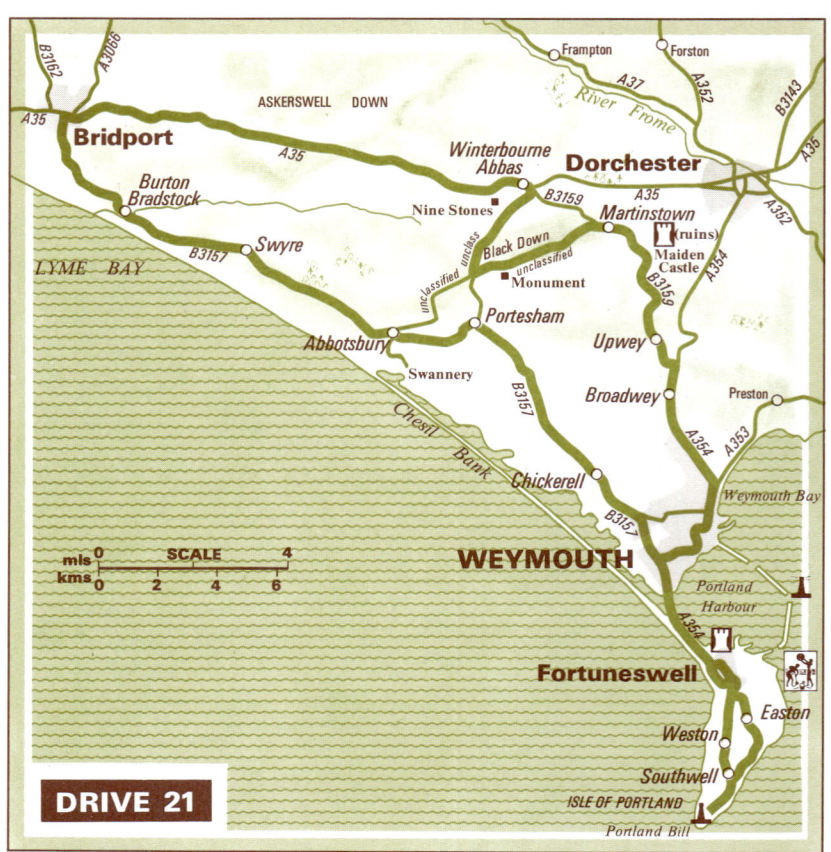

Alongside Chesil Bank

From Weymouth

Drive 21   60 miles

Follow *Portland* signposts to leave Weymouth on the A354, and after crossing the Small Mouth pass *Chesil Bank* to the right. Climb steeply through and beyond Fortuneswell (Portland) with Portland Bill signposts, then continue through Easton and past Avice's Cottage Museum in Wakeham. Continue to Southwell and approach the Eight Kings public house before turning left for Portland Bill. Return to the Eight Kings and turn left for Weston. Proceed to Southwell, and in 1½m approach a church and turn left. Ascend to the summit of Portland Hill and turn left again for the descent into Fortuneswell. Cross to the mainland and in 1m follow the B3157 *Abbotsbury* road to pass through Chickerell to *Portisham*. Continue to Abbotsbury, then drive through Swyre to *Burton Bradstock* and *Bridport*. Take the A35 *Dorchester* road from Bridport to *Winterbourne Abbas*. At the end of the latter village branch right on to the B3159 Weymouth road, then immediately turn right again on to an unclassified road signposted Hardy's Monument. Climb on to heathland before turning left for Hardy's Monument on 776ft Black Down. Descend into *Martinstown*, join the B3159 Weymouth road, and pass below prehistoric Maiden Castle. Cross downland to Upwey and continue to Broadwey; follow the A354 back to Weymouth.

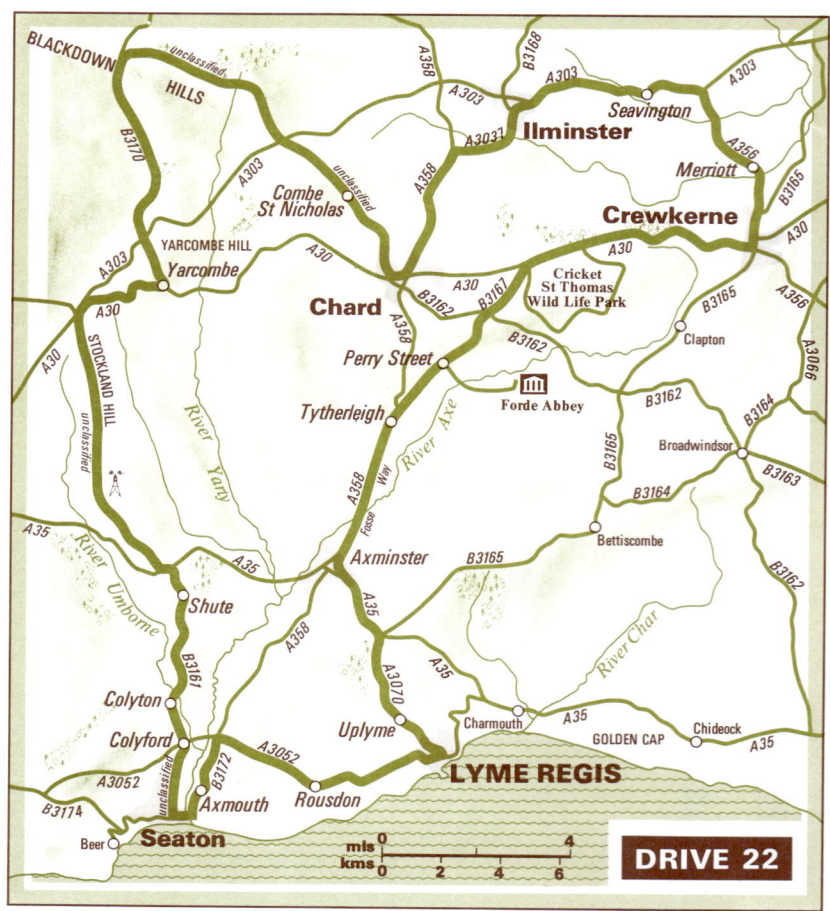

Jane Austen's Dorset
From Lyme Regis
Drive 22   72 miles

Take the A3070 *Axminster* road out of *Lyme Regis* and pass through Uplyme. Continue and turn left on to the A35, then descend into Axminster. Follow the A358 *Chard* road north through the Axe valley, then meet the Somerset boundary and turn right on to the B3167, signposted *Crewkerne*. Proceed to Perry Street and continue along the B3167 to join the A30. Immediately to the right is the Cricket St Thomas Wild Life Park. Continue across 700ft Windwhistle Hill and descend into Crewkerne. Take the A356 *Ilminster* road, later joining the A303 *Honiton* road into Ilminster. Follow the A3037 and A358 to Chard, turn right into the town, and pass the porticoed town hall before turning right on to an unclassified road for Combe St Nicholas. Drive beyond Combe St Nicholas and ascend to 819ft before reaching the A303. Follow signposts indicating *Wellington* along the Blackdown Hills, then turn left on to the B3170 Honiton road. Approach the junction with the A303 and continue forward on an unclassified road before descending Yarcombe Hill. Meet the A30 and turn right with Honiton signposts, then ascend to the junction with the A303. In another ¼m approach crossroads and turn left on to the unclassified Axminster road. Continue along Stockland Hill, later passing a TV transmitting station. Proceed to the junction with the A35 and go forward on to the B3161 towards *Colyton*. Pass through Shute for Colyton, then enter Colyford and turn right on to the A3052; turn left on to an unclassified road and continue to the coast and *Seaton*. Leave Seaton on the B3172 Lyme Regis road, and cross the River Axe to *Axmouth*. Turn right on to the A3052 and ascend before passing through Rousdon. Within another 3m descend steeply into Lyme Regis.

Cranborne Chase to the Blackmore Vale
From Shaftesbury
Drive 23   74 miles

Take the A30 *Sherborne* and *Yeovil* road out of *Shaftesbury* and descend to the Blackmore Vale. Continue to East Stour, then turn left onto the B3092 and enter the Stour Valley. Pass through *Marnhull* and *Sturminster Newton*. Continue on the *Blandford* road, cross the Stour, then turn right on to the A357 and cross Lydlinch Common before turning left on to the A3030. Pass the grounds of Stock Gaylard House to the right before ascending through Bishop's Caundle and passing through Allweston. Drive beyond the latter for 2m and turn left on to the A352 and proceed to Middlemarsh. Climb the outer slopes of 860ft High Stoy Hill to pass through a gap in the hills to Minterne Magna. Within a further 2m branch left into *Cerne Abbas* and drive to the village centre. Turn left on to an unclassified road, then right on to the road for *Piddletrenthide*. Turn right on to the B3143 and continue to Piddlehinton. Within 1½m turn left on to the B3142, pass Waterston Manor Gardens, and continue to *Puddletown*. Leave the latter on the A354 Blandford road and drive to Milborne St Andrew before taking an unclassified road to the left and proceeding to *Milton Abbas*. Continue from the foot of this village by following the Hilton road past Milton Abbey, then drive into Hilton itself. In ¾m branch right for Bulbarrow Hill, then follow Blandford signposts to pass the outskirts of Winterborne Stickland before joining the A354. Cross the River Stour into Blandford; leave the town on the A350 *Warminster* and Shaftesbury road, then continue to *Iwerne Minster* war memorial. Turn right here on to the unclassified Tarrant Gunville road and climb on to *Cranborne* Chase. Turn left on to the Shaftesbury road, and at the crossroads turn right for Ashmore. Keep left at the pond and later join the B3081. Continue and descend Zig-Zag Hill for the return to Shaftesbury.

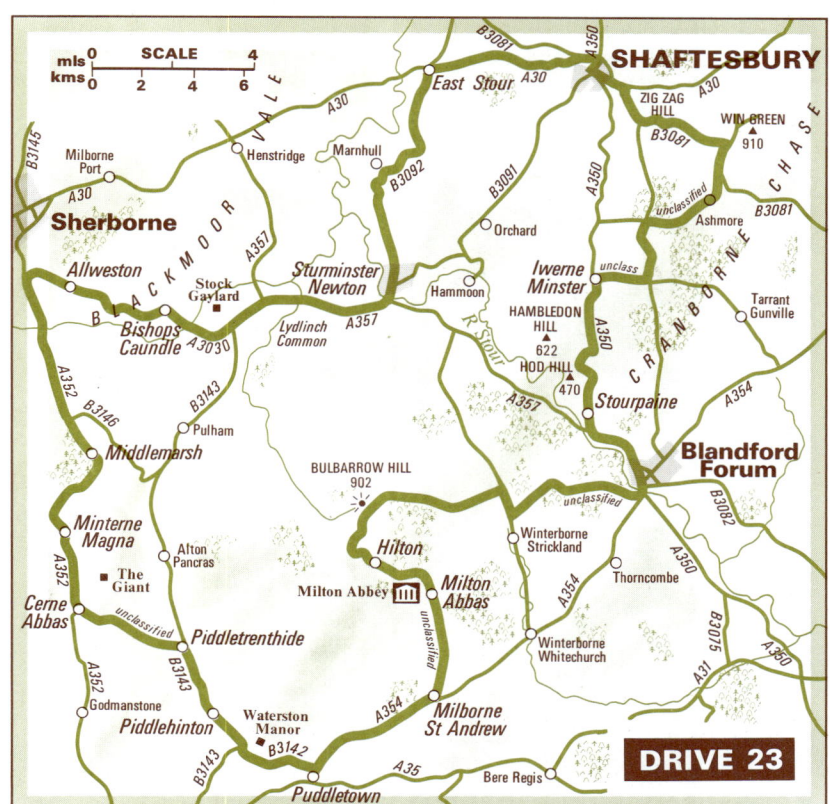

Placenames in *italic* type are worth stopping at; each is listed and described in the main gazetteer section of the book

East Somerset

Through the Avon Valley

From Bath

Drive 24   50 miles

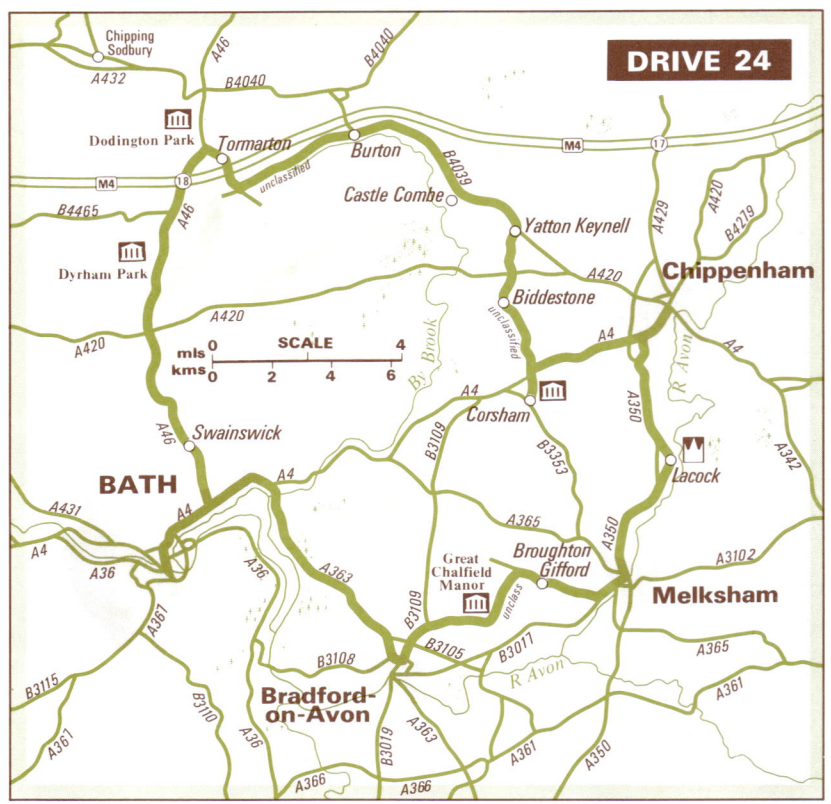

Take the A4 *Chippenham* road from *Bath*, and after 3m branch right on to the A363, signposted *Bradford-on-Avon*. Continue and descend to Bradford-on-Avon. Leave the latter on the B3109, signposted Chippenham and *Corsham*, and after 1¼m approach the Plough Inn and turn right on to an unclassified road. Follow Great Chalfield signposts for 1m, then approach a T-junction and turn right into Broughton Gifford. Follow *Melksham* signposts to join the B3107 and continue to Melksham, then follow the A350 Chippenham road; after 3m turn right on to an unclassified road for *Lacock*. Return to the A350, turn right, and later join the A4 to enter Chippenham. Leave this town on the A4 Bath road, and after 3½m turn left on to an unclassified road to Corsham. Visit the latter, return along the same route, then cross the A4 and continue along unclassified roads to *Biddestone*. Cross the A420 and proceed to *Yatton Keynell*. Turn left on to the B4039 and in 2m turn left again on to an unclassified road to *Castle Combe*. Return to the B4039 and turn left. Drive through Burton and branch left on to an unclassified road signposted Pucklechurch. After 3m approach crossroads and turn right to enter Tormarton. Pass the Portcullis Inn and after ½m turn left with Westerleigh signposts. Continue to a junction with the A46, opposite which is the entrance to *Dodington* Park, then proceed along the A46 towards Bath. After 2½m pass the entrance to *Dyrham* Park on the right, and keeping to the A46 descend through Swainswick and join the A4 in the Avon Valley. Approach traffic signals, turn right, and re-enter Bath.

The Polden and Mendip Hills

From Glastonbury

Drive 25   78 miles

Leave *Glastonbury* from the market cross, following the B3151 alongside the River Brue to *Meare*. After 1½m turn left on to an unclassified road signposted Shapwick and *Bridgwater*, and cross wooded Shapwick Heath. Turn right at the towered church in Shapwick, signposted Bridgwater, and climb through Loxley Wood to the *Polden Hills*. Turn right on to the A39 before crossing a dyke known as King's Sedgemoor Drain, and enter Bridgwater. Leave Bridgwater on the A372 *Langport* road. Continue to Othery and join the A361 with *Taunton* signpost before proceeding through the village. After

continued on page 51

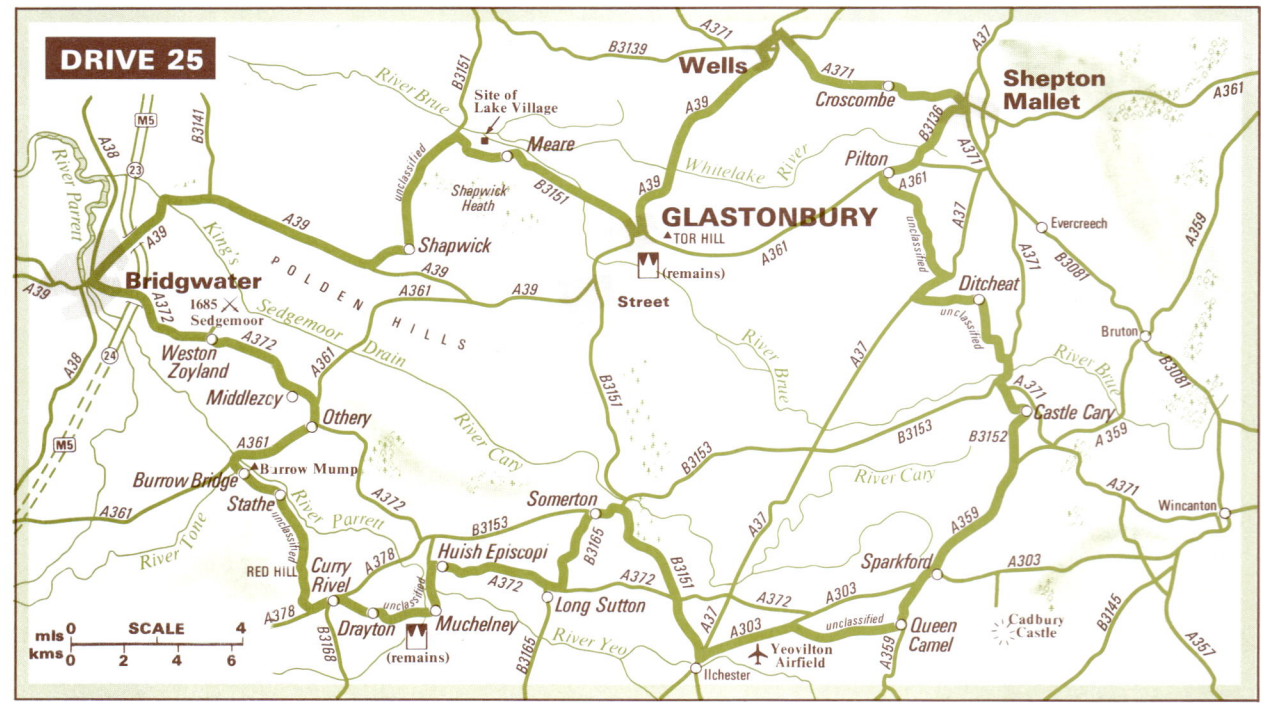

EAST SOMERSET

Cheddar Gorge and Wookey Caves
From Cheddar
Drive 26 65 miles

Take the A371 *Wells* road out of *Cheddar* and drive through Draycott to Easton. On reaching the Easton Inn turn left on to an unclassified road for *Wookey Hole*. Continue past the Wookey Hole Inn and later rejoin the A371 to enter Wells. Follow the A39 *Bath* road and climb up the side of a valley on to the *Mendips*. Pass a television transmitting station on the left and then continue to *Chewton Mendip*. Join the A37 to enter Farrington Gurney, then leave the village and continue for 1m. Turn right to continue on the A39, then pass through a number of villages to Marksbury (Stantonbury Iron Age camp to the right) and Corston. Drive on for ½m before turning right on to the A4 to Bath. Leave the city following signposts marked 'Bristol and the A4'. Pass through *Saltford* and reach a roundabout. Take the first exit on to the B3116 to enter *Keynsham*, then drive to the church and turn right on to the A4175 Bitton road. Cross the River Avon and proceed to Willsbridge. Turn left on to the A431 and follow signposts into Bristol city centre. Follow *Taunton*, *Bridgwater* and 'A38' signposts for 2¾m, then meet traffic signals and turn left on to an unclassified road signposted Bishopsworth, then Withywood. After passing Bishopsworth church branch left along the Withywood and *Chew Magna* road, then ascend *Dundry* Hill. Descend and turn right on to the B3114 to enter *Chew Stoke*. Follow the *West Harptree* road through this village and then skirt Chew Valley Lake. Reach the Blue Bowl Hotel and in 150yds turn right on to an unclassified road with Cheddar signposts. Cross the A368 and ascend the Mendip Hills. On reaching the Wellway Inn turn right, then in ¼m approach crossroads and turn left. Go straight across the next crossroads on to the B3371 and cross the almost treeless Mendip Forest. Later turn right on to the B3135 to descend Cheddar Gorge, and return to Cheddar village.

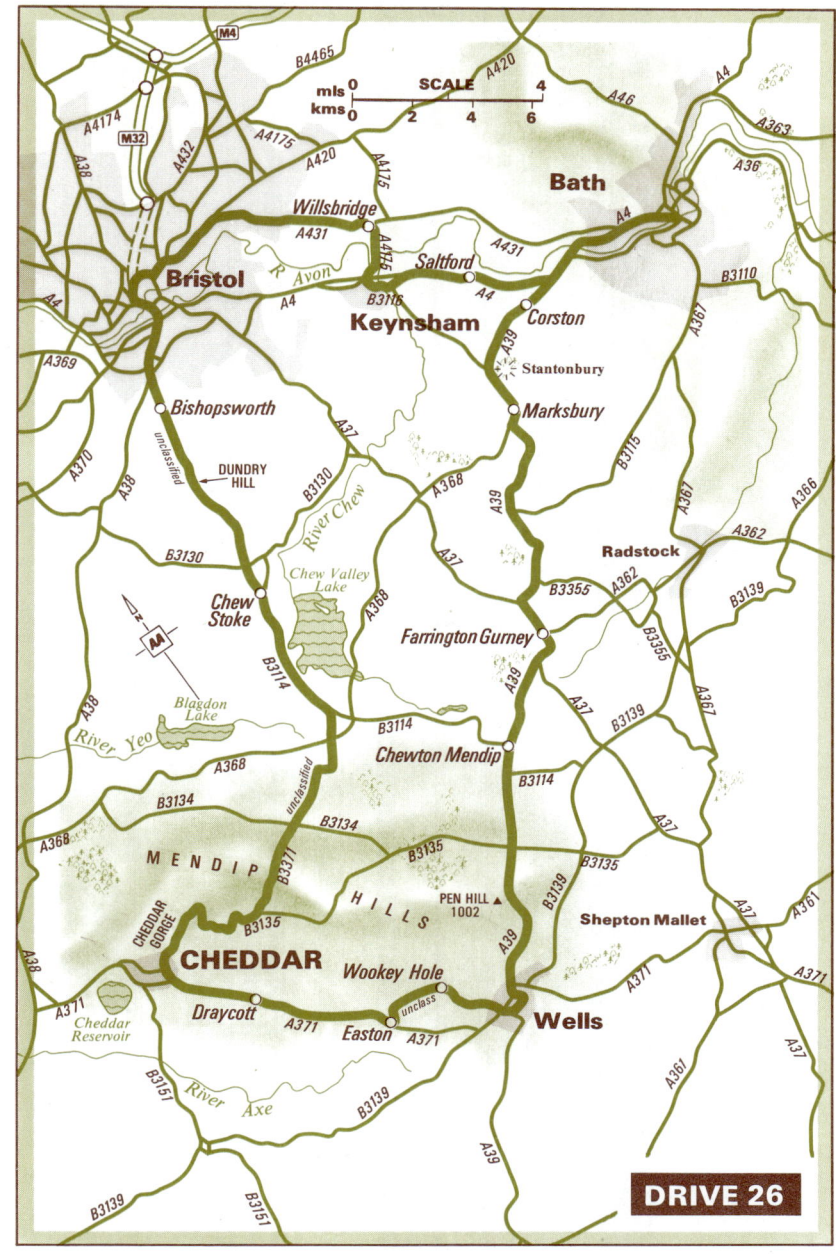

Drive 25 continued

2m pass Burrow Mump and its unfinished church, and cross the River Parrett at Burrow Bridge. Immediately after the bridge turn left on to an unclassified road signposted Langport. Continue alongside the River Parrett and follow *Curry Rivel* signposts. Pass through Stathe and after 1m branch right to cross a railway bridge. Ascend wooded Red Hill and turn left on to the A378 Langport road to enter Curry Rivel. Pass the Bell Hotel and take the first turning on the right on to an unclassified road for Drayton and *Muchelney*. Leave Muchelney and follow the Langport road; cross the River Yeo before entering *Huish Episcopi*, then turn right to join the A372 Wincanton road. Continue through *Long Sutton*. After ½m turn left on to the B3165, signposted *Somerton*. Enter the latter and turn right on to the B3153, signposted *Ilchester*. After 1m follow a descent and at the foot turn right on to the B3151. Later turn right on to the A37, then left to join the A303 *Andover* road. Pass *Yeovilton* Air Base and turn immediately right on to an unclassified road for the village of *Queen Camel*. Join the A359 Sparkford road, pass the church, and after a short distance turn right on to the A303 to proceed into Sparkford. Turn left on to the A359, signposted *Frome*, and after 4m branch left on to the B3152 for Castle Cary. In *Castle Cary* follow *Shepton Mallet* signposts past the Heart and Compass Inn. Later join the A371 and cross a railway bridge. After ½m turn left on to an unclassified road signposted Alhampton and Ditcheat. On entering Ditcheat turn left and follow Glastonbury signposts, then turn right on to the A37 and ascend. Approach the summit and turn left on to an unclassified road signposted East Pennard. Turn right and descend to *Pilton*. Approach crossroads in Pilton and turn left, then proceed to the western end of the village and turn right on to the A361. Continue along the B3136 to Shepton Mallet, then follow the A371 *Wells* road and descend a wooded valley to *Croscombe*. Continue to Wells and follow the A39 Glastonbury road. Cross the dyked Whitelake River and re-enter Glastonbury.

Placenames in *italic* type are worth stopping at; each is listed and described in the main gazetteer section of the book

EAST SOMERSET

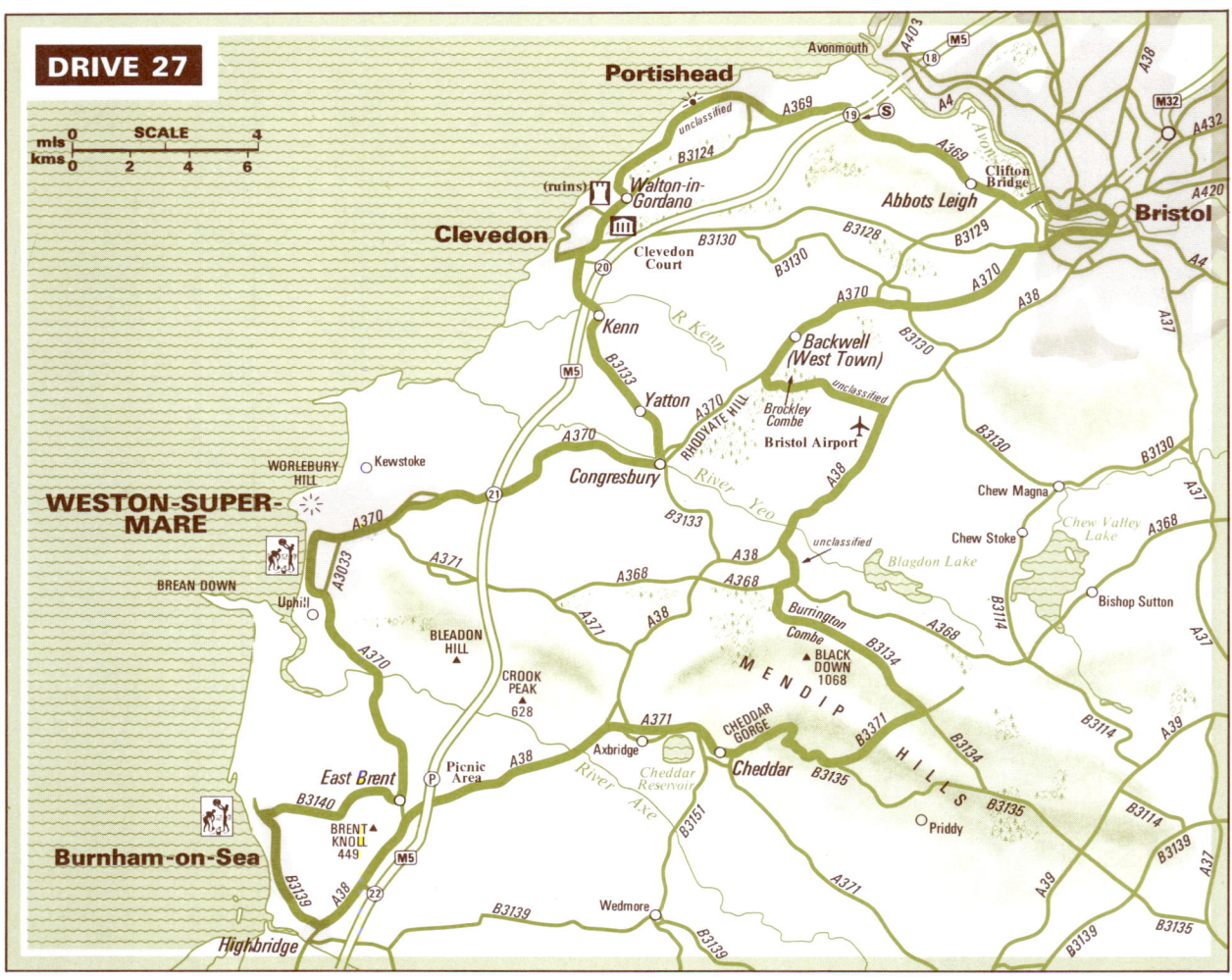

Bristol Channel and the Avon Gorge

From Weston-super-Mare

Drive 27   83 miles

Leave *Weston-super-Mare* on the A370 *Bristol* road and continue to *Congresbury*. From the latter village continue along the A370, and after ¼m turn left on to the B3133 with *Clevedon* signposts. Pass through *Yatton* and *Kenn* to Clevedon, then take the Bristol road before continuing on the B3124 *Portishead* road. Proceed to Walton-in-Gordano and on reaching the post office turn left on to an unclassified road. After another 2m turn left into Nore Road and after 1½m pass the Hole in One Inn. Proceed to Portishead, then leave the town on the A369 Bristol road before climbing to higher ground. Within a further 1¼m pass the George Inn at Abbots Leigh and turn left on to the B3129, signposted 'Clifton via Toll Bridge'. Cross the bridge and enter Bristol city centre. Leave by the A370 Weston-super-Mare road, passing near the docks. Proceed for 7m to Backwell (West Town), then after 1½m approach crossroads and turn left on to an unclassified road for Brockley Combe. Ascend to the top of a long slope and turn right on to the A38, signposted *Taunton*. Pass Bristol Airport, continue for 4m, then meet crossroads and turn left on to the unclassified Burrington road. After ¾m drive forward on to the A368,

signposted Burrington Combe. Take the second turning left on to the B3134, signposted *Wells*, and climb through Burrington Combe into the *Mendip Hills*. Continue along the B3134, approach crossroads, and turn right on to the B3371. After joining the B3135 descend through Cheddar Gorge, past the caves, to *Cheddar*. Enter the village and leave by following *Axbridge* and Weston-super-Mare signposts. Join the A371 and by-pass Axbridge before branching left to join the A38. Continue along the A38 to Highbridge, then turn right on to the B3139 to enter *Burnham-on-Sea*. Proceed to the seafront and continue on this road for 2m, then turn right on to the B3140 with Weston-super-Mare signposts. Pass through East Brent and turn left on to the A370. Complete the drive by re-entering Weston-super-Mare from the south.

Isle of Wight

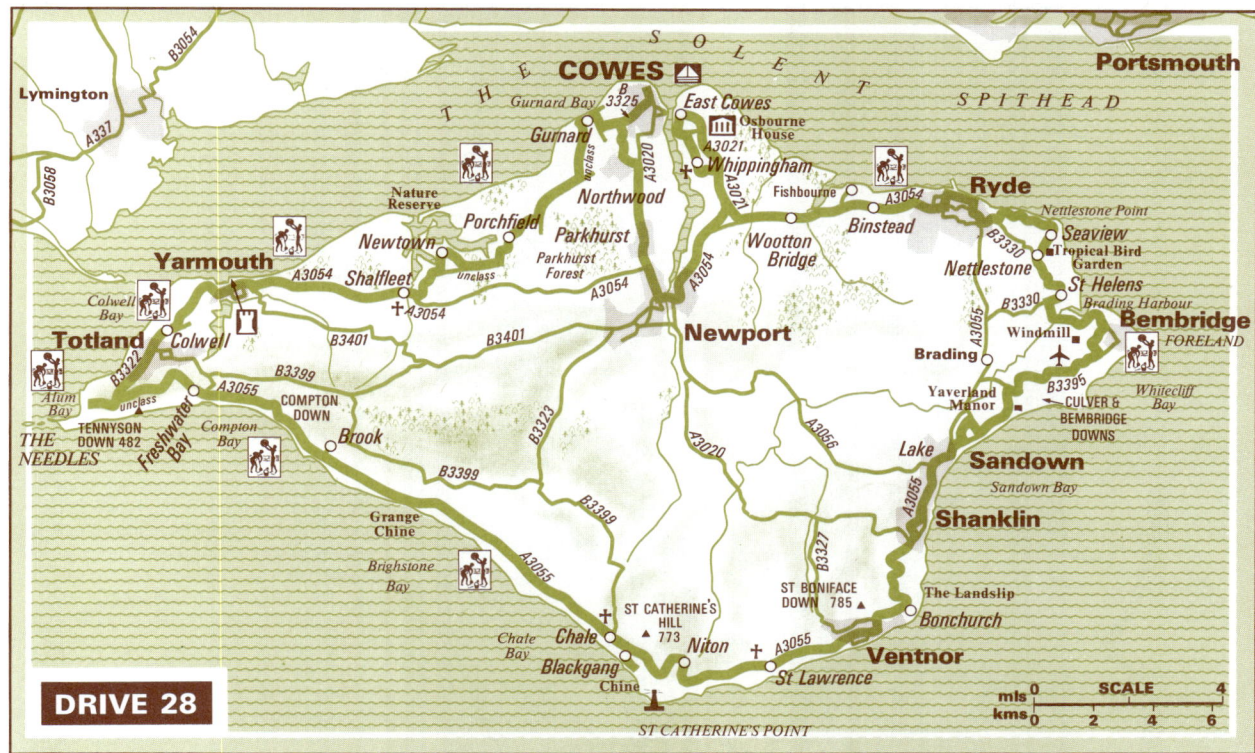

The Island Coast

From Cowes

Drive 28 76 miles

Leave *Cowes* by following Gurnard signposts on to the B3325, and after ¾m continue straight on to an unclassified road to Gurnard. Proceed past the Gurnard Hotel and approach a T-junction. Turn right into Lower Church Road and at the next T-junction turn left, signposted *Yarmouth*. Pass Gurnard Bay, then after 1½m approach another T-junction and turn right. Continue for 1½m and turn right again for Porchfield. Continue through wooded country and after 1½m turn right to Newtown. Proceed for ½m, turn right at a T-junction, and in another ¾m approach the next T-junction and turn right on to the A3054 for *Shalfleet*. Drive to Yarmouth, then follow *Freshwater* signposts and cross the Yar bridge. After 1m bear right, then pass through Colwell to Totland and join the B3322 *Alum Bay* road. Continue for ¼m to the war memorial, then bear right for Alum Bay car park. Return and in ½m branch right on to an unclassified road signposted Freshwater Bay. Pass Tennyson Down on the right before entering Freshwater Bay. Join the A3055, signposted *Chale*, and bear right before ascending to a cliff-top road and skirting Compton Bay. Continue to the edge of Brook and continue for another 2½m with thickly-wooded Grange Chine on the right. St Catherine's Point and St Catherine's Hill can be seen ahead before Chale. Proceed past Chale church, following *Ventnor* signposts, and after ½m turn right on to an unclassified road for Blackgang. Return and after ½m turn right on to the A3055 signposted Ventnor. Pass under St Catherine's Hill to Niton and turn right. Continue along the thickly-wooded Undercliff to *St Lawrence*.

Drive on to Ventnor, then follow signposts to *Shanklin* and pass the Landslip. Continue through Shanklin and Lake to *Sandown*. Proceed to the Sandringham Hotel and turn left on to the B3395, signposted *Bembridge*, for Yaverland. Meet a T-junction and turn right to skirt Bembridge Down, and then pass Bembridge Airport before reaching crossroads and turning left on to an unclassified road. Continue to Bembridge, then follow the B3395 St Helens road around the shore of *Brading* harbour. After 1½m approach a T-junction and turn right on to the B3330 before driving into St Helens. Turn left with *Ryde* signposts and continue to Nettlestone. Branch right on to the B3340, signposted Seaview, and pass the entrance to a tropical bird garden on the right. In ½m keep left, then go forward to a T-junction and turn left and immediately left again. Turn right into Seafield Road for Seaview. Approach a T-junction and turn right, then keep left on an unclassified road along the shore line. After ½m pass through a toll gate and continue for 1m before turning right on to the B3330, then right again on to the A3055 for Ryde. Follow signposts to *Newport* and join the A3054 to pass through *Binstead*. In 1¾m pass the road to Fishbourne car ferry on the right. Drive straight through Wootton Bridge and after 1½m turn right for East Cowes. Reach a T-junction and turn right again on to the A3021, then after 1¼m turn left on to an unclassified road signposted Whippingham Church. Continue past the church to a T-junction and turn left into Victoria Grove. Proceed to the next T-junction and turn left again to join the A3021 for East Cowes. Return along the A3021 Ryde road and pass the entrance to *Osborne House* on the outskirts of the town. After 2m keep right with Newport signposts, then after ½m turn right on to the A3054 and proceed along a flat road to Newport. Follow the Cowes road past Parkhurst Prison and proceed to Northwood. Branch left on to the B3325, then continue to a T-junction and turn right to return to Cowes.

Placenames in *italic* type are worth stopping at; each is listed and described in the main gazetteer section of the book

Hampshire and the New Forest

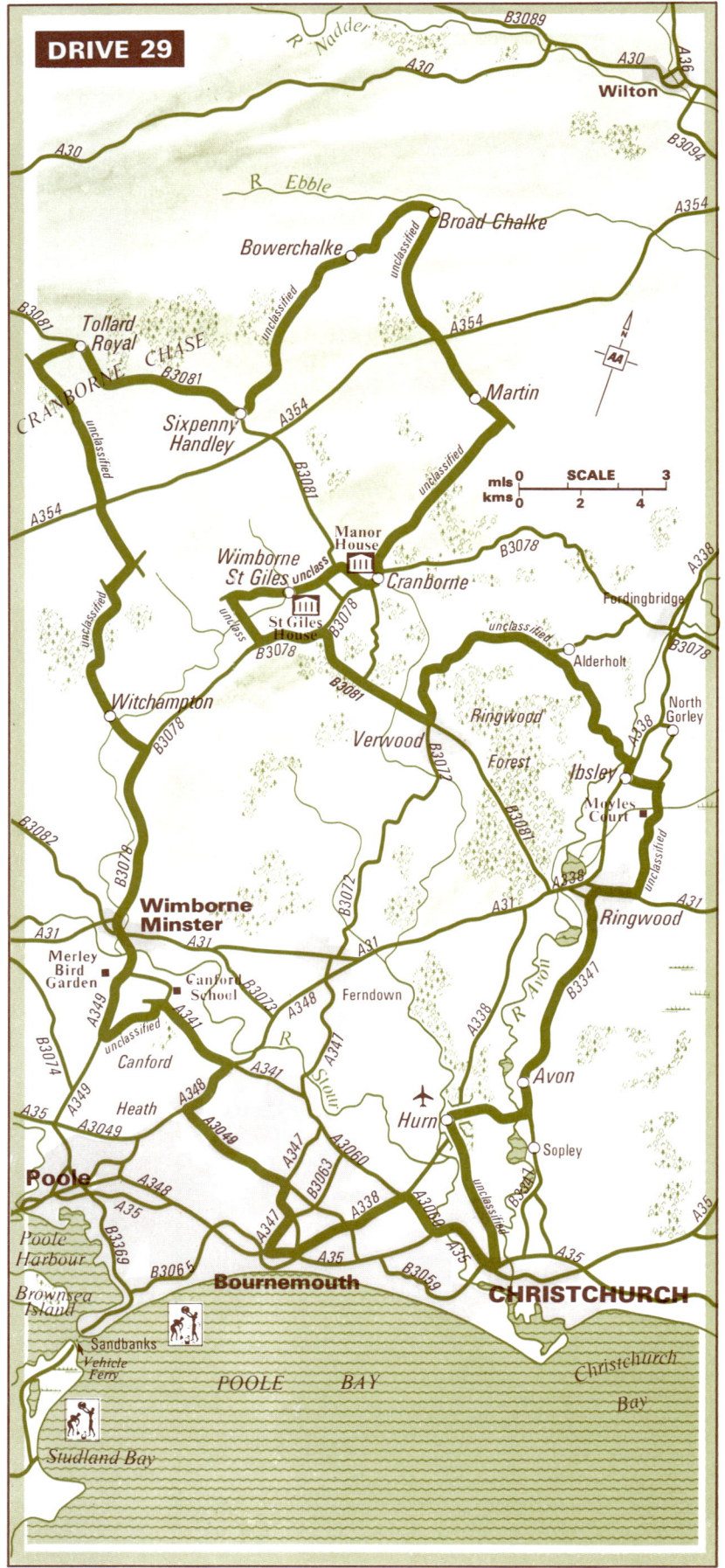

Ringwood Forest and the Wiltshire Downs

From Christchurch

Drive 29 82 miles

Leave *Christchurch* by following *Ringwood* signposts from the roundabout in the High Street, then continue with Hurn Airport signposts to Hurn village. On entering the village keep right for the Sopley and Avon road, and continue for a short distance through the Avon meadows before turning left on to the B3347, signposted Ringwood. Drive into Avon and follow the valley to Ringwood. Enter the town and leave on the A31 *Cadnam* and *Southampton* road, and at the White Hart Inn turn left on to the unclassified North Gorley road. After a short distance enter the New Forest, and after passing the Dame Alice Lisle public house turn left to pass Moyles Court. Continue to the T-junction and turn left. Proceed for ½m along the North Gorley road and on reaching crossroads turn left for Ibsley. Turn right on to the A338, and after passing through Ibsley turn left on to an unclassified road signposted Alderholt. Cross the River Avon, ascend from the meadows, and after 1m turn left along the wooded Alderholt road. Continue to the next junction and keep left, later passing the Churchill Arms public house on the Verwood road. Within 1m turn left into Batterby Drove and continue to Verwood; turn right on to the B3081 *Cranborne* road. After about 2m, in woodland, turn left on to the *Wimborne St Giles* road. Continue through further patches of woodland and turn left on to the B3078 *Wimborne Minster* road. Take the next right turn, signposted Wimborne St Giles, and pass the ruins of Knowlton church on the right before descending into the valley of the River Allen. Cross the Allen and at the next T-junction turn right for Wimborne St Giles. Leave this village by following Cranborne signposts, and proceed along the B3081, an unclassified road, and the B3078 to Cranborne itself. Take the unclassified Martin road out of the village and drive through open countryside before approaching a T-junction and turning left to pass through Martin village. After another 2m cross a main road, signposted *Broad Chalke*, and climb Wiltshire downs. Descend into the Ebble Valley through avenues of beech trees and pass through Broad Chalke before continuing with Bowerchalke signposts into the village of Bowerchalke. Pass through the village and continue with signposts marked 6d Handley. Climb steeply and then descend into *Sixpenny Handley*; turn right on to the B3081 *Shaftesbury* road, and later drive through a fine avenue of trees into *Tollard Royal*. Drive to the telephone kiosk and turn left on to an unclassified road signposted to the church. Ascend to Cranborne Chase, then approach the next T-junction and turn left. Continue with the Wimborne Minster road across pleasant countryside, and follow Ringwood signposts across a main road. Within 1½m approach crossroads and turn right into a road signposted *Witchampton*, and continue through pleasant countryside. Turn sharp left to pass through Witchampton and stay with the Wimborne road. Cross the River Allen and later turn right on to the

continued on page 55

HAMPSHIRE AND THE NEW FOREST

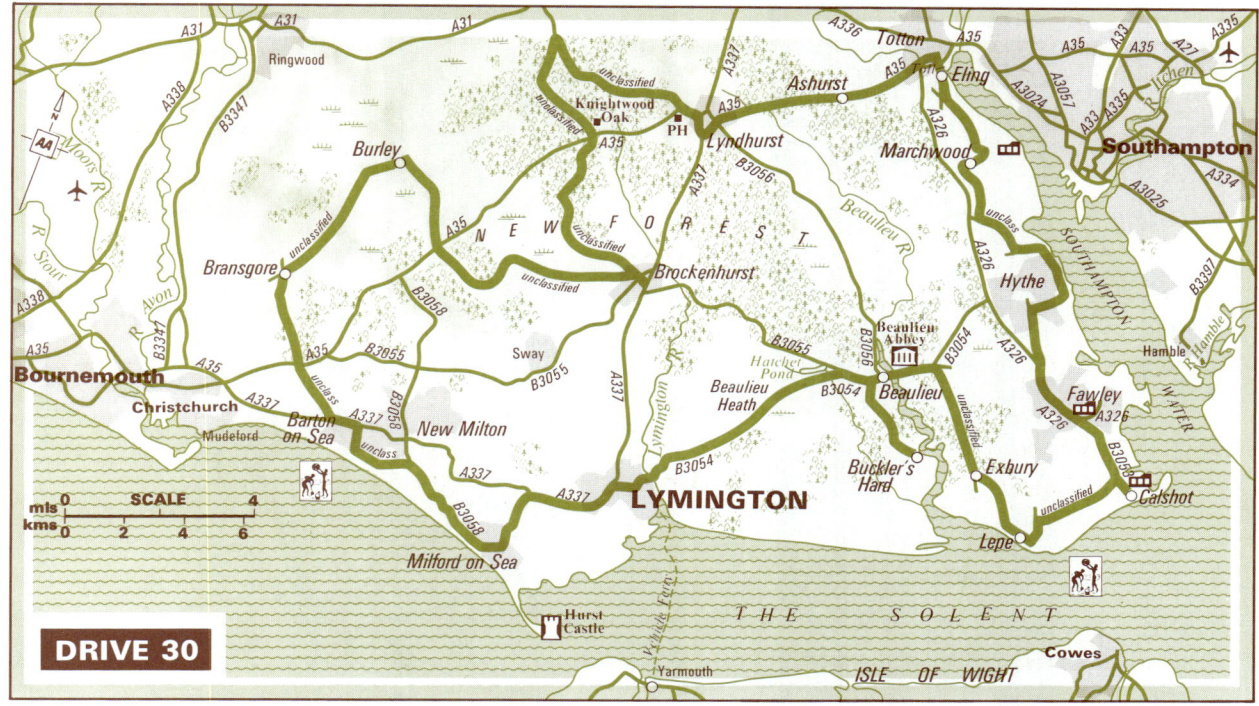

Forest Byroads

From Lymington

Drive 30   74 miles

Drive 29 continued

B3078 to reach Wimborne Minster. Enter the town and follow Town Centre signposts to the Square. Continue with signposts marked 'Poole A349' and cross the River Stour. Stay with the Poole road and pass the Willet Arms public house and Merley Bird Gardens before entering woodland. Continue through the woodland as far as a left turn signposted Canford and *Bournemouth*. Take this turning and drive through woodland along unclassified Arrowsmith Road, with Canford Heath on the right. Approach the next T-junction and turn right, then right again, to join the A341 Bournemouth road. Pass Canford School on the left, and after 2m approach a roundabout; take the third exit and follow signposts marked 'Town Centre'. Proceed to Bournemouth via Winton Bypass. Drive to the town centre, follow Ringwood then *Lyndhurst* signposts to join the A35, and return to Christchurch.

Follow signposts marked 'Beaulieu B3054' from *Lymington* and cross the Lymington River before climbing into the New Forest. Cross Beaulieu Heath to Hatchet Pond. Turn right and after 1m turn sharp right on to the unclassified road to *Buckler's Hard*. Leave this village by returning along the Beaulieu road, and after 2m turn right on to the B3054 to enter Beaulieu itself. Follow Hythe signposts to Beaulieu Abbey and associated places of interest, then continue with the Hythe road and pass through woodland to the Royal Oak Inn; turn sharp right on to the unclassified Lepe road. Proceed with the Fawley Oil Refinery on the left, and after more woodland enter the village of Exbury. Turn left in the village and continue for 2m before bearing left to reach Lepe foreshore. Drive inland and after ¾m turn right on to the Calshot road. Within 2½m turn right with signposts marked 'The Beach', and proceed to Calshot foreshore. Return along the B3053 Totton road and continue to the edge of *Fawley*. Approach the next roundabout and follow Hythe signposts; within 1m turn right into Frost Lane and descend to the shores of Southampton Water. Keep forward to Hythe town centre and follow Totton signposts from the pier. Within ½m approach a T-junction and turn right. Continue for 2m and on the nearside of the next roundabout turn sharp right for the Marchwood road. Pass Marchwood Power Station, drive through the village itself, and continue for 2m before meeting crossroads and turning right on to the Eling road. Cross the small toll bridge that connects Eling with Totton and follow *Lyndhurst* signposts to join the A35. Proceed through Ashurst and cross *New Forest* heathland before driving into Lyndhurst. Follow the *Bournemouth* road from here and drive as far as the Swan Inn before turning right on to the unclassified Emery Down road. Cross a small hill and turn left with signposts indicating Bolderwood. After a further 3m pass a common on the left and turn sharp left on to an unsignposted road. Keep forward, cross a main road, and continue along the Ornamental Drive. Proceed across more heathland before turning left across a ford and driving into the village of *Brockenhurst*. Take the New Milton road from here, then the *Burley* road, and cross heathland. After about 3m the road takes the route of an old railway track and later enters Burley. Continue the drive by leaving this village on the Bransgore road, and on entering Bransgore approach crossroads and turn left with Lymington signposts. Within 2m turn left and then right across a main road. Farther on join the A337 and within ¾m turn right on to the unclassified road for *Barton-on-Sea*. Approach a T-junction within ½m and turn left then right to enter this seaside resort. Drive to the end of the Promenade and turn left to follow *Milford-on-Sea* signposts; before reaching the resort itself turn right on to the B3058. Pass through Milford-on-Sea and continue on the B3058 Lymington road. Turn right on to the A337 before re-entering Lymington.

Placenames in *italic* type are worth stopping at; each is listed and described in the main gazetteer section of the book

HAMPSHIRE AND THE NEW FOREST

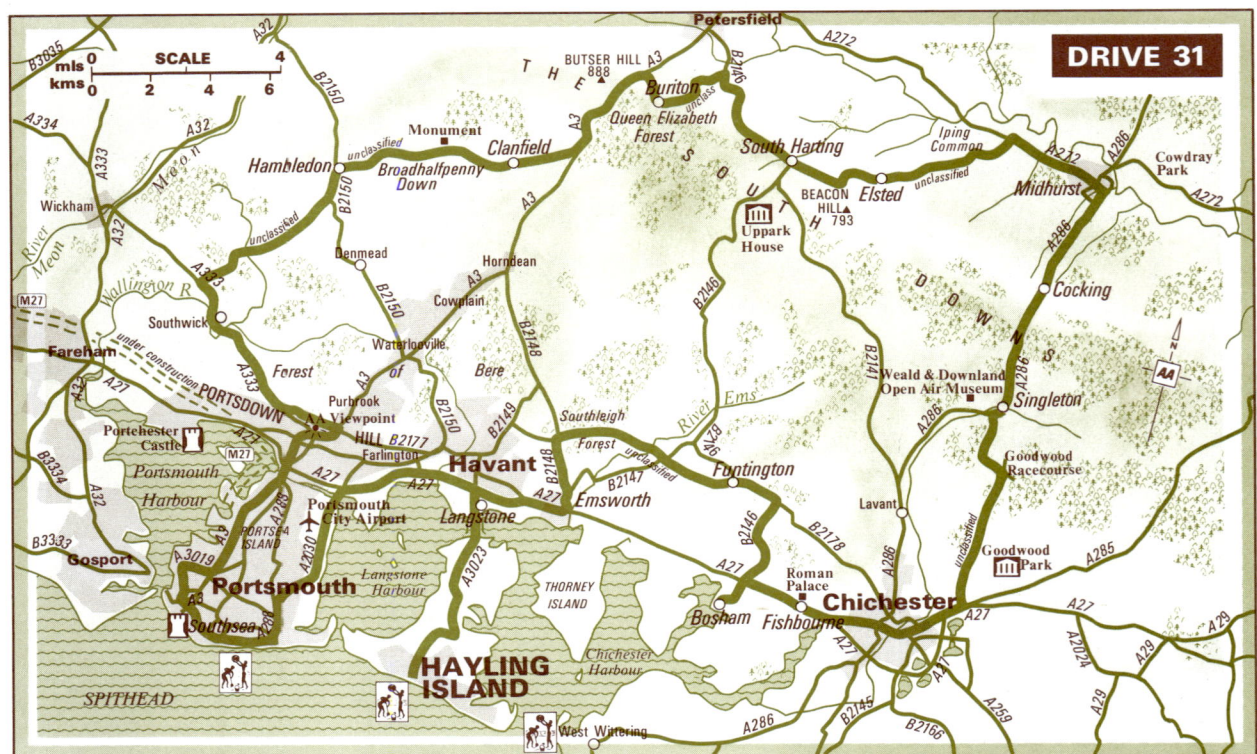

Across the South Downs

From Hayling Island

Drive 31   84 miles

Cross from *Hayling Island* to the mainland on the A3023 via Langstone Bridge, and at the roundabout follow signposts marked 'Chichester A27'. Drive to *Emsworth* and turn left on to the B2148 Horndean road; after a further 2m enter Southleigh Forest and turn right on to the unclassified Funtington road. Continue through Funtington on the B2146, and in 1m turn right with signposts indicating *Bosham*. Cross the A27 on to an unclassified road and drive to the yachting centre of Bosham Quay. Return, and follow *Fishbourne* and Chichester signposts to join the A27. Follow City Centre signposts into Chichester, proceed to the market cross, and leave the town along East Street. Approach a roundabout and take the first exit signposted *Arundel*. Continue to the next roundabout and take the first exit on to the unclassified Goodwood road. Drive past the entrance to *Goodwood* Park and Goodwood House on the right, and climb towards Goodwood Racecourse on the South Downs. Turn left, passing below the 675ft Trundle, and descend. Continue past the entrance of the Weald and Downland open-air museum on the left, and turn right into *Singleton*. Leave the downs and pass through Cocking before entering *Midhurst*. Leave by the A272 *Petersfield* road, and in 2½m turn left at a signpost indicating Elsted and Harting. Follow this unclassified road across Iping Common and drive to the Ship Inn in *South Harting* before following signposts marked 'Petersfield B2146'. In 3m turn left on to an unclassified road for *Buriton*. In a further 1m turn left on to the A3 *Portsmouth* road and continue alongside Queen Elizabeth Forest before taking the second right turning on to the unclassified Clanfield road. Continue beyond Clanfield on the *Hambledon* road and cross Broad Halfpenny Down. Drive into Hambledon, turn left on to the B2150 Denmead road, and in ¾m branch right on to the unclassified *Fareham* road. Approach the A333 and turn left to follow Portsmouth signposts. Ascend *Ports Down* and at the summit turn left along an unclassified road signposted *Havant* and Chichester, passing Duncton Hill on the right. After 1m turn right at a Portsmouth signpost and join the A3. Proceed into Portsmouth city centre and drive to the seafront by following Southsea signposts. Turn left along the Esplanade and cross Southsea Common before passing South Parade Pier and turning left into St George's Road. Pass Eastney Barracks on the right and turn right on to the A2030, signposted Chichester. On approaching the A27 take the roundabout's third exit; two roundabouts later take the third exit on to the A3023 and return to Hayling Island.

HAMPSHIRE AND THE NEW FOREST

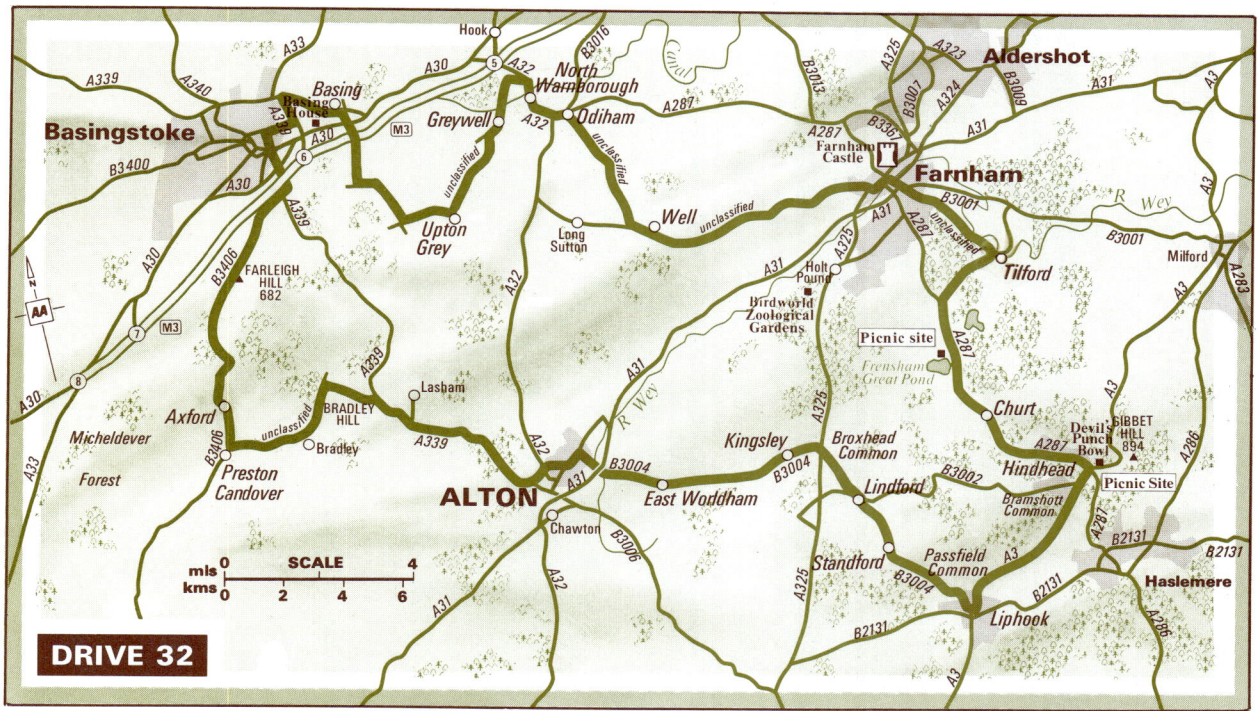

Devil's Punchbowl and North Hampshire

From Alton

Drive 32   84 miles

From *Alton* follow signposts marked 'Farnham A31' then 'Bordon B3004', and pass through Kingsley. Leave the village and continue for 1m before following *Liphook* signposts across Broxhead Common to Lindford. Cross Passfield Common, enter Liphook, and leave by the A3 *Guildford* road. Cross *Bramshott* Common and ascend to *Hindhead*. Take the A287 Farnham road out of Hindhead, pass through Churt, and after crossing the River Wey at *Frensham* turn right on to the unclassified road for *Tilford*. Drive through wooded country and within 1½m approach a T-junction and turn left on to the Farnham road. Cross a level crossing and on meeting traffic signals continue forward into Farnham. Leave the town centre by the *Petersfield* road and within ½m pass the Jolly Sailor Inn before turning right into unclassified Crondall Lane. Ascend and within 1m follow Long Sutton signposts. Pass the Chequers Inn at Well, and within ½m turn right on to the Odiham road. Take the A32 *Reading* road from *Odiham* High Street to North Warnborough and cross the disused Basingstoke Canal. Stay with the A32 for ¾m beyond the village, then turn left on to an unclassified road for Greywell. At the far end of this village turn left with signposts indicating Upton Grey, and at the next T-junction turn right with *Basingstoke* signposts. Continue through sparsely populated countryside and within 2½m turn right to follow signposts for *Basing*. Cross the M3 and A30, and on entering Basing village turn left into Crown Lane and left again at the Crown public house. Drive forward for a short distance, then turn right and continue to a roundabout. Take the first exit and follow Basingstoke signposts into the town centre. Leave the town by the A339 Alton road, and after passing beneath a motorway bridge turn right on to the B3046 with signposts indicating *Alresford*. Drive through Cliddesden and after climbing 682ft Farleigh Hill continue through Axford to the edge of Preston Candover. Turn left on to the unclassified Bradley road and follow Herriard signposts. Cross Bradley Hill, turn right on to the Alton road, and later turn right again on to the A339. Stay with the A339 and return to Alton.

Placenames in *italic* type are worth stopping at; each is listed and described in the main gazetteer section of the book

Wiltshire and Berkshire

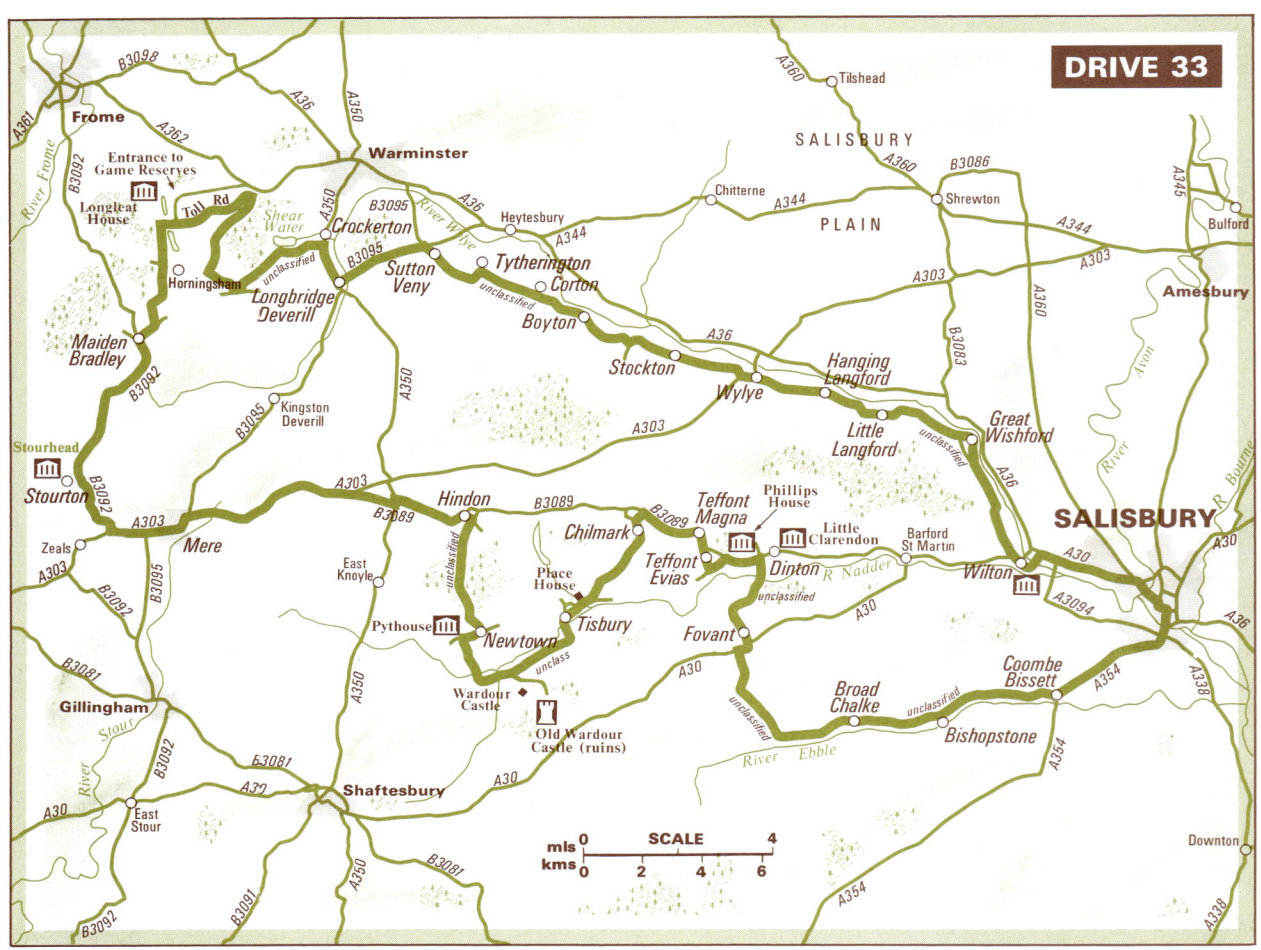

The Wylye Valley and South Wiltshire

From Salisbury

Drive 33   75 miles

From *Salisbury* follow signposts marked 'Yeovil A30' and drive to *Wilton*. Approach a roundabout and take the first exit, passing Wilton House to the left. Continue to the Bell Inn at the far end of the town and turn right on to an unclassified road signposted Great Wishford. Within $2\frac{3}{4}$m turn right into the Wylye Valley and proceed into the village of Great Wishford. Continue to the village church, then turn left and drive to the Royal Oak public house. Turn right here and continue through Little Langford and Hanging Langford for *Wylye*. Keep forward to join the A303, then turn right on to an unclassified road signposted Sutton Veny. Continue through the Wylye Valley and pass *Stockton*. After 1m cross the railway line and turn right for Boyton. Skirt the edge of Corton village and proceed to the edge of Tytherington. Keep left for Sutton Veny and pass through the latter to the crossroads at the far end. Turn left on to the B3095 and drive to *Longbridge Deverill*. Approach crossroads and turn right on to the A350; proceed to the edge of Crockerton and turn left at the Bath Arms into an unclassified road signposted *Horningsham*. Continue through woodland and after a short distance pass Shear Water on the right. After $1\frac{1}{4}$m approach a T-junction and turn right, then take the next turning right with 'Longleat' and 'Heaven's Gate' signposts. Drive on to the outskirts of Horningsham and then turn right to run alongside Longleat Estate, passing the car park for Heaven's Gate viewpoint. After $1\frac{1}{4}$m, before the main road, turn left to enter Longleat Park (toll). Leave the park by following signposts marked 'Way Out/Warminster' and exit the grounds via the Horningsham Gate. Drive to the Bath Arms and go forward over crossroads with signposts indicating *Shaftesbury* and *Maiden Bradley*. Within $1\frac{1}{2}$m approach a T-junction and turn right for Maiden Bradley. Continue to crossroads and turn left on to the B3092, signposted *Mere*. In $5\frac{1}{4}$m turn left on to the A303, signposted *Andover*, and enter Mere. Drive through open countryside for 4m and turn right on to the B3089, signposted Salisbury. Continue to a junction with the A350 and turn left, then immediately right for Hindon. Proceed to the Grosvenor Arms Hotel and turn right on to an unclassified road signposted *Tisbury*. Meet the next crossroads and turn right into an unsignposted road, then take a narrow byroad to Newton. Approach a T-junction and turn right with Semley signposts. After $\frac{1}{2}$m turn left with signposts marked Donhead and Wardour and descend. Within $\frac{1}{2}$m cross the railway and after a short distance turn left with Tisbury signposts to continue past the grounds of Wardour Castle for Tisbury. Enter the town and turn right at the post office, signposted Salisbury, and continue to the end before turning right again. Drive on for $\frac{1}{4}$m and branch left with *Chilmark* signposts, passing Place House on the left and eventually entering Chilmark village. Turn left with Salisbury signposts, then right. Continue to the main road and turn right again on to the B3089 for *Teffont* Magna. Keep right into the village and drive to the far end and the Black Horse public house. Turn right here into an unclassified road signposted Tisbury, and continue into *Teffont Evias*. Within $\frac{1}{4}$m turn left with Salisbury signposts and cross a river bridge before ascending to a main road. Turn right to rejoin the B3089 and proceed to the outskirts of *Dinton*. Approach crossroads and turn right on to the unclassified road to *Fovant*. Drive to the far end of the village and turn right on to the A30. In $\frac{1}{2}$m turn left on to an unclassified road signposted *Broad Chalke*, and continue with hill-figure representations of army badges on the chalk slopes to the left. Ascend on to the down and after $1\frac{1}{2}$m turn left and drive to Broad Chalke in the Ebble Valley. Bear right then left through the village and proceed to *Bishopstone*. Continue to Combe Bisset and turn left on to the A354 for the return to Salisbury.

WILTSHIRE AND BERKSHIRE

Upper Thames and the Marlborough Downs

From Swindon

Drive 34   67 miles

Leave *Swindon* town centre by following Stow and *Banbury* signposts and taking the A361 for Stratton St Margaret. Approach traffic signals and turn left, then right, and continue to the hilltop town of *Highworth*. Stay with the A361 and later pass a riverside park before crossing the Thames into *Lechlade*. Turn right, then right again on to the A417 *Faringdon* road, and in ¾m approach the Trout Inn. By the nearside of the Inn turn left on to the B4449, signposted *Bampton*. Stay with the B4449 for 4m, approach a T-junction, and turn right on to the A4095, signposted Faringdon. After a short distance cross *Radcot* Bridge to reach Faringdon. Leave Faringdon by following signposts marked Swindon A420, and within ½m turn right into Highworth Road (B4019). Proceed for 1¼m before turning left on to an unclassified road and driving into *Great Coxwell*. Turn left on an unsignposted road and within ½m approach a T-junction. Turn right on to the A420, then take the first turning left for the unclassified road to Little Coxwell. Continue to the far end of the village, turn right at the triangle, and drive to Fernham. Turn left on to the B4508 and in ¼m branch right on to an unclassified road to *Uffington*. On the nearside of the village turn right; then take the second turning right, signposted White Horse Hill, and in 1m cross the main road. Ascend White Horse Hill to Uffington Castle, then follow the exit signs and descend. Approach the main road and turn right on to the B4507, then continue with views of the prehistoric white horse on the right. After another 2m approach crossroads and turn right on to the unclassified road signposted *Lambourn*. Ascend the Berkshire Downs into Berkshire and within 4¼m turn right on to the B4001 and continue to Lambourn. Turn right on to the B4000, then take the next turning left on to an unclassified road signposted Baydon. Within 2¼m approach a T-junction and turn right to cross the M4 motorway into Wiltshire before entering Baydon. Proceed as far as the Red Lion public house and turn left for the downland village of *Aldbourne*. Turn left on to A419, signposted *Newbury*, then in 1¾m turn right on to an unclassified road and continue to Ramsbury. Turn right and keep forward through this village, following a pleasant byroad through Axford and *Mildenhall* to *Marlborough*. Leave the latter by following signposts marked 'Swindon A345', then 'Wootton Bassett', on to an unclassified road. Continue along this and after 2m start the gradual climb up to the Marlborough Downs. Descend 1 in 7 Hackpen Hill and within 1¼m turn right on to the A361. Continue for a short distance before descending into *Wroughton*, then drive to the end of the village and turn left for the return into Swindon.

Placenames in *italic* type are worth stopping at; each is listed and described in the main gazetteer section of the book

WILTSHIRE AND BERKSHIRE

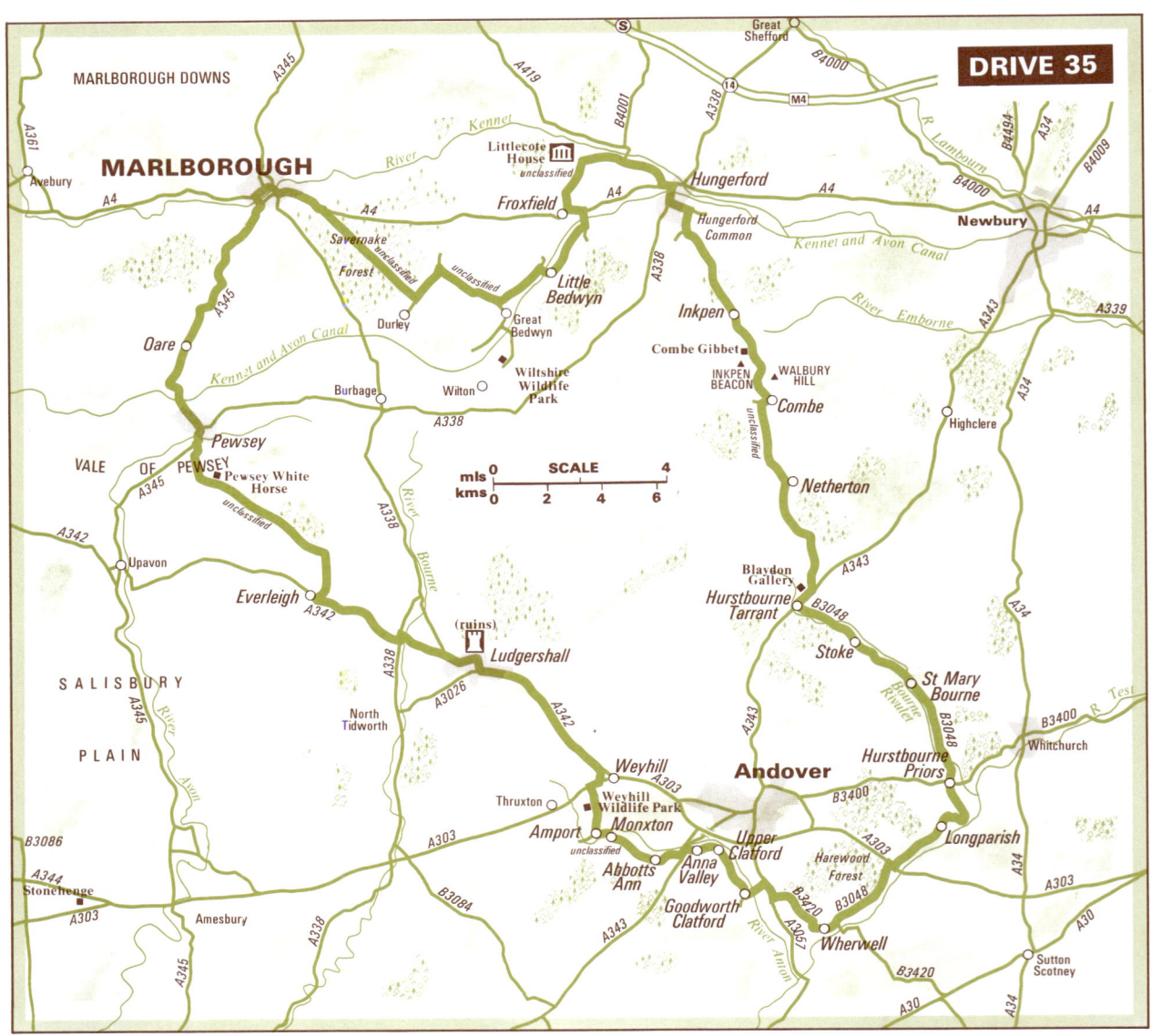

Vale of Pewsey and Savernake Forest

From Marlborough
Drive 35   68 miles

Leave *Marlborough* on the A345 by following *Chippenham* then *Salisbury* signposts. Cross high ground before reaching Oare, then continue through the Vale of Pewsey to cross the Kennet and Avon Canal. Enter *Pewsey* and leave by the Amesbury road. Cross the River Avon before branching left along an unclassified road signposted Everleigh, then turn immediately right. Ascend Pewsey Hill and cross the northern part of *Salisbury Plain* to the edge of Everleigh. Turn left on to the A342 with *Andover* signposts, and after 2m approach the junction with the A338 and turn left then immediately right. Continue into the town of *Ludgershall* and turn left at the T-junction. Drive to the far end of the town and continue to the outskirts of *Weyhill*. Turn right at the crossroads, signposted *Exeter*; turn right again on to the A303 and continue for $\frac{1}{4}$m before turning left on to an unclassified road signposted Zoo. After 1m Weyhill Wildlife Park lies to the right. Proceed to Amport, turn left to Monxton, then on approaching crossroads drive straight on for Abbotts Ann. Turn right, then approach the Eagle public house and turn left. Drive on for a short distance and keep left, then bear right. Meet the main road, turn left on to the A343, and take the next right turning on to an unclassified road signposted the Clatfords. Continue through Anna Valley and Upper Clatford, then through the neighbouring town of Goodworth Clatford. Turn left with Andover signposts and cross the river bridge. Approach the main road and turn right on to the A3057, signposted *Winchester*, before continuing for another $\frac{1}{4}$m and turning left on to the B3420. Descend into the Test Valley and enter the village of *Wherwell*. Keep left, then at the end of the village drive forward on to the B3048 and later pass through the edge of Harewood Forest. Meet the junction with the A303 and turn right and immediately left to pass through the villages of *Longparish* and Hurstbourne Priors. Again turn right and immediately left to follow the Bourne stream and pass through St Mary Bourne and Stoke for *Hurstbourne Tarrant*. Turn right on to the A343, signposted *Newbury*, then within $\frac{1}{2}$m turn left on to an unclassified road signposted Netherton. Proceed along a byroad and after 3m enter the hamlet of Netherton. Continue forward with signposts indicating Combe and *Inkpen*. Climb a gradual ascent and after 2m turn sharp right to the edge of Combe. Keep left and continue the ascent over the shoulder of Inkpen Hill, passing Walbury Hill on the right and Combe Gibbet on the left. Descend steeply and later pass over crossroads to follow *Hungerford* signposts into Inkpen. Approach the T-junction, turn right, then take the first turning left. Continue for $2\frac{1}{2}$m and bear right into a gated road signposted Hungerford. Cross Hungerford Common and proceed to the next T-junction, then turn left and drive into the town of Hungerford. Approach a T-junction and turn right on to the A338. Cross the Kennet and Avon Canal and turn left on to the A4. Within $\frac{1}{4}$m turn right on to the A419, signposted *Swindon*, and in a further $\frac{1}{2}$m re-enter Wiltshire from Berkshire. Within another $\frac{1}{2}$m keep forward along the unclassified Froxfield road, and within $\frac{3}{4}$m

continued on page 61

WILTSHIRE AND BERKSHIRE

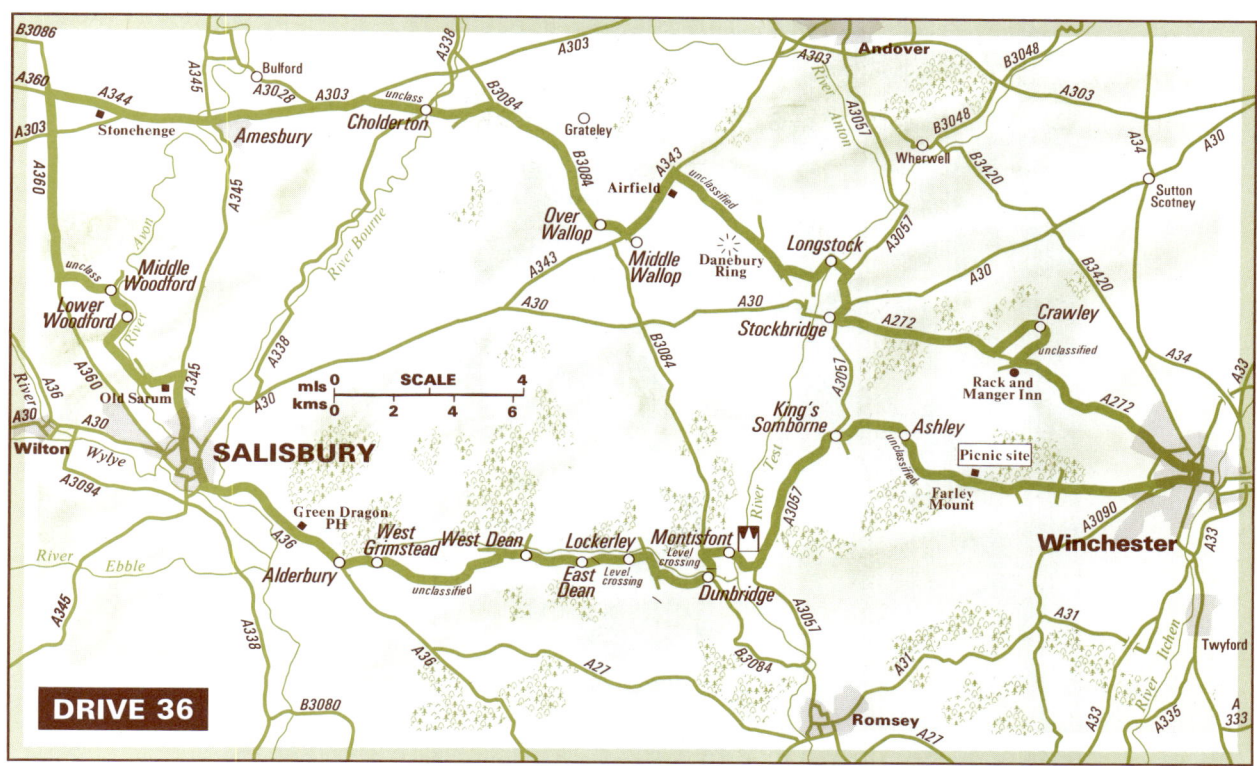

The Test Valley and Stonehenge

From Salisbury

Drive 36   71 miles

Follow *Southampton* signposts to leave *Salisbury* by the A36, and within 2m ascend to pass the Green Dragon public house on the left. Continue to Alderbury and turn left on to an unclassified road for West Grimstead. Continue forward with West Dean signposts and within 3m approach a T-junction. Turn right to reach West Dean, then turn right again with Lockerley signposts and continue beyond East Dean. Go over the level crossing and proceed into Lockerley. Within ½m turn right, and in a further ¼m pass under a railway bridge; turn left with Dunbridge signposts by the nearside of the green, and

Drive 35 continued

pass the entrance to Littlecote House. Continue to Froxfield and turn left to rejoin the A4, passing the Somerset Almshouses. After almost ½m turn right on to an unclassified road signposted Little Bedwyn, then cross bridges before turning right again to follow the line of the Kennet and Avon Canal. Drive to Little Bedwyn and keep right with signposts marked Great Bedwyn. Recross the canal and railway bridge and turn left. At the edge of Great Bedwyn, follow the Marlborough road and after 1¾m turn left with Savernake signposts. After another mile take an unsignposted right turn opposite a set of iron gates and enter Savernake Forest. Continue for 3m before turning left on to the A4 and returing to Marlborough.

continue into Dunbridge. Turn left on to the B3084 in the village, then go over a level crossing and river bridge. In a further ½m turn right on to an unclassified road signposted *Mottisfont* Village. At the next T-junction turn right and pass the entrance to Mottisfont Abbey. In the village keep left, later crossing the River Test and approaching a main road. At the main road turn left on to the A3057 and follow the Test Valley to *King's Somborne*. Drive to the Crown Inn and turn right on to an unclassified road signposted *Winchester.* Take the next turning left, and after ¾m turn right for Ashley. Climb through wooded countryside to Farley Mount and bear left at the fork junction. Follow a pleasant byroad and continue forward over all crossroads for the next 3m; turn left on to the A3090 and enter Winchester. Leave the city by following *Stockbridge* signposts along the A272. Approach the Rack and Manger Inn in 4¾m, and turn right on to an unclassified road signposted Crawley. Drive for 1m to a pond, then turn left and pass through to the far end of Crawley village. Keep left, then within 1¼m turn right to rejoin the A272 before later descending into the Test Valley and proceeding to the edge of Stockbridge. Drive to the roundabout and take the second exit on to the A30, then continue to the next roundabout and branch left on to the A3057, signposted *Andover.* In ¾m turn left on to an unclassified road signposted Longstock, and cross a bridge. Cross the River Test to Longstock, turn left, then continue to the end of the village and turn right on to a narrow unsignposted byroad. Approach a T-junction within ¾m and turn right. Drive across open downland and within another ¾m bear left with Grateley signposts. Proceed for about 2m and meet a main road. Turn left on to the A343 and pass the Army Aviation Centre, then continue

for 1½m to crossroads and turn right on to the B3084. Continue to Over Wallop, and within 3½m turn left on to an unclassified road signposted *Amesbury*. Drive on for about ¼m before bearing right through wooded country to Cholderton. Turn left on to the A338, then within 200yds turn right into an unclassified road. Continue for 1½m before turning left on to the A303 and taking a fast main road to bypass Amesbury. Approach a roundabout and keep forward, then within 1¾m turn right on to the A344, signposted *Devizes*. Pass *Stonehenge* and continue with the A344. Within 1½m turn left on to the A360, signposted Salisbury, and within a further 1m approach another roundabout and take the second exit. Cross part of *Salisbury Plain* and after 3m approach crossroads and turn left on to an unclassified road signposted Woodford. Proceed to Middle Woodford and turn right at the T-junction. Follow the River Avon to Lower Woodford and in 2m cross the river bridge and turn left, then immediately right. Drive on for a short distance before passing the earthworks of *Old Sarum*. On reaching the main road turn right on to the A345 and return to Salisbury.

Placenames in *italic* type are worth stopping at; each is listed and described in the main gazetteer section of the book

Sussex

Beachy Head and the Sussex Weald

From Eastbourne

Drive 37   80 miles

Take the B2103 Beachy Head road from *Eastbourne*, and after ascending turn left on to an unclassified road leading to the summit of Beachy Head. Continue past Belle Tout Lighthouse towards *Birling Gap*, then turn inland to *Eastdean* and left on to the A259 *Seaford* road. Climb to the top of a steep ascent and turn right on to the B2105 Polegate road. Pass *Friston* Forest on the left as the drive continues through Jevington and Wannock to Polegate. Turn left on to the A22, signposted *London*. Pass through *Wilmington* Wood then turn left on to an unclassified road to *Michelham Priory*. Continue to the B2108 and turn right then immediately left, signposted London. Cross flat countryside before turning left on to the A22, then take the next turning right on to the unclassified Horam road. After a while, join the A267 and enter Horam. From here take the *Tunbridge Wells* road to Cross in Hand, and continue through wooded country to Five Ashes. Within ½m turn left on to an unclassified road. Join the B2101 and enter *Rotherfield*, on the eastern edge of *Ashdown Forest*, then keep forward on an unclassified road with *Eridge* signposts. Drive to a T-junction and turn right on to the A26 with Tunbridge Wells signposts, then pass through Eridge. Within 1m turn left on to an unclassified road signposted *Groombridge*, and in another ½m turn right with High Rocks signposts. Within ½m bear right to pass the curious sandstone outcrop known as High Rocks on the right. Drive on for 1½m and at crossroads, turn right into Major York's Road. Cross the common, and on the far side — where there are further outcrops of rock — turn left on to the A26 into Royal Tunbridge Wells. Follow Eastbourne A267 signposts from the town. Proceed to Frant and turn left on to an unclassified road signposted Bells Yew Green. Drive on to the latter and turn right on to the B2169 *Lamberhurst* road. Pass through woodland and turn left on to the B2100 for Lamberhurst, then return by the same road. Continue for 3m and turn left on to the B2099 for Wadhurst. Follow Ticehurst signposts and in 1½m turn right on to the B2181, signposted Burwash Common. Enter Stonegate, turn left on to the unclassified Burwash road, and in another ¾m turn right before crossing the River Rother on the approach to Burwash. Proceed to a junction with the A265 and turn right, then approach a war memorial and turn left on to an unclassified road signposted Woods Corner. Climb to 646ft, and after reaching the Swan Inn at Woods Corner turn right then left on to the Ponts Green road. Descend to the Ash Bourne valley and on meeting the B2204 turn right with *Hailsham* signposts. Continue and turn right on to the A271. Proceed through Boreham Street and in ½m turn left on to an unclassified road. Pass *Herstmonceux* Castle and continue to Wartling. Bear right on to the *Pevensey* road and cross the Pevensey Levels. Reach the A27 and turn right into Pevensey. Continue to Westham and turn left on to the B2191, signposted Eastbourne, before later joining the A259 for the return to the town.

SUSSEX

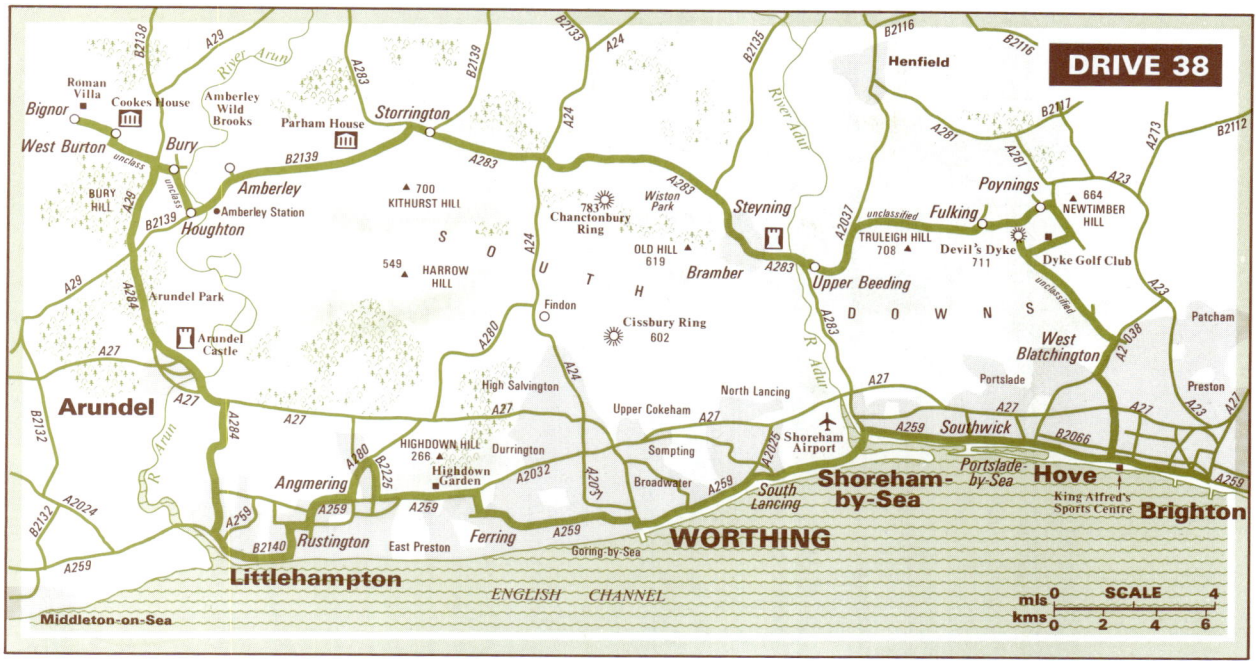

Villages of the South Downs

From Worthing

Drive 38   63 miles

Leave *Worthing* on the A259 *Brighton* road and pass through South *Lancing* to *Shoreham-by-Sea*. Continue through *Southwick, Portslade by Sea,* and *Hove* before driving into Brighton. Return along the sea front towards Hove and pass the King Alfred Sports Centre. Approach traffic signals and turn right into Hove Street, then follow *London* signposts. In 1¾m turn right on to the A2038 and ascend to a crossroads. Take the left turn on to an unclassified road signposted Devil's Dyke, and in ½m keep left and climb to Devil's Dyke. Return, then in ½m turn left with Poynings signposts and pass the Dyke Golf Club. In ¾m turn left again, and ½m farther turn sharp left to descend into Poynings. Turn left and proceed along the foot of the South Downs to Fulking. At the A2037 turn left to Upper Beeding, then turn right on to the A283, signposted *Steyning*. Cross the River Adur into *Bramber*, and continue to Steyning. Stay with the A283 and skirt the grounds of *Wiston* Park before proceeding to the edge of Washington. Approach a roundabout and take the second exit to *Storrington*. Drive to the end of the town and turn left on to the B2139, signposted *Bognor Regis*. Pass a road on the right leading to *Parham* House, continue beyond Amberley station and cross the River Arun. Proceed to *Houghton*, turn right on to an unclassified road signposted 'Roman Villa', and continue along a narrow lane to *Bury*. Approach crossroads and turn left, then meet a main road and turn right then immediately left for West Burton. Continue to *Bignor*, then return through West Burton to the A29. Turn right and ascend Bury Hill. Approach a roundabout and take the second exit on to the A284, signposted *Littlehampton*. Pass through thickly-wooded country and skirt the grounds of Arundel Park on the approach to *Arundel*. Take the A27 Worthing road out of the town, and in 1m turn right on to the A284 for Littlehampton. Follow signposts marked Worthing, then *Rustington* B2140, and continue along the coast to Rustington. Drive to Rustington church and turn right with Worthing signposts, then in ¼m turn left. After a farther ¼m turn left again and approach a roundabout. Take the second exit on to the A259 and in ¾m, at the next roundabout, take the first exit on to the A280 *Horsham* road. Continue to *Angmering* and turn right on to the B2225, passing Pigeon House on the left. Keep right, then in ¾m approach crossroads and turn left on to the A259, signposted Worthing. Pass Highdown Garden on the left before approaching another roundabout; take the third exit, signposted 'To The Town Centre', then pass over a level crossing to a T-junction. Turn left and keep forward through *Goring-by-Sea* for the return to Worthing.

Placenames in italic type are worth stopping at; each is listed and described in the main gazetteer section of the book

SUSSEX

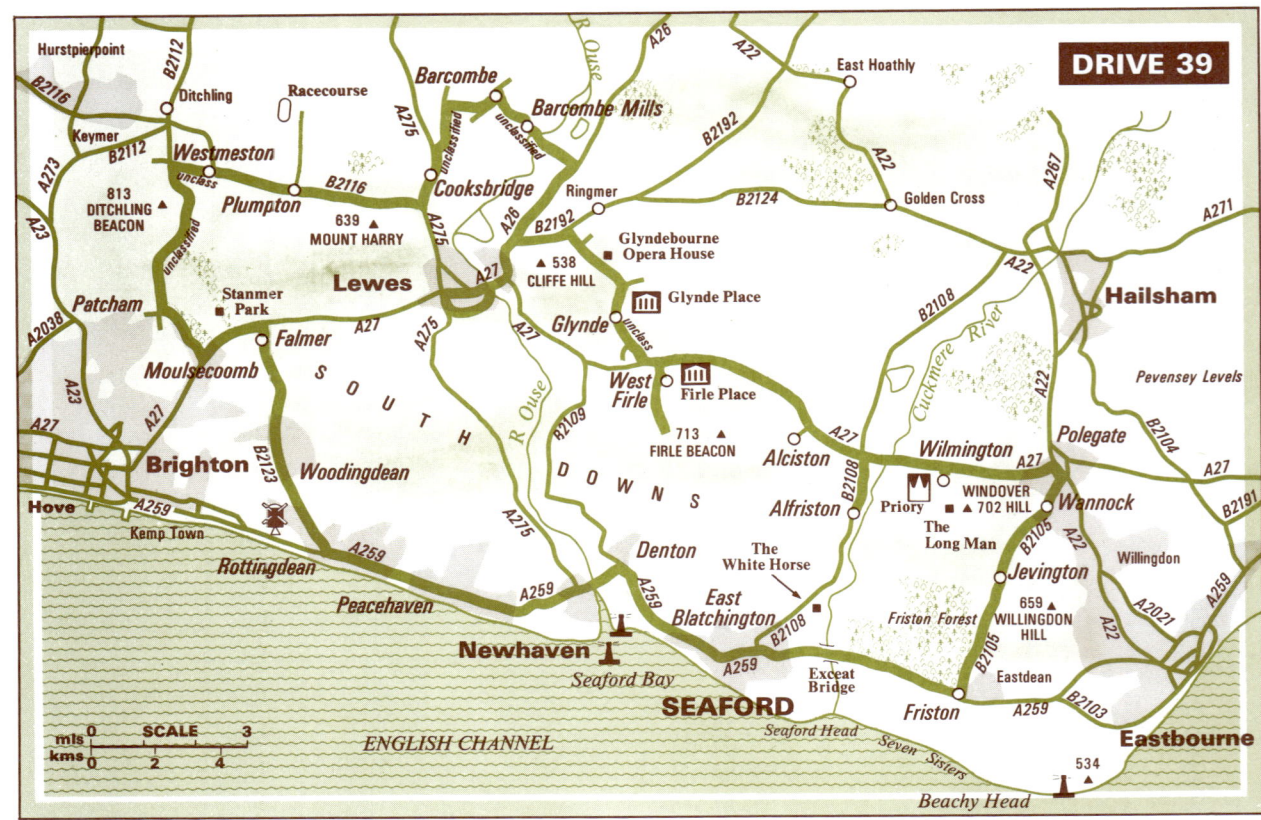

The Downs of East Sussex

From Seaford

Drive 39   59 miles

Follow the A259 *Eastbourne* road out of *Seaford* and descend to cross the Exceat Bridge. Cross the downs to *Friston*, then turn left on to the B2105 Polegate road and pass Friston Forest on the left on the way through Jevington and Wannock to Polegate. Turn left on to the A22, then turn left again on to the A27 *Lewes* road; pass a large figure cut into the hillside turf before reaching the outskirts of *Wilmington*. Drive for 1½m and approach crossroads, then turn left on to the B2108 Seaford road and proceed to *Alfriston*. Return to the A27 and turn left; in 4½m turn left on to the unclassified West Firle road, passing the entrance to Firle Place on the left. Keep forward to ascend Firle Beacon, then return to the A27. Turn left, then in ½m turn right on to an unclassified road and continue into *Glynde*. After about ¾m bear left, signposted *Ringmer*, passing Glyndebourne Opera House on the right. Reach the B2192 and turn left with Lewes signposts, then approach the A26. Turn left into Lewes, then leave on the A26 *Uckfield* road. In 3m turn left on to an unclassified road to Barcombe Mills. Proceed to Barcombe then turn left, signposted Lewes, and in ½m branch right. Keep forward to a T-junction and turn left. Within 1m join the A275 and go over the level crossing at Cooksbridge. In another ½m turn right on to the B2116, signposted Hurstpierpoint. Proceed along the foot of the *South Downs* to *Plumpton*, then skirt the downs to Westmeston. Drive past the church and keep forward on to an unclassified road signposted Underhill Lane. In 1m approach crossroads and turn left to ascend *Ditchling* Beacon. Descend across downland and in 2½m turn left, signposted Moulsecoomb. In 1¼m turn left on to the A27 Lewes road, passing Stanmer Park on the left. Proceed to Falmer and turn right on to the B2123 *Rottingdean* road. Cross downland and pass through Woodingdean before reaching Rottingdean. Turn left on to the A259, signposted *Newhaven*, and proceed through *Telscombe* Cliffs and *Peacehaven* to reach Newhaven. Follow Eastbourne signposts for the return to Seaford.

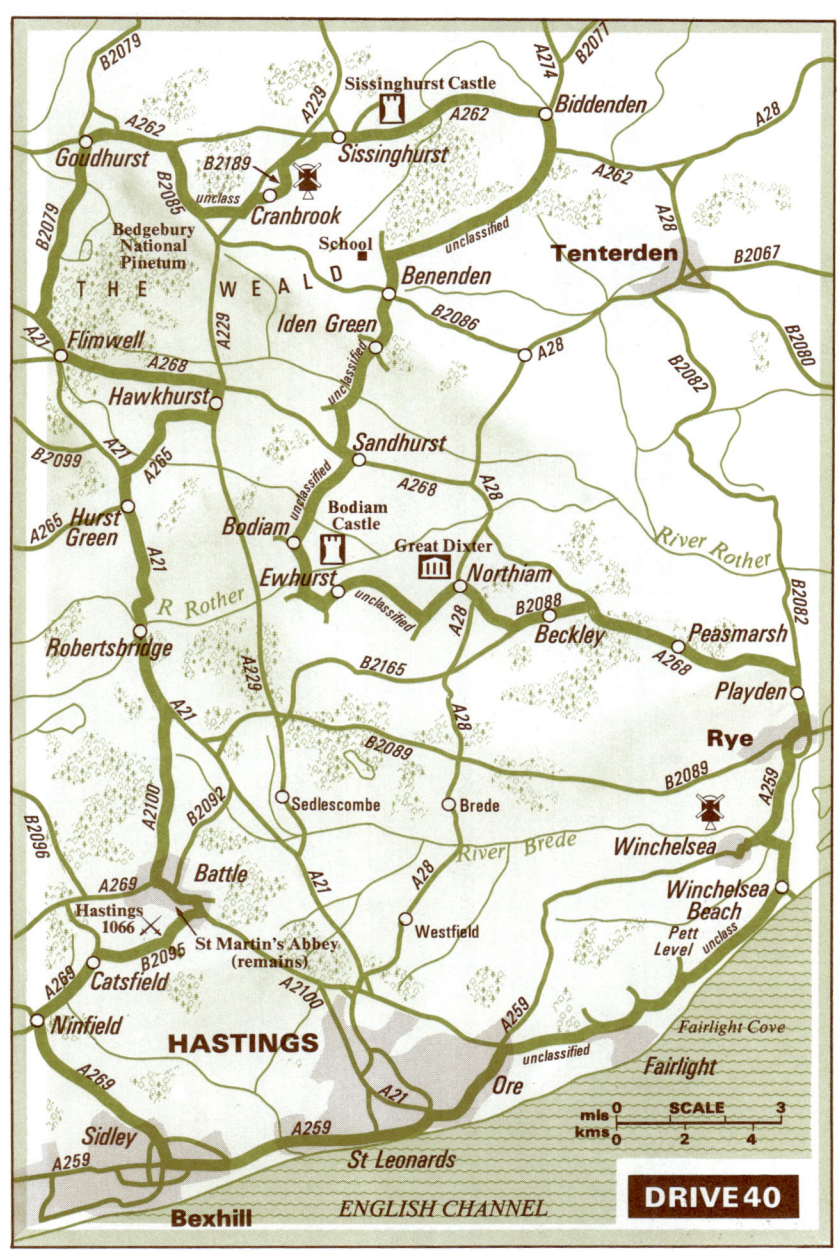

Woodlands of the Eastern Weald

From Hastings

Drive 40   78 miles

From *Hastings* follow signposts marked 'Bexhill' and 'Lewes A259' along the sea front. Pass through *St Leonards* to Bexhill, then take the A269 London road out of Bexhill and continue through Sidley to Ninfield. Turn right in the latter village and continue on the *Battle* road. Proceed to Catsfield, drive to the end of the village, then turn right on to the B2095 with Battle Station signposts. Turn left on to the A2100 and enter Battle. Follow London signposts and pass through woodland to join the A21. Pass through *Robertsbridge* and ascend to Hurst Green, then turn right on to the A265 *Hawkhurst* road. After entering Kent ascend to Hawkhurst, then turn left on to the A268 Flimwell road and continue the ascent to Flimwell in Sussex. Approach crossroads and turn right on to the A21 London road to re-enter Kent. In another 1m turn right on to the B2079, signposted *Goudhurst*, and pass the entrance to Bedgebury National Pinetum. Beyond Goudhurst turn right and follow *Ashford* signposts along the A262. Turn right on to the B2085 Hawkhurst road, and after 2m turn left on to an unclassified road signposted *Cranbrook*. Drive to a main road and turn left then right on to the B2189. Proceed into Cranbrook. Continue along the B2189 with *Staplehurst* signposts, then join the A229. In ¼m turn right on to the A262 Ashford road and pass through *Sissinghurst*. Proceed to *Biddenden* and turn right to continue with the Ashford road. In ¾m go forward on to an unclassified road signposted *Benenden* School. Cross a main road in Benenden and continue through Iden Green. After a while turn left on to the A268 *Rye* road and drive into *Sandhurst*, then turn right on to an unclassified road signposted *Bodiam*. Re-enter Sussex and pass Bodiam church before making a left turn on to the *Ewhurst* road. Pass Bodiam Castle and keep forward to cross the river. In 1m turn left along a narrow lane. Pass through Ewhurst and continue along the *Northiam* road. Enter Northiam and turn right on to the A28 *Hastings* road, then branch left on to the B2088 Rye road. Drive to the end of *Beckley* village and turn right on to the A268 to continue through Peasmarsh and Playden to Rye. From Rye follow Hastings signposts to leave along the A259, crossing flat country then making a sharp ascent to *Winchelsea*. Return to the river bridge and turn right on to the unclassified road to Winchelsea Beach. Follow an embankment to Pett Level, then turn inland and pass the road to *Fairlight* Cove. Continue through Fairlight and turn left on to the A259 into Hastings.

Placenames in *italic* type are worth stopping at; each is listed and described in the main gazetteer section of the book

South of London

North Downs and St Leonard's Forest

From Epsom

Drive 41   71 miles

Leave Epsom from the southern end of the High Street. Enter a roundabout, take the second exit to join the B280, and cross Epsom Common. After 1½m approach traffic signals and continue forward. Continue for 2m and turn left on to the A244 for Oxshott, then turn right on to an unclassified road and proceed to *Stoke D'Abernon*. Turn right on to the A245 for *Cobham*, then left on to an unclassified road signposted Downside and *Ockham*. Cross the river bridge, then turn right and follow Ockham signposts. Drive to the war memorial and turn right on to the B2039 before taking the next turning left on to an unclassified road. Approach crossroads and continue forward into *East Clandon*. Turn left to join the A246 for *East Horsley*, then after ½m turn right on to an unclassified road signposted *Shere*. After another ½m bear left with *Dorking* signposts, then after another 1½m meet crossroads and turn right with *Abinger* signposts. Descend 1 in 6 White Downs Hill and continue for 1m before turning left on to the A25. After ½m turn right on to an unclassified road. Ascend for 1¼m before making a short detour, and turn sharp left to *Friday Street*. Return to the T-junction, turn left, then keep forward with Leith Hill signposts. Continue for 2½m to join the B2126, then keep left for *Ockley*. Turn left on to the A29, and after passing the King's Arms public house turn right on to the B2126. Continue for 1½m then turn left on to the A24 to Capel. Approach the Crown Inn and turn right on to an unclassified road signposted Newdigate. Enter the latter village and turn right. Proceed to *Rusper* and bear left with *Crawley* signposts. Continue for ½m then turn right for Faygate. Pass the Holmbush Inn, turn left with Crawley signposts, then approach the main road and turn left again on to the A264. After 2¾m turn left on to the A23 Crawley Bypass. Follow *London* signposts, and after passing *Gatwick* Airport continue for 1m before meeting a roundabout and taking the first exit on to an unclassified road leading to the villages of *Charlwood* and Leigh. Pass through Leigh and after ¼m pass the Seven Stars public house. Turn right here and continue to Betchworth before approaching a T-junction and turning left then right, signposted *Walton-on-the-Hill*. Meet a roundabout and take the second exit on to B2032. Climb 1 in 6 Pebble Hill on to the downs and on reaching the summit turn left on to the B2033, signposted *Box Hill*. Bear left on to an unclassified road for Box Hill. Descend to the bottom of the hill, then approach a T-junction and turn right with *Mickleham* signposts. Within ¼m turn right again on to an unclassified road signposted Headley. Proceed forward to a T-junction and turn right on to the B2033. Ascend and take the next turning left on to an unclassified road to Headley, signposted Epsom. After 1¾m approach crossroads and turn right. Pass Epsom Downs Racecourse and turn left on to the B290 for the return to Epsom.

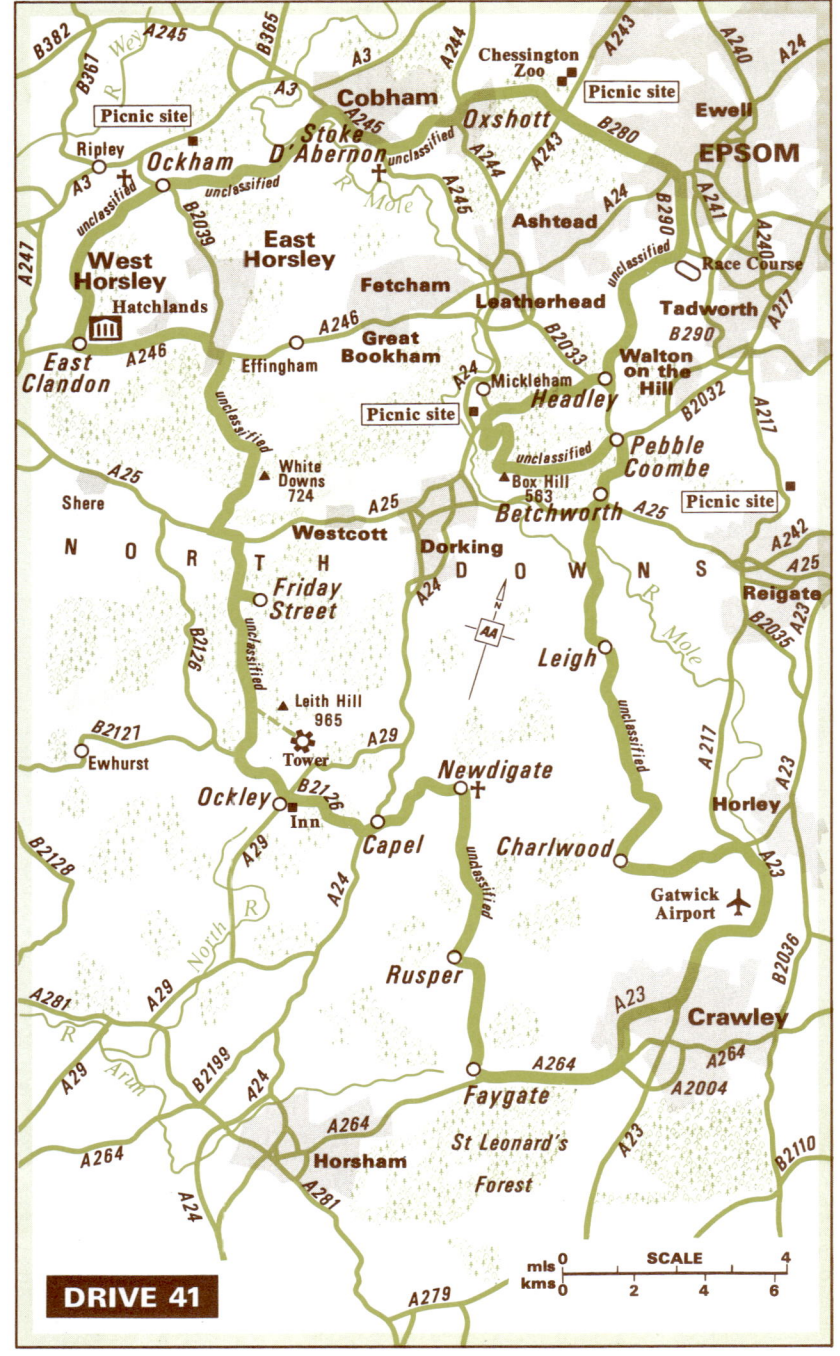

SOUTH OF LONDON

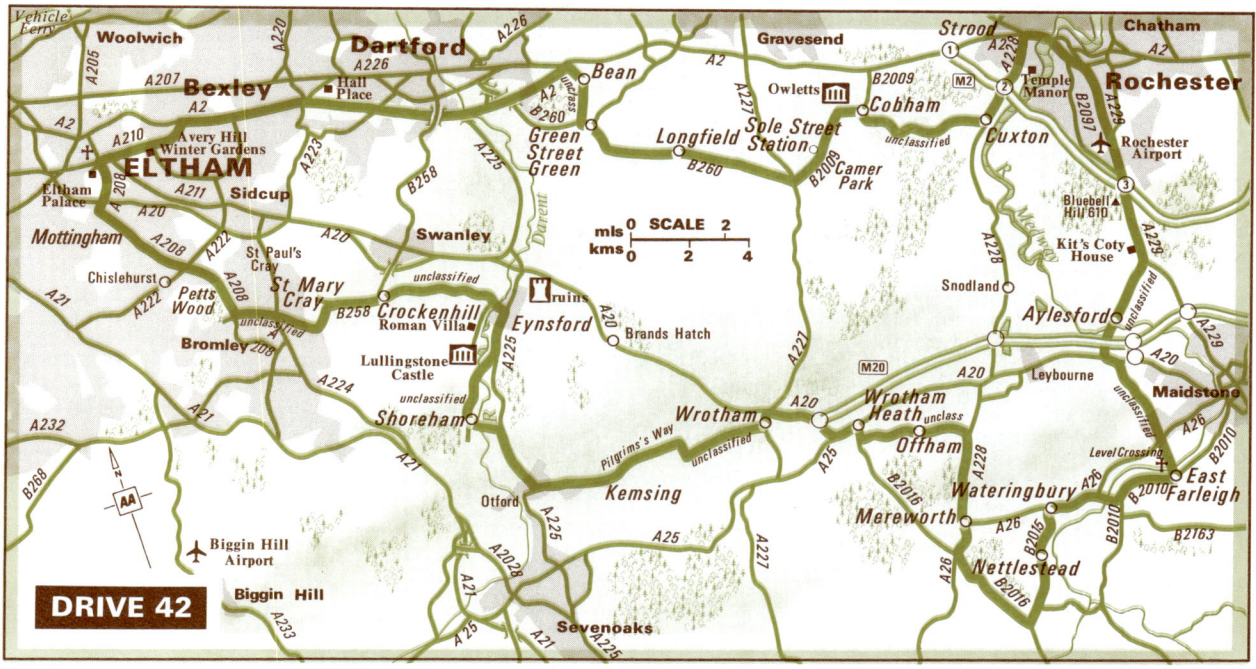

Kent Orchards and the Medway Valley

From Eltham

Drive 42   73 miles

Leave *Eltham* from the church, following signposts marked 'Mottingham/*Chislehurst* A208' for 100yds before keeping left and continuing for ¾m. Cross a main road and proceed to Mottingham. Turn left, pass *Petts Wood*, then in ¾m approach a roundabout and turn left into unclassified Poverest Road. After 1m approach traffic lights and continue forward past the edge of St Mary Cray. Proceed along the Chelsfield Road, then after ¼m bear left into Cockmannings Road. After ½m turn left into Waldens Road, then approach a T-junction at the end of the road and turn right on to the B258 for Crockenhill. Drive to the Chequers Inn and go forward on an unclassified road, following *Eynsford* signposts. Proceed to the second T-junction and turn left; cross the River Darent into Eynsford, drive to the church, then turn right on to the A225 *Sevenoaks* road. Proceed for 1m and turn right on to an unclassified road signposted Castle Farm. Descend, recross the river, and keep left for *Shoreham*. On reaching the Royal Oak public house turn left, then approach a main road and turn right again to rejoin the A225. Continue to the outskirts of *Otford* and turn left on to an unclassified road signposted *Kemsing*. Proceed to *Wrotham*, turn left into the village to join the A227, then approach a roundabout and turn left again. Bear right, meet another roundabout, and take the third exit on to the A20 *Maidstone* road. Continue to Wrotham Heath; approach traffic signals and drive forward, then in ¼m turn right on to the B2016, signposted Paddock Wood. Pass under a railway bridge and turn left on to an unclassified road for *Offham*. Keep forward into a fruit-growing area, then after 1¼m approach crossroads and turn right on to the A228 to *Mereworth*. Join the A26 *Tonbridge* road and within ¾m turn left on to the B2016, signposted East Peckham. After 2¼m turn left again on to the B2015 and pass through *Nettlestead* and *Wateringbury*. Approach traffic signals and turn right on to the A26, then in 1m turn right again on to the B2163 with Coxheath signposts. Drive over a level crossing and the River Medway, then proceed for ½m and turn left on to the B2010. Enter *East Farleigh* and drive to the church. Turn left on to an unclassified road, recross the Medway, then go over a level crossing. Proceed forward over all crossroads, skirting Maidstone, for 2¾m. Approach a T-junction and turn left on to the A20. Take the next right turn on to an unclassified road, then later cross a bridge into *Aylesford*. Enter the village and approach traffic signals; turn right then bear left with *Rochester* signposts, and after 1¼m ascend to the *North Downs*. Reach the Lower Bell public house and turn left on to the A229. Pass Kit's Coty House to the left and climb 1 in 10 Bluebell Hill. Continue to a roundabout and keep left on to the *Chatham* road. Pass Rochester Airport, keep left, then after a while enter Rochester on the A2 London road. Cross Rochester Bridge into *Strood* and approach traffic signals. Turn left on to the A228 with Cuxton signposts, and on entering Cuxton turn right on to an unclassified road signposted *Cobham*. In 2m bear right, and after approaching a war memorial turn left on to the B2009. Enter Cobham and in ½m, after passing Owletts house on the right, turn left with *Meopham* signposts. Continue for ½m beyond Sole Street Station and pass Camer Park on the left. After ¼m approach a T-junction and turn left on to the A227, then in 200yds turn right on to the B260 for Longfield. Proceed along the *Dartford* road to Green Street Green, then pass the White Hart public house and turn right on to an unclassified road for Bean. Within ½m turn left and join the A2 *London* road, then after 6m pass the junction for *Bexley*. In 2¾m turn left into Chester Road, signposted 'Eltham A210'. Within ¼m turn right on to the A210, then after a further ½m drive to traffic signals and continue forward. After a short distance pass the entrance to Avery Hill Winter Gardens on the left. Continue along the A210 for Eltham High Street and the return to Eltham church.

Placenames in *italic* type are worth stopping at; each is listed and described in the main gazetteer section of the book

SOUTH OF LONDON

Royal Parks and Open Heath

From Staines

Drive 43   57 miles

Leave *Staines* town centre cr bypass by following *Basingstoke* and then *Windsor* signposts to join the A308. Pass Runnymede and Old Windsor, then keep left. Approach a roundabout and take the first exit on to the A332, signposted *Ascot*. Enter Windsor Great Park, then continue for 4m before bearing right then left. Approach the Crispin public house and turn right on to the B3034, signposted Winkfield. After $\frac{3}{4}$m turn left on to the A330, signposted Ascot, then after $\frac{1}{2}$m turn right on to the B3034. Go forward over all crossroads to join the A3095, continue for $\frac{1}{4}$m, then turn left to rejoin the B3034. Continue for 1m and cross a humpback bridge; keep left to *Binfield*, then approach crossroads by the Royal Standard public house and turn left on to an unclassified road. After $\frac{1}{2}$m bear right; continue to the main road and turn right on to the A329 for *Wokingham*. Join one-way traffic and bear right through the town. Before reaching the clock tower turn left on to the B3349, signposted Arborfield, and go over a level crossing. After $2\frac{1}{2}$m turn right for Arborfield Cross. Turn right and immediately left on to an unclassified road signposted Swallowfield. Continue for about 2m and turn right, then proceed for $\frac{1}{2}$m and turn left, crossing a river bridge to reach Swallowfield, then turn left with Basingstoke signposts and proceed through the village of Swallowfield. Meet the A33 main road and turn left to Riseley. Bear right and on approaching the Wellington monument turn left on to an unclassified road signposted *Eversley*. Continue for $\frac{1}{2}$m then cross a main road to join the B3011. After $\frac{1}{2}$m branch left on to an unclassified road, and after a further 3m go over crossroads to join the A327 for Eversley Cross. Drive to the Chequers public house and turn left on to the B3016, signposted Wokingham. Continue to *Finchampstead* and turn right. After $\frac{1}{4}$m meet a war memorial and branch right on to the B3348, signposted Crowthorne. Approach a roundabout and take the first exit on to the A321, then after 1m meet crossroads and turn right on to an unclassified road. After $2\frac{3}{4}$m go over a staggered crossroads, signposted *Bagshot*, and at the end of the road turn right on to the A322. Proceed for $1\frac{1}{2}$m before turning left on to the A332 Ascot road, then continue for $1\frac{3}{4}$m and bear right. Approach a roundabout and take the third exit on to the A329, then enter Ascot. Drive forward to the A30 main road and turn left. Proceed for $1\frac{1}{4}$m before turning left again on to an unclassified road, then pass the Sun public house and continue for $\frac{1}{2}$m before turning right for Englefield Green. Cross a main road, continue for 300yds, then bear left to descend Tite Hill to the edge of *Egham*. Rejoin the A30 for the return to Staines.

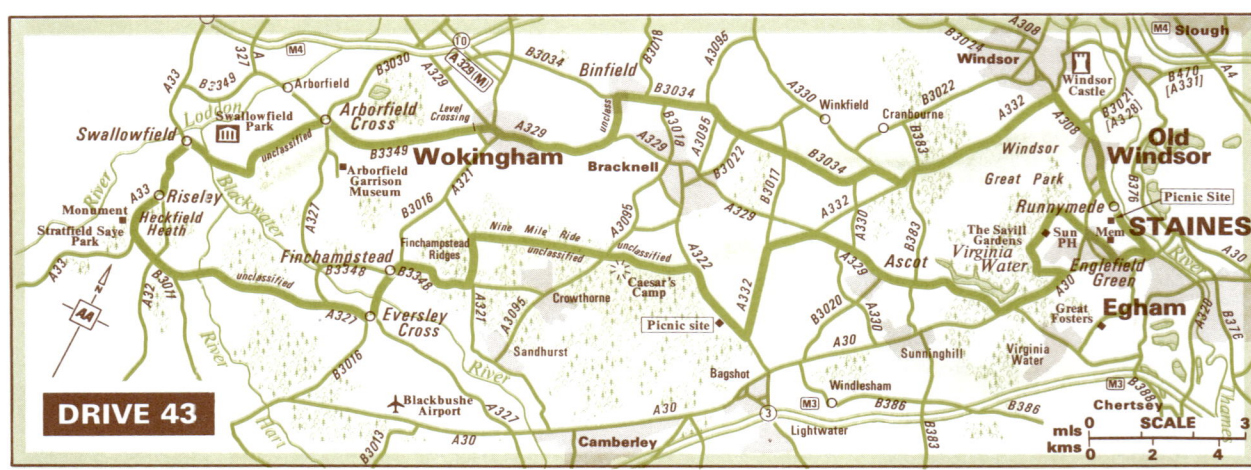

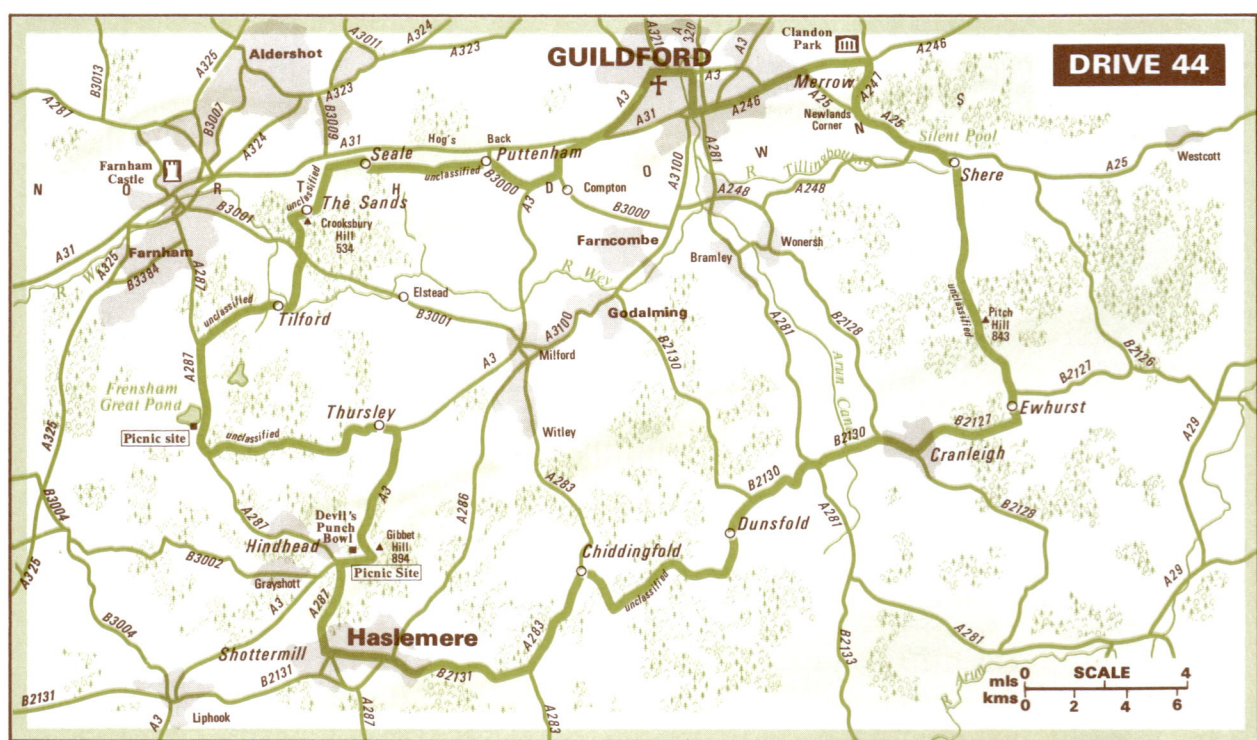

SOUTH OF LONDON

To the Heart of the Sussex Weald

From Purley

Drive 45 57 miles

Take the A23 *Brighton* road out of Purley, then after 1m turn left on to the B2030 with *Caterham* signposts. Climb on to the *North Downs* at Old Coulsdon, then continue 1m before crossing Coulsdon Common. After ¼m proceed forward on to an unclassified road signposted *Chaldon*. Meet a T-junction and turn right on to the B2031, then take the

Along the Hog's Back Ridge

From Guildford

Drive 44 55 miles

Leave *Guildford* town centre with signposts marked 'Other Routes', and after 1m turn left on to the A3 bypass, signposted *Petersfield*. After 1½m go under a road bridge, and after a further 1m pass the turning for *Compton*. Continue for ½m then turn right on to the B3000, signposted *Farnham*, and proceed to Puttenham. Turn left in the village on an unclassified road, then follow a by-road along the southern slopes of the Hog's Back to Seale. Drive to the end of the latter village and turn left. Proceed for ½m before meeting crossroads and turning left for The Sands. Cross a main road with *Tilford* signposts, then proceed for ½m before turning left again, signposted *Elstead*. Drive to the end of Elstead and turn left on to the B3001 before taking the next turning right on to an unclassified road for Tilford. Cross the River Wey twice, following *Frensham* signposts, and after ¼m turn left. Continue for a further 1½m, turn left on to the A287 with *Hindhead* signposts, then proceed to Frensham Great Pond. Proceed for ¾m before turning left on to an unclassified road signposted *Thursley*. Reach the Pride of the Valley Hotel after 1½m, cross the main road, and after 1¾m turn right for Thursley. Continue for ½m then turn right on to the A3 to Hindhead. Follow signposts marked 'Haslemere A287', descend to Shottermill, then keep forward on to the B2131 for Haslemere. Leave this town by following *Petworth* signposts, then after 2½m take a left turn signposted *Chiddingfold*. After ¾m approach a T-junction and turn left on to the A283 for Chiddingfold. Drive to the Crown Inn, turn right on to an unclassified road signposted *Dunsfold*, and at the far side of the green bear right. Continue for 1m, turn left, then proceed to Dunsfold. After a further 1m turn right on to the B2130, signposted *Cranleigh*. Continue 1m farther and bear left, and after ¼m turn right. Go over a staggered crossroads, then after 1¼m turn right on to the B2128 into Cranleigh. Approach an obelisk at the end of the village and turn left on to the B2127; after 2¼m turn left again into *Ewhurst*, then keep forward for the unclassified *Shere* road. After ¾m bear left and cross Pitch Hill. Drive to a T-junction in Shere and turn left, signposted Guildford. Continue to the next T-junction and turn left again to join the A25. Ascend to *Newlands Corner* and turn right on to the A247, signposted *Woking*. Descend for 1m, then at crossroads turn left on to the A246. Drive through Merrow on the return to Guildford.

next turning left on to an unclassified road into Roffes Lane. After 1m turn right, passing The Harrow public house. Descend White Hill and keep forward with Nutfield and Redhill signposts. Continue for 1½m before meeting crossroads, then turn left and proceed to the main road. Turn left again on to the A25 and drive into *Bletchingley*. Proceed to the Prince Albert public house and turn right. Continue to Smallfield, keep forward with Copthorne signposts, and after 1½m turn left on to the B2037, signposted *East Grinstead*. After 1m turn right on to the B2028, signposted *Haywards Heath*, and continue to Crawley Down and Turners Hill. Approach the Crown Hotel, keep forward over crossroads, then after ¾m branch left on to an unclassified road. Continue for 1¾m, then turn right into West Hoathley. Drive to the church and turn left, then at the Vinols Cross Inn turn right and descend to Sharpthorne. After ¾m turn left with East Grinstead signposts and continue past the end of Weir Wood Reservoir before ascending to East Grinstead. Turn right into the town and proceed forward along the High Street. Turn left into College Road, signposted 'A264 *Tunbridge Wells*'.

then descend to a T-junction and turn right. Pass through Hammerwood to Holtye, and on reaching the White Horse public house turn left on to an unclassified road to enter *Cowden*. After ½m cross a main road, signposted *Penshurst*, then after 1m turn left, signposted *Hever*. Approach crossroads and drive straight on, then after 1½m turn right and enter Hever. Return through this village and on approaching a T-junction turn right. After 2m turn right on to the B2026 and cross the River Eden into *Edenbridge*. Pass the Crown Inn and turn left on to an unclassified road signposted Lingfield, then continue to Haxted Mill. Return for 100yds and turn left with *Limpsfield* signposts. Continue for 5m. Approach traffic signals, then drive forward on to the B269 and continue into Limpsfield. Proceed to the end of this village and turn right. Ascend the North Downs and after ¾m turn left on to an unclassified road signposted Woldingham. Descend to Woldingham Station, then after ½m approach crossroads and turn left with Caterham signposts. Continue to a roundabout and take the fourth exit to join the A22 *London* road. Pass through Whyteleafe and Kenley on the return to Purley.

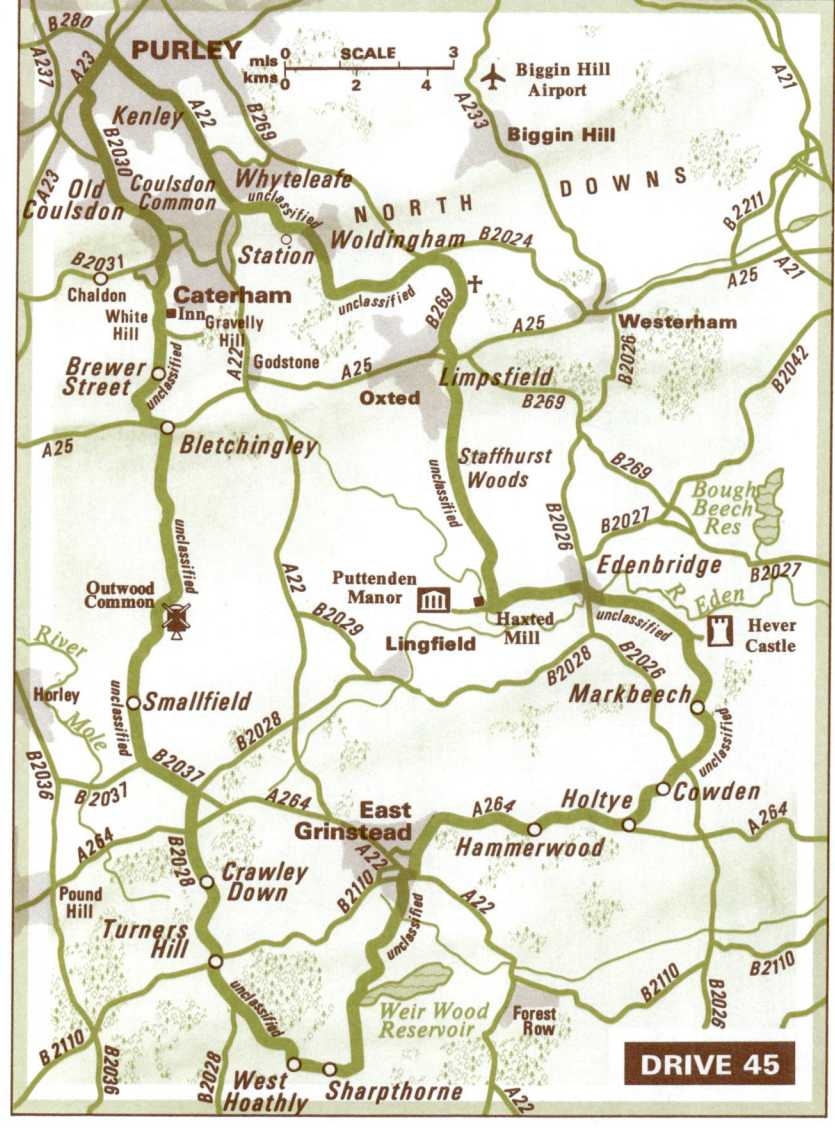

Placenames in *italic* type are worth stopping at; each is listed and described in the main gazetteer section of the book

69

North of London

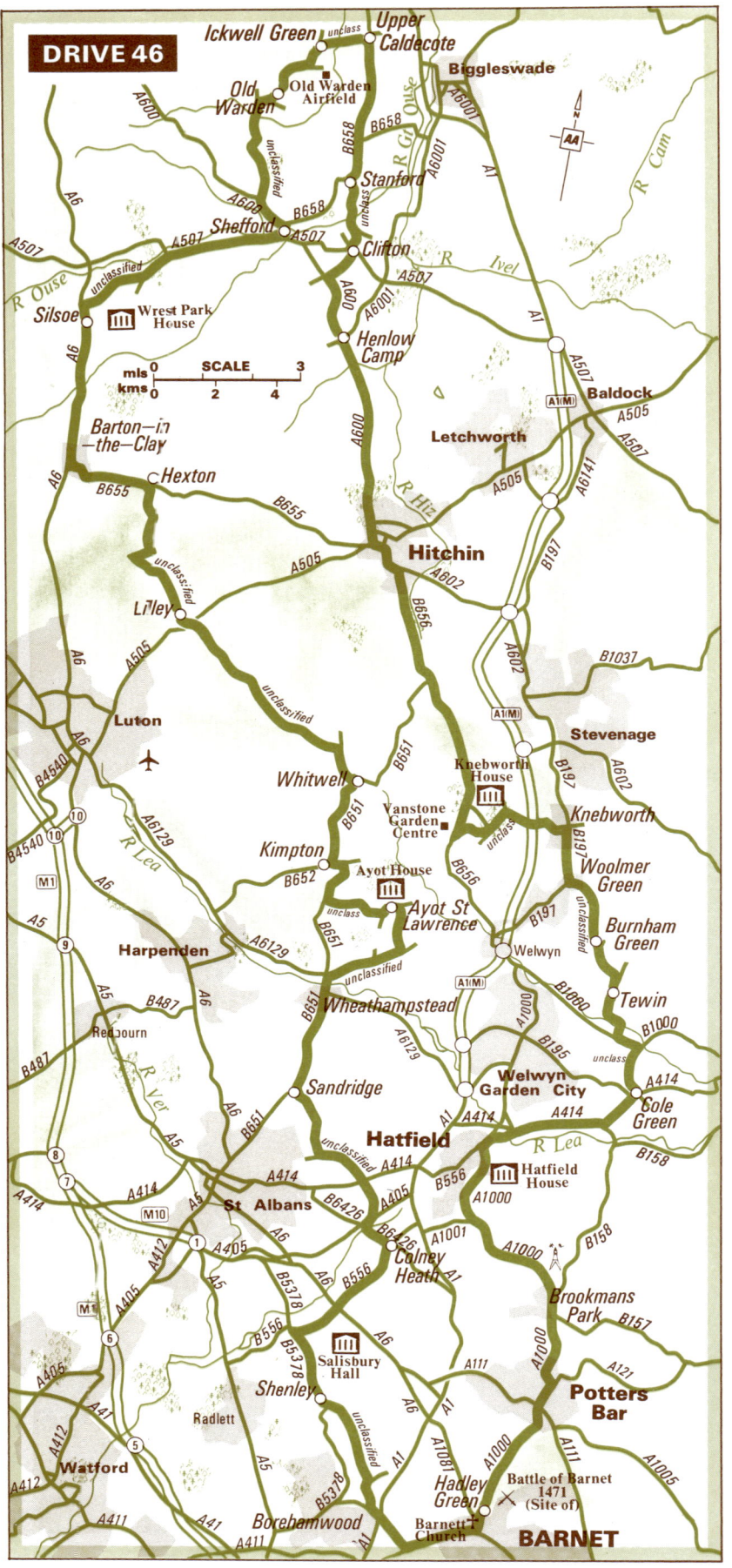

Hadley Woods and the Barton Hills
From Barnet
Drive 46   90 miles

Leave *Barnet* church with signposts marked *Hatfield* A1000. After ½m pass through Hadley Green. Continue to Potters Bar and go over crossroads, passing the BBC radio station at Brookmans Park. In 2m bear left for Hatfield. At the roundabout go forward, and after a short distance pass entrance to Hatfield House on the right. Proceed through Old Hatfield and on reaching traffic signals turn right with *Hertford* signposts. Within ½m cross a flyover and turn left to join the A414. In 2m approach a roundabout and take the first exit. After about 1m reach Cole Green and take the second turning left, signposted *Welwyn* B1000. Continue for 1¼m and turn left to join the B1000. In another ½m turn right on to an unclassified road across the River Mimram, signposted Archers Green, and at the end of this turn right for *Tewin*. Proceed to the green and keep left for Burnham Green; drive over the crossroads for Woolmer Green. Turn right on to the B197 and follow part of the old Great North Road to *Knebworth*. Approach crossroads and turn left on to an unclassified road signposted Old Knebworth. Pass under a railway bridge and turn right. After 1m keep left along the Codicote road and in ½m turn right with Kimpton and Whitwell signposts. Turn right on to the B656, signposted *Hitchin*, and after a short distance pass the Vanstone Garden Centre to the right. Continue to Hitchin, then leave the town on the A600 *Bedford* signposts. Continue to Henlow Camp. Drive to a roundabout and go forward, then in 1½m reach crossroads and turn right on to an unclassified road for Clifton. Turn left then immediately right, signposted Stanford, and in ¼m pass the church and turn left. Proceed for 1m and keep right for Stanford, then turn right on to the B658, signposted *Sandy*. Keep straight on for Caldecot and on meeting crossroads turn left on to an unclassified road to *Ickwell* Green. Turn left, signposted *Old Warden*, and in ½m approach a T-junction and turn right. Take the *Shefford* road through Old Warden, then after ½m approach a T-junction and turn left. Continue for 1m, pass under a railway bridge, and turn left. Follow Shefford signposts and eventually rejoin the A600. Cross a river and enter Shefford village. Proceed to traffic signals and turn right on to the A507, signposted *Ampthill*. In 2m drive forward on to an unclassified road signposted Silsoe, and in another 2m turn left on to the A6 for Silsoe. Continue to Barton-in-the-Clay and turn left on to the B655, signposted Hexton. Climb on to the Barton Hills and drive to Hexton. Approach crossroads and turn right on to an unclassified road leading to Lilley. Keep straight on over all crossroads and enter Whitwell. Turn right on to the B651, signposted *St Albans*, and ascend to the edge of Kimpton. Turn left then right, and in 1m turn left on to an unclassified road for *Ayot St Lawrence*. Turn left into the village and pass the church and Ayot House on the left. Keep right and after 1m approach a T-junction then turn right. In a further 2m meet another crossroads and turn left on to the A6129. Enter *Wheathampstead* and continue along the B651 to *Sandridge*. Turn

continued on page 71

NORTH OF LONDON

Drive 46 continued

left on to an unclassified road, signposted Colney Heath, then in 1½m approach a T-junction and turn left. Drive on for 1m and cross the main road, then in another 1m turn right across the dual carriageway; turn left on to the B6426 for Colney Heath. Proceed to crossroads and turn right on to the B556, signposted London Colney. Continue for 2m, and on reaching a roundabout take the second exit, signposted Radlett. Drive to the next roundabout and turn left on to the B5378 for *Shenley*. Continue to the end of the village and go forward along an unclassified road. In 2¼m join a one-way system and follow Barnet signposts to cross the flyover. Turn right, then in 1m turn left on to the A411 for the return to Barnet.

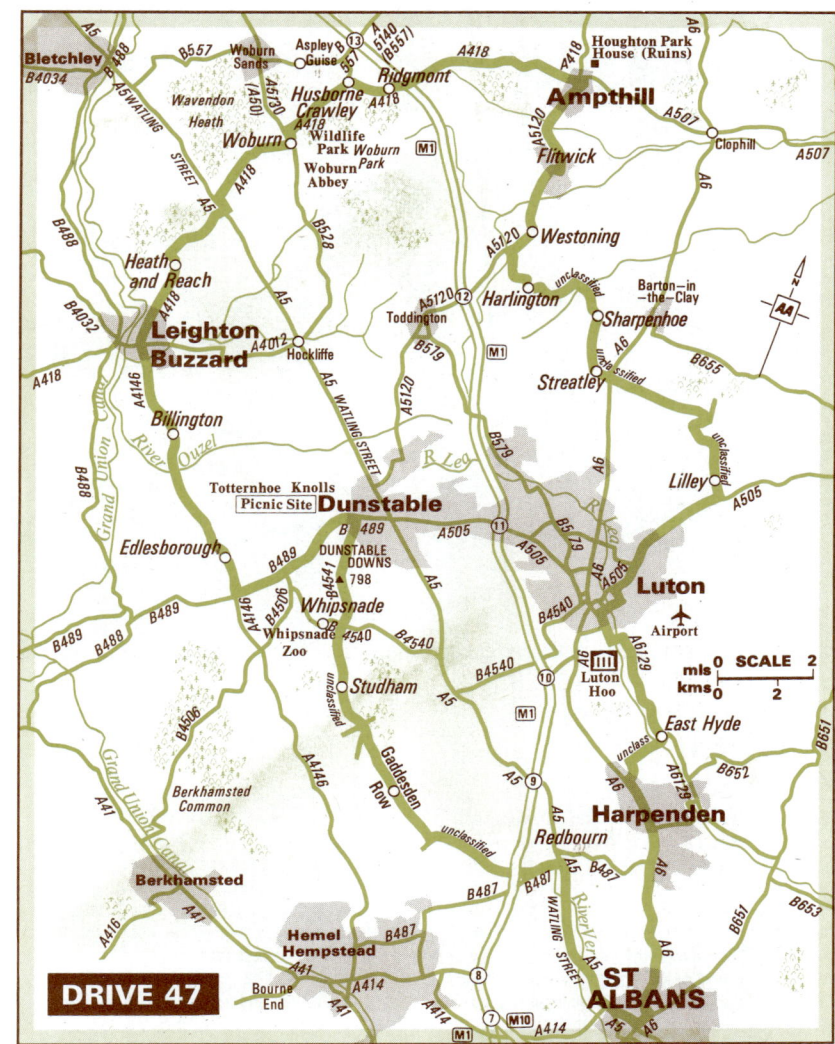

Through Woburn to the Dunstable Downs

From St Albans

Drive 47   65 miles

Take the A6 *Luton* road out of *St Albans* and drive to *Harpenden*. Keep forward through the town and pass under a railway bridge, then within ¾m turn right on to an unclassified road signposted East Hyde. Turn left on to the A6129 signposted Luton. After 3m pass the entrance to Luton Hoo on the left. Continue with the Luton road and on meeting traffic signals go forward. Turn right, then follow signposts marked Hitchin (A505) to avoid Luton town centre. In 1½m turn right on to the A505 Hitchin road. Proceed for 3m, and after passing the Silver Lion public house turn left on to an unclassified road for Lilley. In 2m turn left with Streatley signposts, then in another 2m cross the main road and continue to Streatley. Bear right and pass Sharpenhoe Hill before descending into Sharpenhoe. Turn left, then in 1¾m reach the top of an ascent and keep left for Harlington. Pass the church, approach crossroads, and turn right into Westoning Road. Turn left at the end of the road and pass under the railway bridge. In ¾m approach a T-junction and turn right on to the A5120, signposted *Ampthill*.

Continue through Westoning to Flitwick, then cross the bridge and turn left to Ampthill. Drive to the clock tower and turn left on to the A418, signposted *Woburn*. Follow an undulating road through Ridgmont and Husborne Crawley to Woburn. Leave Woburn by following signposts marked 'Leighton Buzzard A418'. Proceed for 2m and turn left then right across the A5 for Heath and Reach, and Leighton Buzzard. Follow the A4146 *Hemel Hempstead* road through Billington and continue to Edlesborough. Continue for 1m and approach the Travellers Rest public house. Turn left on to the B489, approach *Dunstable*, and on meeting a roundabout turn right on to the B4541. Ascend to Dunstable Downs, bear right at the fork, and in 1¼m approach crossroads and keep forward on to an unclassified road for Studham. Drive to the clock tower and keep straight on, signposted Gaddesden Row; in ½m go over crossroads and bear left, signposted *Redbourn*. Continue through Gaddesden Row and in 2m approach a T-junction and turn left. Pass under a motorway bridge and turn left on to the B487 for Redbourn. Turn right on to the A5 for the return to St Albans.

Placenames in *italic* type are worth stopping at; each is listed and described in the main gazetteer section of the book

NORTH OF LONDON

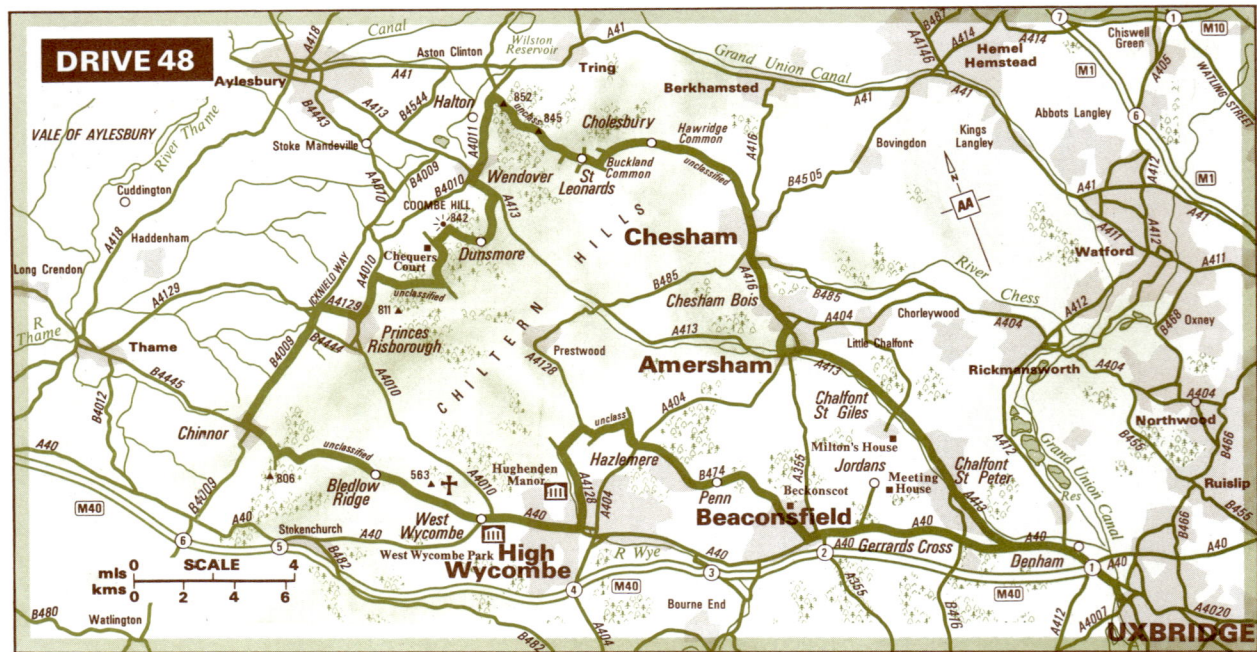

The Buckinghamshire Chilterns

From Uxbridge

Drive 48   67 miles

Follow *Denham* then *Beaconsfield* signposts to leave Uxbridge on the A4020. Proceed to the Denham roundabout and take the third exit on to the A40. Denham village lies off the road to the right. Continue for 2m and approach traffic signals, then turn right on to the A413, signposted *Amersham*. Drive on for 2¼m and go forward to skirt *Chalfont St Peter* and *Chalfont St Giles*. Proceed to Amersham town centre and meet traffic signals by the Crown Hotel; turn right into Church Street. Within 1m approach more traffic signals and turn left on to the A416 to *Chesham*. Bear left then right along a one-way street with *Berkhamsted* signposts, then at a roundabout drive forward for about ¼m and turn right. Proceed to a T-junction and turn left. Within ½m keep forward on to an unclassified road signposted *Tring*, then in 1¾m bear left to climb on to the *Chilterns* for Hawridge Common, Cholesbury, and Buckland Common. Continue to the Horse and Hound public house and keep left, then take the next turning right to St Leonards. Follow the Aston Clinton road and descend Aston Hill to the A4011. Turn left to Halton and *Wendover*, left on to the A413, signposted Amersham, and within ¼m turn left again. Continue for 1½m and turn right on to an unclassified road. Ascend to Dunsmore, then go forward with Kimble signposts to follow a narrow road over a shoulder of Coombe Hill. Descend and turn left with *Great Missenden* signposts. In 1¼m turn sharp right, signposted *Princes Risborough*, and in 1m descend Longdown Hill. Turn left on to the A4010 for *Monks Risborough* and Princes Risborough. Approach Princes Risborough and turn right on to the A4129, signposted *Thame;* in 1m meet crossroads and turn left on to the B4009. Proceed to *Chinnor* and on reaching crossroads turn left. Within ¼m go forward along an unclassified road with *Bledlow Ridge* signposts, then in ½m ascend Chinnor Hill and turn sharp left for the climb to Bledlow Ridge. Descend to *West Wycombe*, join the A40 through the village, and continue to *High Wycombe*. Leave the latter by following signposts marked 'Great Missenden A4128'. Within 1½m pass *Hughenden* Manor on the left, and after about ½m turn right. Ascend, then in ¾m approach the White Lion public house and turn right into Cryers Hill Lane. Proceed to a T-junction and turn left with *Penn* signposts. In 1m reach the end and turn right, then in ½m approach traffic signals and drive straight over crossroads on to the B474, signposted Beaconsfield. Continue through Penn to Beaconsfield. Turn left on to the A40 and follow *London* signposts. Return via the outskirts of Gerrards Cross and the Denham roundabout, taking the A4020 into Uxbridge.

NORTH OF LONDON

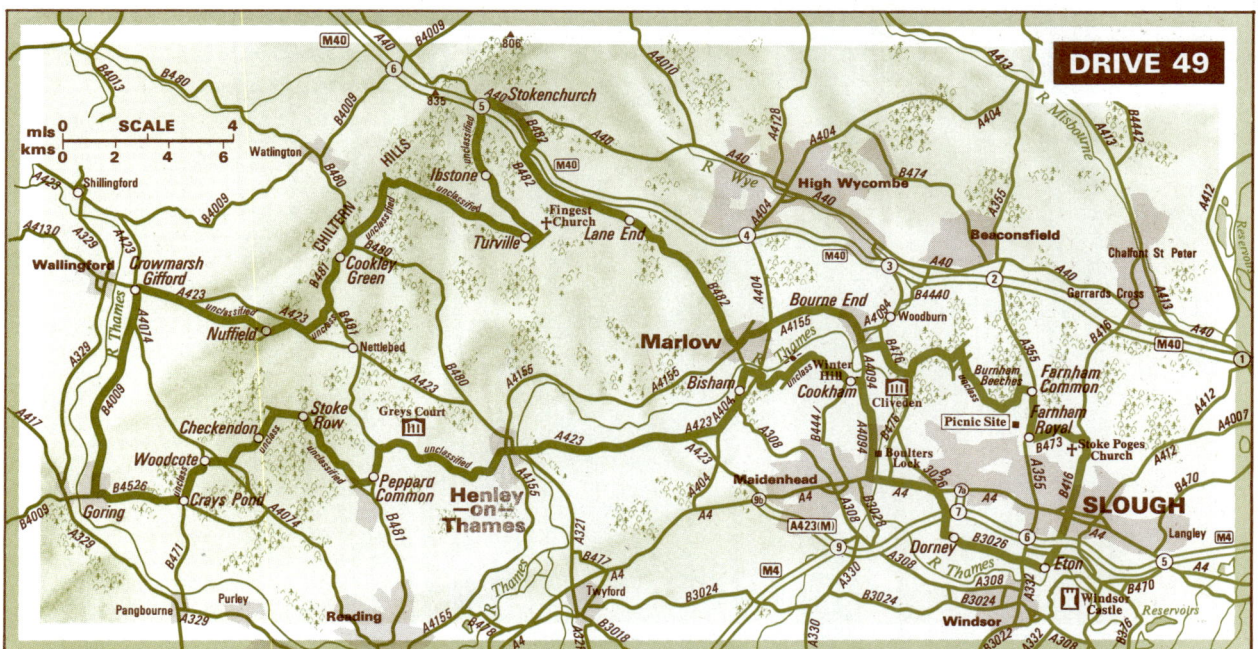

Thames Towns and the South Chilterns

From Slough

Drive 49 80 miles

Leave *Slough* by following signposts marked 'Gerrards Cross B416', and in 1¾m turn left on to the B473, signposted Farnham Royal. At Farnham Royal turn right on to the A355 with *Beaconsfield* signposts and continue to Farnham Common. Turn left on to an unclassified road and follow *Burnham Beeches* signposts. Approach T-junction and turn left to skirt the woods of Burnham Beeches. After 1¾m approach another T-junction and turn right into Dorney Wood Road. Within ½m approach the Beech Trees public house and continue straight on over crossroads. Turn sharp left with Woburn signposts and take the next turning right. Within ¼m bear left with *Taplow* signposts, then after 1m turn right on to the B476, signposted Bourne End and *Marlow*. Descend wooded *Cliveden* Reach, then in ¾m turn left on to an unclassified road. Turn right on to the A4094 into Bourne End, then bear left on to the A4155 and continue to Marlow. Turn right on to the B482, signposted *Stokenchurch,* and ascend on to the Chilterns. Continue to Stokenchurch via Lane End; turn left on to the A40 with *Oxford* signposts, then drive to the end of the village and turn left on to an unclassified road. Cross a motorway bridge for Ibstone. Descend *Turville* Hill and turn right for Turville. Keep forward and ascend a narrow road through the Wormsley Valley. Proceed to the summit and go forward with *Watlington* signposts. After 1¼m turn left, signposted Nettlebed, then in 1¾m pass over staggered crossroads and join the B481. Within another ½m pass through Cookley Green, then in 1¼m turn right on to an unclassified road signposted Nuffield. Meet a main road, turn right on to the A423, then take the next turning left on to an unclassified road. Pass Huntercombe golf course and turn right for Nuffield. Descend to re-enter the *Thames Valley*, then after 2m rejoin the A423 for *Crowmarsh Gifford*. Turn left on to the A4074 signposted *Reading*, and in 1m turn right on to the B4009. Continue to *Goring*; leave by the B4526, signposted Reading, and ascend to the *Chilterns* for Cray's Pond. Approach crossroads and turn left on an unclassified road. Pass the White Lion public house and proceed to Woodcote. Continue to the next crossroads and turn right with Checkendon signposts. In ½m approach a T-junction and turn right then immediately left for Checkendon. Proceed through the latter and in 1m meet a T-junction. Turn right for Stoke Row. Pass the Maharajah's well on the left, then in ½m pass the Cherry Tree public house and turn right with Peppard and Reading signposts. In 2¼m approach crossroads and turn left with Nettlebed signposts. Descend to join the B481, then ascend to Peppard Common. Pass The Dog public house and in ½m turn right on to an unclassified road signposted *Henley*. After 1¼m pass Greys Court to the left, and in 2m descend into Henley. Leave by following signpost marked 'Maidenhead' and 'London A423'. Cross Henley Bridge and ascend with the Marlow road. After 5m branch left on to the A404. Enter a roundabout and take the first exit on to an unclassified road to Bisham. In ¾m, as the drive approaches the Compleat Angler Hotel, turn right into unclassified Quarry Wood Lane and ascend. Meet the summit of the climb and keep left before turning left for Winter Hill. Within ¾m bear left, and in another 1m turn left on to the B4447 for *Cookham*. Turn right on to the A4094, signposted Maidenhead, and in 2m pass Boulters Lock. Continue alongside the Thames to a T-junction and turn left on to the A4 to cross Maidenhead Bridge. In 1½m approach traffic signals. Turn right on to the B3026, signposted *Eton,* and pass through Dorney and Eton Wick. Continue to traffic signals and turn left. Approach a roundabout and keep forward on to the A332 for the return to Slough.

Placenames in *italic* type are worth stopping at; each is listed and described in the main gazetteer section of the book

NORTH OF LONDON

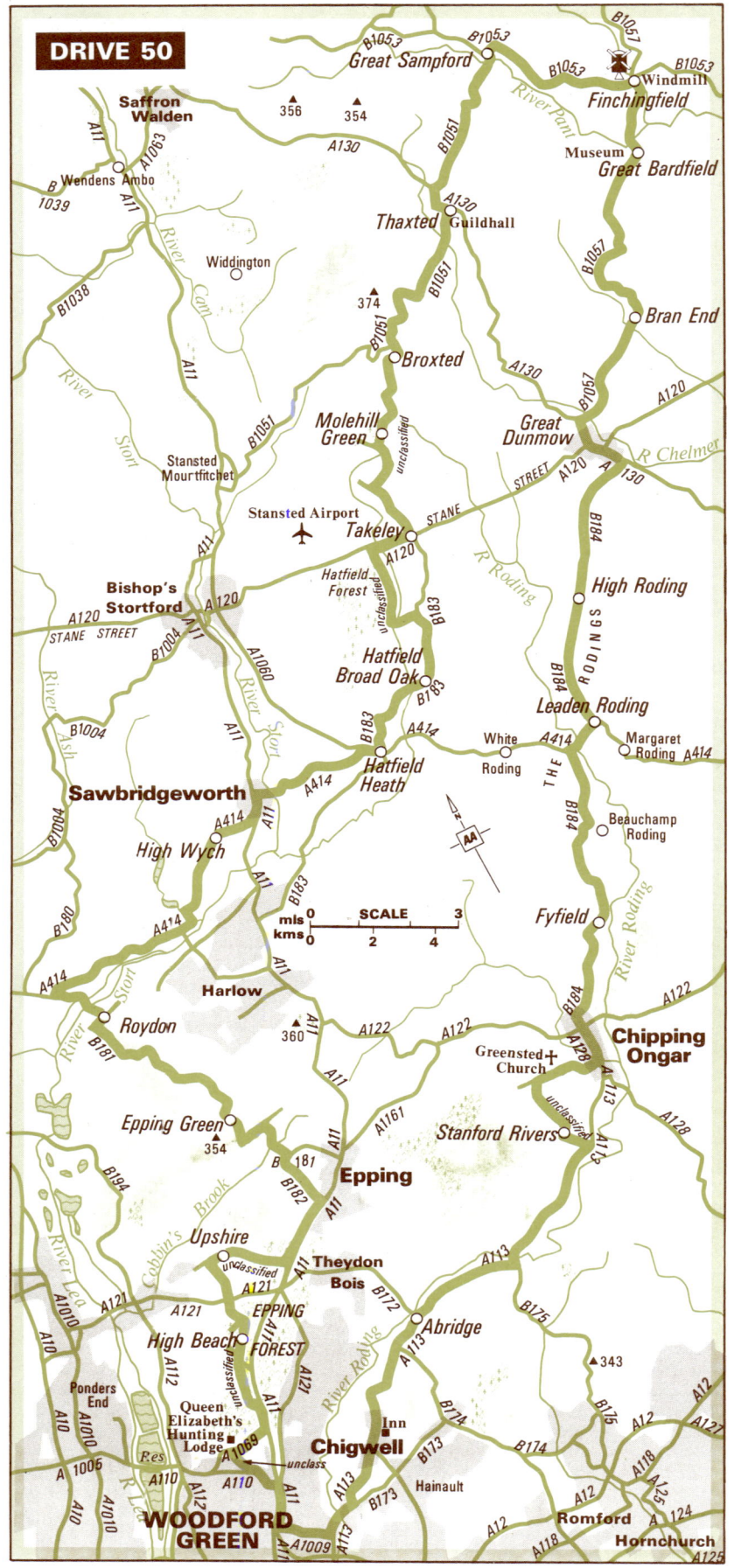

Epping Forest and West Essex
From Woodford Green
Drive 50   88 miles

Take the A11 *Epping* road out of Woodford Green and in ¾m turn left on to the A110, signposted *Enfield*. In another ¾m turn right on to an unclassified road signposted *Chingford* Station, and continue into Forest Side. Approach a T-junction and turn right on to the A1069, passing the Royal Forest Hotel on the way to Epping Forest. Within ¾m approach another T-junction and turn left on to the A11, then take the next turning left along an unclassified road signposted High Beach. In 1m keep left then turn right with Kings Oak signposts for High Beach. Pass the Kings Oak public house and turn right. Descend, then in ¾m cross the main road; continue for 1m and turn right with Epping signposts. Ascend to re-enter the forest, then approach a T-junction and turn left to rejoin the A11. Pass the Bell Inn Motel and take the next turning left on to the B182, signposted *Roydon*. Proceed for 1¼m and turn left on to the B181. After ¾m reach a T-junction and turn left again. Continue through Epping Green to Roydon, then turn left with *Hertford* signposts and go over a level crossing. Within ½m ascend, then turn right with *Chelmsford* signposts to join the A414. After 5m pass through High Wych, then in ¾m meet a T-junction and turn left on to the A11 into *Sawbridgeworth*. Continue to crossroads and turn right on to the A414, signposted Chelmsford. Drive on over a level crossing. Proceed to *Hatfield* Heath and turn left on to the B183, signposted Takeley, for Hatfield Broad Oak. In 1¼m turn left on to an unclassified road signposted Hatfield Forest, then in ¾m keep forward with Takeley signposts and skirt the forest. Later turn right on to the A120 for Takeley and on reaching the Four Ashes public house turn left on to an unclassified road with Broxted signposts. In 1¼m skirt *Stansted* Airport and turn right, then in another 1¼m turn right into Molehill Green. Continue with *Thaxted* signposts through Broxted, then join the B1051 for Thaxted. Turn left on to the A130, continue to the church, and keep right. In ½m reach the Fox and Hounds public house and turn right on to the B1051 for *Great Sampford*. Turn right again on to the B1053 and continue to *Finchingfield*. Drive to the war memorial and turn right on to the B1057 for *Great Bardfield*. Turn right again with *Dunmow* signposts, then continue to Bran End. After 2½m turn left on to the A130 and continue to Dunmow. Turn left again with Chelmsford signposts, then in ¾m turn right on to the B184 with *Ongar* signposts for High *Roding* and Leaden *Roding*. Continue to the King William IV public house and turn right on to the A414, then in 1m turn left on to the B184 for *Fyfield*. Proceed for 2½m and enter a roundabout, then take the second exit on to the A128 into Chipping Ongar. At the end of the High Street turn right on to an unclassified road signposted *Greensted*, and pass the Two Brewers public house. Continue for 1m to reach Greensted church on the right, then in a further ½m turn left, signposted Stanford Rivers. After 1¼m pass the church and proceed to crossroads. Turn left, approach a T-junction, and turn

continued on page 75

Kent and East Sussex

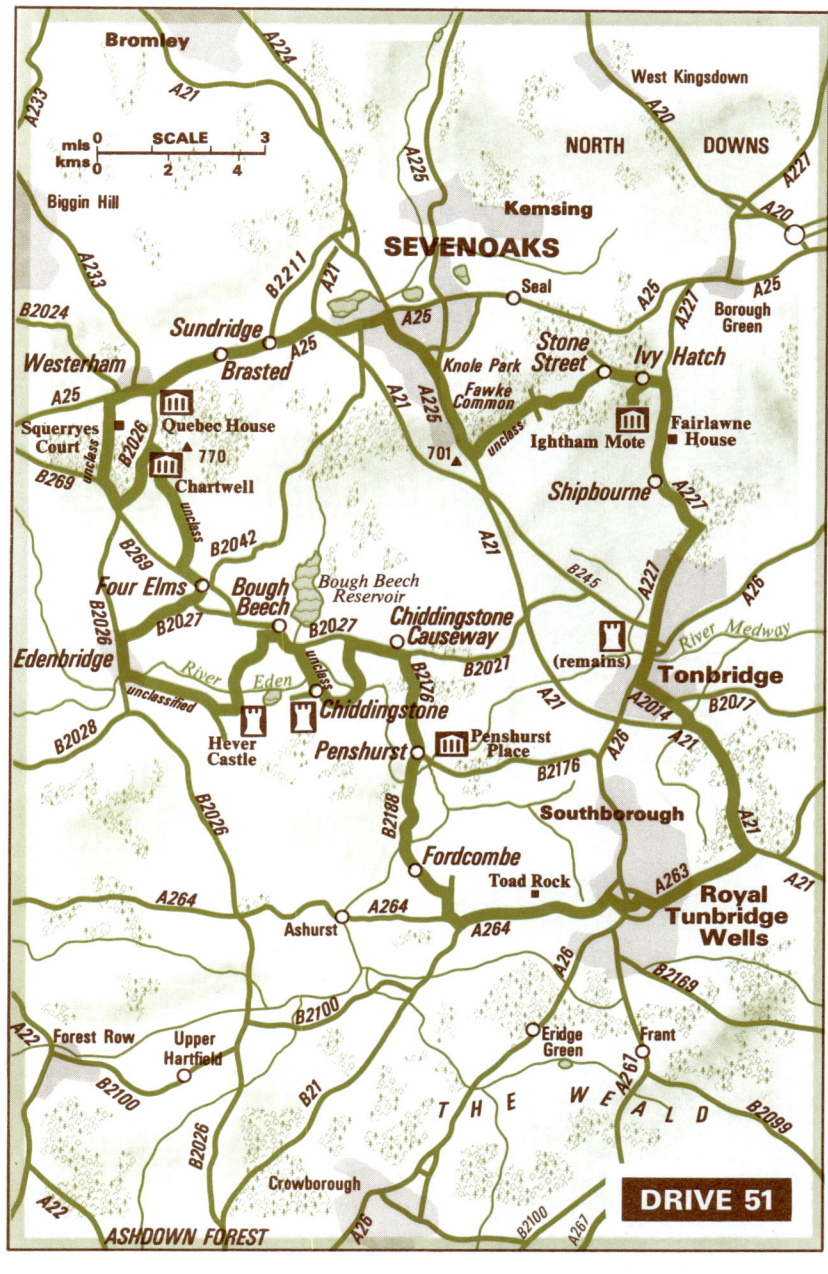

Manors and Castles of West Kent
From Sevenoaks
Drive 51   51 miles

Leave *Sevenoaks* by following signposts marked 'Bromley A21', and in 1m turn left on to the A25 with *Westerham* and Redhill signposts. Pass through the villages of Sundridge and *Brasted* and enter Westerham. Continue on the Redhill road and at the end of this village turn left on to the unclassified road to Squerryes Court. Ascend through wooded country and turn left on to the B269 *Edenbridge* road. In ¾m turn left on to the B2026 Westerham road and climb on to Crockhamhill Common before turning right on to an unclassified road to *Chartwell*. Beyond Chartwell descend into the Eden Valley and turn left on to the B269 *Tonbridge* road. Continue to Four Elms and turn right on to the B2042, signposted Edenbridge, later joining the B2027. After 1½m turn left on to the B2026 and proceed along Edenbridge main street. Cross the river and take the first turning on the left; continue along an unclassified road to *Hever Castle*. Leave the castle and take the Bough Beech road, then go forward on to the B2027 for 200yds before turning right on to the unclassified *Chiddingstone* road. Approach crossroads and turn left to pass through Chiddingstone, then in ½m branch left. Within 1¾m turn right on to the B2027 for Chiddingstone Causeway, and pass the church before turning right and following the B2176 to *Penshurst*. Continue towards *Tunbridge Wells* on the B2188, driving through the Medway Valley and Fordcombe. Later turn left on to the A264. Cross Rusthall Common and continue for approximately ¼m to the Spa Hotel. Turn right into Major Yorks road and cross the common before turning left on to the A26 and entering Royal Tunbridge Wells. From here follow signposts marked 'Hastings A263', and later turn left on to the A21 Sevenoaks road. Pass woodlands before branching left on to A2014, then later take a right turn and enter Tonbridge. Leave Tonbridge by following signposts marked '*Gravesend* A227', and ascend through wooded country to *Shipbourne*. Continue through this village and pass Fairlawne House. At the top of the ascent turn left on to an unclassified road signposted Ivy Hatch. Take the next turning left and descend to *Ightham* Mote. Return and keep left, passing the Plough Inn on the Seal road, then turn left again. Enter the village of *Stone Street* and bear left, passing the Rose and Crown Inn on the Fawke Common and Riverhill road; continue by crossing Fawke Common to the next main road. Turn right on to the A225 and descend to Sevenoaks, passing the entrance to *Knole* Park on the right.

Drive 50 continued

right on to the A113. In 3m meet a roundabout and take the second exit for Abridge. Continue to *Chigwell*, then in 1¾m approach a T-junction and turn right. Within ¾m meet traffic signals and turn right again on to the A1009, signposted *Chingford*. Continue forward and return to Woodford Green.

Placenames in *italic* type are worth stopping at; each is listed and described in the main gazetteer section of the book

DRIVE 52
MAIDSTONE
NORTH DOWNS
SCALE
mls 0 4
kms 0 2 4 6
Leybourne
(remains)
Allington Castle
West Malling
Ditton
Larkfield
(remains)
British Legion Village
St Leonards Tower (remains)
Mereworth
Wateringbury
R Medway
Level crossing
unclass
Yalding
Boughton Monchelsea Place
Sutton Valence
Lenham
Charing
Tonbridge
River Medway
River Beult
R Teise
Collier Street
Paddock Wood
Marden
unclass
Staplehurst
Headcorn
unclassified
Pluckley
River Great Stour
Smarden
Ashford
Brenchley
Matfield
Horsmonden
Royal Tunbridge Wells
R Teise
Owl House
Lamberhurst
Scotney Castle
Goudhurst
M20
M2
A20
A227
A25
A228
B2016
A26
B2015
B2010
A229
A249
B2163
A274
A262
A252
B2077
B2162
B2160
B2017
A21
A263
B2079
A28
B2070
B2169
B2085

DRIVE 53
ASHFORD
SCALE
mls 0 3
kms 0 2 4
THE WEALD
Great Chart
Bethersden
High Halden
Tenterden
Aldington
Ashford Airport
Hythe
Lympne
Level crossing
Station
Ham Street
Royal Military Canal
(disused)
Rolvenden
Rolvenden Layne
unclassified
ISLE OF OXNEY
Wittersham
ROMNEY MARSH
Romney Hythe Dymchurch Railway
Dymchurch
St Mary's Bay
New Romney
Station
Littlestone-on-Sea
Greatstone-on-Sea
Brookland
River Rother
ROTHER LEVELS
Iden
Playden
Canal
WALLAND MARSH
Lydd Airport
Lydd
DENGE MARSH
unclass
Rye
River Tillingham
Camber Castle
Denge Beach
Dungeness
Rye Bay
ENGLISH CHANNEL
A20
A28
A292
B2077
A274
A262
B2070
B2069
B2067
A261
A259
B2082
B2086
B2080
B2081
B2088
A268
B2076
B2075
B2071

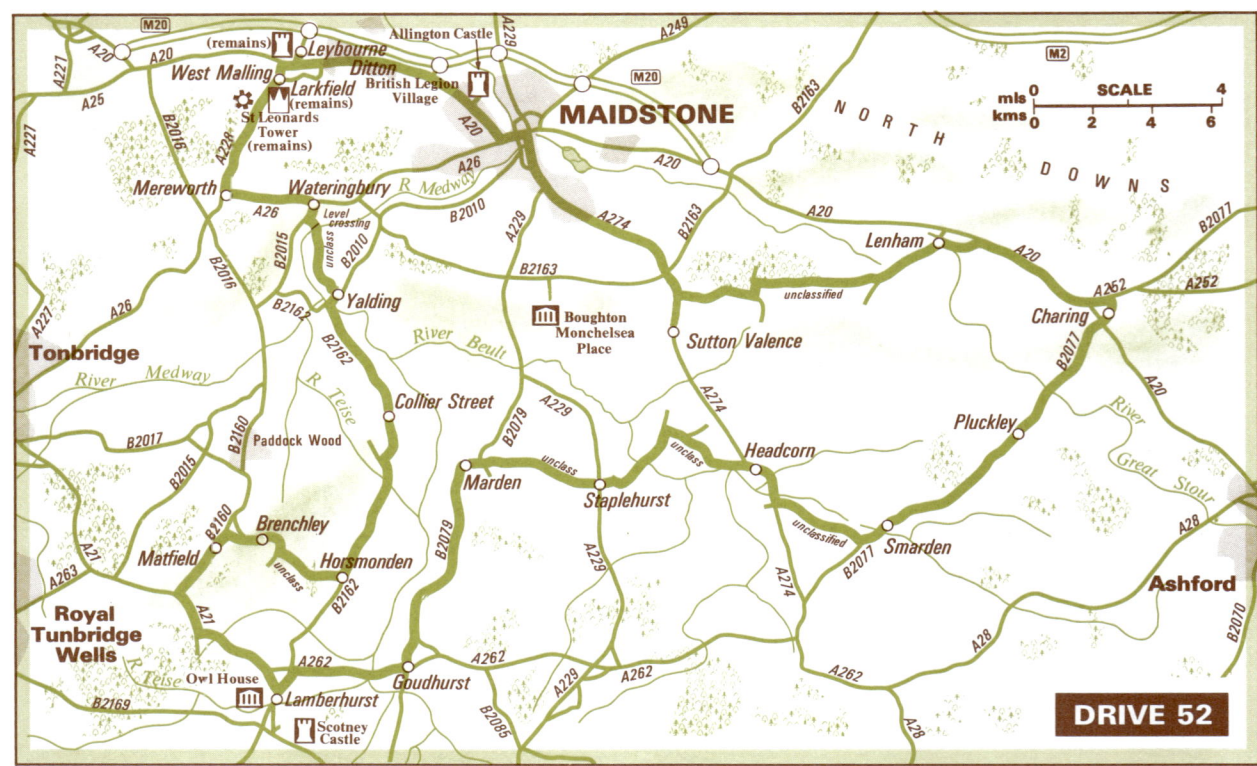

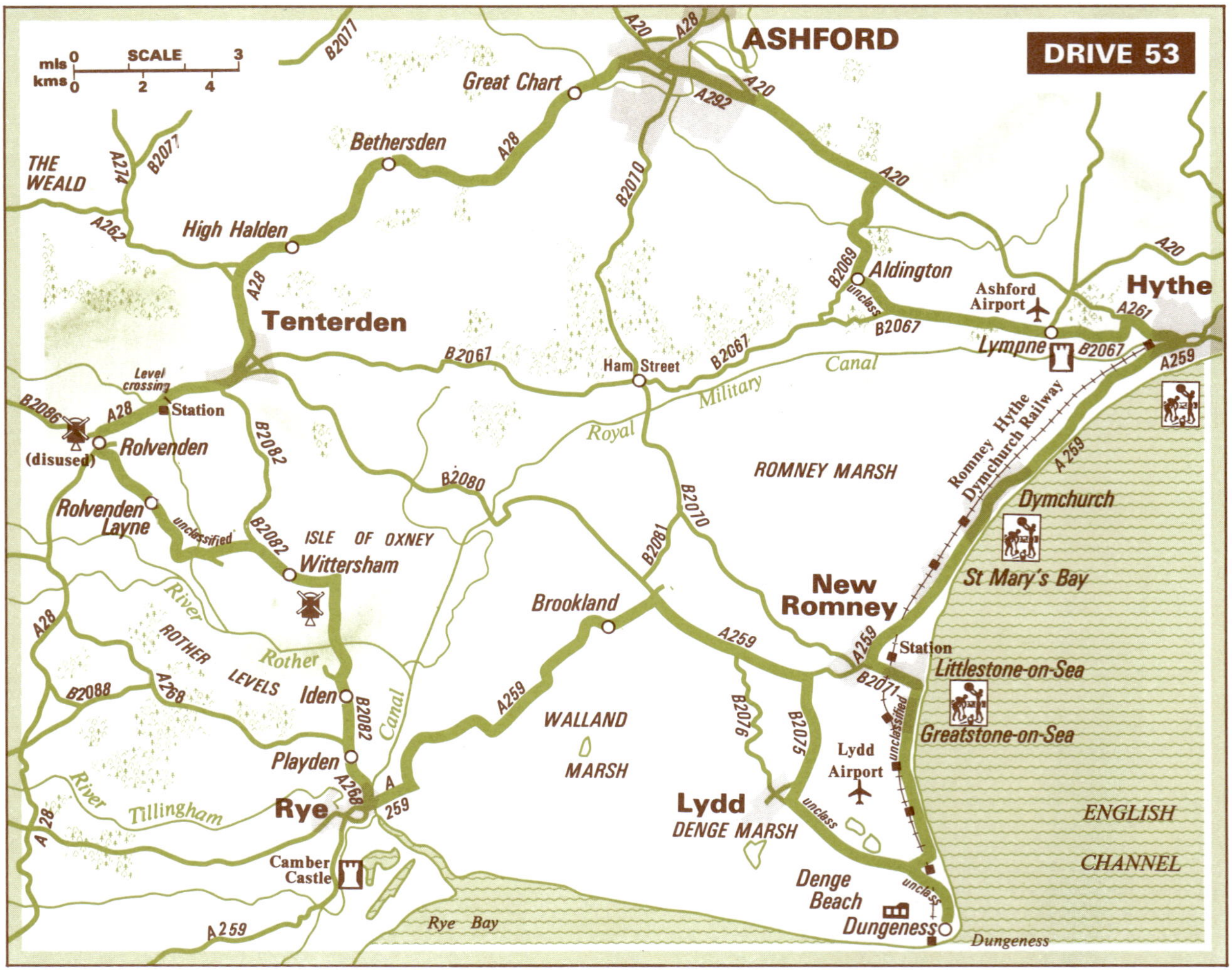

KENT AND EAST SUSSEX

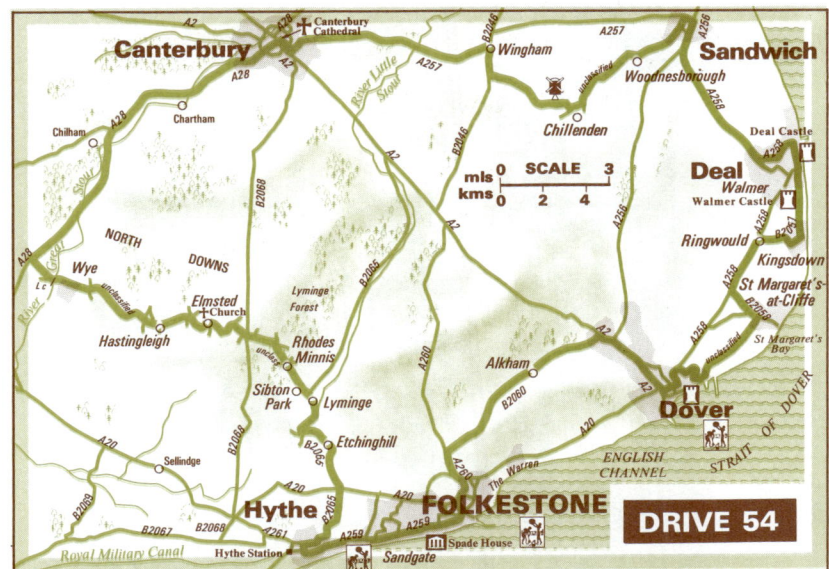

Hops and the Vale of Kent

From Maidstone

Drive 52 72 miles

Leave *Maidstone* by the A20 *London* road. After 2m approach a roundabout and take the first exit on to the A20. Pass through the British Legion Village, Ditton, and Larkfield. Turn left on to the A228 *Tonbridge* road and continue into *West Malling*. Approach the edge of *Mereworth* before turning left on to the A26 Maidstone road. Proceed to the traffic signals in *Wateringbury* and turn right on to the B2015, signposted Paddock Wood. Within ½m approach the Railway Hotel and turn left over the level crossing on to an unclassified road for *Yalding*. Enter Yalding and leave by turning right on to the B2010 Horsmonden road. Cross the River Beult, turn left on to the B2162, then continue through Collier Street to Horsmonden. Turn right on to the *Brenchley* road; from Brenchley continue to Matfield and turn left on to B2160, signposted Pembury. Continue amid the Kentish Weald and turn left on to the A21 *Hastings* road then continue to *Lamberhurst*. Return along the A21, ascend, and turn right with *Goudhurst* and *Ashford* signposts. Continue on the A262. On meeting the Vine Hotel in Goudhurst turn left on to the B2079 Marden road. Pass through Marden and approach the Unicorn public house. Continue straight on to the unclassified *Staplehurst* road, and in 1m drive alongside the railway before turning right then left. Reach the edge of Staplehurst and cross the A229 for the *Headcorn* road. Follow this across the Beult Valley and about 1½m after crossing the railway turn right. Continue and turn right on to the A274 *Tenterden* road. Pass through Headcorn, then ¾m after crossing a railway approach crossroads and turn left on to the unclassified *Smarden* road. Join the B2077 and continue through Smarden on the *Charing* road. Ascend through Pluckley, then cross the A20 to enter Charing. Keep straight on through Charing and turn left on to the A252, signposted Maidstone. Join the A20 and within 3m branch left on to an unclassified road into *Lenham*. Proceed to the village crossroads and turn left on to the Sandway and Platt's Heath road; in 2¼m approach the White Swan and turn right with East Sutton signposts. Continue for 2m, turn left on to the A274, then descend into *Sutton Valence*. Return and continue into Maidstone along the A274.

The Marshlands

From Ashford

Drive 53 73 miles

Leave *Ashford* by the A28 Tenterden road and pass through Great Chart to Bethersden. Continue through High Halden to reach *Tenterden*. Follow the *Hastings* road and descend to cross Newmill Channel at *Rolvenden* Station. Ascend to Rolvenden and drive to the church, then turn left on to the unclassified *Wittersham* road. Pass through Rolvenden Layne and later climb on to the Isle of Oxney and turn right on to the B2082 through Wittersham. Descend to Wittersham Level to cross the River Rother, and pass through Iden. Proceed to Playden to join the A268, and continue to *Rye*. Follow signposts marked 'Folkestone A259' from Rye, then cross Walland Marsh and pass through Brookland. In 1½m reach crossroads and turn right, then in 4m turn right again on to the B2075 *Lydd* road. Drive on to the edge of Lydd before crossing a railway bridge, then branch left on to the unclassified *Dungeness* road. Continue for 3m beyond Lydd before turning right for Dungeness. Return along the unclassified road for 1m, then turn right and follow Greatstone-on-Sea signposts to Littlestone-on-Sea. Turn left on to the B2071 and enter the outskirts of New Romney. At the edge of the town turn right on to the A259 Folkestone road to cross *Romney Marsh*. Proceed to St Mary's Bay and *Dymchurch*, then continue to *Hythe* before turning left on to the A261 Ashford road. Ascend, and after 1m turn left on to the B2067 *Lympne* road. Drive through the village, take the Tenterden road, and pass Ashford Airport. In 2½m bear right on to the unclassified road to *Aldington*; turn right on to the B2069 Ashford road. After ¾m cross the railway and turn left on to the A20. Follow Town Centre signposts and return to Ashford.

Around the Channel Ports

From Folkestone

Drive 54 74 miles

Leave *Folkestone* with 'Hythe A259' signposts, then continue through *Sandgate* and Hythe. Follow *Ashford* and *London* signposts to Hythe Station. Return along the Folkestone road and take the B2065 *Elham* road, then ascend to cross the main road for Etchinghill and Lyminge. Drive to the end of Lyminge and turn left on to an unclassified road signposted Rhodes Minnis. Continue through Rhodes Minnis and after ½m branch left to climb on to the *North Downs*. Cross the B2068 and turn right. Continue to Elmsted church, turn left with *Wye* signposts and proceed to Hastingleigh. Cross downs for Wye, then follow Ashford signposts and cross the river Great Stour. Drive over a level crossing and turn right into the *Canterbury* road. Meet the A28 and turn right along the Great Stour Valley, passing the villages of *Chilham* and *Chartham* before entering Canterbury. Leave the city with *Dover* then *Sandwich* signposts on the A257, then enter *Wingham* and turn right on to the B2046 Folkestone road. Within 1m turn left on to the unclassified road signposted Chillenden. Approach crossroads in Chillenden and turn left for Woodnesborough and Sandwich. Leave Sandwich on the A256 Dover road, later turning left on to the A258 *Deal* road. Pass through Deal and continue with the Dover road before branching left on to the B2057, signposted Kingsdown. Pass *Walmer Castle* and proceed to Kingsdown. Turn inland with Dover signposts for *Ringwould*, then continue on the A258 and turn left on to the B2058 for *St Margaret's-at-Cliffe*. Pass the village church and turn right on to the unclassified Reach Road. Within 3m turn left on to the A258. Enter Dover and leave by following signposts marked 'Canterbury A2'. After 1m pass under the railway bridge, turn left on to the B2060 *Alkham* road, climb through a North Downs valley, then turn left on to the A260 to descend to Folkestone.

Placenames in *italic* type are worth stopping at; each is listed and described in the main gazetteer section of the book

Suffolk and Essex

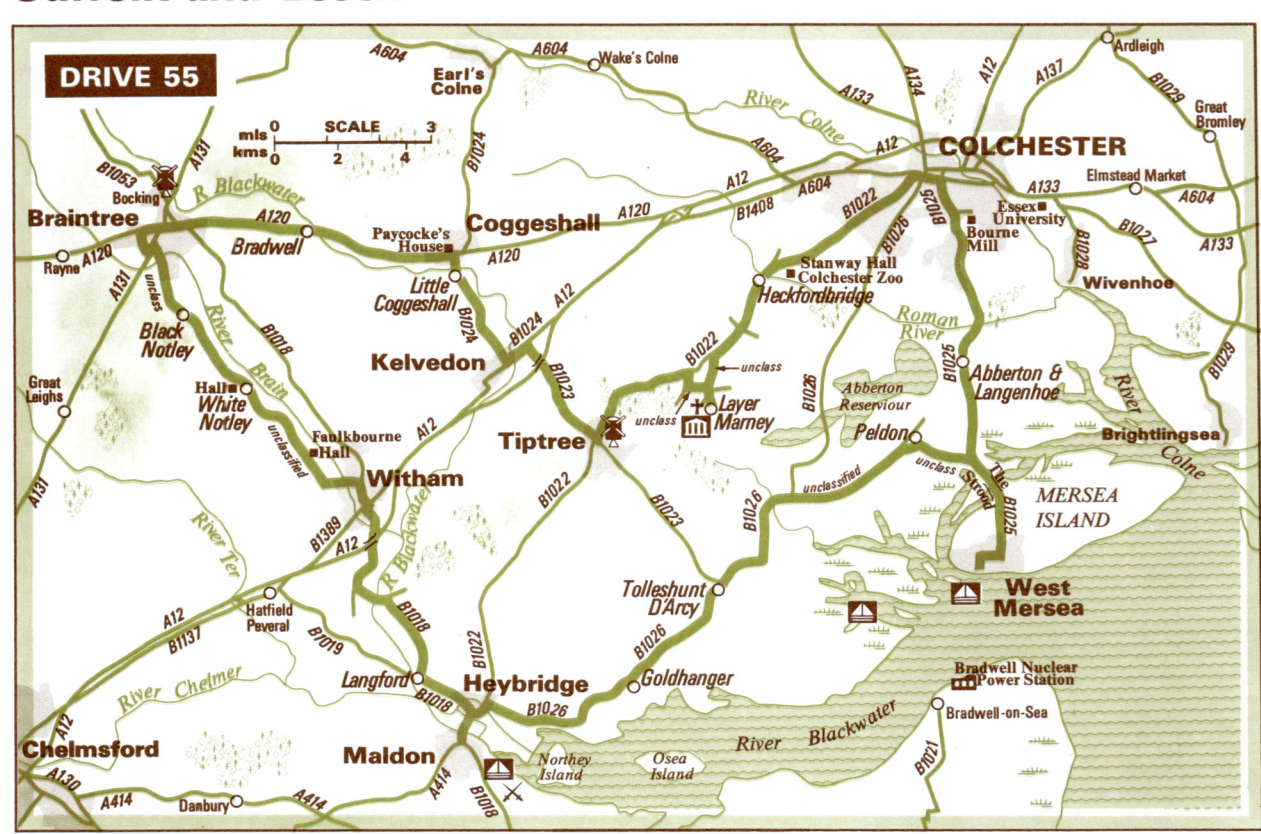

Essex Coast and Dedham Vale

From Colchester

Drive 56 73 miles

Follow signposts marked 'Ipswich', then 'Clacton A133' to leave Colchester, and pass the grounds of Essex University on the right before turning right on to the B1027 St Osyth road. Continue forward on to the B1028, signposted Wivenhoe, and drive into Wivenhoe itself. Drive to the Park Hotel and follow Alresford signposts along an unclassified road. Within ½m turn right and proceed to Alresford. Enter the village, go forward, then turn right on to the B1027 Clacton road. Within 1¼m reach Thorrington and turn right on to the B1029 Brightlingsea road. Continue into the latter town and return on the B1029 to Thorrington. Turn right on to the B1027 to reach St Osyth, then turn right on to an unclassified road signposted St Osyth Beach to reach the village centre and priory entrance. Leave by the Clacton road and after a short distance turn right to rejoin the B1027. Approach a roundabout within 2½m and take the third exit on to the A133 to enter Clacton-on-Sea. Follow signposts indicating the seafront and turn left with Holland-on-Sea signposts. Follow the Promenade to Holland-on-Sea and at the end turn right on to the B1032 Frinton and Walton road. Pass through Great Holland, approach a railway bridge, and turn right on to the B1033. Enter Kirby Cross and continue to Frinton Station crossroads; drive forward for Walton-on-the-Naze. Within 1½m enter Walton, then return along the Frinton road. Drive to the church and turn right on to the B1034 Kirby-le-Soken road. Continue through the latter and within 1m turn right on to the unclassified Harwich road. Within a further 1¾m turn right on to the A134, and keeping to the higher ground pass through the villages of Great and Little Oakley. Enter Upper Dovercourt and at the T-junction turn right on to the A604 to enter Dovercourt and Harwich. Leave Harwich by following Colchester signposts marked 'A604'; within 3m reach Ramsey and turn right on to the B1352 Manningtree road. Continue to Bradfield and turn right to enter Mistley. Drive to the end of this village and keep forward on the Manningtree road, passing the Mistley Towers church ruin on the right. Proceed through Manningtree and within ½m approach Manningtree Station and turn right on to the A137 Ipswich road. After a short distance cross the River Stour and turn left on to the B1070 East Bergholt road. Continue into Dedham Vale and in 1½m drive forward on an unclassified road into East Bergholt. Drive to the church and bear right, then continue

continued on page 79

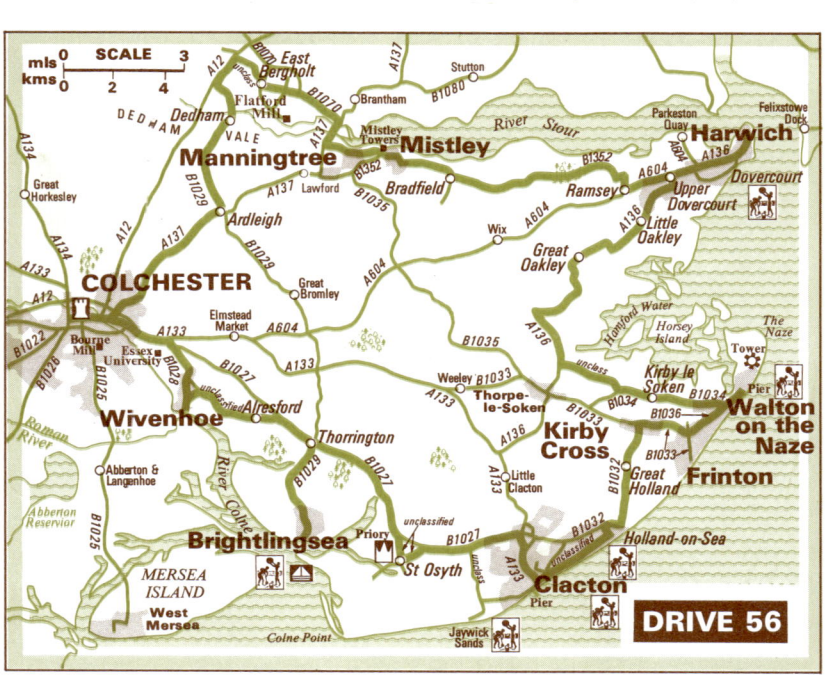

SUFFOLK AND ESSEX

Mersea Island and the Blackwater River
From Colchester
Drive 55   62 miles

Take the B1025 Mersea road out of *Colchester* and within ¾m pass an unclassified left turn signposted Hythe Quay (leading to Bourne Mill). Within another 6m cross an area of marshland to reach the long causeway (known as Strood; flooded at high tide) over a channel dividing Mersea Island from the mainland. Visit *West Mersea* then return across the Strood and in ¾m bear left on to the Peldon/*Tolleshunt* road. Continue to the edge of Peldon village and turn left on to the *Maldon* road. Within 3m continue forward on to the B1026 and proceed into *Tolleshunt D'Arcy*. Stay with the B1026 Maldon road, skirt Goldhanger village, and on reaching *Heybridge* turn left on to the B1022. In ½m turn left again into Maldon, then follow Colchester signposts and return to Heybridge. Turn left on to the B1018 *Chelmsford* road, and at Langford turn right with *Witham* signposts to pass through orchards before crossing the river. Approach a T-junction and turn right. After a short distance enter Witham and continue to the traffic signals for a right then left turn on to the *Braintree* road. Cross a railway bridge, then turn left on to an unclassified road signposted The Notleys. In 1m bear right and follow the shallow River Brain valley. Within ¾m pass Faulkbourne Hall on the right and continue into *White Notley*. Stay on the Braintree road and after a short distance pass through Black Notley to the outskirts of Braintree. Approach a T-junction and turn left, then turn left again at the church before turning right to follow signposts marked Colchester A120 through Braintree. Cross the River Blackwater at Bradwell and continue alongside the river to *Coggeshall*. Leave Coggeshall town centre by turning right on to the B1024 Kelvedon road, and cross the river into Little Coggeshall. Drive to Kelvedon and turn left with Colchester signposts. Within ½m turn right on to the B1023 *Tiptree* road, and at the edge of Tiptree meet a T-junction and turn left again on to the B1022 Colchester road. Within 2½m turn right on to the unclassified Marney Tower road, and in ¼m turn left and approach crossroads. Turn right then bear left to *Layer Marney*. After visiting the village return to the crossroads and continue forward. In ¾m meet the B1022 main road and turn right for Colchester. Proceed through a rural area and pass an unclassified left turn to *Copford* Green. Meet the Angel Inn at Heckford bridge and pass Stanway Hall and Colchester Zoo on the right. Enter suburbs and continue to Colchester town centre.

Drive 56 continued

beyond the Red Lion public house before turning left with Colchester signposts. Within 1m turn left on to the A12, then after a further 1m turn left again on to the B1029 *Dedham* road. Cross the River Stour to enter Dedham, and proceed to Dedham church. Turn right at the church and continue on the B1029 to Ardleigh before turning right on to the A137. Stay with the A137 and return to Colchester.

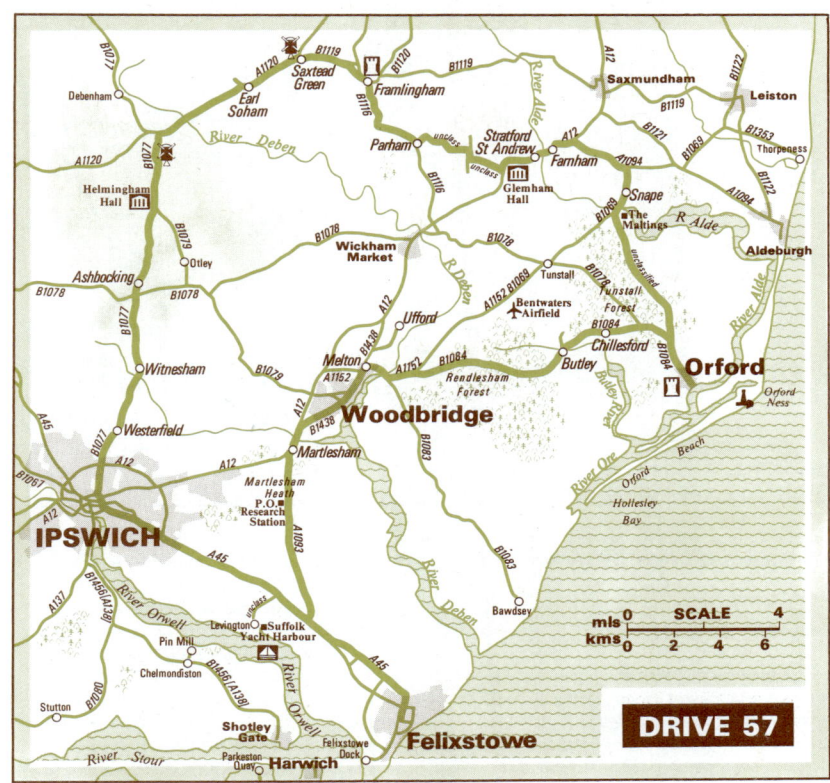

Orford Beach and Framlingham Castle
From Ipswich
Drive 57   70 miles

Leave *Ipswich* on the A45 *Felixstowe* road, and within 5½m pass an unclassified right turn leading to Leavington and Suffolk Yacht Harbour, on the River Orwell. Continue on the A45 to Felixstowe. Return along the Ipswich road for 4½m before turning right on to the A1093 *Woodbridge* road, then pass the Post Office Research Station on Martlesham Heath and turn right on to the A12 to pass through *Martlesham*. Drive under a railway bridge and turn right on to the B1438 for Woodbridge. Leave the latter by the B1438, and on entering Melton turn right on to the A1152, signposted *Orford*. Cross a railway and the River Deben, then bear left. Within ¾m keep forward on to the B1084 and after a short distance enter Rendlesham Forest. Enter *Butley* and bear right before skirting part of Tunstall Forest near Chillesford. Visit Orford, then return along the Woodbridge road for 1½m and drive forward on to the unclassified *Snape* road. Skirt Tunstall Forest for nearly 4m before joining the B1069 and passing the Maltings. Cross the River Alde into Snape, and within ¾m turn left on to the A1094 Ipswich road. Within 2m turn left on to the A12 and continue through Farnham and Stratford St Andrew. After a further 1m approach the entrance to Glemham Hall and turn right on to the unclassified *Parham* road. In 1m approach a T-junction, turn right, then after a short distance turn left and proceed into Parham. From Parham take a right turn on to the B1116 *Framlingham* road and enter Framlingham. Leave by following signposts marked '*Stowmarket* B1119', and enter Saxstead Green. Turn left here on to the A1120 and pass through Earl Soham before turning left again. Within another 3m turn left on to the B1077 Ipswich road, and in 1m pass a post mill on the left. After 1¼m pass *Helmingham* Hall on the right. Return to Ipswich along the B1077, passing through Ashbocking, Witnesham, and Westerfield.

Placenames in *italic* type are worth stopping at; each is listed and described in the main gazetteer section of the book

Suffolk and Essex

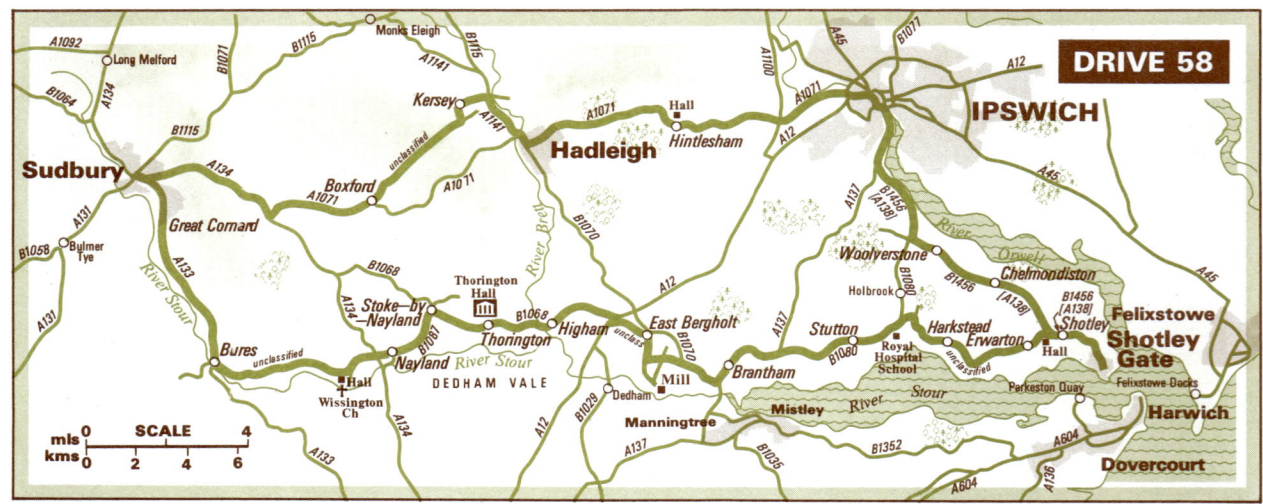

The Stour and Orwell Estuaries

From Ipswich

Drive 58   65 miles

Leave *Ipswich* by following signposts marked 'Colchester', then 'Sudbury A1071'. Pass the grounds of Hintlesham Hall and continue to *Hadleigh*. Turn right on to the Sudbury road and proceed to the end of the town before turning right again on to the A1141 *Kersey* and *Lavenham* road. Follow the shallow valley of the River Brett, then after 1¼m approach crossroads and turn left on to an unclassified road for Kersey. Beyond Kersey church bear right on to the *Boxford* road. Continue to Boxford and turn right on to the A1071 Sudbury road. Within 2½m turn right again on to the A134 and drive into Sudbury. Leave by the A133 *Bures* road and follow the Stour Valley south through Great Cornard and into Bures. Continue to the church and turn left on to the unclassified *Nayland* road in order to remain in the Stour Valley. Within 3¾m pass a right turning leading to Wissington church, and after a further 1m cross the main road on to the B1087 and continue into Nayland. Stay with the B1087 to *Stoke-by-Nayland*, then turn right on to the B1068 Ipswich road. Within 1¾m reach Thorington and pass Thorington Hall on the left. Continue through Higham, cross the River Brett, and in 2m meet a main road and turn right then left on to the unclassified road for *East Bergholt*. Turn right into this village and keep left at the church; in 1m continue forward on to the B1070, signposted Manningtree. After 1½m turn left on to the A137 Ipswich road and drive into *Brantham*. In 1m approach the Bull Inn and turn right on to the B1080 Holbrook road. Pass through *Stutton* and the grounds of the Royal Hospital School before turning right on to the unclassified Harkstead and Shotley road. Pass through Harkstead and Erwarton to rejoin the main road at Shotley before turning right on to the B1456 (A138) to enter Shotley Gate. Return along the B1456 (A138) Ipswich road, passing Chelmondiston and Woolverstone before skirting the river and returning to Ipswich.

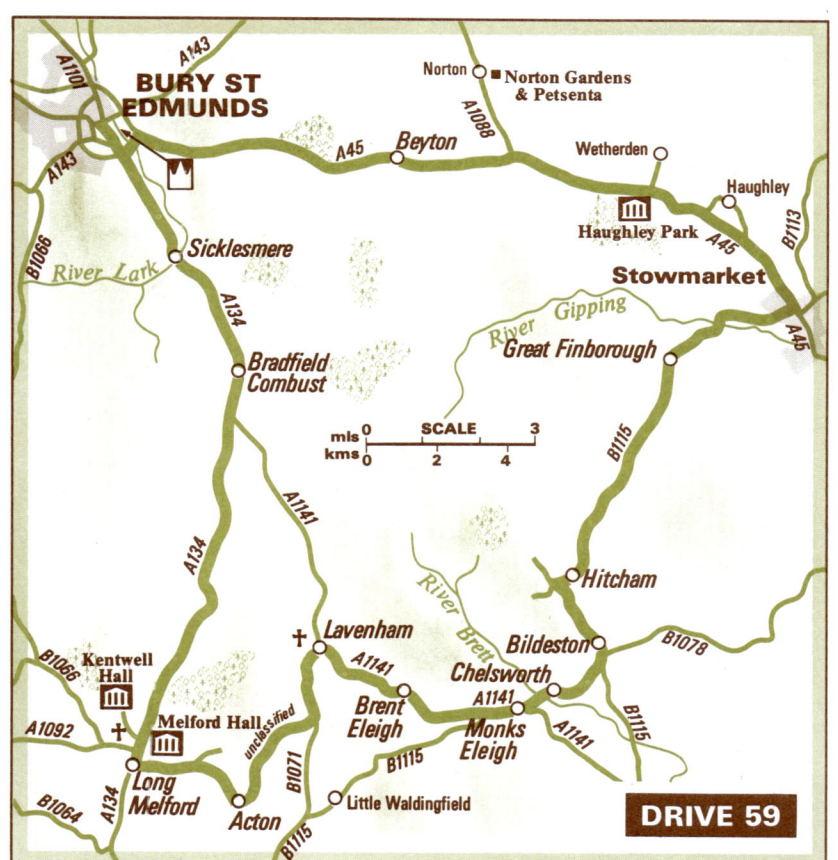

Wool and the Gipping Valley

From Bury St Edmunds

Drive 59   47 miles

Take the A134 *Sudbury* road out of *Bury St Edmunds* and continue through the villages of Sicklesmere and Bradfield Combust to *Long Melford*. Drive to the Bull Inn and turn left on to the unclassified *Lavenham* road. Within 1¼m keep forward to *Acton* before turning left with Lavenham signposts; within 2¼m join the B1071 and drive into Lavenham. Leave the latter by the A1141 *Hadleigh* road to pass through Brent Eleigh and *Monks Eleigh*. Approach the church at the end of the latter and bear left on to the B1115 *Stowmarket* road. Pass through *Chelsworth* and continue into *Bildeston*. Turn left on to the B1115 for *Hitcham*, and stay with this road to continue through Great Finborough; proceed to the Gipping Valley and Stowmarket. Leave Stowmarket by taking the A45 Bury St Edmunds road, and within 4m skirt the grounds of *Haughley* Park on the left. Continue on the A45 and pass through Beyton before returning to Bury St Edmunds.

Cotswolds and the Vale of Oxford

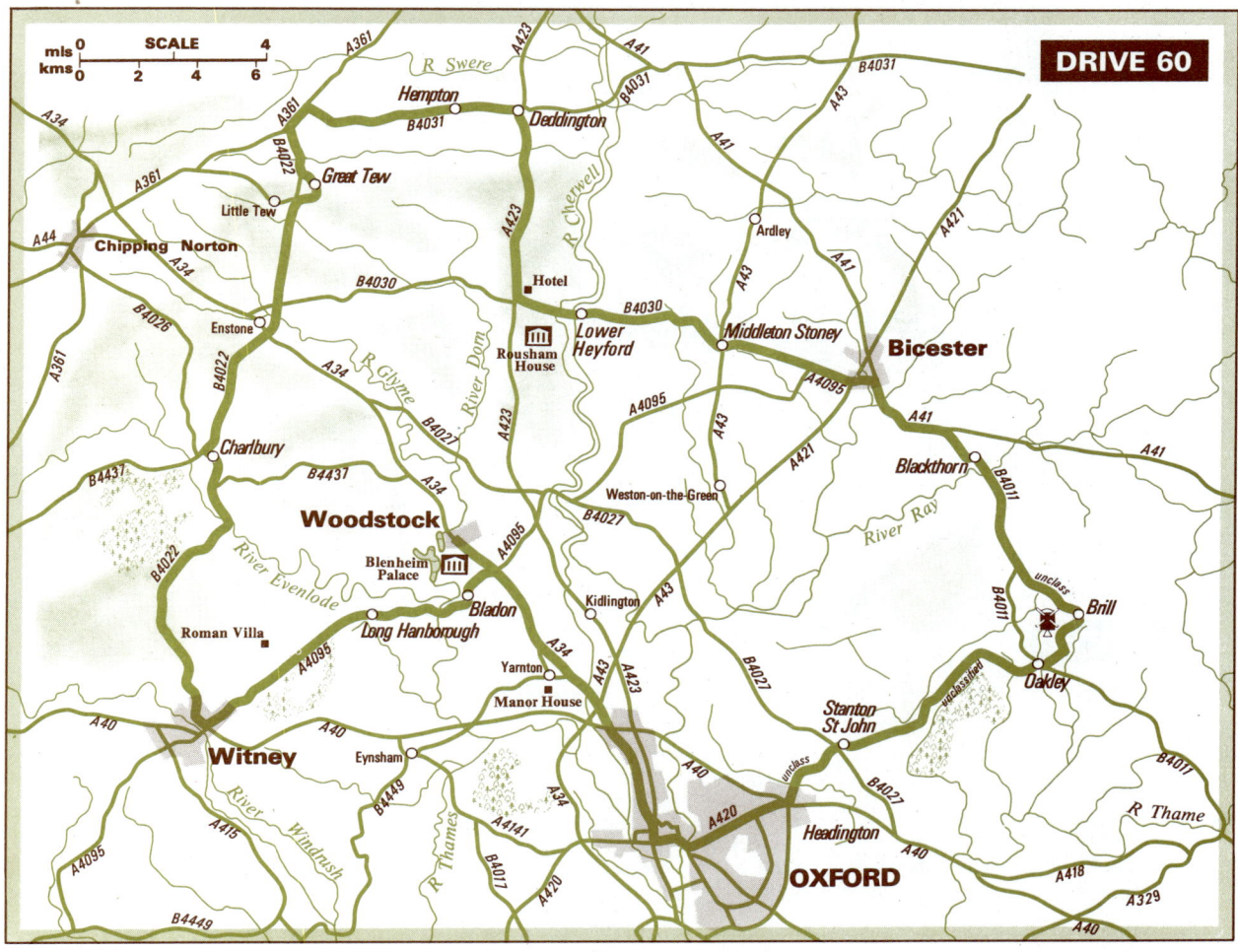

Gleaming Spires to Cottages

From Oxford

Drive 60 71 miles

Leave *Oxford* by following signposts marked 'The East A420', and pass through *Headington*. Continue to a roundabout and take the second exit into unclassified Bayswater road. After ¾m turn right, signposted *Stanton St John*, then drive forward to a T-junction and turn right then left into Stanton St John. Drive to the church, turn left, then follow signposts to Oakley. From the latter approach a main road and turn right on to the B4011. Take the next left turning on to an unclassified road for *Brill*. Proceed to the Sun Hotel, turn left into Windmill Street, and pass an old windmill. Stay on this road to join the B4011 to Blackthorn. Pass through the village and after 1m turn left on to the A41 for *Bicester*. Follow the A421 Oxford road, then turn right on to the A4095 with *Chipping Norton* signposts. Proceed for 1m, then go forward on to the B4030 for Middleton Stoney. At Middleton Stoney cross a main road, continue to the outskirts of *Lower Heyford*, then turn left and cross the River Cherwell. Continue to the Hopcrofts Holt Hotel and turn right on to the A423 for *Deddington*. On reaching this village turn left on to the B4031, signposted Chipping Norton, and pass through Hempton. After 3m keep left and join the A361, then after ½m turn left on to the B4022, signposted Enstone. Continue for 1m and turn left again on to an unclassified road for *Great Tew*. Proceed through the village and after ½m turn right, signposted Little Tew. Drive to crossroads and turn left to rejoin the B4022. After a further 3m drive over staggered crossroads and skirt Enstone before proceeding to *Charlbury*. Continue along the B4022 and later turn right in to *Witney*. Follow the A4095 Bicester road through Long Hanborough to *Bladon*, then drive for a further 1m and approach a roundabout. Turn left on to the A34 for *Woodstock*, then return to Oxford along the A34.

Placenames in *italic* type are worth stopping at; each is listed and described in the main gazetteer section of the book

COTSWOLDS AND THE VALE OF OXFORD

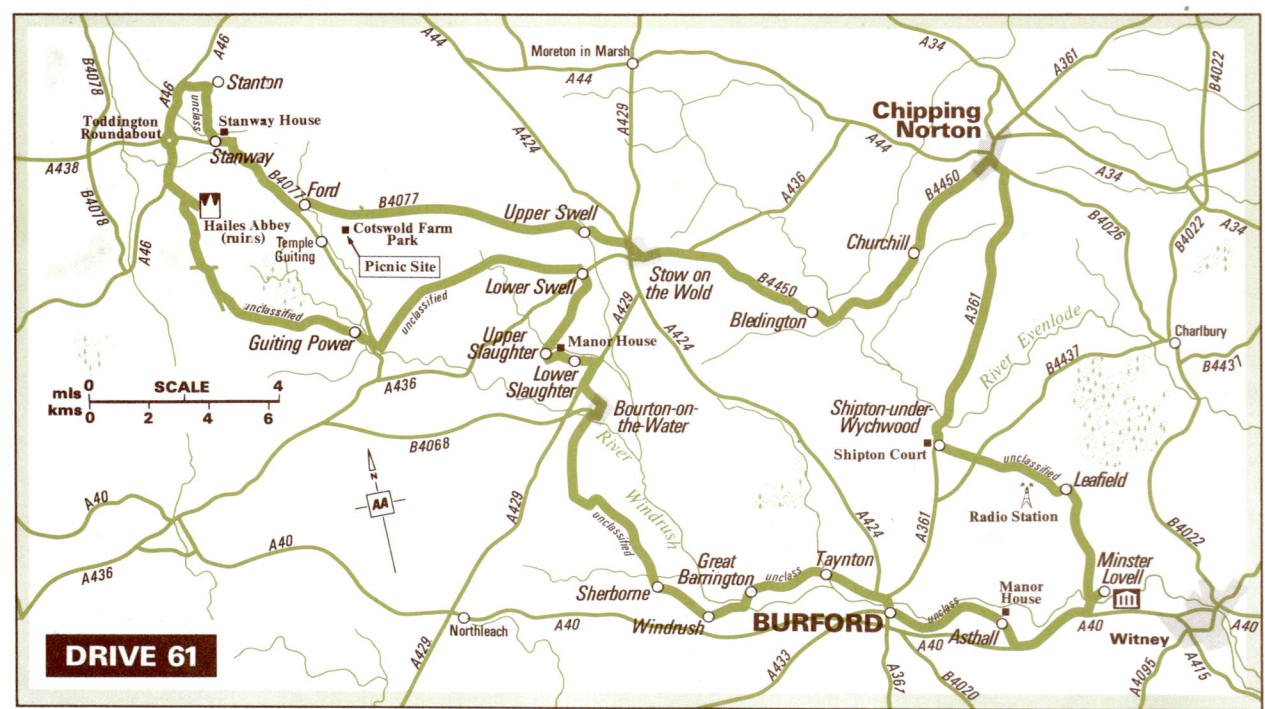

In the Vale of Red Horse

From Moreton-in-Marsh

Drive 62   65 miles

Follow the A44 *Oxford* road from *Moreton-in-Marsh,* and proceed for 2½m and turn right on to an unclassified road for *Chastleton*. Pass through the latter village and after ½m turn left. Cross a cattle grid and turn right on to the A44. Pass the Cross Hands public house and turn left on to an unclassified road. Proceed to the *Rollright* Stones, which stand on the right. Drive past the Stones and after ¾m turn left on to the A34 for a descent to *Long Compton*. Continue to *Shipston-on-Stour*, then turn left on to the B4035 Campden road. Proceed for 1¾m, cross a main road, and continue for a further 1½m through Charingworth and into *Ebrington*. At the end of the latter village keep right, then right again on to an unclassified road signposted 'To The Hidcotes'. After 2¼m turn right again for Hidcote Bartrim. Return to the T-junction and turn left, then take the next turning on the right signposted *Mickleton*. On reaching the main road turn right on to the A46 to enter Mickleton. Drive through the village, turn left, and after ½m continue on to the unclassified road for *Long Marston* and *Welford-on-Avon*. Go forward and later cross the River Avon, then turn left on to the A439 to Bideford-on-Avon. Turn left on to the A4085 with *Broadway* signposts and cross a 15th-c bridge. After ½m turn right for Cleeve Prior and South Littleton. Continue along the same road for a further 1m, then cross over a level crossing and turn left on to the unclassified *Bretforton* road. Proceed for 1¼m, join the B4035, and continue to Weston Subedge. Continue to the Seagrave Arms public house and turn right on to the A46. Pass through *Willersey* and after a while approach a T-junction. Turn right on to the A44 and proceed into Broadway. Drive to the Swan Hotel and turn left on to an unclassified road. Ascend, then bear right into *Snowshill*. Continue to the church and turn left. Ascend to the top of the incline and drive forward over crossroads, signposted *Chipping Campden* and Broadway Tower. After 1¾m turn left with Broadway signposts and proceed to Broadway Tower. Continue for ½m, cross a main road with Mickleton signposts, and after ¾m turn right. Continue for 2½m and on meeting a T-junction turn right on to the B4081 for Chipping Campden. Drive through this town and turn

continued on page 83

COTSWOLDS AND THE VALE OF OXFORD

The Cotswold Villages

From Burford

Drive 61   71 miles

Take the unclassified Asthall road from the Bull Hotel at *Burford*, and at Asthall approach a T-junction, then turn right with *Witney* signposts. Ascend and turn left on to the A40. Proceed for 1¾m to the White Hart public house and turn left on to the unclassified Leafield road. Descend, cross a river bridge, then turn right through *Minster Lovell*. Return to the T-junction and turn right for Leafield. Drive to the war memorial and turn left, then approach the Fox Inn and bear right. After a short distance pass the Leafield Radio Station. Continue to *Shipton-under-Wychwood*, and turn right on to the A361. Cross the River Evenlode and continue to *Chipping Norton*. Follow the B4450 Stow road through *Churchill* and *Bledington* before joining the A436 for *Stow-on-the-Wold*. Follow signposts to *Tewkesbury* and join the B4077 for *Upper Swell*. Continue along the B4077 through Ford, then descend to the *Stanway* war memorial. Approach crossroads and turn right on to an unclassified road. Pass the gateway and grounds of Stanway House and after 1¼m turn right for Stanton. Return and in ¼m bear right, signposted *Cheltenham*. Proceed for ½m and turn left on to the A46. Meet the Toddington roundabout and keep straight on. Continue for 1m and take the second turning on the left on to an unclassified road for *Hailes Abbey*. Return for 200yds and turn left, then climb on to the Roel Hill ridge. Proceed to a T-junction, turn left and then right and continue to Guiting Power. After ½m approach another T-junction and turn right, signposted Andoversford; take the next turning on the left, signposted Stow. Continue to Lower Swell and turn right on to the A436, signposted The Slaughters. Turn left on to an unclassified road for *Upper Slaughter*. Proceed through the village, turn left, and continue to the neighbouring village of Lower Slaughter. Cross a bridge, turn right, then at the end right again on to the A429, and after ½m turn left on to the B4068 into *Bourton-on-the-Water*. Drive to crossroads in the village and continue on the unclassified *Sherborne* road. Cross the river and bear right then ascend. In 3½m turn left into Sherborne. Stay on this road and enter *Windrush*. Keep to the left, then after ¾m approach a T-junction and turn left to Great Barrington. Continue to the war memorial and bear right for *Taynton*. Pass through the latter village and after a while join the A424. Join the A361 and cross a river bridge to re-enter Burford.

Drive 62 continued

left with the B4081, signposted Broad Campden. After ¼m turn left again on to an unclassified road for Broad Campden. Keep right through the village and climb to Blockley. Turn left, then after a short distance turn right on to the B4479. Proceed for 1½m, approach a T-junction, and turn left on to the A44. Pass through *Bourton-on-the-Hill* before returning to Moreton-in-Marsh.

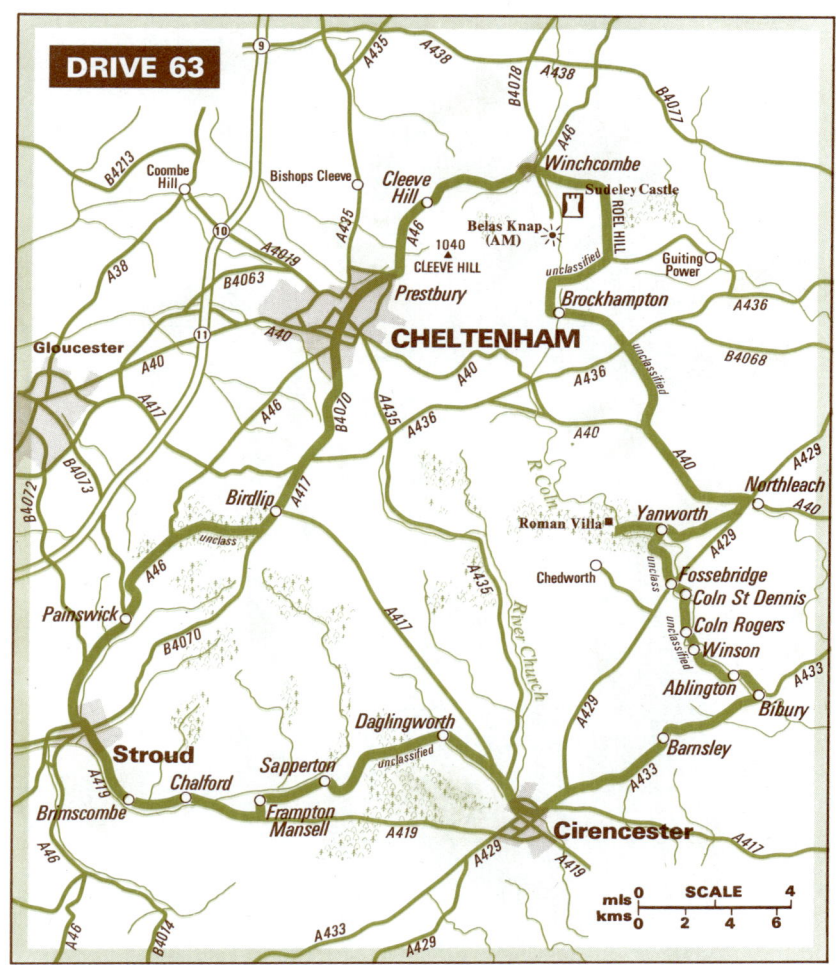

Golden Valley and Cleeve Hill

From Cheltenham Spa

Drive 63   70 miles

Leave *Cheltenham Spa* on the A46 Stroud road. Continue on the B4070, signposted *Birdlip*, and climb to the top of Leckhampton Hill. At the main road turn right, proceed to the roundabout and take the first exit on to the A417. On entering Birdlip turn right on to the B4070, then turn left; after ¾m branch right on to the unclassified *Painswick* road. In 2½m meet a T-junction and turn left on to the A46 and continue to Painswick. Follow the Painswick Valley to Stroud, then take the A419 *Cirencester* road through Brimscombe and *Chalford*. Ascend and after 2m approach the White Horse Inn. Turn left on to an unclassified road for Frampton Mansell. Continue to *Sapperton*, turn right, then approach a T-junction and turn left. After 1m turn right to *Daglingworth*, then continue for 1½m past the village before turning right on to the A417 for Cirencester. Leave Cirencester by following the A433 *Burford* road for Barnsley then *Bibury*. Drive to the Swan Inn in the latter and take an unclassified road through the Coln Valley to *Ablington*. After Ablington turn left, cross a river bridge, and then turn right. Turn right again into Winson, then drive through the village and turn right for Coln Rogers and Coln St Dennis. At the latter village turn left for Fossebridge, left again on to the A429, then right on to an unclassified road. Follow signposts to *Chedworth* Roman villa. Return for 1½m, go through Yanworth, and continue for 2m to the main road. Turn left and follow the A429 to the outskirts of *Northleach*. Approach traffic signals and turn left on to the A40 Cheltenham road. After 2¾m pass the Puesdown Inn, then ¾m farther approach crossroads and turn right on to the unclassified Brockhampton road. Proceed for 2¼m and cross the main road for Brockhampton. After ¼m meet crossroads and turn right, signposted Charlton Abbots. Drive to the next crossroads and turn right again, signposted Guiting Power. Ascend, and at the top of the incline turn left along the Roel Hill Ridge. Continue and descend to *Winchcombe*. Approach a T-junction and turn left. Follow the A46 Cheltenham road and descend to Prestbury before re-entering Cheltenham.

Placenames in italic type are worth stopping at each is listed and described in the main gazetteer section of the book

Wye and Lower Severn

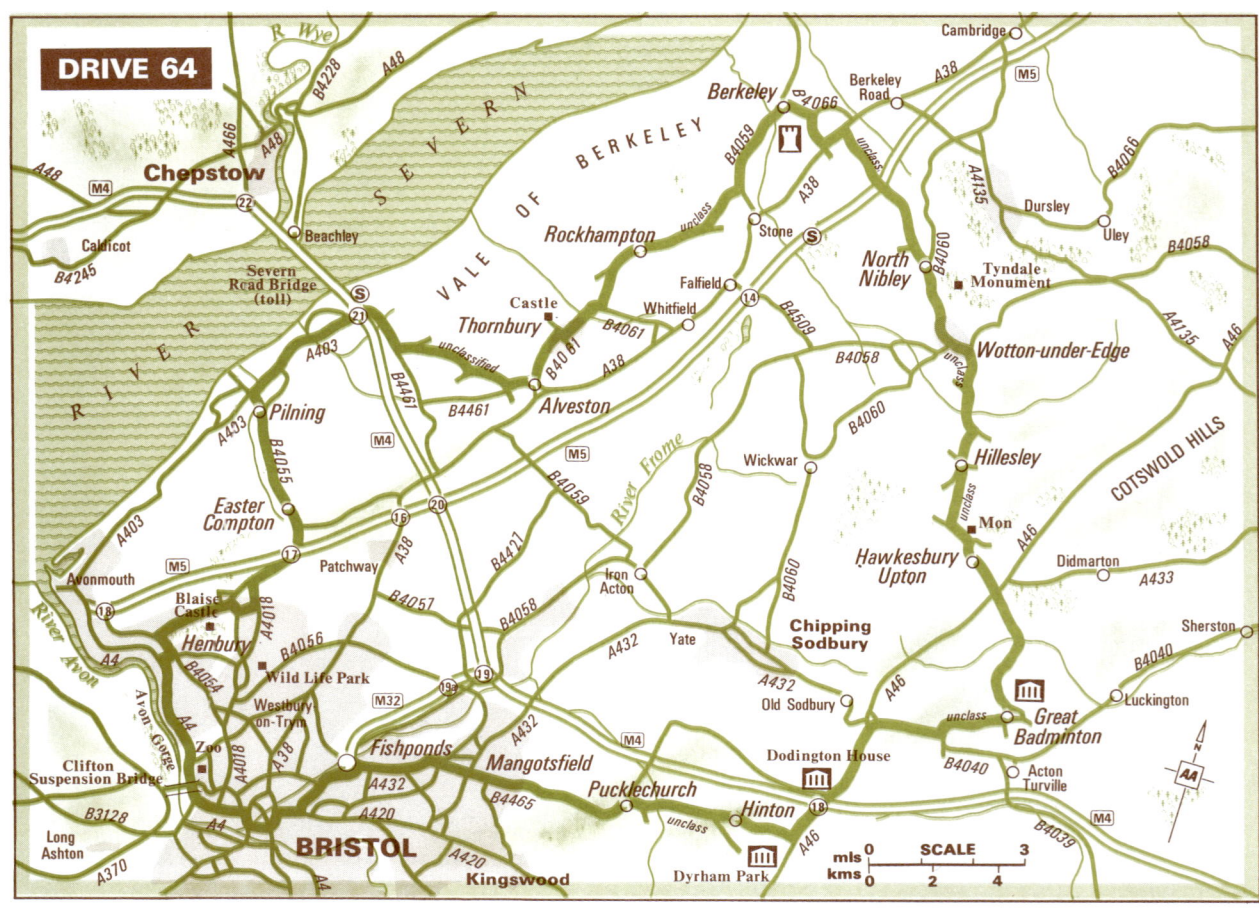

Vale of Berkeley and the Cotswold Hills

From Bristol

Drive 64   62 miles

Follow signposts marked 'M32 *Cirencester*' from *Bristol* city centre, leaving by the A432. Enter the suburb of Fishponds and on reaching the Cross Hands Inn turn right on to the B4465, signposted Mangotsfield. At Mangotsfield church turn right, signposted Pucklechurch. Approach a T-junction in Pucklechurch and turn right on to an unclassified road signposted *Hinton*. Proceed for 200yds then turn left, and continue through Hinton to a main road. Turn left on to the A46, signposted *Stroud*, then after ¾m approach a roundabout and take the second exit to cross the M4 motorway. Continue with the A46 for 1¾m, then approach traffic signals and turn right on to the B4040, signposted *Malmesbury*. In 1½m take the first turning left on to an unclassified road. Continue for 1½m then turn left again for Great Badminton. Proceed for 2¾m and cross a main road to Hawkesbury Upton, then continue for ¾m and pass the Hawkesbury monument. Bear right for Hillesley and follow signposts to reach *Wotton-under-Edge*. From here follow *Gloucester* signpost and join the B4060 to reach *North Nibley*. Drive to the Black Horse public house and turn left on to an unclassified road; proceed for ½m to the church and bear right, signposted *Berkeley*. In 2¾m meet a main road and turn left on to the A38, then after ½m turn right on to an unclassified road. Approach a T-junction and turn left to join the B4066 for Berkeley. Proceed to the Berkeley Arms Hotel and turn left on to the B4509. Drive on for 2m and turn right on to an unclassified road signposted *Thornbury*. Continue past Rockhampton and in 1½m turn right on to the B4061 to reach Thornbury. Drive into the town and turn right. Keep forward on to an unclassified road for Thornbury church, then return and bear right to rejoin the B4061, signposted Bristol. Proceed to Alveston and on reaching the Ship Inn turn right on to the B4461. Within ½m turn right again on to an unclassified road signposted *Aust*. Continue for 2¾m, then rejoin the B4461 to reach a junction with the M4 motorway. Approach a roundabout and follow signposts marked 'Avonmouth A403'. In 3m, turn left on to the B4055, signposted Pilning, then pass through Pilning and Easter Compton. Continue for 1m to reach a roundabout, and take the third exit on to the A4018, signposted 'Bristol West'. Continue for 1½m to the next roundabout and again take the third exit on to the B4057, signposted Blaise Castle. Drive to Henbury and on reaching crossroads turn right to follow one-way traffic past Blaise Castle House. Continue for 1½m, then keep forward to join the B4054 with Shirehampton signposts. After ¼m approach traffic signals and turn right on to the A4162, signposted Avonmouth. Proceed to a T-junction and turn left on to the A4 for the return to Bristol.

WYE AND LOWER SEVERN

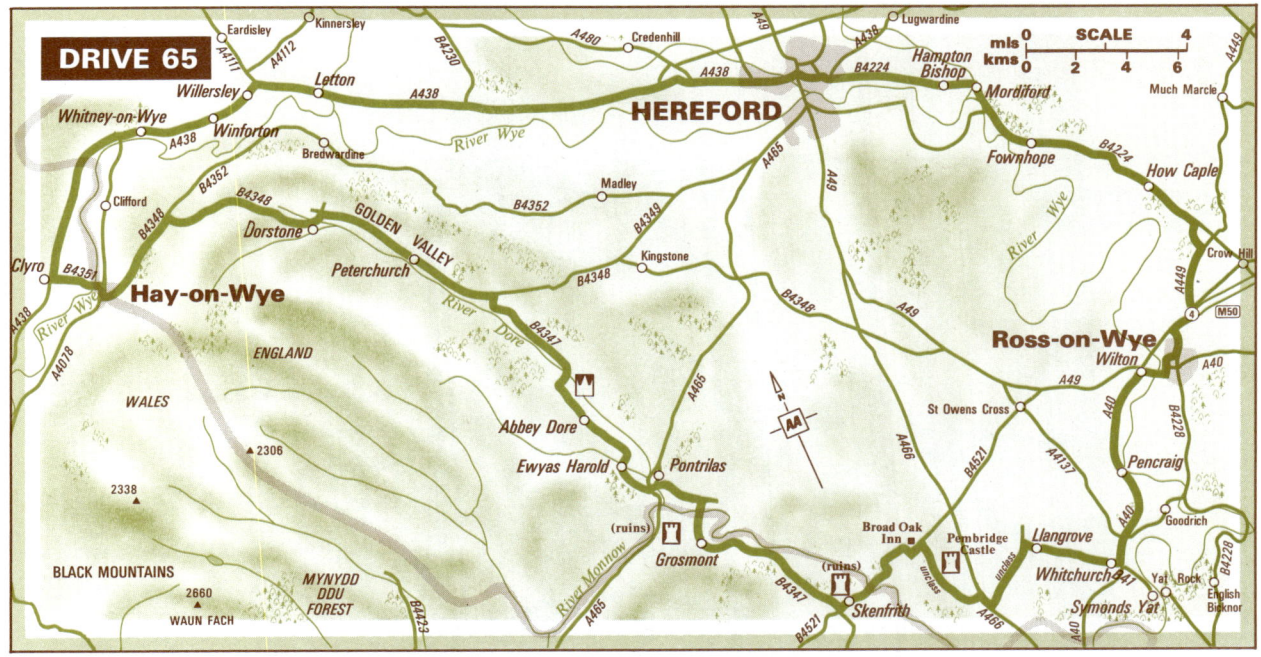

Upper Wye and the Golden Valley

From Hereford

Drive 65   80 miles

Leave *Hereford* by the A438, following Brecon signposts. Pass through Letton and continue for 1¾m before turning left into *Willersley*. Proceed through Winforton and Whitney on Wye and continue to the edge of Clyro. Turn left on to the B4351 and later cross a river bridge. Turn right into Hay on Wye and drive to the Blue Boar Inn before turning left on to the B4348, signposted *Peterchurch*. After 2¼m turn right, continue to the edge of *Dorstone*, and after ¼m approach crossroads. Turn right and continue to Peterchurch, then proceed for 2m and turn right on to the B4347, signposted Pontrilas. Continue to *Abbey Dore* and Ewyas Harold and cross a bridge. In ¾m cross a main road with Monmouth signposts, then cross the River Dore and turn right; proceed for 1½m then after passing the Bridge Inn turn right again. Drive on through Grosmont and proceed for 4¼m before turning left on to the B4521, signposted Ross. Pass the edge of Skenfrith and cross the River Monnow. Continue for 1¾m and on reaching the Broad Oak Inn turn right on to an unclassified road signposted Monmouth. In 2½m approach a main road and turn right on to the A466, then take the next turning left on to an unclassified road signposted Llangrove. After 1¾m turn right into Llangrove. Descend to Whitchurch and turn left to join the A40, signposted Ross. Proceed to the *Wilton* roundabout and take the third exit to enter Ross-on-Wye. Follow *Ledbury* signposts and in 1m turn right on to the A449. Continue to the next roundabout and take the first exit, signposted *Worcester*. Proceed for 1¾m, then branch left to join the B4224, signposted Hereford. After ¼m turn left and pass through How Caple to reach *Fownhope*. Continue through *Mordiford* and Hampton Bishop for the return to Hereford.

Placenames in *italic* type are worth stopping at; each is listed and described in the main gazetteer section of the book

WYE AND LOWER SEVERN

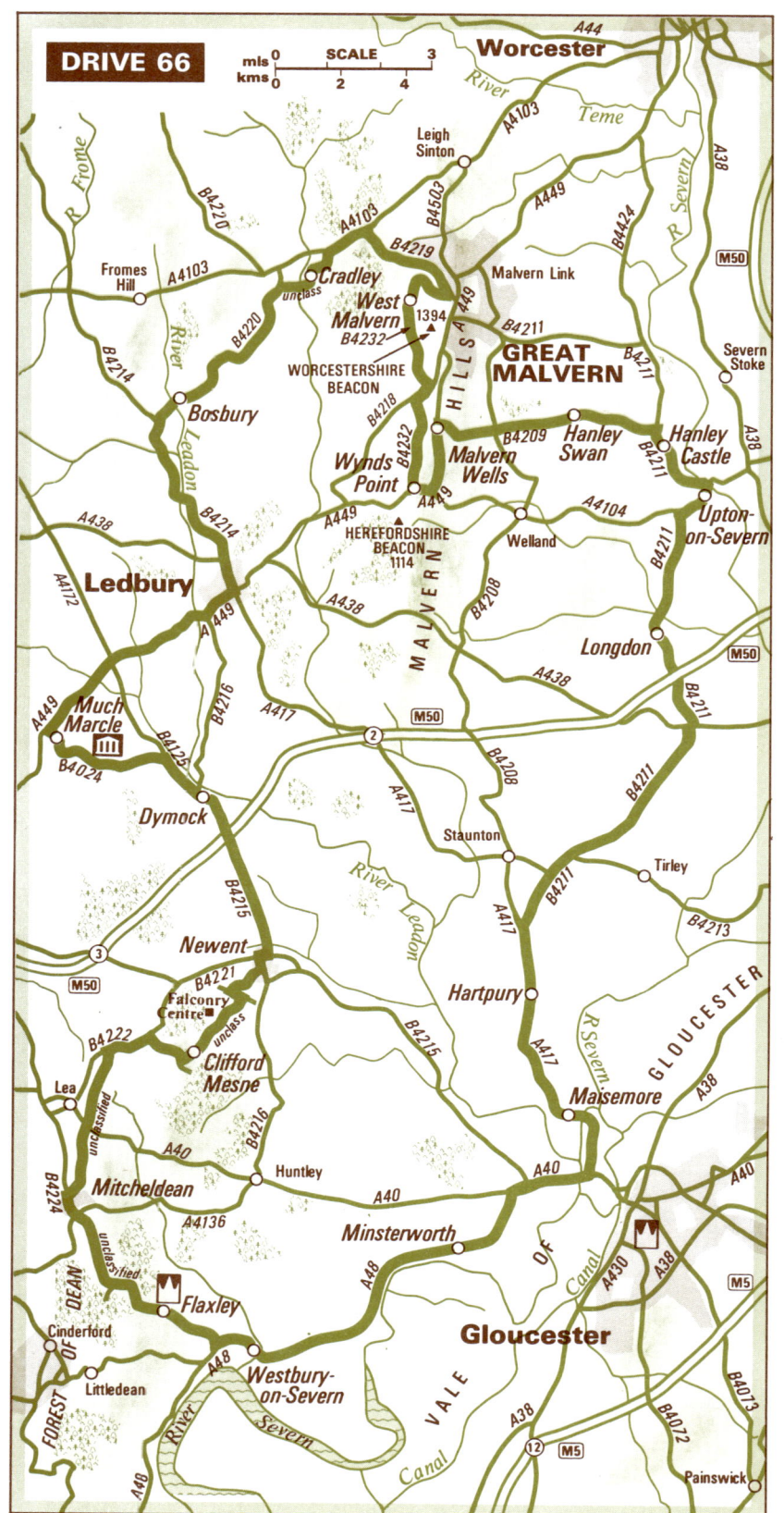

Over the Malvern Hills
From Great Malvern
Drive 66   74 miles

From *Great Malvern* follow signposts marked 'Worcester' then 'Hereford B4219'. After 2m turn left on to the A4103 and continue for 1m before turning left on to an unclassified road to Cradley. Drive beyond the village and turn right with *Bromyard* signposts. Approach a main road and turn left on to the B4220, signposted *Ledbury*. Continue to *Bosbury*, then shortly turn left to join the B4214 and reach Ledbury. Proceed to crossroads and turn right on to the A449, signposted Ross, then continue to *Much Marcle* and turn left on to the B4024, signposted *Newent*. After 2½m approach crossroads and turn right to join the B4215 for *Dymock*. Proceed for 3½m and turn right then left into Newent. Once in the town turn right on to an unclassified road signposted Cliffords Mesne. Proceed for ¾m and turn left then immediately right in order to continue through Cliffords Mesne. From this village ascend with Ashton, Ingham signposts, then after ¾m keep left to join the B4222, signposted Ross. In 1m keep forward on to an unclassified road signposted Mitcheldean, and in 1½m cross a main road. In a further 1½m join the B4224 and drive to the far end of Mitcheldean, then reach crossroads and continue straight forward on to an unclassified road signposted Flaxley and Westbury. Pass Flaxley and after 1½m turn left on to the A48, signposted *Gloucester*. Continue through *Westbury-on-Severn* and Minsterworth, then continue for 2m and reach a roundabout. Take the second exit to join the A40, then shortly turn left on to the A417, signposted Ledbury. Pass through Maisemore to reach Hartpury. Continue for 1¼m then turn right on to the B4211, signposted *Upton-on-Severn*. Proceed for 5m and on meeting a T-junction turn right then left; continue to Longdon. After 2¼m turn right on to the B4104 to reach Upton-on-Severn, then turn left and keep forward with the B4211, signposted Malvern. Reach Hanley Castle and turn left again on to the B4209, signposted Malvern Wells. Pass through Hanley Swan and continue to Malvern Wells, then turn left to join the A449 with Ledbury and Ross signposts. Drive to the British Camp Hotel and turn right along Jubilee Drive on to the B4232, signposted West Malvern. After 2¼m turn right then left for West Malvern and skirt the Worcestershire Beacon before returning to Great Malvern.

West Midlands

The Teme and Severn Valleys

From Kidderminster

Drive 67   76 miles

Take the A456 *Leominster* road out of *Kidderminster*, and within 3m cross the River Severn into *Bewdley*. Drive as far as the local church and turn left on to the B4194, signposted Ribbesford. Continue along the west bank of the Severn, with Ribbesford Woods on the right, and within 2¾m approach crossroads and turn right on to the A451 for *Great Witley*. Drive to the end of this village and turn right on to the A443, then within 1m branch right on to the B4202, signposted *Cleobury Mortimer*. Negotiate the gradual ascent to Clows Top. Approach crossroads and turn left on to the A456, signposted Leominster; after descending turn right to continue along the valley. Approach the edge of *Tenbury Wells* and turn right with Cleehill signposts on to the B4214. Climb out of the valley and continue through attractive hill country before ascending steeply and turning a hairpin bend. Drive to Cleehill and turn left on to the A4117 for the gradual descent into Ludlow. Leave *Ludlow* by returning along the A4117 Kidderminster road, pass under a railway bridge, and turn immediately left into unclassified Fishmore Road. Within 1¼m bear right with Clee St Margaret signposts and ascend. Follow signposts to Clee St Margaret, then cross a ford and turn left with Abdon signposts. Enter Abdon and turn right with Ditton Priors signposts. Within 1¾m bear right with Cleobury North signposts and drive round the north flank of Brown Clee Hill. Continue for about 1½m and turn left for a descent to a T-junction, then turn right. After a further ½m turn left on to the B4364, signposted *Bridgnorth*, and pass through Cleobury North. Later turn right on to the A458 to enter Bridgnorth. Leave the latter town on the B4363 Cleobury Mortimer road and enter Kinlet. Turn left with Bewdley signposts on to the B4194 and approach a T-junction. Turn left and drive through the Wyre Forest into Bewdley, then left at Bewdley on to the A456. Cross the River Severn and return to Kidderminster.

Along the Wenlock Edge

From Shrewsbury

Drive 68   73 miles

Follow the A49 *Leominster* road out of *Shrewsbury* and continue for ½m beyond Baystonhill before turning left on to the unclassified road for *Condover*. Enter Condover and turn left with Pitchford signposts. Within ½m bear left, and in a further 1½m approach crossroads and turn right to continue through Pitchford to *Acton Burnell*. Approach crossroads and turn right with Church Stretton signposts. In 2¾m meet crossroads and turn right before proceeding to Longnor. Bear left through the village and after ¼m turn left to join the A49. Continue for about another 5m, and on meeting crossroads turn right on to the B4371 with signposts marked 'Town Centre'. Enter Church Stretton and drive to the crossroads by the Midland Bank. Turn left on to the B4370 and pass through Little Stretton before turning right on to the A49. Continue to *Craven Arms*, then turn left on to the B4368, signposted *Bridgnorth*, and drive along Corve Dale to pass through Munslow and enter *Shipton*. Bear left on to the B4378 at Shipton, signposted *Much Wenlock*, and pass the manor of Shipton Hall on the left. Drive to Much Wenlock and leave by the A458 Bridgnorth road. Continue through *Morville* and enter Bridgnorth. Take the B4373 out of this town and pass through the North Gate. Within 5½m bear right with *Wellington* signposts and descend into the Severn Gorge before crossing the river to a T-junction. Turn left on to the A4169 (B4380) and pass through *Ironbridge*, continuing forward with Shrewsbury signposts; the famous Iron Bridge itself lies to the left. Continue past Ironbridge Power Station and cross the river. Pass through *Buildwas* and approach crossroads 4m beyond Leighton. Keep forward, passing Roman baths on the left, and within ¾m turn left on to the A5 to cross the River Tern. Enter *Atcham* and continue across the River Severn to re-enter Shrewsbury.

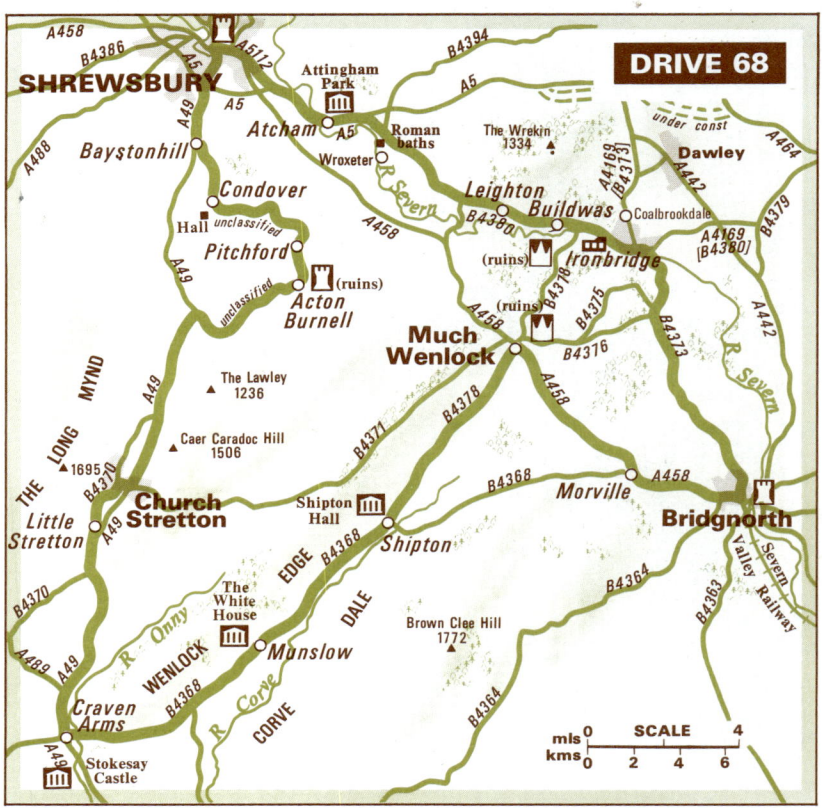

Placenames in *italic* type are worth stopping at; each is listed and described in the main gazetteer section of the book

WEST MIDLANDS

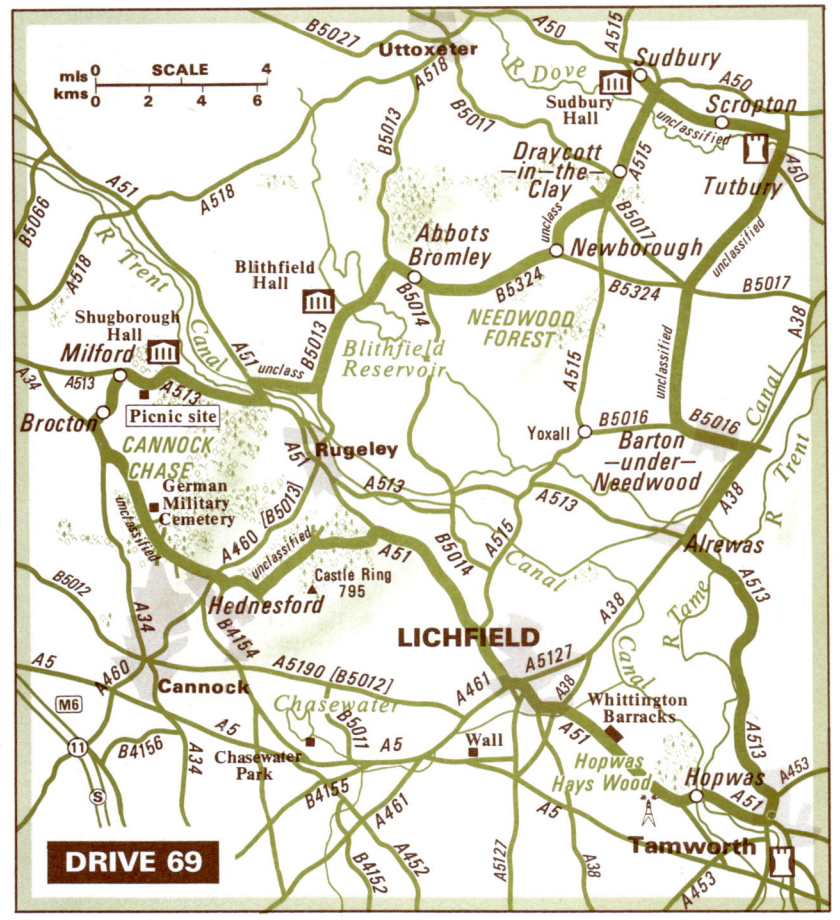

The Woods of Cannock Chase
From Lichfield
Drive 69 67 miles

Leave *Lichfield* by following signposts marked 'Tamworth A51', and pass a TV mast on the right before descending past Hopwas Hays Wood to Hopwas. Continue to Tamworth and follow the A513 Burton and *Alrewas* road to Alrewas; turn right on to the A38 with Burton signposts. Within 1m cross the River Trent before running alongside the Trent and Mersey Canal, and in about 1¾m approach crossroads. Turn left on to the B5016, and continue through Barton-under-Needwood by following Yoxall signposts. Within 1m approach the Bell public house and turn right on to the unclassified *Tutbury* road; within a further 3m cross a main road and pass through Tutbury via the A50 High Street. Cross the River Dove and a level crossing before turning left on to an unclassified road signposted Scropton and Sudbury, and continue for 2m beyond Scropton. Turn left on to the A515 to recross the Dove, and continue through Draycott-in-the-Clay. Ascend to crossroads ¾m beyond the village. Turn right on to the unclassified Newborough road, then at Newborough turn right again on to the B5324, signposted *Abbots Bromley*. Continue through pleasant countryside before turning right on to the B5014 to enter Abbots Bromley. Proceed on the B5014 for about ½m, then turn left on
continued on page 89

The Stour and Edgehill
From Warwick
Drive 70 77 miles

Leave *Warwick* by the A425 *Banbury* road and pass the grounds of the castle park. Within 2¼m join the A41, and after a further 1¼m turn right on to the B4087, signposted Wellesbourne. Leave Wellesbourne by following signposts marked 'Stratford B4086', and within 1m turn right on to the B4088, signposted Charlecote. Pass *Charlecote* Park and after entering the village turn left on to the unclassified Hampton Lucy road, skirting the edge of the park. Cross the River Avon, and after entering Hampton Lucy bear left with Stratford signposts. Within 1½m bear left again, and after ¾m turn left on to the A46 for *Stratford-upon-Avon*. Leave this famous town by the A34 *Oxford* road and follow the Stour Valley to Newbold-upon-Stour. Drive to the end of the village and turn right on to the unclassified road for Armscote, before turning right to *Ilmington*. Turn left and follow Campden signposts to climb Ilmington Down. Descend to crossroads and turn left to *Ebrington*. Join the B4035, signposted Shipston, and later enter Shipston-on-Stour. Leave the latter by following Banbury signposts across the River Stour, and within ¾m approach crossroads and turn left on to the unclassified Honington road. Within a further ¾m turn right with Tysoe signposts, and after 2¾m approach crossroads and continue forward. Enter Upper Tysoe and turn left with Kineton signposts, then right with Shenington and
continued on page 89

88

WEST MIDLANDS

Drive 69 continued

to the B5013, signposted *Rugeley*. Within 1m cross the extensive Blithfield reservoir, and in 2m turn right on to the unclassified *Stafford* road. After a further 1½m approach crossroads and turn left, then left again to join the A51. Cross the River Trent before turning right on to the A513, signposted Stafford, and follow the Trent Valley with the wooded slopes of *Cannock* Chase to the left. Pass the entrance to Shugborough Hall (right) on approaching Milford; enter Milford and turn left on to the unclassified Brocton road and pass through Brocton with Stafford signposts. Keep forward to the main road, then turn left with Cannock signposts on to the A34. Within ¼m turn left on to the unclassified Hednesford road and climb to Cannock Chase. Ascend beyond the next crossroads, and at the following crossroads continue forward to enter the colliery district around Hednesford. In ½m continue forward and descend to crossroads before crossing a railway bridge and turning right then left with Rawnsley and Hazleslade signposts to pass beneath a railway bridge and within ¾m turn left and go over a level crossing. Climb through thick woodland and approach crossroads. Turn right into Startley Lane and descend. Drive forward to the main road and turn right on to the A51 for the return to Lichfield.

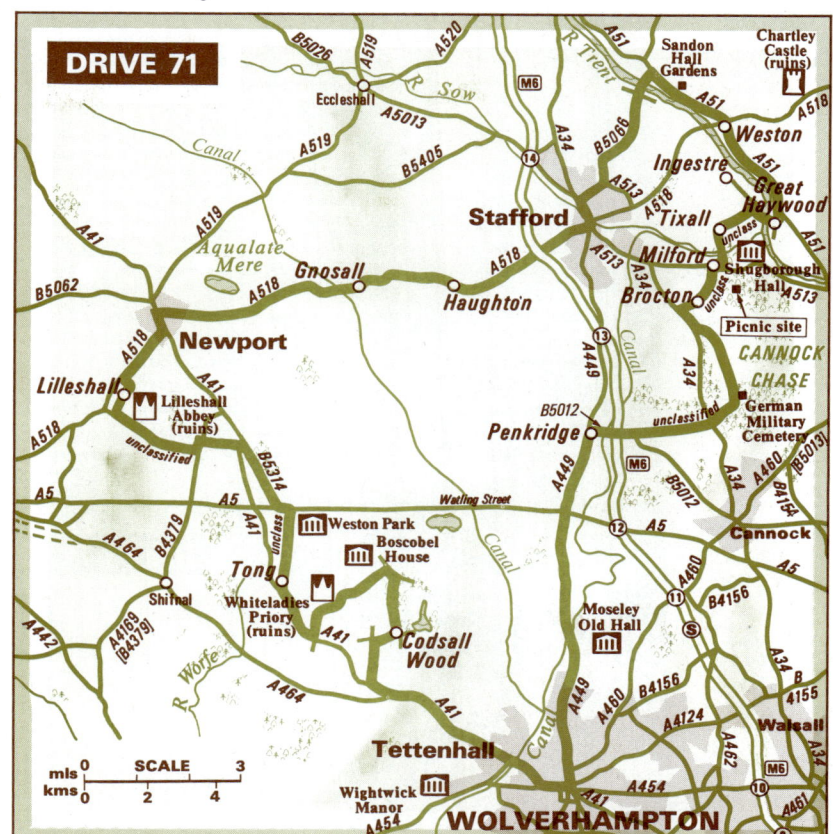

Drive 70 continued

Banbury signposts. Ascend Tysoe Hill to crossroads, then turn left and follow the 700ft ridge of Edgehill. Within 2m proceed forward on the A422, and continue for ¼m before bearing left on to the unclassified road for Edgehill village. After a further 1m bear left on to B4086, signposted Kineton, and descend into Kineton itself. Turn right on to the B4451 with Southam signposts, and on reaching Gaydon turn right on to the A41, signposted Banbury. Within 2m turn left on to the unclassified Fenny Compton road, then keep forward with signposts indicating the Burton Hills. Ascend the Burton Hills with Burton Dassett and Church Hill to the right, then after 1m reach crossroads and turn right. Descend and drive through Avon Dassett to enter Farnborough. Keep left through the latter village and at the far end turn left on to the A423, signposted *Coventry*. Continue to the edge of Southam before turning left at Leamington signposts on to the A425. Pass through Ufton and Radford Semele before entering *Leamington Spa*. Proceed on the A425 for the return to Warwick.

Around the Black Country

From Wolverhampton

Drive 71   71 miles

Leave *Wolverhampton* on the A449 *Stafford* road; enter *Penkridge* and turn right on to the B5012 with signposts indicating *Cannock*. Within 1¼m drive forward on to the unclassified *Rugeley* road, and after a further 2m cross a main road and climb Cannock Chase. Approach the next crossroads and turn left with signposts marked Brocton and Stafford, passing a German military cemetery on the right. Descend through wood and heathland and turn right on to the A34. Within ¼m turn right at crossroads and take the unclassified road to Brocton. Pass through Brocton, continue to Milford, and turn right on to the A513. Branch left on the unclassified Tixall road before crossing the River Sow and Staffordshire and Worcester Canal. Pass through Tixall and follow *Great Haywood* signposts for 1m to the next crossroads. Turn right and cross the River Trent via the Old Essex Bridge, and then cross the Trent and Mersey Canal into Great Haywood. Approach the next T-junction and turn left with *Weston* and *Sandon* signposts. Within ¼m turn left on to the A51 to Weston, and after a while pass the grounds of Sandon Hall on the right. Drive about 1½m to the Dog and Doublet Inn, and turn left with Salt and Enson signposts on to the B5066. Recross the river and canal, then keep forward with Stafford signposts. Descend and turn right to enter the town of Stafford, then leave the town by following signposts marked Cannock, and later 'Telford A518'. Pass through Haughton and *Gnosall* and continue to *Newport;* turn left then right for the A518. Within 2m turn left on to the unclassified *Lilleshall* road and continue to the T-junction at the end of this village. Turn left, and after 3m turn left again on to the B4379 and right on to an unclassified road signposted *London*. Continue to crossroads and drive forward on to the B5314, still with London signposts. Within 2m turn left on to the A5 and then take the next right turning for an unclassified road signposted *Tong*. Pass the entrance to *Weston* Park, enter Tong, and turn left past the village church before turning left again on to the A41, signposted Albrighton and Wolverhampton. Continue for about 1½m and approach crossroads; turn left on to the unclassified Shakerley road. Within ½m turn right and after 2m pass Whiteladies Priory on the left and continue to Boscobel House. Approach a T-junction and turn right, then bear right to follow Codsall signposts to the crossroads at Codsall Wood. Turn right, then at the next crossroads turn left with Kingswood signposts and continue to the main road. Turn left on to the A41 with Wolverhampton signposts, and return to Wolverhampton through Tettenhall.

Placenames in *italic* type are worth stopping at; each is listed and described in the main gazetteer section of the book

WEST MIDLANDS

To the Centre of England

From Coventry

Drive 72   73 miles

Follow the A27 *Rugby* road out of *Coventry*, and within 2m approach the Craven Arms public house and turn left, signposted *Lutterworth*. In another 1¾m pass the entrance to Coombe Abbey Countryside Park, then turn left on to the unclassified *Ansty* road. Within a further 2m approach a T-junction and turn left on to the B4029. After 1¼m cross the Oxford Canal and turn right on to the A46. Continue through Shilton to Wolvey, then proceed forward on the A447 with *Hinckley* signposts. Within 2m approach a roundabout and take the first exit on to the A5, signposted *Tamworth*. Keep forward for 4m before turning right on to the unclassified Higham road. Enter Higham and turn right; drive to the end of the village and keep left on the road signposted *Stoke Golding*. Cross the *Ashby-de-la-Zouch* Canal before entering Stoke Golding. Proceed into the latter and on reaching the T-junction turn right then left, signposted Dadlington. Pass the local church and within 1m approach crossroads and turn left with *Market Bosworth* signposts. Drive through Dadlington and in another ½m cross a main road and pass beneath a railway bridge. After another 1¼m turn right under a railway bridge with Sutton Cheney signposts. Proceed for 1½m and turn left on to a gated road. Continue to Market Bosworth and leave the town by the B585 *Atherstone* road; within another 3¼m turn right on to the A444 road, signposted Burton, and continue through Twycross and *Appleby Parva*. Stay with the A444 and in 1m approach crossroads and turn left on to the A453 Tamworth road. Drive to No Mans' Heath and take the second turning on the right on to an unclassified road signposted Clifton. Enter *Clifton Campville* and proceed to the far end of the village to turn left with Tamworth signposts. At the next crossroads keep forward and continue past the grounds of Thorpe Constantine Hall. Cross the main road into Seckington, then follow *Polesworth* signposts. Within 2m approach a T-junction and turn left with Walton and Grendon signposts. After a further 1m turn right and drive through Polesworth. Cross the River Anker and turn left on to the B5000 with Atherstone signposts; in 3½m turn right on to the B4116 and continue into the town of Atherstone. Once in the town follow signposts indicating *Weedon* and The South to the far end, then leave by turning right on to the B4111 (A4131) with *Nuneaton* signposts. Pass through *Mancetter* and within 1m turn right under a railway bridge and keep forward on the unclassified Hartshill road. Drive to Hartshill and turn left into Victoria Road, signposted Chapel End, and after ¼m cross a main road, signposted Whittleford. Within 1¼m cross a railway bridge, turn right into Church Road, and continue for ½m to the crossroads. Turn right on to the B4102 with *Meriden* signposts, then left to pass through Fillongley and enter Meriden. Approach the roundabout in Meriden, take the first exit, and in 1¼m approach another roundabout and turn left. Within another ¼m turn right to join the A45; after 2m branch left, meet a roundabout, and take the first exit on to the A4114 for the return to Coventry.

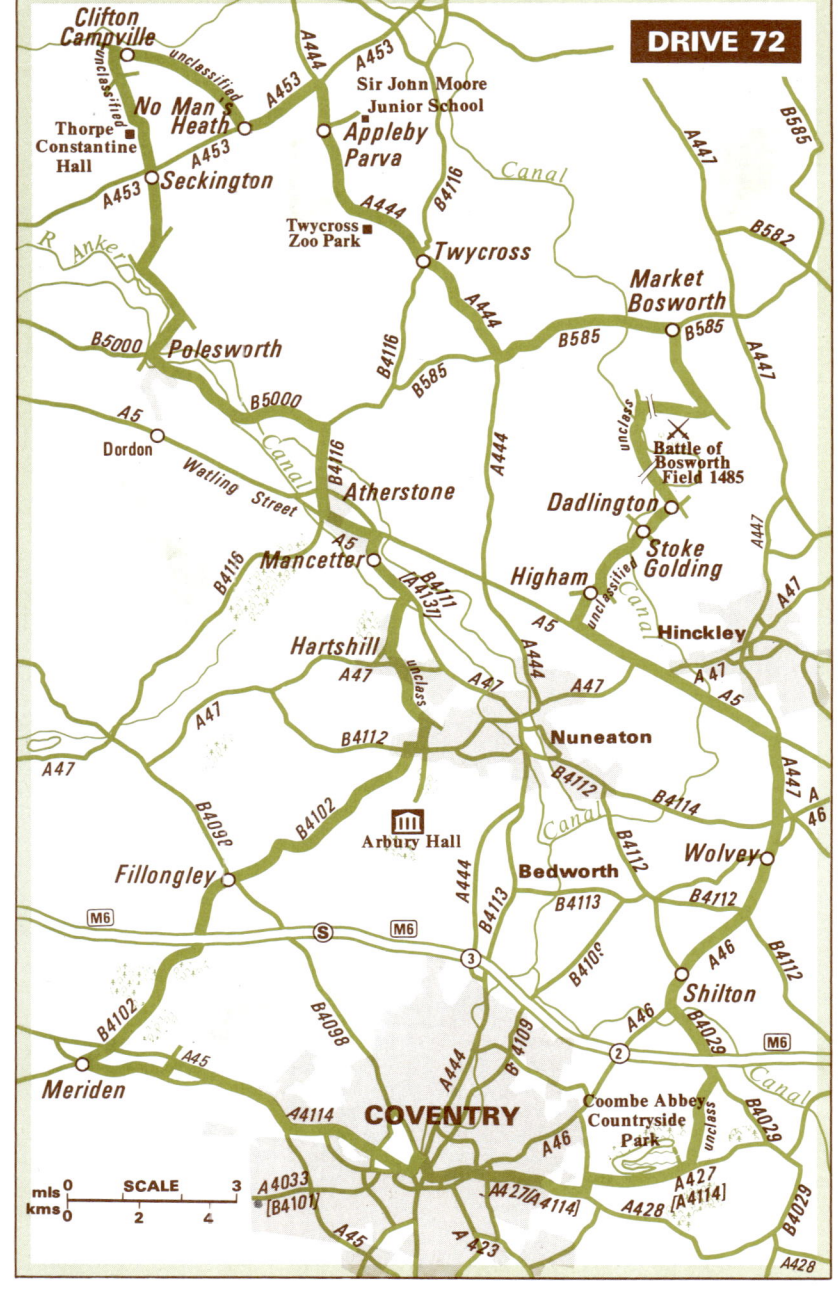

WEST MIDLANDS

Along the Clent Hills

From Bromsgrove

Drive 73   65 miles

Leave *Bromsgrove* by the A38 *Birmingham* road and continue for 2½m before turning right on to the B4096, signposted Rednal. Proceed to the crossroads in Lickey, and turn left on to the unclassified Rubery road. Continue to the next T-junction and turn left on to the road signposted Bromsgrove. Descend to the crossroads and turn right. Proceed for ½m and turn left then right, following Halesowen signposts. Turn right again on to the A38, continue to the roundabout, and take the second exit on to the A491. Within ½m turn right on to the B4551. Follow the gradual climb to *Romsley* and continue as far as the Sun public house; turn left here on to the unclassified Clent road. Follow Clent signposts and after 1¼m turn left and descend into Clent itself. Continue forward with *Belbroughton* signposts and in ¼m cross a main road. Proceed into Belbroughton, continue forward on to the B4188, and in ¼m bear left on to the unclassified *Chaddesley Corbett* road. Pass through the latter village and turn right on to the A448, signposted *Kidderminster*. In ¾m turn right on to the unclassified road to Harvington Hall. Drive to the T-junction in Harvington village and turn left on to the A450. Continue to the roundabout and take the second exit signposted *Worcester*. Continue for 2m, pass beneath a railway bridge, and turn left on to the A449. After ¼m turn right on to the B4193, signposted *Stourport*, and continue into *Hartlebury*. Drive as far as the church, turn left on to the unclassified Worcester road; after ½m turn right on to the A449. Proceed into *Ombersley* and turn left on to the A4133 for *Droitwich*. Follow signposts marked 'Worcester A38' to reach the county town itself. Leave Worcester by following signposts marked 'Evesham A44', and within 2m keep left on to the A422, signposted Stratford. After another 2m pass Spetchley Park and continue through Broughton Hackett and Upton Snodsbury. Pass through Inkberrow and after 1m turn left on to the B4092, signposted *Redditch*. Within a further 1m turn left on to the unclassified Feckenham road, and after another ½m turn left on to the B4090 with Droitwich signposts. Pass through Feckenham and at *Hanbury* turn right on to the B4091, signposted Bromsgrove. Drive through Stoke Prior, cross the Worcester and Birmingham Canal, and pass the Avoncroft Museum of Buildings. Cross a main road to join the A38 and re-enter Bromsgrove.

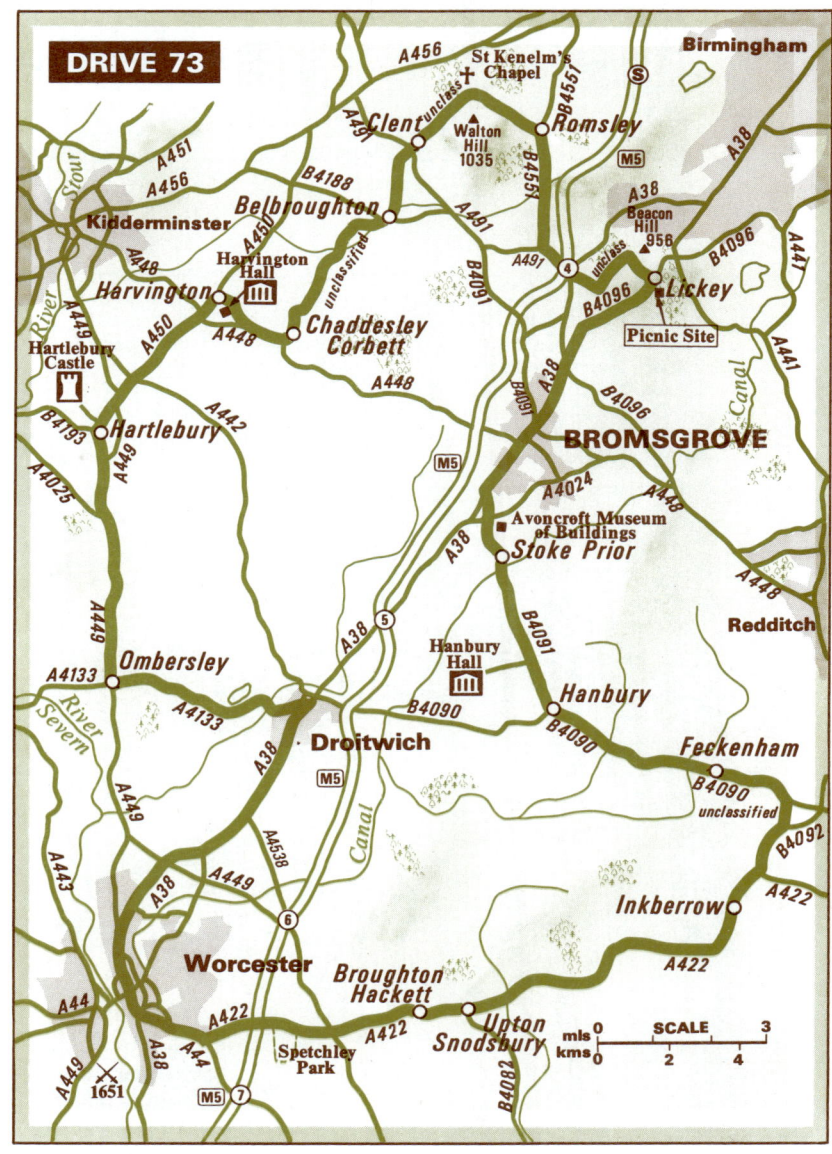

Placenames in *italic* type are worth stopping at; each is listed and described in the main gazetteer section of the book

East Midlands and Fens

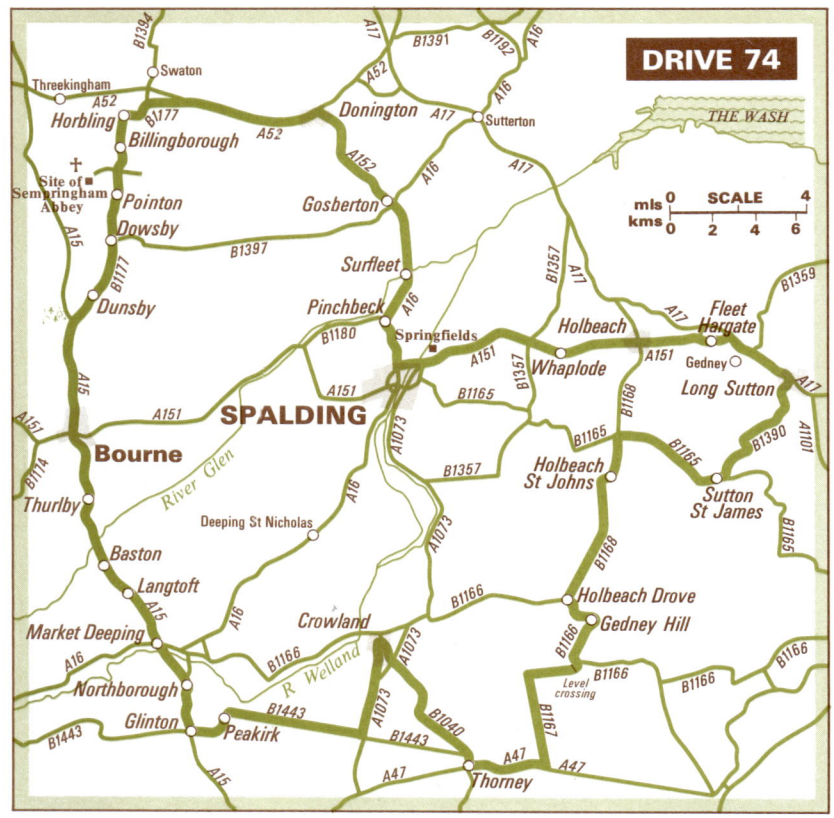

South-West of the Wash
From Spalding
Drive 74   84 miles

Take the A16 *Boston* road to leave *Spalding*, and pass through *Pinchbeck* and *Surfleet* to *Gosberton*. Continue straight on to the A152 *Grantham* road and proceed to *Donington*. Continue on to the A52, and in 4m turn left on to the B1177 *Bourne* road. Pass through the villages of Horbling, *Billingborough, Pointon,* Dowsby, and Dunsby before joining the A15 and reaching Bourne. Proceed south on the A15 *Peterborough* road and pass through Thurlby, Baston, Langtoft, *Market Deeping,* and *Northborough.* Drive on to *Glinton* and turn left on to the B1443 *Thorney* road for *Peakirk.* Proceed for 4m east of the village and turn left on to the A1073 to *Crowland.* Turn right on to the B1040 to Thorney, then turn left on to the B1167, signposted to Gedney Hill. Drive on for 4½m, go over a level crossing, then turn left on to the B1166 to *Gedney Hill* and follow the road to the left. Shortly enter *Holbeach Drove* and turn right on to the B1168. Continue to Holbeach St John's and after 1m approach crossroads and turn right on to the B1165 for Sutton St James. Drive to the end of the latter village, then turn left on to the B1390 *Long Sutton* road. Proceed to Long Sutton and turn left on to the A17 *Sleaford* road. Pass Gedney on the left and continue straight through Fleet Hargate on to the A151 *Spalding* road. Go through Holbeach and *Whaplode,* then cross a canal bridge and re-enter Spalding.

Grafham Water and the Great Ouse
From Cambridge
Drive 75   79 miles

Drive out of *Cambridge* on the A45 *Bedford* road, then in 2¾m pass the American World War II Cemetery. After a short distance turn right on to an unclassified road and pass through *Madingley.* Continue forward to the A604 and turn left, then in 4m turn right on to an unclassified road for *Swavesey.* Pass through *Over* to *Willingham* and turn left on to the B1050. After 2m follow the River Ouse to Earith. Turn left on to the A1123 and pass through Needingworth. Continue for 1½m beyond the latter and turn left again on to the B1040. Enter *St Ives,* cross the river, and in ½m turn right on to an unclassified road for Hemingford Grey. Turn left then right towards Hemingford Abbots, and follow *Huntingdon* signposts to re-join the A604. Proceed to *Godmanchester,* cross the River Ouse, and enter Huntingdon. Stay on the A604 *Kettering* road and pass Hinchingbrooke House on the right before turning left on to the A141. Join the A1 after a short distance, and in ½m take the second turning on the left into *Buckden.* Pass Buckden Palace; approach a roundabout and take the B661 *Kimbolton* road past Grafham Water Reservoir. Continue to *Great Staughton,* turn left on to the A45, then in 4m pass over the A1. Cross a viaduct over the River Ouse and enter *St Neots.* Turn right on to the B1043 and in 4m join the A1. After 3m turn left on to the B1042 for *Sandy,* and at the end of this town turn left again on to the B1042 (A603). Drive past the entrance to Lodge Nature Reserve, then pass a TV mast on the left before entering Potton. Turn left to leave on the B1040 St Ives road and continue through Gamlingay to Waresley. Keep forward on to an unclassified road to Great Gransden. Turn right on to the B1046 and continue past the Crown and Cushion public house. Turn left on to an unclassified road into the village following Caxton signposts. At Caxton turn right then left towards *Bourn,* passing Bourn windmill, then in 1m approach a T-junction and turn right. Pass through Bourn and turn left to join the B1046. Drive through Toft and Comberton to Barton, then turn left on to the A603. Continue for 1m before turning right on to the unclassified road for *Grantchester.* Cross the River Cam before turning left to join the A10 at Trumpington. Continue forward and return to Cambridge.

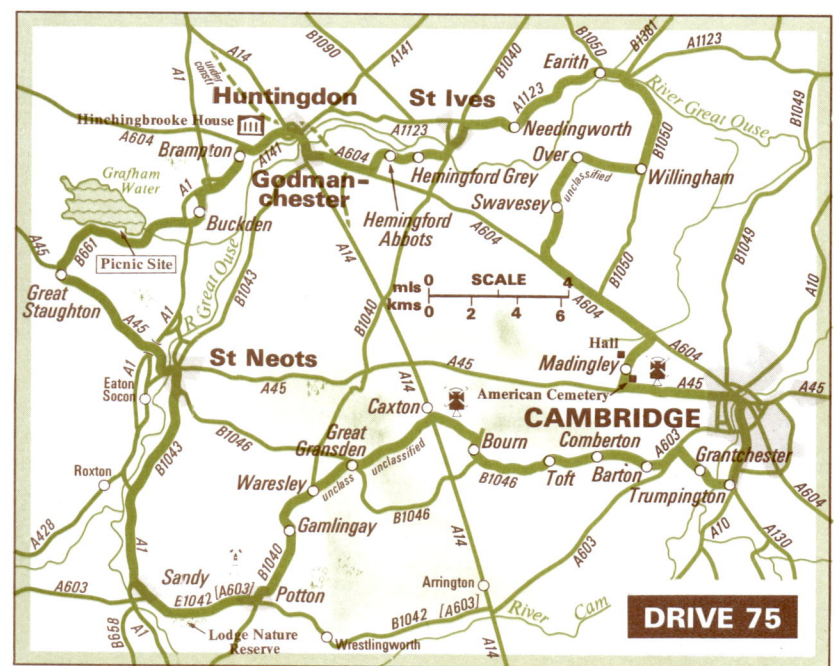

EAST MIDLANDS AND FENS

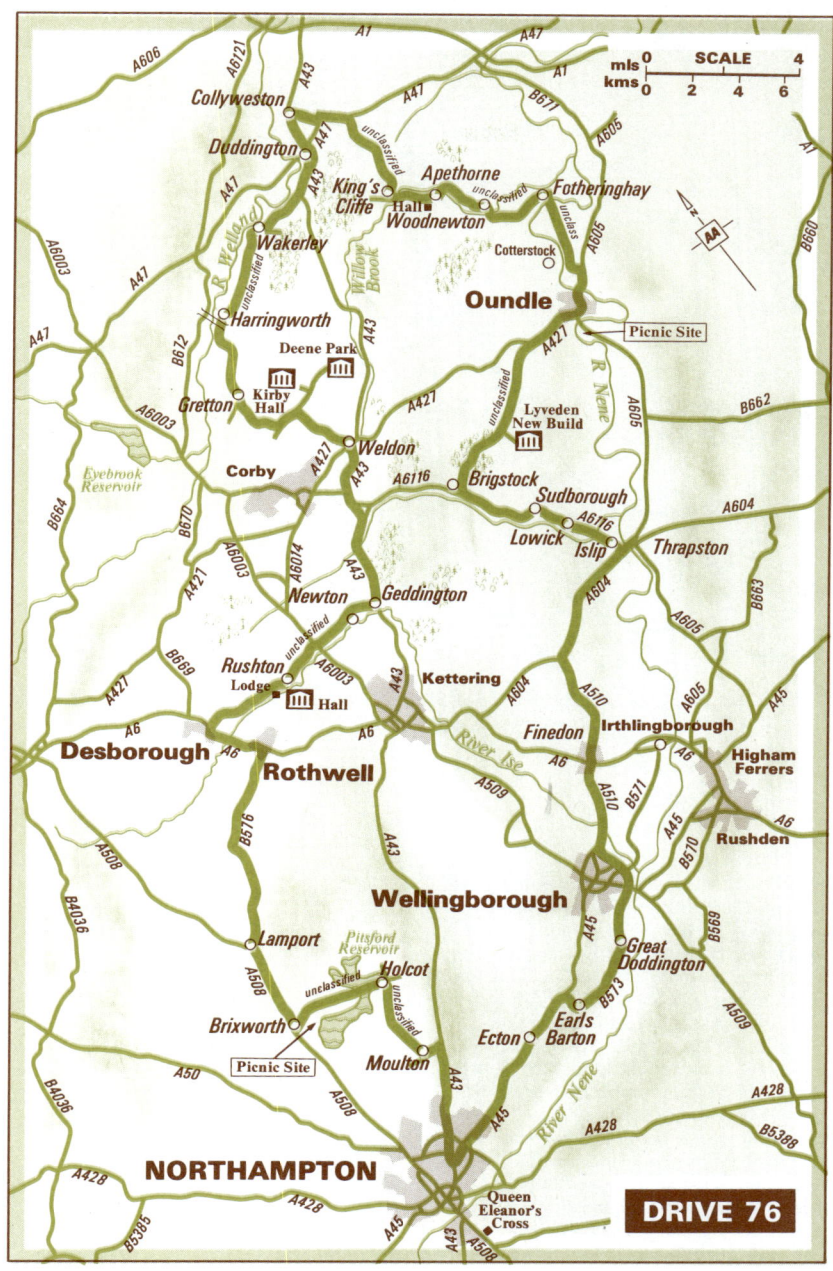

Beside the Nene and Welland

From Northampton

Drive 76   94 miles

Leave *Northampton* on the A45 *Wellingborough* road and drive through *Ecton*. Continue for 1½m beyond this village and turn right on to the B573 before entering *Earls Barton*. Continue to Great *Doddington* and in 1½m meet traffic signals. Drive straight across and follow *Peterborough* signposts to join the A510. Proceed through *Finedon* and in 3¼m turn right on to the A604; after 3½m cross the River Nene and enter *Thrapston*. Return across the river, turn right on to the A6116, then pass through Islip, Lowick, and Sudborough. Approach *Brigstock* and turn right on to a narrow unclassified road signposted Lyveden. Continue for 5m and turn right on to the A427 to enter *Oundle*.

Follow the A605 Peterborough road for 1m then turn left on to an unclassified road and pass Cotterstock village to the left before reaching *Fotheringay*. Leave on the *King's Cliffe* road and pass through Woodnewton and *Apethorpe* to King's Cliffe. Turn right and continue on the *Stamford* road, then shortly turn left on to the A47. Proceed for ¾m then turn right on to the unclassified road into *Collyweston*. Turn left on to the A43, in 1m enter a roundabout, and take the third exit into Duddington. Continue along the A43 and after 1m turn right on to an unclassified road and proceed through Wakerley and *Harringworth*. On reaching *Gretton* turn left and take the *Weldon* road. In 1½m turn left and continue to Weldon village. Turn left into Chapel Road, pass the church on the left and turn right on to the A43. Drive to *Geddington*, approach crossroads, and turn left on an unclassified road to the churches.

Return to crossroads and continue straight across towards Newton and Rushton. Later turn right and then left under a railway bridge before proceeding to Rushton. Enter the latter and turn right at a *Desborough* signpost. At Desborough turn left on to the A6, continue to *Rothwell*, then turn right on to the B576. On reaching Lamport turn left on to the A508, then drive to the Red Lion public house in *Brixworth*. Turn left on to the unclassified Sywell road. Stay on this road to cross the *Pitsford* Reservoir into Holcot, then approach crossroads and turn right with Northampton signposts. Proceed to Moulton, turn left then shortly right to join the A43, and return to Northampton.

Placenames in *italic* type are worth stopping at; each is listed and described in the main gazetteer section of the book

EAST MIDLANDS AND FENS

Whatborough Hill and Naseby

From Market Harborough

Drive 77   90 miles

Take the A427 *Corby* road out of *Market Harborough*. Drive through East Carlton and turn left on to the B670, then proceed to *Rockingham*. Turn left on to the A6003 *Uppingham* road and shortly cross the River Welland and proceed to Caldecott. Leave the latter by driving straight on to the B672, then after 4¼m pass under the Welland railway viaduct. In 2m join the A6121 and pass through *Ketton* to *Stamford*. Follow *Grantham* and *Oakham* signposts and take the A606 to Empingham. Continue to Whitwell and after 1m turn right on to the unclassified *Exton* and Cottesmore road. Skirt Exton Park, then reach Cottesmore and turn left on to the B668. Drive through Burley and descend into Oakham. Follow *Melton Mowbray* signposts, drive over a level crossing, then turn left and left again on to an unclassified road for *Braunston*. Leave Braunston on the *Leicester* road and after 4¾m pass Whatborough Hill on the right. Continue to Tilton and join the B6047 Market Harborough road. In 2m cross a main road, then after 3m reach the top of an ascent and turn right on to an unclassified road signposted Carlton and *Kibworth*. Proceed to Kibworth Harcourt and follow Leicester signposts to join the A6. Take the first unclassified road on the left, signposted Kilby and Wistow, then cross the Grand Union Canal at a series of locks. Continue to the next crossroads and turn left to pass through Fleckney and into Saddington. Turn right for Mowsley and continue to the village. Enter Mowsley and turn right, then right again with Leicester signposts. In 1m turn left on to the A50, then after 1½m turn right on to the B5414 for North Kilworth. Drive to the latter and turn right on to the A427, then left to rejoin the B5414 for South Kilworth. Proceed through South Kilworth and pass *Stanford* reservoir to the left before turning left on to the unclassified Stanford-on-Avon road. Descend to Stanford Hall, continue through Stanford-on-Avon, and within ¼m turn left on to the Cold Ashby road. Re-cross the Grand Union Canal and in 1½m climb Honey Hill to enter Cold Ashby. Turn left on to the B4036 and continue to *Naseby*, then turn left again on to the unclassified Sibbertoft road. Proceed to Sibbertoft and turn right for the Theddingworth road. In 1m bear right for Marston Trussell. Meet a T-junction and turn right and after ¾m turn right again to join the A427. Continue through Lubenham and return to Market Harborough.

EAST MIDLANDS AND FENS

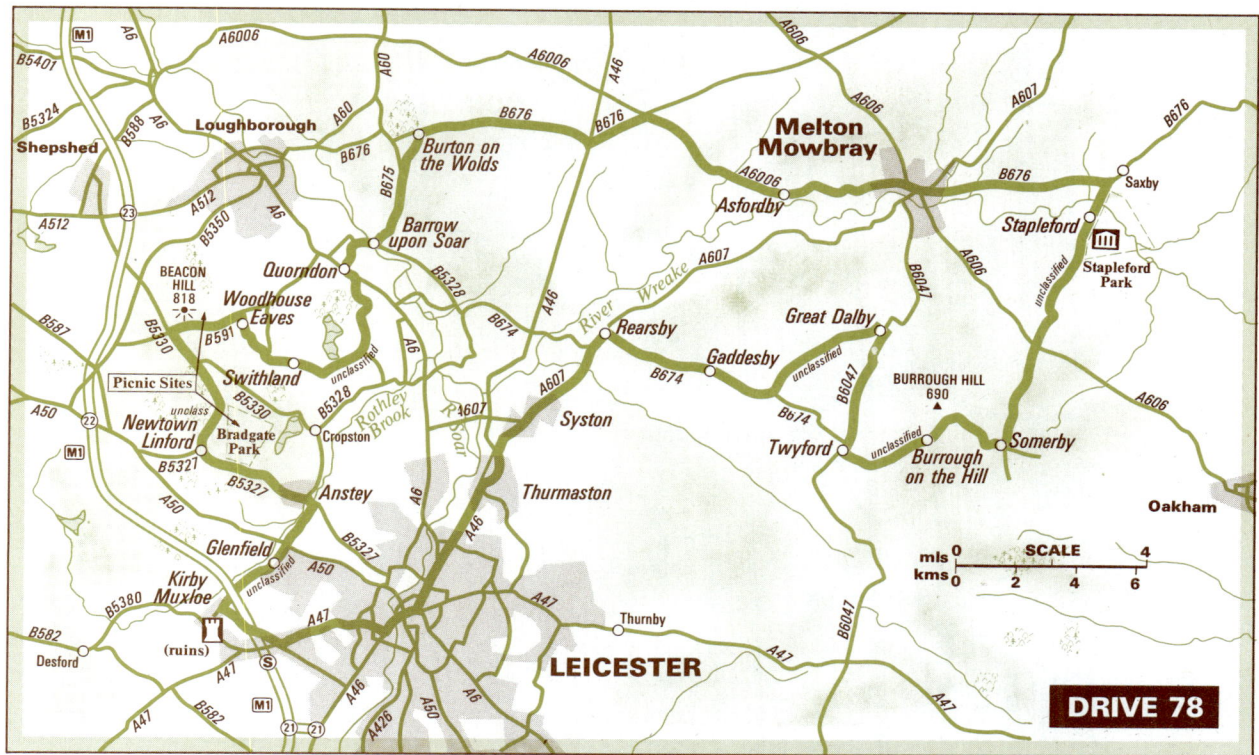

Wolds and Charnwood Forest

From Leicester

Drive 78   68 miles

Leave *Leicester* by the A46 *Newark* road and continue for 4m, then follow signposts marked 'Melton A607' and pass through *Syston*. Continue to Rearsby and turn right on to the B674 for *Gaddesby*. Stay on the B674 and within 1m turn left on to an unclassified road to Great Dalby. Later approach a T-junction and turn right into the village; pass the church, turn right on to the B6047, and proceed into *Twyford*. Turn left on to the unclassified Burrough road and proceed through Burrough-on-the-Hill before continuing to Somerby. Meet a T-junction and turn left with Pickwell and Melton signposts, then in 2¼m cross the A606, signposted *Stapleford*. Pass Stapleford Park on the right and proceed north before turning left to join the B676 to *Melton Mowbray*. Keep on the A6006 *Loughborough* road, passing through Asfordby, and 3½m later turn left on to the B676 to Burton-on-the-Wolds. Turn left again on to an unclassified road then after a short distance join the B675 for *Barrow-on-Soar*. Drive to the end of the village and turn right, then cross the river to Quorndon. Turn left on to the A6 and within 200yds turn right on to the unclassified Cropston and *Anstey* road. Proceed for 2¼m and on approaching crossroads turn right towards Swithland. Cross the end of Swithland reservoir, ascend through the village, and in 1m turn left for Woodhouse Eaves. At the end of the village turn left on to the B591 and ascend. In 1¼m pass a car park and turn left on to the B5330; shortly approach crossroads and drive straight on to the unclassified road for *Newtown Linford*. Leave the latter village by following the B5327 Leicester road to Anstey, then approach a roundabout and turn right to cross Rothley Brook. In 200yds turn right on to the unclassified Glenfield road and 1m farther meet a roundabout and go straight across to enter Glenfield. Follow signposts for *Kirby Muxloe*, approach crossroads at the edge of the village, then turn left towards Leicester, passing the castle on the right. In 1m enter a roundabout and turn left on to the A47 for Leicester.

Placenames in *italic* type are worth stopping at; each is listed and described in the main gazetteer section of the book

Norfolk

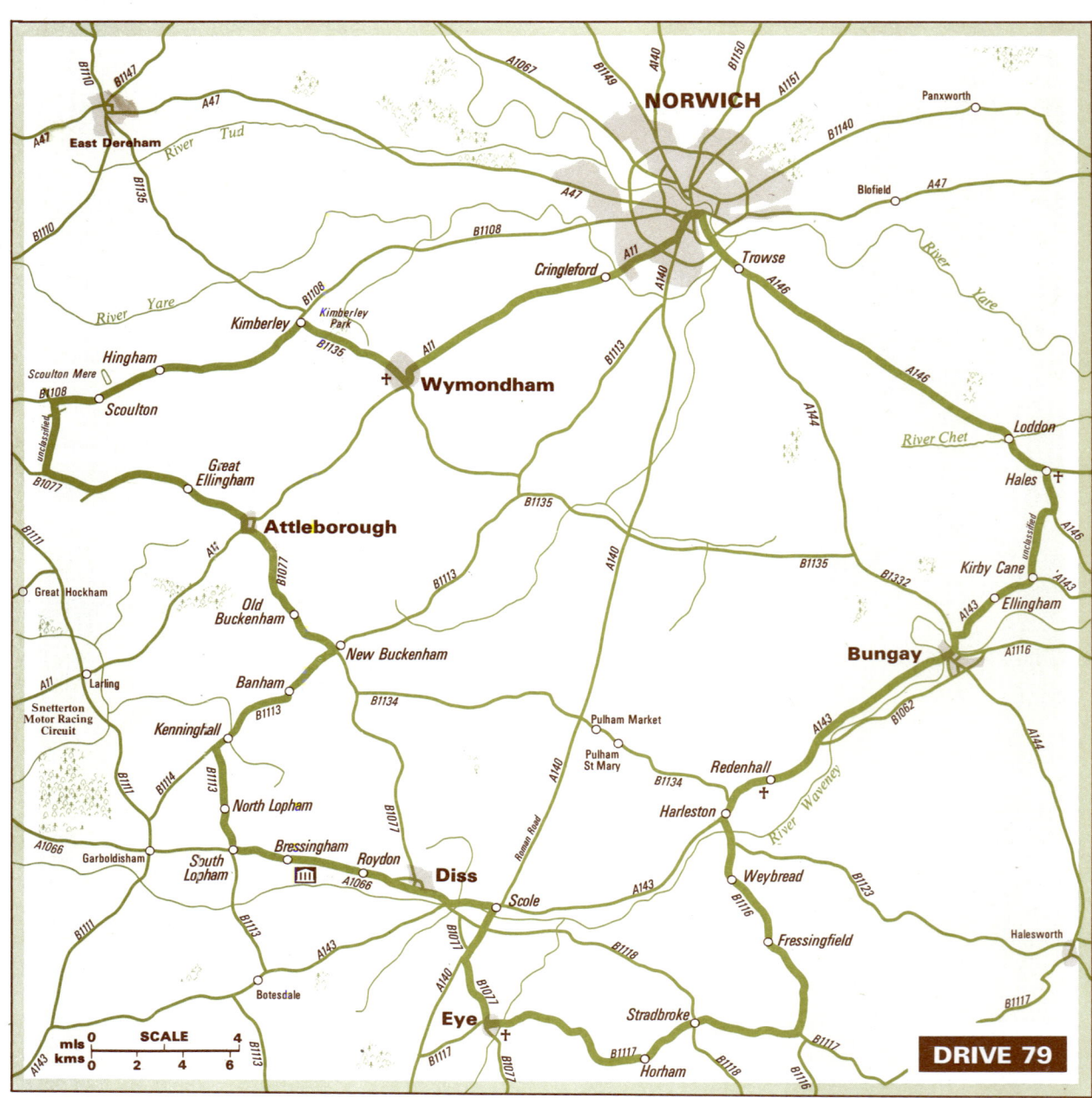

Scoulton Mere and Waveney Valley

From Norwich

Drive 79   95 miles

Leave *Norwich* on the A11 *Thetford* road and pass through Cringleford. In 6m turn right on to the B1135 and enter *Wymondham*, then continue along the East Dereham road and drive into the hamlet of Kimberley, situated in a corner of Kimberley Park. Turn left on to the B1108 and drive through *Hingham*, past Scoulton Mere (right), and through Scoulton. About 1¼m beyond Scoulton approach crossroads and turn left on to an unclassified road signposted Attleborough. Continue to a T-junction and turn left on to the B1077. Proceed through Great Ellingham and enter Attleborough. Leave by the B1077 *Diss* road, drive through Old Buckenham, then continue to crossroads at the edge of *New Buckenham*. Turn right on to the B1113. Proceed through Banham and continue to the far end of Kenninghall. Turn left and drive through North Lopham; continue to South Lopham and join the A1066 to pass through Bressingham. After Roydon keep forward on to the B1132 into *Diss*, leaving the latter on the A1066 *Yarmouth* road, and join the A143 for Scole. On meeting crossroads turn right on to the A140 *Ipswich* road. Cross the River Waveney and in ½m turn left on to the B1077 and continue to *Eye*. Leave Eye on the B1117 *Stradbroke* road and follow a winding road through Horham and over crossroads in Stradbroke. In 2¾m turn left on to the B1116 Harleston road and pass through *Fressingfield* and Weybread before crossing the River Waveney to re-enter Norfolk. Turn right on to the A143 and drive into Harleston. Continue along the Waveney Valley and pass *Redenhall* church before reaching *Bungay*. Leave Bungay on the Yarmouth road, and after passing through Ellingham and Kirby Cane go forward on to an unclassified road signposted *Loddon*. In 2m join the A146 Norwich road, cross the River Chet at Loddon, then continue through Trowse and return to Norwich.

NORFOLK

Windmills and the North East Coast

From Norwich

Drive 80   79 miles

Follow the A47 *Yarmouth* road out of *Norwich* and pass through Thorpe-St-Andrew and Blofield. Proceed to *Acle,* then cross flat marshland beside the River Bure. Enter Great Yarmouth and follow the A149 to *Caister,* then in 1¼m reach the First and Last Inn and turn right on to the B1159 for Hemsby. Continue along a winding route through *Winterton* and West Somerton, then pass the flat area round *Horsey* Mere and Horsey Windmill. Drive to Sea Palling and turn right to continue through Lessingham and *Happisburgh*. In 1½m approach crossroads and turn right for Walcott. On reaching the latter keep straight on to *Bacton*, then turn right. Continue past the North Sea Gas pipe-line terminal on the right, and proceed to *Mundesley*. Drive on to *Trimingham* and climb to higher ground before continuing to *Cromer*. Leave the latter town on the A149 *Norwich* road, and in 2¼m bear left for *North Walsham*. Follow the B1150 Norwich road through wooded Westwick Park and beneath an arched gateway that spans the road. Continue to *Coltishall* and cross the River Bure to Horstead. Drive through wooded country on the return to Norwich.

Placenames in *italic* type are worth stopping at; each is listed and described in the main gazetteer section of the book

NORFOLK

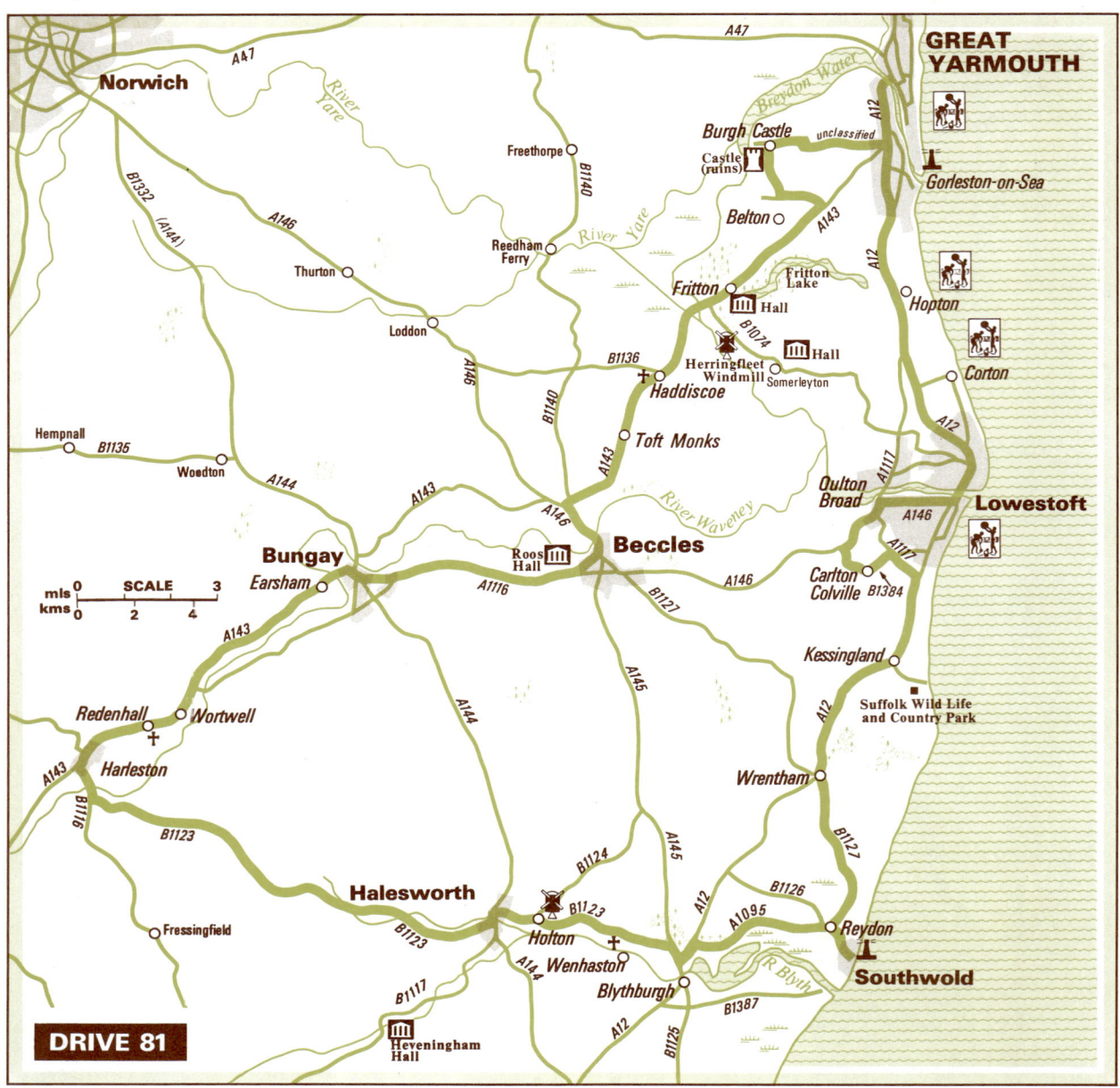

Oulton Broad and North Suffolk Coast

From Great Yarmouth

Drive 81   80 miles

Follow the A12 *Lowestoft* road out of *Great Yarmouth* and drive to the roundabout at the edge of *Gorleston-on-Sea*. Take the third exit on to an unclassified road and continue to Burgh Castle. Leave Burgh Castle on the Belton road; go forward to a T-junction and turn left, then approach a junction with the A143 and turn right, signposted *Diss*. Pass through *Fritton* and cross the River Waveney. Pass through Haddiscoe and Toft Monks and continue to the A146. Turn left, cross the Waveney and enter *Beccles*. Leave on the A1116 *Bungay* road and pass Roos Hall before continuing along the Waveney valley into Bungay. Leave this town on the A143 Diss road, and recross the Waveney. Proceed through Earsham and Wortwell and pass *Redenhall* church before entering Harleston.

Stay with the Diss road to the end of Harleston, then turn left on to the B1116 *Halesworth* road. Cross the Waveney, turn left on to the B1123, and then follow a winding road to Halesworth. Take the B1123 *Southwold* road out of this town and proceed to Holton. Continue through the latter and in 2m pass *Wenhaston* church on the right. Approach a junction with the A145 and turn right, then continue to a T-junction and turn left on to the A12. Skirt an inland lake formed by the River Blyth, then turn right on to the A1095 to cross marshland for Reydon and the coast at Southwold. Return to Reydon and turn right on to the B1127 with *Wrentham* signposts. Drive to Wrentham and turn right on to the A12 Lowestoft road. Continue past *Kessingland* and a right turn

leading to the Suffolk Wild Life and Country Park, then in 2m enter a roundabout and turn left on to the (A1117) *Oulton Broad* road. Proceed to the next roundabout and turn left on to the B1384, then continue to Carlton Colville. Drive on to the A146 and turn right for Oulton Broad. Continue into Lowestoft, then leave the town on the A12 Yarmouth road and skirt the seaside villages of Corton and Hopton-on-Sea. Drive through Gorleston-on-Sea into Great Yarmouth.

NORFOLK

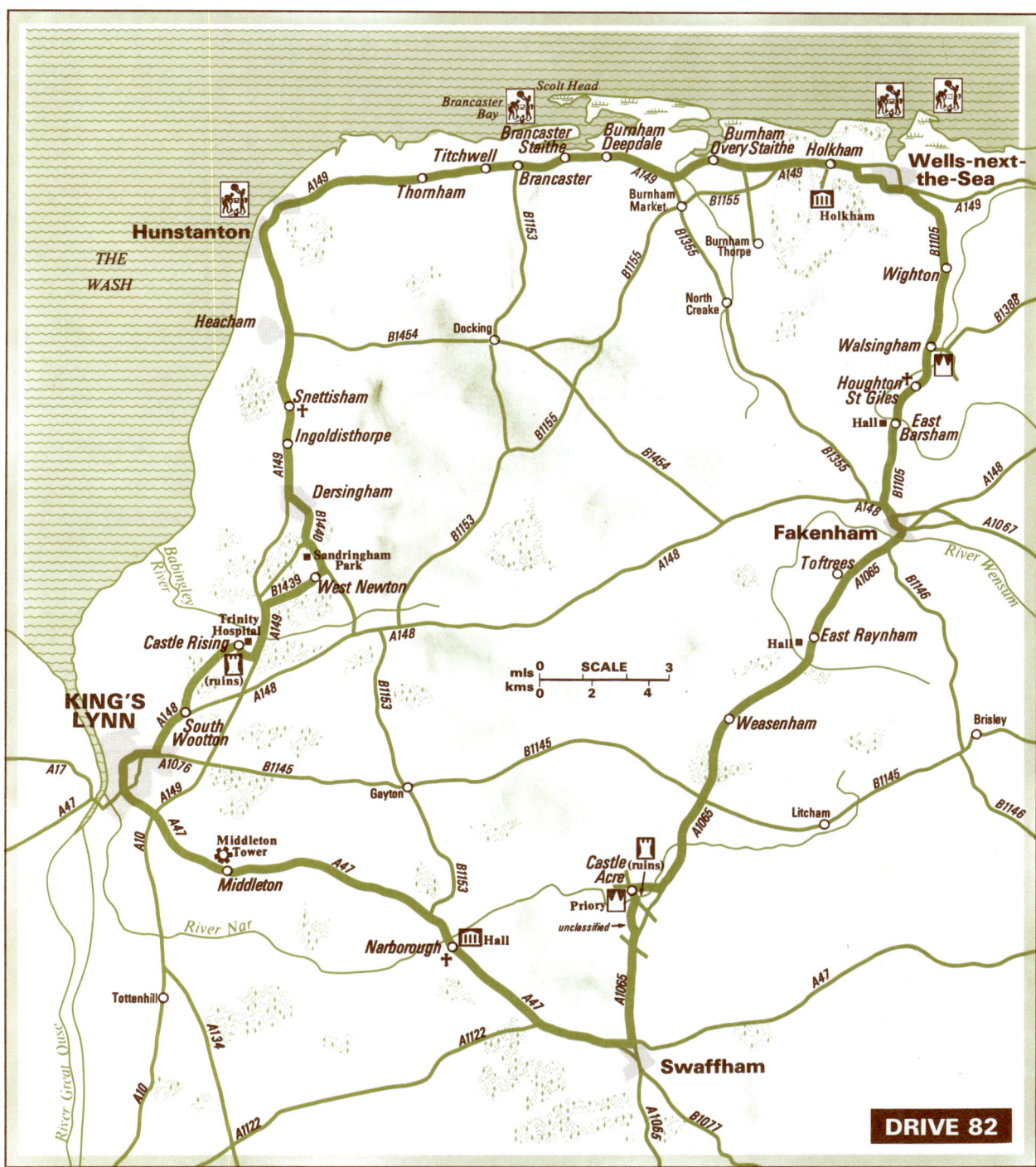

Resorts of North West Norfolk

From King's Lynn

Drive 82 74 miles

Leave *King's Lynn* on the A47 *Swaffham* road, and pass through *Middleton* and *Narborough* before continuing into Swaffham. Leave the latter on the A1065 *Cromer* road, then in 2¾m turn left on to the unclassified road for *Castle Acre*. Drive to the end of this village and turn right with Newton signposts to rejoin the A1065. Pass through Weasenham and *East Raynham*, then continue to *Fakenham* and follow King's Lynn signposts for the A148. In ¾m turn right on to the B1105 *Walsingham* road. Descend through *East Barsham* with East Barsham Hall on the left, and proceed through Houghton St Giles to Walsingham. Continue on the B1105 and pass through Wighton on the way to the coast at *Wells-next-the-Sea*. Enter the resort and leave on the A149 *Hunstanton* road. Continue through *Holkham, Burnham* Overy Staithe, *Burnham Deepdale,* and Brancaster Staithe. Scolt Head bird sanctuary can be reached from the latter. Pass through *Brancaster*, Titchwell and Thornham, then continue to the coast at Hunstanton. Leave this resort on the A149 and proceed through the outskirts of Heacham. Continue through *Snettisham* and Ingoldisthorpe to enter *Dersingham*. Leave Dersingham on the B1440 and climb to attractive woodland surrounding *Sandringham* Park. Keep left at the main gates and in ¾m turn right, signposted King's Lynn, on to the B1439. Drive into West Newton and continue to a main road. Turn left to rejoin the A149, and proceed for 1m before turning right on to an unclassified road for *Castle Rising*. Continue through South Wootton and return to King's Lynn on the A148.

Placenames in *italic* type are worth stopping at; each is listed and described in the main gazetteer section of the book

Lincolnshire Wolds and Nottinghamshire

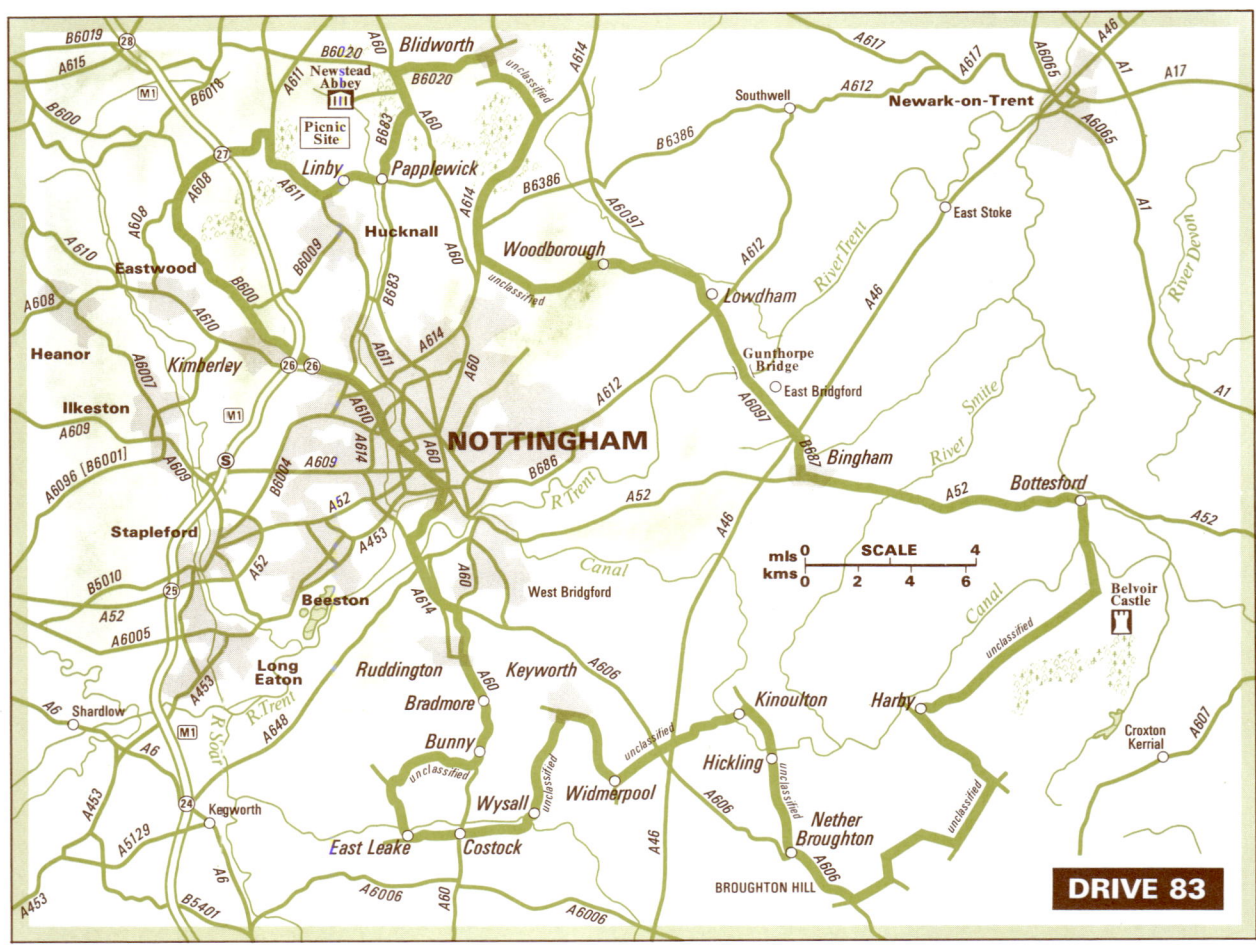

Robin Hood's Sherwood

From Nottingham

Drive 83   89 miles

Leave *Nottingham* by following signposts marked '*Loughborough* A60'. Cross the River Trent and pass through Bradmore and Bunny. Beyond the latter turn right on to an unclassified road signposted *Gotham* and East Leake. Pass under a railway bridge and after $\frac{1}{2}$m turn left. Continue to a T-junction at the centre of East Leake and turn right for the very interesting church. Return to the centre and keep straight on. Continue to Costock, cross the main road, then continue through Wysall and into Keyworth. Turn right and continue to the edge of Widmerpool village, then turn left with Kinoulton signposts. After $1\frac{1}{2}$m cross two main roads and keep forward through Kinoulton. Approach a T-junction and turn right for *Hickling*. Continue to Nether Broughton and follow *Melton* signposts to turn left on to the A606. Ascend Broughton Hill and continue to crossroads. Turn left on to the unclassified Eastwell road, and after $1\frac{1}{4}$m approach a T-junction and turn left again. Continue for 4m and meet crossroads. Turn left with *Harby* signposts and proceed to the edge of Harby; turn right with *Bottesford* signposts, and on entering Bottesford turn left on to the A52. Proceed to *Bingham*, approach traffic signals, then turn right on to the B687. After 1m enter a roundabout and take the second exit on to the A6097. Cross the River Trent and skirt Lowdham before continuing for $1\frac{1}{4}$m and turning left on to the unclassified Woodborough road. Drive to the end of Woodborough and turn left. Ascend on to high ground, then keep forward and shortly turn right on to the A614. In $3\frac{1}{2}$m turn left on to the unclassified *Kirkby-in-Ashfield* road. After $1\frac{1}{2}$m turn right with *Blidworth* signposts. Within a further $\frac{1}{2}$m turn left on to the B6020, signposted Sutton-in-Ashfield, and pass through the edge of Blidworth. In $2\frac{1}{2}$m reach crossroads. Turn left on to the A60, pass *Newstead* Abbey on the right, and after $\frac{1}{2}$m turn right on to the B683, signposted Papplewick. Enter the latter village and turn right on to the B6011, signposted *Linby*. A short distance beyond Linby turn right on to the A611. Drive on for $1\frac{1}{2}$m and turn left on to the A608. After a short distance cross the M1 motorway. Proceed for another $1\frac{1}{2}$m, then join the B600 and continue with Nottingham signposts. Enter Nuthall and on approaching a T-junction turn left. Reach a roundabout and drive forward on to the A610 for the return to Nottingham.

LINCOLNSHIRE WOLDS AND NOTTINGHAMSHIRE

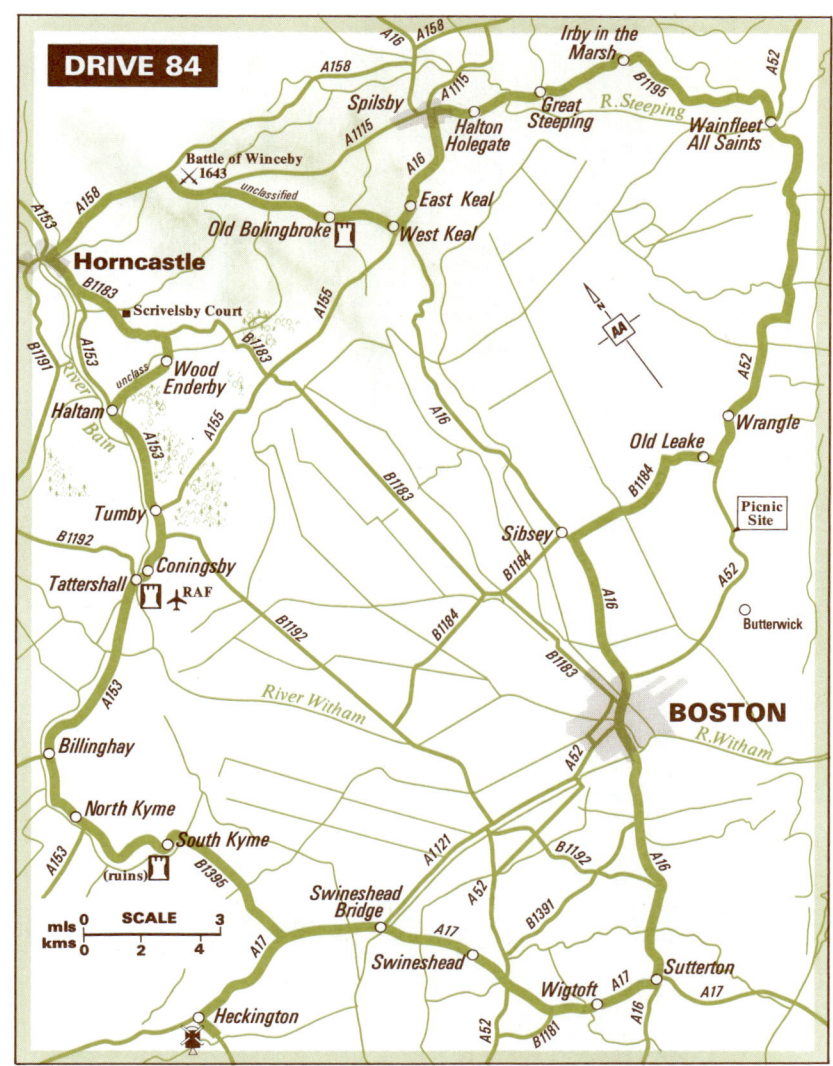

On to the Lincolnshire Wolds

From Boston

Drive 84   77 miles

Leave *Boston* on the A16 *Grimsby* road, and in 1¼m turn left. Continue to the edge of Sibsey and turn right on to the B1184, signposted Old Leake. In 1¼m approach a T-junction and turn right then left; after 1¾m approach crossroads and turn right into Old Leake. Drive to the end of the village and turn left on to the A52, then continue through Wrangle to *Wainfleet-all-Saints.* Keep forward on to the B1195, signposted *Spilsby,* and pass through Irby-in-the-Marsh, Great Steeping, and Halton Holegate. Climb to the south-east corner of the Lincolnshire Wolds and enter Spilsby. Proceed to the church and take the A16 Boston road to pass through East Keal. In ¾m turn right on to the A155, then enter West Keal and turn right again on to the unclassified High Barn road. Ascend past the church, then in 1m turn left and descend into *Old Bolingbroke*. Bear right, approach crossroads and turn right, then after a short distance turn left and pass the church. Continue to the war memorial and bear right with *Horncastle* signposts. Climb Horncastle Hill and in 2½m drive forward on to the A1115; after 1¼m turn left on to the A158 and proceed to Horncastle. Leave the latter on the A153 *Sleaford* road and in 1m turn left on to the B1183, signposted *Boston*. Pass the entrance to Scrivelsby Court on the left, then in 1¼m approach crossroads and turn right on to the unclassified Wood Enderby road. Enter Wood Enderby and turn right with Haltham signposts. Within 1¾m turn left on to the A153 and drive into Haltham, then continue along the Bain Valley and pass through Tumby to Coningsby. Cross the River Brain into *Tattershall*, then leave this village on the A153. Pass through Billinghay and proceed to the far end of North Kyme. Drive forward on the B1395, signposted *Heckington*, then proceed to South Kyme and in 4m turn right on to the A17. Continue to Heckington, then return along the A17 and enter Swineshead Bridge. Cross the railway and South Forty Foot Drain, then proceed through *Swineshead*. In 1m approach a roundabout and take the second exit. Pass through Wigtoft to Sutterton and turn left on to the A16 for the return to Boston.

Placenames in *italic* type are worth stopping at; each is listed and described in the main gazetteer section of the book

LINCOLNSHIRE WOLDS AND NOTTINGHAMSHIRE

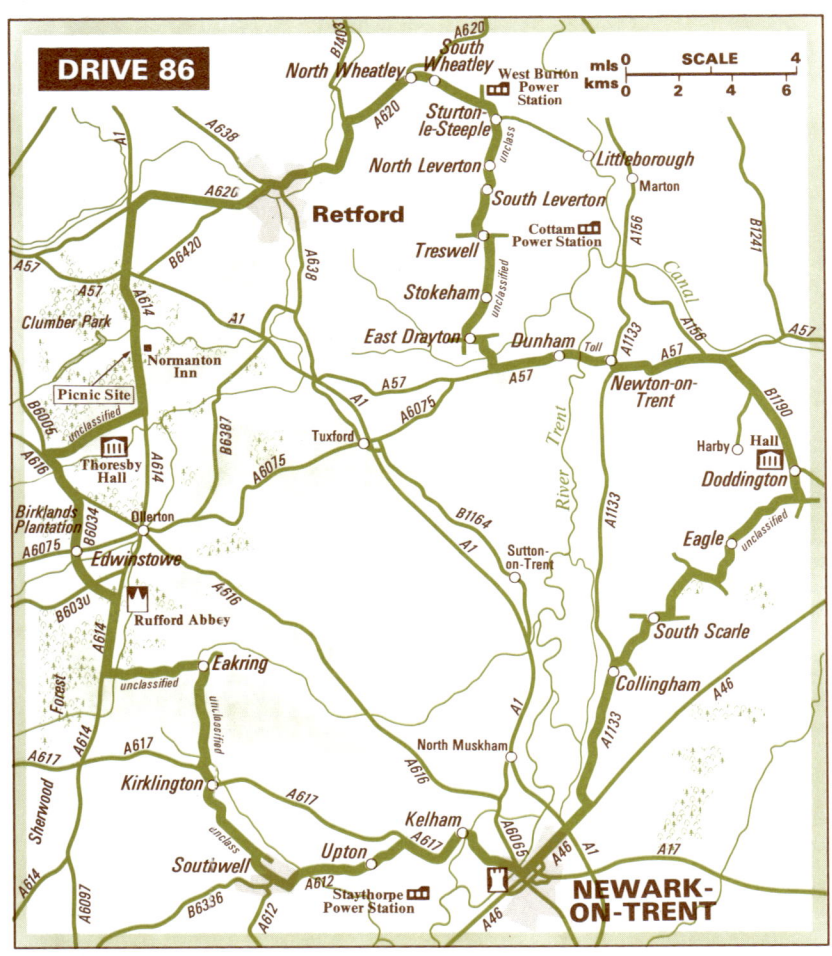

Wolds Villages and the East Coast

From Skegness

Drive 85   78 miles

Take the A158 *Lincoln* road out of *Skegness* and pass through *Burgh-le-Marsh*. Within 2¾m approach a roundabout with Gunby Hall to the left, and continue forward to Candlesby. Pass through Scremby to crossroads and turn right on to an unclassified road to Skendleby. Drive to the end of the village and bear right with Willoughby signposts, then ascend to cross a main road. Descend to the B1196 and turn left, then on approaching *Alford* turn sharp left on to an unclassified road to Well. Return along the unclassified road and on reaching the B1196 turn left into Alford. Leave Alford on the A1104 *Louth* and Lincoln road, then ascend to Ulceby Cross roundabout. Go forward on to the A16 and in ½m turn right on to the unclassified Harrington road. Pass the edge of Harrington and pass through *Somersby* to Salmonby. Turn left with *Horncastle* signposts, then in 2m approach crossroads and turn right, signposted Belchford. Descend into Belchford and turn right, then in 1m climb Belchford Hill; approach a T-junction and turn left with Louth signposts. Continue for 3¼m and approach crossroads. Turn right on to the A153, passing the entrance to Cadwell Park motor-cycle racing circuit on the right. In ¾m branch right on to an unclassified road and pass through Tathwell to crossroads. Keep forward, signposted Legbourne, and in 1¼m turn right on to the A16. In 1¾m turn left on to the unclassified Little Cawthorpe road and descend into this village. Turn right then left with Legbourne signposts and pass the church. Cross a ford and in ½m turn right on to the A157. Continue through Legbourne and within ½m turn left on to the unclassified Manby road. Enter Little Carlton and turn left, then continue past RAF Manby and through Manby. Meet crossroads and turn right on to the B1200. Proceed through *Saltfleetby* and continue to a junction with the A1031. Turn right to drive through Theddlethorpe St Helen, then in 3m turn left on to the A1104 into *Mablethorpe*. Leave this seaside resort on the A52 Skegness road and proceed through Trusthorpe and Sutton-on-Sea. Continue through Huttoft, Mumby, and *Ingoldmells* before returning to Skegness.

Through the Dukeries

From Newark-on-Trent

Drive 86   73 miles

Follow the A46 *Lincoln* road out of *Newark-on-Trent*, then continue for 2½m and approach a roundabout. Follow signposts marked 'Gainsborough A1133' and drive to the far side of Collingham. Turn right on to the unclassified South Scarle road and after ¼m turn left. In 1¼m turn right into South Scarle and follow Swinderby signposts before turning left with Eagle signposts. Proceed for ½m, then bear right and drive through Eagle with Lincoln signposts. Continue for 1½m and turn left, signposted *Doddington*, then drive on for ¾m and turn left again. Enter Doddington and go forward past Doddington Hall on to the B1190. Continue
continued on page 103

LINCOLNSHIRE WOLDS AND NOTTINGHAMSHIRE

Witham Valley Fens

From Lincoln

Drive 87 82 miles

Follow the *Grantham* road out of *Lincoln* and ascend the Edge to Bracebridge Heath. Turn right on to the A607 and after a short distance pass the large RAF base at Waddington on the left. Proceed through Waddington and Coleby into *Navenby*, then turn left on to an unclassified road signposted *Ancaster* and *Sleaford*. Continue for 2½m and on approaching crossroads drive straight across; proceed for 1¾m to the next crossroads and turn right on to the A17. Continue to *Leadenham* and approach traffic signals. Turn left on to the A607 and continue through *Fulbeck*. After ½m beyond the crossroads, for Caythorpe, turn right on to an unclassified road for *Hough-on-the-Hill*. Enter the latter and pass the church before turning left, signposted Barkston and Grantham. After 3m enter the outskirts of Barkston and turn left on to the A607. After ¾m go forward on to the A153 and skirt Honington. Continue for 2½m to crossroads and turn left on to the B6403. Drive through *Ancaster*, then after 3½m turn right on to the A17 and left on to the B1429. Proceed through Cranwell village and after ¾m turn right on to the A15 for Sleaford. Leave this town on the A153 *Horncastle* road and after 2¾m turn right for North Kyme. Beyond North Kyme go forward on to an unclassified road signposted Walcot and Metheringham. Continue for 1¼m and turn left on to the B1189. After 4m turn right on to the B1191, signposted *Woodhall Spa,* then drive through Martin before crossing the Witham Valley fens. Cross the River Witham, passing Kirkstead Abbey on the right, and enter Woodhall Spa. Continue on the B1191 to Horncastle, then leave this town on the A158 Lincoln road. After ½m turn left on to the B1190, signposted Bardney. Drive through Thimbleby, Horsington, and Bucknall, then pass ruined Tupholme Abbey. In 1¾m turn left into Bardney, then cross a railway and the River Witham. Stay with the B1190 and after 2½m bear right to skirt Lincoln 'Edge'. Pass through Washingborough and continue to Lincoln.

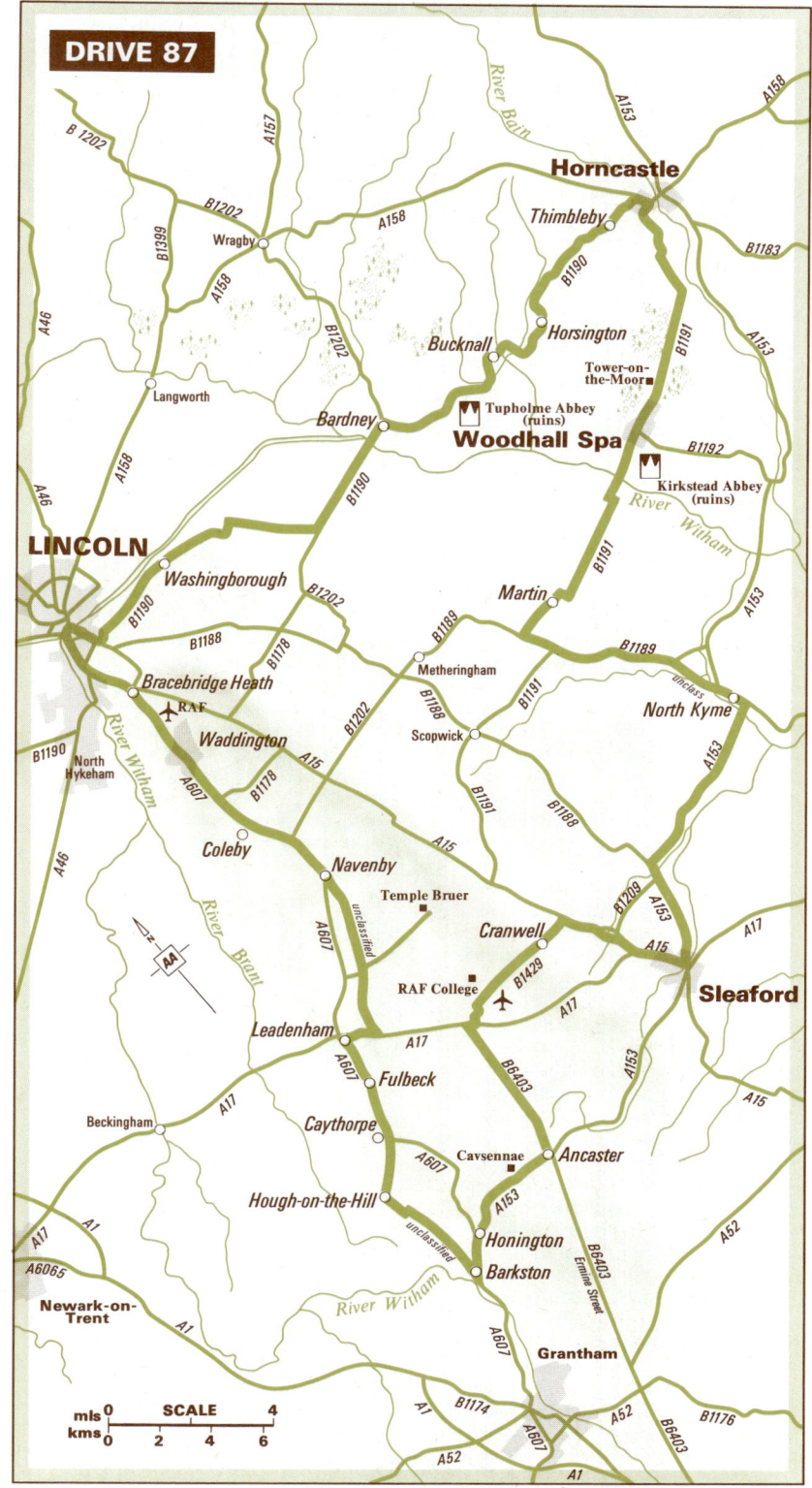

Drive 86 continued

for 3m and turn left on to the A57. Pass through Newton-on-Trent and Dunham, then proceed for 1¾m and turn right on to the unclassified East Drayton road. Proceed for 1m and turn left, then drive to East Drayton church and turn right. Enter Stokeham and turn right then left with Leverton signposts. After 1¼m turn left into Treswell. Turn right and continue through South Leverton, North Leverton, and Sturton-le-Steeple. Follow Gainsborough then Wheatley signposts, then pass through South Wheatley and turn left, signposted *Retford*. Enter North Wheatley and turn left on to the A620. Drive through Retford and follow *Worksop* signposts to stay with the A620. After a short distance turn left, then proceed for 3¾m and turn left again with Newark signposts to join the A1. Continue to a roundabout and follow signposts marked 'Nottingham A614'. After 3¾m turn right on to the unclassified *Thoresby Hall* road. Pass Thoresby Hall and continue for 2m, then turn left on to the A616. Proceed for 1½m then turn right on to the B6034, signposted *Edwinstowe*. Continue through Edwinstowe and drive for 1½m before turning right on to the A614. After 1¾m turn left on to an unclassified road for *Eakring*, then follow Kirklington signposts. After 2¾m turn left on to the A617. Drive to the edge of Kirklington and turn right on to an unclassified road for *Southwell*. Proceed for 2½m and turn right for Southwell town centre (no signs). Leave this town on the A612 and pass through Upton and *Kelham* before returning to Newark.

Placenames in *italic* type are worth stopping at; each is listed and described in the main gazetteer section of the book

Peak District

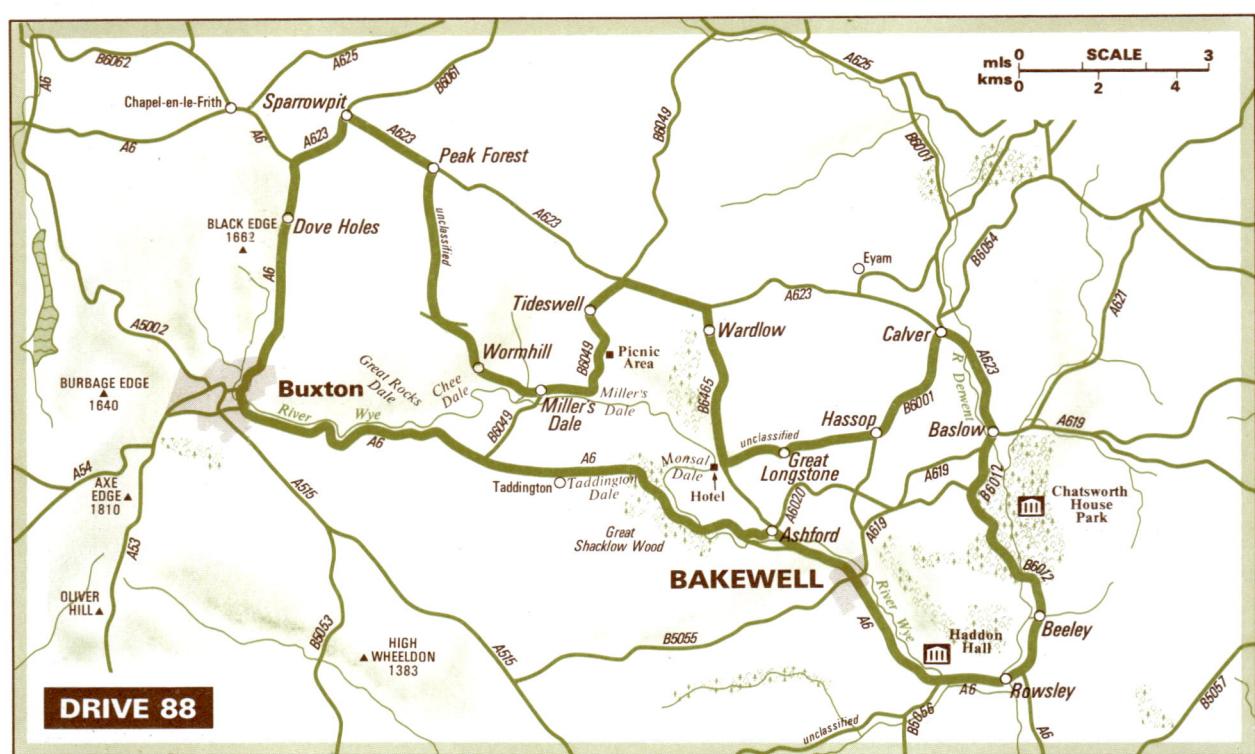

Monsal Dale and the Wye Gorge

From Bakewell

Drive 88   46 miles

Follow the A6 *Matlock* road out of *Bakewell*, and in 2m pass Haddon Hall. Enter *Rowsley* and pass the Peacock Inn on the left. Turn left on to the B6012 with Baslow signposts, and continue through Beeley. Beyond Beeley pass the grounds of *Chatsworth* House on the right before entering the park and passing Chatsworth House. Continue to Baslow and turn left with *Chapel-en-le-Frith* signposts in order to join the A623. Proceed to Calver and at the traffic signals turn left on to the B6001 Bakewell road. Within 2m reach Hassop and turn right on to an unclassified road for Great Longstone. Approach the T-junction in this village and turn right for Monsal Head. Continue to the Monsal Head Hotel and turn right on to the B6465 for views across Monsal Dale. Drive through Wardlow and turn left on to the A623; in 1½m turn left again to join the B6049 and continue into *Tideswell*. Keep with the *Buxton* road and after 1m pass the Tideswell picnic area on the left before descending into *Millers Dale*. Pass a railway viaduct, and just before the river bridge turn sharp right on to the unclassified road for Wormhill. Pass Chee Dale on the left and drive through Wormhill. After the village bear left with Peak Dale signposts, then within ½m turn right and continue to the village of *Peak Forest*. Turn left on to the A623, signposted Chapel-en-le-Frith, and keep left at Sparrowpit. Within 1¼m turn left on to the A6 and proceed towards Buxton. Pass limestone quarries to the left at Dove Holes, then descend into Buxton. Follow Matlock signposts in order to remain on the A6 out of the town, and descend through the woodlands of the *Wye* gorge. Climb away from the valley with Great Rocks Dale to the left, and continue to the edge of Taddington. Descend wooded Taddington Dale and pass Great Shacklow Wood on the right before crossing the River Wye. After ¾m turn left on to the A6020 and enter *Ashford*. Return to Bakewell via the B6465 and A6.

PEAK DISTRICT

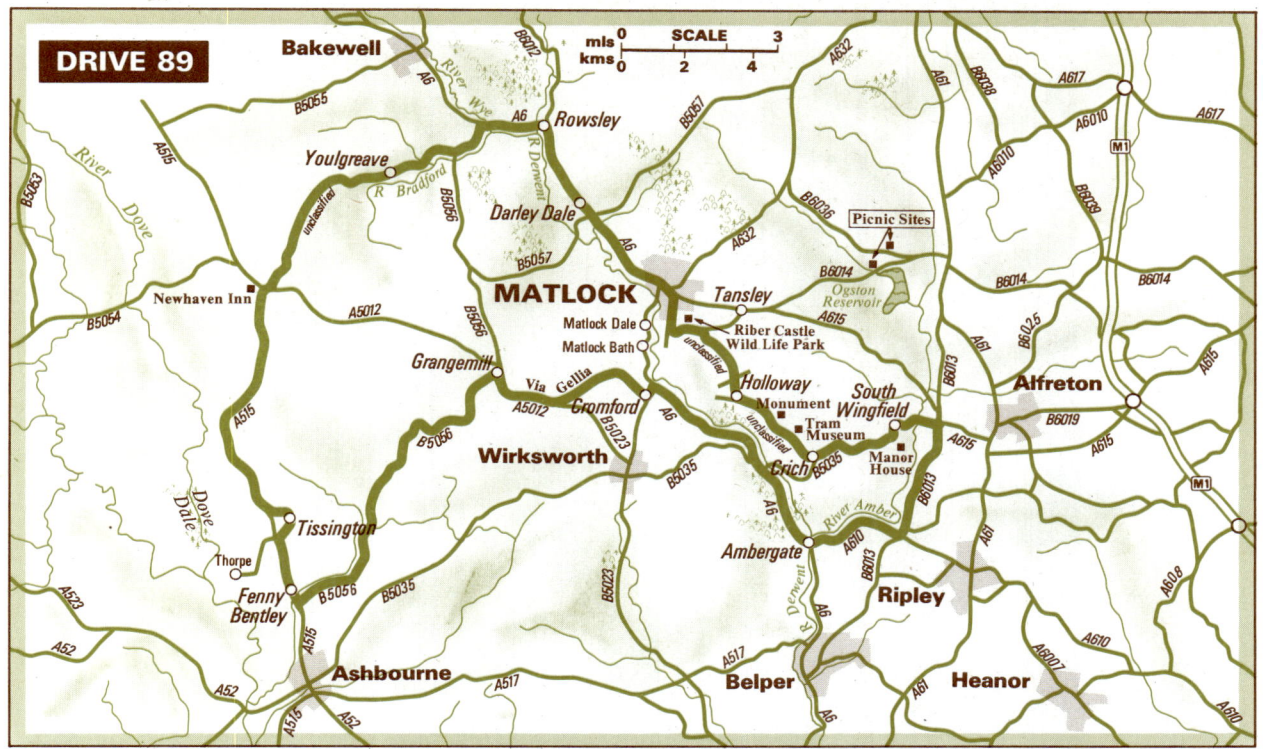

Through the Derwent Valley

From Matlock

Drive 89   51 miles

Leave *Matlock* on the A6 *Buxton* road and pass through *Darley Dale* and *Rowsley*. Within 1¼m turn left on to the B5056 (A524) *Ashbourne* road, and after 1m bear right on to an unclassified road signposted *Youlgreave*. Enter the Bradford Valley, and after passing through Youlgreave continue with the Ashbourne road for about 4½m. Turn right on to the A5012, and left to join the A515. Pass Newhaven Inn, and after 5½m turn left on to an unclassified road for *Tissington*. Leave this village by turning right and passing through attractive parkland before turning left to rejoin the A515. Drive to *Fenny Bentley*, then in ½m turn left on to the B5056, signposted *Bakewell*. Proceed for 8m to Grangehill, then turn right on to the A5012 and descend the wooded Via Gellia to *Cromford*. Turn left then right on to the A6 with *Derby* signposts, and cross wooded country before descending into the River Derwent valley to reach Ambergate. Turn left here on to the A610, signposted *Ripley*, and follow the Amber Valley. Within 2m turn left on to the B6013, signposted *Chesterfield*, then after 3m turn left again to join the B5035 for *South Wingfield*. Drive to the end of this village, passing a ruined manor house before driving on and ascending into *Crich*. From here branch right on to an unclassified road signposted Holloway. Pass the tower of Crich Stand before descending through Holloway. Turn right with Riber and Tansley signposts, then in ½m approach crossroads and continue straight on. Within 2m approach a T-junction and turn left, signposted Riber Village. After ¼m keep left, passing the road to Riber Castle Wildlife Park on the right. Follow a steep descent and negotiate several hairpin bends before reaching the bottom. Turn right and within ¾m turn left on to the A615. Return to Matlock.

Placenames in *italic* type are worth stopping at; each is listed and described in the main gazetteer section of the book

PEAK DISTRICT

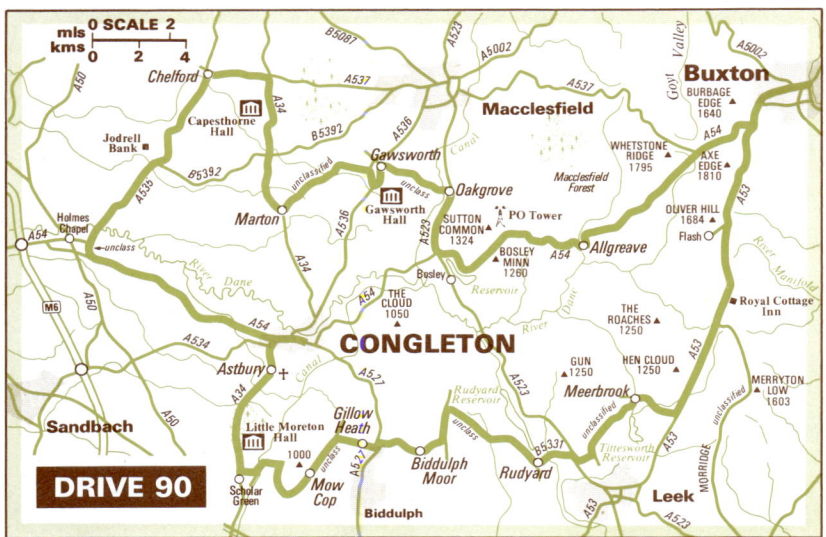

Peak District National Park

From Congleton

Drive 90 67 miles

Proceed along West Street and West Road to leave *Congleton*. Join the A34 *Newcastle* road to continue through *Astbury* and pass Little *Moreton Hall*. Within ¾m reach the edge of Scholar Green and turn left on to an unclassified road signposted Mow Cop. In another ¼m turn left, then after ½m cross a canal bridge and pass beneath a railway bridge. After a further ½m meet a T-junction, turn right, and ascend to Mow Cop. Continue past the towered church and after 1m turn right into unsignposted Mow Lane prior to the descent through Gillow Heath. Approach the main road and turn left, then within 300yds turn right on to an unclassified road signposted *Biddulph Moor*. Ascend to this village, then turn left with *Leek* signposts. Take the next turning right. After ½m approach a T-junction and turn left; continue for 1m and turn right. After 2½m descend to *Rudyard*, then continue with the B5331 Leek road to the next T-junction. Turn right on to the A523 and then left on to an unclassified road signposted Meerbrook. After ½m turn left again. Enter Meerbrook and turn right with Blackshaw Moor/Leek signposts, then cross Tittersworth reservoir. Within 1m approach a main road and turn left on to the A53 Buxton road. Climb on to the moors and enter the *Peak District* national park. Continue beyond the Royal Cottage Inn and after a short distance pass the Manifold Valley on the right. Drive into Derbyshire and continue to the outskirts of Buxton. Turn left on to the A54 Congleton road and ascend with 1,604ft Burbage Edge to the right. After 1m 1,795ft Whetston Ridge rises to the right, and Axe Edge and Oliver hill lie to the left. Descend from moorland and pass through Algreave. After passing close to the Post Office Communications tower skirt Bosley reservoir and turn right on to the A523 *Macclesfield* road. Within 2m reach Oakgrove and turn left on to an unclassified road signposted *Gawsworth*. Immediately cross the Macclesfield Canal, and on entering Gawsworth turn left with signposts marked Gawsworth Church. At the end of the road keep right and pass a pond before continuing past the church on an unclassified road. Approach the Harrington Arms Inn and turn right, then right again on to the A536. After ½m approach crossroads and turn left on to the unclassified road for *Marton*. Continue to the junction with the A34 and turn right with *Manchester* signposts. After 3½m pass the entrance to Capesthorne Hall, then in 1m approach traffic signals and turn left on to the A537 *Chester* road. Enter the Chelford roundabout and turn left on to the A535, signposted *Holmes Chapel*. Jodrell Bank radio telescope can be seen before the road passes the entrance to the Nuffield Radio Astronomy Laboratories. Continue forward with the A535 and within 3m cross the River Dane. In a further ½m approach the outskirts of Holmes Chapel and turn left into Manor Lane (unclassified and unsignposted). Continue to the A54 Congleton road and turn left. Drive through Somerford and re-enter Congleton.

Lancashire and Cheshire

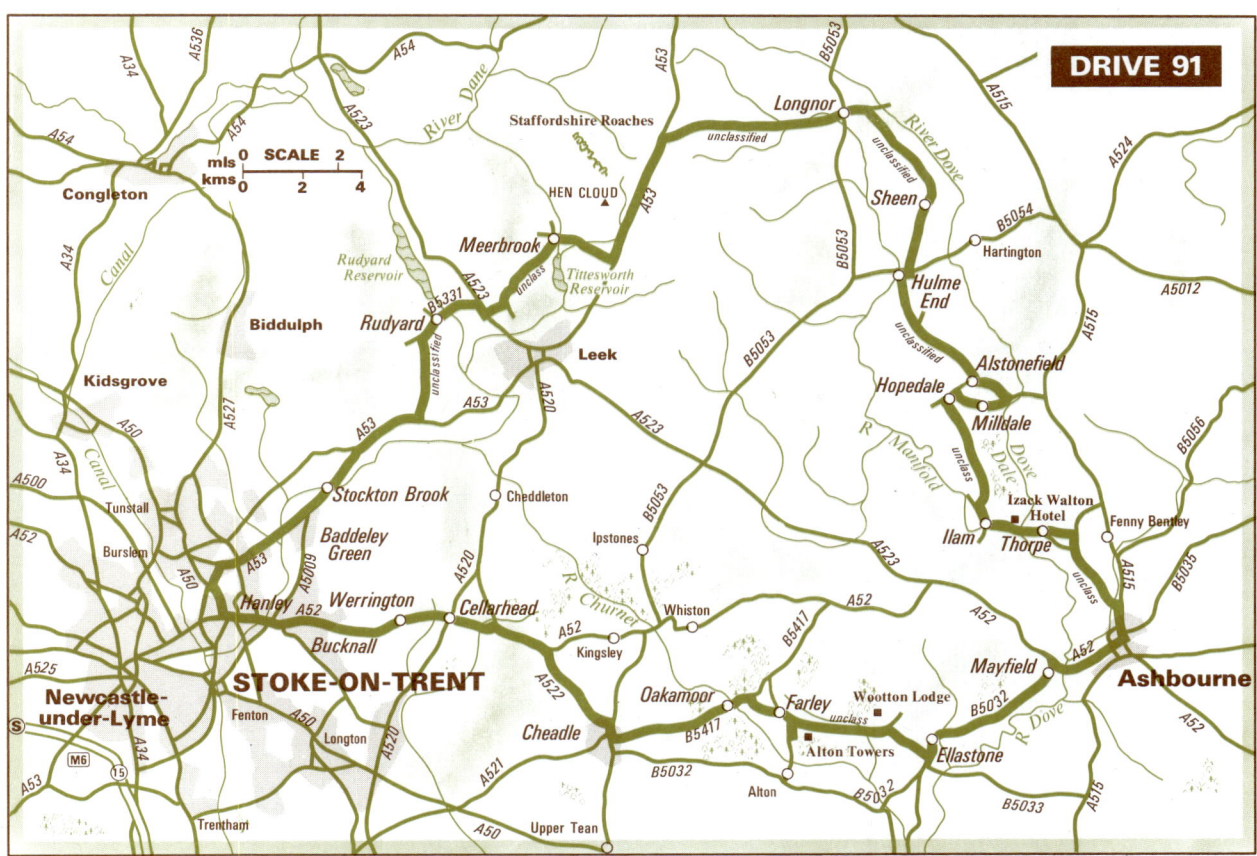

The Potteries and Dove Dale

From Stoke-on-Trent

Drive 91 62 miles

Leave the centre of *Hanley* — part of the *Stoke-on-Trent* conurbation — by following signposts marked 'Burslem A50'. In ¾m turn right on to the A53, signposted *Leek*, and pass through Baddeley Green and Stockton Brook. Proceed for another 2¼m, turn left into unclassified Dunwood Lane, and follow signposts to *Rudyard*. Turn right on to the unsignposted B5331 and in 1m approach a T-junction and turn right on to the A523. Take the next turning left on to an unclassified road signposted Meerbrook. Within another ½m turn left again, then enter Meerbrook and turn right with Blackshaw Moor and Leek signposts. Cross the Tittesworth Reservoir and in 1m turn left on to the A53, signposted *Buxton*. Climb on to moorland and enter the Peak District national park. After 1¾m drive straight on over crossroads and turn right on to an unclassified road signposted *Longnor*. Descend into Longnor, follow *Bakewell* signposts across a main road, and in ¼m branch right on to a road signposted Hulme End. Follow a by-road along a ridge between the Dove and Manifold Valleys and pass through Sheen. In 1½m turn right on to the B5054 and enter Hulme End. Drive to the Light Railway Hotel and turn left on to an unclassified road for *Alstonefield*. Enter the latter and keep left with *Ashbourne* signposts, then continue for 1¼m, and on a descent and turn sharp right with Milldale signposts. Proceed along the Dove to Milldale, turn right to Hopedale, and on reaching the Watts Russell Arms public house turn left with *Ilam* signposts. Within 100yds turn left again, then continue to the war memorial in Ilam. Turn left with *Dovedale* and *Thorpe* signposts and cross the River Dove. Ascend, skirting the village of Thorpe, then in ½m reach the Dog and Partridge Hotel and turn right with Ashbourne signposts. In another 2m join the A515 for *Ashbourne*; leave the latter by following signposts marked 'Uttoxeter (B5032)' on to the A52. Proceed for 1½m and cross a river. Approach the Queen's Arms public house and turn left on to the B5032, signposted *Cheadle*. Pass through *Mayfield* to *Ellastone* and turn left, then take the next turning right on to an unclassified and unsignposted road. Within another ½m approach crossroads and keep straight on with Farley and *Alton* signposts. In another ½m turn left, and in 1¾m turn left again for Alton Towers. Return to the unclassified road, turn left, and in ½m enter Farley. Turn left with Oakamoor signposts, then in 1m turn left again on to the B5417, signposted Cheadle. Cross the River Churnet into Oakamoor, then ascend and continue to Cheadle. Leave the latter by following signposts marked 'Leek A522', then in 2¼m join the A52 and continue through Cellarhead, Werrington, and Bucknall. Within ½m approach traffic signals and turn right. At the next traffic signals go forward with the A5008 and return to Stoke-on-Trent.

Placenames in *italic* type are worth stopping at; each is listed and described in the main gazetteer section of the book

LANCASHIRE AND CHESHIRE

Lancashire Plain and West Pennines

From Southport

Drive 92   74 miles

Leave *Southport* by following signposts marked *'Preston* A565'. After 3m turn right on to the B5246 with *Rufford* signposts and pass through Mere Brow and Holmeswood. Enter Rufford and turn left on to the A59, signposted Preston. In ½m pass Rufford Old Hall on the right, and in another ½m turn right on to the A581, signposted *Chorley*. Proceed for 2¼m and turn left across a bridge into *Croston*. Turn right, then in ¼m approach the war memorial and turn left. After 1m reach a T-junction and turn right; pass the Royal Umpire Museum and continue for 3½m to another T-junction. Turn left and in 300yds turn right to drive into Chorley. Approach traffic signals and turn left on to the A6 with *Blackburn* signposts. Within ½m turn right on to the A674, then turn left. Continue to a roundabout and take the third exit, then in 1½m turn right and proceed to Higher Wheelton. After about 1¾m enter a roundabout and leave by the second exit. Continue for ½m to a T-junction and turn right for Feniscowles, then turn right on to the A6062, signposted Darwen. Within ½m pass under a railway bridge and turn immediately right on to an unclassified road, then left and in 1m reach the Black Bull public house. Continue straight on over crossroads and descend. Proceed for 1m and cross a main road on to the B6231, signposted *Accrington*. Within ½m turn right and ascend to Guide, then approach crossroads near the King Edward VII public house and turn right on to the B6232, signposted *Bury*. Keep left, and after 2m reach the Grey Mare Inn and turn right on to an unclassified road signposted Edgworth. Drive to Edgworth and proceed over crossroads for *Turton*, then approach the main road and turn sharp right on to the B6391, signposted Darwen. Continue north and in 2¾m approach a T-junction. Turn left

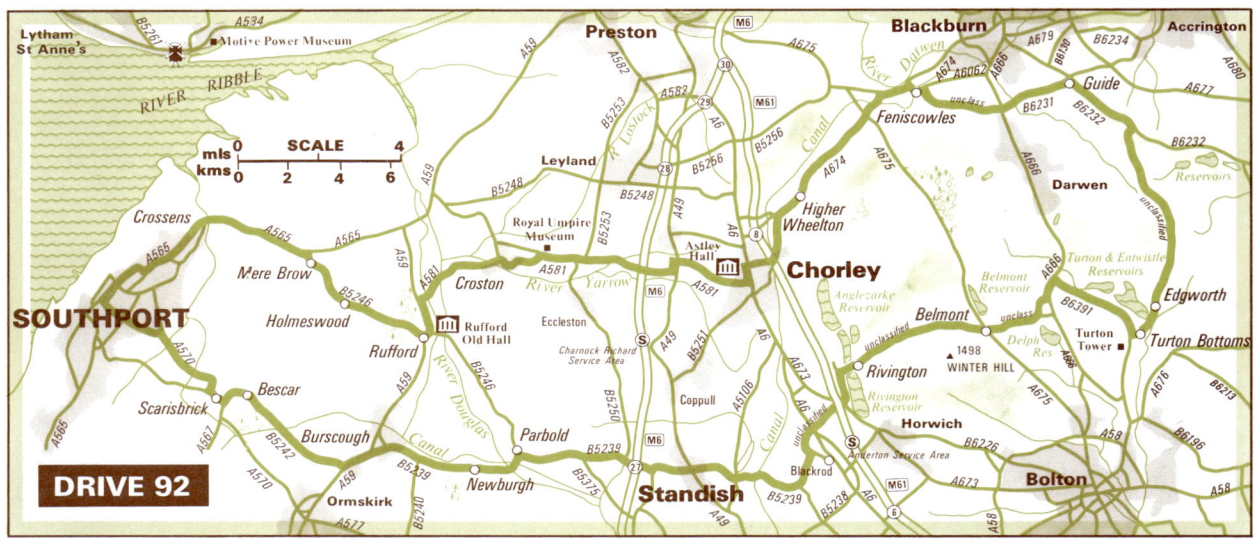

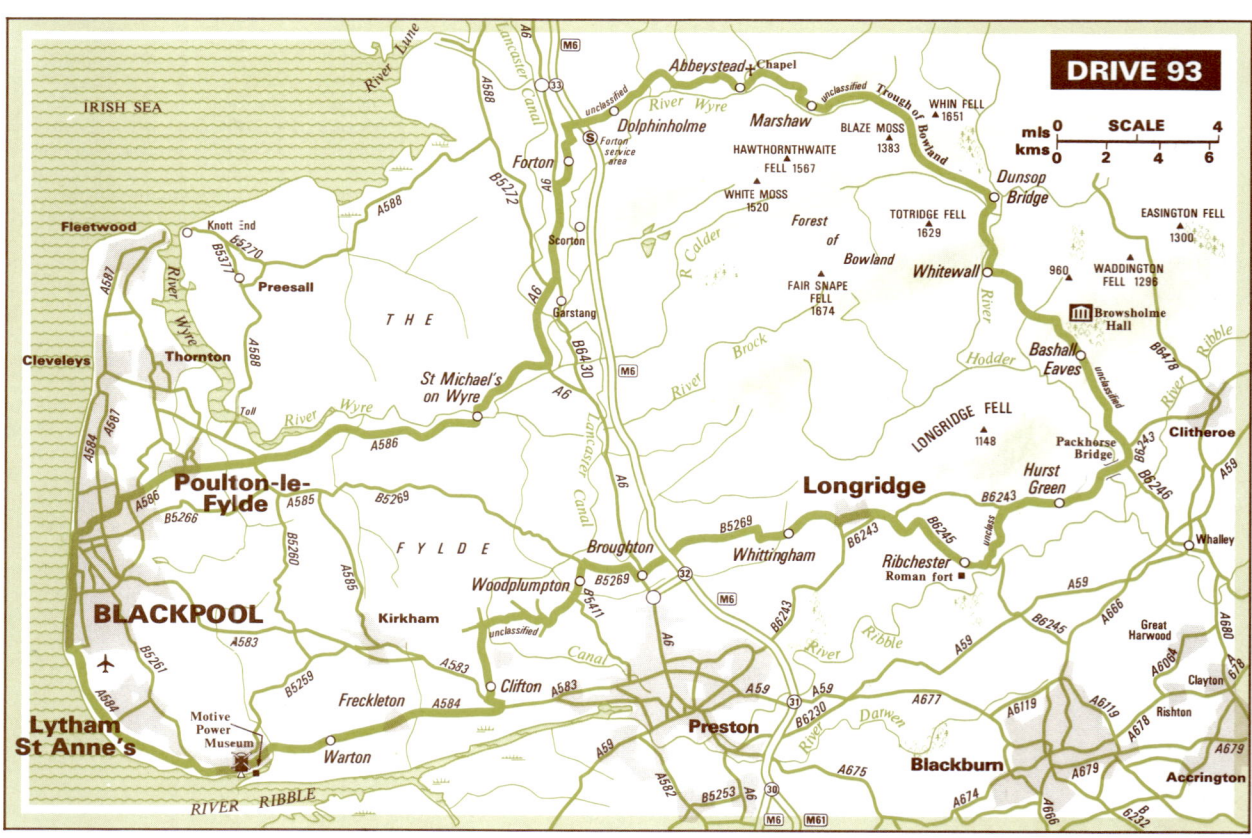

LANCASHIRE AND CHESHIRE

on to the A666, signposted *Bolton*, then in ½m branch right on to an unclassified road signposted Belmont. Take the next turning right, descend, and in 1m cross a main road to the edge of Belmont. Proceed to a T-junction and turn right on to the A675. Take the next turning left on to an unclassified road signposted *Rivington*. Cross moorland and descend to a T-junction; turn left and continue to Rivington. Keep forward with *Adlington* signposts and cross Rivington reservoir. Meet another T-junction and turn left with *Horwich* signposts. Within ¾m turn right on to the A673, then take the next turning left on to an unclassified road signposted Blackrod. Drive on for a further 1m, cross a main road, and in ½m turn right. After 1m keep forward to join the B5239, signposted *Standish*. Proceed for 1½m and reach a T-junction; turn right on to the A5106, and in 200yds turn left on to the B5239 to enter Standish. Meet traffic signals and continue forward, then in 1¼m turn right. Drive to the next roundabout and take the second exit, crossing the M6 to reach the edge of Burscough. Proceed to the end of the latter and join the A59, signposted Southport. Within ¾m turn right on to the B5242. Pass through Bescar and on reaching traffic signals turn right on to the A570. Return to Southport.

Among the Forest of Bowland Fells

From Blackpool

Drive 93   79 miles

Follow signposts marked 'St Anne's A584' to leave *Blackpool* along the coast. Continue through *Lytham St Anne's*, passing a white-painted windmill on the shore, then keep forward with *Preston* signposts and pass through *Warton* and Freckleton. In 2¾m approach traffic signals and turn left on to the A583, then take the first turning right along an unclassified road signposted Clifton. Skirt Clifton, then in 2m reach the Clifton Arms public house and turn right with Broughton signposts. Cross a canal and in 1½m approach a T-junction and turn right. After another ¼m turn left, and in 1¼m follow the B5411 straight ahead into Woodplumpton. Drive to the end of the village, turn right with Broughton signposts, then turn right again on to the B5269. Continue to Broughton and approach traffic signals. Proceed forward with Longridge signposts and pass through *Whittingham* to Longridge. Enter the latter town and go forward along the B6245, signposted *Blackburn*. Within ½m turn right and in ¾m turn right again. Enter *Ribchester* and bear left; in ½m turn left on to an unclassified road signposted Hurst Green. Continue for 1¾m, ascend, then at the top of the incline turn right on to the B6243 *Clitheroe* road. Pass through Hurst Green and cross the River Hodder, then in 1¼m keep forward along the unclassified Bashall Eaves road. Proceed for 1m and on reaching crossroads continue straight on. Follow the Hodder Valley with 1,148ft Longridge Fell on the left and 1,296ft Waddington and 1,300ft Easington Fells to the right. Enter Bashall Eaves and keep forward for 1m before passing the entrance to Browsholme Hall. In a further 1m turn right, signposted 'Whitewell via Hall Hill', then ascend to 750ft before descending to Whitewell in the Hodder Valley. Turn right

Horseshoe Pass and the Dee Valley

From Chester

Drive 94   60 miles

Follow the A483 North Wales road out of *Chester*, passing the Roodee (racecourse) and

Drive 93 continued

with *Lancaster* signposts, cross the River Hodder twice, then follow a tributary through Dunsop Bridge and the valley leading to the *Trough of Bowland*. Continue for 3m then climb to the Trough between 1,383ft Top of Blaze Moss and 1,561ft Whin Fell. Descend alongside the Marshaw Wyre, with 1,567ft Hawthornthwaite Fell to the left. In 1¼m, beyond the junction with the *Scorton* road, 1,839ft Ward's Stone and 1,531ft Grit Fell can be seen to the right. Drive to a chapel on the right and turn left on to the Preston road. Descend to Abbeystead, follow Preston signposts, and in 3¼m pass through Dolphinholme. After ¼m reach a church and bear right, then in 1¼m cross the M6. Approach a T-junction and turn left with Garstang signposts. Pass Forton, and in 1½m turn left on to the A6, signposted Preston. Drive on for 4¾m and turn right on to the A586, signposted Blackpool, then follow the River Wyre. Continue through St Michael's-on-Wyre and *Poulton-le-Fylde*, then return to Blackpool on the A586.

castle before crossing the River Dee via Grosvenor Bridge. Proceed to a roundabout and take the third exit on to the A55. Continue to Saltney and cross into Wales, then continue to Broughton Church. Branch left on to the A5104, signposted Corwen, and in 2¼m turn left. Enter Penyfford and turn right; continue for 2m, cross the River Alyn to Pontblyddyn, then turn left then right and ascend to Llandegla. Turn right then left, and in ¾m enter a roundabout and take the first exit on to the A542 Llangollen road. Cross the Horseshoe Pass on the eastern flank of Llantysilio Mountain, then descend to the Eglwyseg Valley past the pillar of Eliseg and ruined Valle Crucis Abbey. Recross the Dee into Llangollen and follow the A5 *Shrewsbury* road through the Dee Valley to Froncysyllte. Pass Ponte Cysyllte to the left while proceeding to Chirk. Leave the latter by crossing the River Ceiriog back into England, and in 1¼m turn left on to the B5070, signposted *Ellesmere* and Overton. Enter St Martins and join the B5069 to re-enter Wales. Meet the A528 and turn left for Overton-on-Dee, then keep forward and turn right with Bangor-is-y-Coed signposts. Continue to this village then turn left and cross the River Dee. Turn right on to the A525, signposted *Wrexham*, and in 1¼m turn right on to the B5130, signposted Wrexham Industrial Estate. Continue into Holt and join the A534 to recross the Dee. Drive to Farndon and turn left on to the B5130 with Chester signposts. Proceed to Chester via Huntington.

Placenames in *italic* type are worth stopping at; each is listed and described in the main gazetteer section of the book

LANCASHIRE AND CHESHIRE

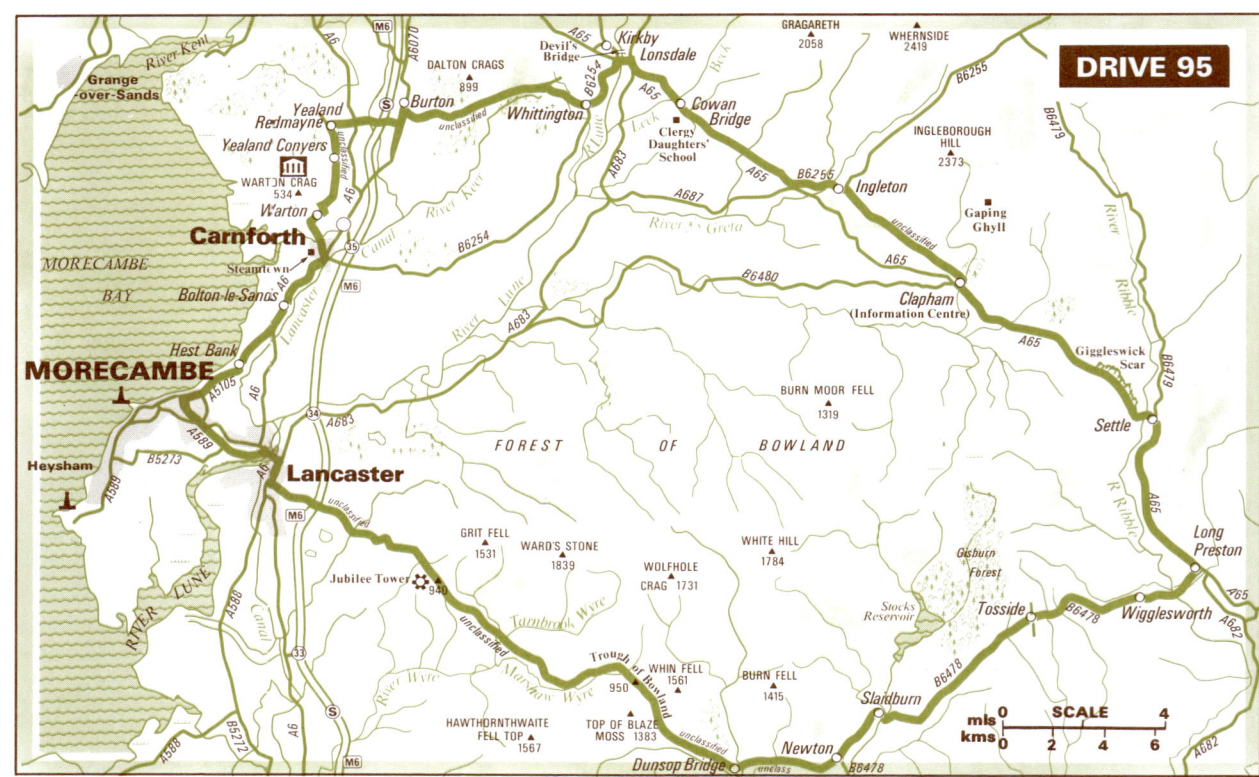

The Craven Heights

From Morecambe

Drive 95   72 miles

From *Morecambe* follow signposts marked 'Hest Bank' and 'The North A5105' to drive along the sea front to Hest Bank. After 1m turn left on to the A6, signposted *Kendal*, and pass through Bolton-le-Sands to enter Carnforth. Turn left on to the unclassified *Warton* road and in ¼m turn left again, passing the station and Steamtown Museum. Continue through Warton and pass a left turn to Leighton Hall before driving through *Yealand Conyers* and into Yealand Redmayne. Proceed to the end of the latter village and turn right with Kendal signposts. In ¾m cross a main road, then pass over the main railway line, a canal, and the M6 motorway. Proceed to the edge of Burton and turn left then right with *Kirkby Lonsdale* signposts. Continue for 3m and bear right before descending into the Lune Valley and entering Whittington. Turn left on to the B6254, signposted Kirkby Lonsdale, and in 1½m enter Cumbria. Within ¼m turn right on to the A65, signposted *Skipton*, and within ½m cross the River Lune to re-enter Lancashire. Pass the Clergy Daughters' School at Cowan Bridge and in 1¾m enter North Yorkshire. Continue for 2m and approach crossroads; turn left on to the B6255, signposted *Hawes*, and proceed to Ingleton. Drive through to the far end of the town on the B6255 Hawes road, then turn right on to the unclassified *Clapham* road. Continue to Clapham, approach the main road, and turn left on to the A65 with Skipton signposts. After about 4m *Giggleswick* Scars can be seen to the left. Stay with the A65 through *Settle*, and on reaching Long Preston turn right on to the B6478, signposted *Slaidburn*. Cross the River Ribble and pass through Wigglesworth. Climb to 850ft at the Tosside crossroads, then keep forward and descend gradually into the Hodder Valley. Enter Slaidburn and turn left with *Clitheroe* signposts. Continue to Newton and drive forward on an unclassified road signposted *Lancaster*. Pass through the Hodder Valley to Dunsop Bridge, and on reaching a T-junction turn right. Ascend to the *Trough of Bowland* and drive between the peaks of 1,393ft Top of Blaze Moss and 1,561ft Whin Fell. Descend alongside the Marshaw Wyre stream and cross the Tarnbrook Wyre. The 1,839ft Ward's Stone and 1,531ft Grit Fell can be seen to the right before the road descends to Lancaster. Enter the latter and then leave by following Morecambe signposts. Cross the River Lune, and on meeting traffic signals turn left on to the A589. Continue forward into Morecambe.

Pennines and Yorkshire Dales

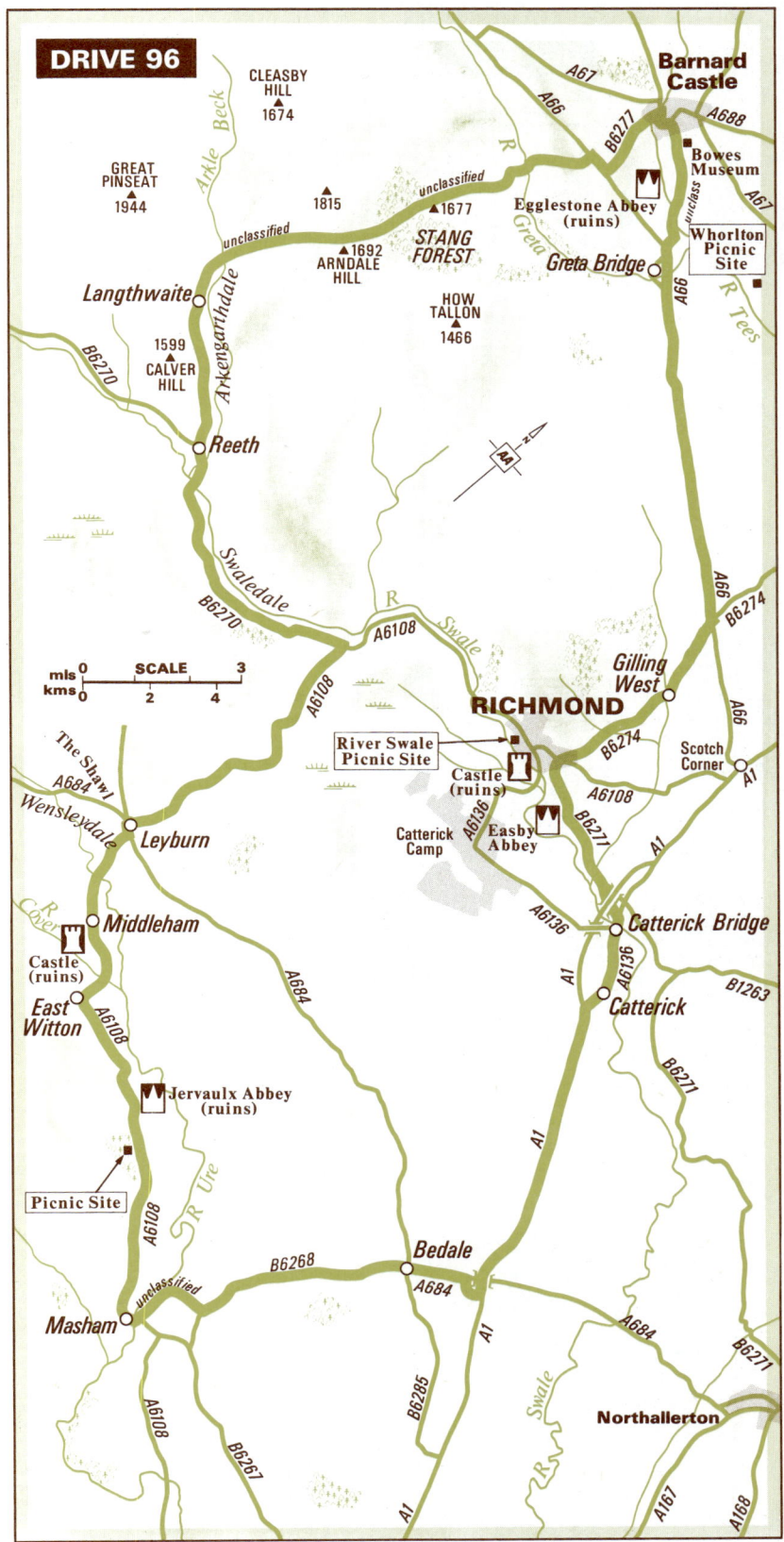

Stang Forest and Northern Dales
From Richmond
Drive 96 71 miles

Leave *Richmond* by following signposts marked 'Scotch Corner A6108', then '*Gilling West* B6274'. Proceed to Gilling West and take the B6274 to cross high ground before turning left on to the A66 *Brough* road. Continue to *Greta Bridge* and in ½m turn right on to an unclassified road signposted *Barnard Castle*. In another 1¼m turn right and cross the River Tees. Pass *Bowes Museum* on the right before entering Barnard Castle. Follow signposts marked 'Brough, Bowes A67', and re-cross the River Tees before turning left on to the B6277, signposted Scotch Corner. Drive through woodland and turn right on to the A66. Take the next turning left on to an unclassified road, signposted *Reeth*, and continue through Stang Forest before descending across Arkengarthdale and bridging Arkle Beck. Proceed along the dale and pass through Langthwaite. Drive into Swaledale and the village of Reeth, and on entering the latter turn left on to the B6270 Richmond road. Descend through Swaledale and approach a junction with the A6108. Turn right and proceed to *Leyburn* by following signposts through several hamlets. Keep forward through Leyburn with *Middleham* signposts, and on reaching the end of the town turn right on to the A6108 and cross the River Ure. Stay on the A6108 *Masham* road and proceed through Middleham and East Witton. Pass *Jervaulx Abbey* ruins on the left and Ellington Firth picnic site on the right before reaching Masham. Follow the *Ripon* road from the latter and recross the river. Turn left on to the unclassified *Bedale* road, then in 1m turn right. In another ¾m turn left on to the B6268, pass through Bedale, and continue along the A684 *Northallerton* road. Drive on for 1½m, then turn right to follow Scotch Corner signposts and eventually join the A1. Continue along a stretch of dual carriageway on the Great North Road, then on reaching a roundabout take the A6136 into *Catterick*. Continue to Catterick Bridge and turn right, cross the Swale, then turn left with Richmond signposts for the B6271. Drive along the B6271 and enter Richmond.

Placenames in *italic* type are worth stopping at; each is listed and described in the main gazetteer section of the book

PENNINES

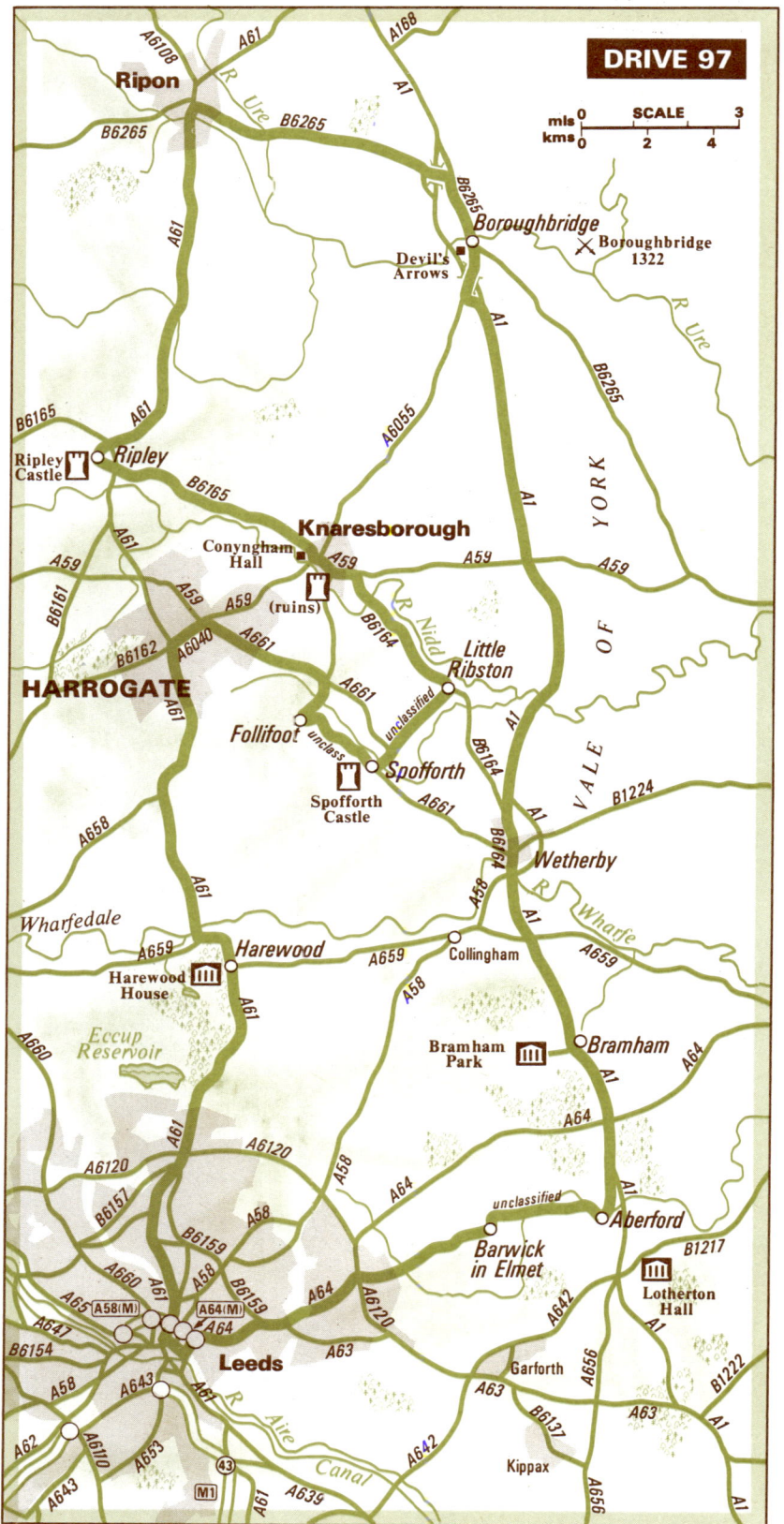

Leeds and the Vale of York

From Harrogate

Drive 97   75 miles

From *Harrogate* follow signposts marked 'Leeds A61', and pass through *Harewood* to continue through the outer suburbs of Leeds. Follow signposts to Leeds city centre, and leave with signposts marked 'York A64'. In 5m reach a roundabout and take the second exit on to an unclassified road, then drive into *Barwick-in-Elmet*. Turn left here and follow signposts to *Aberford*. Leave this village by turning left with *Wetherby* signposts, then 'The North' to join the A1. In 3m pass the entrance to *Bramham* Park, and several miles farther approach a roundabout and take the second exit on to the A661. Cross the River Wharfe into Wetherby, then follow signposts marked 'The North' and *Boroughbridge* to rejoin the A1. Continue along dual carriageway for 10m before turning left on to the A6055 then right into Boroughbridge. Leave the latter on the B6265, signposted 'The North', and cross the River Ure. Continue to a roundabout and keep left on to the *Ripon* road, then in 1½m turn left and cross the Great North Road. Cross the River Ure before entering Ripon. Leave on the A61 Harrogate road and continue to the edge of *Ripley*. Meet a roundabout and take the second exit to enter Ripley. Drive forward through the village to the next roundabout and take the second exit on to the B6165, signposted *Knaresborough*. Enter Knaresborough and follow signposts marked 'York A59' to the end of the town, then turn right along the B6164 Wetherby road and enter Little Ribston. Turn right on to an unclassified road to join the A661 and continue to the Castle Inn at *Spofforth*. Turn right on to the unclassified Follifoot road, passing Spofforth Castle. Drive into Follifoot and turn right, then follow Harrogate signposts to rejoin the A661. Continue on the A661 and return to Harrogate.

Yorkshire Wolds and Moors

Cleveland and the Hambleton Hills

From Helmsley

Drive 98 66 miles

Follow *Stokesley* signposts to leave *Helmsley* on the B1257 and ascend. Within 1½m turn left on to an unclassified road signposted Scawton, then descend steeply through thick woodland before turning right at a *Rievaulx Abbey* signpost. Follow the River Rye to Rievaulx and continue through dense woodland to a junction with the B1257. Turn left on to this road and climb to over 800ft before entering Bilsdale. Continue for 2½m beyond the hamlet of Chop Gate and approach the Hasty Bank viewpoint at the road summit. Descend to Great Broughton and after 2m approach a roundabout; take the second exit and proceed into the market town of Stokesley. Continue by following *Thirsk* signposts and join the A172. Pass through Ingleby Cross and within 1m join the A19. Stay on this road for 1m before branching left on to the A684, signposted *Northallerton*. Enter Northallerton and leave by following Thirsk signposts on to the A168. Within 7m turn right on to the B1448 and enter Thirsk. Follow *Scarborough* signposts on to the A170, crossing a road bridge over the bypass, and ascend after passing through Sutton-under-Whitestonecliffe. Continue to ascend *Sutton Bank* (1 in 4 gradients and hairpin bends), then continue along a high plateau for 3¾m before turning right on to an unclassified road signposted Wass and Coxwold. Go forward at crossroads and cross Wass Moor before descending steeply to the hamlet of Wass. Turn left here for Ampleforth, and at the end of the village bear right with Oswaldkirk signposts. Continue to Oswaldkirk and remain on the B1363, signposted Helmsley. Ascend and turn left on to the B1257 and drive on to Sproxton. Enter the latter village and turn right on to the A170, signposted Scarborough, for the return to Helmsley.

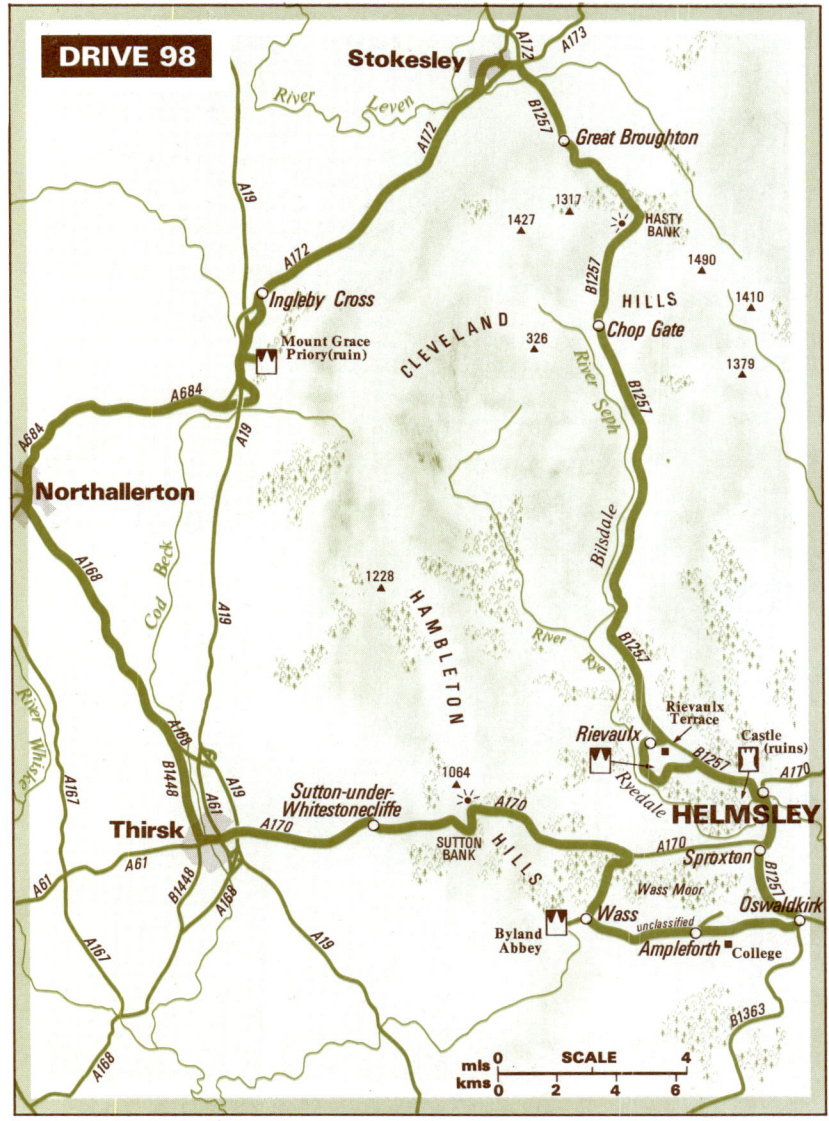

Placenames in *italic* type are worth stopping at; each is listed and described in the main gazetteer section of the book

YORKSHIRE WOLDS AND MOORS

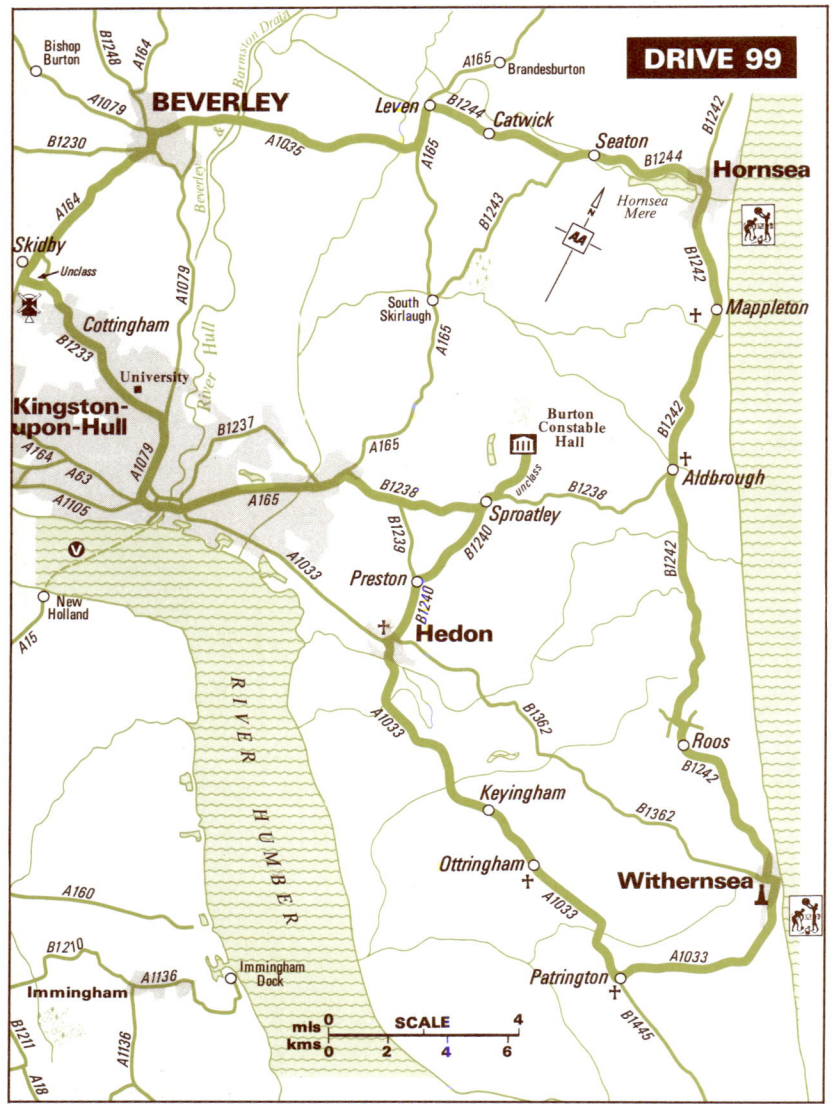

Flat Lands of Holderness
From Beverley
Drive 99   71 miles

Take the A164 out of *Beverley*, following Hessle signposts. Proceed to *Skidby* windmill and turn left on to an unclassified road signposted Cottingham. Continue and later turn right on to the B1233. Drive to Cottingham, pass over a level crossing, and within 1¼m approach a roundabout. Go straight across and pass the University of *Hull*. Within ½m turn right on to the A1079 to enter Kingston-upon-Hull. Leave on the A165 and follow *Hornsea* and *Bridlington* signposts. Approach a roundabout within 3½m and keep forward; meet the next roundabout and take the third exit on to the B1238, signposted *Aldbrough*. In 1¼m keep straight on to *Sproatley*, then bear right and drive to the end of this village. Turn left on to an unclassified road for Burton Constable Hall. Return to Sproatley and turn right; continue to the war memorial and branch left on to the B1240. Enter Preston and turn left again for *Hedon* before turning left on to the A1033, signposted *Withernsea*. Continue through Ottringham and *Patrington* to Withernsea, and approach the Spread Eagle public house before turning left into Hull Road. Proceed to the lighthouse and turn right on to the B1242, signposted Roos and Hornsea. Pass through Roos and within ½m turn left; in a further ¼m turn right and pass though Aldbrough and Mappleton, continuing north to Hornsea. Skirt Hornsea Mere and follow Beverley signposts along the B1244. Pass through Seaton and Catwick and proceed to *Leven*. Turn left on to the A165 and within 1m approach a roundabout and take the second exit on to the A1035, signposted Beverley. Continue through flat countryside before crossing the River Hull and adjacent Beverley and Barmston Drain; re-enter Beverley.

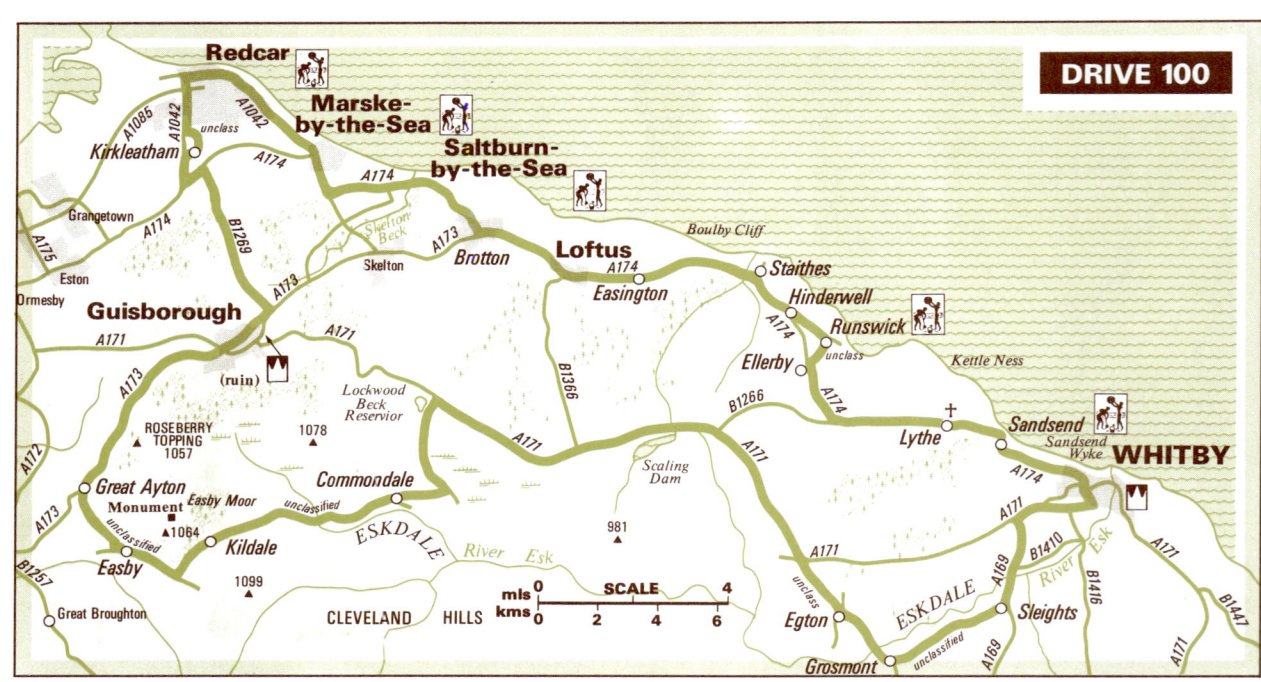

YORKSHIRE WOLDS AND MOORS

Cleveland Moors
From Whitby
Drive 100 71 miles

Follow Saltburn signposts along the A174 to leave *Whitby*, and descend to *Sandsend*. Climb out of the village with 1 in 4 gradients and head towards *Lythe*. Within 3¾m turn right on to an unclassified road and proceed to *Runswick Bay*. Turn left for Hinderwell, and on reaching a T-junction turn right on to the A174. Pass close to the edge of *Staithes*, then continue through Easington for *Loftus* and Brotton. After reaching Brotton

Robin Hood's Bay and Dalby Forest
From Scarborough
Drive 101 73 miles

Follow North Bay signposts to leave *Scarborough* on the A165, and in 1m approach a roundabout and keep left. Continue to Burniston and turn right on to the A171, signposted *Whitby*. Proceed to Cloughton and bear left to drive through woodland before emerging on Fylingdales Moor. Continue for 9½m beyond Cloughton and turn right on to an unclassified road signposted Fylingthorpe and *Robin Hood's Bay*. Descend with 1 in 4 gradients and hairpin bends, then keep straight on through the village of Fylingthorpe to Robin Hood's Bay. The latter's main thoroughfare has restricted access to motor vehicles from May to September, and is narrow and steep. From here follow Whitby signposts on to the B1447. Proceed to Hawsker, bear right, and at the end of the village turn right on to the A171. Descend into Whitby and cross the swing-bridge at the harbour in order to enter the city centre. Leave by the A171, signposted *Guisborough*, and within 2¼m turn left on to the A169, signposted *Pickering*. Continue beyond Sleights and climb on to Sleights Moor. Drive over bleak moorland and pass *Saltersgate* Inn before ascending past the Hole of Horcum gorge. Within 4m approach the Fox and Rabbit Inn and turn left on to an unclassified road signposted *Thornton Dale*. After a further 2m turn left following Low Dalby (Forest Drive) signposts on to a Forestry Commission toll road, and drive to Low Dalby hamlet. Turn left on to the forest drive, signposted Bickley, and follow the narrow road through Dalby Forest. Approach a fire tower and turn left; within another 2m leave the forest drive. Descend a 1 in 8 gradient and within ¾m approach a T-junction and turn right with Scarborough signposts. Enter the hamlet of *Langdale* End and pass the Moorcock Inn. In 1m turn sharp right with Troutsdale and Snainton signposts. Proceed through Troutsdale and descend to Snainton. Approach a T-junction and turn left on to the A170, signposted Scarborough, then pass through Brompton. Immediately after crossing the River Derwent between West and East *Ayton* turn left on to an unclassified road through Forge Valley. Within 2m turn right on to a road marked Private, then after a further 2m pass a pond on the right. Approach a T-junction after another 1m and turn right to re-enter Scarborough.

turn right with Saltburn signposts and ascend. Negotiate a hairpin bend during the steep climb, then pass through *Saltburn-by-the-Sea* and continue on the A174 to *Marske*. Drive forward on to the A1042 with *Redcar* signposts and proceed into Redcar. Continue through this town by following the A1042 with *Middlesbrough* and *Guisborough* signposts. Approach a roundabout at the end of the town and take the first exit, signposted Middlesbrough, before meeting traffic signals and continuing straight on with Guisborough signposts. Within 1½m turn left on to the unclassified road to Kirkleatham. Turn right with Guisborough signposts and in ¼m approach a T-junction and turn left at the roundabout; take the first exit on to the A174 and continue for ½m before turning right on to the B1269. Proceed to another T-junction and turn right on to the A173 to enter the town of Guisborough. Leave by following *Stokesley* signposts and pass 1,057ft Roseberry Topping before reaching *Great Ayton*. Pass the spired church and cross the River Leven, then continue on an unclassified road signposted *Easby*. A monument to Captain Cook can be seen to the left on 1,064ft Easby Moor. Approach a T-junction and turn left for the hamlet of Easby. Follow Kildale signposts and continue for ½m beyond a railway bridge, then turn left to cross open moorland and pass through Kildale and Commondale. After the latter village branch left with Castleton signposts and ascend steeply. Approach a T-junction after 1m and turn left. Pass Lockwood reservoir to the left before reaching another T-junction, then turn right on to the A171 with Whitby signposts. Drive across bleak moorland and within 5m pass Scaling Dam. Within a further 5¼m take the second turning on the right on to an unclassified road, and continue with 1 in 6 gradients to Egton. Continue to the centre of the village, turn left, then descend 1 in 4 gradients to cross the River Esk and enter Grosmont. Bear left with Sleights signposts through this village, then ascend Eskdale's 1 in 4 gradients and continue into Sleights itself. Turn left on to the A169 and later right on to the A171 for the return to Whitby.

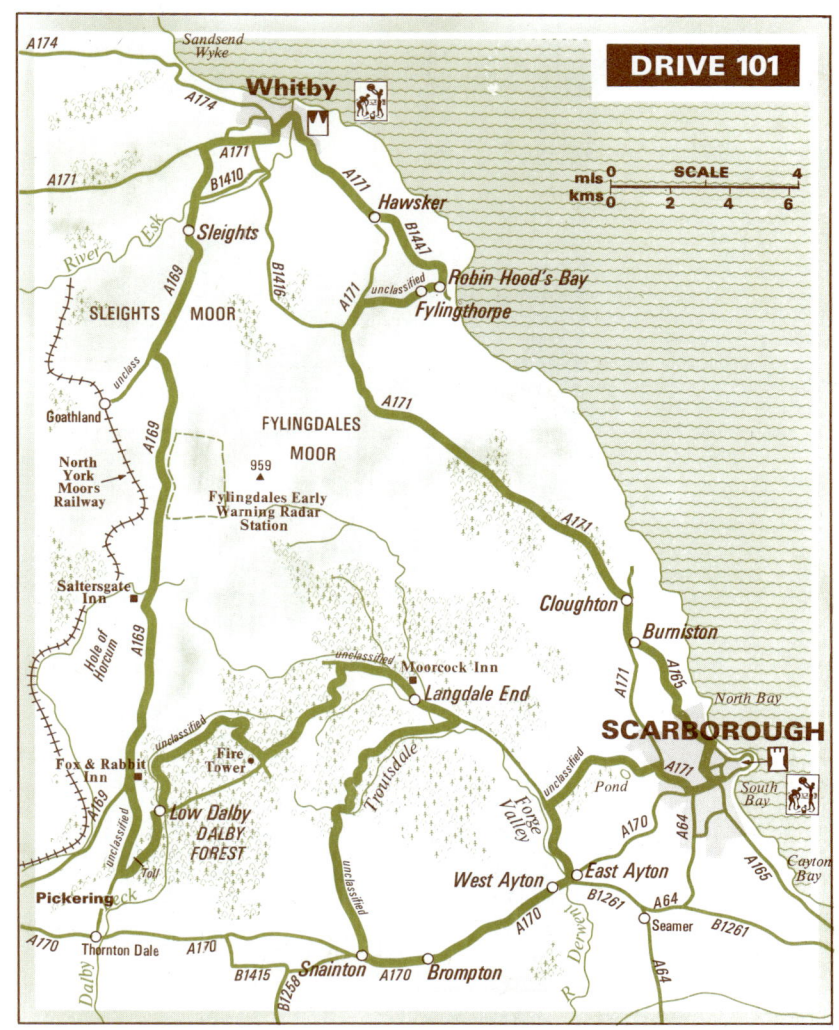

Placenames in *italic* type are worth stopping at; each is listed and described in the main gazetteer section of the book

YORKSHIRE WOLDS AND MOORS

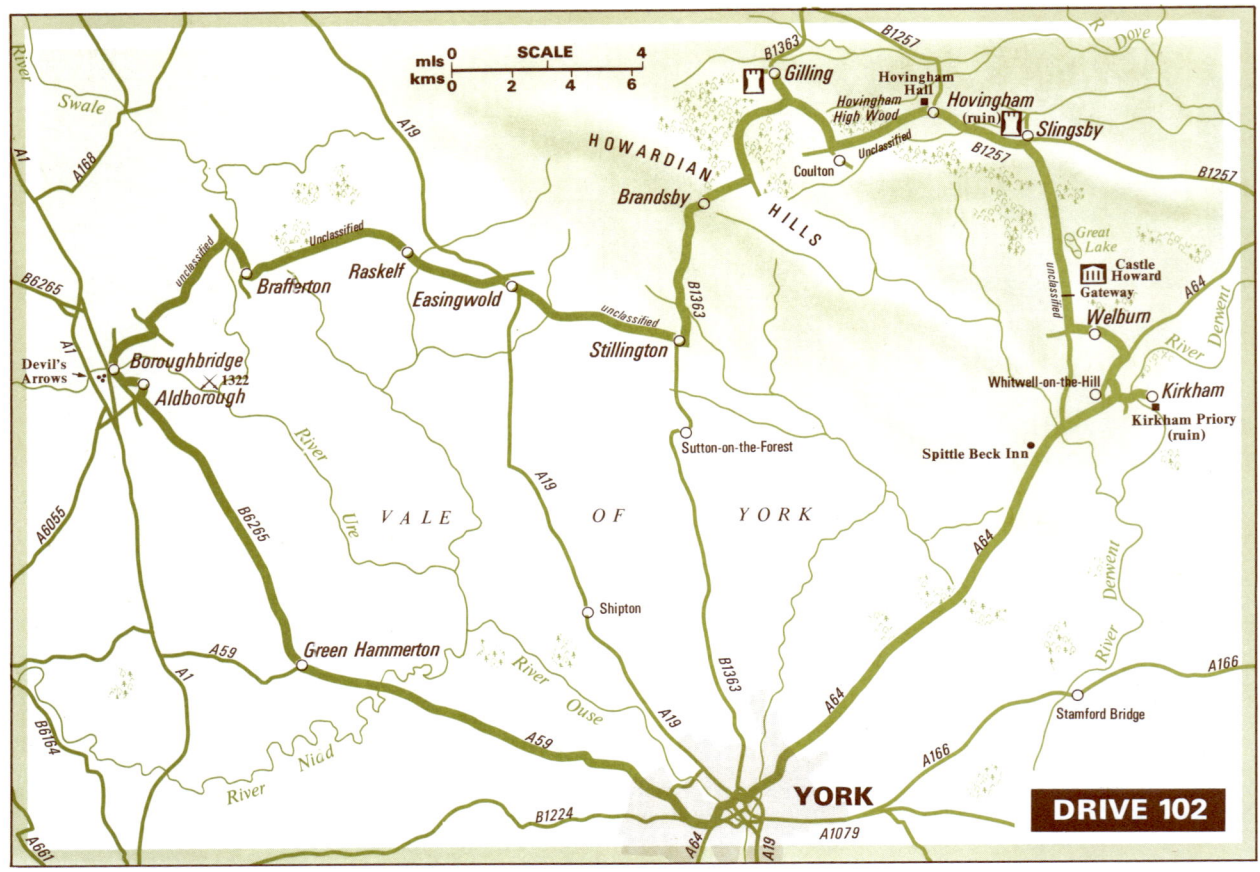

Howardian Hills and Vale of York

From York

Drive 102   68 miles

Follow East Coast and *Malton* signposts to leave *York* on the A64. Continue through agricultural country for 10½m, passing Spittle Beck Inn, then within 1½m turn right on to an unclassified road signposted *Kirkham Priory*. Keep straight on, descend, then drive over a level crossing and the River Derwent to enter Kirkham village. Return to the river and level crossing and ascend. Within ¼m approach crossroads and turn right, then within another ¾m approach a T-junction and turn right on to the A64, signposted *Scarborough*. In ½m turn left on to an unclassified road signposted Welburn/ *Castle Howard*. Pass through Welburn and turn right at the next crossroads. Drive through an arch and wall gateway to pass the entrance to Castle Howard on the right. Continue up into the Howardian Hills and descend to the edge of *Slingsby*. Turn left on to the B1257, signposted *Helmsley*, and proceed to the Worsley Arms Hotel in *Hovingham*. Turn left on to an unclassified road signposted Coulton and *Easingwold*, then skirt the grounds of Hovingham Hall. Drive through Hovingham High Wood, and at the far side approach crossroads and turn right with *Gilling* signposts. Follow this narrow road to a T-junction and turn right again on to the B1363. Proceed to Gilling and return along the B1363 to ascend the Howardian Hills. Descend through *Brandsby* and continue through the Vale of York into *Stillington*. Pass Stillington church and keep forward on to an unclassified road signposted Easingwold. Within 3½m join the A19 and drive to the far end of Easingwold village. Approach crossroads and turn left on to the unclassified Raskelf road. Bear left then right with *Boroughbridge* signposts. Continue to the Oak Tree Inn at Brafferton, then turn right and in 1m cross the River Swale and turn left. Within 2¾m turn left then immediately right, and after 1m approach a T-junction and turn left. Enter a roundabout and take the first exit on to the B6265; cross the River Ure and enter Boroughbridge. Turn left and keep left with York signposts, then continue to the far end of Boroughbridge before branching left on to the unclassified road to *Aldborough*. Drive to the Battle Cross and bear right past Aldborough church to pass the remains of a Roman town. Continue to the B6265 and turn left. Continue through the Vale of York, where the road follows the straight line of an old Roman road, and enter Green Hammerton to join the A59. Within 1¾m cross the River Nidd, then proceed through low-lying country before reaching the suburbs of York. Return to the city centre.

YORKSHIRE WOLDS AND MOORS

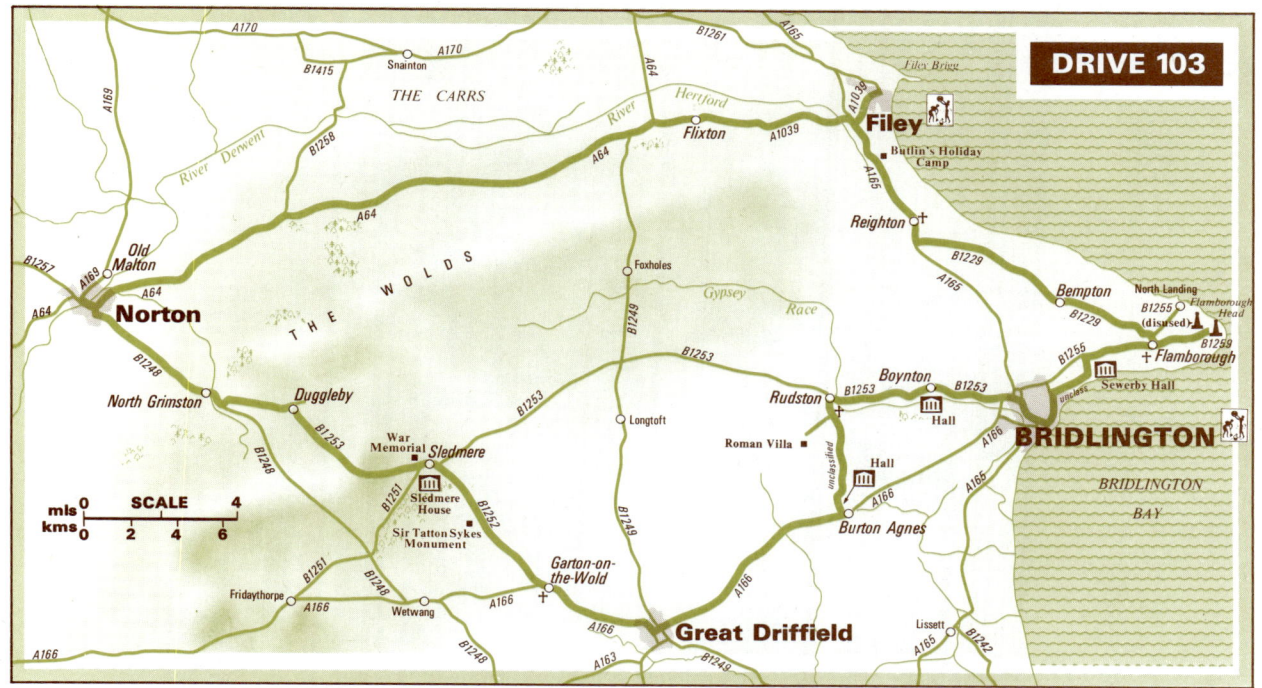

Across the Northern Wolds

From Bridlington

Drive 103   79 miles

Take the B1254 *Flamborough* road out of *Bridlington* and within 1¼m approach a roundabout. Turn right on to the unclassified Sewerby road. Pass the entrance to Sewerby Hall and after ½m turn right on to the B1255. Enter Flamborough and pass the church before turning right on to the B1259, signposted Lighthouse. Pass an old octagonal lighthouse to visit Flamborough Head, then return and turn right into the village of Flamborough. Continue to the far side of the village and bear left to follow *Filey* signposts along the B1229. Proceed through Bempton and within 4¼m turn right on to the A165 with *Scarborough* signposts. Drive into Reighton, pass Butlin's Holiday Camp, then within another 1½m turn right on to the A1039 and continue to Filey. Return along the A1039, signposted *Malton*; in 1m turn right and after ¼m turn left to follow a road along the foot of the wolds. Proceed through Flixton, and 1m after the village approach a roundabout. Take the first exit on to the A64, signposted *York*, and continue to the twin townships of *Norton* and Malton. Leave Malton by returning along the A64 with Scarborough signposts, and cross the River Derwent into Norton. Turn right on to the B1248, signposted *Driffield/Beverley*. Climb on to the wolds and through North Grimston, then tackle a 1 in 7 ascent. Branch left on to the B1253 Duggleby and Driffield road and drive into Duggleby. Leave the village and bear right, then climb to over 600ft. Descend and turn left at the war memorial to enter *Sledmere*, then continue to the end of this village and drive straight on to the B1252. Within 2¼m pass Sir Tatton Syke's monument before gradually descending to a T-junction and turning left on to the A166, signposted Bridlington. Pass through Garton-on-the-Wolds to Driffield, then continue along the A166 Bridlington road to *Burton Agnes*. Turn left on to the unclassified *Rudston* road. Climb back on to the wolds before dropping steeply to Rudston. Drive through the village to the next T-junction, then turn right on to the B1253 and pass a church with a monolith in the churchyard. Skirt *Boynton* on a hilly road and return to Bridlington.

Placenames in *italic* type are worth stopping at; each is listed and described in the main gazetteer section of the book

Northumberland and Durham

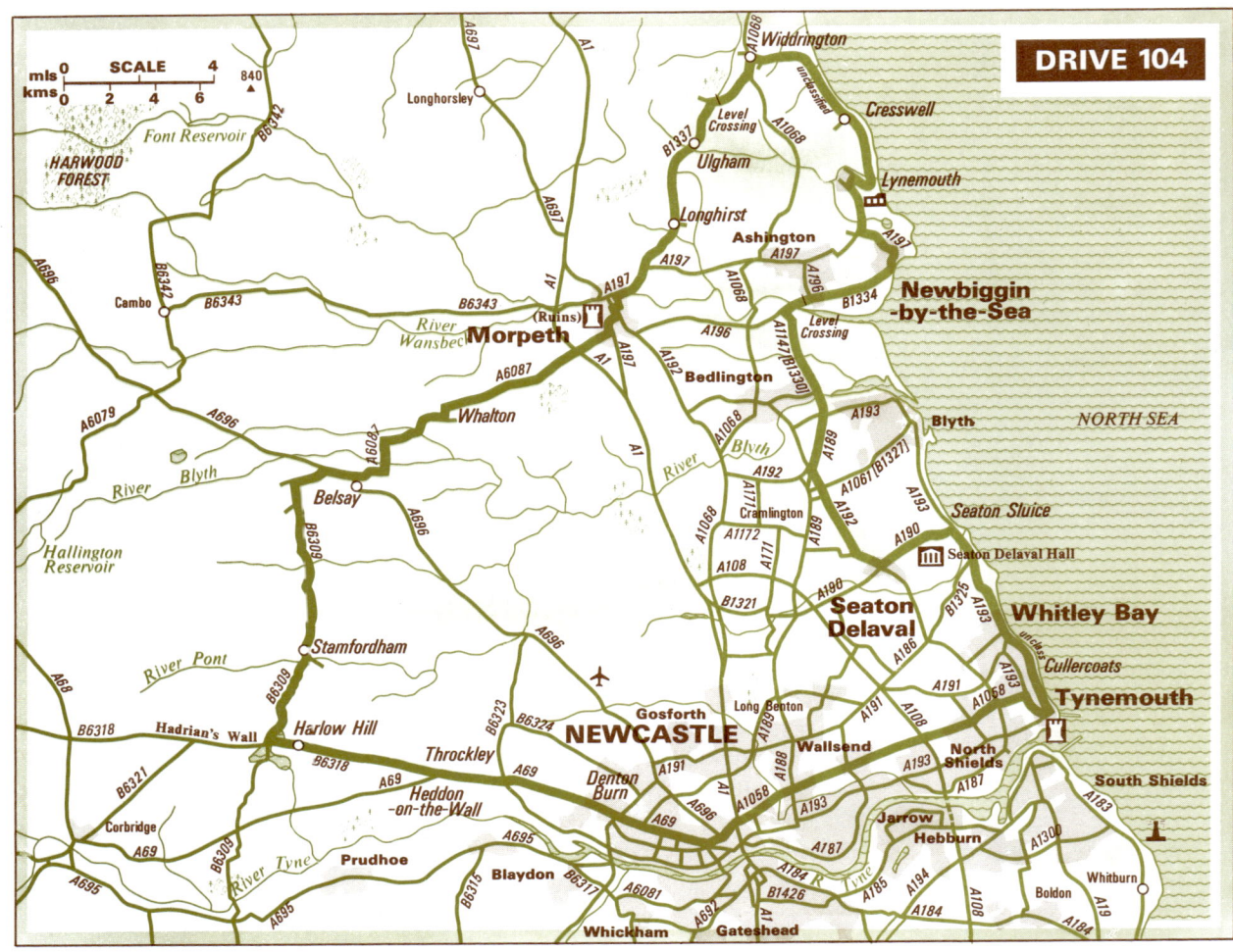

The Tyneside Coast

From Newcastle upon Tyne

Drive 104   76 miles

Take the A1058 *Morpeth* and *Tynemouth* road out of *Newcastle upon Tyne* and after 7m enter a roundabout and leave by the second exit. Continue to another roundabout and keep forward; drive to the next roundabout and take the third exit on to the A193 and proceed into Tynemouth. Approach the Clock Tower and turn left on to an unclassified road, passing the remains of a castle, then pass through Cullercoats to *Whitley Bay*. Continue along the A193 *Blythe* road to Seaton Sluice, then drive for $\frac{1}{4}$m to a roundabout and take the second exit on to the A190. Enter *Seaton Delaval*, approach a roundabout, and take the fourth exit on to the A192, signposted Morpeth. After $2\frac{1}{2}$m meet another roundabout and take the second exit, then at the next roundabout take the fourth exit on to the A189, signposted Ashington. Continue for $1\frac{1}{2}$m and keep forward on the A1147 (B1330). After 3m meet a T-junction and turn right on to the A196. Cross the River Wansbeck and in $\frac{1}{2}$m drive over a level crossing, then continue forward on the B1334 to enter *Newbiggin-by-the-Sea*. Turn left on to the A197 with Ashington signposts, and continue for $1\frac{1}{4}$m before reaching crossroads. Turn right on to the unclassified Lynemouth road, and before entering the village turn right. Approach a T-junction and turn right for Cresswell and Widdrington. Drive to the roundabout in Widdrington and take the first exit on to the A1068. Continue for $\frac{1}{2}$m, then keep forward on to the B1337 with Morpeth signposts. In $1\frac{1}{2}$m bear left for Ulgham and continue to Longhirst. In $1\frac{1}{2}$m join the A197 and proceed to Morpeth church and turn left with the A197, then re-cross the River Wansbeck. After $\frac{3}{4}$m turn right on to the A6087, signposted *Belsay*, and continue through *Whalton* to the edge of Belsay. Turn right on to the A696 and after $\frac{3}{4}$m turn left on to the B6309, signposted *Stamfordham*. Drive to the far end of Stamfordham and turn right, signposted *Corbridge*. Continue on the B6309 for 3m and approach crossroads. Turn left on to the B6318, signposted Newcastle, then pass through *Heddon-on-the-Wall* before joining the A69 and returning to Newcastle.

NORTHUMBERLAND AND DURHAM

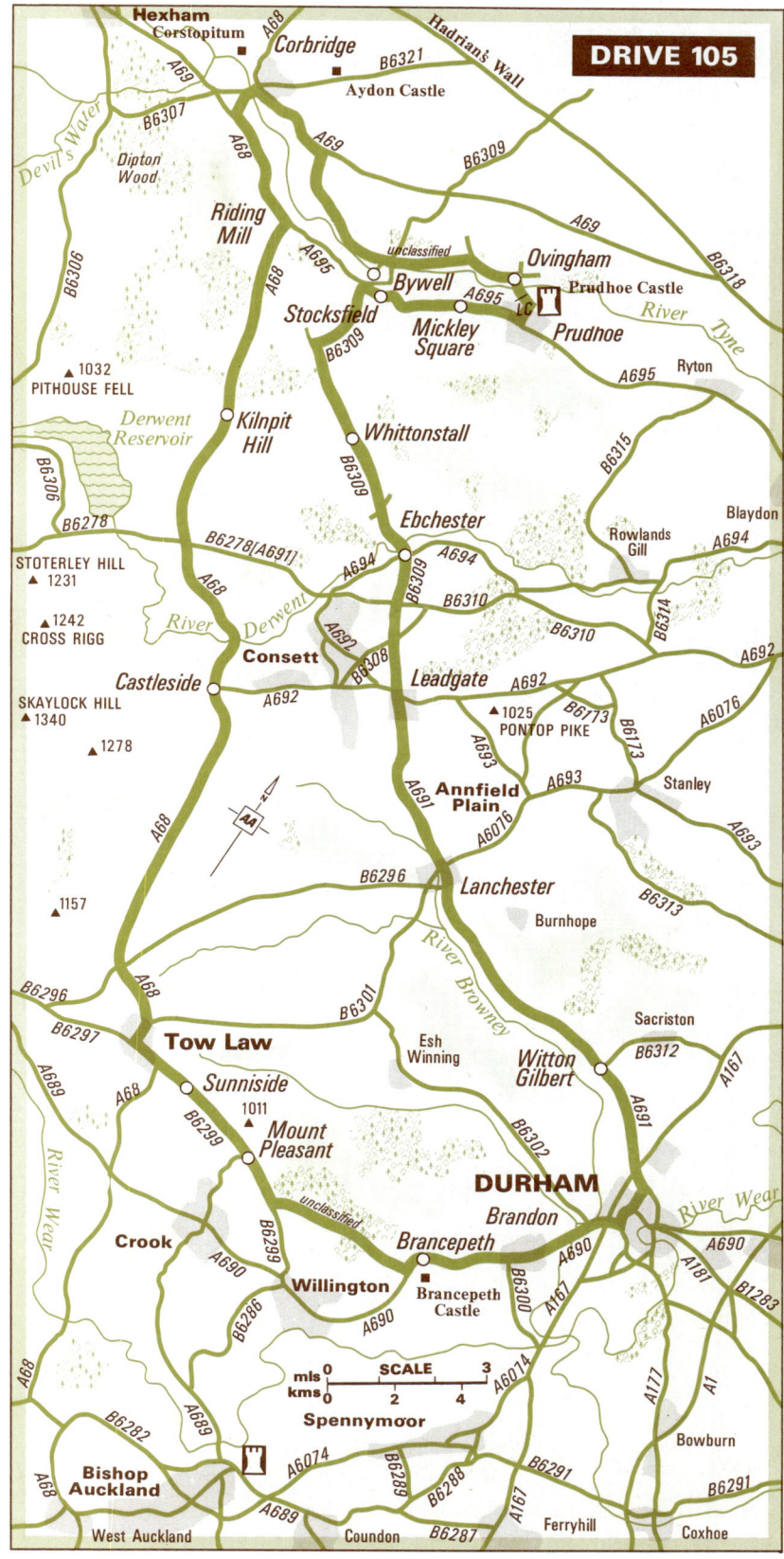

North Durham and the Tyne Valley

From Durham

Drive 105 63 miles

Take the A691 out of *Durham* and follow signposts marked 'Newcastle A1'. Continue for 1m, enter a roundabout, and take the second exit with signposts marked 'A691 *Consett*'. Proceed for ½m to the next roundabout and take the second exit. Pass through Witton Gilbert and skirt *Lanchester* to reach Leadgate. Approach traffic signals and drive forward on to the B6309, signposted *Ebchester*. Enter Ebchester and turn right then left to follow *Corbridge* signposts. Cross the River Derwent and in ½m bear right then left. Continue through Whittonstall and after 2m turn right, signposted Stocksfield. After 2½m approach a T-junction and turn right on to the A695, signposted Prudhoe. Bear right over a railway bridge and enter Stocksfield, then continue through Mickley Square to Prudhoe. Turn left on to an unclassified road signposted Low Prudhoe and continue for ¾m. Drive over a level crossing, then cross the River Tyne to Ovingham. Drive to the church and turn left, then in ¾m turn left again with *Hexham* signposts. After 1½m turn right on to the B6309, and at the next crossroads turn left on to an unclassified road for a short detour to *Bywell*. Return to the crossroads and turn left, signposted Corbridge. Proceed for 2½m and approach a T-junction. Turn left on to the A69 to Corbridge. Follow signposts marked 'Darlington A68' to cross the River Tyne. Enter a roundabout and take the first exit, then continue to Riding Mill and turn right. Pass through Kilnpit Hill and Castleside to Tow Law, then drive to the war memorial and turn left. After ½m keep forward on to the B6299, signposted Willington. Pass through Sunniside and Mount Pleasant, then continue for ¾m before turning left on to an unclassified road signposted Durham. After 3m turn left on to the A690. Drive on through *Brancepeth*, Langley Moor, and Neville's Cross on the return to Durham.

Placenames in *italic* type are worth stopping at; each is listed and described in the main gazetteer section of the book

NORTHUMBERLAND AND DURHAM

Among the Border Forests

From Bellingham

Drive 106 85 miles

Leave *Bellingham* on the B6320, signposted *Hexham*. After ¼m turn left to cross the river, then take the first turning right on to an unclassified road signposted *Kielder*. Continue for 4m, cross a bridge, then turn right and continue through Stannersburn, Kielder Forest, and Kielder. Cross the Scottish border and proceed for 3½m before turning left on to the B6357, signposted Newcastleton. Drive to the far end of the latter village and turn left on to an unclassified and unsignposted road, then cross a river bridge and turn right, signposted *Brampton*. After 3m cross the Kershope Burn to re-enter England. Ascend through the Kershope Forest for ¾m to reach the

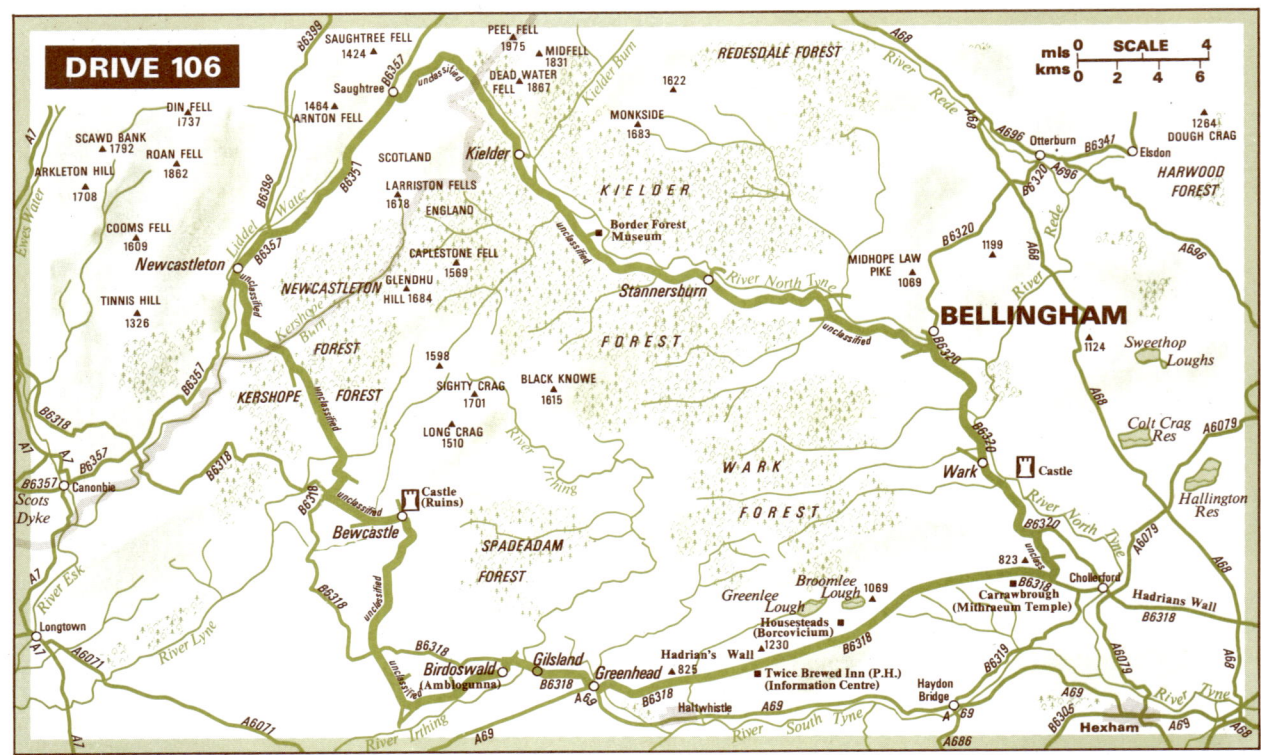

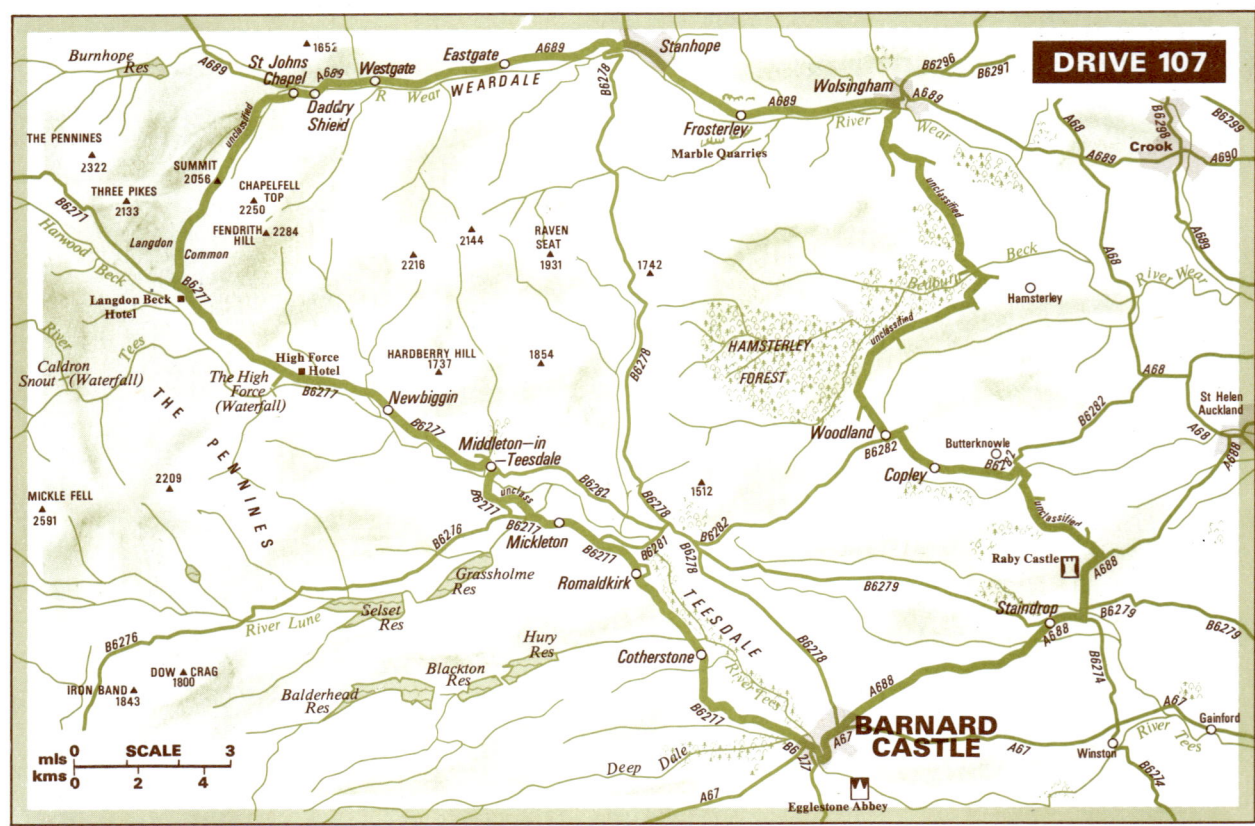

Dog and Gun Inn, then turn left on to a road signposted *Carlisle*. After 4m turn right, and after a further ¾m continue forward on to the B6318. Take the next turning left on to an unclassified road and later enter *Bewcastle*. Turn right on to an unsignposted road and cross a river bridge, then continue for 5m. Cross a main road and after 2¼m approach a T-junction and turn left with Birdoswald signposts. Later pass through Birdoswald, then after ½m ascend and turn right on to the B6318, signposted *Gilsland*. Proceed for 1m and turn right again to enter Gilsland, then turn left with Greenhead signposts and continue for 2m. Approach a T-junction and turn left into Greenhead with *Chollerford* signposts; turn left again to rejoin the B6318 and continue for 15½m before turning left on to an unclassified road signposted *Wark* and Bellingham. Proceed for 1¾m, turn left on to the B6320, then pass through Wark and return to Bellingham.

Through Weardale and Teesdale

From Barnard Castle

Drive 107   58 miles

From *Barnard Castle* follow Bishop Auckland signposts to the end of the town, then turn left on to the A688 and continue to Staindrop. Proceed for 1½m, then turn left on to an unclassified road signposted Cockfield. After ½m keep forward with Butterknowle signposts, then after 2¼m turn left on to the B6282 and continue through Copley to Woodland. Approach a T-junction, turn left, then after 300yds turn right on to an unclassified road signposted Hamsterley. Continue for 4¼m then turn left, signposted *Wolsingham*. In ¾m reach a T-junction and turn left again to cross Bedburn Beck and later the River Wear. Drive to the edge of Wolsingham and turn left on to the A689, signposted *Stanhope*. Pass through Frosterley, Stanhope, Eastgate, Westgate, and Daddry Shield, then reach St John's Chapel and turn left on to an unclassified road signposted Middleton-in-Teesdale. Cross Langdon Common, descend into Teesdale, and on approaching a T-junction, turn left on to the B6277. Continue through *Newbiggin* to Middleton-in-Teesdale, then turn right with Scotch Corner signposts. Cross the River Tees and ½m on keep left on to an unclassified road signposted Barnard Castle. Continue for ¾m and join the B6277, then pass through Mickleton, *Romaldkirk*, and Cotherstone before recrossing the Tees and returning to Barnard Castle.

Peaks, Dales, and the Roman Wall

From Hexham

Drive 108   78 miles

Follow the A6079 out of *Hexham* with *Rothbury* signposts. Cross the River Tyne and continue through Acomb to Wall, then after ¾m approach crossroads and turn left on to the B6318, signposted *Chollerford*. Recross the River Tyne to reach Chollerford, then meet a roundabout and take the first exit, signposted *Carlisle*. Continue with the B6318, then after 11½m pass the Northumberland national park information

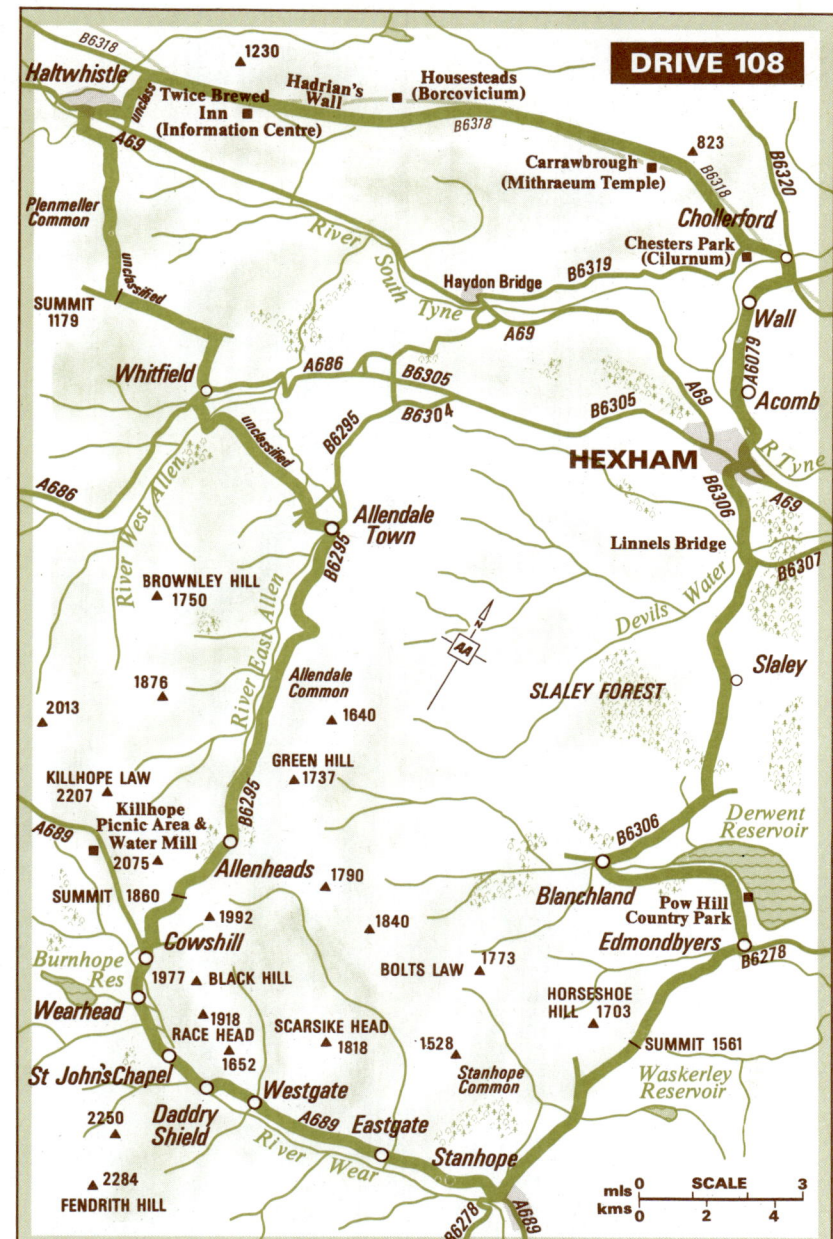

Drive 108 continued

centre and adjacent *Twice Brewed Inn*. Proceed for another 2½m and on reaching crossroads turn left on to an unclassified road signposted *Haltwhistle*. In 1m descend into the South Tyne Valley, then turn right into Haltwhistle. Continue through the latter town, then turn left with Carlisle signposts and shortly turn right on to the A69. In ¼m turn left on to an unclassified road signposted Plenmeller. Cross the River South Tyne, then turn left. Ascend to the summit of Plenmeller Common, turn left, then continue for 2¼m before turning right to descend into West Allen Dale. Meet the A686 at Whitfield and turn right with *Alston* signposts. After ¼m turn left on to an unclassified road signposted Allendale. Cross the West Allen River, and ascend, then continue for 3½m before joining the B6295; cross the East Allen River and ascend to Allendale Town, then turn right with the B6295, signposted Allenheads. Continue over Allendale Common and in 11m join the A689 with *Stanhope* signposts, then proceed to the Grey Bull public house in Stanhope and turn left on to the B6278, signposted Edmondbyers. Later enter Edmondbyers and turn left on to the B6306, signposted *Blanchland*. Drive on and cross the River Derwent before entering Blanchland. Turn right, signposted Hexham, then after 2¾m keep left. Drive through Slaley and cross the Devil's Water via Linnels Bridge before returning to Hexham.

Placenames in *italic* type are worth stopping at; each is listed and described in the main gazetteer section of the book

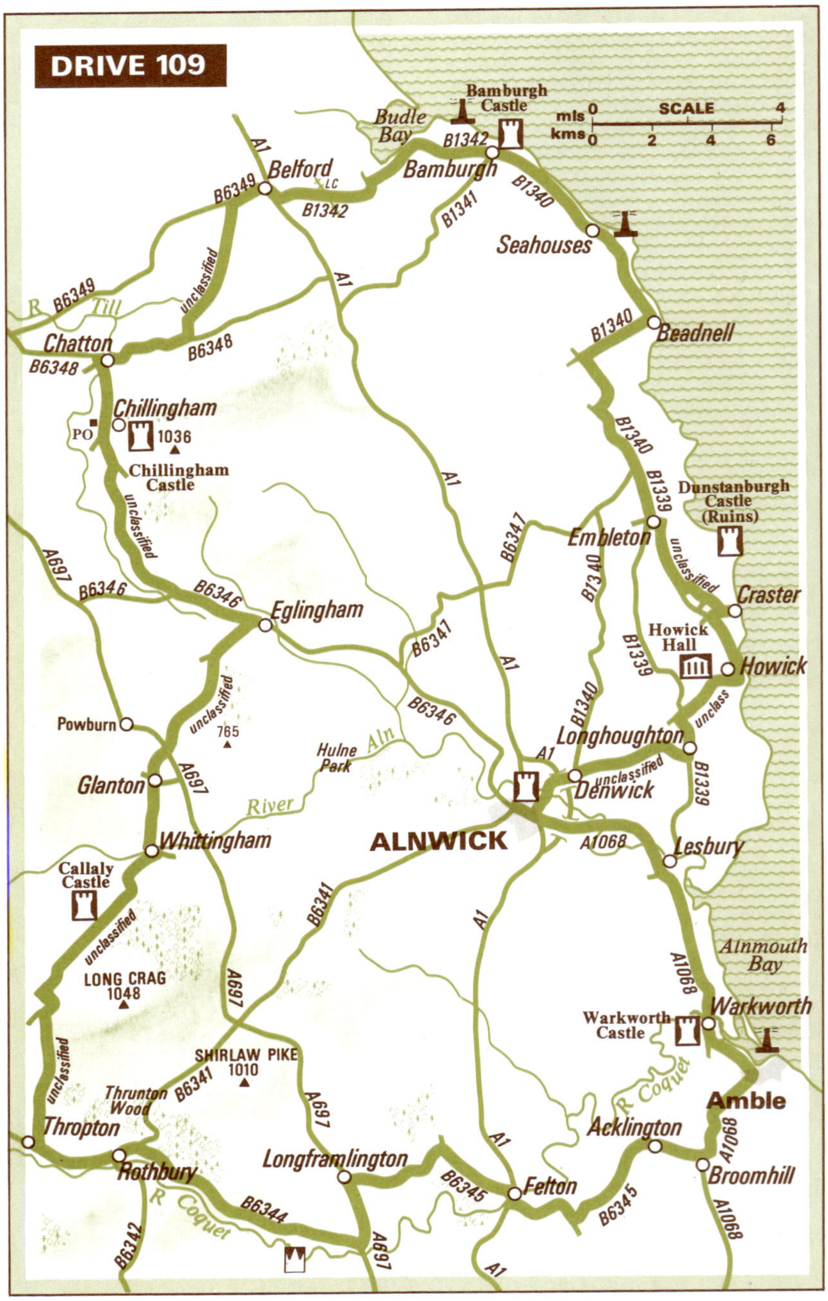

NORTHUMBERLAND AND DURHAM

Along the Northumberland Coast

From Alnwick

Drive 109   84 miles

Leave *Alnwick* by following signposts marked *'Morpeth'* then *'Bamburgh B1340'*. Continue to the far side of Denwick and turn right on to an unclassified road signposted Longhoughton. Proceed for 2½m and turn left to join the B1339 to reach Longhoughton. After a further 1m turn right and continue for ¼m before driving forward on to an unclassified road signposted *Howick*. Continue for 1m and pass the entrance to Howick Hall before turning right. In ½m keep left to reach the coast, then in 1½m approach crossroads and turn right through an archway to *Craster*. Leave Craster and return for ½m before turning right then after ¼m turn right again on to a road signposted *Embleton*. Drive on for ¾m then approach a T-junction and turn right into Embleton. Keep left, drive to the church, then turn right on to the B1339. Continue for 1¼m and keep forward on to the B1340. After another 1½m turn right, proceed for 1½m, then approach crossroads and turn right again. Proceed to *Beadnell* and *Seahouses*; turn right to reach Seahouses war memorial, then turn left to follow a coastal route to Bamburgh. Branch right on to the B1342 with *Belford* signposts, continue for 2½m to a T-junction, and turn left. After 1¾m drive over a level crossing, then in 1m turn right on to the A1 for Belford. On reaching the latter turn left on to the B6349, signposted *Wooler*, then after ¾m left again on to an unclassified road signposted Chatton. In 3m meet a T-junction and turn right on to the B6348. Descend to Chatton, drive to the end of the village and turn left on to an unclassified road signposted *Chillingham*. After 1½m reach Chillingham Post Office and turn left to cross a ford for Chillingham Castle. Return to Chillingham Post Office and turn left, then after 4m drive forward to join the B6346 for Eglingham. Before entering this village turn right on to an unclassified road signposted Beanley and Powburn. After 1m branch left, signposted Glanton, and after 2½m cross a main road for Glanton. Turn right, then take the first turning left for *Whittingham*. Cross the River Aln and turn right with Callaly signposts. Continue for 4½m then turn left with Thropton signposts, and continue to the edge of Thropton. Approach a T-junction and turn left on to the B6341 for *Rothbury*. Keep forward for ½m, then turn right on to the B6344 Morpeth road. After 5½m turn left on to the A697, signposted Coldstream, then continue to the edge of *Longframlington*. Turn right on to the B6354 and continue to Felton. Turn right again on to the A1 and cross the River Coquet. After ¼m turn left on to the B6345 with *Amble* signposts, and continue for 1½m before turning left and continuing through Acklington to Broomhill. Turn left on to the A1068 to Amble. Drive into the village and turn left with Alnwick signposts and continue for 1½m. Approach a T-junction and turn right into *Warkworth*, then after 3½m enter a roundabout and drive forward. Pass through Lesbury and re-enter Alnwick.

122

Lake District

LOCAL ROAD CONDITIONS

It must be emphasized that driving over the Lake District mountain roads and passes is not easy. Anybody venturing into the more difficult regions should be an experienced driver at the wheel of a car which is in perfect condition. Gradients are punishingly steep. Conditions vary according to the weather and the number of people on the road. Most of the narrow roads have passing places, but some of these are unable to cope with the influx of summer traffic and delays are to be expected during peak periods. Bear in mind that it is easier for descending traffic to give way to ascending vehicles.

The following list of roads and passes includes a brief description of each. Some of the passes are known by the alternative names *bank* and *hause*.

Duddon Valley or Dunnerdale
Between Ulpha and Wrynose
Narrow road with a fair surface and several short sharp gradients. Joins a road over Hard Knott and Wrynose passes.

Eskdale to Ulpha
Ascends from Eskdale to maximum height of 890ft. Maximum gradient from Eskdale 1 in 6. Steep descent into Ulpha with maximum gradient 1 in 4.

Great Langdale to Little Langdale via Blea Tarn
Road ascends to 722ft with maximum gradient of 1 in 4. Narrow with occasionally rough surface. Few passing places.

Hard Knott Pass
Between Eskdale and Ambleside
Regarded as an adventure rather than just part of a tour. Maximum gradient of 1 in 3 with numerous hairpin bends. Narrow with a generally fair surface, although rough and loose in places. Maximum height 1,291ft.

Holmrook to Broughton, via Thwaites Fell
Moorland stretch reasonably wide. Passing places throughout; maximum gradient 1 in 5.

Honister Pass
Between Buttermere and Keswick
Well-made road with a good surface, ascending to a maximum height of about 1,176ft. Maximum gradient 1 in 4. Not over-difficult with due care.

Newland Hause
Between Buttermere and Keswick
Well-made road with a good surface. Narrow on the eastern side with awkward bends. Maximum height 1,096ft, maximum gradient 1 in 4.

Red Bank
Between Grasmere and Langdale
Short steep road with a fair surface and some rough patches. Narrow with maximum gradient 1 in 4. Maximum height 523ft.

Stock Ghyll
Between Kirkstone and Ambleside
Long steep descent from 1,476ft. Narrow in places with 1 in 4 gradients.

Whinlatter
Between Keswick and Cockermouth
Road ascends to 1,043ft with maximum gradient 1 in 8. Good surface.

Wrynose Pass
Between Ambleside and Eskdale
Fair surface but narrow and with few passing places. Maximum gradient 1 in 4.

Wast Water, Eskdale, and Birker Fell

From Seascale

Drive 110   56 miles

Take the B5344 *Gosforth* road out of Seascale, then after 2¾m cross a main road and take an unclassified road into Gosforth. Turn right with *Wasdale Head* signposts and in ¼m turn left; after ¾m bear right and ascend. Proceed for 2½m, then bear left to pass under the high crags of Buckbarrow and turn left to follow the shore of Wast Water. Return along the lake shore, and on reaching a Santon Bridge signpost branch left. Continue past Wasdale Hall youth hostel on the left, then after 1¼m turn left and follow a hilly road to Santon Bridge. Turn left, signposted Eskdale, and ascend through Miterdale Forest. Descend and pass a footpath to *Irton* Road Station on the right, then continue to Eskdale. After ½m reach the King George IV Inn and branch right to follow *Ulpha* signposts. Continue on a winding moorland road over Birker Fell and descend through thick woodland to the Traveller's Rest public house. Approach the T-junction and turn right into Ulpha. After ¼m bear left over a river bridge and follow the road through Dunnerdale. Descend through woodland and on meeting a T-junction turn right on to the A595. Cross Duddon Bridge and proceed to Whicham. Proceed to a further T-junction and turn right to continue through *Bootle*. After 4½m descend into the valley of the Esk, then continue past the entrance to Muncaster Castle and Bird Gardens on the left. Drive for a further 1m and take the unclassified road to *Ravenglass*. Return to the A595 and turn left, then after ½m cross the Ravenglass and Eskdale Railway and proceed to Holmrook. Turn left on to the B5344 and return to Seascale.

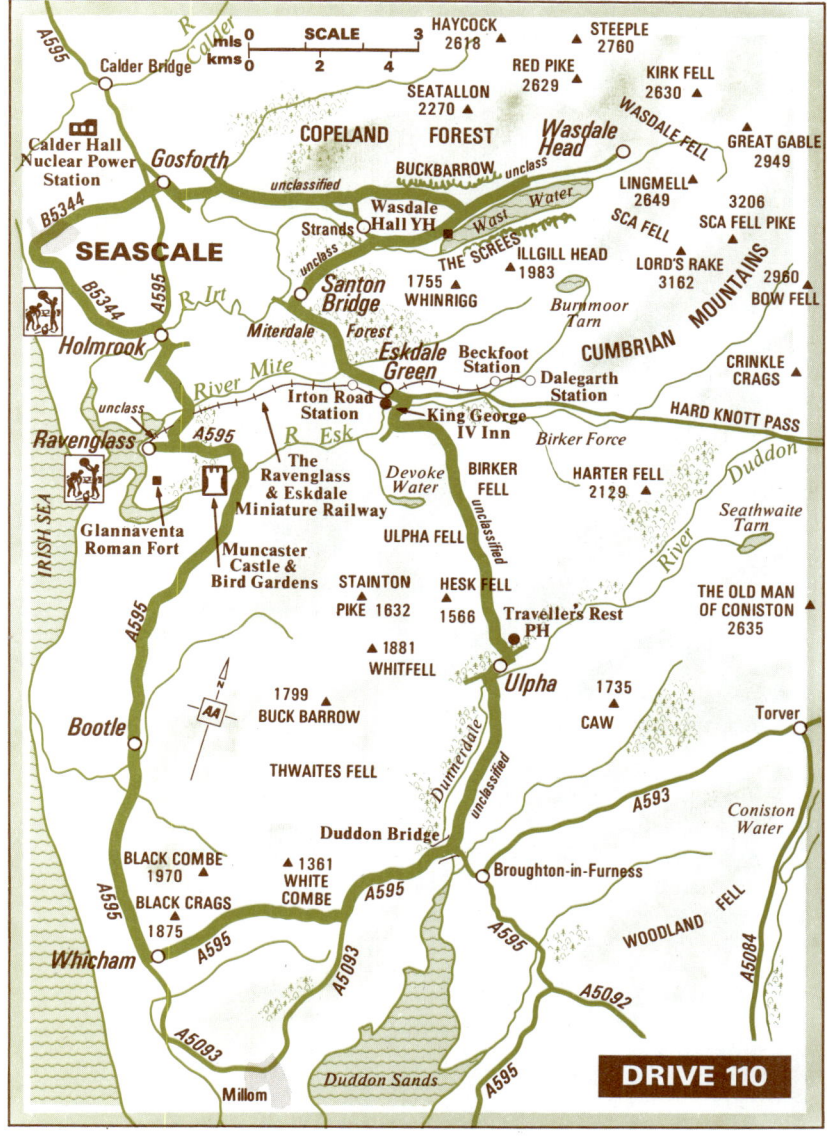

Placenames in *italic* type are worth stopping at; each is listed and described in the main gazetteer section of the book

LAKE DISTRIBUTE

Talkin Fell and the South Tyne Valley

From Carlisle

Drive 111   58 miles

Follow signposts marked 'Penrith A6' to leave *Carlisle*, and pass a television station on the left before continuing for ½m and turning left on to an unclassified road. Proceed to Cumwhinton, approach a T-junction, and turn left on to the B6263 for *Wetheral*. Bear left at Wetheral village green and follow the Eden Valley. Meet a T-junction and turn right on to the A69 before crossing a river bridge. Skirt the grounds of Holme Eden Abbey and continue into Warwick Bridge; proceed to crossroads and turn right on to an unclassified road, signposted Castle Carrock. After 50 yards turn left and follow a secluded by-road for 2¾m before branching left with Talkin signposts. Drive on for 1m and keep left, then pass under a railway viaduct and reach crossroads. Cross the main road and keep forward to pass through Talkin. After ½m turn right on to the road signposted Hallbankgate. Proceed to this village and turn right on to the A689, signposted *Alston*. Left are views of hills extending into Scotland, and right and ahead are the Pennine fells. Drive on to the fells through Tindale and continue through Halton Lea Gate. After 1½m follow the steep wooded slopes of the South Tyne Valley. Pass under a railway bridge and turn immediately left on to an unclassified and unsignposted road. Descend to a T-junction and turn left to continue the descent into the South Tyne Valley. Cross narrow Eals Bridge, then follow the *Haltwhistle* road and ascend steeply. Continue to Rowfoot and turn left at the Featherstone Castle signpost, then drive over a level crossing. Descend through a glade to pass the castle, then continue along the east bank of the South Tyne. Follow Haltwhistle signposts and ascend to a T-junction. Turn left, then after 1¼m pass the ruins of Bellister Castle on the right. Soon, turn left again and cross a river bridge to the outskirts of Haltwhistle. Continue left on to the A69, signposted Carlisle, and after 3¼m pass over a level crossing and enter *Greenhead*. Bear left and in 50yds turn right on to the B6318, signposted *Gilsland*. On reaching a T-junction in Gilsland turn right, signposted Walton. Cross the river and proceed for ¼m, then turn left and continue for 1m. Turn left again on to an unclassified road signposted Birdoswald. Climb close to Hadrian's Wall before descending past Birdoswald. Follow the line of the wall past two Roman turrets and a mile-castle at Banks East. Descend to the banks of the River Irthing and pass the ruins of *Lanercost* Priory. Continue left past Lanercost Bridge, and immediately after crossing the river meet the Bridge Foot Inn and turn left through a gateway. Cross to the far side of Naworth Park and approach crossroads. Turn right on to the A69 for *Brampton*, and proceed through this town to join the B6264. Pass the entrance to Carlisle Airport, then continue through Crosby-on-Eden and return to Carlisle.

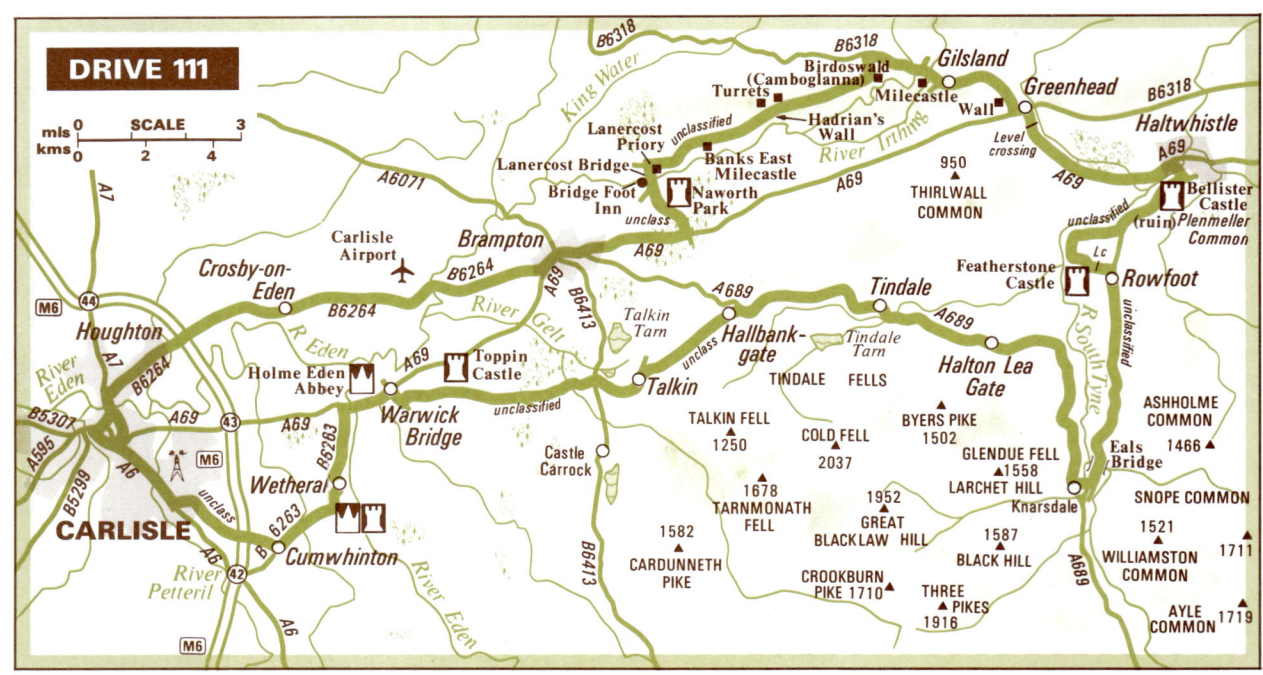

The Fells of Westmorland

From Kendal

Drive 112   70 miles

From *Kendal* follow signposts marked 'The South and *Lancaster*' to leave on the A6. Drive along the River Kent valley for 3½m to pass the entrance to Sizergh Castle; continue along this road and immediately after passing *Levens* Bridge pass the entrance to Levens Hall on the right. After ¼m turn left on to an unclassified road to Leasgill and Heversham. Enter the latter, drive to the church, then turn left with Crooklands signposts and follow a narrow winding by-road. After 1¾m cross a hump-backed river bridge. Proceed for ¾m and approach a T-junction. Turn left on to the B6385 for Crooklands, then turn right on to the A65, signposted *Skipton*. Proceed for 1m and enter a roundabout. Take the first exit, signposted *Kirkby Lonsdale,* and continue to Lupton. Pass through the latter and proceed for 3¾m before turning left on to the B6446. Enter Kirkby Lonsdale and turn right on to the B6254, then left on to the A65. Cross the river and turn immediately left on to the A683, signposted *Sedbergh*. Pass Devil's Bridge on the left and continue through *Casterton* to follow a winding road through the Lune Valley. In 6½m cross a packhorse bridge, then in ½m turn right; later turn right again into Sedbergh, then follow *Brough* signposts and proceed on the A683. Ascend to open moorland. Later meet the A685 and turn right to *Kirkby Stephen*. Drive to the end of the town and turn left on to an unclassified road signposted Soulby. Reach Soulby and cross a river bridge before approaching crossroads and turning left with *Asby* signposts. Follow this lonely road for 3m then ascend and turn right. After 2¼m descend and turn left into Great Asby. Cross the narrow river bridge and approach a T-junction. Turn left, signposted *Orton,* and proceed along a moorland road. Pass a tumulus on the left and descend to the B6260; turn left and pass through Orton and the Lune Valley. Enter a roundabout and take the second exit on to the A685, signposted *Kendal*, into Tebay. Drive parallel to the M6 motorway through the Lune Gorge. Descend through hilly country and pass through Grayrigg before returning to Kendal.

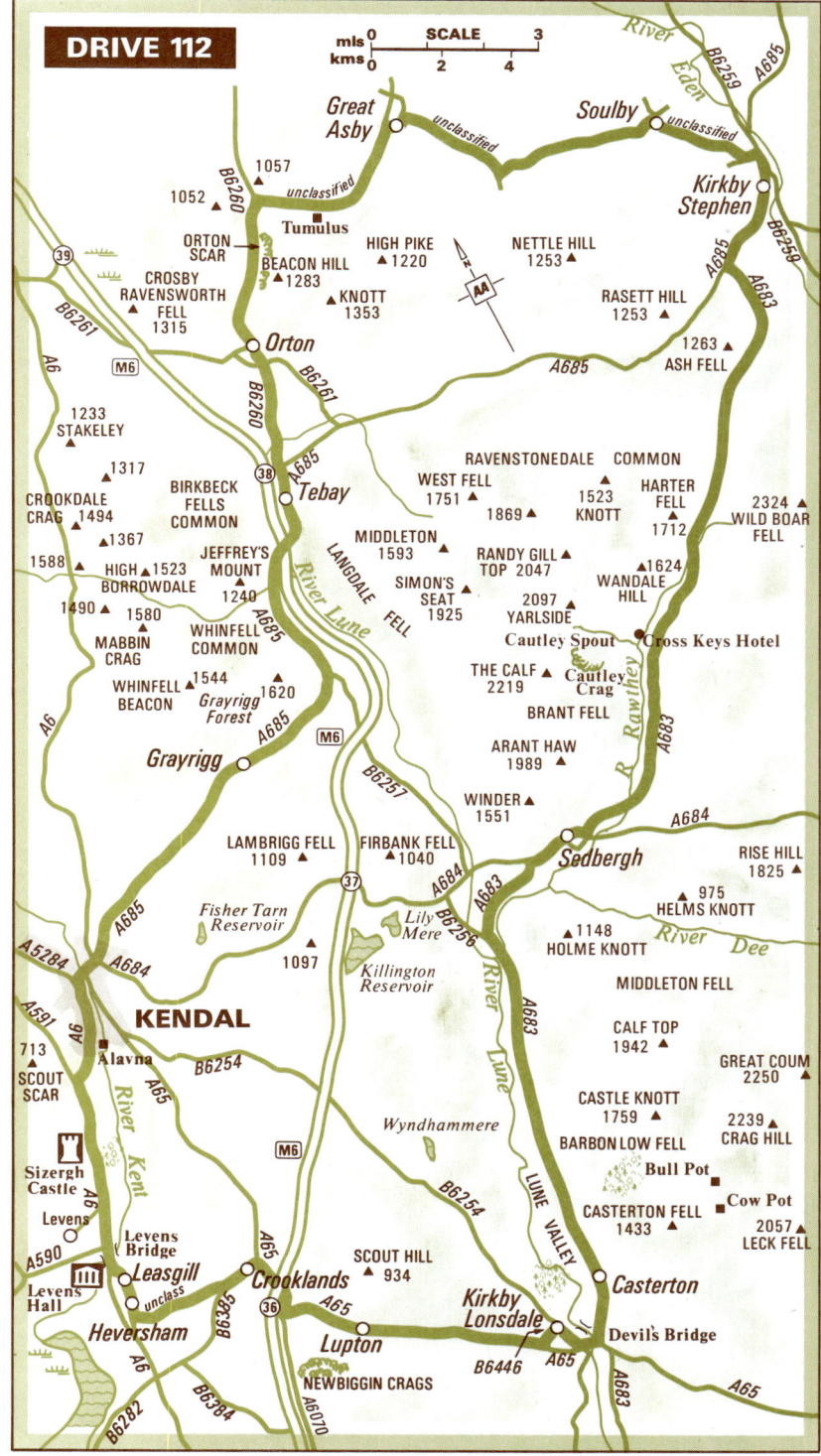

Placenames in *italic* type are worth stopping at; each is listed and described in the main gazetteer section of the book

LAKE DISTRICT

Lakes, Forests, and Honister Pass

From Keswick

Drive 113 65 miles

Take the B5289 *Borrowdale* road out of *Keswick* and drive along the eastern shore of Derwent Water. Continue past the Lodore Swiss Hotel and then enter the broad valley of Borrowdale. Keep to the left bank of the River Derwent and after 1½m pass a track leading left to the Bowder Stone. Borrowdale widens as the road approaches *Rosthwaite*; pass through the latter and continue to *Seatoller*. Leave the latter and ascend on to Honister Pass. Descend to the shore of Lake Buttermere and on reaching the outskirts of *Buttermere* turn right on to an unclassified road signposted Keswick. Ascend to the pass of Newlands Hause, with the left hand edge of the road dropping sheer into a deep valley. Return and turn right on to the B5289 into Buttermere. Follow the eastern shore of Crummock Water and continue into the wide valley of Lorton Vale. Drive to the edge of *Lorton* and turn right on to an unclassified road signposted Keswick. Continue to High Lorton, then turn right and approach a T-junction. Turn right on to the B5292 and start the ascent of Whinlatter Pass. Descend with views of Bassenthwaite Lake and proceed to *Braithwaite*. Turn left on to an unclassified road, and on reaching a T-junction turn left again on to the A66. Pass the outskirts of Thornthwaite and continue to the western shore of Bassenthwaite Lake. Pass between the water and the steep slopes of Wythop Wood, then after 4½m turn right on to the B5291, signposted Castle Inn. Follow the northern end of the lake, proceed for 1m, then turn right with Bothel signposts and cross the Ouse Bridge. Continue to a T-junction at Castle Inn and turn right on to the A591. Take the second turning left on to an unclassified road signposted Bassenthwaite Village. Pass through the village and in 1¾m approach a T-junction, then turn left with *Caldbeck* signposts. Ascend to moorland with Little Tarn and Over Water to the left, then cross open country and approach a T-junction and turn right. Proceed for 1m and join the B5299. Cross a cattle grid, keep left, and continue to Caldbeck. Drive forward on to an unclassified road and enter Hesket Newmarket before bearing left with Mungrisdale signposts. Proceed through farming country for ¾m, branch right, and in another 1m turn left. After 1¾m pass the Horse and Farrier public house and very shortly turn right. Cross open moorland to Mungrisdale, then approach to the A66 with the peak of 2,847ft Saddleback to the right. Meet the T-junction and turn right on to the A66. Pass the edge of *Threlkeld*, then after 1½m turn left on to an unclassified road signposted 'Stone Circle'. After ¼m turn left again and pass Castlerigg Stone Circle on the left. Descend, and later turn left on to the A66, then turn right for the return to Keswick.

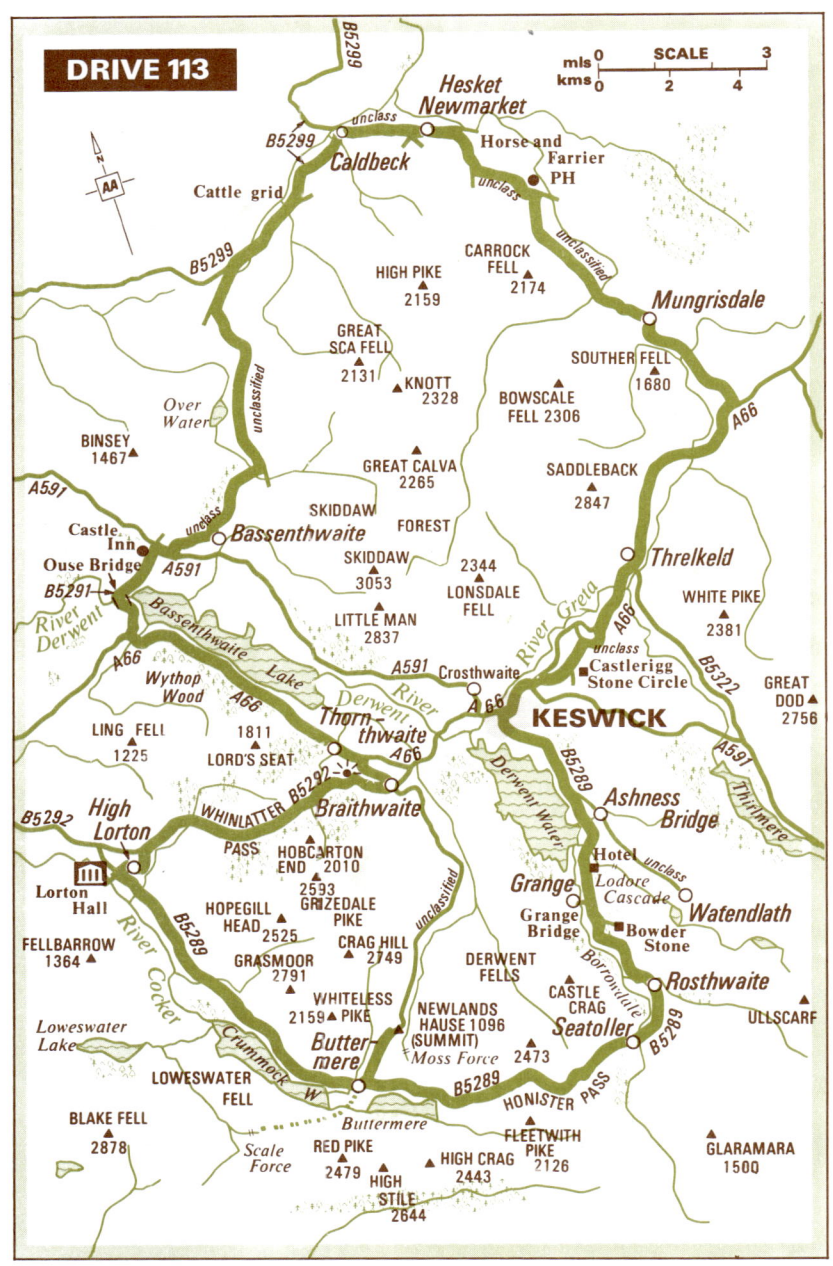

LAKE DISTRICT

Shores of Coniston and Windermere
From Grange-over-Sands
Drive 114   75 miles

Follow the B5277 Lindale road out of *Grange-over-Sands* and drive to Lindale. Turn right on to the A590 with *Lancaster* signposts, continue for 5m and immediately before a river bridge turn left on to the A5074, signposted Bowness. Follow the Lyth Valley, ascend, and pass through *Winster*. After 1¾m approach a crossroads and turn left on to the B5284. After ¼m turn right on to the A592 and visit *Bowness-on-Windermere*. Return along the A592 and in ¾m pass the right turn to Lake *Windermere* ferry. Pass the entrance to Fell Foot Country Park, then follow the eastern shore of Lake Windermere to the far end and meet a T-junction. Turn right on to the A590 into *Newby Bridge*, then turn right on to an unclassified road signposted Lakeside and *Hawkshead* and proceed for another ¼m before turning right again. Continue along the thickly-wooded western shore of Lake Windermere and pass through the small village of Lakeside. After ¾m bear right, then after 2¼m pass Graythwaite Hall Gardens on the left. Branch right, following Sawrey signposts, and in ¾m descend steeply. Drive on for 1¾m and bear left for the climb to *Far Sawrey*. Keep left through the village and turn left to join the B5285, then proceed to Near Sawrey. Leave the latter along the northern shore of Esthwaite Water and continue into Hawkshead. Proceed on to the B5286, signposted *Ambleside*, and follow a winding road through Out Gate to Clappersgate. Turn right on to the A593, cross a river bridge, then turn left into Ambleside. Return along the A593 and pass through Clappersgate. At Skelwith Bridge keep left and cross the river, passing the path leading to Skelwith Force Waterfall on the right. Continue on the A593 to *Coniston* and then turn left on to the B5285, signposted Hawkshead. Skirt the northern end of Coniston Water and keep left and negotiate a long winding ascent through thick woodland. After 1m turn left on to an unclassified road signposted Tarn Hows, and in ½m approach a T-junction and turn left again. Ascend for Tarn Howes, and then descend steeply along a narrow road. On reaching another T-junction turn right on to the B5285. Take the next turning left on to an unclassified road signposted 'East of Lake', then follow the eastern shore of Coniston Water. After 1¾m pass Brantwood on the left. Rocky crags can be seen to the right and Grizedale Forest to the left as the route continues along the shore of the lake. Continue to the far side of the lake and descend into the valley of the River Crake. Furness Fells rise on the left; on reaching a T-junction turn left and proceed to Spark Bridge. Turn left, then after ½m cross a main road with Newby Bridge signposts. Continue to the next T-junction and turn left on to the A590, then follow a level road for 1½m to crossroads. Turn right on to the B5278, signposted Grange-over-Sands, and enter Haverthwaite. Proceed through thickly-wooded country, passing the entrance to Holker Hall on the right, then continue to *Cark* and drive to the Rose and Crown Hotel. Branch left on to the unclassified *Cartmel* road and continue into the latter. Pass Cartmel school and take a right turn signposted *Grange*. After 1m turn left into Grangefell Road and descend to Grange-over-Sands.

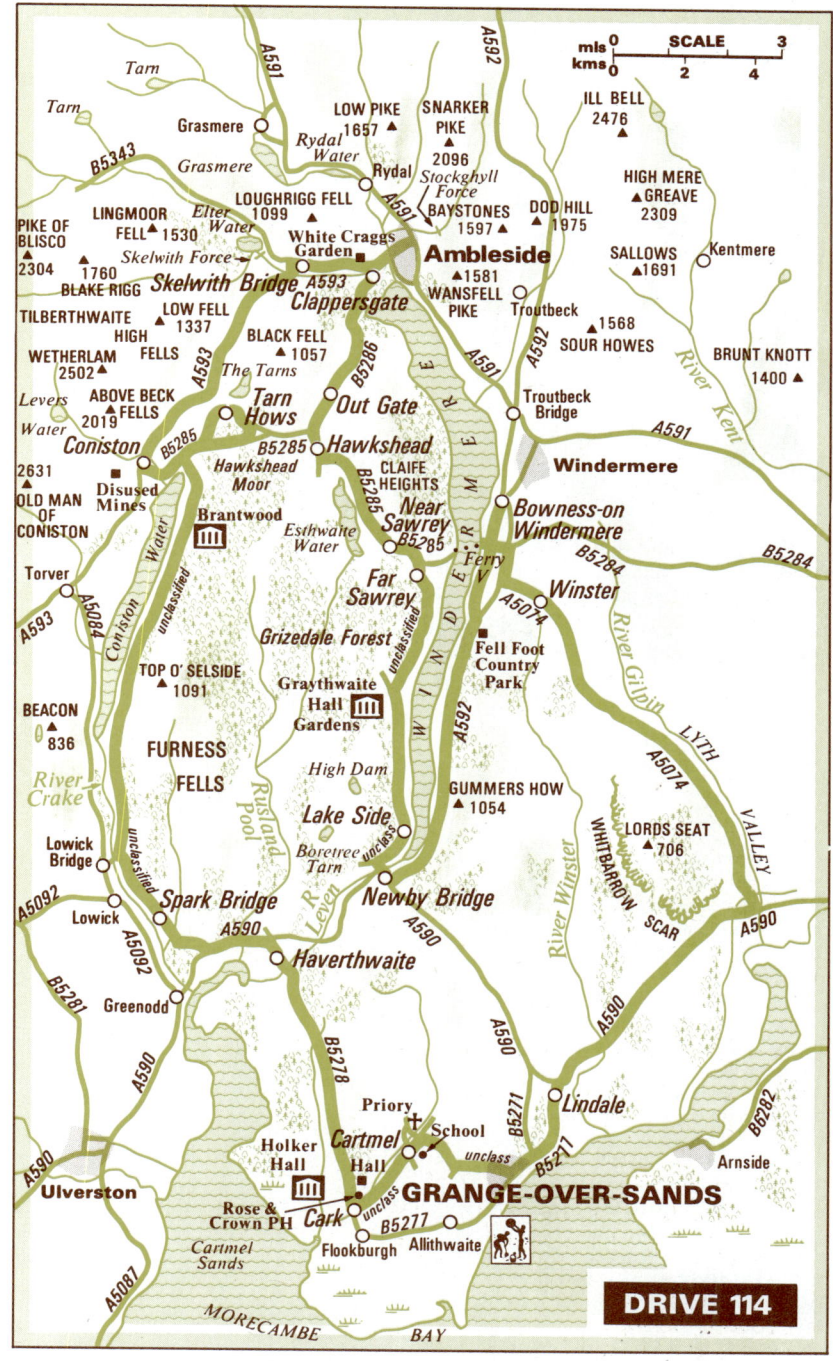

LAKE DISTRICT

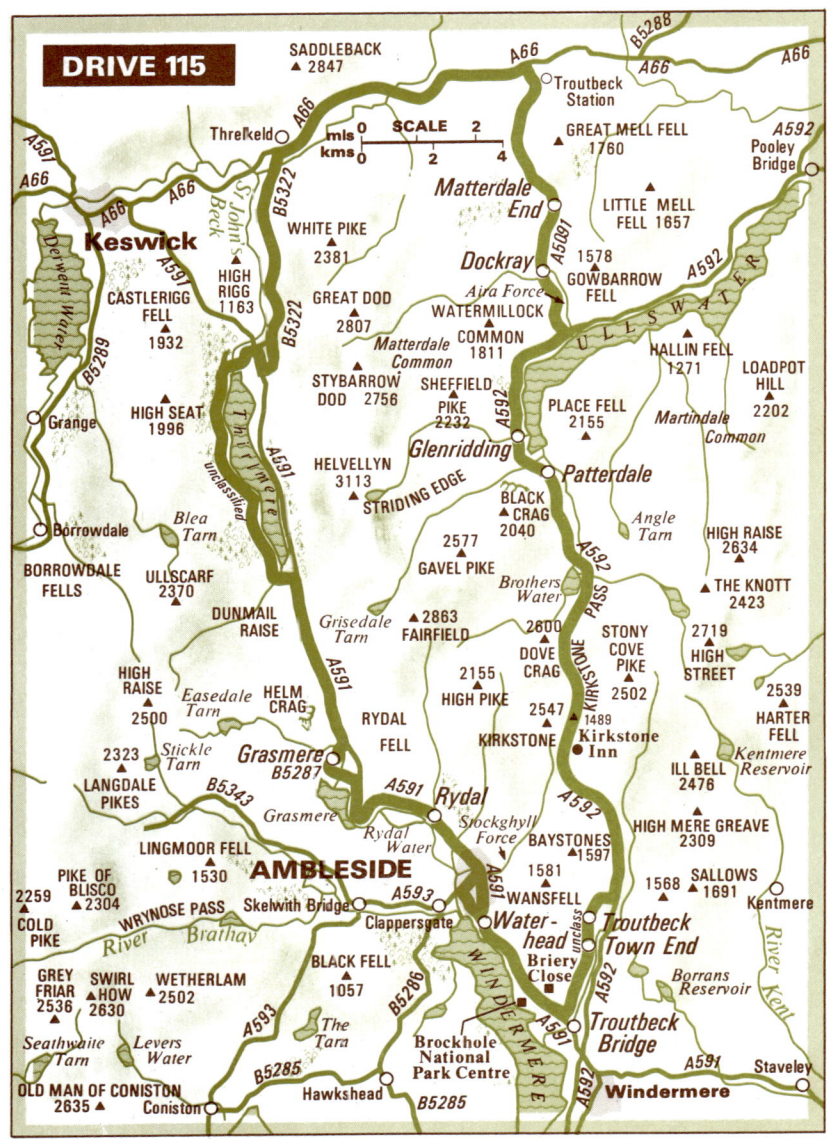

Kirkstone and the Banks of Thirlmere

From Ambleside

Drive 115   47 miles

Leave *Ambleside* on the A591 *Windermere* road and drive through Waterhead. After 1¼m pass a left turn leading to Briery Close, then after a further ½m pass the entrance to Brockhole National Park Centre on the right. Continue for 1m to enter the outskirts of Troutbeck Bridge, then turn left on to an unclassified road signposted *Troutbeck*. Ascend and pass through Town End and Troutbeck. Continue along the side of a deep valley and turn left on to the A592. Follow *Kirkstone* signposts to enter Kirkstone Pass and ascend. Continue over wild mountain country and descend to *Patterdale*. Stay with the A592 and continue through Glenridding. Drive along the wooded shore of Ullswater for 2¼m, then turn left on to the A5091, signposted Troutbeck. Ascend through Dockray to Matterdale, and on reaching the A66 turn left to pass under steep fells. Proceed to the edge of *Threlkeld* and pass directly beneath 2,847ft Saddleback before turning left on to the B5322, signposted Thirlmere. Proceed along St John's Vale and as the valley narrows follow close to the banks of St John's Beck. Approach a T-junction and turn sharp right on to the A591. At the first crossroads turn left on to an unclassified road signposted 'Public Road Round Lake'. Follow the northern shore of Thirlmere and keep left along the western bank of the reservoir. Pass thick woodland above the road to the right, with the massive bulk of 3,113ft Helvellyn on the left. Proceed to the far side of Thirlmere and keep left, then approach a T-junction and turn right on to the A591. Ascend Dunmail Raise. In 2½m turn right on to the B5287 and enter *Grasmere*. Turn left through the village. Drive on for ½m and turn right on to the A591, signposted Windermere. Pass Grasmere Lake and Rydal Water before entering *Rydal*, then continue on the A591 for the return to Ambleside.

The Gazetteer

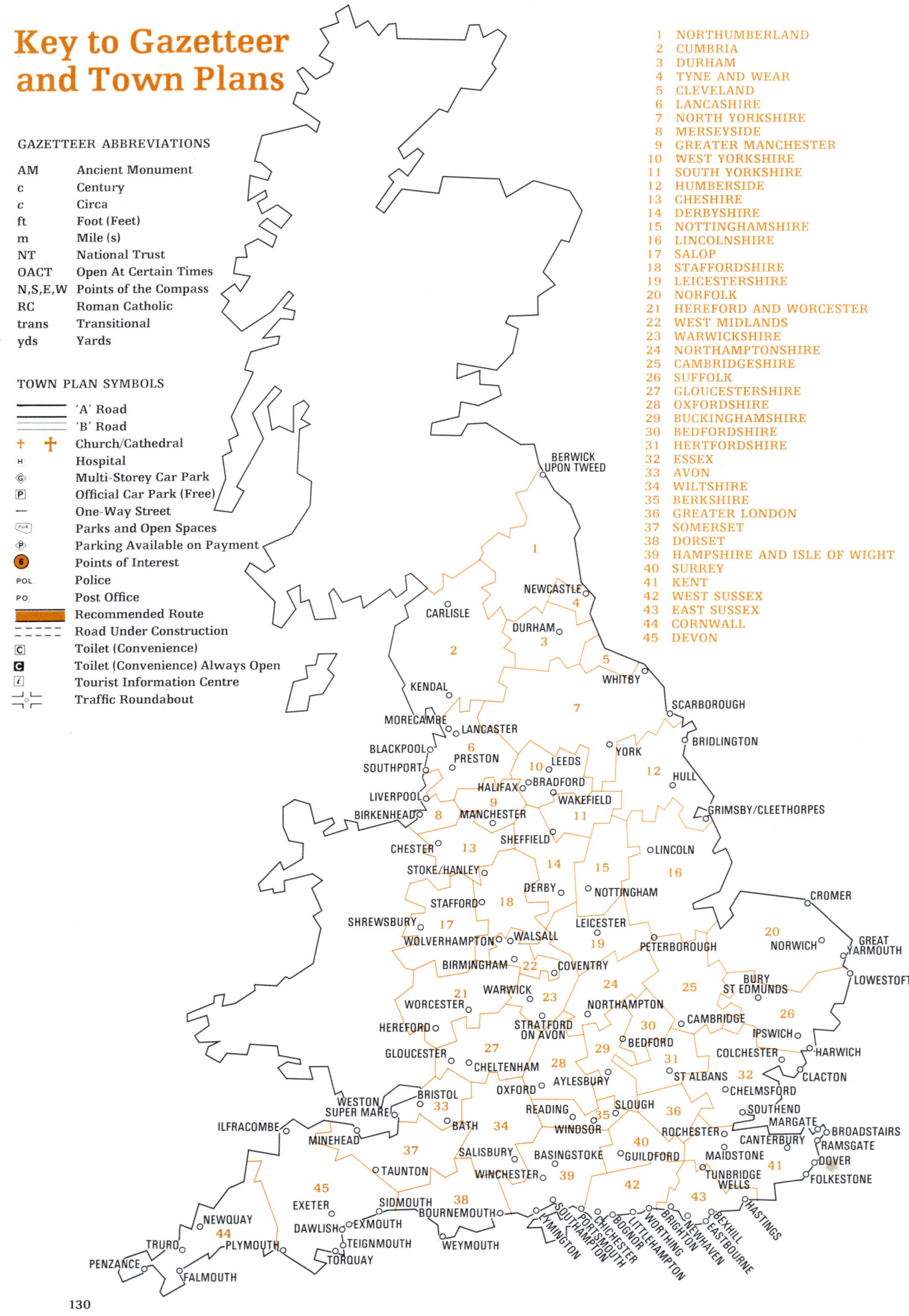

Key to Gazetteer and Town Plans

GAZETTEER ABBREVIATIONS

AM	Ancient Monument
c	Century
c	Circa
ft	Foot (Feet)
m	Mile (s)
NT	National Trust
OACT	Open At Certain Times
N,S,E,W	Points of the Compass
RC	Roman Catholic
trans	Transitional
yds	Yards

TOWN PLAN SYMBOLS

- 'A' Road
- 'B' Road
- † Church/Cathedral
- H Hospital
- Ⓖ Multi-Storey Car Park
- P Official Car Park (Free)
- One-Way Street
- Parks and Open Spaces
- ⓟ Parking Available on Payment
- Points of Interest
- POL Police
- PO Post Office
- Recommended Route
- Road Under Construction
- C Toilet (Convenience)
- C Toilet (Convenience) Always Open
- i Tourist Information Centre
- Traffic Roundabout

1. NORTHUMBERLAND
2. CUMBRIA
3. DURHAM
4. TYNE AND WEAR
5. CLEVELAND
6. LANCASHIRE
7. NORTH YORKSHIRE
8. MERSEYSIDE
9. GREATER MANCHESTER
10. WEST YORKSHIRE
11. SOUTH YORKSHIRE
12. HUMBERSIDE
13. CHESHIRE
14. DERBYSHIRE
15. NOTTINGHAMSHIRE
16. LINCOLNSHIRE
17. SALOP
18. STAFFORDSHIRE
19. LEICESTERSHIRE
20. NORFOLK
21. HEREFORD AND WORCESTER
22. WEST MIDLANDS
23. WARWICKSHIRE
24. NORTHAMPTONSHIRE
25. CAMBRIDGESHIRE
26. SUFFOLK
27. GLOUCESTERSHIRE
28. OXFORDSHIRE
29. BUCKINGHAMSHIRE
30. BEDFORDSHIRE
31. HERTFORDSHIRE
32. ESSEX
33. AVON
34. WILTSHIRE
35. BERKSHIRE
36. GREATER LONDON
37. SOMERSET
38. DORSET
39. HAMPSHIRE AND ISLE OF WIGHT
40. SURREY
41. KENT
42. WEST SUSSEX
43. EAST SUSSEX
44. CORNWALL
45. DEVON

ABBERTON, Essex *9 TM01*
This village includes an old parish church and moated hall. A reservoir to the SW is the habitat of swans and other wildfowl.

ABBEY DORE, Herefs & Worcs *11 SO33*
Abbey Dore is a quiet village at the S end of the River Dore's Golden Valley. The church, once part of Cistercian abbey, has a fine interior and includes the original choir and transepts. A 17th-c screen is housed within the building.

ABBOT'S BROMLEY, Staffs *18 SK02*
Old timbered houses and a market place with a butter cross are features of this small town. The annual Horn Dance (traditional) is held on the first Monday after September 4, and has origins that are almost certainly prehistoric. Six of the twelve men that participate wear headpieces displaying large ancient reindeer antlers, and they dance all day at localities that include the village green, large local houses, and surrounding farms and hamlets. Predominantly Elizabethan Blithfield Hall (OACT), lies 3m W.

ABBOTSBURY, Dorset *6 SY58*
A picturesque village built mainly of stone and thatch, with the ruins of a Benedictine abbey. All that remains of the latter are a notable tithe barn and a gateway. Inside the church is a pulpit which still bears the marks of bullets fired during the Civil War. At the top of a hill is the 15th-c St Catherine's Chapel – a good vantage point for viewing the surrounding countryside. The fishing fleet that used to exist here was blessed at an annual ceremony where children made garlands to be thrown into the sea. Although the fleet has gone, the children still make garlands, but instead of consigning them to the waves they carry them to the local war memorial. A shingle beach at Chesil Bank has sand at low tide, but bathing is dangerous. Other features of the village are the swannery and sub-tropical gardens (OACT).

ABBOTSHAM, Devon *5 SS42*
The village church boasts a Norman font, carved bench-ends, and a 15th-c barrel roof with trade emblems and coats of arms. Nearby is the resort of Westward Ho! which was named after the novel by Charles Kingsley.

ABERFORD, W Yorks *22 SE43*
The rebuilt church still retains its Norman tower, and in nearby Arlington Park a triumphal arch bears the inscription Liberty in North America Triumphant. This arch dates from 1875, and a collection of ornate almshouses were built in 1844.

ABINGDON, Oxon *13 SU49*
At one time the county town of Berkshire but now part of Oxon, Abingdon has connections with several English kings, from Alfred to Charles II. William the Conqueror left his young son Henry here during Easter of 1084, Edward IV's army rested here in June 1471, Henry VIII brought his court for a long stay at Abingdon Abbey to avoid the plague in London, and Charles I held councils of war at local inns.

The surviving abbey buildings are situated near the river and include the Checker Hall, the Checker (*ie* exchequer) itself, and the Long Gallery. The Church of St Helen dates from *c*1260, but the steeple is a later addition. Built mainly in the perpendicular style, the church has five aisles and includes the Lady Chapel, which was built between 1380 and 1390. A feature of the latter is a highly decorated ceiling depicting a tree of Jesse – a kind of family tree showing Christ's descent from Jesse – which is considered unusual. St Nicholas's Church is attached to the abbey gatehouse and was probably built towards the end of the 12thc; a feature is the Jacobean pulpit. Several Georgian and earlier houses can be seen in the town, as well as a number of ancient almshouses. The fine County Hall (AM) was designed by Wren and built by Kempster, his master mason, in 1678. It now houses the Borough Museum.

ABINGER, Surrey *8 TQ14*
This old village is surrounded by wooded hill country and still has its stocks and whipping post. A Jacobean porch is one of the features of the manor house, and the partly-Norman church has been restored after bomb damage. Evidence of human occupation dating back to 8,000BC has been discovered near Abinger Common.

ABINGER HAMMER, Surrey *8 TQ04*
As implied by the name, this hamlet was once a centre for the 17th-c iron industry. An old clock in the main street depicts a smith at his trade. An interesting barn dating from 1620 exists at Fulvens Farm, and fine views may be enjoyed from Abinger Roughs (NT).

ABLINGTON, Glos *12 SP10*
A picturesque village on the River Coln, with a manor house of 1590 which was once the home of Arthur Gibbs. This man's book, *A Cotswold Village*, did much to make this area known and appreciated. Nearby are Ablington House (mid 17thc) and two fine barns.

ACCRINGTON, Lancs *21 SD72*
An industrial town engaged in cotton-weaving, brick-making, and engineering.

ACLE, Norfolk *15 TG41*
Acle is on the River Bure and is a well-known touring centre for the Norfolk Broads. The church is of interest and displays a 12th-c round tower, a 15th-c octagonal belfry, and a 15th-c screen.

ACRISE, Kent *9 TR14*
Set among trees on the North Downs, this village has a rough-flint Norman church, and Acrise Place – a fine Elizabethan manor with Georgian additions.

ACTON, Cheshire *17 SJ65*
The large 13th- and 14th-c church has a fine tower and contains several interesting monuments. One of the latter is the effigy of a canopied knight. Spanning the Weaver Valley to the N is, perhaps, one of Stephenson's finest works – the twenty-arch Dutton-Railway viaduct. Also near Acton is Dorfold Hall, an impressive house built in 1616 (OACT).

ACTON, Suffolk *15 TL84*
A very good brass of a knight in chain mail holding a shield (*c*1302) can be seen in the local church. Another notable monument, and one that might possibly be by Thomas Green of Camberwell, is of a reclining man with his wife at his feet.

ACTON BURNELL, Salop *17 SJ50*
The 13th-c fortified manor house in this village is scheduled as an Ancient Monument (OACT). The first English parliament – that of Edward I – is said to have been held here in 1283. A brass of 1382 can be seen in the early-English church.

ACTON ROUND, Salop *17 SO69*
The hall (*c*1695, OACT), was once a dower house for Aldenham Park which lies 2m NE. Monuments in the small church include one by William Stanton, and the building itself carries a timbered belfry.

ADDERBURY, Oxon *13 SP43*
Attractive ironstone houses are a feature of this village, and include 17th-c Adderbury House. This was once the home of the Earl of Rochester, a dissolute poet who is said to have courted his insane second wife by pretending to be the Emperor of China. The decorated and perpendicular church displays corbels and gargoyles, and has a fine spire.

ADDINGTON, Gt London *8 TQ36*
Addington Palace, once a hunting lodge of Henry VIII, was rebuilt in 1770 and became a residence for the Archbishops of Canterbury. It now houses the Royal School of Church Music. The tombs of five Archbishops lie in 13th-c St Mary's Church, which has been restored. The village cricket club was formed in 1743 and there are excellent golf courses near by.

ADEL, W Yorks *22 SE24*
The Norman village church has notable capitals and a richly-carved south portal and chancel arch. It could be said to be the finest of its period in Yorkshire.

ADLINGTON, Cheshire *18 SJ98*
The hall displays a real mixture of architectural styles, but was originally built between 1450 and 1505. Its Elizabethan black-and-white wing was built in 1581, the south front is Georgian, and there is a Palladian portico. Handel is reputed to have played the organ here (OACT).

AFFPUDDLE, Dorset *6 SY89*
This curious village name is derived from *Aeffa*, the Germanic name for a river and the name of the owner in 987. A number of curious hollows on Affpuddle Heath were, for many years, thought to be man-made. The general opinion these days is that they were caused by natural subsidence. The two largest of these are known as Culpepper's Dish and Culpepper's Spoon. Old bench ends, a carved pulpit of 1547, and a Norman font are features of the 13th-c and later church.

AINTREE, Merseyside *17 SJ39*
Aintree is best known for the nearby racecourses, which are crossed by the Leeds and Liverpool Canal. The world-famous Grand National Steeplechase is held here each year.

AIRTON, N Yorks *22 SD95*
An upper-Airedale village with a triangular green, situated on the famous Pennine Way. The manor house, post office, and Friends' Meeting House all date from the 17thc.

ALBERBURY, Salop *17 SJ31*
The Norman to 15th-c church has a massive saddleback tower which is connected to a ruined 13th-c tower by a wall. Loton Park is a Jacobean and later house; 2m SW is Braggington, a fine 17th-c house that is now a farm.

ALBURY, Surrey *8 TQ04*
In Albury Park there is a partly-ruined Norman church, and the exterior of the house was re-fashioned in the 1840's (OACT). To the N runs the Pilgrims' Way, passing St Martha's Chapel which was largely rebuilt in 1848. The site of a large Romano-British settlement (AM) is at Farley Heath, some 2½m S.

ALCESTER, Warwickshire *12 SP05*
Pronounced Olster, this old market town is situated at the junction of the Rivers Alne and Arrow. Several timbered houses can be seen in the town, and the town hall dates from 1641. Ragley Hall (1½m SW, OACT) is set in a 500-acre park which was landscaped by Capability Brown.

ALCONBURY, Cambs *14 TL17*
NE lie the Monk's-Wood and Woodwalton-Fen nature reserves. The church has a good 13th-c broach spire, and the tower is without a parapet. An elaborate milestone (or obelisk) was erected here on the Great North Road in the 18thc.

ALDBOROUGH, N Yorks *22 SE46*
Remains of the Roman town *Isurium* (AM, OACT) are preserved in the village. The partly 14th-c church has carved stone figures in the vestry, plus examples of old glass. A maypole is sited on the village green.

ALDBOURNE, Wilts *7 SU27*
Pronounced Auburn, this can be considered one of the most attractive villages in Wiltshire. The fine old church was originally 12thc but has subsequently been added to. The ancient manor house of Upper Upham, said to have been visited by John of Gaunt, is sited 3m NW on high-lying Aldbourne Chase.

ALDBURY, Herts *8 SP91*
The village green has a duckpond and still retains the stocks and whipping post. A 15th-c monument surrounded by a stone screen can be seen in the Pendley Chapel of the perpendicular-style church. An avenue of trees stretches across Aldbury Common to the Bridgewater Monument. This was erected to the pioneer of Britain's canal system, the Third Duke of Bridgewater.

ALDEBURGH, Suffolk *15 TM45*
A quiet resort with a pebble beach which allows access for bathing. George Crabbe (Rev), a poet of rural life and author of a collection of tales entitled *The Borough*, was born here. *The Borough* was the inspiration for Benjamin Britten's opera *Peter Grimes*, and the latter work is set in this village. The Moot Hall is a quaint 16th-c building, and the mainly-perpendicular church contains numerous brasses and a bust of Crabbe. Elizabeth Garrett Anderson, the first woman to become mayor and one of the first women doctors, lived at Alde House. The village is known for its annual music festival.

ALDENHAM, Herts *8 TQ19*
Two public schools — Haberdashers' Aske's, and Aldenham — are both situated here. The former is set around the 18th- and 19th-c Aldenham House. The 13th-c and later church houses a notable parish chest, plus various brasses and monuments.

ALDERLEY EDGE, Cheshire *17 SJ87*
This residential district lies at the foot of a 650ft hill (NT). Half-timbered Chorley Hall is 16thc, and the old mill (NT) at Nether Alderley dates from the 15thc (S).

ALDERMASTON, Berks *7 SU56*
An attractive brick-built village close to the Atomic Weapons Research Establishment. The Aldermaston pottery is well known and sells its work all over the country. The River Kennet runs through the top end of the village at Aldermaston Mill.

ALDERSHOT, Hants *8 SU85*
This is an important and well-known military centre. The Heroes' Shrine has a rockery built of material taken from fifty-four bombed boroughs, and there are several service museums within the town. Basingstoke Canal flows to the N, and the parish church displays various monuments and a 15th-c tower.

ALDINGTON, Kent *9 TR03*
Views across Romney Marsh can be enjoyed from this village, and the church has a notable 16th-c tower. Elizabeth the Holy Maid of Kent lived here.

ALDSWORTH, Glos *12 SP11*
Aldsworth is a Cotswold village noted for its original Cotswold breed of sheep, said to be the last to survive. The church has a series of remarkable carved gargoyles.

ALDWORTH, Berks *7 SU57*
The church is noted for its range of De La Beche monuments and a 600-year-old yew.

ALFOLD, Surrey *8 TQ03*
A Norman and decorated church with two 14th-c porches is sited in the village, and the old stocks and whipping post are still in existence. Alfold House is a 16th-c timbered building.

ALFORD, Lincs *19 TF47*
A pleasant marshland town, with a five-sail windmill that is complete but no longer in use. Various Georgian and older houses can be seen, and 2m SW is the Georgian house of Well Vale.

ALFRETON, Derbyshire *18 SK45*
The church is 13th to 15thc, and contains a fine monument dated 1742. An old double lock-up, a small stone cell in which local offenders — usually drunken — were placed overnight to sober up, can also be seen. Large collieries are in evidence near by.

ALFRISTON, E Sussex *8 TQ50*
A pretty village on the River Cuckmere, with a splendid cruciform church (the Cathedral of the Downs), dating from *c*1360. The well-known Star Inn is dated 1520 and has remarkable carvings. A picturesque half-timbered building called the Priests' House (NT) dates from *c*1350 (OACT). One of the smallest churches in the country can be seen across the river at Lullington — a mere 16ft square.

ALGARKIRK, Lincs *19 TF23*
The village name recalls Earl Alfgar, who was killed fighting the Danes in 870. The restored church has a 13th-c tower, 14th-c windows, and double-transept aisles.

ALKBOROUGH, Humberside *23 SE82*
The church is Norman and early English, with a curious whetstone in the churchyard. Cut into the cliff-top turf W of the church is a maze known as Julian's Bower (AM), thought to be 12thc. Views of Trent Falls — where the Trent and the Ouse meet at the Humber estuary — can be enjoyed; they now form part of the Humber national wildfowl reserve.

ALKHAM, Kent *9 TR24*
Carved stone stalls exist in the early-English church, and the old rectory is 18thc. A mile and a half E are the remains of St Radigund's Abbey, founded *c*1200.

ALLERFORD, Somerset *5 SS94*
Thatched cottages and an old, double-arched packhorse bridge are features of this attractive village.

ALLINGTON, Kent *9 TQ75*
Built on the River Medway, Allington includes an imposing 13th-c and later castle that has been well-restored and is now occupied by Carmelites (OACT). Near the castle is a large, newly-established yacht marina.

ALLINGTON, Lincs *19 SK84*
This comprises E and W Allington. The poet George Crabbe was rector of W Allington for some twenty-five years. A beautiful Dutch-gabled manor house of 1660 can be seen.

ALMELEY, Herefs & Worcs *11 SO35*
The timbered 17th-c meeting house is one of the oldest in England, and the church has a 16th-c roof. Contemporary painting can be seen on the front pews.

ALMER, Dorset *7 SY99*
Georgian Charlborough Park stands in vast grounds surrounded by a wall. Inside the park is a tall folly tower dating from 1790, which is described in Thomas Hardy's *Two On A Tower*. Winterbourne Anderson is an early 17th-c moated manor house.

ALMONDSBURY, Avon *12 ST68*
An elaborate four-level intersection, involving the M4 and M5 is located here. In contrast is the fine, partly-Norman cruciform church, with its notable early-English chancel.

ALNE, N Yorks *22 SE46*
The Norman south-doorway of the church displays strange animal carvings; the font and tower arch are also Norman. The pulpit dates from 1626, and a rare maiden's garland has been preserved.

ALNWICK, Northumberland *27 NU11*
A massive Norman castle, principal seat of the Percy family, was built here in the 12thc but lay in ruins for two centuries following Border warfare. It was restored as a residence in the 18th and 19thc's, by the Dukes of Northumberland (OACT).

Old buildings in the town include the Pottergate and Hotspur Gate, the latter displaying the Percy lion emblem. A stepped-cross and old fountain decorate the market place. St Michael's Church is 15thc and preserves a fine 14th-c Flemish chest. The gatehouse is the survivor of a ruined abbey founded in 1147. William the Lion's Stone is a reminder that this Scottish King was captured here in 1172, as Malcolm's Cross, N of the town (restored in 1774) marks the spot where Malcolm Canmore was murdered in 1093. The Tenantry Column of 1816 is surmounted by the Percy lion, and was erected by 1,000 grateful tenants after a reduction of rents.

Partly 13th-c Hulne Priory lies 3m NW in the extensive Hulne Park; 4m SE is the resort of Alnmouth, with one of the oldest golf courses in England (1869) and yachting facilities.

ALRESFORD, Hants *7 SU53*
Pronounced Orlesford, the town lies on both sides of the River Alre – a tributary of the Itchen – as Old and New Alresford. An old fulling-mill spans the streams between the two. Admiral Rodney is buried in the red-brick Church of St Mary at Old Alresford; New Alresford was a medieval wool town, and many of the French prisoners quartered here in the Napoleonic Wars are buried in the churchyard. Mary Mitford, author of *Our Village*, was born in Broad Street in 1787. Several delightful Georgian houses are sited in this street.

ALREWAS, Staffs *18 SK11*
A quiet village with a few black-and-white houses, some dating from the 15thc. The parish church is 12th to 15thc, with a 16th-c roof and a fine old font. A cast-iron bridge spans the nearby Tame, and dates from 1824.

ALSOP-EN-LE-DALE, Derbyshire *18 SK15*
A Peak District national park village, where St Michael's Church has a Norman nave and south-doorway. The old pack-horse crossing known as Viator's Bridge can be seen W in Milldale.

ALSTON, Cumbria *26 NY74*
Possibly the highest in England, this market town is sited in the Pennines at about 900ft. Wide views of the Pennines and the South-Tyne Valley can be enjoyed from here. A covered market-cross is an interesting feature. The Hartside road, to the SW, gives superb views across the Eden Valley and towards the Lakeland fells.

ALSTONEFIELD, Staffs *18 SK15*
A good centre for the Manifold Valley and Upper Dovedale, Alstonefield is built at an altitude of 864ft. The church where anglers Izaak Walton and Charles Cotton worshipped contains some 17th-c woodwork. To the W, near Welton, is the prehistoric double-barrow of Long Low, excavated in the 19thc.

ALTARNUN, Cornwall *5 SX28*
A village set above a stream on the edge of Bodmin Moor. The large 15th-c Church of St Nonna is notable for its imposing tower, fine screen and font, and numerous carved bench-ends. It is known locally as the cathedral of the moors.

ALTON, Hants *8 SU73*
Alton boasts a number of Georgian houses. The Church of St Lawrence bears scars of the Civil War, notably bullet marks in the south door, and houses a brass to Colonel Boles, a Royalist leader who was killed here. A Tudor cottage, former home of Elizabethan poet Edmund Spenser, stands in Amery Street. The Curtis Museum houses agricultural exhibits and items of local interest.

ALTON, Staffs *18 SK04*
Stone-built buildings are a feature of this village, which includes a circular lock-up and the ruins of a 12th-c castle, the latter on a high rock. Alton Towers is a 19th-c gothic mansion by Pugin, surrounded by fine gardens (OACT) and a large park. The latter contains model railways, boating lakes, and a paddling pool. The attractive Chunnet Valley lies NW.

ALTON BARNES, Wilts *7 SU16*
Set below Marlborough Downs in Pewsey Vale, Alton Barnes is overlooked by a stylish white horse which was cut from the turf of 964ft Milk Hill in 1812. The ancient Wansdyke crosses the nearby summit of the downs. A small Saxon nave and a chancel that was rebuilt in 1743 are features of the church.

ALTRINCHAM, Gt Manchester *17 SJ78*
A residential town with some light engineering, situated on the historic Bridgewater Canal near Manchester Airport. Dunham Massey Hall stands in a magnificent deer park, which is open for cars to drive through – although the house is not open to the public. Baguley Hall, with its fine half-timbered hall, stands 2½m NE (AM).

ALUM BAY, Isle of Wight *7 SZ38*
The bay is famous for its multi-coloured sandstone cliffs, and a sand and chalk beach allows access for bathing. One mile SW stand The Needles, a series of eroded chalk rocks that stretch out into the sea, with a lighthouse at the end. Beyond lie Scratchell's Bay and the 200ft chalk Grand Arch.

ALVINGHAM, Lincs *19 TF39*
A rare example of two churches in a single churchyard can be seen here. St Mary's has an 18th-c tower, and St Adelwold's – the only church of this dedication in England – is partly 14thc.

AMBERLEY, Glos *12 SO80*
Splendid views over the Cotswold countryside are available from the high-lying commons of Rodborough and Minchinhampton (both NT).

AMBERLEY, W Sussex *8 TQ01*
A picturesque village of thatched cottages and colourful gardens on the River Arun, which is spanned to the SW by a fine bridge. The castle was built for the Bishops of Chichester, and dates from the 14th and 16thc. The church shows magnificent Norman and early-English work, particularly in the chancel arch. There is a good view of the castle from water meadows known as Amberley Wild Brooks.

AMBLE, Northumberland *27 NU20*
A small seaport and resort with a sandy beach. Druridge Bay lies to the S The stretch of coast N of Amble has been designated an area of outstanding natural beauty. Coquet Island, a breeding ground for eider ducks, lies offshore.

AMBLESIDE, Cumbria *21 NY30*
A well-known Lake District centre near the head of Lake Windermere, Ambleside is popular with walkers and climbers. The church has a memorial window to the poet Wordsworth. A rush-bearing festival that dates from medieval times is held in late July each year. Decorated rushes on wood frames are carried to the parish church, where a brief service is conducted and gingerbread is presented to the rush bearers. Sheep-dog trials take place in September. Bridge House (NT), a curious little building spanning a stream, now serves as a NT information centre. There is a lot of NT property in the area, as well as many fine walks. Climbing is available W at Great Langdale. Stock Gill Force waterfall lies ½m E in a wooded setting, and 3½m S is the Blelham Bog national nature reserve.

AMERSHAM, Bucks *8 SU99*
A fine old country town where a spacious main street is lined with ancient inns and houses. Elmodesham House is an especially-fine Georgian building. The market hall and almshouses are 17thc. Shardeloes Park, an early work by Robert Adam, stands just outside the town on the Aylesbury road. The Chiltern countryside around the town is particularly beautiful in spring, and includes many beech-woods.

AMESBURY, Wilts *7 SU14*
Amesbury is situated on the River Avon, which is crossed here by a five-arched, Palladian-style bridge. Large army and RAF camps exist in the neighbourhood. Amesbury Abbey, set in a park, is mainly 19thc. Beech clumps in the park are said to indicate the positions of English and French ships, as they were at Trafalgar in 1805. The parish church is Norman and early English, with beautifully-

The Needles, Isle of Wight

carved 15th- and 16th-c roofs. John Gay wrote *The Beggar's Opera* here. Woodhenge, the site of a prehistoric wood circle, lies 1½m NE; concrete posts mark the positions of the original wooden uprights, thus indicating the shapes of buildings and the overall site.

AMPTHILL, Beds 14 TL03
An attractive old town with 17th-c almshouses and 18th-c inns. Ampthill Park House was built in 1694 by Lord Ashburnham, a favourite of Charles II, and is now a Cheshire Home for the disabled. It stands near the site of an earlier castle, which is commemorated by a cross with an inscription by Horace Walpole. The 300-acre park (open to pedestrians) is famous for its old oaks. Houghton Park House, the ruins of which stand 1½m NNE, was Bunyan's inspiration for the House Beautiful in his work *The Pilgrim's Progress*. Designed by Inigo Jones or one of his pupils, the house was built for Sir Philip Sidney's sister, the Countess of Pembroke.

AMPTON, Suffolk 15 TL87
This is the birthplace of Admiral Fitzroy, who, in his capacity as superintendent of the Meteorological Department, gave the first official weather forecast in 1861. The 14th- and 15th-c church contains the Royal Arms of Charles I, and the so-called Sealed Book, a copy of the revised Prayer Book of 1661.

AMWELL, GREAT, Herts 8 TL31
Close to Great Amwell, in the Lea Valley, stands a monument to Sir Hugh Myddelton; it was he who began the New River Scheme to provide London with better water in 1609. The church has a Norman apse.

ANCASTER, Lincs 19 SK94
The village lies on the old Roman road of Ermine Street, and was once a Roman station called *Causennae*. A few traces of the latter still remain. Famous Ancaster stone was widely used in medieval times for the building of many Lincolnshire churches. Quarries where this material was extracted lie 2m S of the village.

ANCHOR INN, Salop 11 SO18
Anchor Inn is situated on the edge of Clun Forest. Sweeping views across the Welsh-Border countryside can be enjoyed from nearby Kerry Pole, on 1,500ft Kerry Hill.

ANDOVER, Hants 7 SU34
A town of great antiquity that has taken on a new lease of life as an overspill centre for London's population and industry. The Old Town mill is sited on the River Anton, now converted to modern use, and the town boasts several old inns that were patronized by royalty. James II stayed at the Angel the night before his abdication in favour of William of Orange, and Charles I and George III used the Star and Garter. Remains of iron-age encampments exist on nearby hills and Harewood Forest lies to the E.

ANGMERING, W Sussex 8 TQ00
The Pigeon House, a medieval yeoman's dwelling, belongs to the Sussex Archaeological Trust. Ecclesden Manor dates from 1634. Roman remains have been excavated at Poling, to the W.

ANSTEY, Leics 18 SK50
Old cottages and a fine old five-arch packhorse bridge that is only 5ft wide are features of this village. Ned Ludd, the apprentice who initiated the 19th-c Luddite riots by smashing machinery that had been introduced into the local hosiery to mechanize his job, was born here.

ANSTY, W Sussex 8 TQ22
Legh Manor, an interesting restored 15th-c house in the care of Sussex Archaeological Trust, lies ½m S (OACT).

APETHORPE, Northants 19 TL09
A beautiful stone-built village of old houses, with the great Tudor and later Apethorpe Hall and park. The 13th- to 17th-c church includes the interesting Mildmay Chapel, which houses a monument to Sir Anthony Mildmay, who died in 1617. Above the recumbent effigies on his sarcophagus is a huge tented canopy, held by life-size figures of Charity, Justice, Wisdom, and Piety.

APPLEBY, Cumbria 26 NY62
Appleby is situated in the valley of the River Eden, 3m W of the Pennines. Not only does it lie in a district of great natural beauty, but it has many historic buildings and is an excellent touring centre.

The castle, well-sited above the Eden at the top of the main street, may have been started in the 15thc, but has since been altered and enlarged. It is now a private residence (not open to the public), but was once the home of Lady Anne Clifford, Countess of Pembroke and a prominent opponent of Cromwell. She fortified the castle for the King in 1648, and encouraged the garrison to hold out. Lady Anne died in 1678, and her tomb is in St Lawrence's Church at the lower end of Boroughgate, the main street.

The original church was burnt in 1174 and rebuilt in 1178. St Michael's Church, in Bongate, was restored by Lady Anne and has a hog-back gravestone, the oldest stone monument in the borough – probably dating back to early Norman times. St Anne's Hospital was founded by Lady Anne in 1651 as an almshouse.

The borough council meets in an ancient two-storied Moot Hall in the town centre. A tall 19th-c pillar known as the Low Cross stands near the cloisters in Boroughgate, and outside the castle gates, at the top end of the street, is a similar but older High Cross of the 17thc. Crackenthorpe Hall, 18thc and earlier, stands by the river 2m NW.

APPLEBY PARVA, Leics 18 SK30
The old grammar school of 1687 is considered one of the best of its period, and was erected by Sir William Wilson, with the approval of Sir Christopher Wren (OACT). At Appleby Magna (NW) is a moated and fortified 15th-c manor house which displays its original gatehouse.

APPLEDORE, Devon 5 SS43
A small, picturesque fishing village, with cobbled streets and a sandy beach. There are several little Georgian houses and attractive cottages, and a narrow street climbs steeply from the quay. The largest covered shipbuilding dock in Europe was opened here, on the Torridge estuary, in 1970.

APPLEDORE, Kent 9 TQ92
Once Appledore was sited on an estuary of the River Rother, but so much land has been reclaimed that it now stands inland, overlooking Romney Marsh. The Royal Military Canal runs through Appledore, and there are some pleasant old houses in the wide main street. N is Horne's Place, which preserves behind it a delightful little chapel of 1366 with a panelled roof. The church was rebuilt after the French partly destroyed it in 1380. It belonged to St Martin's Priory, Dover.

APPLEDRAM or APULDRAM, W Sussex 8 SU80
A parish on the Chichester Canal, with waterside walks where many species of wildfowl can be seen. The church contains a good deal of early-English work, and has an ancient chapel screen. Rymans, a 15th-c towered house, stands near by.

APPLETREEWICK, N Yorks 22 SE06
This delightfully-named hamlet is situated on the River Wharfe between Wharfedale and the moors, and lies in the shadow of Simon's Seat (1,592ft). Old houses in the area include Monk's Hall, Low Hall, and High Hall.

ARBURY HALL, Warwickshire 13 SP38
Arbury Hall (OACT) was originally Elizabethan and built on the site of a priory, but it was rebuilt in the 18thc as a gothic mansion. It is set amongst landscaped gardens and wide grounds. Marian Evans, later known as the novelist George Eliot, was born at the estate's south farm in 1819.

Arundel Castle, West Sussex

ARDINGLY, W Sussex *8 TQ32*
Pronounced Ardinglie this pretty village is complemented by its striking scenic situation. The mainly 14th-c church houses notable Culpeper and Wakehurst brasses. Elizabethan Wakehurst Place (NT) stands 1½m N, in 520 acres of gardens, woods, and lakes which are administered by the Royal Botanical Gardens, Kew (OACT). Ardingly College is a well-known public school which lies 1½m S. SW is the great Ouse viaduct, on the main Brighton railway line.

ARKSEY, S Yorks *22 SE50*
The local almshouses date from 1660, and the grammar school from 1683. The Norman and later church houses a 17th-c pulpit and font cover.

ARLESEY, Beds *14 TL13*
A village 4m S of Biggleswade, where the Talbot Chapel of the church (1331) contains an Easter sepulchre.

ARLINGTON, Devon *5 SS64*
Arlington Court (NT, OACT), dated 1820 to 1823, is deceptively plain outside but with a richly appointed interior. Two other interesting features of the hamlet are a heronry and a wild-duck sanctuary. Old horse-drawn vehicles can be seen in the stables.

ARLINGTON, E Sussex *8 TQ50*
A Cuckmere-valley village with a small flint Saxon-and-later church, preserving faint wall-paintings and a double-splayed Saxon window.

ARNCLIFFE, N Yorks *22 SD97*
Delightfully situated in the secluded Littondale Valley, this village includes a wide green and a mile-long limestone cliff named Yew Cogar Scar.

ARNOLD, Notts *18 SK54*
A residential town and dormitory for Nottingham. The 12th-c Church of St Mary, now much restored, has a fine 14th-c chancel with an Easter sepulchre and the tomb of its founder.

ARNSIDE, Cumbria *21 SD47*
This quiet resort on the Kent estuary has a sand and shingle beach. The ruined peel towers of Arnside and Hazelslack are near by.

ARRETON, Isle of Wight *7 SZ58*
A Roman villa has recently been excavated at the Robin Hill county park, Downend. The manor house is a good example of 17th-c work (OACT), and the church shows work from the 11th to 15thc, notably Saxon windows and a fine Tudor porch.

ARUNDEL, W Sussex *8 TQ00*
A charming old town on the River Arun, Arundel pre-dates the Conquest and is dominated by a superb castle (OACT) which guards the gap made by the Arun Valley. Seat of the Duke of Norfolk, the castle is of ancient origin and has a turbulent history. Much of the present structure was rebuilt in the 18thc, and the west-wing between 1890 and 1903. It stands in an extensive park which is open to the public, but not to cars or dogs, and includes Swanbourne Lake.

Another prominent building is the RC Church of St Philip Neri. This was built in 1870 and has recently been raised to cathedral status, with its own bishop. The 14th-c parish Church of St Nicholas was built by Henry Yevele, also architect of Canterbury Cathedral. It is unique in being three-quarters Protestant and one-quarter RC. A wall that separated the two has now been removed; visitors can see the Fitzalan Chapel, and the tombs of many past owners of the castle, through a 600-year-old wrought-iron screen. The museum in the cell-block beneath the town hall contains many items of local interest.

ASBY, GREAT, Cumbria *21 NY61*
The local rectory is unusual in having a fine 14th-c peel tower as its core. The 16th- to 18th-c Gaythorn Hall is 3m W.

ASCOT, Berks *8 SU96*
The Royal Ascot race meeting, started by Queen Anne in 1711, is held each June. It is still attended by members of the Royal family, who are driven in procession down the course before the meeting starts. Ascot is a good centre for walks and drives through Windsor Great Park.

ASH, Kent *9 TR25*
A village with very old cottages and a windmill. The church is 13th to 15thc, with several fine monuments and brasses.

ASH, Surrey *8 SU85*
The restored 12th- to 15th-c church has a tall shingled spire and a 16th-c timbered porch. The hamlet of Christmas Pie lies 3m E.

ASHBOURNE, Derbyshire *18 SK14*
Wide streets and handsome buildings feature in this market town, which is situated on the edge of the Peak District national park. St Oswald's Church has a 212ft spire, which George Eliot thought to be the finest in England. The building dates from the 13th to 14thc (a brass records its dedication by the Bishop of Coventry in 241), and is renowned for a white marble sculpture by Thomas Banks. The subject of this work is Penelope Boothby, a little girl who died at the age of five in 1791.
The former grammar school, now used as a dormitory for the new grammar school, is a fine Elizabethan building dating from c1585. Almost opposite is the 17th-c red brick mansion where Dr Johnson used to stay with his friend and poet, John Taylor. The Spalden and Owlfield almshouses are also of note, and the Green Man is an interesting Georgian inn with a gallows sign spanning the road. A curious and very traditional game of football is played every Shrove Tuesday. A white football is put down in the centre of the town, and an unlimited number of players – local men divided into two teams – try to score in the two goals by any means possible. These goals are the mill wheels at Clifton and Slurston – some three miles apart – and this mammoth game has been known to continue until Ash Wednesday.

ASHBURTON, Devon *5 SX76*
This attractive little town is sited on the River Yeo and includes several old slate-hung houses. In North Street one of these unusual buildings displays representations of playing cards. The decorated to perpendicular church has a fine grey-stone tower, and a characteristic Devon stair-turret.

ASHBURY, Oxon *13 SU28*
A downland village with a 15th-c manor house, now a farm, and a trans-Norman to perpendicular cruciform church with a good south doorway. The first Sunday school was founded here in 1777, first at the church, and later in some cottages.

ASHBY-DE-LA-ZOUCH, Leics *18 SK31*
Grecian-style houses, Georgian shops, and modern office-blocks blend together in unexpected harmony along the wide main streets of this market town.
A county-cricket ground is situated here. The ruins of the castle built by Lord Hastings in the 15thc (AM, OACT) are tucked away behind the main street. St Helen's Church contains a finger pillory, a form of punishment used up to the last century for anyone interrupting the sermon. The Countess of Huntingdon, who led a religious revival in the 18thc and died in 1791, is buried in the Hastings Chapel. Countess of Loudoun lived in the 19th-c manor house facing the castle, and her death (1879) is commemorated by a 70ft cross bearing an inscription by Disraeli. One mile NW is the site of the Tournament Field described in Sir Walter Scott's *Ivanhoe*. The town took the name of the La Zouch family to distinguish it from other Ashbys in the area. The La Zouch's once possessed an earlier settlement on the same site.

ASHBY ST LEDGERS, Northants
13 SP56
The manor house, 16thc and later, has associations with the Gunpowder Plot, which is said to have been hatched in a room over the timbered gatehouse in 1605.

ASHDON, Essex *14 TL54*
A village of great antiquity, with a 16th-c timbered guildhall or church-house, a restored 14th-c church with old woodwork, and the 300-year-old Rose and Crown inn which preserves 17th-c painted decorations. The Bartlow Hills to the N are the site of a group of barrows, thought to be Roman.

ASHDOWN FOREST, E Sussex *8 TQ43*
Some 14,000 acres of sloping heath and moorland, with rocky outcrops and patches of woodland. It is all that remains of the Forest of Anderida, a royal forest which covered most of the country in Roman times. The forest can be explored by minor roads running S from East Grinstead or N from Uckfield to Crowborough. Wych Cross is centrally situated for exploring the region.

ASHDOWN HOUSE, Berks *13 SU28*
This 17th-c mansion (NT) is made of chalk blocks and was probably built by John Webb and the first Lord Craven for Elizabeth of Bohemia (OACT). It stands in a wooded park high on the downs. Alfred's Castle, an iron-age hill fort, lies near by.

ASHFORD, Kent *9 TR04*
On the River Great Stour at its junction with the East Stour, Ashford is the market and business centre of an agricultural area. The parish church of St Mary the Virgin has a massive perpendicular tower. Some medieval houses remain, and there are steam locomotives and rolling stock on display at times in the railway workshop SE of the town centre. The museum of the Intelligence Corps is in Templer Barracks. Godinton House (1628) has carved panelling and attractive formal gardens, and lies 2m NW (OACT). There is a nature reserve 3m N at Hothfield Common, and 4m SE is Mersham-le-Hatch, an 18th-c house (Robert Adam) which is now a school.

ASHFORD-IN-THE-WATER, Derbyshire
18 SK16
A picturesque village on the river Wye, where well-dressing takes place. The church has several maiden's garlands, and there is a fine old bridge and tithe barn.

ASHINGDON, Essex *9 TQ89*
Ashingdon stands on the site of a battle fought in 1016 between Canute and Edmund Ironside. The much-restored church was founded in 1020.

ASHLEWORTH, Glos *12 SO82*
This town has a passenger ferry and quay on the River Severn. A splendid 15th-c tithe barn (NT), the 15th-c Court House, and the half-timbered vicarage are all of interest.

ASHOPTON VIADUCT, Derbyshire
18 SK18
The viaduct carries a road across the great Ladybower reservoir; farther N is the Derwent reservoir (Derwent estate, NT). The 17th-c Derwent packhorse bridge has been re-sited at Slippery Stones, on the Derbyshire and Yorkshire boundary.

ASHOVER, Derbyshire *18 SK36*
A village attractively situated below the hills, with a church which preserves a rare Norman lead font, an old screen, and the Babington Monument of 1518. It is thought that the Crispin Inn may date from 1416.

ASHTEAD, Surrey *8 TQ15*
St Giles Church contains 16th-c stained glass from Flanders. There is an inn with the unusual name of Leg of Mutton and Cauliflower, and Ashtead Park dates from 1790.

ASHTON-IN-MAKERFIELD,
Gt Manchester *17 SJ59*
An industrial town concerned with the manufacture of locks and hinges.

ASHTON KEYNES, Wilts *12 SU09*
A delightful village where the young Thames is spanned by a number of small bridges. The churchyard contains four ancient crosses, and others stand in the village.

ASHTON-UNDER-LYNE, Gt Manchester
18 SJ99
Shopping and commercial centre for SE Lancashire and NE Cheshire, this textile and engineering town lies on the River Tame, close to the Pennines. The church has some notable 15th-c painted glass.

ASHWELL, Herts *14 TL23*
A spacious village of Roman origin, boasting many beamed cottages with decorative external plasterwork (pargeting). The mainly 14th-c church has a small spire on top of the lofty tower, and a carving of the old St Paul's Cathedral in its base. The lych-gate in Mill Street dates from about 1450. A restored timbered house is now the village museum; relics of local Roman, stone-age, and iron-age cultures are all on display here.

ASKHAM, Cumbria *26 NY52*
This attractive village stands on the edge of the great park of Lowther Castle. The old hall is partly 16thc.

ASKRIGG, N Yorks *22 SD99*
A delightful Wensleydale village close to glens and waterfalls. Colby Hall dates from 1633 and is now a farm. The 15th-c Nappa Hall stands 1½m E.

ASPLEY GUISE, Beds *13 SP93*
Aspley Guise is picturesquely situated on hills, and set amid pines and heaths. The Old House is 16thc, and Aspley House is a fine late 17th-c building attributed to a design by Wren.

ASTBURY, Cheshire *17 SJ86*
A pleasant village with a magnificent 14th- to 15th-c church displaying notable Jacobean and earlier woodwork. The rectory is a fine 18th-c house.

ASTHALL, Oxon *13 SP21*
The fine Elizabethan manor house stands on a hill near the trans-Norman to perpendicular church. In the north chapel of the latter is an old stone altar and a fine 14th-c tomb.

ASTLEY ABBOTS, Salop *17 SO79*
The church, dedicated to St Calixtus (Pope from AD217 to AD222), houses some old glass, a maiden's garland, and a Norman font. Binnal, a black-and-white house, dates from 1611. Dunvall Hall is a half-timbered Elizabethan house.

ASTON, W Midlands *12 SP08*
A busy suburb with a university, Aston is sited on the N outskirts of Birmingham. The splendid Jacobean Hall, said to be the original of Washington Irving's *Bracebridge Hall*, is now a museum. Aston Church was rebuilt in 1879 but retains its 15th-c tower; it contains many old monuments.

ASTON CANTLOW, Warwickshire
12 SP15
The mainly early-English church is the one in which Shakespeare's parents are supposed to have been married. In the tower is a medieval clock. The former guildhall is an interesting timbered building

ASTON-ON-CLUN, Salop *11 SO38*
An annual ceremony on May 29 commemorates a local bequest, and is conducted by the decorating of a poplar tree – known as the Arbor Tree – with numerous flags.

ASTON ROWANT, Oxon *8 SU79*
The church is Norman to decorated, with several fine brasses and some ancient glass. To the S rises Beacon Hill (800ft), partly a forest nature reserve, set in the Chiltern escarpment.

ASTON SUBEDGE, Glos *12 SP14*
Attractive views of the Vale of Evesham and its many orchards may be enjoyed from here. The village houses are built of characteristic Cotswold stone, and both the manor farm and old school date from the 17thc. To the S is Dover's Hill, where Dover's games were held between 1612 and 1852; a monument commemorates Captain Dover, the originator of the games.

ATCHAM, Salop *17 SJ50*
A pleasant village on a bend of the River Severn, crossed here by a seven-arch bridge built by John Gwynne in 1768. Another fine bridge, built by Robert Mylne, crosses the nearby Tern. The church is built partly of stones taken from the ruins of Roman *Viroconium* (Wroxeter). It has a Norman doorway, a 13th-c chancel, a 500-year-old timber roof in the nave, and fine tombstones that are even older. The Mytton and Mermaid is a pleasant Georgian inn facing the lodge of Attingham Park. The latter was built for Lord Berwick in 1785 (OACT).

ATHERINGTON, Devon *5 SS52*
This attractive village of old cottages includes a church containing a superb carved rood-screen surmounted by its original gallery (very rare).

ATHERSTONE, Warwickshire *18 SP39*
A small boot and shoe-manufacturing town on the Roman Watling Street. Some of the 18th-c houses are in good condition, and street football is played on Shrove Tuesday.

ATHERTON, Gt Manchester *21 SD60*
An industrial town with collieries and cotton mills. Chowbent Chapel, built in 1721, contains old pews and a three-decker pulpit.

ATTENBOROUGH, Notts *18 SK53*
The house which was the birthplace of General Ireton, Cromwell's son-in-law, is still standing. The church retains grotesque 12th-c nave capitals.

ATTINGHAM PARK, Salop *17 SJ50*
A large NT estate (OACT). The house was designed in the classic style by George Stewart for the first Lord Berwick (1785), and has a notable interior displaying fine furniture and pictures. The grounds were landscaped for the second Lord Berwick by Humphrey Repton.

AUDLEM, Cheshire *17 SJ64*
An ancient market town with a market cross, and a restored perpendicular church showing a fine oak roof. Black-and-white Moss Hall is 17thc.

AUDLEY END, Essex *14 TL53*
Superbly situated in a lake-watered park, this great 17th-c mansion (AM) is only a part of the original structure. The house was built for Thomas Howard, Earl of Suffolk, and contains notable state rooms and some later work by Robert Adam (OACT).

AUST, Avon *12 ST58*
Aust stands on the S bank of the River Severn. The car ferry to Beachley was replaced in 1966 by the Severn Bridge, which carries the M4 to Wales. Aust Passage, clay and limestone cliffs known to geologists and archaeologists as part of the Westbury Beds, has yielded prehistoric animal fossils of great importance.

AVEBURY, Wilts *7 SU06*
A small village on the site of one of the largest stone circles in the world. This ancient structure comprises about 100 standing stones, measures about 1,200ft in diameter, and encloses an area of over 28 acres. The circle is surrounded by a huge ditch more than 40ft wide at the top, and of varying depths. Inside the large circle are two much smaller circles, also formed of standing stones. Each of these is some 300ft in diameter. At one time a 50ft wide avenue of standing stones ran for over a mile to connect with two other concentric circles at Overton Hill, where there is also a large barrow. It is thought the Avebury complex was built during the early bronze age as a kind of open temple.

cont

Elizabethan Avebury Manor (OACT) has a box-hedge garden, and the museum displays a wealth of interesting remains from local archaeological excavations. The church is partly Norman, with a 15th-c tower. Windmill Hill (NT, 2m NW) is the first neolithic camp in England to be fully excavated. The purpose of Silbury Hill (1m S), 130ft high and the largest artificial mound in Europe, is still unknown.

AVELEY, Essex *8 TQ58*
The skeletons of a mammoth and a straight-tusked elephant were found in a local gravel pit in 1964. The restored church contains much Norman work, and a fine Flemish brass of 1370.

AVENING, Glos *12 ST89*
The local church preserves Norman work and two interesting 17th-c monuments. Avening Court is an old house that has been restored. Local inns serve the dish 'pig's face' on Pigs Face Sunday, in mid-September, to commemorate the killing of wild boar.

AVINGTON, Berks *7 SU36*
The interesting little Norman church is almost unspoiled.

AVINGTON, Hants *7 SU53*
A village in the Itchen Valley. The river Itchen forms a lake behind the 17th-c mansion of Avington Park, once occupied by Charles II and Nell Gwynne (OACT). The ballroom ceiling was painted by Verrio. The red-brick 18th-c church has a three-decker pulpit, box pews, and a squire's pew.

AVON DASSETT, Warwickshire *13 SP45*
This village is situated below the Dassett Hills. The rebuilt church has a 13th-c stone coffin in a recess, with a remarkable carving of a deacon. To the NW is the isolated church of Burton Dassett, which displays 13th-c animal carvings.

AVONMOUTH, Avon *6 ST57*
A port of Bristol built round the mouth of the River Avon. The docks are highly mechanized and handle a wide variety of imports and exports. A large bridge carries the M5 across the river (due to open 1975).

AWLISCOMBE, Devon *6 ST10*
The perpendicular church preserves a restored 15th-c stone screen, and Royal Arms of the 17thc. On a buttress of the west door is a stone with the carved outline of a woman's hand, dated 1708 and associated with a local bridal custom.

AXBRIDGE, Somerset *6 ST45*
A very ancient town at the foot of the Mendip Hills in the Cheddar country. Manor House and King John's Hunting Lodge (NT) are two of the numerous old houses. The town hall preserves stocks, bull-baiting gear, and a money-changer's table of 1627. Ambleside Water Gardens and Aviaries (2m SW at Lower Weare) include shrub gardens, ornamental water-fowl, birds, rabbits, and guinea pigs (OACT).

AXHOLME, ISLE OF, Humberside *23 SE70*
A fertile area of flat agricultural land, formerly in the Lindsey district of Lincolnshire, between the River Trent and the Humber estuary.

AXMINSTER, Devon *6 SY29*
This little town on the River Axe gave its name to a kind of carpet which was invented by Thomas Whitty in 1775, and resembled Turkish carpets. Caster Hill House, where they were originally made, can still be seen. When the firm went bankrupt in 1835 the looms were sold to a weaver in Wilton, Wiltshire, now also famous as a carpet town. A new carpet factory was opened here in 1937. In the town centre is a church with a Norman door and a Jacobean pulpit. The original church was founded before 755 and was endowed by Athelstan after his victory over the Danes in 937 – a battle in which five kings and seven earls are said to have fallen. Ashe House (2m SSW) is on the site of the Drake family home, and was the birthplace of the great Duke of Marlborough in 1650.

AXMOUTH, Devon *6 SY29*
A pretty village of thatched cottages on the Axe estuary. The church has a Norman doorway and wall paintings. Stedcombe House dates from 1695. High above, on Hawkesdown Hill, is an ancient settlement. The coast in the vicinity forms an area of outstanding natural beauty, and the coastline E of Axmouth has been shaped by landslips, caused by percolating water washing greensand out from beneath the chalk. On Christmas Day, 1839, the Dowlands Landslip was created by the fall of some 45 acres of arable land, weighing an estimated 800 million tons, and leaving a six-mile gash that stretched almost to Lyme Regis in Dorset. Part of the area is included in the Axmouth to Lyme Regis, Undercliff nature reserve.

AYLESBURY, Bucks *8 SP81*
Now a busy county town, Aylesbury was a stronghold from at least AD571. The statue of John Hampden in Market Square is a symbol of the town's support for the Parliamentary side in the Civil War.

The town centre preserves a little old-world charm, with its narrow Tudor alleyways and 17th-c houses centred around four squares – Temple Square, St Mary's Square, the Market Square, and Kingsbury. Many of the older buildings are situated in St Mary's Square, where mellow terraced houses line three sides. The fourth is occupied by a wooded churchyard and the old church itself. The massive tower dates from the 13thc, and is surmounted by a 17th-c lead clock-tower and spire, visible for miles around. A finely-carved Norman font can be seen in the south aisle. Much of the church was restored between 1848 and 1869, when the striking perpendicular west window was inserted. Next to the church is Prebendal House, an 18th-c building which now serves as a school, but was once the home of John Wilkes, Member of Parliament for Aylesbury (1757 to 1764).

The county museum in Church Street (OACT) is in fine 18th-c buildings, and contains many interesting relics of Buckinghamshire's history. Just off Market Square is the King's Head hotel (NT), which dates from the 15thc and has a splendid old window, a gateway, and a cobbled courtyard. The S side of Market Square is dominated by the county hall, built about 1720 but severely damaged by fire in 1970. Besides these old buildings there are many new ones; Aylesbury is a progressive town, and has attracted several new industries. The new county-council buildings are outstanding.

AYLESFORD, Kent *9 TQ75*
The River Medway is crossed here by a 14th-c bridge (AM). The Friars, an old house (OACT) now tenanted by the Carmelites, retains part of the original friary of 1284. The friars make pottery which can be bought in a shop by the rose garden. One m S, just off the London to Maidstone road, is the British Legion village at Preston Hall. This rehabilitation centre for invalid ex-servicemen was

1 County Hall
2 County Museum
3 King's Head Hotel
4 Prebendal House
5 St Mary's Church

established in 1921. On the Downs (1½m NE) is Kit's Coty House (AM), comprising three standing stones capped by a fourth, the remains of a neolithic burial chamber. A battle was fought hereabouts in AD455, in which the Jute invaders decisively defeated the Britons.

AYLSHAM, Norfolk *15 TG12*
An old market town on the River Bure, still with many attractive Georgian houses. The church, early-English to perpendicular, has a splendid 15th-c font. The old hall dates from 1689. Blickling Hall stands in gardens and a fine park 1½m NW, and has a Jacobean façade. It dates from 1615 (NT, OACT).

AYMESTREY, Herefs & Worcs *12 SO46*
Aymestrey is a quiet village in a picturesque setting. The church has a 15th-c tower and houses a very fine screen.

AYNHO, Northants *13 SP53*
Stone and thatched cottages exist here. Aynhoe Park (OACT), a 17th-c house which was later altered by Sir John Soane, has Cartwright portraits lining the staircase. The school dates from 1671, and the church was built in the style of Vanbrugh in 1723.

AYOT ST LAWRENCE, Herts *8 TL11*
The chief interest in this charming little village lies in Shaw's Corner, George Bernard Shaw's home from 1906 to his death in 1950. The house (NT, OACT), is preserved as it was in his lifetime, and his ashes were scattered over the garden. Lullingstone Silk Farm is at Georgian Ayot House, and was transferred there from Lullingstone in Kent (OACT). Beside the ruins of a 14th-c church is another church, built with a Grecian façade by Nicholas Revett from 1778 to 1789.

AYSGARTH, N Yorks *22 SE08*
A Wensleydale village on the River Ure, with a museum of horse-drawn transport.

Bakewell's famous Saxon cross

A series of waterfalls can be reached by following a lane running N past the church.

AYTON, GREAT, N Yorks *22 NZ51*
This pretty village lies beneath the moors. Captain Cook went to school here, and the old schoolhouse is now a museum. The cottage in which he lived was removed, stone by stone, to Australia. Its place is now marked by an obelisk of Australian stone. Another monument to this famous sailor can be seen to the SE on Easbey Moor. NE rises Roseberry Topping, a 1,057ft landmark in the Cleveland Hills from which the North Sea can be seen.

BABBACOMBE, Devon *5 SX96*
N of Torquay – of which it forms part – Babbacombe is well-known for its attractive bay and beach. A model village is set in four-acre gardens, and a little to the SE is Kent's Cavern, an extensive cave of great archaeological interest. Prehistoric elephant, hyena, tiger, and rhinoceros bones have been found here, plus various weapons of primitive man. Some of these are now in the Torquay Museum.

BABCARY, Somerset *6 ST52*
In 1764 Parson Woodforde, author of the *Diary of a Country Parson*, became vicar of the local church. This building has a 15th-c tower and a Jacobean pulpit. A flower is carved on a window recess, near a stone basin on the south-side of the altar.

BACTON, Herefs & Worcs *11 SO33*
This tiny village is in the Golden Valley. The church houses a monument showing Queen Elizabeth I, and one of her maids-of-honour – possibly a local girl who may have made the exquisite 400-year-old altar cloth.

BACTON, Norfolk *15 TG33*
A small, attractive village on the coast, with zig-zag breakwaters, sands, and bathing. North-Sea gas is brought ashore at this point, and installations have been set up for this purpose. Bromholm Priory is now in ruins, but originated as a 12th-c foundation and was mentioned by Chaucer (½m S).

BACUP, Lancs *21 SD82*
Bacup is a typical mill town of terraces and industrial buildings. Bleak moors that rise to 1,300ft above the town are part of the ancient Forest of Rossendale. A former inn, built in the 18thc, houses the local natural history society's museum. Thieveley Pike Hill rises to 1,474ft at the head of the River Irwell, 2½m N.

BADDOW, GREAT, Essex *9 TL70*
A number of attractive Georgian houses stand in the village, and the exterior of the church is noted for its exceptionally fine Tudor brickwork, including stepped battlements. A few Roman tiles incorporated in the church walls were obviously taken from a building, though no trace of this exists.

BADGEWORTH, Glos *12 SO91*
A village near Cheltenham, where the church is noted for its decorated-style windows with carved ornamentation. To the NE is the smallest nature reserve in England (346sq yds).

BADMINTON, Avon *12 ST88*
Badminton House has given its name to both a summer drink (made of claret, soda, and sugar) and to the familiar game played with net, rackets, and a shuttlecock. The seat of the Dukes of Beaufort for centuries, it is a 17th- and 18th-c Palladian mansion, partly by Kent, with fine paintings and furniture (OACT). Some of the carving is by Grinling Gibbons. Visitors can visit the kennels of the Beaufort Hunt. The three-day Badminton Horse Trials are held in the great park every April.

BAGSHOT, Surrey *8 SU96*
The road through Bagshot was once the coaching road between London and Exeter; the town was a horse-changing stop. Bagshot Park (1879) was the house of HRH the Duke of Connaught and is now an army chaplains' museum (OACT by written permission). Bagshot Heath extends SE to join Bisley Common – of rifle shooting fame – and together they form an expanse of open country that was once notorious for highwaymen.

BAINBRIDGE, N Yorks *22 SD99*
Small stone houses line a picturesque green from which a horn is sounded at 2200hrs in winter. This ancient custom dates back centuries, and began as a way of guiding travellers to the village. Brough Hill is topped by a Roman fort, and Addlebrough Hill rises to 1,564ft in the SE. Semer Water, 2m S, is the largest lake in Yorkshire; a picturesque by-road through the hamlet of Countersett gives striking views of its hilly setting.

BAKEWELL, Derbyshire *18 SK26*
A River Wye town that has given its name to the recipe for a kind of pastry cake, said to have been invented when a cook at The Rutland Arms misunderstood instructions and spread egg mixture over the fruit in a strawberry tart. The river is spanned by a fine old bridge, and the 12th- to 14th-c cruciform church has a famous Saxon cross (AM) in the churchyard. A number of old houses are built of the local brownstone – notably Holme Hall (1626) and Bath House (1697).

In the Old House museum there is a 15th-c screen. The town is a convenient centre for exploring the hills and caves of the neighbourhood, and for visiting the local stately homes of Chatsworth and Haddon Hall. The Wye passes through picturesque Monsal Dale (3m NW), which can be viewed from the B6465 road to Tideswell. On the S side of Lathkill Dale, 3m S of Bakewell, 123 acres of mixed ash and elm woodland have been leased from the Peak Park planning board to form part of the first natural nature reserve in the Peak District national park.

BALDOCK, Herts *14 TL23*
An ancient town with many relics of the past. Old houses can be seen in the side streets, and the High Street displays several fine Georgian buildings. The Wynn almshouses, founded in 1621, were endowed 'To The World's End'.

BAMBURGH, Northumberland *27 NU13*
A quiet resort with bathing from a sandy beach. The massive restored Norman castle (OACT) that dominates the village was once the seat of the first Kings of

Northumbria. Grace Darling was born here in 1815, and is buried in St Aidan's churchyard. In 1838 she and her father rowed out to save five people from a wrecked steamboat, the Forfarshire. There is a Grace Darling museum in the town. The church of St Aidan is mainly 13thc, and has a fine chancel and vaulted crypt of the same period. To the NW lies almost land-locked Budle Bay, the haunt of many wild birds. Farne Islands (NT), situated 4m off the coast, are designated an area of outstanding natural beauty, and are breeding grounds for sea birds. These islands were once the home of St Aidan (died 651) and St Cuthbert (died 687).

BAMPTON, Devon 5 SS92
This town lies on the edge of Exmoor. Ponies are brought in from the moor for a pony fair every October. The church is 14th to 15thc, and has several ancient yew trees in the churchyard. Georgian houses can be seen in the street.

BAMPTON, Oxon 13 SP30
The church of this large village has a fine 13th-c spire and 14th-c reredos. Many old stone houses and Georgian façades can be seen, as well as an ancient school. There is Morris dancing in the streets on each Spring Bank-Holiday Monday. A plum cake is impaled on a sword and carried round the streets during these festivities; those who eat it are said to enjoy good luck.

BANBURY, Oxon 13 SP44
This busy industrial, cattle-marketing, and shopping centre has retained much of its old charm and interest. The town dates back to Saxon times, but only a few buildings constructed earlier than the 17thc survive. Banbury Cakes, made from puff pastry filled with dried, spiced fruit, can still be bought locally. The original Banbury Cross of nursery rhyme fame was destroyed in 1602 by the Puritans, but a replica was erected in its place during 1859. Although the local citizens have been noted for their tendency to destroy ancient buildings (eg blowing up the old church in the 18thc rather than restore it), a number of attractive old houses and inns are still to be seen. The vicarage of 1649 is of particular note.

BANSTEAD, Surrey 8 TQ25
Although it is within easy reach of London, and largely a dormitory for that city, Banstead is still surrounded by rolling downs and open country. Excavations near Burgh Heath in 1952 revealed the foundations of a 12th-c manor at Preston Hawe.

BANWELL, Avon 6 ST35
Named after a well that was believed to have curative powers, the village is noted for a cave which was discovered by a local man in 1824. The bones of several wild animals dating from prehistoric times were found here, and are now on display in the county museum, Taunton. The 14th-c church is close to a Victorianized manor house, with towers and turrets displaying pinnacled buttresses.

BARCHESTON, Warwickshire 13 SP23
A tiny village that is famous as the birthplace of tapestry weaving in England. This craft was started here by William Sheldon in the 16thc. Sheldon tapestry maps of the English counties are highly prized, and examples are preserved in the museums of York and Oxford. The little church has several fine alabaster tombs, and a carved 14th-c font.

BARDFIELD, Essex 14 TL63
There are three attractive Bardfield villages on the River Pant – Great Bardfield, Little Bardfield, and Bardfield Saling. At Little Bardfield there is a 16th-c hall, and St Katherine's Church has a Saxon tower. Great Bardfield has a very fine restored windmill, a 14th-c church (St Mary's) with a 15th-c chancel screen, and several medieval and Georgian houses. A 16th-c museum sells corn dollies, the traditional straw figures that used to be made and placed on hayricks to celebrate a successful harvest. The Bardfield Oxlip (*Primula elatior*), still grows in the district.

BARDON MILL, Northumberland 27 NY76
The only Roman milestone (AM) still in its original position can be seen N at Chesterholm, near the line of the Roman Wall.

BARDWELL, Suffolk 15 TL97
The 15th-c church has a tall west tower, fine flushwork decoration, a chancel of 1553, and some 15th-c stained glass. Early 16th-c Bardwell Hall is built of plaster and brick.

BARFRESTON, Kent 9 TR25
Near Dover, this tiny village boasts one of the finest examples of a Norman church in England. It was built (1080) of flint and stone from Caen, and carries rich stone carvings on its inner walls. The south doorway is especially notable, and the church bell hangs from a wood frame in an ancient churchyard yew tree.

BARKING, Gt London 8 TQ48
This London Borough was formed in 1965 by the merging of Barking and Dagenham. Local industries include Barking power station and Dagenham Docks, plus installations concerned with the manufacture of cars, chemicals, paints, rubber, plastics, and wood products.

The district has been inhabited from very early times. Bronze-age and Roman remains have been found, and both Barking and Dagenham derive their names from early Saxon settlers. There was once a large and powerful abbey at Barking, but this was demolished in 1540, and the roof-lead shipped to Greenwich for repairs to Greenwich Palace. The only part of the structure now remaining is a 15th-c gate-tower. The names of Abbey Road and Abbey Playing Field commemorate its site.

St Margaret's dates from the 13thc and was built within the abbey precincts. It became the parish church of Barking in 1300, and thus survived the Dissolution. Explorer Captain Cook was married here in 1762. The parish church of St Peter and St Paul was also built early in the 13thc, but has been subjected to a great deal of restoration work. Eastbury Manor House is a fine Elizabethan brick structure dated 1572 (NT, OACT). The district is richly endowed with parks and playing fields and, perhaps as a result, has produced some outstanding footballers.

BARLASTON, Staffs 17 SJ83
This is the site of the famous Wedgwood pottery and museum (OACT). The latter displays interesting examples of Josiah Wedgwood's experimental designs, as well as an exhibition of 18th- to 20th-c ceramics. The works were founded at Etruria, between Stoke-on-Trent and Newcastle-under-Lyme.

BARLBOROUGH, Derbyshire 18 SK47
This little village of stone-built red-roofed houses contains Barlborough Hall, a beautiful Elizabethan house built in 1583 and now a RC preparatory school (OACT). The Norman church has been rebuilt, but original arches may be seen between the north aisle and nave. It appears in the Domesday Book, underlined in red.

BARLEY, Herts 14 TL33
The Fox and Hounds inn, rebuilt after a fire, has a picturesque sign spanning the width of the road. A fine example of an early 19th-c post mill can be seen 2m E, at Chishill.

BARNACK, Cambs 19 TF00
The church's Saxon tower is surmounted by one of England's earliest spires. Barnack stone has been used in the construction of many buildings in surrounding villages and towns. Walcot Hall dates back to 1678.

BARNARD CASTLE, Co Durham 22 NZ01
A market town on a bank above the Tees, admired by Sir Walter Scott and by Charles Dickens. The latter may have written *Nicholas Nickleby* at the King's Head Inn. The ruined 12th-c castle has a three-storeyed keep (AM, OACT).

The first castle here was built before 1100 by Guy de Baliol, Lord of Bailleul in Picardy, who was given the land by William Rufus. Soon after 1150, the castle was rebuilt in stone by Bernard Baliol, nephew or great nephew of Guy de Baliol, and the town grew around it.

Bowes Museum is one of the finest in the country, and is housed in a mansion of 1869 which is built in the style of a French chateau. Founded by John Bowes, son of the tenth Earl of Strathmore and Mary Miller of Stainton, it contains an exhibition of past local life and a splendid art-collection. The latter covers paintings, porcelain, tapestry, and furniture.

BARNES, Gt London 8 TQ27
A Thames-side residential district, with Regency terraces and the new buildings of St Paul's School. Several attractive old houses can be seen near the pond and common.

BARNET, Gt London 8 TQ29
This borough has several charming rural areas. Mill Hill is a particular example, with its picturesque weather-boarded houses grouped together on the green ridge that gave the area its name. The Mill-Hill non-conformist public school is well known. An expanse of unspoiled country, once forming part of Enfield Chase and incorporating the delightful Hadley Woods, stretches for 2m from Cockfosters to the village of Monken Hadley. An obelisk on Hadley Green marks the place where the Battle of Barnet was fought in 1471. This was a Yorkist victory in which Warwick the Kingmaker was slain. The tower of the nearby church bears a copper cresset placed there in the 18thc.

cont

This was filled with oil and used as a beacon.

A feature of Hendon (to the S) is the Welsh Harp, an expanse of water near the North Circular road. It takes its name from a neighbouring inn, and is now a popular place for sailing. Barnet Fair is held annually in the first week of September.

BARNHAM, W Sussex 8 SU90
This village has a Norman and 13th-c church, with an early-English oak framework dividing the nave and chancel. Barnham Court is a beautiful 17th-c brick house with Dutch gables.

BARNOLDSWICK, Lancs 21 SD84
Rolls-Royce engines are now made in this old town. The perpendicular church of St Mary-le-Gill, Coates, houses Jacobean pews and a three-decker pulpit. Coates Hall was built c1700.

BARNSLEY, Glos 12 SP00
The church in this pretty Cotswold village has a good 16th-c tower and two ancient carved tables. Sir Isaac Newton's hidden library was discovered at Barnsley Park, a fine late-Renaissance house, in 1927.

BARNSLEY, W Yorks 22 SE30
Mentioned in the Domesday Book, Barnsley was an early coal-mining area and is still the administrative centre of the Yorkshire coalfield. Coal and glass are its main products, but many other industries exist here. The town hall is an imposing building, and the nearby College of Technology is a good example of modern architecture. In St Mary's Church there is an 18th-c organ by Snetzler. Remains of the 14th-c Monk Bretton Priory (AM) can be seen 1½m E; 2m SW is the palatial 18th-c Wentworth Castle – now housing a college of education – in the grounds of which are several obelisks and a folly known as Stainborough Castle. Cannon Hall, 5m NW near Cawthorne, was built c1765 by Carr of York, and is now a museum and art gallery.

BARNSTAPLE, Devon 5 SS53
Barnstaple has been the administrative and commercial centre of North Devon since Saxon times. It celebrated the millenary of its Charter in 1930, and may well be the oldest borough in England. Although an important port and a market for the wool trade for several centuries, shipping declined with the improvement of road transport and the coming of the railway in 1854. Other industries have since led to the town's continued growth, and it has expanded beyond the angle of land between the Taw and the Yeo to which it was previously confined. River Taw is spanned by a 13th-c bridge, built by a London merchant who saw a woman drowned here while attempting to cross the river. This has since been widened.

The Square at the town end of Long Bridge is the hub of the settlement. The Strand runs from here to Castle Street and the site of the ancient castle. Queen Anne's Walk, an 18th-c colonnade on the river side of the Strand, was once the town's merchant exchange. The Tome Stone that can be seen here was used as a money table. Castle House stands in the grounds of the former castle, and was partly built with stones from the previous structure – of which only the mound now remains. The 16th-c Church of St Peter is easily identified by its twisted lead spire, and contains the monuments of many wealthy citizens. The ancient grammar school was endowed in 1646, but is much older. Two of its more notable pupils were Bishop Jewel and John Gay, the latter, author of The Beggar's Opera. This school was once housed in the 11th-c Chantry of St Anne, in the churchyard of St Peter's. Friday is market day, and a variety of stalls sell country produce, wicker-work, and pottery.

Pilton lies N of the river and includes the Church of St Mary the Virgin, a 14th-c building on the site of a priory. Renaissance memorials to members of the Chichester family, a fine carved stone pulpit, an oak screen of a unique type, and a 15th-c font cover are all housed in this interesting building. Arlington Court (NT), built (1822) in fine grounds (OACT), stands 7m NE.

BARNWELL, Northants 14 TL08
The remains of a 13th-c castle can be seen near the attractive Elizabethan manor house. To the SW is Jacobean Lilford Hall, in picturesque gardens.

BARROW, Salop 17 SJ60
The church's Saxon chancel is notable for its arch. The nave and tower are Norman, and the brick south porch dates from 1705.

BARROWFORD, Lancs 21 SD83
A small textile town with several 16th- and 17th-c houses. Ruined Roughlee Hall and 1,831ft Pendle Hill to the NW, are both associated with the Lancashire witches of the 17thc. Two old women who were seized for practising witchcraft implicated several other people, including Dame Alice Nutter of Roughlee Hall. Up until this time the lady's reputation was quite unblemished, but she was unable to prove her innocence. This, coupled with the machinations of relatives eager to appropriate her property, caused her to be brought to trial at Leicester, where she was found guilty and later burned.

BARROW-IN-FURNESS, Cumbria 21 SD26
Situated at the S end of the Furness peninsula, this town is a major engineering and ship-building centre, and includes the building of Polaris submarines among its achievements. The majority of development has been recent, the population increasing from under 700 to over 64,000 in the last hundred years; the town's boundaries now encompass 35sqm and contain four islands.

The largest, Walney Island, shelters the harbour from the open sea and is a residential area in its own right. It is connected to the mainland by a modern opening bridge, and offers the facilities of a seaside resort. The other off-shore islands of Roa, Piel, and Foulney are much smaller. Piel has a fine ruined castle and an inn whose landlord is known as the King of Piel. The industry in Barrow itself is concentrated near the railway and docks, and the visitor can still enjoy miles of unspoilt coastline. N of the town are the magnificent remains of Furness Abbey.

BARROW-ON-HUMBER, Humberside 23 TA02
The church is mainly of the perpendicular style, and an old sundial stands in the churchyard. Ancient earthworks and a large circular mound can be seen 1m NW. A ferry plies between here and Hull.

BARROW-ON-SOAR, Leics 18 SK51
The village sign depicts an extinct aquatic reptile – the plesiosaurus – and was erected in 1953. The old hospital is dated 1694, and there are almshouses of 1825.

BARTHOMLEY, Cheshire 17 SJ75
This village boasts numerous black-and-white houses, and the only English church dedicated to St Bertoline. The building has a massive tower and notable panelled roof. The White Lion inn dates from 1614.

BARTON-ON-SEA, Hants 7 SZ29
This modern resort has low cliffs of soft clay which form part of the Barton Beds, a geological series famous for its vast abundance of Eocene fossils – shells, bones, and shark remains. The narrow sand and shingle beach provides access for bathing.

BARTON STACEY, Hants 7 SU44
The 12th-c and later church has a fine tower in the perpendicular style. Ancient tumuli can be seen in the area.

BARTON TURF, Norfolk 15 TG32
A small Broads village with a church containing one of the most famous painted screens of this district. Barton Broad lies to the E.

BARTON-UPON-HUMBER, Humberside 23 TA02
St Peter's Church has a notable Saxon tower and contains items of old armour. St Mary's Church is of the 13thc, and many early 19th-c houses are to be seen in the town. The S extremity of the new Humber bridge will be sited here.

BARWICK, Somerset 6 ST51
Richly-carved bench-ends dating from 1533 are housed in the church. A number of follies and a curious grotto are contained in Barwick House Park.

BARWICK-IN-ELMET, W Yorks 22 SE43
A maypole still stands on the green, and there are large earthworks in the vicinity. One of the latter was originally a Celtic stockade, and subsequently a Norman fortress. The ancient Kiddal Hall is now a farm.

BASILDON, Essex 9 TQ78
The district of Basildon has an area of 42sqm and is one of the largest in England. The boundaries include the three towns of Basildon, Billericay, and Wickford, plus a number of villages. Basildon New Town is one of the eight new conurbations around London, and was first planned for a population of 50,000. This was in 1949; before development had proceeded very far, the corporation entrusted with the project were planning for double the original estimate, and current forecasts predict a population of 134,000 by 2001.

Large industrial areas are sited alongside the London to Southend arterial road (A127), with the Ford Motor Company's tractor plant sandwiched between them. A third industrial area has been started at Burnt Mills.

BASING, Hants 7 SU65

Basing House was razed to the ground by Cromwell's troops in 1645 after a two-year siege. All that remains are large earthworks, cellars, and a secret tunnel. Among the prisoners taken was the famous architect Inigo Jones. The fine tithe barn in the village served as stable and billet for the Cromwellian army, and the church houses some notable tombs to the Paulets, Marquesses of Winchester. Basing House has recently been taken over by the Hampshire County Council, and at the time of publishing was closed to the public due to its dangerous condition.

BASINGSTOKE, Hants 7 SU65

A development area designed to take overspill from London, Basingstoke is a rapidly expanding industrial centre which includes the new headquarters of the AA.

The district has been inhabited from earliest times, although nearby Basing village claimed greater importance until the construction of the Basingstoke canal in 1789, and later the railway in 1839. The canal, now in a state of disuse, provided access to the Thames and London. An extensive cloth industry had developed by the early 17thc, and some timbered buildings of this period survive in a restored state. One of the town's older buildings is the Church of St Michael and all Angels. This contains work of the 12th, 15th, and 16thc, and displays quaint tower gargoyles. The ruined chapel of the Holy Ghost was erected in the 13thc, and Deane's almshouses in London Street are of the early 17thc.

Outstanding among recently completed buildings is the shopping, sports, and recreation complex. The indoor sports centre was opened in 1970, and has facilities for many activities, including swimming in two pools. May's Bounty is a county cricket ground, and the 17th- to 18th-c house in Hackwood Park (SE) is partly by James Gibbs. This is a venue for point-to-point racing. The Willis Museum is of interest.

BATCOMBE, Dorset 6 ST60

Above the village on Batcombe Down is the isolated Cross-in-Hand pillar which figures in Thomas Hardy's *Tess of the D'Urbervilles*.

BATCOMBE, Somerset 6 ST63

A remote village on high ground, offering delightful views of the surrounding area. The church of 1540 has one of the great Somerset towers, notable because it lacks the usual rich pinnacles. Far from detracting from the effect of the structure, this omission imparts an added grandeur to the tower. The south porch is dated 1629.

BATH, Avon 6 ST76

Perhaps the most elegant city in England, Bath is famous for its history, architecture, and natural hot springs. It was a famous spa in Roman times, when it was known as *Aquae Sulis* (the waters of Sul, a Celtic goddess) and there was a temple dedicated to *Sulis Minerva*. This double dedication to Celtic and Roman gods was probably a shrewd move by the Romans to ensure that the local people remained peaceful. The Roman Baths (AM) are among the city's main attractions. A Roman reservoir below the Pump Room provides half a million gallons of water a day, at a constant temperature of 49degC. Mineral water running into the Great Roman Baths still courses through a lead conduit laid down by a plumber some 2,000 years ago.

The Pump Room is a centre where townspeople and tourists meet for coffee and music. The chandelier and sedan chairs are of interest, and the magnificent clock was presented by its famous maker, Tompion, in 1709. The museum adjoining the Baths displays many interesting relics of the Roman occupation. Nearby is Bath Abbey.

Earlier buildings once existed on this site, and it was here, in a Saxon abbey, that Edgar was crowned in 973. Later a Norman minster was rebuilt; an arch from this period still remains in the south choir-aisle, but the bulk of the building was destroyed by fire in 1137. The present abbey was founded in 1499 by Bishop Oliver King, and an unusual carving on the west front depicts his dream of angels ascending and descending a ladder from Heaven, with an olive tree supporting a crown at the foot. Many restorations have been carried out on the abbey, and the east window, destroyed in an air raid in 1942, was successfully replaced in 1955. Fan-vaulting in the abbey roof is notable.

The development of the city in the 18thc owes a great deal to Ralph Allen, a Cornishman who made a fortune from postal contracts. He acquired the quarries near Bath and encouraged the brilliant young architect John Wood to create spaciously planned projects in Bath Stone. John Wood and his son were responsible for Queen Square, the Circus and Royal Crescent, the Assembly Rooms, and the striking Prior Park, built on Combe Down for Ralph Allen himself. There is a Palladian bridge in the grounds of Prior Park (OACT). Other architects followed, encouraged by Beau Nash, a dandy who brought Bath into vogue for fashionable society. Robert Adam built Pulteney

1 AA Headquarters
2 Chapel of the Holy Ghost
3 Church of St Michael and all Angels
4 County Cricket Ground
5 Deane's Almshouses
6 Hackwood Park
7 Sports Centre
8 Willis Museum

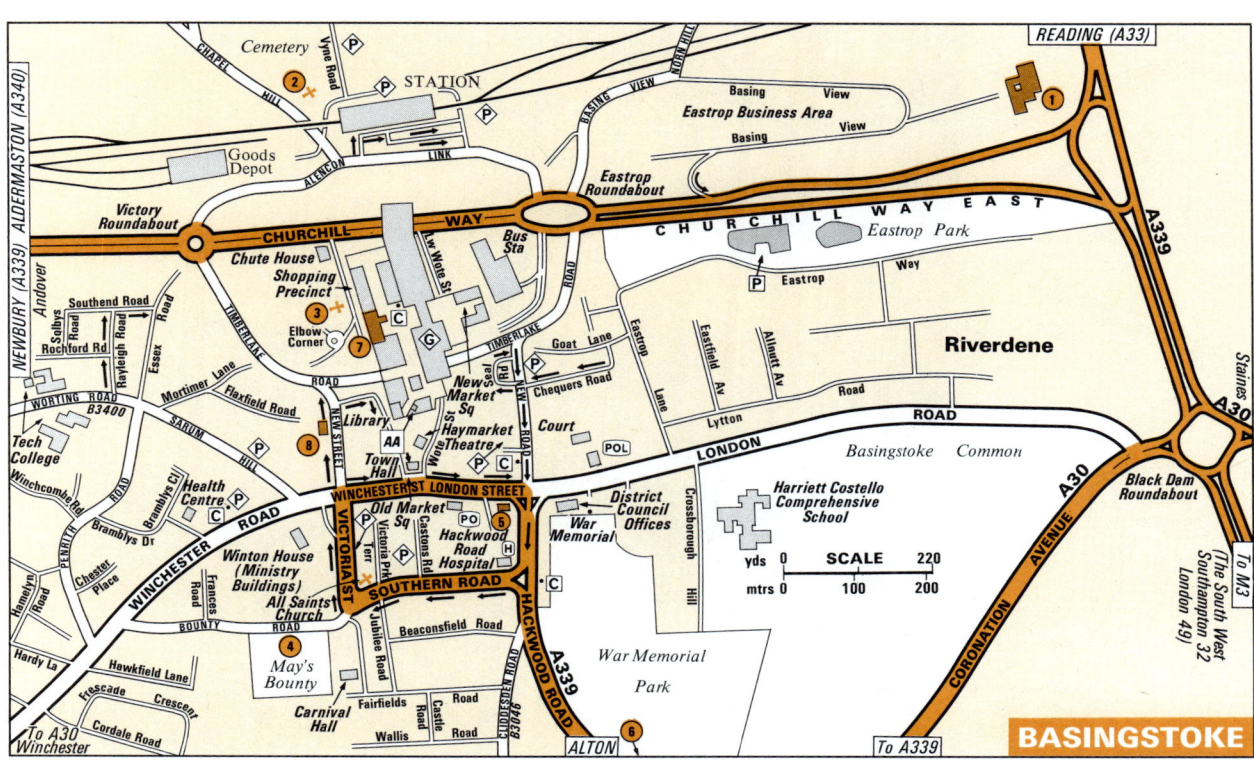

141

Bridge, an enclosed structure with three arches supporting a broad roadway and shops on either side. The tradition of elegance was maintained in Pulteney Street and elsewhere.

The Holburne of Menstrie Museum is a Palladian-style structure designed by C Harcourt Masters in 1795, which now houses a very fine collection of paintings, silver, porcelain, and pottery (OACT). No. 1 Royal Crescent is a house (OACT) which was restored by the Bath Preservation Trust to show how these dwellings looked in their Georgian heyday. Sham Castle was built in 1760 by Ralph Allen to improve the view from his house, and fulfils no other purpose. The guildhall was rebuilt in 1775 by Thomas Baldwin, the city architect who also built Pulteney Street and Bath Street. The latter is famous for its colonnades on both sides. The Assembly Rooms, by John Wood Junior, formed the city's social centre for many years. They were gutted by fire during an air raid in 1942, but have since been successfully restored. The famous Museum of Costume, founded by Mrs Doris Langley Moore, is now housed in this building.

An abundance of trees and flowers is a feature of the city; the Royal Victoria Park covers nearly fifty acres of ground, and includes the Botanical Gardens in which over 5,000 varieties of plants are grown. Linley House is a Georgian building in Pierrepont Place, and is the organizational centre for a yearly festival of music and the arts. The many other annual events that are held here include a county-cricket festival, and races are regularly held on Lansdown race course above the city. The University of Technology, founded in 1966, is situated SE of the city on Claverton Down.

BATHEASTON, Avon 6 ST76
Two notable houses in this area are Middlesex House (1670), and Eagle House (1729). The tower of the restored church is a good example of the perpendicular style. Little Solsbury Hill is a good viewpoint to the NE of the village, and is surmounted by an iron-age camp. The beautiful renaissance manor house of St Catherine's Court is set in terraced gardens 2m N (OACT). Near this is a little Norman to perpendicular church, displaying some old glass and a 15th-c pulpit.

BATLEY, W Yorks 22 SE22
This important industrial town is in the heart of the former West Riding. For centuries it was the centre of this country's heavy woollen industry, and a world centre for shoddy fibre and fabric, made by shredding old cloth. New industries are now replacing the old, providing a more flexible economic background, and

1 Abbey
2 Assembly Rooms
3 County Cricket Ground
4 Guildhall
5 Holburne of Menstrie Museum
6 Lansdown Racecourse
7 Linley House
8 Prior Park
9 Pulteney Bridge
10 Roman Baths and Pump Room
11 Royal Crescent
12 Royal Victoria Park & Botanic Gardens
13 Sham Castle
14 University of Technology

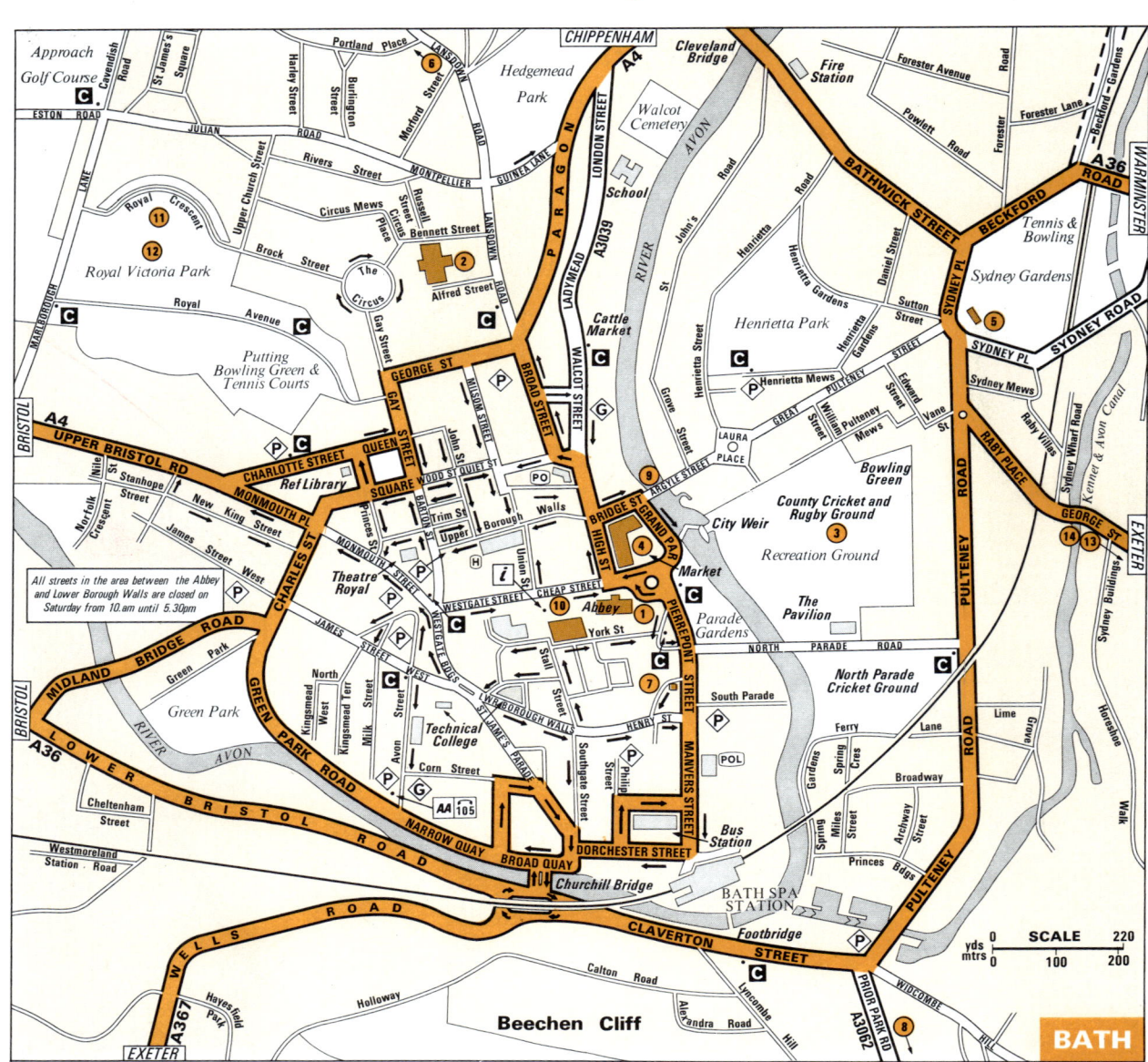

the town is an important shopping and market centre. It is also a centre for sport in the West Riding. Oakwell Hall (1583, OACT) lies 3m NW of Birstall, and was described under the name Fieldhead in Charlotte Brontë's *Shirley*. Extensive collections of local and general interest are housed in Bagshaw Museum, set among the woodlands of Wilton Park.

BATTISFORD, Suffolk   15 TM05
Sir Thomas Gresham, an Elizabethan banker, owned property and estates in this area. Timber from his woods at Battisford Tye was used in the construction of the first Royal Exchange, and the 14th-c church also has associations with this famous gentleman. The notable Everton Brass (1608) was raised to Mary Everton, who died at the age of 100 after having lived under the reigns of six monarchs. An old manor house in the area is reputed to have been built from materials taken from a hospital built by the Knights Hospitallers.

BATTLE, E Sussex   9 TQ71
The town takes its name from the Battle of Hastings, fought around a small stream called Senlac in 1066. William the Conqueror swore to erect an abbey if he won the battle – the living proof of his victory is embodied in St Martin's Abbey, built on the hilltop where the unfortunate Harold was killed. Consecrated in 1094, the abbey flourished until Henry VIII dissolved the monasteries. Part of the remains are now incorporated in a girls' school. A fine 14th-c gatehouse, a roofless refectory, and a 13th-c Abbot's House (OACT) can be seen. Close to the abbey are the Norman Church of St Mary and a fine Deanery (1669). The Pilgrims' Rest, by the main gates of the abbey and once the home of monks, is now a restaurant. The local Historical Society museum is in Langton House.

BATTLEFIELD, Salop   17 SJ51
The church, built by Henry IV to commemorate the Battle of Shrewsbury in 1403, has a carved lych-gate. Timber-and-brick Albright Hussey is a house dating from 1524 and 1601 (OACT).

BAWDSEY, Suffolk   15 TM34
A small yachting centre on the River Deben. A passenger ferry connects with Felixstowe, and also serves the local bathing beach.

BAWTRY, S Yorks   18 SK69
A market town where the former Great North Road enters Yorkshire. The Crown is a fine old coaching inn, and the 18th-c almshouses are of interest. At the N end of the village is a rare example of an animal pound, used to pen stray animals until the owners could be found. Mainly 18th-c Serlby Hall is set in notable gardens 3m SW (OACT).

BEACON HILL, Leics   18 SK51
An AA viewpoint, covering an area of countryside NE from Charnwood Forest to the Leicestershire Wolds.

BEACONSFIELD, Bucks   8 SU99
A busy town with a wide main street, old inns, timbered cottages, and red-brick Georgian houses. The atmosphere still evokes traces of bygone elegance. Bekonscot Model Village and gardens (OACT) include model trains. Edmund Burke, a writer and politician who lived between 1729 and 1797, and Edmund Waller a poet, are buried at the restored 15th-c church. The half-timbered Old Rectory dates from 1543. G K Chesterton lived at Top Meadow, a house on the outskirts of the town. The 17th- to 18th-c Hall Barn stands amidst woods and lakes in a park to the S.

BEADNELL, Northumberland   27 NU22
A small fishing village and holiday resort, with a sandy beach giving access for bathing. Several 18th-c lime kilns are of interest (NT).

BEAL, Northumberland   31 NU04
An embarkation point for the crossing to Holy Island, when the tides allow. The low Kyloe Hills rise SW of Beal, and much of the coast now comprises a national nature reserve.

BEAMINSTER, Dorset   6 ST40
A small town situated in a beautiful natural amphitheatre formed by the surrounding hills. The area is designated one of outstanding natural beauty, and the church's richly-ornamented Tudor tower is perhaps the finest in Dorset. Near by is a plaque which records a time when people, holding posies to ward off the plague, met under a sycamore tree (1665). Beaminster features in Hardy's *Tess of the D'Urbervilles* under the name Emminster. Mapperton Manor House (2m SE) is dated 16thc and later. The little church was rebuilt in the 17thc, and 1m S is Parnham Manor, a Tudor and later house which has been restored.

BEARLEY, Warwickshire   12 SP16
This village is probably little-changed since the day when Charles II rode through after escaping from the battle of Worcester in 1651. An iron aqueduct of 1813 carries the Stratford Canal and towpath over a railway line.

BEARSTED, Kent   9 TQ75
Rapidly becoming a suburb of Maidstone, Bearsted has an attractive village green and a church with a good 15th-c tower. Alfred Mynn, England's first fast bowler, played here; A P Freeman, the famous Kent cricketer, died here in 1965.

BEAULIEU, Hants   7 SU30
Situated on the Beaulieu River in the New Forest, close to a stretch of Solent coastline which is now an area of outstanding natural beauty. Remains of a 13th-c abbey (AM) are of interest, the refectory of which now serves as the parish church and preserves a beautiful early-English readers' pulpit. The National Motor Museum, owned by Lord Montagu, contains a large library and numerous veteran and vintage cars, motor cycles, and bicycles (OACT). The adjacent abbey is open daily all the year round. The gatehouse of the abbey, Palace House, is Lord Montagu's home. Well-known Exbury gardens lie 4m SE and are famous for flowering shrubs (OACT).

BEAUWORTH, Hants   7 SU52
Situated on a lofty ridge S of the village is the Fox and Hounds inn, with a 300ft deep well that was once used to supply water for a former castle. A treadmill is used to raise the water.

BEBINGTON, Merseyside   17 SJ38
A town on the Wirral, largely a dormitory for Birkenhead and Liverpool. The mainly-perpendicular church has early-Norman arches, old woodwork, and an ancient font.

BECCLES, Suffolk   15 TM49
Beccles Quay is a convenient centre from which to explore the waterways of the area, which are well-supplied with landing stages. The Church of St Michael has a detached bell-tower, a massive 14th-c structure rising to a height of 97ft, with a peal of ten bells. A notable south porch, a fine turret with a cupola, and a 16th-c monument are features of the church itself. The town hall dates from 1726. There are several fine Georgian houses and 1m W is the small but graceful Elizabethan mansion of Roos Hall (OACT).

BECKHAMPTON, Wilts   7 SU06
A downland village with a number of horseracing stables in the vicinity. To the E is the well-known West Kennet long barrow (AM), one of England's largest prehistoric burial chambers.

BECKINGTON, Somerset   6 ST85
An old weaving village that retains the charm of its antiquity. The church has a Norman tower, and the Royal Arms of Queen Elizabeth I were carved in stone in 1574. Beckington Castle is a house of Tudor origin, and several fine stone-built buildings include the 16th- to 17th-c abbey. One house has a topiary model of the former battleship Queen Elizabeth. The old manse houses the Lewis Pram museum. NE of the village is Seymour's Court Farm, an Elizabethan building which once served as the home of the Protector Somerset; the gabled porch is an interesting feature. Lullington Church (2½m W) is rich in Norman work, a notable example of which is the beautiful doorway.

BECKLEY, E Sussex   9 TQ82
Among the old buildings in this village is Church House, which displays fine 18th-c brickwork. The 14th-c church has a lych-gate with representations of St George and St Michael beneath canopies.

BECKLEY, Oxon   13 SP51
The Norman to 15th-c church has a tub font – which may be of Saxon origin, a 14th-c tower, and a stone reading desk on a nave column. Beckley Park is a mid 16th-c house with three moats, and the manor was mentioned in King Alfred's will. The old Roman road, which ran through this village on its way to Dorchester, can still be traced as a narrow hedged lane on the edge of Otmoor.

BEDALE, N Yorks   22 SE28
A picturesque market town with many Georgian houses, inns, and an old cross. The 13th- to 14th-c church houses several notable monuments, a lofty tower arch, and a vaulted crypt. Facing the church is the 18th-c hall (OACT).

BEDDINGHAM, E Sussex   8 TQ40
Some 2m E stands Firle Place, mainly of Georgian style and the old home of the Gages (OACT). The brasses and monuments of this family adorn the little church at West Firle. To the SE rises Firle Beacon (718ft), a high point in the South Downs.

BEDFORD, Beds   13 TL04
A county town on the River Ouse, and a thriving industrial and commercial centre, within easy reach of London. The town's recorded history begins in Saxon times. It was prominent in the reign of

King Alfred, and was sacked and burned by the Danes in 1010. A castle built by the Norman Beauchamp family was demolished in 1224, but the mound can still be seen.

Bedford achieved doubtful fame when, at a time of religious persecution, it imprisoned John Bunyan in the county gaol from 1660 to 1672, and again in 1676. A slab in the pavement of Silver Street marks the site of the prison. The tower was the home of John Howard for many years, the great prison reformer of the 18thc. Several Bunyan memorials include the Bunyan Meeting House and Museum, and a statue.

The town also boasts well-known schools and a cluster of early churches. St Paul's Church was originally of the 12thc, but has been greatly restored. It still retains a 15th-c pulpit from which Wesley preached a famous sermon; this is now known as the Wesley Pulpit. St Peter's Church retains some Saxon work in the tower and north wall. Stones in the tower bear scars of a fire caused when the town was sacked by the Danes. St Mary's Church has a Norman tower and a 14th-c chancel, but the rest of the building is mainly 16thc. The fine bridge spanning the Ouse was built in 1813 and considerably widened in 1940. The Cecil Higgins Art Gallery is of great interest, as is also the Bedford Museum.

BEDINGFIELD, Suffolk *15 TM16*
The fine 14th-c church has carved benches and a double hammerbeam roof. Flemings Hall, a moated building, is partly half-timbered and displays a two-storeyed brick porch.

BEDINGHAM, Norfolk *15 TM29*
The church's Norman round-tower is topped by a 15th-c belfry, and the main building houses a good screen, also of this period.

BEDLINGTON, Northumberland *27 NZ28*
A coal-mining town which has given its name to a well-known breed of terrier.

BEDRUTHAN STEPS, Cornwall *4 SW86*
In legend these huge granite blocks were stepping stones for the giant Bedruthan. Cliffs rising high above a sand and rock beach have been judged unsafe, and the descent was closed at the time of publishing (NT). This feature is just one part of a fine stretch of coastal scenery within easy reach of Newquay.

BEECHAMWELL, Norfolk *15 TF70*
A late-Georgian village, with a church displaying a Saxon round tower and housing two old brasses. The ancient Devil's Dyke earthwork is near by. There are two theories as to the origins of this 9m-long structure, plus other earthworks in the vicinity. They were either built by retreating Anglo Saxons after a battle or, more likely, by the East Anglians as a defence against the Mercian raiders of the 7thc.

BEER, Devon *6 SY28*
This small resort and fishing village, with its interesting buildings and quaint narrow streets, was once the stronghold of smugglers. Beer Head is a magnificent chalk promontory which can be reached by public footpath, and the shingle beach is easily accessible for bathing. Bovey House, an Elizabethan building with secret hiding places, lies 2m NW.

BEESTON, & STAPLEFORD, Notts *18 SK53 & 43*
This Trent-Valley residential district was formed by the amalgamation of five parishes and townships, and boasts many flourishing industries of recent development. A factory of 1932 and 1938, belonging to Boots the chemists, is a notable example of modern industrial architecture. The Gregory Rose Gardens are the largest in the country (OACT).

BELBROUGHTON, Herefs & Worcs *12 SO97*
A noted manufacturing area for scythes. Walton Hill, to the NE, is part of the Clent Hills and rises to a height of 1,036ft.

BELFORD, Northumberland *27 NU13*
This little market town's main features are The Hall, by James Paine in 1756, and the remains of an old market cross.

BELLINGHAM, Northumberland *27 NY88*
A small market town which once had an iron industry, situated in the valley of the North Tyne. Some of the metalwork produced here was used in the construction of the Tyne Bridge. The 12th-c church is noted for its massive ribbed-stone roof, which was built partly as a defence against marauding Scots. The water from St Cuthbert's Well, behind the churchyard, is supposed to have healing powers. The Pennine Way passes close to Bellingham Youth Hostel, and much of the surrounding area is part of the Northumberland national park. A track to the N follows Hareshaw Burn to the picturesque waterfall of Hareshaw Linn. Two fine mansions of the area are Lee Hall and Hesleyside, both of the 18thc.

BELPER, Derbyshire *18 SK34*
This settlement on the River Derwent has large cotton mills. A Roman kiln was found here in 1964. The first Turnpike Act for Derbyshire is recalled on a stone at the Hollybush Inn, Makeney (2m S on E bank of the river). The inscription borne by this tablet reads Derby Coach Road 1739.

BELSAY, Northumberland *27 NZ17*
Here, a ruined 14th-c castle stands in the grounds of a 19th-c Grecian-style mansion. The latter is said to be one of the finest examples of its period, but its future is uncertain.

BELSTONE, Devon *5 SX69*
The village lies in a picturesque Dartmoor setting, and still retains its stocks and whipping post. Several prehistoric stone circles are to be seen in this area.

BELTON, Lincs *19 SK93*
The Church of St Peter and St Paul is partly 12th to 13thc, and houses numerous monuments to the Brownlow family. Belton House, attributed to Wren, was built in 1685 and has been the home of this well-represented family for 300 years. Alterations were carried out in 1775 and the interior displays beautiful naturalistic carvings which may be the work of Grinling Gibbons (OACT).

BELVOIR CASTLE, Leics *19 SK83*
This castle stands on a lofty ridge overlooking the Vale of Belvoir (pronounced Beever). The original castle – then a fortress – was presented to the Manners family, later to become the Dukes of Rutland, in the 16thc. The family rebuilt the house several times, and the present structure dates from 1816. It is renowned for its pictures, the Gobelin Tapestries, and a regimental museum of the 17/21 Lancers (OACT). The Belvoir foxhound was bred near

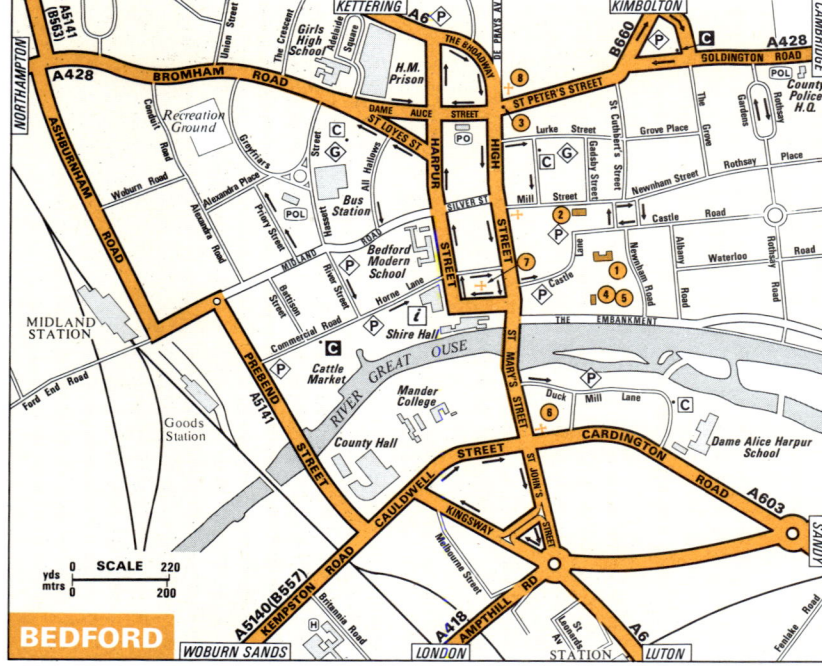

1 Bedford Museum
2 Bunyan Meeting House (museum)
3 Bunyan Statue
4 Castle Mound
5 Cecil Higgins Art Gallery
6 St Mary's Church
7 St Paul's Church
8 St Peter's Church

here in the 18thc and took its name from the castle.

BEMBRIDGE, Isle of Wight *7 SZ68*
An interesting feature of this small yachting resort is the restored 17th-c windmill, and an AA viewpoint is situated on Bembridge Down to the SW. Original drawings and manuscripts by Ruskin can be seen at the Ruskin Art Gallery and Museum, Bembridge School, Whitecliff Bay.

BEMERTON, Wilts *7 SU13*
George Herbert, poet and rector from 1630 to 1632, is buried in the 14th-c Church of St Andrew.

BENENDEN, Kent *9 TQ83*
The village is set amid hop fields, and includes old timbered houses round a picturesque green. Princess Anne was a pupil of Benenden School.

BENINGTON, Herts *14 TL32*
The kings of Mercia once lived here, and Benington Lordship is a Georgian house adjoining a ruined Norman castle. A large neo-Norman 'folly' gatehouse has been added. The village green and 16th-c cottages are attractive.

BENTLEY, Hants *8 SU74*
The church font and tower are Norman, the latter with an 18th-c brick top. A unique stone book under a thatched cover can be seen at the entrance of the village. This relates particulars of the district, and was given by first Chief Scout Lord Baden-Powell. Alice Holt forest lies to the SE.

BENTLEY, GREAT, Essex *15 TM12*
Features of this village are a 42-acre green – one of the largest in the country – and a Norman church. Several 17th-c houses stand behind the pond on the green.

BERDEN, Essex *14 TL42*
The Norman and later church has fine 13th-c chancel windows. Berden Hall and The Priory are both Elizabethan, and a large fortified mound exists in the area.

BERE FERRERS, Devon *5 SX46*
The 14th-c church houses a Norman font, old bench-ends, and 14th-c glass depicting William de Ferrers and his wife Matilda. The village is situated on the River Tavy.

BERE REGIS, Dorset *6 SY89*
King John once had a hunting lodge in this village, hence the name Bere – meaning of the King. The area is Hardy country, and many of the local features figure in his novel *Tess of the D'Urbervilles*. The main characters of the novel were taken from life, and the family was based on the old Dorset family of Turberville. The perpendicular church has a 15th-c lion-rampant crest of the family, and houses several Turberville tombs. The splendid nave roof is carved and painted, and it was at this church that Hardy 'buried' Tess' ancestors.

1 Berwick Bridge
2 Barracks (museum)
3 Castle Remains
4 Church of the Holy Trinity
5 Elizabethan Town Walls
6 Museum and Art Gallery
7 Royal Border Bridge
8 Royal Tweed Road Bridge
9 Town Hall

An iron-age earthwork surmounts Woodbury Hill, to the E, and 3½m SW is Cloud's Hill (NT), the former home of T E Lawrence – alias Lawrence of Arabia (OACT).

BERKELEY, Glos *12 ST69*
In 1327 King Edward II was murdered in this magnificent 12th-c castle, the ancestral home of the Berkeley family for some 800 years (OACT). Many Berkeley monuments can be seen in the early-English church, with its detached tower of 1783 and a Norman doorway beneath a fine rose window. Buried in the church is Edward Jenner, a local man who introduced vaccination and died in the nearby Chantry in 1823. A small Jenner museum may be visited. A nuclear-power station is operating in the area, and 1m N is Wanswell Court, a 15th-c and later house which is now a farm.

BERKHAMSTED, Herts *8 SP90*
A lively market town on the Grand Union Canal. The father of William Cowper was rector of the large partly 13th-c church in 1731 – when William Cowper himself was born. The latter well-known poet and hymn-writer died in 1800. All that can be seen of the Norman castle where Chaucer, Thomas Becket, and the entire court of Henry VIII stayed at different times, are scanty remains. The main structure has entirely vanished. Also of interest are the Sayer almshouses of 1684, the public school founded 1541, and Berkhamsted Common (NT) which lies to the N.

BERKSWELL, W Midlands *12 SP27*
An attractive village that takes its name from a well that can still be seen near the churchyard gate. The predominantly Norman church is one of the most interesting in the county and dates from about 1150. An impressive vaulted crypt lies beneath the chancel, and the much-later gabled and timbered porch is in two stories, access to the upper being by an outside stair. Ram Hall and Blind Hall are two interesting 16th-c houses, and the local stocks have been preserved.

BERRYNARBOR, Devon *5 SS54*
This village lies in the delightful Sterridge Valley, and has an early-English to perpendicular church boasting a 96ft-high west tower. Bowden, an old farmhouse 1m up the valley, was the birthplace of famous Elizabethan churchman Bishop Jewel. Watermouth Castle (19thc) lies 1m N on the coast.

BERRY POMEROY CASTLE, Devon *5 SX86*
Extensive ruins of this fine 13th- and 17th-c stronghold stand in a wooded valley. The castle was founded by Ralph de Pomeroy, a favourite of William the Conqueror, and dismantled during the Civil Wars of the 17thc. The village church to the SW bears the Pomeroy arms on the porch, and houses a good screen.

BERWICK, E Sussex *8 TQ50*
A South-Downs village noted for its modern murals, which were painted by the Bloomsbury Group. This group was made up of the artists Duncan Grant, Vanessa Bell (sister of Virginia Woolf), and her son Quentin. A Saxon barrow can be seen in the churchyard.

BERWICK-UPON-TWEED, Northumberland *31 NT95*
This has been England's most northerly town since 1482, when it finally surrendered to the English Crown after changing hands thirteen times during the period of border warfare between England and Scotland. The approach to the town is dominated by three famous Tweed bridges – the old, or Berwick Bridge of fifteen arches and dating from the 17thc; the Royal Tweed road bridge of 1928; the Royal Border Bridge of 1850, which carries the railway.

cont

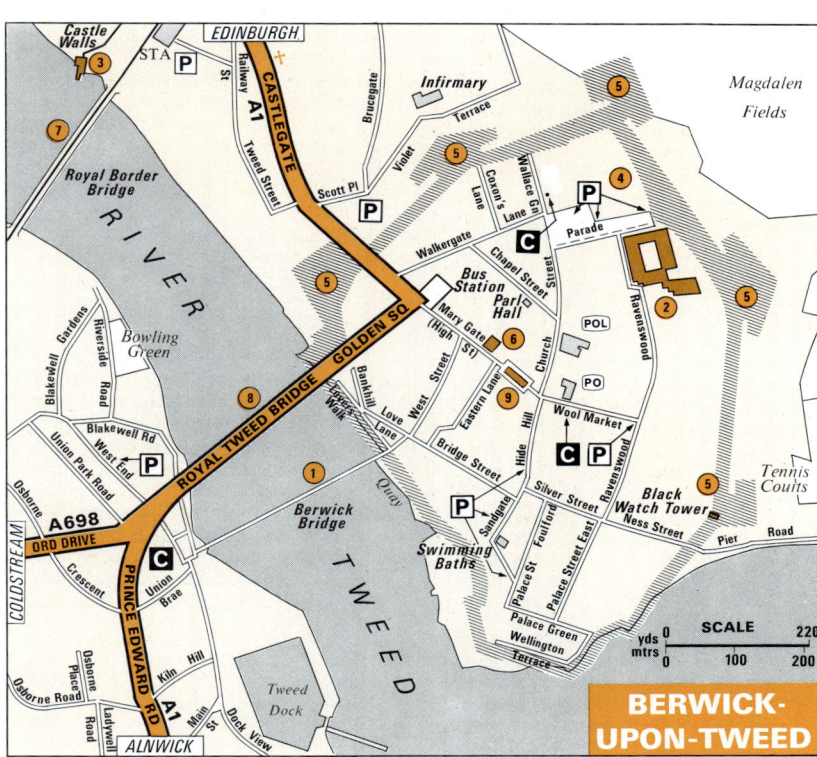

The original circuit was replaced by Elizabethan town walls, which are considered to be the earliest of their period in Europe. They are thought to anticipate the work of French engineer Vauban. Designed as a defence against gunpowder warfare, they are up to ten-feet thick in some places.

The town hall and several houses on the quay are 18th-c Georgian. Berwick is said to have more buildings scheduled for preservation than any other town of its size in England. The parish church (1648 to 1652) was one of the few built in England during the Commonwealth, and was extended in 1855. This latter building work was conducted with stone taken from the demolished castle of which only a few fragments remain.

Barracks (now closed) designed by Vanbrugh between 1717 and 1721 are the earliest to be seen in Britain. They incorporate the museum of the King's Own Scottish Borderers. The town's grammar school dates from 1754, and the local museum and art gallery are also of interest. The coast to the S of Berwick has been designated an area of outstanding natural beauty. An interesting annual feature is the May Day ceremony of Riding the Bounds.

BESFORD, Herefs & Worcs *12 SO94*
Besford has the only timber-framed church in the county, probably dating from the 14thc. A carved rood-loft parapet is only partly original, but is certainly of interest. Inside the church are monuments to the Harwell family. Besford Court is a partly half-timbered house, that was added to in 1912. It is thought to date from *c*1500.

BETCHWORTH, Surrey *8 TQ24*
An attractive village on the River Mole, with a church displaying 12th- and 13th-c work. A long Norman chest can be seen under the tower.

BETHERSDEN, Kent *9 TQ94*
This place is famous for its marble quarries, stone from which was used in the construction of Canterbury and Rochester Cathedrals. The church has a good 15th-c tower.

BETLEY, Staffs *17 SJ74*
A great deal of timber was used in the construction of the church, particularly in the nave arcades. The tower and chancel display 17th-c work. The attractive waters of Betley Mere are worth a visit, and several old houses in the village are half timbered.

BEVERLEY, Humberside *23 TA03*
This flourishing market town was the capital of old Yorkshire's East Riding, and has a Charter dating from 1129. It is also a place of outstanding architecture.

The 13th-c minster is just one of the many notable buildings, all unique in their own ways, that can be seen in the town. Its twin towers are visible for miles around, and it is a superb example of the gothic style of architecture. Earlier churches that existed on this site suffered the depredations of Danish raiders and a series of fires, but rebuilding started in the 13thc and by 1260 the whole of the eastern arm had been constructed in its present early-English style. The replacement of the old nave was started *c*1308, and the architect cleverly managed to blend and combine his new decorated style with the design of the adjacent structure. The full flowering of the 14th-c style can be seen in the execution of the Percy tomb, particularly in the canopy, and in the tracery on the east side of the reredos. The years 1390 to 1420 saw the completion of the twin western towers, the front, the western part of the nave, and the magnificent north porch. The great east window retains its original glass and belongs to the same period. A unique feature is the cathedral clock which strikes bells in both towers. Subsequent additions of note include the sixty-eight choir stalls and a Snetzler organ. The former are the 16th-c work of the Ripon school of woodcarvers, and the latter was built in 1769. This magnificent building is not a cathedral – just a parish church.

The minster is situated at the south end of the main street; St Mary's, at the north end of the street and once the minster's chapel of ease, is just as fine in some respects. It is cruciform in shape, and although retaining some traces of its original Norman structure, has been somewhat altered and enlarged over the years. Thus it too shows a variety of styles. The nave and central tower were rebuilt in 1520, though the chancel ceiling displays earlier 15th-c paintings of the English kings. These have now been repainted by Leslie Moore. The 'minstrel' pillar of the north arcade bears the recorded names of benefactors of the year 1530.

The rest of the town is just as interesting. The 15th-c North Bar is the sole survivor of five ancient gateways that used to allow access through the old town wall. An ornate market cross was built between 1711 and 1714; many good Georgian houses and a few 18th-c shop fronts can also be seen. The guildhall dates from 1762, and much of its fine plasterwork and wood carving was executed by local men. The structure itself was built by William Middleton, a Beverley joiner. The Beverley Arms retains an original Elizabethan kitchen. Lairgate Hall is an 18th-c building, now the Municipal Offices, with an interesting Chinese room (OACT). Races are held from early May to late September, at a racecourse on adjoining Beverley Westwood.

BEVERSTONE, Glos *12 ST89*
The castle was rebuilt in the 13th and 14thc but still preserves some original Norman work. It was held against King Stephen by the Berkeley family. The local Norman to decorated style includes a mid 14th-c Berkeley chapel which contains 17th-c stained glass. To the N stands the lovely Elizabethan and later Chavenage Manor (OACT). Some of the finest beech trees in England can be seen 3m NW near Kingscote.

BEWCASTLE, Cumbria *26 NY57*
Bewcastle is near the site of a Roman fort which served as an outpost of Hadrian's Wall. A famous 7th-c Anglo-Saxon Cross (AM), with Runic inscriptions and patterns, can be seen in the churchyard. Unfortunately the head of the cross is missing. Remains of a medieval castle, built of materials from the Roman wall, also exist in the area. To the NW lies Kershope Forest, part of the Border Forest Park, which crosses the border into Scotland.

BEWDLEY, Herefs & Worcs *12 SO77*
This town on the River Severn, near the fringe of Wyre Forest, has a Georgian church. A large number of its houses are 18thc – particularly those in Load Street. Many of the earlier timber framed buildings have recently been restored with the aid of government grants. Historic Tickenhill House is 18thc and earlier. To the NW is Dowles, a picturesquely-situated old manor house, and 1m S is Ribbesford House, which was rebuilt in 1820. During the Second World War the latter was used as a military academy for the Free French Forces. The church in the park has a remarkable Norman tympanum over the north doorway (the area over a doorway within an arch), and the south arcade is of unusual wooden construction. The new West Midland wild life park is situated outside the town on the Kidderminster road. Kentish Glory moths, a rare species the colour of terracotta, can be seen in Wyre Forest.

BEXHILL-ON-SEA, E Sussex *9 TQ70*
A south-coast resort with a shingle beach which graduates to sand and rock at low tide. Many of the inhabitants are retired people. The De La Warr Pavilion (1935) overlooks the beach, and is built in a strikingly modern style. It is used as an entertainment centre, and contains restaurants, a ballroom, theatre, concert hall, and sun terraces. Festivals of music are held here annually. The restored church in the old village retains Norman features, and has a carved Saxon stone in the tower. Remnants of a submerged forest lie to the E, below Galley Hill. These trees once grew on a land bridge that joined Britain to the Continent.

BEXLEY, Gt London *8 TQ47*
The Greater London Borough of Bexley comprises a region S of the Thames, taking in Erith, Crayford, Sidcup, and numerous villages, as well as Bexley itself. Although the area has been inhabited from prehistoric times, there are few ancient buildings. The most interesting of those remaining is Hall Place (AM), a historic mansion set in beautiful gardens (now a public park) beside the river Cray. The house is made of flint and brick, and the earliest part (*c*1540) was built by Sir John Champneys, Lord Mayor of London. The Red House at Bexley Heath was built for William Morris in 1860, by Philip Webb.

BIBURY, Glos *12 SP10*
Bibury is a village of typical Cotswold houses on the River Coln, well-known for its trout fishing. Arlington Row is a famous group of old cottages (NT) and Arlington Mill, now a museum, is near a bird sanctuary (OACT). The church is partly Saxon to early English, and has eight aumbries in the chancel. Two 18th-c brasses depicting skeletons can be seen. Bibury Court, a beautiful old Jacobean house, now serves as an hotel.

BICESTER, Oxon *13 SP52*
A noted hunting centre on the edge of the Vale of Aylesbury, with a pleasant market square and wide grass verges by the roadsides to make the going easier for horses. The site of Roman Alchester is to the S, on the line of ancient Akeman Street.

BICKLEIGH, Devon *5 SS90*
This pretty village on the River Exe

has a restored thatched roof Saxon chapel. Adjacent to this is a castle gatehouse which has also been restored. Lofty earthworks of the prehistoric Cadbury Castle, a notable viewpoint, lie to the SW.

BICKNOLLER, Somerset *6 ST13*
The interesting local perpendicular church houses a good screen and some interesting bench ends. The village stocks have been preserved.

BIDDENDEN, Kent *9 TQ83*
This picturesque Wealden village includes several weavers' cottages and a fine medieval Cloth Hall which has been restored. Its church has a good 15th-c tower and contains a wealth of brasses. The 'Biddenden Maids' were Eliza and Mary Chulkhurst, a pair of Siamese twins who lived here in the 12thc and bequeathed 20 acres of land to provide an annual dole for the poor. Representations of the sisters are stamped on cakes distributed free every Easter Monday.

BIDDESTONE, Wilts *7 ST87*
Old buildings in this stone-built village include a 17th-c manor with a brick gazebo overlooking the road. The attractive green still has its village pond.

BIDDULPH, Staffs *17 SJ85*
A small industrial town in the moors. The Old Hall, now in ruins, is dated 1558 and was besieged in the year 1643 of the Civil War. Like many other buildings that suffered this fate, it was dismantled after being taken. The later hall dates from 1664 and 1725. The River Trent rises E of the town, on Biddulph Moor.

BIDEFORD, Devon *5 SS42*
Sir Richard Grenville, who was born here in 1541, secured a charter for the town from Queen Elizabeth I. From then on it was the principal port of N Devon until trade declined in the 18thc. The town handled imported American tobacco on a major scale in 1700.

Bideford stands on the River Torridge, which is spanned here by a 677ft-long bridge with twenty-four arches. Some of its 15th-c stonework is still visible. Late 17th-c houses can be seen in Bridgeland Road. The rebuilt church has an ancient tower and contains memorials to the Grenville family. Charles Kingsley wrote *Westward Ho!* in a room at the Royal Hotel (1688), and there is a statue to this author at the gates of the park. The Ship Tun is said to stand on the site of an inn of the same name that featured in the novel. Lundy Island (NT) can be reached by launch.

BIDFORD-ON-AVON, Warwickshire *12 SP15*
Shakespeare is said to have been born here, and the appearance of the village has changed very little since his lifetime. A Tudor house sited here was formerly the Falcon Inn, an interesting wayfarers' haven that included William Shakespeare and Ben Johnson among its clientele. Also of interest are several old houses, a 15th-c bridge, and a church with a 700-year-old tower.

BIDSTON, Merseyside *17 SJ29*
Fine views over the Wirral peninsula are available from Bidston Hill, sited on which are a windmill and an observatory. The latter is used for work on tides and meteorology. A rare example of an old 'plague' wall exists at 17th-c Bidston Hall.

BIGBURY-ON-SEA, Devon *5 SX64*
A resort at the mouth of the River Avon, with Bigbury itself 2m inland. Burgh Island can be reached on foot at mid-tide, and some sand is revealed at low tide.

BIGGIN HILL, Gt London *8 TQ45*
This rambling North Downs village has a famous Battle of Britain airfield. The chapel here commemorates 453 pilots, who were killed while stationed at Biggin Hill during the last war.

BIGGLESWADE, Beds *14 TL14*
Sited on the River Ivel, this village's much-restored church retains a good south porch, and the much-altered Market House still shows some old work.

BIGNOR, W Sussex *8 SU91*
Several old houses exist here. Of particular note is the picturesque village shop, which is featured in many books on architecture. A Roman villa that existed on this site is one of the best known in the country, with remains including fine mosaic floors, Samian pottery tiles, etc (OACT).

BILDESTON, Suffolk *15 TL94*
An attractive village with many old half-timbered houses.

BILLERICAY, Essex *9 TQ69*
Now part of Basildon New Town, Billericay's Mayflower Hall contains memorials to four people who sailed with the Pilgrim Fathers. The ship's purser Christopher Martin was a native of the town. The church is 18thc, with an older brick tower.

BILLESDON, Leics *18 SK70*
A 14th-c cross stands in this hunting centre, and the old school dates from 1650. To the E is Skeffington Hall, largely 17thc, and 4m NW is 17th-c Quenby Hall – considered to be the finest of its period in the county.

BILLESLEY, Warwickshire *12 SP15*
The church dates from 1692 and the hall is early 17thc, with some additions.

BILLINGBOROUGH, Lincs *19 TF13*
An early-English to perpendicular church here has a 150ft spire; also in the village is a 17th-c hall.

BILLINGFORD, Norfolk *15 TM17*
A fine example of a brick-built tower mill survives here.

BILLING, GREAT, Northants *13 SP86*
The church is Norman and later, and the post office occupies a building of 1703. To the S is Billing Aquadrome.

BILLINGHAM, Cleveland *27 NZ42*
A town concerned with the manufacture of chemicals. The town centre was opened in 1963, and the Forum Theatre is one of the newest in England. The early-English church has a fine Saxon tower.

BILSTON, W Midlands *18 SO99*
Bilston, a Black-Country manufacturing town, was the birthplace of poet and writer Sir Henry Newbolt (1862). *Drake's Drum* is one of his more famous works.

BINFIELD, Berks *8 SU87*
All Saints' Church was rebuilt in the 14thc, and displays a curious old hourglass. The poet Alexander Pope sang in the local choir as a boy.

BINGHAM, Notts *18 SK73*
The church is a good example of the early-English to perpendicular periods. It boasts a fine tower and spire, and displays 14th- and 15th-c windows.

BINGLEY, W Yorks *22 SE13*
It was here that the well-known Airedale Terrier was first bred, originally for the hunting of otters. Old mansions in the area include Marley Hall, St Ives, Gawthorpe Hall, and the Georgian Myrtle Grove – now the town hall. The Market House (1753) and cross are now in the Prince of Wales Park. A musical festival is held annually.

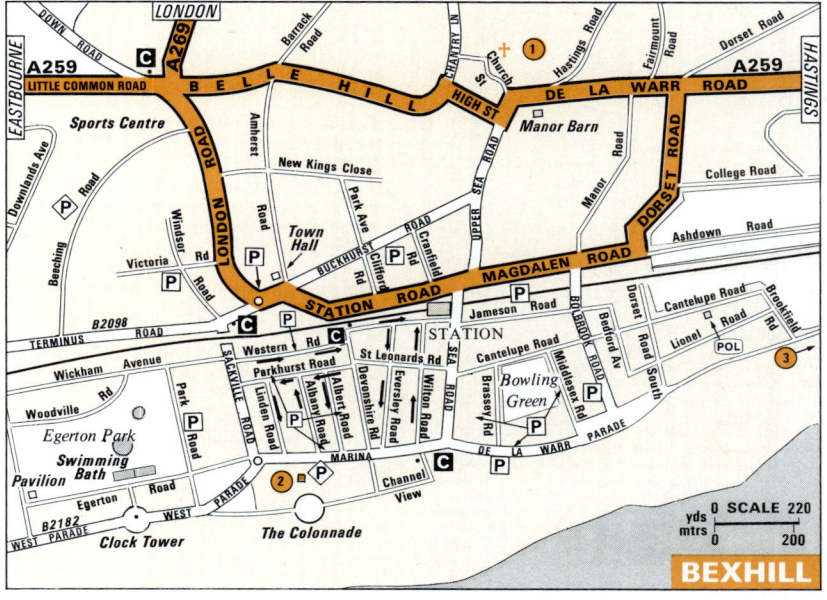

1 Church of St Peter
2 De La Warr Pavilion
3 Submerged Forest

147

BINHAM, Norfolk 15 TF93
Remains of a 12th-c priory (AM) include a fine Norman nave which the village uses as a parish church. Elizabethan Hindringham Hall stands 2m S.

BINLEY, Warwickshire 13 SP37
The church (from 1771) is attributed to Robert Adam because the interior decoration is characteristic of his known style. Overall design includes a western octagonal cupola, Tuscan columns, and a shallow chancel with plaster decoration.

BINSTEAD, Isle of Wight 7 SZ59
A modern abbey and the remains of 12th-c Quarr Abbey can be seen here.

BINTON, Warwickshire 12 SP15
Incidents from Captain Scott's ill-fated expedition to the South Pole are portrayed by a window in the local church.

BIRCHINGTON, Kent 9 TR36
A holiday resort with sand and chalk cliffs. The churchyard contains the grave of Dante Gabriel Rossetti, and a detached bell tower (campanile) can be seen in the park. The Powell-Cotton big-game museum is 1m S in Quex Park (OACT).

BIRDHAM, W Sussex 8 SU80
This village is on Chichester channel, near the Chichester yacht basin which was inaugurated in 1965. The parish church has a low narrow door through which, according to legend, the Devil was kicked out. The exit was blocked up so that he could not re-enter the church. Chichester Harbour, declared an area of outstanding natural beauty in 1964, covers some 29sqm.

BIRDLIP, Glos 12 SO91
Birdlip is situated on the edge of the Cotswolds, at an altitude of 900ft. Magnificent views over the Severn Vale to the distant Malvern Hills can be enjoyed from a road along the escarpment to the NE. A Roman villa (AM) at Witcombe, W of Birdlip, preserves a hypocaust system and several mosaic pavements.

BIRKENHEAD, Merseyside 17 SJ38
An important port and shipbuilding centre on the River Mersey, connected to Liverpool by the Queensway road tunnel, an electric railway line, and a passenger ferry service. The ruined 12th-c priory formed a hub around which the town grew. The Scout Movement originated in Birkenhead in 1908 at YMCA Headquarters, then in Grange Road. St Mary's Church (1821) and Hamilton Square (1826) are architecturally impressive, and the Williamson Art Gallery and Museum includes an interesting shipping gallery.

BIRKIN, N Yorks 22 SE52
Birkin has one of Yorkshire's finest Norman churches. The richly-carved, south-nave doorway and notable vaulted apse are well worth seeing. Fragments of 14th-c glass and a 14th-c monument of a man holding a heart are housed within the building.

BIRLING GAP, E Sussex 8 TV59
A beach of shingle, rocks, and sand allows access for bathing, with the well-known Seven Sisters Cliffs (NT) rising to the W. On the top of the cliffs to the E is the old Belle Tout lighthouse, stark against the distant South Downs. A prehistoric Beaker settlement was founded nearby.

BIRMINGHAM, W Midlands 12 SP08
An important manufacturing city which is second only to London in size, Birmingham specializes in the fabrication of motor-cars, jewellery, and metalwork. As an early industrial city it was popular with a large number of smiths, probably because of the availability of fuel – coal from the N Warwickshire mines. At the time of the Civil War, the city's industry had developed sufficiently to allow the supplying of many thousands of sword blades to the Parliamentary forces. Royalist troops had to look elsewhere for their weaponry. Gun-making and brass-founding were flourishing by 1700, and 1762 saw the setting up of the Soho Manufactory of Boulton and Watt. This opened a whole new conception of manufacturing technique, and Soho plant was a showplace that employed over 1,000 workers.

In spite of its incredible industrial growth, Birmingham was not represented in Parliament until 1832. Its first town council was elected in 1838. The municipal development of the town owes much to the Chamberlain family. Birmingham was made a city in 1889, and its chief magistrate became Lord Mayor. In 1909 the university was founded – some of its fine buildings can be seen at Edgbaston, and in 1966 the College of Advanced Technology was given a charter and became the University of Aston in Birmingham.

Bull Ring is the oldest inhabited area and forms a centre from which the city has gradually expanded through the centuries. It has now been reconstructed on a scale, and to standards, unrivalled in Europe, comprising twenty-three acres of shopping space on several levels. Development of the city centre has been influenced by the construction of an inner ring road, encircling the business and main shopping areas. The whole traffic system of the city has been redesigned, and road-travelling to and from the city has been facilitated by the opening of two new systems – the multi-level junction at Gravelly Hill, popularly known as

cont pg 150

1 Arrowe Park
2 Priory Ruins
3 St Mary's Church
4 Williamson Art Gallery and Museum
5 YMCA Headquarters

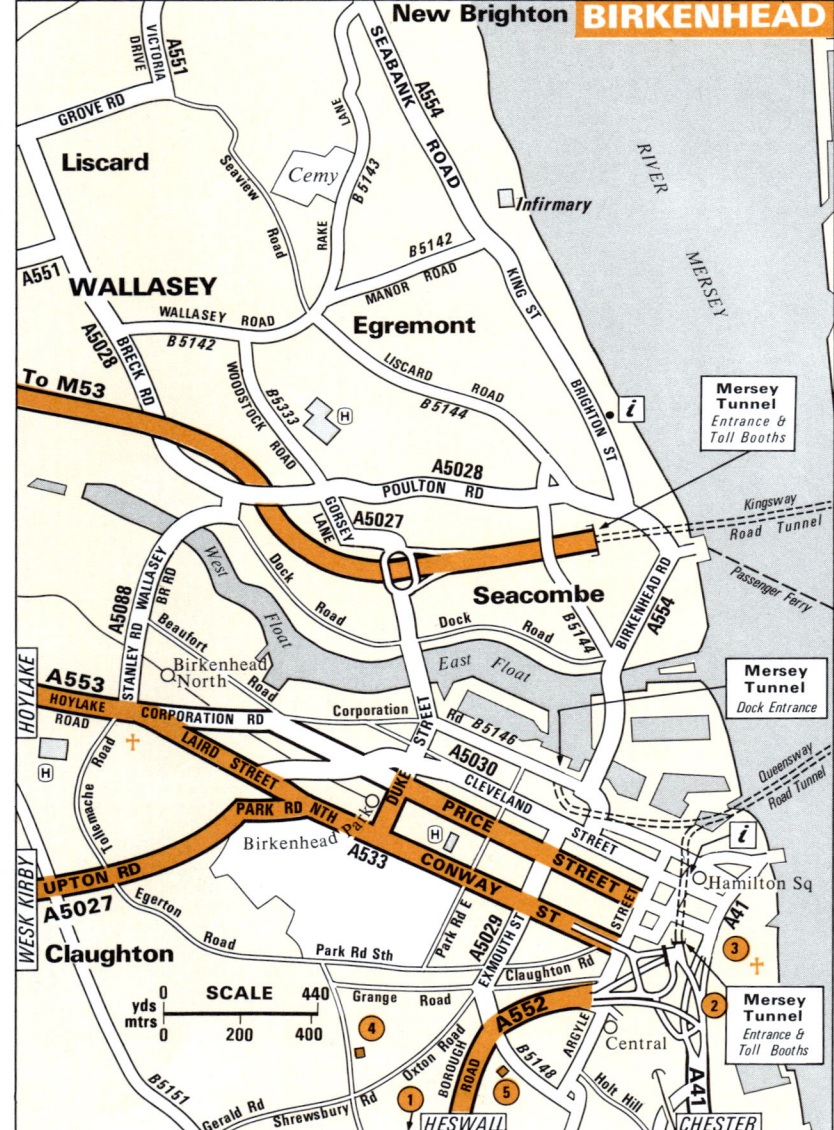

BIRMINGHAM

District Plan overleaf

1. Barber Institute of Fine Arts (D)
2. Birmingham Railway Museum (D)
3. Birmingham University (D)

D – district; C – central

4. Botanic Gardens (D)
5. Bull Ring (C)
6. Council House (museum & art gallery) (C)
7. County Cricket Ground (D)
8. Curzon Street Goods Station (C)
9. Hall of Memory (C)
10. Kennedy Memorial (C)

(Central) BIRMINGHAM

'Spaghetti Junction', and the new Aston Expressway.

St Philip's was built by Thomas Archer in 1711, as a parish church, and became a cathedral in 1905. It has a good baroque tower and four chancel windows by Sir Edward Burne-Jones, who was born near by. St Martin's Church was rebuilt on the original 14th-c plan in 1875 to 1885, and houses ancient tombs of the De Berminghams. The RC Cathedral of St Chad's is by Augustus Pugin, and was the first RC cathedral to be finished after the Reformation. Pugin began St Chad's in 1839, and it was dedicated in 1841. Close by is a mosaic mural in memoriam of Kennedy. The city museum and art gallery forms part of the council house in Victoria Square, and displays fine collections of pre-Raphaelite paintings and recent sculpture. It also includes the unique Pinto gallery of wooden bygones. Further Pinto exhibits are in the preserved Sarehole Water Mill at Hall Green.

A museum of science and industry was opened in 1950, and the Hall of Memory in 1925. The Birmingham Railway Museum has preserved steam locomotives and coaches, and there are plans to preserve the monumental façade of Curzon Street Goods' Station. This was designed by Philip Hardwick, also architect of the wantonly-destroyed Euston Arch of 1836 in London.

Central plan page 149
11 King Edward VI's School (D)
12 Museum of Science and Industry (C)
13 Oratory of St Philip Neri (D)
D district; C central

The town hall (1834), modelled on a classical temple, houses a fine organ and is the home of the City of Birmingham Symphony Orchestra. The first part of the Queen Elizabeth Medical Centre, now a huge complex of buildings, was opened in 1938.

Edgbaston, a suburb 3m from the centre of Birmingham, is the site of the university, the Barber Institute of Fine Arts (OACT), and the county-cricket ground. The Botanical Gardens are also in this area, and King Edward VI's school, founded in 1552, was moved here in 1930.

Cardinal Newman founded the Oratory of St Philip Neri in 1847. Birmingham is also the centre of a canal network linking the city to the Thames, Severn, Mersey, and Humber. The 200th year of Birmingham canal navigation was celebrated in 1969.

BIRSTALL, W Yorks 22 SE22
Birstall itself is part of the town of Batley, and the area is described under various fictional names in Charlotte Brontë's novel, *Shirley*. She called the town Briarfield, and the Elizabethan Oakwell Hall (½m N) Fieldhead (OACT). The Red House, ½m W, appears in her books under the name Briarmains. Charlotte was a pupil of Miss Wooler's school at Roehead from 1831 to 1832, and a teacher from 1835 to 1838. Lord Asquith was born 3m NE at Morley (1852–1928).

14 Queen Elizabeth Medical Centre (D)
15 Sarehole Water Mill (D)
16 St Chad's Cathedral (RC) (C)
17 St Martin's Church (C)

BIRTSMORTON, Glos 12 SO73
The cruciform church is 14thc, with a fine Purbeck-marble table tomb; the picturesque partly 14th-c restored court is moated and timber framed. The latter has a secret hiding place which was used during the Wars of the Roses.

BISHAM, Berks 8 SU88
On the River Thames, with a church displaying a Norman tower and notable range of monuments – including fine Hoby tombs. The Elizabethan Bisham Abbey, now a training centre for physical recreation, incorporates fragments of a 14th-c priory. It is said to be haunted by the ghost of Lady Elizabeth Hoby.

BISHOP AUCKLAND, Co Durham 27 NZ22
A mining town, situated at the junction of the Rivers Wear and Gaunless. The mainly 16th-c castle has been the county residence of the Bishops of Durham since the 12thc, and has a notable 13th-c chapel. Bishops Park has well-kept lawns around two small streams – the Gaunless and the Cordon Burn. The gatehouse to the park is of 1760 and displays a clock of great age.

BISHOP BURTON, Humberside 23 SE93
One of the most delightful of the Wold villages, with cottages picturesquely situated near a wayside pool. A bust of

18 St Philip's Cathedral (C)
19 Town Hall (C)
20 University of Aston in Birmingham (C)

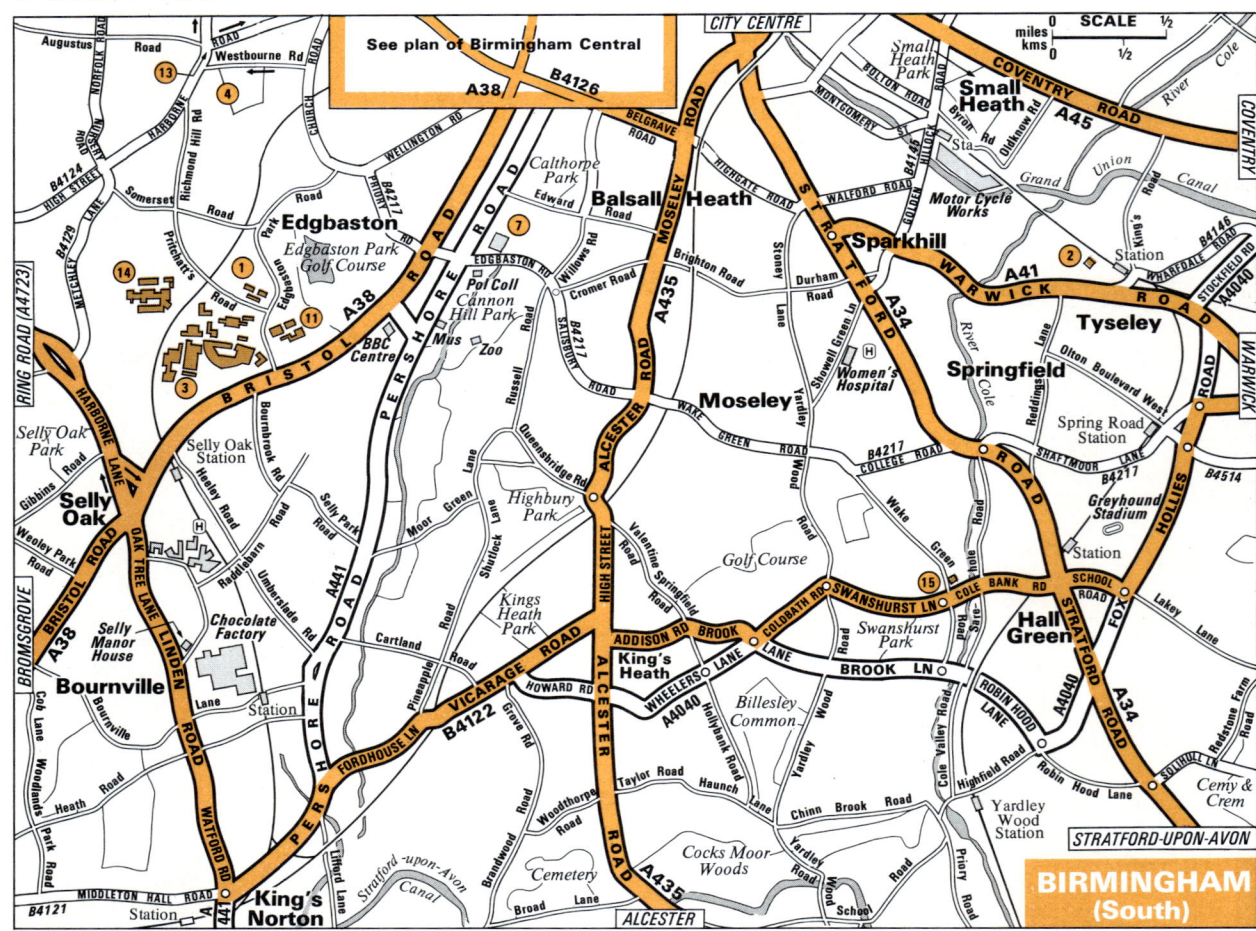

John Wesley, carved from the trunk of a tree under which he preached when at the village, can be seen in the church vestry.

BISHOPSBOURNE, Kent   9 TR15
A delightful Stour-Valley village where Richard Hooker was once vicar of the church (1595–1600), Master of the Temple, and subsequently rector of Boscombe. He was famed for his important book *Ecclesiastical Polity*, and was known as Judicious Hooker because of his exquisite choice of words. Near by is the house in which Joseph Conrad lived until his death in 1924. Bourne Park is a fine Georgian mansion.

BISHOP'S CANNINGS, Wilts   7 SU06
The local church is a fine example of early-English work, and includes a lofty tower and spire. Inside is a rare meditation seat, on which are painted inscriptions about sin and death and the picture of a hand. To the NE, the ancient Wansdyke runs along the crest of the downs, with tumuli and earthworks in the vicinity.

BISHOP'S CASTLE, Salop   11 SO38
A sheep-farming border town on the edge of Clun Forest, with fragmentary remains of a 12th-c castle. The timbered House on Crutches has an overhanging upper storey and is supported on posts. This dates from 1573, and there are several other interesting buildings in the area. The surrounding countryside is of an attractive hilly aspect. Linley estate, where larches were planted as early as 1739, is 3m NE.

BISHOP'S CLEEVE, Glos   12 SO92
A trans-Norman and 14th-c church here has a carved-oak musicians' gallery of the Jacobean period, dated 1604. An old tithe barn is now the village hall, and 2½m NE is 16th-c Dixton Manor, with a towered porch.

BISHOP'S FROME, Herefs & Worcs   12 SO64
The rebuilt church has a good Norman south doorway. The church at Castle Frome (2½m SSW) has a remarkable Norman font with grotesque carvings.

BISHOP'S HULL, Somerset   6 ST22
Bishop's Hull boasts a fine old manor house dating from 1586.

BISHOP'S LYDEARD, Somerset   6 ST12
A beautiful 14th-c cross stands in the churchyard of the perpendicular church. The building itself has a notable sandstone tower, and houses a carved screen.

BISHOP'S STORTFORD, Herts   14 TL42
Original woodcarving can be seen in the 15th-c church, and the old vicarage in South Road was the birthplace of Cecil Rhodes in 1853. The latter building is now a museum. Several old inns, notably the Black Lion and the Boar's Head, are of interest. Hatfield Forest (NT, 3m NE) covers some 1,000 acres and has facilities for boating and fishing.

BISHOP'S TAWTON, Devon   5 SS53
The church has a crocketed octagonal spire which is unique in Devon. Several interesting monuments and some good glass are housed in the building.

BISHOPSTEIGNTON, Devon   5 SX97
A splendidly-carved Norman west porch is attached to the church, and a few remains of a 14th-c bishop's palace can be seen to the NE.

BISHOPSTONE, E Sussex   8 TQ40
The interior of the Saxon to early-English church shows a large amount of Norman work, and the south porch is of Saxon origin.

BISHOPSTONE, Wilts   7 SU02
An Ebble-Valley village with a beautiful, cruciform decorated and perpendicular church, noted for its furnishings.

BISHOP'S WALTHAM, Hants   7 SU51
Remains of a 12th-c bishop's palace (AM) – part of the see of Winchester – are considerable. William of Wykeham died here in 1404.

BISHOPTHORPE, N Yorks   22 SE54
Situated on the River Ouse, where the palace of the Archbishops of York is set in fine gardens and includes a 13th-c chapel.

BISHOP WILTON, Humberside   23 SE75
This attractive Wolds village has a restored early-English to perpendicular church, preserving a fine Norman chancel-arch and south doorway. There are many prehistoric burial-places near by.

BISLEY, Glos   12 SO90
Bisley is a Cotswold hilltop village which includes a partly-Saxon cross. A curious stone monument, which combines a lantern and cross of stone, stands in the churchyard, and Over Court is partly 15thc. There are prehistoric remains and a spring-fed fountain in the vicinity. A well-dressing ceremony is held annually on Ascension Day.

BISLEY, Surrey   8 SU95
A village known mostly for its association with Bisley Camp. A meeting of the National Rifle Association is held 1½m SW each July.

BITTERLEY, Salop   12 SO57
The 14th-c churchyard cross is one of the finest of its period, and the Norman and later church houses a restored screen and loft, and a fine monument. The Elizabethan brick-built house of Crowleasowes is situated ½m N.

BLACK BOURTON, Oxon   13 SP20
Authoress Maria Edgeworth was born here in 1767. The church is noted for its 13th-c wall paintings, restored by Professor Tristram.

BLACKBURN, Lancs   21 SD62
Textiles have been made here since the Flemish weavers first settled here in the 14thc, Blackburn was initially involved in woollens and cotton. Its later diversification of industry helped the town to overcome the worst effects of the cotton-trade depression. Engineering, and the manufacture of electrical apparatus, now employ thousands, and there are three large breweries. The cathedral was formerly St Mary's Church, and was rebuilt in 1820–26 and enlarged in 1937–50. The Lewis Textile Museum illustrates the history and development of the industry (OACT). Much of this history belongs to Blackburn – James Hargreaves, the inventor of the spinning-jenny, was one of the town's weavers. Singer Kathleen Ferrier also was born there.

BLACK COUNTRY
A name usually applied to a strip of country extending approximately from Birmingham to Wolverhampton, which has been largely given over to heavy industry.

BLACKHEATH, Gt London   8 TQ37
This is a high common to the S of Greenwich Park. The introduction of golf into England was effected here by James I in 1608. Morden College for Poor Merchants was built (c1700) by Wren for Sir John Morden, a rich merchant of Aleppo. The carvings are attributed to Grinling Gibbons. A fine example of a Georgian crescent, dating from c1794, is The Paragon. Other good Georgian houses can be seen in Dartmouth Row and Montpelier Row. St Michael's Church has an exceptionally tall and slender spire, dubbed the Needle of Kent, and the Earl of Chesterfield once lived at the early 18th-c Ranger's House. Macartney House, c1720 and later, is associated with General Wolfe. The old manor house is at the top of Croom's Hill (see Greenwich).

BLACKMORE, Essex   9 TL60
The restored 12th- to 15th-c church has some remarkable timbering, notably the tower. The building that stood where Jericho House now stands was a resort of Henry VIII, and is associated with the saying 'Go to Jericho'.

BLACKPOOL, Lancs   21 SD33
Blackpool is a thriving holiday town that began to develop as a recreational resort in the mid 18thc. Each summer the population is increased by some 8 million visitors, and everything the town has to

The tower, Blackpool

offer is operating at its highest peak. Lancashire factories and mines close down for their annual wakes or holidays during this period, so that their workers can enjoy the wealth of available entertainment.

The famous promenade runs beside excellent sands for 7m, allowing beach and bathing access for the millions of trippers. Three piers offer the usual recreations, and the famous tower (518ft) has a ballroom and other amusements. Every autumn sees the lighting up of spectacular illuminated decorations along the shore, and the pleasure beach on the South Shore – also known as the Golden Mile – is packed with funfair distractions. The town also boasts ten theatres. The last remaining trams in Britain run along the front.

East Park Drive has a notable zoo, and facilities for sports including boating, tennis, and golf, set amid richly-planted gardens. County matches are held at the local cricket ground, and all the big teams in League Football have played Blackpool at Bloomfield Road. Annual events include a host of dog shows, horse-trials, bowls tournaments, swimming championships, beauty contests, dance festivals, and political conferences.

BLADON, Oxon *13 SP41*
A modern church is sited on the edge of the great park of Blenheim here, and the churchyard contains the tombs of Sir Winston Churchill and his father, Lord Randolph Churchill.

BLAGDON, Avon *6 ST55*
The miniature 'Cheddar Gorge' in this area (2m SW), is where Toplady wrote the hymn *Rock of Ages*. The church has a perpendicular tower, and the Yeo reservoir lies N.

BLAKENEY, Glos *12 SO60*
A village on the edge of the Forest of Dean national forest park. A well-preserved stretch of the Roman Dean road can be seen 2m NW, at Blackpool Bridge.

BLAKENEY, Norfolk *15 TG04*
This picturesque tidal port is well-favoured by yachtsmen. Extensive salt-marshes are a feature of the neighbourhood. The church, early-English and later, has two towers of which one may have been for a beacon. The nave roof is of an angel-carved, hammerbeam type, the seven-light chancel window is 13thc, and some old screenwork has been retained. The guildhall (AM) is 15thc. A windmill can be seen in the vicinity, and 2m N is a 1,000 acre bird sanctuary at Blakeney Point. The latter can be reached by ferry.

BLANCHLAND, Northumberland *27 NY95*
Stone-built Blanchland is situated in the Derwent Valley. The settlement was planned in the early 18thc, and the building of its cottages followed the ground plan of monastic buildings founded here in the 12thc. The 13th-c church incorporates remains of a 12th-c abbey. An old cross with a traceried head stands in the churchyard. Also of note are a 15th-c gatehouse and an interesting old inn, the Lord Crewe Arms.

BLANDFORD FORUM, Dorset *7 ST80*
Blandford gained its Forum suffix to distinguish it from other towns of this name. The word Forum is the equivalent of the early-English word Chipping, meaning market. A town existed here in early times, but was almost wiped out by fire in 1731. All but about fifty buildings were destroyed, and most of the present houses are of subsequent date. Many of these, including the church, were put up by the Bastard brothers. These local architects had been brought up in the tradition of Wren and, as a result the town enjoys the reputation of being an outstanding illustration of Georgian architecture. A memorial in the form of a Roman temple (1760) recalls the fire. The contemporary church contains a notable mayor's chair.

Early buildings that survived are Ryves almshouses and the Old House, both of the 17thc. Blandford St Mary, across the river, has a decorated and perpendicular church. To the NW, Bryanston House is by Norman Shaw (1890) and now serves as a public school.

BLAYDON, Tyne & Wear *27 NZ16*
An industrial town on the south bank of the River Tyne, formerly known for its collieries, but now engaged in a variety of interests which include fire-clay products, machine tools, paint, engineering, and thermo-plastic manufacture. The song *Blaydon Races* is the folk anthem of Tyneside, and refers to a racecourse that has long since gone. The course is now part of the site occupied by the Stella South Power Station.

BLEDINGTON, Glos *12 SP22*
Bledington is sited on the River Evenlode, with a maypole and a good Norman to perpendicular church containing examples of old glass. The fine old manor house of Icomb Place is situated 2m NW, and Maugersbury Hill forms a good viewpoint at nearly 800ft high.

BLEDLOW, Bucks *8 SP70*
The 13th- and 14th-c church has a Norman font. Beside the church is the Lyde stream, which supplies local watercress beds. The manor house and Forty Green farm (1m NW) are both 18thc, and Bledlow Cross on Wain Hill may be 17thc. Bledlow Ridge affords wide views over the surrounding countryside.

BLENHEIM PALACE, Oxon *13 SP41*
This palatial mansion, by Vanbrugh, was started in 1705 and completed after the death of the Duke of Marlborough in 1722 (OACT). £250,000 of the total cost of £300,000 was defrayed by Parliament as a reward for Marlborough's victory over the French at Blenheim. The palace is rich in furnishings and art treasures, and it was here that Sir Winston Churchill was born in 1874. He was buried in the nearby village of Bladon. The deer-park is always open to pedestrians. The beautiful lake, with an unfinished bridge and a column in honour of the great Duke, was created by Capability Brown. The surrounding trees were planted in groups to represent the Battle of Blenheim.

BLETCHINGLEY, Surrey *8 TQ35*
An attractive village with a broad main street containing several interesting old houses. Of particular note is the 16th-c Whyte Harte inn. The large church is one of the finest in the county. Its Norman tower was built in *c*1090, and increased to its present height *c*1160. The rest is

1 Blackpool Tower
2 Football Ground
3 Zoo

mainly of the 15thc. A notable feature is the large monument (1707) to Sir Robert Clayton, Lord Mayor of London, and his wife. A few traces of the castle – once the home of Henry VIII's divorced queen, Anne of Cleves – still remain. Half-timbered Brewer Street farm (15thc), and the 17th-c buildings of Pendell Court and Pendell House lie ¾m N.

BLETCHLEY, Bucks 13 SP83
A market town and railway junction. The chancel of the church contains a curious portrait engraved on copper. A large New Town planned for the district is being laid out at Milton Keynes.

BLEWBURY, Oxon 13 SU58
Blewbury is noted for half-timbered houses and thatched-top walls. The trans-Norman to perpendicular church houses brasses and some chained books.

BLIDWORTH, Notts 18 SK55
This colliery village in the Sherwood Forest was traditionally the home of Friar Tuck. Blidworth Rocking is a cradle-rocking ceremony – an old church custom – which is still held annually on February 2.

BLISLAND, Cornwall 4 SX07
The Norman to 16th-c Church of St Proteus and St Hyacinth displays fine wagon roofs, with angels. Inside are a Norman and 15th-c font and a carved 17th-c pulpit. Other features of the village are an old manor house and the attractive tree-bordered green. Two prehistoric stone circles can be seen in the area: to the NE are the Trippet Stones, a circle of eight erect rocks; a little more distant are the Stipple Stones, a bronze-age circle with a 13ft central member, at the top of Hawks Tor.

BLISWORTH, Northants 13 SP75
This village includes a 14th-c church with a good screen amongst its many old stone-built cottages. The twin pavilions comprising Stoke Bruerne House (3m SE, OACT), are attributed to Inigo Jones and are all that remain of Stoke Park. This park was twice rebuilt after its burning in 1884. The Waterways Museum is situated on the Grand Union Canal, to the N, near the point where the canal enters a 2m tunnel between Stoke Bruerne and Blisworth.

BLOXHAM, Oxon 13 SP43
Bloxham has an exceptionally fine church, mainly decorated in style, and with a 198ft spire. The east window is by William Morris and Edward Burne-Jones; other interesting items include the west door of the tower, the buttresses, and a 15th-c screen. A few old houses still stand in the village.

BLUNDESTON, Suffolk 15 TM59
Associated with the poet Thomas Gray, writer of *Elegy Written in a Country Churchyard*, this village is also mentioned in Charles Dickens' *David Copperfield*. The mainly early-English church has been restored as a Dickens memorial, and displays a round tower and a fine screen.

BLYTH, Northumberland 27 NZ38
An industrial port serving an expanding industrial area, with bathing from excellent sands. Seaton Delaval Hall, an 18th-c baroque-style structure by Vanbrugh, lies 3m SW of the town. It is, perhaps, this designer's finest work (OACT).

BLYTH, Notts 18 SK68
The church is part of an 11th-c priory and includes an interesting early-Norman nave. The original stone screen across the nave is now built into the east wall of the church. The Angel Inn is of ancient foundation.

BLYTHBURGH, Suffolk 15 TM47
Blythburgh's 15th-c church was built here when the place was a thriving port. It is one of the best known in East Anglia, and displays fine carvings. An unusual feature is a carved portrayal of the Seven Deadly Sins on the benches, instead of the usual poppyheads. Cromwell's troops used the building as a stable, and marks on the pillars show where the horses were tethered.

BOCKING, Essex 15 TL72
Many old houses can be seen here, and the 15th-c church has unusual tower buttresses. Brick-built Panfield Old Hall (Elizabethan) is sited 2m NW.

BOCKLETON, Herefs & Worcs 12 SO56
This village's Norman and later church contains the fine Barnely monument of 1594. Old mounting steps approach the 15th-c lych-gate, and Bockleton Court Farm displays a number of interesting Jacobean features.

BODENHAM, Herefs & Worcs 12 SO55
The partly 13th-c church has a massive tower, and Broadfield Court (N) is of 14th-c and later origin.

BODIAM, E Sussex 9 TQ72
A fine moated castle (NT) was built here in 1386 to discourage French raiders from sailing up the River Rother. Now a hollow shell, the castle was dismantled in 1643 and restored by Lord Curzon in 1925 (OACT). The great gateway is flanked by turrets, and the outer portcullis can still be seen. The nearby Guinness estate is the largest hop farm in Britain.

BODINNICK, Cornwall 4 SX15
Fowey faces Bodinnick across the estuary, and a car ferry plies between the two. Old cottages and the Ferry Inn are of interest. Hall Walk (NT) is a fine viewpoint where memorials to Sir Arthur Quiller Couch, and the dead of the Second World War, are sited.

BODMIN, Cornwall 4 SX06
This is the county town of Cornwall and is sited on the steep edge of Bodmin Moor. St Petroc's Church was rebuilt in 1469 and is probably the largest old church in the county. It houses a fine Norman font, and the waters of St Guron's well, near the churchyard, were once recommended as a cure for eye complaints.

The town includes an interesting county, regimental museum, and the district is rich in Roman and prehistoric remains. Bodmin Beacon (SW) bears a 144ft obelisk to General Sir Walter Raleigh Gilbert, whose ancestors were the Elizabethan sailors Raleigh and Gilbert.

Bodmin Moor (NE) is an area of outstanding natural beauty, and rises to its highest points at Brown Willy (1,375ft) and Rough Tor (1,312ft) (NT). Lanhydrock Park (NT), a restored 17th-c house with a notable gatehouse and picture gallery (OACT), can be seen 2½m S. The beautifully-wooded Glynn Valley contains the Fowey River and lies 3m SE.

BOGNOR REGIS, W Sussex 8 SZ99
Plan overleaf
A popular resort which began life as a Saxon village. The name Regis commemorates a visit by George V, who stayed at Craigweil House (now demolished) during his convalescence in 1929. The Dome House (1793) is now Bognor Training College.

BOLAM, Northumberland 27 NZ08
The church has a late-Saxon tower, and a Norman nave and chancel. On the moors (W) is the 6ft standing stone of Poind and his man. The Roman Devil's Causeway is in the vicinity.

BOLDON, Tyne & Wear 27 NZ36
West Boldon church, particularly the spire, is partly of 13th-c origin. The fine hall dates from 1709, and Scot's House (1½m W) is dated 1798. Mid 18th-c Boldon House is situated at East Boldon.

BOLLINGTON, Cheshire 18 SJ97
On a 920ft hill to the S of this cotton town is White Nancy, a white-painted tower erected as a Waterloo memorial.

BOLSOVER, Derbyshire 18 SK47
The imposing castle (AM) is of Norman origin, but was restored and enlarged in 1613. Some of the panelling and all of the fireplaces are of note, and an interesting range of buildings includes the riding school and gallery. The latter were added after 1617. The church, rebuilt after a fire, houses Cavendish monuments.

BOLTON, Gt Manchester 21 SD70
Bolton, the home of fine spinning and weaving, has been known as one of the great Lancashire cotton centres for many years.

Two very important inventions of the industrial revolution were made by inhabitants of the town: Samuel Crompton, a native, conceived the spinning-jenny; Arkwright, a local barber, designed the water frame. Needless to say both these machines had applications in the cotton industry. Crompton perfected his machine in 1779 at Hall i' th' Wood, a timber and stone house which now houses a folk museum (OACT). He also pioneered the making of textile machinery, plus subsidiary industries like bleaching, dyeing, and fabric finishing. Many factories fell out of use when the cotton industry was re-organized, and over fifty of these have been adapted to other uses. Engineering is now the leading industry in the town.

An interesting old inn in Church Gate is the Old Man and Scythe, a building with its origins in the 13thc. It was here that Cromwell lodged the Earl of Derby for the night of October 14, 1641, before having him beheaded in the market place the next day in retaliation for a Royalist massacre. Behind the 1873 town hall, a modern civic centre (1939) includes a fine library, museum, and art gallery. The striking new Octagon theatre was opened in 1967. Smithills Hall (OACT), a half-timbered building of the 14thc and later, lies 2m NW.

BOLTON ABBEY, N Yorks 22 SE05
Situated on the River Wharfe, which can be crossed here by a footbridge or stepping stones, the 12th-c abbey is strictly a priory. The structure lies in ruins except for the nave, which has been a parish church since c1170.

cont

BOLTON ABBEY/BOSCASTLE

Bolton Hall is a 19th-c mansion incorporating the old gatehouse, which lies W of the abbey. Riverside paths lead through woodland to the Strid (2m N), a gorge where the river rushes through a 12ft channel. Strid is derived from an old-English word meaning turmoil. Farther N are the picturesquely situated ruins of late 15th-c Barden Tower. The quaint circular Beamsley Hospital (1593), a group of almshouses for old women, can be seen 2m SE on the Harrogate road.

BOLTON-BY-BOWLAND, Lancs 21 SD74
A secluded village by Tosside Beck, near the River Ribble, which retains its stocks and a ruined cross. The church is of perpendicular style, and Henry VI took refuge at the Old Hall in the 15thc.

BOLTONGATE, Cumbria 26 NY24
The remarkable perpendicular church contains Scottish-type pointed-stone vaulting. A peel tower is attached to the rectory.

BOLTON PERCY, N Yorks 22 SE54
This place has one of Yorkshire's most memorable village churches, constructed in 1424 and especially noted for its beautiful chancel. It also houses a complete set of Jacobean box-pews.

BOLVENTOR, Cornwall 5 SX17
A small village in the middle of Bodmin Moor, and the location of Jamaica's Inn as featured in Daphne du Maurier's book and film of the same name. Dozmary Pool, situated high on the moors 1½m SE, is the water where King Arthur was given the mystic sword Excalibur – according to legend. It is also associated with the legendary Cornish demon Tregeagle, who was set the endless task of emptying the pool with a limpet shell.

BONCHURCH, Isle of Wight 7 SZ57
An old delightfully-situated village under St Boniface Down (NT), where the Victorian villas where Dickens, Thackeray, and Macaulay stayed are still standing. Near the sea to the NE is a picturesque landslip, and farther N is well-known Luccombe Chine. Algernon Swinburne was buried in the churchyard in 1909.

BOOKHAM, GREAT, Surrey 8 TQ15
Great Bookham church is a building of particular interest. The nave walls are late 11thc, and remains of contemporary frescoes can be seen on the north wall. Round piers with scalloped capitals are features of the 12th-c south arcade, and the lower tower and north arcade are trans-Norman, of the late 12thc. The chancel is dated 1341. Monuments housed within the building are exceptional, and include several to the Slyfield family. The Slyfield Chapel dates from the 15thc. Jane Austen was a frequent visitor at the Old Rectory, and Fanny Burney wrote her novel *Camilla* at Fairfield House, High Street, in 1796. The village hall is a reconstructed 15th-c barn. Polesden Lacey House (NT), designed by Cubitt in 1824, lies 2m S. It is set amid splendid gardens and contains notable works of art (OACT).

BOOT, Cumbria 21 NY10
This village is beautifully situated in Eskdale, facing Lakeland's highest mountains. Prominent to the E at 2,140ft is Harter Fell. Dalegarth Hall is a quaint old farmhouse with typical round chimneys, and Stanley Force is a notable waterfall. The terminus of the Eskdale narrow-gauge railway is near Boot, and an iron girder crossing the river once supported a bridge on the 'Owd Ratty' railway line. This was built by Ratcliffe in the 1870's, to carry ore from the mines at Boot. The Eskdale narrow gauge railway occupies part of this line.

BOOTLE, Merseyside 17 SJ39
Adjoining Liverpool to the N, Bootle has the largest and newest docks on the Mersey Estuary. It is also headquarters of the Post Office Giro Bank.

BORDEN, Kent 9 TQ86
The church has a Norman tower and a fine 16th-c lady-chapel roof. Many old timbered houses can be seen in the area, and restored Borden Hall is partly 15thc.

BOREHAM, Essex 9 TL70
Boreham House dates from 1728 and is now a college. The Norman and later church includes Sussex and Tufnell chapels. New Hall, now a convent, was built by Henry VIII.

BOROUGHBRIDGE, N Yorks 22 SE36
A fine old bridge spanning the Ure marks the meeting of the former W and N Ridings. The Devil's Arrows prehistoric monoliths are large stone monoliths which can be seen in the area. A 250ft well with a modern canopy stands in the market place. The Duke of Lancaster was defeated here by Edward II in 1322, and the pro-Catholic rising of the northern earls came to an end at Tancred's manor house – later the Crown – in 1569.

BORROWDALE, Cumbria 21 NY21
Considered to be the most beautiful valley in the Lake District, with impressive fell scenery on all sides. Glaramara (2,560ft) and Great End (2,984ft) dominate the horizon to the S, and much of the area is NT property. Sir Hugh Walpole lived at Brackenbury.

BORWICK, Lancs 21 SD57
A village with a fine Elizabethan hall, which incorporates an earlier peel tower.

BOSBURY, Herefs & Worcs 12 SO64
An attractive village with half-timbered houses and a Norman and later church of red sandstone. The latter displays several splendid monuments, one of which is signed by John Guldo (1573). The Crown Inn has a panelled room of 1571.

BOSCASTLE, Cornwall 4 SX09
This picturesque Valency-Valley village has a small harbour (NT) guarded by cliffs on either side. The rocky beach has odd patches of sand, and allows access for bathing. St Symphorian's Church, Forrabury, is partly Norman with a tower of 1750. Welltown Manor (SW) dates from c1640. Most of the neighbouring coastal scenery is of a rugged aspect, and the cliffs to the NE – nearing Cambeak – are the highest in Cornwall. High Cliff rises to 731ft, but not in a single sheer drop.

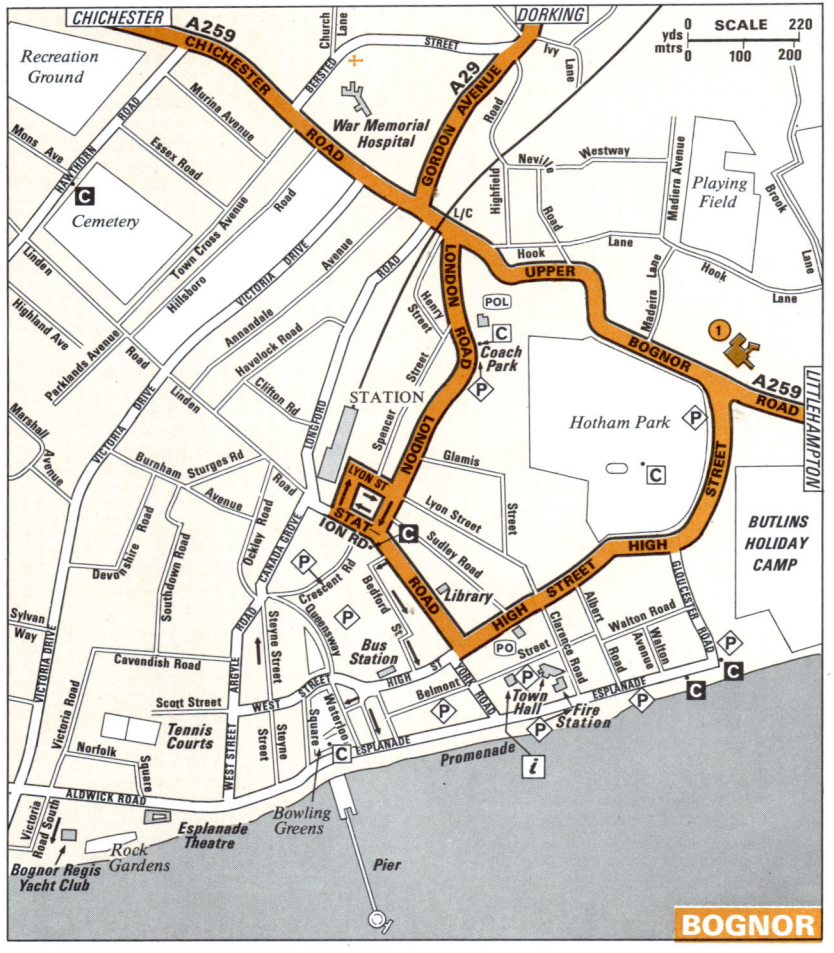

BOGNOR

1   Dome House

BOSCOMBE, Dorset *7 SZ19*
A resort with excellent sands and bathing, forming part of Bournemouth.

BOSHAM, W Sussex *8 SU80*
Pronounced Bozzam, this is a fishing village and yachting centre situated on a creek of Chichester Harbour. The partly-Saxon church has a fine Norman font, and appears on the Bayeux tapestry. Harold sailed to Normandy from here, and Bosham may have been the place where King Canute attempted to command the sea. Various old houses can be seen in the village.

BOSSINEY, Cornwall *4 SX08*
A tiny village adjoining Tintagel, with the distinction of having had Sir Francis Drake as its MP. Wild well-wooded Rocky Valley contains a waterfall and lies to the E.

BOSTON, Lincs *19 TF34*
This ancient seaport on the River Witham is still an important link with the Continent. Its function as a port declined when the opening up of the New World caused the diversion of much of its trade to W-coast ports, and the harbour is partly silted up. It does, however, still deal with cattle, timber, and bananas.

St Botolph is reputed to have founded a monastery hereabouts in 654, and the name Boston is a shortened corruption of Botolph's town. Although started in 1309, the present St Botolph's Church was completed in 1460 and the bulk of the building is of the 15thc. It is an outstanding example of the perpendicular style, and is one of the largest parish churches in England. The 272ft tower is nicknamed the Boston Stump, and is used as a navigational aid for shipping in The Wash. It has a peal of ten, and a carillon of fifteen bells. Of particular note are the south porch, with its fine double doors, the medieval stalls, and several brasses. The south porch is of 14th- and 15th-c origin.

The guildhall of 1450 shows a good example of 15th-c linenfold panelling, restored largely by American help in 1911. It now serves as the Borough Museum. The doors of the cells in which the Pilgrim Fathers were imprisoned during their original attempt to sail to Holland and America, can still be seen. The American town of Boston derives its title from here, the name being taken to the New World by immigrants who sailed from the port with John Winthrop in 1630.

Fydell House, standing next door to the guildhall, is a fine example of Queen Anne architecture (OACT). A modern grammar school preserves its original schoolroom of 1567 as a library, and the refectory of a 13th-c Dominican friary has been restored for use as the Little Theatre. Pescod Hall in Mitre Lane is now a warehouse, but was once the home of a 14th-c merchant. The Maud Foster windmill has been standing on its site at Skirbeck, overlooking the river, for 150 years. Other items of interest include partly-restored black-and-white Shodfriar's Hall, the Hussey and Rochford Towers in Skirbeck, and the many fine old town warehouses.

BOSTON SPA, N Yorks *22 SE44*
An inland resort on the River Wharfe, with saline springs.

BOTHAL, Northumberland *27 NZ28*
A River-Wansbeck village with a castle displaying a fine 14th-c gateway. The restored church is also of the 14thc, and contains fragments of medieval glass.

BOTLEY, Hants *7 SU51*
Situated on the River Hamble, this village comprises old houses along a wide main street. The district is famous for its strawberries. A modern memorial has been raised to William Cobbett, author of *Rural Rides*, who lived here from 1805 to 1817. The land along the river at Curdridge (S) is NT property.

BOTTESFORD, Leics *19 SK83*
Old stocks and a whipping post stand near the remains of an old cross in this village. The interesting decorated to perpendicular church displays some notable monuments, two of which are by Grinling Gibbons. Most of these are to the former owners of Belvoir Castle, the Earls of Rutland.

BOTTISHAM, Cambs *14 TL56*
One of the Cambridgeshire village-colleges of 1937 is situated here, and the village has a fine 13th- and 14th-c church. Anglesey Abbey (NT) was built in 1236 and altered in 1600. Its notable 100-acre gardens have been developed since 1930 (OACT).

BOUGHTON ALUPH, Kent *9 TR04*
The Aluph part of this name refers to a former owner. The 13th- to 14th-c church houses some old glass and displays a fine tower. Boughton Lees manor house (SW) is a 17th-c brick and timber construction.

BOUGHTON MALHERBE, Kent *9 TQ84*
Malherbe is the name of the family that once owned this village. The much-restored village church dates from the 14thc, and contains interesting brasses. A nearby manor house was the birthplace of poet Sir Henry Wotton, in 1568.

BOUGHTON MONCHELSEA, Kent *9 TQ74*
The Monchelsea part of the name relates to the family that once owned Boughton Place, a grey-stone, battlemented Elizabethan house set in an 18th-c deer park (OACT). One of England's oldest lych-gates can be seen at the restored church, and the village itself stands on a ridge.

BOULGE, Suffolk *15 TM25*
Edward Fitzgerald, translator of the *Rubiayat of Omar Khayyam*, is buried in the local churchyard. A rose tree on his grave was grown from the seed of a similar tree growing on the grave of Omar Khayyam in Naishapur.

BOURN, Cambs *14 TL35*
A pleasant village with a much-restored Jacobean hall. The restored church carries a fine west tower, and displays some 15th-c woodwork. An old post-mill, possibly the earliest surviving example of its type in the country (1633), also exists here.

BOURNE, Lincs *19 TF02*
This market town is said to have been the birthplace of Hereward the Wake, the last Saxon to resist the invasion of William the Conqueror. Local water is said to be some of the purest in the country, and numerous watercress beds are to be seen in the area. Tudor cottages exist in South Street, and good Georgian houses can be seen throughout the town. The church nave is trans-Norman, and the Red Hall is Elizabethan. Castle earthworks lie to the S, and the Roman canal known as Car Dyke flows E of the town. Sir William Cecil, Lord High Treasurer to Elizabeth I, was born here in what is now the Burghley Arms Hotel.

BOURNEMOUTH, Dorset *7 SZ09*
Plan overleaf
Bournemouth is a resort set among large gardens and pine clusters, with a very mild climate. Nearly every form of entertainment and outdoor sport is available, and large events include tennis tournaments, county-cricket matches, and league football. The 100ft cliffs that surround the bay are penetrated by deep ravines, or chines, and the beach offers good sand and safe bathing. Two piers and three lifts connect the beaches with street level.

The interesting Russell-Cotes Art Gallery and Museum specializes in Victorian art, and the Rothesay Museum exhibits many early-Italian paintings. The Winter Gardens are the home of the world-renowned Bournemouth Symphony Orchestra, and the East-Cliff rock garden is noted for its collection of geological specimens. Robert Louis Stevenson's association with Bournemouth is commemorated by a memorial garden at his former home in Alum Chine Road.

Bournemouth is an excellent centre for touring in both the New Forest and the Wessex of Thomas Hardy. The latter described this town in his novel, *Tess of the D'Urbervilles*.

BOURTON-ON-THE-HILL, Glos *12 SP13*
This picturesque Cotswold village comprises old cottages and an 11th-c and later church. A fine example of a Winchester Bushel, for weights and measures, can be seen inside the church. Bourton House is 16thc, and 1½m S is the unique Indian-style Sezincote House, a 19th-c building set in fine grounds.

BOURTON-ON-THE-WATER, Glos *12 SP12*
A delightfully situated village, where the River Windrush is crossed by miniature stone bridges. Interesting features include typical Cotswold houses, the Birdland Zoo Gardens, a witchcraft museum, and the New Inn's fascinating model of the settlement.

BOVEY TRACEY, Devon *5 SX87*
Views across Dartmoor are offered by this small town. The church, dedicated to St Thomas à Becket, is traditionally held to have been built by Sir William de Tracey to expiate his part in Becket's murder, in 1170. The original building was burned down c1320, and the present design is perpendicular with a decorated tower. The carved pulpit and screen are outstanding examples of characteristic Devon style. In January 1646, Cromwell took Royalist troops at Bovey by surprise and captured many prisoners. Perhaps it was for this reason that the name Cromwell's Arch was given to an old gateway which once formed part of an early priory. To the W is Yarner Wood reserve, one of the four such areas adjoining the town.

BOVINGTON CAMP, Dorset *6 SY88*
This large military camp includes an

interesting museum of armoured fighting vehicles from the two world-wars (OACT).

BOWES, Co Durham 22 NY91
Remains of the Roman station *Lavatrae* have been found here, and the ruined castle (AM) is of Norman origin. A house at Bowes has been identified with Dotheboys Hall, described in Dickens' *Nicholas Nickleby*. The old pump mentioned in the novel has been preserved. The Roman camp of Rey Cross, 6m W off the A66, includes the remains of a cross described in Scott's *Rokeby*.

BOWNESS-ON-WINDERMERE, Cumbria 21 SD49
Situated on the east bank of Windermere, this resort includes facilities for water-skiing, pony-trekking, etc. The 15th-c church contains some old stained glass and a rare wooden equestrian statue of St Martin. The cylindrical island-mansion of Belle Isle dates from 1774.

BOX, Wilts 6 ST86
Bath stone was once extracted from this area, and the quarries were used as an aircraft factory during the last war. They also served as safe storehouses for national treasures during the same period. The 1¾m Box railway tunnel was built by Brunel, and was dug 300ft below ground level. Shockerwick House, by John Wood the Elder (c1750 and later), lies 2m W. An old lock-up exists in the village.

BOXFORD, Suffolk 15 TL94
A quaint old village of timbered and plastered houses, with a mainly-perpendicular church displaying a fine 14th-c wooden north porch and containing a 17th-c font with doors.

BOXGROVE, W Sussex 8 SU90
Boxgrove's impressive church was built around the remains of Boxgrove Priory, and both the choir and De La Warr chantry (1532) are notable. On a nearby hill is the well-restored mid 18th-c brick tower mill of Halnaker. Old cottages exist in the village.

BOX HILL, Surrey 8 TQ15
A noted beauty spot and viewpoint, so named because of the box trees that used to surround its flanks. These were mostly cut down for wood engraving in the 18thc, but some still exist. The 590ft hill (NT) is an expanse of down and woodland and has been designated an area of outstanding natural beauty. Above Burford Bridge is Flint Cottage, where George Meredith lived from 1867 to 1909, and Max Beerbohm during the Second World War. Little Switzerland beauty spot (NT) lies N of Box Hill.

BOXLEY, Kent 9 TQ75
The local church has a west chapel attached to the tall 15th-c tower, and a memorial to Sir Francis Wyatt, who was Governor of Virginia in 1621. There are also remains of Kent's only Cistercian abbey, founded in 1146, and a splendid medieval tithe barn can be seen near by.

BOYNTON, Humberside 23 TA16
The hall is Elizabethan and later, and the 18th-c church houses a lectern carved with a turkey design. The Stricklands of Boynton are thought to have introduced the bird into England.

BRABOURNE, Kent 9 TR14
The church's Norman window contains some very rare glass of the same period. Fine brasses and a heartshrine can be seen in the chancel.

BRACKLESHAM BAY, W Sussex 8 SZ89
A small resort with a shingle beach that graduates to sand at low tide. There are marine fossils in the area, and a geological bed takes its name from the bay.

BRACKLEY, Northants 13 SP53
The church has an early-English tower, and the 13th-c chapel of Magdalen College was the old chapel of St John's Hospital. Crewe almshouses (1633) and several 18th-c houses can be seen in the long wide main street.

1 County Cricket Ground	3 Football Ground	5 Rothesay Museum
2 East Cliff Rock Garden	4 Russell-Cotes Museum and Art Gallery	6 Winter Gardens

BOURNEMOUTH

BRADBOURNE, Derbyshire 18 SK25
A rich Norman south-doorway and fragments of a sculptured pre-Norman cross can be seen in the 13th- to 15th-c church. The village also has an Elizabethan hall.

BRADENHAM, Bucks 8 SU89
Bradenham is beautifully situated below the Chiltern beechwoods. The fine 17th-c manor house was once the home of Isaac Disraeli, and his famous son Benjamin. A Norman doorway and perpendicular tower are features of the local church.

BRADFORD, W Yorks 22 SE13
Bradford, a centre of the wool and worsted industry for some time, is now a university city. Its parish church became a cathedral in 1920, and the Institute of Technology was raised to university status in 1966. The city's sporting facilities include a county-cricket ground and several football clubs. Its town hall and wool exchange were both built in the Victorian-gothic style by a local firm.

Cartwright Memorial Hall houses a museum and art gallery, and is set in Lister Park which also contains botanical gardens. Another museum is housed in partly 14th-c and partly-Elizabethan Bolling Hall (OACT). Composer Frederick Delius was born in Bradford in 1862. Horton Hall lies SW of the city, and is of the late 17thc. Near by is the slightly earlier Old Hall, and Royds Hall is of mainly 17th-c construction.

BRADFORD ABBAS, Dorset 6 ST51
The local church houses a stone screen and carved bench-ends, and its tower is of note. One of Dorset's finest tithe barns can be seen at Wyke Farm, to the E. This building is a full 268ft in length.

BRADFORD-ON-AVON, Wilts 6 ST86
An ancient bridge (AM) that crosses the River Avon at this point is surmounted by a rare bridge-chapel, and the town is criss-crossed with quaint old alleyways. Old weavers' cottages can be seen in the street called Dutch Barton, and tiny St Lawrence's Church is one of the finest, complete Saxon churches in the country. The latter is thought to have been built by St Aldelm. Several old tombs and brasses can be seen in the Norman to perpendicular parish church, and the church hall dates from the early 16thc.

Barton tithe barn is one of the best preserved in the country, and the nearby medieval bridge is also of particular note. The many 17th- and 18th-c houses in the area include Westbury House and Druce's Hill House. Belcombe Court is a fine Georgian mansion, and John Hall's almshouses date from 1700. The perpendicular-style Hermitage, or Tory Chapel, was restored in 1870, and the Old Priory is of mainly 15th-c origin. The Hall (Kingston Hall) dates from c1600 and was used as a model for the Paris Exhibition of 1900.

BRADING, Isle of Wight 7 SZ68
Brading is sited on a once-navigable inlet, where the interesting church (1150 to 1250) is noted for wooden Oglander monuments housed in a 15th-c chapel. The old town hall preserves stocks and a whipping post, plus a rare bull-baiting ring. A notable Roman villa lies 1m S on the sheltered southern side of Brading Down (OACT). The Oglander family came to Brading in 1607, and lived 1m NW in 16th-c and later Nunwell House (OACT).

BRADNINCH, Devon 5 SS90
King Charles I stayed at the old manor house in 1644, and the bed in which he slept is still in existence. A good painted screen in the 15th-c church is of typical Devon style.

BRADWELL WATERSIDE, Essex 9 TL90
Also known under the names Bradwell-juxta-Mare and Bradwell-on-Sea, this place is sited on the Blackwater estuary and has a sand and shingle beach. Bradwell Lodge is a good 16th-c and later house. There is a nuclear power station in the vicinity, and a marina is being built. On the coast 3m E is the tiny 7th-c Chapel of St Peter-on-the-Wall, built largely of Roman materials from the fort of Oltona. It is accessible only by foot.

BRAINTREE, Essex 15 TL72
Situated on the River Blackwater, at the meeting of two Roman roads, Braintree was once a medieval wool town. Today it is noted for the manufacture of silks, rayons, and metal windows. The 13th-c and later church has been restored with a shingled broach spire.

BRAITHWAITE, Cumbria 26 NY22
A village at the S end of Coledale Valley. To the W the Whinlatter Pass (1,043ft) crosses to Lorton, and farther S the peaks of Grisedale Pike and Hobcarton Pike rise to respective heights of 2,393ft and 2,525ft. On the far side of Coledale Pass is the prominent Eel Crag (2,649ft).

BRAMBER, W Sussex 8 TQ11
Bramber lies on the River Adur, with a ruined Norman castle (NT) that has been owned by the Dukes of Norfolk from the 14th to the 20thc. It was one of the many such places that suffered destruction during the Civil War. Nicholas Barbon (alias Praise-God-Barebones) was born here; in 1680 he introduced fire insurance, following the Great Fire of London in 1666.

BRAMCOTE, Notts 18 SK53
Bramcote Hill, 4½m SW of Nottingham, is a notable viewpoint. Bramcote Hall is a fine old mansion, and near by is the isolated Hemlock Stone.

BRAMFIELD, Suffolk 15 TM47
The Tudor and early-Georgian hall has curved-brick crinkle-crankle garden walls, a type of construction almost unique to Suffolk. The church has a 13th-c round tower and houses a good painted screen, plus the early-English Coke monument.

BRAMHAM, W Yorkshire 22 SE44
Splendid 17th-c Bramham Park is built in the classical style, and is set in gardens featuring canals and temples in the Versailles manner (OACT).

BRAMLEY, Hants 7 SU65
The Norman and later church has a 17th-c tower, and a chapel dating from 1801. The latter houses a tomb that is thought to be by Banks (1777). Notable wall paintings include one which illustrates the murder of Thomas Becket, and a rare example of the Royal Arms of Charles I can be seen. The timbered manor house dates from the 16thc.

BRAMLEY, Surrey 8 TQ04
Unstead Bridge is an old structure which spans the River Wey here. Near by is timbered Unstead Farm, of Elizabethan origin.

BRAMPTON, Cambs 14 TL27
This River Ouse village has strong associations with Samuel Pepys. His parents' cottage, where the famous diarist buried his money in fear of a Dutch invasion, is still standing. An entry in his diary shows how he 'thanked God he had such a pretty spot to retire to'. The decorated to perpendicular church houses a 14th-c screen and stalls, and has fine 15th-c roofs.

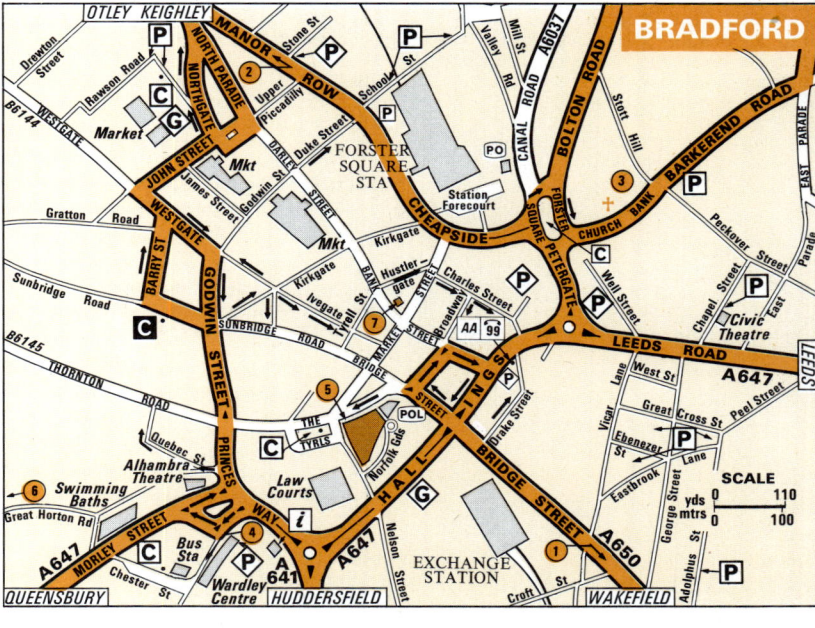

1 Bolling Hall (museum)
2 Cartwright Memorial Hall (museum and art gallery)
3 Cathedral
4 County Cricket Ground
5 Town Hall
6 University of Bradford
7 Wool Exchange

BRAMPTON, Cumbria 26 NY56
An old town on the River Irthing, where the Church of St Martin was built by the Earl of Carlisle. The church's windows are by Burne-Jones and William Morris. Restored Naworth Castle, the 14th-c and later home of the Howards, stands in a fine park 2½m NE. Stretches of a Roman wall can be seen 2m N, and inscriptions scratched by Roman workers can be seen in a quarry near the River Gelt about 2m S.

BRAMPTON BRYAN, Herefs & Worcs 11 SO37
Remains of a 14th-c castle mark the site of a famous siege in the Civil War. The church, destroyed during the siege, was rebuilt in 1656 and has a good hammer-beam roof.

BRAMSHILL, Hants 8 SU76
Splendid Bramshill House stands in a large park and is now a police college. This Jacobean building is regarded as Hampshire's finest old house, and was the ancestral home of the Copes.

BRAMSHOTT, Hants 8 SU83
The church is 13thc and later. Other notable buildings include Bramshott Manor (15thc), Bramshott Vale (Georgian) and Bramshott Place, with its 16th-c gatehouse.

BRANCASTER, Norfolk 15 TF74
This one-time Roman station is now a golfing resort. A lane leads 1m N to a pebble beach which allows access for bathing and yachting. Strong tides make the sea dangerous, and great care must be taken when swimming. Extensive salt marshes are to be found in the area, and Scolt Head Island is a bird sanctuary (NT) and national nature reserve.

BRANCEPETH, Co Durham 27 NZ23
The old castle, now a research centre, has been largely modernized and displays impressive drum towers. A footpath leads to a 13th- and 14th-c church, which is noted for its Neville monuments and some fine 17th-c woodwork given by Bishop Cosin.

BRANDON, Suffolk 15 TL78
This town on the River Little Ouse stands in an area where flint is found in vast quantities. The abundance of this natural building material is immediately evident in the construction of the local buildings, and industry associated with the mineral has existed here since prehistoric times.

Grimes Graves (AM), 3½m NE, are shafts that neolithic man dug through thick layers of chalk to reach the bands of flint. Prehistoric implements, fertility goddesses, and carvings have been discovered here, and it is thought that the mining was done with picks made of deer antlers, by the light of primitive oil lamps. Flint extracted in this way would have been used for the construction of tools and arrowheads. Brandon flints were used by the British during the Napoleonic wars, and have recently been demanded by American enthusiasts of the old muzzle-loading gun. A flint knapping industry, started in prehistoric times, still exists today. The great new state forest of Thetford Chase lies to the E, and a delightful 18th-c hall is set amid Dutch gardens.

BRANDSBY, N Yorks 22 SE57
Both the village hall and church are of 18thc date. The latter, designed by Thomas Atkinson in classical style, features a cupola over the roof. Facing the church is an old rectory (16thc).

BRANDS HATCH, Kent 9 TQ56
Site of the famous motor-racing circuit.

BRANKSOME, Dorset 7 SZ09
Part of Poole, set amid woods and chines W of Bournemouth. The sandy beach affords safe access for safe bathing.

BRANSCOMBE, Devon 6 SY18
This scattered village includes houses of cob and thatch, and offers fine cliff scenery. The Norman to decorated church displays a massive tower, and houses a three-decker pulpit and some Jacobean woodwork. The oak nave-gallery is reached by an outside stairway. Much of Branscombe Estate is NT property.

BRANT BROUGHTON, Lincs 19 SK95
A village on the River Brant, where the church displays splendid examples of early-English to decorated work, and beautiful exterior carving. The chancel is modern. The Friends' Meeting House dates from 1701.

BRANTHAM, Suffolk 15 TM13
The decorated church contains an altarpiece that was painted by Constable.

BRASTED, Kent 8 TQ45
Standing in a fine park adjoining the village is 18th-c Brasted Place. The work of Robert Adam, this fine house was once the home of Napoleon III.

16th c Bishop Percy's house, Bridgnorth

BRATTON, Wilts 7 ST95
The perpendicular church displays large gargoyles on its 15th-c tower. A White Horse (AM) cut into the chalk of Westbury Hill 1½m W, is the oldest of several examples in the county, and one of the best known in England.

BRAUGHING, Herts 14 TL32
Braughing (pronounced Bruffing) was the meeting place for several Roman roads, including Stone Street and Ermine Street. River Quin flows alongside the village green, and the 15th-c church has a good screen. Several 17th-c houses in the village display half-timbering and decorative plasterwork (pargetting). Excavations since 1949 have revealed traces of a large Roman town.

BRAUNSTON, Northants 13 SP56
This canal and boat-hire centre is the meeting place of the Grand Union and Oxford Canals. Locks and a large boatyard can be seen here; to the E is Braunston Tunnel, over 1m long and opened in 1796.

BRAUNTON, Devon 5 SS43
Braunton claims to be the largest village in England, and the sand dunes of Braunton Burrows are noted for their flora and fauna. St Brannock's church has a Norman tower with a later broach spire, and houses 16th-c bench-ends plus a Jacobean pulpit, reading desk, and gallery. Chapel Wood is a small bird sanctuary to the N at Spreacombe, and a 560-acre national nature reserve exists in the area.

BRAY, Berks 8 SU97
The church in this Thames-side village has a perpendicular tower, and a lych-gate which may date from 1448. It is associated with the well-known turncoat Vicar of Bray, thought to be Simon Aleyn, who lived through four reigns and altered his religion to suit the monarch of the day. The 17th-c almshouses known as Jesus Hospital are of interest. Ockwells Manor is a restored 15th-c timbered house (2m W), which has some old glass.

BRAYTON, N Yorks 22 SE63
Brayton church has a notable Norman chancel-arch and south doorway, and the chancel is a beautiful example of decorated style.

BREADSALL, Derbyshire 18 SK33
The Norman to perpendicular church includes a fine tower and spire, and the priory is a modernized Jacobean house.

BREAGE, Cornwall 4 SW62
Notable wall paintings and a Roman milestone are preserved in the 15th-c village church. Colonnaded 15th- to 17th-c Godolphin House stands 3m N (OACT). Tin-mining was once an important local industry, and many derelict mine buildings can still be seen.

BREAMORE, Hants 7 SU11
Pronounced Bremmer, the village contains an excellent Saxon church. Breamore House is of Elizabethan origin, and houses fine collections of paintings, china, and tapestry (OACT). A medieval miz-maze is cut into the turf of Breamore Down.

BRECKLAND
This extensive area of heathland is situated on the borders of Norfolk and

Suffolk. It has recently been the scene of large-scale afforestation, and is rich in bird life. The district has associations with Borrow's *Lavengro*.

BREDE, E Sussex 9 TQ81
An inland village in the Brede Valley, where the early-English and perpendicular church contains the notable 16th-c Oxenbridge Chantry. Brede Place, a fine Tudor mansion sited 1m E, is where J M Barrie had his inspiration for Captain Hook – arch villain of the celebrated fantasy *Peter Pan*.

BREDON, Herefs & Worcs 12 SO93
A River-Avon village with a Norman to perpendicular church, displaying a 14th-c spire and housing the sumptuous Reed monument of 1611. Other interesting features of the village include a fine 14th-c tithe barn (NT), and a curious old milestone in the form of an obelisk. The remains of a Roman camp exist 3½m NE on 960ft Bredon Hill. This hill was made famous in song by A E Housman, and it is crowned by an 18th-c folly named Bell Castle.

BREDWARDINE, Herefs & Worcs 11 SO34
One of the finest of the old River-Wye bridges can be seen here, and the Norman and later church contains effigies of knights in the sanctuary.

BREEDON-ON-THE-HILL, Leics 18 SK42
This crescent-shaped village is built around the site of an iron-age fort. A remarkable sculptured frieze was saved from a Saxon monastery which existed on the site now occupied by the church, and can be seen inside the latter. The original structure was burned down by the Danes in the 9thc. The hill on which the church stands forms a notable viewpoint, and a curious conical lock-up has survived in the village.

BRENCHLEY, Kent 9 TQ64
Brenchley figures largely in Siegfried Sassoon's autobiography, and includes many fine old houses. The Old Palace, or Roberts Mansion, is of note and the Parsonage is of Tudor origin. An avenue of ancient yew trees leads to the door of the church, and the building's screen is dated 1536.

BRENDON, Devon 5 SS74
The East Lyn river is crossed by a medieval packhorse bridge at Brendon. Exmoor and the Doone Valley are within easy reach, and the village is set amid woodlands.

BRENTFORD, Gt London 8 TQ17
This ancient market town was once the capital of Middlesex, and is now part of Greater London. The Grand Union Canal joins the Thames here, and it is thought that Julius Caesar crossed the river by means of the ford that forms part of the town's name. Caesar's stone marks the place where the crossing was supposedly effected, and various Roman remains have been found during recent excavations. Edmund Ironside defeated Danish invaders here in 1016.

St Lawrence's Church was rebuilt in 1762, but retains the original tower; St George's Church has an altar-piece depicting the Last Supper, painted by Zoffany. A fascinating piano museum is housed in a disused church in the High Street (OACT). Syon House, near the river and opposite Kew Gardens, was remodelled by Robert Adam in the 18thc (OACT). The interior displays what is perhaps the finest decorative scheme of his busy and highly successful career. The Gardening Centre was created in the grounds of the house in 1968. Also here is a comprehensive exhibition of London Transport buses and trams, which was transferred from a former museum in Clapham.

Boston Manor (AM) is an interesting three-storey house in a small park, built in 1622 (OACT). To the W is Osterley Park, a fine mansion originally built in 1576, altered in 1711, and magnificently decorated by Robert Adam in 1763 and 1767 (OACT). In Gunnersbury Park (between Acton and Brentford) is an early 19th-c house of the Rothschilds, which now serves as a museum (OACT).

BRENT KNOLL, Somerset 6 ST35
An isolated village with an ancient camp on the 450ft hill from which it takes its name. Sometimes known as South Brent, it is noted for the church, which contains 15th-c carved bench-ends with scenes depicting the Tale of the Greedy Abbot.

Apparently the one-time Abbot of Glastonbury tried to seize revenues from the parish priest. The parson successfully prevented this, and the bench ends were carved to celebrate his victory. The first carving shows a fox in an abbot's clothing, with various animal victims. The second shows a rebellion of geese, led by an ape, and the third portrays the fox abbot hung, with geese pulling on the rope and two watch dogs barking triumphantly.

BRENTOR, Devon 5 SX48
Brentor's early-English church, once the property of Tavistock Abbey, stands at the summit of Brent Tor Hill. According to legend the church was built by a grateful merchant whose ship narrowly escaped being wrecked. The 1,130ft hill is a local landmark offering E views over Dartmoor.

BRENT PELHAM, Herts 14 TL43
A little village which still retains its medieval stocks and whipping post. The 14th-c church has a fine south doorway, and the hall, the Bury, and Beeches are all 17th-c houses.

BRENTWOOD, Essex 9 TQ69
Brentwood grew up in an area where the great forest of Essex had been cleared by fire – hence the name, which means burnt wood. The town was situated on the Pilgrims' Way from East Anglia and the Midlands to Canterbury, and was the first stage on the old coaching road out of London. These factors contributed to the growth of the town. The White Hart is one of the many old inns still to be found in the area, and the grammar school, founded in 1557 and incorporating the Georgian Roden House, is another survival from the past. Though largely a commuter town, Brentwood is still near open countryside.

BRESSINGHAM, Norfolk 15 TM08
Five acres of informal gardens with some 5,000 species of hardy plants have been laid out at Bressingham Hall. This place also displays a collection of locomotives and road engines restored to working order, with some in steam, and a roundabout and steam organ (OACT).

BRETFORTON, Herefs & Worcs 12 SP04
An attractive village below the Cotswold ridge, with several timber-framed houses among its many old buildings. The delightful Fleece inn is an example of timbered construction, and one of the several ancient dovecotes in the area has been made into a cottage.

BREWOOD, Staffs 17 SJ80
The 13th-c and later church contains Gifford monuments, and the remains of William Carlos, who helped Charles II to hide at Boscobel, lie in the churchyard. Several old houses still exist in the town.

BRIDESTOWE, Devon 5 SX58
A Dartmoor village with a much-restored, 15th-c church. A Norman arch which was formerly in the nave has been adapted as a gateway to the church approach. Great Links Tor (1,908ft) rises to the SE.

BRIDFORD, Devon 5 SX88
Bridford lies in the Dartmoor foothills, W of the Teign Valley. The 15th-c church is interesting for its 16th-c carved and painted screen. An unusual feature of the latter is the tiny carved figures displayed on the wainscoting.

BRIDGNORTH, Salop 17 SO79
This ancient market community is split into Upper and Lower Town by the River Severn. The short Castle Hill railway which links the two has a gradient of 2 in 3 – one of the steepest in England. A leaning tower (AM) is the sole relic of the Norman castle that used to stand here; it is out of true by 17deg from the perpendicular, three times the angle of the leaning tower of Pisa. The half-timbered town hall has an upper portion which once served as an old barn, but which was re-erected on the arches of the original structure. A fine 16th-c half-timbered house was the birthplace of Bishop Percy in 1729, and there are 18th-c houses in East Castle Street. The restored north-gate of the town is now a museum, and St Mary Magdalene's Church was built by Thomas Telford – best known for his bridge engineering – in 1794. The Hermitage (AM) is an ancient cave in Bridgnorth's sandstone ridge, believed to have been the retreat of the 10th-c hermit Ethelred, King Athelstan's brother. Other caves exist in the vicinity. The revived Severn-Valley railway operates steam trains in the area.

BRIDGWATER, Somerset 6 ST33
A market and industrial town on the River Parrett, with a town hall dating from c1820. Rows of Georgian houses can be seen in Castle Street. The rebel Duke of Monmouth was proclaimed King here in 1685, before his forces were defeated at nearby Sedgemoor. He surveyed the field from the tower of decorated and perpendicular St Mary's Church, which contains good screenwork. The one-time house of Admiral Blake is now a museum, and Water Gate House is a reminder of the old 13th-c castle. A nuclear power station has been built at Hinkley Point on Bridgwater Bay.

BRIDLINGTON, Humberside 23 TA16
Amenities offered by this popular resort include sands, good bathing, sailing, fishing, and a variety of other seaside entertainments. Two beaches are separated by the harbour. The early-English to perpendicular priory church has two towers, and houses an impressive nave interior and choir stalls, plus the

Tournai marble founders stone. The 14th-c Bayle Gate also survives from the former priory, and contains a small museum. Architectural designer and decorator William Kent was born at Bridlington in 1685. Several 18th-c houses can be seen in the High Street, and Sewerby Hall, N of Bridlington, is a fine Georgian mansion now containing an art gallery and museum (OACT).

BRIDPORT, Dorset 6 SY49

This ancient town has been involved in rope-making for over 750 years. The wide pavements were originally rope-walks, used for the laying-out and drying of new rope, and Bridport is still the principal centre for the production of fishing nets, lines, twines, and cordage in Europe.

The town is described in Thomas Hardy's novels as Port Bredy. West Bay offers the resources of a small seaside resort, plus the interest and excitement of a busy old harbour. The mainly-perpendicular church contains a fine effigy of a knight, and is close to a 16th-c stone house that now houses a museum. Also near by are the Daniel Taylor almshouses, founded in 1696.

Charles II once entered the town in disguise, with a price of £1,000 on his head. He was in flight after the Battle of Worcester, and although the town was full of Cromwellian troops, he paused to call at a local inn. This is now a shop near the Georgian town hall. His escape from here was by a lane off the Dorchester road, now marked by an inscribed stone, and he eventually reached the haven of Normandy.

BRIERLEY HILL, W Midlands 12 SO98

A busy industrial town with iron and glass works. An interesting glass museum is located in the library (OACT).

BRIGG, Humberside 23 TA00

Brigg is a market town in an area that benefited from the draining of the Fens. An ancient – perhaps prehistoric – boat was found here, and the grammar school is partly of 17th-c origin.

BRIGHOUSE, W Yorks 22 SE12

The town lies in the old West Riding woollen district, and is best-known for its carpets and its brass band. The remains of 13th-c Kirklees Priory lie 2m SE, and include a gatehouse of later date. It is said that the priory was where Robin Hood died, and his grave is traditionally in the vicinity.

BRIGHTLING, E Sussex 9 TQ62

A picturesque village where Mad Jack Fuller, a local squire well-known for his construction of follies, built a tomb comprising two domes, two needles, and a pyramid over his grave in the churchyard. An obelisk on Brightling Down (646ft) forms a good viewpoint.

BRIGHTLINGSEA, Essex 9 TM01

This old fishing port on the Colne estuary is now a yachting centre. The beach is mainly of sand and mud, and there are well-known oyster fisheries in the area. Outside the town, the mainly-perpendicular parish church displays a fine 94ft tower, flint flushwork, and several monuments and brasses. Half-timbered Jacobe's Hall is of the 15thc and now serves as an hotel.

BRIGHTON, E Sussex 8 TQ30

Brighton is a resort which enjoys the amenities of a large town within easy reach of London, and is known for its bracing climate. The curious Royal Pavilion was built by Henry Holland in 1787, and later completed in oriental style by John Nash for the Prince Regent. Nash was the architect who laid out Regent's Park. Numerous fine Regency terraces and houses exist as apt memorials to the period when royalty and society enjoyed sea-bathing and high-living in the town. Marlborough House, designed by Robert Adam in 1786, is one of Brighton's finest dwellings. The pebble beach was very popular when the Victorian stone-collecting vogue was at its height.

The resort's amenities include a long promenade, six golf courses within six miles, and facilities for tennis, sailing, skating, and pier-fishing. Fifteen race meetings a year are held at a racecourse N of Kemp Town, and Plumpton Races are held only 13m away. A new yacht marina is under construction E of the resort towards Rottingdean. The Volks electric railway was one of the first of its kind in England, and runs E from Palace Pier to Black Rock. Peter Pan's playground has swings, roundabouts, go-kart racing, and donkey rides for the children.

The Booth Bird Museum is of great interest and Potter's Museum of Taxidermy, formerly in Bramber, is being re-located in Brighton. The Dome Concert Hall occupies former Royal Stables, and an extensive aquarium can be seen near Palace Pier. Several cinemas and theatres operate in the town, and plays are often given a run here before opening in London.

Fashionable shops contrast pleasantly with the picturesque Lanes and their numerous antique furniture and jewellery dealers. An attractive modern piazza adjoins the Lanes, and the sea-front is largely faced with hotels. Stanmer Park (Georgian) forms the nucleus of the new University of Sussex. The Devil's Dyke is a cleft in the 700ft crest of the Downs, N of the town, where impressive views over the surrounding area can be enjoyed. This viewpoint is easily accessible by road.

BRIGSTOCK, Northants 13 SP98

The village church preserves notable Saxon work, and an old cross carries the accession dates ER 1586, AR 1705, VR 1837 and ERII 1953.

BRILL, Bucks 13 SP61

An isolated village some 700ft above sea level, preserving an ancient windmill of 1668 and some old houses. Boarstall Tower is a moated 14th- to 17th-c gatehouse (NT) situated 2½m NW; 3m NE is the fine 18th-c and later Wotton House, remodelled by Sir John Soane after a fire in 1820, and set in a park with a lake (OACT).

BRINGTON, GREAT, Northants 13 SP66

This attractive village has a fine 12th- to 16th-c church containing a Washington brass and tombstone. These monuments commemorate Lawrence and Robert

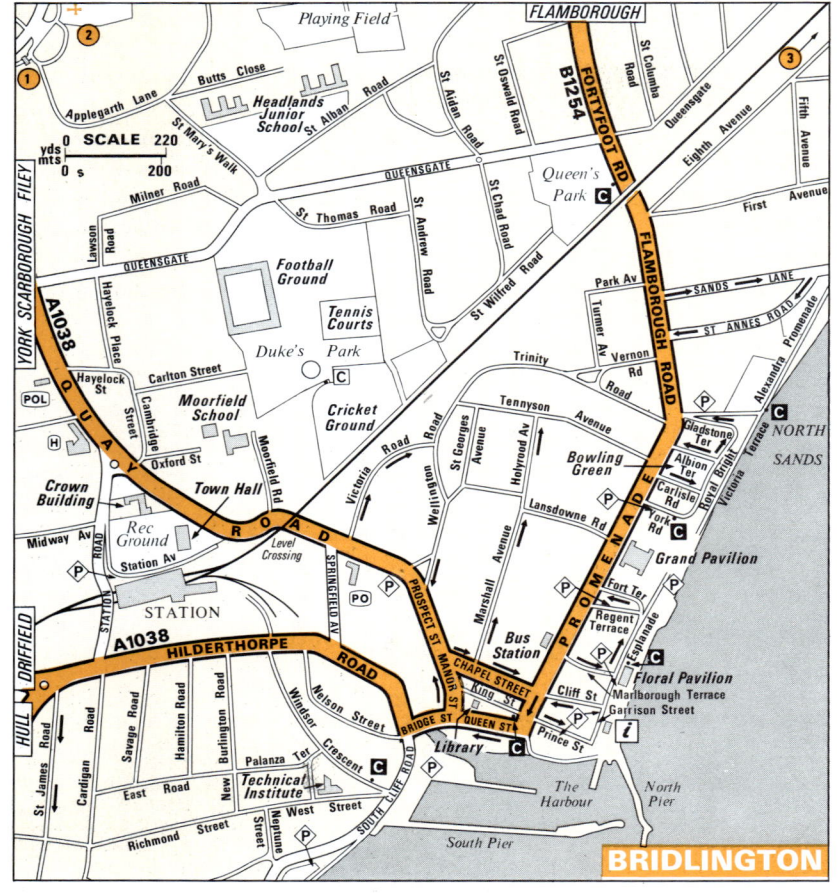

1   Bayle Gate (museum)
2   Priory Church
3   Sewerby Hall (museum and art gallery)

Washington and their families, who were local ancestors of George Washington. Splendid 16th- to 17th-c monuments housed in the Spencer Chapel are said to have been by the same architect as designed the Henry VII Chapel in Westminster. Charles Stuart stayed 1m E at Althorp House, home of the Spencers, which was remodelled with a very notable picture gallery in 1787.

BRINKBURN, Northumberland 27 NZ19
A village on the River Coquet, including the very beautiful 12th-c priory church (AM). This notable example has been restored and displays fine lancet windows, plus the original altar stone with five consecration crosses. It is all that remains of a priory founded in about 1135 by Augustinian canons.

BRINKWORTH, Wilts 12 SU08
William Penn's family once lived here, and the rectory was occupied by Thomas Crisp. The latter came to Brinkworth in 1627, but was persecuted for his Puritan principles and driven from his living. He went to London where he caught smallpox and died.

The 15th-c church contains the remains of old wall paintings, a west gallery, 17th-c Royal Arms, a Jacobean pulpit, and two squints.

BRISTOL, Avon 6 ST57
This famous old city was the first county borough, and has been a port for over 800 years. It is now a resort and manufacturing centre, the seat of a university, and the see of a bishop. It has imported wine from Bordeaux and Spain since the middle ages, and has traded with America since the 17thc — though larger vessels now dock at Avonmouth.

The impressive cathedral was originally the church of an abbey founded in 1148. It is much restored, but displays a fine Norman chapter house, an early-English lady chapel, a 15th-c tower, and 16th-c stalls. The lady chapel shows some of the unique stellar tomb recesses found only in Bristol. The abbey gateway is Norman.

St Mary Redcliffe is a 13th- to 15th-c church which is one of the largest in England. Its massive tower is richly decorated and bears a 285ft spire. The hexagonal north porch (late 13thc), and the carved door and inner porch of 1180, are outstanding. Above the north porch is the muniment room in which Thomas Chatterton pretended to have discovered the Rowley manuscripts. This notorious teenage poet started writing poetry on old parchment found in St Mary Redcliffe, and passing it off as the work of a fictitious monk named Thomas Rowley. People believed him, and he travelled to London intending to make his fortune; his failure to realize this ambition culminated in his committing suicide in a Holborn garret. His birthplace, Chatterton House, is now a museum.

The restored gothic Lord Mayors Chapel displays stellar tomb recesses and can be seen in College Green. Red Lodge (16thc) has a collection of furniture and maps. Cabot Tower in Brandon Hill is a prominent local landmark commemorating John Cabot's expedition from Bristol to discover the mainland of America.

Numerous 18th-c buildings can be seen in the city, but of particular interest is the

1 Aquarium
2 Booth Bird Museum
3 Devil's Dyke
4 Dome Concert Hall (old royal stables)
5 Lanes
6 Marlborough House
7 Peter Pan's Playground
8 Racecourse
9 Royal Pavilion
10 University of Sussex

BRIGHTON

impressive Corn Exchange. Outside this stand the original nails or metal standards upon which merchants once put their payments. It is from this custom that the phrase 'to pay cash on the nail' originates. The Theatre Royal dates from 1766. Queen Square and Dowry Square are 18thc, as are also the Colston and St Nicholas almshouses, and Cooper's Hall. Edward Colston was Bristol's greatest merchant. The Quakers Friars, once a Dominican friary and now a record office, has a fine 14th-c roof.

The Methodist Chapel was built by John Wesley in 1743, and his statue now stands outside. Above it are the rooms where Wesley and his preachers once lived (OACT). Another native of Bristol was the English poet and historian, Robert Southey. St John's Gate is the sole remaining city gate, and above it is the diminutive Church of St John the Baptist. Temple Church is a 14th-c ruin with a leaning tower, and St Stephen's Church, given to the city by merchant and Chief Magistrate John Shipword, has a lofty tower with pinnacles. Redland Chapel dates from 1740, and Redland Court from 1735. Arno's Castle is a curious castellated structure dating from 1750. At the end of Christmas Steps (1669) are the 19th-c Foster almshouses and the Chapel of the Three Kings of Cologne, the latter founded in 1504.

The main building of the university, Great Tower, was opened in 1925. It has a 10-ton bell to strike the hours. The Royal Fort of 1761 was originally a merchant's house, but is now part of the university. The Victoria Rooms, built in 1842 on the lines of a Greek temple, serve a like purpose. Many Georgian houses, some of which are well restored, can be seen in the Kingsdown district.

St Michael's Hill shows restored Georgian architecture, and Orchard Street has retained an air of the same era. Llandoger Trow is a picturesque inn of 1664, which is said to have been the haunt of pirates; it is thought to figure in *Treasure Island*. Of more recent date is the part of Temple Meads Station, built by Brunel in 1839/1840, that still stands. The liner SS Great Britain was also built by Brunel in 1843, and towed back to Bristol from the Falkland Islands in 1970. She was towed up the Avon to her original dock in the floating harbour for restoration.

Of Bristol's modern buildings, the imposing Council House dates from 1935 and 1955. This is where the city's extensive civic insignia and archives are preserved. Another notable piece of contemporary architecture is the new swing-bridge, which cost more than

1	Arno's Castle	11	Foster Almshouses	21	St Nicholas Almshouses
2	Cabot Tower	12	Great Tower	22	St Stephen's Church
3	Cathedral	13	Llandoger Trow Inn	23	Swing Bridge
4	Chapel of the Three Kings of Cologne	14	Lord Mayor's Chapel	24	Temple Church Ruins
5	Chatterton House (museum)	15	Methodist Chapel and Wesley Statue	25	Temple Meads Station
6	Church of St John the Baptist	16	Redland Chapel	26	Theatre Royal
7	Christmas Steps	17	Red Lodge (museum)	27	The Quakers Friars
8	Colston Almshouses	18	Royal Fort	28	University of Bristol
9	Corn Exchange	19	St John's Gate	29	Victoria Rooms
10	Council House (archives)	20	St Mary Redcliffe Church		

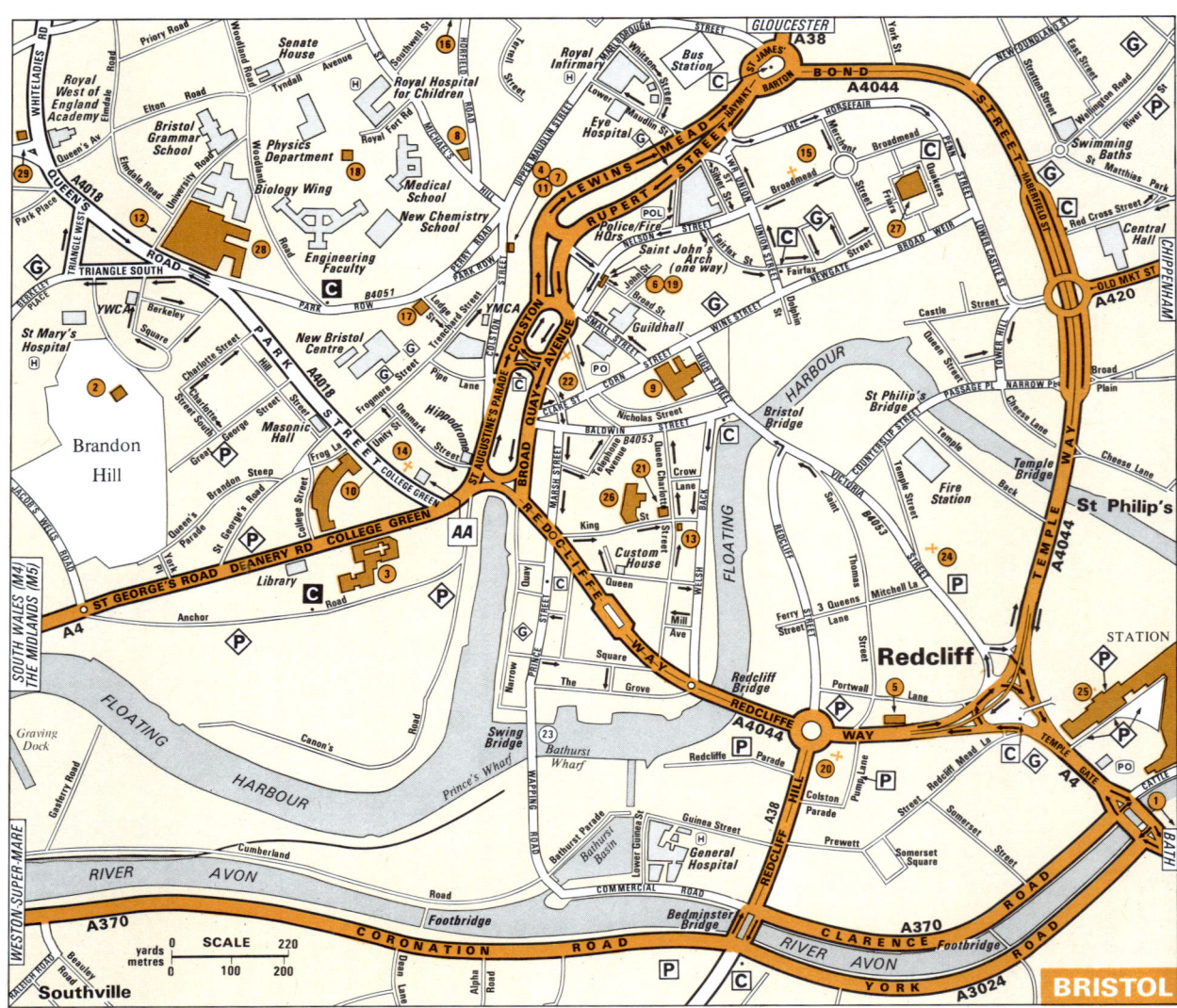

2½ million pounds and was opened in 1965 to give access to the city's docks. Modern Redcliff Way intersects Queens Square (1699) between two arms of the Floating Harbour, to connect the busy centre with Temple Meads. A link from the M4 motorway is gradually being extended into the heart of the city. See also entry for Clifton.

BRITFORD, Wilts 7 SU12
A village in the Avon water-meadows, with a church containing remarkable Saxon arches and a Jacobean pulpit. The fine altar tomb in the chancel is also of note. Triangular Longford Castle, largely of the 16thc and known for its collection of rare paintings, lies 1m SSE.

BRIXHAM, Devon 5 SX95
This fishing town and holiday resort, with its picturesque harbour, is popular with artists. Sands giving access for bathing can be found at Mudstone Bay. Perpendicular St Mary's Church is a little way inland, and has a buttressed tower. William of Orange landed here in 1688, a turning point of English history which is commemorated by a statue on the quay. Berry Head lies to the E, overlooking Tor Bay, and attractive St Mary's Bay is to the SE. Several caves in the area were inhabited in prehistoric times, and Windmill Hill cave is open to the public. H F Lyte wrote the hymn *Abide with Me* when he was vicar of All Saints, Brixham.

BRIXTON, Gt London 8 TQ37
A well-restored windmill, complete with sails, can be seen behind the west side of Brixton Hill. The library has a fine Shakespearian collection which includes several Folios.

BRIXWORTH, Northants 13 SP77
One of the finest Saxon churches in England can be seen here. Built in AD680, the material used in its construction were bricks and tiles scavenged from local Roman buildings. The kennels of the Pytchley Hunt are near by. Cottesbrooke Hall dates from the 18thc, and can be seen 3m NW.

BROAD CHALKE, Wilts 7 SU02
This delightful Ebble-Valley village has a 13th-c church displaying a notable, 15th-c porch and central tower.

BROAD CLYST, Devon 5 SX99
The 14th- to 15th-c church has a tall west tower and houses interesting monuments. Some 2m N is the Killerton estate (5,000 acres), with magnificent gardens (NT, OACT).

BROADHEATH, Herefs & Worcs 12 SO66
Sir Edward Elgar was born in Broadheath in 1857. A small museum of books and musical scores is of interest.

BROADHEMBURY, Devon 6 ST10
Considered one of Devon's loveliest villages, Broadhembury is made up of buildings including the characteristic cob and thatched cottages of the county. The perpendicular church has a 100ft tower, and The Grange is of Elizabethan and Georgian date.

BROADS, THE
This roughly triangular district lies between Norwich, Lowestoft and Sea Palling, and contains over thirty Broads of various sizes. These, together with the many rivers and streams in the area, amount to over 200 miles of navigable inland waterways, unique in Great Britain. Various types of boats can be hired, and motorists are catered for by facilities offered at such places as Wroxham, Horning, Stalham, Potter Heigham, and Acle. Fishing in the area is excellent, but all anglers must have fishing permits and licences; these can be obtained from local post offices. The chief Broads are Wroxham, Barton, Hickling, Ormesby, Rollesby, and Filby; the main rivers are the Bure, Yare, and Waveney. Broadland churches are noted for their medieval painted screens, some of the finest examples of which are at Barton Turf, Ludham, Ranworth and Tunstead.

BROADSTAIRS, Kent 9 TR36
A popular resort with excellent sands allowing access for bathing and fishing. Bleak House was once the home of Charles Dickens (OACT), and tablets mark several other houses in which he lived. Remains of the 16th-c York Gate can be seen, and 1½m N are the chalk cliffs and lighthouse of the North Foreland. The latter gives a wide view over shipping lanes into the Thames estuary.

BROADWATER, W Sussex 8 TQ10
This suburb of Worthing has a fine Norman and early-English church. Near by is a cemetery where the graves of naturalist Richard Jefferies, and naturalist/author W H Hudson, can be seen. Mary Hughes, subject of the nursery rhyme *Mary had a Little Lamb*, was buried here in 1881.

BROADWAY, Herefs & Worcs 12 SP13
Picturesque old houses can be seen in this Cotswold village. The 17th-c Lygon Arms was once a coaching inn, and the fine Tudor House of 1660 is also of note. Norman and later St Eadburgh's Church displays a fine palimpsest brass. Fish Hill rises to 1,024ft above the village, and is surmounted by an 18th-c tower. Near by is an ancient Cross Hands signpost; three innocent people were hanged for a murder committed here in 1661.

BROADWINDSOR, Dorset 6 ST40
Pilsdon Pen, the highest point in the county and a magnificent viewpoint, rises to 909ft near this village. The 894ft Lewesden Hill is near by (NT). Thomas Fuller preached from the Norman to perpendicular church's Jacobean pulpit, and Charles II slept at a local house in September of 1651. Wordsworth lived at Racedown Lodge, W of the village, for two years.

BROCKENHURST, Hants 7 SU20
An attractively-situated New-Forest village, where the Norman church houses a squire's pew. Brusher Mills, responsible for the death of 3,186 New-Forest adders, is commemorated by a monument in the churchyard.

BROCKHAM GREEN, Surrey 8 TQ14
A village below Box Hill, with a green that is considered one of the prettiest in Surrey. The name is a reminder of the numerous badgers (ie brocks) that used to frequent the area.

1 Bleak House
2 Lighthouse
3 York Gate Remains

BROCKLESBY, Lincs 23 TA11
The local church shows decorated-style tracery, an organ of 1773, and Pelham tombs. A large park surrounding the restored 18th-c hall includes a mausoleum by James Wyatt (1792).

BROCKWORTH, Glos 12 SO81
Two Roman roads met near this old town, which is now the site of a large aerodrome. The church has two fine Norman tower arches, and Brockworth Court preserves its old timbering. Cheese-rolling down Cooper's Hill is a picturesque Whit-Monday custom.

BROMFIELD, Salop 12 SO47
The timber-and-stone gatehouse of a 12th-c priory is preserved here, and the chancel of the mainly early-English church was once the priory nave. The curious painted ceiling of the latter dates from 1672.

BROMHAM, Wilts 7 ST96
This village has a church noted for its richly-carved perpendicular-style Baynton Chapel. The grave and Celtic cross of Tom Moore, a poet who lived at Sloperton Cottage for thirty-five years, can also be seen. Other features of the village are a timbered lock-up and 17th-c almshouses.

BROMLEY, Gt London 8 TQ46
Bromley is the largest of the thirty-two London Boroughs created in 1963. It comprises the former boroughs of Beckenham and Bromley, the urban districts of Orpington and Penge, and parts of Chislehurst and Sidcup. It lies in an area which is highly urbanized to the N and W, but which has open countryside to the SE. A plaque in the High Street marks the site of the place where H G Wells was born in 1866. Bromley College, founded and endowed by John Warner in 1666, occupies its original buildings. The parish church has been rebuilt after destruction – apart from its 14th-c tower – by wartime bombing.

BROMLEY, GREAT, Essex 15 TM02
A splendid buttressed and pinnacled tower is a feature of Great Bromley's perpendicular-style church. Also of note are the south porch and double hammer-beam roof.

BROMSGROVE, Herefs & Worcs 12 SO97
An industrial town with a few old gabled houses, and a restored Norman to

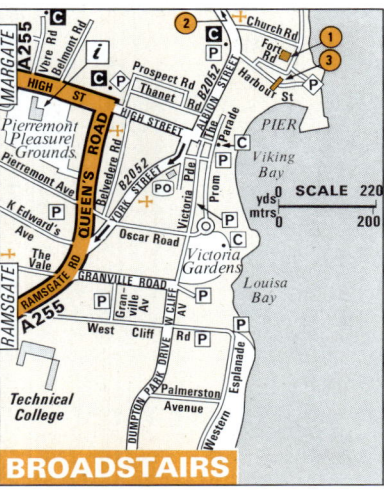

BROADSTAIRS

perpendicular church. The latter displays a 14th-c tower and many interesting monuments. In the churchyard, the tombstone of Thomas Scaife depicts a carved delineation of an early railway engine. The grammar school was founded in 1553. A E Housman was born 1m N at Fockbury in 1859, and 2m SW is 16th- and 18th-c Grafton Manor. Royal Arms of 1567 can be seen over the manor's porch, and the chapel displays some interesting 15th-c work.

BROMYARD, Herefs & Worcs *12 SO65*
Bromyard preserves several old buildings, including Tower Hill House, Bible House, and the timbered Falcon inn. Lower Brockhampton (NT) is a moated 14th-c timbered house with a rare 15th-c gatehouse, standing 2½m E (OACT).

BRONTË COUNTRY
See Hathersage, Haworth, Kirkby Lonsdale, Thornton (near Bradford), and Wycoller.

BROOK, Kent *9 TR04*
Norman arches and windows of the local church are notable, but this building is especially famous for its series of medieval wall-paintings – restored by Professor Tristram. The village also has an interesting agricultural museum.

BROOKE, Norfolk *15 TM29*
A Norman round tower and an octagonal Seven-Sacraments font are features of the local church. Kirstead Old Hall is a beautiful brick-built Jacobean house to the SE, with pedimented and stepped gables.

BROOKLANDS, Surrey *8 TQ06*
This one-time motor-racing track is now used as an aircraft works and aerodrome.

BROOKSBY, Leics *18 SK61*
The Elizabethan manor-house was the birthplace of George Villiers (1592), later to become famous as the Duke of Buckingham. The small perpendicular church contains Villiers memorials.

BROOKWOOD, Surrey *8 SU95*
This is the site of the large London-based Necropolis Company cemetery, and Commonwealth and USA-forces cemeteries.

BROOMFIELD, Essex *9 TL71*
A village where the church displays an early-Norman round tower, incorporating Roman tiles.

BROUGH, Cumbria *21 NY71*
Brough's 12th- to 16th-c church houses many 18th-c brass inscriptions. Brough Castle (¾m S) was originally built by William II, but was subsequently rebuilt by Lady Anne Clifford in the 17thc. It now lies in ruins (AM, OACT). Fox Tower stands in a clearing in Hellbeck Wood 1m NW, offering widespread views over the surrounding area. Mickle Fell, Yorkshire's highest mountain, rises to 2,591ft from Lune Forest (8m N); E is bleak and lofty Stainmore Common. The fells and woods around Brough are fine walking areas, and although used by the army are quite safe when there are no red flags flying.

BROUGHAM, Cumbria *26 NY52*
Pronounced Broom, this River-Eamont village includes the remains of a 12th-c castle (AM), on a Roman site. Brougham Hall is near by, and the 14ft Countess's Pillar was erected in 1656 to commemorate Lady Anne Clifford's last parting from her mother. The little Church of St Ninian's is noted for its old woodwork, and was restored in 1660 by Lady Anne. She also restored the Chapel of St Wilfred.

BROUGHTON, Oxon *13 SP43*
A fine 14th- to 16th-c moated castle with a chapel and gatehouse can be seen here (OACT). The church is mainly of the decorated style, has a good screen, and shows several notable tombs.

BROUGHTON-IN-FURNESS, Cumbria *21 SD28*
This market town overlooks the Duddon estuary, with the beautiful Duddon Valley extending N in the direction of the Lakeland fells. Broughton Tower is a 14th-c peel tower which has been incorporated in an 18th-c house. The Swinside Druidical circle lies to the W.

BRUTON, Somerset *6 ST63*
Bruton is a fine old town where an old pack-horse bridge called Bruton Bow spans the River Brue. The church has two towers, the larger of which is a splendid example of perpendicular style, and an 18th-c chancel. Part of the 12th-c abbey walls can be seen in the street named Plox, and a dovecot survives on a hill above the town (NT). Sexey Hospital dates from the 17thc, and the grammar school from the 16thc. Both occupy stone-built buildings.

BRYMPTON D'EVERCY, Somerset *6 ST51*
The interesting little decorated-style church, has a quaint bell-cote, a 15th-c stone screen, and some interesting tombs. Brympton d'Evercy House is now a school, and is a notable example of 15th- to 18th-c styles. The Tudor and 17th-c dower house is also of interest (OACT).

BUCKDEN, Cambs *14 TL16*
Considerable remains of ancient Buckden Palace belong to the Bishops of Lincoln, and now house a school (OACT). Catherine of Aragon was a prisoner here. Two of the several interesting old inns in the village are the George and the Lion. A fine perpendicular church displays a notable spire and carvings. Laurence Sterne was ordained here in 1736. A new reservoir to the W of Grafham Water provides a 6sqm boating and fishing amenity.

BUCKFAST ABBEY, Devon *5 SX76*
The abbey was founded in the 10thc, refounded two centuries later, and rebuilt on the old foundations by the monks themselves between 1907 and 1938. A magnificent mosaic pavement has been laid inside the church. The House of Shells museum is another interesting feature of the area.

BUCKFASTLEIGH, Devon *5 SX76*
This is a small River-Dart market town, where the steam-hauled Dart Valley railway is a big local attraction. The church is approached by 198 steps, and has an early-English tower and chancel. Local caves have been acquired as a nature reserve, and the modern agricultural museum is of interest. Dart Bridge (AM) lies ¾m N.

BUCKINGHAM, Bucks *13 SP63*
A quiet town on the River Ouse, which has long been replaced by Aylesbury as the county town. The ancient Bull Ring is on Market Hill, and several old houses, including the manor house with its rare twisted chimney, can be seen. The Chantry Chapel (NT) was rebuilt in 1475, but preserves a Norman doorway. It once housed the Royal Latin School, and is now used for meetings. The parish church, town hall, and the old gaol are all 18thc, and Castle House dates originally from c1280. George Gilbert Scott the architect was born 1m SW at Gawcott, and the local church was designed by his father, then the vicar.

BUCKLEBURY, Berks *7 SU57*
Primitive wood turnery is still practised here. Among the examples of carving in the church is an interesting Norman south doorway. Windows designed by Frank Brangwyn are also a feature of this building. A 1m avenue of oaks was planted in the reign of Queen Anne. Bucklebury Common, now a well-known beauty spot 1½m S, was the camping ground of 20,000 Parliamentarians on the eve of the second Battle of Newbury, 1664.

BUCKLER'S HARD, Hants *7 SU40*
A small village sited on the Beaulieu River at the edge of the New Forest. A street of 18th-c old houses lends an air of gentility to the place, and a small, maritime museum is a reminder that wooden warships were once built here – notably, Nelson's Agamemnon in 1781. After launching the ships were towed to Portsmouth for fitting-out. Remains of an old Cistercian chapel, including an exceptionally large barn, are situated S at St Leonards.

BUCK'S MILLS, Devon *5 SS32*
This attractive fishing village lies in a secluded position amid wooded-cliff and rock scenery.

BUDE, Cornwall *5 SS20*
Bude is a popular resort with fine beaches that face the prevailing wind – a fact which caused over eighty shipwrecks between 1825 and 1874. Nowadays these conditions make the area ideal for surfing, and enthusiasts come from all over the country to enjoy this sport. The town has grown up separated from the coastline by ridges of downland, and the two principal beaches are Summerleaze, at the mouth of the Neet, and Crooklets – immediately N of it. A large swimming pool on Summerleaze beach is refilled at every tide, and is ideal for bathers who wish to avoid the long rollers of the open sea. Rock scenery around Bude is particularly notable, and S of the town is a 3m walk along the cliffs. Compass Point and Efford Beacon are excellent viewpoints. Bude Castle, built by the inventor Gurney in about 1840, now houses the council offices. Bude Canal runs E to the Tamar, on the Devon border.

BUDLEIGH SALTERTON, Devon *6 SY08*
This quiet resort at the mouth of the River Otter has a shingle beach providing access for bathing. The second part of the town name is derived from the old English word for salt-works – the monks of a priory founded on the E bank of the river used to produce salt. Several Georgian buildings can be seen in the town. An 18th-c house in Fore Street contains an art gallery and museum.

BUDWORTH, GREAT, Cheshire *17 SJ67*
Great Budworth includes a 14th- to 15th-c church containing 13th-c stalls and quaint carvings.

BUILDWAS, Salop *17 SJ60*
Buildwas is a River-Severn hamlet noted for its ruined 12th-c abbey (AM). Although some attractive scenery can be enjoyed in Coalbrookdale, a large power station dominates most of the district.

BULFORD, Wilts *7 SU14*
This is a military centre situated on the edge of Salisbury Plain. A kiwi cut out of the turf on Beacon Hill, in true white-horse style, was originally executed by New-Zealanders in the First World War.

BULKINGTON, Warwickshire *13 SP38*
A silk-weaving industry was once plied in this village of 16th- and 18th-c houses. The 13th- to 15th-c church has a remarkable font made from a Roman marble column.

BUNBURY, Cheshire *17 SJ55*
Largely decorated and perpendicular in style, the local church contains interesting chapels and monuments to the Calveleys. The curious Image House has associations with witchcraft.

BUNGAY, Suffolk *15 TM38*
The odd name of this town is of old-English origin, and probably meant 'the island of Buna's people'. Remains of a castle built in c1165, and a twin-towered gatehouse of 1294 exist here. The octagonal market cross once held a cage for malefactors. Holy Trinity Church has a round tower, with traces of 11th- to 14th- and 16th-c work. The black-oak pulpit was made in 1558 for five shillings. St Mary's Church is 15thc, and was gutted by a fire that destroyed much of the impressive tower in 1688. The town weather vane above the market depicts lightning and a black dog, perhaps symbolizing the Devil. The ancient office of Town Reeve is still held by the town's civic head. Remains of 14th-c Mettingham Castle lie 2m SE, near a fine old Dutch-gabled hall.

BUNNY, Notts *18 SK52*
A 17th-c school and hall in this attractive village were the work of Sir Thomas Parkyns, known as the Wrestling Baronet. A notable Parkyns monument can be seen at the decorated to perpendicular church.

BUNTINGFORD, Herts *14 TL32*
Many old buildings still stand here, including a 17th-c church, attractive almshouses of 1684, and houses and inns. Corney Bury is a gabled early 17th-c house standing 1m N.

BURBAGE, Wilts *7 SU26*
To the E are remains of former Wolf Hall mansion, where a great banquet in honour of Jane Seymour, Queen of Henry VIII, took place in 1536. The Seymours took the wardenship of Savernake Forest (described under Marlborough) over from the Esturmys.

BURES, Suffolk *15 TL93*
This River-Stour village includes half-timbered houses and a 13th- to 15th-c church. The church font is adorned with painted shields, and a notable monument can be seen in the Waldegrave Chapel of 1514. Chapel Barn is an ancient thatched building from the former priory at Earl's Colne, which contains several tombs. Bevills, c1500 with later alterations, is a brick and timber house; 1½m E is 16th-c Smallbridge Hall, a place once visited by Queen Elizabeth I.

BURFORD, Oxon *13 SP21*
A picturesque Cotswold town, largely comprising one steep main street lined with old houses and inns. A bridge spans the River Windrush at the foot of the hill, and the town's 15th-c almshouses are of interest. The Great House, dating from 1690, stands in Witney Street. Burford's Norman to perpendicular church displays an imposing tower and spire, old screens, and monuments. The south porch is of some note, and the building has macabre associations with the Civil War. In 1649 a body of mutineers was trapped by Cromwell, and many were shut in the church. Three were subsequently shot near the churchyard. Speaker Lenthall, who defied Charles I in the House of Commons, once lived in the restored Elizabethan house now known as The Priory. He is buried in the church. The Old Tolsey (toll-house) is now an interesting little museum. Sir Compton Mackenzie called Burford 'Wychford' in his novel *Guy and Pauline*.

BURFORD BRIDGE, Surrey *8 TQ15*
Situated on the River Mole at the foot of Box Hill, this place includes an hotel where Keats completed *Endymion*, and Nelson said farewell to Lady Hamilton. R L Stevenson also stayed here.

BURGH-BY-SANDS, Cumbria *26 NY35*
Pronounced Bruff, this village has a church with a massive embattled Norman tower standing on the site of a Roman camp. The structure is partly built of Roman stones. Edward I died here in 1307, and a monument to him can be seen 1m N.

BURGHCLERE, Hants *7 SU46*
This place is noted for the modern Sandham Memorial Chapel (NT), which contains paintings by Stanley Spencer. The chapel may be visited at reasonable hours, and the key is available from the adjoining almshouses. Beacon Hill (858ft) is a local landmark to the S, surmounted by an iron-age camp.

BURGH-LE-MARSH, Lincs *19 TF56*
The church has a fine tower and some restored screenwork. A well-preserved five-sailed windmill exists in the area. Gunby Hall, dated 1700, lies 3m NW (NT, OACT).

Well-preserved five-sailed windmill near Burgh-le-Marsh

BURGHLEY HOUSE, Cambs *19 TF00*
This Elizabethan mansion was the home of the Cecils and Exeters for 400 years. It stands in a great park, designed by Capability Brown, on the SE side of Stamford and contains splendid art treasures. The Heaven Room is considered the masterpiece of the painter Verrio (OACT). Burghley Horse Trials are usually held here in the early autumn.

BURITON, Hants *8 SU72*
Edward Gibbon spent his youth in the Georgian manor house. The trans-Norman and later church houses 13th-c mural paintings, and displays a tower which was rebuilt in 1714. Queen Elizabeth Forest is on the nearby South Downs, and 900ft Butser Hill is surmounted by the remains of an iron-age fort. Facilities for motorists include a large public car park at the summit of this hill.

BURLEY, Hants *7 SU20*
The Queen's Head Inn has a remarkable collection of souvenirs, trophies, and weapons.

BURNHAM, Bucks *8 SU98*
Monuments and brasses are housed in the large 13th- to 15th-c church. Remains of Burnham Abbey, founded in 1266 and now restored and in use as a nunnery, can be seen to the S. Nashdom Abbey, by Lutyens in 1910, is the home of a religious order. Huntercombe Manor shows 14th- and 17th-c work.

BURNHAM BEECHES, Bucks *8 SU98*
This area comprises some 600 acres of picturesque well-established woodland, purchased by the City of London in 1879. East Burnham, lying S of the Beeches, is where Sheridan spent his honeymoon and George Grote, the Greek historian, entertained Chopin and Mendelssohn. Dorneywood (NT) has been accepted as an official residence for one of the Ministers of the Crown, and remains at the disposal of the Prime Minister of the day (OACT).

BURNHAM DEEPDALE, Norfolk
15 TF84
A Norman round tower and a particularly fine Norman font are features of the local church. The latter is square, and adorned with carving.

BURNHAM MARKET, Norfolk *15 TF84*
The decorated and perpendicular church has 15th-c sculptured battlements on the tower. Several fine 17th- and 18th-c

houses can be seen around the green at the W end of the town.

BURNHAM-ON-CROUCH, Essex 9 TQ99
This yachting centre on the Crouch estuary is famous for its oyster beds. The beach is mainly of pebbles, although there is a little sand.

BURNHAM-ON-SEA, Somerset 6 ST34
A popular resort, with miles of sandy beach providing access for bathing. Wide views over Bridgwater Bay, part of which is now a national nature reserve, can be enjoyed from here. The church is early perpendicular, and contains part of the white-marble altar which was originally carved for the chapel of Whitehall Palace by Grinling Gibbons. The altar was first moved to Hampton Court, and thence to Westminster Abbey. George IV disposed of it to Bishop King of Rochester, who was then Vicar of Burnham, in 1830.

BURNHAM THORPE, Norfolk 15 TF84
The one-time rectory here was the birthplace of Lord Nelson in 1758. The font at which he was christened is housed in the perpendicular church, which also contains a lectern and rood made from timbers of the Victory, and a fine brass of 1420.

BURNLEY, Lancs 21 SD83
This industrial town was once the largest cotton-weaving centre in the world. Recent diversification of industry is evident by the many new buildings and developments in the area. Of the remaining old structures, the 14th- to 16th- and 18th-c Towneley Hall, now an art gallery and museum, is of interest. Both cricket and football are keenly followed in Burnley, and the town has produced high-calibre players of both sports. High moorland countryside is within easy walking distance of the town.

BURNSALL, N Yorks 22 SE06
A picturesque Wharfedale village, where the fine old grammar school was founded in 1602. The wild gully of Trollers Gill lies NE on the moors.

BURSLEM, Staffs 17 SJ84
This centre of the Potteries district was the birthplace of Josiah Wedgwood in 1730. An Arnold Bennett museum is situated at Cobridge, on the S side of the town (OACT), and both Arnold Bennett and the scientist Oliver Lodge studied at the local Wedgwood Institute. The latter was founded in 1869. An interesting period museum is housed in timbered Ford Green Hall (16thc) at Smallthorne.

BURSTOW, Surrey 8 TQ34
Burstow's restored Norman to 15th-c church has an all-timbered tower, and one of its rectors was Flamsteed, the well-known astronomer (1684 to 1719).

BURSTWICK, Humberside 23 TA22
The mainly-perpendicular church displays the Royal arms of King Charles II under the tower. On the back of this is a remarkable painting depicting the execution of Charles I.

BURTON AGNES, Humberside 23 TA16
A notable Elizabethan hall in this village includes a fine gatehouse (OACT). Near by is a recently-restored Norman manor house (AM).

BURTON BRADSTOCK, Dorset 6 SY48
This village includes many thatched stone-built cottages. The banded cliffs to the E are of geological interest, and the much-restored perpendicular church has an embattled central tower.

BURTON FLEMING, Humberside 23 TA07
An iron-age burial site of unusual construction was excavated here in 1968.

BURTON LATIMER, Northants 13 SP97
The church preserves notable 14th-c wall-paintings of St Catherine. A Jacobean hall can be seen in the area, and the local school dates from 1662.

BURTON UPON TRENT, Staffs 18 SK22
Numerous breweries in this area testify to the unique qualities of the local water. The town is famous for its beer making, but other industries are gradually growing up. St Modwin's parish church is early Georgian, and St Paul's houses an ironwork screen. The town's museum and art gallery is of interest, and Bretby Park (3½m SE) is a large early 19th-c mansion by Sir Geoffrey Wyatville.

BURWASH, E Sussex 9 TQ62
Rudyard Kipling once lived in 17th-c Bateman's (NT, OACT), and the neighbourhood is mentioned in his book *Puck of Pook's Hill*. The oldest iron grave slab in Sussex can be seen in the churchyard. Rampyndene is a fine old house situated in the village street.

BURWELL, Cambs 14 TL56
A straggling village, with a perpendicular church displaying a lofty west tower, a fine palimpsest brass, and some good woodwork. Old houses and two windmills can be seen here, and 2m N is the unspoiled area of Burwell Fen. This fenland is reserved as a sanctuary for flora and fauna typical of the district (NT).

BURY, Cambs 14 TL28
The Norman and early-English church displays a fine tower, and houses a 15th-c screen and 14th-c oak lectern.

BURY, Gt Manchester 21 SD81
This is an industrial town in which textiles are dyed and printed, and woollen yarn is manufactured. Other industries include paper-making and engineering. Sir Robert Peel was born here in 1788, and a statue raised to him can be seen in the market place. The art gallery and museum are of interest.

BURY, W Sussex 8 TQ01
John Galsworthy once lived in this River-Arun village, and Bury Hill is a notable downland viewpoint.

BURY ST EDMUNDS, Suffolk 15 TL86
County town of West Suffolk, this place has been the seat of a bishop since 1914. The name is taken from the shrine of St Edmund, who died as the last king of East Anglia in c870. For a long time this was a place of pilgrimage, and the abbey that was erected here in the 11thc became one of the grandest in England. Its scanty remains include a beautiful 14th-c gateway and a 13th-c Abbot's bridge. A fine Norman, gateway-tower now functions as the cathedral bell tower.

The cathedral is dedicated to St James and includes a fine nave that was begun in 1438, plus a new porch, cloister walk, and chancel. A large graveyard separates the cathedral from St Mary's Church, a good 15th-c building with a magnificent hammerbeam roof.

Moyse's Hall (12thc) may once have been a Jewish merchant's house, and is now a museum. The guildhall preserves a 13th-c doorway. Abbeygate Street includes several old houses and a few Georgian shopfronts. Cupola House is an outstanding town mansion of 1693, and Angel Corner, of 1711, contains a collection of clocks and watches (NT, OACT). The 17th-c town hall was remodelled by Robert Adam and later restored. This, and the fine Unitarian

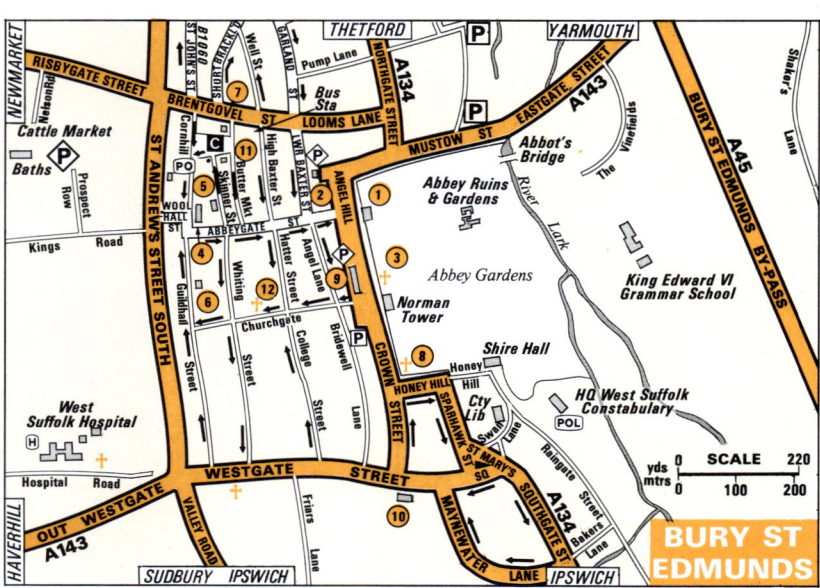

1	Abbey Remains
2	Angel Corner (museum)
3	Cathedral
4	Corn Exchange
5	Cupola House
6	Guildhall
7	Moyse's Hall (museum)
8	St Mary's Church
9	The Athenaeum
10	Theatre Royal
11	Town Hall
12	Unitarian Chapel

Chapel of 1711 are both of architectural interest. The Theatre Royal dates from 1819 and has been restored. Court House and St Margaret's House are early Georgian. The Athenaeum has a façade of 1804, and the Corn Exchange is dated 1861.

BUTLEY, Suffolk 15 TM35
Remains of the priory include a 14th-c gateway which has been converted into a vicarage. The latter is notable for its flintwork. Some Norman work and a good screen are evident in the local church.

BUTTERMERE, Cumbria 21 NY11
Buttermere is finely situated between Buttermere and Crummock Water, near the peaks of High Stile, High Crag, and Robinson. These all rise to about 2,500ft. Sour Milk Ghyll comes down from the lofty hill of Red Pike, opposite the village and above Crummock Water is the 120ft Scale Force waterfall. Much of the area is NT property. A steep road climbs E over Buttermere Hause and Newlands Hause, then through Keskadale to the shores of Derwentwater. Honister Pass (1 in 4) lies between 2,473ft Dale Head and 2,126ft Fleetwith Pike, 2½m SE. It provides access into Seatoller and Borrowdale.

BUTTERTUBS PASS, N Yorks 21 SD89
This wild pass is at an altitude of 1,726ft, linking Wensleydale with Swaledale, reaching a gradient of 1 in 5. Curious holes or Buttertubs lie to the side of the road. Great Shunner Fell rises to 2,340ft in the NW, and Lovely Seat to 2,213ft in the E.

BUXTED, E Sussex 8 TQ42
Iron cannon were first cast here by the Hogge family in 1543, and 16th-c Hog House stands at the entrance to finely-timbered Buxted Park.

BUXTON, Derbyshire 18 SK07
This well-known inland watering-place is sited at an altitude of nearly 1,000ft, and is the highest town of its size in the kingdom. Thermal and chalybeate springs which rise here have been known since Roman times, and were very popular in the Middle Ages. St Anne's Church is early 17thc, and Devonshire Hospital dome is the widest in the world. A fine 18th-c crescent of houses in the town is the work of John Carr of York. The tower on 1,450ft Grin Low provides a splendid viewpoint, and Poole's Hole, a 700 yard-long cave, contains stalactites and stalagmites. The town is a good centre for touring in the Peak District. Picturesque Goyt Valley lies 3½m W, and 3m SW is lofty Axe Edge, and the Travellers' Rest Inn at 1,535ft.

BYFLEET, Surrey 8 TQ06
The church here is partly 14thc, and the grave of George Smith, founder of the Dictionary of National Biography, can be seen in the churchyard. The manor house dates from the late 17thc.

BYLAND ABBEY, N Yorks 22 SE57
Considerable remains of this 12th-c Cistercian abbey (AM) still exist in a delightfully rustic setting.

BYWELL, Northumberland 27 NZ06
A River-Tyne village with twin churches. The Saxon tower of St Andrew's is of note, and the 15th-c castle gatehouse is interesting. Bywell Hall dates back to the 18thc.

CADBURY, Somerset 6 ST62
This area is divided into the two villages of North and South Cadbury. North Cadbury includes an Elizabethan and later manor house, and a fine perpendicular church housing carved bench ends. W of South Cadbury is the hilltop fort of Cadbury Castle, said to have been the site of King Arthur's Camelot. Excavations of this hilltop have shown traces of neolithic and bronze-age occupation, and the Saxon king Ethelred the Unready chose this site to establish a royal mint. The latter was later destroyed by King Canute. Compton Castle (c1825) stands in a picturesque setting to the E of the hill.

CADDINGTON, Beds 8 TL01
Prehistoric flint implements have been discovered here, and the church contains two interesting 15th-c brasses.

CADE STREET, E Sussex 9 TQ62
A pillar in this hamlet marks the spot where Jack Cade was killed by Iden, sheriff of Kent, during the insurrection of 1450.

CADGWITH, Cornwall 4 SW71
The approach to this attractive little village of the Lizard district is by steep lanes, and the pebble beach allows access to sandy coves. The Devil's Frying Pan is a strange tidal chasm running through the cliffs. Above the village is Ruan Minor, where serpentine stone has been used extensively in the construction of the church.

CADNAM, Hants 7 SU21
Sir John Barleycorn is an attractive old thatched inn in this New Forest village. The commons to the N and W are NT property and include those of Cadnam, Penn, Plaitford, and Bramshaw.

CAERHAYS CASTLE, Cornwall 4 SW94
This picturesque 'Gothick' castle is near Portholland, and was built by John Nash in 1808. It stands on the site of an earlier house which was once the seat of the Trevanion family.

CAISTER-ON-SEA, Norfolk 15 TG51
A small resort built on a site once occupied by a Roman walled town, offering a fine sandy beach. Interesting remains of a 15th-c moated castle can be seen, plus a 98ft tower by John Falstaff – a fine example of early brickwork. This tower now houses a large motor museum (OACT), and an adjacent hall has been renovated in Georgian style.

CAISTOR, Lincs 23 TA10
Situated at the far N extremity of the Wolds, this town has a partly-Saxon church displaying a good tower and south doorway. Traces of a Roman camp have been discovered in the area.

CAISTOR ST EDMUND, Norfolk 15 TG20
The town was once sited near the junction of the Rivers Yare and Wensum. As its old name of *Venta Icenorum* indicates, it was the cantonal town of the British Iceni tribes. Excavations have revealed extensive Roman remains. The early-English and perpendicular church houses a fine carved font (c1400) and a mural of St Christopher.

CALBOURNE, Isle of Wight 7 SZ48
One of the two good brasses that can be seen in the 12th- to 13th-c church dates from c1380. Nearby Winkle Street is a well-known beauty spot, comprising low stone cottages with thatched or tiled roofs. A 17th-c water mill can also be seen in the area.

CALDBECK, Cumbria 26 NY33
John Peel, the celebrated huntsman who died in 1854, is buried in the local churchyard. A natural bridge and cave called Fairykirk can be seen near a waterfall ½m W. Extraction of lead and copper used to be a flourishing industry in this area.

CALDER BRIDGE, Cumbria 20 NY00
In the autumn of 1956, Britain's first nuclear power station was opened at nearby Calder Hall by Queen Elizabeth II. The 18th-c mansion of Ponsonby Hall is sited here, and ¾m E are the ruins of 12th-c Calder Abbey (AM, OACT). The latter was originally built by Savignac monks from Furness Abbey.

CALLINGTON, Cornwall 5 SX36
A quiet town with a perpendicular-style church housing monuments, and displaying an ancient churchyard cross. Stone slabs known as cromlechs are among the several prehistoric remains to be found in the neighbourhood. The partly-rebuilt 15th-c New Bridge spans the River Lynher to the SW. Kit Hill is a 1,067ft viewpoint lying 1½m NE, surmounted by an ancient camp, the chimney of an old mine, and a radio mast. A 15th-c chapel 1m E houses Dupath Well, one of the Cornish Holy Wells.

CALNE, Wilts 7 ST97
Calne is a small town of great antiquity, which originally derived its prosperity from weaving. Two centuries ago the Industrial Revolution destroyed this source of revenue, but the bacon-curing industry for which the town is now famous arose in its place. This alternative occupation grew up because droves of Irish pigs passed regularly through the town on their way from Bristol to London.

The interesting 12th-c church has a fine, timbered nave roof and a 17th-c tower. The Lansdowne Arms, a reconstructed coaching house that was famous in the days of Elizabeth I, still displays its large barometer on the outside wall. The poet Coleridge lived here for two years, and Macaulay often visited the town in his capacity as MP. The large Georgian house of Bowood, partly by Adam but now reduced in size, lies 2m W. Joseph Priestley discovered oxygen while staying here as librarian to the Earl of Shelburne.

CALSTOCK, Cornwall 5 SX46
This quiet town is situated on a picturesque stretch of the River Tamar, and is now the centre of an area growing soft fruit. Cotehele House is an interesting granite-built house of 1485 and 1627, standing in lovely gardens (NT, OACT). Mining was once an important local industry, and an underground canal linked Morwellham Quay with Tavistock. Industrial relics of the former copper port are displayed in a recreation and education centre by the quay (OACT).

CAMBER, E Sussex 9 TQ91
The sandy beach adjacent to this bungalow village is sheltered by dunes which, in former days, were constantly shifting in the wind. The Forestry Commission are planting grass and windbreaks to curtail such erosion, and the area is rapidly developing into a major holiday resort. Across the estuary of the River Rother, 3½m W, is 16th-c Camber Castle (AM), a coastal defence fort originally erected by King Henry VIII.

CAMBERLEY, Surrey 8 SU86
This town has extensive connections with the armed forces, and includes the Royal Staff College. Sandhurst lies immediately W. The Chobham Ridges viewpoint is situated 2½m E.

CAMBO, Northumberland 27 NZ08
Founded in 1740, this high-lying moorland village includes the impressive 17th- to 18th-c Wallington Hall (NT) among its more interesting features. This house is set in a 12,000-acre estate that rises to more than 1,000ft in places (OACT), and was given to the NT by Sir Charles Trevelyan in 1942. Alarming stone heads dotted around the grounds are of mythical beasts, and came from London's old Aldersgate after its demolition in 1761.

CAMBORNE, Cornwall 4 SW64
Although most of the deep tin mines in the area are no longer worked, Camborne still has a School of Metalliferous Mining. The local museum displays items of archaeological, historical, mineralogical, and mining interest. Richard Trevithick, a pioneer of steam locomotion, was born at nearby Pool in 1771. Five original Cornish beam-engines were presented to the NT in 1967 (OACT). Remains of old mine engine-houses and chimneys are a feature of this part of Cornwall.

CAMBRIDGE, Cambs 14 TL45
The river upon which this famous university city is built bears two different names; N of the town it is the Cam, and the more S reaches are known as the Granta. The Backs are delightful lawns and gardens that slope down to the Cam behind the colleges, and the river is spanned by a number of fine bridges. Cambridge is sited at a point where several roads once converged upon a ford. This, combined with the fact that the River Cam itself bore a great deal of

Fenland traffic, made the city a natural centre for local trade and a place of great strategic importance. Thus it is not surprising that settlements have existed here since prehistoric times, or that the Romans, Danes, Normans, and Oliver Cromwell (a one-time student of Sidney Sussex College) all used it as a military base.

The origins of the university are obscure, but it is thought that the migration of scholars from Oxford to Cambridge in 1209 – the first year of the university – might have had something to do with it. By 1226 a corporate body had evolved with an elected Chancellor, and 1284 saw the foundation of the first college, Peterhouse, by Hugh de Balsham (Bishop of Ely). Seven other colleges were founded in the first half of the 14thc, and Papal recognition was sought in 1318.

The compactness of the town makes it easier to explore by foot rather than by taking a car through the complicated one-way system. Although restrictions to entry into the interesting parts of the city are minimal, pedestrians must not wander into colleges where notices expressly forbid this, or climb steps and outside staircases unless invited to do so. There are plenty of delightful courts and gardens open to the public, and most of the college chapels and libraries may be visited at specified times.

Trumpington Street enters Cambridge from the S side, and is a veritable storehouse of architectural treasures. Hobson's Conduit was built to carry water from Nine Wells (1610 to 1614). It was named after Thomas Hobson, whose habit of making customers take the horse nearest the door of his livery stable, or go without, gave rise to the expression Hobson's Choice. Further down the street is Addenbrooke's Hospital, opposite the classical frontage of the Fitzwilliam Museum. The latter has period rooms housing paintings, furniture, and ceramics contemporary to each other, plus galleries of early and classical antiquities. Peterhouse lies beyond the museum, and comprises buildings that were constructed after a fire in the 15thc. The windows in the hall include stained glass by Madox Brown, Burne-Jones, and William Morris. Gray the poet was a fellow here before he left for Pembroke College in high dudgeon, after being the subject of a practical joke by students.

Little St Mary's Street leads left towards the river and past the Museum of Classical Archaeology, and Pembroke College, founded by the Countess of Pembroke (1346) is sited opposite Peterhouse. Its old chapel is now used as a lecture room, and the new chapel of 1663 was built with a donation from Bishop Wren of Ely, and designed by his famous nephew Christopher Wren. This was the latter's first design project.

Off Silver Street, which also turns left towards the river, is Queens' Street and the entrance to Queens' College – the most picturesque of the Cambridge colleges and the only one displaying half-timbering (President's Lodge). The name is plural because the foundation enjoyed the patronage of first Queen Mary of Anjou, and then of Elizabeth Woodville (1465), wife of Edward IV. A wooden bridge dubbed the mathematical bridge spans the Cam between the Cloister Court and the college gardens. Its strange name refers to the fact that it was designed in such a way, using mathematical principles, that no nails or similar fixings were required to hold it together. The original of 1749 was replaced by a replica in the early part of this century – built in exactly the same way.

Beyond Silver Street are the buildings of St Catharine's College, founded in 1743 and rebuilt from 1674 to 1757. Recent extensions join it to King's College on King's Parade. Corpus Christi is opposite St Catharine's and is unique in having been founded by two town Guilds. The earliest English example of a medieval academic quadrangle can be seen in the Old Court, and the First Court library houses priceless collections of coins, gems, and manuscripts. Paintings by English artists are hung in the hall, which itself has a painted ceiling. A fine brick gallery connects Corpus Christi with the Church of St Bene't, which displays a Saxon tower and tower arch and originally housed the college.

King's College was founded by Henry VI in 1441, but much of it is of 19th-c date. The Fellows' Building dates from 1724, and the chapel was started in 1446. The latter is considered the crowning glory of the university; work was interrupted by the Wars of the Roses, and the structure was not completed until 1515. Flemish craftsmen spent a further twenty-six years glazing the superb stained-glass windows, and the overall design of the interior is famous for its fan tracery roof and 16th-c organ screen. The altar piece is *The Adoration of the Magi* by Rubens, and was donated in 1959. This chapel is world-famous for its choral singing.

During term time the university sermon is preached in the parish church of Great St Mary, built from 1478 to 1574. The tower was finished in 1608, and an evening curfew is rung from here. Elegant arches support the nave, and the organ was brought from its original home of St James's (Piccadilly), in 1697. Senate House is by Gibbs, also architect of London's St Martin's in the Fields, and nearby Trinity Hall (1350) is noted for its crow-stepped Elizabethan library. Behind the Senate House are a number of old buildings which include the Old Schools. Between these and the river is Clare College, founded by Richard Bradew in 1326, and containing work of the 17th, 18th, and 20thc. Giles Scott designed New Court in 1924, which is considered to be one of the most successful new buildings in Cambridge and contains the Unknown Warrior by Henry Moore.

Trinity College was founded by Henry VIII and is the largest in Cambridge. Great Gate displays statues of various monarchs, and Great Court is claimed to be the largest university court in the world. It contains a fountain by Thomas Neville, master of the college from 1593 to 1615. The library on one side of Neville's Court was built by Wren from 1679 to 1695, and contains bookcases carved by Grinling Gibbons, plus original manuscripts by Milton, Thackeray, Tennyson, Newton, and Byron.

St John's College lies adjacent to Trinity, was founded in 1511, and has superb red-brick gateways linking its red-brick courts. Spanning the river is the well-known Bridge of Sighs. Gonville and Caius (pronounced Keys) lies S of Trinity and is noted for its carved Gate of Virtue and Gate of Honour. It was founded in 1349 and 1558. Magdalene College (pronounced Maudlen) lies N of St John's and was founded in 1542. It is particularly noted for the Pepysian library of c1703, which contains the manuscript of Pepys' diary. Mallory Court recalls the famous Everest climber of the same name.

Other Cambridge colleges are Jesus; Sidney Sussex; Christ's; Emmanuel; Downing; Selwyn; Churchill; Fitzwilliam; Darwin; St Edmund's Hall; University; and the theological colleges, Ridley Hall, Wesley House, Westcott House and Westminster. Women's colleges are Girton, New Hall, and Newnham. University Library was by Sir Gilbert Scott from 1931 to 1934. Local guide books will supply more detailed information about these places.

The interesting Sedgwick Museum of Geology is sited in Downing Street, and the University Botanic Gardens cover more than 40 acres and were founded in 1761 for teaching and research purposes. They are rated second only to Kew and are best visited in the afternoon, when the glass houses are open. The tower in Madingley Road was founded in 1960 for the promotion of teaching and research – particularly in science and technology. At the junction of Bridge Street and St John's Street is the Church of the Holy Sepulchre, one of the very few round medieval churches in England. The much-restored circular

Colleges
1 Christ's College
2 Churchill College
3 Clare College
4 Clare Hall
5 Corpus Christi College
6 Darwin College
7 Downing College
8 Emmanuel College
9 Fitzwilliam College
10 Gonville and Caius College
11 Jesus College
12 King's College
13 Magdalene College
14 New Hall College (women)
15 Newnham College (women)
16 Pembroke College
17 Peterhouse College
18 Queens' College
19 Ridley Hall (theological)
20 St Catherine's College
21 St Edmund's Hall
22 St John's College
23 Selwyn College
24 Sidney Sussex College
25 Trinity College
26 Trinity Hall
27 University College
28 Wesley House (theological)
29 Westcott House (theological)
30 Westminster College (theological)

Churches
31 Church of St Bene't
32 Church of St Mary the Great
33 Holy Sepulchre (round church)

Museums
34 Fitzwilliam Museum
35 Museum of Classical Archaeology
36 Sedgwick Museum of Geology

Other Places of Interest
37 Addenbrooke's Hospital
38 Hobson's Conduit
39 Old Schools
40 Senate House
41 University Botanic Gardens
42 University Library

part originates from the 12thc, and extensions were added in the 15thc. Boat races are held on the river during 'May Week', an event which actually takes place in June.

CAMELFORD, Cornwall 4 SX18
This small town is situated 4m from the coast and was once, according to legend, the site of King Arthur's Camelot. Slaughter Bridge crosses a stream 1m N and is said to have been the scene of Arthur's last battle. The town's Market Hall dates from 1790.

CAMPSALL, W Yorks 22 SE51
An attractive stone-built village with a trans-Norman church displaying a notable west tower. The 15th-c vicarage is of interest, and the hall dates from the 18thc.

CANFIELD, GREAT, Essex 9 TL51
The large mound with a moat and outer bailey that can be seen in this River-Roding village is probably of Norman origin. A notable 13th-c wall-painting has been preserved in the Norman and later church.

CANFORD CLIFFS, Dorset 7 SZ08
This residential district is sited on sandy Poole Bay, between Bournemouth and Poole. The beach is edged by low cliffs, and attractive Compton Acres gardens are well worth a visit (OACT).

CANNINGTON, Somerset 6 ST23
A Quantock-Hills village, with a mainly 15th-c church displaying a fine tower. Brymore House lies W, and was the birthplace of John Pym in 1584. He became a leading statesman under the reign of Charles I. Gurney Street Farm is a fine old house of the 16thc, and Gothelney Manor, dating from c1500, can be seen 2m S. Blackmoor Farm lies 1m SW and is of the same approximate date.

CANNOCK, Staffs 18 SJ91
Cannock Chase, a 26sqm area of woodland now designated an area of outstanding natural beauty, laps the very edge of this coal-mining town. Hilton Hall is the moated home of the Vernons (4m SW), where a lofty tower in the park commemorates the capture of Portobello in 1739.

CANONS ASHBY, Northants 13 SP55
The 13th-c church in this tiny village displays a fine exterior and various monuments to the writer Dryden. Remains of a 13th- and 14th-c priory chapel are included in the structure, and Roundhead troops used the tower as a refuge when attacked by the King's men. Shot marks can still be seen on the walls. Fine gardens surround the beautiful 16th- to 18th-c manor house, a building which is strongly associated with Spenser and Dryden. The first house was built by Sir John Cope, whose daughter and heiress married John Dryden, the first of the family to bear this name. The poet often stayed here with the second baronet (his uncle), and Edmund Spenser frequented the house as a friend of Sir Erasmus Dryden.

CANTERBURY, Kent 9 TR15
Canterbury has been the site of a settlement since prehistoric times. When the Romans invaded they found a community of the Belgae at a ford on the River Stour. This was named *Durovernum*, and quickly expanded to become a town; the present city wall has Roman foundations dating from the third century. After 407, when Britain ceased to be part of the Roman Empire, the invading Angles, Jutes, and Saxons built dwellings within the boundaries of the former Roman city. Several Christian churches were built in the city during the Roman occupation, and the famous mission of St Augustine reached Canterbury in 597. Ethelbert (King of Kent) was converted, and a number of early churches were restored to Christian use. These included St Martin's, and a church on the site of the present cathedral. It was soon after this that Canterbury became the metropolitan city of the English Church.

Long, reasonably-preserved stretches of the town walls survive, and tall overhanging houses can be seen in the lanes leading to the cathedral's main entrance. The original building on the cathedral site was destroyed by fire in 1067, and the present structure was started by Lanfranc, the first Norman archbishop, in 1070. Parts of the crypt, some sections of wall, and the nave ground plan are all that remain of his work. Anselm, who followed Lanfranc, carried out a massive re-building of the choir and east transepts. Archbishop Thomas Becket was murdered in the north-west transept of the cathedral in 1170, and the destruction of the choir by fire some four years later provided an opportunity to construct a worthy setting for the shrine of a new martyr saint. This may be seen in the Trinity Chapel. The rebuilding, which involved the vertical and linear extension of the whole eastern end, was the work of two gifted architects – William of Sens and William the Englishman. It was the first English example of the transition from Norman round to pointed Gothic arches, and has remained substantially unaltered since the end of the 12thc. Other parts of the cathedral that have been changed include the western section, the nave, the south-west tower, and the noble central tower (Bell Harry), all of which were rebuilt or altered between c1400 and c1500.

When the nave was reconstructed by Henry Yevele, the Great Cloister was also rebuilt in its present form. The precincts are entered through the Christ Church gate of 1517. No other important changes were made until 1834, when the Norman tower was pulled down to make way for the present north-west tower, matching the south-west tower of 1424 to 1434, and a new cathedral library was built. This was destroyed in an air raid in 1942 and has been replaced. Many interesting monuments housed in the cathedral include the tomb of the Black Prince, and one of Henry IV and his wife Joan of Navarre. Some of the oldest stained glass in the world can be seen here. Other features of outstanding interest are the Norman crypt, the 12th-c choir with its 14th-c screen, the Corona (or Becket's crown), the slender Norman tower, and John Wastell's great 15th-c Angel Steeple or Bell Harry tower.

King's School is one of the oldest extant, and has a unique Norman exterior staircase. The remains of St Augustine's Abbey (AM) display a gateway of c1309 and are incorporated in a college. St Martin's Church is perhaps the oldest working church in England, and was standing before St Augustine arrived. St Dunstan's shows Saxon work and houses the head of Sir Thomas More, who was executed in 1535. Izaak Walton was married in 13th-c St Mildred's Church. The other city churches also display items of great interest.

Canterbury's interesting West Gate now contains a museum of armour and is the only surviving gate in the city walls. St Thomas's Hospital preserves a Norman hall, Black Friars refectory dates from c1300, and St John's Hospital from 1074. The Roper gateway survives from the house where Sir Thomas More's daughter lived, and 13th-c Greyfriars friary stands in a garden near the Stour. The Weavers are an attractive collection of old houses overlooking the Stour, and the Falstaff is an interesting old inn. Poor Priests' Hospital dates from the 14thc and contains the regimental museum of the Buffs. Recently excavated Roman paving can be seen in Butchery Lane, and remains of the castle and stretches of the city walls lie close to Dane John, an ancient fortification. Preserved near by is the locomotive *Invicta*, built by Stephenson in 1830 for the Canterbury and Whitstable Railway, and one of the earliest in England. Kent University (1961) was designed by Lord Holford and has been founded on the Whitstable road.

Christopher Marlowe the playwright was born at Canterbury in 1564, and R H Barham, author of the *Ingoldsby Legends*, lived at 61 Burgate. The 16th-c House of Agnes on St Dunstan's Street has associations with Dickens' *David Copperfield*. The town suffered greatly from indiscriminate bombing during the Second World War, and subsequent rebuilding has altered some of its character. A county-cricket ground is sited in Canterbury, and Cricket Week, held annually in August of each year, is famous.

CANVEY ISLAND, Essex 9 TQ78
This Thames-estuary island is linked to the mainland by a bridge, and is largely covered by bungalow settlements, with some industry. A small museum is located in a thatched octagonal 17th-c cottage.

CAPHEATON, Northumberland 27 NZ08
An attractive mainly 18th-c village, where the hall of 1668 is by Robert Trollope from Newcastle. It is considered one of the best examples of its period. The grounds were landscaped by Capability Brown.

CARHAMPTON, Somerset 6 ST04
The old custom of 'Wassailing the apple trees', when the villagers drink a toast to the largest apple tree in the cider orchards and throw cider on its trunk, is still observed each January 17. This ceremony is supposed to drive evil spirits from the crop. The restored church has a fine painted screen.

CARISBROOKE, Isle of Wight 7 SZ48
Carisbrooke is the old capital of the island, and was defended by a strong Norman castle, itself built on the site of a Roman fort. An interesting 12th-c priory church with a fine tower of 1474 can be seen in the village, plus a statue of the Madonna and Child by John Skelton (1969). Carisbrooke Castle, where Charles I was imprisoned from 1647 to

1648 and his daughter Elizabeth died in 1650, is ½m away. An archway of 1598 allows access to a stone bridge and a 14th-c gatehouse. The chapel of St Nicholas has been rebuilt, and various domestic buildings have been restored. The museum displays local antiquities, and a 16th-c well is worked by a donkey in a large wheel (OACT).

CARK, Cumbria 21 SD37
The hall in this village dates from the 16thc, and ½m N is the 16th- to 19th-c Holker Hall. The latter is set in a famous deer park and is the home of the Cavendish family. Good paintings and beautiful oak carvings can be seen in the house (OACT).

CARLISLE, Cumbria 26 NY45
Plan overleaf
During the Roman occupation this city was an important military centre which was often raided by the Scottish tribes. It owes its importance to the strategic position it occupies, and the town grew up around the castle built by William Rufus, again as a defence against the Scots. Work started on the stronghold in 1092, and although it was taken by the Scots on several occasions, they never held it permanently. Mary Queen of Scots was a prisoner here in 1568, and the rescue of Kinmont Willie by the Bold Buccleuch in 1596 is commemorated in a ballad. The structure is in good repair and is in use (OACT).

Six western bays of the fine Carlisle cathedral were demolished by the Scots to repair the town wall in 1645, but what remains is not without interest. Two surviving bays of the nave are Norman work from 1123, and now serve as a memorial chapel to the Border Regiment. The small south transept is also 12thc, and contains a Runic inscription. The north transept is 14thc, and the choir, destroyed by fire in 1292, was restored in contemporary style early in the 13thc. A magnificent east window is an outstanding feature of the choir, and is said by some to be finer than that of York Minster. Fine carved woodwork is displayed by the 15th-c stalls, and the 16th-c pulpit is of interest. Good screenwork can be seen in St Catherine's Chapel and on the north side of the chancel.

A good Jacobean mansion in Castle Street houses the Tullie House Museum, where a fine collection of local antiquities and some modern paintings are on display. The spacious market place contains a market cross of 1682, the old town hall of 1717, and a medieval guildhall. St Cuthbert's Church (18thc) has a curious movable pulpit.

CARRAWBROUGH, Northumberland 27 NY87
Here, near the Roman wall-fort of *Procolitia*, are the remains of one of the very few Mithraic temples ever to be found in England. It dates from the 3rdc and was excavated in 1950. The temple was discovered when a dry summer caused the peat covering over the remains to shrink.

CARSHALTON, Gt London 8 TQ26
Now in the midst of suburbia and part of the London borough of Sutton, Carshalton grew up as a town in Surrey. The manor house that once stood on the site now occupied by Carshalton House was where the founder of Oxford's Radcliffe Library died in 1714. The present building was erected for Sir John Fellowes, a governor of the ill-fated South-Seas Company, in 1720. It has since been considerably enlarged, and was purchased by a religious order for use as a convent and school (OACT). A number of Regency houses can be seen by the pond, and the nearby church (partly 13thc) houses a fine organ case and altar-piece by Sir Ninian Comper.

CARTER BAR, Northumberland 26 NT60
This is a notable viewpoint rising to

1	Black Friars Refectory	9	House of St Agnes
2	Canterbury Weavers Houses	10	Invicta
3	Castle Remains	11	King's School
4	Cathedral	12	Poor Priests' Hospital (museum)
5	County Cricket Ground	13	Roman Paving
6	Dane John Fortifications	14	Roper Gateway
7	Falstaff Inn	15	St Augustine's Abbey Remains
8	Greyfriars Friary	16	St Dunstan's Church
17	St John's Hospital		
18	St Martin's Church		
19	St Mildred's Church		
20	St Thomas' Hospital		
21	West Gate (city wall; museum)		
22	University of Kent		

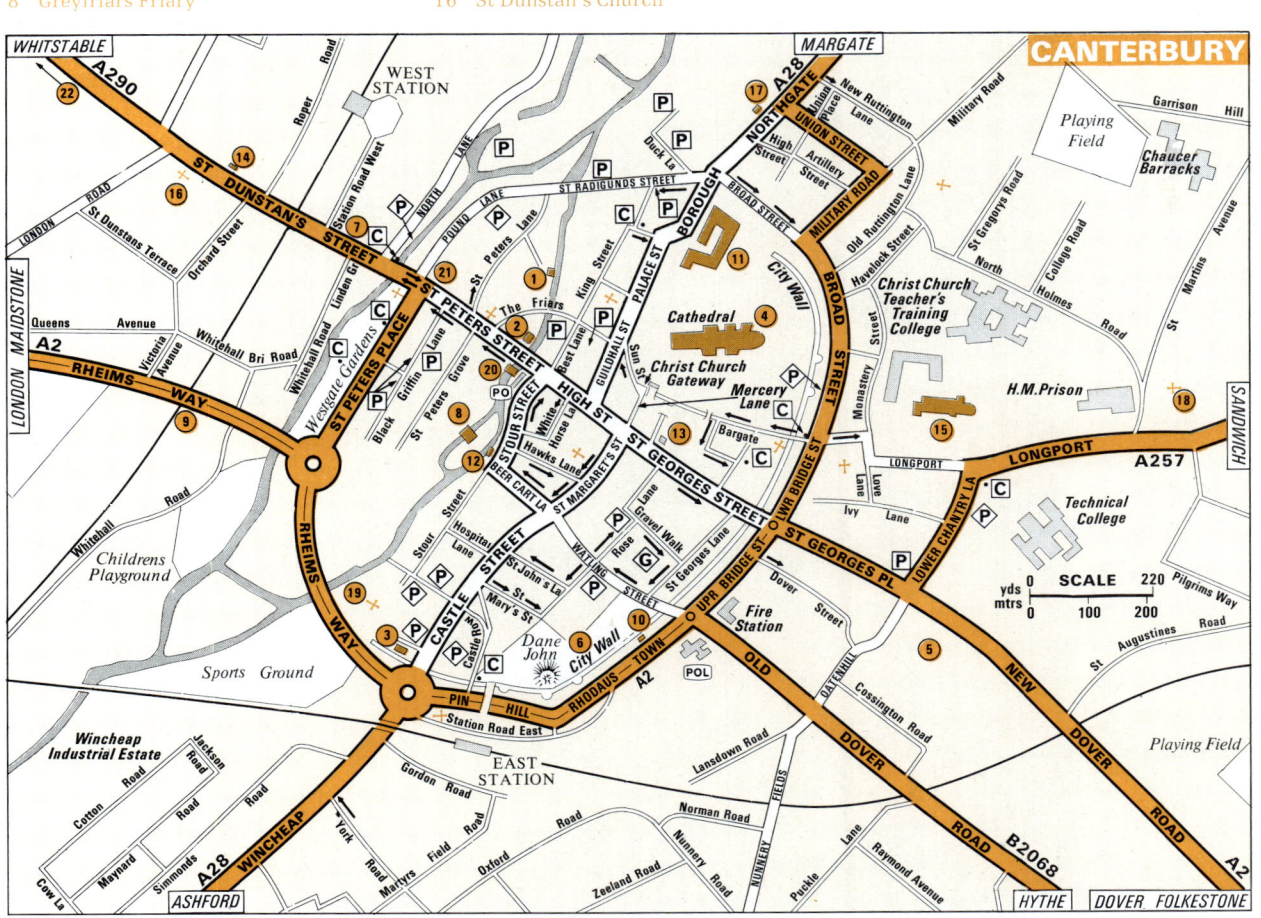

1,371ft on the English-Scottish border, and was the scene of one of the last Border battles in 1575. The contest culminated in a victory for the Scottish Jeddarts over the Redesdale men, in the Battle of Redeswire.

The S approach passes through lonely, now afforested Rede Valley, and past the Catcleugh reservoir which supplies Newcastle with water. Chew Green Roman camp lies E along the Cheviot ridge, on the line of Agricola's Dere Street. The Border national park stretches SW from Carter Bar.

CARTMEL, Cumbria 21 SD37
Whitsun steeplechasing is a popular annual event at this pleasant old town. It was once the seat of an important priory, and the 12th-c priory church displays superb stained glass, a fine 15th-c tower, and a nave and east window of the same period. The gabled gatehouse dates from the 14thc (NT, OACT), and 3m S is the ancient peletower of Wraysholme. Above High Newton, 3m E, is an area of small hills covered in bracken, hawthorn, and holly, providing excellent walking.

CASTERTON, GREAT, Leics 19 TF00
An attractive stone-built village on the route of Ermine Street. The Norman to 13th-c church has a fine priest's tomb, and displays attractive carving on the capitals of its porch columns. John Clare, the rural poet, met his wife Martha while working here. Recent excavations have revealed parts of a Roman town and villa.

CASTLE ACRE, Norfolk 15 TF81
This place is sited on the line of ancient Peddars' Way road (thought to be Roman), which crosses Norfolk. Remains of a Norman castle (AM) include a fine gateway; exceptional 11th-c priory ruins include a Tudor gatehouse and fine Norman arcading (AM, OACT). The parish church has 15th-c painted-screen panels, and a font cover that is 26ft high.

CASTLE BYTHAM, Lincs 19 SK91
A pleasant stone-built village, including earthworks which are all that remain of a one-time castle. Near the partly 13th-c church are the priory and manor house, both of the 17thc. The Clipsham quarries which lie to the W provided stone for the building of Buckingham Palace, and the rebuilt House of Commons.

CASTLE CARY, Somerset 6 ST63
Although predominantly modern, the heart of this market town still contains a number of interesting old buildings. The castle that existed here had a 78ft square keep, the boundaries of which have been marked out on the ground. A picturesque old lock-up in the shape of a beehive can be seen at Bailey Hill, and is said to have been erected for a mere £23. The post office occupies a fine 18th-c house.

CASTLE COMBE, Wilts 6 ST87
A picturesque stone-built village in a wooded valley near Chippenham. The 13th-c market cross and numerous old houses are interesting, and the partly-perpendicular church was rebuilt in 1851. Its old tower survived the alterations, and the interior shows beautiful fan vaulting. The village once had a prosperous weaving industry, and was a centre for the trade.

CASTLE DONINGTON, Leics 18 SK42
A town near the River Trent where the timbered Old Key House has keys hanging from two of the gables. The church is mainly of early-English style, and contains a notable 15th-c brass. East midlands airport and an electric power station are sited here. Iron water-wheels can be seen at King's Mills, and 1½m W is late 18th-c Donington Park, once a motor racing circuit. A museum of old racing cars has recently opened in the area.

CASTLEFORD, W Yorks 22 SE42
This River-Aire manufacturing town is situated on the site of a Roman station. Coal-mining and bottle-making are the chief industries, and the sculptor Henry Moore was born here in 1898. Fairburn Ings nature reserve lies to the NE.

CASTLE HEDINGHAM, Essex 15 TL73
The Norman castle keep was built by the de Veres, and is considered one of the finest in England (AM, OACT). It dominates the little medieval town, where a fine Norman to early-English church shows a late 14th-c screen, a brick tower of 1616, and a double hammerbeam roof over the Norman nave. The 12th-c churchyard cross has been restored, and the town's numerous old houses and inns are of interest.

CASTLE HOWARD, N Yorks 22 SE77
This house is perhaps Vanbrugh's finest achievement. It is a domed mansion that dates from 1699 to 1726, and is set in superb grounds. The building contains numerous art treasures in its palatial interior, and the grounds display Hawksmoor's mausoleum and Vanbrugh's Temple of the Four Winds (OACT).

CASTLE RISING, Norfolk 14 TF62
Although once a port, the sea has long-since withdrawn from this interesting Norfolk village. The much-restored church is of late-Norman origin, and a restored stepped cross can be seen on the green. The massive castle has remarkable earthworks and a fine Norman keep (AM), and 17th-c Bede House, or Trinity Hospital, is of interest. The latter is an almshouse charity for ten elderly women, and the occupants still wear Stuart costume on Sunday.

CASTLETON, Derbyshire 18 SK18
This large Derbyshire village was the setting for Sir Walter Scott's novel *Peveril of the Peak*. Its Peveril or Peak Castle is of Norman origin (AM). Garland day is a traditional celebration commemorating the restoration of Charles II, held annually on May 29.

The church has a Norman chancel arch, 17th-c box pews, and a library of old books. Douglas Museum is interesting, and limestone caverns can be seen in the vicinity. These include the Peak Cavern, the Speedwell Mine, the Treak Cliff Cavern, and Blue John Mine. A mineral known by the name Blue John – a translucent variety of fluorspar banded with red, blue, purple, and yellow – is found in the area. It has been prized for ornament making since Roman times.

Nearby Giant's Hole is 536ft deep. Winnats Pass (NT) is an impressive, rugged defile, and 1½m W is Mam Tor (NT), known as the shivering mountain because of the way shale is constantly being eroded from its face. A Peak

1 Castle
2 Cathedral
3 Guildhall
4 Market Cross and Market Place
5 Old Town Hall
6 St Cuthbert's Church
7 Tullie House Museum

District national park residential study centre, the first of its kind in the country, is at Losehill Park. This was opened in November 1972, by HRH Princess Anne.

CASTLETOWN, Isle of Man *20 SC26*
Castletown is the old capital of the island, and is situated on Castletown Bay and River Silverburn. Castle Rushen, a fine 14th-c medieval fortress, preserves a one-hand clock which was given by Queen Elizabeth I in 1597 (OACT). A nautical museum exhibits The Peggy, a schooner-rigged yacht that may well be the oldest in the country. The Witches Mill and Witchcraft Museum exhibits curious objects used in connection with magic, witchcraft, and the evil-eye.

CASTOR, Cambs *19 TL19*
On the River Nene, Castor was known for its pottery in Roman times. St Kyneburga's Church has a magnificent, richly-carved Norman tower, considered one of the finest in England. An inscription records the dedication of the church in 1124, and there are interesting wall paintings. To the N is Castor Hanglands nature reserve, and 2m NE stands the notable Milton Hall, an Elizabethan and Georgian mansion set in its own park.

CAT AND FIDDLE INN, Derbyshire *18 SK07*
This notable inn is set in lonely moorland at a height of 1,690ft, on the main Buxton to Macclesfield road. Picturesque Goyt Valley lies N, and the equally impressive Dane Valley is to the S.

CATERHAM, Surrey *8 TQ35*
The coming of the railway in 1856 started the growth of this once-quiet upland village; it is now a residential district that fills the valley, and has encroached upon the surrounding downs. Gravelly Hill lies S, and at 778ft offers a good viewpoint that takes in the ancient Pilgrims' Way on its way to Kent.

CATTERICK, N Yorks *22 SE29*
A village mainly known for the large military training area nearby. The good church is of 15th-c origin, and a racecourse is situated 1m N at Catterick Bridge, on the River Swale. Brough Hall (18thc and earlier) lies to the SW, and Hipswell Hall is another interesting old house farther to the W. The Roman military camp of *Cataractonium* was sited nearby.

CATTISTOCK, Dorset *6 SY59*
The rebuilt church in this village is famous for its tower, which boasts a carillon of twenty-five bells from Louvain in Belgium. These were restored after a fire. Chantmarle, a lovely 15th- to 17th-c manor house sited 2m N, is now a police training centre.

CAVENDISH, Suffolk *15 TL84*
Cavendish is an attractive village in the pretty Stour valley, and was once the ancestral home of the Dukes of Devonshire. The old gabled home of the Cavendishes is now the village institute. Good examples of perpendicular work can be seen in the church, which contains a 15th-c brass-eagle lectern.

CAVERSWALL, Staffs *18 SJ94*
A fine Jacobean manor house standing within a dry moat can be seen here. The moat was part of a former castle, and the present building is now a convent. A Chantrey sculpture is housed within the church.

CAWOOD, N Yorks *22 SE53*
This River-Ouse village preserves the gatehouse of a former palace in which Cardinal Wolsey was arrested in 1530 (AM). Its Norman church displays a 15th-c tower.

CAWSTON, Norfolk *15 TG12*
The perpendicular local church has a very fine double-hammerbeam roof showing carved angels with widespread wings, and was built by the Earl of Suffolk in the early 15thc. Attractive red-brick cottages can be seen in the village, and the Duel Stone (NT) at the Woodrow Inn is a reminder of a fight which occurred in 1698.

CERNE ABBAS, Dorset *6 ST60*
The abbey which gives this charming village its name was a Benedictine foundation of 987, and its remains include a beautiful 15th-c gatehouse and a 14th- and 15th-c guesthouse. Abbey House is of the 17thc and later, and a near by 15th-c tithe barn has now been converted into a home. A good buttressed tower and examples of early heraldic glass are displayed by the mainly-perpendicular church, and a number of Georgian and older houses exist in the area. The Cerne Giant (NT) is a 180ft figure cut into the chalk hillside, NE of the village, and is thought to be of Romano-British origin. At Upper Cerne, 1m N of Cerne Abbas, is an old manor house.

CHADDESLEY CORBETT, Herefs & Worcs *12 SO87*
This picturesque village of half-timbered houses includes a 14th-c inn, and a mainly 14th-c church. The carved 12th-c font housed in the church is of particular note. Harvington Hall (OACT) is a moated 16th- to 18th-c house sited 1m NW. It contains secret hiding places and is close to an area of NT land.

CHAGFORD, Devon *5 SX78*
The name of this quiet little Dartmoor town comes from old English, and means a ford in gorse-covered country. This is an excellent description of the region. Near the source of the River Teign, and some 6m SE on the moor, are the Grey Wethers stone circles; the whole area is rich in prehistoric remains. A one-time manor house in the town now serves as the Three Crowns Inn.

CHALDON, Surrey *8 TQ35*
A quiet upland hamlet, where the church preserves some remarkable 12th-c wall paintings. The church bell is thought to date from the 13thc, and is certainly one of the oldest in England.

CHALE, Isle of Wight *7 SZ47*
The beach at Chale is largely formed of sand and shingle, and the local church has a good 15th-c tower. Picturesque Blackgang Chine is close to the village, and beyond the landslip 2m SE is St Catherine's Point, a lighthouse. St Catherine's Hill rises to 781ft behind the community, and is surmounted by the remains of a 14th-c beacon.

CHALFONT ST GILES, Bucks *8 SU99*
The largely-decorated and perpendicular church houses 14th-c paintings, and the churchyard lych-gate is of probable 16th-c date. Bertram Mills, the famous circus owner and organizer, is buried here. Milton's Cottage is a half-timbered building where the poet lived during the plague of 1665. It contains several Milton relics and was where he completed *Paradise Lost* and started *Paradise Regained* (OACT). The Vache is a house of Elizabethan and 19th-c origin, with an 18th-c monument to Captain Cook in the grounds.

CHALFONT ST PETER, Bucks *8 SU99*
Old brasses can be seen in the local church, and 1m E of Chalfont Colony is a 50ft milestone obelisk. This was erected, on its present site above the Misbourne Valley, by Sir T M Gott in 1785, a gentleman from the nearby mansion of Newland. Restoration work was carried out on the obelisk in 1879.

CHALFORD, Glos *12 SO80*
A picturesque village situated near Stroud, above the Frome Valley and disused Stroud Canal. An old round-house which was formerly a lock-keepers cottage now houses a canal museum. The delightful Golden Valley stretches E towards Sapperton.

CHALGROVE, Oxon *13 SU69*
This was the scene of a Civil-War skirmish in which John Hampden was fatally wounded in 1643. The Hampden Monument commemorates this fight. The village church, mainly of decorated and perpendicular styles, contains medieval pictures and a curiously-shaped font.

CHAPEL-EN-LE-FRITH, Derbyshire *18 SK08*
An old-fashioned town in the High Peak country, where a 17th-c cross and old stocks are preserved in the market place. The church was largely rebuilt in the 18thc, and in 1648 served as a prison for 1,500 Scots prisoners, many of whom died. Partly-Elizabethan Ford Hall lies 1½m NE.

CHAPEL-LE-DALE, N Yorks *21 SD77*
This village gave its name to a glacial valley that was formed nearly two-million years ago, and is known for a deep chasm called Weathercote Cave. Waterfalls can be seen near by, and NE lies Colt Park Wood national nature reserve.

CHARD, Somerset *6 ST30*
Judge Jeffreys' notorious Bloody Assize was held in the manor house at Chard after the 1685 Monmouth rebellion. The Chough Inn has an Elizabethan interior, and the mainly-perpendicular church displays a number of interesting monuments. A two-storey portico can be seen on the 19th-c town hall, and the fine old grammar school is partly housed in a building of 1583.

John Stringfellow, supposedly responsible for the 'invention' of the aeroplane in 1848, is commemorated by a plaque set into the wall of a house. Margaret Blondfield was England's first female Cabinet Minister and was born here in 1873. The artist Lucient Pissarro died at South Chard in 1944.

Forde Abbey is a particularly interesting 12th-c to 17th-c house on the River Axe, 3½m SE, which displays a splendid Tudor entrance-tower and Mortlake Tapestries. It is set in a 15-acre garden (OACT). Cricket Court was built by Admiral Pitt in 1820, and Cricket House, 2m E, was rebuilt for Admiral Hood by Sir John Soane in c1801. The town is known for its lace-making.

CHARING, Kent *9 TQ94*
A 14th-c gateway is among the remains of an archbishop's palace which used to

exist here. Cranmer lived at the palace, and Henry VIII stayed here on his way to negotiate with Francis I at the Field of the Cloth of Gold in Artois. The church has a good perpendicular tower, and several delightful Georgian houses can be seen in the area. The Pilgrims' Way passes through Charing.

CHARLBURY, Oxon   13 SP31
Opposite this attractive little town, on the other side of the River Evenlode, is Wychwood Forest. Nearby Cornbury Park was once the home of Elizabeth I's favourite, the Earl of Leicester. The park's fine mansion is of 17th- and 18th-c date, and lies on the outskirts of Wychwood Forest – now a national nature reserve. Ditchley Park is a fine 18th-c house by James Gibbs, which lies 2½m NE and now serves as an Anglo-American conference centre (OACT).

CHARLECOTE, Warwickshire   13 SP25
The main feature here is a restored-Elizabethan hall (NT), which shows a notable gatehouse and is set in a fine park laid out by Capability Brown. The River Avon threads its way through the grounds, which are traditionally associated with Shakespeare's deer-stealing escapade (OACT). One of the notable Lucy monuments that can be seen in the church (rebuilt 1851) is attributed to the famous Italian sculptor Bernini.

CHARLTON, Wilts   12 ST98
Charlton Park is a modernized Jacobean mansion where John Dryden lived during the time of the great plague and subsequent fire of London.

CHARLWOOD, W Sussex   8 TQ24
This pleasant little village on the River Mole includes an 11th- to 15th-c church, housing excellent screenwork and ancient wall-paintings. Charlwood House shows 15th-c timbering.

CHARMINSTER, Dorset   6 SY69
An aisled church of the 12th to 16thc displays original Norman arcades and a good tower. Tudor and later Wolfeton House has a fine gatehouse.

CHARMOUTH, Dorset   6 SY39
The Regency houses in this small resort line the lower slopes of a steep hill, which dips down to the sea and a sand-and-shingle beach. The cliffs are of great geological interest and contain numerous Jurassic fossils. Remains of a large marine reptile that lived many millions of years ago were found in a shale cliff near Lyme Regis by Mary Anning. Mary was the daughter of a carpenter, and found her *Icthyosaurus* in 1811. The soft cliffs are full of fossil ammonites, ancient sea creatures with tightly-coiled shells, that can be broken out of the limestone without too much trouble. Charmouth is described in Jane Austen's *Persuasion*.

CHARNWOOD FOREST, Leics   18 SK41
This wooded tract of upland country lies to the NW of Leicester, and is notable for picturesque outcrops of rock. The highest point is Bardon Hill (912ft), also the highest in the county.

CHARTHAM, Kent   9 TR15
This Stour-Valley village is an angling centre and the site of a large paper mill. The 14th-c church is noted for characteristic Kentish-tracery displayed by its windows, and for a fine brass of 1306. It also has one of the oldest sets of bells in the country.

CHARTWELL, Kent   8 TQ45
Chartwell was the country home of Sir Winston Churchill during his lifetime, and its rooms are kept furnished in much the same way as they were when this great statesman lived here. Part of it now serves as a Churchill museum, and a studio in the garden contains many of his paintings (NT, OACT).

CHARWELTON, Northants   13 SP55
The local church has been restored, but preserves its 14th-c tower and contains brasses and monuments to the Andrews family. An 18th-c façade is displayed by the fine manor house, and a 3ft-wide packhorse bridge spans the River Cherwell.

CHASTLETON, Oxon   12 SP22
Chastleton House dates from 1603, is of Cotswold stone, and is considered a notable architectural example. The interior displays original furniture, fine tapestries and glass, and the actual Bible given to Bishop Juxon by Charles I on the scaffold. The box garden dates from 1700, and the old dovecote is of interest. A fine prehistoric camp can be seen at the top of Chastleton Hill, 1m SE.

CHATHAM, Kent   9 TQ76
The town has a naval dockyard, and is situated on the estuary of the River Medway. Urban developments have caused it to merge with Rochester. St Bartholomew's Hospital retains an 11th-c chapel, and several 18th-c houses can be seen in the town. Dickens spent part of his childhood here.

CHATSWORTH, Derbyshire   18 SK27
Chatsworth House is a palatial mainly 17th-c mansion on the River Derwent. It was built by William Talman for the 1st Duke of Devonshire, and stands in a great park which is crossed by a public road. An earlier house on the same site was designed by the Duke's ancestress, Bess of Hardwick, and was occasionally visited by Mary Queen of Scots. Magnificent gardens contain Britain's tallest fountain, and a fine hunting tower which was part of the original Elizabethan layout (OACT).

CHATTERIS, Cambs   14 TL38
The manor house in this small Fenland town has a cupola; near by is a tall windmill with six fingers. Chatteris House is early 19thc, and a road near the town crosses the Forty Foot Drain dug by Cornelius Vermuyden in the 17thc.

CHAWTON, Hants   8 SU73
Jane Austen's old home in Chawton is a long two-storey red-brick building that partly serves as a museum. Many of the novelist's personal belongings are on show here, including her portrait (OACT). Her mother and sister are buried in the church, but Jane herself lies in Winchester Cathedral. She wrote *Emma* and *Persuasion* while living here. Chawton House is of Elizabethan origin, and has been restored.

CHEADLE, Staffs   18 SK04
The interesting RC church in this old market town was designed by Pugin, one of the architects who worked on the Houses of Parliament. Several picturesque Tudor houses and an old market cross can be seen in the High Street. The Weaver Hills are close to the town, and 2m NE is the Hawksmoor nature reserve (NT). This was founded by the Staffordshire naturalist J R B Masefield, cousin of the poet John Masefield. Nature trails run through the moors, woodlands, and marshes that make up the reserve, and there are opportunities for close study of birds and other wild life.

CHEAM, Gt London   8 TQ26
Once in Surrey, this residential district is now part of Greater London and is situated near the place where Nonsuch Palace once stood. The church stands on a low hill and is notable for a chancel which stands in the yard – a relic of an earlier church. The chancel is known as the Lumley Chapel, and contains elaborate monuments set up by John, Baron Lumley. Lord Lumley was Lord Chamberlain to Elizabeth I, and a founder member of the Society of Antiquaries. The church itself was restored in 1954, and displays a fine plaster ceiling plus two Norman or Saxon windows in the north wall. Opposite the church, in Malden Road, is the charming 16th-c rectory. To the S is Whitehall, a picturesque 16th-c timbered house said to have been used by Elizabeth I to hold council when she visited Nonsuch. Near by is Old Cottage, an oak-framed building that was built *c*1500 and moved to its present site in 1922.

CHEDDAR, Somerset   6 ST45
Every summer the remarkable Cheddar Gorge attracts throngs of visitors to this little Mendip village. The gorge cliffs rise to a height of 450ft in places, and it is best seen on the descent into the village. Several of the numerous caves are open to visitors, and old stone-age artifacts are on display. Famous Cox's and Gough's caves contain fantastically shaped and coloured stalactites and stalagmites. The interesting perpendicular church has a characteristic Somerset tower, and the market cross is an AM. Excavations in the area have revealed the outline of a Saxon Royal palace, with a large 12th-c timbered hall where the Witan (parliament) met. Cheddar cheeses are world-famous and are now made in other parts of the county, and in other countries. There is a motor museum at the foot of the gorge.

CHEDDLETON, Staffs   18 SJ95
Two River-Churnet mills, the north and the south, can be seen here. They have both been well-preserved, and now contain museums displaying much of the original machinery (OACT). One mill was used to grind corn, and the other to grind flint. Both show their low-breast wheels and mechanism.

CHEDWORTH, Glos   12 SP01
Chedworth is noted for countless lilies of the valley, said to have originally been planted by the Romans. An outstanding Roman villa which is considered one of the best preserved examples in England stands in Chedworth Woods (NT, OACT). One of its many features is tessellated paving. The fine Norman to perpendicular church bears quaint gargoyles, and houses a beautifully-carved stone pulpit.

CHEDZOY, Somerset   6 ST33
A low-lying marshland village, where the south transept of the old church bears marks said to have been made by

Monmouth's followers, sharpening their weapons before the battle of Sedgemoor in 1685. A rare tumble-gate provides access into the churchyard.

CHELMSFORD, Essex *9 TL70*
Chelmsford is an agricultural and industrial centre divided into three districts by the Rivers Chelmer and Can. Both rivers are crossed by several bridges, but the main one is the Stone Bridge of 1787 (AM). Although the perpendicular church of St Mary the Virgin became a cathedral in 1914, it is still a typically Essex parish church of the 15thc. The south porch and the tower are its best features.

The Shire Hall is situated so that it faces down Chelmsford High Street, and was built to the design of John Johnson, county surveyor, in 1791. The present buildings housing the grammar school were begun in 1891, but the school itself was founded in 1551. One of its most distinguished scholars was the greatest of the Elizabethan translators, Philemon Holland. Chelmsford museum contains a Roman room, Victorian room, glass room, and numerous exhibits relating to local industry and natural history – plus a beehive with live bees. Springfield, on the NE outskirts of the town, has a mainly Norman church which contains a brass of 1421. Springfield Place, Springfield Dukes, and the rectory are all 18th-c houses.

CHELSWORTH, Suffolk *15 TL94*
A village with old timber-framed houses facing the little River Brett, which is spanned here by a double hump-back bridge of 18th-c date. A tomb recess in the church is of the early 14thc, and displays naturalistic carved foliage.

CHELTENHAM SPA, Glos *12 SO92*
Plan overleaf
This fashionable inland resort is an important centre of education, music, and the theatre. The place developed very rapidly after mineral springs were discovered here in the 18thc, with the result that much of the town is in Regency style. The only alkaline spring in Britain rises in the grounds of Cheltenham Ladies' College.

Among the fine residential terraces and buildings to be seen are the Montpellier Rotunda by Papworth, and the restored domed and colonnaded, Pittville Pump Room. The Cheltenham Music Festival was started in 1944, with the intention of fostering contemporary British music. First performances of works by Benjamin Britten, Sir Arthur Bliss, Malcolm Arnold, and many other British composers have been given here. St Mary's Church is the only medieval building still standing; although it still shows some traces of its Norman origin, it is mainly of decorated and perpendicular styles. It is best known for its 14th-c window tracery, particularly near the rose window in the north transept.

Cheltenham is famous for its many schools; the grammar school now occupies a 19th-c building, but was founded in 1576. Among its pupils was Gustav Holst the composer, who was born here in 1874. Cheltenham Ladies' College (1853) is in Old Well Lane, and Cheltenham College (1841) is in Bath Road.

A steeplechase-course where the important Cheltenham Gold Cup is run every March is at Prestbury Park. The curious Devil's Chimney can be seen on Leckhampton Hill 2m S, and the hexagonal tower of Swindon's Norman church can be seen 1½m N.

CHENIES, Bucks *8 TQ09*
Situated on the River Chess, this attractive village includes a church with a remarkable 16th-c chapel containing monuments and brasses to the Dukes of Bedford. The restored 16th-c manor house has fine chimneys.

CHEQUERS, Bucks *8 SP80*
Beautifully situated below the Chiltern escarpment, this notable 16th-c house lies 1m from Princes Risborough. It contains valuable Cromwellian relics and was given to the nation by Lord Lee of Fareham in 1917 – to be used as a country home for the British Prime Minister of the day. It is not open to the public.

CHERHILL, Wilts *7 SU07*
A stylish white horse cut into the hillside above this village dates from 1780, and is the work of a Dr Alsop from Calne. It is said that he stood more than a mile from his workmen and shouted instructions through a megaphone. The finished work can be seen for some 30 or 40-odd miles. The village itself includes a number of old houses, and the prominent Lansdowne Column can be seen on Cherhill Down, to the S.

CHERRINGTON, Salop *17 SJ61*
The half-timbered manor house in this village was built in 1635, and is an attractive example of the period. It is traditionally the House that Jack Built, and an old dovecote can be seen near by.

CHERTSEY, Surrey *8 TQ06*
A pleasant old-fashioned Thames-side town, where the river is spanned by a seven-arch 18th-c bridge. In the Middle Ages, Chertsey was famous for its wealthy abbey, which was destroyed by the Danes. Remains are scanty.

Old buildings that exist include the quaint partly 17th-c George Inn, and Curfew House of c1729. A curfew bell in the church commemorates Blanche Heriot, who saved her lover's life. Knowing that he was to be executed at curfew, she hung on the clapper of the bell to prevent it being sounded until he was reprieved. The poet Abraham Cowley (1618 to 1667) spent the last two years of his life 'stretched at ease in Chertsey's silent bowers'. An interesting small museum is in the town, and a wooded sandstone knoll known as St Anne's Hill is a prominent landmark and a viewpoint to the NW.

CHESHAM, Bucks *8 SP90*
Chesham lies in the Chess Valley, with attractive Chiltern country to the NW. In Church Street there are some old houses, the town hall is partly 18thc, and The Bury is dated 1712. The early-English to decorated church has a curious 17th-c monument in the chancel.

CHESHUNT, Herts *8 TL30*
Only one wing of the Great House which used to stand here survives, but this contains the original 15th-c hall. Richard Cromwell, son of the Protector, died at Cheshunt in 1712, and the great-grandson of the Protector, another Oliver, owned Cheshunt Park in the 18thc. The Temple Bar stands at the entrance to Theobald's Park, 2m SW, and was built by Wren in 1672. It was originally one of the City of London gates, and was set up here in 1888. There is a possibility that one day it may be returned to London.

CHESIL BANK, Dorset *6 SY58*
This is a 20 to 30ft high pebble ridge, 200yds wide and extending approximately 12m from Portland to Abbotsbury. After Abbotsbury it continues in a diminished form for some 5m farther, to a point near Bridport. It is composed of graduated pebbles of local rocks and

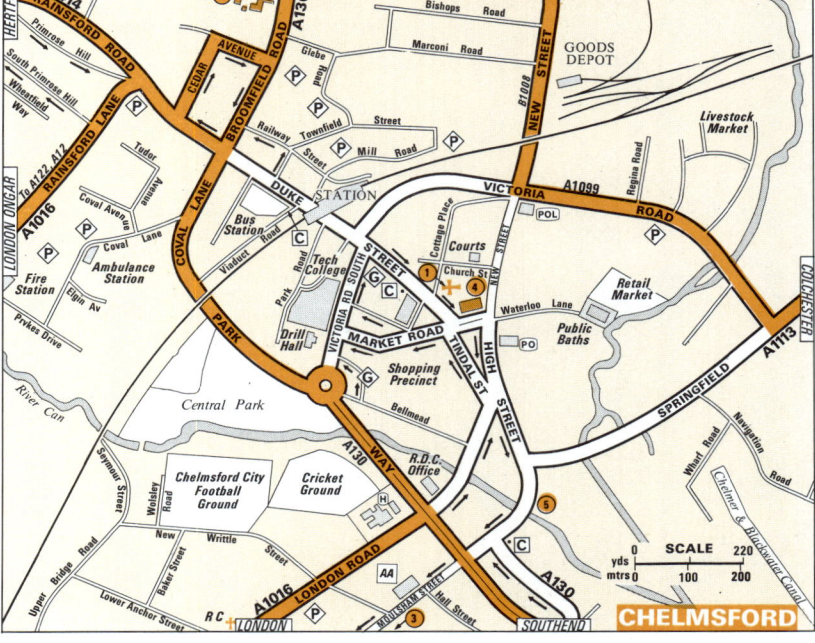

1 Cathedral
2 Grammar School
3 Museum
4 Shire Hall
5 Stone Bridge

CHESIL BANK/CHESTERTON, Warwickshire

material from as far away as Devon and Cornwall. The area is liable to severe storms, and bathing from the bank is dangerous. The bar is separated from the mainland by a channel and tidal lagoon called the East and West Fleet, and lies within an area of outstanding natural beauty. Pebbles from the area were used as ammunition by the iron-age defenders of Maiden Castle, and the variety of debris thrown onto the shore by storms makes the beach a splendid hunting-ground for archaeologists.

CHESSINGTON, Gt London 8 TQ16
The town is best known for the Chessington Zoological Gardens at Burnt Stub, on the Leatherhead road (OACT).

CHESTER, Cheshire 17 SJ46
Chester's medieval appearance is preserved through its walls, numerous timbered houses, and the cathedral. Black-and-white buildings are a definite feature of the city – God's Providence House, Bishop Lloyd's House, and Old Leche House are of particular interest, and a number of good 18th-c houses can also be seen. Chester is the only English city to have preserved its city walls in their entirety, and they offer a 2m circular walk with excellent views of the city and surrounding countryside. The defences on the N and E side of the city follow the line of the original Roman barrier, and are of largely Roman workmanship. The original W and S defences were destroyed and rebuilt in an extended form to take in the castle. At one point the walls overlook the Roodee, a racecourse where the Chester Cup has been run every May since 1540. The Roman camp that was the beginning of Chester was settled by the Twentieth Legion, who sited a fortress here in 70AD. It was the permanent headquarters of one of the Legions until the end of the Roman occupation, some 300 years later, when it fell into the hands of the Saxons and Danes. Ethelred of Mercia rebuilt the fort in 908AD, and the city did not submit to the Normans until William the Conqueror granted it to his nephew, Hugh Lupus, in 1070. The Norman earls of Chester wielded immense power, and the 1stc saw the whole county emerge as a palatinate in which the earls enjoyed powers almost equal to those of the king. Since the year 1301, the eldest son of the reigning monarch has included the title Earl of Chester among his many others.

By the 15thc river traffic to Chester had been seriously interfered with by the silting-up of the Dee. This gradually forced seaborne trade to the little coastal village of Liverpool, but thriving commercial interests had replaced Chester's loss by the 18thc. Houses from this period reflect the city's then-reviving prosperity. The beautiful restored cathedral dates mainly from the 14thc and is built of sandstone. It includes extensive Benedictine monastic remains, and is especially noted for its richly-carved woodwork; the Lady Chapel, the refectory, and the cloisters. St John's Church, although partly ruined, retains excellent Norman workmanship. Interesting timbered inns in the city include The Falcon, King Edgar, and Bear and Billet.

The city's streets follow the basic pattern laid down by the Romans, which can be best recognised in the attractive Rows; these are galleried tiers of shops, with one line at ground level and the other at first-floor height. Each has a footway, and the upper is set back and roofed by the second floor of the building. The castle, now mainly 19thc, was built on a site which bore even earlier fortifications before its construction in 1069. Agricola Tower is a square 13th-c edifice which houses the Regimental Museum of the Cheshire Regiment on its ground floor, and the vaulted Chapel of St Mary de Castro on the first floor. Two courtyards of the castle were removed in 1789 to make room for the Thomas Harrison group of buildings, which include the Grand Entrance and the Assize Courts.

CHESTERFIELD, Derbyshire 18 SK37
This ancient market town dates back far enough to be mentioned in the Domesday Book, but is now an industrial centre which is important for its coal and iron production. In 1266 it was the scene of a battle in which the Earl of Derby was defeated by the forces of the Crown. Much later during the Civil War the Earl of Newcastle and his Royalist troops claimed a victory here over the Parliamentarians.

The railway through Chesterfield was built under the supervision of George Stephenson, who lived NE of the town at Tapton House and died here in 1848. His grave can be seen at Trinity Church. Chesterfield owes a great deal to this great man; it was he who discovered the rich seam of coal lying under the town, and formed a company to work it. His association with the town is commemorated by the Stephenson Memorial Hall.

The only remaining Tudor building in the town can be seen near 14th- and 15th-c All Saints' Church, famous for its twisted spire. Exhibitions of art and pottery are held at Chesterfield Civic Theatre during the summer. A group of conspirators met in Revolution House, some 3m N at Old Whittington (1668), to plot the overthrow of James II and invite William and Mary to ascend the throne. This building now houses nothing more sinister than a museum.

CHESTERFORD, GREAT, Essex 14 TL54
Neolithic, palaeolithic, and Roman finds that have been made in and around this village can be seen in the museum at nearby Saffron Walden. The much-restored church is of the 13th to 15thc.

CHESTER-LE-STREET, Co Durham 27 NZ25
A Roman fort once stood on the site of this mining town, and the monks of Lindisfarne brought the body of St Cuthbert here in 883 after wandering with it for eight years. It stayed here until it was moved to Durham in 995. The interesting church has a 156ft spire, an anchorite's cell, and fourteen effigies of ancestors to Lord Lumley. Lumley Castle (14thc) lies 1m E and is an annexe to the University of Durham; 1½m NE is a college of adult education housed in 18th-c Lambton Castle. The 200-acre Lambton Lion Park can be seen nearby.

CHESTERTON, Cambs 14 TL46
The county gaol and assize courts are contained in this suburb of Cambridge. St Andrew's Church displays a spired tower and includes an imposing nave with old bench ends, and a 15th-c Doom painting over the chancel arch. Sparse remains of a medieval abbey-grange exist near the vicarage, and Chesterton Hall is an interesting Jacobean house.

CHESTERTON, Warwickshire 13 SP35
An isolated windmill on arches, with an unusual domed roof, stands on high ground in this area. It was built as a

1 Cheltenham College
2 Cheltenham Ladies' College
3 Devil's Chimney
4 Grammar School
5 Montpellier Rotunda
6 Pittville Pump Room
7 St Mary's Church

viewing tower for Sir Edward Peyto in 1632; tombs of his family can be seen in the local church.

CHEVIOT HILLS, THE
Much of this lonely range of grassy, mountainous hills forms part of the border between Scotland and England. Flocks of Black-Face and Cheviot sheep graze the slopes, and the country between the Cheviots and Hadrian's Wall is part of the Northumberland national park. The 250m-long Pennine Way from the Peak District ends here. The highest point is the Cheviot, a marshy flat-topped hill rising to 2,676ft which is best ascended from Wooler or Kirknewton. Auchope Cairn (2,382ft) is actually astride the border, and NE of the Cheviot itself is picturesque College Valley. Equally attractive Harthope Valley lies to the E. The main road from Newcastle to Jedburgh climbs to 1,371ft at Carter Bar, affording magnificent views over the Scottish Lowlands.

CHEW MAGNA, Avon 6 ST56
A village 7m S of Bristol, with several streams spanned by ancient bridges; the one over the River Chew dates from the 15thc. An old screen, carved bench-ends, and interesting tombs can be seen in the decorated and perpendicular church, and Church House dates from 1529. The remains of Chew Tower, a castellated folly of 1770, overlook the village. Trout fishing is available at Chew Valley reservoir (see next entry).

CHEW STOKE, Avon 6 ST56
This charming village is 8m S of Bristol, and includes an interesting Tudor rectory. The Queen opened the Chew Valley reservoir to the S in 1956, and this large expanse of water is already well-known for its extensive leisure facilities.

A villa is among the Roman remains that have been excavated at Chew Stoke.

CHEWTON MENDIP, Somerset 6 ST55
The springs that rise at the foot of the Mendip Hills, in this village, supply the vast needs of the Bristol Waterworks. The church here displays one of the finest of the great church towers of Somerset, which is 126ft high, and was completed at the comparatively late date of 1541. The main body of the church is partly Norman, and preserves a rare frid or sanctuary stool. Bronze-age barrows have been excavated in the area.

CHICHESTER, W Sussex 8 SU80
Plan overleaf
This was the important Roman town of *Noviomagus*, and the layout that still exists, a walled enclosure with four main streets, is typical. Many relics of early occupation can be seen in the museum at Little London.

The town is situated on a stretch of rich farmland lying between the salt flats and creeks of Chichester Harbour, and the W end of the South Downs. Substantial portions of the city walls remain; these defences were completed about 200AD, bastions were added in c350AD, and an inner rampart was built as a promenade in the 18thc. The remaining portions of wall are of medieval workmanship, but the foundations and core are Roman. The Saxons arrived in Chichester in the 5thc, when a chieftain named *Aella* is said to have landed at West Wittering and conquered the settlement. He is then supposed to have given it to his son *Cissa*, a name perpetuated as a corruption of *Cissa's Ceaster* (camp) – Chichester.

In 1075 the see which St Wilfred had founded at nearby Selsey in 681 was transferred to the city. The present cathedral was started in 1091 and completed in 1123, but has been considerably altered and extended since. After the spire collapsed in 1861, it was immediately rebuilt, but the north-west tower fell in 1635 and was not rebuilt until 1901. The detached bell tower of 1400 to 1475 is the only such example to be shown by an English cathedral. The partly 13th-c Bishop's palace has a notable chapel, and the chantry was a 13th-c hall and chapel.

Remains of a Greyfriars monastery in Priory Park now serve as a guildhall and house a small museum. A partly-Norman building, which used to be the church of St Olave and rests on Roman foundations, is now a bookshop. St Mary's Hospital is a group of almshouses founded in 1158, including a hall with a timber roof and fine chapel screen. Cawley almshouses date from 1625, and the market cross in the centre of the town is of 16th-c date. A Roman inscription recording the building of a temple to Neptune and Minerva can be seen on the wall of the Council Chambers (built 1731 to 1733), and many fine 18th-c houses exist in the town – particularly in St Martin's Square and the Pallant quarter. Pallant House (also known as Dodo House and now the Rural District Offices), and Westgate House have been ascribed to Wren.

Festival Theatre in Broyle Road was built in 1962 and has an open stage. Important dramatic productions are staged here during the festival season which usually runs from May to September.

Chichester Harbour is a well-known yachting centre and has been designated an area of outstanding natural beauty. Fishbourne Roman Palace, the largest ever to be found in Britain, lies 1½m W.

CHIDDINGFOLD, Surrey 8 SU93
A large green forms the centre of this secluded village of old houses, and the partly 14th-c Crown Inn is of interest. A thorn tree on the green is said to be over 500 years old, and walking sticks and umbrella shafts are still made from local ash saplings.

CHIDDINGSTONE, Kent 8 TQ54
Half-timbered houses are included in this very attractive village (NT), and the local church has a perpendicular tower. An 18th-c castle contains important oriental and art collections, and is set in a park which contains the Chiding Stone.

CHIDEOCK, Dorset 6 SY49
Pronounced Chiddock, this village is picturesquely situated among hills and faces N towards Marshwood Vale. The 619ft Golden Cap is a notable viewpoint and the highest point on the south coast (1m SW).

CHIDHAM, W Sussex 8 SU70
This is an unspoiled village of cottages, farms, and barns, situated near a creek of Chichester Harbour. The restored church is of the 13thc, and an 18th-c manor house can be seen in the area.

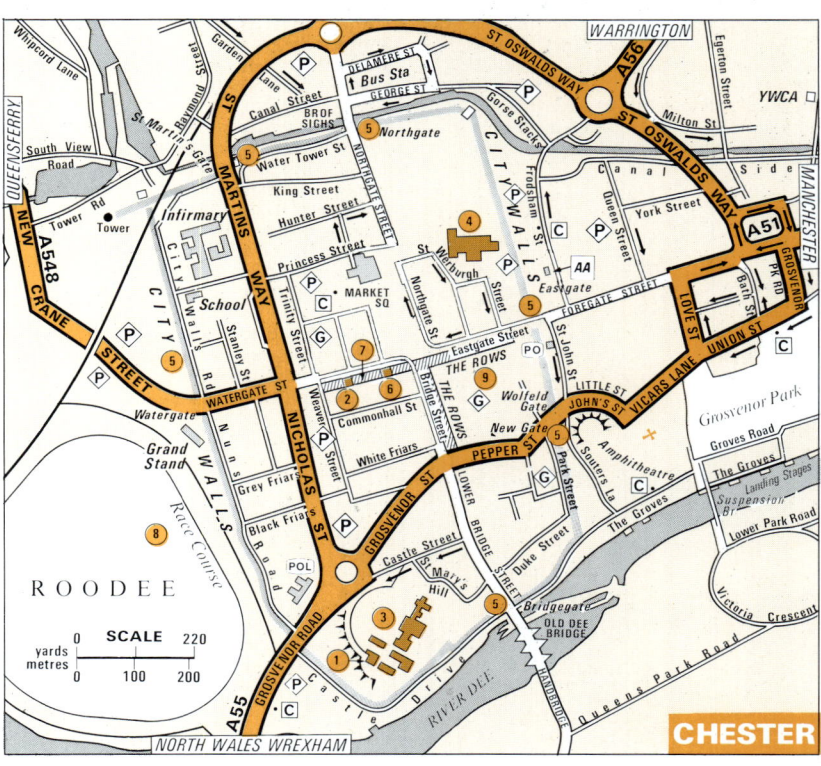

1 Assize Courts
2 Bishop Lloyd's House
3 Castle and Agricola Tower (museum)
4 Cathedral
5 City Walls
6 God's Providence House
7 Old Leche House
8 Roodee Racecourse
9 The Rows

CHIGWELL/CHISLEHURST

CHIGWELL, Essex *8 TQ49*
The ancient King's Head is the public house which Dickens described as the Maypole in his novel *Barnaby Rudge*. The grammar school was founded in 1629, and the headmaster's house displays Georgian influences. The church of St Mary houses brasses to the Archbishop of York (died 1631), Samuel Harsnett, and George Shillibeer. The latter was born in 1767, and is credited as being the founder of the famous London omnibus.

CHILHAM, Kent *9 TR05*
This attractive village includes half-timbered houses and an interesting 15th-c flint church. The latter contains several fine monuments, including a group by Chantrey. The keep of a Norman castle can be seen in the grounds of a fine 17th-c castle which is set in a great park overlooking the Stour Valley (OACT). It is thought that the Woolpack Inn may have been lived in by the master builder of the more recent castle.

CHILLINGHAM, Northumberland *27 NU02*
The magnificent tomb of Ralph Grey (died 1443) and his wife can be seen in the Norman and decorated church, and a famous herd of wild white cattle live in the park (OACT) surrounding a 14th-c and later castle. The grounds of this castle also preserve the well-known Toad Stone, and the ruined castle-tower of Hebburn.

CHILMARK, Wilts *7 ST93*
Thatch and tile are the main roofing materials used in this village, and the early-English church displays a mid 18th-c broach spire. Chilmark stone was used in the construction of Salisbury Cathedral and Wilton House.

CHILTERN HILLS, THE
Most of this range of chalk hills is included in an area of outstanding natural beauty, wooded in the W but mainly bare and windswept nearing Ivinghoe to the E. The range extends in an arc from Goring (in the Thames Valley) to a point near Hitchin, and the woods are comprised mainly of beech trees. One of the highest points is Coombe Hill, rising 853ft above Wendover, and some of the most attractive scenery can be enjoyed around Turville. The North Bucks Way is a new 30m walk from Wolverton to Chequers which has recently been opened for public use.

CHILTON, Bucks *13 SP61*
The high ground upon which this village is built affords splendid views over the surrounding countryside. Fine buildings include a mainly 18th-c hall, an early-English to perpendicular church, and several old cottages. Dorton House, originating from the 17th- and 18th-c, lies 2m N and is now a school (OACT).

CHILTON POLDEN, Somerset *6 ST33*
Cock Hill (NT), part of the low Polden Hills in which this village is sited, is a good viewpoint that lies on the Bridgwater to Glastonbury road. Near by stands a Victorian tower known as Chilton Priory. A national nature reserve can be seen at Shapwick to the SE.

CHINGFORD, Gt London *8 TQ39*
Chingford lies at the SW extremity of Epping Forest, and 2½m NE is a forest museum housed in the picturesquely timbered Queen Elizabeth's Hunting Lodge. Gilwell Park is situated to the W.

CHINNOR, Oxon *8 SP70*
The village lies below the Chiltern Ridge, and includes a good church of the decorated style. This building is noted for its old screen, 14th-c glass, and numerous brasses. Bledlow Cross is a hillside figure cut into the slopes of Bledlow Ridge 1m E.

CHIPPENHAM, Cambs *14 TL66*
Wall paintings can be seen in the church, and the village school dates from 1741. Chippenham Park is of the 17th to 19th-c, and Chippenham Fen is a national nature reserve.

CHIPPENHAM, Wilts *7 ST97*
A pleasant River-Avon town of great age, built mostly of natural stone. Fine old houses can be seen in St Mary's Street, and most of the Old Town (or Yelde) Hall dates from the 15thc. The old lock-up near the town hall is of interest, and although the 15th-c church has been greatly restored it still houses an old chest. The church also displays a striking modern window. Ivy House dates from 1730 and Sheldons Manor (2½m NW), from the 14th to 16thc. Recent times have seen industrial development in the town, mainly on the food-processing side. Bacon is cured here, but there is also a factory involved in the production of railway signals and brakes.

CHIPPING CAMPDEN, Glos *12 SP13*
A beautiful unspoiled Cotswold town of old buildings and houses. These include 14th-c Grevel's House, a 17th-c market hall (NT), and the remains of Campden House which was burnt in 1645. Woolstaplers Hall contains a museum, and the impressive 15th-c wool-church has a 120ft tower. There are several fine brasses housed in the latter, but the one raised to William Grevel (died 1401) is considered outstanding. The town's old almshouses are picturesque. The Cotswold or Dover Games were held 1m N on Dover's Hill until 1862; the hill provides a good viewpoint.

CHIPPING NORTON, Oxon *13 SP32*
The first part of this beautiful little Cotswold town's name is derived from the word cheapening, which was added in the 13thc and means that it was a market or trading place. Old inns like the White Hart and the Crown were once coaching inns, and the numerous stone-built 18th-c houses reflect a former prosperity. The attractive almshouses date from the 17thc, and 3m W is the fine 17th- to 18th-c manor house of Cornwell. The 15th-c parish church is noted for its chancel, tombs, and brasses.

CHIPPING SODBURY, Avon *12 ST78*
Chipping Sodbury and Old Sodbury (2m E) are to be renamed Sodbury. The former is an old market town with an early-English to perpendicular church displaying a lofty pinnacled tower. The 15th-c pulpit is canopied, and a 16th-c cross stands near the church. William Tyndale, translator of the New Testament, is associated with 15th-c Little Sodbury Manor (3m NE). Horton Court (NT) stands 4m NE and preserves a very rare Norman hall.

CHIRBURY, Salop *17 SO29*
The nave of the local church once belonged to the church of an Augustinian priory, and the half-timbered school dates from 1675. Corndon Hill, a local landmark which rises to 1,684ft, lies to the E. Marrington Hall is an Elizabethan half-timbered building 1m SE, which displays a unique sundial.

CHISLEHURST, Gt London *8 TQ47*
This residential area is a dormitory for Central London, and is known for the Chislehurst Caves — underground chalk galleries of indeterminate age. Two Walsingham tombs can be seen in the

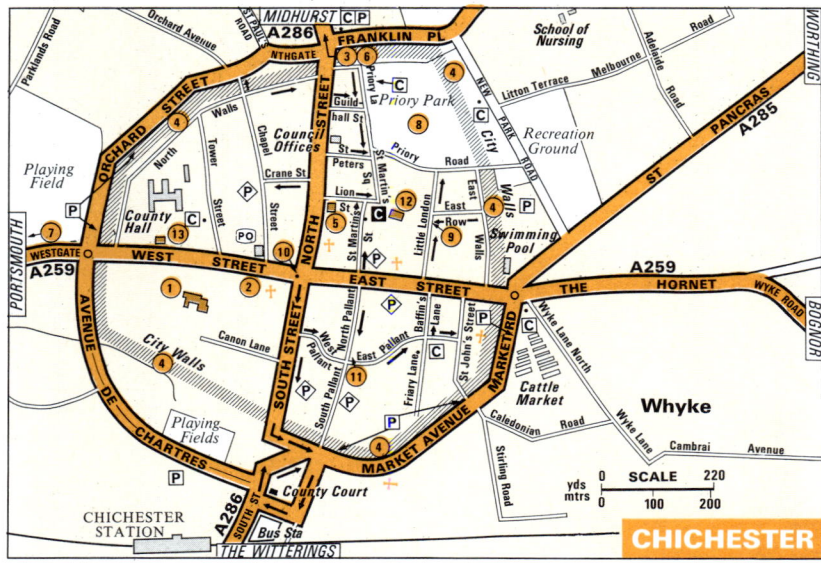

1 Bishop's Palace
2 Cathedral
3 Cawley Almshouses
4 City Walls
5 Council Chambers
6 Festival Theatre
7 Fishbourne Roman Palace
8 Guildhall (museum)
9 Little London Museum
10 Market Cross
11 Pallant (Dodo) House
12 St Mary's Hospital
13 Westgate House

church's Scadbury Chapel, and Camden Place is where the antiquary William Camden died in 1623. The house was also the residence of Napoleon III and the Empress Eugenie in 1871, and a memorial to their son the Prince Imperial can be seen on the large common. He died fighting for the British against the Zulus.

CHISWICK, Gt London 8 TQ27
Situated by the Thames, this was a fashionable residential area in the 17th and 18thc. Chiswick Mall is opposite Chiswick Eyot, and is a riverside street where numerous delightful houses include Kelmscott – the place where pre-Raphaelite artist and author William Morris lived and died. Chiswick House is a magnificent domed mansion which was copied from an Italian villa at Vicenza, and designed by the Earl of Burlington from 1725 to 1729 (AM, OACT). Foreign royalties were formerly received here, and Edward VII once lived in the house as Prince of Wales. Both Charles James Fox and Canning died under its roof. The Duchess of Cleveland, mistress of Charles II, lived at Walpole House. The district was described in Thackeray's *Vanity Fair*, and the painter Pope lived in nearby Hogarth House where he died in 1764 (OACT). The local churchyard contains his tomb. One of the more interesting buildings in Chiswick Square is the late 17th-c Boston House.

CHITTLEHAMPTON, Devon 5 SS62
Chittlehampton boasts what is considered Devon's finest church tower. It dates from 1520 and can be compared with the great Somerset towers farther E. The dedication is to St Hierutha, who was attacked and decapitated by haymakers in his youth.

CHOBHAM, Surrey 8 SU96
The restored church in this pleasant village displays 12th- and 15th-c work, and preserves a rare oak-panelled font. Brook Place is an interesting 17th-c house 1m N, and several attractive cottages can be seen in the village itself. Chobham Common is an area covered with gorse, heather, and pine clumps that lies 2m N, and is considered one of the finest commons in the country.

CHOLLERFORD, Northumberland 27 NY97
The high river bridge that spans the North Tyne at this point dates from 1775. Farther upstream are traces that may indicate the one-time existence of a Roman bridge, and the settlement is close to Hadrian's Wall. Chesters Park contains Roman remains that were found when *Cilurnum* was excavated, plus an interesting museum (AM, OACT). Haughton Castle is a 13th- to 14th-c building set amid beautiful surroundings, 3m N near the North Tyne.

CHOLLERTON, Northumberland 27 NY97
This place comprises little more than a church and the conspicuous remains of 15th-c Cocklaw Tower. Tooling marks on the round pillars in the south arcade of the church indicate that they may be Roman, possibly from the Roman fort at Chesterholme; the altar is certainly Roman. Near Swinburn Castle, 2m N, is the 12ft Swinburn standing stone.

CHORLEY, Lancs 21 SD51
Chorley was once known for cotton-weaving and calico-printing, but has latterly diversified into a wide range of other industries. Situated in the centre of Lancashire, it is on the edge of a large agricultural area and sits at the foot of the Pennines. Henry Tate was born here in 1819, and founded the Tate Gallery in London after making a fortune from sugar. A unique collection of furniture, superb plasterwork, and a fine art collection can be seen in Elizabethan and Jacobean Astley Hall (OACT).

CHRISTCHURCH, Dorset 7 SZ19
Situated on the estuaries of the Avon and Stour, the earliest known record of this town appears in the Saxon Chronicle under its previous name of Twyham. The splendid priory stands behind the quay and displays a mixture of styles from Norman to the Renaissance. Among its more notable features are the chantry chapels and a monument to the poet Shelley. Remains of a Norman castle (AM) and house stand near by on the banks of the Avon. Large carp can be seen in the priory moat, and a popular summer-evening pastime is to sit on the bank of the Avon and watch the salmon running upstream. Red House is of Georgian origin and contains an interesting museum; it is set in attractive gardens containing roses and herbs.

Hengistbury Head lies 2m S, and commands fine seaward views; a sandy beach allows access for bathing at Mudeford, 2m SE. Stanpit Marsh is a local nature reserve.

CHURCHILL, Avon 6 ST45
Privately-owned Churchill Court dominates this stone-built village, and is the seat of the family branch from which the Duke of Marlborough and Sir Winston Churchill descended. Interesting monuments are housed in the perpendicular church. A track to the SE of the village leads to the large iron-age earthwork of Dolbury Camp.

CHURCHILL, Oxon 13 SP22
Warren Hastings was born here in 1732 and later became the first Governor-General of India. The village was also the home of William Smith, the first man to map the rock-strata of England and identify the fossils peculiar to each layer. Some people have called him the father of English geology, and a monolith has been set up to his memory. The restored church displays a fine tower and a fountain-monument to its original builder, Squire Langston. This fountain is a square structure with open arches and pinnacles rising from a basin of flowing water.

CHURCH LANGTON, Leics 18 SP79
This is the chief village of five Leicestershire Langtons, and includes one of the best churches in the county. The rectory is a graceful Georgian red-brick structure which is decorated with vases and displays a prominent Venetian window. Directly opposite is the village green and peace memorial.

CHURCH STRETTON, Salop 17 SO49
A market charter was granted to this small red-roofed town by King John in 1214. The church is partly 12th-c Norman and 17thc, and displays a 14th-c nave roof. A well-worn Saxon fertility-symbol is incorporated in the masonry above the bricked-up Norman north door. This entrance was once known as the Corpse Door, because the dead were taken through it. Stretton Hills surround the village, and the community is sited at the foot of Long Mynd (NT) – a popular gliding area. Approximately 300sqm of these Welsh-Border Hills form an area of outstanding natural beauty. The route of a walk to the heights of Long Mynd follows Cardingmill Valley, which begins on the N outskirts of Church Stretton.

CIRENCESTER, Glos 12 SP00
The name of this town is generally pronounced Sisiter, but locally it is also called Ciren. It was the Roman *Corinium* during the occupation and, after London was the largest town in Britain. Important roads that radiated from this centre are the Fosse Way, Akeman Street, and one of the two Ermine Streets. Extensive archaeological excavations have produced numerous interesting finds, most of which can be seen in the *Corinium* museum.

Nowadays the town is a typical, Cotswold community of local-stone buildings, and a hunting centre. A unique three-storeyed porch, built by the local Guilds in 1500, is an interesting feature of the magnificent parish church. The building itself is 180ft long (one of the largest in England), and largely perpendicular in style with some Norman details. The 134ft tower is of note, and of particular interest are the fan-vaulting of St Catherine's Chapel, the pulpit of 1515, and the brasses and monuments housed in the Trinity Chapel.

Cirencester park (3,000 acres) surrounds an 18th-c house where the yew hedge is said to be the tallest in England. Pope and Swift often visited the park – which is now the summer venue for polo, and generally open for walkers. Thames Head Bridge is situated 4m SW off the Tetbury Road, near Trewsbury Meadow; it is usually accepted as the source of the Thames, and is marked by a statue representation of Father Thames. The Royal Agricultural College lies on the outskirts of the town.

CLACTON-ON-SEA, Essex 9 TM11
Plan overleaf
Natural facilities of this popular seaside resort include excellent sandy beaches. However, many other diversions are available to the visitor, such as swimming pools, a pier, a promenade, a scenic railway, and a holiday camp. Three Martello towers stand near by, and SW are Jaywick Sands. Holland-on-Sea lies E.

CLAPHAM, N Yorks 21 SD76
Ingleborough rises 2,373ft to the N of this attractive moorland village, and is the source of tumbling Clapham Beck. A path leading upstream along the Beck passes through the exotic collection of bushes, trees, and plants at Ingleborough Hall, on its way to Ingleborough Cave. The cave lies 1¼m from the hall and extends – festooned with stalactites and stalagmites – for a ⅓m along underground rivulets and pools. Gaping Ghyll pothole lies 1m farther on, and is a cave where a single fall of water hurtles 365ft to the bottom of the pit.

CLARE, Suffolk 15 TL74
Ancient House, at the churchyard corner in this River-Stour village, displays particularly fine decorative plasterwork. Traces of Clare Castle remain, and the

13th- to 15th-c church preserves a Jacobean gallery pew. Clare Priory, again tenanted by Augustinian friars, dates from the 14th to 17thc and stands in fine gardens (OACT).

CLAVERING, Essex 14 TL43
A brook that feeds the River Stort runs through the collection of old cottages that make up this village. Several mounds surrounded by a dry moat can be seen in a meadow by the churchyard, and are thought to be the remains of Roland's Castle – where Normans arriving in England before the conquest of 1066 defended themselves against indignant Saxons. The church contains 15th-c glass treasures, a carved roof, and a high screen with panels of saints drawn in black on a white ground.

CLAVERLEY, Salop 17 SO79
The black-and-white cottages that are typical of this county are numerous in this village. Roger de Montgomery (died 1094) founded the church. The fine north arcade and the carved font are Norman, but the remainder of the building was constructed between the 13th- and 15th-c. A large mural painting depicts battling knights on horseback, and can be compared with scenes shown in the Bayeux tapestry. A memorial in the shape of a cross was erected in the churchyard to the victims of the Black Death, in 1349. Early-Jacobean Ludstone Hall lies 1m NE.

CLAVERTON, Avon 6 ST76
Ralph Allen, one of the creators of 18th-c Bath, is buried in the local churchyard. A manor house that once existed here has left the remains of a fine terrace layout and little else; the later house was built in Greek-Revival style in 1820, and now contains a museum of early-American domestic life, exhibiting various items of furniture and general artifacts from the USA. Sir Winston Churchill made his first political speech in the grounds of this house in 1897. The Bath University of Technology (founded 1966) stands above the village on Claverton Down, and an 18th-c stone-built lock-up can be seen 2m S at Monkton Combe.

1 Holiday Camp
2 Martello Tower
3 Pier and Scenic Railway

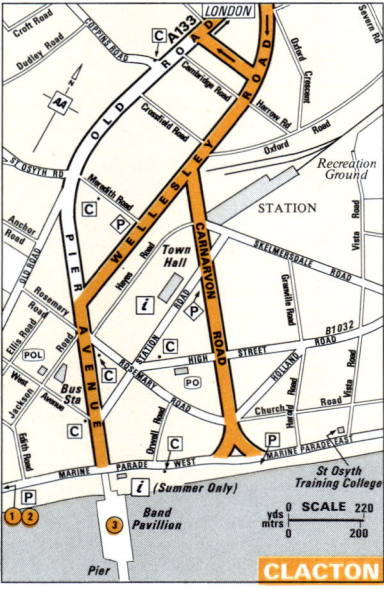

CLAYDON, Suffolk 15 TM14
This village is by the River Gipping, on the Ipswich to Norwich road, with chalk and lime works near by. Mockbeggars Hall has two Dutch gables and a Jacobean front, and the Saxon and Norman Church has a chancel and transepts of 1862; it also contains a Henry Moore sculpture.

CLAYTON, W Sussex 8 TQ31
A South-Downs village, with a partly-Saxon church containing wall paintings. Two windmills known as Jack and Jill date from 1876 and 1821, and a folly built in the shape of a castellated Tudor fortress straddles the entrance to a railway tunnel. The village is a good starting point for walks to Wolstonbury Hill and Ditchling Beacon, both famous viewpoints.

CLEE HILLS, THE
These Shropshire hills are situated at over 1,200ft and form an AA viewpoint offering wide views S across the Teme Valley. Brown Clee Hill rises to 1,790ft in the N and is the highest of the group. A little closer than Brown Clee, and also to the N, is 1,749ft Titterstone Clee Hill; Clee Hill itself rises to 1,531ft and is scarred with quarries.

CLEETHORPES, Humberside 23 TA30
Fine views of shipping entering the mouth of the Humber are available from this popular seaside resort, and good sands allow access for bathing. The town is near Grimsby, and offers all the usual holiday entertainments, including a zoo, fishing, etc. Clee church displays a Saxon tower.

CLEEVE ABBEY, Avon 6 ST04
This is an area where the interesting remains of a Cistercian abbey (AM), founded in 1188, can be seen. A timber roof and good wall paintings make the refectory of particular note. Of equal interest are the picturesque gatehouse and painted chamber.

CLEEVE HILL, Glos 12 SO92
A village near Cheltenham, overshadowed by 1,031ft Cleeve Cloud. This hill is almost the highest point in the Cotswolds and the summit affords magnificent views. Below the hill, to the SW, is the 17th-c and later Tudor mansion of Southam Delabere, now a school. Belas Knap, a well-known prehistoric long-barrow, lies to the E (AM).

CLEOBURY MORTIMER, Salop 12 SO67
The Norman family of Mortimer established themselves here in 1086 and gave this market town its name. A fortress which the family built was later demolished by Henry II, but the earthworks can still be seen near the church. The remains of a market cross stand in front of the 16th-c Talbot Hotel. It was here that the body of Arthur, brother to Henry VIII, was rested during its journey from Ludlow to its burial place in Worcester Cathedral. Half-timbered and 18th-c houses line the main street, and it is thought that William Langland, author of *Piers Plowman*, was born here in the 14thc. A memorial window to Langland can be seen in the trans-Norman to decorated church.

CLEVEDON, Avon 6 ST47
This quiet seaside resort on the Severn estuary was the birthplace of Hartley Coleridge. Arthur Hallam, whose death inspired the poet Tennyson's *In Memoriam*, lived in 14th-c Clevedon Court (NT, OACT), and his body is buried at St Andrews Church. This attractive court was also the working place of Thackeray for a while, and part of *Vanity Fair* was written here. Clevedon itself lies at the junction of two low hill ranges and is a good walking centre. One range sweeps N to Portishead and slopes down to coastal cliffs, while the other runs inland to Bristol and the Avon Gorge.

CLEVELAND
This is a new county in the old North Riding of Yorkshire, extending from the Cleveland Hills to the Tees estuary. A breed of heavy horses known as Cleveland Bays originated here, and the area is also known for its lofty moorlands and iron-mining industry.

CLIFTON, Avon 6 ST57
Brunel's 245ft suspension bridge over the Avon Gorge can be seen near this residential quarter of Bristol. Building of the bridge began in 1836 and finished in 1864. Nearby are the Giant's Cave and a *camera obscura*. Clifton College is a well-known public school, and both Goldney House (1720 and later), and the mid 18th-c Clifton Hall House are now part of Bristol University. A remarkable grotto of 1739 can still be seen in the grounds of the latter. Many fine 18th-c houses exist in the town, and Royal York Crescent displays notable Regency residences. Clifton Zoo is of interest, and Leigh Woods (NT), Clifton Down, and Durdham Down are fascinating country areas for the walker and naturalist.

CLIFTON, Cumbria 26 NY52
Clifton, a little village near Penrith, was the scene of the last battle in England. More of a skirmish than a full-blooded battle, this took place in 1745 between the Duke of Cumberland and the retreating army of Prince Charles Edward. The early-English church houses a good, carved pulpit, and a 15th-c pele tower can be seen at Clifton Hall farmhouse.

CLIFTON CAMPVILLE, Staffs 18 SK21
The 13th- and 14th-c church in this little village is regarded as one of the best in the county. It is particularly noted for the tower and spire, which are supported by flying buttresses. Hasleour Hall is an old gabled house sited 3m W.

CLIFTON HAMPDEN, Oxon 13 SU59
A Thames-side village offering boating and bathing, where Clifton Lock and the Barley Mow inn are situated. The latter figures in *Three Men in a Boat* by Jerome K Jerome.

CLIMPING, W Sussex 8 TQ00
This village lies on the W side of the Arun estuary, and a mile inland from a stretch of undeveloped coastline where fields and trees still sweep right down to the beach. A few wartime installations remain, but these are largely obscured by sand dunes. The village church displays a trans-Norman tower with ten mass-dials on the south face.

CLIPSTONE, Notts 18 SK66
The Duke of Portland's irrigation meadows and canals are situated at Clipstone, which itself lies in the Dukeries and Sherwood Forest district.

Scanty remains of a building called King John's Palace are actually of a 13th-c hunting lodge which was used by the king. Parliament Oak lies 1m NW, and is now thought to be the place where Edward I held his parliament.

CLITHEROE, Lancs *21 SD74*
Although many other industries have now developed here, this was the northernmost of the Lancashire cotton towns. The shell of a Norman castle is prominent on a limestone knoll above the town, and Pendle Hill rises to 1,831ft in the E. George Fox claimed to have had a vision on this summit in 1652, which led him to preach and to form the Society of Friends. The hill has other, more sinister associations, and is in the area where 19 Lancashire women were taken and tried for witchcraft. Robert Neil's historical novel *Mist Over Pendle* describes the area and the events that led up to the trials. Jacobean Browsholme Hall is sited 6m NW, and houses notable panelling, pictures, and furniture (OACT).

CLIVEDEN, Bucks *8 SU98*
The well-known Cliveden Reach is a beautifully-wooded stretch of the River Thames. Stately 19th-c Cliveden House overlooks the river, and is surrounded with fine garden terraces (NT, OACT). Late 18th- and early 19th-c Dropmore House lies to the NE, and 19th-c Hedsor stands in an estate which borders the grounds of the former at so-called Nobleman's Corner. The fine noble trees of Burnham Beeches can be seen to the SE.

CLODOCK, Herefs & Worcs *11 SO32*
St Clodock is a British saint, and was the grandson of King Brychan of Brecknockshire. No fewer than sixty churches are dedicated to various members of his family, and it seems certain that the neighbourhood was the centre of a missionary enterprise in the 5thc. The village stands on the River Monnow and includes a church containing a Norman chancel with a three-decker pulpit and a west gallery. A watermill in the area, built in 1869, still has its wheel and internal machinery.

CLOPHILL, Beds *14 TL03*
This River-Ivel village is situated near Ampthill. Wrest Park is a fine 19th-c mansion sited 2m S, set in a notable, 18th-c garden-layout featuring formal canals and a banqueting house of the same period (AM, OACT). Gilbertine Chicksands Priory stands 4m NW, and is associated with Dorothy Osborne and her famous 17th-c letters to William Temple. The house that now stands here is of 18th- and 19th-c origin, and was erected by Wyatt. A nearby circle of steel uprights is a spectacular local landmark, and part of a USAF base.

CLOVELLY, Devon *5 SS32*
Old buildings, a tiny quay, and the pebble beach combine to form this exceptionally-attractive little fishing village – a place that is popular with artists. The single street is stepped and descends 400ft to the sea. Wheeled traffic is barred from the village, and cars must be parked outside the community. The New Inn is attractive, and good views may be enjoyed from Hobby Drive, Gallantry Bower, and the grounds of Clovelly Court.

CLUN, Salop *11 SO38*
This is the farthest W of the four settlements in the River-Clun Valley. Various finds in the area have shown that Clun originated in the bronze age, and is thus one of the oldest dwelling places in the country. The town is dominated by a hill surmounted by a keep, all that remains of a castle built by the Normans to defend the Welsh border. An old lychgate can be seen at the mainly trans-Norman church. The picturesque almshouses date from 1618, and the Court House from 1780. Clun Forest lies to the W.

CLYFFE PYPARD, Wilts *7 SU07*
An attractive village of thatched cottages, situated on a wooded ridge. The perpendicular church displays old glass, two chalk monuments, and a painted screen. The pulpit dates from 1629.

COALBROOKDALE, Salop *17 SJ60*
This place has been dubbed the cradle of the English iron industry, and the original furnace of Abraham Darby (1708) can still be seen. The first iron bridge was cast here in 1774 – thus the name given to nearby Ironbridge – and is still in use for pedestrian traffic. A local museum of ironfounding is of interest.

COATES, Glos *12 SO90*
The E entrance to the tunnel which took the former Thames and Severn canal is sited here; this guided the canal under the high ground between Coates and Sapperton. Although renovated in the 14thc, the Norman church still shows an original porch with a scratch sundial, and a carved arch. One of the old stone seats that started the saying, 'The weakest must go to the wall', can still be seen around the west end of one aisle. The tower was built some 600 years ago by the priest John Wyatt.

COBHAM, Kent *9 TQ66*
The half-timbered, Leather Bottle Inn that features in *The Pickwick Papers* can be seen in this picturesque village. Cobham Hall is a notable 16th-c and later building that stands in a fine park and now houses a girls' school. The hall has a great-hall which is partly of Elizabethan date, with added Renaissance features in the style of Inigo Jones. Owletts is a large red-brick house dating from the 17thc (OACT), and 1m SW near Sole Street Station is a Kentish yeoman's house of Tudor date (NT).

COBHAM, Surrey *8 TQ16*
Traces of bronze-age and later prehistoric settlements have been found in the area of this scattered, River-Mole village. An inscription on the bridge records the building of a former wooden bridge by Queen Matilda, wife of Henry I, because one of her ladies drowned while crossing the pond. Roman pottery has been found near this crossing. Matthew Arnold lived near by at Pains Hill Cottage, which no longer exists.

COCKERMOUTH, Cumbria *26 NY13*
A ruined Norman castle with a dungeon has been preserved here. The town is small and old, and stands on the Rivers Derwent and Cocker. An 18th-c house in Main Street was the birthplace of Wordsworth in 1770 (NT, OACT), and Fletcher Christian, leader of the mutiny on the Bounty, was born in nearby Moorland Close.

COCKINGTON, Devon *5 SX86*
Situated on the outskirts of Torquay, Cockington is generally visited for its restored thatched cottages and old forge. The public park surrounds a much altered Elizabethan court.

CODDENHAM, Suffolk *15 TM15*
A Roman road runs through this attractive village, which was known by its Roman inhabitants as *Conbretorium*. The church is of 13th-c and later date, and is noted for a 15th-c alabaster panel of the Crucifixion. A school was opened here in the 18thc, to teach the local children 'reading, writing, costing of accounts, and the girls knitting and sewing also'. The timber-framed post office was once an inn.

CODFORD ST MARY, Wilts *7 ST93*
A small Wyle-Valley village on the edge of Salisbury Plain. The chequer-work church displays curious 13th-c tracery in the south chapel, and 2m SW is the beautiful Boyton House of 1618.

COGGESHALL, Essex *9 TL82*
This River-Blackwater town includes a 15th-c church which contains the fine Paycocke brasses and Honywood monument. Paycocke's House is a 16th-c building displaying fine timbering and panelling (NT, OACT). The village is noted for lace making. Little Coggeshall includes restored St Nicholas' Chapel – with curious early brick windows, a Tudor house, and remains of a 12th-c abbey.

COLBY, Isle of Man *20 SC27*
On the outskirts of this village is a house with an inscribed tablet to the compiler of the first Manx dictionary, Archibald Cregeen.

COLCHESTER, Essex *15 TM02*
Colchester is a town of great age, that has developed considerably in recent years. Traditional industries associated with oysters and roses have been partly replaced by diesel engines, lathes, fans, and printing. However, October still sees an annual oyster feast.

The town was founded by the Belgic tribe *Catuvellauni*, and the Romans knew it as *Camulodunum*. Prolific Roman and earlier remains include a temple at Gosbeck's Farm, an iron-age burial in the Lexden tumulus to the W, and kilns for the making of Roman samian tableware – usually imported from Gaul. The burial may have been of *Cunobelinus*, the most powerful king in pre-Roman Britain. The Roman walls that encircled the town are still standing, and the Balkerne Gate is one of the original entrances. Marks on early coins, together with a great deal of similar evidence, indicate that *Camulodunum* once boasted a mint.

The town continued to flourish after the departure of the Romans and was called the fortress on the Colne, or Colchester, by the Saxons. The Normans took stone from existing Roman buildings to build the castle, which has the largest keep in England. An excellent museum at the castle displays a splendid collection of Roman antiquities (OACT). The town was besieged by Cromwell's army in 1648, after which Lucas and Lisle, two commanders of the Royalist defences, were executed as rebels.

Holly Trees is a mansion of 1718 which adjoins the castle park, and now contains a good collection of bygones.

cont

The Minories, a house owned by the Victor Batte-Lay Trust, contains interesting items of furniture and paintings. Siege House (late 15thc) was Fairfax's headquarters during the Civil War, and bullet holes made by the Royalist attackers can still be seen in the structural timbers. Priory Street follows the walls and leads to the ruined Church of St Botolph's Priory. This is an Augustinian foundation that was built on the site of an earlier church, and the ruins comprise the west front and part of the nave. Remains that are preserved are built mainly of Roman brick. Several old churches include Holy Trinity, with its Saxon tower, and the restored St Martin's Church. The latter has a fine 14th-c chancel and includes Roman bricks in its structure. Ancient inns include the Marquis of Granby and the 15th-c Red Lion. Lexden dykes, part of the vast pre-Roman defensive system, can be seen to the W. Materials from St John's Abbey were used to build Bourne Mill (NT), in 1591.

The University of Essex was founded in 1962 and lies 2m SE in Wivenhoe Park; Colchester Zoo is 3m W at Stanway Hall.

COLD ASHTON, Avon   6 ST77
Beautifully situated in the hills above Bath, this village includes a gabled 16th-c manor house with a fine gateway. The church was built c1500, and houses a rare wall pulpit which is reached via stairs set into the wall.

COLDRIDGE, Devon   5 SS60
A Taw-Valley village where the originally-Norman church was mostly rebuilt in the 15thc. A splendid carved screen with three pairs of gates can be seen inside the church, together with a parclose-screen displaying delicate Breton-style carving.

COLESHILL, Bucks   8 SU99
This Chiltern village affords fine views over the surrounding hills and countryside. A derelict tower-windmill of 1856 can be seen here, and Coleshill was the birthplace of the poet Edmund Waller in 1606.

COLESHILL, Warwickshire   12 SP18
The River Cole is crossed by a medieval bridge in this village, and the local church, of 14th-c origin, displays a carved Norman font and fine spire. The old pillory, whipping post, and stocks are preserved on Church Hill. Maxstoke Castle is a 14th-c red-sandstone structure lying to the E, with a great hall built in 1345 by the Earl of Huntingdon.

COLLYWESTON, Northants   19 SK90
This delightful village of ancient stone-built cottages is famous for Colly Weston roofing slates. The manor house dates from 1696.

COLNBROOK, Bucks   8 TQ07
The timber-framed Ostrich Inn in this village dates from the 15thc, and many 18th- and 19th-c houses can be seen in the main street. It is thought that King John may have stopped at a local house, now called King John's Castle, on his way to seal the Magna Carta in 1215. The famous Cox's Orange Pippin apple was first cultivated here.

COLNE, Lancs   21 SD83
Colne is a cotton manufacturing town situated on the River Calder. A rare set of mobile stocks is preserved in the churchyard, and Pendle Hill, associated with the Lancashire witch trials, rises to the W. This hill, the surrounding area, and the events leading up to the trials, are described in the historical novel, *Mist Over Pendle*, by Robert Neil. The moors of Haworth rise to the E, and both are within easy reach.

A museum in the town deals exclusively with the British in India; illustrations, photographs, uniforms, etc give an idea of the British occupation before the transfer of power in 1947. Most of St Bartholomew's Church is of perpendicular style, although it dates back to the 13thc.

COLN ST ALDWYN, Glos   12 SP10
This attractive Cotswold village lies 6½m SE of Northleach on the River Coln. A restored Stuart manor house is of interest, and the church displays a fine tower and carved Norman doorway. Modernized Hatherop Castle is sited to the E.

COLSTERWORTH, Lincs   19 SK92
The church in this River-Witham village houses a sundial carved by the famous scientist, Sir Isaac Newton, when he was a boy. Some Saxon work is evident in the north-nave arcade. Woolsthorpe House is a fine stone-built 17th-c house standing 1m NW, where Sir Isaac was born in 1642 (NT, OACT). A tree in the orchard is said to be a descendant of the one from which the famous apple fell.

COLTISHALL, Norfolk   15 TG21
This shooting and angling centre is situated on the River Bure, 8m NE of Norwich. The Limes is a house dated 1629, and another old building named Little Hautbois stands 2m NW. Several 18th-c houses can be seen in the village.

COLYTON, Devon   6 SY29
A market town in the Coly Valley, approximately 1m inland from the coastal resort of Seaton. Picturesque winding streets and a 600-year-old bridge over the Coly add an almost medieval charm to the place, and the partly-perpendicular cruciform-shaped church houses some particularly interesting Pole monuments in the chantry chapel. The Great House in South Street is the old home of the Yonge family, and was probably built by John Yonge, the merchant adventurer who died in 1612. This house displays good wainscoting, and one room contains the Royal Cipher of James I.

COMBE FLOREY, Somerset   6 ST13
This attractive sandstone-built village lies in the foothills of the Quantock range. The existing manor house dates from c1675 and 1730, and has a gateway that originates from 1593. It was once the home of novelist Evelyn Waugh. Sydney Smith, described as the wittiest man in England, once served as a vicar here. He described life in the country as 'a kind of healthy grave'.

COMBE-IN-TEIGNHEAD, Devon   5 SX97
The perpendicular church in this delightful village contains a restored

1 Balkerne Gate
2 Bourne Mill
3 Castle (museum)
4 Holly Tree Mansion
5 Lexden Dykes
6 Marquis of Granby Inn
7 Red Lion Inn
8 Roman Walls
9 Siege House
10 St Botolph's Priory Ruins
11 St Martin's Church
12 The Holy Trinity Church
13 The Minories
14 University of Essex
15 Zoo

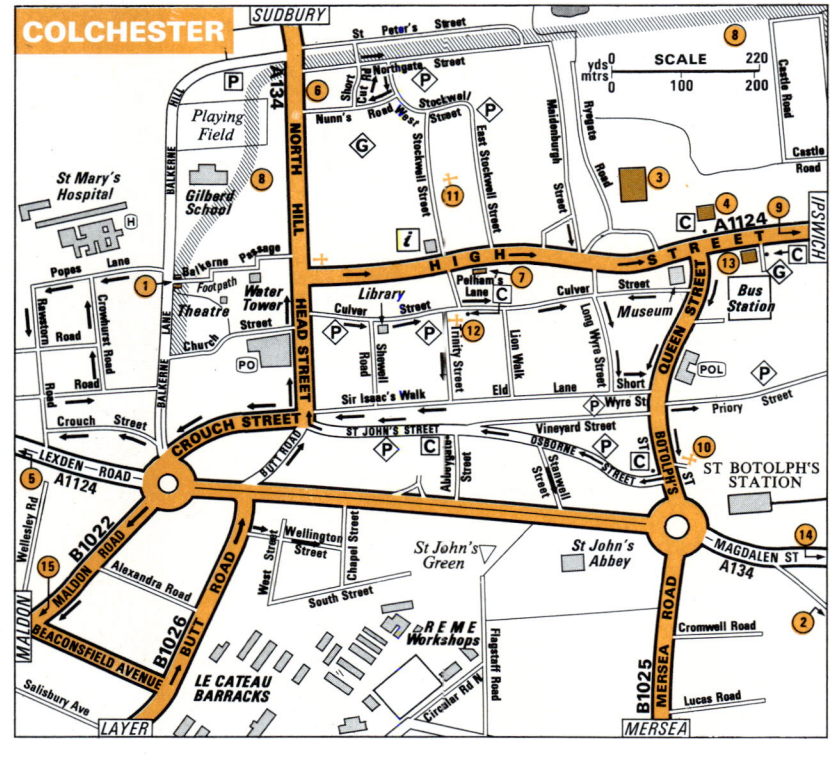

screen, curious old bench-ends, and a Norman font. Bourchier almshouses were founded in 1620, and it is said that the village blacksmith was beating the ironwork for their door while the Mayflower sailed to America.

COMBE MARTIN, Devon *5 SS54*
A straggling village, with a long street descending to a small harbour and sandy bay. The Pack of Cards inn is a strange house which is said to have been built by a man who made his fortune at the card table. It is built like a house of cards, with each storey smaller than the one below it, and numerous chimneys are dotted about all over the place. The church carries one of Devon's tallest towers and contains benches and stalls which display examples of both old and new carving.

Great and Little Hangman (NT) are hills that rise from a lofty cliff area to the NE, now designated an area of outstanding natural beauty. Local silver mines became very important some 700 years ago, when the metal was needed to help pay for the Hundred-Years War. The mines were so rich that 300 men had to be brought from Derbyshire and Wales to help work them.

COMPTON, Surrey *8 SU94*
Very early woodwork and a curious double chancel can be seen in the village's highly-interesting Norman and later church. The Watts Memorial Chapel and Picture Gallery, containing some 150 pictures by Victorian artist G P Watts, can be seen near by.

COMPTON BASSETT, Wilts *7 SU07*
The mainly-perpendicular church is remarkable for its rare double-fronted 16th-c stone screen, which stands on four pilasters featuring canopied stone figures of the twelve Apostles. Near by are 17th-c stables from former Compton House, home of the Heneage family for many generations. The manor farmhouse is dated 1699.

COMPTON BEAUCHAMP, Oxon *13 SU28*
This is a small hamlet lying in a wooded hollow of the Vale of White Horse. The fine early 16th- to 18th-c manor house is gabled and moated. Wayland's Smithy (AM) is a restored prehistoric burial-chamber situated off the ancient Ridgeway, 2m S.

COMPTON CHAMBERLAYNE, Wilts *7 SU02*
Compton House is an old battlemented building which stands just below the church in this pretty Naddar-Valley village. It is associated with John Penruddock, Colonel under the Commonwealth, who led a band of men to Salisbury market place and proclaimed Charles II King in 1655. It was for this action that he was later executed.

COMPTON WYNYATES, Warwickshire *13 SP34*
This beautiful turreted and gabled Tudor manor house is set among modern topiary gardens on the side of a hill (OACT). The Comptons were lords of the manor here before Magna Carta, and the house has many historical associations. The predecessor of the present church was destroyed during the Civil War, and the building that exists today dates from 1663.

CONDOVER, Salop *17 SJ40*
Condover Hall (late 16thc) is a splendid stone-built house set in a large park (OACT). Several old houses can be seen in the village, and half-timbered Pitchford Hall (3m SE) dates from the 16thc. A curious timbered tree-house stands in the grounds. The village church contains fine monuments, and is considered a good example of the trans-Norman and 17th-c styles.

CONGLETON, Cheshire *17 SJ86*
This pleasantly-situated market town manufactures artificial yarn, and serves as a dormitory for Manchester and the Potteries. Several old inns are of interest, and St Peter's Church of 1742 shows a fine Georgian interior. Mow Cop (NT), a fine viewpoint with an 18th-c sham-castle ruin, lies 5m S.

CONGRESBURY, Avon *6 ST46*
The name of this River-Yeo town is pronounced Coomsbury. A rare Somerset spire is born by the largely-perpendicular church, and the vicarage dates from the 15thc. A wild valley called Goblin Combe lies NE in the Ludgate Hills.

CONINGTON, Cambs *14 TL18*
The 15th-c parish church is noted for its tower, and contains monuments erected in 1600 to King David I of Scotland (Earl of Huntingdon) and his son, Henry of Scotland.

CONISBROUGH, S Yorks *18 SK59*
A River-Don village with an interesting, 12th-c castle, probably built by Henry II's half-brother, displaying the oldest circular keep in England (AM, OACT). Norman workmanship is evident in the church, which contains fine capitals and a carved tomb-chest.

CONISTON, Cumbria *21 SD39*
A village at the NW tip of Coniston Water, dominated by the 2,633ft Old Man, in a tranquil setting surrounded by superb scenery on all sides. Dow Crag is a 2,555ft peak to the W, popular with rock climbers, and Brantwood was John Ruskin's home on the E side of the lake. This writer and art-critic is buried in the local churchyard, and the Ruskin Museum contains personal relics. Tennyson lived at Tent Lodge. Coniston Old Hall has characteristic round Lakeland chimneys. A water-speed record of more than 225mph was set-up on Coniston Lake by Sir Donald Campbell in 1956. He died here in an accident, while trying to beat this speed in 1965. Much of the area is owned by the NT, including Yew Tree Tarn on the Monk Coniston Estate. Little Tarn Hows lies 3m NNE (NT).

CONSETT, Co Durham *27 NZ15*
Huge buildings with tall smoking chimneys – the town's ironworks – can be seen from the A68 as the road rises N from the village of Tow Law. Consett has sprung into industrial prominence during the last century, and the works currently produce vast quantities of iron and steel for railways, bridges, ship-building, and other engineering industries all over the world. More than a million tons of steel are produced here each year.

COOKHAM, Berks *8 SU88*
This delightful village faces the wooded Cliveden Reach of the Thames, a fine stretch of river that begins at Cookham Lock and continues downstream past Cliveden. Stanley Spencer the artist lived and worked here and his painting of *The Last Supper* is hung in the partly 12th-c church. Other examples of his work are displayed in King's Hall. Red-brick cottages face the green, and the old 'Bel and the Dragon' inn is of interest. Winter Hill is a good viewpoint lying to the NW.

COOLING, Kent *9 TQ77*
Remains of the 14th-c castle that was once the home of Sir John Oldcastle include an imposing gateway. Sir John was hung as a Lollard, ie a supporter of John Wycliff's belief that churchmen should lead a life of evangelical poverty, and it is said that he was the model for Shakespeare's Falstaff. Dickens describes the churchyard and surrounding flat countryside in his novel *Great Expectations*. High Halstow national nature reserve lies to the E at Northward Hill.

COOMBES, W Sussex *8 TQ10*
A feature of this Adur-Valley village is the number of old barns and farms that can be seen. The chancel of the unrestored Norman church shows wall-paintings that were discovered quite recently. A little 16th-c gabled house near by is the home of the priest of Coombes.

COPFORD, Essex *15 TL92*
Copford church is of particular note. It has an early-Norman nave, chancel, and apse, and displays Roman tiles. The Norman walling is covered with remarkable 12th-c paintings, the size, colour, and arrangement of which have been likened to the paintings in Italian Byzantine churches. Copford Hall is a characteristic Georgian House.

CORBRIDGE, Northumberland *27 NY96*
A 17th-c bridge crosses the Tyne in this pleasant old market town, and the main street is lined with houses and gardens. The church's Saxon tower is of interest, and the churchyard contains a 14th-c pele tower. An unusual cast-iron cross in the market place dates from 1814. The Angel inn is of Georgian and earlier date.

Roman remains of *Corstopitum* (AM), and a museum displaying relics of the occupation here, can be seen 1½m W. A Roman cavalry force was stationed here until 140AD, when the fort was rebuilt to form a military base and depot for operations in Scotland. It was sacked in 197AD and immediately rebuilt by *Severus*. It is thought that the Saxons used the site after the departure of the Romans, because various of their artifacts have been found here.

Dilston Castle is of the 15thc and is sited 1½m SW near Devil's Water, which flows into the Tyne. The fortified manor house of Aydon Castle is of the 14thc and stands 1½m NE (AM).

CORBY, Northants *13 SP88*
This rapidly-developing centre of the steel industry was a village until 1932, and owes much of its prosperity to local deposits of iron ore. It now has its own civic theatre and a new five-acre boating lake. Great Oakley Hall (c1555) lies 3m SW.

CORFE CASTLE, Dorset *7 SY98*
A pretty Purbeck village that takes its name from the ruined castle perched

above it on a peculiarly symmetrical hill. Although the present ruins are Norman, there was an earlier Saxon stronghold on the same site. It was in this previous structure that eighteen-year old King Edward the Martyr was murdered by his step-mother Elfrida in 978, in order that her real son Ethelred could be placed on the throne. King John later used it as a royal prison, and Edward II was imprisoned here in 1326 before his murder at Berkeley Castle. Lady Bankes held the castle against 600 Parliamentary troops in 1643, and Cromwell's men used gunpowder to take it in 1646. Thus the castle was reduced to its present, magnificently-ruined state (OACT). The town hall and museum was partly rebuilt in 1680 and contains relics of past village life. The popular Blue Pool lies 3m NW, with lofty Creech Barrow in the background.

CORHAMPTON, Hants 7 SU62
The interesting church in this little village is largely Saxon, and contains its original stone altar plus 13th-c wall-paintings. An ancient yew stands in the churchyard.

CORNHILL-ON-TWEED, Northumberland 27 NT83
This small Border village is on the River Tweed, and faces across to Coldstream on the Scottish bank. The bridge was built by John Smeaton in the late 18thc, and carries a bronze plate recording the fact that Robert Burns crossed here and entered England for the first time on May 7, 1787. The toll-house on the Scottish side was once notorious for the number of marriages, born of elopements, that took place there.

CORNWOOD, Devon 5 SX65
A village in the Yealm valley, 7½m NE of Plymouth, with a picturesque ravine known as Hawns and Dendles near by. Fardel is a long building incorporating many gables, and Stert displays the Drake crest on its gateposts. These two buildings were the respective homes of the Raleigh and Drake families. Dendles Wood is a national nature reserve.

CORSHAM, Wilts 7 ST87
Corsham is a stone-built market town on the farthest S point of the Cotswolds, near Chippenham. Flemish-style cottages can be seen in the cobbled street, plus the Methuen Arms Inn and the fine baroque 17th-c Hungerford almshouses. Bath stone is the name given to a cream-coloured limestone used extensively for building construction, which is quarried locally. The 12th- to 15th-c church of St Bartholomew houses monuments dating from the 15thc, including some of the Methuen family. Corsham Court is an Elizabethan and Georgian house containing a collection of old masters, and set in a park laid out by Capability Brown (OACT).

COTHELSTONE, Somerset 6 ST13
The beautiful red-sandstone manor house (c1500) has been partly rebuilt, but is still one of the best in the county. It retains its castellated gatehouse, and a roadside arch from which two of the rebels in the Monmouth rising were hanged after the Duke's defeat at Sedgemoor. The house was besieged during the Civil War, and its owner, Sir John Stawell, spent many years in prison before returning home to die. Cothelstone House is sited on a hill above, and dates from 1818. Cothelstone Beacon is a ruined 19th-c folly tower.

COTHERIDGE, Herefs & Worcs 12 SO75
A double avenue of limes that were planted in 1685 approach the church and court in this village. The church is mainly 12thc, and has a massive timber-framed tower of later date. Fine altar-rails and box-pews can be seen inside. The Court is a Georgian house incorporating parts of an earlier gabled building.

COTSWOLDS, THE
The Cotswold Hills extend from the Bath area to N Oxfordshire. Their wooded slopes fall steeply to the Severn Vale in the W, but become bare, and shelve more gently as they join the great Midland plain to the N. A height of nearly 1,100ft is reached near Cheltenham Spa, and the 1,000ft level is again exceeded above Broadway village.

The countryside is patterned with characteristic dry-stone walls, and many towns and villages in the area are constructed entirely of the beautiful locally-quarried silver-grey or yellowish limestone. The Cotswolds were virtually one great sheep-walk from the 12thc onwards, but the introduction of power machinery caused a slow decline in the local wool industry. Cloth manufacturing is, however, still actively conducted around Stroud. Profits from wool helped to build the beautiful old cottages and manor houses which are such a feature of the district, plus the great wool churches at Chipping Campden and Northleach.

Cotswold buildings form a rich part of English architectural heritage, and date mainly from the 16th- and 17th-c. Various towns and villages in this area are listed elsewhere in this gazetteer. The following may be singled out as being worthy of special attention: Bibury Broadway; Burford (Oxon); Chastleton; Chipping Campden; Cirencester; Cleeve Hill; Painswick; Stanton (Glos); Stanway; the Slaughters; Winchcombe.

COUGHTON, Warwickshire 12 SP06
A village near Alcester, Coughton includes a 16th-c church housing old glass, a clock dated 1690, and a rare old bread-rack. One of the rooms at Coughton Court is where the wives of several gunpowder-plot conspirators waited anxiously for news on that fateful November 5 (1605). A noble gatehouse can be seen, and the house was the Throckmorton family-home for many centuries. It contains interesting Jacobite relics (OACT). Coughton lies on the Roman Ryknild Street, and the section to the N of the village is known as Haydon Way.

COVEHITHE, Suffolk 15 TM58
Access from the village to a nearby sandy beach is along cliff paths. The thatched 17th-c church stands within the ruins of a 15th-c structure, the tower of which still stands at its full 100ft.

COVENTRY, W Midlands 13 SP37
Coventry, a city of historical significance and current industrial importance, suffered during both the World Wars. The attention of enemy bombers, particularly in the last war, was attracted by munition factories sited in the city, and during the period from 1939 to 1945 the place was very nearly reduced to rubble. Air-raids became quite commonplace to the citizens of Coventry, but even they did not expect the violent indiscriminate attack which occurred on the night of 14 November, 1940. This, one of the worst bombings of the war, destroyed thousands of homes, offices, and the cathedral.

Until 1700 the city was the centre of the English cloth industry, and several medieval buildings still remain from this period. The 19thc saw a diversification of industry, and the community became first involved in the manufacture of watches and sewing machines, then in later years a leading centre for cycle and motor car production.

The old cathedral walls and 15th-c 295ft tower still stand and adjoin the new cathedral. This latest building was built in pink sandstone to a striking design by Sir Basil Spence. It was completed in 1962, and displays a brilliant baptistery window by John Piper, a vast tapestry by Graham Sutherland, and a bronze of St Michael subduing the Devil by Epstein.

Remains of the Charterhouse, founded by the Carthusians in 1381, comprise a section of the wall that once enclosed a monastery. Blocks of sandstone that make up existing parts of the old city walls and gates have stood for some 600 years. Ford's Hospital is a courtyard of Tudor half-timbered almshouses which were restored after bomb damage; Bond's Hospital, built for the same purpose, was founded 'for as long as the world shall endure'. These and nearby Bablake Old School are all reminders of old Coventry, before the extensive post-war rebuilding scheme. Cheylesmore Manor House, now the Registry Office, dates originally from 1230 and is built over a lane.

The legend of Lady Godiva, who rode naked through the streets of the town to avert her husband's wrath from the people, is thought to date from the 13thc. It was retold by Landor and Tennyson in the 19thc, and a statue of the lady now stands on Broadgate, in the city's new shopping centre. This monument was executed by Reid Dick in 1949. Animated figures on the modern clock tower in Broadgate depict both Lady Godiva and the infamous Peeping Tom.

Other interesting features of the city include several churches, the half-timbered and gabled Golden Cross Inn, timbered houses in Priory Row, and the Herbert Museum and Art Gallery. The Belgrade Theatre was opened in 1958. At Baginton, S of the city, is an interesting reconstruction of a Roman fort. The University of Warwick is situated on the SW outskirts of Coventry, and took its first undergraduates in October 1965.

COVERACK, Cornwall 4 SW71
This attractive fishing village is situated on the Lizard peninsula, and was once a centre for smuggling. The dangerous Manacles Rocks lie off-shore, and can be seen from Chynalis Point to the S. Rocks and shingle make up the beach.

COWDEN, Kent 8 TQ44
A pleasing village of old houses, situated 4m SSE of Edenbridge on the Kent Water. Notable 14th-c timbering is shown by the church tower, and both tower and spire are shingled. Old houses in the area include Crippenden, Waystrode Manor, Bazling Farm, and Scarlett Mill.

COWES, Isle of Wight 7 SZ49
Cowes is a busy port with a good harbour on the River Medina – which separates the town from East Cowes. A ferry and floating bridge connect the two. It is the chief yachting centre in the country, and the headquarters of the Royal Yacht Squadron is situated in Cowes Castle. The Royal London Yacht Club is also based here. Thomas Arnold, headmaster of Rugby School, was born here in 1795. East Cowes Castle was built by John Nash. Steamer and hovercraft services link with the mainland, and the building of hovercraft forms a local industry. Osborne House (1m SE) was the home of Queen Victoria at her death (OACT).

COWFOLD, W Sussex 8 TQ22
Old red cottages make up this village and the early-English and later church houses a famous 15th-c brass. This depicts Thomas Melond, a monk who died some 500 years ago, and is over 10ft high. St Hugh's Monastery lies 1½m S, and was built in this century by Carthusion monks. Its 200ft spire can be seen for miles.

COXWELL, GREAT, Oxon 13 SU29
A vast stone-built tithe barn of 14th-c date stands here, considered the finest in England (NT, OACT).

CRACKINGTON HAVEN, Cornwall 4 SX19
This tiny seaside village offers a small sandy beach and surf bathing. The coastal scenery is very rugged, and the highest cliffs in Cornwall lie to the S; High Cliff soars to approximately 700ft.

CRANBORNE, Dorset 7 SU01
Attractive houses line the broad street of this village, which was the seat of the Chase Court – an organization responsible for controlling hunting rights in Cranborne Chase forest – from 980 to 1102. Its beautiful Jacobean manor house is set in 17th-c gardens (OACT), and displays unusual Renaissance loggias and a brick gatehouse. James I and Charles I were both frequent visitors here. The large parish church displays a perpendicular tower, but is mainly of early-English style. Bokerly Dyke, a structure thought to have been built by Romanized Britons, can be seen on the slopes of Pentridge Hill 4m N. It follows the Hampshire border in the direction of the main Salisbury to Blandford road, part of which follows the same route as the Roman Ackling Dyke.

CRANBROOK, Kent 9 TQ73
A former cloth-weaving town that is now a busy commercial centre, Cranbrook is sited on a hill above the Weald and includes many old houses. One of these is the Elizabethan Old Cloth Hall, once called Coursehorn Manor, which has associations with Queen Elizabeth I. The late-perpendicular church is sometimes called the Cathedral of the Weald, and shows an ancient porch of 1291 plus a fine oak door. The grammar school was founded in the 16thc. Flishinghurst is an interesting 15th- to 17th-c house, and a restored though still impressive windmill is preserved in the town. Old Wilsley House is a 14th-c and later building lying 1m NE, and the fine 18th-c moated manor-house of Glassenbury stands 2m W. The latter is approached by an avenue of fine limes.

CRANLEIGH, Surrey 8 TQ03
The long main street skirting a green forms the spine of this village. A well-known public school is sited here, and good examples of 14th-c work can be seen in the church – which also displays Norman nave pillars. Beyond Vachery Pond, to the SE, is the restored Tudor Baynards Park. A Roman road runs near by.

CRANTOCK, Cornwall 4 SW76
A quiet village opposite Newquay, and near the mouth of the River Gannel. The mainly-Norman church houses good carving; six-holed stocks and an old well can be seen in the churchyard. Kelsey Head (W), and The Chick island are NT property.

CRANWELL, Lincs 19 TF04
Cranwell's mainly early-English church preserves workmanship of Saxon and Norman origin, and houses an ancient screen. The well-known Royal Air Force College was founded in 1920 and lies 1½m W. The extent of a jump made by the once-famous horse Bayard, is marked with two horseshoes by a hedge at Bayard's Leap (2½m W). A stone commemorates the leap.

1. Bablake Old School
2. Belgrade Theatre
3. Bond's Hospital
4. Broadgate (Godiva statue & clock tower)
5. Cathedral and Old Cathedral Ruins
6. Charterhouse Remains
7. Cheylesmore Manor House
8. City Walls
9. Ford's Hospital
10. Golden Cross Inn
11. Herbert Museum and Art Gallery
12. University of Warwick

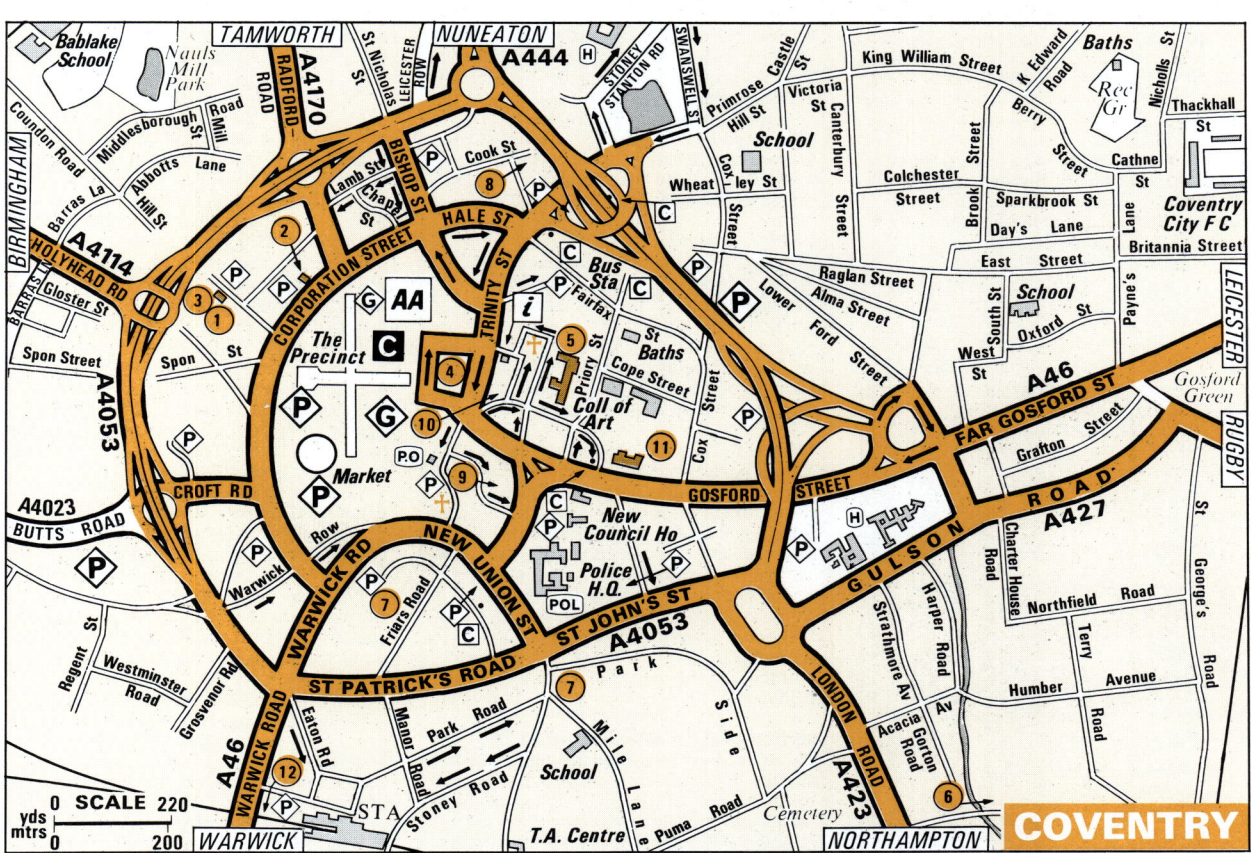

CRASTER, Northumberland 27 NU21
Oak-smoked kippers have made this place famous, although it deserves to be known just for its cliff scenery. The old fort of Crawchester, from which the village's name derives, vanished long ago, but 15th- and 17th-c Craster Tower still exists as part of a farmhouse.

CRAVEN
This Pennine district is situated in the old West Riding of Yorkshire, and extends in a W direction from Skipton to Bowland Forest, beyond Ribblesdale. It is noted for its striking limestone scenery, the best examples of which can be seen around Malham. Numerous deep potholes penetrate the rock below the peak of Pen-y-Ghent.

CRAVEN ARMS, Salop 12 SO48
Important sheep-auctions are conducted in this small market town. An old mileage pillar records the distances to various places. The Craven Arms inn dates from the early 19thc, and Stokesay Castle – a splendid example of a 13th-c fortified manor house – lies ¾m S (AM, OACT). One of its features is a black-and-white Elizabethan gatehouse. The church is separated from the manor by a moat, and displays a 17th-c gallery and three-decker pulpit.

CRAWLEY, W Sussex 8 TQ23
Crawley New Town has spread out from the old town and taken in several villages, but the industrial estate is well separated from the residential area. Pleasant open spaces with green lawns prevent the closed-in atmosphere that often results from high-density building. The 16th-c George Inn displays a gallows sign. St Leonard's (at Tilgate) and Worth are forests situated to the S, and all that now remain of Anderida, a forest which covered the country in Roman times.

CREDITON, Devon 5 SS80
Crediton lies on the River Credy, and the town was the see of a bishop in Saxon times. This was before the christian centre was transferred to Exeter, and tradition says that St Boniface – Winfrid of Crediton – was born here. He later became Bishop of Mainz (Germany), and a statue to him was unveiled by Princess Margaret in 1960. The splendid early-English and perpendicular church is almost a miniature cathedral.

CREGNEISH, Isle of Man 20 SC16
A Manx folk museum can be seen in Harry Kelly's cottage, and the cliffs at Spanish Head reach a height of 400ft. Chasm Cliffs and Sugar Loaf Rock are particularly striking.

CRESWELL, Derbyshire 18 SK57
This area is well-known for its crags and caves. The latter were once occupied by upper-paleolithic cave-dwellers, and have yielded rich stone-age finds.

CREWKERNE, Somerset 6 ST40
Crewkerne has long been a centre of the flax-weaving and sail-making industries, and is a market town in the valley of Rivers Axe and Parrett. Interesting buildings include several old houses, an ancient grammar school, and almshouses of 1604 and 1707. The church is an exceptionally-beautiful mainly 15th-c structure, displaying a notable west facade. Fine gardens surround 14th- to 16th-c Wayford Manor, 3m SW.

CRICH, Derbyshire 18 SK35
A tramway museum is sited in an old quarry here, and displays working exhibits including examples from Czechoslovakia and Vienna (OACT). Crich Stand, a hill rising to 955ft, is surmounted by a memorial to the Sherwood Foresters. Interesting effigies are contained in the Norman to decorated church.

CRICKLADE, Wilts 12 SU09
This name means 'the passage over the Thames by the hill', and Cricklade is the only Thames-side town in Wiltshire. This part of the famous river is little more than a channel. St Sampson's Church was built by the Duke of Northumberland, and its vaulted roof displays sixty-four fine bosses. The tower is also of interest. St Mary's Church is partly Norman. Both churchyards are noted for their medieval carved crosses. Ancient fortifications surrounding the town were partly excavated in 1952, and a museum at the west-end of the main street exhibits items dating from Roman times, through the Saxon period, to the present day.

CROFT, N Yorks 22 NZ20
A River-Tees village near Darlington, where the river is spanned by a fine, probably 15th-c bridge. Tombs and attractive carving can be seen in the church, and the old rectory was the boyhood home of Lewis Carroll (Charles Lutwidge Dodgson), who wrote *Alice's Adventures in Wonderland*.

CROMER, Norfolk 15 TG24
This is a popular holiday resort, where the sandy beach is fringed by lofty cliffs. Other amenities include a zoo and boating lake. Local crabs are justifiably famous, and a small fishing-industry still operates. The 15th-c parish church carries a fine tower which is one of the tallest in Norfolk. Felbrigg Hall dates from the 17thc and stands near by (NT, OACT). A church in the park houses old brasses, and monuments by Grinling Gibbons and Nollekens.

CROMFORD, Derbyshire 18 SK25
The River Derwent runs through this small village, which features a restored bridge-chapel (AM). Richard Arkwright built Derbyshire's first water-powered cotton mill here in 1771, and his remains lie in the church he built in 1792. Willersley Castle dates from the 18thc, and was built as the home of Richard Arkwright. Via Gellia is a wooded area to the W, bearing a name derived from that of the Gell family who lived near by. The Black Rocks, 1m S, are well known to climbers, and Lea Hurst, the former home of Florence Nightingale, lies 3m E.

CRONDALL, Hants 8 SU74
Most of the fine village church is Norman, but the original central tower was pulled down to make way for the existing mid 17th-c brick tower. Inside is a brass dated 1381, said to be the oldest in Hampshire. A nearby prehistoric earthwork is known, misleadingly, as Caesar's Camp.

CROPREDY, Oxon 13 SP44
A village on the River Cherwell, near Banbury. Charles II defeated Waller at Cropredy Bridge in 1644, and the 14th-c church preserves two suits of armour from the battle. It also boasts a fine brass-eagle lectern.

CROPTHORNE, Herefs and Worcs 12 SO94
This attractive village is formed largely about a single main-street running parallel to the winding River Avon. The houses display a variety of different styles, but blend happily to give the village its charm and character. Bredon Hill stands S, and between it and the village are black-and-white cottages scattered among the trees. The church has a Norman tower and part of a rare Saxon cross.

CROSBY, Isle of Man 20 SC37
A little village near Douglas, featuring an interesting motor museum at Glen Vine. Among the exhibits are a very rare Sunbeam Mabley, and a Briggs and Stratton – the only five-wheel car ever made. Greeba Castle, where Sir Hall Caine lived in 1931, is beside Greeba Mountain.

CROSCOMBE, Somerset 6 ST54
This stone-built village faces a horizon of steep wooded hills. An early-Tudor manor-house exists here, and the church shows rich black oak-carving from the 17thc. Over 200 wood panels depict sunflowers, acorns, eagles, shields, and foliage, and even more carving can be seen on the pews, roof, bench-ends, and pulpit. Among the church records are manuscripts showing that seven guilds existed in Croscombe. These were for young men, maidens, and wives; for webbers, archers, fullers, and hogglers. The hogglers were labourers that would meet in church to talk – the only meeting place they had.

CROSTON, Lancs 21 SD41
The 15th-c church contains a curious brass, and the village almshouses are dated 1692. An interesting collection of old coaches can be seen in the Royal Umpire Museum, which also features a collection of birds and rare animals, a pheasantry, and a haunted room.

CROWBOROUGH, E Sussex 8 TQ53
A Wealden golfing-centre situated on high ground at the E extremity of Ashdown Forest. Beacon Hill rises to 792ft in the W. Phie Forest Garden, at Marden Hill, offers panoramic views across Ashdown Forest and has picnic facilities. The forest itself covers some 14,000 acres,

1 Boating Lake
2 Felbrigg Hall
3 Parish Church of St Peter and St Paul
4 Zoo

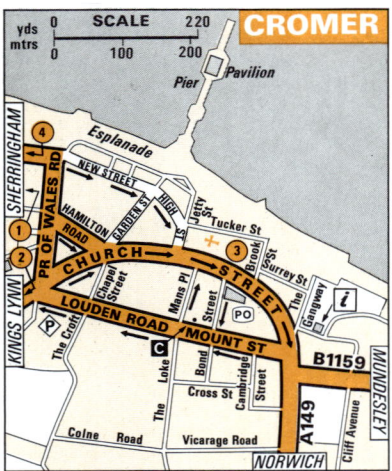

and is the largest remaining part of the ancient and once-vast forest of Anderida. All Saints Church and vicarage date from 1744. The naturalist Richard Jeffries lived in Crowborough, and described the rural scene in a beautiful and sympathetic manner.

CROWCOMBE, Somerset *6 ST13*
Situated below the Quantock Hills, the village is approached by a steep lane from Nether Stowey. To the right of the road is a view of the coast, with the Welsh hills in the distance. The good perpendicular church houses carved Tudor bench-ends symbolizing fertility, and stands opposite the partly-Tudor Church House (AM). Crowcombe Court is an interesting early-Georgian mansion, and Halsway is a fine old house which was partially rebuilt in 1870. The ancient Heddon Oak, known for its wide spreading branches, stands on the Stogumber road.

CROWDEN, Derbyshire *18 SK09*
Situated in Longdendale, Crowden stands on the N side of the Woodhead Reservoirs. Holme Moss is surmounted by a BBC television mast to the N, and stands in front of Black Hill. At 1,908ft, the latter is the highest point in Cheshire. Laddow Rocks are on Featherbed Moss, NW of Crowden, and are well-known among climbers.

CROWFIELD, Suffolk *15 TM15*
The village church has a very rare timber-framed chancel, with the framing exposed both internally and externally.

CROWHURST, E Sussex *9 TQ71*
A village 2m S of Battle, where the rebuilt church still carries its 15th-c tower with the Pelham buckle carved on the door. Near by are the ruins of a late 13th-c manor house, and Hye House is dated 1744. A large old yew stands in the churchyard.

CROWHURST, Surrey *8 TQ34*
The churchyard in this Wealden village contains a very ancient yew tree which measures some 33ft round. Twelve people can sit round a table in the hollow of its trunk; to give an idea of the tree's age, it must have been old when William the Conqueror first came to Britain. The gabled 16th-c Old Mansion bears fine chimneys, and 1m S is the moated and restored, 15th-c and later Crowhurst Place, described as one of the best timbered homes in Surrey.

CROWLAND, Lincs *19 TF21*
A pleasant little town with wide streets, where a partly-ruined 12th-c and later abbey now serves as a parish church. The original foundation in 716 was by King Ethelbald, in memory of St Guthlac. Interesting features include a sculptured west front, and a 15th-c oak screen. The unique 14th-c Triangular Bridge (AM) originally spanned streams of the Welland, but now stands on dry land. It comprises three 14th-c arches meeting at an angle of 120 degrees. A carved figure of the Virgin Mary was placed on the bridge in 1720, and comes from the west front of the abbey. Hereward the Wake is said to have been buried here.

CROWMARSH GIFFORD, Oxon *13 SU68*
This Thames-side village stands opposite Wallingford, and includes a partly-Norman church with windows and doorways of the same period. Jethro Tull (1674 to 1741), a pioneer of mechanized farming, once lived N of here at Howbery Park.

CROXLEY GREEN, Herts *8 TQ09*
Croxley Green is now a suburb of Watford. The well-preserved and ancient tithe barn at Croxley Hall Farm is said to be the second largest in England. Redheath, dated 1712 and now housing a school, lies N.

CROXTON KERRIAL, Leics *19 SK82*
A pleasant little Wolds village of stone houses, situated high enough to afford wide views over the surrounding area. Croxton Abbey was founded in 1150, but has since vanished. Its site has, however, been revealed by excavation in 800-acre Croxton Park, once the hunting seat of the Dukes of Rutland. Also revealed was evidence of earlier occupation, including Saxo-Norman pottery and a coin of *Aethelred II*.

CROYDON, Gt London *8 TQ36*
Croydon has been a London borough since 1965, and displays some of the most advanced architecture, road-building, and town-planning in England. Older buildings that have survived the extensive redevelopment include Archbishop's Palace (14thc, now a school), Whitgift's almshouse (founded 1596), and well-known Whitgift School. The 15th-c parish church was rebuilt after a fire in 1867, and Wrencote is an early 18th-c house in the High Street. Among the more recent buildings are Fairfield Halls and the Ashcroft Theatre.

CRUWYS MORCHARD, Devon *5 SS81*
This village takes its name from the Norman family of *de Crues*, and the Celtic word for great wood. The church contains a rare Georgian screen, plus stall-ends marked with local farm names. A curious revolving lych-gate can also be seen here.

CRYSTAL PALACE, Gt London *8 TQ37*
A high area named after the immense iron-and-glass structure built by Sir Joseph Paxton in Hyde Park, as a hall for the Great Exhibition of 1851. It was rebuilt on its last site near Sydenham, in 1854, and almost completely burnt down in 1936. Part of the grounds now form a public park, with a boating lake, children's zoo, and plaster prehistoric monsters. The BBC transmitting mast at Crystal Palace is over 700ft high, and the National Recreation Centre has a diving pool, swimming pool, a running track where world-class athletes compete, and an artificial ski-slope.

CUCKFIELD, W Sussex *8 TQ32*
Cuckfield is a developing village situated between the South Downs and Ashdown Forest, near Haywards Heath. Elizabethan and later Cuckfield Park shows a fine gatehouse, and now houses a school.

CULBONE, Somerset *5 SS84*
The smallest complete church still in regular use can be seen here. A walk through dense woodlands from Porlock Weir is required of the would-be visitor, and the building displays Norman to perpendicular styles. It measures 33ft by 12ft 18in, and contains a 14th-c screen and old benches.

CULLOMPTON, Devon *6 ST00*
This market town on the River Culm is noted for apple orchards which supply the local cider industry. Much of the town was burnt down in 1839, and Victorian additions stand alongside Georgian houses that escaped the blaze. The exceptionally-fine church has a splendid tower, screen, roof, and fan vaulting. Walronds House dates from the 17thc, and the nearby manor house, now a hotel, dates from 1603 and 1718. Bradfield House is a 16th-c building lying NE, now housing a school.

CUMNOR, Oxon *13 SP40*
A village sited on the side of 520ft Hurst Hill. Cumnor Hall has entirely disappeared, but was the house where Amy Robsart (Lady Robert Dudley) was found dead under tragic circumstances in 1560. The church has a rare contemporary statue of Queen Elizabeth I, and an unusual oak spiral-staircase of 1685.

CURRY RIVEL, Somerset *6 ST32*
Situated 2½m SW of Langport, this village includes a good 15th-c church displaying quaint gargoyles. The park of Burton Pynsent lies on the Taunton Road and contains Burton Steeple, erected by the first William Pitt to the memory of William Pynsent. Elizabethan Midelney Manor lies to the NE, off the Langport road.

DACRE, Cumbria *26 NY42*
A village on the river Dacre, situated 4½m SW of Penrith. The 14th-c castle is now a farmhouse, and the 13th-c church contains a chained Bible dated 1617. Four stone bears that were formerly on the castle keep can be seen in the churchyard.

DAGLINGWORTH, Glos *12 SO90*
The church in Daglingworth displays a great deal of Saxon work. Original Saxon carvings were found in the chancel arch in the 19thc, and three of these are now mounted on the walls of the nave. The church at Duntisbourne Rouse, 1m NW, also shows Saxon work plus a perpendicular saddleback-tower, a crypt, and a 14th-c churchyard cross.

Edgeworth Manor dates from 1685, with 19th-c additions, and lies 4m NW. The church here has a Norman chancel-cornice decorated with hideous faces and quaint tower gargoyles.

DALE ABBEY, Derbyshire *18 SK43*
Tradition has it that a baker from Derby came to live at Deepdale, a nearby area of wild marshland, in about 1130. He cut a dwelling and oratory from living sandstone, and was soon discovered by the owner of the land, Ralph FitzGeremunde. When this gentleman saw the poverty in which the hermit lived, he gave him the site of the hermitage and a tithe of his mill at Borrowash. After this the hermitage expanded and passed first to the Augustinian canons of Calke, who founded a priory on the site, and then to William de Grendon, who replaced the canons with monks. A few remains of the abbey still exist and the font, once used as a flower vase in the garden of Stanton Hall, is preserved in Dale Church. The latter is a curious little building under the same roof as an adjacent house. It contains traces of 13th-c mural paintings and numerous box pews.

DALSTON, Cumbria 26 NY35
A River-Calder village with a restored, partly-Norman church. Dalston Hall is of 15th- to 17th-c date, and carries a fine old tower. The quarries in this area have been worked since Roman times, and the district is splendidly situated for walks through fields and woods. Rose Castle, the ancient summer seat of the Bishops of Carlisle, lies 3m S.

DALTON-IN-FURNESS, Cumbria 21 SD27
This was the birthplace of artist George Romney (1734 to 1802), and his body lies in the local churchyard. A restored tower or castle of the 14thc that stands in the market place was originally built by Furness-Abbey monks as a courtroom; it has belonged to the Duke of Buccleuch's family since 1660 (NT).

DANBURY, Essex 9 TL70
Danbury is a village standing on a 400ft hill, affording a good view of the sailing craft in the Blackwater estuary to the E. The restored church dates largely from the 14thc, and houses some interesting wooden effigies of knights. Griffin Inn is a timber-framed building dating from the 16thc.

DANEHILL, E Sussex 8 TQ42
A village 6m NW of Uckfield, with the delightful little 16th- and 17th-c manor of Colin Godman to the W. The tiny courtyard is a feature of this house.

DARENTH, Kent 9 TQ57
Situated on the River Darent some 2m SE of Dartford, this place includes an interesting 10th- to 12th-c church which was partly built of Roman materials. A good Norman font can be seen inside the building, and the nave is of Saxon origin.

DARESBURY, Cheshire 17 SJ58
The Rev Charles Lutwidge Dodgson, better known as Lewis Carroll, was born here in 1832. Amongst the books that he wrote is the famous *Alice's Adventures in Wonderland*. The church is set among rhododendrons, and has a bright blue, red, and gold window depicting Alice, the Mad Hatter, and other characters that appear in the book.

DARLEY DALE, Derbyshire 18 SK26
The Darley Dale quarries have provided stone for many famous places, including the Thames Embankment and Hyde Park Corner. A number of early sepulchral stones can be seen in the 13th- to 14th-c church, and three ancient stone coffins have been found. The smallest of these was discovered under a pillar in the nave, and contained the remains of a child. The Song of Solomon window by Burne-Jones is notable, and the giant churchyard yew has a trunk measuring some 32ft round. This tree is thought to be at least 600 years old.

DARLINGTON, Durham 22 NZ21
This town is of Anglo-Saxon origin, and was once involved in the wool industry. Work included spinning from local fleeces, the weaving of fine linen, and carpet-making. As the profitability of wool began to drop, Darlington became a pioneering railway centre concerned with the manufacture of wagons, locomotives, tracks, and signals. It then branched out into general engineering, based on the needs of the railway, and particularly into structural work. This included bridge building. All these industries are still represented in the town, plus many more. The museum specializes in transport and local social history. George Stephenson's early steam engine, *Locomotion*, is on show at Bank Top Station. The fine early-English church was built between 1180 and 1220, and has been restored. It displays a 14th-c spire, 15th-c chancel stalls, and a 17th-c, gothic font-cover. Walworth Castle dates from the 16thc and lies 5m NW.

DARTFORD, Kent 8 TQ57
A busy River-Darent town which preserves a gateway from the old palace, a Georgian galleried inn, and several timbered houses. The restored parish church has a Norman tower and contains old brasses. It also houses the tomb of Sir John Spielman (1626), said to have been the first English paper-maker. Paper mills still operate here, and lie about ¾m from the town. A wild bird called the Dartford Warbler was first spotted in 1773 within this area. The Thames road-tunnel to Purfleet lies 2½m NE.

DARTINGTON, Devon 5 SX76
The historian JA Froude (1818 to 1894) was born in this River-Dart village. Dartington Hall is a restored 14th-c manor house comprising ancient buildings grouped round a quadrangle. These are now owned by a trust, which has made the manor a centre for rural education and experimentation, and a cultural centre for the district. Institutions so housed include a school, a college of arts, and an adult education centre. Activities include farming, horticulture, forestry, weaving, and building. The 14th-c banqueting hall is open to the public at certain times, and the entire complex is set amid gardens, courtyards, and terraces.

DARTMOOR
The upland district of Devon is bleak, wild, and often dangerous. Much of it now forms a 365sqm national park, and granite tors rise above the already rugged surface of the moor in many places. High Willhays (2,039ft) and Yes Tor (2,028ft) are the highest points. Heavy rainfall gives Princetown an annual figure of 100in, compared with 35in at Exeter, and the ground is made treacherous by deep bogs in many parts of the area.

An artillery range is often in use S of Okehampton, and visitors should check at the local post office for details of firing days. Two main roads traverse the area, intersecting at Two Bridges, and climbing to well over 1,000ft at different points. Beautiful wooded country fringes the moor along the river valleys of the Teign, Dart, Plym, and Tavy. Near West Okement River is the Black Tor Copse forest nature reserve. Ponies have run wild on Dartmoor for at least 1,000 years, and every autumn sees a round-up where many are captured and sold.

Prehistoric remains and ancient crosses are fairly common, and stone circles can be seen near Gidleigh and the source of the Teign. Some of these monuments are well-known under the name Greyweathers. The enclosure of Grimspound, near Postbridge, is more-or-less circular and surrounded by the remains of a stone wall. Enclosures of this type are probably the oldest recognizable dwelling places on the moor. Their functions depended on cattle raising and some cultivation.

Tin, lead, manganese, and copper were mined here in the middle ages, and the miners ruled their industry through Stannary courts at the towns where the tin was weighed. These included Ashburton, Tavistock, Chagford, and Plympton.

DARTMOUTH, Devon 5 SX85
A market town and fishing port of great historical interest, Dartmouth is sited on the W bank of the River Dart. Many naval expeditions, including the fleet sent by Edward III to assist at the Siege of Calais, sailed from here. A ruined stronghold built by the townspeople in 1537, with an inscribed stone recording the sailing of the *Mayflower* in 1520, can be seen in Bayard's Cove. Also here are 17th-c houses, and the remains of an old Butterwalk, *ie* a colonnaded arcade with carved overhangs, has been restored and now houses a nautical museum (AM).

Dartmouth is a popular holiday resort, offering sandy beaches at Castle and Compass Coves, and boat trips along the beautiful Dart estuary. The town is connected with Kingswear by car-ferry across the Dart, and steamers sail up the river to Totnes. Dartmouth Castle, a Tudor building on the site of an earlier castle, lies about 1m S (OACT). Close by, and at the mouth of the harbour, is the gothic Church of St Petroc (1641). The town church of St Saviour's dates from the 14thc and contains one of the finest carved screens and matching pulpit in Devon.

Kingswear Castle stands on the opposite shore. Both Dartmouth and Kingswear castles were built and positioned so that a thick chain could be stretched across the river in times of war, thus preventing entry by enemy vessels. The British Underwater Centre is located at Warfleet Creek, and the Royal Naval College, by Sir Aston Webb and opened in 1905, lies about 1m N.

DAVENTRY, Northants 13 SP56
Daventry is an ancient town, where the Wheatsheaf Inn of 1610 was Charles I's residence for a week before the Battle of Naseby. The Moot Hall dates from 1769, and the Church of Our Lady of Charity was once the grammar school. The latter originated in *c*1600. The masts of a broadcasting station situated outside the town are a familiar feature of the landscape. Borough Hill, a view-point and the site of an iron-age fort, lies 1m E.

DAWLEY, Salop 17 SJ60
Dawley is on the Shropshire Canal and stands 4m SE of Wellington. A fountain in the library forecourt commemorates Captain Matthew Webb, the first man to swim the English Channel (1875). He died in 1883 while trying to swim through the rapids of Niagara Falls. A new town is being built here as part of the Telford development.

DAWLISH, Devon 5 SX97
This is a quiet seaside resort near the mouth of the River Exe, with a sandy beach and red cliffs. Local architecture is partly Regency and partly Victorian; The Strand was built in the early 1800's, and still retains its elegant Regency character. The main railway-line to Penzance runs along the seafront, and Luscombe Castle was built by John Nash

in 1800. A large national wildfowl refuge is sited at Dawlish Warren.

DEAL, Kent 9 TR35
Deal was a limb of the old Cinque ports, and now prospers as a seaside resort cum fishing centre. Many Georgian houses exist here, and the beach is mainly of pebbles. Goodwin Sands are only 5m offshore, and ships have to pass close inshore in order to avoid them. Deal Castle was built by Henry VIII after he broke with Rome – at a time when fears were expressed that England might be invaded – and was constructed in the shape of a six-petalled flower. An attractive walk may be taken S along the cliffs to St Margaret-at-Cliffe, but the chalk is crumbling in places and great care is required.

DEAN, FOREST OF
This is a large area of wild woodland between the Rivers Wye and Severn. An extensive modern forestry plantation and newly-created national forest park lie within the district. Stretches of Roman road exist in places – notably near Blakeney – and private mine-workings can be seen in the vicinity of Cinderford. St Briavels Castle (S) was the administrative centre of the forest in Norman times; from 1680 onwards the main business was transacted in well-known Speech House, which still retains its Verderers' Court Room. Railway items preserved by the Dean Forest Railway Preservation Society can be seen at Parkend.

DEBENHAM, Suffolk 15 TM16
The River Deben runs beside the main street in this delightful small town. Rush-weaving is a local industry and has, at some time, been carried on in a building by the bridge. Moated Crows Hall is an Elizabethan house, and the local church dates back to the Saxon period.

DEDDINGTON, Oxon 13 SP43
A small market town on the River Cherwell, with many old houses built of honey-coloured stone. Castle Farm is a 16th-c dwelling where it is reputed that Charles I once slept. The tower carried by the interesting 14th-c church was rebuilt after it fell in 1635, and displays a fine north porch.

DEDHAM, Essex 15 TM03
This quiet attractive village lies in Constable country, and was one of the artist's favourite subjects. The High Street boasts several fine houses and two old inns; Sun Hotel is a half-timbered early 16th-c building with stable yard, and Marlborough Head Inn dates from c1500. Many of Constable's paintings feature the tower of the 15th- and 16th-c church. Insignia of the Guilds of Weavers and Millers, who generously endowed the church, are among heraldic shields on the nave roof. Dedham Vale is an area of outstanding natural beauty, and the River Stour flows near the village. Artist Sir Alfred Munnings specialized in painting horses, and lived in Castle House. Many of his paintings are on show here. Southfields, once the home and working headquarters of a prosperous Tudor weaver, is a timbered and gabled building S of the village.

DEENE, Northants 19 SP99
Interesting old cottages are preserved in the village, and the church was restored in memory of the Seventh Earl of Cardigan. Cardigan led the ill-fated Charge of the Light Brigade at Balaclava, and his name is perpetuated in the familiar wool garment. Deene Park, a beautiful 16th-c mansion, is the ancestral home of the Brudenells. It is set in an extensive park which contains rare trees and a large lake (OACT). Thomas Brudenell was created Earl of Cardigan by Charles II.

DEERHURST, Glos 12 SO82
A village on the River Severn, where the highly-interesting Saxon church houses a remarkable carved font and is thought to date from the 7thc. Also contained in the church is a 14th-c brass depicting Sir John Cassey and his wife's dog, Terri. This is a very rare example of a named pet appearing on an old brass. Near by stands Odda's Chapel (AM), a Saxon building dating from 1056. This was erected by the Lord of the Manor, and is attached to a half-timbered house.

DELABOLE, Cornwall 4 SX08
Slate quarries which have been worked for over 300 years have made this village quite famous. Visits to the workings have been discontinued, but a path through Old Delabole allows impressive views into the workings.

DELAMERE, Cheshire 17 SJ56
Woodlands to the N of the village are all that remain of Delamere Forest. An ancient camp which once existed on Eddisbury Hill was, quite possibly, of Celtic origin.

DENBY DALE, W Yorks 22 SE20
This village lies 8m W of Barnsley, and is noted for its once-yearly manufacture of a giant pie. The first of these was baked here in 1788, to commemorate George III's recovery from mental illness, and the 1964 pie was the largest ever. Enough money was raised, by selling portions of this enormous savoury, to pay for a new community centre.

DENHAM, Bucks 8 TQ08
An attractive village where The Savoy, and 17th-c Hills House, are of particular interest. The 14th-c church contains several old brasses, and 17th-c Denham Place is a formal mansion built from 1688 to 1700 for Sir Roger Hill. The latter houses fine tapestries and Dutch friezes.

DENNINGTON, Suffolk 15 TM26
The lovely 14th- to 15th-c church in this village is noted for its lavish parclose screens, a carved and painted 15th-c pyx-cover, and old bench-ends.

DENT, Cumbria 21 SD78
Set in picturesque Dentdale, this River-Dee village comprises old houses grouped around narrow cobbled streets. The church is of late-perpendicular style, and displays good Jacobean woodwork. Adam Sedgwick, a noted 18th-c geologist, is commemorated by a monument. Whernside rises 2,414ft SE of the community.

DENVER, Norfolk 14 TF60
The 13th-c mainly-perpendicular church lost its spire in a great storm of 1895. Denver Hall is a fine old house which was the birthplace of Captain Manby, a contemporary of Nelson and the inventor of ship-to-shore rocket apparatus for life-saving. A series of sluices, some by Rennie, drain the area; Denver Sluice is an important part of the Fen drainage system. Also of interest is a local windmill.

DERBY, Derbyshire 18 SK33
Derby is an ancient county town on the River Derwent, and was once a Roman camp. It was here that Bonnie Prince Charlie stopped while marching to London with a force of 7,000 troops, and decided to advance no farther. As long ago as the Norman Conquest the town had six churches and a population in excess of 2,000. More recent times have seen it develop as a manufacturing town.

Silk mills were established here in 1717, and industry expanded even more with the building of Midland Railway's great locomotive and coach works, now run by British Rail. Factories of the Rolls-Royce company are sited here, and a monument to the engineer Sir Henry Royce stands in the Arboretum park. The cathedral, formerly the parish church, was rebuilt in 1725. It displays a fine 16th-c tower and houses the tomb of famous Bess of Hardwick (Elizabeth, Countess of Shrewsbury). Near the cathedral are The Dolphin, a former coaching inn, and The Bell.

Friargate is a street with several Georgian houses and the ancient Church of St Werburgh. Manuscripts in this church record the marriage of Dr Samuel Johnson to Elizabeth 'Tetty' Porter. St Peter's Church was mentioned in the Domesday Book, and houses a Flemish chest. A 16th-c building in St Peter's churchyard was once Derby School. This is where John Flamsteed, the first English Astronomer Royal, was educated. The county hall has a façade

1   Luscombe Castle
2   The Strand
3   Wildfowl Refuge (Dawlish Warren)

dating from 1660, and the town hall dominates the market place. The latter building is no longer the seat of local government; since 1949, this has occupied a fine complex of buildings beside the river at Morledge. St Helen's House is a notable mid 18th-c building now housing a school, and the 18th-c bridge over the river carries a restored 14th-c brigg, or bridge chapel. The nearby birthplace of 19th-c philosopher Herbert Spencer is marked by a tablet.

Painter Joseph Wright was another native of Derby, and some of his paintings are hung in an art gallery annexed to a museum. The latter has a Prince Charlie room, and the Arboretum contains a plague stone as a reminder of the time when Derby was devastated by disease. The town museum contains a scale working-layout of the former Midland Railway, and the Industrial Museum, housed by the Old Silk Mill in Sowter Road, contains a Rolls-Royce aero-engine collection and an introduction to local industries (OACT).

Royal Crown Derby porcelain works still produces the fine bone china for which it has long been famous. A few remains of Darley Abbey lie 1m N, and the town's amenities include first-class cricket and football grounds.

DERBY HAVEN, Isle of Man 20 SC26
A small village to the E of Castletown Bay, including Derby Fort (1645) and the remains of a 12th-c chapel on St Michael's Isle. Ronaldsway Airport lies ½m N.

DEREHAM, Norfolk 15 TF91
Also known as East Dereham, this market town has an 18th-c town hall and several houses of the same period. The early-English to perpendicular church displays a detached bell-tower, and contains a 16th-c Flemish chest, painted ceilings, and the tomb of the poet Cowper. Several pargetted cottages of 1502 have been restored, and may have been the early home of Bishop Bonner. They now house a museum which exhibits items of local archaeological interest, plus summer displays of rural crafts. An ornate gallows town-sign was erected in 1954 to celebrate Dereham's 1,300 years of history. Dumpling Green lies 1½m S and was the birthplace of George Borrow, the rural poet, in 1803.

DERE STREET
This is the name given to a Northumberland branch of Watling Street, the Roman road that links Corbridge with the Scottish border and continues beyond into the Cheviots, E of Carter Bar.

DERSINGHAM, Norfolk 14 TF63
A village 8½m from King's Lynn, where the decorated and perpendicular church preserves a notable 14th-c chest. A fine barn of 1671 can also be seen, and the village belongs partly to the Royal Estate of Sandringham.

DESBOROUGH, Northants 13 SP88
The church here has a 14th-c tower and 15th-c screen. A Saxon mirror and necklace found in the area are now in the care of the British Museum.

DEVIZES, Wilts 7 SU06
Devizes is a pleasant old market town surrounded by rich agricultural country. It once lay on the boundary between three manors; hence the name as a corruption of *ad divisas*, meaning 'at the boundary'.

A castle was constructed at this unenviable location, and had an understandably turbulent history. At one time it formed part of the dowry of the queens of England, and although it was demolished after the Civil Wars, a little of the old building survives in the present 19th-c castle. The latter is now a block of flats. St John's Church was built for the castle in c1150, and St Mary's for the town in about the same period. Both display fine Norman work, and the former has an impressive tower. The Bear Inn was visited by Fanny Burney in 1730, and the landlord was the father of painter Sir Thomas Lawrence. The museum in Long Street has a rich and important collection of local antiquities, including finds from Wiltshire neolithic, bronze-age, and iron-age sites. Many good Georgian houses stand in this stone-built town, and timbered houses of c1500 can be seen in St John's Alley.

An ornamental market cross carries an inscription telling the tale of Ruth Pierce, a woman who died suddenly in 1753 after cheating in the local market. Brownston House and the old town hall are both interesting buildings, and Greystone House, in the High Street, is dated 1731. The Kennet and Avon Canal passes close to the town, and rises with the aid of twenty-nine locks by Rennie. Little traffic now uses this waterway, but it is stocked with coarse fish as an amenity for anglers. Restoration of the canal is planned for the future.

DEVONPORT, Devon 5 SX45
This important naval dockyard was founded on the Hamoaze, the estuary of the Tamar, in 1691. The estuary leads into Plymouth Sound, and the town is now a part of Plymouth. Royal William Victualling Yard at East Stonehouse is largely by John Rennie, and includes a statue of William IV. A town hall of 1821 is by John Foulston, who was also responsible for a number of other buildings in the area. Gun Wharf dates from 1718 to 1725, and the Royal Naval Hospital from 1761. The parish church was built in 1771, and Government House (Mount Wise) in 1795. Devonport was the birthplace of Captain Scott in 1868 and a monument to him can be seen at Mount Wise. Stoke Damerel is the mother church of Devonport, and contains a plaster pulpit from the Great Exhibition of 1851. Ships' masts have been used to form the nave-supporting pillars. A car ferry to Torpoint in Cornwall plies from Gun Wharf, and the seaward view encompasses distant Eddystone Lighthouse.

DEWSBURY, W Yorks 22 SE22
Dewsbury is the centre of the old West Riding heavy-woollen industry, and is situated on the River Calder. It also conducts a number of other industries. The rebuilt church shows some 14th-c glass and Saxon and Norman stones. Thornhill parish church is largely of 15th-c date (restored), and houses Runic inscriptions and ancient glass. Part of the Moot Hall dates back to the 13thc.

DIDCOT, Oxon 13 SU59
An important railway junction 4½m SE of Abingdon, where the decorated and perpendicular church retains two rood-loft doorways. A large new power

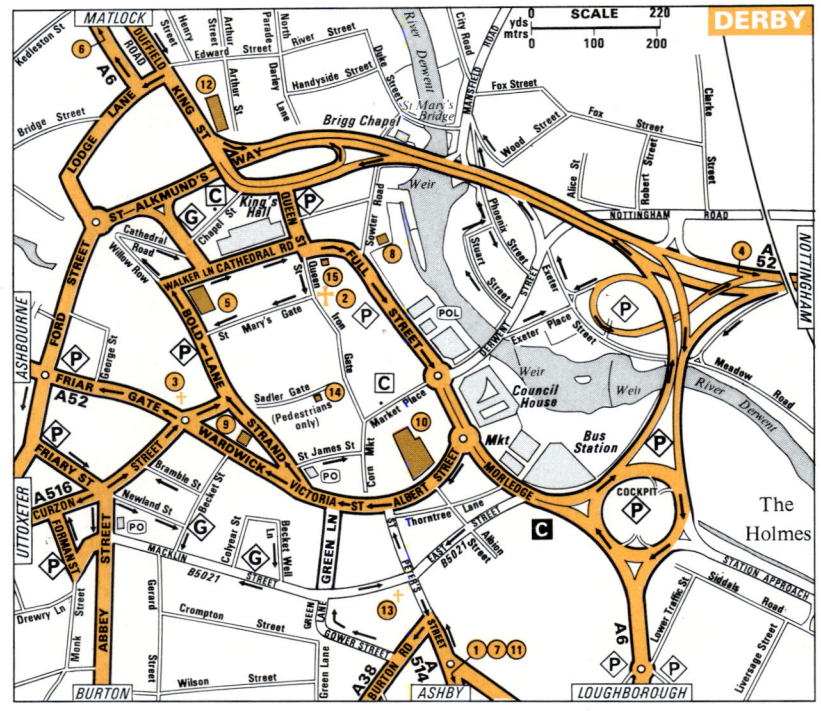

 1 Arboretum and Plague Stone
 2 Cathedral
 3 Church of St Werburgh
 4 County Cricket Ground
 5 County Hall
 6 Darley Abbey Remains
 7 Football Ground
 8 Industrial Museum
 9 Museum and Art Gallery
10 Old Town Hall
11 Royal Crown Derby Porcelain Works
12 St Helen's House (school)
13 St Peter's Church & ex Derby School
14 The Bell Inn
15 The Dolphin Inn

station operates in this area, and a Great Western Railway museum is of interest.

DIDDLEBURY, Salop *12 SO58*
A Corvedale village where pre-Conquest work can be seen in the church, including typical herringbone masonry. Elsych is an Elizabethan house lying 1m SW.

DILWYN, Herefs & Worcs *12 SO45*
This attractive village of timbered black-and-white houses includes Luntley Court (1674), with its old dovecote. The church contains notable 15th-c screenwork and a knight's tomb which dates from c1300.

DINTON, Bucks *8 SP71*
The village church has a Norman doorway, and the adjacent manor house displays a great deal of 16th-c work. Dinton folly is a hexagonal structure dating from 1769. Old stocks and a whipping-post have been preserved.

DINTON, Wilts *7 SU03*
Three beautiful houses lie on the outskirts of this hillside village. Dinton Park surrounds the 19th-c Philipps House (NT), now a YMCA rest home, and the building itself has a white neo-Grecian façade. Hyde's House (NT) is Tudor and 18thc, and ¼m E is ivy-covered Little Clarendon (NT), dating from the 15thc and open on application. Adjoining the latter is 17th-c Lawes Cottage (NT), one-time home of composer and friend of John Milton, William Lawes.

DISLEY, Cheshire *18 SJ98*
Lyme Park (NT) is set in a beautiful deer park of over 1,300 acres, some 2½m SW of Disley. The Elizabethan house, altered in 1726 and 1817 (OACT), has a fine Palladian frontage, Jacobean rooms, and an interesting collection of pictures and furnishings. A nearby hilltop is surmounted by a 15th-c church which displays a beautiful timbered nave roof, decorated with bosses and angels. Stained glass in the east window is German, and originates mainly from the 16thc. Another feature of the church is a monument to Thomas Legh of Lyme Park.

DISS, Norfolk *15 TM17*
Diss is an old market town that was built round the edge of a six-acre lake. Its decorated and perpendicular church contains two 15th-c chancel chapels built by local trade guilds. Thelveton Hall dates from 1592, and lies 4m NE. Attractive shops, old inns, and a mixture of Tudor, Georgian, and Victorian houses can be seen in the town.

DITCHLING, E Sussex *8 TQ31*
An old village of 16th-c houses, including one that Henry VIII gave to Anne of Cleves. The cruciform church is mainly of early-English style, and preserves a chest of the same period. Sir Frank Brangwyn, the eminent painter, died here in 1956. Ditchling Beacon (813ft), lies 1½m S and is one of the highest points in the South Downs. A road climbs almost to the summit, from which an extensive view can be enjoyed. Ditchling Gibbet stands on a common 2m N, as a reminder of a pedlar's execution after being convicted of triple murder in 1734.

DITTISHAM, Devon *5 SX85*
Wooded river-scenery adds a certain charm to this pleasant River-Dart village, and a 15th-c church houses a contemporary pulpit carved in the shape of a wine glass. Greenway House is associated with Sir Walter Raleigh, who spent boyhood holidays here with his step-brother Humphrey.

DOBCROSS, Gt Manchester *22 SD90*
A village of old weavers' cottages, 6½m NE of Ashton-under-Lyne. This was one of the places where weaving machinery was first manufactured.

DODDINGTON, Lincs *19 SK87*
The hall is an Elizabethan structure set in fine gardens, with an approach guarded by a picturesque gabled gatehouse (OACT). Fine china and furnishings can be seen inside the house.

DODINGTON, Avon *12 ST78*
Dodington House lies to the N and was built for Christopher Codrington by James Wyatt in 1813 (OACT). The fine park that surrounds it is by Capability Brown, and contains two lakes and a number of rare trees. Wyatt, who died as the result of an accident in the same year, designed the Palladian-style house as an almost perfect square, with a west portico built so that a carriage could be driven through to the main entrance. The church, also by Wyatt, is in the Greek style.

DONCASTER, S Yorks *22 SE50*
Doncaster, known as *Danum* under the Romans, was subsequently a Saxon settlement before the Norman occupation. It is now well-known as a busy industrial town.

The parish church of St George was rebuilt by Gilbert Scott in 1854, and displays a 170ft tower. The Mansion House, by James Paine, is a fine Georgian building and one of the three mansion houses in England originally intended as mayoral residences (the other two are in London and York). It was built from 1745 to 1748, and the ballroom has an ornamental ceiling and Adam-style white-marble fireplaces. A cross standing by a stretch of the former Great North Road was re-erected in 1793. Both the museum and art gallery are of interest, and the former exhibits many Roman relics. The famous St Leger horse-race is run on Town Moor racecourse, 1½m SE, in the second week of September. Cusworth Hall lies 1½m SW, and is an 18th-c house now serving as an industrial museum. It shows fine chimney-pieces and a chapel, and is set in extensive grounds that are open all year.

DONINGTON, Lincs *19 TF23*
The school in this ancient market town was founded in 1701, and the early-English to perpendicular church carries a fine tower and spire. A tablet commemorates Captain Matthew Flinders, who was born here in 1774 and became a pioneer of Australian exploration.

DONINGTON LE HEATH, Leics *18 SK41*
This manor house is built of Charnwood stone and, dating back to the 13th-c, is one of the oldest in England. It has been well-restored by Leicestershire County Council and contains a collection of old furniture (OACT).

DONNINGTON, Berks *7 SU46*
Remains of Donnington Castle (AM) include a 14th-c gatehouse. The building was defended during the Civil War, and its outworks presented a formidable barrier to the attackers. Laying siege to this castle proved so difficult that the second battle of Newbury was provoked. Restored Elizabethan almshouses can be seen in the village, and Donnington Grove is a notable gothic-revival house of about 1795. Donnington Castle House is of 17th- and 18th-c construction.

DORCHESTER, Dorset *6 SY69*
A pleasant, bustling town on the River Frome, called *Durnovaria* by the Romans and Casterbridge in Thomas Hardy's novels. Fascinating Roman remains that include several mosaics have been excavated in Colliton Park. The main-road routes were originally laid down by the Romans, and the County Museum in High Street West displays a fine collection of prehistoric and Roman antiquities. Hardy's manuscript for *The Mayor of Casterbridge* can also be seen here.

The six Tolpuddle Martyrs were sentenced to transportation in the Old Crown Court of the Old Shire Hall (1834), for demanding a wage increase. This was at a time when unions and fraternities were barred by law. Ironically, this building now forms a Tolpuddle Memorial. Other notorious legal proceedings that have taken place in this town are associated with the bloody Judge Jeffreys. His harsh sentencing of Monmouth rebels at the Bloody Assize of 1685 gave him a place as one of the butchers of history. More than 300 prisoners were tried, of whom 292 were sentenced to death and seventy-four hung within the city walls. Jeffreys was 1st Baron of Wem and later became Lord Chancellor, but after the fall of James II he was sent to the Tower, and eventually died in confinement. His lodgings still exist in West High Street, and the chair and table he used can be seen in the Council Chamber. The Assize was held in a courtroom that is now part of the Antelope Hotel.

Other interesting buildings in Dorchester include an old grammar school, 17th-c Napper's Mite almshouses, and the King's Arms. The almshouses now form a small shopping precinct. Dorset Military Museum is housed in the Keep, and covers nearly 300 years of military history. A monument to William Barnes, a poet who wrote in the local dialect, stands outside 15th-c St Peter's Church; the latter displays a 13th-c doorway, 14th-c Easter-Sepulchre, and a 90ft tower. The suburb of Fordington includes Norman and later St George's Church, notable for its tower.

Prehistoric Maiden Castle, considered the finest fort of its kind in Britain, is a gigantic earthwork occupying 120 acres 1½m SW. It was probably built originally as a defence against neighbouring tribes, but has been altered and enlarged several times. The original bank-and-ditch system was multiplied to counter increased use of the sling in warfare. Some 5,000 people could live inside the ramparts at the fort's greatest extent. Maiden Castle was of great strategic importance during the Roman invasion, and was captured by *Vespasian's* legions. A Roman temple has been discovered within the fortifications.
cont

Other prehistoric remains near Dorchester include Maumbury Rings, originally a henge monument of the bronze age, and later converted into an amphitheatre by the Romans. Boundary Camp is another hill fort, situated ½m from the town, and covering an area of some 20 acres.

DORCHESTER, Oxon 13 SU59
A pleasant village dating back to the bronze age, situated on the River Thame near its junction with the Thames. It served both as a Roman station and subsequently as a sizeable Saxon town. The exceptionally interesting trans-Norman to decorated abbey contains 13th-c glass and preserves a fine Jesse window. Another of the windows has been restored as a memorial to Sir Winston Churchill. The White Hart is a picturesque old inn in a street of old half-timbered and brick houses.

DORE, S Yorks 18 SK38
Dore lies 5m SW of Sheffield, near the Derbyshire border. It was here that Ecgbert, Saxon king of Wessex, received the submission of the Northumbrians in 829. This forged England into a single kingdom for the first time in history, an event now commemorated by an inscribed tablet.

DORKING, Surrey 8 TQ14
Bow-fronted shop windows facing on to narrow streets are a feature of this ancient market town, which is pleasantly set in the Surrey hills. The High Street follows the line of Roman Stane Street, and the Saxons had a village here. Charles Dickens stayed at 15th-c White Horse Inn, and the hotel at Burford Bridge is where Nelson and Lady Nelson finally separated in 1800. Leith Hill stands 4m SW, and at 965ft is the highest point in SE England. The view from the tower at the top (NT) includes thirteen counties, and in fine weather both St Paul's Cathedral and the English Channel near Shoreham can be seen. Milton Court is a 17th-c gabled building which stands 1m W, and the English composer, Ralph Vaughan Williams, lived at White Gates. George Meredith, novelist and poet, is buried in the nearby churchyard.

DORMSTON, Herefs & Worcs 12 SO95
Moat farm is a gabled black-and-white farmhouse that is considered one of the most attractive in the county. An interesting old pigeon-house stands near by. A timbered 16th-c tower displayed by the church is characteristic of the region.

DORSTONE, Herefs & Worcs 11 SO34
This village lies at the head of the Golden Valley, 5½m E of Hay. The rebuilt church has some old glass, and preserves a 13th-c tower arch. Arthur's Stone (AM), the remains of a neolithic long barrow, lies 1m N on Merbach Hill. Remains of Snodhill Castle (c1200) can be seen to the SE, and Snodhill Court Farm is a 17th-c house.

DOUGLAS, Isle of Man 20 SC37
Douglas is the chief town of the Isle of Man, and a well-known holiday resort. Its extensive sands and fine 2m promenade run along the wide bay, and contribute to the town's popularity among holiday makers.

Horse-drawn trams, known locally as toast-racks, are still a feature of the resort. Electric trains run N to Port St Mary and Port Erin. The House of Keys is the site of the Manx Parliament, the Tynwald, whose Scandinavian origins are earlier than those of Westminster. It stands on Prospect Hill, and the nearby Manx National Museum displays local antiquities, natural-history, and folklore collections. Offshore Conister Rock bears a tower of refuge for shipwrecked mariners, and was erected by Sir William Hillary in 1832. Sir William was founder of the National Lifeboat Institution. A mansion called The Nunnery stands S of the town and was rebuilt in the 18thc; it includes a chapel of earlier date. Castle Mona Hotel was originally the residence of the Duke of Atholl, the last Lord of Man; Fort Anne Hotel is sited on Douglas Head, and was once the home of Sir William Hillary. The famous Tourist Trophy motor-cycling races are held in June, and the Manx Grand Prix is held in September.

DOULTING, Somerset 6 ST64
A village situated 2m E of Shepton Mallet, noted for its quarries. Stone from here was used in the construction of Wells Cathedral. A fine old tithe barn is also of particular interest, and a good cross can be seen in the churchyard.

DOVEDALE, Derbyshire & Staffs 18 SK15
Dovedale is a beautifully-wooded ravine in the Peak District, through which the River Dove flows. It is partly-owned by the NT, and is accessible only by foot. Dr Johnson greatly admired its scenery, and this particular stretch of the river is associated with the famous anglers, Izaak Walton and Charles Cotton. Picturesque features of the ravine include formations variously named The Twelve Apostles, Lion Rock, Viator's Bridge, and Tissington Spires. Beyond these are the Dove Holes. A continuation of the dale to the N leads to lovely Wolfscote and Beresford Dales.

DOVER, Kent 9 TR34
This ancient town was once the walled Roman city *Dubris*, and the chief of the ancient Cinque Ports. These ports were given certain privileges, and were expected to supply a certain number of ships for the royal fleet in return. Dover is now well-known as a cross-Channel ferry terminus. The skyline above the town is dominated by Dover Castle, an extensive Norman and later building which is one of the best known structures of its type in England (OACT).

Built on a magnificent site that shows evidence of occupation or fortification from prehistoric times, the castle commands the harbour, and was an important link in England's defence system for hundreds of years. Kings in the Middle Ages spent vast sums on its fortification, and it naturally became the most important building in the town.

The Pharos is a lighthouse of Roman origin which stands within the walls of the castle, near the Saxon church of St Mary de Castro. St Edmund's Chapel, 12th- and 13th-c, is one of the smallest in England. The town hall incorporates the 13th-c Hall of Maison Dieu. Near by is Maison Dieu House, which dates from 1665. An interesting museum is situated beside the town hall. A granite memorial in the shape of an aeroplane can be seen in North Fall meadow. This was raised to Louis Bleriot, the first man to fly an aeroplane across the Channel. He landed here in 1909 after his historic flight.

Shakespeare's Cliff is a famous 350ft landmark of white chalk. The North Downs (included in an area of outstanding beauty) finish here, and Dover is the destination of many cross-Channel swimmers.

DOVERCOURT, Essex 15 TM23
Dovercourt has good sandy beaches, and is situated on the Stour estuary. The churchyard contains the grave of Captain Fryatt, a First World War hero.

DOWN AMPNEY, Glos 12 SU09
A Tudor manor house is the village venue for an annual art exhibition (OACT), and the partly-Norman church shows a Jacobean screen and several medieval effigies of knights and ladies. Composer Vaughan Williams was born in the local vicarage, and the canopied village cross was restored in 1578.

DOWNE, Gt London 8 TQ46
This attractive village is situated on a ridge of the North Downs, and contains many flint cottages. Down House lies to the S, and was the former home of scientist Charles Darwin. It was he who formulated the theory of evolution, and the house is now a museum. The church contains interesting brasses.

DOWNHAM, Lancs 21 SD74
An attractive, stone-built village which includes a Tudor hall. The church has a 14th-c tower, and Pendle Hill rises to the S. The latter was once associated with Lancashire Witches, and is described in Robert Neil's book *Mist Over Pendle*. The district in which it stands is an area of outstanding natural beauty.

DOWNHAM MARKET, Norfolk 14 TF60
A small market town situated on the River Ouse, in an area where a drainage scheme was started by Charles I's Dutch engineer Vermuyden. The original idea was to rid the land of excess water, in an attempt to provide resources needed for agricultural development. Part of this development included the building of a new market town, which was to be called Charlemont. Flood tides destroyed the project, but modern techniques are now succeeding where Vermuyden pioneered.

DOWNTON, Wilts 7 SU12
Downton lies on the River Avon, some 7m SE of Salisbury. The flint-and-stone church is of trans-Norman to perpendicular style, and carries a fine tower. An old cross can be seen in the village street. The Moot is a 17th-c house, with grounds including earthworks which are said to have been the meeting place of a Saxon parliament.

DRAX, N Yorks 22 SE62
This River-Ouse village is now dominated by a power station. The church is mainly Norman and contains a screen of later date. Camblesforth Hall (W) dates from c1700, and the grammar school was founded in 1669.

DREWSTEIGNTON, Devon 5 SX79
The eastern fringe of Dartmoor borders the boundaries of this attractive village. A house dating from the 16thc can be seen near the 15th-c granite-built church, and the latter displays a two-storeyed embattled porch. Spinsters Rock is a notable cromlech situated some 2m to the W, and near by are Cranbrook Castle and Prestonbury. Both of these

are prehistoric forts. Fingle Bridge is a beauty spot 1m SE on the River Teign, and 2m SW stands Castle Drogo, a modern structure designed by Sir Edwin Lutyens. The latter is sometimes described as the last stately home to be built in England.

DRIFFIELD, GREAT, Humberside 23 TA05
This agricultural town has a church which displays a lofty perpendicular tower and late trans-Norman nave. An interesting private museum exhibits local antiquities.

DROITWICH, Herefs & Worcs 12 SO86
Medicinal properties of this spa town's brine-baths were known to the Romans. This people called it *Salinae*, the place of salt. Rock salt was worked here from Saxon and Norman times to the present century, but the industry has now moved 4m to Stoke Prior.

Medieval churches in the town include St Andrew's and St Peter's. The former has a small chapel to St Richard de Wych, patron saint of Droitwich, and the latter is of Norman to perpendicular origin and contains a fine monument dated 1616. It was in St Peter's that Edward Winslow, one of the Pilgrim Fathers, was baptized in 1595. A more recent church is famous for striking mosaics which depict the life of Sir Richard. Salwarpe Court lies 2½m SW and is a fine half-timbered Elizabethan house. Westwood Park (2m E) is also Elizabethan, but has been built to an unusual plan and includes a picturesque gatehouse.

DRONFIELD, Derbyshire 18 SK37
A small town with a number of 18th-c houses, 6m NW of Chesterfield. The partly 14th-c church houses a good Jacobean pulpit and a curious brass (c1390) of two brother priests.

DROXFORD, Hants 7 SU61
Izaak Walton fished in the River Meon here, and the 13th- to 15th-c church shows four mass-dials. The railway station was used as the allied HQ before the 1944 Normandy landing, during the last war.

DUDDINGTON, Northants 19 SK90
The River Welland flows among the attractive houses that make up this village, and the old watermill of 1664 is one of the best-known in this county.

DUDLEY, W Midlands 18 SO99
Dudley is known as a centre of the iron industry, and rises on ridges to a height of 800ft above sea level. Impressive remains of a 13th-c and later castle (AM) include walls up to 8ft thick, plus large 16th-c additions. Its location makes it a splendid viewpoint and a zoo is kept in the grounds. Many of the zoo animals are accommodated in pits that were made during mineral extraction. Remains of a priory are sited in a wooded valley below Castle Hill. Several striking new buildings in the town include the town hall of 1928, council houses of 1935, and arts centre of 1947. Wren's Nest Hill lies NW of the town, and is well-known among geologists and fossil collectors. It is now protected as a national nature reserve.

DUFFIELD, Derbyshire 18 SK34
Foundations of a large Norman castle (NT) exist here, and the hall is of Elizabethan origin, with Victorian additions. It now houses a school. George Stephenson's 147ft sighting tower stands on Chevin Hill, and a number of Georgian buildings can be seen in the town.

DUFTON, Cumbria 26 NY62
Situated below the Pennine escarpment, this pretty village lies in the shadow of prominent Dufton Pike. An extraordinary cleft in the hills is known as High Cup Nick and lies 3m E. It displays the dark bands and columns of rock that make up the Great Whin Sill, and provides a splendid view towards Eden Valley and the Lakeland fells. The hamlet of Knock is 2m NW, and a steep road climbs for 4½m to the summit of Great Dun Fell (2,780ft), probably England's highest motoring road. The immediate approach to the summit is not accessible, as it is the site of an RAF radar station.

DUKERIES, THE
The Dukeries is the name given to a Nottinghamshire area between Worksop and Ollerton, so called because it includes the great ducal parks of Clumber, Rufford, Thoresby, and Welbeck. Part of Sherwood Forest is included in the area. A small section to the S of the lake in Clumber Park (NT) is open daily, and the entrance is off the A614 Ollerton to Bawtry Road, 200yds S of Normanton Inn. The modern church, by Anthony Salvin, is approached by a lime-tree

1 Castle, Pharos Lighthouse, and Church of St Mary De Castro
2 Louis Bleriot Memorial
3 Maison Dieu House
4 Museum
5 Shakespeare's Cliff
6 St Edmund's Chapel
7 Town Hall and Hall of Maison Dieu

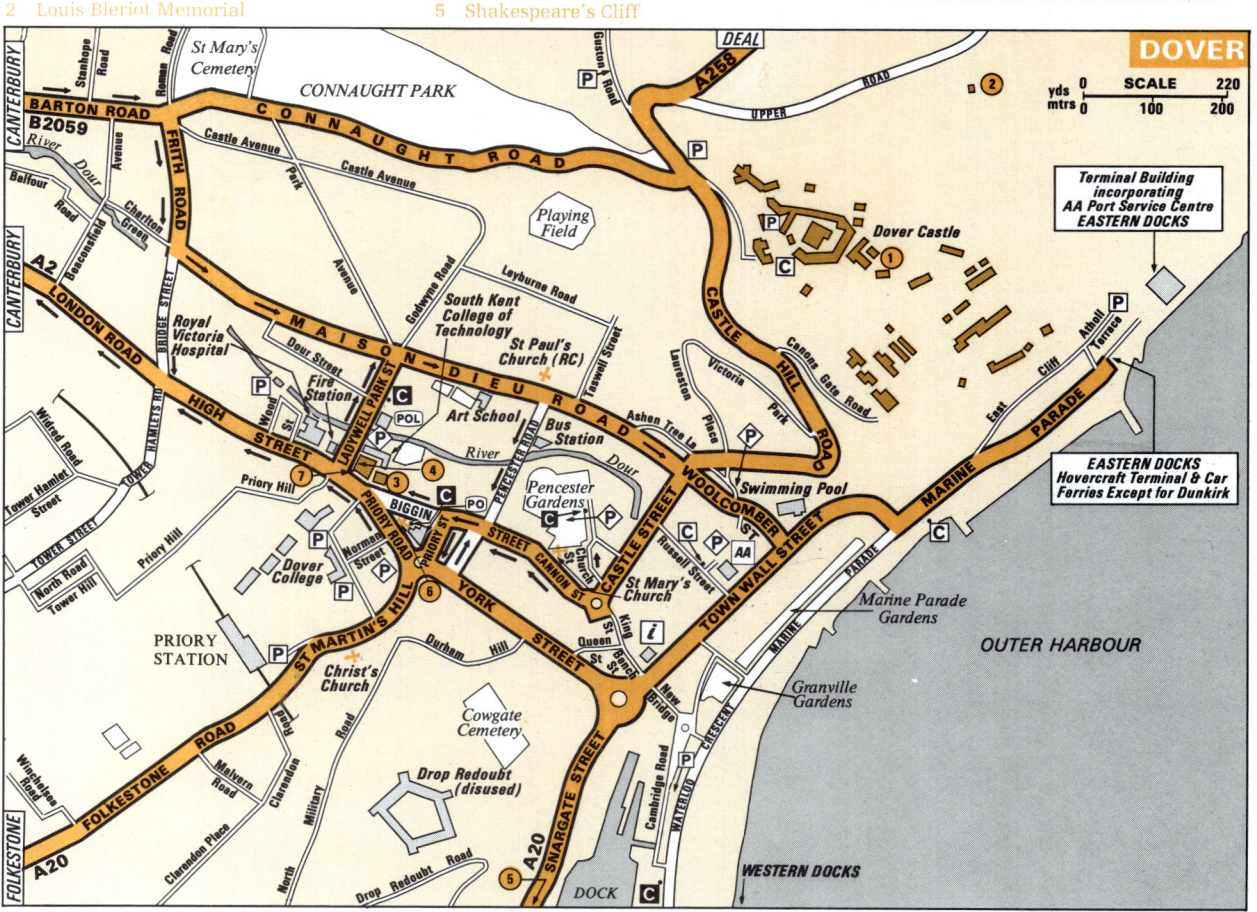

avenue. Rufford Abbey has been demolished, except for the 12th-c monastic remains, and its fine park lies off the A614 2m S of Ollerton.

The most important of the Dukeries' surviving mansions are Thoresby and Welbeck. The former is a Victorian hall standing in its own park near Budby (OACT). Welbeck Abbey is a 17th-c house with curious underground passages and rooms, standing in a lake-watered park between Cuckney and Worksop (not open).

DULVERTON, Somerset 5 SS92
Beautifully situated on the River Barle, on the borders of Exmoor, this is a fishing resort and tourist centre. Tarr Steps (AM, NT) is the local name for a prehistoric stone clapper-bridge over the River Barle, 5m NW below Winsford Hill.

DULWICH, Gt London 8 TQ37
Dulwich Village contains many of the Georgian houses that exist in this residential suburb, and Dulwich College Art Gallery was the first public art gallery to be opened in London. Sir John Soane was responsible for the building, which houses a famous collection of pictures. Dulwich College is a public school to the S, and numbers P G Wodehouse among its past pupils.

DUMMER, Hants 7 SU54
The small early-English to perpendicular church has a rare panelled 15th-c canopy over the chancel arch, which was probably part of a former rood. George Whitefield once preached from the late 14th-c pulpit, and the manor house is of 18th-c origin. Lying to the S is the partly 17th-c Grange.

DUNCHIDEOCK, Devon 5 SX88
A little village near Exeter, where the small red-sandstone church displays a particularly fine screen. Haldon House was built 1m S on the site of Sir Lawrence Palk's 18th-c home. Sir Lawrence was governor of Madras, and it was he who built the curious Belvedere Tower which stands on a hill near the house (OACT).

DUNDRY, Avon 6 ST56
Dundry stands high above the S side of Bristol, in a situation affording remarkable panoramic views. Interesting fossils have been found on Dundry Hill. The Tudor church tower incorporates an elaborate parapet, and a large dole table stands in the churchyard.

DUNGENESS, Kent 9 TR01
This place is most famous for the large nuclear-power station that has been erected on its bleak shingle promontory Sharing this isolated site are an old and new lighthouse, and the foreshore slopes so steeply into the sea that large ships can sail close inshore. A 12,000-acre, national nature and bird reserve has been established here, and the bird observatory has recorded more than 200 local and visiting species in ten years. Fishing is excellent, but strong currents make bathing and boating hazardous.

DUNMOW, GREAT, Essex 14 TL62
One of the first lifeboats was tested on the local Doctor's Pond, by its inventor Lionel Lukin, in 1785. The customary Dunmow Flitch trial, now carried out at Great Dunmow, was originally associated with the former priory of Little Dunmow. Every four years the town holds this mock trial, and a flitch or side of bacon is presented to any married couple who have not had a brawl in their home, nor wished to be unmarried, for the last 12 months-and-a-day. The town hall is partly Tudor.

DUNSFOLD, Surrey 8 TQ03
A Wealden village where the cruciform-shaped church is approached through tunnels of clipped yews. It is of the decorated period and contains interesting ancient woodwork. The 13th-c benches are of particular interest. Burningfold is one of the old houses still existing in this area, and displays 16th-c timbering.

DUNSFORD, Devon 5 SX88
Cob-and-thatch cottages are a main feature of this pretty Upper-Teign village. The winding street climbs to a medieval church and the Teign flows through a wooded gorge which is a noted beauty spot. Great Fulford (about 2m NW) is a fine Elizabethan house which has been the seat of the Fulford family since at least the 12thc.

DUNSTABLE, Beds 14 TL02
This is where the Roman Watling Street crossed the older Icknield Way, and where the Romans built a station called *Durocotrivae*. Henry I caused the woods in the neighbourhood to be cut down in the early 12thc, so that robbers could be cleared from them. He also founded an Augustinian priory in c1132. Very fine Norman work remains from this, including the nave arcade and the west front. Divorce proceedings of Henry VIII against Catherine of Aragon took place here, and Cranmer pronounced judgement during a church sermon in 1553. More recent buildings in the town include Queensway Hall – built from 1938 to 1964 and forming part of a new civic centre – and the ultra-modern Windsock public house. Dunstable Downs (NT) lie W of the town and afford fine views. They are also noted for gliding.

DUNSTANBURGH CASTLE, Northumberland 27 NU22
This ruined 14th-c castle overlooks the North Sea and is in an area of outstanding natural beauty. (AM, NT, OACT). It was started by the Earl of Lancaster and later enlarged by John of Gaunt. Defensive walls surrounded it, and the entire complex covered 11 acres. Yorkists took this stronghold in the Wars of the Roses, after which it was dismantled.

DUNSTER, Somerset 5 SS94
Dunster is a village with several old houses in the wide main street, a delightful Yarn Market (AM), and the panelled Luttrell Arms (15th- and 17thc). There is also an old watermill with a double wheel. The fine mainly-perpendicular priory church has a richly-carved screen, three chapels, and monuments to the Luttrells. Conygar Hill tower overlooks the village and dates from 1775. It is a landmark for shipping. Two families only have owned the 11th-c and later castle – the Mohuns and the Luttrells – and it is noted for its great staircase (OACT).

A circular dovecote which is most probably of 12th-c origin retains its original revolving ladder, and the fine shingled Nunnery House is another feature of the village. Old Butter or Rockhead Cross (AM) can be seen on the Alcombe road. Gallox packhorse bridge (AM) spans the River Avill.

DUNWICH, Suffolk 15 TM47
Part of this town was washed away by the sea in the 12thc, and the low cliffs are still crumbling away. A port existed here in medieval times, and the town was the birthplace of Sir John Downing. Downing Street in London was named after this person. Westleton national nature reserve, part of the Minsmere bird reserve, lies 2m S. Dunwich folk museum contains items of local interest, such as coins and objects washed up on local beaches (OACT).

DURHAM, Co Durham 27 NZ24
Durham grew up around its cathedral, which is set on a high rock and is surrounded on three sides by the River Wear. Three of the six bridges that span the Wear are of historical interest – the Elvet, Prebends', and Framwellgate.

Nothing remains of the original Saxon cathedral, and the present Norman building – one of the largest English churches – was begun in 1093 by Bishop William of Calais. The nave was completed early in the 12thc, and the Galilee porch, containing the tomb of the Venerable Bede, a little later on. This was the first church to use ribbed vaulting on any scale, and the cathedral has many other interesting features; these include the 13th-c chapel of the Nine Altars and a sanctuary door-knocker on the door. The latter is a reminder that Durham was a place of refuge in the Middle Ages. Puritans used the cathedral to hold Scottish prisoners during the Civil War.

The interesting castle, like the cathedral, was built on a neck of land that once guarded the city approaches. It has a notable crypt chapel, and a richly carved doorway. Durham University has grown up around the cathedral and castle, and occupies most of the buildings in the city centre – including the castle, which is still open to the public. The grammar school was founded in 1541, and its buildings date from c1661. Other ancient houses include Bishop Cosin's Hall and the Bishop's Hospital.

Gulbenkian Museum of Oriental Art is unique; it is the only museum in Britain devoted solely to this subject, and the many fascinating and beautiful items exhibited include Chinese jade, Tibetan paintings and sculpture, and Egyptian antiquities. There are several old churches of interest in the town, among which is partly-Norman St Giles', which houses a wooden effigy of 1591. Notable Ushaw College of 1808 lies 4m W and was founded to succeed a college at Douai.

DURNFORD, GREAT, Wilts 7 SU13
An Avon-Valley village with flint-and-stone cottages, situated below Ogbury Camp. The church displays a fine Norman chancel arch and font, Royal Arms of 1678, and a timbered 15th-c porch. The manor house and Little Durnford Manor are both 18thc.

DURSLEY, Glos 12 ST79
This Cotswold town lies in delightful surroundings, and is involved in the manufacture of machinery. The arcaded town hall dates from 1738, and 2m NW is Stinchcombe Hill, a fine viewpoint.

DURWESTON, Dorset *7 ST80*
Durweston lies in the Stour Valley, 2m NW of Blandford Forum. Its rebuilt church displays a fine perpendicular west tower, and Hanford House, to the NW, dates from 1604. Bulbarrow Hill is an AA viewpoint rising to 920ft in the W.

DYMCHURCH, Kent *9 TR12*
An old smuggling port with an ancient sea wall, on the edge of Romney Marsh. Vast stretches of good sands, and good shore fishing and shrimping in the shallows can be enjoyed here. The church is partly Norman, notably the doorways and chancel arch. New Hall was rebuilt in the 16thc, and contains the Old Court House and a tiny prison that was in use until 1866. A light railway runs to Hythe and S to New Romney and the lighthouses and nuclear power station at Dungeness. A number of Martello towers, built originally to defend the coast against Napoleon, can be seen along the shoreline. One of these, at Dymchurch itself, has been restored as a museum and is open to the public (AM). 'Martello' comes from *Cap Mortella* in Sicily.

DYMOCK, Glos *12 SO63*
Countryside around this village is noted for its orchards and early-spring displays of daffodils. The church has a fine Norman doorway with carved tympanum, and John Kyrle, known as the Man of Ross, was born in the White house in 1634.

DYRHAM, Avon *6 ST77*
The Norman to perpendicular church in this ex-S Gloucestershire hamlet is noted for a brass dated 1401, and a monument dated 1581. Dyrham Park (NT, OACT) was built from 1692 to 1702 by William Blathwayt, Secretary of State and Secretary for War. It stands on the site of an earlier house which belonged to his wife's family, the Wynters. The east front is an unaltered example of William Talman's design; the west front is a few years earlier, and documents show it to be the work of a S Houduroy, a Huguenot. Panelling, furniture, wall-hangings, and pictures all illustrate the Dutch taste of the period.

EAGLESFIELD, Cumbria *25 NY02*
A parish 2½m SW of Cockermouth, which was the birthplace of John Dalton in 1766. He published the *New System of Chemical Philosophy* in 1810, in which the atomic theory was first propounded – a feat commemorated by a tablet on a local house. Fletcher Christian, leader of the mutineers in the famous mutiny on The Bounty, was born at Moorland Close in about 1753.

EAKRING, Notts *18 SK66*
This village lies 5½m NW of Southwell. Its interesting Norman and later church contains a brass to the Rev W Mompesson, one-time vicar of the plague village Eyam. Royal Arms of Charles II and Queen Elizabeth I can also be seen in this building. The latter were taken from a house in the village.

EALING, Gt London *8 TQ18*
A large grass common is crossed by the old Oxford road in this residential area. Attractive Walpole Park surrounds Pitshanger Manor, which was rebuilt by Sir John Soane in 1801 for his own use. Sir John was a famous architect who also founded the Soane Museum in Lincoln's Inn Fields, Central London. Pitshanger is now a public library, but there are plans to move the library and restore the house to its original state. Questor's Theatre in Mattock Lane has been described as the finest amateur theatre in London.

EARDISLAND, Herefs & Worcs *12 SO45*
Eardisland is a pretty village comprising many timbered black-and-white houses. One of the best examples of this building style is Staick House, which dates from the 14thc and later. Old dovecotes can be seen near the river and at Burton Court. The latter is of 14th- to 18th-c origins (OACT), and its manoral records go back to 1332. These are kept in Hereford Library.

EARDISLEY, Herefs & Worcs *11 SO34*
Several timbered black-and-white buildings and a partly-Norman church exist in this village. The church displays later additions, and contains a curious cup-shaped font of *c*1150. This is decorated with carvings which show men fighting with spear and sword, a large lion, and other figures and ornaments.

EARLS BARTON, Northants *13 SP86*
The magnificent Saxon church-tower is one of the finest in England, and was probably built in the late 10thc. It is thought to have once formed part of the defences of a nearby Norman castle. The Normans added a small nave and chancel to the tower, and the church was further enlarged in the 14th and 15thc.

EARLS COLNE, Essex *15 TL82*
This village is sited in the Colne Valley, some 2½m SE of Halstead. Mainly 18thc Colne Priory stands on the site of a Benedictine priory, and the restored 14th-c church carries a fine tower. Colneford House dates from 1685 and displays good external plasterwork (pargetting).

EARL STONHAM, Suffolk *15 TM15*
Four hour-glasses sit on the 17th-c pulpit in the village's 13th- to 15th-c church, and the magnificent hammer-beam roof is decorated with angels.

EARTHAM, W Sussex *8 SU90*
A downland village where the poet William Hayley made Eartham Hall a rendezvous for some of the leading writers and artists of the late 18thc. Blake and Southey were frequent guests, and Southey wrote of Hayley – 'Everything is good about him except his poetry' – perhaps rather unkindly. Hayley is chiefly remembered for his epitaphs. The tiny church has a Norman chancel, but the rest of the old work is mainly of 13th-c origin.

EASBY, N Yorks *22 NZ50*
Easby is a hamlet in a richly-wooded part of Swaledale. Interesting remains of a 12th-c and later abbey (AM) stand in a lovely setting near the mainly early-English church. Notable frescoes of biblical scenes can be seen in the latter.

EASHING, Surrey *8 SU94*
Eashing Bridges, below the hamlet, have small round arches which cross separate channels of the River Wey. They originate from the 13thc, and are said to date from King John's reign (AM). Half-timbered cottages of the 16thc stand near the bridges, and both the former and latter are NT property.

EASINGWOLD, N Yorks *22 SE56*
This little town lies 2½m NE of Alne, and displays a pleasant combination of mellow red-brick buildings and cobblestones. A bull-ring can be seen in the Market Place. The mainly gothic church has old roofs and houses an ancient parish coffin.

EAST BARSHAM, Norfolk *15 TF93*
A village 2m N of Fakenham, known for its early-Tudor brick and terra-cotta manor. The fine chimneys are twisted and otherwise decorated, and the approach is guarded by an imposing two-storey gatehouse. It is said that Henry VIII stayed here on his way to the shrine of Our Lady of Walsingham.

1 Bishop Cosin's Hall
2 Bishop's Hospital
3 Castle
4 Cathedral
5 Elvet Bridge
6 Framwellgate Bridge
7 Grammar School
8 Gulbenkian Museum of Oriental Art
9 Prebend's Bridge
10 St Giles' Church
11 University of Durham

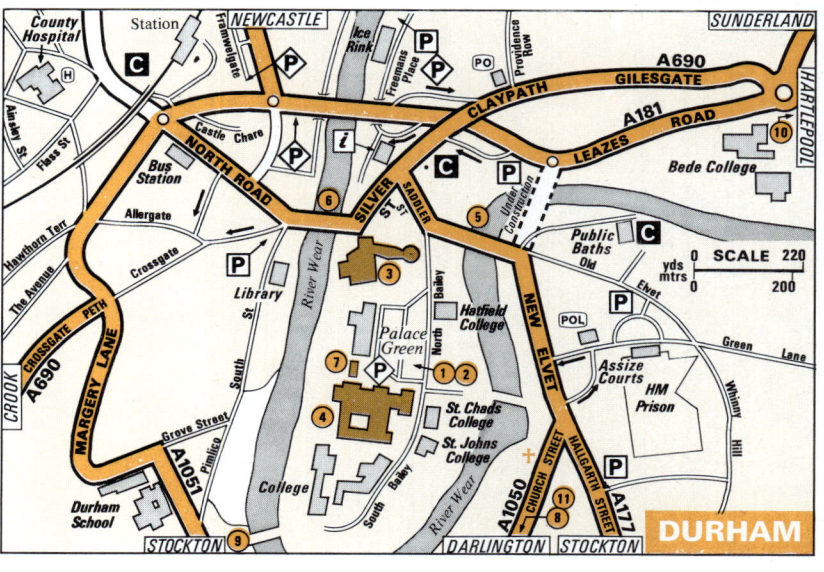

EAST BERGHOLT, Suffolk 15 TM03
John Constable was born in this Stour-Valley village in 1776. Several plastered cottages of Elizabethan origin blend happily with a host of other attractive houses and beautiful gardens. Most of the village is built along a ridge above the river. An external bell-cage displayed by the 14th- and 16th-c church is remarkable; the church tower was never finished, and the bells hang in a 16th-c wooden frame. The unfinished tower was begun by Cardinal Wolsey. Stour was the home of the late Randolph Churchill, and is set amid beautiful gardens (OACT). Little Wenham Hall (AM) shows some of the earliest 13th-c brickwork in England, and lies 4m N.

EASTBOURNE, E Sussex 9 TV69
Eastbourne is a popular seaside resort which lies in a sheltered position below Beachy Head. It has a good sunshine, temperature and rainfall record, and the beach is mainly shingle. Amenities include boating, bowls, tennis, horse-riding, fishing, dancing, a theatre, and indoor swimming pools at Devonshire Baths.

Several fine parks here include the Devonshire and the Hampden, and areas of grass and flower beds border the promenade. Also on the sea front is the Wish Tower, originally a Martello tower built as a defence against Napoleon in 1804, which now serves as a museum. The name Wish is a corruption of Wash — a stream that once ran here.

Other places of interest include the picturesque old Lamb Inn, the Towner Art Gallery, and 18th-c Compton Place. The 600ft pier dates from 1872 and 1888. Beachy Head (575ft) is accessible on foot by an easy walk. South Downs bridleway extends W from here to a point beyond South Harting, on the Hampshire border. The old Belle Tout lighthouse stands on a cliff top W of the resort.

EAST BUDLEIGH, Devon 6 SY08
An attractive hillside village, just N of Budleigh Salterton. Thatched cottages follow the hill's incline, and footbridges cross a brook to houses lower down the slope. The church contains a variety of carved bench-ends, plus a memorial to the Raleigh family. Sir Walter Raleigh was born at Hayes Barton, a thatched and plastered house 1m to the W, in 1552 (OACT). Bicton Gardens lie about 1m N of East Budleigh, and were laid out by Le Notre, the Frenchman who designed the gardens at Versailles (OACT).

EASTCHURCH, Kent 9 TQ97
Lord Brabazon and the Hon C S Rolls flew over this lonely Isle of Sheppey village in the early days of aviation, and the first British aerodrome was established near by in 1909. The church of 1432 displays early-perpendicular design, and contains a 60ft screen. A few remains of 15th-c Shurland Castle can still be seen.

EAST CLANDON, Surrey 8 TQ05
A village of brick-and-timber houses and large old barns. The church is largely of 13th-c date, but was badly restored in the 19thc. Hatchlands is a fine 18th-c house which was built for Admiral Boscawen, showing interiors by Robert Adam – his first commission (NT, OACT). This admiral was victorious over the French fleet at Louisberg in 1758.

EAST CLAYDON, Bucks 13 SP72
Among the old houses in this village, many of them timbered, is the Elizabethan White House. Claydon House lies 2m W and was the mid 18th-c home of the Verneys. It was built on the site of an earlier house by the 2nd Earl Verney (NT). A Florence Nightingale museum is one of the house's features (OACT), and the building itself contains unique Chinese-style decor and splendid rococo state-rooms. The latter display wood carvings by Lightfoot.

EAST COKER, Somerset 6 ST51
Ashes of poet T S Eliot were rested in the local perpendicular church in 1965. East Coker gave its name to the second of Eliot's *Four Quartets*, and the poet's New England family came from this village. Coker Court is a modernized 15th-c house. Hymerford House was the birthplace of the explorer William Dampier in 1652. He wrote of his adventures in *Voyage Round the World*.

EASTDEAN, W Sussex 9 TV59
This small downland village has a 12th- to 15th-c church which houses a curious old font, and displays an 11th-c tower with 3ft-thick walls. There are seaward walks to Birling Gap (1m), and inland walks to Jevington.

EAST FARLEIGH, Kent 9 TQ75
A village where the River Medway is spanned by a fine medieval bridge. West Farleigh Hall is a good 18th-c house.

EAST GRINSTEAD, W Sussex 8 TQ33
This market town has a charter dating from 1221, and preserves a number of timber-framed houses. Sackville College is a beautiful Jacobean almshouse with a picturesque courtyard. It was founded as a home for the poor and disabled by the Earl of Dorset, and is built in sandstone. Old Surrey Hall preserves a timbered 15th-c hall amid 20th-c alterations and lies 4m ENE.

EASTHAM, Merseyside 17 SJ38
Eastham stands at the W entrance to Manchester Ship Canal, on the River Mersey, and has docks which are now capable of taking 30,000-ton tankers. The old church includes the Stanley Chapel, dating from Tudor times.

EAST HAM, Gt London 8 TQ48
The interesting parish church of St Mary Magdalene is mainly of Norman construction, and contains several ancient monuments. One of these was raised to Edward, Earl of Westmorland. The west tower is of early 16th-c date, and fragments of 13th-c wall-paintings can still be seen inside. The antiquarian William Stukeley is buried in the churchyard.

EAST HENDRED, Oxon 13 SU48
An exceptionally pretty downland village of timbered cottages. The clock on the church tower dates from 1525, and a rare 14th-c Crusader's lectern can be seen inside the building. Champ's Chapel is a former shrine which has been used as a granary, and near it stands a half-timbered building which was once the priest's house. Hendred House, the seat of the Eyston family, has a private chapel where mass has been celebrated since 1291. This contains relics of St Thomas More and St John Fisher.

EAST HOATHLY, E Sussex 8 TQ51
A village 4½m SE of Uckfield, in a locality known for the manufacture of trugs. The trugs are baskets, hand-made from broad bands of willow attached to an ash or chestnut frame. A good perpendicular tower is displayed by the local church, which also carries a Pelham Buckle on its Tudor doorway.

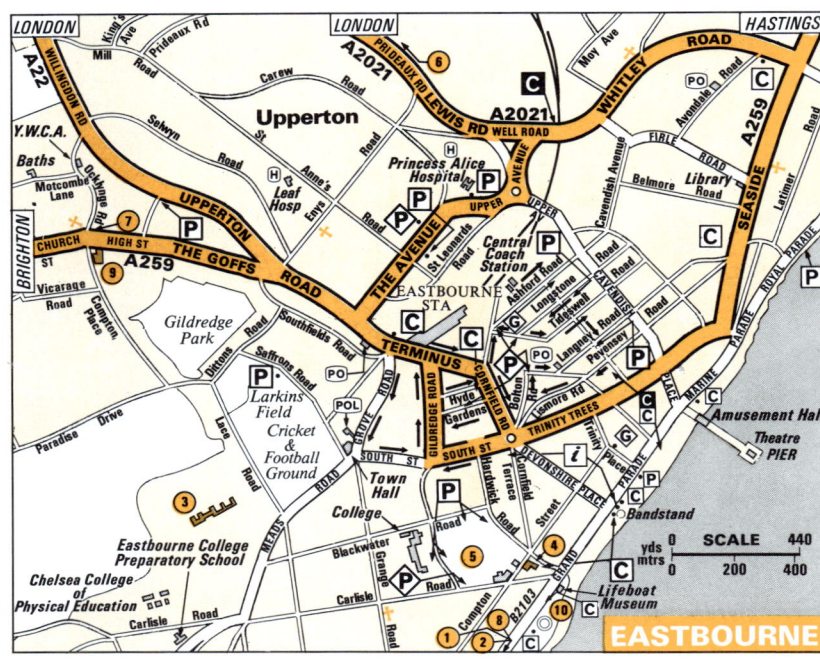

1 Beachy Head
2 Belle Tout Lighthouse
3 Compton Place
4 Devonshire Baths
5 Devonshire Park
6 Hampden Park
7 Lamb Inn
8 Lighthouse (off Beachy Head)
9 Towner Art Gallery
10 Wish Tower (museum)

EAST HORSLEY, Surrey 8 TQ05
Most of this village originates from the 19thc, and is almost entirely flint-built. The restored partly 13th-c church houses several old brasses, among which is one of 1478. East Horsley Towers is a curious 19th-c mansion which now serves as offices for the Electricity Board.

EAST KNOYLE, Wilts 7 ST83
Sir Christopher Wren, the famous architect of St Paul's Cathedral, was born here in 1632. Clouds is a fine mansion by Philip Webb, built in 1879.

EASTLEACH, Glos 12 SP10
The twin Cotswold villages of Eastleach Martin and Eastleach Turville are divided by the River Leach. They are entirely unspoiled, and include a number of old houses and a picturesque clapper bridge. Each has an ancient church; the one at Eastleach Martin boasts five ancient sundials, and the Eastleach Turville church displays a gabled tower and fine porch. Carving over the door of the latter shows Christ in glory, attended by cherubim and seraphim.

EAST LULWORTH, Dorset 7 SY88
The 16th-c castle in this attractive village is part of the Weld estate. It was burned out in 1929, and only a shell now remains. The grounds, however, hold a round building dating from 1786, which was the first English RC church to be built by royal permission after the Reformation. George III consented, on the condition that it did not look like a church. Ring's Hill, or Flower's Barrow, is a prehistoric camp which overlooks the magnificent scenery around Worbarrow Bay 1¾m S (only accessible at certain times). Some roads leading to East Lulworth are on army training ground; red flags are flown when the area is closed for shooting practice.

EAST LYNG, Somerset 6 ST32
A small perpendicular tower carried by the local church is a good example of this style. King Alfred's Athelney monument is ¾m E, and 2m NE is Burrow Bridge. The latter is noted for the hill, or Mump, which is crowned by an unfinished church and affords a wide view over the surrounding area. Also here is an exhibition of Victorian engines, housed in a pumping station.

EAST MEON, Hants 7 SU62
This compact downland village below Park Down is where the angler Izaak Walton once stayed to fish the River Meon. The river runs beside the main street, and the village is still a good centre for trout fishing. Old Winchester Hill rises to 653ft to the SW, and is partly a national nature reserve. The Norman church carries a mid 12th-c tower and preserves a rare black-marble Tournai font. Stained glass by Sir Ninian Comper can be seen in the E window, and 14th-c Court House stands near by.

EASTNOR, Herefs & Worcs 12 SO73
Eastnor Castle, the early 19th-c work of Sir Thomas Smirke, is finely furnished and stands in a beautiful park (OACT). A few traces of Bronsil Castle can be seen. Remains of an iron-age hill fort (NT) exist on Midsummer Hill, and comprise the enclosure and a number of hut sites.

EASTON-ON-THE-HILL, Northants 19 TF00
An attractive stone-built village situated 2m SW of Stamford, where a 13th-c and later church contains two stone screens. The rectory is of Georgian origin, and the pre-Reformation Priest's House is now a parish hall (NT).

EAST PORTLEMOUTH, Devon 5 SX73
This small village is sited on the Kingsbridge estuary and has a sandy beach. The church houses a notable painted screen. An epitaph to a girl burnt at the stake in 1782, for poisoning her employer, can be seen in the churchyard. This is said to have been the last punishment of its kind in England. A passenger ferry plies to Salcombe. Prawle Point and Gammon Head are areas of fine cliff scenery lying to the SE.

EAST QUANTOXHEAD, Somerset 6 ST14
A delightful village grouped around a pond. Early 17th-c Court House is a seat of the Luttrell family, who have lived in the district for 800 years. The church contains old bench-ends.

EAST RAYNHAM, Norfolk 15 TF82
A parish on the River Wensum, standing at the edge of a fine park surrounding Raynham Hall. This house is a magnificent 17th-c building which has been ascribed partly to Inigo Jones. It is said to be haunted.

EASTRY, Kent 9 TR35
Eastry lies 2½m SW of Sandwich. The large early-English church displays a good tower, and old chalk caves can be seen near by.

EAST STOKE, Notts 19 SK74
Situated on the Fosse Way and the River Trent, this village saw the battle of Stoke Field in 1487, and the virtual end of the Wars of the Roses.

EAST WELLOW, Hants 7 SU32
The restored mainly early-English church has several notable wall-paintings preserved on the nave and chancel walls. These show a knight, St Christopher, and the murder of Thomas Becket. The pulpit dates from the early 17th-c, and other good examples of old woodwork can be seen. Florence Nightingale is buried in the churchyard.

EASTWOOD, Essex 9 TQ88
Fine Norman doorways displaying particularly interesting ironwork can be seen in the church, which also contains a Norman font. A curious timbered priest's chamber exists in the north aisle.

EASTWOOD, Notts 18 SK44
A mining town in the heart of agricultural country, Eastwood was the birthplace of D H Lawrence and appears in his novels as Eberwich. He was born at 8A North Street; the contrast provided by peaceful countryside, so close to the pithead machinery of Eastwood, is said to have influenced his outlook.

EATON SOCON, Cambs 14 TL15
This large River-Ouse village now forms part of St Neots. The White Horse Inn is partly of 13th-c origin, and was visited by both Pepys and Dickens. The latter mentioned it in *Nicholas Nickleby*. The old lock-up is divided into two compartments. Farther upstream is a good area for riverside walking.

EBBSFLEET, Kent 9 TR36
Situated on Pegwell Bay, the beach at Ebbsfleet shows good wide sands at low tide. Hengist and Horsa reputedly landed here in 449AD, as did St Augustine in 597AD. The latter's disembarkation is commemorated by a cross. A replica of the Viking ship Hugin, which crossed the North Sea in 1949, rests at the site of Saxon landings near the hovercraft terminal. There is a huge power station near by.

EBCHESTER, Co Durham 27 NZ15
The much-restored parish church is partly 11thc, and Roman bricks were used in its construction. R S Surtees,

16th-c Lulworth Castle, East Lulworth

author and creator of the fictional character Jorrocks, spent part of his youth at 17th-c Harnsterley Hall. He is buried near by.

EBRINGTON, Glos *12 SP14*
Stone and thatched cottages make up this delightful Cotswold village, and the local church displays a fine Norman doorway. Hidcote Bartrim lies 2m N, where the beautiful formal gardens of Hidcote Manor, and a gabled 17th-c house are both of interest (NT, OACT).

ECCLES, Gt Manchester *17 SJ79*
This is an industrial and engineering town on the Manchester Ship Canal, where the famous waterway is spanned by Barton swingbridge. The latter carries the Bridgewater canal of 1758. Monks Hall Museum is housed in a Tudor building, with 17th-c additions, and displays interesting local items. These include a steam hammer made at the local Bridgewater foundry by engineer James Nasmyth. The restored church is 14th to 19thc, and an old market cross can be seen in the town. Most Eccles cakes – large spicy mince-pies, are made in Manchester.

ECCLESFIELD, S Yorks *18 SK39*
The 15th-c church is known as the Minster of the Moors, and houses fine contemporary woodwork and a tomb of 1638. Whitley Hall dates from 1584 and later.

ECCLESHALL, Staffs *17 SJ82*
The early-English to perpendicular church carries a fine tower rising to almost 100ft. Monuments to former Bishops of Lichfield can be seen in the building, and the ruined castle was formerly the residence of these Bishops. The 15th-c tower of Ranton Abbey lies 4m S.

ECKINGTON, Derbyshire *18 SK47*
A large squint and a Sitwell monument of 1625 are housed within the trans-Norman to perpendicular church. Renishaw Hall (S) was originally built by George Sitwell in 1625, and later enlarged; it was the early home of Osbert, Sacheverell, and Edith Sitwell.

ECKINGTON, Herefs & Worcs *12 SO94*
A good 16th-c bridge spans the River Avon here, and the interesting church is of 12th-c and later date. Elizabethan Woolas Hall lies 2m E under 960ft Bredon Hill, and 2m S is Bredons Norton Manor with a gateway of 1585.

ECTON, Northants *13 SP86*
Ecton is the ancestral home of the Franklin family. Benjamin Franklin's father left here for New England in 1685, and the 13th- to 14th-c church contains old monuments.

EDALE, Derbyshire *18 SK18*
An unspoilt River-Noe village which provides a good base for walks in the Peak District. Much of the delightful Vale of Edale is owned by the NT, and the already dramatic scenery is dominated by Crowden Head, 2½m NW. One of the many tough walks leads W through Upper Booth, past Edale Cross, and N to 2,088ft Kinder Scout, the highest point in the Peak District. The 250m Pennine Way starts in this area. Much of the moorland is preserved for grouse shooting.

EDBURTON, W Sussex *8 TQ21*
A village 3½m E of Steyning, where the little 12th- to 13th-c church includes Saxon and Norman stones, and houses a panelled lead font. Truleigh Hill rises 700ft in the South Downs.

EDENBRIDGE, Kent *8 TQ44*
Several old houses can still be seen in the town's main street, and the Norman to perpendicular church carries a massive 13th-c tower crowned by a spire of later date. The old Crown Inn of 1507 has a gallows sign, and interesting Haxted Mill and museum lies on the Lingfield road.

EDENHALL, Cumbria *26 NY53*
The famous Luck of Eden Hall is the name given to a precious glass goblet which was owned by the Musgraves, residents of a former Eden Hall, for centuries. It is now preserved in the Victoria and Albert Museum, London. The River Eden flows through the area, and the local 13th- to 15th-c church displays some old glass.

EDENSOR, Derbyshire *18 SK26*
The houses making up this 19th-c village display many different shapes and styles, and were all built in the same decade. Cavendish monuments of the 17thc can be seen in the 19th-c church, which was rebuilt by Sir Gilbert Scott. They include a memorial to Lord Frederick Cavendish, who was murdered in Ireland in 1882. Also remembered is Sir Joseph Paxton of Crystal Palace fame. The village is sited on the River Derwent, at the edge of lovely Chatsworth Park – the one-time prison of Mary Queen of Scots.

EDGWARE, Gt London *8 TQ19*
Edgware is a residential district. St Lawrence's Church, Whitchurch (Little Stanmore) is dated 1715, and contains an organ on which Handel played when staying at the nearby mansion of Canons. The mansion has since been rebuilt, but the church retains a 16th-c tower and is noted for its ceiling and wall paintings by Italian artist Laguerre. Also of interest are the Chandos tombs, and the churchyard tomb of the Harmonious Blacksmith.

EDINGTON, Wilts *7 ST95*
A fine early-perpendicular cruciform-shaped collegiate church can be seen here. The college was founded by William of Edington in 1351, and the church consecrated ten years later. Many fine monuments from the 15thc onwards are housed within the church; of particular note are one of c1630, adorned with angels, children, and recumbent effigies, and one by Chantrey. A 17th-c panelled plaster ceiling covers the nave, and the priory is probably of 16th-c origin.

EDITH WESTON, Leics *19 SK90*
Edith was Edward the Confessor's Queen, and was given this corner of old Rutland. Part of an old village cross can be seen, and the spired 12th-c church displays fine Norman carving; a one-hand clock is situated beneath the tower and modern reredos. Lyndon Hall (SW) has associations with Gilbert White of Selborne.

EDLESBOROUGH, Bucks *8 SP91*
The mainly-decorated church stands on a mound. It is known for its exceptionally-fine woodwork, and a unique rose brass of 1412.

EDMONTON, Gt London *8 TQ39*
The graves of Charles Lamb and his sister Mary can be seen at the much-restored church. Lamb Cottage stands in Church Street, and was where Keats lived from 1810 to 1816. Salisbury House dates from c1600, and is partly timbered.

EDWINSTOWE, Notts *18 SK66*
An attractive village on the River Maun, Edwinstowe is near the older parts of Sherwood Forest and the Dukeries. Robin Hood and Maid Marian are said to have been married in the largely 13th-c church. A mausoleum to the Ward family can be seen here, and interesting old oak trees include the Major Oak, said to have sheltered Robin Hood.

EGGINTON, Derbyshire *18 SK22*
The 14th-c church in this River-Dove village contains examples of old glass. A medieval bridge was built by the Abbot of Burton to carry traffic to the abbey, and was widened in 1775. The hall is 18thc. Brindley's 23-arch Monks Bridge aqueduct carries the Trent and Mersey Canal over the Dove, and was built in 1777.

EGHAM, Surrey *8 TQ07*
Runnymede (NT) is a broad riverside meadow where King John sealed the draft of Magna Carta in 1215, lying ½m NW of this Thames-side community. Two memorial buildings, entrance pillars designed by Lutyens in 1929, and two kiosks can be seen here. A Magna Carta memorial in the shape of a classical temple was presented by the American Bar Association in 1957, and stands at the foot of Cooper's Hill. Above the hill is the striking Royal Air Force Memorial, commemorating the 20,000 airmen who died in the Second World War with no known grave. Great Fosters, a 16th-c house now serving as a hotel, lies 1½m SW. The Royal Holloway College of 1887 was built to resemble the French Loire-valley mansion of Chambord, and is situated 1m W.

ELHAM, Kent *9 TR14*
Pronounced Eelham, this attractive village includes several old houses and is sited in a valley. The 13th-c church shows a 14th-c chancel arch and houses a yew chest. Good modern fittings blend with the building's original character.

ELING, Hants *7 SU31*
Eling lies on an inlet at the head of Southampton Water, and has a toll-bridge that may well be the smallest in England. It is the property of Winchester College. Several old headstones displaying ship carvings are contained in the restored church.

ELKSTONE, Glos *12 SO91*
The remarkable Norman and later church in this village displays a carved south-doorway and a fine chancel. Musician gargoyles decorate its perpendicular west tower, and a fine Georgian rectory also exists near by.

ELLAND, W Yorks *22 SE12*
A woollen-manufacturing town in the Calder Valley, 3m SE of Halifax. Elland Old Hall and Elland New Hall are both old houses.

ELLASTONE, Staffs *18 SK14*
A village beautifully situated below the Weaver Hills, near the River Dove.

Wootton Lodge is a fine early 17th-c building sited some 2m W. The area is strongly associated with George Eliot's *Adam Bede*; Ellastone becomes Hayslope in the chief scene of the book, and the Bromley Arms appears in the narrative as the Donnithorne Arms.

ELLEL, Lancs 21 SD45
The 18th- and 19th-c silk-spinning mill that is sited here was begun in 1792. It is said to be the oldest in England. Ellel Grange was built in the mid 19thc, to an imposing Italianate style; its grounds contain a church of 1873.

ELLESBOROUGH, Bucks 8 SP80
A village 2½m W of Wendover, with the Chiltern height of 813ft Pulpit Hill rising to the S. Cymbeline's Mount is an ancient fort which overlooks the mansion of Chequers.

ELLESMERE, Salop 17 SJ33
This is a small market town which stands in a district of small lakes known as meres. Although largely rebuilt, the church still has a fine 15th-c carved roof in the Oteley chapel. The pedimented town hall dates from 1833, and half-timbered Lee Old Hall (16thc) lies 1½m S. Hardwick Hall is a notable Georgian house of 1733, lying 1¾m to the W.

ELLESMERE PORT, Cheshire 17 SJ47
An industrial port on the S bank of the River Mersey, at a point where the Manchester Ship Canal is joined by the Shropshire Union Canal. Stanlow oil-refineries lie to the E, and several other flourishing industries exist in the town.

ELLINGHAM, Hants 7 SU10
A River-Avon village where the 13th- to 19th-c church is notable for a partition over the screen, carrying the Commandments, the Creed, and the Royal Arms of 1671. Moyles Court, a 17th-c house once owned by Dame Alice Lisle, lies 1m E. Dame Alice was beheaded by order of Judge Jeffreys after the Monmouth rebellion in 1685. She is buried in the local churchyard.

ELMLEY CASTLE, Herefs & Worcs 12 SO94
This picturesque village of half-timbered cottages lies at the foot of Bredon Hill. The 12th- to 15th-c church is interesting, and houses many fine monuments.

ELMORE, Glos 12 SO71
Elmore is on the River Severn, and the nearby Stone Bench is considered the best place from which to watch the Severn Bore. Elmore Court is a country mansion with Elizabethan, Stuart, and Georgian features, containing collections of period furniture and tapestries (OACT).

ELSDON, Northumberland 27 NY99
This isolated village was once the Norman capital of Redesdale, and is grouped around a large village green that displays a pinfold, or cattle pound. A rare 15th-c fortified parsonage built onto a pele tower is an interesting feature of the village.

ELSING, Norfolk 15 TG01
Elsing's fine 14th-c church was built by Sir Hugh Hastings in c1340, and houses a magnificent brass to this gentleman. The octagonal font cover is almost of the same period as the building, and the

Magna Carta Memorial standing in the Runnymede meadows near Egham

stained glass figures also date from the 14thc. Elsing Hall lies 1m SW and is a late 15th-c partly half-timbered house, surrounded by a moat.

ELSTEAD, Surrey 8 SU94
The River Wey runs beside this village, and the attractive water-mill is partly Tudor. An ancient restored five-arch bridge spans the river. Fine 14th-c timbering is shown by the church, and Hankley Common lies to the SW.

ELSTOW, Beds 13 TL04
John Bunyan lived in Elstow when it was a village; it is now almost a part of Bedford. Bunyan originally followed his father's footsteps and became a tinker, but was religiously converted by a vision while playing a ball game called tip-cat. He subsequently became a popular preacher. He was persecuted after the Restoration, and wrote *Pilgrim's Progress* while in prison. The church is of Norman and later date, and displays a detached tower. One of the rare English abbess's brasses can be seen in the church, and Bunyan was baptised here. The Moot Hall dates from the 16thc and is now a museum of rural life.

ELTHAM, Gt London 8 TQ47
The Great Hall of Eltham Palace preserves a magnificent restored 15th-c oak roof, and a fine stone bridge spans the moat (OACT). Eltham Lodge, dated 1663 and built by Hugh May, is now a golf clubhouse. The picturesque buildings of Well Hall, also moated, are the remnants of an Elizabethan manor house of 1568. The churchyard contains the remains of Thomas Doggett, an Irish comedian who founded the well-known Thames Watermen's Race for Doggett's Coat and Badge. This was originally to commemorate the accession of George I in 1714, and takes place on the river each summer. Severndroog Castle is a triangular structure which stands ½m NE.

ELTON, Cambs 19 TL09
The hall in this River-Nene village was rebuilt in c1660, and shows later additions. The present Jacobean structure was built by Sir Thomas Proby, and contains a fine collection of pictures and a library. A Tudor gatehouse and vaulted crypt are all that is left of a house destroyed during the Commonwealth period. A notable tower is a feature of the decorated and perpendicular church, which also houses monuments to the Probys and old, possibly Saxon, crosses.

ELVASTON, Derbyshire 18 SK43
Elvaston church has an interesting Stanhope monument of 1610. An early 19th-c castle in the area is famous for its topiary work and gardens, which are open as part of a country park.

ELVEDEN, Suffolk 15 TL87
Elveden Hall is in 19th-c oriental style, constructed partly of marble, and crowned with a copper dome. A 113ft stone column with 148 interior steps can be seen, and the house was formerly the home of the Maharajah Duleep Singh. He restored the church in various styles, and is buried in the churchyard. The tower and cloisters were built in memory of Lady Iveagh in 1922.

ELY, Cambs 14 TL58
Bede says that this place acquired its name because of the large number of eels caught in the fens, but the actual Isle of Ely disappeared when the Fens were drained in the 17th and 18thc. A superb cathedral that dominates the surrounding Fenland was begun in 1083. It is notable for the octagonal lantern tower and choir stalls, both designed by Alan de Walsingham. The west front and tower, the lady chapel, the prior's door, and the chantry chapels are also of interest.

The Bishop's Palace dates from the 15thc and later, and across the green is the Chantry, a 17th- to 18th-c house. The ancient grammar school incorporates a gateway house known as Ely Porta, and the beautiful Prior Crauden's Chapel – in decorated style – is now the school chapel. Hereward the Wake held out against the Normans until 1071 on this island, and was only defeated when a road that the army could use was built across the marshes. St Mary's Church displays Norman to perpendicular styles, and has a fine north doorway. Near by is the old vicarage, once a tithe house, which was the home of Oliver Cromwell and his family for ten years.

EMBLETON, Northumberland 27 NU22
A pele tower is incorporated in a 14th-c fortified vicarage in this village. The church is of 13th-c and later date, and has a 14th-c tower. It is associated with the statesman and naturalist Viscount Grey of Fallodon, who died at Fallodon Hall in 1933. Good beaches lie 1m from here.

EMNETH, Norfolk *14 TF40*
The fine church is of 12th- to 15th-c date, and is noted for the nave roof, some old glass, and a 15th-c screen. Dial House is 1½m SE and dates from the early 18thc.

EMSWORTH, Hants *8 SU70*
This is a small harbour and yachting centre at the mouth of the River Ems. Oyster fisheries are cultivated near by, and Thorney Island (2m S) is reached by a causeway.

ENBORNE, Berks *7 SU46*
A village 2m SW of Newbury, near the site of the first Battle of Newbury, which was fought in 1643. The Royalist Lord Falkland was killed here, and a monument to the fallen Royalist troops lies 1m S on the Andover road (NT).

ENFIELD, Gt London *8 TQ39*
Enfield was once a straggling parish in the county of Middlesex, but is now a Borough of Greater London. It retains some patches of open country, including several well-wooded parks, and is associated with the essayist Charles Lamb. He lived at several houses in the town, one of which was in a terrace of good 18th-c buildings called Gentlemen's Row. The area is well-blessed with literary associations. Keats attended school here while living in Edmonton with his grandmother, and Leigh Hunt – poet and politician – was born in High Street, Southgate. Thomas Hood, who wrote a poem entitled *The Song of the Shirt*, lived in the area for several years.

Forty Hall is an interesting 17th-c house that was built for Sir Nicholas Raynton, Lord Mayor of London, and set in a park containing cedars and a lake. It is now a museum. Broomfield House stands in Broomfield Park, between Southgate and Palmers Green, and houses an art gallery. The parish church of St Andrew contains interesting monuments and brasses, plus an organ case of 1572. Near by is a mid 16th-c grammar school.

ENNERDALE BRIDGE, Cumbria *21 NY01*
The River Ehen flows through this hamlet, and Ennerdale Water is at sufficient height to provide magnificent views towards the Pillar mountain, at the lonely head of the valley. Parts of the valley have been afforested, and Great Borne rises to 2,019ft at the W end of the lake. The River Liza flows into the lake from Ennerdale; excellent footpaths run N, S, and W of this water. Impressive views of surrounding fells can be enjoyed from the area.

EPPING, Essex *8 TL40*
Epping Forest was used for hunting by Saxon, Norman, and Tudor kings, and was bought for the nation about 100 years ago. It comprises beautiful woods and rough heathlands, the habitat of great hornbeam trees. The hornbeam is native only to SE England, and produces exceptionally hard wood. Its name has roots in the Anglo Saxon period and means horny (wooded) tree. The timber from such trees was used for ox-yokes and cog wheels in the machinery of windmills and watermills.

EPSOM, Surrey *8 TQ26*
Epsom is a pleasant market town and residential area within easy reach of London, which was well known for its medicinal springs in the 18thc – hence Epsom salts. Buildings of the period still stand in Church Street. The famous Epsom Downs racecourse, where the Derby and Oaks are held, lies 1½m SE. The Derby has been run here since 1780. A bridleway for riders and walkers stretches for 5m along an old Roman road leading to Box Hill.

EPWORTH, Humberside *23 SE70*
This town is situated on the low-lying Isle of Axholme and was the birthplace of John Wesley, the founder of the Methodist Church. His father Samuel Wesley was the rector of Epworth. Their home was rebuilt after a fire in 1709, and still contains furniture associated with the Wesley family (OACT).

ERIDGE GREEN, E Sussex *9 TQ53*
Eridge Castle is a modern structure which stands in an extensive park. A notable outcrop of sandstone known as Bowles Rocks occurs in the area, and has nearly-vertical 70ft ascents which are used as training for mountaineers. The Bowles Mountaineering and Outdoor Pursuits Centre teaches rock climbing and other outdoor activities.

ERMINE STREET
Ermine Street is the Roman road running from London to Lincoln (*Lindum*), by way of Royston and Huntingdon, and thence to the Humber estuary. The name Ermine or Ermin Street is also given to another road, connecting Silchester (*Calleva Atrebatum*) with Gloucester (*Glevum*). This route stays E of Swindon and, after crossing the Fosse Way and meeting Akeman Street at Cirencester, descends Birdlip Hill to enter the Severn Vale at Gloucester.

ERPINGHAM, Norfolk *15 TG13*
The name of this River-Bure village recalls the Erpingham family. Sir Thomas Erpingham landed at the now-extinct Ravenspur (Humberside) with Henry IV in 1399, and built the Erpingham gate at Norwich. A 14th-c Erpingham brass is a notable feature of the church, which also displays a fine tower. Hanworth Hall is a 17th- and 18th-c house lying 3m N.

ESCOMB, Co Durham *27 NZ13*
One of the finest Saxon churches in England can be seen here. It was built in the 7thc, probably with materials from a Roman station, and is considered one of the most important survivals of early-christian architecture in Britain. The nave and chancel are separated by an arch which displays original period work on the side supports.

ESHER, Surrey *8 TQ16*
The name of this popular residential area (and dormitory for London) is pronounced Ea-sher. Although developed, it retains a village green and several 18th-c houses. A 15th-c gateway known as Wolsey's Tower (or Waynflete's Tower, after its builder) is all that remains of a mansion to which Cardinal Wolsey retired after his fall from favour. It stands in the grounds of Esher Place, which is near the River Mole and now serves as a trades union college.

Claremont House was originally built by Vanbrugh, but was rebuilt on its present site by Capability Brown for Lord Clive of India. It was occupied by Prince Leopold until he became King of the Belgians, and was the home of the exiled French Imperial family. It later became the private property of Queen Victoria; it now serves as a girls' school (OACT). The hill above bears a belvedere tower dating from 1717. The old parish church of 1540 contains a three-decker pulpit, and a double-chambered pew which could only be entered from outside the building. The latter was occupied by Queen Victoria. Sandown Park is a well-known and newly rebuilt racecourse situated near by. A tall circular milestone known as the White Lady, stands NE on the London Road.

ETCHINGHAM, E Sussex *9 TQ72*
A village on the River Rother, where the fine decorated-style church dates from 1366 and displays windows and brasses of the same period. The remains of Sir William de Etchyngham, founder of the church, are buried here. A fine Jacobean façade can be seen at Haremere Hall.

ETON, Berks *8 SU97*
Eton College, across the bridge from Windsor (no cars allowed), is a famous public school originally founded by King Henry VI in 1440. The notable chapel houses paintings and brasses, and Lupton's Tower is an impressive structure. Manuscripts preserved in the library include the original of Gray's *Elegy*. Upper School is attributed to Wren, and the playing-fields sweep towards the Thames. The Eton Wall game is a unique annual event played each St Andrew's Day (November 30).

ETRURIA, Staffs *17 SJ84*
Etruria owes much of its fame and development to Josiah Wedgwood (1730 to 1793), who founded his great pottery there in 1769. It is situated on the Trent and Mersey Canal.

ETWALL, Derbyshire *18 SK23*
The picturesque range of 17th-c almshouses near the restored church was built by Sir John Port, founder of Repton College. A Jesuit priest named John Gerard was born here, and died under torture in the Tower of London during the Elizabethan period.

EUSTON, Suffolk *15 TL87*
This place gives its name to Euston Station, because the London rail terminus was built on the estate of the Duke of Grafton who then owned Euston Hall. The present hall dates from the 18thc and replaces a former structure that was destroyed by fire. Inside the park gates is a rebuilt church of 1676, with a reredos that might have been by Grinling Gibbons. A well-carved pulpit can be seen inside the church.

EVERCREECH, Somerset *6 ST63*
A village 3½m SE of Shepton Mallet, where the church has one of the best perpendicular towers in the county. The nave's wooden roof shows original colouring.

EVERSLEY, Hants *8 SU76*
The novelist Charles Kingsley was once rector of this church, and is buried in the churchyard. The building itself is of brick construction, rebuilt in 1735. Warbrook to the SW, and Farley Hall to the NW, are fine mansions of the Wren period. Bramshill House is a notable Jacobean mansion of 1612, set in fine gardens and now serving as the Police Staff College. It was the former home of the Cope family and ranks as Hampshire's finest old house (not open).

EVESHAM, Herefs & Worcs 12 SP04
Evesham is sited on the River Avon, in the centre of the famous fruit and vegetable growing district the Vale of Evesham. The area is particularly notable in early spring, when it is a mass of blossom. Ruins of the abbey (AM) include a fine perpendicular bell tower and a half-timbered gateway on an original Norman stone base. A cross has been erected in memory of Simon de Montfort, slain in the battle of Evesham which was fought to the N of the town in 1265. Two interesting churches are All Saints', with the beautiful Lichfield chantry, and St Lawrence's, with fan vaulting. Fine old houses include half-timbered and Georgian buildings. Walker Hall and Church House both date from the 15th and 16thc. The Almonry is a 14th- to 16th-c house in Vine Street, now containing a museum. The Tudor Round House (or Booth Hall) is also of interest. The Avon is navigable for small craft at this point, and an annual regatta is held in May.

EWELL, Surrey 8 TQ26
An attractive residential area 1m NE of Epsom. Remains of Henry VIII's Nonsuch Palace are sparse, but a small museum exists on the site.

EWELME, Oxon 13 SU69
This is the little village where Henry VIII spent his honeymoon with Catherine Howard. The couple stayed at the local manor house, home of Alice, Duchess of Suffolk, whose 15th-c tomb is a perfect example of medieval workmanship. An exceptionally interesting group of 15th-c buildings in the village comprise the church, the almshouses, and an old school. Jerome K Jerome, author of *Three Men in a Boat*, died in 1927 and lies in the local churchyard. Watercress beds and streams border the main street.

EWERBY, Lincs 19 TF14
The splendid 14th-c church in this village carries a west tower and fine, broach-spire rising to 172ft. Old bench-ends, a good screen, and a late 14th-c effigy are housed within the building.

EWHURST, Surrey 8 TQ04
An attractive village with several old houses, situated below the Surrey Hills near Hurt Wood. A fine Norman doorway is displayed by the church, but much of the structure was rebuilt after the tower collapsed in 1838. As implied by the name (meaning yew-wood) the district has always been heavily forested. Ewhurst is a good point from which to start the ascent of Pitch Hill, 1m to the N.

EXETER, Devon 5 SX99
Formerly the Roman city of *Isca Dumnoniorum*, this River-Exe university city includes a mainly-decorated cathedral which preserves two remarkable Norman transeptal towers. Some of the other notable features in the building include a minstrels' gallery displaying angels carrying musical instruments; an interesting stone screen; a wealth of carved roof bosses; several good chantry chapels; fine wood carving; and a 14th-c clock. A door in the north transept includes an unusual cat hole. Other old churches in the area include St Mary Steps, which displays a curious old 16th-c clock.

Guildhall dates from 1330, 1446, and 1593 (AM). Wynard's Hospital was founded in 1436, and restored St Nicholas' Priory (AM) is an interesting building of Tudor date. Parts of the Norman Rougemont Castle and sections of the city walls have survived. Mol's Coffee House dates from the 16thc. Fine panelling is preserved in 15th-c Tucker's Hall, and numerous Georgian and Regency houses and terraces exist in the city. A rare 14th-c half-timbered merchant's house was removed from its original site in 1961, and now stands near the river. Customs House was built in 1681, and remains of Polsloe Priory exist. The Maritime Museum on Town Quay is probably the finest in England (OACT), and the Albert Memorial Museum and Art Gallery is of interest.

EXFORD, Somerset 5 SS83
This well-known fishing resort and stag-hunting centre lies in the E of Exmoor, and stands on the River Exe. A 5m path leads N through Exford Common to Dunkerly Beacon – the highest point on Exmoor.

EXMOOR
A royal forest some ten centuries ago, Exmoor now forms a 265sqm national park of which approximately two-thirds lie in Somerset and one-third in Devon. Three types of countryside predominate – coastal, grassy-moorland, and heathland. Bronze age peoples settled here, and some Roman material has been found in the area. In spite of this, settlers did not make much impression on the landscape until John Knight bought 10,000 acres in 1815, for £50,000. He and his successors enclosed and reclaimed a large area.

Exmoor Forest covers an area of approximately 20,000 acres. The annual rainfall exceeds 80in in places, and the highest point is 1,705ft Dunkerly Beacon (NT). Below this and to the N is the beautiful wooded Horner Valley.

Lorna Doone country, an area of picturesque combes, is situated near the Bristol Channel and includes Badgeworthy Valley and the Hoccombe (Doone) Valley. Ponies and red deer run wild on Exmoor, and an annual pony fair is held at Bampton.

EXMOUTH, Devon 6 SY08
Plan overleaf
A well-known seaside resort with excellent sands, situated on the estuary of the River Exe. A passenger ferry links with Starcross, and Georgian houses stand in an area called The Beacon, where Lady Nelson lived. A circular 18th-c house called A La Ronde stands 2m N, and includes a gallery decorated with thousands of sea-shells (OACT). Near by are the picturesque Point in View almshouses, and chapel built to a similar plan.

EXTON, Leics 19 SK91
Exton is a village of thatched stone-built cottages standing in one of the largest ironstone extraction areas in Britain. The restored church has a fine 14th-c tower and spire, and one of the notable monuments housed within the building is by Grinling Gibbons. The old hall was damaged by fire in 1811, and a

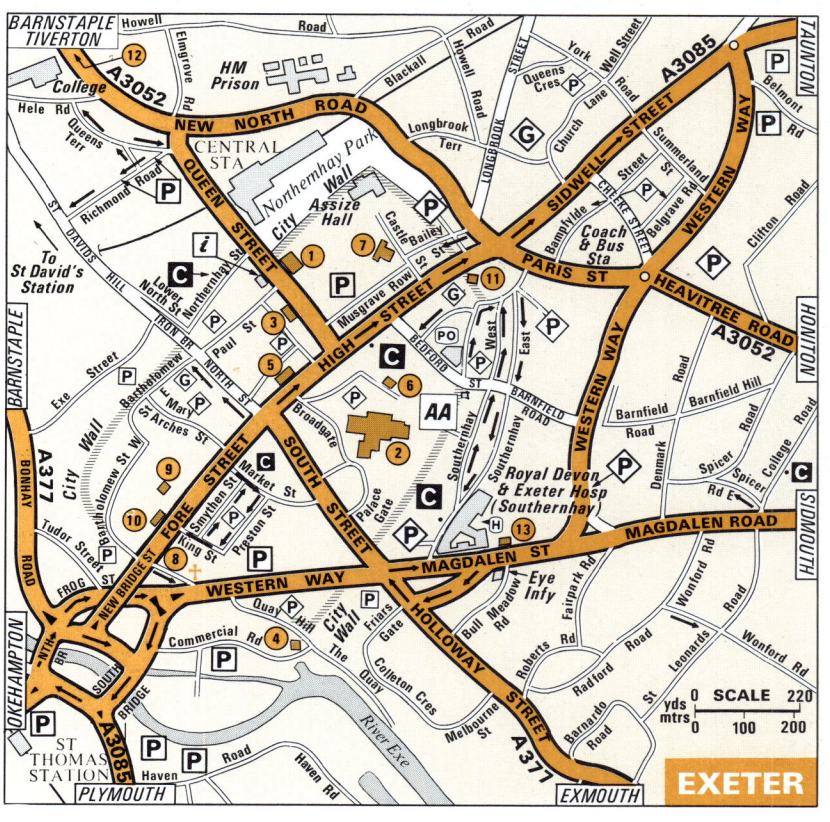

1 Albert Memorial Museum and Art Gallery
2 Cathedral
3 Civic Hall
4 Customs House
5 Guildhall
6 Mol's Coffee House
7 Rougemont Castle Remains
8 St Mary Steps (church)
9 St Nicholas' Priory
10 Tucker's Hall
11 Underground Passages (OACT)
12 University of Exeter
13 Wynard's Hospital

modern building has been erected in the park.

EYAM, Derbyshire *18 SK27*
This village stands at an altitude of 800ft, and is pronounced Eem. It is the notorious plague village of 1665 to 1666, when three-quarters of its 350 inhabitants were killed by the disease. Services to fend off the plague were held by the Rev W Mompesson in Cucklet Dell, where an annual commemoration is still conducted on the last Sunday in August. A notable Runic cross (AM) stands in the churchyard. The church itself dates from the 13th to 15thc, and contains a Mompesson chair dated 1665. An elaborate sundial can be seen on the chancel wall and the Riley graves contain the remains of seven members of one family (the Hancocks) who died of the plague in 1665 (NT).

Eyam's village stocks have been preserved, and the manor house is a fine structure of 1676. Also in the area is an interesting Georgian rectory. Local lead mines are now closed, but large fluorspar workings have been opened.

EYE, Herefs & Worcs *12 SO46*
Eye is a name derived from the old English word for island. The local church displays a fine old porch of carved oak, and the 17th-c manor house was built for Ferdinando Gorges, a former slave-trader. The latter is noted for its wood and plaster-work (OACT).

EYE, Suffolk *15 TM17*
Remains of a castle demolished by Cromwell's army can be seen here, plus several old houses. A lofty 15th-c flint tower and good rood screen are displayed by the church, and the timber-framed Guildhall is of early 16th-c date.

EYNSFORD, Kent *8 TQ56*
An attractive village where a 15th-c bridge spans the River Darent. The 12th-c and later church has a chancel apse and carved perpendicular font. Remains of a castle (AM) include a defensive ditch and flint-rubble walls.

EYNSHAM, Oxon *13 SP40*
The River Thames is spanned by the fine Swinford Bridge to the SE. This structure dates from 1807 and has a toll-house. A 20ft cross in the market square dates from the 14thc.

EYTON, Herefs & Worcs *12 SO46*
This village stands on the River Lugg. Eyton Court displays a 16th-c black-and-white wing, and the church shows a beautiful 15th-c rood screen and loft.

FAILSWORTH, Gt Manchester *22 SD90*
A typical cotton town, now forming part of the Manchester conurbation.

FAIRFORD, Glos *12 SP10*
An attractive River-Coln town with an old mill on a stretch of river notable for its trout fishing. John Keble was born here in 1792, and the church has 15th- to 16th-c stained-glass windows said to be the finest of their period in England. The British prototype Concorde was first tested on an RAF airfield S of the town, in 1969.

FAIRLIGHT, E Sussex *9 TQ81*
The rocky coast from which this place lies slightly inland is not suitable for bathing. Sandstone cliffs rise to 400ft at Fairlight Glen, and are heavily wooded almost to sea level. E of the glen are the Fire Hills, so called because of the mass of brilliant yellow gorse which covers them each year.

FAIRSTEAD, Essex *9 TL71*
The Norman church in this remote Essex village incorporates Roman bricks mingled with pebbles and flints in its construction. A 13th-c tower is carried by the building, and inside are wall paintings of the same period.

FAKENHAM, Norfolk *15 TF92*
An attractive market town where the decorated and perpendicular church displays a good tower and houses a carved screen. Also here are several interesting Georgian buildings, and the restored Elizabethan Thorpland Hall lies 3m NE.

FALMOUTH, Cornwall *4 SW83*
Falmouth is a leading holiday resort with a mild climate. The bay forms an excellent base for yachting, and the beaches allow access for safe bathing.

Shipping from all over the world uses the harbour, which is the largest in the county and includes a dry dock capable of handling tankers of up to 90,000 tons. There is a safe anchorage on the estuary of the Fal. Falmouth began to develop as a port after Sir Walter Raleigh recommended its natural strategic advantages to Sir Peter Killigrew. It became a station for the Mail Packet Service in 1688, and by 1827 had 39 overseas-mail vessels.

Henry VIII's Pendennis Castle overlooks the harbour entrance and provides a good viewpoint (OACT). Arwenack House, a long 17th-c building in Grove Place, incorporates a little of the old Killigrews' house. An east window in the 17th-c church of King Charles the Martyr, dedicated to Charles I, depicts the king holding the execution axe. Attractive 18th- and 19th-c buildings can be seen in the older part of the town; the Customs House and Grove Hill House are two good examples. Steamers sail up the Fal to Truro and also along the winding River Percuil.

FAREHAM, Hants *7 SU50*
This old market town is also a port and is situated at the head of a small creek. Thackeray lived in the town as a boy, and several good Georgian houses can be seen on the Wickham road. Other interesting buildings include the former 19th-c Corn Exchange, and Bishopwood – a thatched house of *c*1800.

FARINGDON, Oxon *13 SU29*
Dairy produce including fine bacon has made this market town famous. The church shows styles ranging from trans-Norman and early-English periods, and contains old monuments and brasses. It lost its spire during the Civil War. Several interesting inns still exist here, plus numerous other old buildings including the 18th-c Market Hall. Faringdon House was built by the Poet Laureate Henry Pye in 1780. A folly in the park was added by Lord Berners in 1935, and was built to provide work and thus relieve local unemployment. Buscot Park is 3½m NW (NT, OACT), and 18th-c Buckland House stands 5m NE.

FARLEIGH HUNGERFORD, Somerset *6 ST85*
A River-Frome village where remains of a 15th-c castle include a chapel housing monuments to the Hungerford family, and a collection of antiquities. The chapel originally served as the parish church (AM, OACT).

FARNBOROUGH, Hants *8 SU85*
Farnborough and its neighbour Aldershot are both leading military centres. It was the birthplace of British air power, and has been the home of the Royal Aircraft Establishment (originally His Majesty's Balloon Factory), since 1906. The well-known air display, attended by spectators from all over the world, is held towards the end of summer every second year.

Farnborough Hill is an interesting old mansion of 1800, set in the midst of private grounds and now housing a Convent College. It was once the home of the Empress Eugenie, who built the Church of St Michael's Abbey in which a mausoleum for her husband (Napoleon III) and her son can be seen. Both were killed during the Zulu War of 1879, and she was also buried there after her death in 1920. Monastic buildings adjoin the church.

The last great fist fight was fought between Tom Sayers and John Heenan in the grounds of the ancient Ship Inn in 1800. It lasted over two hours, and the referee stopped it as a draw. A fine 15th-c wooden porch can be seen at the entrance of the ancient parish church, which also houses a screen and pulpit of 17th-c date.

1 Lady Nelson's House
2 Ornate Shell Gallery, A La Ronde
3 Point in View Almshouses

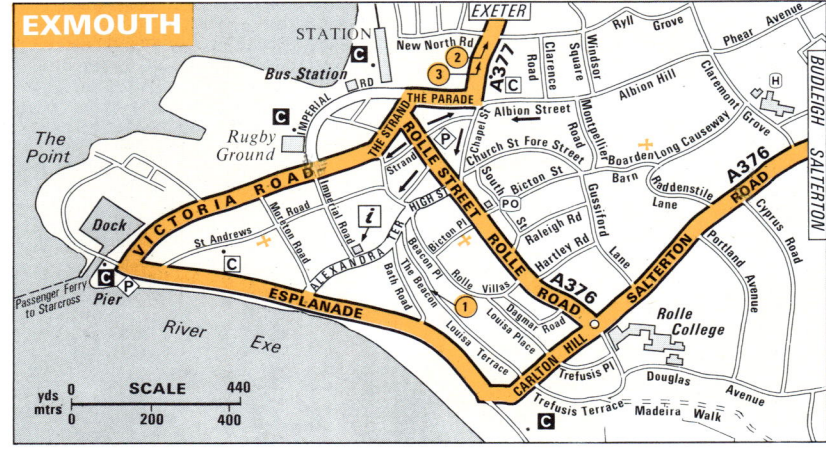

FARNHAM, Surrey *8 SU84*
Farnham is one of the most outstanding examples of a small red-brick country town in England. Its good fortune is largely due to the efforts of preservationists who have made every effort to ensure that necessary new buildings blended in, and that old buildings were protected. The town's essentially Georgian character is also preserved by the lack of motor traffic – a by-pass keeps all through-traffic well away from the town centre. Castle Street and West Street are excellent examples of Georgian street architecture; the latter includes Willmer House and Sandford House, two particularly outstanding examples. Willmer House contains an interesting museum (OACT).

Wide Castle Street climbs to Farnham Castle, where a 12th-c shell keep adjoins the impressive 15th- to 17th-c former residence of the Bishops of Guildford. It is noted for its Great Hall and brick tower, and is now a centre for International Briefing (OACT). On the opposite side of the road is The Grange, a lovely Queen Anne house in outstanding gardens.

William Cobbett, author of *Rural Rides*, was born here and is buried near the porch of the 12th-c and later church. A lofty tower is a feature of the building. Charles I spent a night at the restored Elizabethan Vernon House on the way to his execution. Both the Bush and William Cobbett are old coaching inns; Cobbett was born in the latter. The modern RC Church of St John is notable. Jonathan Swift is associated with 17th- and 18th-c Moor Park (1½m SE), and the Birdworld Zoological Gardens lie 3½m SW at Holt Pound (OACT).

FARNINGHAM, Kent *8 TQ56*
One of the most attractive villages within easy reach of London, Farningham was once an important stop for coaches travelling the Dover Road. Fine 18th-c houses, an old mill by the River Darent, and an interesting inn are some of the interesting buildings to be seen here. The old manor house was once the home of Captain Bligh of The Bounty. The famous Brand's Hatch motor-racing circuit is near here, situated close to the site of a Roman villa.

FARNWORTH, Gt Manchester *21 SD70*
A typical Lancashire industrial town involved in coal-mining, iron-founding, and the manufacture of cotton goods. The Church of St Luke is a 12th-c foundation of mainly decorated and perpendicular styles. Among its many monuments are memorials to the Bold family by Pietro Tenerani, Sir Francis Chantrey, and a firm called Franceys of Liverpool.

FAR SAWREY, Cumbria *21 SD39*
This hamlet lies between Windermere and Esthwaite Water. Hill Top was the 17th-c home of Beatrix Potter (NT, OACT).

FAVERSHAM, Kent *9 TR06*
Once a flourishing port, this quiet old market town includes many interesting houses, particularly in Court Street and Abbey Street. The latter leads to Faversham Creek. Specifically notable buildings include the arcaded town hall, the Freemason's Hall (once a school), a house in Court Street where James II was held in 1688, and the old Ship Inn.

The site of a Cluniac abbey and tomb of King Stephen its founder were discovered here in 1965. Near by is the house of Thomas Arden (1540), whose murder by his wife's hand became the subject of a play, *Arden of Faversham*.

Manufacture of gunpowder was once a local industry, and the last of the town mills has been preserved (OACT). The large partly early-English church contains carved late 15th-c stalls, numerous brasses, and an Easter Sepulchre of 1535. Davington Priory lies ½m NW and is partly Norman; the domestic buildings have been restored. Lees Court is a partly-rebuilt 17th-c house attributed to Inigo Jones, lying 4m S.

FAWLEY, Bucks *8 SU78*
Fawley Court is one of the few secular buildings attributed to Wren, and stands to the SE in grounds landscaped by Capability Brown. The church has a 13th-c tower and the chancel, rebuilt in 1748, contains fittings from a former mansion belonging to the Duke of Chandos. This mansion used to stand at Canons, near Edgware.

FAWLEY, Hants *7 SU40*
This Fawley stands on the edge of the New Forest and close to Southampton Water, in an area completely dominated by a large petroleum refinery. The church, damaged during the war, incorporates examples of Norman work. Calshot Castle was originally built by King Henry VIII for coastal defence, and lies 3m SE. Eaglehurst is a Regency house lying to the SW. Lofty Eaglehurst Tower was built in the 18thc, and may once have been used to store smuggled wines.

FEERING, Essex *15 TL82*
Feering church displays remarkable Tudor brickwork. A few thatched cottages are included in the village, and Houchin's Farm (1600) is a picturesque timbered and weather-boarded house lying 2m N.

FELIXSTOWE, Suffolk *15 TM33*
A resort near the estuaries of the Orwell and Stour, where the beach comprises shingle, pebbles, and a little sand. The Church of St Peter and St Paul in Church Road, Old Felixstowe, retains a 14th-c doorway and old bench-ends. Landguard Fort was originally built in the mid 16thc, but was rebuilt in the two following centuries. Felixstowe Dock is an oil-tanker terminal and container port about 2m S, with a car-ferry service to Rotterdam.

FELMERSHAM, Beds *13 SP95*
This attractive River-Ouse village includes charming stone-built houses, a tithe barn, and a picturesque inn among its more interesting features. The church – particularly the west font – is a fine example of early-English work, and contains a delicate perpendicular screen.

FELPHAM, W Sussex *8 SZ99*
An old cottage in Felpham was once occupied by the poet William Blake. The place itself offers good sands, bathing, and fishing, and is now a suburb of Bognor.

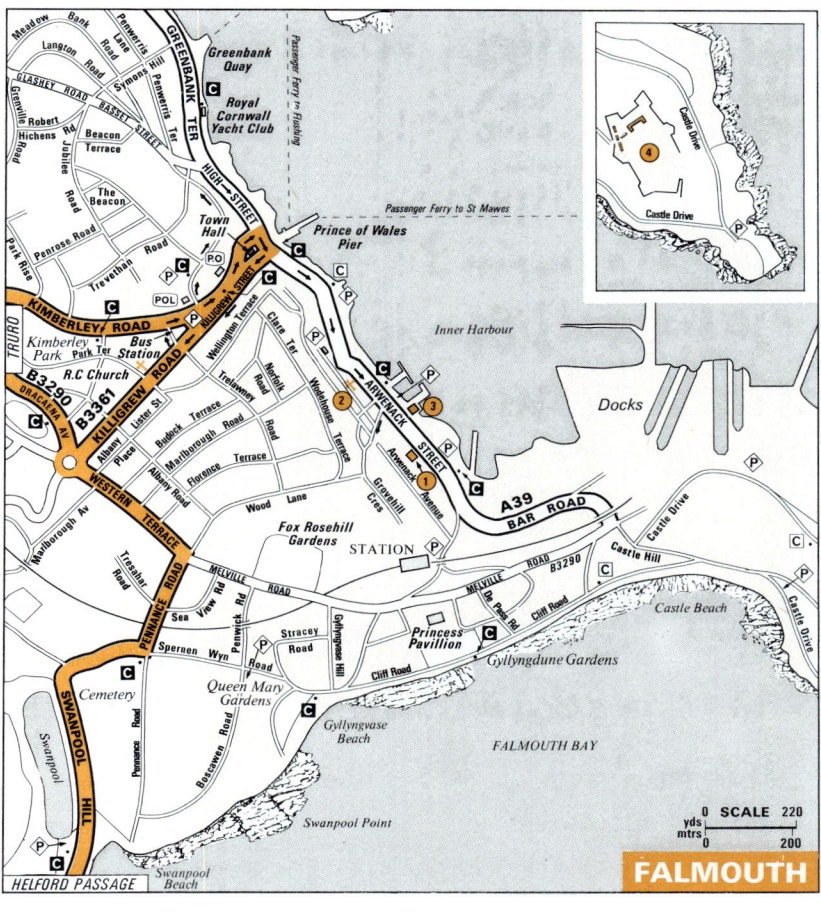

1 Arwenack House
2 Church of King Charles the Martyr
3 Customs House
4 Pendennis Castle

Mid 2nd-c mosaic from the Roman palace at Fishbourne

FELSTED, Essex *14 TL62*
Also spelt Felstead, this village of old houses has a mainly trans-Norman church. The public school was founded in 1564 by Lord Rich, a sumptuous monument to whom can be seen in the church's Rich chapel.

FENNY BENTLEY, Derbyshire *18 SK15*
A good screen of c1500 and the curious Beresford monument are interesting features of the gothic church. Remains of an ancient tower are incorporated in the fine 15th-c manor house.

FENNY STRATFORD, Bucks *13 SP83*
This place is now part of Bletchley, and boasts a marina on the Grand Union Canal. Fenny Poppers are the local name for carronades which are fired on 11 November in the churchyard. This is to commemorate Dr Browne Willis's founding of the church in 1730. A carronade is a short large-calibred ship's gun. Six of these were presented to the church by the doctor, and on the traditional day are used to produce gunpowder explosions every four hours.

FENSTANTON, Cambs *14 TL36*
The Roman road *Via Devana* leads NW from Cambridge on a line which brings it very close to this village. Notable examples of the decorated style are displayed by the chancel east window of the church. Capability Brown lived here for twenty-five years, and he, his wife, and their eldest son are buried in the church. Also of interest are a clock tower and a quaint old lock-up.

FENS, THE
The Fens are a flat and fertile district extending from N of Cambridge to the Wash, and including the extensive Bedford Level W of Wisbech. The area was once very marshy; Vermuyden, Rennie, and Telford are famous names connected with the giant reclamation scheme which started in the 17thc, and nowadays the whole district is well-drained by criss-cross systems of canals and dykes. The area W of King's Lynn, known as the Marshland, is famous for its numerous medieval churches.

FEOCK, Cornwall *4 SW83*
Rare seven-holed stocks can be seen in the churchyard of this prettily-situated village. The Trelissick estate includes a partly 19th-c mansion set in a fine park (NT, OACT). The King Harry car ferry crosses the River Fal NE of Feock.

FERRYBRIDGE, W Yorks *22 SE42*
This place includes a fine bridge over the River Aire, which was built by Carr of York in 1789 and is now used by pedestrians only. Near by is a large new power-station. An interesting prehistoric round barrow is situated to the NW of St Andrew's Church.

FIFIELD BAVANT, Wilts *7 SU02*
The tiny local church houses a Norman font and is one of the smallest in England (35ft by 14ft). Norrington Manor dates from the 14th to 17thc, and now serves as a farm (3m SW).

FILEY, N Yorks *23 TA18*
This is a golfing resort with a sandy beach allowing access for bathing and fishing. A jagged reef called Filey Brigg lies to the NE below Carr Naze cliff. The church is mainly early-English, and displays a massive tower and fine south doorway. It is planned that a 70m footpath, to be known as Wolds Way, will terminate here after crossing the high Wolds from North Ferriby on the Humber estuary. Another path links Filey with Saltburn-on-the-Sea, pushing its 90m course along the coast, thence inland across high moorlands to Helmsley. The latter is known as Cleveland Way.

FILLEIGH, Devon *5 SS62*
The rebuilt church of 1732 contains two brasses for one man, both dated 1570. Castle Hill is a fine house that has been rebuilt since 1934. The great park in which it is set also contains a Sitka spruce which has attained a girth of 25ft.

FILLINGHAM, Lincs *19 SK98*
Fillingham lies below a ridge known as The Cliff, and includes several old cottages. John Wycliffe was rector here from 1361 to 1368, and the church was largely rebuilt in 1777. Fillingham Castle is sited on The Cliff, and dates from 1770.

FINCHALE, Co Durham *27 NZ24*
Finchale Priory stands by the bank of the River Wear; it is a 13th-c building considered to be the most important monastic survival in this county. The tower, cloisters, and refrectory are later than the basic structure, and date from the 14thc.

FINCHAMPSTEAD, Berks *8 SU76*
An early-Norman font and a brick tower dating from 1720 are features of the local church. Finchampstead Ridges (NT) form a notable viewpoint 1m NE, and a splendid double-avenue of tall sequoia pines borders the Crowthorne road to the E. Nine-Mile Ride follows the line of a former Roman road 2m N, and passes through delightfully wooded country.

FINCHINGFIELD, Essex *14 TL63*
This is perhaps the most picturesque village in Essex; its duckpond and stream, village green, and church on a hill give it an air of having just materialized from a children's storybook – a feeling enforced by numerous old houses. A postmill still stands in the village, and 1m N is a fine 16th- to 18th-c house known as Spains Hall.

FINDON, W Sussex *8 TQ10*
A village sited in a downland valley, Findon lies 2m W of a well-known earthwork called Cissbury Ring (NT). This is the largest iron-age entrenchment in the South Downs.

FINEDON, Northants *13 SP97*
The church at Finedon shows good 14th-c work, and displays a tower and spire that rise to 133ft. The nave has an unusual carved strainer-arch, and the Old Bell Inn is one of the earliest known. Wellington tower is a circular edifice commemorating the Iron Duke's visit to General Arbuthnot, lying 2m NE.

FINGEST, Bucks *8 SU79*
A curious double-saddleback roof surmounts the local church's fine Norman tower. The area is notable for its fine Chiltern beech-wood scenery.

FINGRINGHOE, Essex *15 TM02*
This pleasant village lies near the Colne estuary, and includes several old houses. An earthquake of 1884 revealed interesting wall-paintings in the 15th-c church.

FISHBOURNE, W Sussex *8 SU80*
Fishbourne lies just W of Chichester, on a site where the largest Roman palace ever to be found in this country was excavated. Tesellated pavements, mosaic floors, and a museum lie under a roof which allows the whole of one wing to be kept open for public view. The large formal garden has been arranged on the same ground plan and planted with the same shrubs and trees as the Roman original.

FITTLEWORTH, W Sussex *8 TQ01*
A medieval bridge spans the River Rother here, and a watermill is just one of the picturesque old buildings to be seen in the village. The Swan Inn has a gallows sign.

FLADBURY, Herefs & Worcs *12 SO94*
The Ferry Inn and Cropthorne mill are interesting features of this attractive River-Avon village. Notable brasses are housed within the 14th-c church.

FLAGG, Derbyshire *18 SK16*
Flagg is situated on the edge of the curious Flagg Bowl, one of the sights of the county. Steeplechases are held here on Easter Monday, and the Peak dry-stone wall contest takes place once every three years.

FLAMBOROUGH, N Yorks *23 TA27*
An old octagonal lighthouse (AM) standing near the sea at Flamborough is made of chalk, and the local church preserves a rare 15th-c rood screen and loft. A naval battle was fought near here in 1779, between the frigate Serapis and the American Bonhomme Richard, the latter under Commodore Paul Jones. Fine chalk cliffs can be seen at the North Landing and 4m E at Flamborough Head.

FLAMSTEAD, Herts *8 TL01*
The Norman to 15th-c church in this pretty village shows 15th-c screenwork and notable medieval wall-paintings. The community also boasts 17th-c almshouses. Beechwood lies 1½m SW on the site of a former nunnery, and displays a beautiful brick front of 1702.

FLASH, Staffs *18 SK06*
Flash lies at 1,518ft in the Peak District national park, and is usually acclaimed as the highest-situated village in England. Axe Edge rises immediately to the N.

FLATFORD MILL, Suffolk *15 TM03*
A River-Stour watermill dating from the 18thc, one of several owned by the father of painter John Constable. The mill, mill house, and picturesque Willy Lott's Cottage (all NT) are portrayed in Constable's paintings; the artist worked here for a year.

FLEET, Lincs *14 TF32*
A thatched lych-gate covers the approach to the restored 14th-c church, which also displays a detached tower and spire, and curious gargoyles.

FLEETWOOD, Lancs *21 SD34*
This large fishing port lies on the Wyre estuary and Morecambe Bay, and is a popular resort offering 4m of beach, bathing from good sands at low tide, and a large indoor swimming pool. A wonderful panoramic view of the Lake District mountains can be enjoyed from Mount Pavilion. A steamer service plies to the Isle of Man, and the town includes large fish docks.

FLETCHING, E Sussex *8 TQ42*
Edward Gibbon (died 1794) is buried in the Sheffield mausoleum of the church; the main building houses two notable brasses, and a restored 14th-c screen.

FLETTON, Cambs *19 TL19*
The Norman and decorated church at Fletton displays Saxon carving on the south-chancel wall. Large brickworks are a feature of the district.

FLITTON, Beds *14 TL03*
The De Grey mausoleum is a remarkable feature of the village's 15th-c church, and contains tombs and brasses from the 16thc onwards.

FLORE, Northants *13 SP66*
The ancestors of John Adams, who followed George Washington as President of the USA, are said to have lived in the thatched Adams Cottage. A River-Nene watermill can be seen near by, and the 13th- to 15th-c church displays old brasses and 15th-c screenwork. The village school is noted for its May Day festival.

FOLKESTONE, Kent *9 TR23*
An ancient town and Cinque port 'limb', Folkestone is now a harbour for cross-Channel steamers and a popular holiday resort. The Old Town near the harbour is picturesque; fishing boats still sail from the Inner Harbour and bring back catches to be sold in the Fish Market.

The Leas is a wide grassy promenade running along the clifftop, connected by lift to the seafront. Many attractive, wooded walks slope down to the beach, and several Martello towers can be seen along the coast. A few old houses exist near the harbour, and impressive Victorian terraces along the Leas are interspersed with striking new buildings. Much of the old town was destroyed by heavy bombing during the last war. A road running downhill from The Leas to the harbour is named the Road of Remembrance, and has rosemary bushes planted along the side. This forms a memorial to the many soldiers who marched down the hill to embark on troopships, but did not return after the war.

The Warren lies E and is an interesting strip of coast between high cliffs and the sea; it is a noted habitat of rare plants, hundreds of trees, and is an area rich in fossil remains. Remains of two Roman villas have been excavated here. The parish church of St Mary and Eanswith is of early-English to perpendicular origins and displays later additions. It houses a casket of early relics, and includes an aisle commemorating William Harvey, who discovered the circulation of the blood and became physician to James I. He was born near by in 1578. A museum of local interest is situated at Grace Hill, and the New Metropole Arts Centre holds exhibitions at the W end of The Leas. Spade House, now a museum, was once the home of H G Wells; some of his best known works were written here.

The ancient fortifications of Caesar's Camp, 2m N on the North Downs, were once assumed to be Roman. It is now thought that they may be of early-Norman construction.

FOLKINGHAM, Lincs *19 TF03*
An impressive old coaching-inn is a reminder of this town's one-time importance. A tall 15th-c tower is carried by the early-English and later church, which also preserves the stocks and whipping-post. Earthworks mark the site of a former castle, and several late-Georgian houses can be seen.

FONTHILL BISHOP, Wilts *7 ST93*
An attractive village on the outskirts of Fonthill Park, 1m N of Fonthill House. The house recalls a once-sumptuous mansion created by James Wyatt for Willam Beckford, author of *Vathek*. Wellingtonia firs near Fonthill have attained heights of up to 165ft.

FORD, Northumberland *27 NT93*
The castle at Ford was rebuilt in the 18thc, but retains two 14th-c towers.

FORD, W Sussex *8 TQ00*
A River-Arun village which includes several old farm buildings. The 11th-c church is set among trees, well away from roads, and has a brick south porch of 1637. Several faded 15th-c wall-paintings can be seen inside.

FORDHAM, Cambs *14 TL67*
Fordham Abbey dates from c1710, and the early-English to perpendicular church includes an unusual lady chapel.

FORDINGBRIDGE, Hants *7 SU11*
A village near the edge of the New Forest, where an old bridge spans the River Avon. Augustus John the painter died here in 1961, and a memorial was raised to him in 1967. The restored church includes an interesting 15th-c chapel. Hale Park (4m NE) dates from 1715 to 1770, and was designed by Thomas Archer.

FORDWICH, Kent *9 TR15*
This was once Canterbury's River-Stour port, but nowadays the river is navigable only by canoe. The church is partly Norman and preserves a rare heart shrine. A sculptured tomb also housed in the building may have been the one in which St Augustine once lay. An old ducking-stool is preserved in the ancient timbered town hall (AM).

FORTHAMPTON, Glos *12 SO83*
This is a picturesque village of black-and-white cottages and ancient barns. Forthampton Court preserves 14th- or 15th-c work, and the mainly 14th-c church displays a remarkable wall-painting and old woodwork. Stocks and a whipping-post have also been preserved.

1 Church of St Mary and Eanswith
2 Fish Market
3 Martello Towers
4 Museum
5 New Metropole Arts Centre
6 The Lees

FOSSE WAY
Excavations have shown that this famous Romanized road was built partly on earlier tracks. It crosses England diagonally from a point near Axminster to Lincoln, passing through the towns of Bath, Cirencester, and Leicester – all one-time Roman stations. Much of its course is followed by the present-day A46 and A429, but certain stretches are now only recognizable as rough tracks.

FOTHERINGHAY, Northants 19 TL09
The site of the vanished castle where Mary Queen of Scots was executed in 1587. An imposing perpendicular church displays a lantern tower, but is only a portion of the original collegiate church that once stood here. A fine 18th-c bridge spans the River Nene, and a picturesque old hostel, built in the 15thc by Edward IV, is now a farmhouse. Mary's executioner is said to have spent the night prior to the execution here. Southwick Hall is a partly 14th-c building lying 4m SW.

FOULNESS, Essex 15 TR09
This Thames-estuary island is a lonely stretch of land occupied only by birds, wildfowlers, and a few scattered farms. The wildlife here was threatened by the development of a new London airport, but plans for this have since been suspended. The marsh areas are prolific with bird life for most of the year.

FOUNTAINS ABBEY, N Yorks 22 SE26
Remains of this beautiful 12th- to 15th-c Cistercian abbey (AM) lie within the park of Studley Royal, on the River Skell. The whole structure is notable, but of particular interest are the nave, tower, and lay-brothers' quarters. These ruins are among the best preserved in the country, and display an imposing system of medieval drains and waterworks. Near by stands the early 17th-c Fountains Hall, built with stones from the abbey (OACT).

FOVANT, Wilts 7 SU02
The chancel of the 15th-c church contains a brass of 1492, depicting the rector of the period. Military badges carved in the chalk of the nearby Down were executed by troops training for the first World War.

FOWEY, Cornwall 4 SX15
Fowey, pronounced Foy, stands at the estuary of a River bearing the same name. It has a harbour, several quaint streets, and bathing at sandy Readymoney Cove. The town hall of 1792 retains several 14th-c windows, and St Catherine's Fort (AM) was built by order of King Henry VIII. Tudor Place House has been restored. The Church of St Fimbarrus, with its Rashleigh monuments, is largely of 14th-c origin. Quiller-Couch lived and wrote here, using the town under the name Troy Town in many of his books.

The sign of the King of Prussia Inn commemorates a famous Cornish smuggler, John Carter, who operated some two centuries ago. Menabilly is a house dating from 1600, 1770, and c1820, lying in fine grounds that originate from the latter period.

FOWNHOPE, Herefs & Worcs 12 SO53
A village on the banks of the River Wye, where the church has a Norman tower and an Elizabethan mansion called the Court displays timbered construction. Two prehistoric camps can be seen in the neighbourhood.

FOXTON, Leics 18 SP79
Scanty remains of an inclined plane, or lift, exist at this point on the Grand Union Canal. It was built in 1900 but abandoned ten years later for technical reasons. The 'staircase' currently comprises ten locks. A village church dates back to the 13thc, and the nearby manor house is partly medieval.

FRAMLINGHAM, Suffolk 15 TM26
Extensive remains of a castle that was largely rebuilt in the 16thc can be seen here (AM, OACT). It was originally built by Roger Bigod, 2nd Earl of Norfolk, in about 1190. The chimneys and towers are notable, and picturesque almshouses which include fragments of the great hall in their construction stand within the walls. Mary Tudor lived here for a time and the castle became a rallying point for her supporters. The church contains a splendid range of mid 16th-c Howard monuments. Thomas Howard was made Duke of Norfolk. Several old houses and a well-known school are additional features of the town.

FRAMPTON-ON-SEVERN, Glos 12 SO70
A delightful village grouped around Rosamund's Green, one of the largest village greens in England. An old timbered manor farm includes a fine barn, and 18th-c Frampton Court was built by a pupil of Vanbrugh.

FREISTON, Lincs 19 TF34
Marshes and creeks are features of the countryside around this coastal village. The fine church was originally the nave of a 12th-c priory church, and houses a lofty perpendicular font cover. White Loaf Hall stands E and dates from 1613 and 1614.

FRENSHAM, Surrey 8 SU84
Well-known Frensham Ponds cover over 100 acres and provide an excellent amenity for fishing and sailing. The River Wey runs through here, and the crest of the common carries a line of large bowl barrows. The restored church houses a Norman font and a curious old pot, said to be the witches' cauldron owned by a Mother Ludlam. She lived in a nearby cave in the Middle Ages. The church itself displays 14th- to 15th-c work.

FRESHWATER, Isle of Wight 7 SZ38
Tennyson memorials are housed in the church, and a column to the poet stands on lofty High Down. The Church of St Agnes is an interesting thatched building. Freshwater Bay is suitable for bathing, and has sand at low tide. Freshwater Cave can be explored at low tide, and the Arched and Stag Rocks are notable. Farringford House stands 1m SW and was once owned by Tennyson; he wrote Crossing the Bar on his way to the island.

FRESSINGFIELD, Suffolk 15 TM27
The Fox and Goose Inn is a picturesque timbered and plastered building. Old carved bench-ends are housed in the 14th- and 15th-c church.

FRIDAY STREET, Surrey 8 TQ14
Friday Street is a picturesque hamlet of red cottages, where a lovely lake is backed by pine trees (partly NT). The name of the inn, the Stephen Langton, is unusual; it recalls the Cardinal who was Archbishop of Canterbury from 1207 to 1288, and who played a leading role in drawing up Magna Carta. Severell's Copse is a 59-acre patch of woodland (NT) stretching from a hillside by the lake to Leith Hill.

FRIERN BARNET, Gt London 8 TQ29
The Campe almshouses in this residential district date from 1612. *Friern* is an Old English form of friars, and the place once belonged to the Hospital of St John of Jerusalem.

FRINTON-ON-SEA, Essex 9 TM21
A quietly fashionable resort with facilities for bathing, golf, fishing and tennis tournaments.

FRISTON, E Sussex 8 TV59
Friston is a downland village with a partly-Norman church containing the Selwyn tomb and a strangely-carved black-oak chair. Friston Place is a restored Tudor house with a curious donkey-well in the garden. The area is noted for gliding.

FRITHELSTOCK, Devon 5 SS41
The west front of an Augustinian priory, founded c1220, is still standing here. The parish church displays a lofty tower, wagon roofs, and Royal Arms of 1677.

FRITTON, Norfolk 15 TG40
Several wall-paintings inside the local church are of note. The building itself has a Saxon tower and the chancel shows Norman work. Under the thatched roof of the chancel is a trap door, said to have been the access to a smugglers' hiding-place. Fritton Decoy, near the partly-ruined St Olave's Priory (AM), is an attractive little lake lying ½m E.

FRITWELL, Oxon 13 SP52
This large village includes a beautiful Jacobean manor house of 1619, which has a history of past tragedies. Two Norman doorways are preserved in the early-English to perpendicular church.

FROCESTER, Glos 12 SO70
Frocester Court has a timbered gatehouse and was visited by Queen Elizabeth I in 1574. Frocester Hill is an AA viewpoint, and the village is known for its very fine old tithe barn.

FRODSHAM, Cheshire 17 SJ57
The picturesque Bear's Paw Inn dates from 1632, and restored Frodsham church is partly Norman. The latter contains old screenwork and a fine north chapel.

FROME, Somerset 6 ST74
The name of this busy market town is pronounced Froom, and its main industry is the manufacture of cloth and carpets. It is criss-crossed by steep narrow streets and its well-restored richly-decorated church contains numerous chapels. Cheap Street has a central watercourse running down the middle of the road, and the Bluecoat School dates from about 1720. Old almshouses stand by a bridge spanning the River Frome. Most of the old houses here date from the 18thc. Orchardleigh Park, with its Victorian mansion, lies 4m N. An island in the lake bears a small restored church of great interest, particularly notable for its examples of ancient glass and a fine priest's doorway.

FROYLE, Hants 8 SU74
Froyle's red-brick church is of Georgian date, but retains its late 13th-c chancel. Isington Mill, a nearby restored building, is the home of Field Marshal Lord Montgomery.

FRYERNING, Essex 9 TL60
Roman tiles are incorporated in the fabric of the church, and the west tower is a fine example of 15th-c brickwork.

FULBECK, Lincs 19 SK95
A pretty village in a wooded setting, Fulbeck has a restored church containing a fine trans-Norman font and many monuments. The hall dates from 1733 and is the seat of the Fanes.

FULBOURN, Cambs 14 TL55
To the SE of the village is the line of 3m-long Fleam Dyke, a massive 7th-c earthwork built to defend East Anglia from the Mercians. SW are the low Gog Magog Hills, from which Cambridge can be seen. The village itself is attractive, and includes a good early-English to perpendicular church.

FURNESS ABBEY, Cumbria 21 SD27
Exceptional pink-sandstone remains of this 12th-c and later abbey lie in an attractive Cumbrian setting (AM, OACT). Originally a Savignac house, the abbey was taken over by the Cistercian order and became one of the richest Cistercian houses in England – second only to Fountains Abbey. Most of this wealth was in property. A great deal of the building remains, including one end of the church and the east side of the cloister, with its adjoining chapter house.

FURNEAUX PELHAM, Herts 14 TL42
A pleasant village where windows by Morris and Burne-Jones can be seen in the early-English to perpendicular church. The nearby hall is a fine Elizabethan structure.

FYFIELD, Oxon 13 SU49
Interesting monuments can be seen in the restored church, and a 14th-c manor house stands in the village. The Fyfield or Tubney Elm, an actual shoot from the original tree, is associated with Matthew Arnold's *Scholar Gipsy*.

FYLDE, THE
The Fylde is a flat Lancashire district extending from the Wyre estuary, near Fleetwood, towards the estuary of the Ribble farther S. The district comprises about half of the ancient Hundred of Amounderness, and preserves numerous windmills.

GADDESBY, Leics 18 SK61
The fine 13th- to 14th-c church contains an equestrian statue depicting Colonel Cheney on the battlefield at Waterloo. By J Gott, this is one of the few pieces of its kind to be found in an English church. The south side of the church is richly decorated with stone carvings.

GADS HILL, Kent 9 TQ77
An inn in Gads Hill is associated with Shakespeare's Falstaff; it was here in *Henry IV part I* that Falstaff met the rogues in buckram. Gads Hill Place is an 18th-c red-brick building that was the former home of Dickens. He died here in 1870. The Swiss Chalet, formerly in the garden, was the studio where Dickens worked on his last novel. It now stands at Eastgate House, Rochester.

GAINFORD, Co Durham 22 NZ11
The restored church is attractively situated above the River Tees, and dates largely from the 13thc. An old Elizabethan hall has been restored.

GAINSBOROUGH, Lincs 19 SK88
Gainsborough is associated with George Eliot's *Mill on the Floss* and appears under the name of St Ogg's. A three-arched bridge spans the River Trent and links the town with Nottinghamshire on the opposite bank. Gainsborough Old Hall (AM, OACT) dates from the 15th to 16thc, and is one of the largest medieval buildings open to the public in England. Richard III, Henry VIII, and the latter's fifth wife Katherine Howard stayed at the house. All Saints' church displays a 15th-c tower, but the majority was rebuilt in classical style in 1745. The Trent tidal wave (eagre) can be seen at certain times.

GAMLINGAY, Cambs 14 TL25
This village has a row of old almshouses that were built in the year of the Great London Plague. The church is mainly of 15th-c date; it houses an oak screen with fine tracery dating from the last years of the 14thc, plus stalls with armrests showing animals and birds, bishops and angels.

GANTON, N Yorks 23 SE97
An attractive village at the foot of the Wolds, $7\frac{1}{2}$m SW of Scarborough. A fine view of the Vale of Pickering can be enjoyed from the churchyard.

GARBOLDISHAM, Norfolk 15 TM08
The decorated and perpendicular church displays a good tower, and the old hall dates from c1700. An ancient 2m-long earthwork called the Devil's Dyke lies $1\frac{1}{4}$m W.

GARROWBY, Humberside 23 SE85
Situated on the edge of the Wolds, at a height of 800ft, Garrowby is a splendid viewpoint. A 20ft memorial cross to King George VI can be seen here, and Garrowby Hall is of late 19th-c date.

GARSDON, Wilts 12 ST98
Both the church and former manor house have associations with the family of George Washington. The bells in the church tower were given by Richard Moody, a servant of Henry VIII, who received the manor as a gift. He later sold it to the Washingtons. A tomb of 1640 can be seen in the church, showing the stars and stripes that were later adopted in the design of the American flag.

GARWAY, Herefs & Worcs 12 SO42
A small village on the River Monnow, where the church has been rebuilt and shows fine Norman work in the chancel. The massive semi-detached tower is of interest, and near by is a circular 14th-c dovecote which once belonged to the Knights Templars. Surrounding countryside is largely unspoiled and of great rural beauty.

GATESHEAD, Tyne & Wear 27 NZ26
Gateshead is a Tyneside town traditionally involved in the building and repair of ships, but it also conducts a wide range of additional industries.

It is linked to Newcastle upon Tyne by five notable bridges: the swing bridge (1874 to 1876) was one of the earliest opening bridges in the country; the high-level bridge was built (1846 to 1849) to a design by Robert Stephenson, and carries road and rail traffic; Redheugh bridge is also high-level, was originally built in 1871, and reconstructed in 1901; King Edward Railway Bridge (1906) carries main-line trains from the S to Newcastle upon Tyne and Scotland. The last and most recent is the Tyne Bridge of 1928, perhaps the most majestic of them all, which crosses the river with a single span of 531ft. It is 1,800ft long and stands 200ft above the river at its highest point.

Much of Gateshead was completely destroyed in a fire of 1854. The parish church originates from the 12thc, but a large part of the present building was constructed in 1855. Nave arcades of the 14thc are interesting, and the church houses several handsome pews that date from 1634. The Team Valley trading estate to the SW dates from 1936.

GATWICK, W Sussex 8 TQ24
This is the site of London's second airport, which was enlarged to cope with the increasing volume of modern air traffic. A spectators' enclosure includes car parking facilities. Access to the airport is via an adjoining main-line railway station, and the A23 London to Brighton road. The latter is to be eventually supplemented by the M23 motorway.

Gateshead's majestic Tyne Bridge of 1928

GAWSWORTH, Cheshire 17 SJ86
The fine village church displays a perpendicular tower, quaint gargoyles, and a notable range of monuments to the Fittons of Gawsworth Hall. A picturesque 15th-c black-and-white rectory is of interest, and Gawsworth Hall is an Elizabethan half-timbered house (OACT). The grave of Maggoty Johnson, an eccentric dramatist of the 18thc, lies in a nearby spinney.

GAYHURST, Bucks 13 SP84
Gayhurst House is a splendid late 16th- to 18th-c building that once belonged to Sir Francis Drake. The leaders of the infamous Gunpowder Plot, including Guy Fawkes, used to meet here. A park that surrounds the house contains a church that was completely rebuilt in 1728. This houses a monument to Sir Nathan Wright and his son, attributed to Louis Roubiliac, depicting two standing figures in period dress and wigs. Tyringham Hall dates from the late 18thc and lies on the far side of the River Ouse. It was designed by Sir John Soane and Sir Edwin Lutyens, and displays a fine bridge.

GEDDINGTON, Northants 13 SP88
An attractive, stone-built village where one of the three surviving Eleanor Crosses has been preserved. Originally there were twelve of these memorials, all of which were raised by King Edward, in memory of Queen Eleanor (1290). The cross (AM) is built over a well. Geddington's church contains fine old screenwork, and a feature of the village is the ancient much-repaired bridge. A magnificent park surrounds 17th-c Boughton House (½m E), a building that has been called the English Versailles.

GEDLING, Notts 18 SK64
The largely 13th-c church displays a fine 14th-c tower and spire. Graves of Arthur Shrewsbury and Alfred Shaw, both famous cricketers, can be seen in the churchyard.

GEDNEY, Lincs 14 TF42
Gedney's fine marshland church shows early-English to perpendicular styles, and carries a notable west tower. Other interesting features include a 14th-c porch and a good 15th-c nave clerestory. A 14th-c brass to a lady can be seen, plus several alabaster effigies.

GERRARDS CROSS, Bucks 8 TQ08
A residential district with a modern Byzantine-style church of 1859, and an area of common land.

GESTINGTHORPE, Essex 15 TL83
The local church has been restored and displays an embattled brick tower, a double-hammerbeam roof of c1500, and a restored 15th-c screen. A notable feature is a memorial to Polar explorer Captain Oates, who died in an act of supreme self-sacrifice with the intention of saving his companions' lives.

GIGGLESWICK, N Yorks 21 SD86
Situated in limestone country on the River Ribble, Giggleswick includes a perpendicular church dedicated to St Alkelda. The carved pulpit is of 1680 and an ancient reading-desk can be seen. The school was founded in the 16thc. Giggleswick Scar lies 1m N.

GILLING EAST, N Yorks 22 SE67
This parish is beautifully situated between the Hambleton and Howardian Hills. The castle, now a school, includes a 14th-c keep and a magnificent Elizabethan dining-room. The latter's original ribbed-plaster ceiling has been preserved, and the room is considered one of the finest in England. The west front is ascribed to Vanbrugh (OACT).

GILLINGHAM, Dorset 6 ST82
A River-Stour town in an area that was once a royal manor and forest, Gillingham now pursues a number of industries that include brewing, pottery, and flour milling. The school was founded in 1526, and several good Georgian houses exist in the town.

GILLINGHAM, Kent 9 TQ76
The name of this industrial town is pronounced Jillingham; it is linked to Chatham and includes paper mills sited on the Medway estuary. Will Adams, a sailor who founded Japan's sea-power, was born here and has a memorial clock on Chatham Hill. The Royal Engineers' museum is situated in the suburb of Brompton.

GILLINGHAM, Norfolk 15 TM49
A village 1½m NW of Beccles where the hall is of 17th- to 18th-c date. The church is of pure early-Norman origin.

GILSLAND, Northumberland 26 NY66
This small town stands on the River Irthing and was once a spa with sulphur and chalybeate springs. Sir Walter Scott met and became engaged to Charlotte Margaret Carpenter here in 1797. A Roman Wall and the fort of *Amboglanna* exist in the area, and remains of Triermain Castle lie on the Canonbie road (to Scotland). Cramel Linn waterfall is a picturesque feature of the surrounding countryside.

GITTISHAM, Devon 6 SY19
Thatched cottages and a 14th- to 15th-c church containing a fine Beaumont monument can be seen here. Joanna Southcott, famous for the numerous curious prophecies she made during the late 18thc, was born here.

GLASSON DOCK, Lancs 21 SD45
A Lune-estuary port with 18th-c quays and walls, and a large basin on the Lancaster Canal. These installations are of great interest to industrial archaeologists. Yachts and coastal vessels still use the port.

GLASTONBURY, Somerset 6 ST43
According to legend, Joseph of Arimathea landed on the Somerset coast with the Holy Grail and made his way inland to Glastonbury. He and his followers reached Wearyall Hill on Christmas morning, where he stuck his staff in the ground while he rested. The staff took root and flowered, a sign that his travels were over, and that he should found a religious house. St Patrick is said to have retired here and been adopted as Abbot in the 5thc. Even more legends tell how King Arthur lived here and was buried with his wife Guinevere on the Isle of Avalon.

Little of the abbey's early history is actually known, but it was probably of Celtic origin with Saxon additions. St Dunstan, a Somerset man, was a monk at Glastonbury and became abbot in 943. He repaired the damage wreaked by marauding Danes. Under King Edgar it became a famous centre, and was still further enlarged after the Norman Conquest. From then until 1524 it continued to expand, but after the Dissolution fell into ruins and was used as a source of building stone. Remains of the abbey now comprise St Mary's Chapel, the abbey church, and the monastic buildings (OACT). St Mary's Chapel (1186) is a beautiful ruined shell, with an underground chapel to St Joseph beneath it. Another notable feature is the Abbot's Kitchen, with a famous flowering thorn tree near by (said to be from a cutting of the one planted by Joseph of Arimathea). The Tribunal, once the Abbot's courtroom, and the George Inn both date from the 15thc. The abbey tithe-barn is a fine example.

Other churches in the town include St John and St Benign – both with good perpendicular towers – and the St Mary almshouses in Magdalene Street date partly from the 13th and 14thc. A museum in the Tribunal exhibits finds from the prehistoric lake dwellings at Meare and Godney. Fine views can be enjoyed from a tower on Tor Hill (NT).

GLEMSFORD, Suffolk 15 TL84
The 15th-c church houses a notable carved font of the same period, and a beautiful old timbered house stands in the village.

GLINTON, Cambs 19 TF10
A stone-built village 3m SE of Market Deeping, with a 17th-c manor house. The old church has a tall slender spire, and 2m SW is Woodcroft Castle. The latter is a 13th- to 14th-c moated structure which is reputedly haunted.

GLOSSOP, Derbyshire 18 SK09
This industrial town has built up its prosperity around cotton and woollen mills, and is a good centre for exploring 2,088ft Kinder Scout. Snake Pass runs SE towards the High Peak District and Sheffield. Remains of the Roman fort called Melandra Castle lie NW, and the line of a Roman road runs E of the town – known at this point as Doctor's Gate.

GLOUCESTER, Glos 12 SO81
Gloucester was once the Roman *Colonia Glevum*, a fortified city guarding the roads into Wales. It is now the county capital and stands on the River Severn. Many industries operate in and around the town, and a 16m canal that was completed in 1827 links Gloucester with docks at Sharpness on the Bristol Channel. This virtually makes Gloucester a seaport. The town shares an airport with Cheltenham; it is sited at Staverton, 4½m from both towns.

The fine cathedral is of Norman to early perpendicular design, and marks the birth of this latter style in England. A 14th-c east window is of interest, and of particular note are: the tomb of murdered King Edward II; the crypt; the choir stalls; the noble central tower; and the lovely old cloisters. The Close is entered by two old gateways, and displays several Georgian buildings. A cross to the memory of Bishop Hooper, who was martyred in 1555, can also be seen here. Attractive 18th-c and older houses include Raikes House, named after Robert Raikes – a founder of Sunday Schools. The timbered Parliament House is of 15th-c date.

Local antiquities and Roman relics are exhibited in the city museum. A regimental museum is housed in a 17th-c building adjacent to 15th-c Bishop Hooper's Lodging, now a museum of English rural life.

Ancient churches include St Mary de Lode, which rests on a Roman pavement and has a Norman tower; the Norman to perpendicular St Nicholas, with a tower leaning 3ft 7in out of true; and Renaissance-style St John's. St Mary-de-Crypt has associations with the Calvinist preacher George Whitefield, and contains the grave of Robert Raikes. Slight remains of Llanthony Abbey can be traced near the river. The New Inn is a famous 15th-c galleried pilgrim's hostel, and the United Hospital almshouses include St Mary Magdalene's and St Margaret's chapels. The former preserves some Norman work. Remains of the Blackfriars include some of the earliest library buildings in the country. The King's Board is a 14th-c Friars pulpit that can be seen off London Road in Hillfield Gardens.

County-cricket is played at the local ground, and the Three-Choirs music festival takes place every third year. Matson House, 2m S below Tuffley Hill, was the headquarters of King Charles I when he was besieging Gloucester during the Civil War. It is of 16th-c origin.

GLYNDE, E Sussex 8 TQ40
Glynde is a South Downs village facing 718ft Firle Beacon. John Ellman bred the famous Southdown sheep here in the 18thc. The 18th-c classical-style church is sited near Elizabethan Glynde Place (OACT). The latter contains fine bronze, picture, and needlework collections. It was originally a 16th-c quadrangular house of flint-and-brick, but Richard Trevor (Bishop of Durham) rebuilt much of it in 1752, and added a stable block. Partly-Tudor Glyndebourne lies 1m N, and includes a modern opera house.

GNOSALL, Staffs 17 SJ82
The church in this small town is a large Norman cruciform-shaped building. Its impressive central tower was added in the 15thc, and the east window shows good decorated tracery.

GOADBY MARWOOD, Leics 19 SK72
A village 5m NE of Melton Mowbray with a 14th-c church displaying good windows, and an 18th-c hall. Many Roman coins were found here in 1953.

GOATHLAND, N Yorks 23 NZ80
This small moorland village of grey-stone houses lies near waterfalls including Mallyan Spout and Nelly Ayre Force. Lilla Cross, which may date from the 7thc, lies E near the Whitby to Pickering road. The North York Moors steam-hauled railway has been partially re-opened as a private venture. Enormous white globes can be seen 5m SE of Goathland. These are part of the Early Warning Station on Fylingdales Moor, a link in the country's radar-defence chain.

GODALMING, Surrey 8 SU94
Part of the river in this colourful River Wey town is called the Godalming Navigation and owned by the NT. Its restored Norman to 14th-c church displays a lofty lead-covered spire, and old houses of Tudor and Stuart periods can be seen in the area. The 17th-c almshouses are of interest, and the attractive town hall of 1814 now houses a museum.

Farncombe is situated on the NE outskirts of the town, and includes almshouses displaying tall chimneys. Charterhouse School lies 1m N, and Peper Harow, a fine Georgian house, is sited 3m W. The outbuildings of Peper Harow Farm include a good example of an early 17th-c granary standing on pillars. Winkworth Arboretum is a hillside with rare trees and shrubs planted around a lake (NT). Its situation affords fine views over the North Downs.

GODMANCHESTER, Cambs 14 TL27
Pronounced Gumchester, this River-Ouse town includes 16th- and 17th-c timbered and plastered houses, an Elizabethan grammar school, and a fine 13th- to 14th-c church housing notable carved choir-stalls of the 15thc. The so-called Chinese bridge dates from 1827. Excavations on the line of Ermine Street have proved that the town was once a Roman station. Farm Hall and Island Hall are both Georgian.

GODMERSHAM, Kent 9 TR05
A little village on the River Stour, where the restored partly early-English church contains a stone carved with an early image of Thomas Becket. Godmersham Park stands in extensive grounds and dates back to 1732. Jane Austen often stayed here with her brother, and used it as the background for her novel *Mansfield Park*. Juliberry's Grave is a stone-age barrow.

GODSHILL, Isle of Wight 7 SZ58
This pleasant village has a 14th-c and later church. The latter is set on a hilltop, and is noted for its chancel tombs and a wall painting. Appuldurcombe House (AM) is a ruin lying 1m S, but the grounds laid out by Capability Brown still exist (OACT).

GODSTONE, Surrey 8 TQ35
An attractive village green and a fine Elizabethan inn called the White Hart, formerly the Clayton Arms, form part of this village. A sarsen-stone in the churchyard recalls S F Taylor (died 1908), known as the father of rambling.

GODSTOW, Oxon 13 SP40
Godstow's old bridge over the Thames, and the picturesque Trout Inn, contribute to the village's character. Ruins of the 12th-c nunnery where Fair Rosamond, mistress of Henry II, is said to have been buried still exist.

GOLDSBOROUGH, N Yorks 22 SE35
Goldsborough is near the River Nidd and has a restored Norman church showing fine nave roofs and several old tombs. The hall is Jacobean; S is Ribston Hall (1674), which is noted for its rich Harlequin Saloon.

GOMERSAL, W Yorks 22 SE22
This town is situated 1½m from Cleckheaton. The Manor House, Pollard Hall, Red House and Spen Hall, are all interesting old houses of the area. The district featured in Charlotte Brontë's *Shirley*, in which the Red House appears as 'Briarmains'.

GOMSHALL, Surrey 8 TQ04
Gomshall is pronounced Gum-shal, and the village lies under a ridge of the North Downs, S of Netley Heath. Netley Park was built in 1790, and now serves as a Holiday Fellowship guesthouse (NT). An old water wheel is preserved at Gomshall Mill, on the River Tillingbourne (OACT).

GOODRICH, Herefs & Worcs 12 SO51
Imposing ruins of moated Goodrich Castle, built in the 12thc as a defence against Welsh raiders, stand on a wooded

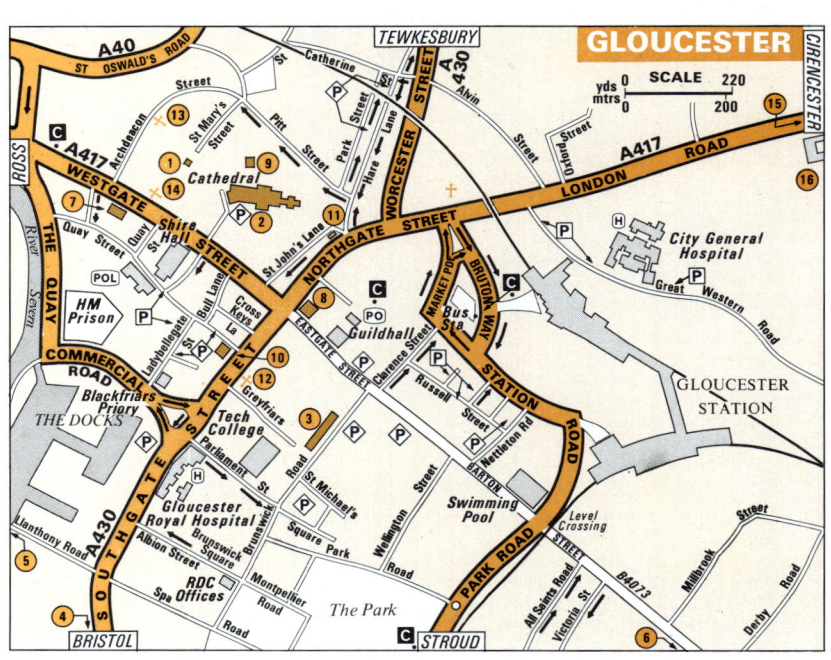

1 Bishop Hooper's Cross
2 Cathedral
3 City Museum
4 County Cricket Ground
5 Llanthony Abbey Remains
6 Matson House
7 Museum of English Rural Life (Bishop Hooper's Lodging) & Regimental Museum
8 New Inn
9 Parliament House
10 Raikes' House
11 St John's Church
12 St Mary de Crypt Church
13 St Mary de Lode Church
14 St Nicholas' Church
15 The King's Board
16 United Hospital Almshouses

hill overlooking the River Wye. It was the home of the Talbots (Earls of Shrewsbury) until it was destroyed by Cromwellian troops during the Civil War. The instrument of this destruction was Roaring Meg, a mortar that is now preserved at Castle Green near Hereford Cathedral. Thomas Swift's house was built in 1636 by Dean Swift's grandfather.

GOODWOOD, W Sussex *8 SU81*
The well-known racecourse located in this part of Sussex lies in a delightful downland setting. Goodwood House, built by James Wyatt from 1790 to 1800, contains a good collection of pictures. It shares a fine park with a curious Shell House of 1739, and an early 18th-c Palladian temple known as Carne's Seat. Birdless Grove is comprised of beeches, and is so named because it is said that no bird ever sings there (OACT). The Trundle, a 677ft hill surmounted by the well-defined earthworks of an iron-age hillfort, affords good views of the racecourse.

GOOLE, Humberside *22 SE72*
Goole was laid out in the early 19thc, at the confluence of the Rivers Ouse and Don and on the Aire and Calder Navigation Canal. The latter has extensive docks and a water tower said to be the largest in England. A large railway swing-bridge of 1868 crosses the 770ft-wide channel of the Ouse, 2m NE.

GORING-BY-SEA, W Sussex *8 TQ10*
The shingle beach here gives way to sand at low tide. Richard Jefferies the naturalist died here in 1887. Late 19th-c Castle Goring was the work of Biagio Rebecca, and lies N on the A27.

GORING-ON-THAMES, Oxon *13 SU58*
An attractive Thames-Valley village situated in a gap between the Chilterns and the Berkshire Downs. The mainly-Norman church contains a bell dating from c1290. Ancient Icknield Way crosses the river here to meet the Ridgeway.

GORLESTON-ON-SEA, Norfolk *15 TG50*
Now part of Yarmouth, this popular resort is sited at the mouth of the River Yare. A small harbour exists, and good sands allow access for bathing. St Andrew's parish church is of 13th- to 15th-c origin. It displays a tall tower and houses a fine military brass.

GORRAN HAVEN, Cornwall *4 SX04*
The Church of St Goronas lies slightly inland from this small fishing village and displays a 15th- to 16th-c west tower rising to a height of 110ft. A few old bench-ends can be seen inside. The Dodman is a rocky 400ft headland situated 2m S (NT), affording magnificent views and surmounted by an iron-age fort.

GOSBERTON, Lincs *19 TF23*
The restored early-perpendicular cruciform-shaped church displays a tower-gargoyle in the shape of an elephant.

GOSFORTH, Cumbria *21 NY00*
Curious hog-back tombs are preserved in the church, and figures from Norse mythology and the Crucifixion are represented on the ancient, very notable, churchyard cross.

GOSFORTH, Tyne & Wear *27 NZ26*
Gosforth was once an important mining town, but is now a residential centre. St Nicholas Church dates from 1799 and c1818. The Barretts of Wimpole Street, parents of Elizabeth Barrett Browning, were married here in 1805. Salters Bridge is of partly-medieval construction.

GOSPORT, Hants *7 SZ69*
A sheltered residential town with good beaches at Stokes Bay and Lee-on-the-Solent. Trinity Church is of 17th-c date and contains an organ that once belonged to the Duke of Chandos. It comes from Canons in Edgware (Middlesex), and is the original on which Handel is said to have played. The naval hospital at Haslar, facing Spithead, was built largely in the 18thc. Fort Brockhurst (AM) is of mid 18th-c date, and is being restored to house a military museum. It is one of five similar structures built in the area. A passenger ferry links Gosport and Portsmouth.

GOTHAM, Notts *18 SK53*
Famous for the legendary Wise Men of Gotham – who are said to have tried to make a hedge round a cuckoo, and to have sailed out to sea in a bowl. Gypsum mines are located in the area, and several monuments can be seen in the 13th- to 14th-c church.

GOUDHURST, Kent *9 TQ73*
An attractive Wealden village, including old houses and a fine 15th-c church. The latter is notable for its Culpeper monuments and brasses, and the tower which was rebuilt in the 17thc provides a fine viewpoint. Finchcocks, a notable example of 18th-c brickwork, lies 2½m SW. Farther E is the 15th-c half-timbered house of Pattenden. The National Pinetum, established by the Forestry Commission in 1925, can be seen 2m S at Bedgebury (OACT).

GRAFFHAM, W Sussex *8 SU91*
This South-Downs village lies 4m SE of Midhurst. The church was rebuilt by Street in the 19thc as a Wilberforce memorial. Wooded slopes of the Downs rise from the outskirts of Graffham, and Lavington Common lies to the E (NT).

GRAFTON REGIS, Northants *13 SP74*
The historic Queen's Oak marks a place where Edward IV first met his future Queen, Elizabeth Woodville, nearly 500 years ago. The Norman and later church carries a 15th-c tower. Inside is a monument by Flaxman, and an altar tomb engraved with a Woodville portrait. The manor house is of 16th- and 17th-c origin.

GRAIN, ISLE OF, Kent *9 TQ87*
Yantlet Creek used to separate this Thames-estuary island from the mainland, but it has now been walled across. Large oil refineries are sited near the Medway estuary.

GRANGE, Cumbria *21 NY21*
River Derwent is spanned by a double bridge in this well-known Borrowdale village. A narrow pass to the S is called the Jaws of Borrowdale, and is dominated by 900ft Castle Crag (NT). The summit of Grange Fell is known as the King's How, and provides a splendid viewpoint (NT).

GRANGE-OVER-SANDS, Cumbria *21 SD47*
A rocky wooded shore fringes this quiet Morecambe-Bay resort. A modern mansion was built by John Wilkinson, the inventor of iron ships, who died here in 1808.

GRANTCHESTER, Cambs *14 TL45*
The Cam or Granta – this river bears two names – flows through Grantchester, which is associated with the poet Rupert Brooke. He lived in the old vicarage before the first world war. Byron's Pool was named after another famous poet, Lord Byron, and the church includes a beautiful decorated-style chancel.

GRANTHAM, Lincs *19 SK93*
Grantham is a town of ancient origin, a railway junction, and a farming and hunting centre. It once served as a staging point between London and Lincoln, and was thoroughly sacked during the Wars of the Roses. Several fine coaching inns are still to be seen, plus an attractive market square.

The magnificent church carries a 281ft 14th-c spire, and houses a chained library of 83 books which was presented by a local rector in 1598. The famous Angel Inn is partly 14thc, and was where King Richard III signed the death warrant of the Duke of Buckingham in 1483. The Beehive Inn stands in Castlegate, and has an actual beehive as a sign; George Inn dates from the 18thc.

Grantham House stands near the church and dates from the 14th to 18thc (NT). Princess Margaret, daughter of Henry IV, stayed here on her way to marry James IV of Scotland. Boothby Pagnell is a very rare Norman manor house lying 5m SE in the grounds of a modern building. Grantham Castle, or Harlaxton Manor, lies 3m SW and is also a very notable example of its period (19thc).

GRAPPENHALL, Cheshire *17 SJ68*
Fragments of old glass can be seen in the local church, which was re-fashioned in 1539. The figure of a grinning cat can be seen above the tower's west window, and may possibly be the original Cheshire Cat. Old cottages can be seen in the village, and the stocks have been preserved.

GRASMERE, Cumbria *21 NY30*
Grasmere Lake is a sheet of water 1m long by ½m wide, and the village is a good centre for touring the Lake District.

Dove Cottage at the S end of the village was the home of poet William Wordsworth for thirteen years (OACT). The Wordsworth Museum is also of interest, and contains manuscripts and personal relics (OACT). An annual rush-bearing ceremony derives from a period when rushes were collected as floor-covering for houses and churches. Rush bearings are bundles of elaborately-decorated rushes which are ceremonially carried to the church. A service is then held, followed by celebrations that include the distribution of local gingerbread to the rush bearers.

Grasmere Sports are held in a beautiful natural arena near the village each August. The wrestling, in traditional Cumberland and Westmorland style, is the most important item. This is followed closely by the Guides Race, a punishing event in which young men race up a steep crag and along a ridge, then down again to the arena. The mountain valley of Easedale lies NW. It includes a tarn, and is backed by 2,414ft Sergeant Man, and 2,500ft High Raise.

GRASSINGTON, N Yorks *22 SE06*
A charming Upper-Wharfedale village, where a predominantly-medieval bridge

spans the River Wharfe. Narrow streets meet in a little cobbled square. The old hall is of partly 13th-c origin, and stands in a lovely garden behind the square. Nearby Grass Woods have been scheduled as a nature reserve.

GRAVELLY HILL, W Midlands 18 SP19
Gravelly Hill's elaborate road interchange involves the M6 motorway, the Aston Expressway into Birmingham, and the A38 Derby to Bristol road. It has been dubbed Spaghetti Junction by motorists, owing to its complexity.

GRAVENEY, Kent 9 TR06
A village facing the Swale marshlands, 2¾m NE of Faversham. The Norman and later church houses a 15th-c screen, a fine 13th-c chest, and notable brasses of 1370 and 1436.

GRAVESEND, Kent 9 TQ67
This flourishing residential, industrial, and commercial centre is sited on the River Thames, and is connected to Tilbury by passenger ferry. Ships coming up-river exchange coastal for river pilots here, an operation that can be watched from riverside gardens.

Three Dawes is an old inn near the town pier, built in such a way as to include several tunnels, and was possibly used by smugglers. Weather-boarded houses exist in the Main Street, and a large cement works operates in the area. Two windows in the 18th-c St George's Church – now the Chapel of Unity – commemorate the Red-Indian Princess Pocahontas who saved the life of John Smith in Virginia. She later married an Englishman, and died here during a visit to England. Her grave is in the church, and her statue stands in the former churchyard.

GRAYS, Essex 9 TQ67
Grays is now a largely-residential town, within easy reach of London. The church of 1846 incorporates 12th- and 13th-c work, and the Thurrock museum features local history and archaeology. Exhibits include finds of early and late bronze-age date, plus Romano-British glass, bronzes, and Roman coins.

GREAT
Places incorporating the prefix Great (eg Great Malvern), are listed under the actual place-name – ie Malvern, Great.

GREENHEAD, Northumberland 26 NY66
A little village 3m NW of Haltwhistle, Greenhead lies S of the Roman Wall and close to a series of ravines known as the Nine Nicks of Thirlwall. Thirlwall Castle (14thc) lies in ruins. Maiden Way is a Roman track which extends S from here to a point near Penrith.

GREENHITHE, Kent 9 TQ57
Sir John Franklin led an expedition to find the North-West passage from here in 1845, and never returned. The training ship Worcester is dated 1905, and is moored near by on the Thames.

GREENSTED-JUXTA-ONGAR, Essex 8 TL50
A unique Saxon nave wall of split-oak trunks can be seen in the nave of the village church; the brick choir was added c1500.

GREENWICH, Gt London 8 TQ47
British sea-power and the historic town of Greenwich are inseparable. Cutty Sark, a famous old clipper that shipped tea from China in the 19thc, is in dry dock near the pier, and Gipsy Moth IV, sailed single-handed round the world by Sir Francis Chichester, is berthed near by.

The Old Royal Observatory is part of the National Maritime Museum, and stands in Greenwich Park. The latter was laid out by Le Nôtre, a famous French gardener. Current observatory work is now conducted at Herstmonceux Castle in Sussex, but interesting astronomical and navigational exhibits can be still seen in the Greenwich installation. The Airy Transept Circle Room and Wren's Octagon Room of 1675 are of particular interest.

The Royal Naval College has variously served as Greenwich Hospital and a palace for royalty. A Tudor building that once stood here was the birthplace of Henry VIII and his two daughters, Elizabeth and Mary. The existing complex was designed by Sir Christopher Wren, and added to by such famous architects as John Webb, Hawksmoor, Vanbrugh, and Ripley. The chapel was rebuilt in the late 18thc, and the famous Painted Hall has a ceiling by Sir James Thornhill. The National Maritime Museum is in Queen's House, by Inigo Jones, and exhibits an exceptionally interesting collection of paintings and models concerning British seafaring.

Several Georgian buildings on the W of the park include Roger's House, the one-time home of Lord Chesterfield. Georgian and older houses can also be seen in Croom's Hill, and Vanbrugh Castle was built by the architect for his personal use. The latter now serves as an RAF school. Jacobean Charlton House is a splendid building standing E of the park, which contains a library and museum. It includes contemporary stables and garden house (OACT).

GRESHAM, Norfolk 15 TG13
Foundations of a fortified manor house that was held by Margaret Paston in 1450, as related in the Paston Letters, are still in existence. Features of the decorated-style church are a round tower and fine Seven-Sacraments font. Barningham Norwood Church lies 1½m SW, and displays a notable range of Palgrave monuments. Farther SW is beautiful old Barningham Hall, built in 1612 by Sir William Paston.

GRETA BRIDGE, Co Durham 22 NZ01
Dickens stayed at the fine old Morritt Arms Inn in 1838, and the hamlet has many other associations with artists of various types. Rokeby House, sited near the junction of Rivers Tees and Greta, is an 18th-c building that was painted by Turner and has associations with Sir Walter Scott. Near by, the 15th-c Mortham Tower stands in a picturesque setting above the Greta. This river flows through beautifully-wooded Brignall Banks, to the SW.

GRETTON, Northants 19 SP89
An attractive stone-built village situated some 9½m NW of Oundle. Kirby Hall is a partly-restored 16th- to 17th-c house lying 3m SE (AM). Some of the latest additions to the building have been ascribed to Inigo Jones; all that remains of the main part of the house is the façade and one or two restored rooms. It is, nevertheless, very fine and the gardens have been restored to an attractive layout (OACT). The village stocks and whipping post were last used in the mid 19thc.

GREYSTOKE, Cumbria 26 NY43
The Victorian castle in this village incorporates a medieval building and stands in a large park. The Church of St Andrew is a large structure of mainly 15th-c origin, featuring misericords, stained-glass fragments of the 15thc in the east window, carved stalls, and fine alabaster effigies. Greenthwaite Hall is 17thc and lies ¾m SW.

The Cutty Sark tea clipper, Greenwich

GRIMSBY, Humberside *23 TA20*
Grimsby has one of the largest fish markets in the world, with adjoining facilities for curing and freezing. Its docks are a national centre for the trade, and catches from Arctic waters are landed here. Several fine churches include 13th-c St James, an early-English structure in which the clerestory and triforium are combined. The 350ft tower supplying power to the docks is a prominent landmark.

GRIMSTHORPE, Lincs *19 TF02*
The partly 13th-c castle, of which four towers survive, was extensively added to in 1541, 1722, and again in 1810. Sir John Vanbrugh was involved in the second period of work, and the immense park was landscaped by Capability Brown.

GRIMSTON, Norfolk *14 TF72*
Decorated and perpendicular styles are evident in the large church, which also displays a lofty tower, good stalls, and carved bench-ends. Traces of a Roman villa have been found S of the village.

GRINDLEFORD BRIDGE, Derbyshire *18 SK27*
This noted beauty spot is 2½m SE of Hathersage. Cliff-like Froggatt Edge lies S, while Froggatt Wood – 76-acres of broken woodland and pasture – is situated below the escarpment (NT). Longshaw Park is a NT estate 2m NE, comprising 1,097-acres of moor and woodland. Village settlements with the remains of stone defending-walls and hut sites exist at Lawrence Field and Sheffield Plantation. Totley railway tunnel runs for 3½m, and is the second longest in England.

GRINTON, N Yorks *22 SE09*
A Swaledale village where the notable church houses old screenwork and a Norman font with a 15th-c cover. Sometimes known as the Cathedral of the Dales, this church was first built by the Normans but most of the existing structure is of perpendicular style. Remains of 12th-c Marrick Priory have been restored as a Young People's Adventure Centre, and can be seen 2m SE. The 15th-c tower of Ellerton Abbey is near by.

GRISTON, Norfolk *15 TL99*
A quaint inscription on the church font records the tower's restoration in 1568, and the building displays examples of 14th-c glass. Wayland Wood, associated with the Babes in the Wood legend, lies to the NW.

GROOMBRIDGE, E Sussex *8 TQ53*
This exceptionally-attractive village of 18th-c tiled cottages is grouped round a triangular village green. Groombridge Place, a moated late 17th-c house, has been attributed to Wren. It is a country house of the Restoration period, and contains interior panelling from an Elizabethan manor house which once stood on the same site. The local church is of early 17th-c date. Harrison's Rocks are situated 1m S at Birchden Wood, and serve as a climbers' practice ground. The mid-Georgian house of Penn's Rocks lies 2m SSW.

GROTON, Suffolk *15 TL94*
John Winthrop left Groton – his birthplace – in 1629, and became the first governor of Massachusetts. The village name is now carried by a famous American school.

GRUNDISBURGH, Suffolk *15 TM25*
Bast's is a notable timbered house – one of the many to be seen in this village. The community lies 3m NW of Woodbridge, and includes a 15th-c church with a fine hammerbeam roof. The latter also features a good screen and a brick tower dated 1751 to 1752.

GUILDEN MORDEN, Cambs *14 TL24*
A remarkably fine double screen is a feature of the village's church, which also displays a stairway and upper-doorway which gave access to the former rood-loft. Morden Hall (15thc) is a good example of a moated timber-framed house. Iron-age and Romano-British finds have been excavated from a nearby prehistoric cemetery.

GUILDFORD, Surrey *8 TQ04*
Modern developments have changed much of this old River-Wey town, but many interesting old buildings still exist – particularly in the High Street. In contrast to these are the new buildings of the University of Surrey (1970), and Sir Edward Maufe's new cathedral. The latter is perched at the top of Stag Hill, and the former exists in the same area.

The guildhall was built on the site of a medieval guildhall in 1683, and the clock hanging over the street bears the same date. A 16th-c grammar school preserves several chained books. Jacobean Abbot's Hospital is a fine building that was erected as a home for twelve old men of Guildford; it still houses old people. Remains of Guildford Castle are sparse and comprise the ruined Norman keep, with a small museum (AM, OACT). Near the castle is a house in which Lewis Carroll died in 1898. This fact is recorded by an inscribed plaque. The Yvonne Arnaud Theatre opened in 1965, and has since attracted many actors and actresses.

Old churches in the town include St Mary's which is partly Saxon and 13thc. St Nicholas' Church is fairly modern (1870), but retains the 15th-c Loseley Chapel. An 18th-c riverside-crane with a 20ft treadwheel lies off Friary Street, and the waterworks incorporates a water-mill of 1760 and later (off Quarry Street). Semaphore House, a relic of a 19th-c Napoleonic

1 Fish Market

2 St James' Church

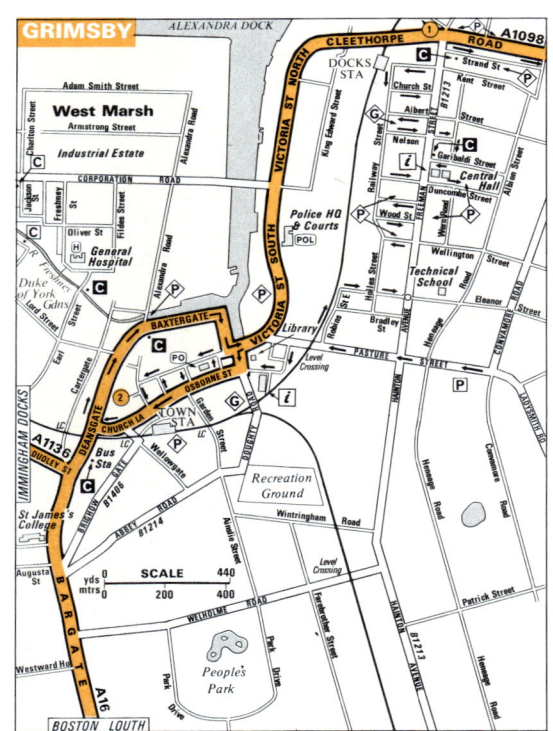

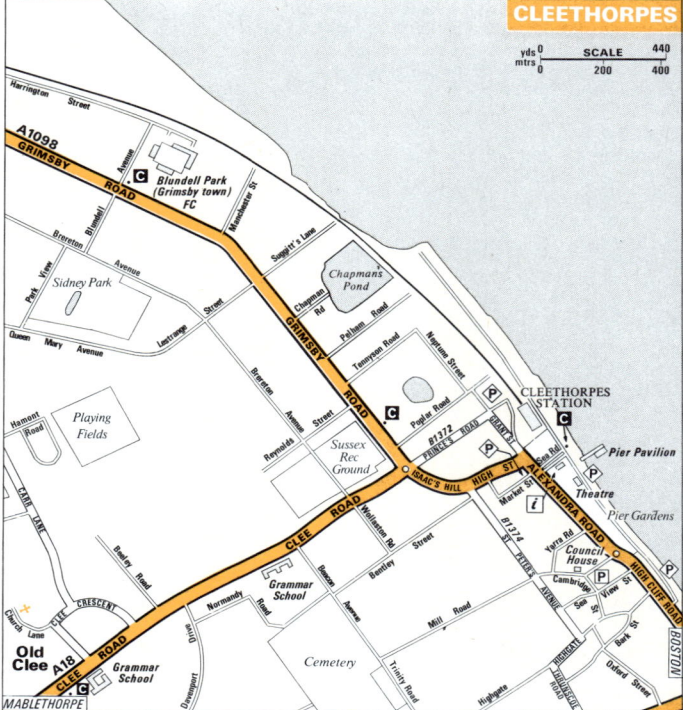

station linking London and Portsmouth, stands on Pewley Hill. Stoke Park is usually the venue for the annual Surrey County Show. Sutton Place, $3\frac{1}{2}$m NE, is probably the most striking old building outside the actual city. It is a magnificent 16th-c house of brick and terracotta. The gardens are on show in the spring. Loseley House lies 2m SW, and is of Elizabethan origin (OACT).

GUILSBOROUGH, Northants *13 SP67*
Burne-Jones and Morris decorated the local church's chancel windows in memory of Countess Spencer. Also in the village is a fine 17th-c gabled house which is built of ironstone and was once a school.

GUISBOROUGH, Cleveland *22 NZ61*
Ruins of a 12th-c Augustinian priory can be seen in this attractive market town, overshadowed by the Cleveland Hills. They stand near a restored late 15th-c church and comprise a 12th-c gatehouse and dovecote, plus the late 13th-c east end of the building. Included is a window decorated with carved vines. The priory was founded by Robert de Brus in 1119, whose family originally came to England with William the Conqueror and made their home at nearby Skelton.

GUISELEY, W Yorks *22 SE14*
The restored church in this village preserves Norman workmanship and a tower of the 15thc. A Saxon cross can be seen in the churchyard. Charlotte Brontë's parents were married here in 1812. The rectory is a fine old house, and Jacobean and later Hawkesworth Hall lies 2m W.

GULVAL, Cornwall *4 SW43*
A small village surrounded by narcissi, daffodil, and violet fields, and where the ancient industry of mead-brewing has been revived. The remarkable iron-age Chysauster village of stone huts can be seen 2m N on Gulval Downs (AM, OACT).

GUNTON, Norfolk *15 TG23*
The Adam church was built by Sir William Harbord in 1769, and is one of the best of its period in Norfolk. It displays a portico of Tuscan columns, and the west gallery is supported by Corinthian columns. Extensive Gunton Park surrounds a late 18th-c mansion.

GWEEK, Cornwall *4 SW72*
Gweek is a name derived from *gwic*, the Cornish word for village. The community is situated at the head of the Helford River inlet. About 4m SE is the hamlet of Halligye and the fine old mansion of Trelowarren, near one of the curious Cornish *fogous* (refuge caves).

GWITHIAN, Cornwall *4 SW54*
Situated on St Ives Bay, Gwithian includes an ancient chapel possibly dating from the 8thc or earlier Godrevy Point lies 2m N, and is the W extremity of a five-mile cliff range (NT) which includes Hell's Mouth and Reskajeage Downs. Some of the most impressive cliff scenery in Cornwall is located here.

HACCOMBE, Devon *5 SX87*
This is one of the smallest parishes in England, and lies 3m SE of Newton Abbot. The Georgian mansion (no longer a private house) stands adjacent to the little 14th-c chapel of St Blaise, which houses several notable monuments.

A horseshoe fixed to the door recalls a wager between Carew and Champernowne, relating to a horse-swimming contest in Tor Bay. The road approach to the village is rough and narrow.

HACKNESS, N Yorks *23 SE99*
A River-Derwent village in a beautiful Yorkshire setting. On one side lie moors and on the other are forests, broken here and there by areas of pastureland. The Georgian hall is of interest, and the early-English to perpendicular church contains fragments of a Saxon cross bearing a Runic inscription.

HADDENHAM, Bucks *8 SP70*
Most of the houses in this little village, 3m NE of Thame, are made of wichert – chalk marl compressed with straw. The church of St Mary is of 13th-c origin and contains a Norman font plus medieval glass in the north chapel. Bone House carries a curious knuckle-bone design on the façade.

HADDON HALL, Derbyshire *18 SK26*
This famous 12th- to 15th-c house is situated on the River Wye in a lovely, woodland setting (OACT). Although originally a fortified dwelling, Haddon Hall was never fought over and is one of the finest examples of medieval architecture in existence. The old chapel contains a Norman font plus 15th-c wall paintings. A minstrel gallery is a feature of the banqueting hall, and a raised platform at the opposite end originally served as a stage for the high table. The 16th-c ceiling is painted, and the Long Gallery is reached by semi-circular steps of solid oak, cut from the roots of one tree. Dorothy Vernon and Sir John

1	Cathedral	6	Lewis Carroll's House	
2	Grammar School	7	Loseley House	
3	Guildford Castle Remains (museum)	8	Semaphore House	
4	Guildhall	9	St Mary's Church	
5	Jacobean Abbot's Hospital	10	St Nicholas' Church	
11	Stoke Park			
12	Sutton Place			
13	University of Surrey			
14	Water Mill			
15	Yvonne Arnaud Theatre			

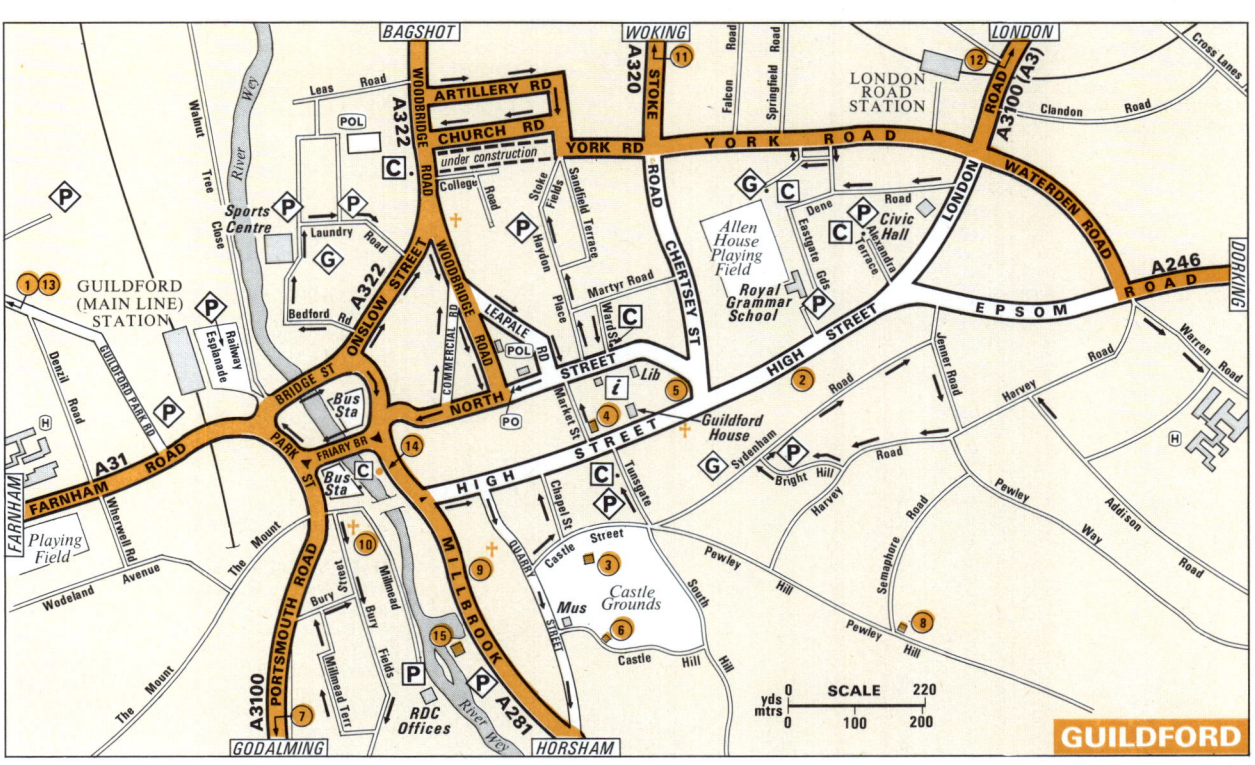
GUILDFORD

Manners are said to have eloped from here during the lady's sister's wedding party, towards the end of the 16thc. An old packhorse bridge spans the nearby river.

HADLEIGH, Essex 9 TQ88
Remains of a 13th-c castle (AM), rebuilt in the 14thc as the residence of Edward III, were the subject of a painting by Constable. Its towers are immense and the walls some 9ft thick at the base. Excellent views over the Thames estuary and the Kent coast can be enjoyed from here. Hubert de Burgh was the original builder of this structure, and after Edward Henry VIII made it the home of Anne of Cleves. The church is mostly Norman and displays remains of a wall painting of Thomas Becket.

HADLEIGH, Suffolk 15 TM04
This market town was once a centre of the East-Anglian cloth trade. The High Street shows a remarkable architectural mixture – timber, brick, and plasterwork – with some examples of the plaster decoration known as pargetting.

Two overhanging storeys are features of the fine timbered Guildhall, and several other medieval houses exist in the town. The tall Deanery Tower, built in 1495 and situated in the churchyard, is all that remains of the deanery. Georgian houses can be seen in the area.

The 14th- and 15th-c Church of St Mary contains monuments by Charles Regnart (c1793), and Eric Gill (c1935). The brasses are also of interest. A 14th-c bench-end depicts a wolf holding the decapitated head of St Edmund. This is a representation of a legend that recalls how the body of St Edmund was decapitated and the head thrown in a thicket, whereupon the saints' followers found it being guarded by a grey wolf.

HADLOW, Kent 9 TQ64
Hadlow lies in one of Kent's hop-growing districts. A large park in the area contains a curious 170ft folly tower dating from 1840. The mansion has been demolished. Features of the rebuilt church include a 14th-c timbered tower and spire.

HADSTOCK, Essex 14 TL54
Hadstock's church dates back to Saxon times. It shows 14th-c additions and carries a 15th-c west tower, but the most interesting items are a Saxon oak door (very rare), and Saxon windows with their original wooden frames. It is believed that the church may have been built to celebrate King Canute's victory over Edmund Ironside in 1016.

HAILES ABBEY, Glos 12 SP02
The ruins of this Cistercian Abbey, founded in 1246 by the Earl of Cornwall (AM, NT), are of interest; a small museum on the site contains a collection of early tiles and other relics of the abbey. Hailes church, mainly 14thc, has an ancient timbered belfry, a 15th-c screen, and wall-paintings.

HAILSHAM, E Sussex 9 TQ50
A pleasant country town below the Downs, where the 15th-c church stands in the middle of a busy street. It has a perpendicular tower with a splendid arch, and fragments of sculptured capitals can be seen in a niche above an unused piscina. The vicarage and council offices both occupy 18th-c houses.

HAINTON, Lincs 19 TF18
This Wolds village lies 7m SE of Market Rasen, and its partly-Norman church contains the notable Heneage Chapel. Numerous monuments and brasses are housed within the latter.

HALE, Merseyside 17 SJ48
The 17th-c manor in this Mersey-estuary village was formerly the rectory, and the 18th-c church preserves its old tower. John Middleton, a local giant who died in 1623 and was over 9ft tall, is buried in the churchyard. His existence is recalled by the village inn sign.

HALESOWEN, W Midlands 12 SO98
An industrial town on the River Stour near Birmingham, involved in coal-mining and the manufacture of iron and steel. The 12th-c church dominates the valley and contains a monument to William Shenstone. The latter was an 18th-c poet who lived at The Leasowes, a house standing in grounds which he laid out himself. The remains of a 13th-c abbey lie 1m SE.

Deanery Tower of 1495, Hadleigh (Suffolk)

HALESWORTH, Suffolk 15 TM37
A market town on the River Blyth, 9m SW of Beccles. The church is mainly of perpendicular style and houses a good font and brasses. Several old houses exist in the area.

HALFORD, Warwickshire 13 SP24
This village of fine grey-stone houses is pronounced Ha-ford. The local manor house displays a pleasant mixture of styles, from early half-timbering to the 16thc. Interesting features of the small church include a three-light window with a pointed arch, which was obviously brought from a larger church. An old bridge spans the River Stour here.

HALIFAX, W Yorks 22 SE02
Halifax is an important clothing-manufacturing town in the old West Riding of Yorkshire, which has also developed a variety of other industries. It contains the headquarters of the largest building society in the world, and has an international reputation for the making of toffee and carpets.

The perpendicular church was mostly completed in 1490 and preserves a notable tower. It houses a curious life-sized figure known as Old Tristram, holding an almsbox. The town hall was designed by Sir Charles Barry (who also designed the Houses of Parliament), and was opened in 1863. Many interesting exhibits are displayed by the Bankfield Museum and Art Gallery, and West Yorkshire Folk Museum is in 15th-c Shibden Hall, to the NE. Piece Hall was erected in Thomas Street as a cloth-market in 1779, and now serves as a wholesale fruit and vegetable market. Lofty Wainhouse tower of 1871 to 1874 was built as a dyeworks chimney, and later topped by a Renaissance-style pinnacle. It now forms a notable landmark and viewpoint. Part of the original gibbet has been preserved in Gibbet Street.

To the N is the Victorian Akroyd estate, which was built round the Haley Mills of 1837. Copley Mill and estate, across the Calder, was a similar venture. Holdsworth House dates from 1633 and stands on the town's NW outskirts.

HALLAMSHIRE
Hallamshire was the South Yorkshire Domesday district of Hallam, an ancient lordship which covered Sheffield and the district immediately N and W.

HALLATON, Leics 19 SP79
An old village set in pleasant hill-country. Stone-built cottages dating from the 17th to 19thc form an attractive terrace, and a quaint conical market-cross stands near the conduit. A good 13th-c broach spire is displayed by the church. A curious local custom is Easter Monday's hare-pie scramble. This entails the distribution of hare-pie portions to local residents – originally as a token rent for a field.

HALLSANDS, Devon 5 SX83
This fishing village is sited on Start Bay, and has a shingle beach allowing access for bathing. Start Point and lighthouse lie 2m SE. Wild cliff scenery can be enjoyed 4m SW at Prawle Point.

HALSALL, Lancs 21 SD31
The Leeds and Liverpool canal runs through this village, which lies between

Ormskirk and Southport. The 14th- to 15th-c church has been well-restored and shows a good chancel in the decorated style, plus examples of old woodwork. The choir vestry, erected in 1592, was formerly a grammar school.

HALSTEAD, Essex 15 TL83
A good 14th- to 15th-c flint church in this upper-Colne valley market town contains Bourchier monuments. Also in the area is a fine example of an 18th-c three-storied weatherboarded mill. Gosfield Hall is a Tudor and later mansion lying 2½m SW (OACT).

HALTON, Lancs 21 SD56
The village church carries a 15th-c tower and contains a Roman altar. Other interesting features in this building are several ancient stones, and an 11th-c churchyard cross with curious carvings of Norse legends.

HALTWHISTLE, Northumberland 26 NY76
River South Tyne flows through this mining town, which preserves an interesting towerless 13th-c church founded by William the Lion in 1178. Three notable carved 14th-c gravestones can be seen in the sanctuary. Outside the town are the ruins of Bellister Castle, and Blenkinsopp Castle of 1339 lies 3m SW. Featherstone Castle is an ancient structure which was rebuilt in Jacobean times, lying 3½m SW.

HAMBLE, Hants 7 SU40
Noted for yachting on the Hamble River and the Solent, Hamble is also the mooring for Mercury – a training ship anchored in the estuary. The church has a fine Norman north doorway.

HAMBLEDEN, Bucks 8 SU78
A delightful Thames-Valley village 3m NE of Henley-on-Thames. Notable features include a 17th-c manor house, an old mill, and a Georgian rectory. Roman remains are exhibited by a small museum, and the restored church is described as a miniature cathedral. A fine monument dating from 1633 can be seen in the latter, and the oak nave-altar may be part of a bed-head screen originally made for Cardinal Wolsey – a unique survival.

HAMBLEDON, Hants 7 SU61
It is claimed that one of the very first games of cricket was played here on Broadhalfpenny Down (1½m NE) in 1774. A stone commemorating this stands opposite the Bat and Ball Inn, and the pub itself contains interesting old relics of the game. Saxon workmanship forms much of the church's construction, although most of this is now hidden by later building. The flint-and-chalk manor farm dates partly from the 13thc and the rectory is a 17th-c house. A vineyard and winepress on Mill Down supply grapes for English wines (OACT).

HAMPDEN, GREAT, Bucks 8 SP80
Hampden House was rebuilt in 1754, and was the home of John Hampden for many years. It now houses a girls' school. Hampden opposed Charles I's Ship-Money tax, fought for the Parliamentary Army, and died after the Battle of Chalgrove. He is buried in the churchyard. The church dates mainly from the 13thc and contains Hampden family monuments.

HAMPSTEAD, Gt London 8 TQ28
Beautiful old houses and the vast expanse of Hampstead Heath combine to make this NW suburb of London an extremely pleasant area. It was a popular spa resort in the 18thc, and its old buildings are interesting on two counts – because of their historical associations, and their connections with famous people.

Keats House was the poet's home (OACT), and is a Regency building that was built the year after the Battle of Waterloo. One half of the house was shared between Keats and a friend, and the other by Mrs Brawne and her children. Keats became engaged to the eldest child, Fanny, while living here. Manuscripts and relics are on show, and the garden is where Keats wrote *Ode to the Nightingale*. Fenton House is probably the oldest in Hampstead, and dates from c1693. It is a beautifully brick-built structure with a lovely walled garden and wrought-iron gates, and is situated in Hampstead Grove. It contains pottery, porcelain, furniture, and musical instruments (NT, OACT).

Many enchanting little streets run through Hampstead, but probably the most attractive is Church Row, leading from Heath Street to the 18th-c parish church of St John's. John Constable the famous painter lived in Hampstead for many years and is buried in the churchyard. George du Maurier lived near Fenton House and is buried in ground opposite Constable. Hollybush Hill is surmounted by weatherboarded Romney's House, built by the artist George Romney. The novelist John Galsworthy wrote *The Forsyte Saga* at nearby Grove Lodge.

Hampstead Heath affords views over London and with the surrounding open space makes up a 790-acre area of unspoiled, semi-wild heathland. Grassy slopes and wooded areas are the habitat of many species of wild life, and the heath is considered the best breathing space that Londoners possess. A famous group of ponds includes White Stone, a water situated at London's highest point (440ft) where Shelley sailed paper boats to amuse children, and George du Maurier, owner of a St Bernard, splashed through the winter ice to rescue a drowning dog. The view includes Hertfordshire ridges, the Surrey Hills, Windsor Castle and the Chilterns in clear weather. A flagstaff marks the highest point of the heath, and close by is Jack Straw's Castle, an old inn patronized by Dickens and Thackeray. It was rebuilt after the last war, and is thought to be named after

1 Bankfield Museum and Art Gallery
2 Folk Museum (Shibden Hall)
3 Gibbet Remains
4 Holdsworth House
5 Parish Church of St John the Baptist
6 Piece Hall
7 Town Hall
8 Wainhouse Tower

one of Wat Tyler's men of the Peasants' Revolt. Spaniards Road runs from here, to Spaniards Inn and toll house. The latter is said to have been built by a Spanish ambassador in the 18thc. Legend has it that Dick Turpin the highwayman was a frequent visitor there. Certainly the heath was once the haunt of highway robbers.

HAMPTON COURT, Gt London *8 TQ16*
This magnificent palace is set in beautiful extensive grounds, and was built by Cardinal Wolsey. He offered it to Henry VIII in 1526, and the palace became a favourite country residence of the king. Five of his wives lived there and it remained a royal residence until the death of George II in 1760.

Most of the original house exists, including the whole of the west front, but the remainder of the external façade dates from the accession of William III (1689), when Sir Christopher Wren was commissioned to enlarge and improve the building. The astronomical clock in Clock Court was built for Henry VIII – the dial is original, but the mechanism was renewed in the 19thc. A closed tennis-court, where the king played royal or real tennis, lies next to the palace. The nearby maze has been popular for hundreds of years, and the Great Vine planted in the 18thc still bears large bunches of grapes. Mantegna cartoons can be seen in the Orangery. Beautifully laid-out gardens contain the Banqueting House, and the palace houses magnificent collections of tapestries, furniture, and clocks.

Paintings include works by Holbein, Lely, Tintoretto, and Titian. Home Park surrounds the palace, and to the N is Bushy Park, with its beautiful chestnut trees. Sir Christopher Wren died at the Old Court House on the Green in 1723. Nearby stables date from the mid 16thc.

HAMPTON-IN-ARDEN, W Midlands *12 SP28*
Several picturesque houses with overhanging upper-storeys can be seen in this old-world village. It lies in the ancient Forest of Arden – the setting for Shakespeare's *As You Like It* – and features an interesting packhorse bridge. The local church stands on a hill near the bridge, and fragments of old glass in a chancel window are composed into panels of delicately-drawn birds.

HANBURY, Herefs & Worcs *12 SO96*
The red-brick hall dates from c1710 and contains paintings by Sir James Thornhill (NT, OACT). Inside are a staircase and hall, also painted by Thornhill, and the Long Room displays plaster decoration. The church has an 18th-c tower and contains monuments to the Vernons. Mere Hall is a fine half-timbered 15th- to 17th-c structure situated 2m SSW.

HANDCROSS, W Sussex *8 TQ22*
This is the highest point (504ft) on the main London to Brighton road. The fine gardens at Nymans (NT, OACT) contain rare conifers, shrubs, and plants including hydrangeas, magnolias, camellias, and roses. About 570 acres of wood and farmland are included in the overall park.

HANDFORTH, Cheshire *17 SJ88*
A little village 5m SW of Stockport. Handforth Hall is a particularly fine black-and-white half-timbered house dating from the 16thc.

HANLEY, Staffs *17 SJ84*
This pottery town is one of the Five Towns now amalgamated with Fenton, to make Stoke-on-Trent. Novelist Arnold Bennett was born in Hanley in 1867, and his early home at 205 Waterloo Road is now a Bennett museum (OACT). The City Museum and Art Gallery is situated in Broad Street, and has a famous collection of ceramics, including Staffordshire figures.

HANSLOPE, Bucks *13 SP84*
Hanslope is a village of thatched cottages lying some 4½m NE of Stony Stratford. The Norman church is noted for its lofty 15th-c embattled tower and spire, supported by flying buttresses; this can be seen from three counties. Numerous weird gargoyles stare from the walls of the church, and a carved priest's doorway is of interest.

HAPPISBURGH, Norfolk *15 TG33*
Pronounced Haze-burgh, this pretty fishing village lies among sand dunes and offers a sandy beach and safe bathing. A lighthouse warns shipping of the treacherous off-shore Haisboro' Sands. The church carries a lofty tower and displays a perpendicular-style screen.

HARBLEDOWN, Kent *9 TR15*
Pilgrims following the ancient Pilgrims' Way into Canterbury would look forward to this place as their last halt. A lepers' hospital was founded in 1084, rebuilt in 1674, and now serves as almshouses. A few interesting relics are preserved in the latter. The church is of largely-Norman origin, and contains medieval benches.

HARBY, Notts *19 SK87*
Queen Eleanor, wife of King Edward I, died here in 1290. A number of memorial crosses were raised to her by her husband – the Eleanor Crosses – of which three have survived. Memorials to the Queen can be seen in the modern church.

HARDHAM, W Sussex *8 TQ01*
The 11th-c church is well-known for its series of 12th-c wall-paintings, which are considered to be some of the finest to have been preserved in this country. They were re-discovered in 1866. Sparse remains of the Augustinian Hardham Priory lie near the Arun water-meadows, and are incorporated in a farm.

HARDRAW, N Yorks *21 SD89*
A Wensleydale hamlet, with the 100ft Hardraw Force waterfall to the N. This is considered one of the finest in England – especially after heavy rain – and is accessible on foot from the local inn.

HARDWICK HALL, Derbyshire *18 SK46*
Robert Smythson built this magnificent Elizabethan house for the famous Bess of Hardwick (Elizabeth, Countess of Shrewsbury), whose initials E S (Elizabeth Shrewsbury) are cut in the stonework of the parapet (NT). Four large towers mark each corner, and the interior is lit by huge windows. The Great Chamber, perhaps the finest in England, contains notable tapestries and a plaster frieze. Remains of an older hall in which Bess of Hardwick was born in 1520 lie in the park (OACT).

HARDY COUNTRY
This name is used to describe a part of Dorset associated with Thomas Hardy's novels – in particular the area extending E from Dorchester to Wareham, near bare heaths which the novelist described as Egdon Heath. Part of this district is now an area of outstanding natural beauty. Many placenames in Hardy's novels are pseudonyms for the real names. See Beaminster, Dorchester (Dorset), Higher Bockhampton, Puddletown, Stinsford, Wareham, and Wool.

HAREFIELD, Gt London *8 TQ09*
The much-restored decorated-style church preserves many interesting monuments and brasses, the finest being to the Countess of Derby, dated 1636. Picturesque Elizabethan red-brick almshouses are also of interest.

HAREWOOD, W Yorks *22 SE34*
Ruins of a castle exist in the grounds of 18th-c Harewood House, the magnificent home of the Earls of Harewood. The building work is largely by Carr of York, Robert Adam, and Sir Charles Barry. Its interiors are outstanding (OACT). A notable series of monuments in the perpendicular church include one to Chief Justice Gascoigne, dated 1419. Arthington Nunnery House, dated 1585, lies 2m W.

HARLOW, Essex *8 TL41*
Harlow is the site of one of the largest new towns, the well-planned centre of which is known as The High. St Andrew's Church at Netteswell is partly Norman and has a 15th-c brick outside panel depicting the carved emblem of Abbot Rose of Waltham. The River Stort, a tributary of the Lea, is navigable for small boats at this point.

HARLYN BAY, Cornwall *4 SW87*
A fine sandy bay allows access for bathing, and Treyarnon Bay lies W beyond Trevose Head. The latter has a lighthouse. An ancient burial-ground has an interesting museum and is situated near Harlyn.

HARPENDEN, Herts *8 TL11*
A residential district with a well-known co-educational school. The former Bull Inn, Bowers House, and The Hall, are old buildings of interest. Rothamsted agricultural research station was founded in 1843 and lies 1m SW.

HARPLEY, Norfolk *15 TF72*
The interesting mainly-decorated church is noted for its old bench-ends, an ancient doorway, and the angel-carved roof. Houghton Hall is a notable 18th-c house by Colin Campbell, 2m N. A partly 13th-c church stands in the park and houses memorials to the Walpoles.

HARPSDEN, Oxon *8 SU78*
A parish and village in SE Oxon, 1m SW of Henley-on-Thames. Harpsden Court is partly Tudor, and the church houses a fine 16th-c brass.

HARRIETSHAM, Kent *9 TQ85*
A number of old houses and the 18th-c Mark Quested almshouses can be seen in this village. Stede Hill is a 17th-c house above the North Downs line of the Pilgrims' Way. The church has a fine perpendicular tower and Norman font.

HARRINGWORTH, Northants *19 SP99*
The 13th- to 14th-c church has a pulpit dated 1605, and the 14th-c village cross has a top of 1837. A late 17th-c manor farm exists, and the eighty-two arch brick-built railway viaduct spanning the

Welland Valley dates from 1874 and 1879. The latter is a notable landmark.

HARROGATE, N Yorks 22 SE35
Harrogate is a well-known inland spa-resort and conference centre, and a handy vantage point for Wharfedale and Nidderdale. It lies at a height of between 400 and 600ft above sea level, and has mineral springs which are still used by sufferers from rheumatic diseases.

Many attractive open spaces in the town include Valley Gardens and the Harlow Car Trial Gardens – the latter a centre for experimental horticulture, controlled by the Northern Horticultural Society. These two are joined by a path. The 200-acres of common known as The Stray border the S side of the town. Most of the town is built in fine Yorkshire stone, and the Royal Pump Room is now a museum of local history. St Wilfrid's is an imposing modern church, and the Regency mansion of Rudding Park lies 3m SE.

HARROW, Gt London 8 TQ18
Harrow-on-the-Hill stands high above the surrounding plain, and its restored 11th-c church with a prominent 13th-c spire can be seen for miles. Several 18th-c houses exist in the vicinity. The famous public school was founded in 1571 by John Lyon, a yeoman of the parish, and granted a charter by Elizabeth I. Former pupils of Harrow School include Sir Robert Peel, Lord Byron, and Sir Winston Churchill. Grims Dyke House, Harrow-Weald, was once the home of Sir William Gilbert of the famous Gilbert and Sullivan partnership. A fine new civic centre has been constructed at Wealdstone.

HARROWAY
Generally considered to be the oldest of the ancient trackways, the Harroway starts from Marazion in Cornwall and crosses S England to Dover. Part of its route is across Dartmoor, and several primitive clapper-bridges can be seen in the area. Salisbury Plain was the junction-centre for this and other tracks coming from different directions, and parts of the Harroway later became the medieval Pilgrims' Way.

HARTFIELD, E Sussex 8 TQ43
A village to the N of Ashdown Forest, with a church displaying an old lych-gate.

HARTINGTON, Derbyshire 18 SK16
Beresford Dale and the Upper Dove lie W of this attractively-situated village. The Fishing House is dated 1674, and Hartington Hall is a restored 17th-c house containing fine oak panelling. Although restored, the 13th-c and later church displays a good two-storeyed porch. The interesting Newhaven Inn lies 2½m E on the Ashbourne-Buxton road.

HARTLAND, Devon 5 SS22
Hartland Abbey is an 18th-c house lying to the W; still farther W is 350ft Hartland Point, with a lighthouse and fine cliff scenery. The perpendicular church carries a magnificent tower, and houses a carved Norman font and richly-carved screen. It lies 1½m W at Stoke. Beyond Stoke is Hartland Quay, approached by a steep winding descent from which the first surprise view of the savagely-contorted cliffs is said to be the finest of its kind in England. St Catherine's Tor (S) is being slowly eroded by the Atlantic waves, and the fine Spekesmouth waterfall can be reached on foot from here. Other waterfalls are to be found on the lonely cliff-bound coast, ending by the Cornish border at Marsland Mouth. The district is now designated an area of outstanding natural beauty.

HARTLEBURY, Herefs & Worcs 12 SO87
The castle, built originally in 1268, has a 15th-c hall and includes many 18th-c alterations. It is the former home of the Bishops of Worcester (OACT), and the 17th-c wing is now a folk museum.

HARTLEPOOL, Cleveland 27 NZ53
This town is situated on Hartlepool Bay, and incorporates former West Hartlepool. The old parish church has a 13th-c nave and chancel arch, and remains of the medieval town-walls include a gate. Coal, iron, shipbuilding, and a nuclear power station are important local industries. The Gray Art Gallery and Museum is of interest, and All Saints' Church, Stranton, carries a perpendicular tower. The town hall dates from 1866. Castle Eden is a fine 18th-c house lying 8½m NW off the Durham road, and Castle Eden Denes form a local nature reserve.

HARTLEY WESPALL, Hants 7 SU65
A Loddon-Valley village 5m NE of Basingstoke. The church has a remarkable 14th-c timbered west wall, considered more typical of the West Midlands than of Hampshire. It houses a curious 17th-c tomb showing a skeleton.

HARTWELL, Bucks 8 SP71
A village 2m SW of Aylesbury, where the E-shaped Jacobean mansion of Hartwell House displays an east front of 1759 to 1761. Inside is an early 17th-c staircase, and Louis XVIII of France lived here from 1807 to 1814. It now functions as the House of Citizenship (OACT). A notable Georgian church of 1753 to 1756 shows remarkable fan vaulting.

HARWELL, Oxon 13 SU48
Harwell is a pleasant village with a 13th-c and later church. The Atomic Energy Research Establishment is sited 2m SW.

HARWICH, Essex 15 TM23
This busy seaport and sailing centre lies at the mouths of the Stour and Orwell. Continental traffic is dealt with at Parkeston Quay. A number of the local houses date from the 16th, 17th, and 18thc and an 18th-c council chamber can be seen in the guildhall. A unique naval treadmill crane is preserved on the green. Christopher Jones, the captain of the Mayflower, was one of the famous sailors born here. The Redoubt is a circular 180ft-diameter fort surrounded by a moat and built in 1808 to defend the port against Napoleon's invasion. The walls are 8ft thick (OACT).

HASELEY, GREAT, Oxon 13 SP60
This attractive village includes old houses and a good early-English to perpendicular church which is noted for its 14th-c chancel. John Leland the 16th-c antiquary was rector here for ten years. Haseley Court is of Queen Anne and Georgian styles and is set in fine gardens.

1 Guildhall
2 Naval Treadmill
3 Redoubt (fort)

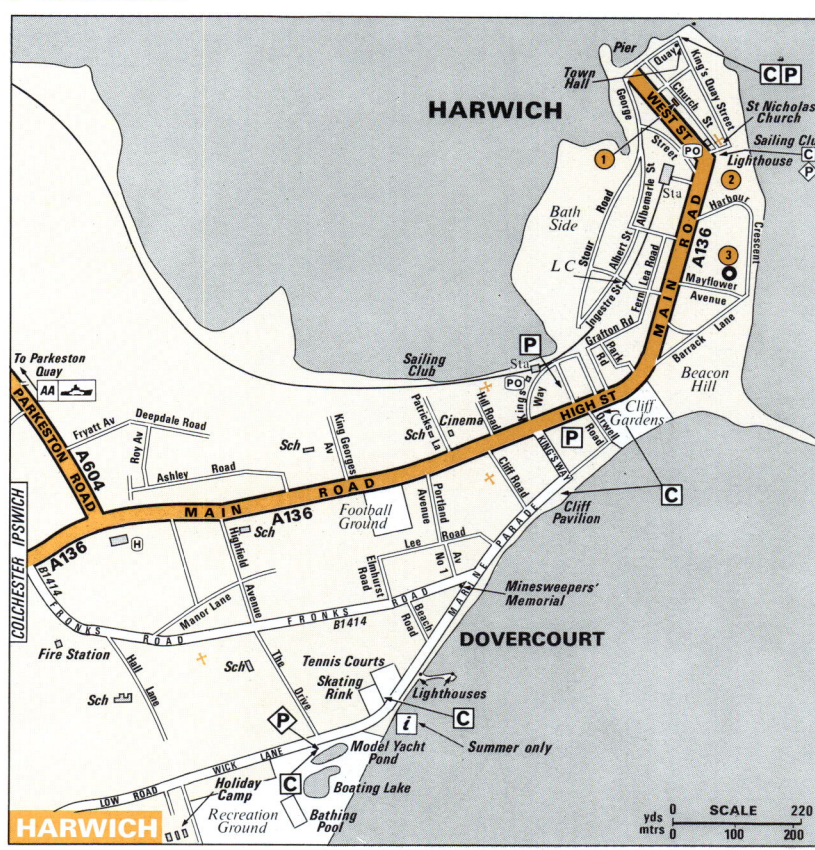

HASLEMERE/HATHERSAGE

HASLEMERE, Surrey *8 SU93*
Haslemere lies in beautiful surroundings under the northern slopes of 918ft Blackdown (part NT). Blackdown is designated an area of outstanding natural beauty, and Tennyson's former home Aldworth stands on its slopes. A memorial window to Tennyson, by Burne-Jones, can be seen in the church.

Attractive old houses exist near the town hall, which was rebuilt in 1814, and the educational museum was initiated by surgeon Sir Jonathan Hutchinson in 1888. The workshops of Arnold Dolmetsch, where harpsichords, various stringed instruments, and recorders are made, can be seen in King's Road (OACT). An interesting museum of antique instruments is housed at Jesses, Graywood Road, and is owned by the founder (OACT). Barfold Copse is a small bird-sanctuary.

HASLINGDEN, Lancs *21 SD72*
A cotton town and the centre of the cotton-waste industry, surrounded by extensive moors. A rare plague stone is preserved near the church.

HASLINGFIELD, Cambs *14 TL45*
The early-decorated church in this River-Cam village carries a very fine perpendicular tower. Interesting monuments are to be seen inside. Chapel Hill is a good viewpoint to the S.

HASTINGS and ST LEONARDS, E Sussex *9 TQ80*
These popular twin resorts offer 5m of shingle beach and sand at low tide. The Old Town lies between the East and West Hills, and its picturesque old houses are dominated by the ruins of a Norman castle built by William the Conqueror in 1086 (OACT). Hastings was one of the original Cinque Ports. Many parks and open spaces feature throughout the towns, and a model Tudor village can be seen in White Rock Gardens.

The miniature train that runs along the front at Rock-a-Nore passes a lifeboat station and several old net-houses, *ie* tall huts once used for drying fishing nets. The track ends near the Fishermen's Museum, once a church, which houses the last of the Hastings luggers to be built for sail. A lift connects Rock-a-Nore Road to the top of East Hill (250ft).

All Saints' and St Clement's are of perpendicular style, and the church of St Mary Star of the Sea was built mainly by Coventry Patmore, the poet. Many fine houses exist in the town, particularly in the High Street and All Saints' Street, and include the half-timbered Cloudesley Shovel house. Stylish Pelham Crescent dates from 1824, and was built by Joseph Kay. St Clement's Caves were reputedly the one-time haunt of smugglers, and are situated on the E slope of West Hill (OACT). The town hall dates from 1880, and the pier from approximately the same period. The White Rock Pavilion (built 1913) contains the Hastings Embroidery which was prepared for the 900th anniversary of the Battle of Hastings, by the Royal School of Needlework. This tapestry records 81 great events of British history since 1066.

Facilities for many sports, amusements and pastimes are provided by the towns, and an annual chess tournament attracts leading players from all over the world. At Hollington (2m N) is the well-known 13th-c restored Church-in-the-Wood. Cliffs border the sealine to the E, and Fairlight and Ecclesbourne Glens are noted beauty spots. For details concerning the Battle of Hastings (1066), see Battle.

HATFIELD, Herts *8 TL20*
This ancient market town lies to the E of the A1000, adjacent to Hatfield New Town. Since the latter was built in 1946 the population of the area has doubled, but the old town is still full of charming old buildings. Fore Street has a row of Georgian houses stepped up the hillside, and several other interesting old buildings can be seen in Park Street and Church Street. Magnificent Hatfield House was built for Robert Cecil, 1st Earl of Shaftesbury, and stands in a great park. Its superb great-hall is richly appointed with panelling, carving, and several unique paintings (OACT).

Tudor Palace was constructed entirely of brick – a startlingly new fashion for the period – and stands in the grounds of Hatfield House. Elizabeth's Oak, said to be where Elizabeth I received news of her accession, is also in the park. The Cecil family's Chapel is included in the local church. Sir Robert Cecil's tomb was ordered before his death, to make sure of a good likeness. Great Nast Hyde is a 17th-c house lying 2m SW.

HATFIELD, S Yorks *22 SE60*
Old brick houses are a feature of this pleasant little village, and the fine trans-Norman and later church displays a perpendicular central tower. It also shows a good screen. Much of the district was under water until drained in 1626 by Cornelius Vermuyden, the Dutch engineer who did so much work in the East Anglian Fens.

HATHERSAGE, Derbyshire *18 SK28*
Robin Hood is associated with this Peak District village, which is beautifully situated on the River Derwent. Hathersage appears in Charlotte Brontë's *Jane Eyre* under the name Morton, and Eyre brasses can be seen in the local church. An additional particularly-notable brass dates from 1459. The old halls of Highlow, Offerton, and North Lees all lie in this area, and the latter, together with Moorseats House is

1 All Saints' Church
2 Castle Ruins
3 Church of St Mary Star of the Sea
4 Church-in-the-Wood
5 Cloudesley Shovel House
6 Fishermen's Museum
7 Lifeboat Station
8 Miniature Railway
9 Model Tudor Village
10 Pier
11 St Clement's Caves
12 St Clement's Church
13 Town Hall
14 White Rock Pavilion

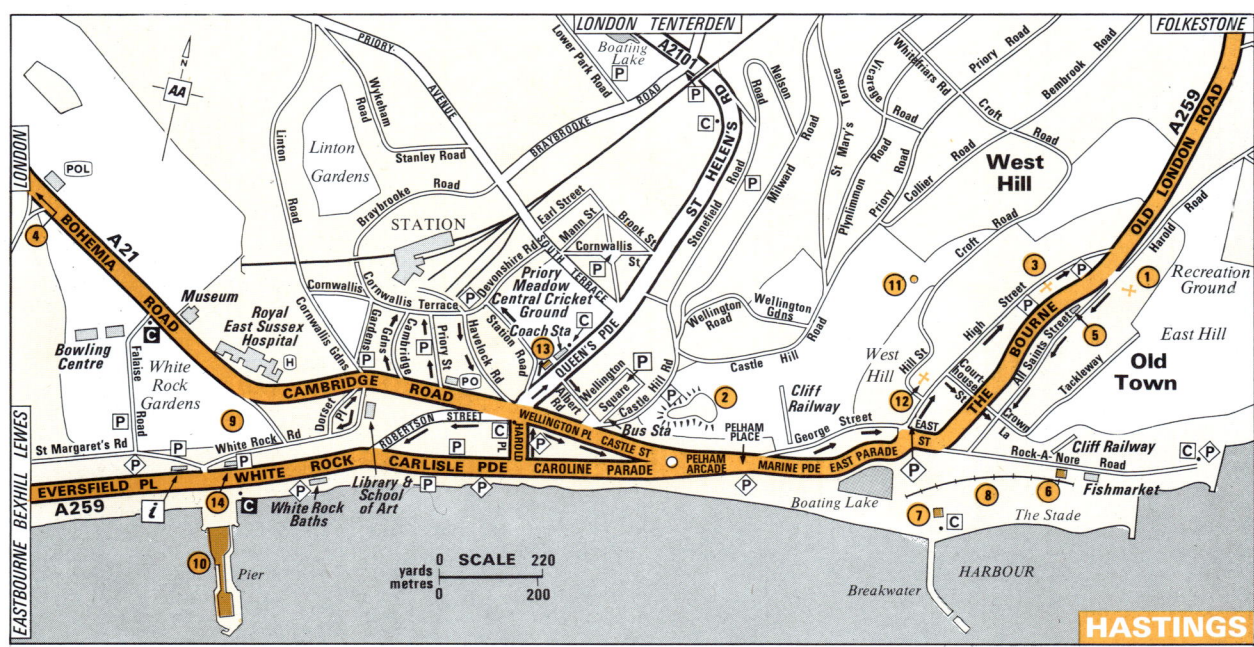

associated with *Jane Eyre*. Stanage Edge lies 3m N, and 1,500ft High Neb is well-known to rock climbers. Below Millstone Edge, 2m SE on the Sheffield road, is Surprise View. The iron age hill-fort of Carl Wark lies to the N.

HAUGHLEY, Suffolk   15 TM06
A village 2½m NW of Stowmarket, where a large mound marks the site of a former Norman castle. Haughley Park dates from 1620 (OACT). The decorated and perpendicular church displays a good nave roof, and the porch contains over thirty 18th-c leather buckets.

HAUXTON, Cambs   14 TL45
Cambridge lies 4m NE of this little River-Cam village. Much of the church is of Norman origin, and it has a 13th-c wall-painting of Thomas Becket, thought to be one of the earliest in England.

HAUXWELL, N Yorks   22 SE19
Hauxwell lies 4m NE of Leyburn and includes a Norman church. A Saxon cross in the churchyard is inscribed *Crux Sancti Jacobi*, recalling a 7th-c missionary known as James the Deacon. The local hall dates from the 18thc.

HAVANT, Hants   8 SU70
A rapidly-developing coastal town facing Hayling Island and the enclosed waters of Langstone Harbour.

HAVERHILL, Suffolk   14 TL64
Although a rapidly-expanding overspill town, Haverhill still retains the 19th-c Court House, Corn Exchange, and town hall. On the parapet of the 14th- and 15th-c church tower is a representation of a wild man holding a bludgeon.

HAWES, N Yorks   21 SD88
Hawes is situated on the River Ure, between two of England's highest passes and near the 850ft head of Wensleydale. Fleet Moss, at some 1,900ft, is the highest in Yorkshire and leads S to Wharfedale, affording a superb view of the Craven passes from its summit. Buttertubs stands at 1,728ft and leads N to the lonely head of Swaledale. By-roads from Hawes lead E to Semer Water, considered the most picturesque lake in Yorkshire, and W to the notable waterfall of Hardraw Force.

HAWKEDON, Suffolk   15 TL75
The local church stands on a wide village green and displays a fine south porch. Carved poppy-head bench-ends are of interest inside. The 16th-c hall has Georgian additions, and two notable timbered 15th-c houses – Thurston Hall and Swan's Hall – stand S at Thurston End.

HAWKHURST, Kent   9 TQ73
Once a smuggling stronghold, this ancient town includes several old houses and a green called The Moor. The church is of decorated and perpendicular style, and carries a 75ft tower.

HAWKSHEAD, Cumbria   21 SD39
A picturesque village with a 16th-c church. A grammar school of the same period counts the poet Wordsworth among its pupils. The old Court House contains the Lakeland Folk Museum of Rural Crafts, displaying forestry, textile, and farm exhibits (NT). The head of Esthwaite Water, in the Lake District national park, lies to the E; near by is the national nature reserve of North Fen. Wetherlam rises 2,502ft from the fells to the NW.

HAWORTH, W Yorks   22 SE03
Situated on the edge of rugged moors, this bleak village is famous for its Brontë associations – notably the parsonage in which the family lived. This building now houses the Brontë Parsonage Museum. Emily Brontë died here in 1848, and Charlotte in 1855. Both were buried at St Michael's Church, in which a Brontë chapel was dedicated in 1964. The Black Bull Inn was once frequented by their brother Branwell. Keighley and Worth Valley railway is a revived steam line with a railway museum, exhibiting the largest private collection of veteran standard-gauge steam and diesel locomotives in the country, at Haworth Station.

HAWTON, Notts   19 SK75
The church has a famous 14th-c Easter Sepulchre, which is said to show some of the best stone-carving in the country.

HAXEY, Humberside   19 SK79
Strip-cultivation is still practised in this old farming centre, which was once the capital of the flat country known as the Isle of Axholme. A restored perpendicular church displays a good 15th-c nave roof. Throwing the Hood is a curious old custom akin to Rugby football, played in costume on the twelfth day of Christmas (6 January).

HAYDOCK, Merseyside   17 SJ59
Haydock Park racecourse lies some 2½m NE of the town itself, which lies roughly halfway between Liverpool and Manchester.

HAYES, Gt London   8 TQ08
Once a straggling village in Middlesex, Hayes is now an industrial and residential district of Greater London. St Mary's Church has a timbered 16th-c porch, and contains brasses and a wall painting.

HAYFIELD, Derbyshire   18 SK08
This small textile-manufacturing town is a good centre for walks and climbs on 2,088ft Kinder Scout (The Peak).

HAYLE, Cornwall   4 SW53
A port and market town on the estuary of the Hayle River, in St Ives Bay. The beach offers fine sands and dunes.

HAYLING ISLAND, Hants   8 SU70
Comprising an area of 4sqm, this island resort offers holiday camps, caravan sites, good sands, and bathing. A passenger ferry plies to and from Portsmouth, and a bridge connects to Havant on the mainland. St Peter's Church in North Hayling shows old woodwork and preserves three bells cast in about 1350, still set in their original frames. The Hayling Billy Inn has a real locomotive preserved as an inn sign – the one that used to travel between the island and the mainland before the railway bridge was closed. Chichester Harbour offers excellent sailing facilities, and the island's coast is known for its fishing.

HAYWARDS HEATH, W Sussex   8 TQ32
A modern residential town on the main railway line from London to Brighton.

HAYWOOD, GREAT, Staffs   18 SJ92
Fine Essex Bridge spans the River Trent with fourteen arches here (AM). It formerly had forty-three, but was rebuilt in 1679. The Trent and Mersey, and Staffordshire and Worcestershire canals meet here. Shugborough Park was the birthplace of Admiral Anson, and incorporates the Staffordshire County Museum. It includes an interesting triumphal arch (NT, OACT).

HEADCORN, Kent   9 TQ84
Both the church and the Cloth Hall date from the 15thc; the former shows old screenwork and fine roofs. Magnificent half-timbered houses in the area include Headcorn Manor and Hawkenbury, both used as cloth halls by Flemish-immigrant weavers in the 17thc. An ancient oak tree stands near the church.

HEADINGTON, Oxon   13 SP50
Headington church preserves a fine Norman chancel arch. The area has been associated with morris dancing for many years, and this tradition is revived every Whit-Monday. Many of the Oxford Colleges were built of Headington stone.

HEANOR, Derbyshire   18 SK44
An industrial town which is mainly involved with coal, iron, and pottery.

HEATH CHAPEL, Salop   12 SO58
This largely unspoiled Norman church is considered one of the best examples of its period.

HEATHFIELD, E Sussex   9 TQ52
Heathfield Park is a William-and-Mary period house, with late 19th-c alterations. The grounds contain the 55ft Gibraltar tower, and the area was well-known for cannon-making in the days of the old Sussex iron industry.

HEBDEN BRIDGE, W Yorks   22 SD92
A mill town on the River Calder and Hebden Water, near the hill-top village of Heptonstall (NW). Picturesque Hardcastle Crags (NT) lies some 3m farther.

HECKFIELD, Hants   8 SU76
Heckfield's parish church preserves a notable 13th-c chest. A table to Neville Chamberlain, who died in the parish in 1940, can also be seen. Stratfieldsaye Park lies 2m NW and was rebuilt in 1795. It was given to the first Duke of Wellington by Parliament. A Wellington Monument can be seen on Heckfield Heath.

HECKINGTON, Lincs   19 TF14
The magnificent decorated-style church in this parish is considered one of the finest of its period in England. Also in the area is the only example of an eight-sail tower mill ever to have been preserved (OACT).

HECKMONDWIKE, W Yorks   22 SE22
A market town 2m NW of Dewsbury, involved in the manufacture of carpets and blankets. The name means the *wie*, or dwelling, of someone called Heakmund.

HEDDON-ON-THE-WALL, Northumberland   27 NZ16
The village church has a vaulted stone-roofed Norman sanctuary. Cottages known as Frenchmen's Row date from 1796, and were occupied by French priests fleeing from the Revolution. A sundial commemorates their departure in 1802. Near the River Tyne is the Tide, or Kissing Stone of 1783, which shows the arms of Newcastle and has marked the jurisdiction of the port for over 600 years. A 100yd section of Hadrian's Wall is still visible.

HEDON, Humberside 23 TA12
One of Yorkshire's best towers is displayed by the splendid early-English to perpendicular church. The whole building is known as the King of Holderness. Ravenspurne Cross was brought here from Kilnsea and recalls the landing of Bolingbroke (Henry IV) in 1399, at the long-since vanished village of Ravenspur. This extinct community was sited on the Humber estuary.

HEIGHINGTON, Co Durham 27 NZ22
Several greens are interspersed among the 18th-c houses of this village, which is built on a 450ft escarpment.

HELFORD, Cornwall 4 SW72
Helford village is beautifully situated S of the Helford River, and is connected to Helford Passage by passenger ferry. The small harbour was used for export of tin in the 18thc, but now it is a centre for yachtsmen and anglers.

HELMINGHAM, Suffolk 15 TM15
Imposing restored Tudor Hall is completely surrounded by a moat, and entry is by means of a drawbridge. The gardens are also moated and form part of an ancient deer park (OACT). Monuments to the Tollemaches can be seen in the church, which has a fine perpendicular tower.

HELMSHORE, Lancs 21 SD72
A local museum of early textile machinery is housed in a former blanket mill, where an early 19th-c water-wheel was replaced by electric motors in 1954. The East Lancashire Railway Preservation Society had, until recently, a museum here; this is now located at Bury.

HELMSLEY, N Yorks 22 SE68
Helmsley is a delightful stone-built town, with an old cross in the market place. The ruined 12th-c castle (AM) stands in the grounds of Duncombe Park, which now houses a school. It is thought that the castle was built by Walter l'Espec, founder of nearby Rievaulx Abbey. Notable temples, a 152ft lime tree, and a 148ft ash can be seen in the park.

HELPRINGHAM, Lincs 19 TF14
Situated 5m SE of Sleaford and at the edge of the Fens, this Kesteven village includes a fine early-English to perpendicular church.

HELPSTON, Cambs 19 TF10
John Clare the peasant poet was born here in 1793, and is buried in the churchyard. A plaque marks the cottage where he lived, and a cross has been erected in his memory.

HELSBY, Cheshire 17 SJ47
Helsby Hill (462ft, part NT) is a notable viewpoint which is well-known as a practice-ground for climbers. Traces of an iron-age camp have been found here, and Ince Manor, 4m W, was fortified in 1399.

HELSTON, Cornwall 4 SW62
An ancient Stannary town where locally-mined tin used to be weighed and taxed. The picturesque Furry Dance is held annually on May 8. A plaque on a house in Wendron Street marks the birthplace of Bob Fitzsimmons, the only Englishman to have held the world heavyweight boxing championship. Coinagehall Street is delightful, and 18th-c houses can be seen in Meneage Street. The River Cober flows into Loe Pool (1m S), which is separated from the sea by a bar.

HEMEL HEMPSTEAD, Herts 8 TL00
Recent times have seen a rapid expansion of this River-Gade town, which now includes a large and successful new town. The old part retains several Tudor cottages, and 17th- to 18th-c cottages can be seen in the High Street. The church retains a great deal of fine Norman work, and the prominent lead spire rises to 200ft. A Roman villa has been discovered in Gadebridge Park. Piccott's End lies 1m N, and may once have been a pilgrims' hostel. It is some 500-years old and contains remarkable medieval paintings (OACT).

HEMINGBROUGH, N Yorks 22 SE63
The magnificent local church carries a 120ft stone spire, and examples of old woodwork are outstanding. Wressell Castle is the only remaining fortified building in the old East Riding and lies 3m ENE. It dates from about the late 14thc, and was once the home of the Perrys.

HEMINGFORD, Cambs 14 TL27
Hemingford Abbots and its twin Hemingford Grey are picturesquely situated on the River Ouse. The former includes a church with a fine spire, and the latter has a rare partly 12th-c manor house. Other features are a water-mill and several old cottages.

HEMPSTEAD, Essex 14 TL63
Highwayman Dick Turpin was supposedly born at the Crown Inn, possibly in 1705. The church contains the tomb of William Harvey (died 1657), who discovered the circulation of blood.

HENDON, Gt London 8 TQ28
Once a straggling village in Middlesex, Hendon is now part of Greater London. The restored church contains a Norman font and is where Raffles, the founder of Singapore, is buried. The Daniel almshouses of 1686 have been restored, and the old house of Church Farm now contains a museum. Hendon Hall currently serves as a hotel, but once belonged to the actor-manager David Garrick. It displays a notable portico.

HENFIELD, W Sussex 8 TQ21
A rambling village 4m NE of Steyning, where the partly 13th-c church contains several interesting brasses. The eves of 16th-c timbered Cat House are adorned with metal cats. The area also boasts the 18th-c Wood Mill watermill (OACT).

HENGRAVE, Suffolk 15 TL86
The hall is a magnificent Tudor house, with a notable south-front gatehouse and an interior courtyard. Old monuments and a Norman round tower are displayed by the church. West Stow Hall is an ancient house with a curious arcaded gatehouse, lying 2m N.

HENLEY-IN-ARDEN, Warwickshire 12 SP16
This small town of old houses lies in the ancient Forest of Arden district — though little of the forest remains today. Oak-timbered buildings lining the main street date from the 15th, 16th, and 17thc, and the finely-timbered guildhall dates from 1448. The church shows good 15th-c window tracery, and part of an ancient market cross has survived. Beaudesert church displays a fine chancel arch and an enriched chancel window, both of which are Norman.

HENLEY-ON-THAMES, Oxon 8 SU78
A well-built residential town and popular Thames-Valley resort. The famous regatta is held annually in the first week of July. Thames and Isis are represented on the bridge of 1736, and the decorated and perpendicular church contains numerous monuments. Numerous Georgian and older houses can be seen in the town.

HENSTRIDGE, Somerset 6 ST71
Henstridge's rebuilt church contains the Tudor Carent tomb. The Virginia Inn has a humorous historical association with Sir Walter Raleigh; it is said that the gentleman's pipe was extinguished with a stoup of beer, cast by his servant in the belief that he was on fire.

17th- and 18th-c buildings in the High Street at Hemel Hempstead

HEYDON, Norfolk *15 TG12*
A most attractive village where the local church houses a 15th-c screen and pulpit. An Elizabethan hall is also of interest.

HEYSHAM, Lancs *21 SD46*
Sailings to Northern Ireland and the Isle of Man originate from this port, and good sands offer access for bathing. Ruined St Patrick's Chapel, a Celtic church which probably dates from the 5thc, is thought to have been founded by Irish missionaries. It shows curious rock-hewn coffins as graves. St Peter's Church displays remains of ancient crosses in the churchyard, and the old hall at Higher Heysham dates from 1598.

HEYTESBURY, Wilts *7 ST94*
This village lies in the lovely Wylye Valley. Its old buildings include the rebuilt Hospital of St John – an almshouse of 1449 which was founded by the Hungerford family, and displays their arms. An old lock-up is also of note, and the restored early-English and perpendicular church contains a fine stone screen with fan-vaulting on both sides. Heytesbury House dates from 1782. Knook is a fine old manor house to the SE. Battlesbury and Scratchford Camps lie to the NW.

HICKLING, Norfolk *15 TG42*
Typical of the Norfolk Broads, this village includes a restored perpendicular church displaying fierce tower gargoyles. Remains of a 12th-c priory are of interest, and the hall dates from the 18thc. Hickling Broad lies 1m S of the village and is the largest of the Broads. Part of its 1,200 acres comprises a national nature reserve.

HICKSTEAD, W Sussex *8 TQ22*
Hickstead is well-known as the scene of outdoor show-jumping – notably the annual British Jumping Derby. It lies on the main London to Brighton road.

HIGHAM, Kent *9 TQ77*
A Thames-marshlands village, where the church displays a traceried door and a restored 16th-c screen. Across Higham Marshes are the remains of Shornmead Fort, built by General Gordon in the 19thc. A 4,000yd canal tunnel between Higham and Frindsbury was built from 1819 to 1824. The architect, William Twiney Clark, also built an iron bridge across the Danube at Budapest.

HIGHAM FERRERS, Northants *13 SP96*
Features of the splendid early-English to decorated church include a lofty crocketed spire, a fine west door, and good chapels and screens. Near by are the 15th-c chantry chapel (or school, AM) and a fine old Bede House. An ancient stepped-cross can also be seen.

HIGHCLERE, Hants *7 SU46*
The modern castle of 1842 was designed by Sir Charles Barry, and stands in a superb park. Sidown Hill (872ft) lies S and 874ft Pilot Hill to the W.

HIGHCLIFFE, Dorset *7 SZ29*
A resort with a shingle and sand beach, bordered by 100ft clay, sand, and shingle cliffs. Highcliffe Castle is a modern structure which, until recently, was occupied by a religious order. It was rented by the Kaiser in 1907.

HIGH CROSS, Leics *13 SP48*
Venones, a Roman settlement at the intersection of two famous Roman roads – Watling Street and the line of the original Fosse Way – used to exist here. An ivy-shrouded pillar was erected at this junction in 1712, and at one time was thought to mark the centre of England.

HIGH EASTER, Essex *9 TL61*
An attractive village of old houses, where the church displays good 15th-c brickwork and a fine oak nave roof. Roman tiles were used in the construction of this building.

HIGHER BOCKHAMPTON, Dorset *6 SY79*
The thatched cottage (NT) in which Thomas Hardy was born in 1840 stands in this village. The approach is difficult for cars.

HIGH ERCALL, Salop *17 SJ51*
Civil War damage of 1645 is evident on the otherwise fine tower of High Ercall's trans-Norman church. Remains of the churchyard cross incorporate a sundial. The hall dates from 1608. It was garrisoned for the King and repelled many fierce assaults before finally surrendering in 1646. Delightful almshouses in the village were founded in 1694.

HIGH FORCE, Co Durham *27 NY82*
High Force is a notable waterfall where the Tees plunges 70ft, and is particularly impressive when the river is in flood. It lies partly within the 6,500-acre national nature reserve of Upper Teesdale. Mickle Fell, Yorkshire's highest mountain, rises 2,591ft in the SW; NW are the Whin-Sill outcrop of Falcon Clints and the waterfall of Caldron Snout, which falls 200ft in a 450ft stretch of cataracts and rapids. The latter is only accessible on foot. Still farther NW are the 10,000 acres of ground that make-up the Westmorland national nature reserve of Moor House. Dufton Fell rises to 2,403ft in the background. Birkdale Farm lies near Maize Beck, beyond Caldron Snout, and claims to be the most isolated in England. A large reservoir has been built in the area.

HIGHGATE, Gt London *8 TQ28*
This northern suburb of London is situated on high ground adjoining Hampstead Heath and the beautiful Kenwood estate. Older parts of the area, like its neighbour Hampstead, retain the aspect of an 18th-c village.

The 18th-c Kenwood House is by Robert Adam, and forms part of the Iveagh Bequest. It is notable for its splendid library (OACT).

Highgate village boasts many literary associations. Samuel Coleridge lived at number 3 The Grove, from 1816 until his death in 1834. His remains lie under the vaults of the school chapel, and a monument to him can be seen in St Michael's Church. Andrew Marvell, Lord Bacon, and Leigh Hunt all lived in the district. The site of Marvell's house is marked on the wall of Waterlow Park, itself almost opposite the exceptionally-fine 17th-c Cromwell House.

Attractive Georgian houses can be seen in the Grove and South Grove. On the left side of Highgate Hill, at the corner of Salisbury Road, is the well-known Dick Whittington Stone. Traditionally it was here that Whittington rested with his cat prior to entering London for the first time. He became Lord Mayor of London in the middle ages.

HIGH HAM, Somerset *6 ST43*
High Ham lies on high ground to the S of Sedgemoor. The local perpendicular church displays a splendid carved screen, perfect rood stairs, and curious gargoyles representing Darby and Joan. An old windmill in the district has a unique cap of thatch (NT). Low Ham lies 1m S, and includes a 17th-c church – unusual in that it has no churchyard. A 4th-c Roman mosaic pavement has been excavated here.

HIGHWORTH, Wilts *12 SU29*
An old hilltop town with several 17th-c houses, and a perpendicular church which displays a good tower. The town's situation affords fine views over the surrounding area. Hannington Hall, 2m NW, is of Elizabethan origin.

HIGH WYCOMBE, Bucks *8 SU89*
Well-known for the manufacture of furniture – especially chairs – High Wycombe is a prosperous town situated in a gap of the Chiltern Hills. The 13th-c church has been greatly restored, and contains a fine mid 18th-c monument by Scheemakers. A notable modern window commemorates famous women. Little Market House originated in 1604, but was rebuilt by Robert Adam in 1761. The guildhall dates from 1757, and the remains of St John's Hospital are of the late 12thc. Bassetbury Manor is 17thc and later. Bassetbury Mill, Bowden Mill, and Pann Mill all retain original wheels. The mansion of Wycombe Abbey is now a girls' school, and was built by James Wyatt in 1795.

Collections of domestic chairs, old tools, and chair-making apparatus are on display in a museum in Castle Hill House. This house is surrounded by grounds containing a moated folly. At Terriers, on the Amersham road, is a notable modern church by Sir Giles Gilbert Scott. Terriers House dates from the late 17thc.

HILLESDEN, Bucks *13 SP62*
This secluded Vale of Aylesbury village includes a church noted for its screen, its examples of old glass, and an ornate outside stair-turret to the vestry.

HILLINGDON, Gt London *8 TQ08*
Once a manor and parish in Middlesex, Hillingdon is now part of Greater London. The church tower dates from 1629, and the building itself houses fine brasses and tombs. Cedar House is a beautiful red-brick building which dates from 1580 and later. Charles I spent several uneasy hours at the Red Lion Inn, by the church, in 1646.

HILLMORTON, Warwickshire *13 SP57*
Several 16th- to 18th-c houses and part of a 14th-c market cross can be seen in this village. The restored 13th- to 16th-c church houses interesting old effigies. In contrast is the nearby Post Office wireless station.

HILPERTON, Wilts *7 ST85*
A stone-built village characteristic of the region, which includes a small lock-up with a domed roof. The rebuilt church retains its spired 14th-c tower.

HEREFORD, Herefs & Worcs *12 SO54*
Once the Saxon capital of West Mercia, this ancient county town is sited on the River Wye. The river is spanned by old and new bridges. It was an early religious centre and has been the seat of a bishop since 672AD. The restored cathedral is mainly Norman and decorated in style, and of special interest are the carved stalls, the 14th-c Mappa Mundi, King Stephen's 800-year-old chair, the chapels and tombs, and the library of rare chained books. Cloisters leading to the ancient Bishop's Palace contain a rare 12th-c timbered hall, and the nearby College of Vicars Choral dates from 1472.

Of the other interesting churches in the area the oldest is 12th- to 14th-c St Peter's. This has medieval roofs and stalls. All Saints' is of early-English to perpendicular style, displays carved stalls, and houses a library of chained books. David Garrick the actor was born at the Raven Inn, and Nell Gwynne is said to have also been born in the city. Several old almshouses include the picturesque Coningsby Hospital of 1614. Half-timbered Old House dates from 1621 and now contains a museum. The Shire Hall, by Smirke, displays a Grecian style and dates from 1819.

A preaching cross stands near the 14th-c Black Friars, or Dominican Friary and a modern cross surmounts the White Steps (AM) on the Hay road. Vestiges of the former town walls exist, and earthworks from the former castle, once a stronghold against the Welsh, can still be seen. The Three Choirs festival of music is held at Hereford every third year. The great 17th- and 18th-c mansion of Holme Lacy lies 5½m SE, and displays some of the finest plaster ceilings in England. Numerous Scudamore monuments are contained within the church. The RC Abbey and College of Belmont is situated 2½m SW.

HERNE, Kent *9 TR16*
Herne is a quiet country village lying inland from Herne Bay. The 14th-c church has a good tower, described by Ruskin as perfect. A memorial has been raised to Nicholas Ridley, the martyr Bishop who was once vicar here. A local windmill dates from 1781.

HERNE BAY, Kent *9 TR16*
This popular resort has a shingle beach which offers some sand at low tide. Excellent fishing and sailing may be enjoyed here, and there is a long pier.

HERRINGFLEET, Suffolk *15 TM49*
The local thatched church retains an early-Norman round tower. An old smock mill and fine old barn are of interest, and 16th- to 19th-c Somerleyton Hall stands in a park to the SE (OACT). Tapestries, pictures, and carvings by Grinling Gibbons can be seen inside the mansion, and the grounds hold a children's farm and miniature railway.

HERSTMONCEUX, E Sussex *9 TQ61*
Herstmonceux includes a beautiful moated 15th-c castle which has been restored in recent years. It has housed the Royal Observatory, from Greenwich, since 1948. The Isaac Newton telescope can be seen from a special gallery, and the gardens are attractively laid out (OACT). Trug baskets are manufactured in the village, and the mainly trans-Norman church is noted for its brick-built Dacre chapel. Herstmonceux Place is a Georgian house.

HERTFORD, Herts *8 TL31*
An ancient county town on the River Lea, with sparse remains of the original Norman castle of c1100. The present castle dates from 1500 and 1800. A number of old houses dating from the 16th to 18thc are still standing, and Shire Hall, by James the brother of Robert Adam, dates from 1768 to 1769. Lombard House was once the home of Chauncy, the county historian, and dates from the 17thc. Christ's Hospital School for girls is of note. The restored Friends Meeting House dates from 1670, and Hale's Grammar School from the 17thc. Situated on the N outskirts is the small Norman church of Bengeo. Balls Park is a good mid 17th-c house with later additions, now serving as a training college (1m S).

HESSETT, Suffolk *15 TL96*
A fine decorated to perpendicular church here is notable for its rich embattled parapets. Also of note are the porch and several wall-paintings. The window to St Nicholas shows a golfclub, and the 14th-c vestry was once an anchorite's cell. The latter still has its own squint and altar.

HEVER, Kent *8 TQ44*
Hever's 13th-c and later moated castle has associations with Henry VIII and Anne Boleyn. It was the latter's girlhood home, and the surrounding grounds are beautiful (OACT). A tomb and brass to Anne Boleyn's father can be seen in the early-English and later church, and the village inn displays a rare sign depicting Henry VIII. The River Eden flows through the area.

HEXHAM, Northumberland *27 NY96*
An attractive old town on the River Tyne, and an excellent centre for walkers exploring the Roman wall. The very interesting priory church is larger than some cathedrals, and contains a Saxon crypt. Much 13th-c workmanship is evident, and other items of particular interest include the night staircase of the canons; a beautiful wooden pulpitum; a rare pre-Conquest frid-stool (or throne); the restored Acca's Cross; and fragments of painted choir screens. A carved Roman stone and several altars of the same period can also be seen, and parts of the priory building still exist. The 15th-c Moot Hall and 14th-c prison – or Manor Office – are of note. A 13th-c bridge spans Halgut Burn, and modern Beaufront Castle stands 2m NE.

HEYBRIDGE, Essex *9 TL80*
Chelmsford lies 9m W of this village, and the River Blackwater flows through the area. Heybridge Hall dates from the 17thc, and the mainly-Norman church displays a fine tower. A mill and the Georgian mill-house are attractive. Access to Heybridge Basin, at the mouth of the river, is by canal towpath. This has been an anchorage for yachts and eel boats for many years.

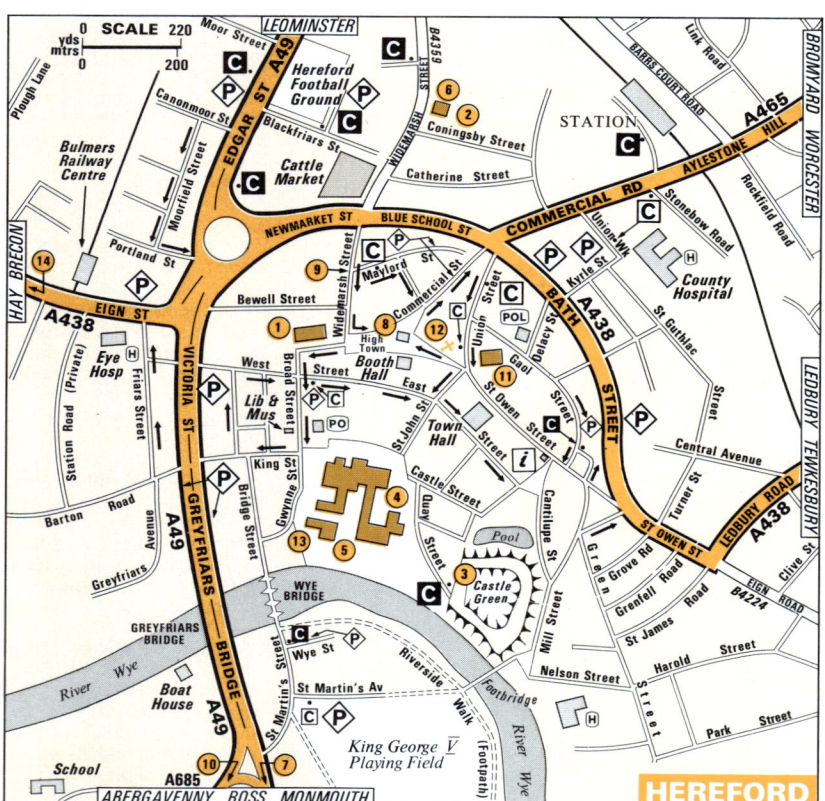

1 All Saints' Church
2 Black Friars (Dominican) Friary
3 Castle Site
4 Cathedral and Bishop's Palace
5 College of Vicars Choral
6 Coningsby Hospital
7 Holme Lacy Mansion
8 Old House (museum)
9 Raven Inn
10 RC Abbey and College of Belmont
11 Shire Hall
12 St Peter's Church
13 Town Wall Remains
14 White Steps

HILTON, Cambs 14 TL26
A rare turf maze of 1660, with a stone pillar at its centre, can be seen here.

HIMLEY, Staffs 17 SO89
Himley church is Georgian, and the Crooked House is a curious old inn. Holbeche (Holbeach) House is where the fleeing Gunpowder Plot conspirators made their last stand after their failure in 1605.

HINCKLEY, Leics 18 SP49
Engaged in the manufacture of hosiery and shoes, this place has the distinction of having had the country's first stocking frame installation (1640). Bosworth Field was the site of a great battle in 1485 – part of the Wars of the Roses – in which King Richard III was killed (5m N). The decorated and perpendicular church has a good roof.

HINDHEAD, Surrey 8 SU83
This delightful inland resort and residential town stands at about 850ft in an area of outstanding natural beauty. Gibbet Hill lies ¾m NE, and is a noted viewpoint (NT). Near by is a deep combe known as the Devil's Punchbowl, where an unknown sailor was murdered in 1786 (NT). The murderers were hanged by the side of the Punchbowl, where an inscribed stone recalls the event. Waggoners' Wells is a noted beauty spot 1½m SW (NT).

HINDLEY, Gt Manchester 21 SD60
Galleried All Saints' Church was rebuilt in 1766, and the interior contains panelling and woodcarving. The town is involved in the coal-mining industry.

HINDLIP, Herefs & Worcs 12 SO85
The predecessor of the present Hindlip Hall was famous for its secret hiding-places, which were used by two of the Gunpowder Plot conspirators in 1605.

HINGHAM, Norfolk 15 TG00
Emigrants who left this district in the 17thc, including the Puritan rector Robert Pack, founded a Hingham in New England after safely crossing the Atlantic. The fine 14th-c church shows some 16th-c glass, a remarkable 15th-c tomb, and a bronze bust of Abraham Lincoln. The famous president's ancestors lived here. Good 18th-c houses exist in the town.

HINTON ST GEORGE, Somerset 6 ST41
A picturesque village where the church is notable for its perpendicular tower and range of Poulett monuments. Scratch sundials are carved on the buttresses. Hinton House is a fine old mansion.

HITCHAM, Suffolk 15 TL95
Delightful old timbered houses can be seen in this village, and the decorated to perpendicular church shows a 15th-c hammerbeam roof plus a canopied piscina.

HITCHIN, Herts 14 TL12
Hitchin is an old market town with a large perpendicular-style church displaying a fine porch and good screenwork. A number of Georgian and older houses can be seen, particularly in Tilehouse Street and Bridge Street. Also of interest are the Cooper's Arms and Sun inns, and the Biggin almshouses. Hitchin Priory dates from 1770 and 1771, and incorporates fragments of a 14th-c Carmelite house. It retains its moat. Skynner almshouses are situated in Bancroft, and date from 1760 and 1698.

The Hall at Holkham, one of the largest Palladian mansions in England

The town was the birthplace of the poet George Chapman in 1559, and of Sir Henry Bessemer in 1813. Bessemer is famous for his early work on the commercial manufacture of steel. Wooded Barton Hills lie 6m W and include the prehistoric hill fort of Ravenburgh Castle. The ancient Icknield Way ran to the S, and its route traverses Telegraph Hill. The latter provides a good viewpoint at 602ft.

HOCKLEY HEATH, W Midlands 12 SP17
Packwood House, a 16th- to 17th-c building with a yew garden planned to represent the Sermon on the Mount, lies some 2½m E (OACT). Baddesley Clinton is a splendid moated 15th-c house lying 4m SE.

HODDESDON, Herts 8 TL30
Georgian houses and inns line the spacious High Street of this town. The Golden Lion is of interest, and Jacobean Rawdon House is now a convent. A gatehouse survives among other remains of Rye House, a place where the plot to murder Charles II was hatched in 1683 (1m E). It is proposed that the land around Rye House should become part of the Lea Valley regional park.

HODNET, Salop 17 SJ62
The mainly-decorated church shows a fine octagonal tower, and retains a Norman priest's doorway. Several attractive half-timbered houses can be seen in Hodnet, and a half-timbered tithe barn at Home Farm dates from 1619. Modern Hodnet Hall stands in lovely gardens (OACT). Picturesque Hawkstone Park, with the ruined Red Castle and a mansion belonging to a religious order, lies 2½m NW.

HOLBEACH, Lincs 14 TF32
An ancient market town, Holbeach is one of Lincolnshire's bulb-growing centres. The fine church is of decorated and perpendicular styles and displays a lofty spire, a fine north porch, and good windows.

HOLBETON, Devon 5 SX65
The local church is notable for its very fine 16th-c parclose screens and 19th-c carved bench-ends. Flete is a modern mansion near the River Erme.

HOLCOMBE ROGUS, Devon 6 ST01
Holcombe Court is a towered Elizabethan house, and the church houses the carved 17th-c Bluett pew. Cothay is a beautiful little manor house of Tudor origin, lying 3¼m E. A gatehouse guards its approach, and the main building is surrounded by a moat. Greenham Barton, an early 15th-c house, stands near by.

HOLDENBY, Northants 13 SP66
Charles I was taken from Elizabethan Holdenby House by Cornet Joyce, of the Parliamentary army, and removed to London in 1646. Sir Christopher Hatton was born in the old house in 1540, and later became Lord Chancellor under Queen Elizabeth I. Hatton Garden in London is named after him. Although rebuilt, the house still retains imposing gateways of a former outer court, which bear the date 1583.

HOLDERNESS
This is the name given to a flat area of country in the SE corner of the old Yorkshire East Riding (Humberside). It extends from the Wolds to the Humber and Spurn Head, and is famous for its great medieval churches.

HOLKHAM, Norfolk 15 TF84
One of the largest Palladian mansions in England stands here in a great park, and was once the home of Coke of Norfolk. He is famous for his agricultural developments. The house dates from the 18thc and contains a superb hall by William Kent (OACT). State apartments are splendidly appointed with fine pictures and furnishings. A tomb in the church houses the remains of the second Countess of Leicester, who died in 1870.

HOLLAND
The smallest of the three old county divisions lying around the Wash, Holland is a fertile area of fen and marshland. Canals and dykes drain the land for farming; these, plus a series of fine medieval churches, are the main features of the districts.

HOLLINGBOURNE, Kent 9 TQ85
Situated under the North Downs close to the Pilgrims' Way, this place includes the restored half-timbered 16th-c

Godfrey House among its many old buildings. The church houses fine monuments to the Culpepers, plus notable embroidered hangings. The manor house is of brick construction. Eyhorne Manor is a 15th-c half-timbered building to the SW (OACT).

HOLMBURY ST MARY, Surrey *8 TQ14*
Holmbury Hill (875ft) and Pitch Hill (844ft) are notable viewpoints, and the area is now designated one of outstanding natural beauty. The village itself is picturesquely situated in the Surrey Hills, under Hurt Wood.

HOLME HALE, Norfolk *15 TF80*
The 14th- to 15th-c church has a restored angel-carved roof, and a 15th-c screen with rose-window tracery.

HOLME PIERREPONT, Notts *18 SK63*
A new Trent-side water-sports centre is located here, with a straight six-lane rowing course of 2,000 metres.

HOLMES CHAPEL, Cheshire *17 SJ76*
Jodrell Bank (3m NE) houses the steerable pencil-beam radio telescope which was built for Manchester University – once the largest in the world (OACT). A good sandstone tower is carried by the partly-decorated church, which also preserves old woodwork.

HOLMFIRTH, W Yorks *22 SE10*
Bleak moorland butts up to this rather grim town. Holme Moss lies to the SW, and is surmounted by the BBC North of England television transmitter. Black Hill rises to 1,909ft near by, an altitude that makes it the highest point in Cheshire.

HOLNE, Devon *5 SX76*
Holne was the birthplace of Charles Kingsley in 1819 and lies high above the River Dart. The river is spanned by a 15th-c bridge at this point. A small perpendicular church houses a fine painted screen, and a pulpit with an hour glass. Beautiful wooded scenery can be enjoyed N near Holne Chase.

HOLT, Norfolk *15 TG03*
Gresham's school was founded in 1555 by Sir William Gresham, Lord Mayor of London and founder of the Royal Exchange. The original Tudor school building stands in the town square, though the school itself is now established ½m along the Cromer road. Home Place is a large mansion dated 1903 and 1905.

HOLT, Wilts *7 ST86*
The Courts is a house with a fine façade dating from c1700 (NT), standing in good gardens (gardens OACT). Great Chalfield Manor is a magnificent moated 15th-c house lying 1½m N, which is faced by a tiny 13th-c church displaying a quaint bell turret (NT, OACT).

HONITON, Devon *6 ST10*
This town gave its name to Honiton lace, a material now largely produced in neighbouring villages. The Hospital of St Margaret is of 14th-c origin and was refounded as a leper hospital c1530. It includes a chapel. Marwood House dates from 1619, and the long main street shows several pleasant Georgian houses. A 17th-c black-marble tomb to Thomas Marwood, physician to Queen Elizabeth, can be seen in the perpendicular church. He died at the age of 105 in 1617.

Allhallows School has a perpendicular chapel and is dated 1770. An 80ft tower, erected outside the town by Bishop C Copleston of Llandaff affords wide views of the surrounding area.

HOOK NORTON, Oxon *13 SP33*
Hook Norton church has a strangely-carved Norman font. The door in the 13th-c porch has hinges of 1739, recording the names of the blacksmith and churchwardens of the time.

HOOTON PAGNELL, S Yorks *22 SE40*
Situated on high ground, Hooton Pagnell affords good views of the district and has a Georgian church containing an 18th-c pulpit. The hall retains its 14th-c gatehouse.

HOPE, Derbyshire *18 SK18*
Sheepdog trials are held every August in this lovely Hope-Valley village, which is sited at the entrance to the Vale of Edale. The church is an interesting restored 14th-c structure, containing a quaint brass of 1685 and 17th-c stall backs. The churchyard contains the shaft of a Saxon cross.

HOPE COVE, Devon *15 SX63*
Bolt Tail is the start of a 5m track from here, past Soar Mill Cove to Bolt Head (NT). It is considered one of the finest cliff-walks in England. Grand cliff scenery may be enjoyed beyond Bolberry Downs. Hope Cove itself is a fishing village with good sands.

HOPE-UNDER-DINMORE, Herefs & Worcs *12 SO55*
The restored church has a sculptured, 13th-c font and fine Coningsby monuments. Dinmore Hill is a viewpoint lying 1m S, overlooking the Lugg Valley. Below and to the W is 16th-c Dinmore Manor. Near by is the 12th- to 14th-c Hospitallers' Church, where the chapel and gardens are of particular note (OACT). Hampton Court, 1m SE, is a fine castellated house of 15th-c origin, but has been greatly restored.

HOPTON CASTLE, Salop *11 SO37*
Half-timbered cottages are a feature of the village. A square keep is all that is left of a Norman castle which was the scene of a Civil-War siege during the 17thc.

HORBURY, W Yorks *22 SE31*
John Carr was born here, and is buried in the Church of St Peter and St Leonard, which he built in the 18thc.

HORLEY, Oxon *13 SP44*
The old church in this attractive stone-built village preserves fine doorways and a wall painting of St Christopher.

HORLEY, W Sussex *8 TQ24*
Over-restored is a fair description of the local church's state, but it does still retain some interesting features. These include a fine knight's effigy of c1315 and a 15th-c brass. The Six Bells is an old timbered inn. Tinsley Green lies 3m S and is known for its marbles contests. Crullings, formerly Smallfield Place, is a fine old house some 3m E. The River Mole runs through the area.

HORNCASTLE, Lincs *19 TF26*
This town is on a River-Baine site once occupied by a Roman settlement. Its church is of 13th-c and later date and has been extensively restored. Inside the building is the Dymoke brass of 1519, and a chest dating from 1690. Borrow's *Romany Rye* features the town. Scrivelsby Court lies 2m S and is the traditional home of the King's Champion. A curious lion gateway can be seen, but the rest of the house is now demolished. A 16th-c gatehouse has been converted into the new court.

HORNCHURCH, Gt London *8 TQ58*
Once part of Essex, this residential district is now part of Greater London. A stone and copper bull's head is mounted over the east end of the 13th- to 15th-c church's chancel, and the late-Georgian house of Langtons is of interest.

HORNING, Norfolk *15 TG31*
Noted as a touring centre for the Broads, Horning lies 4m WNW of the remains of St Benet's Abbey. These ruins include a 15th-c gatehouse.

HORNINGSHAM, Wilts *6 ST84*
The thatched nonconformist chapel here is the oldest in England, and was built by Scottish artisans in 1566. They constructed the chapel while working on the great Elizabethan mansion of Longleat.

HORNSEA, Humberside *23 TA24*
Hornsea pottery is famous throughout the country and the workshops are open to visitors. An interesting bird sanctuary is sited at Hornsea Mere, and the resort offers excellent sands. A battlemented, 14th-c tower is retained by the perpendicular church; a market cross stands in the churchyard, and a cross shaft stands in Southgate.

HORSEY, Norfolk *15 TG42*
Incursions of the sea have caused periods of severe flooding along this part of the coast. The village has a thatched church with a Norman round tower and an octagonal 15th-c belfry. Its screen also dates from the 15thc; the area boasts a windmill.

HORSHAM, W Sussex *8 TQ13*
Market town, railway junction, and residential centre, Horsham includes an early-English and perpendicular church with a 175ft shingled spire. The nave roof is rich with bosses, and The Causeway, leading to the church, is lined by fine old houses. One of these is the fascinating Causeway House museum. Denne House, 17thc and later, stands in a park. Two nearby forests are St Leonards at Tilgate and Worth to the E. Both contain ancient hammer-ponds dating from the days of the Sussex iron industry. Percy Bysshe Shelley was born 2m NW at Field Place, a 15th- to 18th-c house, in 1792. Christ's Hospital is a famous boys' school lying 2m SW; it was once located in London but moved here in 1902. One of its features is a very fine Verrio painting measuring 85ft by 14ft (OACT).

HORSTED KEYNES, W Sussex *8 TQ32*
Tudor houses can be seen grouped around the village green, and the Norman and later church has a shingled broach-spire. A station of the revived Bluebell railway exists here.

HORTON, Dorset *7 SU00*
A local folly look-out tower stands 120ft high, and dates from 1700. Monmouth Ash Farm lies 2m SE near the ash tree where the Duke of Monmouth was captured after the rebellion of 1685.

HORTON-IN-RIBBLESDALE, N Yorks 21 SD87
Pen-y-ghent rises to 2,273ft E of this picturesque moorland village, and Alum Pot (4m NNW) is one of the best-known of the Craven potholes. Ling Gill national nature reserve is located near the source of the River Ribble.

HORWICH, Gt Manchester 21 SD61
Cotton mills, railway engineering works, and collieries are the town's main industries. Nearby Rivington reservoirs supply water to Liverpool.

HOUGH-ON-THE-HILL, Lincs 19 SK94
The village church is noted for its Saxon tower, which has a 15th-c top storey. Its Saxon portion includes a curious turret containing a newel stairway. Brandon Old Hall lies 2m NW and is dated 1637.

HOUGHTON, Cambs 14 TL27
Houghton is situated on the River Ouse, and has an outstanding water-mill of timber construction on a stone base. It is let to the Youth Hostels Association (NT).

HOUGHTON, W Sussex 8 TQ01
An inscription on the George and Dragon Inn recalls the visit of Charles II in 1651. A fine bridge spans the Arun at this point.

HOUGHTON-LE-SPRING, Tyne & Wear 27 NZ35
This industrial town is in a colliery district and includes the Kepier Grammar School of 1574 among its features. Local almshouses date from the 17th c, and the mainly 13th-c church has a curious 15th-c two-storey building between chancel and transept. This was erected for the use of a guild. Houghton Hall is of Jacobean date.

HOUNSLOW, Gt London 8 TQ17
Once a famous Middlesex coaching place on the London to West Country road, Hounslow is now a completely modern town forming part of Greater London. Hounslow Heath was a notorious haunt of highwaymen in the coaching era.

HOUSESTEADS, Northumberland 27 NY76
Borcovicium to the Romans, Housesteads is situated on Hadrian's Wall. Remains of a wall-fort can be seen, and an NT museum is of interest. Several picturesque little lakes lying N of the wall include Crag Lough. The wall itself climbs away from here over steep craggy heights, attaining an altitude of over 1,000ft above sea level.

HOVE, E Sussex 8 TQ20
Hove is joined with Brighton and shows a number of fine Regency houses. The shingle beach includes some sand at low tide. Roman remains from Southwick can be seen in the museum, and All Saints' Church is a modern structure noted for its richly-carved screen and high altar.

HOVERINGHAM, Notts 18 SK64
One of the county's largest sand and gravel producing areas lies within this district. A very unusual feature is the 23ft steel-sculpture of a mammoth which faces the office block of a gravel firm. A corn mill of 1778 retains its wheel.

HOVETON ST JOHN, Norfolk 15 TG31
A Broadland village situated NW of Wroxham Broad and Hoveton Great and Little Broads – partly a national nature reserve. Hoveton House is of 17th-c origin, and the old hall dates from 1700.

HOVINGHAM, N Yorks 22 SE67
Hovingham stands around a green, and the church has a Saxon tower. Notable statuary is housed in the 18th-c hall.

HOWDEN, Humberside 23 SE72
Interesting monuments are contained within the 13th- to 14th-c church, which also carries a fine tower. The chancel, however, is in ruins. A statue to the chronicler Roger of Hoveden, who was the rector here until his death in c1200, can also be seen. Portington Hall lies 3m NE and dates from 1582.

HOWICK, Northumberland 27 NU21
Howick stands on a fine stretch of coast near 120ft black cliffs where the Great Whin Sill meets the sea at Cullernose Point. Howick Hall, associated with the Greys, is an 18th-c house standing in fine gardens (OACT).

HOXNE, Suffolk 15 TM17
St Edmund was reputedly taken by the Danes on a bridge over the little River Dove, and Hoxne is thus associated with his martyrdom. The River Waveney runs through the area, and the perpendicular village church carries a lofty tower.

HOYLAKE, Merseyside 17 SJ28
Excellent sands and safe bathing are offered by this resort. Hilbre Point and Island lie to the W, and remains of a submerged forest are visible NE near Dove Point at low tide.

HUBBERHOLME, N Yorks 22 SD97
A remote village picturesquely situated in the wilds of Upper Wharfedale and Langstrothdale Chase. The church is one of two in Yorkshire to retain a carved medieval rood-loft.

HUCKLOW, GREAT, Derbyshire 18 SK17
Gliding competitions are held in the district, and Bradwell Dale is the site of Hazlebadge Hall (NW).

HUCKNALL, Notts 18 SK54
The tomb of Lord Byron lies in the church, and Eric Coates the composer was born here in 1886. The church tower is of 12th-c date, and the district is involved in the coal-mining industry.

HUDDERSFIELD, W Yorks 22 SE11
Huddersfield is an important cloth and woollen centre in the old West Riding. The Tolson memorial museum, on the Wakefield road, illustrates the growth and development of the cloth industry. Victoria Tower crowns 900ft Almondbury Castle Hill, which is also the site of an early iron-age camp. Almondbury lies 1½m SE and includes a large perpendicular church with numerous roof bosses, a fine font cover of the same period, and several monuments. Wormald's Hall dates from 1631, and 3m SE is Woodsome Hall – a delightful Tudor House serving as a golf clubhouse.

HUGHENDEN, Bucks 8 SU89
Disraeli's grave can be seen in the churchyard. Hughenden Manor, which was remodelled in 1862, was his old home. It now contains a museum (NT, OACT).

HUGHLEY, Salop 17 SO59
The timber-framed hall dates from c1600. Hughley church has a tower of 1701, and a carved 15th-c screen.

HUISH EPISCOPI, Somerset 6 ST42
A superb 15th-c tower, considered one of the finest in the country, is displayed by the local church. The south doorway is Norman and examples of glass by Burne-Jones can be seen.

HULL, Humberside 23 TA02
Plan overleaf
Officially known as Kingston-upon-Hull, this fishing port is sited at a point where the River Hull flows into the Humber and includes extensive docks.

Holy Trinity Church is of decorated and perpendicular style, and is one of the largest parish churches in England. It is particularly notable for the fine perpendicular font, the tower, and early brickwork. A tall column surmounted by a statue commemorates William Wilberforce; the Wilberforce House and museum are of great interest. Maister's House is of the mid 18th c, and contains a notable staircase (NT). The grammar school was rebuilt in 1583. St Mary's Church preserves its brick tower of 1697, which was later encased in stone, under which is a path for pedestrians.

The Land of Green Ginger is a curious local street name. Trinity House dates from 1753, and the Maritime and

King George Dock, Hull

Transport museums are worth a visit. Hull is connected to New Holland by the Humber ferry, which is to be replaced by the largest bridge in Europe. A modern university has been founded in the town.

HUNGERFORD, Berks 7 SU36
On the River Kennet, this town is known for the picturesque Hock-tide ceremony which takes place on Tuesday of Easter week, featuring the Tutti-men. The town hall has a horn which is said to have been presented by John of Gaunt. He also gave the town fishing rights on the Kennet, and the area is still a popular resort for anglers. In memory of John of Gaunt, a red rose is presented to any sovereign passing through the town. Outside the church is a curious old five-barred stile.

Littlecote is a fine 16th-c house lying 2½m NW, with a notable great hall and armoury (OACT).

HUNSDON, Herts 8 TL41
An attractive village including 17th-c cottages and a church which is noted for its north porch, Jacobean screens, and tombs.

HUNSLET, W Yorks 22 SE33
Middleton Colliery Railway preserves working locomotives in this old West Riding mining town, which had the first line to be authorized by Parliament (1758).

HUNSTANTON, Norfolk 14 TF64
A Washside resort. Chalk cliffs displaying coloured strata rise to 60ft, and are capped by soft turf. Restored St Mary's Church houses a 16th-c screen and notable brasses. At Old Hunstanton, 1m N, is a moated Tudor and later mansion.

HUNTER'S INN, Devon 5 SS64
This is a North Devon beauty spot set deep in a valley leading to steep hog-back cliffs, where the Heddon River flows seawards to Heddon's Mouth (partly NT). Splendid coast views are available from the footpath which follows the E side of the ravine to climb lofty Highveer Point.

HUNTINGDON, Cambs 14 TL27
Cromwell and Pepys were scholars at Huntingdon grammar school. The building has a restored Norman exterior and now houses a Cromwell museum.

George Inn has a galleried yard, and a 13th-c bridge spans the Ouse to Godmanchester (AM). Numerous fine Georgian houses include Cowper House, where the poet of this name once lived.

Of the two old churches: St Mary's is early-English to perpendicular, with interesting interior fittings; All Saints' is said to have been rebuilt in 1620, and has Cromwellian associations in the shape of the font at which he was baptized. A coffin containing the body of Mary Queen of Scots was rested at the latter church during its final journey to Westminster Abbey. Hinchingbrooke House is a Tudor and later building containing Cromwell relics, lying 1m W. The town hall dates from 1745.

HURLEY, Berks 8 SU88
A Thames-side village where the largely-Norman church contains two Lovelace tombs. Remains of a 13th-c priory include a dovecote. Hall Place is of early 18th-c date and displays notable stuccowork. Harleyford Manor was built by Sir Robert Taylor in 1775.

HURSLEY, Hants 7 SU42
The church was rebuilt by John Keble, who was vicar from 1836 to 1866 and is buried in the churchyard. Keble College Oxford was founded to his memory in 1869. Oliver Cromwell's son Richard was buried in the old church, and a Cromwell monument is under the tower of the present building.

HURSTBOURNE TARRANT, Hants 7 SU35
Cobbett described the village under its old name of Uphusband in his *Rural Rides*, and there are associations with W H Hudson. The Bladon gallery houses an exhibition of crafts.

HURSTPIERPOINT, W Sussex 8 TQ21
This town lies below the South Downs and is well-known for its public school. The fine Elizabethan mansion of Danny Park lies to the SE (OACT).

HURWORTH, Co Durham 22 NZ31
An attractive Teesside village, with Georgian houses grouped around the green. The manor house dates from 1728 and a striking railway bridge from 1840.

HUTTON-LE-HOLE, N Yorks 22 SE78
Picturesque Farndale, protected as a reserve for wild daffodils, stretches away to the N from this delightful village. The Ryedale Folk Museum contains many interesting bygones, including a reconstructed Elizabethan glass furnace.

HYTHE, Kent 9 TR13
Hythe was one of the ancient Cinque Ports, and is now a well-known resort. The Royal Military Canal was built from 1804 to 1806, and extends W towards Appledore and Rye. It was intended as a defence against an expected Napoleonic invasion.

St Leonard's is a Norman to early-English church which includes a crypt where hundreds of human skulls and bones are stacked. The chancel of c1210 is notable for its Purbeck and Bethersden marble shafts. Old houses still exist in narrow streets near the church. Three Martello towers were built along the front to repel Napoleon. Hythe is the E terminal-point of the well-known Romney, Hythe, and Dymchurch narrow-gauge railway.

ICKENHAM, Gt London 8 TQ08
Ickenham now forms part of Greater London. The parish church is of 14th- and 16th-c date. An old moated manor house is of interest and Swakeleys is a fine Dutch-gabled Jacobean mansion with ornamental chimney stacks. Pepys the famous diarist praised a carved screen that is still there.

ICKLESHAM, E Sussex 9 TQ81
Icklesham church is noted for its Norman tower and nave. An 18th-c windmill exists on Hog Hill.

ICKLINGHAM, Suffolk 15 TL77
A village on the River Lark, with Roman remains and ancient tumuli in the vicinity. All Saints' Church is a thatched Norman to perpendicular structure with good interior fittings.

ICKNIELD WAY
This ancient Romanized track extends from East Anglia to SW England, the middle stretch lying between Royston and the Berkshire Downs. The latter section is, perhaps, the best known. It crosses Watling Street at Dunstable, and divides into the Lower and Upper Icknield Way for a few miles in the Chilterns W of Ivinghoe. The Way crosses the Thames near Goring, and later follows the foot of the Berkshire Downs; ancient Ridgeway follows the crest of the latter. The track is negotiable only by foot for most of its extent.

ICKWELL, Beds 14 TL14
May Day revels are held round a maypole which is preserved on the village green. Thomas Tompion, the

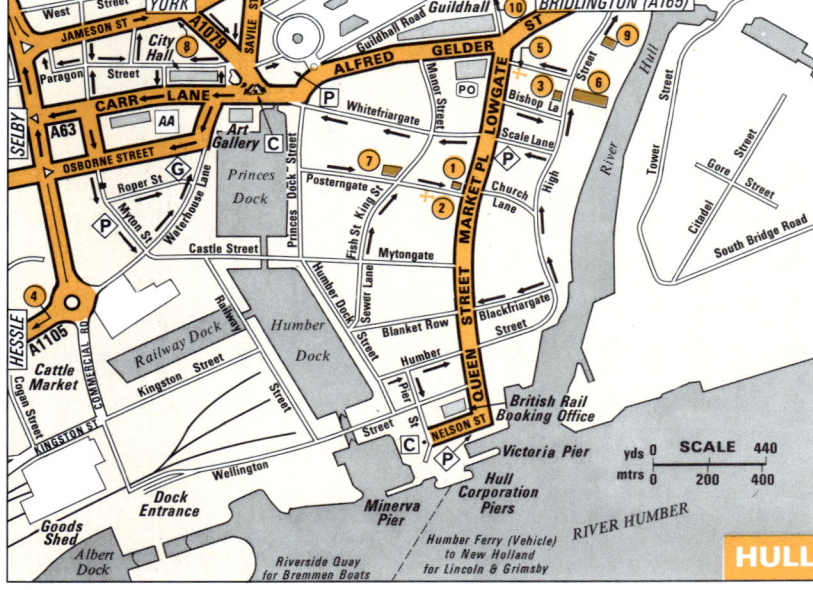

1 Grammar School
2 Holy Trinity Church
3 Maister's House
4 Maritime Museum
5 St Mary's Church
6 Transport Museum
7 Trinity House
8 University of Hull
9 Wilberforce House (museum)
10 William Wilberforce Statue

famous clockmaker who lived between 1639 and 1713, once worked in the village. Ickwell Bury is a partly 17th-c house with an old dovecote.

ICKWORTH, Suffolk 15 TL86
The 18th-c mansion of Ickworth is a vast elliptical rotunda, containing a collection of Regency furnishings, silver, and pictures. It is considered one of the most remarkable in England (NT, OACT). Earls of Bristol, former owners, are commemorated in the 13th-c church.

IDSWORTH, Hants 7 SU61
Restored Norman to 18th-c St Hubert's Chapel contains Royal Arms of 1824 and a wall-painting depicting Salome performing a sword-dance.

IFFLEY, Oxon 13 SP50
Iffley has a richly-carved Norman church which is a very famous example of its type. Built c1170, its many notable features include the west front, north doorway, and chancel arch – all of which are outstanding.

IFIELD, W Sussex 8 TQ23
Two interesting table-tombs can be seen in the early-English to decorated church, and the churchyard contains the grave of Mark Lemon, a founder and first editor of *Punch* magazine. Ewhurst Place is an ancient moated farm.

IGHTHAM, Kent 9 TQ55
Pronounced Item, this place has a mainly 14th-c church containing 17th-c pews, the 14th-c Cawne monument, and a sundial of 1669 in the churchyard. Oldbury Hills lie SW and were where Benjamin Harrison made important flint discoveries in the 19thc. Ightham Court is of 16th- to 18th-c date, and 2¼m S lies Ightham Mote, considered one of the loveliest 14th- to 16th-c moated manor houses in the country (OACT).

ILAM, Staffs 18 SK15
A small village on the River Manifold, forming a convenient base from which to explore the picturesque Manifold Valley and Thor's Cave near Wetton Mill. Apes Tor forms part of Ecton Hill and is of geological interest (NT). Ilam Hall is a 19th-c house which now serves as a Youth Hostel (NT).

The church contains a Chantrey sculpture, has rare maidens' garlands, a carved Norman font, and the 13th-c Shrine of St Bertram. Two Saxon crosses can be seen in the churchyard.

ILCHESTER, Somerset 6 ST52
A Roman community that became prominent in the Middle Ages, Ilchester is a quiet country town on the River Yeo. Roger Bacon, one of the greatest scholars of the 13thc, was born here in c1214. The market cross dates from the 17thc and is topped by a sundial. The restored church carries an octagonal tower.

A 13th-c octagonal mace that is preserved in the town hall is the oldest in England. Lytes Cary is a Tudor manor house lying 3m NNE (NT, OACT).

ILFRACOMBE, Devon 5 SS54
This one-time fishing port is now a popular holiday resort. Summer steamers cruise along the coast and connect Ilfracombe with Swansea, Cardiff, Bristol, and Lundy Island. A zoo is sited on the old Barnstaple road.

Chambercombe Manor, to the SE, is a lovely 15th- and 16th-c house (OACT). The church displays good wagon roofs and an Elizabethan pulpit, and dates from the 15th- and 16th-c.

ILKESTON, Derbyshire 18 SK44
Ilkeston is engaged in mining and the manufacture of iron and concrete pipes. On the lighter side, there are also concerns producing lace and hosiery. The restored church preserves an early 14th-c stone screen.

ILKLEY, W Yorks 22 SE14
Standing on the site of a Roman fort, this well-known inland resort and residential town is sited by the River Wharfe. It stands very high (up to 750ft) and it is surrounded by the fine scenery of Ilkley Moor. Near Heber's Ghyll is the unique Swastika Stone, a carved relic of the bronze or iron age. All Saints' Church has three Saxon crosses in the churchyard, and the Old Manor of 16th-c date is now a museum. An old bridge across the Wharfe is now reserved for pedestrians and cyclists only. Heathcote was designed by Lutyens in 1906.

ILMINGTON, Warwickshire 12 SP24
The rectory and manor house are both of 16th-c origin, and Foxcote is a fine early-Georgian house. Ilmington Down touches 854ft, and is possibly the highest point in Warwickshire.

ILMINSTER, Somerset 6 ST31
Ilminster church carries a very fine, perpendicular-style central tower. Inside is the tomb of the Wadhams, founders of Wadham College in Oxford. The grammar school is dated 1586, and is now a school for girls. Jordans is a house on the Taunton road which was the home of J H Speke, the discoverer of Lake Victoria Nyanza – the source of the Nile. Barrington Court is a splendid Tudor mansion built of Ham Hill stone lying 4m NE (NT). A former stable block dates from 1670, and a remarkable ten-faced sundial exists in the grounds (OACT).

1 Chambercombe Manor   2 Parish Church   3 Zoo

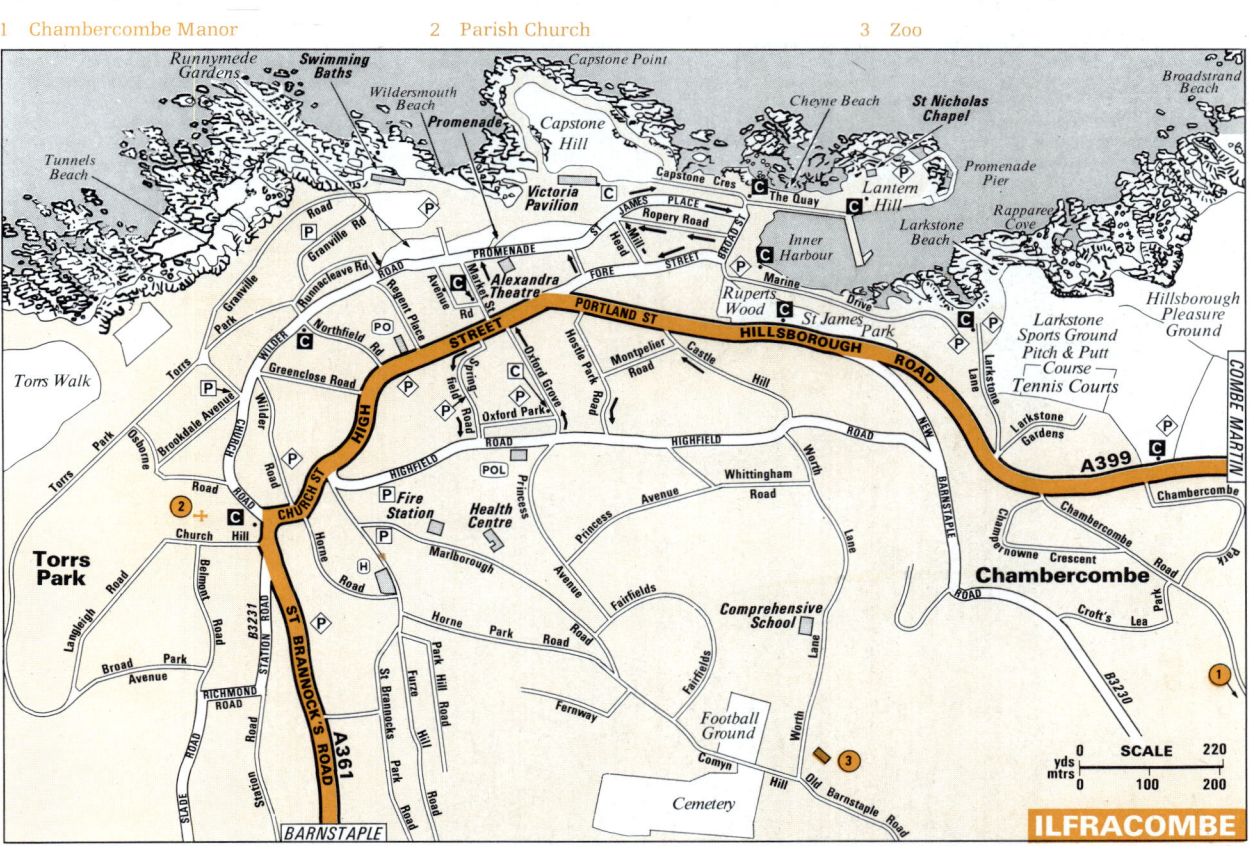

IMMINGHAM, Humberside *23 TA11*
Immingham is a port 6m from Grimsby. At South Killingholme Haven, NW of the docks, is a monument to the Pilgrim Fathers who sailed from here to Holland in 1608.

IMPINGTON, Cambs *14 TL46*
A pleasant village where the restored decorated and perpendicular church preserves a half-timbered south porch. Village College, the forerunner of many present-day school buildings, was built by Walter Gropius and Maxwell Fry between 1934 and 1937. Impington Hall was the seat of the Pepys family and was often visited by the famous diarist.

INGATESTONE, Essex *9 TQ69*
The local church carries a magnificent brick-built tower, and houses a range of monuments to the Petres. The hall is of late 16th-c date, with some alterations, and mounts interesting exhibitions of pictures and Essex documents (OACT). A fine brick-built barn shows crow-stepped gables, and a windmill at Mill Green has been restored.

INGESTRE, Staffs *18 SJ92*
The classical-style church dating from 1677 is usually ascribed to Wren. The interior shows plaster roofs, a good screen decorated with Royal Arms, plus monuments by Sir Francis Chantrey and Richard Westmacott the Younger. The hall, now an arts centre, dates largely from 1613 and 1820.

INGLEBY GREENHOW, N Yorks *22 NZ50*
Situated in a wooded area, this settlement includes a restored Norman and 18th-c church showing grotesquely carved nave capitals. An Elizabethan manor house is of interest. Urra Moor rises to 1,489ft in the S, and is the highest point in the Cleveland Hills.

INGLESHAM, Wilts *12 SU29*
Near the junction of the River Thames with the Severn canal and River Cole is a lovely little trans-Norman and early-English church. Its main features include box pews, a 15th-c screen, and a Norman carving of a madonna. A quaint circular lockhouse is a relic of the now disused Thames and Severn canal.

INGLETON, N Yorks *21 SD67*
A noted Craven-country centre, and a useful base from which to visit local caves and waterfalls. Thornton Force and Pecca Falls are particularly notable. Ingleborough rises to 2,373ft in the NE, and has part of its lower slopes riddled by the White Scar Caves. Farther E is the well-known Gaping Ghyll pothole, which has the longest main shaft in Britain (360ft) and a 500ft-long main chamber.

INGOLDMELLS, Lincs *19 TF56*
The church displays a 13th-c porch, a brass of 1520, and some good examples of woodwork.

INGRAM, Northumberland *27 NU01*
Ingram stands on the River Breamish and includes a 13th-c church with a rebuilt tower. Remains of an ancient village exist on Ingram Hill, and farther up river – near the waterfall of Linhope Spout – is the prehistoric 20-acre village of Greave Ash. Hedgehope Hill, one of the highest of the Cheviots, rises to 2,348ft.

INKPEN, Berks *7 SU36*
This pretty village boasts a fine old rectory, plus a church that was used by the Templars. Ancient Wansdyke is thought to start near by. Inkpen Beacon and Walbury Hill are both around 1,000ft high and rise to the S. Combe gibbet, a rare example of its kind, is preserved on the summit of the former. These are the highest chalk downs in England.

IPPLEPEN, Devon *5 SX86*
One of Devon's finest churches can be seen here. It is notable for its lofty tower, splendid carved screen, and carved oak pulpit.

IPSDEN, Oxon *13 SU68*
Charles Reade the author was born at the manor house in 1814. Two palimpsest brasses of 1525 can be seen in the church, and Wellplace Bird Farm shows many species of both birds and animals (OACT).

IPSWICH, Suffolk *15 TM14*
Ipswich is the largest town in Suffolk, and the county town of East Suffolk. It stands at the head of the Orwell estuary and is a thriving port, an important farming centre, and an area of continual industrial expansion and development. Connections between this town and Europe have existed for centuries. Cardinal Wolsey was born here; Gainsborough the painter lived here for a while. In spite of necessary recent development, a few earlier buildings survive – particularly the churches. St Margaret's Church displays a hammerbeam roof and the Royal Arms of Charles II; St Lawrence's Church has a flint-panelled tower and 15th-c stone screen; St Peter's retains a rare 12th-c black-marble Tournai font; St Mary-le-Tower, the civic church, has a 176ft tower and fine carved woodwork which includes a pulpit by Grinling Gibbons.

Ancient House, or Sparrowe's House, is a picturesque building dated 1567. Wolsey's Gate of 1536 and the Pykenham Gate of c1471 are both of interest. The 16th-c Christchurch Mansion is set in its own park and now houses a museum displaying, among other things, the famous Pownder brass from the former Church of St Mary Quay. Timber-framed houses can be seen in Fore Street and Silent Street, and the Great White Horse Inn features in Dickens' *Pickwick Papers*. Friar Street includes the Unitarian Meeting House, a plaster and timbered structure of c1700 which is considered a notable example of its kind. A museum of archaeology and natural history can be visited, and several partly-weatherboarded houses exist on Albion Wharf. Good Georgian houses stand in Lower Brook Street. Suffolk Yacht Harbour is being developed some 7m S, on the Orwell at Levington.

IRLAM, Gt Manchester *17 SJ79*
An industrial town on the edge of Chat Moss, with a steelworks quay on the Manchester Ship Canal.

IRON ACTON, Avon *12 ST68*
A beautiful though mutilated 15th-c cross stands in the churchyard, and the church's Poyntz chapel is of interest. Part of Elizabethan Iron Acton Court is incorporated in a farmhouse.

IRONBRIDGE, Salop *17 SJ60*
Close to Coalbrookdale, Ironbridge is situated at a point near the beginning of one of the River Severn's most attractive stretches. The first large cold-blast iron bridge to be erected in England was built here in 1779, and foot passengers still use it to cross the Severn. An iron-founding museum and the site of Abraham Darby's original furnace are also of interest. Darby was the designer of the bridge. A railway bridge of 1859 stands near an old iron

1 Albion Wharf
2 Christchurch Mansion
3 Great White Horse Inn
4 Pykenham Gate
5 Sparrowe's or Ancient House
6 St Lawrence's Church
7 St Margaret's Church
8 St Mary-le-Tower
9 St Peter's Church
10 Suffolk Yacht Harbour
11 Unitarian Meeting House
12 Wolsey's Gate

company's wharf, and Elizabethan Benthall Hall lies 2m SW on a site mentioned in the Domesday Book (NT, OACT).

IRTHLINGBOROUGH, Northants 13 SP97
The local church has a fine detached and restored 14th-c tower, crowned by an octagon. The River Nene is spanned here by a 14th-c bridge.

IRTON, Cumbria 21 NY00
A finely-carved 10ft sandstone cross can be seen in the churchyard, and probably dates from c950. The hall is a mansion built around an old pele tower.

ISLE ABBOTS, Somerset 6 ST32
The carved perpendicular church tower is one of a group of three, near Taunton, considered among the finest in Somerset. Low-lying country surrounds the village, which is sited on the River Isle.

ISLEHAM, Cambs 14 TL67
The Norman chapel (AM) of a former Benedictine priory has survived here, and the church is of 14th- and 15th-c date. Features of the latter include an ancient lych-gate, a nave roof of 1495, a 15th-c eagle lectern, and several old brasses and monuments.

ISLE OF MAN
The Isle of Man was known to the Romans as *Mona*, and is about 33m long by 12m broad.

It was annexed by England in the 13thc but has its own parliament, or Tynwald, and its own laws and taxes. The mild climate and miles of sandy beach make it a popular holiday place. Off the extreme SW corner of the island is the Calf of Man (NT), a small island nature reserve which is not accessible to visitors during the breeding season. Snaefell rises to 2,034ft, and is the highest point in the island. Access to the summit is by means of a mountain railway. Annual TT motor-cycle races take place in the N part, and have brought the island considerable fame. The motor-cycle circuit roads are closed to traffic during the races.

Steamers ply between Liverpool and Douglas, and near the latter is an airport. Resorts and places of interest are listed under their respective headings.

ISLE OF WIGHT
Vectis or *Ictis* to the Romans, this delightful island measures some 22m long by 13m wide and can almost be considered as a microcosm of typical English scenery. It is separated from the mainland by two channels – the Solent and Spithead.

The notable coastline includes picturesque chines and land-slips between Shanklin and Chale, the prominent white chalk cliffs known as The Needles (SW), and the coloured sands of Alum Bay. Several ranges of downs give height to the interior of the island, and its sheltered position ensures a mildness of climate which makes it a popular holiday venue. About half the area of the island has been declared an area of outstanding natural beauty, including much of the coast and downs.

Three car ferries operate from the mainland: Portsmouth to Fishbourne; Lymington to Yarmouth; and Southampton to Cowes. Several passenger ferries are also available, including hovercraft, and an airport is situated at Sandown. Places of interest are listed under their own headings.

ISLES OF SCILLY
The Isles of Scilly lie some 28m W of the mainland, off Land's End; the distance from the steamer's embarkation point at Penzance is nearly 40m. This ferry docks at St Mary's. Five of the larger islands are inhabited, and some 140 smaller islands support no population at all.

Only St Mary's, which has 14m of roads, is of interest to motorists. An exceptionally mild winter is a favourable feature of this group, and the islands are best known for the early cultivation of spring flowers, mostly daffodils and narcissi. These are gathered between Christmas and May, and sent to the mainland. Many species of sea birds breed in the islands, and porpoises, seals, and dolphins can be seen in the surrounding waters. Sandy beaches and coves give access for bathing. A large number of chambered bronze-age cairns exist in the group. St Mary's is the largest island of the group and serves as the main port. The quay is situated in the island's capital, Hughtown. A partially-restored church at Old Town contains numerous memorials to ships wrecked in the local rock-strewn waters, and New Church in Hughtown was built in 1835. The latter preserves a coloured lion figurehead from Sir Cloudesley Shovel's flagship, which was wrecked here in 1707.

Granite-built houses of the late 18th and early 19thc can be seen, and Star Castle, dating from 1593 and displaying a fine gateway, stands on Garrison Hill. It now serves as a hotel. Local scenery is picturesque and a lighthouse stands to the S on rocky Peninnis Head. A modern abbey at Tresco stands on the site of a 10th-c Benedictine Priory, dedicated to St Nicholas. Notable subtropical gardens and a unique collection of ships' figureheads are of interest (OACT). Remains of Cromwell's Castle date from 1651, and traces of King Charles's Castle, c1635, also exist. These recall the island's association with the Civil War, when Charles II took refuge in 1651. Dover Fort, above Old Grimsby, is of 16th- or 17th-c date. An edifice named the Day Mark on St Martin's is a signalling tower which was erected in 1683. Prehistoric remains have been discovered here and on St Agnes. The old lighthouse was built in 1680.

All Saints' Church on Bryher dates from 1742 and was enlarged in 1822. Samson is an uninhabited inland W of St Mary's, which has many prehistoric remains. Beyond the SW extremities of the group stands the lonely 160ft Bishop's Rock Lighthouse, the place where Sir Cloudesley Shovel drowned.

ISLEWORTH, Gt London 8 TQ17
Formerly part of Middlesex, Isleworth stands on the left bank of the Thames between Twickenham and Brentford. The London Apprentice is a fine Georgian inn sited near the river, and several Georgian houses can be seen in the area. Syon House was founded as a monastery in 1415, and remodelled in the 18thc. It faces across the Thames and contains Robert Adam's finest interior work (OACT). England's largest gardening centre includes a remarkable conservatory of 1820 and is contained in Syon Park.

Also here is the London Transport Company's museum of old vehicles, etc.

IVER, Bucks 8 TQ08
Coppins was the home of the Duke and Duchess of Kent, and two fine Georgian buildings in the area are Iver Grove of 1722 and Bridgefoot House. The 12th- to 15th-c church contains interesting monuments.

IVINGHOE, Bucks 8 SP91
Scott took the name *Ivanhoe* for his famous novel from this village. The 13th- to 14th-c church is noted for its carved nave pillars. Some 2,500 acres of the neighbouring treeless Chiltern Hills are NT property, and include the fine viewpoint of Ivinghoe Beacon, 1½m NE. Pitstone post-mill is a completely restored building which dates from c1627 and forms a local landmark (NT).

IVYBRIDGE, Devon 5 SX65
A River-Erme village near delightful woodlands. Brunel designed the local railway viaduct.

IVYCHURCH, Kent 9 TR02
Ivychurch is a village in the Romney Marsh area. Its church is of mainly-decorated style and carries a lofty tower. It has been called the Cathedral of the Marshes, and contains examples of ancient woodwork.

IWERNE COURTNEY, Dorset 7 ST81
Also known as Shroton, this village lies in the shadow of 623ft Hambledon Hill. A largely 17th-c church is the work of Sir Thomas Freke, whose tomb can be seen in the north chapel. The fine mid-18th-c house of Ranston is interesting.

IWERNE MINSTER, Dorset 7 ST81
Just outside the village is the site of a Roman villa. The Norman to 17th-c church displays a perpendicular-style stone spire. Clayesmore School lies near by, and Cranborne Chase is to the E.

IXWORTH, Suffolk 15 TL97
Two interesting mills – a fine water-mill and a tower windmill – can be seen in this River-Thet village. The perpendicular church carries a panelled tower, and the partly-Georgian abbey shows remains of an ancient priory (OACT).

JARROW, Tyne & Wear 27 NZ36
An industrial town on the River Tyne, Jarrow is involved in coal-mining and ship-building. Its name is associated with the unemployment and social unrest of the Twenties, and the Venerable Bede lived and died at the former monastery. The parish church shows examples of Saxon work, and preserves Bede's chair and a dedication plate of the year 684.

JERVAULX ABBEY, N Yorks 22 SE18
Pronounced Jervo or Jarvis, the interesting remains of this 12th-c Cistercian abbey are situated beside the River Ure in Lower Wensleydale.

JURBY, Isle of Man 20 SC39
Noted for the 1,000-acre Curragh, or moor, Jurby is the place where Sir Hall Caine spent part of his childhood. A Viking tomb was excavated in the SW, near Ballateare, in 1946. The ramparts of Ballachurry Fort, 4m ESE, were constructed in c1640.

KEDINGTON, Suffolk *14 TL74*
Interesting monuments, a three-decker pulpit, a wig-rack, and a screen dated 1619 can be seen in the decorated and perpendicular church. A single-handed clock is displayed on the tower face, and a fine 18th-c rectory exists nearby.

KEDLESTON, Derbyshire *18 SK34*
The Norman to perpendicular church contains Curzon monuments, and Kedleston Hall is a fine 18th-c house by such famous people as Matthew Brettingham, James Paine, and Robert Adam. It is considered one of Adam's finest creations and is situated in an extensive park (OACT).

KEELE, Staffs *17 SJ84*
Keele Hall is now the University of Keele, specializing in multi-disciplinary courses. It was founded in 1962.

KEEVIL, Wilts *7 ST95*
Talboys is a restored 15th-c half-timbered house. The manor house is a stately 17th-c gabled building, and the local church was largely rebuilt in the 17thc.

KEGWORTH, Leics *18 SK42*
A village on the River Soar, 5½m NW of Loughborough. The church is a good example of decorated work and includes fine windows.

KEIGHLEY, W Yorks *22 SE04*
Pronounced Keethly, this manufacturing town stands at the junction of the River Aire and the River Worth. A stepped market cross is of interest. East Riddlesden Hall lies 2m NE and displays circular windows characteristic of this part of Yorkshire (NT, OACT). A fine old barn stands near by. West Riddlesden Hall dates from 1687.

KELHAM, Notts *19 SK75*
The interesting church in Kelham houses an early 18th-c monument to Lord Lexington. This work is executed in marble and is mounted on a free-standing tomb.

KELMSCOTT, Oxon *12 SU29*
This greystone village is situated on the River Thames, and includes the small trans-Norman and later church where William Morris is buried. He lived at the nearby Elizabethan manor house. Although his private printing press was called the Kelmscott Press, it actually operated in Hammersmith, London.

KELSALE, Suffolk *15 TM36*
Among the timbered houses to be seen in this village is the picturesque guildhall, now used as a school.

KEMPLEY, Glos *12 SO62*
St Mary's church, though small, is of considerable interest. Good Norman work is preserved in the building, and notable mid 12th-c wall-paintings can be seen on the chancel walls and vault. These are considered the most complete series to be found in any English parish church.

KEMPSEY, Herefs & Worcs *12 SO84*
The interesting 13th- to 15th-c church displays examples of old glass.

KEMPSFORD, Glos *12 SU19*
A central tower built by John of Gaunt, and weather vanes on all the crocketed pinnacles are features of the perpendicular church.

KEMSING, Kent *9 TQ55*
Kemsing lies 2½m NE of Sevenoaks and includes a partly-Saxon church with a shingled tower. Other features of the structure include a beautiful stained-glass window, a splendid altar canopy, and a good chancel showing a screen and a 14th-c priest's brass. St Edith's Well is near the peace memorial. The Pilgrims' Way lies a little to the N, and St Clere, a fine Georgian house, stands to the E.

KENCHESTER, Herefs & Worcs *12 SO44*
Castra Magna, the most important Roman station in the county, was sited here. Most of the relics discovered during excavations are displayed in the Hereford Museum.

KENDAL, Cumbria *21 SD59*
Shoes and snuff are made in this pleasant River-Kent town. Remains of a Norman castle which was the birthplace of Catherine Parr in 1512 can be seen (AM). George Romney the portrait painter was born here in 1734 and a collection of his works hangs in the Mayor's Parlour. Abbot Hall is an 18th-c house with an art gallery, and the Borough Museum is of interest. Early-English and perpendicular styles are evident in the church, which has a tall square tower, double aisles, and a 16th-c brass in the Bellingham Chapel. Picturesque old yards can be found in the town, and the Castle Dairy dates from 1564. An obelisk of 1814 commemorates William Pitt. Restored Sizergh Castle lies 3m S, and displays an ancient pele tower plus fine Elizabethan work (NT, OACT). SW is the 713ft viewpoint of Scoat Scar.

KENILWORTH, Warwickshire *13 SP27*
Famous Kenilworth Castle stands on a grassy slope and includes a Norman keep (AM). John of Gaunt remodelled the castle as a palace in the 14thc, and the great gatehouse dates from 1570. Much of the action in Scott's *Kenilworth* is set in this area. The rebuilt church preserves a Norman west doorway.

KENSWORTH, Beds *8 TL01*
Situated at 600ft on the Dunstable Downs, this village is well-known among gliding enthusiasts. The Norman church shows a chancel arch and two doorways as good examples of the period.

KENTISBEARE, Devon *6 ST00*
The perpendicular church has a magnificent carved screen, and the west tower is patterned with red and grey stone in a chequer-board design. Near by is a medieval priest's house containing a minstrels' gallery and oak screens.

KENTON, Devon *5 SX98*
A picturesque old village situated on the Exe estuary. The exceptionally fine red-sandstone perpendicular church has a notable rood screen and modern loft. It also displays a fine tower and south porch. A completely restored Celtic cross is of considerable interest. Powderham Castle is a partly 14th-c rebuilt structure lying ½m E (OACT).

KERSEY, Suffolk *15 TM04*
An unspoiled village of interesting old houses with a shallow water-splash at the centre. The perpendicular church shows a flint tower and south porch. Kersey fabrics are said to have taken their name from here. An interesting bygone is the stallion's tail hanging from the eaves of a local veterinary surgeon's house.

KESSINGLAND, Suffolk *15 TM58*
The lofty tower carried by Kessingland's church, which was built in the 17thc, is used as a navigational aid for shipping. A lion gargoyle decorates the tower, and the nave is roofed with thatch. The place itself is a fishing village with a good beach.

KESTEVEN
This name is given to the undulating W portion of Lincolnshire, which is threaded by the River Witham and includes fenland to the E. Grantham is a good base from which to tour the area.

KESTON, Gt London *8 TQ46*
Roman remains that include a mausoleum have been excavated at Keston Court Farm. A windmill of 1716 can be seen on the common.

KESWICK, Cumbria *26 NY22*
Keswick's situation – on the River Greta at the far N extremity of the beautiful Derwentwater – makes it a popular centre for tourists interested in exploring the Lake District. It has been a market town since very early times.
Coleridge and Southey lived at Greta Hall, and Shelley stayed in the town. The museum displays a scale model of the Lake District, and relics of Sir Hugh Walpole. The Moot Hall was rebuilt in 1813. Notable monuments can be seen in the parish church at Crosthwaite plus twenty-one consecration crosses. Southey, and a co-founder of the National Trust Canon Rawnsley, are buried in the churchyard. Portinscale lies at the N end of Derwentwater. Castle Head rises to 529ft, and Friars Crag has a Ruskin memorial. Both are notable viewpoints (NT). Other viewpoints include Walla Crag, Falcon Crag, and Ashness Bridge. The Castlerigg prehistoric stone circle stands 1½m E of Keswick (NT), and Bassenthwaite Lake is backed by 3,054ft Skiddaw 4m NW.

KETTERING, Northants *13 SP87*
Footwear is manufactured in this River-Ise town, and a mainly 15th-c church displays a 177ft tower and spire. A Roman industrial centre was situated N of the town, and various relics have been excavated. The local art gallery is of interest. Facilities for bathing, model yachts, and sailing are available 2m SE at Wicksteed Park.

KETTLEWELL, N Yorks *22 SD97*
One of the most attractive of Upper Wharfedale's villages, Kettlewell is picturesquely situated among stone-walled moors. Great Whernside rises to 2,310ft near by.

KETTON, Leics *19 SK90*
Well known for the production of cement, this town has a splendid largely early-English church, carrying a notable tower and spire. Local stone-quarries are famous.

KEW, Gt London *8 TQ17*
Conducted river trips and facilities for boating are available in this River-Thames area. The Royal Botanic Gardens were originally laid out by Princess Augusta, mother of George III, and are of considerable interest. They cover some 300 acres and contain rare plants, palm-houses by Decimus Burton, a 214ft Douglas-fir flagstaff, a mid 18th-c Pagoda by Sir William Chambers, and various museums (OACT). Kew Palace is where Queen Charlotte died in 1818, and is a Dutch-gabled structure (OACT).

KEWSTOKE, Avon *6 ST36*
Views across Sand Bay take in the Welsh coast. Remains of 13th-c Woodspring Priory include an old barn and lie 2m N (NT). A 15th-c pulpit is housed within the Norman to perpendicular church, and the building's 15th-c tower is linked to a farm.

KEYNSHAM, Avon *6 ST66*
Cocoa and chocolate are made in this industrial River-Avon town. The church displays a 17th-c tower, the Bridges monument of 1661, and a good screen. Albert Mill has a wide exterior water-wheel that is still in working order.

KEYSOE, Beds *14 TL06*
The decorated and perpendicular church has a lofty spire. A tablet on the tower records that William Dickins almost fell to his death while repointing the steeple in 1718, but was miraculously saved.

KIBWORTH, Leics *18 SP69*
This place consists of Kibworth Harcourt and Kibworth Beauchamp. A fine house dating from 1678 and a largely decorated church with a restored screen stand at Kibworth Harcourt. Restored, 17th-c Carlton Curlieu Hall lies 2m NE, and 2m S is Gumley Hall of 1764.

KIDDERMINSTER, Herefs & Worcs *12 SO87*
A well-known carpet-manufacturing town on the Staffordshire and Worcestershire Canal. Sir Rowland Hill, of penny-post fame was born here in 1795. The few old houses include Caldwell Hall tower. A statue has been raised to the preacher Richard Baxter. St Mary's parish church has been rebuilt, but contains interesting monuments and several 15th-c brasses. The lady chapel dates from the 16thc. The canal was designed by Brindley.

KIDLINGTON, Oxon *13 SP41*
Pleasant stone-built cottages and almshouses dated 1677 can be seen here. Good woodwork is displayed by the early-English to perpendicular church. Beautiful early-Jacobean Water Eaton is a manor house standing on the W bank of the River Cherwell, 3m SSE off the Oxford road. Near it is a small chapel of 1610.

KIDSGROVE, Staffs *17 SJ85*
This manufacturing town stands to the N of the old Trent and Mersey Harecastle canal-tunnel. This was designed by Brindley, and later superseded by one by Telford. Brindley was buried in Kidsgrove churchyard in 1772.

KIELDER, Northumberland *26 NY69*
A great state forest has been planted, and a village built here on the slopes of the Cheviot Hills. Conifers are grown here to supply timber for industry, and Kielder Forest forms part of the Border forest park which extends into Scotland. Kielder Castle was built as a shooting lodge in 1775. A small Border Forest museum is of interest. Peel Fell rises to 1,975ft in the N, and is surmounted by a cairn from which the North Sea and the Solway Firth are sometimes visible.

KILBURN, N Yorks *22 SE57*
Kilburn's church preserves good examples of Norman work, and is well-known for workshops which produce modern ecclesiastical woodwork. This work is easily recognizable by the mouse trademark, first used by the late Robert Thompson. An example of this – a perfectly-carved three-dimensional representation of a mouse – can be seen in the church. A white horse is cut into a nearby hillside.

KILDWICK, W Yorks *22 SE04*
Situated in an unspoiled part of Airedale, Kildwick includes a church known as the Lang Kirk of Craven. This dates from the 14th- to 17th-c, and houses an ornate font cover. Fine 17th-c Kildwick Hall is now an hotel and has an 18th-c garden-house. A notable old bridge spans the River Aire.

KILKHAMPTON, Cornwall *5 SS21*
A north-Cornwall village situated on the main road from Bideford to Bude. The 12th- to 15th-c church includes a rich Norman south doorway and contains a great array of carved bench ends. Purcell played the organ that still exists in the building, and the Grenville chapel is rich in monuments.

KILLINGWORTH, Tyne & Wear *27 NZ27*
The new garden-city that has been founded here includes many buildings which have won their designers awards. Dial Cottage, home of railway-pioneer George Stephenson, stands by the main road from the S.

KILMERSDON, Somerset *6 ST65*
This prettily-situated village stands on an 800ft hill to the W of Ammerdown Park. A memorial column surmounted by a glittering lantern stands near by. The church carries a fine perpendicular west tower, and has a triangular lych-gate of 1900. A footpath known as Jack and Jill Lane leads to a covered well, and is associated with the nursery rhyme.

KILNSEY, N Yorks *22 SD96*
Kilnsey is situated in one of the most attractive reaches of Wharfedale, near the entrance to Littondale. Overhanging Kilnsey Crag is popular with climbers, and one of the notable sights of the Yorkshire Dales national park.

KILPECK, Herefs & Worcs *12 SO43*
The beautiful little Norman church is rich with sandstone carving, reminiscent of Celtic craftsmanship, and is one of the finest remaining buildings of its period. The south doorway and west window are outstanding. Earthworks from a vanished castle can be seen in the area.

KIMBOLTON, Cambs *14 TL06*
A long main street lined with old houses runs through this attractive village, and the mainly restored early-English church houses memorials to the Montagus. Vanbrugh designed most of the imposing early 18th-c castle, but the interior courtyard dates from about 1690. The portico was executed by Robert Adam in *c*1765 (OACT).

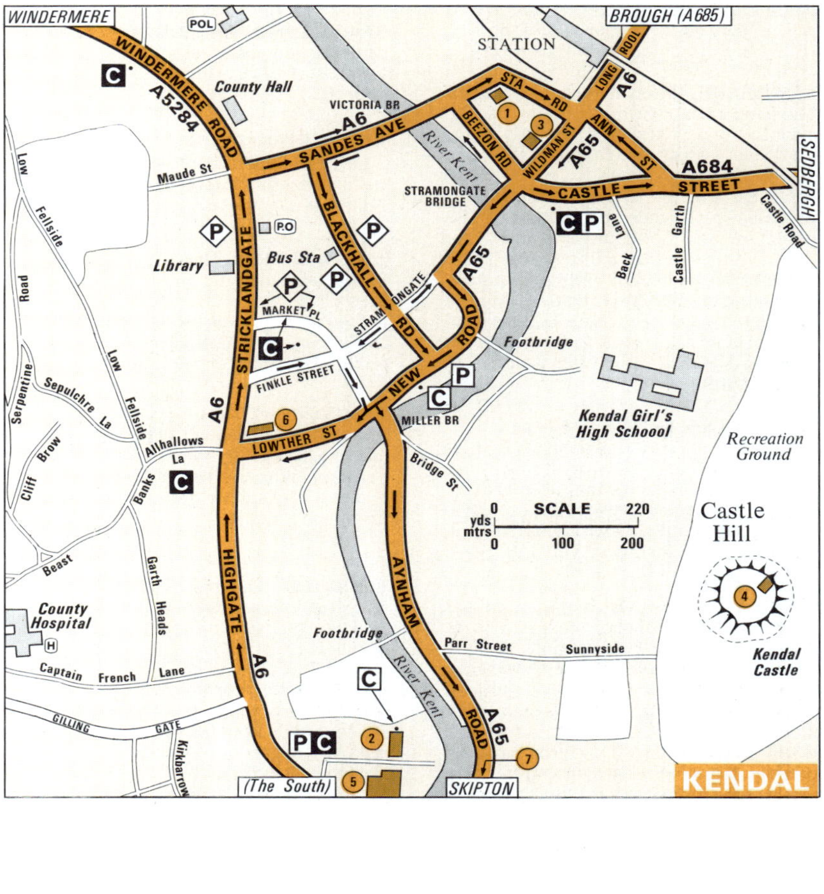

1 Borough Museum
2 Abbot's Hall (art gallery)
3 Castle Dairy
4 Castle Remains
5 Church of the Holy Trinity
6 Mayor's Parlour
7 Sizergh Castle

St George's Guildhall, King's Lynn

KIMMERIDGE, Dorset *7 SY97*
Thatched-roof cottages make up this village, and are grouped near a small bay ringed by low cliffs of black shale. The former quay was destroyed in a gale of 1745, and its replacement is now derelict. Two notable houses SE of the village are the mainly 18th-c Encombe and 17th-c and later Smedmore (OACT). Ruined Clavel coastguard tower is situated on the cliffs, and was once a summerhouse belonging to Smedmore.

KINETON, Warwickshire *13 SP35*
Old inns, 17th-c cottages, and a church re-fashioned in the 18thc can be seen here. The Battle of Edgehill was fought $1\frac{3}{4}$m SE in 1642, a site now marked by two stones which were erected in 1949. Farther S is Edge Hill, or Radway tower, built by Sanderson Miller in c1750. It is a fine viewpoint. Upton House is a 17th-c and later building lying $5\frac{1}{2}$m SE (NT, OACT). Compton Verney House dates from the 18thc and is partly by Robert Adam. It stands in a lake-watered park 2m NE.

KINGSBRIDGE, Devon *5 SX74*
This place is situated in the South Hams, at the head of a picturesque estuary leading to Salcombe. St Edmund's Church has a 13th-c tower and displays flamboyant screen-work; Dodbrooke Church is 16thc. The grammar school dates from 1670 and later, and The Shambles is a late 16th-c arcade. Bowringsleigh, a fine Tudor mansion lying $1\frac{1}{2}$m W, was altered in the 19thc.

KINGSBURY, Warwickshire *18 SP29*
An old hall stands by the Norman church; 17th-c Flanders Hall and early 18th-c Hurley Hall lie to the SE.

KINGSBURY EPISCOPI, Somerset
6 ST42
Old houses and an octagonal lock-up can be seen in the village. The perpendicular church carries a lofty richly-carved tower, one of the finest in Somerset.

KINGSCLERE, Hants *7 SU55*
This town lies amid downland, and has a largely-Norman restored church. The Kingsmill monument is a notable feature of the latter. King John's Hill rises 754ft in the S, and still farther S is the line of the Roman Portway.

KING'S CLIFFE, Northants *19 TL09*
Almshouses founded in 1668 are a feature of this beautiful village. The William Law Library has a sundial, and takes its name from a religious writer born here in 1686. This fact is recorded by an inscription. The church has a Norman tower with a 13th-c spire and houses a fine 14th-c font cover.

KINGSGATE, Kent *9 TR37*
Margate lies $2\frac{1}{2}$m W of this resort, which is situated near the North Foreland. Good sands are almost covered at high tide, and lofty chalk cliffs border the coast.

KING'S HEATH, W Midlands *12 SP08*
Joseph Chamberlain died at Highbury Hall, now a hostel, in 1914. Cannon Hill Park lies farther N and houses the Midland Arts Centre and museum. Near by is a Boy Scouts memorial and the 15th-c half-timbered Golden Lion Inn.

KINGSLAND, Herefs & Worcs *12 SO46*
The local 13th-c church contains the curious Volca chamber. The battle of Mortimer's Cross was fought $\frac{1}{2}$m N.

KING'S LANGLEY, Herts *8 TL00*
Remains of a former royal palace can be seen here, and the River Gade and Grand Union Canal run through the area. The restored perpendicular church contains the 14th-c tomb of Edmund de Langley, brother of Richard II. Also of interest is an altar-tomb to Sir Ralph Verney, decorated with effigies and dated c1500.

KING'S LYNN, Norfolk *14 TF61*
Remains of old city walls and a single 15th-c south gate (AM) are all that remain of the defences that used to protect this ancient River-Ouse port. It is still a beautiful old town however, and was called Bishop's Lynn until the bishop's property became the King's.

Greyfriars' Tower (AM) is of interest, and many Georgian and older houses – particularly in the Tuesday and Saturday market-places – can be seen. Clifton House has a curious five-storeyed tower. A panel with a heart design, above a building in the Tuesday Market Place, is said to be associated with the burning of a witch in oil. St George's Guildhall (NT) is now a theatre, and the King's Lynn Music Festival is well known. A picturesque chequerwork front is still retained by the old town hall, and the fine Custom House is of 17th-c date.

Norman and later St Margaret's church houses two notable 14th-c Flemish brasses. St Nicholas's Chapel is of decorated and perpendicular styles, with an angel-carved roof. The 15th-c octagonal Red Mount Chapel (AM) includes a tiny fan-traceried chapel.

Duke's Head Hotel is a notable building designed by Henry Bell, who also built the Custom House. Dutch-gabled Thoresby College, c1500, was founded as a college for priests and retains old doorways. Hampton Court is of 14th- to 18th-c date and stands in Nelson Street. Old warehouses can be seen on the quays, and the Corn Exchange dates from 1854.

KING'S NORTON, Leics *18 SK60*
A notable church originating from between 1757 and 1775 is approached by a fine iron gate which once belonged to a local hall. The early 18th-c Fortrey obelisk stands in the churchyard.

KING'S NORTON, W Midlands
12 SP07
King's Norton includes a church with a fine 15th-c tower and crocketed spire, near which stands an ancient timbered grammar school. The former Saracen's Head Inn, an old timbered house, is now a church meeting-place. The Worcester and Birmingham and the Stratford canals cross here.

KING'S PYON, Herefs & Worcs
12 SO45
Black-and-white roofs are a feature of the local church. Buttas Farm lies 2m S, and preserves a richly-carved timbered gatehouse dating from 1632. This is considered one of the finest in existence.

KING'S SOMBORNE, Hants *7 SU33*
Marsh is a notable early 20th-c house by Lutyens. A 13th-c font exists in the church.

KING'S STANLEY, Glos *12 SO80*
Stanley Mill dates from 1812, and forms the centre of an interesting group of mill buildings. Stanley House dates from 1593.

KING'S SUTTON, Northants *13 SP43*
Pinnacles and flying buttresses make the lovely 15th-c church splendid, and a gabled manor house exists in the area. Oxford Canal and the River Cherwell are on the Oxford border to the W.

KINGSTEIGNTON, Devon *5 SX87*
Situated at the head of the River-Teign estuary, Kingsteignton has a restored perpendicular church with a library of chained books. Clay is extracted in the area, and a number of potteries operate in this district.

KINGSTON, Somerset *6 ST22*
Kingston is also known as Kingston St Mary or Kingston-on-the-Quantocks, and the local church's beautiful 15th-c tower is considered one of the best in the county. The manor house is of Elizabethan and early 18th-c date. Hestercombe is a late 19th-c house, standing in gardens laid out by Gertrude Jekyll and Lutyens. It now serves as a fire-service headquarters.

KINGSTON, E Sussex *8 TQ30*
An attractive South-Downs village where the restored decorated-style church has a tapsel gate giving access to the churchyard. Both the Old Manor and 18th-c Hyde Manor are of note; Swanborough Manor once belonged to Lewes Priory, and is of 12th- to 15th-c date (SE). An interesting sign-post can be seen at the Juggs Arms.

KINGSTON LISLE, Oxon *13 SU38*
The Norman to decorated church contains old wall-paintings, plus examples of Jacobean woodwork. The 18th-c manor house is situated in a fine park. The curious Blowing Stone, a perforated Sarsen stone described in *Tom Brown's Schooldays*, lies to the S of the village.

KINGSTON-ON-SOAR, Notts *18 SK52*
Gypsum mines are worked in this area. A rebuilt church is notable for its very rich Babington chantry. Of particular interest is the curious rebus, Babe-in-Tun. A rebus is the representation of a name by pictures suggesting its syllables. There are said to be over 200 examples on the Babington monument. Kingston Hall is of 19th-c date.

KINGSTON UPON THAMES, Gt London *8 TQ16*
Still regarded as the county town of Surrey, this is also part of Greater London. A Coronation Stone is preserved near the guildhall, and is said to have been used at the crowning of at least six Saxon Kings. The restored All Saints' Church houses monuments and brasses, and Lovekyn's Chapel dates from 1367. The guildhall of 1935 and the county hall of 1892 and 1930 are impressive. Clattern Bridge spans the Hogsmill River and dates from the 12thc. Cleave's Almshouses date from 1668, and Tiffin's School was founded in the early 17thc. The latter was re-housed in modern buildings in 1930.

KINGSWEAR, Devon *5 SX85*
Standing by the River Dart, Kingswear is connected to Dartmouth by car ferries. The revived Dart Valley steam-operated railway branch runs from Paignton and terminates here. The local castle is of Tudor origin.

KINGTON, Herefs & Worcs *11 SO25*
A small town on the River Arrow, set in delightfully hilly scenery. The interesting old church includes a good early-English chancel. John Abel designed the old grammar school of 1625, but this has subsequently been greatly altered. Both the market hall of 1885 and 1897, and the former town hall of 1845 are of interest. An old corn mill and miller's house exist in the area. Hergest Ridge lies to the W and gives fine views; Hergest Court, the former 15th-c home of the Vaughans, is now a farmhouse. Stanner Rocks lie 3m NW.

KINNERSLEY, Herefs & Worcs *11 SO34*
The imposing castle is mainly Jacobean, and the church displays a 14th-c tower topped by an unusual gable. Inside is the notable Smalman monument.

KINTBURY, Berks *7 SU36*
This Kennet-Valley village includes a partly Norman church, and 17th-c and later West Woodhay manor house stands 2m S. The latter is ascribed partly to Inigo Jones.

KINVER, Staffs *12 SO88*
Kinver Edge (NT) lies ½m SW of this small border town, and is a notable viewpoint surmounted by an ancient camp. A curious rock-dwelling on the hill is known as Holy Austin Rock. Part of a rare Norman rood-loft staircase has survived in the decorated and perpendicular church. The Staffordshire and Worcestershire canal winds through the area, set in attractive wooded countryside near the River Stour. Sandstone cliffs, numerous locks, and unusual weirs are features of this waterway.

KIPLING COTES, Humberside *23 SE94*
A horse race said to be the oldest and longest in England, dating from 1519, is run here every year in the latter half of March. The present course is 4m long and has been used since 1667.

KIRBY MUXLOE, Leics *18 SK50*
Lord Hastings, Grand Chamberlain to Edward IV, built the 15th-c brick castle or fortified manor house (AM). It stands within an encircling moat and is considered a fine example of its type.

KIRDFORD, W Sussex *8 TQ02*
Glass foundries were once a feature of this neighbourhood, and the Petworth marble used in many Sussex churches was quarried here. The fine 13th- to 15th-c church displays 13th-c glass and twisted 17th-c altar rails.

KIRK BRADDAN, Isle of Man *20 SC37*
Sunday services are held in a field adjoining the ancient church, and a number of ancient crosses exist here.

KIRKBURN, Humberside *23 SE95*
This small Wolds village includes a remarkably interesting Norman church, displaying a rich south doorway and carved font.

KIRKBY-IN-ASHFIELD, Notts *18 SK55*
The brick rectory dates from 1717 and the manor house from 1622. An old horse gin and capstan are being preserved by the National Coal Board at the Bentinck Colliery training centre. Newstead Abbey and Sherwood Forest both lie to the W.

KIRKBY LONSDALE, Cumbria *21 SD67*
The nearby River Lune is crossed by means of Devil's Bridge (AM), probably dating from the 13thc. A market cross has been re-erected in the Horsemarket, and a small stone building standing near by was a former check house for locally-made wares.

The church shows good Norman work, particularly in the carved nave capitals. An inscribed plaque near the churchyard describes Ruskin's view, which was painted by Turner, and an octagonal gazebo affords wide views. The town was used in Charlotte Brontë's *Jane Eyre* under the name of Lowton, and the authoress herself was a scholar at Clergy Daughters' School, Cowan Bridge. Whelprigg Manor lies 4m NE near an early-Christian carved cross. Farther N lies picturesquely-wooded Barbondale.

KIRKBYMOORSIDE, N Yorks *22 SE68*
Picturesque Farndale valley lies to the N of this attractive little town, and is now protected as a reserve for wild daffodils. The Black Swan is an old interesting inn.

KIRKBY STEPHEN, Cumbria *21 NY70*
The fine 13th-c and later parish church includes the Musgrave and Wharton chapels, plus a number of ancient carved stones. Cloisters in the market place date from 1870. More picturesque river-scenery can be enjoyed on the S outskirts of the town at Stenkrith, where there are also several potholes. Nine Standards Rigg rises to 2,008ft in the SE, and is crowned by a row of nine cairns near the summit. Mallerstang Valley is a wild area lying to the S, containing 15th-c Wharton Hall (AM) and sparse remains of Lammerside and Pendragon Castles.

KIRKDALE, N Yorks *22 SE68*
Situated in a charming wooded setting, Kirkdale includes a church where the porch carries a rare Saxon sundial. Kirkdale Cave measures 100yds long and was an important discovery of 1821. Rich pre ice-age remains were found in the cave.

KIRKHAM, N Yorks *22 SE76*
Remains of the 12th-c abbey (AM) include a fine late 13th-c chapel and a lavatorium. Howsham Hall is a Jacobean and late 18th-c house lying 4m S.

KIRK HAMMERTON, N Yorks *22 SE45*
The local 19th-c church is formed from a highly-interesting little Saxon church which shows various 19th-c additions.

KIRKLEATHAM, Cleveland *27 NZ52*
The present church dates from 1763, and the large mausoleum from 1740. The 17th-c Turner Homes are very interesting and include a museum and chapel. Free School (Old House) dates from 1708 to 1709. Sword dancing is a feature of the area.

KIRK MICHAEL, Isle of Man *20 SC39*
Eight runic crosses are preserved at the parish church of this small seaside resort. Bishopscourt, the residence of the Bishops of Sodor and Man, lies about ½m N. It includes a theological college and a chapel that is the official pro-cathedral.

KIRKNEWTON, Northumberland *27 NT93*
A remarkable chancel and diminutive south transept are included in the old church, both probably built with a view to defence. The ancient Northumbrian town of *Gefrin* is recalled by a roadside monument. St Paulinus baptized people in the River Glen. The valley of the College Burn starts here and leads first to narrow Hen Hole, and thence to the 2,676ft summit of The Cheviot. Coupland Castle, a 16th-c structure near a 19th-c house, lies 2m NE of Kirknewton.

KIRKOSWALD, Cumbria *26 NY54*
Attractive buildings of red sandstone make up the bulk of this village, and sparse remains of a 13th-c castle are of interest. The church belfry stands on a nearby hill, and the college dates from 1696. A nunnery lying to the NW was built in 1715.

KIRKSTALL ABBEY, W Yorks *22 SE23*
Extensive remains of this interesting, mainly trans-Norman Cistercian Abbey (AM) lie by the River Aire. The former gatehouse is now known as Kirkstall Abbey House, and contains an interesting museum of old craftsmanship. The monks originally came from Fountains Abbey and pioneered the exploitation of iron ore in this area. Their craft works included tanning, pottery, spinning, and weaving.

KIRKSTEAD, Lincs *19 TF16*
Sparse remains of a former abbey lie to the E. Nearby St Leonard's Chapel preserves part of a screen dating from 1210, one of the oldest to have survived.

KIRKSTONE PASS INN, Cumbria *21 NY40*
This lonely inn stands at the summit of well-known Kirkstone Pass at an altitude of 1,476ft, and is one of the highest in the country.

KIRTLING, Cambs *14 TL65*
The great brick gate-tower that can be seen here is said to be the finest in the country, and is a survival of the moated mid 16th-c Kirtling Tower. Queen Elizabeth I was entertained in the latter. Norman work is evident in the church, which includes two ornate 16th-c memorials among its North-family monuments.

KIRTON IN LINDSEY, Humberside *19 SK99*
Formerly a manor of importance, Kirton in Lindsey has been held by Piers Gaveston, the Black Prince, and Queen Anne of Bohemia. The restored church carries a notable 13th-c tower and displays a good south doorway.

KNAPTON, Norfolk *15 TG33*
One of the finest hammerbeam angel-carved roofs to be seen in East Anglia is displayed by the decorated and perpendicular church. The unusual font cover dates from 1704.

KNARESBOROUGH, N Yorks *22 SE35*
Picturesquely situated on the River Nidd, this attractive old town includes the ruined 14th-c castle of John of Gaunt, and a petrifying well. Legend has it that the prophetess Mother Shipton was born in a local cave of the same name. Eugene Aram's cave is said to be the place where Aram hid the remains of his victim Daniel Clark. St Robert's Chapel comprises chambers hewn out of solid rock, on the N bank of the Nidd, and dates from the late 18thc. It is known as Fort Montagu.

The decorated and perpendicular church houses good monuments, and the Old Manor House has Civil War associations. Well-known zoological gardens exist in the grounds of Conyngham Hall, and a linen mill dating from 1785 can be seen on Waterside.

KNEBWORTH, Herts *14 TL22*
Knebworth Park includes the Old Church and 16th- to 19th-c Knebworth House – the former home of Bulwer Lytton. Both house and park now form part of a large new country park, with various amenities (OACT). The modern church is sited on the former Great North Road and was designed by Sir Edwin Lutyens.

KNOCKHOLT, Kent *8 TQ45*
Knockholt Beeches are a prominent local landmark, and the place itself stands at over 700ft on the North Downs. Chevening Place is a fine 17th- to 18th-c building which has been presented to the nation. A splendid monument by Chantrey can be seen in Chevening church.

KNOLE, Kent *8 TQ55*
This famous mansion was started in 1456 by Thomas Bourchier, Archbishop of Canterbury, and displays large 17th-c additions. It contains splendid state rooms and remains the home of the Sackvilles. A vast deer park surrounds the house, and the entire estate lies adjacent to Sevenoaks (NT, OACT).

KNOWLE, W Midlands *12 SP17*
Grimshaw Hall is a beautiful old timbered house displaying an unusual three-gabled porch. The fine perpendicular church was once collegiate, and preserves the 15th-c timbered hall of the collegiate house.

KNOWLTON, Kent *9 TR25*
Knowlton Court is an Elizabethan and Georgian house which is associated with Dorothy Osborne and her 17th-c letters to William Temple. The perpendicular church has a Jacobean three-decker pulpit. A good example of an old post-mill stands to the NW.

KNOWSLEY, Merseyside *17 SJ49*
Palatial Knowsley Hall is a 17th- to 19th-c mansion set in a 2,500-acre park. It is the home of the Earls of Derby. Knowsley Safari Park is contained within the estate, and the 18th-c and later Croxteth Hall stands in another fine park to the SW.

KNUTSFORD, Cheshire *17 SJ77*
An attractive residential town which includes a few black-and-white houses, Knutsford was the *Cranford* of Mrs Gaskell's book of the same name. This authoress is buried behind the Unitarian Chapel of 1688. The parish church is of the 18thc, and the Sessions House dates from 1818. Tatton Park (NT, OACT) and Tabley Hall are two 18th-c mansions situated on the outskirts of the town. The former is set in an extensive park to the N, and the latter lies SW. Attractive Rostherne Mere is situated 4m N.

KYNANCE COVE, Cornwall *4 SW61*
Perhaps the best-known in Cornwall, this cove is surrounded by remarkable serpentine rock scenery, including caves and cliffs (part NT). It is accessible on foot from a large car park near The Lizard. A little to the NW, the cliff-top path leads to spectacular cliffs known as Pigeon Hugo and The Horse.

LACOCK, Wilts *7 ST96*
Lacock has a fine 14th-c barn, an old lock-up, a stepped cross, and many old buildings in styles ranging from grey-stone houses to thatched cottages (NT). Although the present house dates from 1540 and later (NT, OACT), the abbey was actually founded in the 13thc. The more recent building was the birthplace of W H Fox-Talbot, a pioneer of photography, who made the first photographic prints in 1833 and was subsequently awarded the Royal Society medal. Two old houses to the E are Bewley Court and Bowden Park; the latter is dated 1796 and was designed by James Wyatt.

LAINDON, Essex *9 TQ68*
Although engulfed by Basildon's New-Town development, Laindon still has a village church which preserves fine carved-wood decoration. Laindon Hall, now a farm, dates from the 15thc. Also from this period is a rare two-storied priest's house. Laindon, or Langdon, Hills rise to 378ft in the S, and form a good viewpoint.

LAKE DISTRICT, THE
The Lake District is a compact 900sqm area of beautiful national-park countryside. It includes lakes, tarns, and the highest mountains in England. About sixty areas of still water exist here, the largest of which is Windermere. This lake measures 10m long by 1m wide and extends from Ambleside to Newby Bridge; the next biggest, Ullswater, stretches from Pooley Bridge to Patterdale. Bassenthwaite and Derwentwater come farther down the scale, with Skiddaw rising in the background. The important Lakeland centre of Keswick lies on the latter.

Ennerdale Water is reached via Ennerdale Bridge, and Wast Water is surrounded by rugged screes; these are the wildest lakes in the area. A road which runs along the far side of Wast Water leads to Wasdale Head, and thus to Scafell and Great Gable. Lesser-known lakes include Loweswater, near a village of the same name, and Esthwaite Water, near Hawkshead. Thirlmere lies under the lower slopes of Helvellyn, near the tiny church of Wythburn. This and Haweswater, beyond the remote Mardale valley, have both been converted into reservoirs.

Numerous small tarns, exist in the area, some of which are situated high up on the fells. Two of the best-known are Tarn Hows near Coniston, and Blea Tarn S of Great Langdale. Scafell Pike, monarch of the fells, rises to 3,210ft and is neighboured by Broad Crag and Ill Crag. Helvellyn is famous for the Striding Edge arete (see Patterdale), and the peaks of Skiddaw, Great Gable, and Pillar – with the famous Pillar Rock. Excellent rock-climbing is offered by most of the peaks. Many of the other hills in this area exceed 2,500ft, and the lower peaks include noteworthy Langdale Pikes. Fine passes include Kirkstone, with its isolated inn; grim Honister, to the W of Seatoller; and Whinlatter, rising to the E of Lorton. The more difficult Wrynose and Hardknott passes link Ambleside with Eskdale and the Cumberland coast.

Newlands Hause lies on the direct road from Keswick to Buttermere. Delightful Borrowdale is threaded by the River Derwent and can be considered the loveliest of Lakeland's many valleys. Great and Little Langdale also offer charming scenery, plus the spectacular bonus of Dungeon Ghyll waterfall, and the pretty Blea Tarn. Eskdale valley extends from Ravenglass towards the Hardknott national forest park, and lesser-known Duddon valley – known as Dunnerdale – lies N of Broughton-in-Furness. Nearly 90,000 acres of the Lake District, including some of the high fells – notably the Scafell group, are owned or protected by the NT.

Road conditions vary considerably according to weather and local circumstances. Many Lakeland roads are narrow, winding, and hilly, with gradients of up to 1 in 4. The most difficult route is that between Ambleside and Eskdale, across the Wrynose and Hardknott Passes. Wrynose has a maximum gradient of 1 in 4, but is narrow and has few passing places. Hardknott is more difficult because of steep gradients (max 1 in 3) on numerous hairpin bends. The road is narrow, with a predominantly good surface except for a few rough patches. It cannot be too strongly emphasized that driving over these passes, particularly Hardknott, is not easy. However, an experienced driver at the wheel of a car in excellent running order should experience only the minimum of difficulty. The Hardknott section can be avoided if need be, by following the Duddon valley down to Ulpha and then taking the mountain road over Birker Moor, past Devoke Water, to Eskdale. Both Honister Pass and Newlands Hause have well-made roads, with gradients of up to 1 in 4 and several awkward bends. Careful driving is enough to safely negotiate these sections. The Kirkstone Pass has a long ascent and descent, but Stock Ghyll, the narrow direct road from Ambleside to high Kirkstone Pass Inn, rises continuously for 2½m. The longer route by way of Troutbeck Bridge is much easier.

Lakeland's characteristic flocks of Hardwick sheep are a hardy breed noted for their wonderful homing instincts. They graze on the many fells and live in a semi-wild state. Keswick, Ambleside, Grasmere, and Windermere – or Bowness-on-Windermere – are the best-known touring centres. The Lakes are famous for their literary associations, and the names Coleridge, Ruskin, Southey, and Wordsworth are inseparably entangled with the district – in which they all lived or stayed. Many other eminent writers have had contacts with the area.

LAKENHEATH, Suffolk 14 TL78
An important USAF base has existed here since 1941. The church houses a notable 13th-c font, a 16th-c angel-carved roof, many fine old bench-ends, and Royal Arms of Charles II. A memorial to Lord Kitchener can also be seen.

LALEHAM, Surrey 8 TQ06
This pleasant Thames-side village includes a church containing various, interesting monuments. Other features of the building include Norman arcades, a tower dated 1732, and the early-Tudor Lucan chapel. Matthew Arnold (1822 to 1880) was born here, and is buried in the churchyard. Laleham Abbey was the home of the Lucan family, including the Crimean War general Lord Lucan.

LAMBERHURST, Kent 9 TQ63
Bayham Abbey includes 13th-c remains, and is situated in the grounds of a modern house 2m W of this village. Scotney Castle is a picturesque ruin 1½m SE (NT, OACT). The later castle dates from the 19thc.

LAMBOURN, Berks 7 SU37
Lambourn is in a downland situation, and includes a large Norman to perpendicular church containing several old brasses. Much of the town's character is provided by a number of Georgian houses and an ancient cross. Fawley, which lies E, was named Marygreen in Hardy's *Jude the Obscure*.

LAMERTON, Devon 5 SX47
Collacombe Barton was once the home of the Tremaynes, and dates from 1574. It is noted for its hall. Horsebridge spans the River Tamar and dates from 1437; it is one of the oldest bridges in Devon.

LAMORNA VALLEY, Cornwall 4 SW42
This delightful valley is popular with artists, and leads to a rocky cove which has natural pools large enough for bathing. The Pipers standing stones and the stone circle of the Merry Maidens lie near the head of the valley. A *fogou*, or refuge hole, exists near Boleigh.

LANCASTER, Lancs 21 SD46
Plan overleaf
Lancaster is a county town on the Lune, where the river is spanned by the Sherton Bridge. A number of Georgian houses and an impressive castle are features of the area. John of Gaunt, Duke of Lancaster and father of Henry IV, enlarged the castle, and Elizabeth I added fortifications against the Armada. It now houses the county courts and a prison (AM, OACT). The gatehouse is its most prominent feature. St Mary's Church contains notable woodwork, including superb 14th-c stalls which were formerly at Cockersand Abbey.

A cathedral (RC) and art gallery are also of interest. Shire Hall (18thc) is part of the castle, and the old town hall now houses a regimental museum. Ashton Memorial overlooks the town from Williamson Park. A university has been founded 2½m S at Bailrigg. Rennie's fine aqueduct of 1796, built to carry the Lancaster Canal across the River Lune, stands N of the town.

LANCHESTER, Co Durham 27 NZ14
The interesting Norman to perpendicular church houses a Roman altar and columns, plus a fine late-Norman chancel arch.

LANCING, W Sussex 8 TQ10
The Norman to decorated church contains an Easter Sepulchre. Lancing College is a well-known modern public school which has a fine chapel rising to 94ft. This is one of the highest in England.

LANDKEY, Devon 5 SS53
Landkey church carries a fine perpendicular tower. Various monuments can be seen inside. Acland Barton dates partly from c1475, and Codden Hill is a fine viewpoint to the S.

LAND'S END, Cornwall 4 SW32
Land's End is England's most westerly point. The distance from here to John O'Groats, in the N of Scotland, is about 873m. During clear weather the Isles of Scilly – some 28m to the W – are visible. Whitesand Bay lies to the N, and is part of a section of fine coastal scenery; SE is Nanjizal Bay, which can be reached via a cliff-path from which splendid granite-rock scenery can be viewed. Pordenack Point and several remote sandy and rocky bays can be seen on the way. The coastal area around Land's End is now designated one of outstanding natural beauty.

LANERCOST, Cumbria 26 NY56
Remains of a 12th-c priory (AM) include a nave which now forms the parish church, showing notable 13th-c work, fine tombs to the Dacres, and a 13th-c cross. The priory was founded for Augustinian canons by Robert de Vallibus, and was built largely of stones from the Roman wall.

LANGDALE, Cumbria 21 NY30
A delightful Lakeland valley, overshadowed by lofty fells which include Bow Fell and Crinkle Crags. The waterfall of Dungeon Ghyll is notable, and a large part of the area is NT-owned or protected. Above the fall rise well-known Langdale Pikes, plus Gimmer and Pavey Ark – all familiar to climbers. Lonely Stickle Tarn lies below, and 2,510ft High Raise forms a splendid viewpoint farther N. Blea Tarn lies S of the valley in Little Langdale, and is situated high in the fells below the 2,304ft Pike of Blisco. Elterwater and the nearby Loughrigg Tarn lie 1m SE of the village.

LANGFORD, Oxon 12 SP20
The very interesting village church is of early-Norman and later date. Its trans-Norman work is notable, and two representations of the crucifixion appearing on the south porch may be of Saxon workmanship.

LANGLEY MARISH, Berks 8 TQ07
Picturesque old almshouses built in two ranges date from 1617 and 1675 respectively. The interesting church is noted for its 17th-c brick tower, Charles I Royal Arms dated 1625, a double-colonnade of wooden Tuscan pillars, and the remarkable Kederminster library of 1623. Langley Park is an 18th-c house.

Sheep are the ideal answer to the problem of farming rugged Lake District heights

LANGPORT/LAXEY

LANGPORT, Somerset *6 ST42*
The River Parrett flows below the main street of this old market town, and the perpendicular church houses some old glass. A curious hanging chapel over an arch, built for a medieval craft guild, can be seen E of the church. The guildhall dates from 1733.

LANGWATHBY, Cumbria *26 NY53*
A quiet village on the River Eden, 4m NE of Penrith. The church was rebuilt in 1718 and contains 17th-c armour. The lower slopes of the Pennines, beyond the line of the Roman Maiden Way, bear curious mounds or terraces known as the Hanging Walls of Mark Antony.

LANIVET, Cornwall *4 SX06*
Two fine crosses, a coped stone, a cross slab, and a pillar slab are all features of the local churchyard. The large church displays a lofty tower and a 14th-c font. A ruined tower from a former priory is also of interest.

LANREATH, Cornwall *5 SX15*
An old court in this attractive village dates from c1610. The restored mainly-perpendicular church is noted for its painted screen, carved chancel-stalls, and fine carved-wood Grylls monument of 1623. A sign by Augustus John hangs outside the Punch Bowl Inn.

LANSALLOS, Cornwall *5 SX15*
The 15th-c church displays an embattled tower and some fine woodwork. Lantivet Bay lies to the S, and shows rugged cliff scenery (NT).

LAPFORD, Devon *5 SS70*
A hilltop village above the River Yeo, Lapford comprises a steep street of thatched cottages and several Georgian houses. The millionth acre planted by the Forestry Commission is marked by a tablet and includes trees planted by Queen Elizabeth II and Prince Philip. A magnificently carved screen, probably 16thc and certainly one of the best in the county, can be seen in the church.

LAPWORTH, Warwickshire *12 SP17*
Near the junction of the Stratford and Grand Union Canals, this village includes a particularly-interesting 13th- to 15th-c church. Of greatest note is the partly-detached tower of c1400, surmounted by a rebuilt spire. An Elizabethan altar table and a carving by Eric Gill can be seen in the north chapel of the chancel. At Kingswood, the actual place where the canals meet, are the NT workshops. Shakespeare Hall is a Jacobean and later building lying 3m SE.

LASSINGTON, Glos *12 SO72*
Lassington church carries a Saxon to Norman tower and houses a fine pulpit of 1636. Ancient Lassington Oak stands on a nearby hillside, forming a good viewpoint.

LASTINGHAM, N Yorks *22 SE79*
The trans-Norman and later church in this moorland village preserves a notable crypt, which was built as a shrine for St Cedd. Also of interest are various fragments of old crosses.

LATIMER, Bucks *8 TQ09*
Largely made up of attractive cottages, this delightful Chess-Valley village has associations with Charles I. He is said to have visited a building which used to stand on a site now occupied by Latimer House. The latter is dated 1863 and was erected by Blore.

LAUGHTON, E Sussex *8 TQ41*
Vaults in the restored church contain Pelham tombs, and remains of Laughton Place lie 2m SW. The famous Pelham Buckle can be seen above the windows of a surviving 16th-c tower.

LAUGHTON-EN-LE-MORTHEN, S Yorks *18 SK58*
One of Yorkshire's finest parish churches can be seen here, and is notable for its pre-Conquest work. The tall 15th-c tower and spire form a landmark that can be seen for miles around.

LAUNCESTON, Cornwall *5 SX38*
Launceston is a pleasant, very ancient town situated on hills. The ruined Norman castle (AM) has an imposing keep, and a gateway survives from the former town walls. St Mary Magdalene's church shows remarkable 16th-c granite carving on the exterior, and fine woodwork inside. St Thomas's church houses the largest Norman font in Cornwall.

A Norman doorway which came from the old priory is incorporated in the White Hart, and Georgian houses are to be found in Castle Street. St Stephen-by-Launceston lies 1½m N and was the mother church of the town. It has a battlemented chapel and dates from Norman and 15th-c periods. The River Kensey is crossed here by two bridges – one medieval, and one dating from the 18thc. Trecarrel Manor dates from c1500 and lies 4m S.

LAVENHAM, Suffolk *15 TL94*
One of the loveliest old wool towns in England, Lavenham is rich in timbered houses. The guildhall (NT) and Wool Hall are particularly outstanding, and a De Vere house dates from the late 15thc.

Shilling Old Grange was once the home of Jane Taylor, who wrote *Twinkle, Twinkle, Little Star*. The clerestoried wool church is of decorated and perpendicular styles, and carries a grand 141ft tower. Inside are the fine Spring chapel of 1525 and some good screenwork. A hand-operated fire engine dating from 1725 has been preserved. An old cross (AM) stands in the marketplace, and several interesting inns include the Angel and the Swan (now incorporating the old Wool Hall).

LAVERSTOKE, Hants *7 SU44*
Paper for Bank of England notes is made at the mill in this Test-Valley village.

LAWFORD, Essex *15 TM03*
The church in this River-Stour village includes a splendid 14th-c chancel. A timber-framed hall of 1583, with a Georgian front of about 1756, lies to the N.

LAXEY, Isle of Man *20 SC48*
Situated on the E coast of the island, this harbour town is the starting point of an electric mountain-railway to Snaefell. The famous Lady Isabella is a big pump-wheel constructed to keep the lead mines free from water. Although the workings are now closed, the wheel is still kept turning (OACT). Laxey Glen is picturesque, and waterfalls can be seen in the Dhoon Glen. Farther N, near Glen

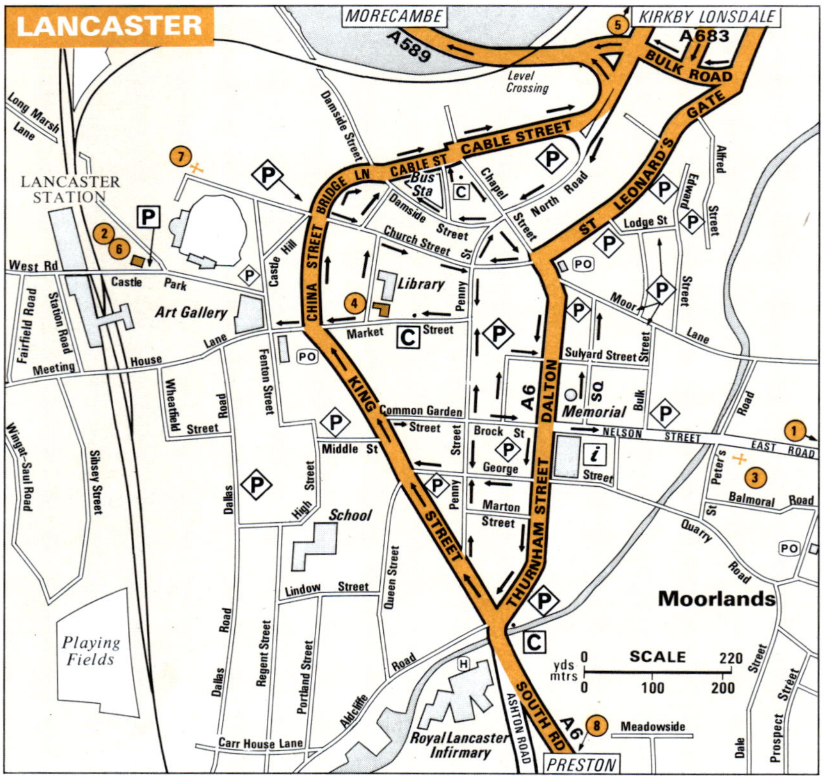

1 Ashton Memorial
2 Castle
3 Cathedral (RC)
4 Regimental Museum (Town Hall)
5 Rennie's Aqueduct
6 Shire Hall
7 University of Lancaster

Mona, is the notable Cashtal yn Ard gallery-grave.

LAXFIELD, Suffolk *15 TM27*
The local church shows a fine perpendicular flint tower, plus a Seven-Sacraments font. Also of interest is a restored 15th-c guildhall.

LAXTON, Notts *18 SK76*
Laxton is one of the few villages where the open three-field system of cultivation is still practised. Arable land is divided into three parts, and farmed on a three-year rotation basis. St Michael's church includes a fine nave clerestory, the De Everingham monuments, and a screen dated 1532. A large Norman motte-and-bailey castle stands near by.

LAYER-DE-LA-HAYE, Essex *15 TL92*
There are fine views over Abberton reservoir to the S. This water is the haunt of thousands of wildfowl. Near the reservoir is an old house called Blind Knights, associated with a former hospital to which returning Crusaders were sent if they had eye injuries. The 14th-c church displays a timbered south porch.

LAYER MARNEY, Essex *9 TL91*
The hall has an enormous 16th-c multi-storeyed gatehouse which was erected by Lord Marney. It is one of the tallest in England. The main house was originally to be built N of the gatehouse, but was never completed. Only a portion of the house exists (OACT). Terracotta decorations displayed by the battlements and windows are typical early-Renaissance motifs of Italian character. The church, rebuilt in the 16thc, is notable for its brick and terra-cotta work – particularly the Marney tombs.

LAZONBY, Cumbria *26 NY53*
A fine old bridge and quarries that date from the Roman period are of interest.

LEADENHAM, Lincs *19 SK95*
Decorated and perpendicular styles are displayed by the church, which also carries a lofty spire. The Old Hall dates from c1700. Temple Bruer is a restored 13th-c tower from a former church of the Knights Templar (AM), and can be seen 5m E at Temple Farm.

LEAMINGTON SPA, Warwickshire *13 SP36*
This inland spa is situated on a branch of the River Leam, and the Grand Union Canal. Natural springs in the area are said to be medicinal, and the Royal Pump Room and baths are of interest. Queen Victoria granted a Royal prefix to the town after a visit in 1838. A number of fine Regency houses can be seen, and the Jephson Gardens are attractive. The modern parish church has a 145ft tower, and the town hall dates from 1833. A former town hall was built in 1831.

LEATHERHEAD, Surrey *8 TQ15*
Several old houses and inns can be seen in this busy River-Mole town. An old bridge is of interest, and the church dates partly from the 12thc. A long 13th-c chest is preserved inside. Hope, the author of *The Prisoner of Zenda*, is buried in the churchyard. Thorndike Theatre was opened in 1969.

LEATHLEY, N Yorks *22 SE24*
Old stocks and a mounting block are preserved outside the walls of the Norman to perpendicular church. The hall and almshouses date from the early and late 18th-c respectively. Almscliff, situated on high ground to the NE, is famous as a training ground where some of England's best-known rock climbers have begun their careers. Reservoirs which supply the city of Leeds are situated in the Washburn Valley, to the NW.

LECHLADE, Glos *12 SU29*
Lechlade is the limit for large craft ascending the River Thames from the E. The local perpendicular church has a fine priest's door and displays strange figures on its tower buttresses. Halfpenny Bridge is an old structure which spans the Thames here, and St John's Bridge lies ½m E where the Leach and Thames meet. Berkshire, Gloucestershire, and Wiltshire all meet at this point.

LEDBURY, Herefs & Worcs *12 SO73*
Black-and-white houses and inns give this town its character. Market Hall is of timbered construction (AM). Also of interest are a group of almshouses, and the 16th-c and later Ledbury Park. Features of the large Norman to perpendicular church are a detached tower, a fine decorated north chapel, and a number of monuments. Outside the town is a prominent railway viaduct that dates from 1859. Pixley lies 4m NW and includes a little church with a remarkable ancient screen.

LEEBOTWOOD, Salop *17 SO49*
Lawley Hill dominates this village. Attractive half-timbered houses can be seen, and of particular interest is the thatched Pound Inn. Features of this building include an outside beam dated 1650, and fine interior panelling. The 13th-c church stands just W of the village, and contains pews displaying 17th-c woodwork. The 17th-c red-brick manor house at Longnor, to the N, shows what is thought to be the oldest example of Chinese wallpaper in England. This is hung in the dining-room.

LEEDS, Kent *9 TQ85*
Stone-built Battle Hall dates from the 14thc, and is just one of several old houses that exist in this village. A massive Norman tower is carried by the church, and 12th-c and later Leeds Castle is a restored building situated 1½m NE on lake-girdled rock-strewn knolls. Henry VIII's first wife Catherine of Aragon lived at the castle; the diarist John Evelyn guarded French and Dutch prisoners of war here in 1665.

LEEDS, W Yorks *22 SE33*
Plan overleaf
Fabrics, footwear, and engineering items are made in this important university city. Although progressive, Leeds still retains some of its old buildings. Several churches are numbered among these.

St Peter's has a restored pre-Conquest cross, and St John's Church is noted for its wealth of 17th-c woodwork. The grammar school was founded in 1552, and the city market dates from 1857 and 1904. The Corn Exchange dates from 1861 to 1863. Two impressive local buildings are the town hall of 1853, and the more recent civic hall of 1933.

A triennial music festival is held in the city, and the local art gallery is of interest. Temple Newsam lies on the SE outskirts; it is a splendid 17th-c house containing a collection of works of art, and was the birthplace of Lord Darnley (OACT). The county-cricket ground at Headingley is a traditional Test Match pitch. Leeds United Football Club is well-known as one of the country's big teams, and the city also has a good reputation in Rugby League circles.

Roundhay Park covers 775 acres, and is one of the best in the country. Beyond the busy shopping area, by The Headrow, are the Quarry Hill flats. These were built in 1938 and were one of the first large-scale residential complexes to be completed prior to post-war developments. The Leeds and Liverpool and Aire and Calder canals meet in the city. Characteristic containers on the latter are known as Tom-Pudding boats, and are towed by tugs in strings of up to nineteen.

LEEK, Staffs *18 SJ95*
Important silk mills operate in this industrial town. St Edward's church is of decorated and later styles and carries a fine pinnacled tower. A Saxon or Danish pillar exists in the churchyard. A tablet to canal engineer James Brindley recalls his work on a local mill during the mid 18thc. Picturesque Rudyard Lake is a 2m-long reservoir lying 3m NW. Spectacular 1,658ft Staffordshire Roaches and Hen Cloud are millstone-grit formations well-known to climbers, and lie 5¾m N.

LEE-ON-THE-SOLENT, Hants *7 SU50*
This small resort has amenities including a shingle beach and a bathing pool. It faces the Isle of Wight, and is the site of an air base.

LEICESTER, Leics *18 SK50*
Plan overleaf
Leicester is a county town and university city, sited on the River Soar and Grand Union Canal and involved in various industrial operations. During the Roman occupation it was a walled station known as *Ratae Coritanorum*. Various Roman relics can be seen in the museum, and Roman pavements exist under the former Central Station and below a shop fronting St Nicholas's Church. Other remains were excavated between 1936 and 1939, from sites extending over a large area; nearby Jewry Wall Museum and the Roman Baths (AM) display examples of Roman masonry.

St Martin's is now the cathedral and shows early-English to perpendicular styles. It retains old doorways, a carved chancel-roof, and good modern woodwork. The Saxon to early-English St Nicholas's church incorporates Roman materials, and has a Norman doorway. St Mary's church retains good Norman work, and carries a tall crocketed 14th-c spire. Beautiful Norman sedilia can be seen in the chancel of the latter. Bow Bridge is traditionally associated with King Richard III. Remains of a Norman castle lie near a timbered gateway and Tudor house, and 17th-c Court House conceals fragments of a fine Norman hall.

Other features of interest include the picturesque Newarke turret gate; the Magazine Gate (AM) containing a regimental museum; and the very-fine, timbered 15th-c guildhall (AM). Trinity Hospital Chapel is of decorated style. Near by are the Newarke Houses, the Chantry House of 1511, and Elizabethan

Skeffington House. The county rooms are of 1792, and the town hall of 1874 date. The Corn Exchange dates from 1851 and 1855, and New Walk is a promenade that was planted in 1785. Belgrave Hall is a Georgian house that now contains a period museum. Concerts are held in the fine De Montfort Hall. A racecourse lies S of the town, and a war memorial of 1923 by Lutyens can be seen in the Victoria Park.

A locomotive museum stands near the racecourse, and the ambitious new Museum of Technology – for the East Midlands – has been opened in Corporation Road. Botanic gardens owned by the university are of note. Cardinal Wolsey died in Leicester Abbey in 1530, and the remains of this building now form part of Cavendish House in Abbey Park. Fine early-Georgian Scraptoft Hall belongs to Leicester Training College and stands 4m E.

LEIGH, Gt Manchester 17 SJ69
Pronounced Lee, this industrial town is a centre for coal and cotton industries. It is also involved in the production of cable and brick-making machinery. The East Lancashire roads run near the town, and Leigh itself is situated on the Leeds and Liverpool and Bridgewater canals.

LEIGH-ON-SEA, Essex 9 TQ88
Fishing and smuggling were popular local occupations when this Thames-estuary residential resort was a small hamlet. Southend lies to the E, and cliffs afford fine views over the surrounding area. St Clement's church is of 15th-c origin and carries a good tower.

LEIGHS, GREAT, Essex 9 TL71
The Norman round-tower carried by the local church is one of six existing in the county, and the 14th-c chancel contains a lovely Easter Sepulchre. Little Leighs, or Leez Priory, retains two superb Tudor brick gatehouses of a former mansion, and lies 2m NW. Two 16th-c barns are also of interest.

LEIGHTON BROMSWOLD, Cambs 14 TL17
Furnishings inside the church are notable, and the building has associations with George Herbert the poet. It carries a tower of 1634 and displays a 13th-c chancel. Near by is the partly-moated gatehouse from an uncompleted mansion. It dates from 1616 and now forms the vicarage.

LEIGHTON BUZZARD, Beds 13 SP92
The River Ouzel runs through this market town. Several old inns and a restored 15th-c market cross are of interest, and the largely early-English church carries a good tower and spire. Victorian buildings include the former town hall of 1851 and the Corn Exchange. Linslade, formerly in Buckinghamshire, is now amalgamated with Leighton Buzzard. The combined towns are sometimes known as Leighton Linslade. Mentmore, a palatial modern mansion 4m to the S, was based on the design of Nottingham's Elizabethan Wollaton Hall.

LEIGH-UPON-MENDIP, Somerset 6 ST64
One of the finest church towers in the county can be seen here. It is of 15th-c date and displays rich carving. Inside the church are fine carved bench-ends, and the west window contains lovely 15th-c glass. Soho is a little hamlet lying N, the name of which was used for the Duke of Monmouth's password in the bloody and abortive rising of 1685.

LEINTWARDINE, Herefs & Worcs 12 SO47
Standing near the junction of the Rivers Teme and Clun, Leintwardine features a 13th- and 14th-c church displaying a massive battlemented tower, medieval carved roofs, and 15th-c carved chancel-stalls. General Tarleton, who fought in the American War of Independence, is buried here. Mid 17th-c Heath House lies 2m NW. To the NE of Downton-on-the-Rock, 2½m SE of Leintwardine, is a delightfully wooded gorge through which the River Teme flows. Downton Castle is a picturesque late 18th-c structure.

LEISTON, Suffolk 15 TM46
Remains of 14th-c Leiston Abbey, parts of which have been a Diocesan retreat centre since 1953, lie about 1m N of the village. Saxmundham is 4m W.

LELANT, Cornwall 4 SW53
A golfing resort on the River Hayle, near the head of St Ives Bay. The Norman and perpendicular church displays an 18th-c sundial; SW is 400ft Trencrom Hill.

LENHAM, Kent 9 TQ85
Fine medieval houses can be seen in this small town, and the 13th- to 15th-c church has an old double-arched lych-gate. The pulpit is notable among the many examples of fine woodwork to be seen inside the church. Honeywood is dated 1621, and two other features of the town include a tithe barn and an old lock-up. Early 18th-c Chilston Park lies to the S. A large white cross on the North Downs was raised to the dead of both world wars.

LEOMINSTER, Herefs & Worcs 12 SO45
This town has produced fine wool since the 13thc, and Hereford cattle are exported all over the world from here. It stands at the junction of the Rivers Pinsley and Lugg, and its many black-and-white houses include the fine Grange Hall by John Abel. This was re-erected in 1856. The former Corn Exchange dates from 1858, and the town hall from 1855. Bargate almshouses were built in 1736. The interesting Norman to perpendicular priory church has a double nave, fine decorated-style windows, and preserves a ducking-stool. Wharton Court, a 17th-c stone-built house surrounded by a moat, lies 2m S. Berrington Hall lies 4m NE and was by

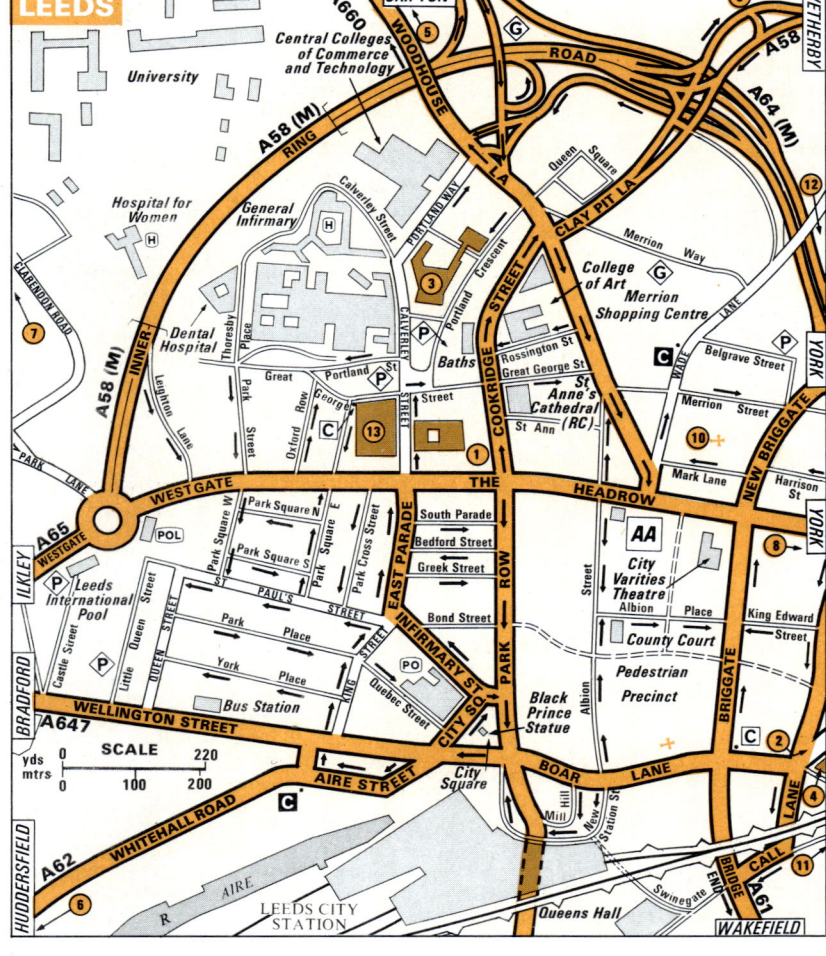

1 Art Gallery
2 City Markets
3 Civic Hall
4 Corn Exchange
5 County Cricket Ground
6 Football Ground
7 Grammar School
8 Quarry Hill Flats
9 Roundhay Park
10 St John's Church
11 St Peter's Church
12 Temple Newsam
13 Town Hall

Henry Holland in 1778. It affords fine views towards Wales (NT, OACT).

LETCHWORTH, Herts 14 TL23
Letchworth, the first garden city, was planned and founded by (Sir) Ebenezer Howard in 1903. Its design and construction has had a great influence on the subsequent development of town planning. Letchworth Hall is Jacobean and serves as an hotel.

LEVENS, Cumbria 21 SD48
Levens Hall is an Elizabethan mansion which has been added to a 14th-c pele tower. Its topiary gardens are probably the finest of their kind in England, and were designed in 1689 by a Frenchman called Beaumont. The Plant Centre sells a wide variety of container-grown shrubs. Also of interest is a collection of steam-driven traction engines (OACT).

LEVERINGTON, Cambs 14 TF41
The early-English to perpendicular church carries a 162ft tower and spire. Inside are examples of old glass, a perpendicular font, and the tomb of Oliver Goldsmith's Tony Lumpkin from *She Stoops to Conquer*. The hall is a good 18th-c and earlier house, displaying mullioned windows, gables and a fine staircase (QACT).

LEWANNICK, Cornwall 5 SX28
Lewannick includes a rebuilt church which contains a rare cresset stone, once used to hold lamp-tallow and wicks. Also of particular interest are two Ogham-inscribed stones. Ogam, or Ogham, is an ancient Celtic alphabet comprising strokes placed at angles to a long base line. It is thought the two stones were gravestones, originally raised to people who died some 1,400 years ago.

LEWES, E Sussex 8 TQ41
This county town of East Sussex lies in a downland setting on the River Ouse. Mount Caburn rises to the E, and Mount Harry and Blackcap to the NW.

The castle (AM) is of Norman and later origin, and the Barbican House contains a museum. St Michael's Church carries a curious round tower. St Anne's Church and St John's Church (Southover) are both partly Norman; the former has a notable font of the same period, and the latter houses an engraved stone which covers the grave of one of William the Conqueror's daughters. Most of the old houses are of 18th-c date, and are best seen in Keere Street – where remains of the town wall also exist – and in the High Street. A house belonging to Ann of Cleves exists in Southover, and is dated 1559. It now contains a folk museum which includes a remarkable collection of ironwork. The 18th-c market tower contains the town bell.

John Evelyn the diarist attended Lewes grammar school from 1630 to 1637, and occasionally lived in Southover Grange (1572). Remains of St Pancras Priory, founded in 1095 and once the most important Cluniac house in Britain, exist in the area. Dr Gideon Mantell was a well-known geologist who lived in the High Street. His house displays capitals in the form of ammonite fossils. Bull House, once the home of Tom Paine the pamphleteer, is a half-timbered 15th-c building noted for its carved satyrs.

Large processions take place here on Guy Fawkes night. The Snowdrop Inn commemorates an avalanche of 1836, in which people inhabiting local cottages were killed. A battle took place to the W of the town in 1264, when Henry III was defeated by Simon de Montfort and his baron army. An obelisk to local martyrs stands E on Cliffe Hill.

South Malling and its 17th-c church, late 17th-c deanery, and Malling House of 1710 lies N of the town. Excavations on Itford Hill, 4m S on the right bank of the Ouse, have revealed interesting relics of the late bronze age.

LEYBOURNE, Kent 9 TQ65
A village 5m NW of Maidstone, where the restored church contains a rare heart shrine in the north aisle. Remains of a Norman castle include a fine old gateway, and now form one wing of a modern house. Bradbourne House, a notable example of early 18th-c brickwork, lies 1½m SE. It now serves as the East Malling Fruit Research Station.

LEYBURN, N Yorks 22 SE19
Situated above the River Ure in Wensleydale, this old market town is near a 2m-long limestone scar known as The Shawl. The latter provides a noted walking area and viewpoint. To the E is 18th-c Constable Burton Hall, and the Elizabethan house of Walburn Hall lies 4m N on the Richmond road.

LEYSDOWN, Kent 9 TR07
Views across the widening Thames estuary towards Foulness island and the Maplin Sands are available from this developing Isle-of-Sheppey resort. The beach allows access for bathing, and the cliffs of Warden Point lie NW.

LICHFIELD, Staffs 18 SK10
This city is of great age and considerable architectural distinction. The cathedral, although much-restored, is still a fine

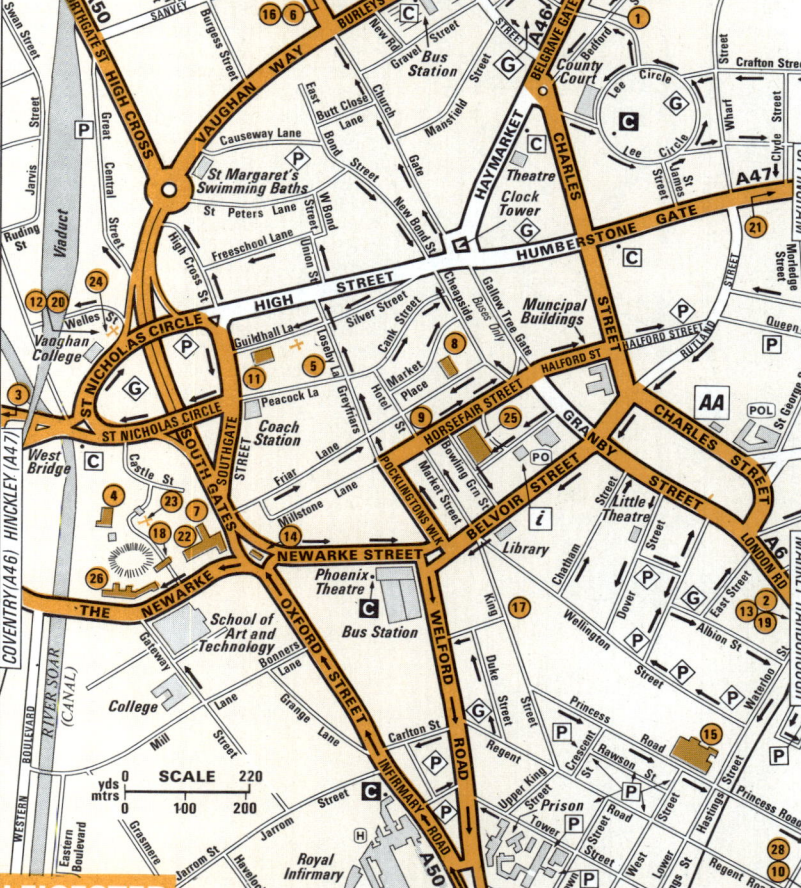

1 Belgrave Hall (museum)
2 Botanic Gardens
3 Bow Bridge
4 Castle Remains
5 Cathedral
6 Cavendish House
7 Chantry Ho (Newark Houses Museum)
8 Corn Exchange
9 County Rooms
10 De Montfort Hall
11 Guildhall
12 Jewry Wall Museum
13 Locomotive Museum
14 Magazine Gate (regimental museum)
15 Museum
16 Museum of Technology
17 New Walk
18 Newark Turret Gate
19 Racecourse
20 Roman Baths
21 Scraptoft Hall
22 Skeffington Ho (Newark Houses Museum)
23 St Mary's Church
24 St Nicholas' Church
25 Town Hall
26 Trinity Hospital Chapel
27 University of Leicester
28 War Memorial

example of early-English and decorated styles. Its three spires form a notable landmark, and are known as the Ladies of the Vale. Lady chapel contains lovely 16th-c Herkenrode glass, and Chantrey's famous group named Sleeping Children exists in the choir aisle. Old buildings exist in The Close and include the former Bishop's Palace, which was built in the 17thc and later enlarged.

Dr Johnson's parents lie in St Michael's church, which bears a 15th-c tower. St Chad's church with its very ancient tenor bell, and St John's Hospital with its eight tall chimneys, are both of interest. Stowe Pool is picturesque. Dr Johnson was born in an old house in Market Square, now a Johnson Museum (OACT), and the Swan Inn has various associations with this famous man.

Timbered 16th-c Lichfield House stands in Bore Street and has been restored. Other notable personages born in Lichfield include Elias Ashmole, Joseph Addison, David Garrick, and Erasmus Darwin. Remains of the friary are now incorporated in a school. Several ancient customs are observed each year: the Old Fair on Shrove Tuesday; St George's Court on April 23; the Court of Arraye on Whit-Monday; the Sheriff's Ride on or about September 8; and the Johnson Celebrations on the Saturday nearest September 18.

LIDDINGTON, Leicester 19 SP89
Uppingham lies 2m NW of this attractive village. The fine old hospital, or Bede House, was formerly a palace of the Bishops of Lincoln and contains an attractive panelled hall (AM). The garden turret is pierced by an opening for pedestrians. Beautiful workmanship of c1635 is displayed by the chancel of the local church.

LIDGATE, Suffolk 14 TL75
It is thought that a 15th-c brass in the local Norman and later church may have been raised to John Lidgate, the early-English poet. He was born in Suffolk House, a timber-and-brick building of the period, in 1375. Extensive castle earthworks can be seen here.

LILLESHALL, Salop 17 SJ71
An enormous 17th-c Leveson monument can be seen in the largely 13th-c church, and remains of 12th-c Lilleshall Abbey (AM) lie 1¼m S. The modern hall stands in extensive grounds, and is now a national recreation centre.

LIMPLEY STOKE, Wilts 6 ST76
Attractively situated in the Avon Valley to the S of Bath, this small spa is S of an aqueduct which carries the Kennet and Avon Canal across the river and railway. A curious Saxon arch can be seen in the church.

LIMPSFIELD, Surrey 8 TQ45
Old houses in this pleasant Holmesdale-Valley village include the notable 16th- to 18th-c Detillens (OACT). The restored church dates from the 12thc and later. The composer Frederick Delius, who died in 1934, is buried in the churchyard. Access to the church is by a 14th-c lych-gate.

LINBY, Notts 18 SK55
Papplewick Castle Mill of 1785 is associated with James Watt, and two village crosses are respectively of medieval and 17th-c origin. Papplewick Hall lies E and dates from 1787. The Hall is a Georgianized structure.

LINCOLN, Lincs 19 SK97
The old town of Lincoln rises from the N bank of the River Witham, on a slope crowned by the splendid cathedral 1072.

Newport Arch (AM), the only surviving Roman example to span an English street, is a relic of the walled Roman city *Lindum Colonia*. The cathedral dates from the 11th to 15thc, has a fine west front, stately triple towers – of which the central tower is a grand 14th-c example – St Hugh's Choir, and the lovely Angel Choir at the east end. The famous Lincon Imp is also in the structure's E section. A choir screen and two rose windows are notable; other features include fine wood-carving, old glass, and a notable 13th-c Chapter House. Of particular interest are the black marble Tournai font, and the best-preserved of four existing copies of Magna Carta. An important collection of Diocesan plate, the first of its kind in an Anglican cathedral, can be seen. Wren built the library and north Cloister Walk in 1674.

The Close, known as Minster Yard, contains the Cantalupe Chantry House, Vicars' Court, a fine tithe barn of 1440, the Bishop's Palace, and the Exchequer Gate. The castle is of 11th-c and later origins (AM, OACT). Also of interest are the 12th-c Jew's House, Aaron the Jew's House, and John of Gaunt's Stables which were once the Guildhall of St Mary (AM). High Bridge carries the High Street over the Witham and has several old houses (AM), and of particular note

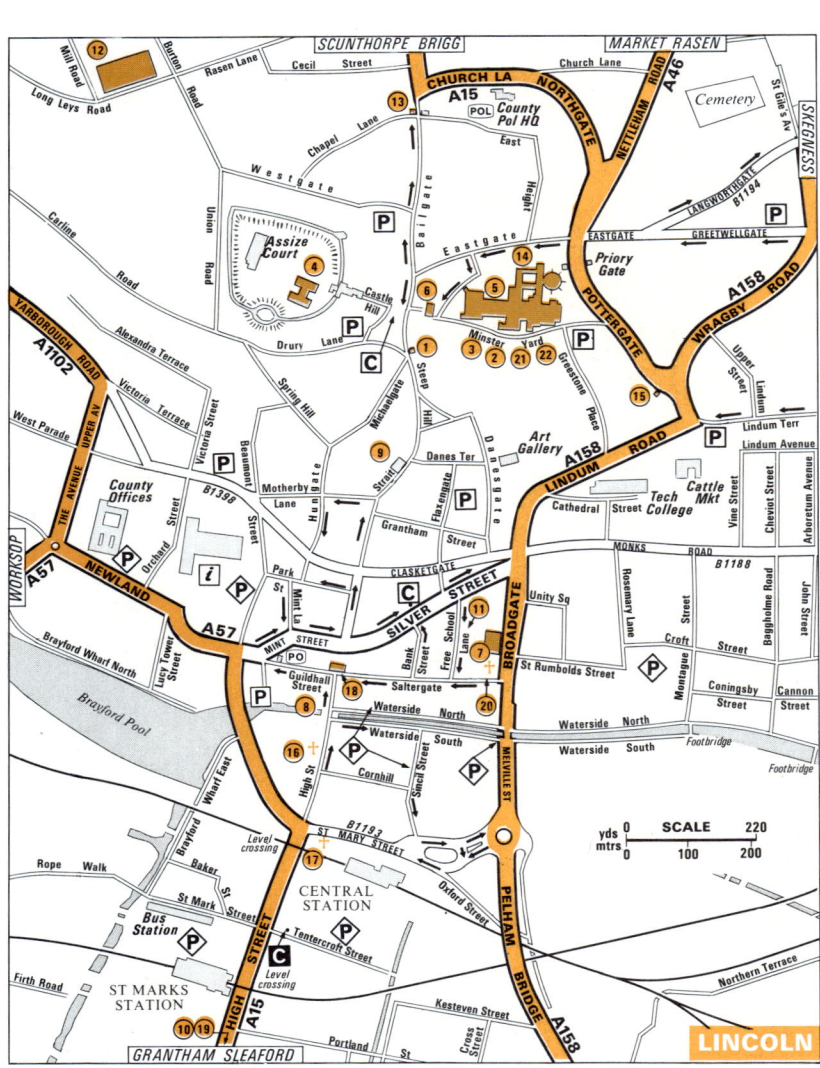

1 Aaron the Jew's House
2 Bishop's Palace
3 Cantalupe Chantry House
4 Castle
5 Cathedral
6 Exchequer Gate
7 Greyfriars (museum)
8 High Bridge
9 Jew's House
10 John of Gaunt's Stables
11 Library
12 Museum of Lincolnshire Life
13 Newport Arch
14 North Cloister Walk
15 Potter Gate
16 St Benedict's Church
17 St Mary-le-Wigford's Church
18 Stonebow
19 St Peter-at-Gowt's Church
20 St Swithin's Church
21 Tithe Barn
22 Vicar's Court

are the Potter Gate and Stonebow (AM).

The Greyfriars was once used as a school and now houses a museum. Three of the parish churches – St Benedict, St Mary-le-Wigford, and St Peter-at-Gowts – have Saxon towers. The modern church of St Swithin preserves a Roman altar stone. A museum of Lincolnshire life has been opened in the former Burton-Road barracks.

LINDFIELD, W Sussex 8 TQ32
Considered one of Sussex's loveliest villages, Lindfield includes numerous old houses and a green. Old Place and Pax Hill, the latter to the NE, are interesting old buildings. Great Walstead and timbered East Mascalls are old manor houses to the E.

LINDISFARNE, Northumberland 31 NU14
Also known as Holy Island, Lindisfarne is now designated an area of outstanding natural beauty, and is partly a national nature reserve. A channel that separates the island from the mainland is covered at high tide. The abbey remains are of late-Norman date and incorporate a small museum. This building is described in Scott's *Marmion* and stands near the 12th- to 13th-c parish church, which displays an inscribed pillow stone. Remains of St Cuthbert's Cross are known as the petting stone and exist in the churchyard.

Sir Edwin Lutyens was responsible for the restoration of a small 16th-c castle that stands on a rocky point of the island (NT, OACT).

LINDSEY
Lindsey is the largest of Lincolnshire's county divisions, occupying over half the total acreage and comprising the high Wolds of the N and the coastal marsh lands. The N sector fringes the Humber estuary and has now been incorporated in the new county of Humberside.

LINDSEY, Suffolk 15 TL94
The 14th-c village church lost its tower in 1836, and now has a weather-boarded bell-turret. A little to the SW at Rose Green is the thatched 13th-c St James's Chapel (AM), with a Tudor doorway.

LINGFIELD, Surrey 8 TQ34
Largely rebuilt in the 15thc, the collegiate church houses notable monuments, brasses, and carved stalls. A number of old houses exist in Lingfield, plus a restored cross near the quaint village lock-up. The college dates from c1700, and New Place from 1617. Pollard Cottage originates from the 15thc. A racecourse is situated outside the town.

LINKINHORNE, Cornwall 5 SX37
One of the highest towers in Cornwall is borne by the 15th-c granite-built church, rising to a height of 120ft. Near the village is the well-preserved 15th-c holy well of St Melor.

LINTON, Cambs 14 TL54
Timbered and plastered houses are a feature of this picturesque River-Granta town. The 13th-c and later church houses interesting monuments and brasses, and near by is the half-timbered Trinity Guildhall. The village college is one of a Cambridgeshire group which was inaugurated at Sawston in 1930. It dates from 1938.

LIPHOOK, Hants 8 SU83
A remarkable collection of old steam-driven fair vehicles and a miniature railway exist in the wooded gardens of Hollycombe, on the Midhurst road. The Royal Anchor is a fine old coaching-inn.

LISKEARD, Cornwall 5 SX26
Local miners once brought their metal to this Stannary town for weighing, assaying, and taxation. The much-restored mainly 15th-c church displays a 17th-c carved pulpit, and a tower of 1902. A bull ring can be seen in the castle park, and its situation affords wide views. Dobwalls Forest Miniature Railway, utilizing steam-hauled trains, lies to the W on the Bodmin road.

LITTLE BADDOW, Essex 9 TL70
The church has a 14th-c tower, a monument of 1639, and a 15th-c painting of St Christopher. Near by stands the 14th- and 15th-c timbered Old Hall.

LITTLE BARDFIELD, Essex 14 TL63
Little Bardfield church carries a partly-Saxon tower and contains an organ of c1700. The hall is 16thc and later, and almshouses of 1774 are of interest.

LITTLE BERKHAMPSTEAD, Herts 8 TL20
Stratton's Observatory is a tall brick tower built by Admiral Stratton in 1789. Bishop Ken, who ministered to Charles II at his death and attended Monmouth's execution, was born in this village. He was one of the seven Bishops to be sent to the Tower in 1688, and died in 1711. Bayfordbury, to the NE, is of late 18th- and early 19th-c date.

LITTLEBOROUGH, Gt Manchester 22 SD91
A cotton manufacturing town with a number of old weavers' cottages, Littleborough includes the Town House of c1798. An interesting stretch of paved Roman road known as Blackstone Edge, perhaps the finest example of its kind to have survived in England, can be seen on the moors 2m E. However, its ancestry is a subject for debate. Both Celia Fiennes in 1698, and Daniel Defoe in 1724, visited the area and recorded their journeys. Defoe described the bleak Pennine moors as the Andes of England.

LITTLEBOROUGH, Notts 19 SK88
King Harold and his army crossed the River Trent by a local ford on their way to the Battle of Hastings in 1066, and a passenger ferry has plied across the river here since Roman times. The small Norman church shows herringbone masonry.

LITTLE BREDY, Dorset 6 SY58
Delightful views down the Bride Valley can be enjoyed from this estate village. Notable archaeological sites in the area include the Kingston Russell stone-circle, the remarkable Poor-Lot bronze-age cemetery, and a well-preserved Celtic field system.

LITTLEBURY, Essex 14 TL53
Littlebury is a small River-Cam village. The rebuilt church has a good 15th-c wooden font cover. Gatehouse Farm is of Tudor origin, and the ancient earthworks of Ringhill Camp lie 1m S.

LITTLE EASTON, Essex 14 TL62
The mainly-perpendicular church in this River-Chelmer village contains medieval paintings, old brasses, and Maynard monuments. The manor house is of 16th- to 18th-c date and includes an old barn.

LITTLE GADDESDEN, Herts 8 SP91
This attractive village includes a perpendicular church which houses several interesting monuments. John o' Gaddesden's House dates from the 15thc or earlier, and the manor house is partly Elizabethan. Ashridge House, rebuilt in 1808 by James Wyatt, lies ¾m S. The latter now serves as the Ashridge Management College (OACT), and is a large gothic-revival mansion which includes a 13th-c crypt, a main hall with a hammerbeam roof, and fan-vaulting in the main tower and chapel. It stands in magnificently wooded grounds which were landscaped by Capability Brown. The estate is largely NT property and includes 700ft Ivinghoe Beacon – a fine viewpoint. Also in the area are the Bridgewater Monument, Frithsden Beeches, and Aldbury and Berkhamsted commons.

LITTLE GIDDING, Cambs 14 TL18
Nicholas Ferrar came to Little Gidding in 1625, to found a community which would lead a life of prayer and good works. He and his family rebuilt the little church of St John the Evangelist, founded a school, and looked after the poor and needy. The beliefs of the community inspired one of T S Eliot's *Four Quartets*. The tiny church contains Ferrar memorials, plus a notable example of Charles I's Royal Arms. This heraldic work is embroidered in silk and gold thread. A late 15th-c brass eagle lectern can also be seen in the church.

LITTLE GLEMHAM, Suffolk 15 TM35
The church has a good Norman doorway and houses 18th-c monuments. Queen Anne furniture can be seen in the large 17th-c hall, and the house itself stands in 350-acre grounds (OACT).

LITTLE HADHAM, Herts 14 TL42
Little Hadham is an attractive village with a fine red-brick Elizabethan hall standing a little to the E. The church, mainly of 13th-c origin, displays a notable timbered south porch.

LITTLEHAMPTON, W Sussex 8 TQ00
Littlehampton once served as an important port on the River Arun. Amenities for the holiday-maker include good bathing, sands, river boating, and a fair. The local museum is devoted to marine and sailing exhibits. Across the Arun, 3m W at Atherington, is the tiny early-English chapel of Bailiff's Court.

LITTLE HEMPSTON, Devon 5 SX86
A rare 14th-c manor house lies next to the 15th-c church in this village. A characteristic Devon tower and an old screen are features of the latter building.

LITTLE HORKESLEY, Essex 15 TL93
Josselyns is a well-restored 16th-c half-timbered house. The church was rebuilt after being destroyed during the last war, and contains five brasses. A cross of 1412 is particularly notable.

LITTLE MALVERN, Herefs & Worcs 12 SO74
Little Malvern church was formerly part of a Benedictine priory and dates from 12th- to 15th-c periods. It houses an interesting 14th-c screen. The neighbouring 15th-c court was probably the prior's lodging, and includes an east window containing 15th-c stained glass depicting Edward IV and his family.

LITTLE MAPLESTEAD, Essex 15 TL83
The curious round church is the smallest of four examples still in existence, and dates from the 13thc. Later restoration is evident, and it formerly belonged to the Knights Hospitallers. Dynes Hall lies 2m SW and dates from Elizabethan and Queen Anne periods.

LITTLE MARLOW, Bucks 8 SU88
Situated near the River Thames, Little Marlow includes a gabled Jacobean manor house and a Norman to 15th-c church displaying examples of 15th-c glass. Edgar Wallace was buried here in 1932.

LITTLE MISSENDEN, Bucks 8 SU99
Chiltern countryside surrounds this village, and the partly early-English church contains notable medieval wall-paintings. The manor house is of Jacobean origin and Missenden House dates from 1729.

LITTLEMORE, Oxon 13 SP50
Littlemore, 2½m SE of Oxford, includes a gothic-revival church with rich screenwork and a pinnacled font cover, and is associated with Cardinal Newman, once vicar of the parish.

LITTLE MORETON HALL, Cheshire 17 SJ85
Perhaps the finest of its type in England, a beautiful black-and-white gabled house was built here between 1559 and 1589. Its approach is guarded by a gatehouse, and the building is surrounded by a moat. Main features include a notable long gallery, great hall, and carved gables. Furniture and pewter of the same period are displayed inside (NT, OACT).

LITTLEPORT, Cambs 14 TL58
The River Ouse runs through this Fenland town, which was the scene of rioting when the marshes were first drained. Five fenmen were hanged and several others transported as a result of this unrest. A lofty tower is carried by the perpendicular church.

LITTLE SALKELD, Cumbria 26 NY53
Well-known 'Long Meg and Her Daughters' is a bronze-age stone circle which, next to Stonehenge, is the largest in the country. It is dominated by the peak of 2,930ft Cross Fell, the monarch of the Pennines.

LITTLE STONHAM, Suffolk 15 TM16
Magpie Inn lies on the Ipswich to Norwich road, and has an interesting gallows sign. Clock House is of partly 14th-c date.

LITTLE THURLOW, Suffolk 14 TL65
Sir Steven Soane's fine 16th-c monument lies in the church. He built the village's beautiful red-brick almshouses, and founded the school in 1614.

LITTLETON, Surrey 8 TQ06
Millais painted the window of this pretty hamlet's church, and the building itself preserves twenty-four faded colours of the Grenadier Guards. Restored choir stalls, pews, and a screen of c1500 are also of interest. The tall brick-built tower is of 16th- to 18th-c date. Queen Mary Reservoir is one of the largest in England.

LITTLETON, Herefs & Worcs 12 SP04
Littleton includes three small Avon-Valley villages – North, Middle, and South Littleton. Middle Littleton includes a notable complex of buildings comprising a manor house, tithe barn, dovecote, and ancient church; the latter incorporates the embattled Smith chapel of 1532. South Littleton shows a beautiful old house dated 1721, near the Norman to 14th-c church. A carved Norman font is a feature of the latter.

LIVERPOOL, Merseyside 17 SJ39
Plan on page 268
Liverpool is an important shipping, university, and cathedral city situated on the Mersey estuary. A settlement has existed here for some time – the north bank of the Mersey bore a community as long ago as the 1st-c AD. This had grown into a thriving fishing village by 1200, and was granted a charter by King John. Much later the town expanded with the onset of heavy trade with the West Indies, and also became connected with the slave trade. However, it was not until the introduction of steamships in the 1840's that Liverpool began to take on its present form.

The famous dockside frontage extends for 7m and forms one of the finest systems to be found anywhere. The landing stage is the largest floating quay in the world, and stretches for ½m on floating pontoons. Leeds and Liverpool Canal terminates here. The 17-storey Royal Liver Building rises to 295ft, and displays two towers surmounted by legendary liver birds. It is flanked by the Cunard building and the Dock Board offices, and the three buildings combine to form an impressive waterfront.

The new Anglican Cathedral by Sir Giles Gilbert Scott was begun in 1904 and displays notable stained glass and a fine organ. In striking contrast is the new RC Cathedral of Christ the King, designed by Sir F Gibberd in 1959 and consecrated in 1967. Features of the latter include a stained-glass tower and a central white-marble altar. Sir Edwin Lutyens conceived a plan for this building in 1933, but the only part of his design to reach fruition was the remarkable crypt which is of particular note.

Restored Bluecoat Chambers are situated in School Lane and date from 1714. St George's Hall of 1854 was designed by Harvey Lonsdale Elwes, at the age of 24. John Wood of Bath designed the town hall in 1749, which was later enlarged by James Wyatt. The restored museum and Walker Art Gallery are also notable. The old parish church of St Nicholas was rebuilt in 1952, except for the tower of 1815, and stands in a memorial garden facing Pierhead. Several good Georgian houses can be seen in the town.

Gladstone was born at 62 Rodney Street, and Felicia Hemans at 118 Duke Street. The Queensway road tunnel of 1934 runs under the Mersey, and was duplicated by the Kingsway tunnel in 1971. Both link with Birkenhead. Liverpool has two leading football teams and is traditionally the home of comedians and other entertainers. The airport lies SE near Speke.

LIZARD, Cornwall 4 SW61
Lizard Point is the southernmost point of England. It takes its name from the Cornish *lis*, meaning place, and *ard*, meaning high. Splendid cliff walks are available in the area and the coastal scenery is magnificent. Sandy beaches can be found at Housel Bay, ½m E, and also in several charming coves. The most notable scenery is around Kynance Cove, immediately to the NW. Cornish heath grows in profusion here and the cliffs are coloured with the green, red, and purple of serpentine rock. A number of caves exist along the coast. Goonhilly Downs lie inland, and are the site of the Post Office's satellite radio-tracking station. The Lizard country is now designated an area of outstanding natural beauty. Landewednack Church dates from the 15thc, has a tower built of local serpentine, and houses an inscribed 15th-c font.

LLANYBLODWELL, Salop 17 SJ22
A bridge across the River Vyrnwy dates from 1710, and the Horseshoe Inn is of 16th-c origin. The church houses a fine screen and displays a detached tower and spire. Excavations have taken place on the site of Owen Glendower's former castle, 4m N at Sycharth.

LOCKINGTON, Leics 18 SK42
This village includes a highly-interesting church containing notable wooden fittings and prominent Royal Arms of 1704.

LODDON, Norfolk 15 TM39
Loddon's fine 15th-c church contains a screen displaying painted panels, and the church at ½m N Chedgrave has a notable enriched Norman doorway. Crossways Farm is dated 1669.

LODORE FALLS, Cumbria 21 NY21
Situated at the S extremity of Derwentwater, Lodore Falls lie near the River Derwent. Bowder Stone is a curious 2,000-ton formation sited 1¼m S.

LODSWORTH, W Sussex 8 SU92
This attractive village includes a much-restored church with a tower dating from c1300. The Dower House dates from 1728, and nearby Great House is contemporary. Walling of 13th-c origin can be seen at the manor house.

LOFTHOUSE, N Yorks 22 SE17
Lofthouse lies in Upper Nidderdale, near the notable How Stean Gorge. Access to the latter is by foot. Scarhouse and Roundhill Reservoirs lie farther N and high up in the moors. Gouthwaite reservoir lies to the SE and is drained by the River Nidd.

LOFTUS, Cleveland 22 NZ71
Loftus is a hill-side town which is involved in the production of iron and steel. Boulby Cliff rises nearly 700ft to the NE, and is one of the highest in England.

London

LONDON

Modern London is the culmination of 2,000 years of incredible history, the result of some 20 centuries of crushing setbacks and spectacular recoveries. It has suffered the maraudings of hostile peoples, the depredations of fire, and the indiscriminate slaughter wreaked by recurring plagues. Yet after each blow it has risen to even greater strength than before.

The name *Londinium* has Celtic roots and suggests that an early British settlement existed here before the coming of the Romans. Julius Caesar surveyed the coast in the years 55 and 54BC, but it is not certain that he ever ascended the Thames this far. The known history of London began with the serious Roman occupation of AD43, when Aulus Plautius started his seven or eight year rule of the country under the Emperor Claudius. The site chosen by the invading forces was a natural stronghold, a little mound rising above miles of flat marshland at a point where the river was narrow enough to be bridged. This mound, now known as Cornhill, was later to become the nucleus of the City of London and the heart of the capital.

Less than a century after the establishment of the community, *Londinium* boasted a $3\frac{1}{8}$m wall enclosing some 330 acres of ground, a bridge over the Thames, its own forum, the largest basilica outside Rome itself, and six main road gates. The bridge was the only permanent link with the south bank of the river until the completion of Westminster Bridge in 1750. Although the development of the community was rapid, it was not entirely trouble free. Its early growth was disturbed by the hostile British, in particular the attacks made by Queen Boadicea and her Iceni tribesmen in AD60.

Construction work in the City *ie* the excavation of deep foundations for new buildings, has revealed much of *Londinium* – in several cases a good fifteen feet below the present surface level.

AD410 saw the degeneration of the Roman Empire and the consequent evacuation of Roman forces from Britain. Their departure marked the beginning of a 61-year period of obscurity for London, which the *Anglo-Saxon Chronicle* tells us was alleviated by the Saxon invasion in AD471. It relates that Hengist and his son Eric fought the British at Crayford, after which some 4,000 Britons lay dead on the battlefield and the residue of the army fled to London. The Saxons seem to have occupied London for the early part of the 6thc, although archaeological evidence of their culture is very sparse. Traces of a Saxon church have been discovered in the crypt of St Bride's, Fleet Street. The Venerable Bede wrote that London was the ecclesiastical capital of the East Saxons, and a market for overland and sea-faring traders in c720. He also stated that St Augustine sent Mellitus from his Canterbury mission to preach to the East Saxons, and that Ethelbert, the Christian King of Kent, built a church dedicated to St Paul. In spite of these efforts the inhabitants of London appear to have remained unconverted for a further 50-odd years.

Vikings from Denmark and Norway sailed up the Thames to plunder London at the end of the 8thc, but Alfred recovered the city in 886 and reconstituted it as a burh – a fortified town garrisoned by men who held certain privileges within the community and surrounding land. Alfred's son-in-law, the Mercian alderman Ethered, was placed in charge of the burh. London stood unconquered during later Danish invasions, and the city prospered under the influence of traders from France, the Low Countries, and Rhineland. It grew to become the largest city in the realm – bigger than Alfred's then capital Winchester – and its importance can be measured by the fact that nearby Kingston became the place of coronation. Kingston was superseded by Westminster, and the great abbey forms the sepulchre of the last of the old English kings – the saintly Edward the Confessor. Harold, not of the royal line but nevertheless the most powerful man in England at the death of Edward, succeeded to the throne. He successfully defended the country against various would-be invaders, but died during his last battle against William of Normandy in 1066.

This was a turning point in the history of both London and England, and the last conquest of England by a foreign power.

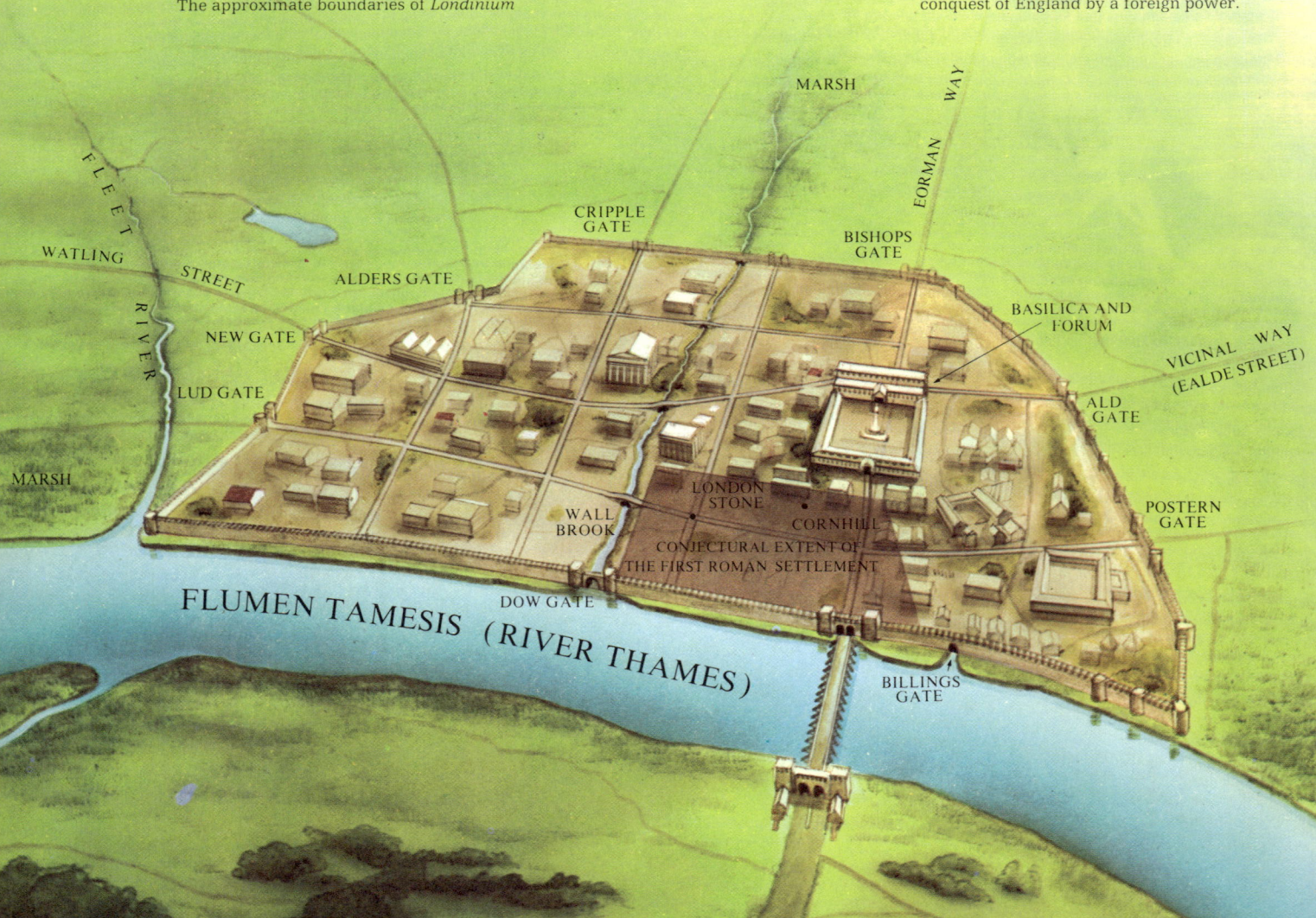

The approximate boundaries of *Londinium*

LONDON

William became Lord of the Normans and King of the English, and was crowned in Westminster Abbey on Christmas Day of 1066; London was his capital and seat of power. A great many of the Normans that settled in London had commercial interests on the continent, and were largely responsible for the foundation of London crafts and trades. They also initiated changes in adminstration that took place in the City during the 12thc.

Civic improvement was usually as a result of royal concessions – in exchange for money or goodwill – and the capital just after the Conquest was more like a shire of various parishes, manors, and estates than a municipal body. This gradually changed as the capital expanded. A mayor and corporation evolved, and the Conqueror's son Henry I granted the City of London its first Charter. Henry II succeeded to the throne after Stephen, nephew of Henry I, and would only concede the citizens' right to plead in their own court. Richard I followed suit, but the first year of King John's reign saw the Sheriffwicks of London and Middlesex restored to the people. Confirmation of this was by charter in 1215, with the proviso that each mayor – then an officer of the Crown – should be presented to the king. Henry Fitz Alwyn was the first Mayor of London and held office for about nineteen years. A new mayor was elected annually.

An Act of 1585 divided the administrative and legislative part of the capital into wards, each of which had a burgess with powers similar to those held by the aldermen's deputies in the City of London. This was a great step towards the welding of the city into a cohesive body, but the latter half of the 16thc also saw less healthy influences. Suppression, currency inflation, and unemployment reacted against the economies of London and the country as a whole, but this disastrous situation eventually proved to lift the capital to an even higher stage of development. It compelled City of London merchants to restore the currency, launch an all-out export drive to the known world, and sail far and wide in the search for new markets. These merchant adventurers were so successful in their enterprise that they had a profound effect on several centuries of the country's future. London was again prosperous and set upon a course which could only lead to even greater wealth.

The next major setbacks occurred in the 17thc. First the Great Plague of 1665 swept through the population, leaving thousands of victims in its wake and bringing all trade and communication with the outside to a standstill. Then in 1666 a bakery oven in Pudding Lane started the Great Fire, a conflagration which raged through the capital along the already devastated trail of the plague, destroying some four-fifths of the City of London.

Rapid development of past centuries had produced a random hotch-potch of buildings crowded round narrow crooked streets and rife with all types of vermin. Although a great disaster, the fire at least offered the opportunity for London to take a long look at its central area and re-develop it in a manner befitting so great a city. Unfortunately this opportunity was not grasped with the enthusiasm which it merited, a failing that has been shown by the administration of London on the three occasions that the city could have been totally re-designed. After the fire Wren planned a great new layout but was over-ruled and only allowed to rebuild the city churches. The second stage was after Nash had been appointed Chief Commissioner of Woods and Forests in 1806. He completely replanned the West End from Buckingham Palace to Regent's Park, but the only examples of this ambitious scheme to have survived are the splendid Regent's Park Terraces. The third and last opportunity arose after the devastation of the second world war; but there was no Wren, no Nash, and nobody of sufficient ability to replace them. Hopes for a planned London vanished and the indiscriminate erection of huge tower blocks in widely separated areas became the order of the day. Possible exceptions are a few of the East End housing complexes and the City's Barbican development – although the latter is still not finished after some 25 years of work. The opportunity to give London a planned new look may never present itself again.

The committee formed for the post-fire rebuilding included Sir Christopher Wren and comprised six members – three appointed by the king and three by the Corporation. Parliament passed various Acts to facilitate the operation and the next decade saw a new red-brick City of London rise from the ashes of the old. This was dominated by Wren's masterpiece in Portland stone, St Paul's Cathedral. Of the 87 churches destroyed by the fire, Wren personally rebuilt or replaced some 49.

Commercial interests soon recovered from the plague and fire. By the 19thc the complete face of the capital had again changed, with business and manufacturing premises growing from the foundations of older buildings, wide new roads replacing little streets, and the opening of the City and South London line in 1890 – London's first true 'tube train'. The last really great disaster suffered by the capital was the massive indiscriminate bombing of the *blitzkrieg* during the 1939 to 1945 world war. Buildings which had survived the various onslaughts of the last four centuries were utterly destroyed, and thousands of civilians died. But London today is the most recent example of the capital's regenerative power; the bombsites have gone and late 20thc multi-storey building has dominated the historic skyline.

Ever since the capital first crossed the boundaries of the square mile still known as the City, it has continued to push its limits farther and farther into the surrounding countryside. Villages, hamlets, parishes, towns, and cities all became absorbed in the inexorable expansion of London, and later Greater London – a county in its own right. The largest organizational change to take place in recent years was in 1965, when the 87 municipal authorities were merged into 32 Greater London Boroughs. The new divisions encompass all of the old plus some 4,000 acres that used to form the Green-Belt buffer between urban development and the open countryside.

In spite of this rapid growth London has retained its wealth of commons, parks, and open spaces, which are still probably unequalled by any other city in the world.

Places of interest located in London – just a few out of the thousands – are listed below under general headings. They appear in alphabetical order and are located to the special map section that follows this gazetteer. Areas on the edge of Greater London *eg* Blackheath, Chiswick, Greenwich, Hampstead, London (Heathrow) Airport, Highgate, and Twickenham, are listed as individual entries in the main gazetteer of this book.

ABBEYS, CATHEDRALS, AND CHURCHES

CHAPEL OF THE SAVOY vK

Once linked to the old Hospital of St John, built by Henry VII on the site of medieval Savoy Palace, this 16th-c chapel royal has always had close links with the English monarchs. Among its many features are a rich ceiling patterned with quatrefoils, an ancient piscina, and a fine reredos covering the east wall. Included with the latter are canopied statues of St Peter and St Paul, and a 14th-c Madonna which had been hidden beneath the dirt of centuries. Two little representations of Tudor ladies that can be seen kneeling on the chancel walls are survivors of a fire that swept through the chapel in 1864. The curious bronze lectern was raised to Laurence Irving, the actor-son of Sir Henry Irving. Two artists are commemorated by an ornate medieval-style font, and a beautiful bronze relief is in memory of author and actor Henry Esmond. Notable windows include a particularly striking tribute to Richard D'Oyly Carte – the man largely responsible for bringing Gilbert and Sullivan to the public; it has a musical theme.

Other famous people commemorated here include the explorer Richard Lander, Archibald Cameron, who was executed some years after helping Charles Stuart to escape from Culloden, and the 17th-c poet George Wither. The latter lies here and was executed by the Stuarts for selling his country home to provide Cromwell with a troop of horse. The chapel was adapted for the Royal Victorian Order in 1940.

ST BARTHOLOMEW-THE-GREAT vJ

This mainly-Norman church is the oldest in London – apart from the Tower – and has been restored. It was founded by Rahere and once served as the ritual choir of a priory church, and the founder's fine tomb displays a coloured effigy under a rich canopy. A window to Prior Bolton dates from the 16thc. The Elizabethan gateway was discovered by accident during the last war, when a bomb damaged the facade and revealed hitherto unsuspected timbering.

The church lay in an advanced state of neglect for some years, and was variously used as a stable, smithy, and Benjamin Franklin's printing shop. Its restoration was largely due to the efforts of four people – the two architects Sir Aston and William Webb, a Mr Frederick Dove, and a rector who managed to raise some £100,000 during his rectorship.

Nearby Bartholomew Close is where Milton lay low in 1660, where Hogarth the artist was born, and where both Benjamin Franklin and Washington Irving had lodgings. Also nearby is Cloth Fair which contains a rare example of a 17th-c brick-built house (restored), displaying wooden bay windows.

LONDON

St Clement Danes, restyled by Wren in 1680

ST BRIDE'S vJ
A beautiful steeple designed by Sir Christopher Wren surmounts this Fleet Street church, rising to 226ft in tiers of open arches and carrying twelve 18th-c bells. The iron gates were erected in memory of Valentine Knapp by the Newspaper Society, and open on to a churchyard planted with the familiar London plane trees. White and gold are the predominant colours in the great nave and chancel, and the interior of the church is beautifully decorated. Gilded roses and cherubs adorn the arches, lines of flowers curve across the rounded roof, and one of the panelled galleries carries the splendid organ. Box pews accommodate the congregation.

Many famous people are associated with the church and its immediate locality, mostly of publishing and literary reputation. One of the most important is Wynkyn de Worde, whose remains lie in the church. He was a pupil of the great Caxton and came to Fleet Street some 400 years ago to continue his teacher's work in the field of printing; the 600 books he left behind testify to his success. Richard Lovelace and the historical chronicler Richard Baker lie here, in the company of the printer John Nichols and printer/writer Samuel Richardson. Also buried in and near the church are 1,200 victims of the Great Plague – all from the City. The poet Milton lived near St Bride's for a while, and Samuel Pepys was born in the parish.

The present structure is one of the 49-odd churches rebuilt or replaced by Wren to compensate for those destroyed during the Great Fire of London. However it is not now the original Wren church, having been beautifully restored inside after bomb damage. A white-marble font bowl on a grey stem is the only visible link between this and the previous building.

ST CLEMENT DANES vL
A curious though unauthenticated story is attached to the name of this church. Legend has it that the early St Clement's came to be known as the church of the Danes after Hardicanute succeeded his father as king. The remains of this, the second Danish king, are said to lie in the church's foundations. As soon as Hardicanute attained the throne he removed the remains of Harold from the abbey and threw them into the Thames; the story then claims that the body was rescued and re-interred in St Clement's.

Although the Great Fire did not come as far as the church, it was demolished except for the tower in 1680 and rebuilt by Wren. He recased the tower with new stone and surmounted it with obelisks, but the present clock chamber and spire were added in the 18thc by Gibbs. This is the spire of nursery-rhyme fame and its eleven bells ring out the well-known tune *Oranges and Lemons*.

One of the main features of the church is its wealth of carved woodwork. Roses and thistles appear on the vaulting of the apse, and the oak casing round the pillars on which the galleries rest is adorned with festoons and cherubs. The low screen to the chancel displays praying angels, and the stalls show more angels plus portrayals of the Four Evangelists. Also of interest are a 17th-c rector's desk, an iron-banded and studded chest of the 16thc, and a pulpit attributed to Grinling Gibbons.

A brass set into one of the pews shows where Dr Johnson sat, and a portrait plaque commemorates the founder of the first English picture-daily, William Thomas. St Clement's has been well restored as the memorial church of the Royal Air Force and displays the crests of some 900 squadrons in the flooring. It has also long been the adopted church of the London flower sellers.

ST GILES viD
John Milton the poet and Martin Frobisher the explorer are both buried in this church, and Oliver Cromwell was married here. A statue of Milton stands in the churchyard and bears lines from *Paradise Lost*, with scenes from *Paradise Lost* and *Comus* on the pedestal. The oldest surviving monument is dated 1575, and the remains of John Foxe – author of the *Book of Martyrs* – lie near by. Foxe survived the age of religious persecution by fleeing the country, and his book was to be found chained next to the bible in many English churches. John Speed, the famous early cartographer, is also buried here.

The first church to exist on this site was built by Alfune, a friend of Rahere the King's Jester, in the reign of William Rufus. Since then it has been rebuilt twice, and the existing structure is some 400-years old. Lancelot Andrewes, later to become bishop three times running and a contributor to the Authorized version of the Bible, was vicar here; another local vicar was Samuel Annesley, whose daughter became the mother of famous John Wesley.

Part of a bastion from the Roman London Wall is preserved in the churchyard, and the excavated gate of a Roman fort can be seen near by. The latter is below ground level and can be visited.

ST JOHN ixH
This remarkable church was built in baroque style by Thomas Archer between 1713 and 1728, and has been known as Queen Anne's footstool. It sustained considerable damage during the last war, but has been well restored and is now used for secular purposes including concerts. Its Greek-cross plan incorporates four corner towers.

Numerous fine examples of Georgian town houses can be seen in the neighbouring Barton, Cowley, and Lord North Streets.

ST MARGARET'S ixE
This 15th-c church is the official place of worship for the House of Commons, and stands adjacent to the world-famous Westminster Abbey. It is particularly noted for its fashionable weddings – Samuel Pepys, John Milton, and Sir Winston Churchill were all married here. A brass plaque states that Sir Walter Raleigh was buried here, but this is uncertain; he was executed outside in Palace Yard, and his body certainly did lie here for a while, but it is thought that his widow may have removed the corpse to Beddington in Surrey.

The building is surprisingly austere for such notable associations. It has no screen and includes a plain clerestory and eight bays, but the lack of luxurious decoration is made up by the massive host of memorials that line the walls. The old east window was originally ordered to be made by Ferdinand and Isabella of Spain, and part of it portrays Catherine of Aragon – Isabella's daughter – and her fiance Prince Arthur. Arthur died before the window was ready and Catherine married Henry VIII, who sent it to Waltham Abbey where it stayed until brought to St Margaret's in the 18thc. Facing this is the west window, a tribute from America to Raleigh, the founder of Virginia. Many other persons are commemorated by windows, including the courageous Admiral Blake whose body Charles II caused to be removed from here, John Milton, Caxton the pioneer of printing, and Goldsworthy Gurney – the Cornishman who pioneered road steam coaches.

The front pew has always been reserved for the use of the Speaker of the House of Commons.

ST MARTIN-IN-THE-FIELDS ivL
Although the fields of St Martin's have long been replaced by roads, buildings, and the paving of Trafalgar Square, their memory lingers on in the name of this superb church. Designed in 1726 by the Wren protege James Gibbs, it is the parish church of Buckingham Palace and displays one of the most impressive classical porticoes in London. A bust of Gibbs, executed by Rysbrack, can be seen inside the building. George I was very impressed with his new parish church – so much so that he gave the workmen 100 guineas and became the first churchwarden.

Inside are many interesting architectural features, not the least being the highly decorated roof which curves down in an ellipse. Gibbs considered this shape to be more acoustically sound than any other. Royal boxes are situated above the sanctuary, on either side of the east Ascension window, and it is thought that the stairway leading to the carved and inlaid pulpit may be by Grinling Gibbons. A marble urn on a twisted pedestal serves as a font and is surmounted by a font cover of 1689; the St Martin's that existed here before the present structure saw the christening of Charles II, Francis Bacon, and the founder of Georgia USA, General Oglethorpe.

The crypt was used as a shelter for the homeless between 1930 and 1945, and is almost a church in itself. The Children's Chapel, a domed and colourful little place, is one of its main features. Also of interest are the old whipping post from Trafalgar Square, a model of the church by Gibbs, and several fine sculptures. Famous people buried at St Martin's include Nell Gwynn, the dramatist and soldier George Farquhar, the French sculptor Louis Roubiliac, and Robert Boyle. The latter is famous for his numerous scientific experiments and discoveries. He was a co-founder of the Royal Society and is most universally known for the formulation of Boyle's Law for gases. His interment took place in 1691. H R L (Dick) Sheppard, vicar here from 1914 to 1927, became a well-known radio personality.

St-Martin-in-the-Fields, designed 1726 by James Gibbs

ST MARY-LE-BOW *vi G*
Bow Bells have been famous for centuries, and tradition has it that any Londoner born within range of their sound is a Cockney. They rang curfew times some 600 years ago and, as every Christmas pantomime reminds us, were supposedly the inspiration which helped Dick Whittington over the last leg of his trek to London. Whittington was three times Lord Mayor of London.

A church has existed here since the 11thc, and its name comes from the period of William the Conqueror when the early building was constructed on arches. The present structure was built by Sir Christopher Wren and can be considered one of his finest achievements, but an ancient vaulted crypt still exists under almost the entire length of the building. Some Saxon workmanship is also evident. The structure was almost completely rebuilt – apart from the tower – after second world war damage.

A balcony on the tower was incorporated in memory of an old gallery that used to lean against the earlier building, from which monarchs from the period of Edward I used to watch pageants in Cheapside. The spire is of particular note and is said to have absorbed nearly half of the total building cost. Features of the square interior include a carved Jacobean pulpit, a painting said to be by Salvator Rosa, and an elaborately carved font thought to have been designed by Wren. A tablet to John Milton can be seen on the outside wall of the church, bearing lines by Dryden.

ST PAUL'S *iv M*
Inigo Jones built this church in 1638 and called it the handsomest barn in England. Although it was extensively rebuilt in 1795, the main portico facing E still supports the overhanging roof. St Paul's is the Harvest Festival church of the nearby market and has also been adopted by actors; memorials to several stage celebrities can be seen inside. London's first *piazza* or square faces the church and was originally laid out for the Duke of Bedford by Inigo Jones.

ST PAUL'S CATHEDRAL *vi G*
Other churches have unquestionably stood on the site which is now graced by this Wren masterpiece – although the actual number is uncertain. If it is assumed that it was King Ethelbert's foundation of c604 that was burnt down in 1086, then a feasible number would be two with the present building as the third. The cathedral's predecessor is generally known as Old St Paul's and was begun by Bishop Maurice in 1087. The project was so vast that work went on well into the 13thc, and the heavy Norman architecture became merged with the lighter and more decorative gothic style. This was one of the country's great medieval churches and the religious heart of London; it contained remains of St Erkenwald, King Ethelred, and Bishop William, all of which were recovered from a Saxon cathedral.

Various alterations were conducted during the Reformation, and a fire in 1561 destroyed the spire which was never replaced. The building gradually sank into a steadily worsening condition, with the public using it as a short cut and traders selling their wares in the nave. Plans to stop this desecration included a restoration scheme to be carried out by Inigo Jones. This great architect started the work by adding a Corinthian portico to the west front, but was prevented from continuing by the outbreak of the Civil War. Then, in 1666, the Great Fire of London dealt the last blow and caused irreparable damage to the building.

Sir Christopher Wren had been instructed to examine the cathedral's state of decay and the extent of damage sustained during the war just a few days before the fire. Instead he found himself demolishing the building – with gunpowder, incidentally – planning a new cathedral to form the heart of a devastated City. The foundation stone was laid in 1675 and the next 35 years were taken up with the massive task of construction. December 1697 saw the first service, a thanksgiving for the Treaty of Ryswick (war against Louis XIV of France) held in the choir. Morning Chapel, now known as St Dunstan's, was opened in 1699 and the last stone of the fabric was positioned in 1710. At this stage Wren was taken off the job and his ideas for the mosaic decoration of the inside of the dome never reached fruition. Instead the task fell on the shoulders of Sir James Thornhill who produced the present monochrome paintings.

The dome has a diameter of 112ft and the predominant material used in the construction of the cathedral is Portland stone. The overall height of the structure, from the ground to the top of the surmounting cross, is 365ft. Numerous monuments inside the building include a carving of the poet John Donne by Nicholas Stone – the only monument to have survived the Great Fire. Tombs of famous soldiers, sailors, and artists, including Nelson, Wellington, Jellicoe, Reynolds, and Turner exist in the crypt. A small charge is levied for entrance to the crypt, Whispering Gallery, Stone Gallery, and Golden Gallery; the latter two afford superb views over London and

LONDON

St Paul's Cathedral, designed by Wren and completed 1710

the Thames. Second world war bombing resulted in damage to the choir and the destruction of the High Altar, but restoration work has rectified most of this. Notable works of art in the cathedral include carvings by Grinling Gibbons, ironwork by Jean Tijou, and an organ commissioned from Schmidt in 1694. Both the restored Chapter House of 1712 and the Deanery of 1670 still stand as built by Wren.

ST STEPHEN vi K
Another of Wren's works sufficiently impressive to be considered one of the great architect's masterpieces, St Stephen's displays a dome which can only be thought of as a smaller version of that carried by St Paul's Cathedral. This rests on arches and pillars over the church's central space, and is adorned with rich panelling and extravagant decoration. It was constructed as an experiment before the larger version at St Paul's, and many experts believe it to be the finest in the world.

Most of the woodwork in the building survives from the period of Wren's lifetime, and the ornate font cover has been attributed to Grinling Gibbons. The pews are the exception and are of more recent date. Benjamin West executed the fine painting of the Burial of St Stephen, and many notable monuments exist in the church. Sir John Vanbrugh the architect (1664 to 1726) is buried in the vaults.

St Stephen's rather austere tower may be partly medieval, and is adorned with a lantern supported by slim pillars.

SOUTHWARK CATHEDRAL xi B
This old cathedral, considered by some to be the finest example of gothic architecture in London after Westminster Abbey, stands near the south end of London Bridge. It has been a 7th-c Saxon Sisterhood, a 9th-c college for priests under St Swithin, and a 12th-c priory. The priory was succeeded by an English building – the choir and Lady Chapel of which survive – and the structure has variously served as a bakehouse, pig-fattening shed, and police court. It was saved from complete degeneration by the Oxford Movement in the 19thc, who restored it and elevated its status to that of a cathedral with a see extending almost to Chichester.

The fine tower, which stayed aloof from most troubles affecting the main body of the church, has a history all of its own. The only contemporary pictures of the Great Fire were sketched from here by Wenceslaus Holland, and guns trained on Sir Thomas Wyatt's rebels from the summit stopped their advance. It is a battlemented and pinnacled structure with two 13th-c and two 16th-c stages carrying twelve bells.

Restoration of the church interior was the responsibility of Sir Arthur Blomfield. This enlightened architect studied original drawings of the building before commencing, and then built a new nave in perfect harmony with the 13th-c east half of the church. Thanks to him the north wall preserves a Norman priest's doorway plus a recess and priors'. doorway of the same period. Examples of 13th-c arcading are also of interest. Several carved columns and a large font are also Norman, and the latter stands on the original Norman floor level – three feet below that of the present.

Remains of a German bomb which penetrated the roof and left scars and pits on the west wall are preserved in a glass case, along with various Roman relics discovered on the site of the church. Sumptuous decorations and superb monuments adorn the interior. The Harvard Memorial Chapel recalls the baptism of John Harvard, founder of the American university that bears his name.

TEMPLE CHURCH v L
Consecration of the round part of this trans-Norman to early-English church took place in 1185. It is the largest of the four round churches existing in England, all of which were built by the Crusaders in the style of Jerusalem's Holy Sepulchre. The consecration was conducted by Heraclius, patriarch of Jerusalem, while he was visiting London in the hope of trying to persuade the king to mount a new crusade. Recumbent effigies of crusaders are a feature of the interior.

The refashioned porch contains a beautiful Norman doorway displaying various shafts, mouldings, and carvings typical of the period's best. The door itself is some 400-years old and displays notable ironwork. Inside, a circle of pointed arches surrounds the nave before continuing as a straight avenue down the choir – a section built some 50 years after the round part of the building. The actual round is covered by a conical roof lined with old paintings, and has a seat with an arcade of 60 pointed arches and capitals running round the wall. Each capital is different, yet all their carved heads display the same remarkable strength of expression. The effigies, many depicted in chain mail and with their weapons, lie on the floor of the round. These include Geoffrey de Mandeville, the Earl of Essex who fought against King Stephen and sacked Cambridge. He died while besieging a castle, and because he was excommunicated by the Pope could not be buried in consecrated ground. The corpse was sealed in lead and hung in a tree until absolved by the church, when it was brought to the Temple and placed in a magnificent tomb of Sussex marble near the door. Near by is the Earl of Pembroke, Regent of England while Richard was in Palestine, and his two sons. Lord de Ros also lies here and may have been at Runymede during the sealing of Magna Carta.

Various other monuments here are of interest, and beneath the floor are the remains of a 13th-c chapel.

WESTMINSTER ABBEY ix E
The first church on this historic site was built by the last of the old English kings, Edward the Confessor. He died within ten days of consecrating the church, and the Benedictine monks for whom he built it buried him within its walls. The actual spot in which he was interred is only a short distance away from the place where his remains now lie.

Remains of the original building comprise the foundations and little else. Some 600 years of building, re-building, and alteration have completely altered the abbey's appearance. The general shape of

LONDON

Westminster Abbey's early-English appearance originated in the 13thc, but was sympathetically sustained during 14th-c building operations

the building is largely due to the first major re-building operation, which was initiated by Henry III in the 13thc. It was he who demolished the Confessor's original structure and gave the new abbey its early-English style. The king was unable to complete the work and building operations continued into the 14thc, conducted by Master of the King's Works Henry Yevele. Yevele followed the original design to the letter, which accounts for the main body of the building appearing to originate from one period. Henry VII built the splendid chapel, and his tomb was commissioned from Torrigiani between 1472 and 1528 by Henry VIII. Sir Christopher Wren and the famous architect Hawksmoor worked on the two main towers during the 18thc.

The interior of the abbey defies any brief description; its historical significance and architectural magnificence are enough to fill several volumes, and the amount of space available here cannot do full justice to its importance. The following notes are intended to serve only as a brief introduction as to what the building offers, and are by no means exhaustive.

All but two of our monarchs have been crowned here since the reign of Edward II, and the Coronation Chair of English oak has been used for this purpose since that time. It incorporates the Stone of Scone, on which the Scottish kings were once crowned, which was appropriated by Edward I in 1297 to demonstrate Scotland's subservience to the English monarchy. One of the most magnificent chapels is that of Henry VII, the Chapel of the Order of Bath. It was built between 1503 and c1512, has been used as a royal burial place, and displays some of the finest work to have survived from this period of English history. It is particularly noted for its fan vaulting and contains the tombs of Elizabeth I and Mary Queen of Scots – plus some 68 other royalties.

Edward the Confessor's Chapel and the Sanctuary lie within the confines of the Ambulatory, which is surrounded by many fine chapels containing the remains of famous members of the nobility and church. Near Poets' Corner, a place where the remains of poets from as far back as Chaucer lie, is a curious altar tomb that used to stand in the Confessor's Chapel. This dates from 1270 and is worth noting for its decoration of mosaic and circles. It was moved from the chapel about 650 years ago to make room for Richard II, and contains the remains of Henry III's deaf and dumb daughter plus other royal children.

A Battle of Britain window in the Royal Air Force Chapel depicts the badges of sixty-three fighter squadrons who participated in the aerial defence of London during the last war. Two recent monuments out of the hundreds that can be seen in the abbey are the Tomb of the Unknown Warrior, commemorating the dead of the first world war, and the Churchill Stone of 1965.

English parliaments met in the nearby Chapter House until 1547, and the building displays a tiled floor and interesting wall-paintings among its many examples of 13th-c work. Westminster School was founded by Edward III and is contained in both Ashburnham House and a collection of buildings adjacent to the abbey. The former is known for its 17th-c staircase.

WESTMINSTER CATHEDRAL *viiiJ*
A modern building in Byzantine style, this RC cathedral was built between 1895 and 1910. John Bentley designed the structure but did not live to see it completed.

Its main feature is a slim campanile built with contrasting bands of stone and brick, rising to 280ft above London. This used to be a well-known feature of the city's skyline, but giant modern developments have now dwarfed its elegant proportions. A lift allows access to the top and a view which is still superb. An octagonal lantern surmounts the tower. Inside is a sculpture by Eric Gill, executed in marble and entitled the Stations of the Cross. Plans to decorate the cathedral walls with mosaic designs have been abandoned. The tombs of Cardinals Wiseman and Manning lie in the crypt. The building was formerly partly obscured by other structures, but recent demolition work has now made it easily visible for the first time.

FAMOUS BUILDINGS

BANQUETING HOUSE *ixB*
This Inigo Jones building stands on the site once occupied by Cardinal Wolsey's house. Henry VIII took possession of the earlier building after Wolsey fell from power, and enlarged it as a royal palace. It was destroyed by fire in 1619, and replaced by the present classical-style building by Jones. Under George I it became a royal chapel, a purpose which it continued to fulfil until the Royal United Services Museum was housed here in 1894. The museum moved from here in 1962 and the Banqueting House was restored to its original function.

The magnificent 115ft-long hall displays a ceiling painting commissioned from Rubens by Charles I in 1634. A few years later in 1649, this king was compelled to step onto the scaffold of execution from one of the windows of the old palace. Restoration includes the dais and chair which was occupied by the king.

BUCKINGHAM PALACE *viiiF*
Buckingham Palace is the London residence of the reigning sovereign, and takes its name from a house that was built here by the Duke of Buckingham and Chandos in 1703. A mulberry garden was planted here to encourage the cultivation and working of silk in the reign of James I, and Buckingham's red-brick house was the first known residence to occupy the site. George III bought it as a dower house for Queen Charlotte in 1761. Remodelling started in 1825, when George IV commissioned John Nash for the alterations, and continued until 1913. The Marble Arch which now stands at Hyde Park once served as an entrance to the palace.

Queen Victoria made the house her London residence, by then again altered by John Nash, and George V employed Sir Aston Webb to reface the east front in 1913. The building's current aspect of quiet grandeur is due to the last architect.

Although the state rooms are strictly out of bounds to the public, access is allowed to the Queen's Gallery and Royal Mews. Pictures and other works of art from the extensive royal collection can be seen in the former, and the Queen's royal carriages can be seen with various vintage cars belonging to the royal family in the latter. Nash designed the stables and coach houses in 1825. Regular investitures held by the Queen to bestow decorations allows guests of the recipients to see more of the building than would normally be possible.

CHARTERHOUSE *vF*
Originally founded as a Carthusian monastery in 1371, this complex of buildings became the private dwelling of a nobleman after the Dissolution of the monasteries in 1537. Thomas Sutton, whose tomb lies in the chapel, bought the Charterhouse estate in 1611 as a hospital and school for 80 old men and 40 boys. The school which was housed here is now situated at Godalming and has become a noted public school.

cont

LONDON

Sir Aston Webb's Admiralty Arch of 1910

Extensive bomb damage sustained during the last war revealed that the original monastery had been considerably extended since the 16thc. War damage has now been carefully repaired, and the great chamber and early-English great hall are of particular interest. The former is considered by some to be one of the finest Elizabethan rooms in England, and displays a marvellous carved panelled mantelpiece and a beautiful ceiling. The great hall was built by the monks in the 15thc and boasts fine wall panelling plus a remodelled hammerbeam roof. Symbolic figures on pedestals carry lines of columns and the black-oak screen shows rich carving. The hall is lit by four large windows which were set in the walls by the Duke of Norfolk some 17 years prior to the Spanish Armada. Apart from Sutton's tomb, the chapel contains many other notable features. These include monuments by Nicholas Stone, James Ryder, and Bernard Janssen, and a fine pulpit of 1613. Ryder carved 24 of the wooden pew heads in 1613. One of the best preserved of the earlier monastic buildings is Wash House Court.

COUNTY HALL   ixF
A modern building dating from 1921 to 1932, County Hall is the administrative headquarters of the Greater London Council and has a 750ft river frontage. It has not yet been completed.

GOVERNMENT OFFICES   ixB
The following government buildings exist in or around Whitehall – Admiralty, Foreign Office, Home Office, Privy Council, Treasury, War Office, etc. The reconstructed houses at 10 and 11 Downing Street are mainly of 18th-c date, and are the official residences of the Prime Minister and Chancellor of the Exchequer of the day. Downing Street was named after Sir George Downing, Secretary to the Treasury in the reign of Charles II. The Prime Minister's house was originally conferred on Robert Walpole, popularly considered the first to hold this office, by George II. Number 14 Downing Street no longer stands, but it is said that Nelson and Wellington met for the only time at this house. Edward Lutyens designed the Cenotaph, which stands in the middle of Whitehall, after the first world war.

Opposite Horse Guards Avenue is a series of offices which were built to a design originally conceived in 1935. These stand on the site of the Tudor Whitehall Palace and include the wine cellars of the former building. This part of Whitehall, known as Parliament Street, was built through the Privy Gardens of the palace in 1752.

GRAY'S INN   vH
This Inn of Court features a hall of 1560, and 18th-c library, and an interesting chapel. Its buildings surround fine gardens and access to the court is by a gate of 1594. The latter has unfortunately had its original finish rendered over with cement. The big garden, called The Walks, is where Sir Walter Raleigh supposedly planted a catalpa tree which he brought from the West Indies. The tree exists, but its origin is doubtful.

Francis Bacon was treasurer of the Inn and may have laid out the gardens during the reign of Queen Elizabeth I; his statue stands on a lawn in South Square. Features of the square include three rows of 17th-c houses, and it is divided from the other square by a block containing the chapel and hall. The chapel has also been refaced, but includes two 400-year-old blocked windows and a 300-year-old oak pulpit.

One of the windows displays two Jacobean glass shields, and the east window includes modern representations of Bishop Juxon, and Archbishops Laud and Whitgift. The hall is noted for its excellent hammerbeam roof, and has windows which display heraldic glass of the 16th and 17thc. The walls are lined with Queen Anne panelling bearing heraldic painting, and Elizabeth I is said to have given the oak screen at the west end. Shakespeare's *Comedy of Errors* was acted here during Christmas of 1594.

GUILDHALL   viG
All that remains of the complex of buildings that once made up the City of London's guildhall is the largely 15th-c Great Hall. The other structures, which included various chambers, vestibules, and lobbies were destroyed or damaged during the last war. The most important of these were the 19th-c Council Chamber and the Aldermen's Court Room. It is ironic that the latter should have escaped the Great Fire of 1666, only to fall victim to the *blitzkrieg*. The recent administrative block was designed by Sir Gilbert Scott and has been occupied since 1958.

The roof of the Great Hall was rebuilt in 1954; the original suffered at the same time as the adjacent buildings were destroyed. The two stained glass windows that can be seen are the only survivors of the raids, and the early 18th-c figures of Gog and Magog were utterly destroyed. Replacements for these were commissioned from David Evans by Alderman Sir George Wilkinson, who was Lord Mayor at the time of their destruction. These semi-mythical giants are featured in the Old Testament and were known as Gogmagog and Corineus in the Elizabethan period. According to legend they represent conflict between Ancient Britons and Trojan invaders in *c*1000 BC. The result of this trouble was supposed to have been the foundation of New Troy, the capital city of Albion and legendary predecessor of London. The representations that were destroyed were set up in 1708, but dummies of the two were carried in midsummer pageants in the 15th and 16thc.

Art treasures previously exhibited in the Guildhall Art Gallery were removed for the period of the last war, and thus escaped the bomb damage that would have resulted when the gallery was destroyed. Part of the gallery has been restored, and these works are again displayed. The Guildhall Museum was formerly housed at the Royal Exchange but is now contained in the Podium. It displays a small collection of clocks and Roman remains, and is due to be moved to the new Museum of London which is being built on a site near by.

HORSE GUARDS   ixB
This is the headquarters of the Household Brigade, also known as the Horse Guards or Life Guards. The front of the building is famous and includes an 18th-c arch surmounted by a clock tower. Horse Guards dates from 1753 and occupies the Tilt Yard of Whitehall Palace. It was built to a design by William Kent. Mounted sentries guard here during the day, and the picturesque Trooping of the Colour is conducted at Horse Guards Parade on the Queen's official birthday. The Old Admiralty of 1725 and 1760 stands near by and displays an Adam façade of 1760. The well-known Admiralty Arch of 1910 was by Sir Aston Webb and leads to The Mall.

HOUSES OF PARLIAMENT (NEW PALACE OF WESTMINSTER)   ixF
Officially known as the New Palace of Westminster, the Houses of Parliament buildings that exist today were designed by Sir Charles Barry and were started in 1840. The House of Lords was occupied by 1847, and the official opening by Queen Victoria took place in 1852. Sir Charles died before the building work was completed, and the latter part of the construction was under the supervision of his son E M Barry.

The original Palace of Westminster was a royal residence from the reigns of Edward the Confessor until Henry VIII, and comprised a walled and moated area of some 12½ acres. Henry VIII dispensed with the palace after it was damaged by fire in 1515 – having by then acquired the unfortunate Wolsey's house and built St James' Palace. Its Chapel of St Stephen was given to the House of Commons by Edward VI in 1547, but another fire destroyed this and the remainder of the palace – except for Westminster Hall, the Crypt Chapel, and

LONDON

The Houses of Parliament, designed by Sir Charles Barry and officially opened by HM Queen Victoria in 1852

the cloisters – in 1834. It is said that the fire was caused literally by red tape – the burning of exchequer tally sticks. The hour bell of the present clock tower was named Big Ben after Sir Benjamin Hall, First Commissioner of Works when the clock was installed in 1858. It weighs 13½ tons and the tower rises to 320ft. Victoria Tower stands at 336ft and is situated S of Old Palace Yard – where Guy Fawkes was executed. Central Tower, an octagonal structure rising some 300ft above the Central Hall, is crowned by an open lantern surrounded by rich ornamentation. The entire building is in a rich gothic style, and displays numerous fine carvings and statues both inside and out. Situated in the north end of the building, the House of Commons was restored in 1950 and incorporates the Churchill Arch.

KENSINGTON PALACE viiA
Kensington Palace was the birthplace and early home of Queen Victoria, who lived here until her accession in 1837. It was also the one-time residence of Queen Mary. William III purchased it in 1689, and it served as a residence for the reigning sovereign until 1760. Before this purchase the building was known as Nottingham House and belonged to the Earls of Nottingham. Wren extensively remodelled it as Kensington Palace in the 17thc, and work by Wren, William Kent, and Grinling Gibbons can be seen in the State Apartments. A notable example of Wren's work is the Orangery of 1704. The palace currently houses the London museum, but this is expected to move to the City.

LAMBETH PALACE ixJ
Originally conceived in the 13thc, this ecclesiastical palace has been adapted and rebuilt on numerous occasions and to many styles. It flourished through Magna Carta, Tudor and Stuart times, fell into ruins after the Commonwealth, was later restored, and finally partly rebuilt during the 19thc. The bombing raids of the last war also took their toll of this ancient foundation, but an interesting gateway of 1490 has come through virtually unscathed. This red-brick construction is situated at the SE corner of the grounds which surround the present building, and is considered one of the finest examples of Tudor brickwork extant. It was built by Archbishop Morton, and is nicknamed Morton's Tower. Lambeth Palace has been the London residence of the Archbishops of Canterbury since c1230. The oldest part that can be seen today is the north side of the cloisters, with the undercroft of the chapel. The chapel itself has been extensively restored after bomb damage but originated in the 13thc.

The Great Hall houses the library and is a long classical building which was erected by Archbishop Juxon soon after the Restoration. Among its interesting exhibits are a first edition of More's *Utopia*, and a cookery book which belonged to the wife of Archbishop Tenison. A notable feature of the Great Hall is its hammerbeam roof, restored in 1948.

LANCASTER HOUSE viiiC
State Apartments in this fine 19th-c town mansion are open to the public when not in use by the government. The building, designed by Benjamin Wyatt, can be considered one of the finest examples of Victorian town architecture extant. It was originally built for the Duke of York, but later passed into the possession of the Dukes of Sutherland. The latter owners commissioned Sir Charles Barry to remodel the staircase hall in 1827.

LINCOLN'S INN vH
This famous Inn of Court boasts two fine halls – the restored Old Hall of c1492 and 1624, and a new hall and library housed in a Tudor-style building dating from the 19thc. The old gateway in Chancery Lane dates from 1518 and bears the arms of Sir Thomas Lovell, the Earl of Lincoln – from whom the inn takes its name – and Henry VIII.

Inside the arch and on the right-hand side is the chapel, one of the few of Inigo Jones' attempts at the gothic style of architecture. The opening in 1623 was marked by a sermon from the famous Dr Donne, and the pillared crypt was a known meeting place in the lifetime of Pepys. John Thurloe, Oliver Cromwell's secretary, lived at the inn and was buried here in 1668. Fine stained glass can be seen in the chapel, plus the tomb of ex-Prime Minister Spencer Perceval. Perceval is the only British Prime Minister to have been assassinated.

Opposite the chapel is the Old Hall, built in the 15thc and restored in 1928. Chancery trials were held here prior to the erection of the Law Courts in the Strand, and the walls are lined with fine paintings. Nearby New Hall was built by the architect of Euston Station, Philip Hardwicke, in c1843. One of its more prominent features is a fresco occupying the whole of the west hall. This was executed in 1859 by G F Watts and is entitled Justice. This is the largest hall in the Inns of Court.

LIVERY COMPANIES' HALLS vJ&M/viG
Of the 36 Livery Companies' Halls that once stood in the City, only two came through the last war completely unscathed. These were of the Apothecaries and Vintners. Those of the Founders, Ironmongers, and Armourers and Braziers suffered only slight damage, 11 more sustained more serious blows, and 20 were utterly destroyed. Several of these historic buildings have since been restored.

LONDON STONE viL
A new building occupying the site of bombed St Swithin's Church carries the London Stone in one of its walls. This stone is reputed to have been the *Millarium* of Roman London, from which all road distances were measured. Other sources claim that it was a stone-age monument before this, and that the existing block is only a fragment of the original. History relates that it was a great stone fixed into the ground at the time when Jack Cade and his Men of Kent marched through the capital, and that Cade smote it with his sword as a token of London's conquest.

MANSION HOUSE viL
George Dance built Mansion House between 1739 and 1752, and it has served as the official residence of the Lord Mayor since occupied by Sir Crisp Gascoigne in 1753. The building stands on the site of the old Stocks Market – which took its name from the stocks which once stood here – and includes the smallest Police Court in England. Its largest apartment is the notable Egyptian Hall, where a sparse Lord Mayor's banquet was held after bomb damage to the Guildhall.

POST OFFICE TOWER ivD
Well-known as the tallest building in London, the GPO Tower of 1965 rises to 619ft and houses radio-telephone and telephone-exchange equipment. The famous revolving restaurant is situated at a height of about 500ft, and the public viewing gallery affords spectacular views over the capital.

ROYAL EXCHANGE viH
This is at least the third building to occupy this site. The first was built by Sir Thomas Gresham and opened in 1568; it acquired the Royal prefix by command of Elizabeth I after her visit in 1571. The building was destroyed during the Great Fire of 1666 and its successor was burned down in 1838. Queen Victoria opened the present building in 1844.

cont

LONDON

The three buildings were all designed on a similar basis – a square surrounding an open quadrangle. The latest, by Sir William Tite, had this open area roofed over in 1882. The walls of the quad are decorated with paintings of scenes in British history, and the statue of Wellington outside the Exchange was executed by Chantrey. No actual exchange business has been conducted here for some 40 years.

ROYAL FESTIVAL HALL
ix C (adjacent halls x A)

Built on a Thames-side site on the South Bank, the modern Royal Festival Hall dates from 1951 and includes an auditorium which can accommodate some 3,400 people. Smaller halls attached to the main body of the building include the Purcell Room, Queen Elizabeth Hall, and Hayward Art Gallery. Additional features are the two restaurants and a recital room.

ROYAL HOSPITAL, CHELSEA *viii K*

Charles II commissioned Wren to build this hospital in 1682, and it was originally intended for aged and invalid soldiers. Grinling Gibbons executed the statue of Charles II that stands in one of the quadrangles, and the hall contains a painting of the king with the hospital in the background. Also in the hall are a collection of captured flags, and the table on which the Duke of Wellington's body lay in state.

More flags, plus carvings by William Emmet and a fine altar-piece, can be seen in the chapel. Interesting stones can be seen in the graveyard, including one to William Hiesland who reputedly lived to 112 and married after his 100th birthday. The hospital gardens are the annual venue for the Chelsea Flower Show. Also in the grounds is a recently opened building housing the National Army Museum.

ST JAMES' PALACE *ix A*

This rectangular brick-built palace was erected by order of Henry VIII and has been the birthplace of many of our sovereigns. It first became the royal residence after Whitehall Palace was destroyed by fire in 1698, and all court functions were held here until George III started to use his newly-acquired Buckingham Palace (*c*1761). The English Court is still officially the Court of St James. All that is left of the original building is a fine 16th-c gateway, and the present palace is occupied by various Court officials. The Royal Chapel preserves a ceiling dating from 1540, and nearby Queen's Chapel of 1623 and 1627 was by Inigo Jones. The latter building stands in Marlborough Road.

Adjoining Clarence House was rebuilt between 1825 and 1829 by John Nash, by order of the Duke of Clarence – later to ascend the throne as William IV. This is now the residence of HM the Queen Mother.

SOMERSET HOUSE *v K*

The site on which Somerset House stands was once occupied by a royal palace in which Queen Elizabeth I resided and the body of Oliver Cromwell lay in state. The south façade of the present building faces the Thames and was by Sir William Chambers; it dates from between 1777 and 1786, but displays examples of later work. King's College, part of the University of London, is housed in the 19th-c east wing and a large part of the building is occupied by the Registrar General's organization. A recent decision to open some of the interior will allow public access to several splendid Georgian rooms – perhaps housing a theatrical museum.

STAPLE INN *v H*

Staple Inn was so called because it was a house of the merchants of the wool staple before becoming an Inn of Chancery in the reign of Henry V. The entrance is beneath a row of gabled Elizabethan houses which have been restored many times, and are claimed to be the oldest in London. Its hall of 1581 had a fine hammerbeam roof but was destroyed by bombing during the last war; it was rebuilt to the original design.

The inn passed out of the ownership of the law fraternity in 1884 and became co-owned by the government and the Prudential Assurance Company. Dr Johnson had chambers in the inn during the year 1759.

THE TEMPLE *v L*

The Temple Bar Memorial stands on the boundary between the City and Westminster, and marks the place where Wren's bar (or gateway) stood before it was removed to Cheshurst in 1878. Farther along is Wren's classical gateway guarding the entrance to the Temple, comprising the Inns of Court known as the Inner and Middle Temple. These two legal societies occupied the complex after the original owners, the Knights' Templars.

Middle Temple Lane passes Brick Court and the site of a house in which Oliver Goldsmith lived from 1764 until his death, and continues to Middle Temple Hall of 1572. *Twelfth Night* was performed here in 1602; the exterior was dressed with stone in 1757 and the entrance tower rebuilt in 1832. It is thought that the hall was used mainly for recreation, a theory strengthened by the discovery of about 100 dice under the floorboards in the 18thc. Features include part of a serving table fashioned from the timbers of Drake's ship the Golden Hind, some original stained glass, and numerous fine paintings. Restoration work was conducted after war damage, and the hall was re-opened by HM the Queen Mother in 1949.

Fountain Court, as mentioned in Dickens' *Martin Chuzzlewit*, lies to the right and the Middle Temple library a little to the SW. Hare Court connects Middle and Inner Temple Lanes, and contains a memorial to Oliver Goldsmith. Pump Court contains houses after the style of those built subsequent to the Great Fire, a type of dwelling in which the Temple is particularly rich. Temple Church is described under the section on London churches. Wren's court and cloisters on the east side of Pump Court were extensively damaged during the last war but have been well restored. To the right is the site where the Inner hall and library stood before their destruction by bombs in May of 1941. A new library was opened in 1958, and a foundation stone for the new hall was laid by HM Queen Elizabeth II in 1952. The hall opened in 1957.

TOWER BRIDGE *xi C*

This is the most easterly and certainly the most spectacular of London's River Thames bridges. Dating from 1886 to 1894, it cost a million and a half pounds to build. The twin bascules weigh 1,000 tons apiece, and are raised by hydraulic power to enable ships to enter the Pool of London between here and London Bridge. The upper part of the structure, which links the two great towers, is 112ft above the surface of the river and was formerly accessible to pedestrians. In the Pool is moored the preserved cruiser HMS Belfast, now a naval museum.

TOWER OF LONDON *vi M*

Although universally known as the Tower, this famous complex of buildings is really a castle of the concentric type. Two fortified curtain walls mark the boundaries of the inner and outer wards, and the entire structure is encircled by a deep moat. The outer wall, which describes an irregular square, is divided from the inner by a narrow lane. Tower Wharf stands between the south section of the moat and the River Thames, and the entire area occupied by the castle comprises some 84 acres.

White Tower is the central point of the castle and probably gave the structure its name. It was built in an angle of the old Roman wall by William the Conqueror, and the present curtain walls were erected between 1189 and 1306. It is thought that most of the outer work was by order of Henry III *c*1272. Features including Wakefield Tower and the water-gate (Traitor's Gate) also date from this approximate period, and many alterations were made by subsequent sovereigns. The present appearance of the building is largely due to the restoration work of Anthony Salvin, architect and authority on medieval strongholds.

Popular memory recognises the Tower as a prison, but it has been much more in its long history. At various times it has served as a fortress, royal palace, arsenal, munitions factory (*eg* longbows for Agincourt), state prison, garrison, map-survey headquarters (thus Ordnance Survey), mint, library, and treasury; but its tragic associations as a prison outweigh the past merit of its other functions.

Prisoners to be confined here ranged from upstarts eager to promote themselves from the lower echelons of the aristocracy, to heads of the church and state. They usually entered the tower by the water-gate, and were conducted to their quarters to await ransom, execution, or interminable incarceration. Two traditional places of execution are Tower Hill and Tower Green, the latter of which is situated near the White Tower in the inner yard. A brass plate here records the executions of Anne Boleyn (1536), Catherine Howard (1542), Lady Jane Grey (1554), and the Earl of Essex. 'Bloody' Tower includes the room in which the little Princes are said to have been smothered, and served as a prison for archbishops Cranmer and Laud, and Sir Walter Raleigh. Wakefield Tower houses the famous Crown Jewels and was where Henry VI was allegedly murdered by Richard Duke of Gloucester.

Also in the inner yard is the Royal Chapel of St Peter and Vincula, possibly London's oldest church. This is of early-Norman date and contains the remains of many execution victims, including Sir Thomas More and the Jacobite Lords who died between 1746 and 1747.

Tower Wharf displays numerous guns of various periods and nations, and is where salutes are fired on royal anniversaries. A stair linking the wharf to the

19th-c Tower Bridge, the most easterly of the London Thames bridges

foreshore came from the P & O liner Rawalpindi, sunk by German battle cruisers in 1939.

WESTMINSTER HALL *ixF*
Lying adjacent to the Houses of Parliament, this magnificent hall was originally built by William II in 1097. Richard II gave the building its present shape in 1399 and ironically was deposed just after its completion.

It functioned as law courts from the 13thc till 1882, and the trials of such famous and unfortunate men as Sir Thomas More (1530), Sir Thomas Wyatt (1554), Earl of Essex (1601), Guy Fawkes (1606), Strafford (1641), and Charles I (1649) were held here. Oliver Cromwell was installed as Lord Protector at Westminster Hall in 1653, and it was here that the body of Sir Winston Churchill was laid in state for mourning. War damage to the splendid medieval oak hammerbeam roof, perhaps the finest in Europe, has been repaired with timber taken from a park in Sussex.

MUSEUMS AND ART GALLERIES

APSLEY HOUSE *viiiB*
Known as No. 1 London, this house contains a Wellington museum and was once the Duke of Wellington's home. Adam originally designed the building but alterations were effected by the Duke; the Waterloo Gallery is by Wyatt.

BRITISH MUSEUM *ivH*
Items displayed in this world-famous museum include two copies of Magna Carta, numerous examples of ancient sculpture, a variety of prints and drawings, and the well-known Elgin Marbles. Special displays include the Egyptian and Babylonian Rooms, and the King Edward VII Gallery. Prior permission must be obtained by anybody wishing to use the extensive library and reading room.

BRITISH MUSEUM OF NATURAL HISTORY *viiH*
Many different animal, plant, aquatic, fossil and mineralogical specimens are excellently mounted and displayed here. Of particular note are the gigantic re-assembled dinosaur fossils and a life-sized model of a blue whale.

DICKENS' HOUSE *vE*
Charles Dickens lived and worked here from 1837 to 1839; he wrote the *Pickwick Papers*, *Oliver Twist*, and *Nicholas Nickleby* at this house, and many of his personal belongings are preserved here.

DR JOHNSON'S HOUSE *vH*
The famous Dr Johnson lived here from 1748 to 1758, while his well-known dictionary was being compiled in the attic.

GEOLOGICAL MUSEUM *viiH*
Exceptionally comprehensive collections of fossils and minerals, ordered in well-displayed groups, can be seen here. The museum is also the headquarters of the Geological Survey of Great Britain.

GEORGE INN *xiB*
This is the last galleried inn to have survived in London. It was built in 1677, partly demolished in 1889, and is open only during licensing house (NT).

IMPERIAL WAR MUSEUM *xG*
Relics, models, and pictures of the two world wars can be seen in buildings which once housed the Bethlem Hospital.

LONDON MUSEUM *viiA*
Currently housed in the former apartments of Princess Beatrice (Kensington Palace), the contents of this museum trace the life of London from its early origins to the present day. The displays and exhibits are to be housed in a new building at the Barbican.

MADAME TUSSAUD'S *iiiE*
Opened in 1802 by a descendant of the original Swiss founder, this fascinating collection of waxworks includes effigies of many living and dead celebrities. These include the notorious as well as the famous, and the macabre Chamber of Horrors portrays infamous criminals from various periods and places.

The more recent Planetarium is housed in an adjacent building and includes a great copper dome, on the inside of which representations of the heavens are projected.

MUSEUM OF LONDON TRANSPORT
(see Isleworth)
Situated in Syon Park, Isleworth, this collection includes road and canal relics. Included are old trams, carriages, and buses.

NATIONAL GALLERY *ivL*
All the important European schools of painting are represented here, and the paintings are sympathetically hung in well-appointed galleries.

NATIONAL PORTRAIT GALLERY *ivL*
Visitors to this gallery can enjoy superb works of art, and stand face to face with some of the most important people of history.

PUBLIC RECORD OFFICE MUSEUM *vH*
Historical documents displayed here include the Domesday Book and letters supposedly written by Guy Fawkes.

ROYAL ACADEMY OF ARTS *ivK*
Works by living artists are shown here during an annual summer exhibition, and details of other exhibitions are announced as required.

SCIENCE MUSEUM *viiE*
Properly known as the National Museum of Science and Industry, this institution illustrates the historical development of its subjects. Some of the most important exhibits include the locomotives Puffing Billy (1813), Stephenson's Rocket, and the Sans Pareil. A modern extension to the building houses more recent engines.

SIR JOHN SOANE'S MUSEUM *vG*
Interesting collections of antiques, pictures, and sculptures are displayed in a fine house dating from 1813.

TATE GALLERY *ixH*
In contrast to the National Gallery, the Tate displays works of painting and sculpture by well-known modern artists. These include items purchased with the aid of the Chantrey Bequest.

VICTORIA AND ALBERT MUSEUM *viiH*
Art and crafts of different countries and periods are shown in this national museum of industrial art. The large library is also of interest.

WALLACE COLLECTION *iiiH*
A collection of mainly-French origin, including paintings, armour, and furniture, which was opened in 1900.

WESLEY'S HOUSE AND MUSEUM *viE*
John Wesley, founder and prime mover of Methodism, lived and died in this house. The building now contains a museum of his personal relics.

ZOOLOGICAL GARDENS *iiiB*
Good wildlife collections can be seen here. Of note are the aviary, aquarium, and Mappin Terraces. The zoo is the HQ of the Zoological Society. Much of the complex follows the original layout put forward by Decimus Burton in 1827.

Map of Inner London

Scale: seven inches to one mile

Legend

Referencing to the London Map
This map employs an arbitrary system of grid reference. Pages are identified by Roman numerals and divided into twelve squares. Each square contains a blue letter; all references give the page number first, followed by the letter of the square in which a particular item can be found. Reference for the Houses of Parliament is **ixF**, meaning that the relevant map is on page **ix** and that the building appears in the square designated **F**.

One-way streets and banned turns shown on this map are in operation at time of going to press. Some of these are experimental and liable to change. Only the more important banned turns are shown – some of which operate between 7am and 7pm only – and are usually signposted on the roads concerned. No waiting or unilateral waiting restrictions apply to many streets. All such restrictions are indicated by official signposts.

Based on Ordnance Survey maps with the sanction of the Controller of Her Majesty's Stationery Office. Crown Copyright Reserved.
© The Automobile Association 1974.

PLACES OF INTEREST IN LONDON

Place	Ref	Place	Ref	Place	Ref	Place	Ref	Place	Ref
Admiralty	ix3	City of London Club	viH	Imperial College	viiE	Percival David Foundation	ivE	St Stephen's	viK
Admiralty Arch	ixB	Clarence House	ixA	Imperial War Museum	xG	Peter Pan Statue	iiL	Sanderson and Sons Ltd	ivG
Albert Memorial	viiE	Cleopatra's Needle	vK	Inns of Court and Chancery	vL	Petticoat Lane		Science Museum	viiE
Apothecaries' Hall	vM	Clock Museum	viH	Inner Temple	vL	(Middlesex Street)	viJ	Serpentine (Hyde Park)	viiC
Apsley House	viiiB	Clothworkers' Hall	viL	Innholders' Hall	viK	Pewterers' Hall	viG	Seymour Hall	iiiG
Armourers' and Braziers' Hall	viH	College of Arms	viK	Institute of Archaeology	iiiB	Physical Energy Statue	viiB	Schomberg House	ixA
Ashburnham House	ixE	Congress House (TUC)	ivH	Ironmongers' Hall	viH	Pipe Museum	ixA	Shell Centre	xA
Bakers' Hall	viL	Corn Exchange	viM	Jewel Tower	ixE	Planetarium	iiiE	Sir John Soane's Museum	vG
Baltic Exchange	viH	County Hall	ixF	Jewish Museum	ivB	Pollock's Toy Museum	ivD	Skinners' Hall	viK
Bank of England	viH	Courtauld Institute		Kensington Palace	viiA	Polytechnic	iiiJ	Smithfield (Central Market)	vJ
Bank of England Extension	viG	Picture Gallery	ivE	Lambeth Palace	ixJ	Port of London Authority	viM	Somerset House	vK
Banking Museum	viL	Covent Garden Market	ivM	Lancaster House	viiiC	Post Office Tower	ivD	Southwark Cathedral	xiB
Banqueting House	ixB	Crafts' Centre	ivH	Leadenhall Market	viL	President	vL	Speakers' Corner	iiiL
Barbican Development Scheme	viD	Crewe House	viiiB	Leathersellers' Hall	viH	Prince Henry's Room	vH	Spencer House	viiiC
BBC	iiiJ	Cutlers' Hall	ivJ	Lincoln's Inn	vJ	Public Record Office Museum	vH	Spitalfields Market	viF
Bear Gardens Museum	xC	Cuming Museum	xJ	Livery Companies' Halls	vJ&M/viG	Queen's Gallery		Staple Inn	vH
Bedford College	iiiE	Daily Mirror Offices	vH	Lloyd's	viL	(Buckingham Palace)	viiiF	Starcross School	vA
Belfast	xiC	Design Centre	ivL	London Bridge	viL	Regent's Park Barracks	iiiC	State House	vH
Bermondsey Town Hall	xiF	Dickens's House	vE	London Museum	viiA	Roman Bath	vL	Stationers' Hall	vJ
Big Ben	ixF	Discovery	vL	London Postal Museum	vJ	Roman Fort	viG	Stock Exchange	viH
Billingsgate Market	viL	Dolphinarium	ivH	London Silver Vaults	vH	Rotten Row (Hyde Park)	viiC	Tallow Chandlers' Hall	viK
Bluecoat School	ixD	Dr Johnson's House	vH	London Stone	viL	Round Pond		Tate Gallery	ixH
Borough Market	xiA	Drapers' Hall	viH	London Tourist Board	viiiE	(Kensington Gardens)	viiA	Temple of Mithras	viK
Bowater House	viiE	Duke of York Column	ixB	Lord's Cricket Ground	iiB	Royal Academy of Arts	ivK	Thames Television	ivB
Brewers' Hall	viG	Eros Statue	ivK	Lord's Cricket Museum	iiB	Royal Academy of Music	iiiF	Temple Church	vL
British Museum	ivH	Euston Tower	ivB	Lost Property Office (LTE)	iiiE	Royal Albert Hall	viiE	The Temple	vL
British Museum of		Faraday Building	vM	Madame Tussaud's	iiiE	Royal College of Medicine	iiiJ	Thorn House	ivL
Natural History	viiH	Finsbury Town Hall	vB	Mansion House	viL	Royal College of Music	viiE	Tower Bridge	xiC
Brompton Air Terminal	viiJ	Fishmongers' Hall	viL	Marble Arch	iiiL	Royal Courts of Justice	vH	Tower of London	viM
Brompton Oratory	viiF	Founders' Hall	viL	Marlborough House	ixA	Royal Exchange	viH	Transport House	ixH
Buckingham Palace	viiiF	Foundling Hospital Art		Marylebone Town Hall	iiiE	Royal Festival Hall	ixC	Toy Museum	ivD
Building Centre	ivH	Treasures	ivF	Mercers' Hall	viG	Royal Hospital Chelsea	viiiK	Trinity House	viM
Bush House	vK	Freemasons' Hall	ivJ	Merchant Taylors' Hall	viH	Royal Institute	ivK	United States Embassy	iiiL
Butchers' Hall	viG	Geological Museum	viiH	Middle Temple	vL	Royal Institute of British		University College	ivE
Carlton House Terrace	ixB	George Inn	xiB	Middlesex Guild Hall	ixE	Architects	iiiF	University of London	ivE
Carpenters' Hall	viH	Girdlers' Hall	viG	Monument (the)	viL	Royal Mews	viiiE	Vickers Tower	ixJ
Caxton Hall	ixE	Goldsmiths' Hall	viG	Mount Pleasant Postal		Royal Mint	viM	Victoria and Albert Museum	viiH
Cenotaph	ixB	Government Offices	ixB	Sorting Office	vE	Royal School of Needlework	viiE	Vintners' Hall	viK
Central Criminal Court		Gray's Inn	vH	Music Box Gallery	iiiH	Royal Society of Arts	ivM	Wallace Collection	iiiH
(Old Bailey)	vJ	Grey Coat Hospital	ixH	National Army Museum	viiiK	RoSPA House	viiiD	Watermen's Hall	viL
Central Hall	ixE	Grocers' Hall	viG	National Gallery	ivL	Saddlers' Hall	viG	Wellington	vL
Central Markets (Smithfield)	vJ	Guards' Museum	ixD	National Portrait Gallery	ivL	St Bartholomew-the-Great	vJ	Wellington Barracks	ixD
Centrepoint	ivH	Guildhall	viG	National Postal Museum	vJ	St Bride's	vJ	Wellington Museum	
Chapel of the Savoy	vK	Guildhall Museum	viG	Nelson's Column	ixB	St Clement Dane's	vL	(Apsley House)	viiiB
Charterhouse	vF	Haberdashers' Hall	viG	New Scotland Yard	ixE	St George's Cathedral	xD	Wesley's House and Museum	ivE
Chelsea Barracks	viiiK	Hayward Gallery	xA	Nuffield Foundation	iiC	St Giles'	viD	West London Air Terminal	viiG
Christ Church	viiD	HM Customs and Excise	viL	Old Bailey		St James's Palace	ixA	Westminster Abbey	ixE
Chrysanthemum	vL	Holborn Town Hall	ivJ	(Central Criminal Court)	vJ	St John's	ixH	Westminster Bridge	ixF
Churchill Gardens	viiiM	Home House	iiiH	Old Curiosity Shop	vG	St John's Gate	vF	Westminster Cathedral	viiiJ
City and Guilds College	viiE	Honourable Artillery		Oval		St Margaret's	ixE	Westminster Hall	ixF
		Company HQ		(Surrey County Cricket Ground)	xK	St Martin-in-the-Fields	ivL	Wigmore Hall	iiiJ
		Horse Guards	ixB	Painters' Hall	viK	St Mary-le-Bow	viG	Winfield House	iiiA
		House of St Barnabas	ivH	Panmakers' Hall	viH	St Paul's	ivM	York Water Gate	ivM
		Houses of Parliament	ixF	Patent Office	vH	St Paul's Cathedral	viG	Zoological Gardens	iiiB

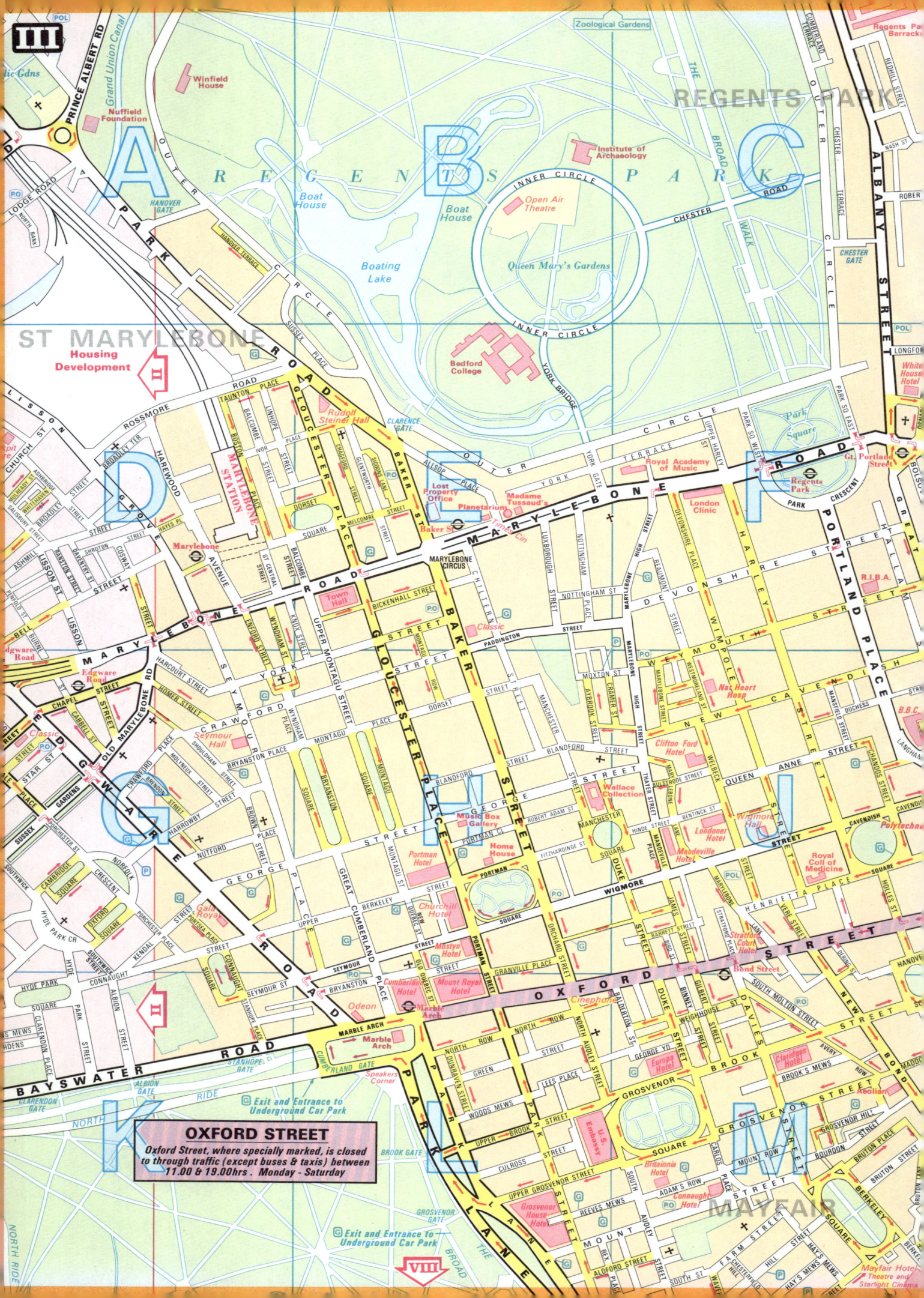

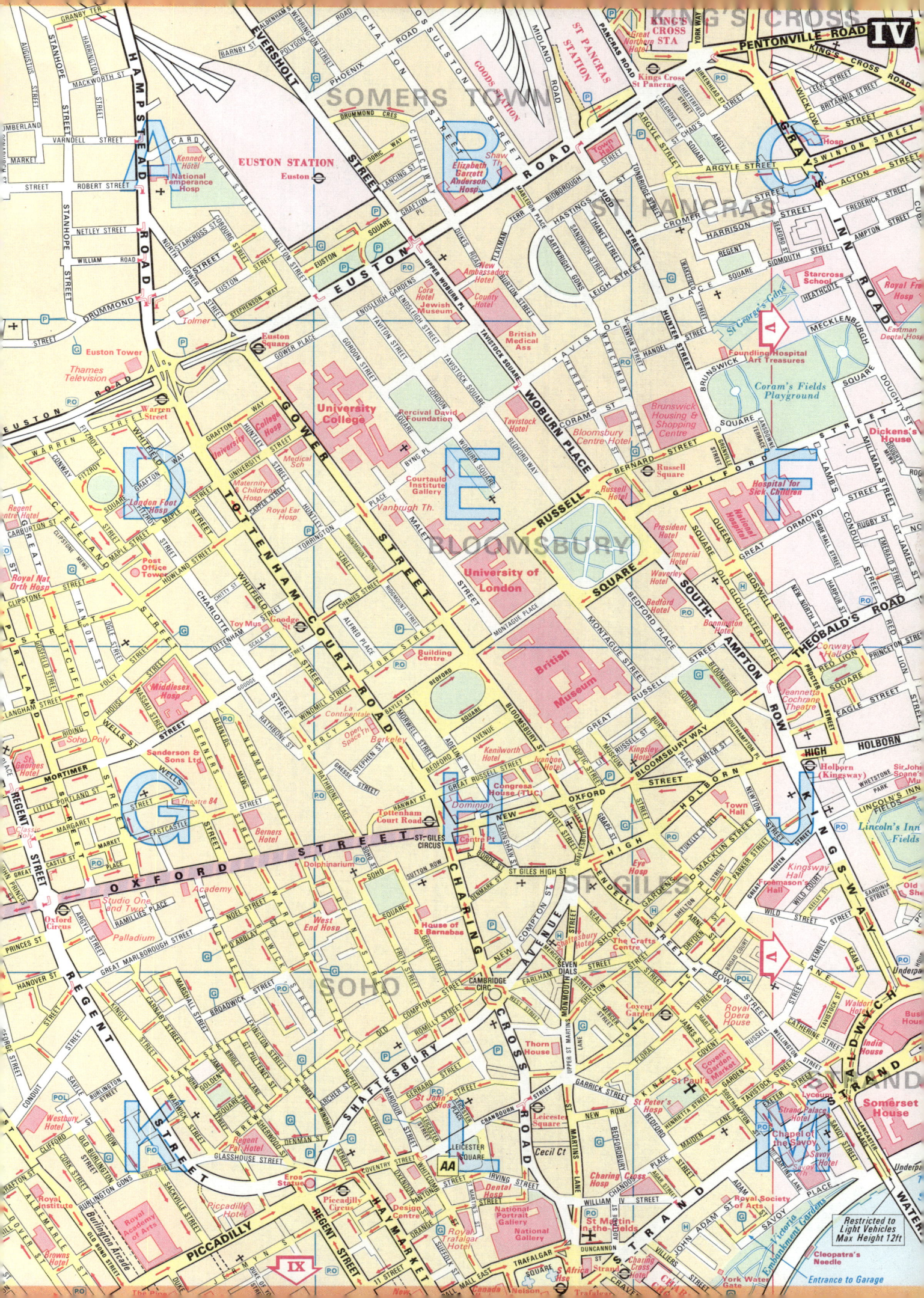

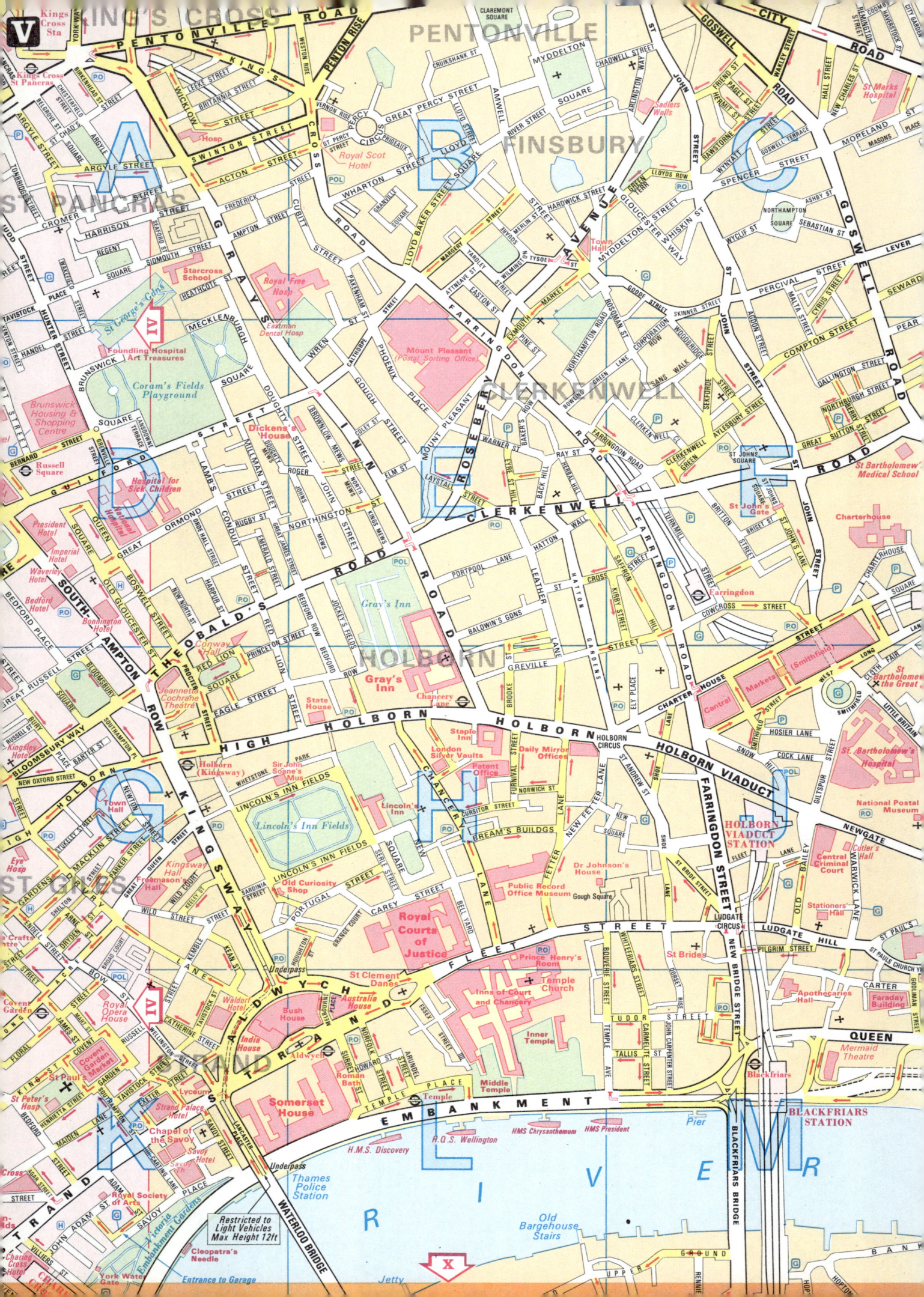

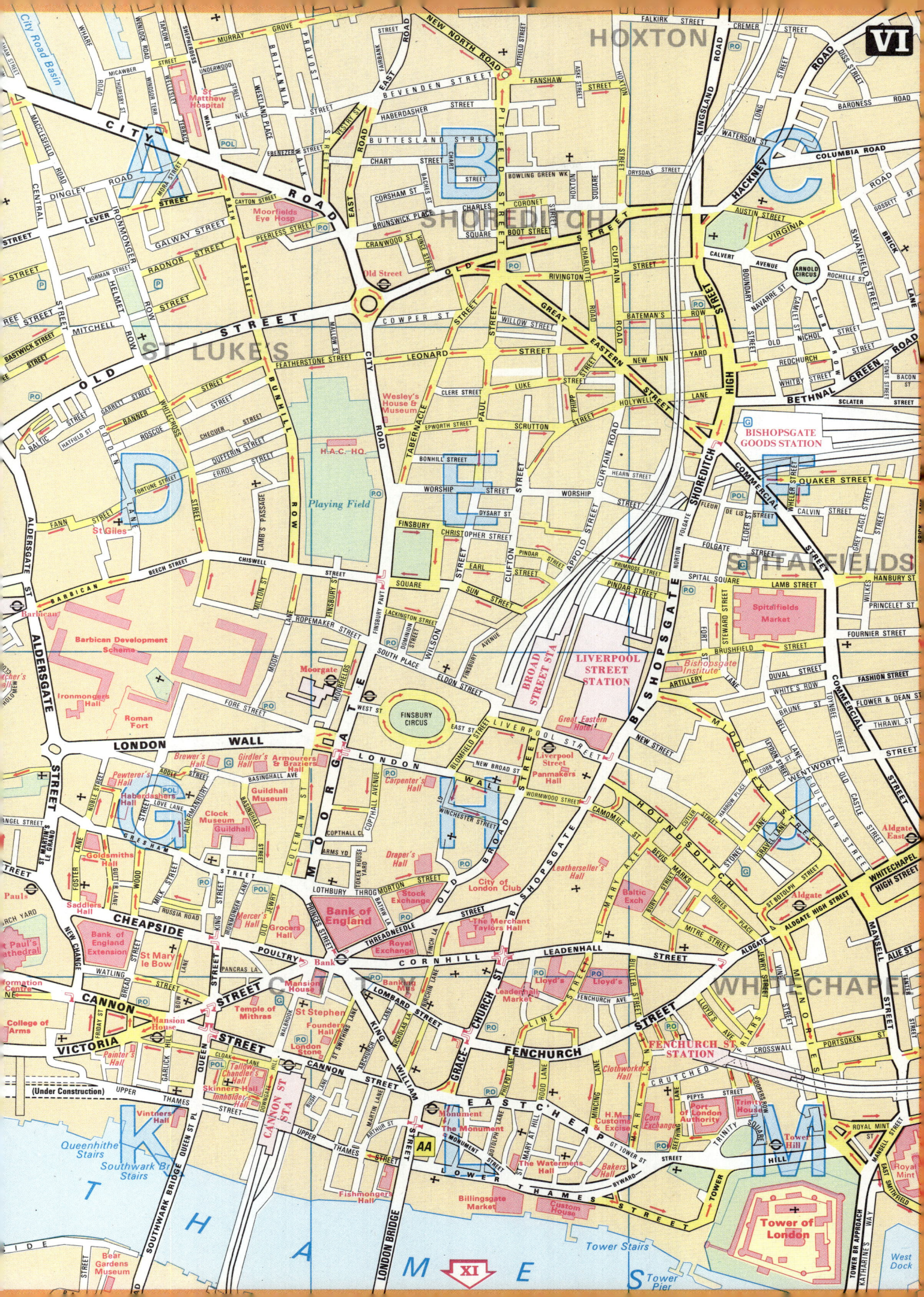

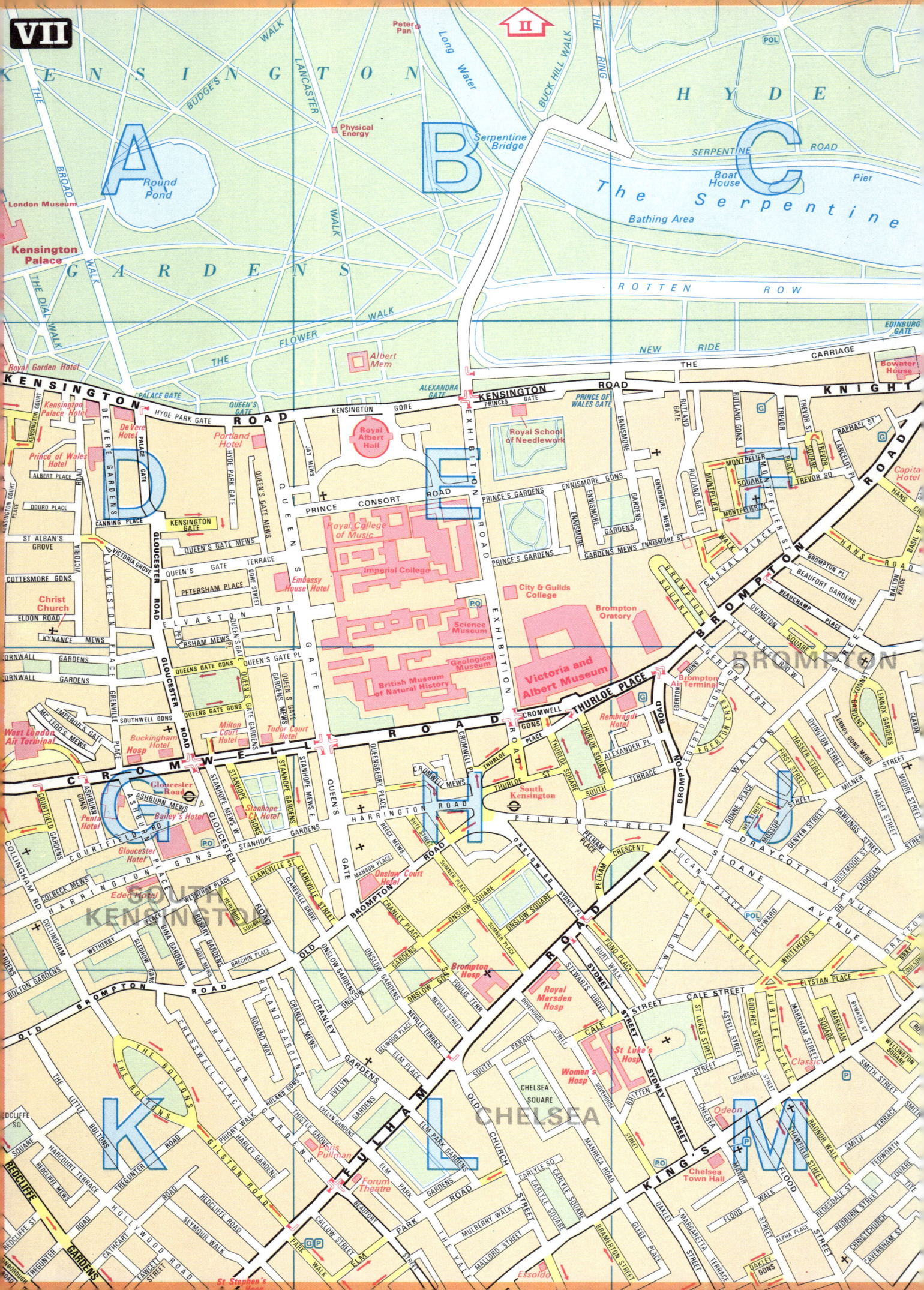

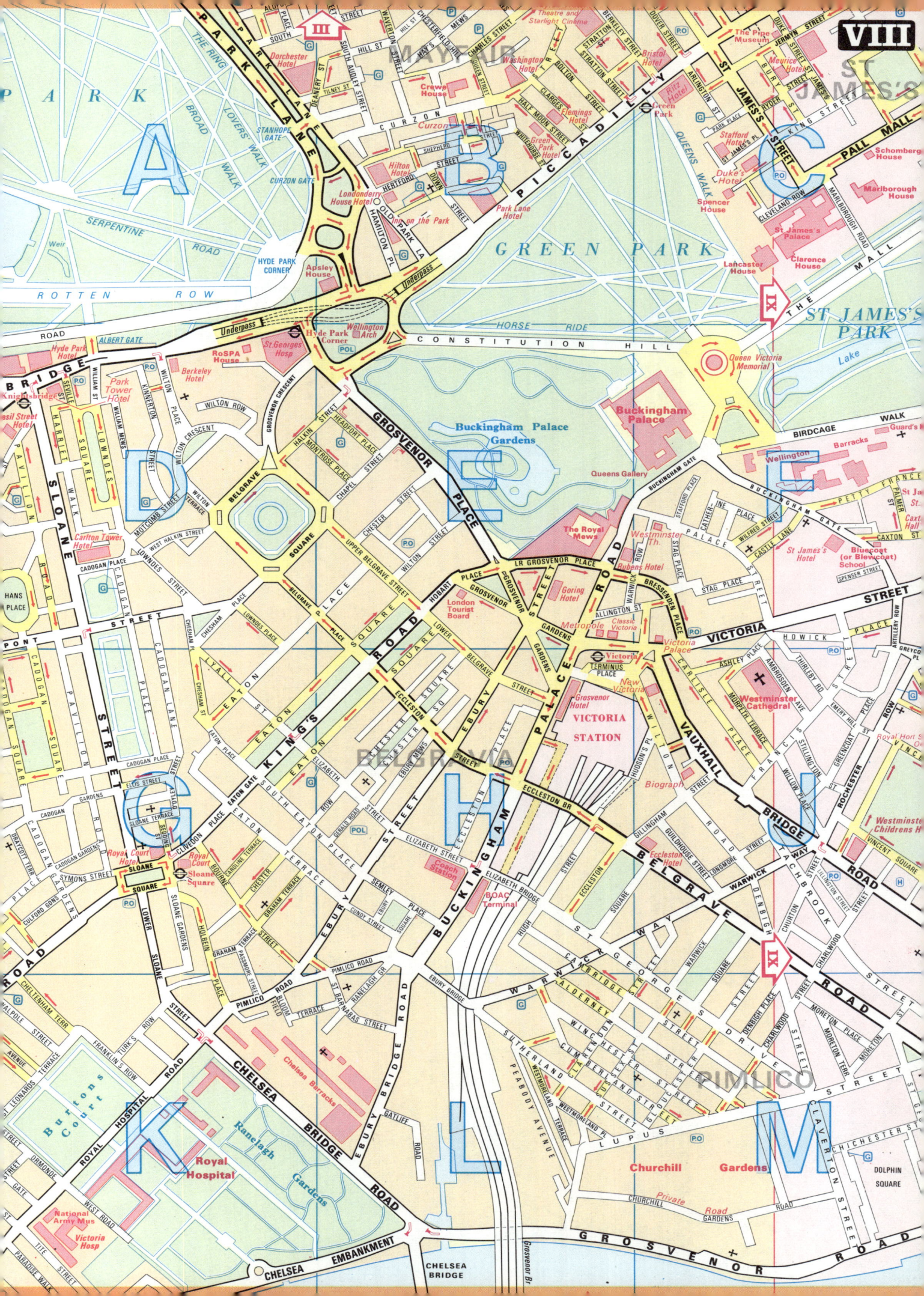

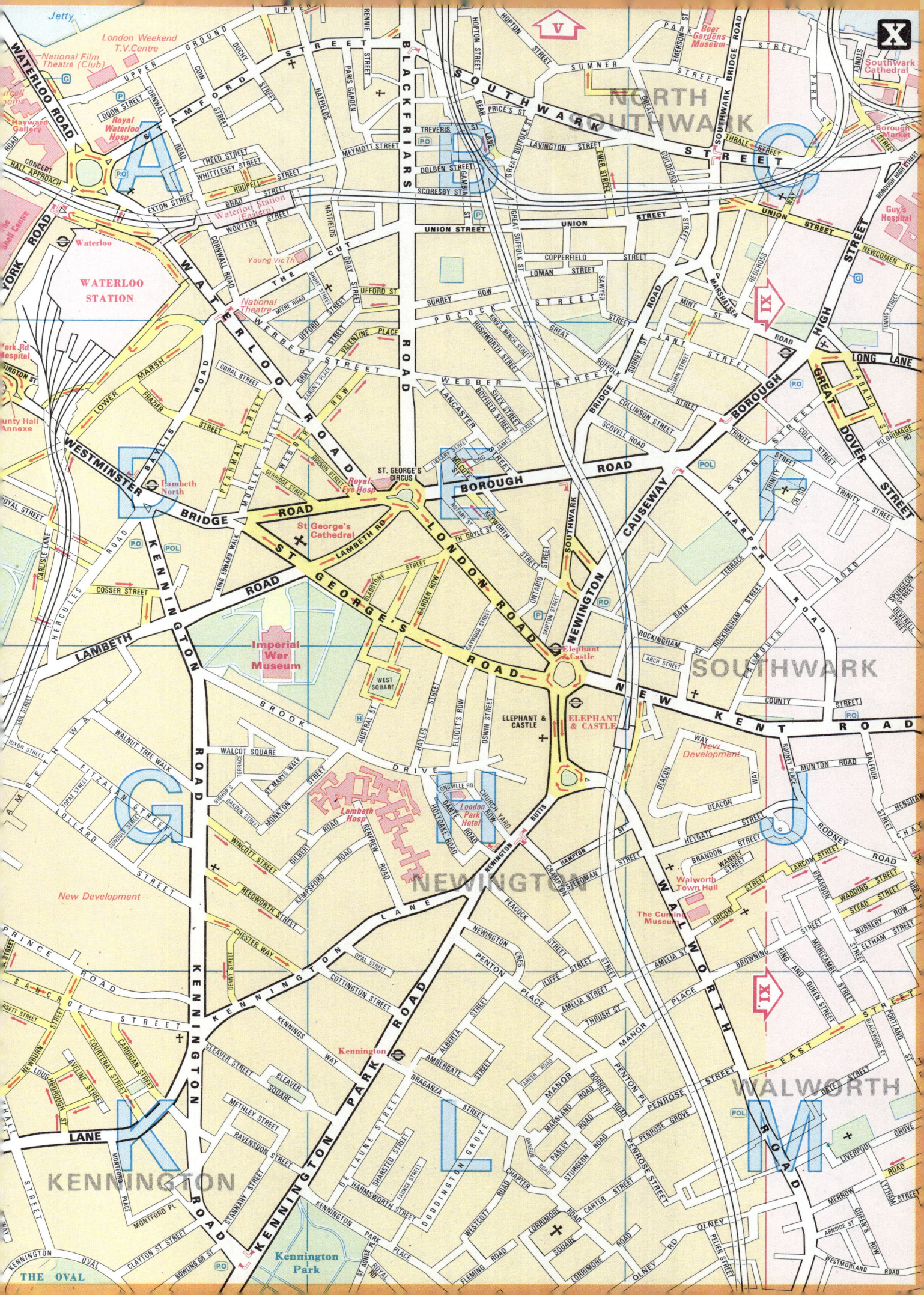

HYDE PARK AND KENSINGTON GARDENS

*You will see me any morning in the park
Reading the comics and the sporting page
(Particularly I remark
An English countess goes upon the stage);
T S Eliot Portrait of a Lady.*

Men reading newspapers, men attempting to sleep under newspapers, men and women just strolling, newspapers deserted on benches or stuffed, neatly folded, into litter bins. This is Hyde Park: linked to Kensington Gardens, a stone's throw from Green Park and St James's, preserved as open land – as were the others – by Henry VIII's penchant for hunting.

Prior to the Dissolution – 'when the light of the Gospel having dawned upon the king through the beautiful eyes of Anne Boleyn, the king drove the poor monks from their snuggeries and claimed the church land' – the Manor of Hyde belonged to the Abbey of Westminster. In Stuart times it was used for horse racing, and a long tradition of equestrian pursuits can be traced from the present day. The 1½m of sandy track frequented by horsemen is known as Rotten Row, a corruption of the French *Route de Roi*.

*Horsed in Cheapside, scarce yet the
    gayer spark
Achieves the Sunday triumph of the park;
Scarce yet you see him, dreading to be
    late,
Scout the new road, and dash through
    Grosvenor Gate:
Anxious – yet timorous too – his steed to
    show
The hack Bucephalus of Rotten Row.*

So wrote Sheridan in *Pizarro*, and undoubtedly he touched a nerve causing many a blush to rise to the cheeks of the young men of fashion who paraded, elegantly attired, up and down the Row on Sundays after church.

The Serpentine, formed from pools of the lost River Westbourne, runs with only one bend through the park. Queen Caroline, consort of George IV, commissioned the damming of the stream and though she wanted the lake to be serpentine by nature as well as by name her designer let her down. For many years the king believed that Caroline had used her own money to finance the construction of the Serpentine; not until after her death did he discover that for this and other projects to improve the park and the adjoining Kensington Gardens, Robert Walpole had granted her £20,000 from the royal revenue.

At one point the Serpentine is spanned by Rennie's Bridge, built in 1826 by Sir John and George Rennie. From the bridge, despite modern development, there is still a fine view to the towers of Westminster. It may also be possible to observe from here those intrepid bathers who swim in the Serpentine on every day of the year. Always popular with devotees of water pursuits, the Serpentine in the mid 19thc was far from being the clear and beautiful lake of today. At a meeting designed to draw attention to the filthy state of the water a Dr Cadogan commented that on numerous trips to Africa he had never seen waters so polluted and so full of animal and vegetable matter as the Serpentine. A young nobleman who had been rowing on the lake was seized with a fever attributed to the noxious gases stirred up by the action of his oars on the thick slime of the lake bed. But this was just one of many accidents – and some suicides – seen by the lake. Shelley's first wife, Harriet Westbrook, drowned herself there in 1816. Her bereaved husband could frequently be seen in Kensington Gardens, sailing paper boats on the Round Pond. Legend has it that they were made from five-pound notes!

Shelley was one of those respectable gentlemen who fulfilled the qualifications for visitors to the gardens. They were opened in the 1790's to all save sailors, soldiers, and liveried servants 'nor indeed anyone whose appearance the gatekeepers did not consider respectable'. As Surtees said, 'none of the great unwashed were to be seen in the park in those days'. But despite the undoubted gentility of those entitled to enter the park, a less predictable element also managed to find its way there. In the reign of George III not a week passed without a robbery and in the 70's, 80's and 90's a bell was rung to 'muster people returning to town'. When the party thus gathered seemed large enough to be safe from robbers, the ladies and gentlemen would set off on their hazardous journey through the gloomy park to the comparative safety of the streets.

Hyde Park and Kensington Gardens, more than any other London parks, are noted for their statuary. The Achilles Statue by Westmancott, cast in bronze from captured French cannon and erected in 1822 to the Duke of Wellington and his companions in arms 'by their countrywomen', is neither Achilles nor the Duke, but an adaptation of the statue of the horse-tamers on the Quirinal in Rome. Others, such as the Peter Pan statue, its animals' heads worn smooth by constant stroking, are almost places of pilgrimage. There are statues or memorials to W H Hudson, the naturalist, Edward Jenner, the discoverer of vaccination, J H Speke, the explorer, William III, Lord Byron and, of course, the Albert memorial. A motley crew perhaps, but each adds to the unique character of the open space that is Hyde Park and Kensington Gardens.

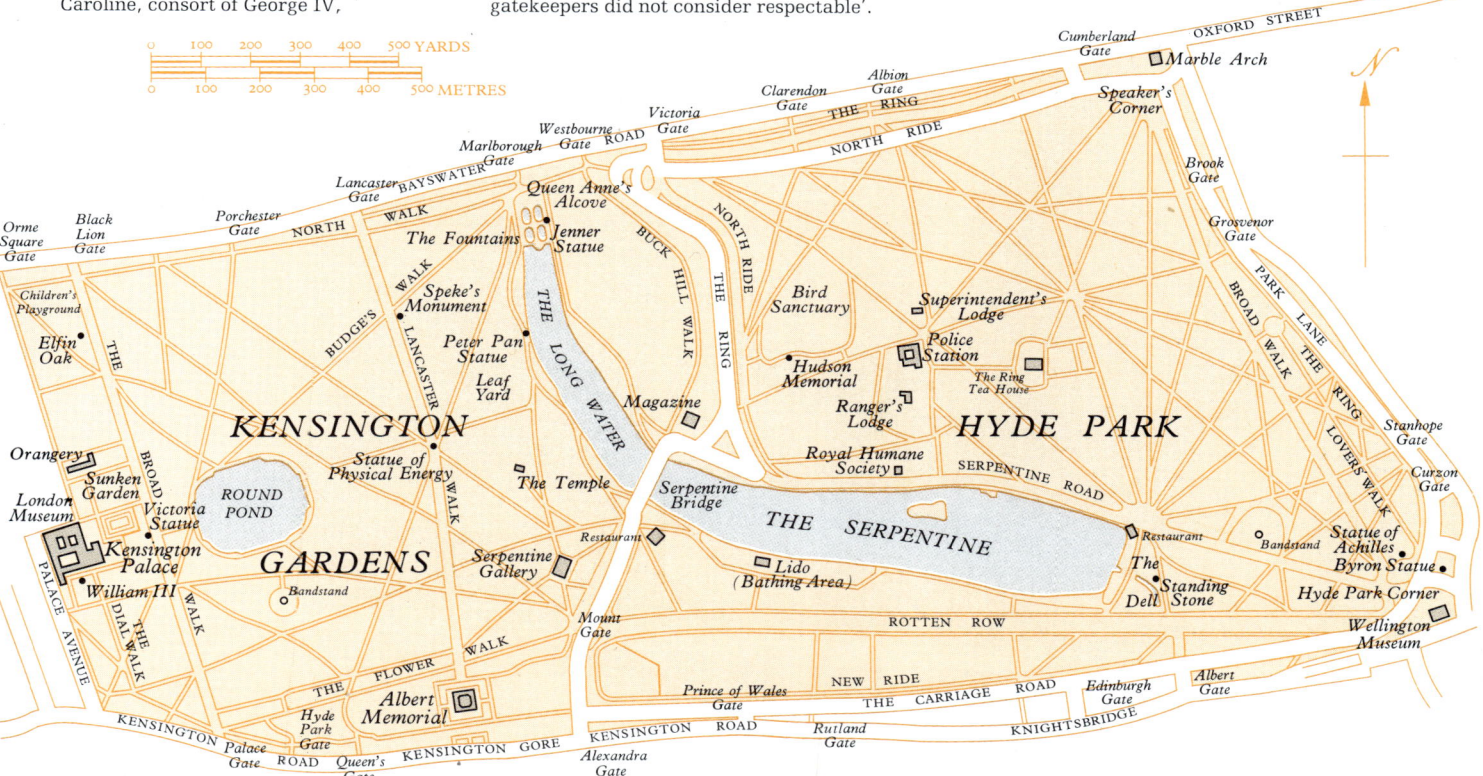

LONDON

ST JAMES'S PARK

It was a saying of Lord Chatham that the parks were the lungs of London;
W Windham of William Pitt, Earl of Chatham, in a speech in the House of Commons, 30 June 1808.

Sometime in the 12thc, on a tract of swampy meadowland belonging to the Abbots of Westminster, was founded by fourteen maidens 'that were leprous' a hospice for lepers, dedicated to St James the Less. They vowed to emulate this exceptionally pious saint since it was said of him by St Jerome that he prostrated himself so much in prayer that 'the skin of his knees and forehead were hardened like a camel's hoofs'.

Backing on to the hospice was the Palace of Westminster, but Henry VIII disliked the 'leprous eyesore' to such an extent that he took over the hospital and, giving the sisters generous compensation in the form of Chatisham and other properties in Suffolk, built St James's Palace on the site. The grounds were converted into a royal chase and stocked with deer for the king's hunt. As late as the 17thc, according to Samuel Pepys, it was possible to 'run down a stout buck' there. Other features – described as 'necessaries' in an act passed by Parliament to limit the size of Henry's chase – included a tilting ground and a bowling alley.

This royal pleasure ground was enhanced in the days of James I by a menagerie. As fond of sport and hunting as any of his predecessors, James also took a great pleasure in his animal collection and the park housed an odd selection sent from all corners of the globe. The House of Savoy sent a leopard, and the Great Mogul despatched two antelopes. From the Czar of Muscovy came sables and hawks, and from others came a wild boar, crocodiles, ducks, and a cormorant specially trained for use in fishing. There was also an elephant whose keeper earned £250 a year and insisted that his charge be given a gallon of wine each morning in the winter months.

Between the reigns of James I and Charles II the park fell into decline – Charles I walked through it once only, on his way to his execution, and casually remarked about a tree that his brother had planted. Gradually the menagerie disappeared, and Charles II replaced the animals with birds. It is popularly considered that Birdcage walk, forming the southern boundary of the park, is so called because Charles II kept his aviaries there. He is also credited with having played the game – not unlike croquet – called *paille-maille*, from which both Pall Mall and The Mall derived their names.

It was Charles who transformed the still swampy chase into a garden, commissioning the French designer Le Nôtre to do the work. Le Nôtre canalized the pool that watered the marshy land from the Tyburn and arranged a series of formal walks after the strict geometry of French fashion. And thus the park remained until the very nearly disastrous Peace Celebrations of 1814. In neighbouring Green Park the festivities inspired an advertisement that appeared in a newspaper on the following day:

'LOST . . . the beautiful Green Park . . . it is supposed to have been removed by Mr John Bull who was seen there last night with a pretty numerous party, and who has left a brown park in exchange . . .'

In St James's a pagoda was built on a Chinese bridge spanning Le Nôtre's canal. Designed by John Nash, it was to be the main attraction of the celebrations. As it turned out such was indeed the case; shortly after the beginning of the fireworks display the top three storeys of the pagoda caught fire – to the entertainment of a vast assemblage who crowded in from Green Park and blocked the route for firemen wishing to fight the blaze. By the following morning, most desolate among the general desolation of the park was the charred bridge carrying the burned stump of the pagoda.

Around the year 1827 the park was redesigned by Nash, who favoured a much more sweeping, romantic woodland scene and created the lake replacing stiff formality with weeping willows. The birds, introduced by Charles II were then, as now, a feature of the park. The ornamental ducks are supposed to be descended from Charles II's, and the North American Pelicans draw fascinated observers. In the 17thc John Evelyn noticed among the other birds a Balearian Crane wearing a wooden leg that it used 'as well as if it had been natural'. The unfortunate bird's benefactor was a soldier.

At one time the park was accounted a 'verge of the Royal Court', an odd title that meant it could provide sanctuary from creditors, and a man was not allowed to draw a sword there. This law did not stop the 'Mohawks', who terrorized the town for some years in the early 18thc. Mohawks aimed to cut the faces of their victims – 'tattoo' them – and to this end they would stand round a man in a pack, pricking at him with rapier or dagger, sometimes making him spin like a dancer to evade their cuts. Mohawks, together with Hawkubites, took over the night-time park from earlier groups like the Muns, Hectors, and Nickers. The latter used to break windows with halfpennies.

Undoubtedly St James's Park is a safer place now than it used to be, but perhaps in some ways it is less colourful. Queen Caroline, for example, saw a boy circle the 93-acre park five times in less than three hours, and a calico-printer from Wandsworth hopped a hundred yards of The Mall in 46 jumps. In 1793 a girl of eighteen months crawled it in 23 minutes, doubtless a profitable exercise for her parents. She did it, as the papers commented, 'to the great admiration of thousands'.

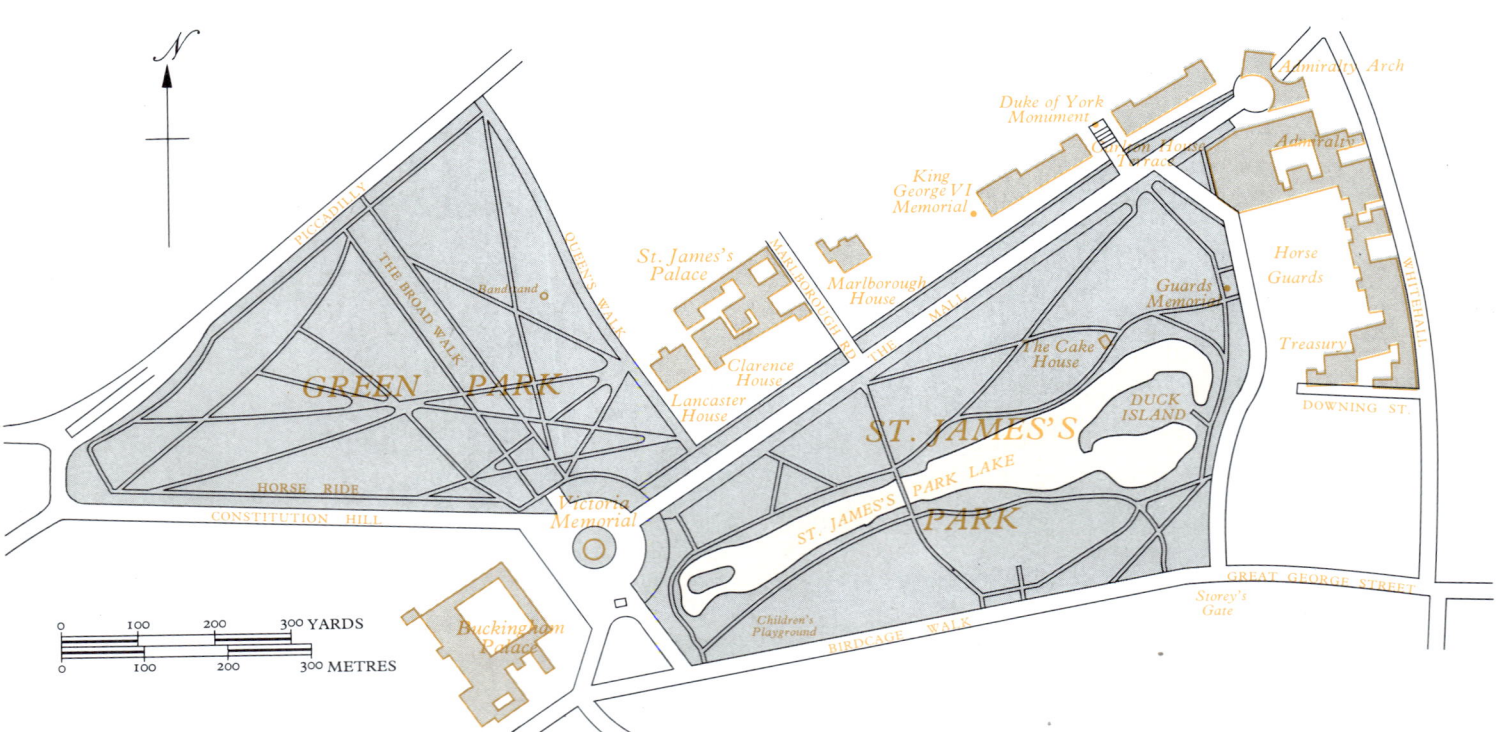

REGENT'S PARK

Live with proud peacocks in green parks;
W H Davies.

Another of John Nash's great achievements, Regent's Park displays a unique blend of rural and architectural character – from the winding lake with its several arms and the islets providing nesting places for numerous wild fowl, to the elegant terraces in the style that became known as 'Regency'. The lake now is nowhere more than four feet deep: the depth was reduced after a disaster in 1867 when the frozen surface was crowded with skaters. The ice broke and more than two hundred fell into the freezing waters; 40 people were drowned.

The design of the park was commissioned in 1814 by the Prince Regent – hence its name – and it was intended to follow a grand plan of villas and gardens accessible only to those holding tickets issued by the Royal Household. (It was opened to the public in 1838.) The Prince Regent wanted to have a fine palace built there, and Nash's elegant terraces were designed to surround this never-built edifice. Still, these beautiful rows of houses sheltered many famous men, among them the composer Ralph Vaughan Williams and the novelist H G Wells. Another, less well-known resident of Clarence Terrace, was George R Sims, dramatist and journalist; he always dated his contributions, rather quaintly, from 'opposite the ducks'.

Before Nash's grand design the park was known as Marylebone Park and was leased to the Duke of Portland. Like many of London's open spaces it was stocked with deer and served as a hunting ground and royal chase. At that time there was no canal. This, a branch of the Grand Union Canal, was also designed by John Nash, and in Regent's Park runs through an almost sylvan setting and carries a considerable volume of pleasure craft. Two roads run within the park – the Outer Circle cuts through the zoological gardens for part of its journey and the Inner Circle – enclosing Queen Mary's Gardens which were formerly maintained by the Royal Botanical Society and are still of considerable interest – also runs round the open-air theatre which wages annual war against the fickle English weather.

The zoo is undoubtedly the finest feature of the park, but among buildings of interest are Bedford College, part of the University of London, and Winfield House. The latter was once the home of Barbara Hutton, the Woolworth millionairess, and is now the residence of the American ambassador. It replaced St Dunstan's Lodge, which gave its name to the famous St Dunstan's Institution for men blinded in the 1914–18 war. Officially the Gardens of the Zoological Society, the London Zoo now occupies about 36 acres at the northern end of the park. It was opened in 1828, two years after the foundation of the Zoological Society by Sir Stamford Raffles and Sir Humphry Davies, and covered five acres. The collection at this time comprised three animals: a deer, a white-headed eagle, and a griffon vulture. They were tended by a single keeper whose uniform consisted of a top hat, striped waistcoat, tail-coat, breeches, and wellington boots with painted tops! In 1831 the animals previously in the Royal Menagerie at the Tower of London were added to the collection; in 1836 four giraffes were purchased at a cost of £2,300; and in 1835 the first chimpanzee ever to be seen in Britain arrived.

The Zoological Society set out to encourage the 'advancement of zoological science' and to introduce into this country 'such subjects of the animal kingdom as might be of utility, and a source of interest and gratification'. With over 6,000 inhabitants in the zoo and visitors totalling more than two million each year it seems certain that it has achieved at least the latter aims. Much of the zoo has been redesigned in recent years and new animal houses are constantly being built, although some of the original buildings by Decimus Burton, who laid out the first zoo, are still in use. Many of the new buildings are designed by Sir Hugh Casson.

The London Zoo has a fine record for the raising of rare animals in captivity, including the takin from Tibet and the giant panda. Now, among the thousands of rare and beautiful mammals, reptiles, birds, and insects, giant pandas are represented once again. This time by the two young pandas presented to Mr Edward Heath by the Republic of China in the spring of 1974. It is to be hoped that, unlike the much-publicized Chi-Chi and An-An of the 1960's, they may prove compatible and provide yet another triumph for the largest and most comprehensive animal collection in the world.

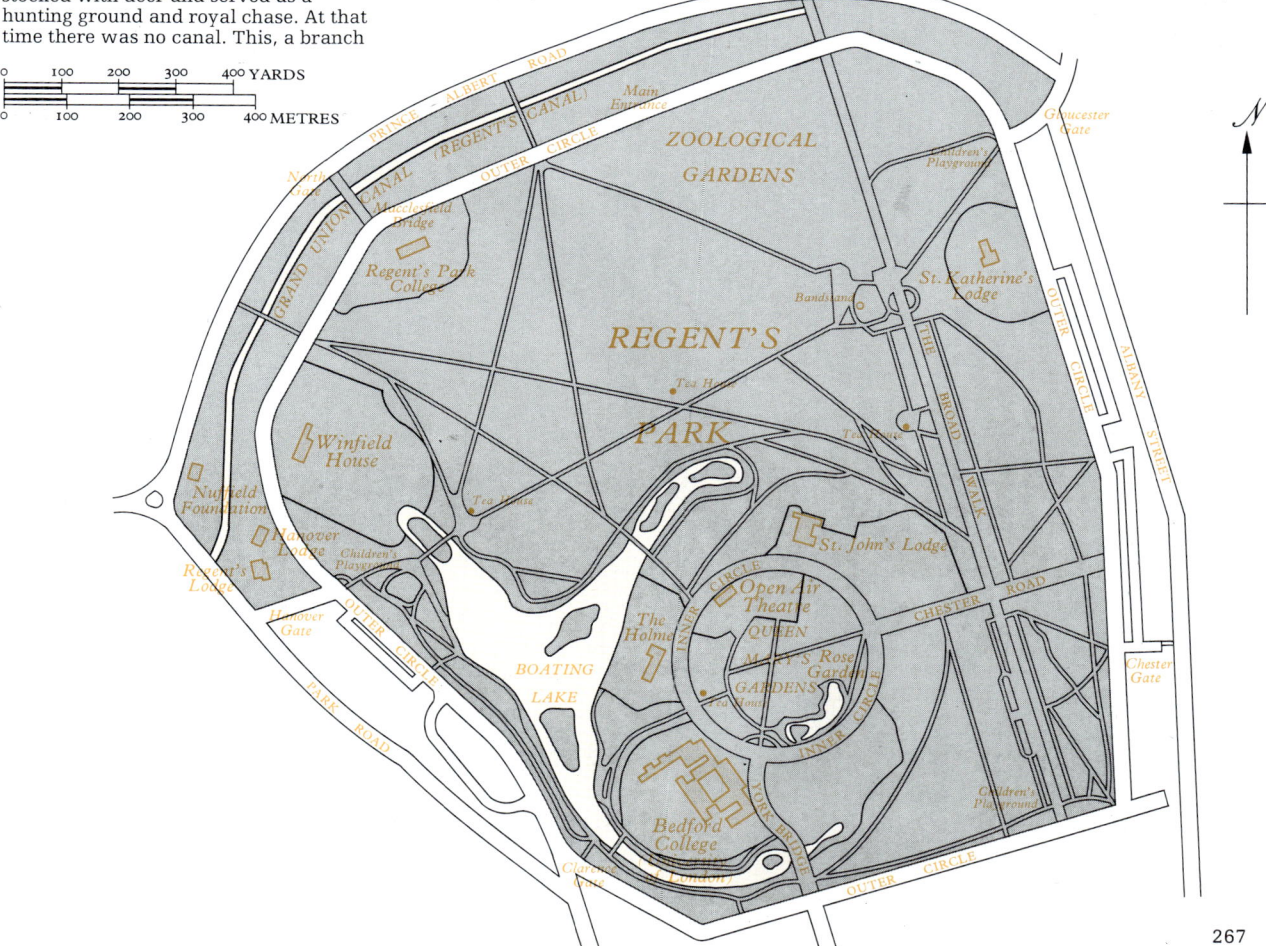

LONDON (HEATHROW) AIRPORT/LONG COMPTON

LONDON (HEATHROW) AIRPORT, Gt London *8 TQ07*
This great airport is situated off the A4 Bath road and is linked to the M4 motorway. A public enclosure and roof terraces are open daily, and parking facilities are available.

LONG ASHTON, Avon *6 ST57*
An important Fruit Research station has existed here since 1903. Ashton Court is a large 15th- to 19th-c mansion with a 300ft frontage. The grounds contain the Domesday Oak, which is thought to be 800 years old. The church contains a striking 15th-c monument to Sir Richard Choke, a judge. It is adorned with a recumbent effigy, angels, heraldry, and includes a canopy.

LONGBRIDGE DEVERILL, Wilts *7 ST84*
Gabled 17th-c almshouses existing in this attractive village were built by Sir John Thynne of Longleat House. Old helmets hang in the church tower, and the building itself contains Norman arches and a Norman font. The village lies near the Somerset border in rolling downland.

LONG COMPTON, Warwickshire *13 SP23*
The restored church displays Norman doorways and a thatched church-room

1 Bluecoat Chambers
2 Cathedral (Anglican)
3 Cathedral of Christ the King (RC)
4 Cunard Building
5 Dock Board Offices
6 Felicia Heman's House
7 Football Ground
8 Gladstone's House
9 Kingsway Tunnel
10 Queensway Tunnel
11 Royal Liver Building
12 St George's Hall
13 St Nicholas's Church & Memorial Garden
14 Town Hall
15 Walker Museum and Art Gallery

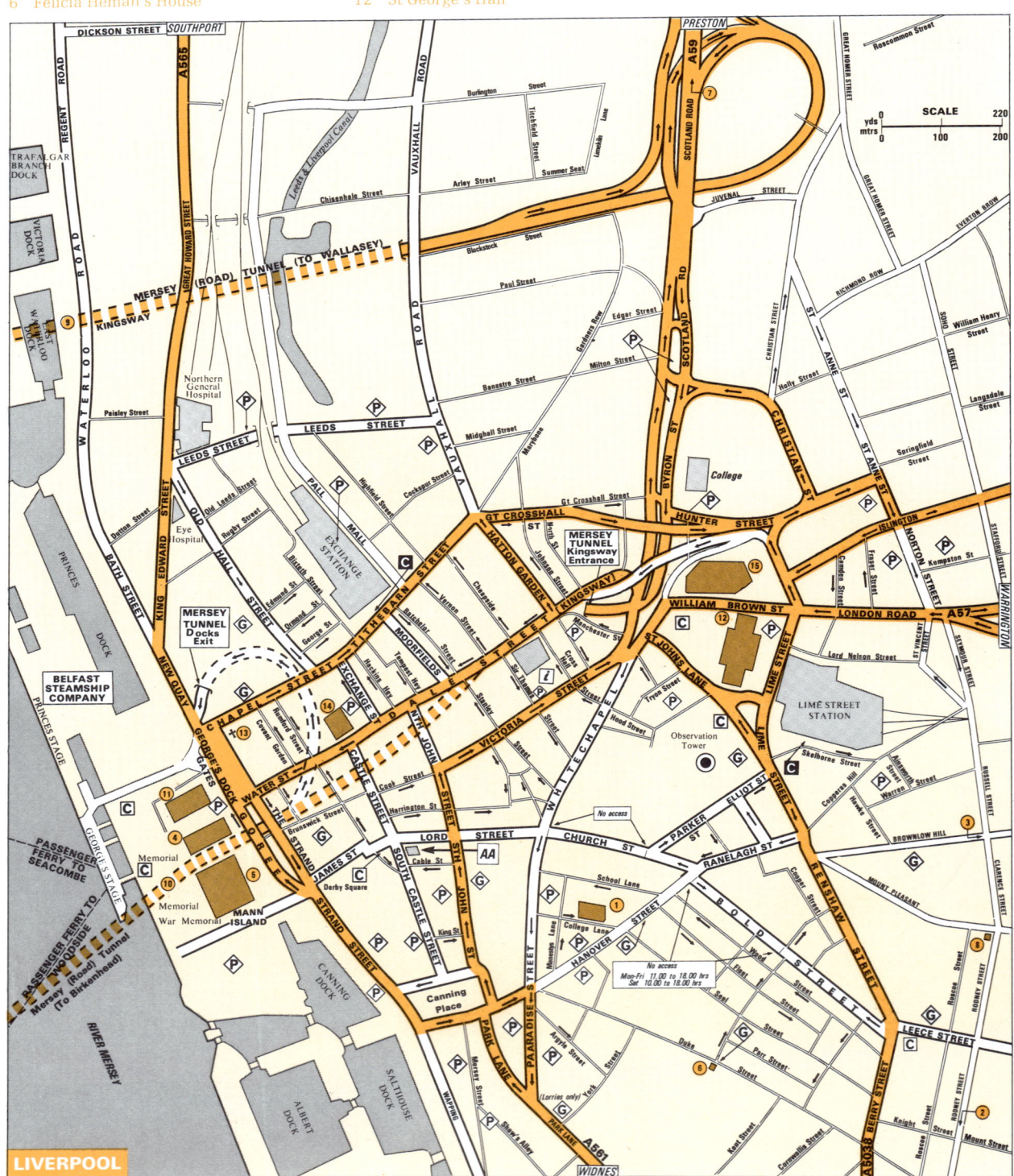

LIVERPOOL

above the lych-gate. Little Wolford includes a beautiful partly half-timbered manor house dated 1557 and 1671 (3m NNW). Several old houses exist in the area.

LONG CRENDON, Bucks *13 SP60*
Cottages dating from the 17thc can be seen in this attractive village, and the perpendicular church includes a spiral staircase in a nave pier. The Court House is a partly half-timbered 14th-c structure. It was once a staple hall, and was probably first used as a wool store. The village also boasts a beautiful old timbered manor house with an entrance guarded by a stone gatehouse. Notley Abbey dates from the 15thc and later, and stands 2m NE with an old dovecote.

LONGDON-UPON-TERN, Salop *17 SJ61*
Designed by Telford in 1794, the cast-iron aqueduct that exists here was built to carry the Shropshire Union Canal across the River Tern. It is the earliest example of its type. The restored church dates from 1742, and the Tudor hall is a fragment of a much larger building.

LONG EATON, Derbyshire *18 SK43*
Once a straggling village, this industrial town owes its development to the growth of roads, canals, and railways – and in particular to the introduction of lace-making mills. Many new industrial operations have been introduced in recent years.

LONGFORD, Derbyshire *18 SK23*
Monuments to the Cokes and Longfords can be seen in the Norman to 14th-c church. The hall is mainly-Tudor house which was remodelled c1700, and has been restored. A plaque recalls the opening of the first English cheese factory.

LONGFRAMLINGTON, Northumberland *27 NU10*
A mainly-Norman church shows notable chancel arch and south porch of the period. The track of a Roman road known as the Devil's Causeway extends SW from here, to reach the Roman Wall near Stagshaw Bank.

LONG ITCHINGTON, Warwickshire *13 SP46*
St Wulfstan was born here in c1012, and the mainly-decorated church houses a good screen. Lightning destroyed the spire during a service in 1762.

LONGLEAT, Wilts *6 ST84*
This great Renaissance house of 1556 was built by Robert Smythson, for Sir John Thynne. Macaulay described it as 'perhaps the most magnificent house in England', and has fine state rooms and numerous art treasures. The large park which surrounds the house contains Shearwater, and the viewpoint of Heaven's Gate. A lion reserve features monkeys and other foreign animals, and is one of the best-known in England (OACT). The grounds were landscaped by Capability Brown.

LONG MARSTON, Warwickshire *12 SP14*
King's Lodge is associated with King Charles II, who stopped here while fleeing in disguise from the battle of Worcester. Morris Dancing is a notable feature of the village.

LONG MARSTON, N Yorks *22 SE45*
Cromwell defeated the Royalists in the 1644 Battle of Marston Moor, the field of which lies about 1m N of the village.

LONG MELFORD, Suffolk *15 TL84*
Long Melford is a particularly attractive village with an impressive main street. Its medieval character is preserved through such features as the 15th-c Bull Inn, a picturesque green, an old brick-built conduit, and an almshouse or hospital founded by Sir William Cordell in 1593 and greatly restored in the 19thc.

The community's splendid perpendicular church includes a lady chapel of 1496, 15th-c stained glass, a great range of windows, and a rebuilt tower. Notable monuments exist in the Clopton chantry. A typical crinkle-crankle (or undulating) brick wall can be seen in the churchyard of the congregational church. The church itself dates from c1724. Melford Hall (NT, OACT), and Kentwell Hall are both Elizabethan structures. The former displays a curious gazebo, and moated Kentwell Hall is approached by a long avenue of lime trees. Melford Place, of mainly 18th-c date, includes the old chapel of St James.

LONGNOR, Staffs *18 SK06*
Longnor is a moorland village situated between the Rivers Dove and Manifold. The church was rebuilt in 1780, but retains an early-Norman font. There is a monument to William Bellinge, who fought at Ramillies and died at the age of 112 in 1791.

LONGPARISH, Hants *7 SU44*
Longparish is an attractive Test-Valley village. A 9ft font cover and a 15th-c tower are features of the local church. Harewood Forest lies to the W, and contains a memorial known as Deadman's Plack. This recalls the murder of King Athelwold by King Edgar.

LONG SUTTON, Lincs *14 TF42*
This pretty market town includes an interesting mainly-perpendicular church. The latter's main feature is a 162ft, detached early-English tower with a timber-and-lead spire – considered one of the finest in existence. The nave is of stately trans-Norman origin, and there is a medieval brass eagle lectern.

LONG SUTTON, Somerset *6 ST42*
A lofty 13th-c tower with an early lead spire is carried by the perpendicular church. Interesting woodwork includes the screen, loft, and nave roof. Court House is of early Tudor and 17th-c date, and the manor house originates from the 17thc. The Friends Meeting House is dated 1717.

LONGTHORPE, Cambs *19 TL19*
Longthorpe Tower is a 13th-c fortified house containing remarkable 14th-c wall-paintings (AM, OACT). Aerial photography has revealed the outlines of a large Roman fort in the area. Thorpe Hall, a fine 17th-c house lying to the E, is attributed to John Webb.

LONGTON, Staffs *18 SJ94*
Longton is a pottery town which is associated with Arnold Bennett's novels about the Five Towns.

LONGTOWN, Cumbria *26 NY36*
This River-Esk market town has a little industry. The local 17th-c church displays an 8ft cross in the churchyard, and is situated at Arthuret. Netherby Hall, famous for Young Lochinvar's elopement with the Graham family heiress – as described by Sir Walter Scott in *Marmion* – lies N of Longtown. Partly 14th- and 15th-c Scaleby Castle has associations with the Civil War, and lies 6m SE.

LONGVILLE-IN-THE-DALE, Salop *17 SO59*
Situated on the W slopes of Wenlock Edge, Longville-in-the-Dale includes two fine old houses – Wilderhope and Lutwyche. These lie above the village, along the Edge. The first-named has Civil War associations and now serves as a Youth Hostel (NT, OACT). It displays fine plaster ceilings of 17th-c origin.

LONG WITTENHAM, Oxon *13 SU59*
The Barley Mow Inn is associated with Jerome K Jerome's *Three Men in a Boat*. A good lead font can be seen in the Norman to perpendicular church, plus examples of Jacobean woodwork and a timbered porch. The Pendon Museum includes railway exhibits and displays scenes from the Vale of White Horse and Dartmoor. The Sinodun Hills include Wittenham Clumps, a wooded hill rising to the SE surmounted by a large iron-age hill fort.

LONGWORTH, Oxon *13 SU39*
Several brasses and a Jacobean screen are features of the ancient church, and an old manor house stands near by. This village was the birthplace of R D Blackmore, author of *Lorna Doone*.

LOOE, Cornwall *5 SX25*
The twin fishing towns and holiday resorts of East and West Looe are joined by a modern bridge spanning the Looe River. West Looe church displays a detached bell tower. East Looe features quaint streets and a pillory preserved outside the 16th-c guildhall. An interesting museum and woolly monkey sanctuary are sited E at Murrayton. Looe Island lies offshore, and the area has developed into a well-known shark-fishing centre. The name is of Celtic origin and means a pool or inlet of water.

LOPPINGTON, Salop *17 SJ42*
Loppington church was damaged during the Civil War, but contains interesting Jacobean woodwork. A very rare iron bull-baiting ring has been preserved in the road facing the local inn.

LORTON, Cumbria *26 NY12*
Situated in the pastoral Vale of Lorton, this River-Cocker village includes a church displaying a good stained-glass window. Lorton Hall dates from the 17thc and retains the ancient pele tower in which Malcolm III and Queen Margaret stayed in 1089. Charles II was here in 1650 (OACT). To the E is 1,043ft Whinlatter Pass.

LOSTWITHIEL, Cornwall *4 SX15*
Once the capital of Cornwall and a centre of the tin trade, Lostwithiel is sited on the River Fowey. A medieval bridge (AM) spans the river, and the 14th- to 15th-c church retains a 13th-c tower surmounted by an octagonal lantern. An ancient cross is also of interest.

Duchy House includes remains of the Stannary Court, and is of 14th-c date. An old building which formerly served as the Malt House bears an inscription recording its 3,000 year lease, commencing in 1652. Georgian buildings in the area include the grammar school of 1781. The guildhall dates from 1740. Restormel Castle is a well-known 12th- to 13th-c ruin. It lies 1m N and has retained its circular keep (AM). The beautifully wooded Glynn-Valley stretch of the Fowey river is situated 6m N. Boconnoc is a fine mansion set in a large park some 3m ENE. It was here that Lord Chatham, the first William Pitt, spent his boyhood. A Civil War battle was fought near by.

LOUGHBOROUGH, Leics 18 SK51
Hosiery and engineering are two of the industries with which this River-Soar town is involved. It is also an educational centre, and is situated on the Grand Union Canal. One of its more famous features is the bell foundry. The large parish church of All Saints is of decorated and perpendicular style, and carries a splendid tower. A notable bell-ringing feat took place here in 1919, when 5,041 changes were rung in a Victory Peal. Burton chapel is notable, and the war memorial in Queen's Park has a carillon of forty-seven bells. A well-known technological university is situated in the town.

LOUTH, Lincs 19 TF38
The church's 295ft perpendicular tower and spire is dated 1506, and can be considered one of the finest in England. Tennyson attended the grammar school, and his first book was published here. Fine 18th-c houses can be seen in Westgate and Upgate. A plaque in Eastgate marks the passage of the Greenwich Meridian line. The curious old Corn Exchange is of interest. Motor racing takes place at nearby Cadwell Park. Little Cawthorpe Manor, dated 1673, incorporates Dutch gables and lies 3m E. The RAF flying college of Manby is situated 5m E.

LOWER BRAILES, Warwickshire 13 SP33
Curious carvings and gargoyles on the south-aisle parapet of the 14th-c church are of interest. The building itself is known as the Cathedral of the Felden, and carries a 120ft tower.

LOWER HEYFORD, Oxon 13 SP42
Rousham is a 17th- and 18th-c house, situated near the River Cherwell. The garden lay-out was by William Kent, and is the only one of his gardens to have survived in its entirety (OACT).

LOWER PEOVER, Cheshire 17 SJ77
This attractive village includes a rare black-and-white timbered church. The Old School dates from 1710, and Peover Hall, situated 3m E at Over Peover, is of mainly 16th-c date. The latter includes notable stables of 1654 (OACT).

LOWESTOFT, Suffolk 15 TM59
Popular as a holiday resort, this fishing port offers natural amenities which include sandy beaches, bathing, and both sea and river fishing. Lake Lothing is linked to Oulton Broad and lies SW. A notable part of the attractive old town is an area criss-crossed by narrow lanes known as the Scores.

Lowestoft's large parish church dates from the 15thc and carries a 14th-c spired tower. Inside is a brass lectern of 1504 and good windows. The Sparrows' Nest is a picturesque park and theatre situated beyond the High Lighthouse. George Borrow wrote most of his books at his home on Oulton Broad, but the house has since been demolished. East Anglia Transport Museum specialises in trams and trolley buses, and is situated at Carlton Colville. Lowestoft Ness is England's most easterly point.

LOWESWATER, Cumbria 26 NY12
This village lies between a lake of the same name and Crummock Water. Carling Knott rises to 1,784ft behind Loweswater lake, and Grasmoor to 2,791ft in the E. The latter is the district's highest mountain. Crummock Water lies a little to the SE and is overshadowed by 1,668ft Mellbreak.

LOWICK, Northants 13 SP98
Lowick's interesting church has a 15th-c tower with an octagonal lantern, and houses numerous contemporary monuments. The famous old Lowick Oak stands in the village. Splendid 14th- to 18th-c Drayton House stands 1m SW and is considered one of the best mansions in the county.

LOWTHER, Cumbria 26 NY52
Lowther Castle was built in 1811 by Smirke, and is now a mere shell surrounded by a great park. A recently-opened wild life park is of interest (OACT). Lowther family tombs exist in the mausoleum of the partly-Norman church, and other notable features include an old cross, a mounting-stone, and three hogback graves.

LUCCOMBE, Somerset 5 SS94
Dunkery Beacon rises from the borders of this picturesque NT-owned village. It attains a height of 1,707ft and is part of the vast Holnicote estate (NT).

A perpendicular tower and barrel-roof with carved bosses are features of the local church. Somerset's only thatched church, 15th-c Tivington chapel, lies 2m NE off the A39. Part of the building is used as a private dwelling. An old pack-horse bridge has been preserved 1½m NW near West Luccombe. Densely-wooded Horner Valley contains an old mill; Cloutsham Combe is noted for stag-hunting meets; both areas lie to the SW.

LUCTON, Herefs & Worcs 12 SO46
Black-and-white cottages can be seen in the village, and Lucton School displays a charming façade. The latter was built by a London vintner, John Pierrepoint, in 1708. Lucton Mill dates from the 18thc and ceased working in 1940 (AM, OACT).

LUDDENDEN FOOT, W Yorks 22 SE02
Kershaw House is dated 1650 and displays a fine rose window. The Lord Nelson Inn was frequented by Branwell Brontë, brother of the Brontë sisters.

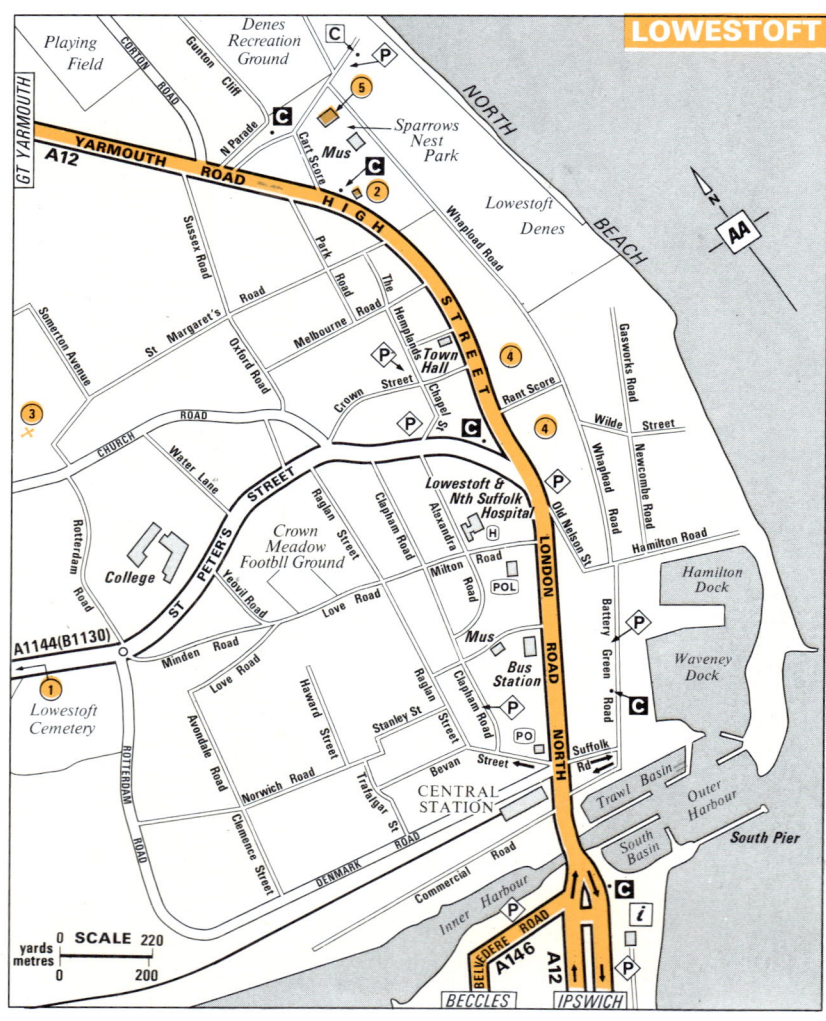

1 East Anglia Transport Museum
2 High Lighthouse
3 Parish Church of St Margaret
4 Scores
5 Sparrows' Nest

LUDGERSHALL, Bucks 13 SP61
John Wycliffe was vicar here in 1368. Carvings of human faces are displayed by the pier capitals, and a Tudor brass in the chancel portrays three women – one of whom is said to have lived through nine reigns.

LUDGERSHALL, Wilts 7 SU25
Part of the old market cross and fragmentary remains of the castle are preserved here. The cruciform-shaped church is partly Norman and contains a notable 16th-c tomb. Biddesden House is a mansion of 1772, lying 2m E.

LUDHAM, Norfolk 15 TG31
Ludham is a Broads village where the mainly-perpendicular church is noted for its painted screen and rare Royal Arms of Queen Elizabeth I. There are 18th-c houses in the market place, and the hall embodies part of an old abbey grange.

LUDLOW, Salop 12 SO57
A picturesque old town on the Rivers Corve and Teme, Ludlow includes a grand ruined late 11th-c Norman castle containing a round chapel (AM, OACT). Milton's *Comus* was first performed here in 1634. Ludford Bridge (AM) is of interest, and the many old houses include the half-timbered Feathers Hotel of 1521. Two other inns of note are The Angel and The Bull, and the Reader's House is a particularly fine building.

Ludford House and Lane's Hospital are of interest. Hosyer's almshouses were founded in 1486 and rebuilt in 1758. The grammar school dates from the 14thc, and the Broad Gate is the only original town gate to survive. Broad Street is considered one of the handsomest streets in England. The guildhall dates from the 15thc. The mainly-perpendicular church displays a fine screen and loft, beautifully carved stalls with misericords, many interesting monuments, and some old glass.

The ashes of A E Housman, author of *A Shropshire Lad*, are buried in the churchyard. The butter cross dates from 1744, and the Tolsey preserves 15th-c half-timbering. An excellent view of the town can be enjoyed from Whitcliffe. Ludlow makes an excellent touring centre for the Welsh Marches.

LULLINGSTONE, Kent 8 TQ56
The mainly 18th-c castle at Lullingstone is the home of the Hart Dykes, and includes a fine 16th-c outer gateway. The original manor house that occupied this site was in existence at the time of the Domesday Survey. A Roman villa, now permanently under cover, has been excavated near the castle. Exhibits include richly tessellated pavements (AM, OACT). The 14th- to 16th-c church features old glass, interesting brasses, tombs, and a good 16th-c screen.

LULLINGTON, E Sussex 8 TQ50
This little Cuckmere-Valley village is noted for its minute 16ft-square church, one of the smallest in England. It dates from the 13thc and formed the chancel of a larger church.

LULWORTH COVE, Dorset 6 SY87
Almost land-locked by the surrounding cliffs, this beautiful small bay is part of an area rich in Thomas Hardy associations. Stair Hole displays curiously contorted rock strata, and is of considerable geological interest. The well-known natural rock arch of Durdle Door is accessible from the cliffs by footpath. Swyre Head faces the cliffs of the White Nothe, and lies W.

LUNDY ISLAND, Devon 4 SS14
Lundy is situated about 12m from the Bristol Channel coast, and is accessible from a number of ports during the summer – including Bideford. Remains of Marisco Castle are of interest, and the Shutter Rock is associated with Kingsley's *Westward Ho!* Puffins and countless other sea birds breed here. A 400ft slab in the granite cliffs is known as the granite slide. Some of the finest sea-cliff climbing in England is available on the island.

LURGASHALL, W Sussex 8 SU92
This attractive village includes an 11th-c and later church housing a font of 1661. A 16th-c timbered external gallery attached to the church was once used as a school.

LUSTLEIGH, Devon 5 SX78
Dartmoor national park laps the W borders of this village. Thatched Wreyland Hall is dated 1680, and the perpendicular church houses a fine screen. Lustleigh Cleave is a beautiful area to the NW, through which the River Bovey flows.

LUTON, Beds 14 TL02
The Vauxhall car factory is in Luton, and engineering is one of the town's main industries. Screens, brasses, and a notable font cover can be seen in the large perpendicular-style Church of St Mary. The Wardown Park museum is famous for its lace. An airport is situated in the area. Luton Hoo, a restored Adam mansion in a fine park by Capability Brown, stands 2m S. The house can be described as palatial and contains rich art collections (OACT). Remains of 15th-c Someries Castle lie 1½m SE.

LUTTERWORTH, Leics 13 SP58
John Wycliffe, who preached against the abuses of papal politics, is associated with the early-English to perpendicular church. He died here in 1384 and is commemorated by an obelisk. His remains were exhumed, burned, and cast into the little River Swift in 1414. The church contains Fielding monuments and brasses.

LYDBURY NORTH, Salop 11 SO38
Close to the old hall is a rare cockpit. The 12th- to 15th-c church carries a massive 13th-c tower and contains a 15th-c screen which bears the Ten Commandments. This inscription is dated 1615. Plowden Chapel dates from the 14thc, and Clive of India once lived in the 18th-c mansion of Walcot. The gardens and grounds of the mansion are notable and include a Douglas fir which has grown to 122ft. Elizabethan Plowden Hall lies 2m E, and contains secret hiding-holes and a notable chapel.

LYDD, Kent 9 TR02
Once a coastal town, Lydd now lies 3m inland and is said to have the lowest rainfall in England. An explosive called Lyddite was first tested here. The partly 14th-c church carries a 130ft tower, and sustained bomb damage during the last war. It is sometimes described as the Cathedral of Romney Marsh. Dungeness, famous for its lifeboats and nuclear-power station, lies 4m SE across Denge Marsh. Two lighthouses exist here.

LYDDEN, Kent 9 TR24
Rally-cross motor racing is held at Lydden Hill. Although of 12th-c origin, the flint church has been severely-restored.

LYDFORD, Devon 5 SX58
One of England's largest civil parishes, Lydford includes the greater part of Dartmoor. The River Lyd flows through a deep gorge (NT), and is spanned here by a bridge. Remains of a Norman castle (AM) have an interesting history; the lower floor was formerly a prison, and the upper floor later became a Stannary Court administering local tin mines. Great Links Tor rises to 1,908ft NE.

LYDIARD TREGOZE, Wilts 12 SU18
The exceptionally interesting 14th- to 17th-c church is noted for its superb St John-family monuments. These include the gilded Golden Cavalier. Other features include 17th-c altar-rails, a triptych in a cabinet, and ancient heraldic glass. Nearby Lydiard Park is a mansion of 1743, and is now the property of Swindon Corporation (OACT).

LYDIATE, Merseyside 21 SD30
Lydiate includes the Scotch Piper, an inn which may be the oldest in Lancashire. It is dated 1320 and incorporates a tree within its fabric. The roof is thatched.

LYDNEY, Glos 12 SO60
Roman remains have been found in Lydney Park, and a restored 14th-c cross is of interest. Oak from the Forest of Dean was used to build warships here in the 17thc. Early-English and perpendicular workmanship is evident in the church, which carries a rebuilt spire. A restored steam railway which is the property of the Dean Forest Preservation Society runs 4m to Parkend, where rolling stock is on display.

LYFORD, Oxon 13 SU39
Lyford is a village in the Vale of White Horse, which includes Georgian almshouses built round a courtyard. Lyford Manor of 1617 and 1631, and Lyford Manor farm of 16th- and 17th-c origin, are interesting old houses. An attractive house near the church is dated 1717.

LYME REGIS, Dorset 6 SY39
A steep main street runs down to the harbour in this small Lyme-Bay resort, and the shingle beach offers a little sand at low tide. The Duke of Monmouth landed on The Cobb to begin his revolution against James II in 1685.

Georgian houses exist in the town, and the restored mainly-perpendicular church contains a 17th-c canopied pulpit and a brass of 1890. Other notable features are the gallery of 1611, a double lectern, and a memorial window to Mary Anning, the amateur geologist.

Local almshouses date from 1549, and the town has links with Jane Austen's novel *Persuasion*. Picturesque Dowlands landslip occurred in 1839, and lies 4m SW. Part of it lies within the Axmouth-Lyme Regis undercliffs nature reserve. The area is rich in fossils. Jurassic ammonites and the occasional reptile bone are found in the blue Lias cliffs of

Lyme Regis – where Mary Anning found the *Ichthyosaurus*, and various cretaceous shells are packed in the narrow greensand strata of the landslip.

LYMINGTON, Hants 7 SZ39
This holiday resort and yachting centre is situated on the Lymington River where it flows into The Solent. The harbour master's office of 1833 was once a bath house, and the porch of Pressgang Cottage, a former inn, was the headquarters of an 18th-c pressgang. A car ferry connects Lymington with the Isle of Wight town of Yarmouth. Much of the church is Georgian, and many 18th-c houses grace the streets. Historian Edward Gibbon was once MP for the town. A lofty obelisk commemorates Admiral Sir Harry Burrard-Neale, who died in 1840.

LYMM, Cheshire 17 SJ68
Stocks and an old market cross are preserved here. The Bridgewater Canal, flows near by.

LYMPNE, Kent 9 TR13
A massive Norman tower is carried by the restored Norman to early-English church. Parts of the restored castle are Norman, but much is of 15th-c date. Port Lympne is a large house dated c1912, and slight remains of Stutfall Castle lie to the S. To the W, at Court-at-Street, are sparse remains of Bellerica Chapel. This was associated with Elizabeth Barton the 16th-c Holy Maid of Kent, who was executed at Tyburn.

LYMPSHAM, Somerset 6 ST35
Lympsham church carries a notable tower, and both the manor house and village cross date from the early 19thc.

LYNDHURST, Hants 7 SU20
Ponies and attractive woodland scenery make this New Forest village a popular place for tourists. Huge Knightswood Oak is thought to be about 600 years old, and has a girth of more than 21ft; Mark Ash Wood shows fine beeches, typical of the Forest. Millais, Leighton, and Burne-Jones ornamented and decorated the 19th-c church, and the grave of Mrs Hargreaves – the original Alice of Lewis Carroll's *Alice's Adventures in Wonderland* – is in the churchyard. The old Queen's House is still used for Forest Court sessions.

LYNEHAM, Wilts 7 SU07
Old screenwork and a fine tomb of 1731 exist in the church, and a large yew faces the south door. Tockenham lies E and dates from the 17thc, with modern additions.

LYNMOUTH, Devon 5 SS74
This picturesque little resort is situated at the mouth of the East and West Lyn Rivers, and includes a small harbour and a shingle and rock beach. The 19th-c Rhenish tower that stands on the shore was rebuilt after bad floods of 1952. Old lime-burning kilns have been converted into a shelter, and a cliff lift can be taken to Lynton. Steep and long Countisbury Hill rises to the E and includes some of the highest cliffs in England (NT). A lighthouse at Foreland Point (NT) is set amid beautiful surroundings. Wooded Watersmeet Valley (NT) is where the East Lyn and Hoar Oak waters converge, and lies $1\frac{3}{4}$m ESE.

LYNSTED, Kent 9 TQ96
Several fine 15th- to 17th-c timbered houses still stand here, and an Elizabethan manor house is of interest. The restored decorated and perpendicular church displays a wooden belfry and spire and houses interesting brasses. It also contains monuments by the first-known great English sculptor, Epiphanius Evesham.

LYNTON, Devon 5 SS74
Beautifully situated on the heights above Lynmouth, Lynton is connected to the latter by cliff lift. Old St Vincent's Cottage is now an Exmoor museum. The spectacular Valley of the Rocks lies W and leads to Lee Abbey, which lies on a well-wooded stretch of coast displaying lofty cliffs. Views towards Woody Bay and the distant Highveer Point can be enjoyed from here.

LYONSHALL, Herefs & Worcs 11 SO35
Remains of a moated 11th-c castle exist here, and the mainly 13th-c church contains carved chancel stalls.

LYTHAM ST ANNES, Lancs 21 SD32
A popular residential resort at the mouth of the Ribble estuary, Lytham St Annes is laid out on garden city lines. Natural amenities include sand at low tide and medicinal baths. An old windmill stands near the shore. The area boasts four championship golf courses. Lytham Hall is a fine 18th-c house by Carr.

LYTHE, N Yorks 23 NZ81
The restored Saxon, Norman, and later church contains memorials to the Mulgraves. Slight remains of 11th-c Mulgrave Castle exist in the wooded grounds of a modern castle. Lythe Bank is a steep 1 in $4\frac{1}{2}$ hill leading towards the coast.

MABLETHORPE, Lincs 19 TF58
Mablethorpe is a resort with sand dunes, golf courses and excellent bathing. It also caters for sea and river anglers.

MACCLESFIELD, Cheshire 18 SJ97
This silk manufacturing town is criss-crossed by steep streets, and includes 18th- and 19th-c mills. The market cross and Brocklehurst museum in West Park are of interest. St Michael's Church houses interesting monuments and the curious pardon brass. Macclesfield Forest lies E of the town.

MADELEY, Salop 17 SJ60
Octagonal St Michael's Church was designed by Telford and built in 1796. A fine old court includes a stately gateway – which is now converted into cottages – plus a remarkable sundial. King Charles took refuge in the Upper House in 1651. Ironworks operate in the district, and the churchyard contains 19th-c cast-iron tombs.

MADELEY, Staffs 17 SJ74
The mainly-perpendicular church contains two good brasses and the fine Egerton tomb of 1522. An old hall is dated 1647, and sparse remains of Heighley Castle lie $1\frac{1}{2}$m N.

MADINGLEY, Cambs 14 TL36
This attractive village includes a fine old hall of 1543 and later, in which King Edward VII lived as an undergraduate. It is now used as a university hostel. An American second world war cemetery is situated near the village, and a restored windmill stands in the area.

MADRON, Cornwall 4 SW43
Built of granite, the 14th-c and later Church of St Madernus is the mother-church of Penzance. Several monuments and a partly-painted screen can be seen inside. Ding Dong mine is a nearby abandoned tin working. Fine shrubs and a remarkable walled garden containing sub-tropical plants are features of mainly-modern Trengwainton (NT, OACT). Lanyon Quoit lies 2m NW and was re-erected in the 19thc; 3m NW is the curious perforated Men-an-Tol. Both of these are notable cromlechs. Near the latter is the *Maen-Scryfa* stone (AM), which bears an inscription in Roman capitals and may date from the 5th or 6thc.

MAIDEN BRADLEY, Wilts 6 ST83
Long Knoll rises to 945ft and forms part of a ring of hills surrounding this downland village. Priory Farm incorporates part of an old hospital, and the church retains a fine 17th-c monument.

MAIDENHEAD, Berks 8 SU88
Situated on one of the finest reaches of the Thames, this well-known resort and residential district includes an 18th-c road bridge and a railway bridge by Brunel among its more notable features. Almshouses date from 1659, and the Henry Reitlinger Bequest contains an

1 Admiral Sir Burrard-Neal Obelisk
2 Church of St Thomas the Apostle
3 Harbour Master's Office
4 Pressgang Cottage

interesting art collection (OACT). Boulter's Lock, a boating rendezvous and well-known beauty spot, is 1½m NE.

MAIDEN NEWTON, Dorset 6 SY59
Maiden Newton is a village in the Frome Valley, where the church displays a Norman chancel arch and an original wooden Norman door. An 18th-c chapel and picturesque old mill house are also of interest.

MAIDEN WAY
This Roman road extends N from a point E of Penrith, and crosses the Pennines near Melmerby Fell to reach the valley of the South Tyne. It passes N of Alston and then follows the river N before heading towards the line of the Roman Wall near Greenhead.

MAIDS' MORETON, Bucks 13 SP73
Now almost a suburb of Buckingham, Maids' Moreton still retains a few old cottages and an exceptionally fine perpendicular church. Notable features of the latter include the tower, windows, and stone seats.

MAIDSTONE, Kent 9 TQ75
Although this county town has some industry – eg brewing and paper-making – it is still the agricultural centre of Kent. It has grown up on both sides of the River Medway, and includes several interesting buildings.

All Saints' perpendicular church displays stallwork in the choir. Near by are the remains of a 14th-c college. The Archbishop's Palace is of mainly-Elizabethan origin, and was once a residence of the Archbishop of Canterbury. It stands facing the Medway, near an ancient barn which now houses a museum of old carriages. Chillington Manor is an Elizabethan house now serving as a museum and art gallery, which contains relics of William Hazlitt, a native of the town.

The town hall dates from 1763 and a fine pargeted house of 1611 stands at No. 78 Bank Street. Several 18th-c houses can be seen in the town, and hop gardens are cultivated in the neighbourhood. Mote Park is a 558-acre area which was bought from Lord Bearsted in 1929. Loose Wool House dates from the 15thc and lies 2m S.

MALDON, Essex 9 TL80
Oyster beds are a well-known feature of this picturesque port and yachting harbour, which lies at the mouth of the Rivers Chelmer and Blackwater. The town hall is of 15th-c origin, and the yard of the Blue Boar Inn is interesting. All Saints' Church carries a unique triangular 13th-c tower, and the south aisle of c1340 is notable. Remains of 12th-c Beeleigh Abbey are incorporated in a picturesque partly-timbered house lying 1¼m W.

MALHAM, N Yorks 22 SD96
This hamlet is extremely popular with summer-weekend trippers, and is situated on the 250m-long Pennine Way in picturesque Craven country. Malham Cove is a spectacular limestone amphitheatre where 300ft cliffs crowd round the source of the River Aire. Nearby Gordale Scar includes waterfalls which can be reached only by foot. Malham Tarn, a lonely sheet of water in a moorland setting, lies 4m N (NT). Charles Kingsley wrote part of *The Water Babies* at Tarn House, which is now leased to the Field Studies Council.

MALMESBURY, Wilts 12 ST98
A pleasant hill-top town above the River Avon, Malmesbury includes a splendid partly-ruined abbey church which shows Norman and decorated workmanship. The richly-carved south porch is particularly outstanding, and a rare watching loft or musicians gallery is situated above the nave arcade. A window recalls the monk Elmer, who attempted to fly with artificial wings.

Below the 14th-c tower of former St Paul's Church is a tombstone of 1703 which bears a curious inscription, recalling the mauling of Hannah Twynnoy by a tiger. The Green Dragon Inn preserves a 14th-c window, and a fine 15th- or 16th-c octagonal market cross (AM) is of interest. Old houses in the town include St John's Almshouses and the fine Bell Inn. John Aubrey, the county antiquary, was educated at the local grammar school during the 17thc. Thomas Hobbes was born at Malmesbury in 1588, and became known as a philosopher. Joseph Addison represented the town as MP from 1710 to 1719.

MALPAS, Cheshire 17 SJ44
Characteristic black-and-white houses can be seen in this small town. Good screens are housed in the Cholmondeley and Brereton Chapels of the 14th- and 15th-c church, and the surrounding area is mainly agricultural farmland.

MALTBY, S Yorks 18 SK59
This old village is situated in a valley and ringed by a complex of more recent buildings. The church has retained its Norman west tower, which shows herring-bone masonry. Hellaby Hall is of c1700 date and lies 1m W. Remains of 12th-c Cistercian Roche Abbey can be seen 1½m SE (AM). The 18th-c Sandbeck Park is near by.

MALTON, N Yorks 23 SE77
Once the site of a Roman station, this River-Derwent market town is situated at the foot of the Wolds. Both St Michael's and St Leonard's churches contain Norman work, and Malton Lodge is an interesting old mansion. Langton Wold, to the SE, is noted for the training of race-horses.

Old Malton (1m NE) has an early-English to perpendicular church – the surviving remains of an ancient priory (AM). The great 18th-c mansion of Castle Howard, seat of the Howard family, lies 6m W. It was built by Vanbrugh and stands in a magnificent park containing numerous statues, a domed temple, and a splendid mausoleum designed by Nicholas Hawksmoor (OACT). The Flamingo Park of Kirby Misperton Hall is sited on the Pickering road to the N of Malton, and is a 350-acre area which incorporates the Yorkshire Zoo (OACT).

MALVERN, GREAT, Herefs & Worcs 12 SO74
Great Malvern is the most important of several local towns which bear this name. The combination of these communities forms a well-known inland resort on the slopes of the Malvern Hills, dominated by the splendid 1,395ft

cont pg 275

1 All Saints' Church
2 Archbishop's Palace and nearby Carriage Museum
3 Chillington Manor (museum and art gallery)
4 College Remains
5 Loose Wool House
6 Mote Park
7 Town Hall

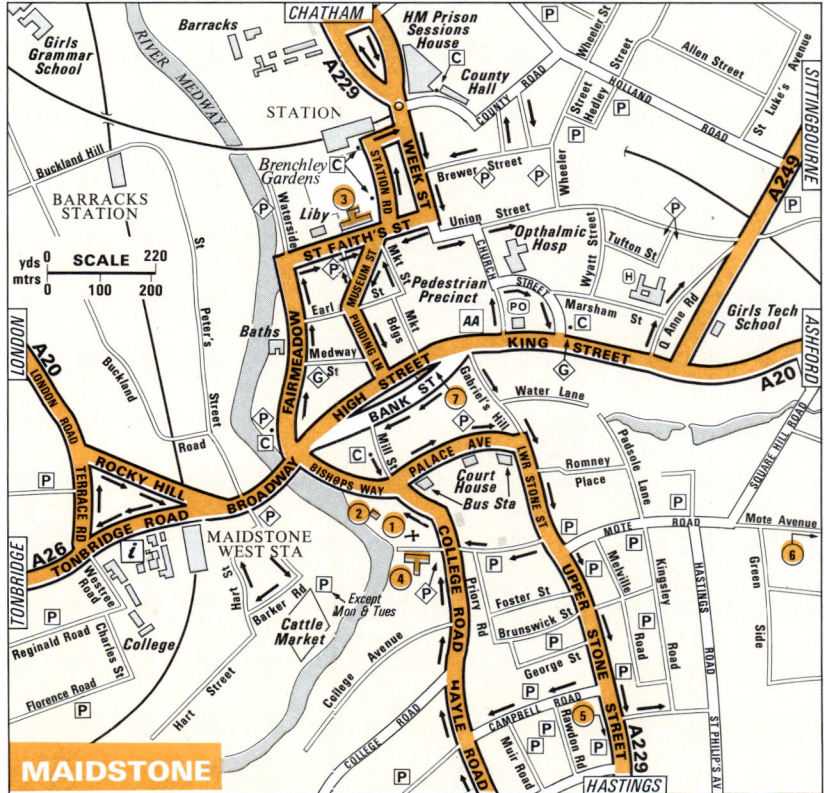

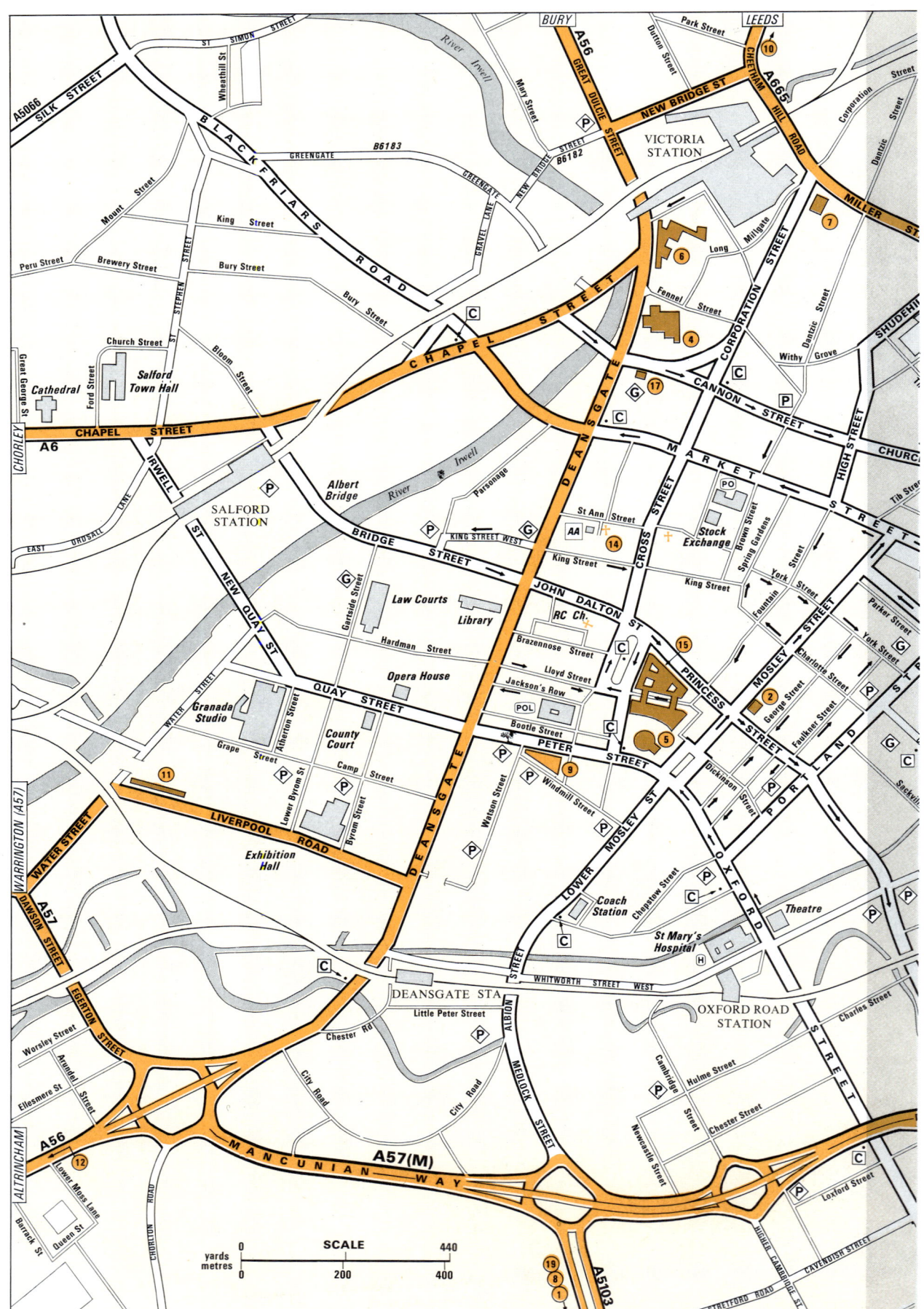

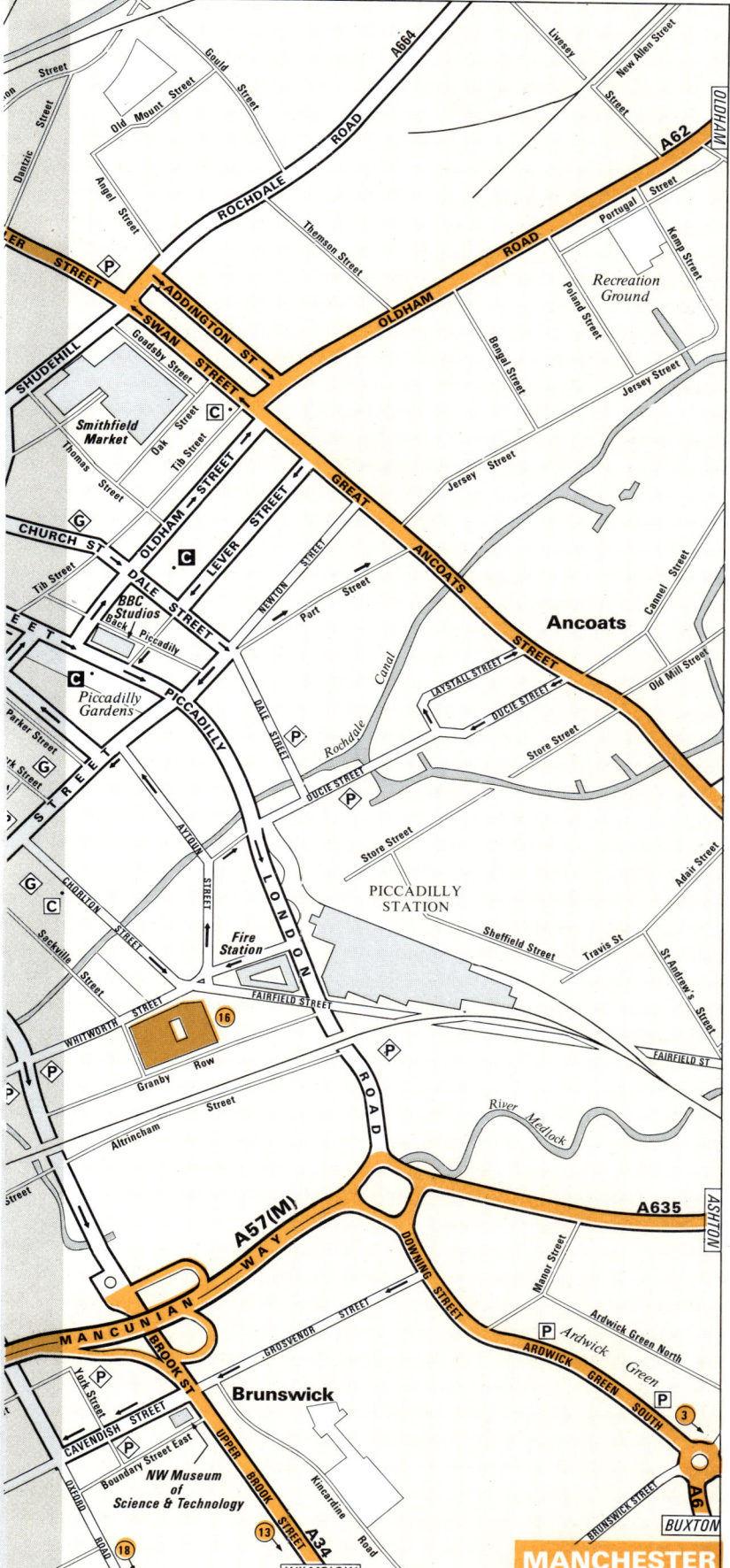

viewpoint of Worcestershire Beacon. St Anne's Well, one of the medicinal springs that gave the resort its reputation and past prosperity, gushes from the Beacon's slope.

Some 40sqm of these hills are currently designated an area of outstanding natural beauty. The fine Norman and perpendicular priory church contains a great deal of old glass, plus remarkable encaustic tiles. Malvern College is a well-known school, and local drama festivals are famous for the performances of plays by George Bernard Shaw. Jenny Lind is buried in the cemetery, and Sir Edward Elgar rests in the RC cemetery 4m S at Little Malvern. Elizabethan Madresfield Court lies 2m NE and is surrounded by a moat.

MANACCAN, Cornwall *4 SW72*
This hillside village is sited on the Lizard peninsula S of the Helford River estuary. The Norman and later church has a fine Norman south doorway, and a fig tree growing from one of the walls. The village was known as Menstre in 1275.

MANATON, Devon *5 SX78*
Situated on the E slopes of Dartmoor, Manaton includes a church displaying an old screen and statuettes. Prominent Hound Tor lies to the S; Bowerman's Nose is a curious outcrop of rock to the SW. Becky Falls can be seen about $\frac{1}{2}$m S, and the noted River-Bovey beauty spot of Lustleigh Cleave is $\frac{3}{4}$m W.

MANCETTER, Warwickshire *18 SP39*
Robert Glover and Joyce Lewis, two 16th-c martyrs, are associated with this village. An old black-and-white manor house is picturesque, and the 13th- to 15th-c church contains fine medieval glass. Michael Drayton was born 2m S at Hartshill in 1563. Remains of a Norman castle exist in the area.

MANCHESTER, Gt Manchester *17 SJ89*
Mancunium to the Romans, this great cotton and university city is linked to the sea by the 36m Manchester Ship Canal. The latter was completed in 1894, and includes fine modern docks. Extensive rebuilding and re-distribution of road traffic has changed the city beyond all past recognition. The mainly-perpendicular cathedral was formerly the parish church, and displays a fine tower and notable woodwork. Bomb damage included the destruction of the lady chapel and one of the two organs.

cont

1 Airport
2 Art Gallery and Museum
3 Belle Vue Zoological Gardens
4 Cathedral
5 Central Library
6 Chetham's Hospital (school & library)
7 Co-operative Insurance Building
8 Fletcher Moss Museum (Old Parsonage)
9 Free Trade Hall
10 Heaton Hall (museum)
11 Liverpool Road Station
12 Old Trafford County Cricket Ground
13 Platt Hall (museum)
14 St Anne's Church
15 Town Hall
16 University of Manchester & John Ryland's Library
17 Wellington Inn
18 Whitworth Art Gallery
19 Wythenshawe Hall (museum)

The city as a whole suffered greatly during the last war, and many of its notable buildings sustained irreparable damage. One of these was the Free Trade Hall, but this has since been rebuilt. Of surviving buildings, the interesting 15th-c Chetham's Hospital is particularly notable for its famous library – claimed to be the first public library in Europe. This structure now houses a school. St Ann's church dates from 1709, and important manuscripts exist in John Ryland's Library, which now forms part of the university. Whitworth Art Gallery displays old textiles; the art gallery and museum and the Central Library are also of note. Half-timbered Wellington Inn is one of the city's few remaining survivals of its particular style and period. Thomas de Quincey was born in Manchester in 1785.

The town hall was by Waterhouse, and dates from 1869. The new Co-operative Insurance buildings rise to 400ft. The halls of Platt, Heaton, and partly half-timbered Wythenshawe now house museums and stand in public parks. The Old Parsonage of c1800 is now the Fletcher Moss museum, and is situated at Didsbury. Old Trafford is the famous location of a county-cricket ground. Manchester is also the home of two famous football teams and the famous Halle Orchestra. Belle Vue Zoological Gardens are of note. Liverpool Road Station (built in c1830) is the oldest passenger station in the world, and is being preserved. Manchester airport is sited S of the city at Ringway in Cheshire.

MANKINHOLES, W Yorks 22 SD92
Stoodley Pike rises from the high moors to the E, and the village was once a thriving woollen centre. A number of 17th-c houses still exist here. Some of the ancient packhorse tracks that radiate from here preserve original stone guide-posts.

MANSFIELD, Notts 18 SK56
Hosiery mills and collieries are the main industrial involvements of Mansfield, and the town is situated at the edge of Sherwood Forest. St Peter's Church tower is of Norman origin, and the Moot Hall dates from 1752. Bentinck memorial was built in 1849. A large railway viaduct is of interest to the industrial archaeologist. King's Mill, associated with Henry II and the Miller of Mansfield, has been rebuilt and stands 1m SW.

MAPLEDURHAM, Oxon 7 SU67
A delightful Thames-side village situated on one of the most attractive reaches of the river. Old almshouses and a water-mill are of interest, and the Tudor manor house was fortified for the King during the Civil War. It was taken in 1643 by the Earl of Essex. Galsworthy's *Forsyte Saga* features the house (OACT). The local church is of restored late-perpendicular style, and includes the interesting Blount chapel.

MARAZION, Cornwall 4 SW53
Natural amenities offered by this small, Mount's-Bay resort include good sands and fishing. The town is of ancient origin and also serves as a port. Views of St Michael's Mount can be enjoyed from here. Goldsithney, lying a little to the E, includes an interesting museum of musical instruments (OACT).

MARCH, Cambs 14 TL49
March is the principal town in the Isle of Ely, and once stood on the River Nene. The river has since been diverted to form a straight route from Peterborough to Wisbech. The 15th-c Church of St Wendreda is famous for its double-hammerbeam roof, which is enriched with numerous carved angels. This is perhaps the finest of its kind still in existence. One of the largest mechanized railway goods yards in England operates here.

MARDEN, Herefs & Worcs 12 SO54
It is thought that the open well belonging to the mainly 14th-c church may mark the site of St Ethelbert's murder of c794. Amberley Court dates from the 14thc and is now a farm (2m E).

MARGARETTING, Essex 9 TL60
This place was known as Ing in the 11thc, but acquired the prefix of Margarett some two centuries later. The church is notable for its ancient timbering. The belfry is particularly good, and is supported on ten posts – in a similar fashion to the better-known Blackmore. Two porches, the tower, a 15th-c Jesse window, and a fine 15th-c octagonal font are also of considerable interest. A moated Tudor and 18th-c house known as Killigrews stands in the area.

MARGATE, Kent 9 TR37
Margate was once a port of some importance, and is now a popular resort offering a harbour, fishing, golf, and excellent sands. Impressive chalk cliffs extend to Birchington in the W, and beyond the North Foreland to Broadstairs in the SE. The restored flint-built parish church of St John houses many brasses, and a nearby 18th-c grotto displays shell-studded walls. The jetty and pier are by Rennie. Newly-restored Theatre Royal has its roots in the year 1787, and is one of the oldest in the country. Salmestone Grange retains 13th- and 14th-c work (OACT). Droit Building is situated at the pierhead and displays a plaque recalling the exodus from Dunkirk during the second world war.

MARHAMCHURCH, Cornwall 5 SS20
Thatched cottages surround a large square in this pretty village. One of its more notable features is a curious inclined plane, from which Bude Canal barges were raised or lowered by means of a continuous chain. The church shows a good 14th-c tower and preserves a rare cresset stone.

MARKET BOSWORTH, Leics 18 SK40
Dr Johnson was once an usher at the school, which is dated 1593, and the town is much the same size as it was when he worked here. The perpendicular church houses a 14th-c font and an ancient chest. The early 18th-c hall is now a hospital. Bosworth Field, the site of the famous battle where King Richard III was slain in 1485, is 2m S. Shenton Hall lies 3m SW and dates from 1629 and the 19thc. A fine gatehouse is displayed at the house.

MARKET DEEPING, Lincs 19 TF11
Market Deeping is situated at the edge of the Fens and stands on the River Welland. Although there is no longer a market at this ancient town, several fine old houses indicate its one-time importance. A restored perpendicular church preserves its rood-loft doorway, and the 13th-c rectory is the oldest inhabited parsonage in England (OACT).

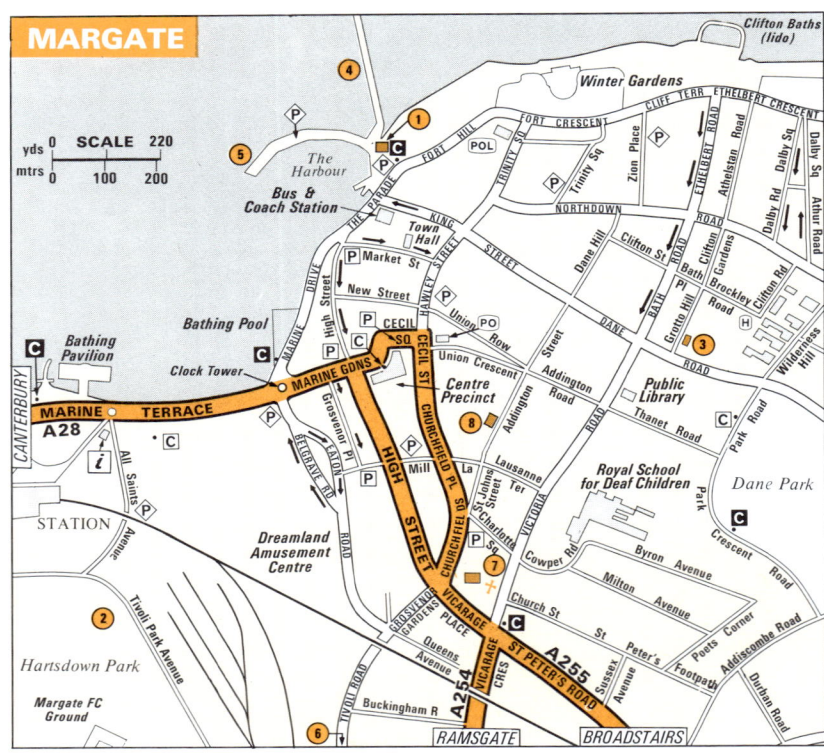

1 Droit Building
2 Golf Course
3 Grotto
4 Jetty
5 Pier
6 Salmestone Grange
7 St John's Church
8 Theatre Royal

Deeping St James lies 1¼m E, and includes a fine Norman to perpendicular church. The building is noted for its transitional nave arcade and 18th-c spired tower. The town's 15th-c cross incorporates an old lock-up.

MARKET DRAYTON, Salop *17 SJ63*
This ancient town stands on the River Tern and the Shropshire Union Canal. Georgian and older houses can be seen in Shropshire Street, and several curious manorial customs are maintained. The Albert Schafer Postage Stamp Room is a remarkable curiosity forming part of the Lord Clive Chambers. Although the church has been greatly restored, it retains a good trans-Norman west doorway. The grammar school was founded in 1558 and numbers Lord Clive among its past pupils. Several local legends relate events that are supposed to have taken place during his boyhood, and he is buried 2m SW at Moreton Say. Buntingsdale Hall is a fine 18th-c house standing 2m SW. A cross marking the site of a battle fought on Blore Heath in 1459 can be seen 2½m NE. This was a Wars of the Roses encounter where the Yorkists emerged victorious over the Lancastrians.

MARKET HARBOROUGH, Leics *13 SP78*
The River Welland flows through this hunting centre, and the decorated and perpendicular church of St Dionysius displays a good tower. It is thought that the latter may have been founded by John of Gaunt. A timbered house supported on wooden pillars stands in the town, and dates from 1614; it was once the grammar school. The town hall dates from 1788, and the former Corn Exchange from 1858. Dingley Hall is an Elizabethan and later house with a notable gatehouse, lying 2½m E.

MARKET OVERTON, Leics *19 SK81*
Formerly in the tiny county of Rutland, this village includes a church which displays a notable Saxon chancel arch. Stocks and a whipping post are also preserved.

MARKET RASEN, Lincs *19 TF18*
An old market town on the W edge of the Lincolnshire Wolds, to which several Georgian houses add a characteristic touch of elegance. The Centenary Chapel of 1861 stands in Union Street, and displays a notable façade. Many Roman remains have been found in and around the town, and a well-known racecourse exists in the area. A belt of blown sand to the E has provided a localized habitat for heather and conifers.

MARKET WEIGHTON, Humberside *23 SE84*
Situated at the foot of the Wolds, Market Weighton includes a trans-Norman to perpendicular church which displays arcades dating from the 13thc. Weighton is pronounced Weeton.

MARLBOROUGH, Wilts *7 SU16*
High downs rise to the N and S of this attractive old River-Kennet town, and the broad High Street is one of the widest in England. Many old houses and inns are preserved here, and the Five Alls Inn displays an interesting sign.

Marlborough College is a public school at which William Morris was once a pupil, and incorporates 18th-c Castle House –

The Marlow suspension bridge of 1829

once a coaching inn. St Peter's Church displays a lofty late-perpendicular tower where the curfew bell is still sounded each night. St Mary's Church was rebuilt in the 17thc, but preserves a fine Norman door and contains fragments of Roman sculpture. A 12th-c black-marble font exists in Preshute Church, ½m SW.

Fyfield Down national nature reserve covers high ground 3m W, and includes numerous sarsen stones – known locally as Grey Wethers. More sarsen stones, plus a dolmen known as Devil's Den, can be seen at Lockeridge Dene (NT).

Savernake Forest lies to the SE and is the habitat of deer. The A4 Bath Road traverses the forest, which measures 16m in circumference. Grand Avenue extends for 4m. Ailesbury Column commemorates the recovery of King George III from a mental disorder, and 18th-c Tottenham House, now a school, stands near by. The line of the ancient Wansdyke runs through the forest and the Kennet and Avon Canal flows through the Vale of Pewsey on Savernake's fringe. The white horse that can be seen on the Downs between Pewsey and Marlborough has been re-cut.

MARLOW, Bucks *8 SU88*
The notable suspension bridge spanning the Thames at Marlow has been strengthened twice since its original erection in 1829. Marlow Place dates from 1720, and is a particularly good example of the many Georgian houses that exist here. Shelley's house stands in West Street. This was where he composed the *Revolt of Islam*, and where Mrs Shelley wrote *Frankenstein*.

The Jacobean Old Vicarage in St Peter's Street retains a 14th-c hall. Interesting monuments are contained within the modern parish church, and St Peter's Church preserves an object said to be the mummified hand of St James the Apostle – brought here from Reading Abbey. An old fire engine of 1731 is preserved in the council offices.

MARNHULL, Dorset *6 ST71*
Well-known to Thomas Hardy enthusiasts as Marlott, Marnhull was the birthplace of the fictional heroine of *Tess of the d'Urbervilles*. Near the Crown Inn, called the Pure Drop in Hardy's novel, is the area where Tess and Angel Clare first met at the Club-Walk dance. The church's pinnacled tower overlooks the pastoral expanse of Blackmore Vale.

MARPLE, Gt Manchester *18 SJ98*
This largely-residential town is situated in the Goyt Valley. An aqueduct carries the Peak Forest Canal, joined here by the Macclesfield Canal, across the valley. John Bradshaw, a former owner of the Jacobean hall, was Chief Justice of the county in 1647. He also has the dubious distinction of having served as president of a court that sentenced Charles I to death.

MARSDEN, W Yorks *22 SE01*
Rapes Highway, an ancient trackway from Denshaw, ends at an old pack-horse bridge in the town. Nearby Marsden Moor covers some 6,000 acres (NT). Standedge railway and canal tunnel extend underground for over 3m, and the Huddersfield Canal tunnel is situated at 644ft – the highest canal level in England. The latter is also the longest to have been bored in the country, but its deterioration has progressed so far that it is no longer navigable.

MARSHFIELD, Avon *6 ST77*
Standing high up in the Cotswolds at an altitude of 633ft, this small stone-built town is noted for its mummers. The Nicholas Crispe almshouses are gabled and date from 1625.

MARSKE-BY-THE-SEA, Cleveland *27 NZ62*
Marske Hall is of Jacobean origin, and the resort provides amenities including sea bathing from good sands, and golf.

MARSTON MORETAINE, Beds *13 SP94*
Marston is the tun or village by a marsh; Moretaine is a family name derived from Mortain in Normandy. A restored 16th-c manor house is surrounded by a moat and displays good half-timbering. It is now used as a farm. The local perpendicular church has a detached tower.

MARTHAM, Norfolk *15 TG41*
A green and several 18th-c houses are included in this Broads village. The early-perpendicular church displays a splendid tower, and the Broads of Ormesby, Rollesby, and Filby lie to the E.

Part of the 4m causeway built by Maud Heath in the 15thc

MARTINSTOWN, Dorset 6 SY68
This was the area that suffered England's highest recorded rainfall on July 18 and 19, 1955 – 11 inches in the period of a single day.

MARTLESHAM, Suffolk 15 TM24
Martlesham is a village sited on a creek of the River Deben. The decorated and perpendicular church has a heptagonal wagon roof, and the Red Lion Inn displays a curious sign that was taken from a Dutch ship in 1672. Martlesham Heath, the site of a famous pre-war airfield, lies to the S and is now destined for extensive industrial development.

MARTLEY, Herefs & Worcs 12 SO75
A pleasant Teme-Valley village where the 12th- to 15th-c church displays a tower of the latter period, plus notable medieval wall-paintings. A fine old rectory includes a 14th-c hall. Sir Charles Hastings, founder of the British Medical Association, was born at Martley in 1794. Berrow Hill rises to 602ft and provides a good viewpoint.

MARTOCK, Somerset 6 ST41
Numerous old stone and thatched houses, plus a 14th-c manor house, can be seen here. A lofty nave and splendidly carved roof are features of the mainly-perpendicular church. Treasurer's House is a 13th- to 15th-c building which was once the home of the Treasurer of Wells Cathedral. It preserves a fine hall of c1370.

MARTON, Cheshire 17 SJ86
Marton Great Oak is said to be one of the largest in the land, and the quaint church is a 14th-c timbered structure. An aeroplane collection and armoury can be seen 3m N at the fine Jacobean-style mansion of Capesthorne Hall (OACT).

MARYPORT, Cumbria 25 NY03
Cliffs to the N of this old coal and iron port bear the remains of a Roman station. The town itself stands on the Solway Firth, at the mouth of the River Ellan, and offers good sands and bathing.

MARY TAVY, Devon 5 SX57
Mining was a flourishing industry in the area around this Dartmoor village during the 19thc. Wheal Betsy (NT) and Wheal Friendship are industrial plants which have partially survived from this period, and the engine house of the former has been preserved.

MASHAM, N Yorks 22 SE28
A huge market place is a feature of this River-Ure town, and the largely-perpendicular church includes a tower with an octagon surmounted by a spire. Swinton Park estate lies to the SW, and contains an 18th- or 19th-c structure known as Druid's Temple. The house itself dates from the 17thc and later. Low Barton Hall is a 15th-c and later house lying NE.

MASSINGHAM, GREAT, Norfolk 15 TF72
Ponds exist on the several greens in this village, and a village pump has survived. A rare arcaded and pinnacled 13th-c porch is the main feature of the local 14th- and 15th-c church.

MATCHING, Essex 8 TL51
Matching includes a marriage feasting house. This is of timber and plaster construction, and is a rare example of its type. The nearby church contains a pulpit of 1624, and the old moated hall preserves a dovecot.

MATFEN, Northumberland 27 NZ07
Houses from the 18th and 19thc face the village green, and the church and town hall both date from the 19thc.

MATLOCK, Derbyshire 18 SK36
This well-known inland resort and spa is situated on the River Derwent, amid lovely scenery on the edge of the Peak District national park. The Heights of Abraham rise to 1,000ft, and 600ft High Tor is a dominant landmark of the area.

Rutland and Cumberland Caverns are disused lead mines, and the ruins of curious 19th-c Riber Castle (1850) stand on a hill to the SE. Riber Castle fauna reserve covers 40 acres, and Riber Hall and manor house are both interesting old buildings. John Smedley founded his great hydro at Matlock Bank in 1853, a huge edifice which is now used as the headquarters of the Derbyshire County Council. The prominent Rockside Hydro of 1905 is now part of the College of Education. Elizabeth Snitterton Hall lies 1½m NW and is not open to the public. An ancient bull ring is set in the nearby roadway, and is a rare example.

MATLOCK BATH, Derbyshire 18 SK25
Medicinal springs and baths have made this River-Derwent town famous, and the area includes petrifying wells. Matlock Bath sprang from the Old Bath of 1698, and flourished until the Regency period. Ruskin stayed here in 1829. St Baptist Chapel stands in Cliff Road and was built by Sir Guy Dawber in 1897; it contains High Church furnishings of interest.

MAUD HEATH'S CAUSEWAY, Wilts 7 ST97
Maud Heath was a Wiltshire market woman who bequeathed her savings to build a 4m causeway from Wick Hill to Chippenham in 1474. The route ran via her home village of Langley Burrell, and she went to the expense of providing this paved way to save travellers – including herself – the trouble of negotiating the badly rutted track which formerly served as the only communication. A tall column at Wick Hill is surmounted by a statue of Maud Heath. A pillar of 1698 bears a sundial, and stands near a 64-arched bridge which carries the causeway near Kellaways.

MAUGHOLD, Isle of Man 26 SC49
Sir Hall Caine is buried here, and the churchyard Cross House contains 42 old crosses – many with runic inscriptions. Ancient Maughold Cross depicts the Legs of Man, and Maughold Head is a notable viewpoint.

MAWGAN PORTH, Cornwall 4 SW86
Mawgan Porth stands at the entrance to the Vale of Lanherne, also called the Vale of Mawgan, in an area of pleasantly-varied scenery. St Mawgan was a disciple of St Patrick. A small bay lying between Watergate Bay to the S and the well-known rock stacks of Bedruthan Steps to the N allows access for safe bathing.

MAXSTOKE, Warwickshire 12 SP28
The impressive moated castle of Maxstoke dates from the 14thc and contains the chair on which Henry VII was crowned at Bosworth Field. The castle is perfectly preserved, and the great gatehouse is its finest external feature. Remains of a priory (AM) dating from the same period are partly incorporated in a farm house.

MAYFIELD, Staffs 18 SK14
Situated on the River Dove, Mayfield includes a Norman and perpendicular church with a tower dating from 1515. Thomas Moore wrote most of *Lalla Rookh* at Mayfield cottage. The old hall is a picturesque structure of some interest.

MAYFIELD, E Sussex 9 TQ52
Old houses in this attractive small town include the notable timbered Middle House of 1576. The mainly-perpendicular church displays a 16th-c screen and a tall spire. Remains of an Archbishop's palace exist in the area, the oldest part being a fine 14th-c hall roof, now incorporated in a modern convent.

MEARE, Somerset 6 ST44
Remains of a prehistoric lake village have been excavated near this River Brue settlement, the finds from which are being kept in museums at Glastonbury and Taunton. The 14th-c manor house is now a farm, and a curious ancient Fish House is where the abbey fisherman of Glastonbury once lived (AM, OACT).

Medieval ironwork exists on the door of the 14th- to 15th-c church, and a carved 15th-c pulpit is housed within the building.

MEAVY, Devon 5 SX56
The village green bears an ancient oak and village cross. Drake once lived at a nearby farm. Marchant's Cross is over 8ft high and stands on the Cornwood road to the SE.

MEDMENHAM, Bucks 8 SU88
A Thames-side village where the decorated and perpendicular church shows a timbered chancel arch. Of special note is the picturesque Dog and Badger Inn. The ruined abbey is now incorporated in an old house, but was formerly connected with the notorious Hell Fire Club of c1750. This strange association was founded by Sir Francis Dashwood, who rebuilt West Wycombe church. Lodge Farm has a 17th-c exterior (NT). Culham Court, a structure dated 1771, lies W across the river.

Ruined Medmenham Abbey incorporated in an old house

MELBOURNE, Derbyshire 18 SK32
Melbourne church is a splendid example of Norman work. Of particular note is the nave. Two of the three towers carried by the building are incomplete, and a fine tithe barn stands opposite. Melbourne Hall is of 16th- to 18th-c date, and was once the seat of Lord Melbourne (OACT). Notable gardens contain a superb and well-restored pergola, designed by the 18th-c master-craftsman in ironwork Robert Bakewell. Thomas Cook, who pioneered popular travel, was born in the town in 1808. He arranged his first tour in 1841 – from Loughborough to Leicester.

MELDRETH, Cambs 14 TL34
The interesting Norman to perpendicular church displays good 14th-c windows and an old screen. Stocks and a whipping post are preserved.

MELKSHAM, Wilts 7 ST96
The much-restored church has a priest's room over the porch and stands near an old tithe barn. The latter is now used as a school. An 18th-c bridge spans the River Avon, and 17th- and early 18th-c houses can be seen in Cannon Square. An attempt was made to utilize a local chalybeate spring in 1815, the idea being to turn Melksham into a spa town. This project failed, and the remains of the original Pump Room are incorporated in a modern bungalow on the Devizes road.

MELLING, Lancs 21 SD67
Attractive 17th-c houses displaying curved Dutch-style gables can be seen in this attractive village. The largely-perpendicular church contains a raised chancel and Saxon gravestone. A curious earthwork exists in the vicarage garden.

MELLOR, Gt Manchester 18 SJ98
Mellor church displays a 15th-c tower, a Norman font, and an exceptionally-fine 14th-c wooden pulpit which has been restored. The latter was carved from a single block of oak, and is possibly the oldest in England.

MELLS, Somerset 6 ST74
This stone-built village has a perpendicular church which is noted for its lofty tower, interesting south porch, and Horner chapel. Opposite is a Tudor manor house associated with Little Jack Horner, displaying gabled roofs and mullioned windows. New St contains 15th-c houses built by Abbot Selwood, and Mells Park was rebuilt by Lutyens in 1923. Several prehistoric camps exist near the village.

MELMERBY, Cumbria 26 NY63
Lying E of the Eden Valley near 2,331ft Melmerby Fell, this village is the starting point of the spectacular Hartside road. The road climbs to almost 1,900ft below the 2,930ft Cross Fell, on its way to Alston, affording splendid views towards the Lake District fells.

MELTON MOWBRAY, Leics 19 SK71
Stilton cheeses and pork pies have helped to put this well-known hunting centre on the map. The fine Church of St Mary, of early-English and perpendicular periods, shows a good tower and west porch. The clerestory of 48 windows was added to the nave and transepts in the 16thc. The 17th-c Hudson Bede House is partly a museum, and Anne of Cleves House is of ancient origin.

MELVERLEY, Salop 17 SJ31
Open benches – a delightful survival from the past – and a massive screen are features of the 15th-c half-timbered church. Breidden Hills rise to over 1,200ft from the Welsh border, to the SW.

MENDIP HILLS
The Mendips are a rather bleak range of hills extending SE from Axbridge to a point beyond Shepton Mallet. The highest point is 1,068ft Black Down, and important Roman lead workings existed between Blagdon and Cheddar. A small amphitheatre can be seen at Charterhouse. Known caves in the area have been explored, and the famous Cheddar Gorge cuts through the hills on the W side. Less spectacular Burrington Combe (see Blagdon) cuts into the N escarpment. The small cathedral city of Wells lies at the foot of the hills in the S.

MENDLESHAM, Suffolk 15 TM16
An attractive village where the 15th-c flint-built church contains pieces of 17th-c armour, finely carved bench-ends, and a 17th-c font cover. A memorial to men of the American Air Force stands on a former airfield.

MEOPHAM, Kent 9 TQ66
Four famous Kent and Surrey players are portrayed by a sign hanging outside the Cricketers' Inn. John Tradescant was born here in 1608. This famous botanist and his father formed Tradescant's Ark, a museum which preceded the famous Ashmolean at Oxford. A restored windmill in the area may date from 1801. Nurstead Court preserves part of its rare original 14th-c timbered hall, and lies 2m N.

MERE, Wilts 6 ST83
Salisbury Plain borders this downland village. The Ship is a 17th-c inn with a fine 18th-c wrought-iron sign; the George is now modernized, but the old inn housed a disguised Charles II after the 1651 battle of Worcester. The perpendicular church displays a good screen and lofty tower. William Barnes the Dorset poet held his school in the Tudor Chantry. Woodlands is a notable 14th-c and later manor house which stands 1m S.

MEREVALE, Warwickshire 18 SP29
Remains of an abbey date from 1148, and the chapel at its gates is now used as the parish church. The latter contains early-English and decorated work, including examples of old glass. Merevale Hall includes the Dugdale library and was rebuilt in 1840.

MEREWORTH, Kent 9 TQ65
Mereworth's domed 18th-c castle is modelled on a famous Italian villa, and is one of the two surviving examples in England. The other is London's Chiswick House. It stands in a finely-wooded park. The 18th-c church preserves old brasses, and the grave of Admiral Lucas – the first VC – is in the churchyard. Mereworth Woods are extensive and Yotes Court dates from 1658.

MERIDEN, W Midlands 12 SP28
Sometimes held to be the exact centre of England, this village has a medieval cross on the green which claims this distinction. Archery contests are held for one of the oldest archery societies in England, the Woodmen of Arden, which was formed here in 1785. A cyclists' war memorial and an old cross are also of

interest. Forest Hall is dated 1788 and stands W of the village; it was originally built as the headquarters of the Woodmen of Arden.

MERSEY TUNNELS, Merseyside *17 SJ38*
The 2½m long Queensway tunnel links Birkenhead with Liverpool, and was opened by King George V on July 18, 1934. Two lines of traffic are carried in each direction by the main tunnel. It is now duplicated by the Kingsway Tunnel of 1971.

MERSTHAM, Surrey *8 TQ25*
Features of the restored partly 12th-c church include interesting brasses and a cornerstone from Old London Bridge, carved with three Royal leopards. Quality Street shows several old houses, and the fine mansion of Gatton Park stands in wide grounds to the SW. The latter now houses a school. Merstham church was gothicized in 1834, as a result of a Grand Tour by Lord Monson. Continental glass and woodwork, and a family pew with a fireplace, are features of this building. Gatton was a pocket borough which returned two members of Parliament until 1832. The curious little town hall was where the elections took place, and stands on a mound.

METHWOLD, Norfolk *14 TL79*
Fine brick and timber work and a gable beautifully ornamented in three tiers are features of the former rectory. The 14th- and 15th-c church displays a tower with a crocketed spire – an unusual architectural style for Norfolk – plus a hammerbeam nave roof.

MEVAGISSEY, Cornwall *4 SX04*
Mevagissey is a name derived from two saints – St Mevan and St Issey. The latter is another form of Ida. Two harbours are included in this picturesque resort and fishing port. It was once famous for smuggling, and for the building of fast sailing boats that could outrun the Excise cutters. An old boatbuilder's workshop now houses a Folk Museum. Interesting monuments of 1617 and 1632 are housed within the church, as well as a carved Norman font. Fine coastal scenery may be enjoyed to the S, towards the headland of The Dodman.

MICHELHAM PRIORY, E Sussex *9 TQ50*
A priory was originally founded here in 1229, on an earlier moated site. The subsequent Tudor and later house has been restored and stands in a delightful setting by the River Cuckmere. Notable features include an early 14th-c gatehouse and an eight-bay bridge over the moat (OACT).

MICKLEHAM, Surrey *8 TQ15*
Fanny Burney was married at the restored church in 1793, and George Meredith in 1864. Yews from an ancient Druids' grove can be seen in Norbury Park and the house dates from 1774 and later. Lord Beaverbrook died at Cherkley Manor in 1964. Box Hill stands 1m SE, and an interesting ruined chapel can be seen at West Humble some 2m S (NT). Local countryside includes several particularly attractive spots.

MICKLETON, Glos *12 SP14*
Medford House is the name of a beautiful Renaissance building which stands in this village, and it has often been the subject of illustrations in architectural text books. Also of interest is a fine gabled house of Tudor origin. The partly-Norman church originates from the latter part of its period, and carries a 90ft 14th-c broach spire – a rarity in the district. Meon Hill rises 637ft from the Cotswolds in the NE.

MIDDLEHAM, N Yorks *22 SE18*
Situated on the River Ure at the E extremity of Wensleydale, Middleham includes an impressive ruined castle which was once a Neville stronghold. Remains comprise a massive 12th-c keep within 13th-c curtain walls. Near the castle is the curious old Swine Cross. The church houses old glass, and 1½m SW is the 17th-c Braithwaite Hall which now forms part of a farm (NT). Scanty remains of Coverham Abbey lie 1¾m SW, at the entrance to delightful Coverdale. The fine old mansion of Danby Hall stands 2½m E.

MIDDLESBROUGH, Cleveland *22 NZ51*
Large iron and steel works and extensive docks on the Tees estuary form the bulk of this iron town's industry. The RC cathedral, the Dorman Museum of natural history and local antiquities, and the art gallery are all of interest. A transporter bridge of 1911 spans the Tees to the N, and is one of the two still in operation. The vertical-lift Newport Bridge of 1934 crosses the river to the W. Middlesbrough is a remarkable example of rapid 19th-c industrial growth, and thus a rich hunting ground for the industrial archaeologist. An imposing hall dates from this period. A modern theatre and a college of technology are important modern innovations.

MIDDLETON, Derbyshire *18 SK25*
The Butterley beam engine here was originally used for hauling mineral traffic up the Middleton incline of the former Cromford and High Peak mineral railway. It has been preserved in an engine house of 1825, and part of the actual line is being converted into a footpath.

MIDDLETON, Gt Manchester *21 SD80*
Silk and cotton were manufactured in this town from the early days of the textile industry. Timbered Boar's Head Inn is an interesting 17th-c building, and the church was rebuilt in the 16thc. The church tower displays a curious, wooden gabled belfry-cap which was added in 1709. A window of 1524, by Sir Ralph Assheton, recalls this man's command of local archers who fought at Flodden Field in 1513. Ashton brasses and the 16th-c chancel screen are also of interest.

MIDDLETON, Norfolk *14 TF61*
Major Everard-Hutton was one of the famous Six Hundred at Balaclava, and is remembered by a memorial in the local church. Some 2m NNW is Middleton Tower, the splendid 15th-c red-brick gatehouse of a former mansion.

MIDDLETON CHENEY, Northants *13 SP44*
The restored church houses notable stained glass by Burne-Jones, Ford Madox Brown, and William Morris. Thenford Hall dates from 1765.

MIDDLETON-IN-TEESDALE, Co Durham *27 NY92*
Delightfully situated in Teesdale, this place is an excellent centre for touring the famous waterfalls of Cauldron Snout and High Force. It was once a lead mining centre and includes a church with a detached 16th-c bell tower – unique in this part of England. Large reservoirs are sited on the moors to the W, beyond which rises 2,591ft Mickle Fell. The latter is the highest point in Yorkshire.

MIDDLEWICH, Cheshire *17 SJ76*
Salt extraction from brine springs forms a local industry of some importance, and a Civil War battle was fought here in 1642. The church displays an embattled tower.

MIDHURST, W Sussex *8 SU82*
Old houses and the fine partly 15th-c Spread Eagle Hotel help this picturesque little town to retain its character. Yew trees in the Close Walk are about 90ft tall. Cowdray House originated in the early 16thc, but was burnt out in 1793. It was noted for the fine Buck's Hall, but is now just a picturesque ruin (OACT). The modern mansion stands in an extensive park which is the venue for polo matches. It is traversed by the main Petworth road.

MID LAVANT, W Sussex *8 SU80*
Kingley Vale national nature reserve is noted for its yews, which may be anything from 1,000 to 2,000 years old, and lies NW under 624ft Bow Hill. Nearby burial mounds include graves which could contain Saxon and Danish kings.

MIDSOMER NORTON, Somerset *6 ST65*
This is the chief centre of the Somerset coalfield. The town hall dates from 1860, and 18th-c Ston Easton Park lies 3m W.

MILBORNE PORT, Somerset *6 ST61*
Saxon work can be seen in the church, which also boasts a fine Norman transept arch and tympanum to the south doorway. The town hall dates from the 18thc, and Ven House is a beautiful Queen Anne mansion of c1700. An unusual feature of the latter is its brick construction in an area where stone is the predominant building material.

MILDENHALL, Suffolk *14 TL77*
This pleasant ancient town lies on the edge of the Fenland, and includes an early-English to perpendicular church carrying a 113ft tower. A beautifully angel-carved roof is another notable feature of the latter. The manor house is of 17th-c date, and 1m W is the restored Elizabethan Wamil Hall. An old market cross is of interest, and an aerodrome and RAF station lie N of the town. The Mildenhall Treasure, a superb hoard of 4th-c Roman silver turned up by the plough in 1942, is now in the British Museum.

MILDENHALL, Wilts *7 SU26*
Pronounced Minall, this place is situated N of Savernake Forest on the River Kennet. Notable polished oak fittings of 1816 can be seen in the early-English to perpendicular church. Folly Farm exists on the site of the Roman *Cunetio*, where a late Celtic vessel known as the Marlborough Bucket was found. This is

now preserved in Devizes museum. Poulton House dates from 1706.

MILFORD-ON-SEA, Hants *7 SZ29*
A resort with low soft cliffs, a shingle and sand beach, and views of the Isle of Wight Needles. The mainly early-English church has a picture by Perugino at the west end of the south aisle. Hurst Castle is a 16th-c edifice lying 2½m SE, where King Charles I was imprisoned in 1648. It is reached on foot over shingle, or by boat from Keyhaven (AM).

MILLER'S DALE, Derbyshire *18 SK17*
Miller's Dale is beautifully situated amid some of the most striking wooded-cliff scenery of the Peak District national park (NT). Equally picturesque Chee Dale, with Topley Pike at its far extremity, lies W. The River Wye flows through both.

MILLOM, Cumbria *21 SD18*
Situated on the Duddon estuary S of the Lakeland Fells, Millom is a modern town built round large ironworks which closed in 1960. Remains of the castle are now partly in use as a farm, and the Norman to 15th-c church stands near by. The latter houses fine Huddleston monuments. Traces of stone circles lie to the NW of the town, and there is an excellent sandy beach 1½m SW at Haverigg.

MILTON, Oxon *13 SU49*
Considered an excellent example of its period, the 17th-c manor house incorporates 18th-c wings. The chapel and library are decorated in gothic style (OACT). Orchards flourish near by in an area where potash was formerly worked.

MILTON ABBAS, Dorset *6 ST80*
This delightful 18th-c model village was moved from its original site by the first Earl of Dorchester between 1752 and 1787. The church of 1786 and later was built by Wyatt, and the 18th-c manor house was formerly the rectory. Milton Abbey, by Chambers and Wyatt, is now a school and retains the ancient Abbot's Hall. The beautiful abbey church dates from the 14th to 15thc and displays fine tower vaulting, a 15th-c sacrament-house, and a lovely altar screen. A hill behind the abbey is surmounted by the Norman chapel of St Catherine. The beautiful Tudor manor of Bingham's Melcombe lies 4m NW, and features an ancient bowling-green and grand yew hedge. Bulbarrow Hill rises to 902ft 4m NNW and is one of the highest hills in the county (AA viewpoint).

MILTON ABBOT, Devon *5 SX47*
Endsleigh estate includes a Wellingtonia fir that has grown to a height of 165ft, and lies by the River Tamar near the W extremity of Dartmoor national park. Greystone bridge is dated 1439 and spans the Tamar to the W.

MILTON BRYANT, Beds *13 SP93*
A fine thatched barn exists at the manor house of this high-lying village. The church houses a font and chancel windows of the Norman period, a Saxon coffin lid, a Chantrey sculpture, and a memorial window to Sir Joseph Paxton. Paxton was born here in 1801 and was the designer of the famous – if ill-fated – Crystal Palace in South London. The palace was erected in 1851 and burnt down in 1936. He also designed part of Birkenhead Park.

MILTON COMBE, Devon *5 SX46*
A strangely-named inn known as the 'Who'd Have Thought It' exists here. Old cottages can be seen in the area, and the River Tavy flows nearby.

MILTON ERNEST, Beds *14 TL05*
Coloured roof bosses and screenwork, and a 13th-c tower are features of the local church. A rare item preserved inside is a bread rack of 1729. This was originally used to carry loaves destined for the parish poor. The vicarage and almshouses date from the 17thc. The 19th-c hall is William Butterfield's only example of a country house.

MILTON KEYNES, Bucks *13 SP83*
Developments associated with the construction of a large New Town are destined to engulf this village. A few 17th-c thatched cottages exist here, and the decorated church is noted for its very fine south doorway and porch.

MILVERTON, Somerset *6 ST12*
Delightful Georgian houses can be seen in this ancient village, and the church is notable for its array of old carved bench-ends. The Parsonage dates from the late 15thc. Milverton was once a woollen centre, and several local people took part in the disastrous Monmouth rebellion of 1685.

MINCHINHAMPTON, Glos *12 SO80*
Minchinhampton is a S Cotswold country town which is known for its famous golf course. The restored cruciform-shaped church has a 14th-c octagonal tower and contains many brasses. Market Hall is pillared and dates from the 17thc. A legendary cure for infantile rickets is attached to the perforated Long Stone (AM). Tom Long's Post, where a highwayman is said to have killed himself to avoid capture, stands on the lofty common. Both this and Rodborough common (3m NW) belong to the NT and afford wide views.

MINEHEAD, Somerset *5 SS94*
Good sands, bathing, and a small harbour help to make this resort popular with holiday makers. Fishermen's Chapel dates from 1630 and has been restored Old almshouses exist in Market House Lane and a model village can be seen on the sea front. The picturesque old village includes the church, which displays a lofty perpendicular tower and a fine carved screen. North Hill is a good viewpoint to the W. Views are also afforded by a road which traverses high ground on its way towards Selworthy.

The town is in a noted stag-hunting district, and makes a good centre for touring Exmoor and the Brendon Hills. A curious hobby-horse dance is performed annually on May Day. Bratton, an attractive village 1½m W, includes the old house of Bratton Court.

MINSTEAD, Hants *7 SU21*
A New Forest village where the Trusty Servant Inn shows a notable sign. The church has a brick tower of 1774, a three-decker pulpit, a pew fireplace, and a double tier of galleries. Arthur Conan Doyle is buried in the churchyard. Picturesque gardens at Furzey are filled with heather, bulbs, rock gardens, and shrubs and trees that flower throughout the year (OACT).

1 Almshouses
2 Bratton Court
3 Church of St Michael
4 Fishermen's Chapel
5 Model Village

MINSTER-IN-SHEPPEY, Kent *9 TQ97*
Sand and shingle make up the beach at this small resort, and amenities include bathing and golf. It takes its name from the sacking of a Saxon nunnery by Danish marauders in 835. The restored church dates from the 13th to 15thc and includes a notable 14th-c palimpsest brass, plus an effigy of Sir Robert de Shurland who is described in the *Ingoldsby Legends*. It stands on the highest ground in Sheppey, thus offering extensive views over the Medway and Thames estuaries.

MINSTER-IN-THANET, Kent *9 TR36*
King Egbert founded the interesting church in 670, and it was later sacked by the Danes. The Canterbury Abbey of St Augustine's took it over and rebuilt the church, the impressive Norman nave of which is still standing. Carved 15th-c choir stalls are of interest. Minster Abbey retains 12th-c work, and is one of the oldest inhabited houses in England. Benedictine nuns now occupy it (OACT). A fine old barn and brewhouse are also of interest.

MINSTERLEY, Salop *17 SJ30*
The curious little local church was built in 1692 – one of the few dating from this period – and retains several rare maidens' garlands. The hall is a fine old black-and-white house. A lofty ridge known as the Stiperstones, with the Devil's Chair rocks on the summit, rises 4m S.

MINSTER LOVELL, Oxon *13 SP31*
Beautifully situated on the River Windrush just to the N of the A40 highway, Minster Lovell comprises attractive stone-built Cotswold cottages and the fine partly-timbered Old Swan Inn. The perpendicular church carries a central tower which displays a carved and vaulted roof. Ruins of a 15th-c manor house stand in the area (AM, OACT), and are connected with two local legends. One states that Lord Francis Lovell, while fleeing after the abortive Lambert Simnel Rising of 1487, hid in a secret room known only to one servant. The servant is said to have died suddenly leaving the Lord trapped. Lovell's skeleton was supposedly discovered in 1718. The legend of the Mistletoe Bough Chest is also attributed to the house and relates how a young Lovell bride hid in a chest on her Christmas wedding night, and was unable to open the lid.

MIRFIELD, W Yorks *22 SE21*
Mirfield is a town in the Yorkshire woollen area, and includes the one-time school of Roe Head – which was attended by the Brontës. The College of the Community of the Resurrection is situated here. Of antiquarian interest are the stone stocks and a cross known as the Dumb Steeple.

MISSENDEN, GREAT, Bucks *8 SP80*
Separated from the main community by a by-pass, the decorated-style village church is approached by a bridge over the modern road. The building has been restored, but retains its strange gargoyles. Abbey Mansion incorporates part of a former abbey and Chequers lies 5m NW.

MISTLEY, Essex *15 TM13*
St Mary's Church dates from 1735; although it has lost its nave Robert Adam's two square towers are still standing. The 18th-c Swan fountain recalls Mistley's abortive attempt to become a small spa. The Stour estuary is noted for its swans.

MITFORD, Northumberland *27 NZ18*
Remains of a Norman castle exist in this village, which is delightfully situated in the wooded Wansbeck Glen. The restored church shows a lovely 13th-c chancel and a fine priest's doorway.

MOBBERLEY, Cheshire *17 SJ77*
The fine decorated and perpendicular church displays a 16th-c tower and a good carved rood loft. Mobberley was the birthplace of George Mallory, a climber of Mount Everest who disappeared with Andrew Irvine as they were approaching the summit of the peak in 1924. His father and grandfather both preached at the church, which has a Mallory memorial window.

MOCCAS, Herefs & Worcs *11 SO34*
Moccas Court is a notable Georgian mansion with rich Adam-style interior decoration, and is surrounded by a park (OACT). The small Norman Church retains a rare east apse, and the River Wye runs through the area.

MODBURY, Devon *5 SX65*
Two old conduits, several slate-hung houses, and a perpendicular church carrying a rare Devon spire are features of this South Hams town. The church was rebuilt in 1621.

MOIRA, Leics *18 SK31*
Considerable remains of an early 19th-c furnace exist here. Colliers' houses of the period are still standing, and the large brickworks also date from the 19thc.

MOLLINGTON, Oxon *13 SP44*
Old stone-built cottages and a decorated and perpendicular church housing a carved font are features of this small village. Wide views towards Edgehill are afforded by the grounds of Farnborough Hall, a house which lies 3m N and displays fine interior plasterwork (NT, OACT).

MONKEN HADLEY, Gt London *8 TQ29*
The restored perpendicular church preserves a rare cresset, or beacon, on the tower turret. Mount House is a fine 18th-c building, and Livingstone's house is situated at Hadley Green. Delightful Hadley Woods are near by, and several Georgian houses face the old Great North Road.

MONK FRYSTON, Cleveland *22 SE52*
A four-stage Saxon tower is carried by the little local church. The 14th-c gatehouse (AM) from former Steeton Hall lies 2m NW, and is noted for its series of 53 carved grotesque and heraldic corbels. Monk Fryston Hall now serves as a hotel.

MONKS ELEIGH, Suffolk *15 TL94*
A pleasant village where the decorated and perpendicular church is noted for its tower and carved pulpit. The weatherboarded mill and Georgian mill-house are attractive, and several old houses exist in the area.

MONKSILVER, Somerset *6 ST03*
Sited W of the Quantock escarpment, this village has a gargoyle-adorned church containing a wonderful series of 15th-c carved bench-ends. The towered Elizabethan manor house of Combe Sydenham lies $\frac{1}{2}$m SE, and a road runs along the crest of the Brendon Hills to the SW at a height of over 1,200ft.

MONKS RISBOROUGH, Bucks *8 SP80*
An interesting old church preserving a Norman font and a good 15th-c screen can be seen in this pretty village. Prominent Whyteleafe Cross stands 1m SE on the Chiltern Ridge, overlooking the track of the Icknield Way, and is the finest of two examples sited in the hills. Its dimensions were first recorded in 1742, but it seems to have been much enlarged at a later date. Its upkeep was traditionally the duty of the Earls of Buckingham.

MONKWEARMOUTH, Tyne & Wear *27 NZ35*
Monkwearmouth is a rather dull suburb of Sunderland, situated on the N bank of the River Wear. St Peter's church displays much pre-Conquest work, including a five-stage tower of several dates, and preserves the wall of a monastery church which was founded in 674. The Venerable Bede entered this foundation in 680 at the age of seven. The former station is of great architectural interest, and was designed by Dobson in 1848. It is being preserved as a transport museum.

MONTACUTE, Somerset *6 ST41*
This beautiful stone-built village preserves the perpendicular gatehouse of a small priory, and the Norman to perpendicular church has a good tower. Montacute House is a splendid Elizabethan building of 1580 which was built in golden Ham-Hill stone by the Phelips family. Lovely gardens and Jacobean pavilions grace the surrounding grounds, and the 189ft-long gallery is the longest in England (NT, OACT).

MORCOTT, Leics *19 SK90*
The late-Norman church displays a notable tower, and the Priest's House is of 17th-c date. Also from this period are the manor house, North Luffenham Hall, and South Luffenham Hall. Old cottages of grey limestone exist here, and a restored windmill is of interest.

MORDIFORD, Herefs & Worcs *12 SO53*
Before the tower of the local Church of the Holy Rood was built in 1811, the west gable carried a 12ft figure of the Mordiford dragon, a fearsome local monster. The rectory is of Georgian origin, and a bridge over the Wye incorporates old arches.

MORECAMBE, Lancs *21 SD46*
Many diversions apart from the usual sun and sea bathing can be enjoyed at this popular Morecambe Bay resort. These include golf, an oceanarium with dolphins, and distant views of the Lake District mountains. The winding estuary of the River Lune lies SE.

MORETON, Dorset *6 SY88*
Modern etched glass is a notable feature of the local church, and the body of T E Lawrence – alias Lawrence of Arabia – lies in the churchyard. He was killed in a motorcycling accident which occurred near here in 1935. Clouds Hill, the cottage to which T E Lawrence retired on leaving the RAF, lies 2M NE (NT, OACT).

MORETONHAMPSTEAD, Devon 5SX78
The E edge of Dartmoor National Park sweeps down to the borders of this quiet market town, which forms a good centre for touring the moor. Picturesque colonnaded almshouses of 1637 (NT) can be seen in the town. Some of the loveliest stretches of richly-wooded Teign valley lie to the N, and 3½m SW is the strange isolated rock known as Bowerman's Nose.

MORETON-IN-MARSH, Glos 12 SP23
Fosse Way is an ancient route which is still used in this small market town – it forms the wide main street. The town itself lies at the edge of the N Cotswolds, and includes a Curfew Tower incorporating an old lock-up. King Charles I slept at the White Hart Hotel in 1643. The well-known Four Shire stone lies 2m E and marks the meeting of Oxfordshire, Warwickshire, and formerly an isolated part of Worcestershire, boundaries.

MORETON PINKNEY, Northants 13 SP54
Thatched 17th- and 18th-c houses are a feature of this attractive stone-built village. The 13th-c church contains a beautiful restored chancel.

MORLEY, W Yorks 22 SE22
Engaged in the manufacture of woollen cloth, this former West Riding town was the birthplace of the first Earl of Oxford and Asquith in 1852.

MORPETH, Northumberland 27 NZ28
An attractive little town in the valley of the River Wansbeck, Morpeth has an interesting largely 14th-c church displaying examples of old glass. Slight remains of a castle include a 14th-c gatehouse. The 15th- to 18th-c Clock Tower, with its quaint figures at the angles, was once a prison. Court House was built by Dobson in 1852, and near the Skinnery footbridge is an old lamp still lit by sewer gas. The town hall of 1714, by Vanbrugh, has been altered. Cockle Park Tower is a restored structure lying 4m N, and 18th-c Netherwitton Hall is sited 6½m NW. Even farther NW is Nunnykirk Hall of 1825, considered one of Dobson's best designs.

MORTEHOE, Devon 5 SS44
Impressive slate rock scenery can be enjoyed toward the lighthouse at Bull Point, N of this small resort. Morte Point (NT) is a viewpoint and the focus of an area of outstanding natural beauty. Good sands and bathing are offered by numerous rocky coves. The best known of these is Barricane Bay, which has a shell beach. A finely situated church carries an old tower and houses forty-eight carved bench-ends plus a notable 14th-c tomb chest. Morte Bay (NT) extends S past Woolacombe to the massive cliff of Baggy Point (NT).

MORTIMER'S CROSS, Herefs & Worcs 12 SO46
Situated in delightful Welsh-Border country, Mortimer's Cross stands on the River Lugg. An inscribed obelisk was erected in 1799 to commemorate a Wars of the Roses battle that was fought in 1461, in which the Yorkists defeated the Lancastrians.

MORTLAKE, Gt London 8 TQ27
This well-known residential area is on the River Thames, and has a brewery. It is the finishing point of the annual Oxford and Cambridge Boat Race which begins at Putney. Famous Mortlake tapestry works which operated here in the 17thc are recalled by a tablet in a passage near the church. A curious tomb in the shape of a tent is in memory of the explorer Sir Richard Burton, who died in 1890.

MORVAL, Cornwall 5 SX25
To the S of this hamlet, at a height of over 700ft, is the prehistoric hill fort of Chun Castle. Rugged coast scenery exists to the NE, running from Bosigran Cliff in Porthmoina Cove to Gurnard's Head. Part of the area, including several fine rocks and viewpoints on Rosemergy and Trevean cliffs, belongs to the NT. Bosigran's granite cliffs are the best known for sea-cliff climbing in Cornwall, and were the scene of intensive commando training during the last war.

MORVILLE, Salop 17 SO69
The former collegiate church preserves a great deal of Norman work, and a whipping post from the village stocks survives. Morville Hall is an Elizabethan mansion which was altered in the 18thc (NT).

MORWENSTOW, Cornwall 5 SS21
Rev Stephen Hawker lived in this secluded village for forty years, and it was here that he wrote the ballad *And shall Trelawny die?* Hennacliff rises 400ft beyond the village. The church displays rich Norman work and 15th-c carved bench-ends. The nearby rectory has curious chimneys designed to represent towers of churches that Hawker particularly liked. A figurehead from the brig *Caledonia*, wrecked here in 1842, is preserved in the churchyard. Fine coastal scenery exists between here and the Devonshire border at Marsland Mouth, a little to the N. Elizabethan Tonacombe manor house lies 1m S.

MOSSLEY, Gt Manchester 22 SD90
Cotton-manufacturing and coal-mining are the town's main industries. It is sited on the edge of lofty moorlands, in the Tame valley near the W Yorkshire border.

MOTTISFONT, Hants 7 SU32
The Test, one of the finest game fishing rivers in the south of England, runs through this small village. Remains of a former priory are incorporated in the partly 18th-c abbey that now exists. The latter is noted for its collection of Rex Whistler paintings (NT, OACT). Norman work and old glass can be seen in the church.

MOTTISTONE, Isle of Wight 7 SZ48
Coloured pillars and a Mottistone memorial chapel are features of the much-restored partly 12th-c church.

cont

1 Golf Course   2 Oceanarium

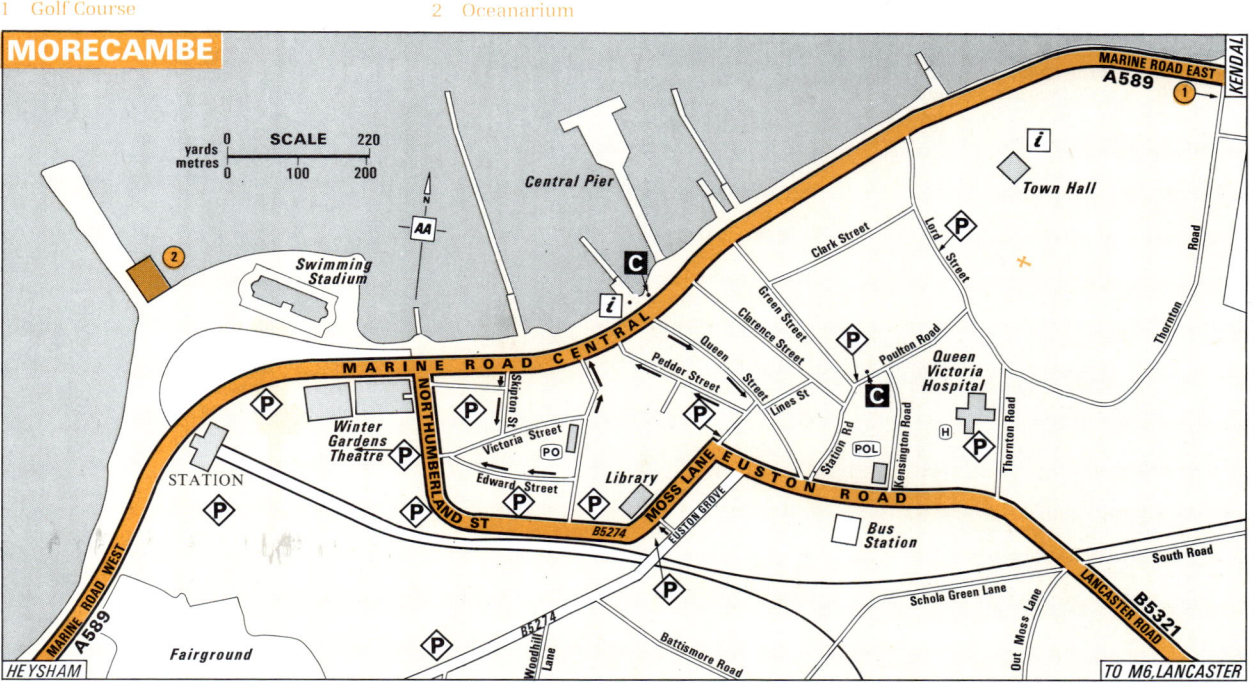

Two huge stones which probably formed part of an ancient dolmen, can be seen on the downs and are now known as the Long Stone. Brighstone Down rises to 701ft in the NE, and overlooks the island's entire S coastline. Mottistone manor house dates from the 16thc.

MOUNT GRACE PRIORY, N Yorks 22 SE49
Interesting remains of a Carthusian priory which was founded in 1398 can be seen situated below the W slopes of the Hambleton Hills. Part of the buildings were made into a house in 1654, after the priory was dissolved in the reign of Henry VIII (AM, NT, OACT).

MOUNTNESSING, Essex 9 TQ69
Mountnessing church carries one of the timber belfries which are so characteristic of Essex. Parts of the nave date from the 17th and 18thc, and the chancel was altered in 1805. A brick-built Georgian hall and a post-mill are features of the village.

MOUSEHOLE, Cornwall 4 SW42
Pronounced Mou'sl, this delightful small port and harbour is situated on Mount's Bay and shelters a pilchard-fishing fleet. The Spaniards landed here in the 16thc and burnt down all the village except the Keigwin Arms, which is no longer an inn. Dolly Pentreath, who claimed to be the last surviving exponent of the Cornish language, died here in 1777. The coast to the S, leading towards Lamorna Cove, is attractive.

MUCHELNEY, Somerset 6 ST42
Rivers Yeo and Parrett flow through Muchelney, and interesting remains of a 15th-c abbey exist here (AM). Excavations have uncovered a 7th-c Saxon chapel under the ruins of Norman monastic work. The perpendicular church preserves an early 19th-c barrel organ, plus 17th-c nave roof paintings. The thatched 14th-c Priest's House is notable (NT, OACT).

MUCH HADHAM, Herts 8 TL41
Perhaps the loveliest and least spoilt village in the county, Much Hadham is graced by a partly-Georgian street and was a manor of the Bishop of London for some 900 years. Numerous old houses include the 17th-c and earlier palace. Both The Lordship and The Hall are 18thc, and the church carries a massive embattled tower. The 15th-c south porch is also of note, and Moor Place dates from 1779.

MUCH MARCLE, Herefs & Worcs 12 SO63
The 13th- to 15th-c church contains a series of interesting monuments. Near the village are the old houses of Hellens and Homme; the former boasts a pigeon house of 1641 and a collection of old carriages (OACT).

MUCH WENLOCK, Salop 17 SO69
This small country town is situated at the NE extremity of lofty Wenlock Edge, and is associated with the poetry of A E Housman. Callow Hill, at the S end, is surmounted by a tower known as Flounder's Folly. Old houses and inns include several half-timbered buildings – notably Raynald's Mansion of 1682. The manor house is dated 1577, and the fine timbered guildhall rests on wooden pillars and preserves movable stocks.

The church is of Norman to perpendicular style and houses a curiously-carved Jacobean pulpit. Wenlock Abbey is a 7th-c foundation that was refounded as a Cluniac house in 1050. Remains of the latter are largely early-English and the Chapter House exhibits fine Norman arcading. Near by is old Prior's Lodge, a particularly interesting building with a two-storeyed gallery.

MUDEFORD, Dorset 7 SZ19
Mudeford lies on a bay where the River Avon flows into Christchurch harbour, and offers a sand and shingle beach. Hengistbury Head provides views along many miles of coast, and lies 1½m S.

MUKER, N Yorks 22 SD99
A remote Upper-Swaledale village set among high moors and fells, dominated by 2,340ft Great Shunner Fell. The latter rises above the lofty Buttertubs Pass, which runs S to Wensleydale.

MULLION, Cornwall 4 SW61
Mullion is a Lizard-peninsula village where the church is noted for its old carved bench-ends, a rare dog door, and fine wagon roofs. Mullion Cove lies 1m SW, and together with the picturesque harbour (NT) forms one of the most scenic areas of the wild Cornish coast. Serpentine rock scenery is particularly notable.

The cliffs range continues S towards remote Predannack Head, near which is even more of the remarkable coastal scenery. To the N of Mullion Cove are Polurrian and Poldhu Coves. On the cliff top near the latter is the Marconi Memorial (NT), commemorating the first long-distance morse signal. The signal was transmitted over the ocean to Newfoundland. The name Mullion is derived from St Melon.

MUNDESLEY-ON-SEA, Norfolk 15 TG33
This small resort offers golf, good sands, bathing, and cliffs and has associations with Cowper. The latter stayed at a Georgian house in the area.

MUNDFORD, Norfolk 15 TL89
A restored church in this Breckland village contains a curious 14th-c font, plus a modern screen and loft. The Stanford battle-practice ground area lies E and is strictly non-accessible.

MUSBURY, Devon 6 SY29
The restored village church houses a fine Drake monument of 1611. Shute Barton house is a fascinating complex of greystone buildings dating from the 14th to 16thc and situated 3m NW (NT). It shows a battlemented tower and fine detached gatehouse, and stands near 18th-c Shute House – now a school.

MYDDLE, Salop 17 SJ42
Remains of a 13th-c castle comprise a circular tower. The church was rebuilt in 1744, and displays an early 17th-c tower plus a timbered lych-gate.

MYLOR, Cornwall 4 SW83
This village overlooks the Carrick Roads, N of Falmouth harbour. An interesting old church shows two Norman doorways, an old screen, and an Elizabethan pulpit. The tallest of several ancient crosses to be seen in Cornwall is set among yews in the churchyard.

NAILSWORTH, Glos 12 ST89
Old houses and woollen mills that exist here include several of Georgian date, and all are of considerable archaeological interest. Nailsworth Ladder is a hill with a 1 in 3 gradient, used for testing cars. The Friends Meeting House dates from 1680, and W H Davies – the tramp poet – died at Nailsworth in 1940.

NANTWICH, Cheshire 17 SJ65
Noted for cheeses and once famous for its salt works, Nantwich includes a fine mainly 14th- and 15th-c church showing an octagonal tower and beautifully carved stalls. Welsh Row is a particularly good place to see some of the many black-and-white houses that exist in the area, and the local almshouses date from 1638. Churche's Mansion is half-timbered and dates from 1577 (OACT). The timbered Crown Inn is most attractive, and 18th-c Doddington Hall stands 5m SE in a park. Near by is the tower of a former 14th-c castle, bearing curious Jacobean figures.

NARBOROUGH, Norfolk 14 TF71
Several fine brasses and a standing effigy to Clement Spelman, Recorder of Nottingham, can be seen in the church. Spelman died in 1679. An old hall displays a mainly-Tudor brick front and a Georgian bay window. The line of the Devil's Dyke lies to the S, and the 14th-c gatehouse to Pentney Priory can be seen.

NASEBY, Northants 13 SP67
Situated on high ground near the start of the Rivers Avon, Nene, and Welland, Naseby includes a churchyard which contains a huge copper ball. This is said to have been brought back from the siege of Boulogne in 1544 by Sir Charles Allington. The Battle of Naseby was fought in 1645, 1½m N, and was where a Cromwellian victory decided the fate of Charles I. A stone column has been erected to mark the site.

NAVENBY, Lincs 19 SK95
Stone and pantiled houses are a feature of this pleasant village, and the restored church contains a good decorated-style chancel. An Easter Sepulchre is decorated with carvings of figures, including three Roman soldiers. Somerton Castle dates from 1281 and lies 2½m NW. Built originally by Anthony Bek, Bishop of Durham, it later served as the prison of King John I of France. It preserves two towers which adjoin an Elizabethan farmhouse erected within the moat.

NAYLAND, Suffolk 15 TL93
Many old houses of 15th- and 16th-c date exist in this attractive River-Stour village. Alston Court is an old half-timbered courtyard house dating from the 15th to 17thc. The perpendicular church has a Constable painting hanging over the Communion table. The building's spire fell in 1832, but has recently been replaced by a replica.

NEEDHAM MARKET, Suffolk 15 TM05
This small town is often visited solely for its church, which includes a unique 15th-c wooden hammerbeam nave roof – one of the wonders of East Anglia. Shrubland Park lies 3m SE in magnificent gardens laid out by Sir Charles Barry, and is an Italianate mansion now serving as a health clinic. Constable used to paint the views which this area affords over the Gipping Valley.

NENTHEAD, Cumbria 27 NY74
Nenthead is situated on Alston Moor, in the lonely high Pennines, at an altitude of nearly 1,500ft. Cumbria and Durham meet 1½m E at a place near the highest classified road in England. This climbs to 2,056ft at one point. Nearby Killhope Water Mill boasts one of the largest mill-wheels in the country.

NESTON, Cheshire 17 SJ27
Largely a residential town, Neston is situated on the Wirral peninsula near the estuary of the River Dee. Nelson's Lady Hamilton was born at nearby Ness, in a cottage that still survives. The Dublin packet used to sail from adjacent Parkgate.

NETHERAVON, Wilts 7 SU14
This is the centre of an extensive military district and the site of an RAF station. A Saxon or early-Norman tower is carried by the church. The writer Rev Sidney Smith was once curate here. Netheravon House dates from the late 18thc.

NETHERBURY, Dorset 6 SY49
Marshwood Vale lies W of this pleasant little River-Brit village. The fine perpendicular church contains a modern brass to Admiral Hood, and the old houses of Strode and Melplash Court stand near by.

NETHER STOWEY, Somerset 6 ST13
The Ancient Mariner was written in this Quantock village by Samuel T Coleridge, and his cottage still stands (NT, OACT). He was later joined here by Wordsworth. Stowey Court includes an 18th-c gazebo or garden house, and Dodington manor house of 1581 lies 2m NW.

NETHER WINCHENDON, Bucks 8 SP71
Thatched and colour-washed cottages exist in this attractive Vale of Aylesbury village. The church contains old pews and a Jacobean three-decker pulpit. Nether Winchendon House is of Tudor to 18th-c date (OACT).

NETLEY, Hants 7 SU40
Wounded soldiers from the Crimean War were brought along Southampton Water to receive treatment at a great military hospital especially built here between 1856 and 1857. This no longer exists. Interesting remains of a large 13th-c Cistercian abbey include an Abbot's House of the period. A convalescent home is now housed in 19th-c Netley Castle.

NETTLECOMBE, Somerset 6 ST03
Nettlecombe Court is a beautiful Elizabethan house, and the village itself lies almost hidden in the Brendon Hills off the Watchet to Bampton road. The nearby church has a Seven Sacraments font, heraldic glass from the 15thc, and a rare chalice of 1479.

NETTLESTEAD, Kent 9 TQ65
This Medway village includes an early 15th-c church which retains a 13th-c tower that belonged to its predecessor. Notable 15th-c stained glass and a fine tomb of the period can be seen inside. Nettlestead Place boasts an old barn, and is of 14th- to 15th-c origin.

NEWARK-ON-TRENT, Notts 19 SK75
An intersection of the Fosse Way and former Great North Road occurs near this ancient town. The ruined 12th- to 15th-c castle overlooks the Trent branch, and is noted for its towered gatehouse (AM).

King John died here in 1216, and the castle was besieged on three occasions during the Civil War. The splendid parish church is of early-English to perpendicular styles, and features good screenwork, a large Flemish brass, and a lofty 252ft tower and spire. Notable structures in the town include fine 18th-c houses, a wide market-square, and several old inns. The Clinton Arms, formerly the Kingston Arms, often received Lord Byron as a guest, and Gladstone once made a speech here. A stone flung at him by hecklers smashed one of the pub's windows. The Olde White Hart, with its overhanging 14th-c façade, is a fine example of its type.

Jeanie Deans, the heroine in Scott's *Heart of Midlothian*, spent a night at the former Saracen's Head on her way from Scotland to London. This inn now houses a bank. Prince Rupert stayed at the timbered Governor's House prior to the Civil War period. The replica of a bear-baiting post has been set up in the market place, and the town hall of 1773 was built by Carr of York. Beaumond Cross has proved a puzzle to archaeologists for many years, and its origins are still obscure. Civil War fortifications known as the Queen's Sconce lie S of the town (AM).

NEWBIGGIN-BY-THE-SEA, Northumberland 27 NZ38
Excellent sands and bathing are available here, and the coast is of a largely rock and sand aspect. Good views are afforded by Newbiggin Point. The church, with its rare Northumberland spire, is a landmark for sailors.

NEW BRIGHTON, Merseyside 17 SJ39
Sibelius the Finnish composer conducted in New Brighton in 1899. This was the first performance of his works in England. The resort lies at the mouth of the Mersey, and offers such amenities as good sands, sea bathing, and an open-air swimming pool.

NEW BUCKENHAM, Norfolk 15 TM09
Sparse remains of a Norman castle exist here, and the old market house preserves an original pillory. The flint church has a splendid south porch and contains a font of 1619. Old Buckenham Church lies to the NW, and displays an octagonal 14th-c tower and thatched roofs.

NEWBURN, Tyne & Wear 27 NZ16
Stephenson's early locomotive The Rocket was first tested here. The church has an early Norman tower, and the Roman wall lies just N of the village.

NEWBURY, Berks 7 SU46
Newbury is a prosperous town that was once engaged in the cloth trade. It is situated on the River Kennet and the Kennet and Avon Canal, and the church was rebuilt in the 16th-c by famous Jack o' Newbury. Jack was a local clothier who led 150 men to the battle of Flodden in 1513. A feature of this church is an ornate buttressed tower.

Newbury's Jacobean Cloth Hall (museum)

The Jacobean Cloth Hall has been restored and is now a museum exhibiting relics of the Civil War. Georgian and older houses, some of which have had modern shop fronts added, can be seen in the town. A delightful 18th-c bridge spans the river, and St Bartholomew's Hospital – once a school – displays perpendicular-style windows. Two Civil War battles were fought outside the town, first in 1643 and then in 1644. Newbury is said to have been the last place in England to have made use of stocks (1872).

The famous racecourse is situated outside the town, and the commons of Greenham and Crookham lie to the SE. Elizabethan Shaw House lies about ¾m NE and is now a school. Relics from the second battle of Newbury are preserved in the latter. Many famous people were entertained by the builder of 18th-c Sandleford Priory, Mrs Montagu; her social gatherings of 1781 gave rise to the expression Blue Stockings, and the priory lies 2m S of the town.

NEWBY BRIDGE, Cumbria 21 SD38
Furness Fells and an old bridge over the River Leven are just two features of this village's delightful setting. Rusland Wood national nature reserve covers 30 acres and lies to the W. Windermere's S extremity is near by, and roads on both banks allow unrestricted views of this famous water. A deer museum is sited SW at Bouth.

1 Assembly Rooms
2 Bagpipe Museum
3 Castle and Black Gate (museum)
4 Cathedral
5 Church of All Saints
6 Customs House
7 Dominican Friary Remains
8 Earl Grey's Monument
9 Guildhall
10 Hancock Museum
11 Jesmonde Dene Park & Chapel of St Mary
12 Jesus Hospital
13 King Edward Railway Bridge
14 Markets
15 Museum of Antiquities
16 Plummer Tower (town wall; museum)
17 Racecourse
18 Scotswood Suspension Bridge
19 St Andrew's Church
20 Station
21 Stephenson's High Level Bridge
22 St John's Church
23 Theatre Royal
24 Trinity House
25 University of Newcastle

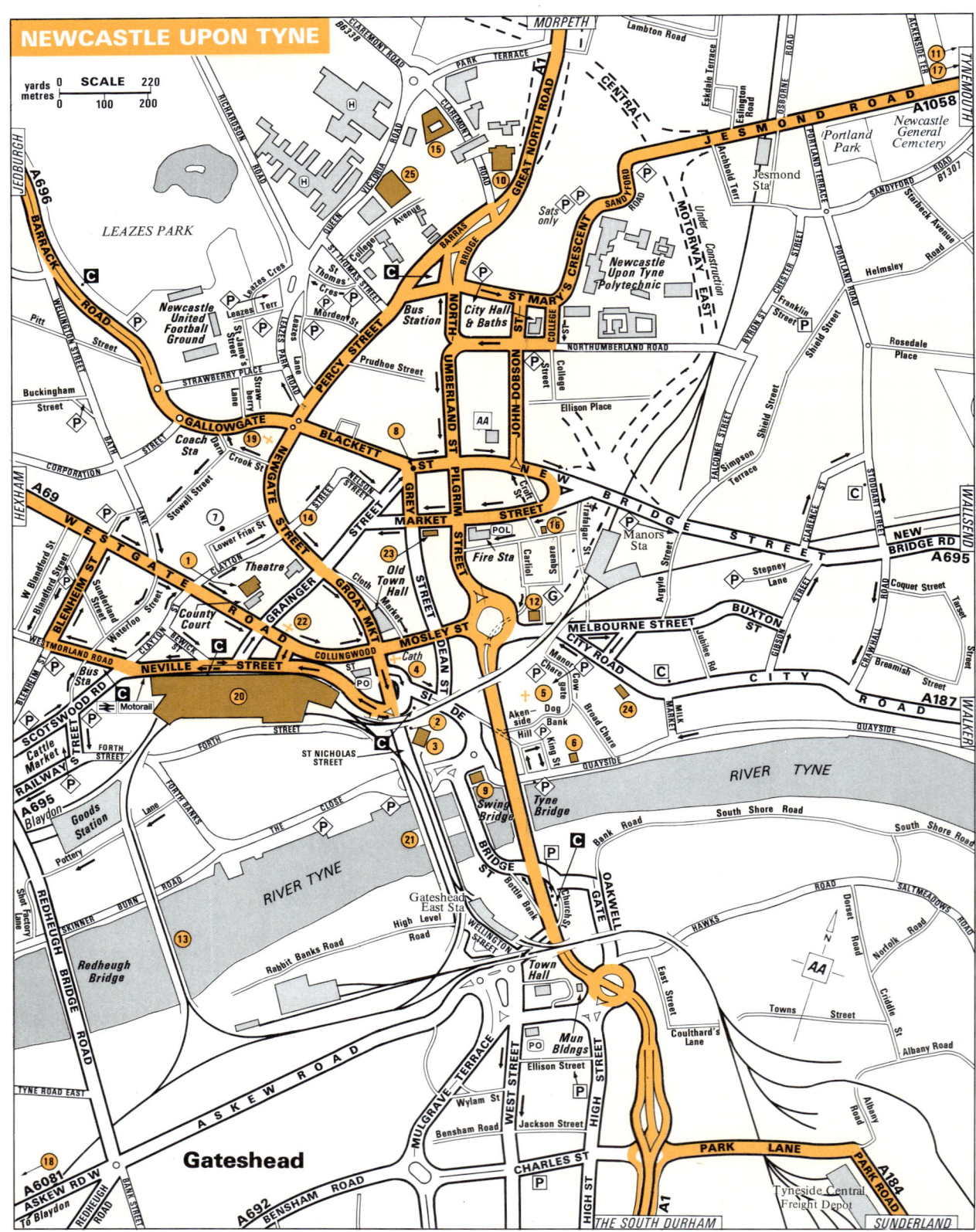

NEWCASTLE-UNDER-LYME, Staffs
17 SJ84
This old industrial town lies W of the Potteries, and includes a rebuilt church which preserves an early-English tower and old lectern. The local museum and art gallery is in Brompton Park.

NEWCASTLE UPON TYNE, Tyne & Wear
27 NZ26
County town of Northumberland, Newcastle upon Tyne was once a station on the Roman Wall, known as *Pons Aelii*. It is now an important university and manufacturing city, traditionally noted for the production of coal, armaments, ships, and locomotives. The old industries still survive, but are supplemented by modern involvements such as electrical engineering and petro-chemical works.

The well-known River Tyne is spanned by three bridges: Stephenson's High Level Bridge of 1849; the King Edward Railway Bridge of 1906; the splendid single-span bridge of 1928, which was opened by King George V. Scotswood Suspension Bridge dates from 1829 to 1831. The guildhall of 1658 was recased in 1796.

The cathedral, once the parish church, shows mostly decorated and perpendicular work. It is noted for its rare crown spire, resembling that of St Giles' in Edinburgh. Several interesting chapels include one in the crypt. The organ was rebuilt in 1811, and is housed in a case dating from 1710. The castle displays a restored 12th-c keep (AM), and the 13th-c Black Gate houses a collection of local antiquities. A newly-opened Bagpipe Museum is of great, if rather specialized, interest. Roman remains can be seen in the Museum of Antiquities, which is situated in the University Quadrangle.

Sections of the town walls bearing turrets have survived, and the Plummer Tower is now a museum. John Dobson and Richard Grainger were the two well-known architects who were largely responsible for the planning of buildings and streets in the city during the early 19thc. This particularly applies to Grey Street, which contains a Theatre Royal of 1837, by Green. Eldon Square and Leazes Terrace are excellent compositions, and the new Civic Centre opened in 1968 is outstanding.

The Church of All Saints' was rebuilt in the 18thc and houses a notable brass. St John's Church is of Norman to decorated style, and displays a fine 17th-c pulpit. Trans-Norman St Andrew's Church contains a 15th-c font canopy. Other interesting foundations in this town include the remains of a 13th-c Dominican friary, Jesus Hospital of 1681, Trinity House and its old hall and chapel, and the Custom House of 1766 and later. Dobson designed the notable mid 19th-c station, and Grainger designed the markets in 1835. Assembly Rooms date from 1779, and a tall monument to the 2nd Earl Grey from 1838. Bessie Surtees eloped with the future Lord Eldon, later Lord Chancellor of England, from a first-floor window of a fine five-storied house of timbered construction in 1772. The latter is situated at Sandhill. Jesmond Dene is a picturesque park which contains the remains of a 12th- to 15th-c chapel of St Mary, and the Hancock Museum exhibits items of zoological interest. A racecourse exists in the area.

NEWENT, Glos *12 SO72*
Several 18th-c houses and a timber-framed 16th-c market hall are interesting local features. Wild daffodils grow here in great profusion during the spring. Pauntley church is a Norman and perpendicular building which lies 3m NE in an isolated position by the River Leadon. It shows an interesting triptych reredos. Dick Whittington, later to be Sir Richard Whittington and Lord Mayor of London three times, was born here. May Hill is a fine viewpoint lying 3m SW, from which ten counties are said to be visible (NT).

NEW FOREST
This beautifully-wooded district lies between the River Avon and Southampton Water, and comprises about 140sqm of undulating forest and heathland. It is partly-owned by the Crown. The name New Forest was first coined by William the Conqueror in 1079, who made it a Royal hunting area. Certain parts have been scheduled as forest nature reserves, and about 1,000 acres of commons NW of Cadnam are NT property. Verderers responsible for administering the forest laws hold their Courts at the Queen's House in Lyndhurst, formerly the home of the Lord Warden. Small herds of ponies run wild in the forest, and the local deer include red, roe, and fallow. Adders are found in certain areas. Some of the loveliest areas are near Lyndhurst and Brockenhurst.

NEWHAVEN, E Sussex *8 TQ40*
Although the beach at Newhaven is mainly shingle, some sand is revealed at low tide. The port is sited on the mouth of the River Ouse, and is linked to Dieppe by cross-Channel ferry. A chancel formed in the lower stages of the tower, with an east apse, is a unique Norman feature of the church. Bridge Hotel was the home of Louis Philippe and his Queen after the 1848 French Revolution, and dates from the 17thc. Firle Beacon rises to 718ft in the NE, and the South Downs dominate the horizon behind the town.

NEWINGTON, Kent *9 TQ86*
Newington is situated amid cherry orchards and includes a very fine 15th-c church tower displaying banded stone and flint. The church itself houses 14th-c screens and old paintings.

NEWLAND, Glos *12 SO50*
Remains of the Newland Oak, a tree measuring some 44ft around the girth, can still be seen here. The Forest of Dean fringes the village borders, and the local 13th- to 14th-c church is sometimes called the Cathedral of the Forest. It contains interesting monuments and brasses; a cross of 1443 portrays a figure of a Free Miner of the Forest. A churchyard tomb shows a 15th-c forester in hunting costume.

NEWLANDS CORNER, Surrey *8 TQ04*
Views across the Weald towards the distant South Downs are offered by this famous 567ft North Downs beauty spot. The Pilgrims' Way runs to the S.

NEWLYN, Cornwall *4 SW42*
Popular with artists, this picturesque fishing village lies off Mount's Bay and

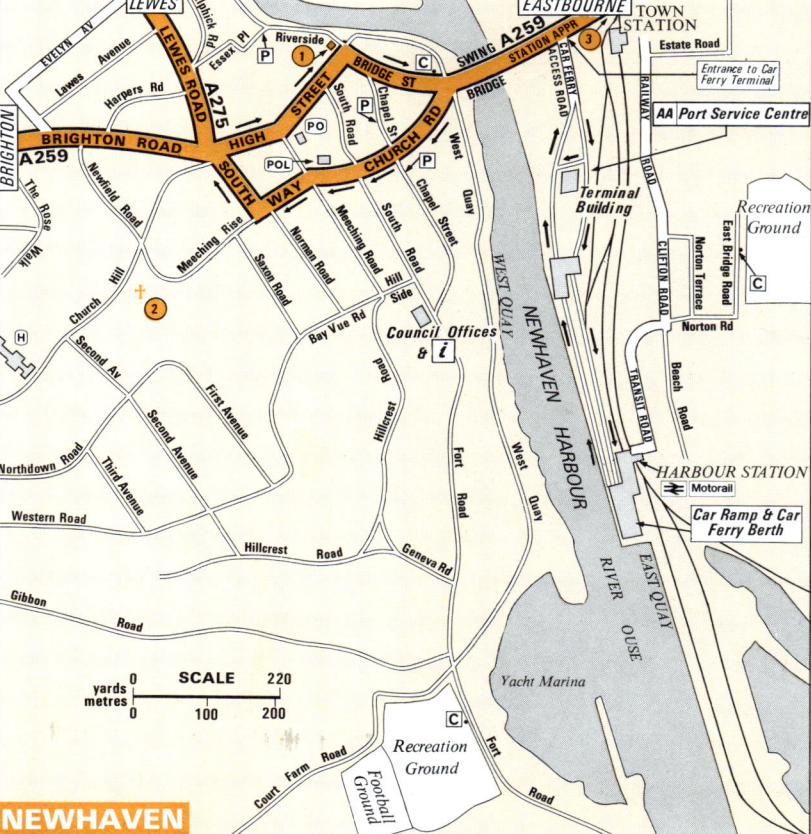

1 Bridge Hotel
2 Church of St Michael
3 Firle Beacon

offers a sandy bathing-beach. The Passmore Edwards picture gallery is of interest, and fittings by local artists can be seen in the church.

NEWMARKET, Suffolk 14 TL66
As well as being a famous horse-racing centre, Newmarket contains the headquarters of both the Jockey Club and the National Stud. The former occupies a prominent modern building, and the latter owns a 500-acre site (OACT). Various courses for early-morning training gallops exist on the Heath.

Nearby Devil's Ditch, actually part of Cambridgeshire, is a well-defined earthwork of ancient origin measuring some 7m in length. King James I and King Charles I and II were associated with the town. Houses where the Duke of Queensbury and Nell Gwynne resided are of interest, and the station is a Victorian baroque building of 1848.

Newmarket Town Plate is one of the oldest races extant, and attracts mainly women riders. It is usually held on the second Thursday of October. The One Thousand and Two Thousand Guineas are held in spring, and both the Cesarewitch and Cambridgeshire are in October.

NEW MILLS, Derbyshire 18 SK08
Textile printing is this town's main industry, and it is sited at the edge of the Peak District national park. Many 19th-c buildings of industrial, archaeological, and railway interest exist here.

NEWNHAM, Northants 13 SP55
The River Nene rises near this attractive village. Several old buildings are of interest, and the fine 15th-c church displays a painted Jacobean wall monument.

NEWNHAM-ON-SEVERN, Glos 12 SO61
Facing the winding Severn estuary, this attractive little town lies on the edge of the Forest of Dean national forest park. Views S across the estuary encompass the Cotswold Hills.

NEWPORT, Essex 14 TL53
Some of the old buildings in this River-Cam village display fine timbering, the Monks Barn being a particularly notable example. Interesting Crown House has a richly-pargetted front and dates from 1692. The flint church is of the 15thc carries an imposing tower, and houses a good screen plus an exceptionally fine 13th-c chest. A Georgian house known as The Links was a former House of Correction, or Workhouse, and was built in 1775.

NEWPORT, Isle of Wight 7 SZ48
Newport, a busy town situated at the head of the River Medina estuary, is the island's capital. The 19th-c church preserves the tomb of the second daughter of King Charles I, plus a carved Jacobean pulpit from an earlier church. Among several 17th-c houses existing in the town, Chantry House of 1612 and Hazard's House of 1684 are of particular note. A fine shell porch displayed by God's Providence House is dated 1701. Other features of the town are an old grammar school, a Roman villa, a guildhall, and the town hall. The last two were designed by John Nash. Monuments and memorials to Queen Victoria and her family can be seen in several places.

NEWPORT, Salop 17 SJ71
Newport's much-restored church carries a 14th-c tower, the grammar school was founded in 1656, the old guildhall dates from 1615, and the town hall from 1859. Beaumaris House is dated 1724. The town stands on the Shropshire Union Canal. Aqualate Mere is situated across the Staffordshire border, a little to the NE.

NEWPORT PAGNELL, Bucks 13 SP84
Old parchment works in this River-Ouse settlement are of interest, and the iron-built Tickford bridge of 1810 spans the River Ouzel. The county library occupies a fine 17th-c house. The largely-decorated church carries a 17th-c tower, and exceptionally lovely Chicheley Hall, an 18th-c building attributed to Thomas Archer, lies some 2m NE. It faces a church displaying a 15th-c central tower and 18th-c chancel.

NEWQUAY, Cornwall 4 SW86
Fine cliff scenery can be enjoyed N beyond Watergate Bay, and this well-known holiday resort has a harbour. Excellent sands, surf bathing, and golf are among local amenities. An old Huer's Hut, a shelter for somebody on the lookout for approaching pilchard shoals, is a quaint survival from the past. The Gannel estuary and village of Crantock lie to the S of Fistral Bay and Newquay. Trerice, a lovely Elizabethan manor house lying 5m SE, displays unique curly gables (NT, OACT).

NEW ROMNEY, Kent 9 TR02
The harbour of this ancient Cinque Port, now 1m from the sea, was destroyed by a storm in 1287. The fury of this storm was so great that it actually changed the course of the River Rother. Until this disaster occurred ships could anchor near the Norman to decorated church. Features of the latter include a rich Norman tower, an imposing nave, and interesting brasses. The town's mayor is still elected within the church. A museum of relics from the narrow-

1 Golf Course   2 Huer's Hut   3 Trerice Manor

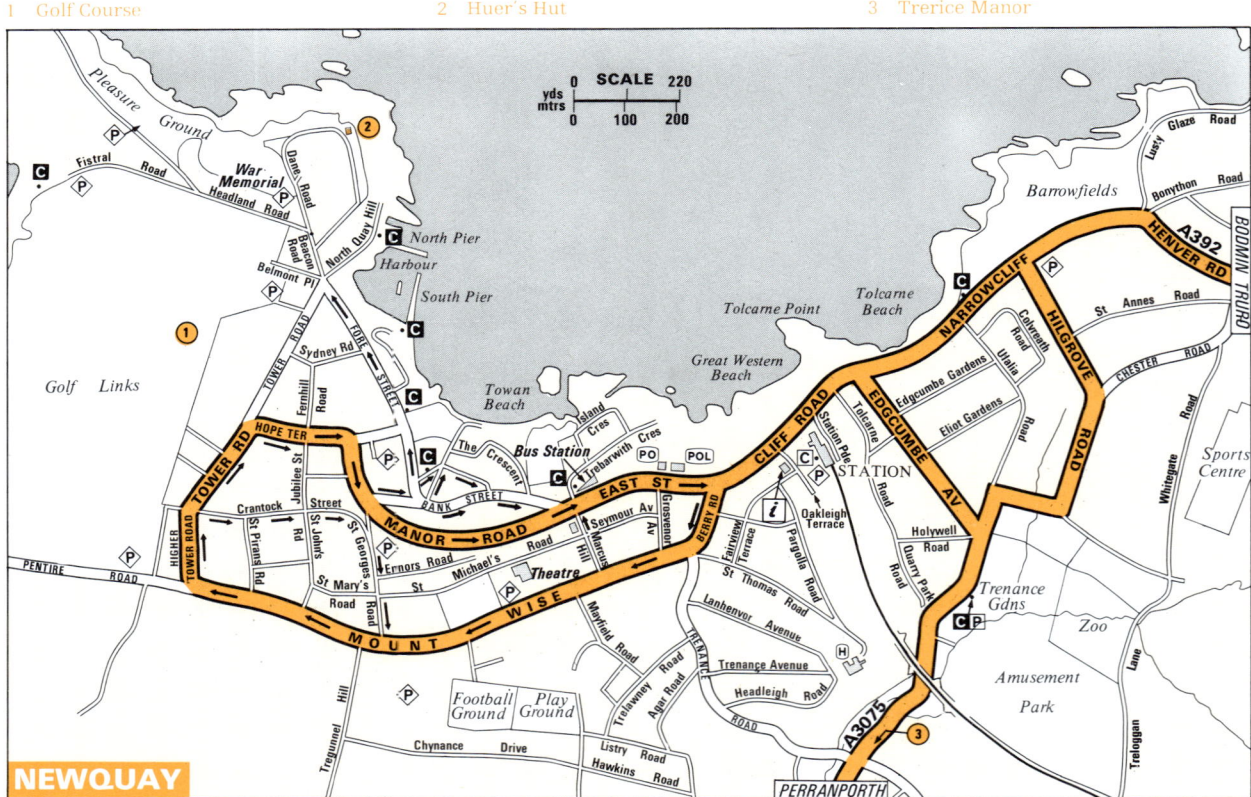

gauge Romney, Hythe and Dymchurch railway is now housed in the station, which also contains a very good model railway display.

NEWSTEAD, Notts *18 SK55*
The abbey was founded in the 12thc and converted into a residence in 1540. It became the ancestral home of Lord Byron, and was given to the city of Nottingham in 1931. The west front of the old priory church, plus the cloisters and chapter house, have survived. Relics of the poet and of Dr Livingstone, who stayed here in 1864, can be seen inside (OACT). Attractive gardens that surround the building are always open. Near by is the ancient Pilgrims' Oak in Sherwood Forest.

NEWTON ABBOT, Devon *5 SX87*
Cider-apple orchards are cultivated to the S of this Teign-estuary town, and Newton Abbot is an important railway junction and agricultural centre. Only the tower of the old Church of St Leonard remains. Jacobean Forde House, visited by Charles I in 1625 and William of Orange in 1688, lies ½m ESE. Picturesque early 15th-c Bradley Manor includes a fine hall and chapel and lies ½m ESE (NT). A well-known pottery operates in the town.

NEWTON FERRERS, Devon *5 SX54*
Picturesquely situated on a richly-wooded creek of the Yealm estuary, this yachting and boating centre stands opposite Noss Mayo. Sandy coves at Stoke (1¾m S) allow access for sea bathing.

NEWTON HARCOURT, Leics *18 SP69*
A small Elizabethan manor house is a delightful feature of this village. Wistow Hall, where King Charles I slept after the battle of Naseby in 1645, is also of Elizabethan origin and lies to the S.

NEWTON-LE-WILLOWS, Merseyside *17 SJ59*
This community comprises two towns – Newton-le-Willows and Earlestown. The former includes a picturesque 16th-c hall, and a stone marking the spot where Mr Huskisson was killed while talking to the Duke of Wellington in 1830. The occasion that brought the two men together was the opening of the world's first passenger-carrying railway. This ran between Liverpool and Manchester.

NEWTON LONGVILLE, Bucks *13 SP83*
Thatched and timbered cottages and an Elizabethan manor house can be seen here. The church retains 12th-c arcades, and the village is situated on the S fringe of Bletchley.

NEWTON ST LOE, Avon *6 ST76*
The local partly 14th-c church displays a perpendicular west tower and houses 18th-c monuments. Newton Park is a fine Georgian house of 1762, standing in grounds that include a lake and the remains of an old castle. These ruins comprise a notable tower and inner gateway, and the house itself is now a college. The Free School dates from 1698.

NEWTOWN LINFORD, Leics *18 SK51*
Charnwood Forest borders this attractive village; and the remains of 16th-c Bradgate House lie to the S. Bradgate park forms an 850-acre country park to the N, which incorporates moorland and rocky hills and is neighboured by lovely Swithland Woods. Lady Jane Grey, England's nine-day Queen, was born at the house in 1537. The ruined sham tower of Old John dates from 1786.

NITON, Isle of Wight *7 SZ57*
Records kept in the local church show that King Charles II landed at Puckaster Cove, near St Lawrence, on 1 July 1675. The building itself carries a 16th-c tower. A disused medieval lighthouse overlooks Chale Bay and Blackgang Chine from the high downland vantage point of St Catherine's Hill. The hill rises to 781ft in the W and is the second highest point on the island. Below this, at 136ft St Catherine's Point, is a powerful modern lighthouse which is visible from the French coast (OACT).

NORBURY, Derbyshire *18 SK14*
The exceptionally interesting 14th-c church is noted for two main features – a wealth of Fitzherbert monuments and examples of 14th-c stained glass in the chancel. A 17th-c manor stands near a recently well-restored house of 1250, perhaps the earliest of its period in Derbyshire.

NORHAM, Northumberland *31 NT94*
Scott's *Marmion* is associated with this River-Tweed town and the fine keep which has survived from a former Norman castle (AM, OACT). A notable Norman chancel can be seen in the church. Other old structures in the town include a restored 13th-c cross and a few old houses. Union Suspension Bridge spans the Tweed 4m NE, and was the first of its type. It was originally erected by Sir Samuel Brown in 1820.

NORTHALLERTON, N Yorks *22 SE39*
Lying to the E of the River Wiske, Northallerton is so situated as to afford distant views of the Cleveland and Hambleton Hills. A 12th- to 14th-c church displays a fine 15th-c pinnacled tower and Jacobean font. The Golden Lion is an old coaching inn, and the site of the 1138 Battle of the Standard is 2½m N.

NORTHAM, Devon *5 SS42*
Northam is situated on the outskirts of Bideford at a point near the widening Torridge estuary. An inscribed stone at Bloody Corner recalls one of King Alfred's battles against Hubba the Dane, in the 9thc. The north aisle of St Margaret's Church is dated 1593.

NORTHAMPTON, Northants *13 SP76*
Plan overleaf
This county town stands on the River Nene and is well-known for the manufacture of footwear. St Peter's Church displays rich Norman work, considered the finest in the county, and of particular note are the carved capitals and chancel arch. St Sepulchre's Church is one of the four round churches still extant, and dates from the 12thc and later. It contains a 6ft-high brass dated 1640, which may well be the largest in England. St Giles's Church retains Norman work, and the central tower is of 17th-c date. All Saints' Church is largely of 17th-c origin, and displays a splendid portico carrying a statue of Charles II. St Matthew's fine modern church contains a sculpture by Henry Moore.

Sparse remains of a castle gate exist by the station, and Cromwell's house – or Hazelrigg Mansion – was built in 1662. The Welsh House has a façade of 1595, carrying a Welsh inscription and recalling the days when Welsh drovers brought their cattle here along the medieval Welsh Lane. This trackway runs NW of the town. Sessions House, the county hall, is of late 17th-c date; the ornate town hall is of the 19thc. Pugin designed the RC cathedral, which was opened in 1864, and part of the 12th-c Hospital of St John survives in Bridge Street as the RC St John the Baptist Church. Abington Park is dated 15th to 18thc and now houses a museum. Delapre Abbey contains the county records and dates mainly from the 17thc.

One of the Eleanor Crosses, erected by Edward I to Queen Eleanor in 1290, can be seen 1½m S at Hardingstone. Hunsbury Hill iron-age camp lies 2m SW. Parts of the Northampton district are destined for New Town development.

NORTHBOROUGH, Cambs *19 TF10*
A notable 14th-c and later manor house in the village shows a fine gatehouse. John Claypole, husband to Cromwell's daughter Elizabeth, lived here. She is buried in the local church, which features a large south chapel.

NORTH BOVEY, Devon *5 SX78*
North Bovey is beautifully situated on the E of Dartmoor, near the River Bovey. Two important features are the village green and delightful Ring of Bells Inn. The perpendicular church bears interesting bosses in the chancel roof, and houses a screen with statuettes. A number of wayside crosses are preserved in the neighbourhood.

NORTH CERNEY, Glos *12 SP00*
A charming Cotswold village in the Churn Valley, where the interesting Norman to perpendicular church displays a curious saddle-back tower and fine stone pulpit. A 14th-c cross exists in the churchyard.

NORTH CREAKE, Norfolk *15 TF83*
The decorated and perpendicular church shows a fine hammerbeam roof, a notable brass of c1500, and carved Royal Arms of 1635. Creake Abbey was founded in 1206 and its remains include a notable 14th-c chapel (AM). The latter lies 1m N.

NORTH CURRY, Somerset *6 ST32*
Nearby Lillesdon Court Farm and Slough Farm are both interesting old houses. The mainly-perpendicular cruciform-shaped church carries an octagonal central tower, and the village itself is situated on the low-lying area of W Sedgemoor.

NORTH DOWNS
This range of chalk hills starts near Reigate in Surrey, and extends across Kent to meet the sea in sheer chalk cliffs at Dover. Various rivers have cut valleys through the soft rock – notably the Medway, and the highest point is sited near Woldingham. This point rises 900ft and has a great chalk pit at its base; it forms an excellent viewpoint. Between the North and South Downs lies the Weald, and the Surrey ridges of the range are now included in an area of outstanding natural beauty.

NORTH ELMHAM, Norfolk *15 TF92*
Remains of a Saxon cathedral and Bishop's castle have been excavated

NORTH ELMHAM/NORTH PETHERTON

from the ruins behind North Elmham church. The bishopric was founded in 673, and the existing church displays a fine 14th-c tower and groined west porch. The north-aisle windows display 14th-c glass.

NORTHFLEET, Kent *9 TQ67*
Manufacture of Portland cement forms this Thames-side town's main industry. The restored mainly 14th-c St Botolph's Church stands on a hill and retains some Saxon work. Its notable 14th-c screen is considered the oldest in Kent. Remains of the Roman town *Vagniacae* have been excavated S at Springhead, on the Dover road.

NORTHIAM, E Sussex *9 TQ82*
A tall tower surmounted by a rare 16th-c Sussex spire is carried by the interesting local church. An oak on the village green is said to be one beneath which Queen Elizabeth I is supposed to have dined. Brickwall shows a 17th-c timbered front and is now a school (OACT). Great Dixter, also timbered, dates from c1450 and includes a splendid great hall (OACT).

NORTHILL, Beds *14 TL14*
The largely-decorated church was formerly collegiate, and carries a massive tower which displays a one-hand clock. Thomas Tompion, known as the father of English clock-makers, was born here in 1639. He was buried at Westminster Abbey in 1713. Several thatched cottages can be seen in the area.

NORTHLEACH, Glos *12 SP11*
Northleach is a small Cotswold town situated on high ground E of the Fosse Way, between the verdant valleys of the Coln and Windrush. It displays typical stone-built houses and almshouses, and the former 18th-c gaol still stands. The splendid perpendicular wool church is notable for memorial brasses to woolstaplers, a fine clerestory, and a famous pinnacled parvis. The latter is a south porch containing an upper room with a fireplace.

NORTH LEIGH, Oxon *13 SP31*
One of the two interesting chapels incorporated in the local church shows fine fan-tracery. The church itself carries a Saxon tower, and contains a doom painting in the chancel. The best Roman villa in the county lies NE and displays tessellated pavements (OACT).

NORTH MIMMS, Herts *8 TL20*
North Mimms's church is a good example of decorated work, and preserves several interesting monuments and brasses. A nearby Jacobean hall dates from c1600 and shows later additions. It is set in a lovely garden which was originally designed by William Robinson, a pioneer of modern English gardening, between 1838 and 1935. A stone sited NE at Welham Green marks the spot where Lunardi made his first balloon landing (1784).

NORTHMOOR, Oxon *13 SP40*
A 13th-c church retains 14th-c effigies and inscribed balustrading of 1701. An Elizabethan parsonage house and fine old dovecote are also of note. Bablockhythe lies 2m NE on the River Thames, and has a passenger ferry.

NORTH NEWTON, Somerset *6 ST23*
King Alfred's Jewel was found here in 1693 and now resides in the Ashmolean Museum, Oxford. The rebuilt church preserves an ancient tower and a good screen.

NORTH NIBLEY, Glos *12 ST79*
Stinchcombe Hill rises 700ft to the N of this attractive Cotswold-ridge village. A tall monument sited on Nibley Knoll viewpoint was raised to William Tyndale, the 16th-c translator of the Bible.

NORTH PETHERTON, Somerset *6 ST23*
One of the finest perpendicular church towers in the county can be seen in this small town. It is richly adorned with carving and dates from c1510. Halswell House, dated 1689, stands 3m NW in fine grounds.

1 Abington Park (museum)	6 Delapre Abbey (records office)	11 St Matthew's Church
2 All Saints' Church	7 Eleanor Cross	12 St Peter's Church
3 Castle Gate Remains	8 Hazelrigg Mansion (Cromwell's house)	13 St Sepulchre's Church
4 Cathedral (RC)	9 St Giles's Church	14 Town Hall
5 County Hall (sessions house)	10 St John the Baptist Church (RC)	15 Welsh House

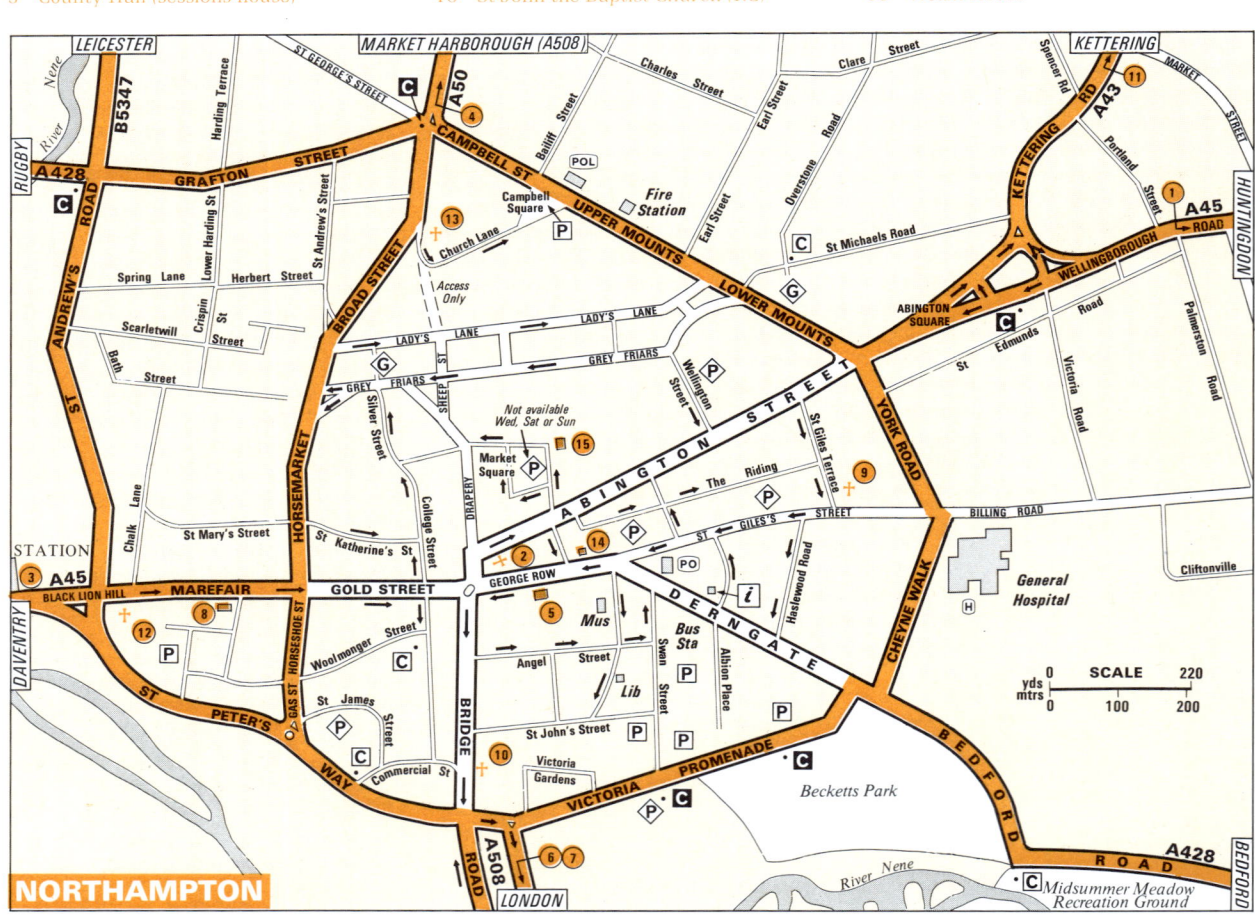

NORTH SHIELDS, Tyne & Wear
27 NZ36

North Shields is a Tyneside port which is linked to South Shields by car ferry. John Dobson, architect of many Newcastle buildings, was born at the Pineapple Inn in 1787.

NORTH SOMERCOTES, Lincs *19 TF49*

Eight shafts support the notable 15th-c font in the restored trans-Norman to perpendicular church. Also of interest are remains of a painted screen. Locksley Hall is a restored 15th-c house which contains interesting old glass. Tennyson wrote a poem entitled *Locksley Hall*.

NORTH STOKE, Oxon *13 SU68*

Medieval wall paintings and the grave of Clara Butt, the famous singer, can be seen in North Stoke's Thames-side church.

NORTH TAWTON, Devon *5 SS60*

The church of St Peter has a tower with thick rubble walls and a 17th-c clock. Broad Hall is dated 1680, and preserves older fragments of 15th-c origin. Cottles Barton, dated 1567, is a thatched Elizabethan house lying 1m S.

NORTHUMBERLAND NATIONAL PARK

This national park covers the bleak upland districts of the county, from the Cheviot Hills to the Roman Wall. The former rise to 2,676ft – the second highest point in England outside the Lake District and the Cross Fell range in the Pennines. Adjacent to the W boundary is the Border forest park, most of which is in Scotland.

NORTH WALSHAM, Norfolk *15 TG23*

A market town where the fine decorated church features a painted screen, a tall font cover of 15th-c date, and a 17th-c monument to Sir William Paston. Paston founded the grammar school in 1606, and Nelson once attended classes here. The restored market cross dates from 1550.

NORTHWICH, Cheshire *17 SJ67*

Northwich is an important salt-producing town, where dissolving rock-salt has created underground caverns and subsidence. Salt mining involved the extraction of artificially produced brine, and contributed greatly to the damage. A few timbered houses can be seen here, and many buildings are leaning at unnatural angles.

Perpendicular St Helen's Church is situated at Witton, to the E of the town. It carries a fine tower showing gargoyles, plus old screenwork and a splendid oak-built tie-beam roof adorned with nearly 400 bosses. A little to the NW is the unique electrically-controlled Anderton vertical canal lift. This is used to transfer barges from the River Weaver to the Trent and Mersey canal. Vale Royal is a stately house near the River Weaver, standing 3m SSW in a large park. The former abbey of 1277 was dissolved by King Henry VIII, and a later building was plundered by Cromwellian troops.

NORTH YORK MOORS NATIONAL PARK

Much of this 600sqm park covers high, heather-clad moorland. It extends from the Cleveland and Hambleton Hills towards the picturesque North Yorkshire coastline, and includes attractive valleys leading to the Vale of Pickering.

NORTON, Cleveland *27 NZ42*

Norton is an attractive village with 18th-c houses grouped around a wide green. The partly-Saxon church has a central tower and is the mother church of Stockton.

NORTON, Suffolk *15 TL96*

Carved misericords and other good examples of woodworking can be seen in the local decorated and perpendicular church. Both the rectory and Little Haugh Hall are of partly 18th-c date, and the latter is notable.

NORTON, S Yorks *18 SK38*

Sir Francis Chantrey was born here in 1781, and is famous for the Chantrey bequest for works of art. Many of the exhibits in London's Tate Gallery were acquired with the aid of this bequest and an obelisk has been raised here to his memory. He designed the frontal terrace of the fine Georgian Oakes Park mansion (OACT).

NORTON FITZWARREN, Somerset *6 ST12*

The restored decorated and perpendicular church houses a fine carved screen and old bench-ends. The village itself lies in the Vale of Taunton Deane.

NORTON-IN-HALES, Salop *17 SJ73*

People who were found to be working after mid-day on Shrove Tuesday were formerly bumped on the Bradling stone, a boulder standing near the church on the village green. The rebuilt church contains the fine Cotton monument of 1606.

NORTON ST PHILIP, Somerset *6 ST75*

One of the earliest and finest examples of its type in England, the 15th-c stone-and-timber built George Inn has included Pepys, Cromwell, the Duke of Monmouth, and Judge Jeffreys among its former patrons. An attempt was made on Monmouth's life here during the rebellion of 1685. The restored church has a curious west tower.

NORWICH, Norfolk *15 TG20*
Plan overleaf

Norwich is a cathedral city and county town on the River Wensum, and was once a centre of the worsted trade. It now specializes in footwear and is involved in a number of other industries.

The interesting largely-Norman cathedral carries a lofty decorated tower and spire rising to 315ft. The Norman nave and the later roof bosses in the nave and cloisters are remarkable. Also of interest are the 15th-c choir stalls, the Norman bishop's throne, the presbytery, and the beautiful cloisters. Nurse Edith Cavell's grave has been moved to a new site on St Martin's Palace Plain. The Bishop's Palace was extensively added to between 1858 and 1859, but originated from the 12th to 15thc. Delightful old houses exist in the Close.

Pull's Ferry and the old Inn stand by the river, near a former water gate. Erpingham and Ethelbert Gates are of note (both AM). Over thirty old parish churches exist in Norwich – more than in any other English city. The largest of these is St Peter Mancroft, with its notable tower; the 15th-c church of St Andrew displays a remarkable series of thirteen carved shields; St Michael Coslany shows notable flint work in the Thorp chapel; St John the Baptist is impressive.

A massive Norman castle dating from c1130 was refaced between 1834 and 1839. It now houses a museum and picture gallery, showing much work by the well-known Norwich school (AM). Robert Kett was executed near here in 1549 for his part in the Rising. St Andrew's Hall of c1460, the beautiful 15th-c Strangers' Hall, the former Church of St Peter Hungate, and the flint-faced Bridewell all house museums or art galleries.

The chequered-flint guildhall of 1407 shows later additions. This and 15th-c Suckling House, are both outstanding old buildings. The city hall of 1932 and 1938 stands in St Peter Street. Many other 19th- and 20th-c buildings are of interest, but space does not permit full descriptions of these. The Music House is mainly Elizabethan, but preserves some Norman work. It is now a centre for amateur musicians. The Maids Head Hotel is one of the oldest in England, and the fine Octagon Chapel dates from 1756. The Old Meeting House originated in 1693. Many old houses can be seen in Elm Hill, Ber Street, Oak Street, and King Street. Portions of the former city walls and towers remain, and the Cow Tower is sited near the ancient Hospital of St Helen. Nelson was a pupil at the old grammar school. The fine rebuilt 18th-c Maddermarket Theatre is notable, and the Georgian Assembly Rooms of 1754 were by a local architect named Thomas Ivory. These have been restored. Augustine Steward's House stands in Tombland Alley, and characteristic Georgian houses can be seen in St Giles' Street.

Earlham is an old hall on the W outskirts of Norwich, now the property of the city and part of the newly-founded University of East Anglia. The buildings of the latter are considered among the finest of post-war universities. Elizabeth Fry, the first great prison reformer, once lived in Earlham Hall.

The view of Norwich from Mousehold Heath is famous and it was here that Kett and his rebels were defeated in 1549. The old Dolphin Inn at Heigham has been restored. Several iron-built bridges existing in the town include Duke's Palace Bridge of 1822, and the iron-and-stone Coslany Bridge of 1804.

NOSELEY, Leics *18 SP79*

The local chapel was made collegiate in 1274, and contains notable 15th-c stalls plus interesting monuments and examples of old glass.

NOTTINGHAM, Notts *18 SK54*
Plan on page 269

A county, university, and manufacturing town on the River Trent, Nottingham specializes in the hosiery, lace, bicycle, and tobacco industries. Much of the early hosiery machinery was destroyed by the Luddite gangs in the early 19thc.

The 17th-c castle is a notable viewpoint which now houses a museum and art gallery, and preserves dungeons and a gateway from the original castle. Below are several good Georgian houses – notably in Castle Gate. Perpendicular St Mary's Church carries a fine tower and displays Royal Arms of 1710, plus interesting monuments. St Peter's Church preserves 13th-c work and boasts two fonts – one of the 15thc, and one of the 17thc. Other churches in the area are of lesser interest. The cathedral (RC) was designed by Pugin. Early 18th-c Bromley House contains a library, and Marshal Tallard once lodged at Newdigate House. The Unitarian Chapel has associations with both Byron and Coleridge, and the town was the birthplace of William Booth, founder of the Salvation Army. King Charles I raised his standard on Standard Hill, near the castle, at the start of the Civil War. Famous Nottingham Goose Fair is held during the first week in October, in the Forest Recreation Ground. Two old local inns, the Salutation and the Trip to Jerusalem, are picturesque. The Playhouse of 1963 is a notable modern theatre – just one of the many interesting modern buildings to be seen in the city. A splendid Norman font can be seen in the Church of New Lenton, situated in a suburb of the same name.

Bendigo, the famous 19th-c boxing champion, was buried in St Mary's cemetery (Bath Street) in 1880. The Royal Children Inn displays a remarkable whale's shoulder-blade sign. Wollaton Hall, one of the largest 16th-c mansions in England, was the work of Robert Smythson and now houses a museum. The county-cricket ground at Trent Bridge is well-known, and a racecourse exists in the area. Attenborough local nature reserve (200-acres) lies 5m SW.

NUNEATON, Warwickshire 18 SP39
Bricks, woollen goods, and hats are manufactured in this town, and coal is worked in the area. St Nicholas' Church was founded in the 12thc and displays an old roof and the notable Constable tomb of 1560. St Mary's Church, largely rebuilt, preserves part of a former nunnery. Associations with George Eliot include a memorial garden of 1953. She was born 3m SW at Arbury Hall in 1819.

This Elizabethan and 18th-c house has a stable block of the former period, and shows work which was possibly by Wren (OACT). Astley Castle is a restored fortified 12th- to 16th-c manor house lying within a moat 4m SW.

NUNEHAM COURTENAY, Oxon 13 SU59
The 18th-c hall stands in a large wooded park belonging to the University of

1	Assembly Rooms	12	Edith Cavell's Grave	22	Octagon Chapel
2	Augustine Steward's House	13	Erpingham Gate	23	Pull's Ferry
3	Bishop's Palace	14	Ethelbert Gate	24	Old Meeting House
4	Bridewell Hall (museum)	15	Former Church of St Peter Hungate (museum and art gallery)	25	St Andrew's Church
5	Castle (museum and art gallery)			26	St Andrew's Hall (museum)
6	Cathedral	16	Grammar School	27	Stranger's Hall (museum)
7	City Hall	17	Guildhall	28	Suckling House
8	Coslany Bridge	18	Hospital of St Helen	29	Town Walls
9	Cow Tower	19	Maddermarket Theatre	30	University of East Anglia
10	Dolphin Inn	20	Maid's Head Hotel		
11	Duke's Palace Bridge	21	Music House		

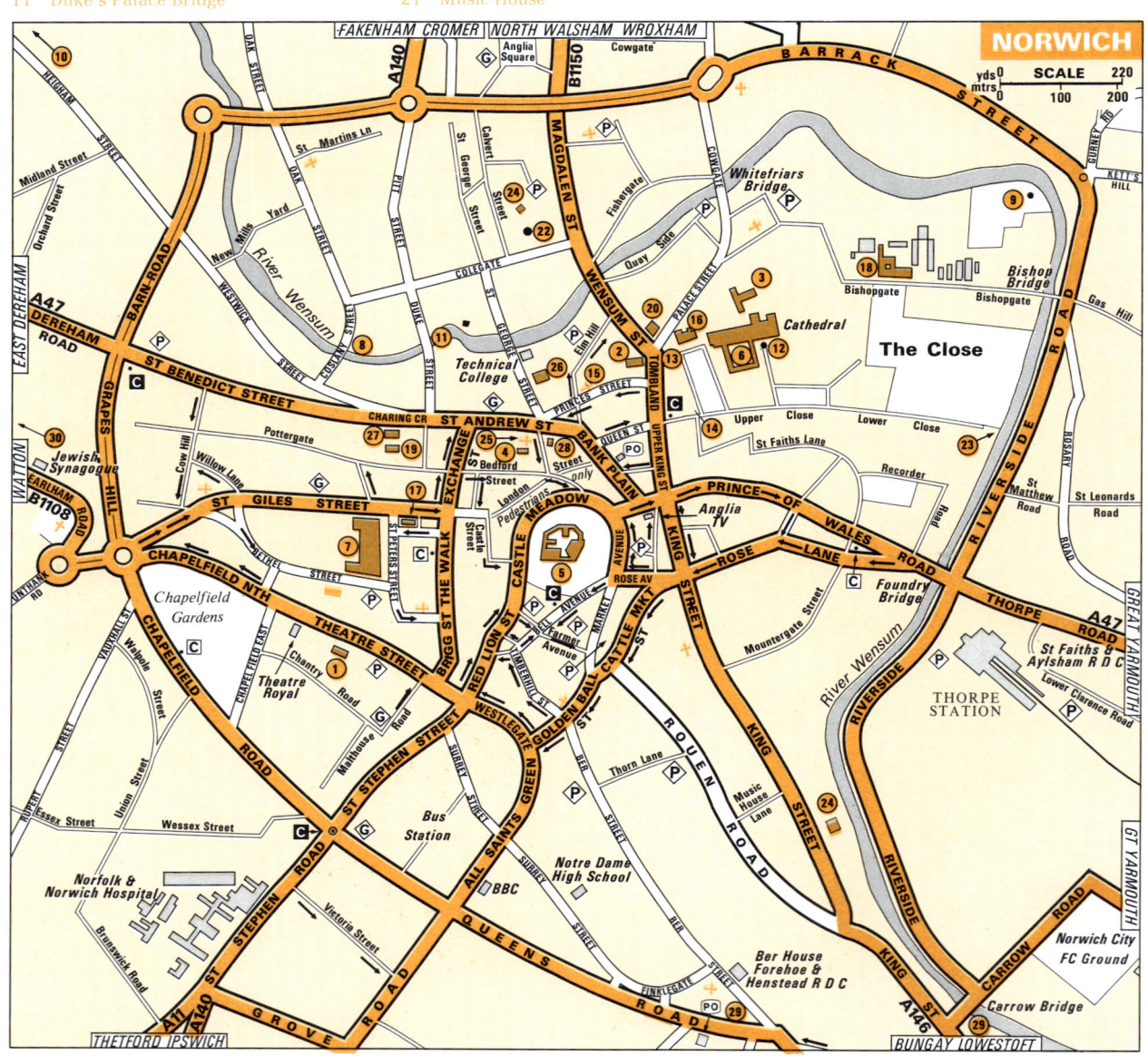

Oxford, adjacent to the River Thames. A highly-ornamented conduit which formerly stood at Carfax in Oxford is preserved in these grounds. Also in the park is a classic-style church, built in the 18th-c by the first Earl of Harcourt.

NUN MONKTON, N Yorks *22 SE55*
Situated at the junction of the Rivers Nidd and Ouse, this attractive village is the proud possessor of a maypole. The nave of an original nunnery survives in the parish church and shows beautiful early-English work. The west front is particularly good. A pilastered hall stands in fine gardens and dates from *c*1690.

NUNNEY, Somerset *6 ST74*
Modelled on the French Bastille, the fine 14th-c castle in this delightful village includes a moat which may be the deepest in England. It was besieged in the Civil War (AM). The church carries a good perpendicular tower, and houses effigies of the Delameres. The manor house dates from *c*1700. The actual village is sited on the E fringe of the Mendips.

OAKHAM, Leicester *19 SK80*
Oakham was formerly the capital of Rutland, once the smallest county in England, and is a well-known fox-hunting centre. The fine 12th- to 15th-c church displays unusual and interesting carved nave-capitals. The original grammar school was founded in 1587 and stands in the churchyard. An old butter cross with stocks has been preserved. Remains of the town's castle include a splendid Norman banqueting hall, where a unique collection of horse shoes is nailed to the wall. These were traditionally contributed by members of the royal family, or of the peerage, visiting the lordship for the first time (AM, OACT). Jeffery Hudson, a famous dwarf who was served up in a pie to Charles II, was born at Oakham in 1619. Another native was Titus Oates (1649 to 1705). Hayne House dates from *c*1700, and Flore's House is of 13th- to 15th-c date. The impressive late 17th-c house of Burley-on-the-Hill displays fine colonnades and lies 2m NE. Egleton is 1½m SE, and the south doorway of its little church shows a remarkable carved Norman tympanum. Nether Hambleton Hall is a beautiful early 17th-c house situated 3m ESE, and Cold Overton Hall is a 17th-c house standing 3½m NW.

OARE, Somerset *5 SS84*
A hamlet in a lovely Doone Country setting, Oare is strongly associated with Blackmore's *Lorna Doone*. This fictional

1 Attenborough Nature Reserve
2 Bromley House (library)
3 Castle (museum and art gallery)
4 Cathedral (RC)
5 Church of New Lenton
6 County Cricket Ground
7 Forest Recreation Ground (Goose Fair)
8 Newdigate House
9 Playhouse
10 Racecourse
11 Royal Children Inn
12 Salutation Inn
13 St Mary's Church
14 St Peter's Church
15 Trip to Jerusalem Inn
16 Unitarian Chapel
17 University of Nottingham
18 Wollaton Hall (museum)

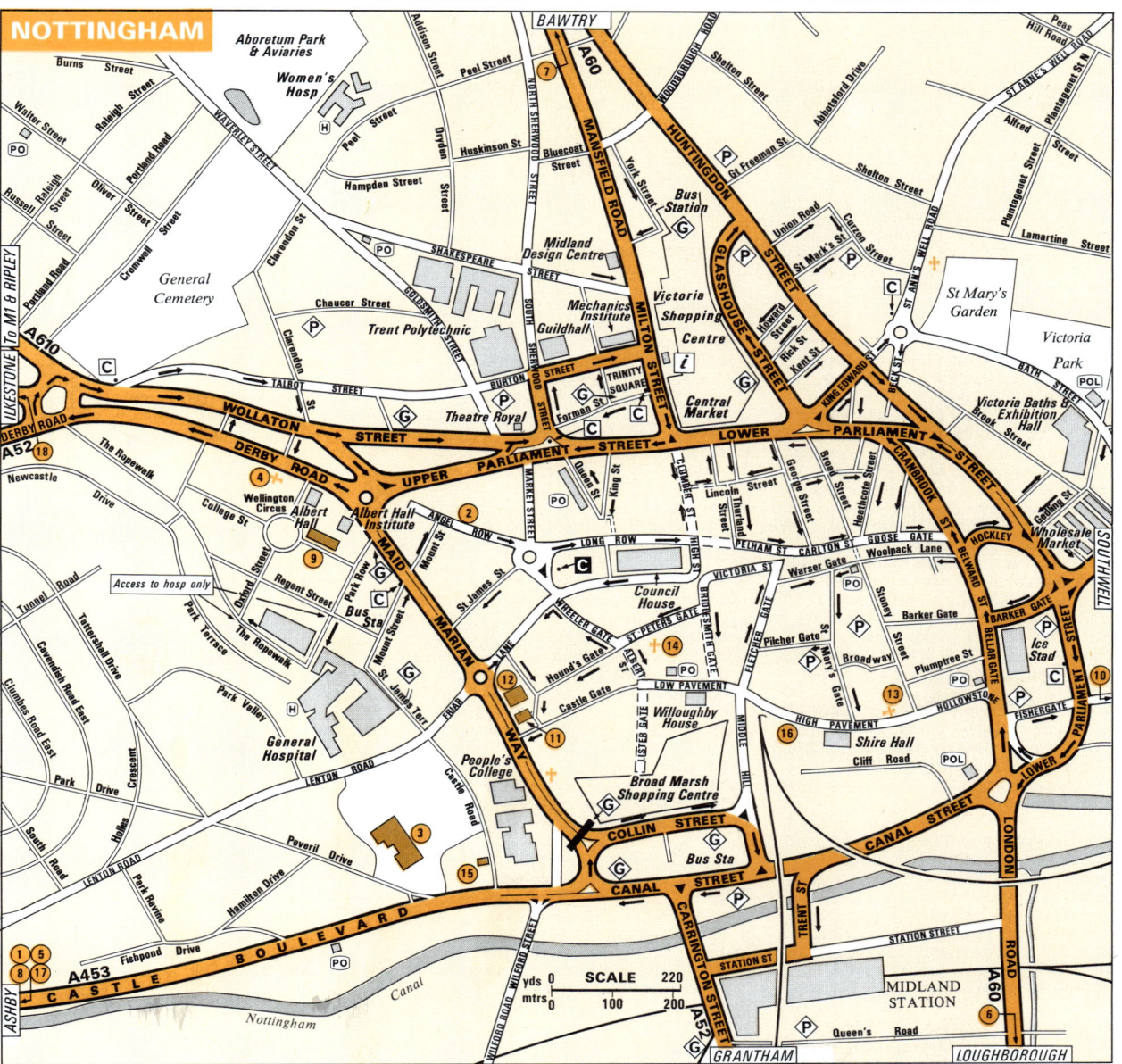

heroine's wedding and subsequent murder are described as having taken place in the village's tiny perpendicular-style church. Both Badgworthy Water Valley and the well-known Doone Valley are picturesque Exmoor national park combes.

OCKHAM, Surrey *8 TQ05*
Ockham village church is almost hidden among the trees of Ockham Park, and preserves a remarkable east window of seven lancets. This feature dates from the 13thc.

OCKLEY, Surrey *8 TQ13*
This village is situated on the Roman Stane Street and is grouped around a wide green. Fine old farms exist in the area. Ethelwulf of Essex defeated and wreaked slaughter among the Danes at a site close to the village in 851. The church tower dates from 1700 and a timbered 15th-c porch is of interest. A sign showing King Charles II in the arms of Nell Gwynne hangs outside the King's Arms Inn.

ODCOMBE, Somerset *6 ST51*
Tom Coryate, the 17th-c poet and traveller who is best known for the introduction of the table fork, was born here. The mainly decorated and perpendicular church houses a 15th-c font cover.

ODELL, Beds *13 SP95*
Once a market town, this attractive River-Ouse village includes scanty remains of an ancient castle on a mound by the river. This was replaced by a mansion in 1632, and a modern house now occupies the site. An embattled west tower and good screenwork are features of the decorated and perpendicular church.

ODIHAM, Hants *8 SU75*
Most of the houses in this town are Georgian, but the fine old George Inn was first licensed in 1540. The stocks and whipping-post have been preserved, and the priory, formerly the rectory, is partly 15th and 17thc. Numerous old brasses, 15th-c screenwork, and a pulpit and galleries of the Jacobean period are features of the largely 14th-c church. The church tower is a 17th-c brick construction and a curious old pest-house which still stands in the churchyard dates back to the great plague of 1665. Remains of Odiham Castle, sometimes known as King John's Castle, lie 1m W near the derelict Basingstoke Canal. It was besieged by the Dauphin of France in 1216.

OFFENHAM, Herefs & Worcs *12 SP04*
Thatched cottages, old dovecotes, and a tall maypole crowned by a cockerel are features of this attractive village. It faces an orchard-covered hillside across the River Severn.

OFFHAM, Kent *9 TQ65*
A quintain has been preserved on the village green. This is a post that used to serve as a mark in tilting (jousting), and is probably the sole surviving example in the country. The church shows Norman work, and the characters TS (1621) are cut into the chancel arch. Hop fields are cultivated in the area.

OKEHAMPTON, Devon *5 SX59*
Okehampton is the market town for a large farming area and is situated N of the highest point in Dartmoor national park. To the W of 2,028ft Yes Tor and 2,039ft High Willhays is picturesque West Okement Valley. The parish church retains its perpendicular tower, and the chapel of St James carries a 14th-c tower. The town hall dates from 1685 and Oaklands is a house of c1830. A little to the W are the ruined chapel, keep, and hall of a 13th- and 14th-c castle (AM).

OLD BOLINGBROKE, Lincs *19 TF36*
Slight remains of the castle where King Henry IV was born in 1366 exist in this Wolds village (AM). John of Gaunt may have rebuilt the partly 14th-c church, which carries a tower adorned with fierce gargoyles. Several 18th-c houses and shops stand near the church.

OLDBURY, W Midlands *12 SO98*
This Black Country town is involved with chemical, steel, and brick industries.

OLDBURY-UPON-SEVERN, Avon *12 ST69*
A nuclear power station has been erected here, facing the estuary above the Severn Bridge.

OLDHAM, Gt Manchester *22 SD90*
Cotton spinning has helped to make this town famous, and the imposing town hall of 1841 and 1880 is a copy of the Temple of Ceres, near Athens. Oldham Wakes, or holidays, commence on the penultimate Saturday of June. Sir Winston Churchill was first elected to Parliament as MP for Oldham in 1900. An art-gallery and museum are of interest.

OLD SARUM, Wilts *7 SU13*
This is the site of an ancient cathedral city, where foundations of a former cathedral and castle are surrounded by Norman earthworks. The see was transferred to Salisbury in 1220, after which the site gradually became deserted. The cathedral was demolished in 1331, and the materials employed in its construction were transported for use in the present building. A pillar erected in 1931 recalls that Old Sarum returned two members of Parliament, until the 1832 Reform Bill. A Roman track known as the Portway linked Old Sarum with Silchester (*Calleva Atrebatum*).

OLD WARDEN, Beds *14 TL14*
Remains of an abbey include a fine Tudor chimney, and the interesting Shuttleworth Collection of historical aircraft and veteran cars is situated in the confines of a small airfield. Flying displays are occasionally held here (OACT). Thatched cottages can be seen, and the area produced the first Warden pear.

OLLERTON, Notts *18 SK66*
Ollerton is a good centre for touring the Dukeries and Sherwood Forest. Picturesque Bilhagh glades lie to the W.

OLNEY, Bucks *13 SP85*
Boots are made in this pleasant little River-Ouse town. Strong associations with Cowper include the house in which he lived from 1768 to 1786, which now houses a Cowper and Newton museum. The church is a good example of decorated style, and carries a fine spire. Cowper Memorial Chapel dates from 1879. The well-known Shrove Tuesday pancake race has a counterpart at Liberal in Kansas, USA.

OMBERSLEY, Herefs & Worcs *12 SO86*
Features of this picturesque village include half-timbered houses of 16th- and 17th-c date, plus the delightful King's Arms Inn. Charity School is dated 1729, and a fine mid-Georgian rectory is of interest. Ombersley Court was refaced in the early 19thc, but originated from the William and Mary period. Thomas Rickman, a noted scholar, built the galleried early 19th-c church.

ONCHAN, Isle of Man *20 SC47*
Onchan stands on a northern headland of Douglas Bay. Government House is the official residence of the Governor, and lies on the outskirts. Local scenery is particularly fine.

ONGAR, Essex *9 TL50*
Also known as Chipping Ongar, this place stands on the River Roding and includes the mound and moat of a Saxon Castle. The King's Head is an inn of 1697 which stands opposite the old Corner Shop of 1642. David Livingstone did his missionary training at the Congregational church between 1838 and 1839. A restored church at High Ongar preserves a doorway displaying rich Norman workmanship.

ORFORD, Suffolk *15 TM45*
The quay of this fishing village is separated from the sea by the River Ore, beyond which lies Orford Ness. An interesting moated 18-sided castle was built by King Henry II in 1165, and houses a collection of arms (OACT). Features of the mainly 14th-c church include old woodwork, screens, and a ruined chancel showing Norman work. Orfordness-Havergate national nature reserve has the distinction of being one of the few places where the rare avocet, a wading bird – can be seen.

ORLETON, Herefs & Worcs *12 SO46*
Black-and-white houses exist here, and the church displays a Norman nave, a timber porch of 1686, and a fine Norman font. King Charles I is said to have stayed at 16th-c Orleton Court in 1645, and Alexander Pope was a later visitor to the house.

ORMSKIRK, Lancs *21 SD40*
Gingerbread is a well-known product of this market town, and the surrounding area is mainly agricultural. The mainly-perpendicular church carries two west towers, one of which bears a spire, and contains interesting effigies in the Derby Chapel. Georgian houses include the notable buildings of Burscough Street, which include 18th-c Knowles House. Remains of 13th-c Burscough Priory lie 2m NE. Lathom House is a surviving portion of Leoni's 1734 mansion and can be seen 3m E. Much of the house was destroyed during the Civil War.

ORPINGTON, Gt London *8 TQ46*
Residential district and dormitory for London, Orpington includes a church which displays traces of pre-Conquest work. The priory is an old clergy house of 14th- and 15th-c date, now housing the Priory Museum of local interest.

ORSETT, Essex *9 TQ68*
The Norman to 15th-c flint church features interesting monuments, plus a Norman nave and south doorway. Orsett House is of Georgian red-brick construction, and Hall Farm has a half-timbered wing of Tudor construction.

ORTON, Cambs *19 TL19*
Plans to re-develop Orton as a New Town for over 25,000 are expected to be implemented from 1975. Part of the scheme includes the provision of special bus roads.

ORTON, Cumbria *21 NY60*
This attractive village lies N of the River Lune, below Shap Fells. Its church shows 15th-c work and a fine tower, and an old hall in the area is of interest.

OSBORNE HOUSE, Isle of Wight *7 SZ59*
Queen Victoria died in this 19th-c mansion in 1901. The State apartments, Swiss Cottage, and bathing machine have all been maintained as they would have appeared in Victoria's day (OACT).

OSMINGTON, Dorset *6 SY78*
Views from Osmington encompass Weymouth Bay, Portland, and the chalk cliffs of Ringstead Bay to the E. A figure of King George III on horseback has been cut out of the turf of downs lying to the N. Osmington Mills, a noted area for lobsters and crabs, lies 1¾m SE on the coast.

OSMOTHERLEY, N Yorks *22 SE49*
Black Hambleton rises to 1,289ft E of this stone-built village, and is the highest point of the Hambleton Hills. Interesting features of Osmotherley include an old village cross and a stone table on five pillars which was once used as a pulpit by John Wesley. A Methodist chapel of 1754 can be seen here, and the church displays a 15th-c tower and porch.

OSPRINGE, Kent *9 TR06*
This attractive little place includes a 15th-c half-timbered Maison Dieu, which now houses a museum (AM). It stands on a site once occupied by a hospital built by Henry III in 1234. The rebuilt church has two Norman doorways.

OSWESTRY, Salop *17 SJ22*
The name of this ancient Welsh-Border market town means The Tongue of Land Belonging to Oswald. St Oswald was slain here by Penda in 642. Traces of the castle remain, and the guildhall museum preserves a 'Scold's bridle'. The church houses Yale monuments and displays a lych-gate of 1631. Llwyd Mansion is a fine old house with an eagle crest.

Croeswylan Stone is part of an old cross which is said to commemorate a market held during a local plague of 1559. Various legends are attached to St Oswald's Well, which is situated near a school founded in 1407. Sir Walford Davies the musician was born here in 1869. Remains of Offa's Dyke can be seen W of the town, and traces of Watt's Dyke lie to the N and E. Old Oswestry is an important iron-age hill fort covering 68 acres and situated 1m N. Brogyntyn mansion dates from the 18thc and lies 1m NE. Aston Hall, a *c*1780 building by Robert Mylne, stands 3m SE.

OTFORD, Kent *8 TQ55*
Thomas a Becket once lived in this River-Darent village, and remains of an old Archbishops of Canterbury palace are of interest. The palace was rebuilt in 1501, and Henry VIII came here on his way to the Field of the Cloth of Gold in France. The restored Norman to decorated church contains a Jacobean font and a notable marble monument of 1687.

OTHAM, Kent *9 TQ75*
This village comprises picturesque old houses, and is set amid orchards and hop gardens. Three fine timbered houses – Wardes, Synyards, and Stoneacre – are of particular note. Stoneacre is a splendid yeoman's house of about 1480, with 16th-c additions (NT, OACT). Gore Court and Rumwood are interesting houses situated near by.

OTLEY, W Yorks *22 SE24*
Otley is an industrially-orientated market town situated on the River Wharfe at the foot of 925ft Otley Chevin. The latter offers a panoramic view of Lower Wharfedale. A cruciform-shaped decorated and perpendicular church displays a good west tower, several monuments, and a Georgian pulpit. The curious railway tunnel memorial in the churchyard was raised to men who lost their lives building Bramhope tunnel, between 1845 and 1849. A Victorian maypole stands at Cross Green.

Thomas Chippendale the furniture designer was born at Otley in 1718. The grammar school was founded in 1611, and Weston Hall is of Elizabethan and later date. Fine old Farnley Hall is of Elizabethan date, but shows Georgian additions by Carr of York. It is associated with the Fairfax family and was visited by J M W Turner. The attractive Washburn Valley stretches to the N.

OTTERBOURNE, Hants *7 SU42*
Charlotte Yonge the authoress lived here and was buried in the local churchyard in 1901. Cranbury Park is a fine 18th-c mansion surrounded by a park, and the River Itchen flows through the area.

OTTERBURN, Northumberland *27 NY89*
Situated in the Rede Valley of the Northumberland national park, Otterburn lies 5m NW of Steng Cross and its lonely gibbet. The Battle of Otterburn was fought 1½m NW in 1388, and is commemorated by the Percy Cross and numerous ballads.

OTTERDEN, Kent *9 TQ95*
The brick church was rebuilt in 1753, and Otterden Palace is a restored Tudor and Georgian mansion (OACT).

OTTERTON, Devon *6 SY08*
A mile to the W of this delightful village of cob and thatched cottages, at a crossroads with the A376, is a curious brick-built mile-post of 1743. This carries four sets of directions couched in Biblical phrases. Mainly 19th-c Bicton House stands NW in grounds which were originally laid out by the famous French designer Le Notre in 1735. The garden now incorporates an avenue of monkey puzzles, a narrow-gauge railway, and a countryside museum (OACT). Two elaborate Rolle monuments can be seen in Pugin's mausoleum of 1850. Detached red-sandstone stacks are a feature of picturesque Ladram Bay, 1m NE.

OTTERY ST MARY, Devon *6 SY19*
Samuel Taylor Coleridge was born in this River-Otter town in 1772. W M Thackeray spent several holidays here, and described the town under the name of Clavering St Mary in *Pendennis*. The magnificent collegiate church was modelled on Exeter Cathedral by Bishop Grandson, and dates largely from 1337. Notable features include twin transeptal towers, fan-vaulting in the Dorset aisle, a stone screen, 14th-c stalls, and a curious Elizabethan clock. The carving of an elephant appears on a nave pier of the Dorset aisle. Cadhay, a fine Tudor house with Georgian additions, lies 1m NW (OACT).

OUGHTERSHAW, N Yorks *21 SD88*
This is the last hamlet that a road through the wild reaches of Upper Wharfedale encounters before climbing over the lonely moors of 1,900ft Fleet Moss. Fine views of the high Pennine peaks can be enjoyed before the steep descent to Hawes, in Wensleydale. Several of England's highest and most isolated farms are located W of the pass's summit at Cam Houses.

OULTON, W Yorks *22 SE33*
The Nookin is a half-timbered house of 1611. The John of Gaunt Hotel stands to the NW, and claims to be the place where its namesake killed the last wild boar in Yorkshire.

OULTON BROADS, Suffolk *15 TM59*
George Borrow wrote many of his works at his home – now demolished – in this

Old Oswestry, an important iron-age hill fort

Broads yachting centre. The hovercraft was first tested on these waters by Christopher Cockerell. Oulton High House is of Elizabethan origin, and the Norman to perpendicular church houses a fine 15th-c font.

OUNDLE, Northants *14 TL08*
Old houses and the picturesque Talbot and White Lion inns, are interesting features of this delightful stone-built town. The early-English to perpendicular church carries a lofty crocketed spire, and displays 14th-c screenwork. The south porch is particularly beautiful. The Latham almshouses date from 1611.

Cotterstock Hall, 2m NE, is a 17th-c house where Thomas Dryden wrote his *Fables* (gardens OACT). Lyveden New Building lies 5m SW, and is built in the form of a cross. Its shape is meant to symbolize the Passion, and the building was constructed by Sir Thomas Tresham in c1600. It was left incomplete because the Treshams became involved in the Gunpowder Plot. Lyveden Old Building is of Elizabethan date and now serves as a farmhouse.

OUTWELL, Norfolk *14 TF50*
The combination of Outwell and Upwell forms a 2m street in the Fenland district. The early-English to perpendicular church displays a 14th-c angel-carved nave roof. Only the towered 16th-c gatehouse of former Beaupre Hall, lying N of the village has survived.

OUTWOOD, Surrey *8 TQ34*
Outwood's post-mill of 1665 is one of the best preserved examples in existence. Harewoods Estate is a 2,000-acre area of unspoilt woods and farmland, which was given to the NT in 1955. Outwood Common is part of the protected area.

OVER, Cambs *14 TL37*
Boating and fishing can be enjoyed on the River Ouse, which flows near this Fenland village. The church shows fine decorated work and curious gargoyles, and the vicarage dates from c1720.

OVERSTRAND, Norfolk *15 TG24*
Cliff walks extend NE from here to Cromer, and sandy beaches are available for sea-bathing.

OVERTON HILL, Wilts *7 SU16*
An avenue of stones leading from the famous prehistoric circle at Avebury ends at the twin circles that make up this monument. The present complex is thought to date from the early bronze age, but excavations have produced evidence of a previous, probably timber-built, neolithic structure. See also Avebury.

OVINGDEAN, Sussex *8 TQ30*
Situated inland from a range of chalk cliffs, this downland village includes a little church with an early-Norman nave and chancel.

OVINGHAM, Northumberland *27 NZ06*
Pronounced Ovinjam, this village boasts a church with a notable pre-Conquest tower. The grave (1828) of Thomas Bewick, a well-known late 18th-c engraver, can be seen in the churchyard. An old pack-horse bridge is also of interest.

OXBURGH, Norfolk *14 TF70*
Oxburgh Hall is a fine towered 15th-c building standing within a moat. It is the seat of the Bedingfield family (NT, OACT). The church is noted for its Bedingfield Chapel, which displays rich terra-cotta work. The building collapsed in 1948 but has since been partially restored.

OXFORD, Oxon *13 SP50*
Oxford is an ancient university town on three main waterways – Rivers Cherwell, Thames, and the Oxford Canal. This reach of the Thames is locally known as the Isis, and the canal, which links with the Coventry Canal, terminates here after a circuitous route of some 80m. The city name means 'the ford for Oxen' (over the Thames), and the first reference to the community appears in the Saxon Chronicle of 912. Other sources indicate that the borough was thriving for some four to five centuries before this, but such claims remain unsupported by any firm evidence. The origins of the university are similarly confused by colourful local legend. Although the idea that its foundation was due to the mythical British King Memphric – or at least by Alfred the Great – is appealing to the romantic, such stories remain doubtful and entirely unauthenticated. It is much more likely that the foundation developed from the monastic schools of St Frideswide's Priory, or as a result of the expulsion of students from Paris. The university received papal recognition in 1214.

In contrast to Cambridge, which retains the atmosphere of a country town, Oxford has had its image somewhat altered in recent years. Much of this change is due to the establishment of a huge British Motor Corporation works at Cowley, on the outskirts of the city. This gigantic complex evolved from a cycle shop which was originally opened by William Morris, later to become Lord Nuffield.

Early students who came to Oxford for the lectures were accommodated in numerous halls administered by graduates, and it was not until the reign of Elizabeth I that the undergraduates were accepted by the colleges themselves. These foundations became corporate bodies with their own rights and privileges in the Middle Ages. Restrictions to entry into the many interesting parts of this fascinating city are minimal, but the best way to see it is in the company of a university member. College life is active and colourful, but persons whose attraction to Oxford lies mainly in the architecture should visit during the long summer vacation. University activities are few at this time, and access to colleges is consequently even easier.

High Street enters the city from the E and terminates at Carfax – the junction of four main streets and the centre of the old community. Known locally as the High, this street is crowded with notable features. Magdalen, pronounced Maudlen, lies at the E end of the High between the Cherwell and Longwall. It is one of the university's richest colleges, and was founded by William of Waynflete in 1448. The splendid tower dates from 1492 to 1507 and is famous for the May morning hymn, sung annually from the summit at Sunrise on May 1. Of particular interest are the Founder's Tower, the open-air pulpit, and a Jacobean screen preserved in the hall. Opposite Magdalen are the oldest botanic gardens in England, dating from 1621 and displaying a gateway of c1630 by Nicholas Stone. A little farther towards Carfax and on the N side of the road is St Edmund Hall. This unique survival of the early residential societies for undergraduates was founded in 1220 and controlled by Queen's College from 1557 to 1937. It is now elevated to full college status. The dedication is to St Edmund of Abingdon, an archbishop of Canterbury who taught at Oxford c1195 to 1200, and its main features include a dining hall of 1659. The chapel displays early glass by Burne-Jones and William Morris, and an ancient well exists in the quadrangle.

St Edmund's W side is flanked by picturesque Queen's Lane and faces across the Lane to Queen's College. Although founded in 1340, much of the latter was rebuilt in the 18thc. Parts of the complex have been ascribed to Wren, and the notable library dates from c1690. Almost opposite Queen's on the S side of the High is University College, said by some authorities to be the oldest in Oxford. It claims Alfred the Great as its founder, but was first endowed in 1249 by William, archdeacon of Durham. It was controlled by the university until 1200 and moved to its present site c1332. Notable features include two quadrangles, a 17th-c façade, and a chapel containing 17th- to 18th-c glass plus various contemporary fittings. Adjacent to Queen's and at the junction of the High and Catte Street is All Souls' College, founded in 1437 and consisting entirely of fellows. Hawksmoor's twin towers are preserved in the Great Quadrangle.

New College lies behind All Souls' and can be considered one of Oxford's finest colleges. It was founded by William of Wykeham in 1379 and is noted for its chapel, hall, and cloisters. Parts of the old city walls exist in the gardens. Farther N are the beautiful 17th-c buildings of Wadham College, founded by the Wadhams from 1610 to 1613.

Forming the centre piece of the High, the university church of St Mary the Virgin carries a beautiful 13th- to 14th-c tower and spire. Its porch of 1637 is supported by twisted pillars, and Amy Robsart was buried in the choir in 1560. Adjacent Brasenose College is immediately distinguished by the 16th-c brazen nose carried by its gateway. The college dates from 1509 and features a 16th-c hall, plus a chapel and library dating from the 17thc. Oriel College, founded in 1324 and re-founded in 1326, stands opposite St Mary the Virgin on the S side of the High. Farther W on the corner of Turl Street and the N side of the High is the city church of All Saints, an imposing 18th-c edifice displaying a fine tower and great panelled ceiling.

The continuation of the High from the junction at Carfax is called Queen Street, the start of which is marked by St Martin's Tower – a 14th-c relic of the former St Martin's church. Queen Street continues W and forks into New Road and Castle Street. The former leads to Nuffield College, which was endowed by Lord Nuffield in 1937 and built on the site of the old Oxford Canal Wharf. Opposite are the County Hall, Assize Courts, and prison, all built on the site of a Norman and medieval castle claimed to have been the birthplace of King Richard I in 1157. Remains of the structure include St George's tower and crypt and the castle mound.

cont pg 274

Colleges

1. All Souls' College
2. Balliol College
3. Brasenose College
4. Christ Church College
5. Corpus Christi College
6. Exeter College
7. Hertford College
8. Jesus College
9. Keble College
10. Lady Margaret Hall (women)
11. Lincoln College
12. Magdalen College
13. Manchester College (theological)
14. Mansfield College (theological)
15. Merton College
16. New College
17. Nuffield College
18. Oriel College
19. Pembroke College
20. Queen's College
21. Regent's Park College (theological)
22. Rhodes House
23. Somerville College (women)
24. St Anne's College (women)
25. St Anthony's College
26. St Catherine's College
27. St Edmund Hall
28. St Hilda's College (women)
29. St Hugh's College (women)
30. St John's College
31. St Peter's College
32. Trinity College
33. University College
34. Wadham College
35. Westminster College (theological)
36. Worcester College
37. Wolfson College

Other Places of Interest

38. All Saints' Church
39. Ashmolean Museum
40. Bishop King's Palace
41. Blackfriars Priory
42. Bodleian Library
43. Botanic Gardens
44. Campion Hall
45. Carfax
46. Castle Remains (county hall, assize court, prison)
47. Cathedral (chapel of Christ Church College)
48. Clarendon Building
49. Divinity School
50. Folly Bridge
51. Golden Cross Hotel
52. Martyrs' Memorial
53. New Theatre
54. Oxford Playhouse
55. Queen Elizabeth House
56. Radcliffe Camera
57. Sheldonian Theatre
58. St Benet's Hall
59. St Martin's Tower
60. St Mary Magdalen Church
61. St Mary the Virgin
62. St Michael's Church

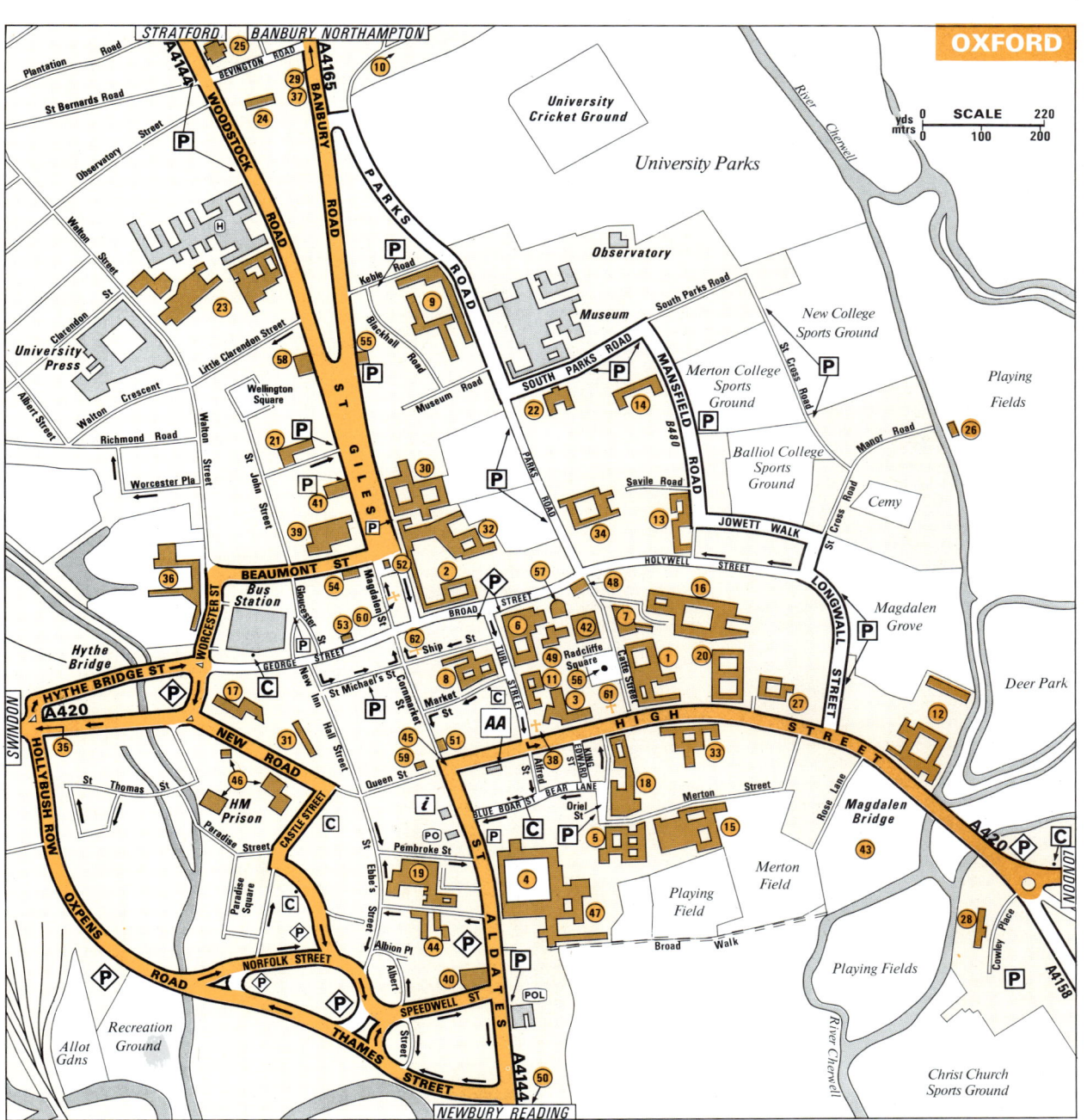

Cornmarket Street runs N from Carfax, passing the Golden Cross Hotel and St Michael's Church on the right before meeting George Street, Magdalen Street, and Broad Street at a crossroads. The Golden Cross was formerly an inn, and has included Bishops Ridley, Latimer, and Cranmer among its guests. St Michael's carries a Saxon tower.

George Street contains the New Theatre and runs W towards Worcester College and Gardens (Worcester Street). This college, founded in 1714, incorporates Gloucester Hall of 1283 and is particularly noted for its exquisite gardens. Original drawings and designs by Inigo Jones are preserved in the library.

Magdalen Street is a N extension of Cornmarket Street and passes St Mary Magdalen church before joining St Giles near the Martyrs Memorial, erected by Giles Scott in 1841. The Ashmolean Museum stands at the junction of St Giles and Beaumont Street, facing the Oxford Playhouse across the latter. It is one of the oldest museums in Europe and houses priceless treasures which include the unique King Alfred's Jewel. Adjacent is the Dominican Blackfriars Priory, and on the opposite side of St Giles are Trinity College and St John's College. Trinity, founded between 1554 and 1555, incorporates parts of the old Durham College of 1380 – notably the library. Sir Thomas Pope was the founder and his alabaster tomb exists in the college chapel. Wren designed the Garden Quadrangle, and delightful gardens include the Lime Walk of 1713. St John's was founded in 1555 and includes a hall c1502. Farther N on the W side of St Giles is the Benedictine St Benet's Hall, standing opposite 17th-c Queen Elizabeth House.

Broad Street runs E from the crossroads, parallel to the more S High Street, and includes the Sheldonian Theatre, Bodleian Library, plus Balliol and Exeter colleges among its many features. Sheldonian Theatre was designed by Wren and presented to the university in 1669. The adjoining Clarendon Building dates from 1712 to 1713. Bodleian Library is the oldest in the world, and in extent is second only to the British Museum in the Commonwealth. A right turn into Catte Street at the end of Broad Street leads past the Radcliffe Camera. This was by James Gibbs between 1713 and 1749, and the view from its Dome is considered remarkable. Brasenose Lane runs W from Catte Street, past the S side of the Bodleian and the adjacent Divinity School. The latter, a splendid example of 15th-c workmanship, is particularly noted for its arched roof adorned with pendant bosses.

St Aldate's Road runs S from Carfax, passing Christ Church College before crossing 19th-c Folly Bridge. Known as The House, this college was founded by Wolsey in 1525, refounded by Henry VIII in 1532, and again in 1546. Some of its many notable features are the 18th-c Peckwater Quadrangle; Tom Tower, built over Wolsey's Gate by Wren in 1682; the Great Bell which weighs over 7 tons and rings 101 strokes at 2105hrs every night. The latter originally came from Osney Abbey. Tom Quad is the largest in Oxford, and the fine hall of 1529 is of great interest. The college chapel lies on the W side of the complex and now serves as Oxford Cathedral. It is of mainly-Norman origin and carries a very early 13th-c tower. Particularly notable features include a groined perpendicular choir roof, the decorated-style Latin Chapel, and the magnificent early-English Chapter House. Pembroke College of 1624 lies opposite Christ Church on the E side of St Aldates. On the same side but a little farther S is Bishop King's Palace, a picturesque building carrying the Royal Arms of Edward VI. This was built by Robert King, the last Abbot of Osney Abbey and first Bishop of Oxford. Its present form dates from 1628, and it houses the Roman Catholic Chaplaincy to the university. Nearby Campion Hall is a building of 1936 by Lutyens.

Although the city includes many other colleges and buildings of outstanding interest, space does not permit a full description of each. Persons interested in acquiring more information should consult local guide publications. Most of the features described here lie in or near the centre of Oxford; the part of the city most rich in architectural treasures is an area bordered by Broad Walk (S), Longwall (E), Worcester Street (W), and Keble Road (N).

Colleges not described here include: Balliol, 1260 and 1266; Merton, 1264; Exeter, 1314 and re-endowed 1566; Lincoln, 1427; Corpus Christi, 1516; Jesus, 1571; Hertford, refounded 1874; Keble, 1870; St Peter's, 1929 as a hall; Rhodes House, in memory of Cecil Rhodes in 1929; St Anthony's, endowed 1948 by M Antonin Besse of France; St Catherine's, opened early 1963; Wolfson, the newest college in Oxford. Women's colleges include Lady Margaret Hall, St Anne's, St Hilda's, St Hugh's and Somerville. The colleges of Manchester, Mansfield, Regent's Park, and Westminster are all theological. Numerous museums and galleries exist in the city, plus many fine churches, houses, and inns.

Eights week is a famous river spectacle held annually at the end of May.

OXTED, Surrey 8 TQ35
Situated below the wooded North-Downs ridge, Oxted's restored church includes a 15th-c doorway, good woodwork, many old brasses, and glass of both ancient and modern origin. Timbered houses in the village include the Old Bell Inn, and a strikingly modern church is of brick construction.

OZLEWORTH, Glos 12 ST79
This secluded S Cotswold village stands on a high spur jutting into the level Vale of Severn. A remarkable Norman hexagonal tower is carried by the church, and the manor house is of late 18th-c date.

PACKINGTON, Warwickshire 18 SK31
The hall stands in a 700-acre park and dates from 1693 and 1772. The Old Hall which lies to the NE and was built in 1679 was visited by both Charles I and Charles II. The church, situated between the halls, was built by Joseph Bonomi in 1789. Handel composed part of the *Messiah* on its organ.

PADBURY, Bucks 13 SP73
Attractive half-timbered 17th-c and Victorian estate cottages can be seen here. Unusual 14th-c circular windows exist in the clerestory of the church.

PADDLESWORTH, Kent 9 TR13
Wide panoramic views are afforded by this small village, which lies at nearly 700ft in the North Downs. The tiny Saxon church is of flint-and-stone construction, and displays Norman additions.

PADIHAM, Lancs 21 SD73
Cotton-manufacturing and coalmining are conducted in this River-Calder town. Restored 17th-c Gawthorpe Hall lies 1m E, and is built around an old pele tower. The 19th-c additions were by Sir Charles Barry (NT, OACT). Huntroyde lies 1m NW and is partly Elizabethan, but most of the building dates from the 19thc.

PADSTOW, Cornwall 4 SW97
Padstow stands on the Camel estuary and includes an ancient harbour. Natural amenities include excellent sands and sea bathing, and a curious Hobby-Horse dance is held annually on May Day. An interesting Bird Garden is situated in Fentonluna Lane. The mainly-decorated church contains Prideaux monuments, and Prideaux Place is an Elizabethan mansion in one of the oldest deer parks to be found in Britain. Quaint old streets slope down to the harbour. Pepper Hole, Butter Hole, and the narrow rock cleft of Tregudda Gorge can be seen on the coast to the N.

PADWORTH, Berks 7 SU66
The pure Norman church dates from c1150, and late 18th-c Padworth House contains plasterwork by Joseph Rose.

PAGHAM, W Sussex 8 SZ89
Pagham Harbour is a local nature reserve situated on the flat Manhood Peninsula. The Norman to early-English church has been restored, and the east window contains 16th-c French glass. Barton Farm, 1m N at Nyetimber, dates partly from the 12thc.

PAIGNTON, Devon 5 SX86
This popular Tor-Bay resort offers a harbour, good sands, golf, and bathing among its many amenities. St John the Baptist Church is notable for its richly-carved 15th-c Kirkham chantry. A tower from a former episcopal palace still stands near the church. Oldway, a 19th-c house which displays rooms modelled on the Palace of Versailles, now contains a museum. The 15th-c Kirkham House was once a Priest's, or Chantry House (AM, OACT). A local zoo is also of interest. Dart Valley steam-operated railway now operates a service to Kingswear, for Dartmouth. Railway exhibits are to be displayed in a museum which has yet to be opened.

PAINSWICK, Glos 12 SO80
A beautiful little Cotswold town, Painswick lies in a hillside setting and includes many characteristic stone-built houses. Iron spectacle stocks have been preserved. About 100 yews are said to grow in the churchyard, and an annual clipping ceremony is held. Also here are several inscribed clothiers' tombs, testifying to a former clothing industry that once flourished. The 15th-c church contains the fine 17th-c Seaman tomb. King Charles I stayed at the old panelled Court House c1600 (OACT).

Painswick House dates from the 18th and early 19thc, and Falcon Inn preserves a rare bowling-green. A few old cloth mills are still to be seen S of the town.

Painswick Hill lies 2m N and forms a fine viewpoint. It is surmounted by an ancient earthwork called Kimsbury Camp (AM). Bull Cross, another splendid viewpoint lying 2m SE on the Stroud to Birdlip road, affords views across the valley to Painswick.

PAKEFIELD, Suffolk   15 TM59
Coastal erosion is a local problem, and the village is constantly threatened. The nave and aisle of the interesting church were probably meant for separate congregations. The roof has been re-thatched after bomb damage.

PAKENHAM, Suffolk   15 TL96
The tower of the Norman and decorated cruciform church carries an octagonal lantern. Newe House is a fine manor house of c1602, and a notable brick-built tower mill exists here (OACT).

PALGRAVE, Suffolk   15 TM17
A fine carved porch, painted hammerbeam roof, and a good Norman font are features of the 14th-c church. An inscribed waggoner's tombstone of 1787 can be seen in the churchyard.

PAMBER END, Hants   7 SU65
Parts of a former priory, comprising the restored Norman tower and early-English choir, are now in use as the parish church. Fragmentary remains of Norman wall paintings have been uncovered inside, and several ancient tombstones are of interest.

PANGBOURNE, Berks   7 SU67
This small town is sited on a pleasant reach of the River Thames at a point where it is joined by the River Pang. Kenneth Grahame, the well-known writer of children's books, lived at Pangbourne. He died in 1932. A nautical college is situated in the town.

PAR, Cornwall   4 SX05
Excellent sands and bathing are available here, and Par is a centre of the china clay industry. It lies on St Austell Bay.

PARADISE, Glos   12 SO81
It is said that this Cotswold hamlet was named Paradise by Charles I, who stayed here during his attack on Gloucester and described it as the most delightful spot he had ever seen. A local inn is appropriately named the Adam and Eve. Cranham Woods lie to N, near the restored 16th-c Prinknash (pronounced Prinnash) Abbey. The latter is now the home of Benedictine monks from Caldy Island, and is famous for its grey metallic-looking pottery. Henry VIII and Anne Boleyn came here in 1535. A new abbey was completed by the monks in the spring of 1972.

PARHAM, Suffolk   15 TM36
Parham Hall is a picturesque 16th-c moated house which now serves as a farm. Sir Thomas Palmer, who sailed with Drake to Cadiz, initiated the building of the mansion. The decorated and perpendicular church houses a 14th-c screen and contains the parish stocks.

PARKGATE, Cheshire   17 SJ27
Now a shrimping village on the Dee estuary, Parkgate was once the important port of Chester. Handel is said to have composed parts of the *Messiah* in the former George Hotel, now a private house. Impressive views across the estuary to the Welsh hills can be enjoyed from here.

Rich table tombs from Painswick churchyard

PARRACOMBE, Devon   5 SS64
Situated in an area of steep hillsides, this village is now by-passed by a modern road. The old church of St Petrock shows a curious screen, a tympanum repainted in 1758 with the Royal Arms, and 18th-c box pews beneath a row of hat pegs. A restored water-mill in the Exmoor national park may be the only example of its type in the area.

PASSENHAM, Northants   13 SP73
Two splendid tithe barns from the 17th-c manor house stand with an old mill near the River Ouse. The 13th-c to 17th-c church houses a 17th-c pulpit, plus a west gallery and stalls of the same period.

PASTON, Norfolk   15 TG33
Letters from the Paston family have provided graphic pictures of 15th-c English life. The thatched decorated-style church contains monuments and wall-paintings, and a fine Paston barn is still standing.

PATCHAM, E Sussex   8 TQ30
One of the oldest doom paintings extant can be seen in the local church, and the interesting Shelley monument is made of chalk. Patcham Place dates from the 18thc and displays a façade of black tiles. Southdown House is of Georgian origin. The restored windmill is considered a good example of its type. Hills of the South Downs rise in the background, and include the domed Indian Chattri memorial of the 1914-18 war.

PATELEY BRIDGE, N Yorks   22 SE16
Pateley Bridge is a Nidderdale village, and the best part of the dale lies to the NW beyond pretty Gouthwaite reservoir. A former 17th-o flax mill boasts one of the largest breast wheels in England and now functions as the Watermill Inn. Greenhow Hill lies 2m W, and a 1 in 6 climb to Bewerley Moor – the extensive views are worth the trouble. Farther W is the remarkable Stump Cross Cavern.

PATRICK, Isle of Man   20 SC28
A granite font of 1714 and a sundial supported by the Three Legs of Man, are features of the local church. Glen Maye lies S and contains a waterfall.

PATRINGTON, Humberside   23 TA32
The magnificent decorated-style cruciform church is known as the Queen of Holderness. Its tower, spire, Easter Sepulchre, and carvings are all outstanding.

PATRIXBOURNE, Kent   9 TR15
Patrixbourne church is one of the finest in Kent. Of Norman origin, it is especially noted for a south doorway which is complete with a carved tympanum. The village stands on the River Stour.

PATTERDALE, Cumbria   21 NY31
Situated in a beautiful Lakeland valley at the head of a fell-girdled Ullswater, Patterdale stands in an area which is extensively protected and administered by the NT. This includes Gowbarrow Park and the waterfall of Aira Force. Kirkstone Pass rises to 1,476ft in the S, and the approach skirts picturesque Brotherswater. Deepdale Valley leads SW to 2,756ft St Sunday Crag, and 2,863ft Fairfield. Grisedale leads W to 3,118ft Helvellyn, which is well known for the famous Striding Edge and neighbouring 3,033ft Lower Man. A cairn on Helvellyn commemorates the first landing of a light aircraft on an English peak.

PAUL, Cornwall   4 SW42
George Borrow visited the 15th-c church, and noted the helmet, cuirass, and swords preserved inside. Dorothy Pentreath, who died in 1777 and was one of the last to speak the ancient Cornish language, is buried here.

PAULL, Humberside   23 TA12
Paull lies on the Humber estuary and includes a shipyard from which small vessels are still launched. A former lighthouse of 1836 stands in a row of houses, and the 15th-c church carries a central tower. A font of the same period can be seen inside.

PAXTON, GREAT, Cambs   14 TL26
Notable pre-Conquest work is preserved in the local church, plus late Norman transepts and a chancel arch. Elizabethan Toseland Hall lies 2½m SE. Great Paxton is situated in the Ouse Valley, where the river describes a succession of wide curves.

PEACEHAVEN, E Sussex   8 TQ40
Greenwich meridian line runs through the area and is marked by the Meridian Monument. A concrete strip at the base of the monument marks the actual line.

cont

Chalk cliffs overshadow a shingle bathing beach, and the South Downs dominate the inland horizon.

PEAK DISTRICT AND DALES
The Peak District incorporates a national park covering some 540sqm. Wild gritstone uplands of the High Peak include 2,088ft Kinder Scout, the south bastion of the long Pennine chain. The Peak is another name for this flat-topped mountain, and the area is popular with walkers from the Manchester and Sheffield areas. Farther N, beyond Snake Pass, Bleaklow Hill rises to 2,060ft and is the second highest in the Peak District.

The great Ladybower and Derwent reservoirs lie beyond Ashop Dale and the end of the Snake Pass. These features are backed by the lofty ridge of Stanage Edge, rising above Hathersage. Lose Hill and Mam Tor (NT) separate the beautiful Vale of Edale from Castleton, with its famous caves, and the Hope Valley. The limestone country of the Dales is patchworked with stone-walled fields and occupies a triangular area between Buxton, Ashbourne, and Matlock. All the latter towns are good touring centres for the district.

Picturesque Dovedale divides Derbyshire from Staffordshire, and is threaded by the River Dove which flows S from Beresford, near Hartington. It is considered the loveliest, and is certainly the best-known, of the Dales. Some of its finest scenery is NT protected. Among various other dales are Miller's Dale (NT); nearby Chee Dale (NT) to the S of Tideswell; beautiful Monsal Dale, which contains the River Wye and is situated NW of Bakewell; lesser-known Lathkill Dale, to the N of Youlgreave. Two of the finest houses in Derbyshire, Chatsworth and Haddon Hall, lie in the Bakewell district, and the church at Tideswell has been called the Cathedral of the Peak.

The 250m-long Pennine Way commences at Edale and runs N to the Cheviots and the Scottish border.

PEAK FOREST, Derbyshire 18 SK17
The site now occupied by a modern church once bore a chapel of 1657 which became famous for runaway marriages. Eldon Hole, a huge 200ft-deep rift connected with a fine stalactite cave, can be seen between Peak Forest and Castleton.

PEAKIRK, Cambs 19 TF10
Waterfowl Gardens (OACT) situated here are connected with the well-known Wild Fowl Trust near Slimbridge in Gloucestershire. St Pega's Church, a unique dedication, contains 14th-c wall-paintings.

PEASLAKE, Surrey 8 TQ04
A delightful village below the N slopes of the Surrey Hills, with picturesque Hurt Wood to the SE.

PEDDAR'S WAY
This ancient track crosses Norfolk from a point 2½m NE of Hunstanton, to about 4m E of Thetford. It is thought to be Roman or pre-Roman. Parts of it still exist as a green or unsurfaced road, and it can be easily distinguished N of Castle Acre.

PEEL, Isle of Man 20 SC28
This pleasant resort is sited on a sheltered harbour. St Peter's Church is a pre-Reformation building which was rebuilt in 1816. Ruins of the 13th-c and later cathedral exist on St Patrick's Isle, and are to be restored. Portions of an episcopal palace and round tower also exist. The castle ruins are associated with Scott's *Peveril of the Peak* and *Lay of the Last Minstrel*.

PEMBRIDGE, Herefs & Worcs 11 SO35
This picturesque village includes several half-timbered houses – notably Clear Brook – and an ancient market hall. The New Inn shows fine black-and-white work. The spacious 14th-c church has a quaint detached timber-built belfry, probably dating from the 14thc.

PENDEEN, Cornwall 4 SW33
The 15th-c farmhouse of Pendeen Pan has a façade of 1670. Dr Borlase the Cornish antiquary was born here in 1696. The modern church is a copy of Scotland's Iona Cathedral. One of the Cornish *fogous* (hiding holes) can be seen in the area, and a lighthouse stands on a nearby headland. The latter forms part of a rugged stretch of coastline, and numerous derelict mine shafts exist near by. Splendid views are available from the road which terminates here.

PENHURST, E Sussex 9 TQ61
Ashburnham Chapel has been rebuilt, but is still a notable part of the 14th- to 15th-c church. Also of interest are a 15th-c screen and pulpit, plus contemporary glass showing the Pelham arms. An old gabled manor farm exists in the area. Surrounding countryside is unspoiled and well-wooded.

PENISTONE, S Yorks 22 SE20
A grim little town with large steel works, Penistone lies N of extensive moorland and several reservoirs. Interesting features of the area include Cat Hill Farm of 1634, Bullhouse Hall of 1655, an old barn of *c*1630 at Gunthwaite Hall, and a Dissenters' Chapel of 1692 near Bullhouse Hall.

PENKRIDGE, Staffs 18 SJ91
Early-English to perpendicular features are shown by the local church, plus a tower dating from *c*1400 and several monuments.

PENN, Bucks 8 SU99
Good views of the Chiltern beechwoods are available to the E of this village, and the flint church houses monuments and brasses to the Penn family.

PENNINES, THE
These lofty hills and moors form the spine of England, and extend N from Kinder Scout in Derbyshire to the Cheviot foothills at the Scottish border. Their highest peak is 2,930ft Cross Fell, situated between Appleby and Alston in Cumbria. A 250m footpath known as the Pennine Way now traverses the range from end to end. The new M62 motorway crosses the bleak Pennine moors to link Manchester with the West Yorkshire woollen towns. Notable Scammonden Bridge is on this route.

PENRITH, Cumbria 26 NY53
Penrith Beacon rises above this old market town and affords wide views of the Pennine and Lake District mountains. A ruined 14th-c castle (AM) can be seen, and two strange monuments known as the Giant's Grave and the Giant's Thumb exist in the churchyard. An old plague stone is preserved in Bridge Lane, and the Gloucester Arms is an interesting old inn. King Arthur's Round Table and Mayborough are prehistoric structures lying 1½m S (both AM). Yanwath Hall shows a fine medieval pele tower incorporated in a farmhouse and lies 2½m S beyond Eamont Bridge, off the Ullswater road.

PENRYN, Cornwall 4 SW73
This Penryn-River port is mainly granite-built and stands close to Falmouth on a large sheltered inlet called the Carrick Roads. Penryn's sheltered position gives it a mild climate, and many sub-tropical plants flourish. Late-Georgian houses are a feature of the town.

PENSFORD, Avon 6 ST66
Pensford lies in the Chew Valley and includes a curious little domed lock-up known as the Round House. The impressive railway viaduct dates from 1873. The slender perpendicular tower carried by Publow Church can be seen from here.

PENSHURST, Kent 8 TQ54
Rivers Medway and Eden flow through this picturesque village, and the interesting Sidney Chapel can be seen in the restored decorated and perpendicular church. Attractive Leicester Square includes Tudor cottages and an interesting arch. Penshurst Place is a famous 14th-c and later mansion, with a notable great hall of 1341. It was the birthplace of Sir Philip Sidney in 1554 (OACT), and includes extensive grounds and a toy museum.

PENTLOW, Essex 15 TL84
The restored apsidal Norman church displays a 14th-c round tower. A timber-framed 16th-c hall is of interest, and the polygonal Bull's Tower of the rectory dates from 1858.

PENZANCE, Cornwall 4 SW43
This holiday resort and port is situated at the head of Mount's Bay. Georgian and Regency houses are to be seen in Chapel Street, and the town hall contains a geological museum. The Market House dates from 1836, and a market cross and natural-history museum can be seen in Penlee Park. Sub-tropical plants are grown in the Morrab Gardens. Both steamer and helicopter services ply between here and the Isles of Scilly. Richard Trevithick, the famous builder of early locomotives, was engineer at the nearby Ding Dong Mine in 1797. Sir Humphry Davy invented the miner's safety lamp and was educated at the local grammar school.

PERIVALE, Gt London 8 TQ18
The weatherboarded tower carried by the church is probably unique to the Greater London area, and dates from the 16thc.

PERRANPORTH, Cornwall 4 SW75
Excellent sands, sea bathing, and fine rock scenery are offered by this popular resort. Holywell Bay lies N beyond Perran Beach, and Penhale Point offers particularly notable rockscapes. Extensive sand dunes exist near Perranporth. Some 1¾m N is the reputedly 6th-c St Piran's Church. This was dug out of the sands in 1835, and is now preserved in a shell. Access is by foot (AM). St Piran's Round is an ancient amphitheatre lying 1½m NE (AM).

PERSHORE, Herefs & Worcs *12 SO94*
Pershore stands on the River Avon, W of the Vale of Evesham. Both old (17thc) and new bridges span the river, and the district is noted for its Pershore plums. Springtime blossom in the local orchards is a beautiful and spectacular sight. The fine Norman to 14thc abbey church contains a 13th-c presbytery with remarkable vaulting and carries an interesting tower. St Andrew's Church houses 12th- to 15th-c work, and has a leaning north-nave arcade. Many 18th-c houses feature in the town. A notable modern building situated SE of the town houses the Institute of Horticulture. The 1,000th anniversary of the town's original charter, given to the abbey by King Elgar, was celebrated in 1972.

PERTENHALL, Beds *14 TL06*
A fine perpendicular tower is carried by the local church, surmounted by a broach spire. Old pews, an old screen, and a knight's effigy are housed within. The manor house was built by Bishop Fox, the founder of Oxford's Corpus Christi College, in 1588.

PETERBOROUGH, Cambs *19 TL19*
Plan overleaf
Originally this ancient River Nene town grew up around a medieval monastery. Railway involvements and the Fletton brickfields stimulated it to even greater growth in the 19thc, and it quickly became a thriving industrial town.

Old features of the town include the cathedral, a magnificent example of Norman and early-English styles, displaying some work of later periods. Of particular note are the west front, the painted nave ceiling, the nave arcades, and fan tracery in the 15th-c retrochoir. Both Catherine of Aragon and Mary Queen of Scots were buried in the cathedral, although the remains of the latter now lie in Westminster Abbey. A curious picture of Old Scarlett, the verger who buried the two queens, is also of interest. Numerous monastic relics incorporated in the archdeacon's house include a guest hall.

Other interesting items displayed by the town include the Knight's gateway, the Bishop's Palace, and the west gateway of Norman and 14th-c origin. St John's Church dates from the 15thc, and houses old screens plus a painting of Charles I. The old town hall, or guildhall, is a fine building dated 1671. The museum in Priestgate contains Roman remains and relics of John Clare, a poet who lived in the area.

PETERCHURCH, Herefs & Worcs *11 SO33*
A wooden panel representing a fish with a golden chain round its neck hangs over the south door of the exceptionally interesting Norman church. The village itself lies in the delightful Golden Valley.

PETERLEE, Co Durham *27 NZ44*
One of England's post-war New Towns, Peterlee was founded in 1948. A notable parish church of 1957 is of interest.

PETERSFIELD, Hants *8 SU72*
The restored church is of mainly-Norman origin. Its nave and chancel are separated by a Norman wall, which was once the west arch of the long-vanished central tower. Notable old houses can be seen in Sheep Street, Dragon Street, and College Street. Old Churcher's College is now an office block, but dates from 1723.

Butser Hill (S) is part of a South Downs area scheduled as one of outstanding natural beauty. It rises to almost 900ft, and is the highest point in the range. A small country park and viewpoint are now located at the summit. Richly-wooded Stoner Hill is a local beauty spot on the Alresford road.

PETERSHAM, Gt London *8 TQ17*
Situated by the River Thames on the outskirts of Richmond Park, Petersham boasts what is perhaps the finest grouping of individual 17th- and 18th-c houses in London. A quaint Georgian church stands in a churchyard which contains the grave of Captain George Vancouver, who gave his name to Vancouver Island. He embarked on his great four-year voyage in 1791. Douglas House, Rutland Lodge, Montrose House, and Sudbrook House are particularly fine, and the latter was the work of James Gibbs between 1726 and 1728. Jacobean Ham House is considered the most beautiful in the district. It is an annexe of the Victoria and Albert Museum, and houses a collection of furniture (NT, OACT).

Strong associations with the Duke of Lauderdale and Charles II's Cabal Ministry of 1682 exist. Ham Common lies S and includes several attractive 18th-c houses.

PETERSTOW, Herefs & Worcs *12 SO52*
Situated to the W of the River Wye, Peterstow includes a Norman to 15th-c church displaying a panelled Jacobean pulpit. Gillow Manor, 2½m NW, retains a 14th-c tower.

PETHAM, Kent *9 TR15*
The church is situated below Chartham Down, and dates mainly from the 13thc. Kenfield is dated c1700, and 18th-c Swarling Farm lies a little N. Features of the latter are a granary of 1779 and several typical oasthouses. Views of the North Downs can be enjoyed from the village.

PETTS WOOD, Gt London *8 TQ46*
Some 90-acres of woodland were acquired by the NT as a memorial to William Willett, of Summer-Time fame. The gentleman is commemorated by a stone sundial and was buried in nearby Chislehurst churchyard.

PETWORTH, W Sussex *8 SU92*
This old-world town has many 16th- and 17th-c houses, including Thompson's almshouses of 1618. Rebuilt St Mary's Church contains Percy monuments. The town hall is of early 19th-c date, and Somerset Lodge dates from 1653. Adjacent Somerset Almshouses, or Upper Hospital, were founded in 1746. Petworth House was presented to the NT by Lord Leconfield in 1947 (OACT), and is a magnificent 17th- and 19th-c mansion. Notable pictures, carvings by Grinling Gibbons, and a 13th- and 17th-c chapel are of great interest. Boundary walls of the great park in which the house stands extend into the town itself.

PEVENSEY, E Sussex *9 TQ60*
William the Conqueror landed here in 1066, and the Roman *Anderida* existed on this site. The Norman to 13th-c castle stands within Roman walls, and is surrounded by a moat (AM, OACT). An exceptionally long chancel is a feature of

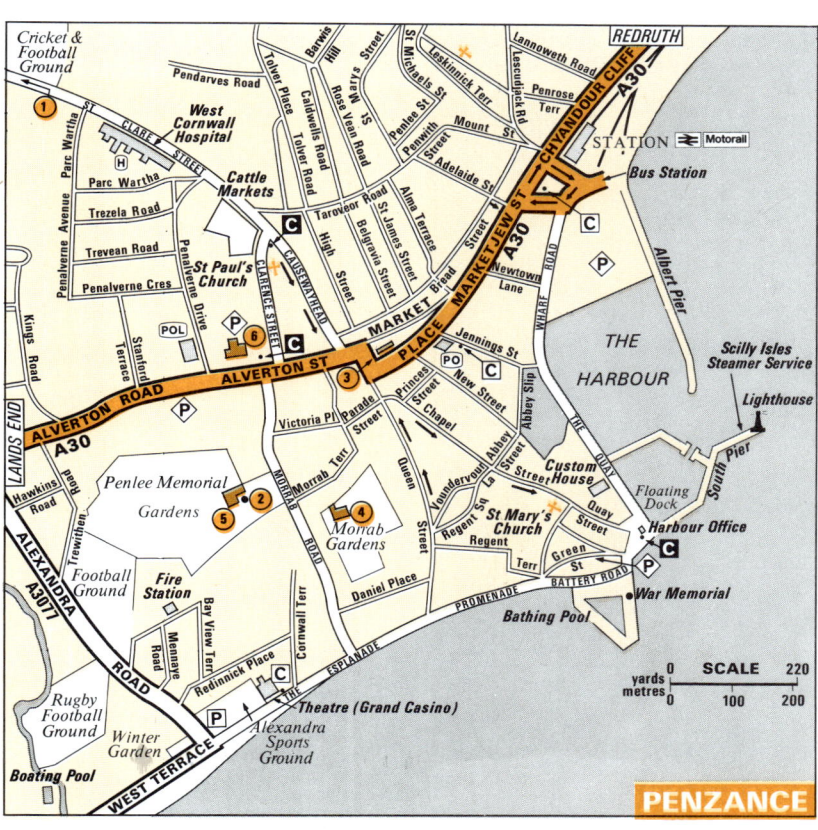

1 Ding Dong Mine
2 Market Cross
3 Market House
4 Marrab Gardens
5 Natural History Museum
6 Town Hall (geological museum)

the early-English church; other buildings of interest include the tiny Court House, and the possibly 14th-c Mint House. Pevensey Bay has a shingle beach with sand at low tide. A Martello tower stands here, and the fine 17th-c Court Lodge lies 4m NE near Hooe, off the Hastings Road.

PEWSEY, Wilts *7 SU16*
Some 188 acres of Pewsey Downs national nature reserve surround 964ft Milk Hill, and the village itself lies on the River Avon in Pewsey Vale. The church carries a perpendicular tower and houses good modern woodwork. A small glazed recess in the nave pier contains feathers which are connected with an old superstition regarding angels. A statue of King Alfred is sited near the river, and the village has made a feature of the Town Criers' championship.

PICKERING, N Yorks *23 SE78*
Both the moated Norman castle and largely-Norman church are of interest. The former (AM) includes a mound surmounted by a shell keep, and the church is famous for its 15th-c frescoes. The Beck Isle museum and art gallery displays folk items relating to the North Yorks moors. Kelhead Springs lie about ½m NW, and the newly afforested Allerston State Forest, including Staindale Forest, is NE.

PIDDINGHOE, E Sussex *8 TQ40*
This River-Ouse village is situated below the South Downs, and includes a church with a Norman round tower and a dolphin weather vane on the spire. An old barrel-organ has been preserved inside.

PIDDLETRENTHIDE, Dorset *6 SY79*
A village attractively situated below the Dorset Downs, Piddletrenthide gets its name from the River Piddle – or Trent. The 15th-c church has a tower which is considered one of the best in the county.

PILGRIMS' WAY
Pilgrims journeying to the Canterbury shrine of Thomas Becket used this route. Those who came from abroad landed at Southampton and proceeded via Winchester, Alton, Farnham, Puttenham, Guildford, Shere, Dorking, Reigate, Titsey Hill, Otford, Wrotham, Snodland, Kit's Coty House, Charing, and Harbledown. At Harbledown they were joined by those coming from London and the N by way of Watling Street. In places the route coincides with good roads, in others with by-roads, and in some places it is a mere track. It follows the southern slope of the North Downs for the most part, keeping to higher ground to avoid marshes which then existed below the Downs. The long North Downs Footpath incorporates part of the Pilgrims' Way. Experts differ as to the exact line followed by the route in some places – particularly near Guildford. The area around Guildford includes the restored St Martha's Chapel, and ruins of St Catherine's Chapel.

PILTDOWN, E Sussex *8 TQ42*
What was perhaps the most famous hoax in English archaeological history was perpetrated here. A famous archaeologist and palaeontologist claimed to have discovered the skull of a creature which provided a link between ape and man. This was in 1912, and it was not until 1953 that investigations proved the so-called discovery to be a fake. The jaw and canine tooth of a modern ape had been added to fragments of a genuine 50,000-year-old skull.

PILTON, Devon *5 SS53*
Barnstaple faces Pilton over the River Yeo, and the two places are almost contiguous. The local church once belonged to a Benedictine priory, and is noted for its fine Elizabethan font cover, a late-perpendicular stone pulpit, the Raleigh Chapel and parclose screen, and the Chichester monuments.

PILTON, Somerset *6 ST54*
The perpendicular church displays an angel-carved roof, a beautiful 15th-c screen enclosing a small chapel, and medieval embroidery. Near by is a fine old cruciform-shaped tithe barn, which has been restored after damage by lightning (AM).

PINCHBECK, Lincs *19 TF22*
On the River Glen in a district of bulb-fields, Pinchbeck includes a fine restored church carrying a massive slightly-leaning perpendicular tower. An imposing nave is also of interest, and the old rectory and stables make a fine 18th-c group. Village stocks have been preserved.

PINHOE, Devon *5 SX99*
Pinhoe is a small town which is almost a suburb of Exeter. The perpendicular church has a notable screen. A curious figure of a man in Queen Anne dress is shown on the 18th-c almsbox, with the inscription 'The Poor Man of Pinhoe'. Beacon House stands near the church and is of Queen Anne origin.

PINMILL, Suffolk *15 TM23*
Yachts are moored at this picturesqely situated Orwell-estuary village, which stands on the outskirts of Chelmondiston village. Curious Cat House dates from 1793 and stands W in Woolverstone Park. It was once used in connection with smuggling. Farther to the NW on the banks of the Orwell is the tall brick-built Freston Tower. This dates from 1549 and may well be the earliest folly still in existence. Ewarton Hall is a restored Elizabethan structure with a pinnacled Jacobean gateway, standing 2½m SE.

PINNER, Gt London *8 TQ18*
Situated on the River Pinn, this residential area includes a church with a good perpendicular tower. The curious arched pyramidal Loudon tomb of 1843 stands in the churchyard, and the Queen's Head Inn dates from 1705.

PIRTON, Herefs & Worcs *12 SO84*
This scattered village has a picturesque church showing a half-timbered belltower, plus work from the 12th to 15thc. The rectory is a Queen Anne house, and Pirton Court is a gabled timber-framed house with traces of a former moat, lying about ½m SW.

PIRTON, Herts *14 TL13*
Among old houses lying N of wooded Barton Hills are the Rectory and Hammond farms, Old Hall of 1609, High Down of *c*1600, and Pirton Grange of 1600 to 1700 date. The last named lies more to the NW. Knocking Hoe lies a little to the SW across the Bedfordshire border, and is a small national nature reserve.

PITSFORD, Northants *13 SP76*
Pitsford reservoir was opened by HM the Queen Mother in 1956, and holds some 4,000,000,000 gallons of water. A road crosses its central portion, allowing excellent views to the left and right. A carved Norman doorway and 14th-c font are features of the local church.

1 Archdeacon's House (monastic remains)
2 Bishop's Palace
3 Cathedral
4 Knight's Gateway
5 Museum
6 Old Town Hall
7 St John's Church
8 West Gateway

PITY ME, Co Durham 27 NZ24
The name of this Great North Road hamlet is thought to be a corruption of *Petit Mer* a name originally given to a small lake by French monks.

PLAISTOW, W Sussex 8 TQ03
Half-timbered Plaistow Place dates from the 16thc, and characteristic brick and tile-hung cottages can be seen in the village.

PLAXTOL, Kent 9 TQ65
Old Soar Manor is of partly 13th-c date and includes a chapel (AM, NT, OACT). It is joined to a privately-owned 18th-c farm. The restored church of 1649 displays a reredos. Fairlawne is a fine house built by Sir Christopher Vane, who also planted the great yew grove in 1684. It is traditionally haunted by Sir Harry Vane, whom Charles II had beheaded in 1662.

PLAYFORD, Suffolk 15 TM24
Sir George Felbridge, builder of the *c*1400 church, is remembered by a good brass of the same approximate date. An obelisk commemorates Thomas Clarkson of slave-trade abolition fame, who died at the moated Elizabethan and later hall.

PLESHEY, Essex 9 TL61
Pleshey is a name derived from the Norman-French *pleissis*, meaning a portion of forest surrounded by a pleached fence. The village lies within a circular mile-long entrenchment which is considered one of the finest in England. Included is an oval 12th-c keep mound, measuring 900ft in circumference and 50ft high (AM). A brick-built 15th-c bridge spans the moat.

PLUMPTON, E Sussex 8 TQ31
Steeple-chasing is a well-known local feature, and an agricultural college stands near moated Plumpton Place. A V-shaped plantation of trees on the nearby down commemorates Queen Victoria's Jubilee in 1887.

PLYMOUTH, Devon 5 SX45
Seaport, important naval station, and dockyard, this town comprises Plymouth, Devonport, and Stonehouse. Fishing and bathing can be enjoyed from the pebble and sand beach. Sir Francis Drake played his historic game of bowls on the famous Hoe. This overlooks Drake's Island in Plymouth sound, which is now a Youth Adventure training centre (NT). Sir Francis Chichester ended his epic round-the-world voyage here in 1967.

Smeaton's Tower was the old Eddystone Lighthouse, and Drake is commemorated by a statue. The Pilgrim Fathers sailed from Sutton Pool in the Mayflower, in 1620. The Royal Citadel dates from the 17thc (AM), and an aquarium is situated near by. St Andrew's Church was damaged by bombs, but has retained its fine 15th-c tower and the 17th-c Prysten House. The Old and New Custom Houses – the latter of 1810 – can be seen near by in Sutton Harbour. Buildings designed by Foulston during the early 19thc are of interest, and a well-restored Elizabethan house exists in New Street.

Most of the city centre has been rebuilt since the war and the central portion – where Royal Parade is bisected by the broad Armada Way – includes one of the finest shopping centres in England. A small zoo is situated in the Central Park, and the new civic centre carries a 200ft tower which affords wide views over the town. Across the Sound is 16th- to 18th-c Mount Edgcumbe, a rebuilt house set in fine grounds (OACT). Captain Scott, the famous Antarctic explorer, was born at Devonport in 1868. He died during his last expedition in 1912. The Tamar Bridge was opened in 1961, and connects St Budeaux with Saltash; a car ferry links Devonport with Torpoint.

PLYMPTON, Devon 5 SX55
Almost part of Plymouth, Plympton comprises Plympton St Mary and Plympton St Maurice. The former includes a fine decorated and perpendicular church displaying a lofty tower and two-storeyed south porch. Borringdon is a fine 16th- to 17th-c house lying 1m N. Plympton St Maurice preserves a ruined Norman shell-keep on a mound, and the perpendicular church carries a tower that was rebuilt in 1466. A 16th-c guildhall is of interest, and Reynolds was born in the 17th-c grammar school in 1723. Plympton House dates from *c*1700. Saltram is an 18th-c mansion on the Plym estuary, containing beautifully decorated rooms by Robert Adam (OACT).

PLYMSTOCK, Devon 5 SX55
The local church carries an embattled tower and houses a Norman sandstone font with a 16th-c cover. Good screenwork and a fine 17th-c Harris monument are also of interest.

PLYMTREE, Devon 6 ST00
Henry VII, his son Arthur, and Cardinal Morton are portrayed on a splendid carved and painted screen in the perpendicular church. Hayne House and Fordmore are both of late 17th-c date.

POCKLINGTON, Humberside 23 SE84
Strangely carved nave capitals can be seen in the local church, which also carries a perpendicular west tower. The village is situated on the edge of the Wolds. Waterlilies are a feature of Burnby Hall Gardens (NT, OACT).

POLEBROOK, Northants 14 TL08
Polebrook's fine 13th-c church is noted for its tall spire, one-hand clock, a 15th-c screen, and four mass dials.

POLDEN HILLS
This low range of hills extends SE from a point near Bridgwater, to the neighbourhood of Glastonbury. Although they rise to less than 300ft they dominate the surrounding marshy levels, and provide widespread views over the surrounding district. The A39 traverses the crest for some miles and affords excellent views. Ivythorn and Walton Hills are among several areas of NT property.

POLESWORTH, Warwickshire 18 SK20
Part of an ancient Benedictine nunnery is still standing, and the parish church is a fragment of the original church. Features of the latter include a 14th-c door with good ironwork, and a stone effigy of an abbess – said to be unique – probably dating from the 13thc. A picturesque old school stands in the small town. Pooley Hall was rebuilt in 1509, and preserves an old chapel.

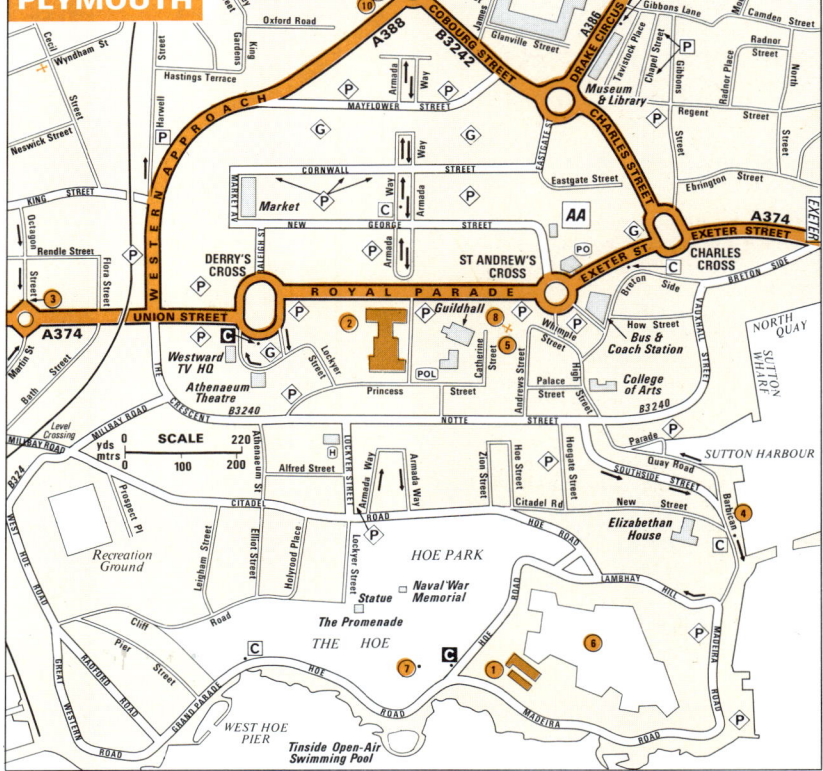

1. Aquarium
2. Civic Centre
3. Mount Edgcumbe
4. Old Customs Houses
5. Prysten House (St Andrew's Church)
6. Royal Citadel
7. Smeaton's Tower
8. St Andrew's Church
9. Tamar Bridge
10. Zoo

18th-c Customs House and the Town Beam at Poole

POLING, W Sussex 8 TQ00
Thatched flint-and-brick cottages stand in this secluded village, and the church incorporates a Saxon nave, 14th-c chancel, and a good 15th-c brass. Roman remains have been excavated in the area.

POLPERRO, Cornwall 5 SX25
Narrow streets and quaint old houses give this picturesque fishing village its famous character. The old home of Dr Jonathan Couch, the grandfather of Sir Arthur Quiller-Couch, houses a smugglers' museum. The curious House on Props is of interest. Rugged coast scenery can be enjoyed in this district, which is one of the most-visited areas of Cornwall. A fine natural pool lying W of the harbour is used for swimming.

POLSTEAD, Suffolk 15 TL93
Maria Marten was murdered in the Red Barn in 1827, and her grave is in the churchyard. Although famous for this notorious act, this Box-Valley village shows other features which are notable in their own right. The Gospel Oak is said to be 1,000 years old. Roman bricks were used in the construction of the Norman church, which carries a 14th-c stone spire unique in Suffolk. An interesting monument of 1630 is sited above the pulpit. The mainly-Georgian hall preserves 16th-c half-timbering.

POLZEATH, Cornwall 4 SW97
Polzeath is a small resort situated on Padstow Bay and the widening Camel estuary, offering excellent sands and sea-bathing. Pentire Head, a notable viewpoint to the W of Portquin Bay, lies N (NT).

PONTEFRACT, W Yorks 22 SE42
Once known as Pomfret, Pontefract includes historic Norman castle ruins of great interest. These include a round tower and dungeons, plus a small museum. King Richard II died here, and the castle was besieged on three separate occasions during the Civil War. This turbulent period also saw the partial destruction of All Saints' Church. The tower survived with its interesting octagonal lantern, and contains a remarkable recently-restored double-spiral staircase. The parish Church of St Giles was rebuilt in the 17th c but retains a 14th-c arcade. The butter cross dates from 1734, and an old pump in the market place was given by Queen Elizabeth I. The town hall is of late 18th-c origin. Pomfret Cakes are small locally-made liquorice lozenges. Liquorice for these is no longer grown here, and now comes from Turkey. Coalfields and a racecourse exist in the area.

PONTELAND, Northumberland 27 NZ17
The restored 12th- to 14th-c church displays 14th-c glass. An ancient pele tower stands in the village, and the Blackbird Inn is of 17th-c date.

PONTESBURY, Salop 17 SJ30
Mary Webb, authoress of *The Golden Arrow*, lived here for a while. The rebuilt church contains interesting memorial tablets, and 1,047ft Pontesbury Hill overlooks the valley of the Rea.

PONTON, GREAT, Lincs 19 SK93
Anthony Ellys was a Calais merchant who built the notable church tower in 1519. Most of the houses in this River-Witham village are stone-built, and the lovely early 16th-c manor house now serves as the rectory.

POOLE, Dorset 17 SZ09
Natural amenities of this port include a sand and shingle beach, sea bathing, and fishing. Numerous local buildings are of historical interest, and include an old postern gate and 15th-c almshouses.

Old Town House, or Scaplen's Court, is of 14th- to 15th-c date. The fine guildhall displays an unusual double external-staircase, and dates from 1761. The customs house includes the Town Beam and is of 18th-c origin. Other houses of the same date exist, but some situated in the centre of the town have become derelict. The finest are Poole College of 1749, and Beech Hurst of 1798. The Town Cellars, or Wool House, dates from 1433. St James's Church dates from 1819 to 1820, and the rectory from 1786. A tiny town gaol was built in 1820, and well-known Poole Pottery is situated on the quay.

Clay for pottery was formerly exported from here in large quantities. Disused tracks and rail-links led to a number of loading points, and were used to convey the material from Poole quay. A marina is being developed in the harbour.

Marconi conducted wireless experiments in the district from 1898. Poole Harbour is popular with yachtsmen, and contains Brownsea Island (NT). The latter boasts a rebuilt castle and a nature reserve; it was site of the first Scout Camp under Baden-Powell in 1907, and is accessible by boat from Poole Quay or Sandbanks during the summer.

POOLEY BRIDGE, Cumbria 26 NY42
Situated in the Lake District national park, Pooley Bridge is a River-Eamont village at the N end of Ullswater. A minor road follows the S shores of the lake to Howtown, on the edge of Martindale Common, and a pier serves the local steamer.

PORLOCK, Somerset 5 SS84
Old houses and the picturesque Ship Inn are features of this attractive village resort. The mainly-perpendicular church has a truncated shingle spire and houses several fine effigies. The Harington monument is particularly notable, and a medieval clock has been preserved. Notorious Porlock Hill rises with a maximum incline of 1 in 4 at the W end of the village, and carries a steep road with numerous hairpin bends. This can be avoided by an easier toll road. Blackford Farm includes a rare Norman dovecote and lies 3m E off the A39.

PORLOCK WEIR, Somerset 5 SS84
Natural amenities of this small village include a pebble and shingle beach, and notable wooded-cliff scenery. The harbour is picturesque.

PORT CARLISLE, Cumbria 26 NY26
Glasson Moss national nature reserve covers 140 acres of this Solway-Firth area. The harbour dates from 1819 and a canal link to Carlisle was cut four years later.

PORTCHESTER, Hants 7 SU60
Known to the Romans as *Portus Castra*, Portchester is situated on Portsmouth Harbour and includes a notable Norman castle built by Henry II. The latter stands within the Roman walls of an ancient fort (OACT). The Norman church once belonged to a former priory of Austin canons, and stands in the outer ward. It is a remarkably unspoiled example of period work, and displays a particularly notable west front. Royal Arms of Queen Elizabeth I (1577) and Queen Anne can be seen inside. A Nelson monument overlooks Portchester from the heights of Portsdown, and the hills carry a line of partly-disused forts.

PORT ERIN, Isle of Man 20 SC16
A sheltered bay offers excellent sands and bathing, and Bradda Head lies to the NW. The Meayl Circle, with six pairs of burial chambers, lies SW.

PORTHCURNO, Cornwall 4 SW32
Some of the finest granite rock scenery of the West Penwith district can be visited from here. Deep-sea communication cable leaves the water at Porthcurno Cove, and the open-air Minack Cliff theatre is unique.

PORTHLEVEN, Cornwall 4 SW62
Shipbuilding yards and a harbour exist at this small resort, and a sandy beach allows sea bathing. Loe Bar separates freshwater Loe Pool from the sea and lies SE.

PORT ISAAC, Cornwall 4 SW98
This fishing village has a small harbour and a rather uncomfortable beach of rocks and pebbles. Beautiful coastline, much of it protected by the NT, leads W past Portquin Bay to the 6m-distant Pentire Head. Port Gaverne is situated at the head of a small bay to the E.

PORTISHAM, Dorset 6 SY68
The mainly-perpendicular church houses a 15th-c screen. A 70ft monument to Admiral Hardy is sited 2m NE on one of Dorset's finest viewpoints, the lofty Black Downs. The latter is accessible by road. The Grey Mare and her Colts are fine large stones in an ancient circle, which lie 3m NW.

PORTISHEAD, Avon 6 ST47
Portishead is a small resort with a dockside area, situated on a wooded hillside overlooking the Bristol Channel. Redcliffe Bay offers a pebble beach and sea bathing. The church displays a perpendicular tower and retains a musicians' gallery. Near by is an ancient manor house known as The Court, and Tudor Capernore Court is now a farm. Local tides rise as much as 45ft in March and are almost the highest in the world.

PORTLAND, Dorset 6 SY67
An important naval harbour and breakwater situated on this narrow limestone peninsula measures some 6,000ft long and was built by convicts between 1849 and 1872. West Bay lies to the N, and Chestil Bank to the W.

Thomas Hardy described the area as the Gibraltar of Wessex, and used it in his novels under the name of Isle of Slingers. Portland Bill includes a lighthouse which is now used as a birdwatching station, plus the notable Pulpit Rock. A good cliff walk extends along the W side. Portland Castle was built by King Henry VIII in 1520 (AM), and the remains of the Bow and Arrow Castle date from the 11thc.

Pennsylvania Castle was built in 1800 for John Penn, the one-time governor of Pennsylvania and grandson of the state's founder. Avice's Cottage faces the castle and houses a museum of local interest. It is featured in Hardy's *The Well-Beloved* (OACT). The prison is now a Borstal institute, and the principal village of Easton includes St George's Church of 1754 to 1766. Portland stone is a famous building material which was used by Wren for St Paul's cathedral. Many deserted quarries, quays, and derricks are still to be seen. The present output of stone is conveyed mainly by road.

PORTLOE, Cornwall 4 SW93
Nare Head lies SW of this attractive fishing village, and the rocky coast scenery is very fine. Portloe itself lies on Veryan Bay and offers sea bathing from good sands.

PORTREATH, Cornwall 4 SW64
Fine cliff scenery can be enjoyed at Reskajeage Downs and Hell's Mouth (NT) to the W. A road along the crest covers many fine seaward viewpoints, where cliffs drop sheer to the sea.

PORT ST MARY, Isle of Man 20 SC26
The ancient Giant's Quoiting Stone lies on the road to Port Erin, and 2½m off the SW shore is a little islet called the Calf of Man (NT).

Henry II's Norman castle at Portchester

PORTSCATHO, Cornwall 4 SW83
Many artists make a point of coming to paint this attractive fishing village and its surrounding scenery. It is situated on Gerrans Bay, and includes wide sandy beaches.

PORTSDOWN, Hants 7 SU60
The natural chalk rampart of 400ft Portsdown Hill affords fine views (AA viewpoint) of the Isle of Wight, over Portsmouth and the waters of Langstone and Portsmouth Harbour. Several partly disused forts were built along the crest by Lord Palmerston in 1860, to offset the threat of a French invasion. As the attack was expected from the N their offensive was directed inland. Fort Wydley has now been opened as a 1944 D-day memorial museum.

PORTSLADE-BY-SEA, E Sussex 8 TQ20
The old village lies 1m inland and has a Norman to early-English church with an oak bible box of 1756 in the nave. To the N of the churchyard, in the grounds of a convent, are the remains of a mid 12th-c flint-built manor house. Shoreham harbour lies W.

PORTSMOUTH AND SOUTHSEA, Hants 7 SU60/SZ69
Plan overleaf
Gosport faces this important seaport and naval dockyard across the waters of Portsmouth harbour. Whale Island lies N of the dockyard and is the Naval Gunnery School. Extensive Langstone Harbour lies E, adjacent to Hayling Island.

Frequent bombing raids during the last war caused the partial demolition of the fine 19th-c guildhall. This was restored in 1959. The cathedral formerly served as the parish church, and preserves 12th-c transepts and chancel. The nave and tower were rebuilt in 1693 and large-scale alterations were started after 1927. Building of a new nave has just begun. The Dockyard covers about 300 acres and includes many 18th-c buildings. Nelson's famous Victory, which was launched originally in 1765, lies here in dry dock. An adjacent Naval Museum is of interest.

Cumberland Fort dates from 1746 and 1786, and the new Eastney Beam-Engine House forms the nucleus of an industrial archaeology museum. The interesting Royal Marines Museum is housed in Eastney Barracks. Former military barracks in Alexandra Road house a museum and art gallery. Cumberland House Museum incorporates an aquarium. Included in the High Street is the Square Tower, dating from the time of King Charles I. The Round Tower and Point Battery date from 1485 and later. Nearby Sally Port opens onto the harbour. The Duke of Buckingham was murdered in Buckingham House in 1628. Restored Garrison church dates partly from the 13thc, and the grave of Sir Charles Napier – whose famous capture of Scinda was announced by a telegram worded: *Peccavi* (I have sinned) – lies outside the west door. St George's Church dates from 1754. St James's Gate of 1687 and the Land Port of 1698 give access to the United Services Recreation Ground.

Charles Dickens was born at a house in Commercial Road in 1812. His father was a dockyard clerk, and the house now contains a museum. Meredith was born in the town in 1828, and Nelson spent his last night ashore in the former George Hotel – demolished by a bomb during the last war. I K Brunel, the great engineer, was born at Portsmouth in 1806. St Mary's churchyard contains the Royal George memorial of 1782, which commemorates the loss of Admiral Kempenfelt and 800 men. Sir Alec Rose arrived at Portsmouth after a single-handed round-the-world journey in 1968.

A car ferry connects with the Isle of Wight and there is also a passenger hovercraft service. The airport lies NE on Langstone Harbour. Access to Gosport is by passenger ferry only. Southsea is Portsmouth's seaside resort. An extensive common extends the length of the front, and contains a restored castle from the period of King Henry VIII. This now houses a military and naval museum. Incorporated in the layout is a restored lighthouse of 1828, and numerous flower beds provide a blaze of colour in the summer. Features of the Esplanade include a prominent Naval Memorial, and the anchor of Nelson's Victory. South Parade pier lies farther E.

PORT SUNLIGHT/POTTERSPURY

PORT SUNLIGHT, Merseyside *17 SJ38*
This 500-acre model village was built by Lord Leverhulme between 1851 and 1925, for the employees of a well-known industrial firm. The Lady Lever art gallery and museum is noteworthy.

POSTBRIDGE, Devon *5 SX67*
The East Dart River flows through this village, which is situated at an altitude of nearly 1,100ft on bleak and beautiful Dartmoor. A primitive clapper bridge can be seen in the area, and the notable prehistoric enclosure of Grimspound lies 4½m NE on Hamildon Down. This is considered the finest of its type on the moor. Hut circles have been traced 2m S near Bellever Tor.

POTTER HEIGHAM, Norfolk *15 TG41*
This is a well-known centre for touring the Broads district. The church carries a characteristic round tower and houses a rare 15th-c brick font. An old three-arched bridge spans the River Thurne 1m SE.

POTTERIES, THE
Famous for its china and earthenware, this district lies around Stoke-on-Trent. Stoke, together with Burslem, Hanley, Longton, and Tunstall, make up the Five Towns of Arnold Bennett's novels.

POTTERNE, Wilts *7 ST95*
A beautiful 14th-c and later central tower is displayed by the village's early-English church. Two medieval fonts are contained in the building, and one has an inscription which may be of Saxon origin. This is now kept as a museum piece. Porch House is a half timbered 15th-c structure (OACT).

POTTERSPURY, Northants *13 SP74*
Features of the church include a

1. Anchor of Nelson's Victory
2. Castle (military & naval museum)
3. Cathedral
4. Charles Dickens's Birthplace (museum)
5. Cumberland Fort
6. Cumberland House Museum and Aquarium
7. Garrison Church
8. Guildhall
9. Land Port
10. Military Barracks (museum and art gallery)
11. Naval Memorial
12. Naval Museum
13. Royal George Memorial
14. Royal Marine Museum (Eastney Barracks)
15. St George's Church
16. St James's Gate
17. Victory

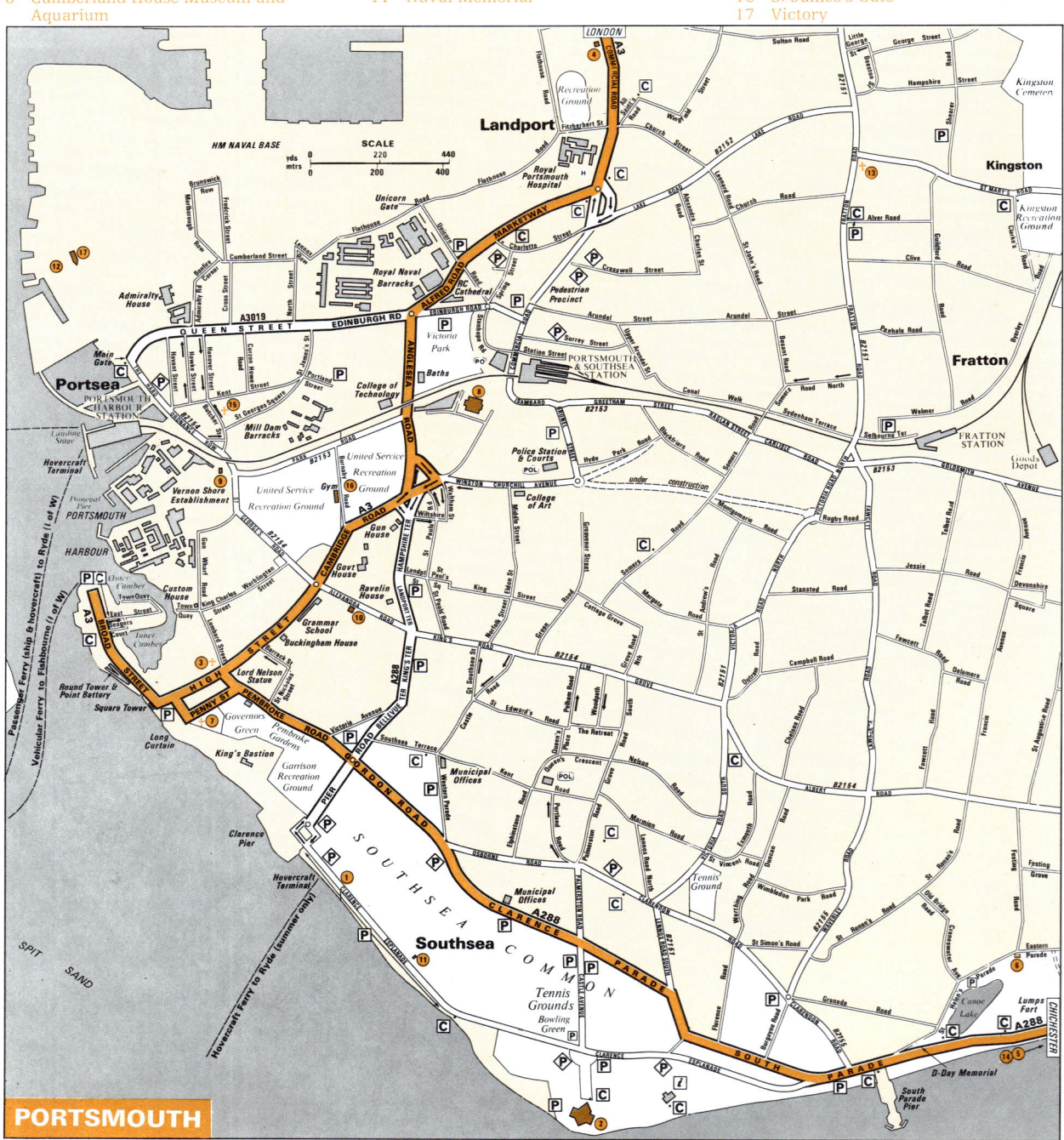

PORTSMOUTH

perpendicular west tower and a chapel of 1780. Potterspury Lodge lies to the NW and dates from 1664 and later. Wakefield Lodge is a mid 18th-c structure lying SW.

POULTON, Glos *12 SP10*
Several 17th- and 18th-c houses can be seen in this attractive Cotswold village. A mound at a crossroads N of the village is known as Betty's Grove, and is said to contain the body of Elizabeth Bastoe who died in 1786.

POULTON-LE-FYLDE, Lancs *21 SD33*
Stocks, a whipping-post, a stepped Jacobean pillar, and ancient fishstones, can be seen in the market place of this Fylde-district town. Prices were once fixed on the fishstones.

POUNDSTOCK, Cornwall *5 SX29*
Faded frescoes on the north wall of the church are interesting, and the nearby two-storeyed 14th-c guildhall is now used as a barn. Penfound Manor, situated off the A39 near Bangors Cross, is mentioned in the Domesday Book. It displays Elizabethan and Stuart features.

POWICK, Herefs & Worcs *12 SO85*
Rivers Teme and Severn join here, and an ancient bridge over the former was the scene of a Civil War battle in 1651. The 12th- to 15th-c church is built of red stone, and contains old woodwork plus an 18th-c monument by Scheemakers.

PRAH SANDS, Cornwall *4 SW52*
Natural amenities include a sandy bathing beach with dunes around on a shallow bay. A tower remains of 16th-c Pengersick Castle. Picturesque Prussia Cove, a former haunt of smugglers, lies 2½m W and is sheltered by Cudden Point.

PRESCOT, Merseyside *17 SJ49*
Once famous for the production of clocks and watches, this industrial town includes a church which was rebuilt in the 17th and 18th c. The latter displays a fine nave roof, plus a tower and spire by Nicholas Hawksmoor. Georgian houses exist in the market place, and the Old Court House of 1755 is also located here.

PRESTBURY, Cheshire *18 SJ97*
Several black-and-white houses, including the former vicarage, are a feature of this attractive village. The latter building has a little gallery above the porch, and the 13th-c church contains an 18th-c oak screen and an interesting oil painting. A restored Saxon churchyard cross and a small Norman chapel with a beautifully carved doorway are also of interest.

PRESTON, Dorset *6 SY78*
Old thatched cottages can be seen here, and the perpendicular church houses a carved sundial and a 17th-c stone figure of a former vicar in the chancel. Near by are the remains of a Roman villa.

PRESTON, E Sussex *8 TQ30*
Now a N suburb of Brighton, Preston includes an early-English church with a few wall-paintings. A nearby Georgian manor house is dated 1739 and contains a collection of furniture and silver (OACT).

PRESTON, Lancs *21 SD53*
Preston lies on the River Ribble and is an important cotton-spinning, engineering, and dock town. Both the Old Pretender and the Young Pretender were proclaimed King in the Market Place, in 1715 and 1745 respectively. Sir Richard Arkwright the inventor was born in Stonygate in 1732. The Harris library and museum contains prehistoric timbers from Bleasdale. The famous Preston Guild festival takes place here approximately every 20 years.

PRESTON, Leics *19 SK80*
Situated in an attractive part of the country which was formerly Rutland, Preston includes a Norman to perpendicular church housing sanctuary lamps and candlesticks from Damascus. A picturesque gabled Elizabethan manor house stands in the village.

PRESTON, Suffolk *15 TL95*
The 13th- to 14th-c church is notable for its 15th-c flint porch, a massive carved Norman font, and a grand example of the Royal Arms of Queen Elizabeth I.

PRESTON BROCKHURST, Salop *17 SJ52*
Black-and-white cottages surround the village green, and a 17th-c manor house is situated here. Remains of a fine unfinished mansion, dated 1606 and burnt by the Parliamentarians in 1645, lie 2m SE at Moreton Corbet. Parts of a castle dated 1573 and 1576 are also of interest (AM). The 17th-c playwright, William Wycherley was born 2m W at Clive Hall.

PRIDDY, Somerset *6 ST55*
A lonely high-lying Mendip village, Priddy was once the centre of an extensive lead-mining district. Priddy Nine Barrows is the name given to bowl barrows on Ashen Hill. Both these and the Priddy Circles, near the Castle of Comfort Inn, are of archaeological interest. A thatched stack of sheep-pen hurdles on the green is supposed to prove the village's right to hold a fair. This fair was transferred from Wells in 1348 at the time of the Black Death.

PRINCES RISBOROUGH, Bucks *8 SP80*
Several picturesque old houses can be seen here, including a 17th- and 18th-c manor house (NT, OACT). The Chiltern escarpment fringes the edge of the village.

PRINCETOWN, Devon *5 SX57*
Princetown is situated on one of Dartmoor's highest points, and is famous for its convict prison. This is due for demolition. The church of 1813 was built by convict labour, and Tor Royal is a mainly 18th-c house. North Hessary Tor rises to 1,600ft and Great Mis Tor to 1,761ft. Both are prominent landmarks.

PRIORS MARSTON, Warwickshire *13 SP45*
Stone-built houses and a Georgian church tower are features of the village. Both the Oxford Canal and the route of an ancient Welsh drovers' road run near by.

PRITTLEWELL, Essex *9 TQ88*
Popular Southend-on-Sea has grown from part of this old village. Remains of a 12th-c priory include a beautiful doorway, and the prior's house is now a museum. Near by stands the original 18th-c Crow Stone, marking the City of London's most eastern point of River Thames jurisdiction. A successor to the stone stands at Westcliff. The mainly 15th-c church displays a fine tower, plus chequered flint-and-stone battlements.

PROBUS, Cornwall *4 SW84*
The richly-carved church tower dates from 1523 and is considered the best example in the county. It closely resembles the better-known Somerset towers.

PUDDLETOWN, Dorset *6 SY79*
Features of the fine mainly-perpendicular church include a panelled nave roof and a Jacobean gallery. Stretches of open heath lie between Puddletown and Wareham, and form the Egdon Heath of Thomas Hardy's novels. Athelhampton Hall is a notable 15th- and 16th-c house, with some restorations, lying 1m E (OACT). Waterston Manor is an Elizabethan and later house which is described by Hardy as Weatherbury in *Far from the Madding Crowd*. It is set in lovely gardens (OACT).

PUDSEY, W Yorks *22 SE23*
Eminent cricketers Herbert Sutcliffe and Sir Leonard Hutton were born in this woollen-district town. The Fulneck Moravian Museum was originally founded in 1457 as a Protestant Episcopal Community, and contains Victoriana etc (OACT).

1   Harris Library and Museum
2   Market Place

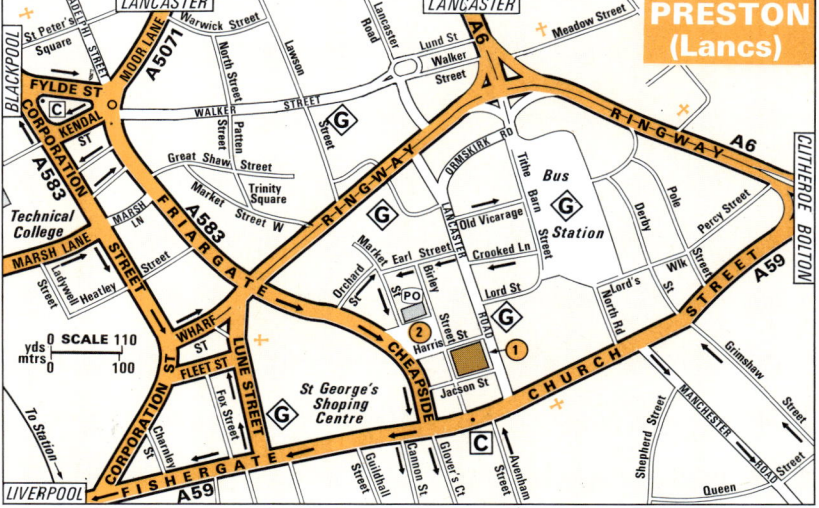

PULBOROUGH, W Sussex 8 TQ01
Attractive half-timbered and stone-built houses can be seen in this pleasant town, and several old bridges span the River Arun. The large early-English to perpendicular church contains a massive 12th-c font, and shows a delightful 14th-c lych-gate.

PURBECK, ISLE OF
Purbeck is the name given to a Dorset peninsula extending from Lulworth Cove to Poole Bay, which is traversed in the W by the Purbeck Hills. The coastal scenery at the point where the Purbecks meet the sea is some of the most spectacular in England, and of great geological interest. A large part of this district is now designated an area of outstanding natural beauty, but a portion of the coast around Worbarrow Bay has not yet been acquired from the army and is largely inaccessible. Purbeck stone is a well-known building material, and numerous quarries exist in the area. See Studland and Swanage.

PURTON, Wilts 12 SU08
The perpendicular cruciform-shaped church carries a central tower and spire in addition to a pinnacled west tower. Close to the church is a fine old manor house which includes a two-storeyed dovecote. A notable L-shaped tithe barn is also of interest, and Elizabethan Restrop House lies 1m W.

PYECOMBE, W Sussex 8 TQ21
Shepherds' crooks are manufactured in this South Downs village, and the Norman and early-English church contains a Norman lead font. Newtimber Place is a moated 17th-c house (OACT).

QUADRING, Lincs 19 TF23
The fine mainly-perpendicular church displays a good tower and spire, and houses a notable font.

QUAINTON, Bucks 13 SP72
Grassy hills affording an exceptionally wide view of the surrounding area sweep down to the boundaries of this pretty village. Part of a 15th-c market cross, a windmill, and delightful 17th-c almshouses can be seen here. An interesting collection of steam locomotives and rolling stock is situated at the former railway station.

QUANTOCK HILLS
This wooded hill ridge and noted stag-hunting district extends towards Taunton from St Audries Bay on the Bristol Channel. The highest point is 1,262ft Will's Neck, and a number of picturesque combes exist in the range – notably on the E side. The newly-afforested Quantock Forest covers some 3,000 acres, and is designated an area of outstanding natural beauty.

QUARLEY, Hants 7 SU24
Bells contained in a ground-level wooden canopy are an interesting feature of the towerless church. An iron-age camp surmounts the 562ft viewpoint of Quarley Hill.

QUATT, Salop 12 SO78
A Queen Anne dower house stands in this Severn-Valley hamlet. Dudmaston Hall is a house of the same period, set in a fine park. The church of 1763 contains Wolryche monuments. Some 3m SE is Coton Hall, which was once the home of American General Robert E Lee's ancestors. It was remodelled in 1820.

QUEENBOROUGH, Kent 9 TQ97
The name of this Isle of Sheppey industrial town is derived from Queen Philippa, wife of Edward III, whose fortress of 1366 has almost entirely vanished. An old guildhall retains its dungeons, and a steamer service formerly operated between here and Flushing. The River Swale flows through the town.

QUEEN CAMEL, Somerset 6 ST52
The mainly 15th-c church carries a good tower, and houses an exceptionally fine carved screen.

QUEEN CHARLTON, Avon 6 ST66
Queen Charlton church carries a Norman tower; it is thought that a Norman arch re-erected opposite the 18th-c manor house may have been the former south doorway of the church.

QUENINGTON, Glos 12 SP10
Two very notable and richly-carved Norman doorways are housed in the village's much-restored church. The area forms part of the picturesque Cotswolds and is watered by the River Coln.

QUETHIOCK, Cornwall 5 SX36
The 13th-c and later church of St Hugo includes a saddle-backed staircase tower rising to the foot of a west tower above the nave. The Kyndon brass of 1471 is notable, and a wheel-headed 14ft-high cross is of interest.

QUIDENHAM, Norfolk 15 TM08
Mainly-decorated in style, the church carries a round tower and the chapel of St Mary was restored by American airmen. Queen Boadicea is said to be buried in a nearby mound.

QUORN, Leics 18 SK51
Quorn gives its name to what is probably the most famous Hunt in England. The Norman to decorated church includes two stone screens and the Farnham Chapel among its more notable features.

RACTON, W Sussex 8 SU70
Gounter monuments dating from the 16th 17th and 18thc can be seen in the church. Racton Tower is a tall folly which cost Lord Halifax £10,000 to erect in 1770. To the NW is the rebuilt house of Stansted Park, surrounded by a park and the remains of the Forest of Bere. It was reconstructed in 1903.

RADCOT, Oxon 13 SU29
The 14th-c bridge over the Thames is the oldest to span the river. A Civil War skirmish won by Prince Rupert took place here.

RADLEY, Oxon 13 SU59
Buildings comprising the public school, which was founded in 1847, include an early 18th-c manor house. The 15th-c church is noted for its fine heraldic glass, which includes arms of Henry VI and Richard III. The 17th-c chancel stalls are also of interest.

RADWINTER, Essex 14 TL63
The partly-rebuilt church contains a 16th-c Belgian reredos, and retains a remarkable 14th-c timbered south porch. The Old Rectory dates from the 16thc; both this and the church were restored by Eden Nesfield.

RAINHAM, Gt London 8 TQ58
Rainham's well-restored church is a notable example of Norman work. It includes a fine priest's door and houses an old chest which may date from the 14thc. Near by stands an exceptionally-fine four-square early 18th-c hall (NT).

RAMSBOTTOM, Gt Manchester 21 SD71
A textile-manufacturing town overlooked by Peel Tower and Grant's Tower. The latter commemorates the Grant Brothers, who were great benefactors to the town. They are portrayed in Dickens' *Nicholas Nickleby* as the Cheeryble Brothers.

RAMSBURY, Wilts 7 SU27
This River-Kennet village includes Jacobean and Georgian buildings, and the early-English church carries a perpendicular tower and displays ancient sculptured stones. The fine Manor House dates from 1677 and is attributed to John Webb, the son-in-law of Inigo Jones.

RAMSEY, Cambs 14 TL28
Remains of the Benedictine Abbey founded here in 969 include early-English arches and a fine perpendicular-style gateway (NT). A modern house now stands on the site. The parish church is mostly Norman, and has a tower carrying the date of 1672.

St Mary's Church, Reading

RAMSEY, Essex *15 TM23*
A well-carved south doorway of 15th-c origin is displayed by the 12th-c and later church. An Elizabethan pulpit is also of interest. A post-mill lies W of the church, and Elizabethan Roydon Hall stands 2m W.

RAMSEY, Isle of Man *20 SC49*
Natural amenities offered by this resort include excellent sand, sea bathing, and brine baths. The Albert Tower is a good viewpoint, and North Barrule rises to 1,842ft in the S. This overlooks the road to 2,034ft Snaefell, the highest point on the island.

RAMSGATE, Kent *9 TR36*
Chalk cliffs fringe excellent sands at this popular resort and fishing port. St Augustine's RC abbey church is considered Pugin's masterpiece and is where the great architect was buried. St George's Church displays a Dunkirk window. Many boarding schools, two piers, and several fine Regency-period crescents are also of interest. Pegwell Bay and the Hovercraft terminal at Ebbsfleet lie to the S.

RANWORTH, Norfolk *15 TG31*
Situated between Ranworth and South Walsham Broads, this village includes a church which is famous for its 14th- or 15th-c painted screen. This is considered one of the finest in the country. Also of interest is a cantor's desk of 1500, and a notable 15th-c choir book displaying an illuminated text.

RAUNDS, Northants *13 SP97*
Boots and shoes are manufactured in this small town, which is situated in the industrialized Nene Valley. The very fine mainly 13th-c church carries a 133ft tower and spire, and houses notable 15th-c wall paintings.

RAVENGLASS, Cumbria *21 SD09*
Ravenglass stands at the mouth of the Rivers Esk, Mite, and Irt, and was once a port. The beautiful Eskdale Valley runs towards Scafell and the high fells, and contains a narrow-gauge railway. Hardknott, one of the national forest parks, includes a Roman fort and lies 11m ENE. Remains of another Roman fort, *Glannaventa*, lie S and include red sandstone walls. Muncaster Castle preserves an ancient tower and lies 1m E. Fine gardens afford views of the Lake District fells (OACT), and nearby Roman ruins known as Walls Castle are of interest. A white tower on the fells recalls the discovery of King Henry VI after his defeat at the battle of Hexham in 1464. He took shelter with the Pennington family of Muncaster Castle, and was found by shepherds.

RAVENSCAR, N Yorks *23 NZ90*
Access to the small rocky beach is by an exceptionally steep descent through lofty cliffs. Lonely Fylingdales Moor extends inland. The 40m Lyke Wake Walk, opened in 1955, runs W over the moors to Mount Grace Priory.

RAYLEIGH, Essex *9 TQ89*
Rayleigh Mount is the site of a former Norman castle (NT). The 15th-c church has a good west tower and a timber arch to the south chancel chapel. A circular thatched cottage, probably built by 17th-c Dutch settlers, stands near the station.

RAYNE, Essex *14 TL72*
Several old houses include the 16th-c hall, which preserves a Tudor doorway and now serves as a farm. The church has a Tudor brick tower of c1510.

READING, Berks *8 SU77*
Plan overleaf
Reading is sited on the River Kennet near its confluence with the Thames. It is a university town which includes scanty remains of a once-famous Norman abbey where King Henry I was buried (AM). The restored abbey gateway is now a museum, but was once a school; Jane Austen was a pupil here in 1786. The flint walls of the former chapter house contain a stone tablet inscribed with notes of the most remarkable piece of early part-song music known. This was written by a monk in c1240 and is entitled *Sumer is i-cumen in*. Churches in the town include St Lawrence's, with a 111ft tower, a 16th-c font at which Archbishop Laud was baptized, and interesting monuments; St Mary's, with a carved oak gallery of 1631, and a rebuilt organ from the great London Exhibition of 1851; the largely 14th-c Grey Friars Church with fine flintwork and a beautiful west window. Reading's museum exhibits a large collection of Roman relics from the excavation of *Calleva Atrebatum*, Silchester. The guildhall and art gallery are also of note. An interesting museum of English rural life is housed in the mansion in Whiteknights Park, and operates under the patronage of the university. The buildings of the university are of partly 19th-c origin, and partly of post second world war date. Oscar Wilde wrote *De Profundis* in 1897 while committed to Reading gaol. The residential district of Caversham stands on the far side of the Thames.

RECULVER, Kent *9 TR26*
Remains of an ancient monastic church stand near the walls of the 3rd-c Roman fort *Regulbium* in an area known as the Saxon Shore (both AM). The church was in use until the 19thc, and its twin towers are still an important navigational landmark (OACT).

REDBOURN, Herts *8 TL11*
Norman work and a good 15th-c screen are preserved in the church. Several Georgian houses exist in the area, and an extensive green lies W of the main street.

REDCAR, Cleveland *27 NZ62*
This well-known resort offers extensive sands and sea bathing. The Museum of Fishing and Shipping is of interest, and a racecourse lies near by.

REDDITCH, Herefs & Worcs *12 SP06*
Needles are manufactured in this town, and the construction of a New Town has been started. Restored Forge Mill lies N and formerly served Bordesley Abbey. Its machinery and water wheel are of interest.

REDENHALL, Norfolk *15 TM28*
The church in this Waveney-Valley village displays a magnificent 15th-c tower with notable flint flushwork. Royal Arms of Queen Anne are also of interest.

REDMIRE, N Yorks *22 SE09*
A Wensleydale village, Redmire is so situated as to form a notable viewpoint. Redmire Force, a waterfall on the River Ure, lies 1m SSW. Grim 14th-c Bolton Castle was the one-time home of the Scropes, and lies 1¼m NW. Mary Queen of Scots was imprisoned here for periods during 1568 and 1569 (OACT).

REDRUTH, Cornwall *4 SW64*
William Murdock the inventor lived in this important mining town and had the first gas-lit house in the country. The house has been restored as a memorial. The area has associations with John Wesley the methodist, and George Fox — the founder of the Society of Friends. St Euny's Church dates from 1768. A local museum of mineral specimens is of interest. Prehistoric Carn Brea Castle lies 2m SW at an altitude of 750ft (AM), with the Dunstanville monument of 1836 near by.

1 St Augustine's Abbey Church (RC)
2 St George's Church

REEDHAM, Norfolk 15 TG40
A ferry crosses the River Yare at Reedham, and the local church is notable for its prominent 15th-c tower, old pews, and the Berney Chapel. Halvergate Marshes and the isolated 19th-c Berney Arms marsh windmill (OACT) lie NE.

REEPHAM, Norfolk 15 TG02
Three churches once stood in a single churchyard here. Reepham Church is decorated in style and houses a notable 14th-c tomb; neighbouring Whitwell Church shows decorated and perpendicular work, and contains a carved Jacobean pulpit. Georgian houses exist in The Square.

REETH, N Yorks 22 SE09
This picturesque Swaledale village lies in a moorland setting near the point where lonely Arkengarthdale Valley turns to the NW. Lead-mining was a former local industry.

REIGATE, Surrey 8 TQ25
Situated below the North Downs and linked to Redhill, this pleasant market and residential town includes a few 18th-c houses. Sparse remains of a Norman castle are surrounded by a park which also features caves. Picturesque Market House is dated 1708, and the large 12th- to 15th-c parish church has been much restored. The grave of Lord Howard of Effingham, who commanded the English fleet that defeated the Armada, can be seen here. Reigate Priory is a fine house which was rebuilt in 1779 and now incorporates a small museum.

Colley Hill is a good viewpoint situated N on the Downs (part NT), close to a section of the Pilgrims' Way. Church services are occasionally held in a converted windmill of 1765 on Reigate Heath. Another windmill, dated 1824, can be seen on Wray Common.

REPTON, Derbyshire 18 SK32
Well-known for its pre-Conquest work, the local church includes a crypt which is considered one of the finest of its period. The public school, originally a grammar school, was founded in the 16thc and preserves parts of an ancient priory. The 17th-c hall now serves as the headmaster's house. An old market cross is also of interest.

RETFORD, Notts 18 SK78
East Retford church displays Victorian stained glass and has been greatly restored; the grammar school was founded in 1552. Broad Stone stands in the market place and is the base of a former cross. West Retford lies on the other side of the River Idle, and includes a church displaying a fine early 14th-c tower and broach spire. The south porch is also of note. West Retford Hall is a Queen-Anne house.

RETTENDON, Essex 9 TQ79
This village lies between the River Crouch and Hanningfield Reservoir. The church carries a 15th-c tower and is noted for its Humphrey monument of 1727. A Tudor barn exists near Victorian Rettendon Place. The gardens of Hyde Hall are exceptionally beautiful.

RIBCHESTER, Lancs 21 SD63
Once a Roman station on the River Ribble, Ribchester boasts a fort of the period and a museum. (NT, OACT). White Bull Inn displays a curious sign. The mainly early-English to perpendicular church includes the notable Dutton and Hoghton Chapels, and two round stone pillars – possibly of Roman origin – supporting an 18th-c oak gallery. Norman Stidd Chapel and nearby almshouses of 1728 lie NE.

RICHBOROUGH, Kent 9 TR36
Massive walls from the Roman fort *Rutupiae*, an original fort of the Saxon Shore, survive in Richborough. Many relics have been found here, and interesting displays are mounted in the local museum (OACT). Sections of the old town walls, plus a Roman amphitheatre, can be seen in the area.

RICHMOND, N Yorks 22 NZ10
Beautifully situated above the River Swale at the foot of Swaledale, Richmond includes a splendid Norman castle which is one of the earliest in England (AM). It displays a massive keep and walls. Greyfriars Tower is a perpendicular structure which survives from an earlier monastery. The Norman and later parish church houses choir stalls that were formerly in Easby Abbey.

Many Georgian and older houses and a well-restored little Georgian theatre of 1788 can be seen here. The Market Place is one of the largest in the country and contains an 18th-c obelisk. Green Howards Museum is housed in Trinity Buildings, and a museum of Horsedrawn Transport is situated in Queen's Road. One of the town's former postern gates leads into Bargate. Richmond is associated with the *Lass of Richmond Hill*, a well-known song. Temple Lodge is dated 1769, and includes the Culloden Tower of 1746.

RICHMOND-UPON-THAMES, Gt London 8 TQ17
A noted Thames-side resort, this residential district includes remains of a Tudor royal palace where Queen Elizabeth I died in 1603. These comprise a gateway and a building known as Wardrobe Court. Many Queen-Anne and Georgian houses still exist here, notable examples of which include Maids of Honour Row, Trumpeters' House, The Wick, and Asgill House; the latter was designed by Sir Robert Taylor. Well-known Star and Garter Home for disabled soldiers overlooks the river.

The restored parish church dates mainly from 1750 and contains monuments to Edmund Keen, James Thompson and Miss Braddon. A view of the river from the terrace is famous. Richmond Park covers over 2,000 acres, measures some 10m in circumference, and is traversed by motoring roads. Herds of deer live in the park, which also contains the 18th-c White Lodge by Roger Morris. This building is strongly associated with the royal family, and both Queen Victoria and King Edward VII lived here at times. It now houses the Royal Ballet School.

RICKINGHALL, Suffolk 15 TM07
Rickinghall Inferior Church carries a Norman round tower with a pinnacled 15th-c parapet. Rickinghall Superior Church dates from the 14th to 15thc, and contains a 14th-c font.

RICKMANSWORTH, Herts 8 TQ09
This River-Colne town includes the Royal Masonic school for girls, and a partly 15th-c vicarage. William Penn lived at Basing House. On the S outskirts is the great early 18th-c mansion of Moor Park. This was designed by Leoni, and displays splendid frescoes by Amiconi and Sir James Thornhill. It is now the clubhouse of a well-known golf-course (OACT).

RIDGEWAY, THE
The Ridgeway is an ancient trackway, considered to date from pre-Roman times, extending some 20m along the crest of the Berkshire Downs above the Kennet Valley. A newly-opened long-distance footpath now follows much of the route.

1 Abbey Gateway (museum)
2 Abbey Remains
3 Art Gallery
4 Grey Friars Church
5 Guildhall (museum)
6 Museum of English Rural Life
7 Reading Gaol
8 St Lawrence's Church
9 St Mary's Church
10 University of Reading

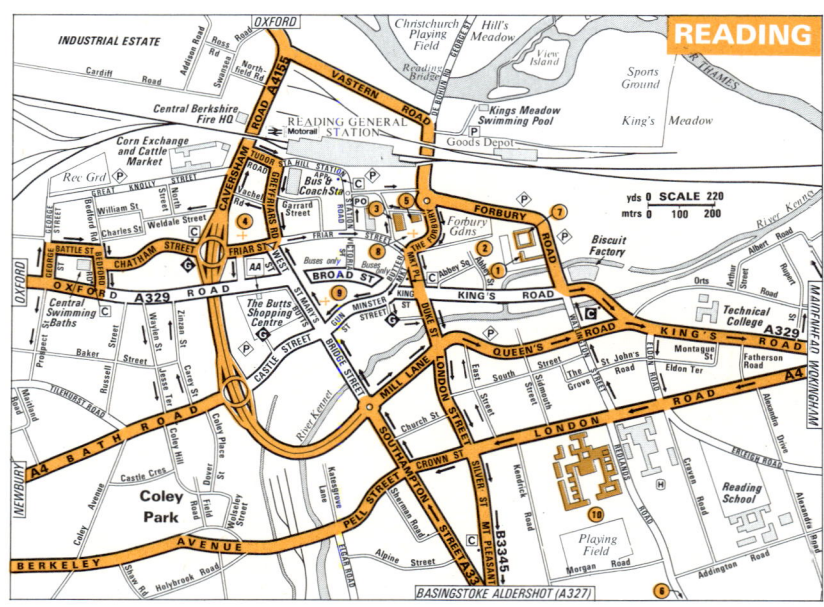

RIEVAULX ABBEY, N Yorks *22 SE58*
Beautiful and interesting remains of this 12th- to 13th-c Cistercian abbey lie amid impressive wooded surroundings in Ryedale (AM). Rievaulx Terrace boasts 18th-c garden temples, and affords a particularly fine view (NT, OACT).

RINGMER, E Sussex *8 TQ41*
Gilbert White lived in Delves House and described a tortoise, which a local signpost near the church recalls, in his diary.

RINGSFIELD, Suffolk *15 TM48*
The village church is well-known as the location of the grave of Princess Caroline Murat, a grandchild of Napoleon's sister. The building itself is thatched and displays a rare Elizabethan exterior brass.

RINGWOOD, Hants *7 SU10*
Salmon fishing can be enjoyed – at a price – in this River Avon market town. It is situated at the W extremity of the New Forest, near the place where the Duke of Monmouth was captured at the close of the 1685 rebellion.

RINGWOULD, Kent *9 TR34*
The mainly 12th- to 14th-c church carries an unusual west tower displaying fine Jacobean brickwork. Several bronze-age barrows exist on Free Down.

RIPLEY, N Yorks *22 SE26*
Cromwell stayed at the 16th-c and later castle – home of the Ingilby family – on the evening before the 1644 battle of Marston Moor. A fine 15th-c gatehouse is of interest (OACT). The decorated and perpendicular church houses noteworthy tombs and brasses, and a weeping cross stands in the churchyard. Stocks can be seen below the village cross.

RIPLEY, Surrey *8 TQ05*
Situated on the Portsmouth road, this pleasant village contains several Georgian and older buildings. The Anchor and the Talbot are two inns of particular note.

RIPON, N Yorks *22 SE37*
An old town on the River Ure, Ripon boasts a mainly 12th- to 15th-c cathedral. Of particular note are the early-English west front, the choir screen of 1480, the Saxon crypt, and beautiful wood carvings. The latter include portrayals of animal subjects on the misericords, and an elephant-and-castle bench end of 1494.

A 90ft-high cross stands in the market place, and the nearby town hall of 1781 was the work of James Wyatt. Remains of two ancient Hospitals – St Anne, or the Maison Dieu, and St Mary Magdalen – are of interest. The Wakeman's Horn is blown each night at 2100hrs, at the same time as the curfew is rung in the Minster tower. The 13th-c Wakeman's House now contains a museum. Thorpe Prebend house dates back to the 15thc, and partly-moated 14th-c Markenfield Hall, which lies 3½m SSW, is of exceptional interest (OACT). Two fine 18th-c houses in the area are Newby Hall 4m SE, and Grantley Hall 5m SW. The former is an Adam house which is noted for its statue gallery and Gobelin tapestries, and stands in splendid gardens (OACT). Grantley Hall is now a college.

RISLEY, Derbyshire *18 SK43*
The church dates from 1593 and was built as the private chapel for an old hall which has since been replaced by a Georgian house. Near by stands the Latin House of 1706, and the school buildings of 1718.

RISSINGTON, Glos *12 SP11*
This name covers a trio of upland Cotswold villages. Great Rissington is the most southerly and includes a restored church with a chapel which was furnished in 1940. The manor house is also restored. Little Rissington includes several interesting old houses. Wyck Rissington has a village green, and boasts a small Norman and early-English church housing twelve wooden chancel medallions. The latter may date from the 16thc. Near the church is a maze of 1953.

RIVINGTON, Lancs *21 SD61*
Rivington lies at the foot of 1,498ft Winter Hill, and above the village is 1,190ft Rivington Pike. A stone tower dating from 1733 surmounts the Pike and forms a notable viewpoint. Two large reservoirs in the area supply Liverpool. The local church was altered in the 17thc, and houses a restored perpendicular screen and an early 16th-c pulpit. Rivington Hall, rebuilt in 1744, stands in Lever Park and belongs to Liverpool Corporation.

ROBERTSBRIDGE, E Sussex *9 TQ72*
The timber-framed Seven Stars Inn and several old houses are notable features of this River-Rother town. Slight remains of a 12th-c Abbey exist 1m E at Abbey Farm. Salehurst lies 1m NE, and includes a largely-decorated church which is noted for its fine tower and a font displaying carved salamanders.

ROBIN HOOD'S BAY, N Yorks *23 NZ90*
Considered one of the most picturesque fishing villages in England, this small resort is set among lofty cliffs and offers sand at low tide. North Yorks Moors national park lies SW above the Derwent Valley; nearby Fylingdales Moor is the location of an Air Ministry Early-Warning Station.

ROCESTER, Staffs *18 SK13*
Situated between the Rivers Churnet and Dove, Rocester includes a 19th-c church with an ancient cross in almost perfect condition in the churchyard.

ROCHDALE, Gt Manchester *21 SD81*
Cotton manufacturing is the main industry of this important town. The modern town hall is imposing, and the much-restored St Chad's church contains fine woodwork. Examples of the latter include carved Tudor pews and a notable monument.

The famous Lancashire poet Tim Bobbin is buried in the parish churchyard of the Friends' Meeting House, and Rochdale Pioneers founded one of the earliest co-operative societies in 1844. The town has a further claim to fame as the birthplace of Gracie Fields. Characteristic weavers' houses, with their top stories lined by long horizontal windows, still exist here.

ROCHE, Cornwall *4 SW96*
The interesting village church is dedicated to St Gonandus and was originally built by the Normans. Although it was largely reconstructed during the 19thc it still contains a remarkable trans-Norman font, and a curious old cross stands in the churchyard. A Cornish holy well can be seen near by. Hensbarrow Beacon is an excellent viewpoint rising to 1,027ft behind the church. Ruins of a 15th-c chapel exist on a 680ft spur of the Beacon and appear to be part of the unusual outcrop of granite rocks into which the structure was originally built. The large iron-age hill fort of Castle-an-Dinas stands at 703ft and is approximately 5½m NW of the village.

ROCHE ABBEY, S Yorks *18 SK58*
Ruins of this Cistercian abbey lie in the River Ryton Valley, and include the transepts, chancel, and main gateway of the old abbey church (OACT). The abbey was founded in 1147. Adjacent Sandbeck Park is of interest, and the church 2¼m SW at Laughton-en-le-Morthen shows a fine perpendicular spire and pre-Conquest doorway.

ROCHESTER, Kent *9 TQ76*
Rochester is a Medway town of great age and interest. The mainly-Norman cathedral features a large early-English crypt, two exceptionally beautiful doorways, and 14th-c wall-paintings on the choir walls. The doorways are of Norman and decorated styles respectively, and the building has suffered many later alterations and restorations. The lady chapel is now the chapel of the King's School – one of the oldest foundations in England. Tombs of a number of medieval Bishops are preserved, and examples of very early woodwork survive in the choir.

cont

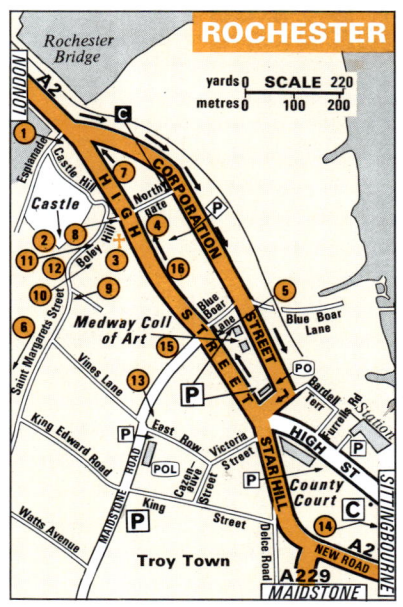

1 Bridge Chapel
2 Castle
3 Cathedral
4 Corn Exchange
5 Eastgate House
   (museum and Dickens's Swiss Chalet)
6 Fort Clarence
7 Guildhall
8 Jasper's Gate
9 King's School
10 Minor Canon Row
11 Old Bishop's Palace
12 Old Hall
13 Restoration House
14 St Bartholomew's Chapel
15 Town Wall Remains
16 Watts Charity Hospital

A section of the 73½m Hadrian's Wall

Three old gateways include the interesting Jasper's Gate, and the Old Bishop's Palace is mainly of 18th-c date. Fort Clarence dates from 1812. Minor Canon Row is an attractive group of old houses, and St Bartholomew's chapel is the surviving relic of a once-famous leper hospital. The castle displays an impressive 12th-c 100ft-high keep (AM). Slight traces of the former town walls remain. Eastgate House is of Elizabethan origin and was described by Dickens in his novel *Edwin Drood*. This now contains a museum, and its grounds include the novelist's Swiss chalet. Restoration House is associated with King Charles II and dates from the Elizabethan period and later (OACT). Dickens described this in his *Uncommercial Traveller*.

Watts Charity Hospital, or Seven Poor Travellers' Hostel, dates from 1579 but has been refronted. The Corn Exchange has a clock which was donated by Sir Cloudesley Shovel in 1706. James II stayed at a house now occupied by Lloyds Bank in 1688, just prior to his abdication. The Old Hall on Boley Hill is a timber-framed house which is noted for its painted Tudor decoration.

A 17th-c guildhall has a ship vane on the roof and contains a collection of pictures plus a notable plaster ceiling. A much-restored bridge chapel now serves as the boardroom of the Bridge Wardens, and is situated on the Esplanade. Good sections of the town wall are visible from here. Other interesting old buildings exist in the area, and the town's associations with Dickens are even more numerous than already indicated. The original Borstal corrective prison for youths, established in 1902, lies 1m SE.

ROCHESTER, Northumberland *27 NY89*
Roman stones were extensively used to build the gable of the old school porch, including two large catapult balls. A Roman station called *Bremenium* includes the remains of walls and gateways, and lies about ½m N.

ROCHFORD, Essex *9 TQ89*
This ancient market town has a mainly 15th-c church which is notable for its fine brick-built tower. A surviving portion of the mid 16th-c hall where Anne Boleyn once lived stands near the church.

ROCK, Cornwall *4 SW97*
The Camel estuary divides Rock and Padstow. The Church of St Michael, at Porthilly, is now the south chapelry of St Minver. It has been rescued from the sands, and displays good wagon roofs plus an early-Norman font.

ROCK, Herefs & Worcs *12 SO77*
A splendid doorway can be seen in the Norman church of *c*1170, and old stocks and a whipping post are preserved on a nearby road. Bowerscourt Farm is a beautiful black-and-white L-shaped house which once stood inside a moat. Wyre Forest and the Abberley Hills lie on opposite sides of the village.

ROCKBOURNE, Hants *7 SU11*
Excavations of a local Roman villa are still in progress, but to date have revealed seventy-three rooms. A large museum on the site contains pottery, coins, and jewellery (OACT).

ROCKINGHAM, Northants *19 SP89*
Several thatched cottages exist here, and the village is well-situated for views over the Welland Valley. Charles Dickens was a frequent visitor at the Norman and Elizabethan castle (OACT). An interesting old cross stands in the village.

RODE, Somerset *6 ST85*
Tropical Bird Gardens at Rode cover approximately 17 acres of ground and include a collection of domestic animals (OACT).

RODINGS, Essex *9 TL51*
Several villages in the River-Roding valley, sometimes known as Roothings, include this suffix in their name. The prefixes are Abbess, Aythorpe, Beauchamp, Berners, High, Leaden, Margaret and White.

RODNEY STOKE, Somerset *6 ST45*
Interesting Rodney monuments, including one of 1478, can be seen in the church. Two other notable features of the building are a screen and pulpit of 1625. The village is situated under the Mendip escarpment near a national nature reserve.

ROGATE, W Sussex *8 SU82*
Rogate's restored Norman and early-English church contains an ancient chest and a brass candelabra of 1776. Scanty remains of 12th-c Dureford Abbey exist in the area. Attractive Rogate Common lies 1m N, and provides fine views of the wooded ridges of the South Downs.

ROLLESBY, Norfolk *15 TG41*
This Broads village lies near 200-acre Rollesby Broad, which is linked to Ormesby and Filby Broads. A round tower is carried by the church, and the 15th-c chancel pinnacles carry carvings of dogs.

ROLLESTON, Notts *18 SK75*
Kate Greenaway lived in this pleasant village as a child. The partly 13th-c church preserves two carved Saxon stones and a number of incised slabs.

ROLLRIGHT, GREAT, Oxon *13 SP33*
Norman doorways and a perpendicular screen can be seen in the local church, which dates from both these periods. The tiny perpendicular church of Little Rollright lies 2½m SW and houses two fine 17th-c tombs. Well-known Rollright Stones form a prehistoric stone circle 2m WSW, and are situated on a lofty ridge offording panoramic local views. King's Stone lies across the road from the main complex and is an outlier of the circle.

ROLVENDEN, Kent *9 TQ83*
A hop-district village of tiled and weather-boarded houses, Rolvenden includes a large 14th-c and later church. The latter contains a curious upstairs pew, originally meant for the lord of the manor's use. A fine old post-mill, considered the oldest in Kent, was restored in 1956. Frances Burnett, who wrote *Little Lord Fauntleroy*, lived at Great Maytham Hall which was designed by Sir Edwin Lutyens in 1910 (OACT).

ROMALDKIRK, Co Durham *27 NY92*
An attractive Teesside village, where the interesting restored 12th-c and later church shows Norman nave arcades and a carved font.

ROMAN WALL
This giant feat of building is known as Hadrian's wall, and is one of the most famous of our ancient monuments. It was built after the Emperor Hadrian's visit in AD121 or 122, to defend the Roman province of Britain against inroads from the N. It is 73½m in length and runs from Wallsend on the River Tyne, to Bowness on the Solway Firth. The main structure comprises a continuous stone wall with a vallum, or earthwork, at short but varying distances to the S. Forts, mile-castles, and turrets are incorporated in the wall at regular intervals along its length.

Where it runs to the W of the North Tyne the wall is preserved to a considerable height; elsewhere it has been badly robbed for its stone. Several picturesque little lakes, notably Crag Lough, lie N of the wall near Housesteads. It is here that the fortification follows 1,000ft high ridges of the Great Whin Sill rock outcrop. Interesting museums connected with the Roman occupation – and particularly the wall – are sited at Chollerford and Housesteads. Countryside between the wall and the Cheviot hills forms part of the Northumberland national park.

ROMNEY MARSH, Kent *9 TR03*
Romney Marsh is a level tract of land measuring about 17m long by 12m broad, bounded by the Royal Military Canal in the W and N and linked to Walland and Denge Marshes in the S – near the coast. The area was once completely covered by the sea, and still lies below sea-level at high tide. Drainage operations started with the Dymchurch and Rhee Walls in Roman times, and most of the land has been reclaimed. The Royal Military Canal is not really part of the drainage system, but was originally built as a defence against an expected Napoleonic invasion. Romney Marsh is now famous for its pasturage and the fine quality of the wool from its sheep. Tulip growing is a newly-developed local industry. The narrow-gauge steam-hauled Romney, Hythe and Dymchurch railway traverses the seaward fringe of the Marsh.

ROMSEY, Hants *7 SU32*
Game fishing offered by the River Test, upon which Romsey stands, is the finest in the country. Abbey Church was founded in the 10thc and displays splendid Norman cruciform-construction. The abbess's doorway is notable and a carved possibly-Saxon crucifix can be seen outside against the south transept wall. A remarkable 16th-c painted wooden reredos is displayed in the north transept. King John's House is a 13th-c flint building which was rediscovered in 1927. Several old inns and a statue of Lord Palmerston stand in the market-place. Broadlands, an 18th-c house sited in a fine park to the W, was the former home of Lord Palmerston: HM the Queen and the Duke of Edinburgh spent part of their honeymoon here.

ROMSLEY, Herefs & Worcs *12 SO97*
Situated on high ground between the Clent and Lickey Hills, Romsley includes the 12th- to 15th-c chapel of St Kenelm. A fine 12th-c doorway surmounted by a carving is one of the features displayed by the latter.

ROOKLEY, Isle of Wight *7 SZ58*
About 1m NW across the River Medina is 18th-c Gatcombe House (NT). Sheat Manor is of Jacobean origin (NT).

ROSEDALE ABBEY, N Yorks *22 SE79*
Scanty remains of the 12th-c priory lie between lofty moors in the picturesque Rosedale Valley. The lonely Ralph Cross lies on high moors in the North Yorks Moors national park, some 5m NW. White Cross, or Fat Betty, is another old cross existing in the area.

ROSSENDALE
Formerly a large forest, Rossendale now forms a partly moorland and partly industrialized area in the triangle of Lancashire bounded by Burnley, Rawtenstall, and Bacup.

ROSS-ON-WYE, Herefs & Worcs *12 SO62*
Ross-on-Wye is an excellent touring centre for the Wye Valley, and is situated in a district which has been locally known as Archenfield since Saxon times. The town stands on a bend of the river, and offers a fine view from The Prospect – which adjoins the churchyard. The decorated and perpendicular church houses Rudhall monuments, and the churchyard cross recalls a plague of 1637.

A 17th-c market hall (AM) stands in High Street, opposite the residence of John Kyrle. The latter was called the Man of

Richly carved capital from Romsey Abbey

Ross by Alexander Pope, and was a local philanthropist who gave Ross-on-Wye its first public water supply. A round tower stands near the site of a former bishop's palace. Five sets of almshouses include Webb's Hospital and Rudhall's, which dates from the 17thc. The Ross Spur M50 motorway gives access to the town from the M5. Picturesquely timbered 16th-c Wythall lies 3m SSW near Walford, and 18th-c Hill Court stands in the area.

ROSTHERNE, Cheshire *17 SJ78*
This attractive village is situated near well-known Rostherne Mere, now a national nature reserve. Interesting monuments are housed within the church, which also displays an entrance dated 1640.

ROSTHWAITE, Cumbria *21 NY21*
Fine mountain views can be enjoyed from this Borrowdale village, which is set in the Lake District national park. The valley of Langstrath Beck lies S and separates 2,560ft Glaramara from 1,873ft Eagle Crag.

ROTHBURY, Northumberland *27 NU00*
Picturesquely situated on the River Coquet and backed by Simonside Hill, Rothbury includes a rebuilt church which is noted for its fine font. This particular feature has a stem fashioned from a carved pre-Conquest cross, surmounted by a bowl of 1664. Cragside is a modern mansion in magnificent grounds (OACT). Across the river is the former rectory, incorporating partly 14th-c Whitton Tower.

ROTHERFIELD, E Sussex *9 TQ52*
This pleasant village is sited at an altitude of more than 500ft, and is at the source of the River Rother. The fine church carries a tall shingled spire, and houses a 17th-c carved pulpit, a font cover of 1533, and old choir stalls. Dr Jex Blake, who became the first lady doctor in 1877, spent her last 12 years in the village.

ROTHERFIELD GREYS, Oxon *8 SU78*
The restored early-English church contains a notable 14th-c brass. The interesting Knollys Chapel of 1605 contains fine tombs. Greys Court is an Elizabethan and modernized house which stands in the quadrangle of an earlier castle. It includes a 200ft-deep well, and is associated with the legend of the Mistletoe Bough Chest. This is a sad tale about a bride who hid in a chest during Christmastide festivities, and was unable to get out (NT, OACT). This legend is also applied to a house in the village of Minster Lovell.

ROTHERHAM, S Yorks *18 SK49*
An old bridge with a restored 15th-c chapel (AM) spans the River Don in this industrial town. The fine perpendicular church features a lofty spire plus good bench-ends and stalls. Clifton Park stands in its own park, and was designed in 1782 by Carr of York. It now contains a museum. Wentworth Woodhouse is a palatial 18th-c mansion set in a great park 5m NW, with one of the longest frontages in England. Hoober Stand rises to 100ft and was erected in honour of King George II in 1748. Keppel's Pillar is about 150ft high and was raised to England's naval glory in the late 18thc.

ROTHLEY, Leics *18 SK51*
Rothley Temple is an Elizabethan house which incorporates part of an ancient religious building. Lord Macaulay was born in the house in 1800.

ROTHWELL, Northants *13 SP88*
Thousands of bones and skulls lie in the crypt of the 13th- to 15th-c church. The fine Elizabethan market house was built by Sir Thomas Tresham, and completed from the original plans by the late J A Gotch (AM). The hospital is a picturesque Elizabethan building, and the manor house dates from the Queen Anne period. Elizabethan Rushton Hall was also the work of Tresham (OACT), and the surrounding park contains the curious and unique Triangular Lodge (AM).

ROTTINGDEAN, E Sussex *8 TQ30*
Rudyard Kipling, whose works included the famous *Jungle Book*, lived at The Elms. The church has windows by Burne-Jones, who is buried in the churchyard, and he lived in a house at North End. A few old houses remain in the High Street and The Grange is now a museum of toys. An 18th-c smock mill is sited on the South Downs behind the village. Famous Roedean girls' school lies 2m NW near St Dunstan's Training Home of 1939.

ROUS LENCH, Herefs & Worcs *12 SP05*
Half-timbered cottages and an old manor house which is famous for its clipped yews are features of this village. The partly 12th-c church displays a richly-carved Norman south doorway.

ROWLANDS CASTLE, Hants *8 SU71*
Only the earthworks remain from a castle that once stood in this Forest of Bere village. Red Hill is an area on the SW outskirts, where a pillar records the review of second world war invasion troops prior to D-day by King George VI.

ROWLSTONE, Herefs & Worcs *11 SO32*
Rich Norman carvings, including several curiously reversed figures of saints, can be seen in the church. Also of special interest are unique 14th-c carved-iron candle brackets.

ROWSLEY, Derbyshire *18 SK26*
Rowsley lies in the Peak District national park and includes a 17th-c bridge spanning the Wye. Although the railway is now closed, a station of 1849 by Sir Joseph Paxton still stands. The beautiful stone-built Peacock Inn dates from 1652.

ROWTON MOOR, Cheshire *17 SJ46*
A Civil War battle was fought near here in 1644. Saighton Grange lies 2m SSW, and is a fine house which dates partly from c1489 but includes modern additions.

ROYDON, Essex *8 TL40*
St Peter's Church houses a good font of c1300, and the parish cage, stocks, and whipping post have been preserved. Ruined Nether Hall is of Tudor origin and belonged to the Colt family. This and a neighbouring timber-framed Tudor farmhouse stand 1½m SW.

ROYSTON, Herts *14 TL34*
Royston Downs extend W from here, and Royston itself lies at the crossing of the ancient Icknield Way and Ermine Street. The restored partly 13th-c church houses several brasses. Royston Cave is situated near the post office and contains curious figures. Old houses and inns of the town are noteworthy.

ROYSTON, S Yorks *22 SE31*
Built originally by the monks of Monk Bretton Priory, the church carries a splendid 15th-c tower which is noted for its rare pentagon-shaped oriel window.

RUARDEAN, Glos *12 SO61*
The 180ft 15th-c tower and spire of the church forms a local landmark in the surrounding Forest of Dean national forest park. A carved Norman doorway in the church has a well-preserved tympanum.

RUDFORD, Glos *12 SO72*
Windows, a south doorway, and a chancel arch — all of Norman date — are preserved in the little local church. A cross commemorating a battle of 1643 lies NW at Barber's Bridge, on the River Leadon. Thomas Gambier and Sir Hubert Parry are associated with 17th-c Highnam Court, which lies 2m SE.

RUDGWICK, W Sussex *8 TQ03*
Attractive old cottages and houses exist in this Wealden village, and the 14th-c church retains a 13th-c tower. Naldrett House and Garlands are among the best of the farms, and lie a little to the S.

RUDSTON, Humberside *23 TA06*
A Roman villa was excavated here in 1933, the fine pavements from which were later transferred to a museum in Hull. The Norman to decorated church has a beautiful chancel. An enormous monolith stands in the churchyard, and the village was once the home of novelist Winifred Holtby.

RUDYARD, Staffs *18 SJ95*
Rudyard Kipling's first name was taken from here, and Rudyard reservoir extends N for 2m from the village.

RUFFORD, Lancs *21 SD41*
The old hall (NT) is a fine Tudor and later black-and-white building displaying notable woodwork, a great hall, and a museum (OACT).

RUFUS STONE, Hants *7 SU21*
William Rufus was slain by an arrow from an unknown assailant in this part of the New Forest in 1100. Sir Walter Tyrrell has been suspected by tradition, although there is no proof of his guilt. The tree which deflected the arrow has long-since perished, but a stone marks the spot.

RUGBY, Warwickshire *13 SP57*
Important railway and engineering works are situated here, and Rugby is also a noted hunting centre. The famous public school was founded in 1567, and Rugby football originated here in 1823. A statue in the school commemorates Thomas Hughes (1822 to 1896), the author of *Tom Brown's Schooldays*. Rugby station was renamed Mugby Junction in one of Dickens' works.

The restored parish church has both a 14th-c tower and a modern tower and spire. The RC Church of St Marie is by Pugin and displays a 200ft spire. Rupert Brooke the poet was born at Rugby in 1887. Masts of the GPO radio station form a notable landmark to the E of the town. They rise to a height of 820ft and are said to comprise the tallest structure in Britain.

RUGELEY, Staffs *18 SK01*
Wooded Cannock Chase lies to the W of this Trent-Valley town. William Palmer, a notorious poisoner, lived here and was hanged in 1856. The partly-demolished Elizabethan house of Beaudesert stands in a large park 4m SSE.

RUISLIP, Gt London *8 TQ08*
Woods and a common help to keep this residential area from becoming too urbanized. A local reservoir is partly protected as a nature reserve, and partly developed as a Lido offering facilities for boating, bathing, and water ski-ing. The restored church contains a four-shelved bread cupboard of 1697 and some 15th-c wall-paintings.

RUNCORN, Cheshire *17 SJ58*
Runcorn is situated on the River Mersey, and was connected to Widnes by a transporter bridge before the new road bridge was built. Large chemical and alkali works exist here, and a New Town is being developed in the area.

RUNSWICK BAY, N Yorks *23 NZ81*
A steep winding descent leads to a rocky and sandy beach, offering bathing and fishing. Kittle Ness, a headland across the bay to the E, is a notable viewpoint.

RUSCOMBE, Berks *8 SU77*
William Penn the founder of Pennsylvania died here in 1718. The actual house is no longer standing. The church displays a 17th-c tower and brick-built nave, but the flint chancel is of 13th-c workmanship.

RUSHBROOKE, Suffolk *15 TL86*
Old woodwork is preserved in the church, plus the only known example of the Royal Arms of King Henry VIII to exist in this type of building. The former hall is no longer standing.

RUSHBURY, Salop *17 SO59*
This delightful Apedale village is situated on the slopes of Wenlock Edge. A rare partly 13th-c house, which was formerly the home of a King's Forester, lies 2m S in the grounds of a farm at Upper Millichope.

RUSHDEN, Northants *13 SP96*
Footwear is manufactured in this Nene-Valley town. The beautiful decorated and perpendicular church carries a fine tower and spire, and displays a curious strainer arch in the nave.

RUSPER, W Sussex *8 TQ23*
Several old cottages in this attractive village are of half-timbered and tile-hung construction. A massive 16th-c church tower is notable, and the last traces of a Benedictine monastery that once stood here vanished in 1781.

RUSTINGTON, W Sussex *8 TQ00*
Sir Hubert Parry lived in this pleasant village and died here in 1918. The Norman to early-English church carries a fine tower.

RUYTON-OF-THE-ELEVEN-TOWNS, Salop *17 SJ32*
The old manor that existed here formerly comprised eleven townships and gained a charter in 1301. The church has an early-Norman chancel, and very slight remains of the former castle exist in the churchyard. Also of interest is a sundial of 1725. Telford built the bridge which spans the River Perry.

RYDAL, Cumbria *21 NY30*
Rydal lies at the E end of Rydalwater in the Lake District national park; the River Rothay links Rydalwater to the larger Windermere, and the area is dominated by Nab Scar and Loughrigg Fell. Wordsworth lived at Rydal Mount for thirty-seven years, and died there in 1850 (OACT). Dora's Field is famous for its daffodils and was given to Dora, nee Wordsworth, by her famous father. Rydal Falls are included in the grounds of the hall. Nab Cottage, dated 1702, is associated with De Quincey and Hartley Coleridge.

RYDE, Isle of Wight *7 SZ59*
This well-known resort overlooks the Solent and offers excellent sands, bathing, and fishing. Views of the mainland are afforded by a nearby hilltop, and regattas are held here. The railway to Shanklin has been electrified, utilizing ex-London-Transport rolling stock. The new and interesting Norman Ball Collection of veteran and vintage cars exists at the airport (OACT).

RYE, E Sussex *9 TQ92*
Although one of the two Ancient Towns attached to the original Cinque Ports, Rye is now some 2m inland from the

receding sea. It is a picturesque hill town with steep cobbled streets, and is sited on the River Rother. Its associations with the sea have by no means ended, and a new quay for cargo vessels has recently been constructed at Rye Harbour, on the narrow estuary.

The Norman to perpendicular church has good screens, and a notable clock with a curious free-swinging pendulum dating from 1560. Remains of a friar's chapel now form the Church House. Peacock's School, associated with Thackeray's *Denis Duval*, dates from 1636. Old houses can be seen in Mermaid Street, Church Square Watchbell Street, and High Street. Particularly noteworthy buildings include Stone House, the restored 15th-c Old Hospital, St Anthony's, and Fletcher's House. Lamb House is a lovely 18th-c building where Henry James lived from 1898 until his death in 1916. (NT, OACT). The arcaded town hall dates from 1742 to 1744. The Mermaid Hotel of 1420, and the Old Flushing Inn are of interest.

The fine Landgate dates from the 14th-c and is the sole remaining town gate (AM). Ypres Tower was a prison and now houses a museum. A rebuilt windmill and a martello tower also exist here. The Royal Military Canal extends NE from Rye, towards Walland Marsh on the Kentish border. It was originally built as a defence against an expected Napoleonic invasion.

RYHALL, Leicester 19 TF01
The fine church is of 13th- to 14th-c date, and carries a notable west tower and spire. Elizabethan and later Toletethorpe Hall has a medieval gatehouse.

RYKNILD, (or ICKNIELD) STREET
This Roman road starts in the Cotswolds at a point N of Bourton-on-the-Water. It runs to Cow Honeybourne, where it is known as Buckle Street, and then passes through Bidford-on-Avon to reach Alcester. Beyond Alcester is a section known as Haydon Way. It was formerly joined by a branch from Worcester near the outskirts of Birmingham. It then ran N to cross Watling Street at Wall and continued NE in a straight line towards Derby, partly on the line of the present A38. Beyond here the route is uncertain, but it may have extended as far N as Aldborough in North Yorkshire, just off the Great North Road.

RYME INTRINSICA, Dorset 6 ST51
The church in this curiously-named village bears the rare dedication of St Hippolyte, and displays a nave and tower of c1530. Old thatched cottages can be seen in the village.

RYSTON, Norfolk 14 TF60
Kett's Oak recalls the ill-fated rising of 1549. The hall dates from the 17thc, and the partly-Norman church houses monuments to the Pratts.

RYTON, Tyne & Wear 27 NZ16
Collieries exist in the vicinity of this attractive Tyneside village. A notable 120ft spire dating from the 13thc is a feature of the local church, which contains fine 17th-c woodwork.

RYTON-ON-DUNSMORE, Warwickshire 13 SP37
A police training college is situated here. The church has a 14th-c tower, Norman doorways, and a curious brass showing a skeleton and coffin. Knightlow Hill lies 1m SE; it is here, in a field off the Daventry road, that the 14th-c Wroth Silver stone is sited. The annual Wroth Silver payment to the Lord of the Manor is made by 25 parishes of the Knightlow Hundred every St Martin's Day. Farther SE is Dunsmore Heath, where the Earl of Warwick is supposed to have slain the fabulous Dun Cow.

SAFFRON WALDEN, Essex 14 TL53
This delightful town once specialized in the growing of a saffron crocus – in autumn. A number of Georgian houses of timbered, brick, plastered, and pargetted construction exist here, and the former Sun Inn is outstanding (NT). Timbered Cross Keys Inn and the restored Rose and Crown, with its Shakespearean associations, are both attractive. Slight remains of a 12th-c castle are of interest, and the local common includes a maze.

The very fine perpendicular church displays an imposing nave, interesting monuments and brasses, and a lofty spire which was added in 1831. The museum exhibits items of anthropological and archaeological interest. Magnificent 17th-c Audley End is a mansion lying 1m W (AM). It is only a portion of the original structure, and stands in a superb lake-watered park (OACT). Old almshouses at nearby Audley End have been restored as St Mark's College. Hales Wood, now a national nature reserve, lies 3m NE on the Ashdon road.

ST AGNES, Cornwall 4 SW75
A sandy beach and sea bathing are among the natural facilities offered by this resort. Trevaunance Cove is attractive and the majority of the coastal scenery is very fine – in spite of several old mine workings. John Opie the painter was born here in 1761. The view from St Agnes Beacon (NT), which attains 700ft and is easily accessible from a motor road, is one of the most extensive in Cornwall.

ST ALBANS, Herts 8 TL10
Plan overleaf
Important remains of the Roman town *Verulamium* exist mainly in a public park, and include an amphitheatre, a good modern museum, and a hypocaust (AM, OACT).

The fascinating cathedral has an exceptionally long nave and dates originally from the Norman period. Considerable restorations by Lord Grimthorpe in 1879 include the Victorian west façade. Roman bricks and tiles have been used in the main fabric of the building and the massive tower. Of particular interest are the remains of wall-paintings, the Shrine of St Alban, the watching loft, and the restored 15th-c screen. The 14th-c abbey gateway is part of the ancient St Alban's School; both this and an ancient clock tower are of note.

Several fine old almshouses include the notable Marlborough group of 1736. The ancient Fighting Cocks Inn is one of the oldest in the country, and there are numerous good Georgian houses in the city. Romeland House is one of the finest of the latter. Fishpool Street contains many old houses, and the City Museum describes the natural history and geology of SW Hertfordshire.

Among the old churches that exist here are: perpendicular St Peter's, with old glass; St Stephen's, displaying a little Norman work and an inscribed 16th-c lectern; St Michael's, with its well-known monument to Francis Bacon. Bacon died here in 1626 and lived at Gorhambury House. Ruins of the old house exist near the present late 18th-c mansion (OACT). To the S lie slight remains of Sopwell Nunnery. Two great battles in the Wars of the Roses were fought at St Albans in 1455 and 1461.

ST ANTHONY-IN-ROSELAND, Cornwall 4 SW83
This settlement stands on a creek of the Percuil river opposite St Mawes, with Zone Point to the S. Nearby St Anthony Head (NT) is just one part of the fine coast scenery that can be enjoyed hereabouts.

ST AUSTELL, Cornwall 4 SX05
China clay is extracted and worked in this area. The 13th-c and later church carries a fine perpendicular tower and displays a carved Norman font with a modern cover. The Market House of 1791, the Menagew Stone in Fore Street, and the Menacuddle Holy Well are of interest. St Austell Bay and the small

15th-c Old Hospital, Rye

port of Charlestown lies to the SE, and extensively sandy beaches are available – particularly at Carlyon Bay.

ST BEES, Cumbria *20 NX91*
Fine cliffs exist near St Bees Head, and bathing sands are offered by this small resort. The grammar school was founded in the 16thc and the restored church preserves a fine Norman doorway.

ST BLAZEY, Cornwall *4 SX05*
Monuments housed in the restored church are of interest. Beautifully wooded Luxulyan Valley is spanned by the 660ft-long 100ft-high Treffry Viaduct of 1839 and lies 4m NW.

ST BRIAVELS, Glos *12 SO50*
Bread and cheese is traditionally distributed among the local people on Whit Sunday after the service. The church is of Norman and later origin. The keep of the restored castle fell in 1752; the structure itself dates from the 12thc and is now a Youth Hostel. Wide views towards the Wye Valley and the Forest of Dean national forest park are available from here, and the castle was the Norman administrative centre of the forest.

SAINTBURY, Glos *12 SP13*
This lovely Cotswold village lies below the high ridge of the escarpment, and includes an old cross. The spired church shows a Saxon mass dial and preserves old glass in the east window.

ST BURYAN, Cornwall *4 SW42*
The 15th-c church has a fine tower which is a known local landmark. Older parts of the carved screen can be considered the finest in Cornwall, and a 13th-c monument bears an inscription in Norman-French. The stone circle of Boscawen-un, known locally as the Nine Maidens, lies 2m NE off the Penzance road (AM).

ST CLEER, Cornwall *5 SX26*
Situated on the edge of Bodmin moor at an altitude of 700ft, St Cleer affords wide views over the surrounding district. The church carries a fine 15th-c tower and a wooden chancel arch. A good example of a Cornish Holy Well can also be seen. Picturesque Golitha Falls are on the River Fowey, and Trethevy Quoit and King Donert's Stone stand near by (AM). The Hurlers lie 3m NW, and Cheesewring ½m farther in the same direction; both are curious rock groups.

ST COLUMB MAJOR, Cornwall *4 SW96*
The mainly 14th-c church carries a fine tower, houses old bench-ends, and contains the Arundell brasses. An old moated rectory in the area is of interest.

ST COLUMB MINOR, Cornwall *4 SW86*
The fine 13th- to 14th-c church tower is one of the tallest in the county. Rialton is a 15th-c monastic manor house which now serves as a farm, and has a holy well in the courtyard. The old millhouse is notable.

ST ENDELLION, Cornwall *4 SW97*
Quaint ringers' rhymes are displayed on an 18th-c panel under the tower arch of the old church, and the wagon roofs are enriched with angel carvings. The village itself lies inland from Port Isaac and Portquin Bay.

ST GERMANS, Cornwall *5 SX35*
This St Germans-River town lies amid lovely woodland scenery. Norman work is preserved on the west front and carved porch of the church, which until the mid 11thc was the Cathedral of Cornwall. The nearby mansion of Port Eliot was built by Sir John Soane in the early 19thc. Unusual open galleries below a row of gables can be seen on old almshouses.

ST HELENS, Merseyside *17 SJ59*
Glass-making and coal-mining are the main industries with which this town is involved. The Pilkington Glass Museum is of exceptional interest. Sir Thomas Beecham, the famous musical conductor, was born here in 1897.

ST IPPOLLITTS, Herts *14 TL12*
Also known under the name Ippollitts – without the St prefix – this rare dedication is said to refer to a saint skilled in the treatment of horses. The rebuilt church is of mainly decorated and perpendicular origin, and houses an interesting brass of 1594. The Olive Branch is an attractive half-timbered inn.

ST IVES, Cambs *14 TL37*
This River-Ouse town has a 15th-c bridge (AM) and a rare restored bridge chapel. A statue of Cromwell can be seen on Market Hill, and the ex-Lord Protector is also associated with an old barn which stands in the area. A fine collection of local items can be seen in the Norris museum. The perpendicular church has a rebuilt spire which was erected after an aircraft crashed into the old one. Well-known St Ives Fair first took place in 1110.

ST IVES, Cornwall *4 SW54*
St Ives is a well-known resort with a harbour which is especially popular with artists. Excellent Porthminster sands lie ½m SE. The 15th-c church carries a tower rising to almost 120ft, and a lantern cross can be seen in the churchyard. Old houses and quaint alleys add to the interest of the town, and the Barnes museum of photography is of note. Smeaton designed the pier, and a hill to the SE bears the pyramidal Knill monument of 1782. This was raised by a former mayor. A number of prehistoric remains and cromlechs exist in the neighbourhood.

ST JOHNS, Isle of Man *20 SC28*
The world's largest open-air parliament is held on Tynwald Hill, and the Manx laws are proclaimed annually on July 5. A Manx national shrine is planned for the village. Picturesque Glen Helen lies 2m N.

1 Cathedral
2 City Museum
3 Fighting Cocks Inn
4 Gorhambury House
5 Marlborough Almshouses
6 Roman Remains and Museum
7 Romeland House
8 Sopwell Nunnery Remains
9 St Michael's Church
10 St Peter's Church
11 St Stephen's Church

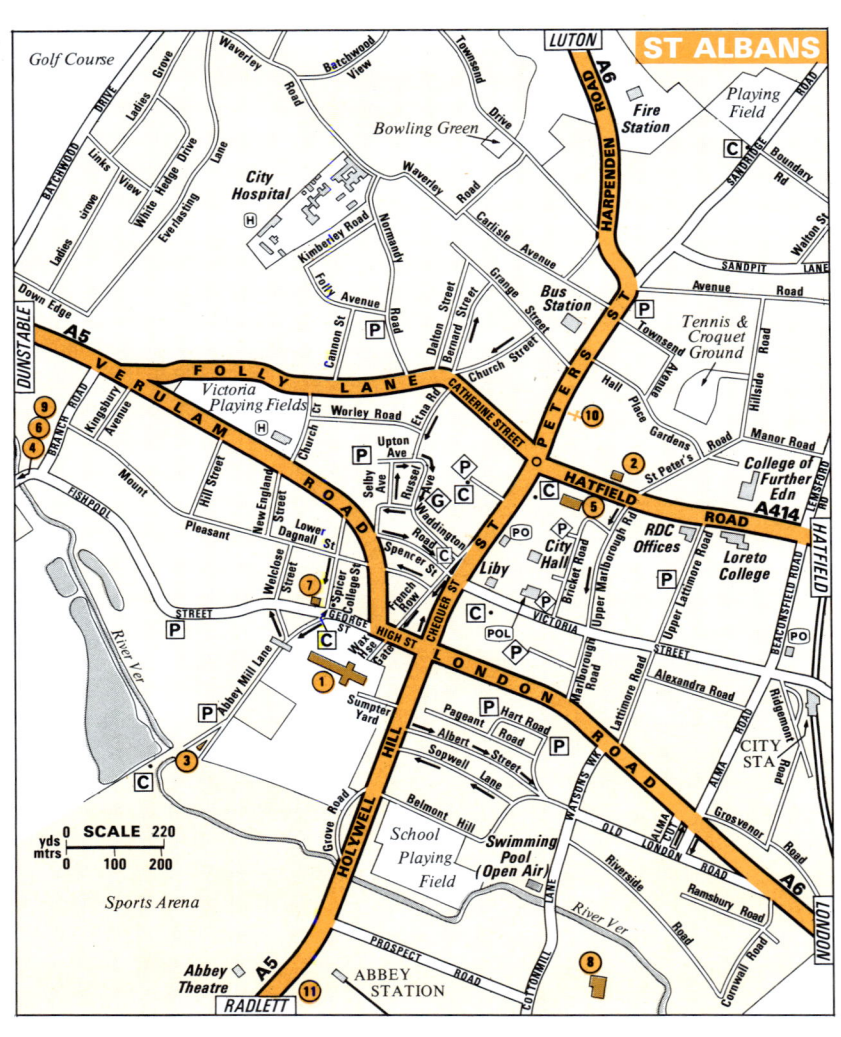

ST JULIOT, Cornwall 4 SX19
This church is sited in the Valency Valley and was planned by Thomas Hardy while he was studying as an architect. Some of his sketches can be seen on the walls, and two old crosses exist in the churchyard.

ST JUST, Cornwall 4 SW33
Land's End airport lies near this village, which is also known as St Just-in-Penwith. A notable wall-painting can be seen in the old church, plus a 5th- or 6th-c inscribed stone found near Cape Cornwall. Ancient tin mines lie NW at Botallack, and the dangerous Brisons Rocks lie off Cape Cornwall to the NW. The headland forms a splendid viewpoint.

ST JUST-IN-ROSELAND, Cornwall 4 SW83
A creek of the Carrick Roads adds even more charm to this village's beautiful setting. The 15th-c church has one of the loveliest churchyards in England, containing masses of flowering shrubs and trees.

ST KEVERNE, Cornwall 4 SW72
The 13th- to 15th-c church carries a rare Cornish spire. Porthoustock lies 1¾m NE, with Manacle Point to the SE and the dreaded Manacles Rocks offshore. The Post Office Satellite Tracking Station stands on Goonhilly Downs in the Lizard Peninsula, and a nearby bronze-age burial chamber known as the Three Brothers of Grugwith is the largest of its kind in Cornwall (AM).

ST KEW HIGHWAY, Cornwall 4 SX07
St Kew village lies a little to the N. The church has good wagon roofs and is noted for its 15th-c stained glass. A rare inscribed Ogham stone is of interest, and the tall vicarage is of Georgian origin. Trewarne is a fine 17th-c manor house to the NE.

ST LAWRENCE, Isle of Wight 7 SZ57
Before the addition of the chancel, the old church was one of the smallest in England. Picturesque Undercliff, one of the best known pieces of coastal scenery on the island, lies near the coast. King Charles II landed 2m SW at Puckaster Cove during a storm in 1675.

ST LEONARDS-ON-SEA, E Sussex 9 TQ80
This resort offers a shingle and sand beach and is now part of Hastings.

ST LEVAN, Cornwall 4 SW32
The local church is dedicated to St Selevan and contains a Norman font and old woodwork. Porthgwarra Cove is reached by a lane leading off the Land's End road, and provides access to the spectacular granite headland of Tolpedn-Penwith. Also known as the Chair Ladder, the latter is well known among sea-cliff rock climbers. A notable blow-hole can also be seen here.

ST MARGARET-AT-CLIFFE, Kent 9 TR34
Situated on 400ft cliffs above St Margaret's Bay, this village includes a church which is considered a very notable example of late Norman work. Of particular interest are the nave, tower, doorways, and chancel arch. Early ship carvings exist on some of the piers in the nave. The last windmill to be erected in Kent stands here and dates from 1929. Dover Patrol Memorial stands on the cliffs, and the South Foreland lighthouse lies 1½m S.

ST MAWES, Cornwall 4 SW83
Beautifully situated on the Roseland peninsula, St Mawes faces Falmouth across the Carrick Roads; it is linked to the latter by passenger ferry. The Percuil River winds inland to the E, and the resort offers good sands and yachting. King Henry VIII built the castle as a coastal blockhouse in 1542 (AM).

ST MAWGAN-IN-PYDAR, Cornwall 4 SW86
The 13th-c and later church displays notable bench-ends, Arundell brasses, and carvings. Elizabethan Lanherne lies 1m N and was formerly the home of the Arundells. It now houses a convent. A richly-decorated cross stands near the entrance.

ST MELLION, Cornwall 5 SX36
Interesting monuments to the Corytons exist in the church. Early 19th-c Pentillie Castle includes a Regency estate office and lies SE near the River Tamar. A former owner of the castle was buried N of the house in a tower on Mount Ararat.

ST MERRYN, Cornwall 4 SW87
A finely-carved font standing in St Marina's Church was originally housed in the ruined church of St Constantine. Medieval Cataclewse quarry is famous for the quality of its stone. Parish stocks have been preserved.

ST MICHAEL'S MOUNT, Cornwall 4 SW53
Situated ¾m offshore from Marazion in Mount's Bay, this famous Cornish feature can be reached by foot via a causeway at certain times, or by boat. The castle which stands at the 250ft summit displays a 14th-c chapel and contains a collection of armour and furniture (NT, OACT). Below this is the village and a small harbour.

ST NEOT, Cornwall 5 SX16
Bodmin Moor rises behind this St Neot-River village. The church is famous for some of the finest 15th-c painted glass in England, and an old well is of interest.

ST NEOTS, Cambs 14 TL16
One of the finest towers in the county is carried by the notable 15th-c church, and well-carved roofs can be seen inside. The attractive market square contains old houses and inns. Neighbouring Eynesbury lies S and includes a church noted for its old bench-ends and 17th-c tower.

ST NICHOLAS-AT-WADE, Kent 9 TR26
Features of the restored church include a prominent decorated tower, carved Norman nave capitals, a pulpit of 1615, and several notable brasses. Attractive Dutch-gabled brick cottages and several old barns exist in the area.

ST OSYTH, Essex 9 TM11
St Osyth lies on a creek of the River Colne. Remains of the 12th-c priory are incorporated in a 16th-c mainly-flint mansion, which also boasts an imposing gateway (OACT). A Lombardy poplar in the grounds is said to have been brought here from Italy by Lord Rochford in 1758. The local church carries a massive 15th-c tower, and contains a 16th-c nave, brick arches, and many effigies. Three Martello towers still stand in the vicinity. St Clairs, a moated house with a 15th-c gateway, stands 1m SE.

ST PAUL'S WALDEN, Herts 14 TL12
HM the Queen Mother was baptized in the restored 14th-c church. The chancel was remodelled in 1727 and has a notable screen. St Paul's Walden Bury mansion was built in 1765, and is partly by Robert Adam.

ST PETER'S, Kent 9 TR36
Originally built in 1070, the fine church includes a 15th-c chancel roof. Its 16th-c tower was used as a signalling station in Napoleonic days. The village is now linked to Broadstairs. Whitfield Tower lies N on the highest point of Thanet, and is a navigating beacon.

ST TUDY, Cornwall 4 SX07
The church of St Uda is noted for its three carved 16th- and 17th-c slate monuments. A rare carved Saxon tomb lid can also be seen. Captain Bligh of the Bounty was born at Tinten Manor, which now serves as a farm.

ST VEEP, Cornwall 4 SX15
An ancient British earthwork known as the Giant's Hedge runs through the parish. It stands at 7ft high in some

The harbour at St Ives (Cornwall)

places, and measures 20ft in width. Stocks are preserved in the 14th- to 15th-c church, which is dedicated to St Ciricus and St Julitta.

ST WEONARDS, Herefs & Worcs *12 SO42*
Mynors Chapel displays 16th-c glass, and the church itself carries a 15th-c tower. The 14th-c manor house of Treago lies about ½m SW.

SALCOMBE, Devon *5 SX73*
Salcombe is beautifully situated at the mouth of delightful Kingsbridge estuary, in the South Hams district. In includes a harbour and offers sea bathing from sandy beaches. J A Froude the historian is buried here. A passenger ferry links Salcombe with East Portlemouth, and a round tower from a ruined Tudor Castle is still standing. Splendid cliff scenery can be enjoyed 2½m S around Bolt Head (NT), beyond Starehole Bay and the Mew Stone. A 5m cliff walk from here to Bolt Tail (NT) is considered one of the finest in England.

SALFORD, Gt Manchester *17 SJ79*
Separated from Manchester by the River Irwell, Salford operates extensive docks on the Manchester Ship Canal and includes a university. A magnificent modern RC cathedral stands in the town, and the famous conductor Sir Charles Halle is buried here. Sir Edward Watkin, the originator of the projected Channel Tunnel, was born in the city.

Half-timbered Bull Inn and the old mansion of Kersal Cell are of interest. Ordsall Hall is of partly 15th-c origin and preserves much of its old timbering. It is associated with William Harrison Ainsworth's *Guy Fawkes*, and has recently been opened as a local museum. A replica of a coal mine was installed at the Buile Hill Park Science museum in 1958.

SALISBURY, Wilts *7 SU12*
Thomas Hardy called this famous city Melchester in his novels. The River Avon runs through Salisbury, and the cathedral was started in 1220 – following the abandonment of Old Sarum.

It is almost entirely built in the early-English style; the upper part of the tower and the spire are of the decorated period. The combination of tower and spire rise to 404ft – higher than any other similar structure in England. A dial-less clock dates from 1326 and is probably the oldest in this country. The latter has been restored. A copy of Magna Carta is kept in the library. This building, the chapter house, and the cloisters are particularly notable.

The Close is considered the best in the country, and contains houses of various styles from the 14th to 18thc. Especially notable are the King's House, Maimesbury House (OACT), the College of Matrons, and Mompesson House (NT, OACT). The North Canonry and Old Deanery are well-known for their gardens (OACT), and Bishop's Palace is now the Choir School. The Meridian stone in the wall of the close was executed by Wren while engaged in restoring the cathedral.

Poultry Cross (AM) is of the 14thc, and several old gates and bridges exist in the city. Joiners' Hall (NT) dates from the 16thc, John Halle's House from the 15thc, and the Church House in Crane Street is of late perpendicular style. Salisbury includes many old inns; the Haunch of Venison, the half-timbered Rose and Crown, and the staircase of the former Plume of Feathers are all notable. John a Port's House is a 15th-c timber-framed structure.

St Thomas's Church is of early-English to perpendicular style and contains a fine doom painting. St Martin's Church exhibits the same period styles and houses beautiful modern painted glass. St Edmund's Church is a perpendicular structure with a tower of 1655. The guildhall dates back to 1797, and the fine Council House is of 18th-c origin. Salisbury and South Wilts museum contains extremely interesting displays. Holy Trinity Hospital is a rebuilt 18th-c structure, and the old Hospital of St Nicholas stands near the ancient Harnham Bridge. Picturesque Harnham Mill is situated on the River Nadder.

A famous view across the Avon to the cathedral can be enjoyed from the bridge. Scanty remains of the once-famous Clarendon Palace exist 2m ESE, and Saxon burials were excavated here between 1949 and 1951. A racecourse lies in the area.

SALISBURY PLAIN
Most of this undulating plateau is under cultivation, but parts around Bulford and Tidworth have been given over to military use. The plain extends towards Salisbury from Pewsey Vale, and includes chalk downs, ancient trackways, and prehistoric remains. The most spectacular of the latter is, of course, Stonehenge. Attractive river valleys of the Avon, Bourne, and Wylye lie on the fringe of the plain, and main roads from Amesbury to Devizes and Warminster allow an appreciation of some of the area's most characteristic scenery.

SALKELD, GREAT, Cumbria *26 NY53*
A fortified 14th-c tower carried by the local church is one of several to be seen in this once-lonely part of the country. Such defences were required for protection against frequent raids from the Scottish side of the nearby border. The River Eden flows to the W.

SALLE, Norfolk *15 TG12*
Perhaps the finest period church in Norfolk exists here, but it is now isolated and lacks a congregation to fill it. It is of perpendicular date, carries a lofty tower, and displays a finely carved nave roof and font cover. Pronounced Saul.

1	Cathedral
2	Choir School (Bishop's Palace)
3	Church House
4	Clarendon Palace Remains
5	College of Matrons
6	Council House
7	Guildhall
8	Harnham Bridge and Hospital of St Nicholas
9	Harnham Mill
10	Haunch of Venison Inn
11	Holy Trinity Hospital
12	John a Port's House
13	John Halle's House
14	Joiners' Hall
15	King's House
16	Malmesbury House
17	Mompesson House
18	Museum
19	North Canonry
20	Old Deanery
21	Plume of Feathers
22	Poultry Cross
23	Racecourse
24	Rose and Crown Inn
25	St Edmund's Church
26	St Martin's Church
27	St Thomas's Church

SALTAIRE, W Yorks *22 SE13*
Saltaire was founded by Sir Titus Salt as an Aire-Valley New Town for the manufacture of alpaca, in 1850. A stone lion by Milnes exists here, and was originally intended for London's Trafalgar Square.

SALTASH, Cornwall *5 SX45*
Rivers Tamar and Tavy meet to the N of Saltash, and the area is dominated by Brunel's great Royal Albert Bridge of 1859. The ferry to St Budeaux in Devon has been replaced by a road bridge which was opened in 1961. Old houses still exist here, and a partly-Norman church houses a fine silver chalice of Tudor origin. Mainly-perpendicular St Stephens Church lies 1m W and contains a Norman font. Shillingham lies SW and dates from c1700. Remains of Trematon Castle include a roofless keep, and a modern house is built within the ancient walls. Brick-built Ince Castle is of 1540 and later date and stands 4m SW near the River Lynher.

SALTBURN-BY-THE-SEA, Cleveland *27 NZ62*
Excellent sands are a feature of this popular resort, and fine cliff scenery can be enjoyed in the district. A 90m footpath is planned for the area, and will take a coast and moorland route SE from here to Filey.

SALTDEAN, E Sussex *8 TQ30*
This small resort is built on chalk cliffs, and offers a rocky shingle beach and sea bathing. Other amenities include a bathing pool and golf course.

SALTERSGATE, N Yorks *23 SE89*
A peat fire which has been burning for over 100 years warms a lonely inn in this part of the North York Moors national park. A curious ravine known as the Hole of Horcum lies S near Bridestones Moor nature reserve (NT). and the long wooded gorge of Newtondale lies W. Pickering Beck and the revived Pickering to Grosmont railway run through the gorge, but it is not traversed by road. Fylingdales Moor extends to the NE.

SALTFLEETBY ALL SAINTS, Lincs *19 TF49*
Good screenwork and a 13th-c reredos can be seen in the church. A new nature reserve has been established along a sandy crest to the S.

SALTFORD, Avon *6 ST66*
Saltford lies on the River Avon and offers boating and golfing facilities. The restored Tudor manor house incorporates Norman work and is said to be the oldest inhabited house in old Somerset.

SALTON, N Yorks *22 SE77*
An exceptionally fine little Norman church can be seen in this Vale of Pickering village. The old parish chest displays 13th-c ironwork.

SALTWOOD, Kent *9 TR13*
The 12th- to 14th-c castle has been greatly restored and was where the murder of Thomas a Becket was planned in 1170. The mainly-Norman church contains a carved oak chest measuring some 8ft in length.

SALVINGTON, W Sussex *8 TQ10*
A fine post-mill near this South Downs village may have been the first to take out insurance against fire. One of its beams is said to carry the 1774 seal of the insurance company.

SAMLESBURY, Lancs *21 SD53*
A two-decker pulpit and many 17th- and 18th-c box-pews exist in the church, which was rebuilt in 1558. High Hall is a notable much-restored timber-framed house displaying a 15th-c hall and an interesting collection of old cabinets.

SAMPFORD COURTENAY, Devon *5 SS60*
This delightful village of cob and thatched cottages stands near the River Tawe and faces S towards 1,799ft Cawsand Beacon, in the Dartmoor national park. The perpendicular church has a pinnacled west tower.

SAMPFORD GREAT, Essex *14 TL63*
Great Sampford Church includes a splendid 14th-c chancel. Little Sampford is a neighbouring village which contains several fine old houses, the moated medieval manor house of Tewes, and two notable farms *ie* Oldhouse and Clockhouse.

SANCREED, Cornwall *4 SW42*
Part of a richly-carved screen and two beautifully decorated old crosses are features of the 14th-c church. The iron-age village site of Carn Euny, with an interesting *fogou* or subterranean hiding-hole, lies 1m W; S is the bronze-age standing stone known as the Blind Fiddler. Attractive Drift Reservoir and dam are situated E of Sancreed.

SANDBACH, Cheshire *17 SJ76*
Old black-and-white houses, notably the gabled Old Hall which now serves as an inn, exist in this salt-mining town. Two remarkable carved crosses which may date from the 7thc stand side by side in the market place. A public right of way runs through the arches of the restored perpendicular church's 19th-c tower.

SANDBANKS, Dorset *7 SZ08*
As implied by its name, this Poole-Harbour resort offers excellent sandy beaches. A car ferry connects Sandbanks with Shell Bay for Swanage and the Purbeck Hills.

SANDFORD ORCAS, Dorset *6 ST62*
The beautiful stone-built manor house includes a gatehouse and is of Elizabethan origin (OACT). Another lovely house of the period is Jerrards, and the 13th-c later church contains a fine monument to William Knoyle.

SANDFORD ST MARTIN, Oxon *13 SP42*
This attractive village includes an old manor house and a churchyard containing the curious tomb of Lord Deloraine, half-hidden in a grassy mound.

SANDGATE, Kent *9 TR23*
Good sea bathing from a pebble beach is offered by this resort. The reconstructed 16th-c castle was slightly damaged by the sea during gales. H G Wells wrote *Kipps* and *The History of Mr Polly* while living at Spade House (OACT).

SANDHURST, Berks *8 SU86*
The Royal Military Academy is situated here, and includes grounds containing the Victory Memorial from Luneburg Heath in Germany.

SANDON, Essex *9 TL70*
Sandon church is of 12th- to 16th-c date, and incorporates Roman tiles and bricks in its fabric. The fine south porch and massive west tower are fine examples of early brickwork. A huge oak is a feature of the village green.

SANDON, Staffs *18 SJ92*
The restored church is of mainly-decorated style and carries a 15th-c tower. Inside are a Jacobean pulpit and sounding board. Sandon Hall dates from the 19thc and stands in a large park. A 75ft column erected in honour of William Pitt the Younger stands in the park, and the gardens are particularly fine (OACT).

SANDOWN, Isle of Wight *7 SZ58*
An excellent sandy beach ensures constant popularity with holidaymakers. Culver Cliff is a prominent chalk formation standing 2½m NE, and the Yarborough monument stands NE on Bembridge Down. The Museum of Isle of Wight Geology is an interesting feature of the town, and a zoo exists in the area. An airport is situated near by.

SANDRIDGE, Herts *8 TL11*
The greatly restored church displays a chancel arch of Roman brick, 12th-c nave arcades, and a remarkable stone screen of 14th-c date.

SANDRINGHAM, Norfolk *14 TF62*
Sandringham House, the country residence of the Royal Family, is set in beautiful gardens (OACT) and dates from the 19thc. King George V died here in 1936, and King George VI in 1952. The Norwich entrance gates were given by the City of Norwich as a wedding present to Edward VII, then Prince of Wales, in 1863. A church in the park contains Royal memorials and a silver altar. More than 300 acres have been developed as a country park and a Big Game Museum is now open. A Royal Car museum exhibiting vintage Daimlers is also of interest.

SANDSEND, N Yorks *23 NZ81*
Situated in a picturesquely hilly setting, this small resort offers excellent sands and sea bathing. Remains of 11th-c Mulgrave Castle lie 1½m W in the grounds of a partly 18th-c house.

SANDWICH, Kent *9 TR35*
This River-Stour town is the oldest Cinque Port, but is now situated some 2m from the sea. The Barbican and Fishergate remain, and many old houses and inns can still be seen in the town. The guildhall dates from 1578 and St Bartholomew's Hospital guest house is of 15th-c date. Manwood Court dates from 1564, and the Old House is a fine Tudor building. St Mary's church preserves an ancient Peter's Pence box. St Clement's church shows a splendid Norman tower and displays carving of the same period. A famous golf course is sited here.

SANDY, Bedfordshire *14 TL14*
Low wooded hills rise to the E of this large River-Ivel village, and the Lodge bird reserve covers more than 100 acres (OACT). Hazells Hall is an 18th-c building displaying fine façades, which lies to the NE.

SANDY LANE, Wilts *7 ST96*
Features of this high-lying model village are its thatched cottages, an 18th-c inn, and a small thatched church. A Roman road in the neighbourhood became part of the later Wansdyke.

SANTON DOWNHAM, Suffolk *15 TL88*
Thetford Forest lies near this Breckland village, and the Forestry Commission headquarters is located here. A 2m forest trail has been laid out.

SAPPERTON, Glos *12 SO90*
Sapperton is beautifully situated at the head of the wooded Golden Valley, and the churchyard is so situated as to afford a good view of the area. Although the local church has been extensively rebuilt it still shows fine woodwork and several notable monuments. Characteristic Cotswold cottages are a common feature of the area. The disused 29m Thames-Severn canal passes through the parish in a 2½m-long tunnel. Lovely 14th- to 17th-c Daneway manor house is built of Cotswold stone and stands 1m NW.

SARNESFIELD, Herefs & Worcs *11 SO35*
The tower carried by the 13th-c church was formerly used as a dovecote, and contains over a hundred nesting-places. The tomb of 17th-c builder and craftsman John Abel can be seen in the churchyard.

SARRATT, Herts *8 TQ09*
This pleasant village includes a green, plus a partly late-Norman church displaying an unusual saddle-back tower.

SARRE, Kent *9 TR26*
Attractive Dutch-gabled houses can be seen in this Thanet village. Names of many well-known people are inscribed on the walls of the 16th-c Crown Inn, which is noted for the manufacture of cherry brandy.

SAUNTON SANDS, Devon *5 SS43*
Braunton Burrows lies E of this wide stretch of fine sands, and forms the habitat for numerous wild flowers and plants. They are of particular interest to botanists.

SAWBRIDGEWORTH, Herts *8 TL41*
Numerous monuments and brasses exist in the decorated and perpendicular church. A number of fine Georgian and older houses give this town its character, and Pishiobury – to the S – was by James Wyatt in 1782. Hyde Hall dates from 1806 and stands NE of the town.

SAWLEY, Derbyshire *18 SK43*
Features of Sawley church include a 15th-c spired tower, a Norman chancel arch, a stone screen, and interesting brasses and monuments to the Boothes. Rivers Trent and Derwent meet here, and there is a yacht marina at Shardlow.

SAWSTON, Cambs *14 TL44*
Monuments and brasses are preserved in the Norman to perpendicular church. Sawston Hall is an exceptionally fine 16th-c manor house containing a number of secret hiding-places. Mary Tudor took refuge here in 1553.

SAWTRY, Cambs *14 TL18*
This place is associated with William Sawtry. He was burnt at the stake for his beliefs in 1401, thus becoming one of the first English martyrs. A splendid brass of 1404 can be seen in the church.

SAXBY, Leics *19 SK82*
A Saxon cemetery has been found here, and the church and rectory both date from 1789.

SAXMUNDHAM, Suffolk *15 TM36*
A red-brick dovecote on Hunts Hall estate is the largest in Suffolk. The decorated and perpendicular church displays a good hammerbeam roof that was rediscovered quite recently. Knoddishall Red House lies 2½m E and is dated 1678.

SAXTHORPE, Norfolk *15 TG13*
Mannington Hall, a moated 15th-c flint house which is reputedly haunted, lies 2m NE on the River Bure. Cromwell is said to have stayed here. Wolterton Hall is a fine house dating partly from 1727, lying in fine gardens (OACT) 3m ENE.

SCARBOROUGH, N Yorks *23 TA08*
Scarborough is a very popular resort which is well-situated on two sandy bays divided by a headland. Ruins of the 12th-c castle (AM) form a fine viewpoint, and the largely early-English church contains interesting chantry chapels. Anne Brontë is buried in the churchyard. The King Richard III House and Wood End are of interest, and the latter now houses a museum.

Scarborough and St Thomas's museums are also of note. The Three Mariners was formerly an inn dating back to 1300, but is now a showplace. A planetarium is situated in the north gardens. Scarborough has associations with Smollett's *Humphrey Clinker*, and the town forms a good centre for touring the North York Moors national park; the Wolds; for tunny-fishing in the North Sea; and for the fine Yorkshire coastline.

SCARISBRICK, Lancs *21 SD31*
The ornate 19th-c hall was built by the Pugin and is a striking example of Victorian opulence. It now houses a school.

SCOLE, Norfolk *15 TM17*
The well-known White Hart is a fine old coaching house dating from 1655; its famous carved sign is unfortunately a thing of the past. Curious bottle cottages that exist here are associated with Waterloo.

SCORTON, N Yorks *22 NZ20*
Archery contests are held in this village, and the Jacobean Kiplin Hall lies some 3m SE. This house was the birthplace of Lord Baltimore, founder of the USA State of Maryland, and incorporates a naval museum with model ships on the lake (OACT).

SCOTT WILLOUGHBY, Lincs *19 TF03*
Materials from an older church were used to build the present gothic structure of 1826. It may well be the smallest church in the county.

SCROOBY, Notts *18 SK69*
William Brewster, the originator of the Pilgrim Fathers' movement, once lived in an old house of which scanty remains still exist. Wolsey stayed at the now-vanished palace of the Archbishops of York.

SCULTHORPE, Norfolk *15 TF83*
Features of the interesting church include a carved Norman font, a 14th-c tower, an organ case of 1756, several old brasses, and a Burne-Jones window. It was rebuilt by Sir Robert Knollys, a veteran of the Hundred Years War.

1 Castle Ruins
2 Church of St Mary
3 King Richard III House
4 Planetarium
5 Three Mariners Inn
6 Wood End (museum)

SCARBOROUGH

SCUNTHORPE, Humberside 23 SE81
Scunthorpe lies near the River Trent and is the centre of the extensive Frodingham iron and steel industry. The Regional Museum for north-west Lincolnshire is sited here.

SEAFORD, E Sussex 8 TV49
This resort has a shingle beach which gives way to sand at low tide. The restored Norman and early-English church carries a good partly-perpendicular tower. The Seven Sisters cliffs (NT) can be seen from the chalk cliff of Seaford Head. Lullington Heath nature reserve is situated in the neighbourhood, and the delightful South-Downs Cuckmere Valley is NE.

SEAHAM HARBOUR, Co Durham 27 NZ44
Seaham lies N of this important North-Sea coal port, and includes a church of Saxon and later date. The hall is from the late-Georgian period.

SEA HOUSES, Northumberland 27 NU23
Motor boats can be hired for visiting the Farne Islands bird sanctuary, now designated an area of outstanding natural beauty (NT). Sea Houses itself offers good sands and bathing.

SEATHWAITE, Cumbria 21 SD29
This remote little place is situated in the lovely Dunnerdale valley. The grave of Wonderful Walker, who was parson here for 67 years, can be seen in the churchyard. He was born in 1709 and is featured in Wordsworth's *Excursion*. Birks Bridge spans the River Duddon to the N of this village, and remote 2,140ft Harter Fell rises in the W. Steep Wrynose Pass lies at the head of the valley.

SEATOLLER, Cumbria 21 NY21
Seatoller lies on the River Derwent in the beautiful valley of Borrowdale, in the Lake District national park. Sprinkling Tarn has an average rainfall figure of over 185ins, and Seathwaite Farm (NT) – 2m farther – is one of the wettest inhabited places in England. The plumbago mine here was extensively worked in the 17th and 18thc. Honister Pass lies 2m W, at an altitude of 1,191ft. It leads to Buttermere and reaches a gradient of 1 in 4.

SEATON, Devon 6 SY29
A small resort in Lyme Bay, Seaton is situated on the estuary of the River Axe. There are fine cliff walks in the area and the beach is composed mainly of pebbles.

SEATON BURN, Northumberland 27 NZ27
Blagdon Hall is a late 18th-c house standing to the NW, off the Great North Road. Cale Cross, removed from Newcastle upon Tyne in 1807, stands near the north lodge.

SEATON CAREW, Cleveland 27 NZ52
Georgian houses exist in this resort, and the beach is composed of firm sand.

SEATON DELAVAL, Northumberland 27 NZ37
The Norman to 14th-c church retains its Norman chancel arch. Seaton Delaval Hall, an imposing 18th-c mansion which is considered to be Vanbrugh's masterpiece (OACT), lies 2m ENE.

SEATON ROSS, Humberside 23 SE74
A cottage in this village has a sundial which measures 12ft in diameter – perhaps the largest in England. Another sundial, dated 1825, can be seen on the church.

SEDBERGH, Cumbria 21 SD69
Moors and lofty fells ring the valley in which Sedbergh is sited. The restored church of trans-Norman to perpendicular date contains several fine monuments and good modern woodwork. The grammar school was first founded in the 15thc and is now a public school. A Friends Meeting House dating from 1675, which contains galleries on three sides, lies 1½m SW at Brigflatts. Partly 14th-c Middleton Hall stands 4½m SSW. Near by, on the W side of A683, is a 5ft inscribed cylindrical pillar which is thought to be a Roman milestone. Kirkby Stephen road is paralleled by the River Rawthey; 5m NE off the road are Cautley Crags with the noted Cautley Spout waterfall.

SEDGEBERROW, Herefs & Worcs 12 SP03
Old thatched and timber-framed cottages exist here. The 14th-c church was dedicated in 1331, and includes a strongly buttressed nave. Its large modern screen is also of interest.

SEDGEFIELD, Co Durham 27 NZ32
The main structure of the church is early-English, and Bishop Cosin's 17th-c woodwork is especially notable. Cooper almshouses date from 1703.

SEDLESCOMBE, E Sussex 9 TQ71
Oaklands, a mansion to the SE of this attractive village, includes the English Pestalozzi children's village. Several old houses exist in the area.

SEEND, Wilts 7 ST96
This former weavers' village includes a good group of Georgian houses. The partly-timbered manor house was originally fortified in the 14thc, and the church shows a good pinnacled tower. A 15th-c aisle displays weird animal gargoyles.

SEFTON, Merseyside 21 SD30
Early 16th-c woodwork, an interesting range of monuments, and the Molyneux brasses are features of the notable local church. The restored screen is also of interest.

SELATTYN, Salop 17 SJ23
An 18th-c tower and woodwork of the same period exist in the church. Fine Tudor roofs are of note, and a magnificent wagon roof with more than 200 traceried panels showing carved bosses can be seen in the chancel.

SELBORNE, Hants 8 SU73
Gilbert White, the 18th-c author of the *Natural History of Selborne*, lived at The Wakes. This house now contains the Oates Memorial Library and museum. He is buried in the church, which has a window depicting St Francis of Assisi and the Birds. An old yew tree measures some 28ft in girth, and a good view can be enjoyed from the Hanger. Selborne Hill is NT protected.

SELBY, N Yorks 22 SE63
A wooden toll bridge over the River Ouse dates from the late 18thc. Corunna House is of the same period and several good Georgian houses exist in The Crescent. An iron swing bridge of 1891 replaces one of 1840. A large number of sea-going vessels, mostly of about 500 tons in size, now come up the river. The late-Norman to perpendicular abbey church was restored after a fire, and includes a fine Norman doorway in the north porch. The choir preserves beautiful screens.

SELLAFIELD, Cumbria 20 NY00
Calder Hall nuclear power station is situated across the River Calder. This was a pioneer enterprise.

SELLY OAK, W Midlands 12 SP08
Bishop's Croft dates from 1760 and later, and used to be known as Harborne Hall. Remains of 13th-c Weoley Castle exist in the area. The group of Selly Oak Colleges was founded in 1879 by George Cadbury, and a domed Serbian Byzantine church was erected here in 1968. The Dudley Canal joins the Birmingham and Worcester Canal at Selly Oak.

SELSDON, Gt London 8 TQ36
Nearly 200 acres of the former Selsdon Park estate are now preserved by the NT, and are of particular interest to bird and flower enthusiasts.

17th-c Daneway House, Sapperton

Anne Hathaway's cottage at Shottery, in the Shakespeare Country

SELSEY, W Sussex *8 SZ99*
Selsey is a small resort situated near Selsey Bill, in what is known as the Manhood peninsula. Excellent sands are available at low tide. The chancel of Old Selsey church is still standing. The original nave was removed to the village in c1860, and a new chancel added.

SELWORTHY, Somerset *5 SS94*
Old cottages, a 15th-c tithe-barn, and almshouses known as Selworthy Green exist in this delightful village. The church is considered a good example of perpendicular style and houses Chantrey monuments plus an 18th-c gallery. Good views of Dunkery Beacon are available from here, and the grand viewpoint of Selworthy Beacon rises to 1,013ft. The whole area is part of the Holnicote estate (NT).

SEND, Surrey *8 TQ05*
A church situated near the River Wey Navigation (NT) is of 13th- to 15th-c origin. It contains an old screen and a Tudor gallery. Send Grove is 18thc and the manor dates from the 17thc.

SENNEN, Cornwall *4 SW32*
This small village is situated on Whitesand Bay, and has a sheltered harbour lying in a cove. The sands and bathing are excellent. The church of St Senana claims to be the furthest W in England, and the rugged coast scenery which stretches from Land's End to Cape Cornwall can be seen from here.

SETTLE, N Yorks *21 SD86*
A small market town in Ribblesdale, Settle is dominated by the Castleberg rock. A 17th-c house known as The Folly is of interest.

SEVENHAMPTON, Glos *12 SP02*
Stone-built houses make up this delightful Cotswold village. The 13th-c and later church includes old windows and contains a brass of 1497. The manor house is of Jacobean origin.

SEVENOAKS, Kent *8 TQ55*
Sevenoaks is a residential town which includes a perpendicular church carrying a good west tower. Chantry House is 17thc and the Red House dates from 1686. Several Georgian houses still stand. The grammar school was founded in 1432 and rebuilt in 1727. Cricket has been played on The Vine since 1734. Knole is a great mansion standing in a vast deer park on the outskirts of the town (NT, OACT). It includes a Tudor hall and notable state rooms.

SEVERN STOKE, Herefs & Worcs *12 SO84*
Dunstall Castle, a folly of 1750, stands a little to the SE of Severn Stoke. Croome D'Abitot lies 2m E and has a notable 18th-c Adam mansion which is now a school. The church of 1763 contains 17th-c monuments.

SEWSTERN LANE
Known also as The Drift, this partly-Roman track links Great Casterton with Long Bennington. Its route thus avoids Grantham and existed as an alternative to the Great North Road. Only parts now survive in road form. Earls of Rutland once used this way to travel from Belvoir Castle to London.

SHAFTESBURY, Dorset *7 ST82*
Shaftesbury stands on the edge of a 700ft-high plateau and overlooks Blackmore Vale. Canute died here in 1035, and the town's old name of Shaston was used by Thomas Hardy in his novels. Slight remains of the abbey (AM) and also a few old houses still exist. Abbey Ruins museum preserves relics excavated from the area. St Peter's church includes a remarkable crypt and a finely-vaulted porch. Grosvenor Hotel boasts the well-known Chevy Chase sideboard, which was carved by Gerrard Robinson between 1857 and 1863. Picturesque Gold Hill affords wide views. Zigzag Hill climbs the downs, 2½m SE and allows an excellent view over Cranborne Chase.

SHAKESPEARE COUNTRY
This name is generally given to the Avon-Valley countryside. Its centre is the town of Stratford-upon-Avon, birthplace and burial-place of the famous poet, and a mecca of all lovers of his works.

Many of the surrounding villages have Shakespearian associations. Prominent among these are Shottery, where the cottage of Shakespeare's wife Anne Hathaway is situated, and Wilmcote, the birthplace of Shakespeare's mother, Mary Arden. Charlecote Park (NT) is a fine Elizabethan mansion standing in a park which was the traditional scene of the poet's youthful deer poaching. Bidford-on-Avon includes a Tudor house which was formerly the Falcon Inn, a place said to have been frequented by Shakespeare.

Among towns situated on or near the Avon are Warwick, with its great castle and wealth of antiquities; Kenilworth, famous for its historic castle; Evesham, sited in an immensely fertile vale which is a mass of fruit-blossom in early spring. Portions of a once-famous abbey are preserved at the last named. The ancient Forest of Arden, setting for the poet's *As You Like It*, lies N and is now little more than a name. Several places in the area, including Henley-in-Arden and Hampton-in-Arden, show a great deal of charm and character.

SHALDON, Devon *5 SX97*
Linked to Teignmouth by a bridge over the Teign estuary, this pleasant little resort offers a harbour, sandy beaches, yachting facilities, bathing, and golf. Several Regency houses still stand, and The Ness is a good viewpoint.

SHALFLEET, Isle of Wight *7 SZ48*
This place lies at the head of the Newtown River estuary, on the Solent. Its fine church preserves details dating from the 11thc onwards, and the tower walls are 5ft thick. A sculptured tympanum can be seen over the Norman doorway.

SHALFORD, Surrey *8 TQ04*
Old houses and a picturesque 18th-c water-mill (NT) on the River Tillingbourne are features of Shalford. The Tillingbourne joins the Wey here, and the ancient village stocks are preserved. Pilgrims' Way lies to the N, near Chantries woods and the two 17th-c Cyder Cottages. The ruined 14th-c chapel of St Catherine's stands near by. Shalford was once the scene of a famous fair.

SHANKLIN, Isle of Wight *7 SZ58*
This popular resort is built partly on cliffs, and a lift provides access to the beach. Amenities include excellent sands, bathing, fishing, and golf. The restored 12th-c and later church preserves a fine chest of 1512. A newly electrified railway from Ryde uses former London Transport coaches and ends here. The old village includes the picturesque Crab Inn and delightfully wooded Shanklin Chine. A fountain near the Crab carries lines which were written by Longfellow while visiting the island. Shanklin Down rises to 779ft in the SW, and a very fine coastal walk can be taken to Luccombe Chine and Bonchurch.

SHAP, Cumbria *21 NY51*
Views of the lakeland fells are afforded by this lofty moorland village. Ruins of the 14th-c abbey lie 1m W (AM) and an unusual sulphur well exists in the same area. Two ancient concentric stone circles can be seen 2½m SE at Oldendale, and 1m SW is a small pre-Reformation building known as Keld Chapel (NT).

SHARDLOW, Derbyshire *18 SK43*
Shardlow's fine hall is dated 1684 and 1726. The River Trent is crossed by Cavendish Bridge to the SE, which was damaged by floods in 1947. A slate tablet showing the toll charges levied from the demolished toll house can be seen

near by. A new viaduct now replaces the bridge, and the junction of the Trent and Mersey Canal and the River Trent occurs in the area. Shardlow is now becoming known for a yacht marina which is slowly replacing its former importance as an inland port. Old warehouses and cranes remain from the earlier period.

SHARPNESS, Glos *12 SO60*
Docks exist where the Gloucester and Berkeley canal, built by Telford in 1827, meets the Severn estuary. One of the largest iron railway bridges in the world formerly spanned the estuary to the N.

SHAUGH PRIOR, Devon *5 SX56*
Situated below the Dartmoor foothills in the Plym Valley, Shaugh Prior lies SE of 200ft Dewerstone Crags. The church is noted for its wooden 16th-c font cover.

SHEBBEAR, Devon *5 SS40*
Near the ancient oak in the village square is a boulder which is turned over annually on Guy Fawkes day, after a peal has been rung on the church bells. An Elizabethan pulpit and Norman doorway are features of the church.

SHEEPSTOR, Devon *5 SX56*
Burrator Reservoir lies near by under Sheeps Tor. Rajah Brooke of Sarawak lies in the churchyard, which is close to St Leonard's Well. Remains of Eylesbarrow mine, the last to smelt tin on Dartmoor, exist in the area.

SHEERNESS, Kent *9 TQ97*
Sheerness lies at the mouth of the River Medway where it joins the Thames, and offers a shingle bathing beach. It was formerly a naval dockyard and is now a developing port which retains the 18th-c Naval Terrace. A mutiny took place here in 1797.

SHEFFIELD, S Yorks *18 SK38*
A university and industrial city on the River Don, Sheffield is known for the manufacture of steel and cutlery. It and its environs once formed the manor of Hallamshire.

The interesting cathedral was originally the town's parish church. It is of partly 14th- and 15th-c origin and contains fine monuments in the Shrewsbury Chapel. Georgian houses stand in Paradise Square. The former girls' Charity School in St James' Row dates from 1786. Also of interest are the Graves Art Gallery, the City Museum and restored Mappin Art Gallery, and the 19th-c Cutlers' Hall. The new Crucible Theatre was opened in 1971. Parts of the early 18th-c Abbeydale works, where scythes were made by water-wheel power until 1933, are being preserved (OACT).

Mary Queen of Scots was held between 1570 and 1584 at both the vanished castle and in a Tudor manor house of which there are still slight remains. A notable survival of the latter is the 16th-c Turret House. Parts of 12th- to 14th-c Beauchief Abbey are preserved on the SW outskirts of the city. Beauchief Hall dates from 1671 and 1836. The restored timber-framed Bishop's House of c1500 stands by Meersbrook Park. Tinsley viaduct measures ¾m in length and has two levels with eleven carriageways. It lies NE of the city on the M1 motorway.

SHEFFIELD PARK, E Sussex *8 TQ42*
A small museum is housed in a station of the revived steam-hauled Bluebell railway. Sheffield Park gardens (NT) and the lake-watered park of 150 acres are particularly fine (OACT). The 18th-c house is partly by Wyatt.

SHEFFORD, Beds *14 TL13*
Southill Park is a notable Regency house to the N, which was rebuilt by Henry Holland in c1800. It was once the home of Admiral Byng, who was shot in 1757 for neglect of duty.

SHELFORD, GREAT, Cambs *14 TL45*
Gog Magog Hills rise gently some 2m NE.

Excavations of the Wandlebury earthworks have revealed the outlines of two large male and female warriors with a horse and chariot, which may be about 1,800 years old.

SHELSLEY WALSH, Herefs & Worcs *12 SO76*
This Teme-Valley village includes a restored church which preserves a fine 15th-c screen. The adjacent manor house is a 17th-c timber-framed building. Motor car and motorcycle hill-climbs are held here.

SHELTON, Norfolk *15 TM29*
A rare 15th-c brick-built church exists here and contains several fine monuments plus examples of old glass.

SHENFIELD, Essex *9 TQ69*
The restored 15th-c church preserves notable timbering which includes an interesting south porch, the tower, and the nave arcade. Shenfield Place dates from 1689 and was designed by Robert Hooke, a contemporary of Wren.

SHENLEY, Herts *8 TL10*
Nicholas Hawksmoor was a well-known architect who lived at Porters Park. He was buried in the local churchyard in 1736, and the house now serves as a hospital. Moated Tudor and 17th-c Salisbury Hall (OACT) lies 2m N off the Barnet to St Albans road. The prototype mosquito aircraft is on view here.

SHEPPERTON, Surrey *8 TQ06*
St Nicholas' Church carries a brick tower of 1710 and houses an early 19th-c gallery and box pews. The delightful rectory dates from c1700. The village square is attractive, and the River Thames flows to the S.

SHEPPEY, ISLE OF, Kent *9 TQ96*
This fertile Thames-estuary island extends from the Medway to the Swale estuary, and is linked to the mainland by a lift bridge.

SHEPTON MALLET, Somerset *6 ST64*
Shepton Mallet church carries a lofty perpendicular tower and displays a very notable panelled nave roof. The ornate market cross dates from c1500, and remains of the medieval Shambles – a 15th-c timbered shed – lie near by. Several good 17th- and 18th-c houses exist, and a row of gabled 17th-c houses in Great Ostry is particularly notable. Late 17th-c Monmouth House and the mid-Georgian Sales House can be seen in Draycott. Mendip exhibits and prehistoric remains are on show at the local museum. This town is now the permanent home of the Bath and West show.

SHERBORNE, Dorset *6 ST61*
An interesting River-Yeo town, where winding streets contain old houses dating from the 15thc onwards. The picturesque

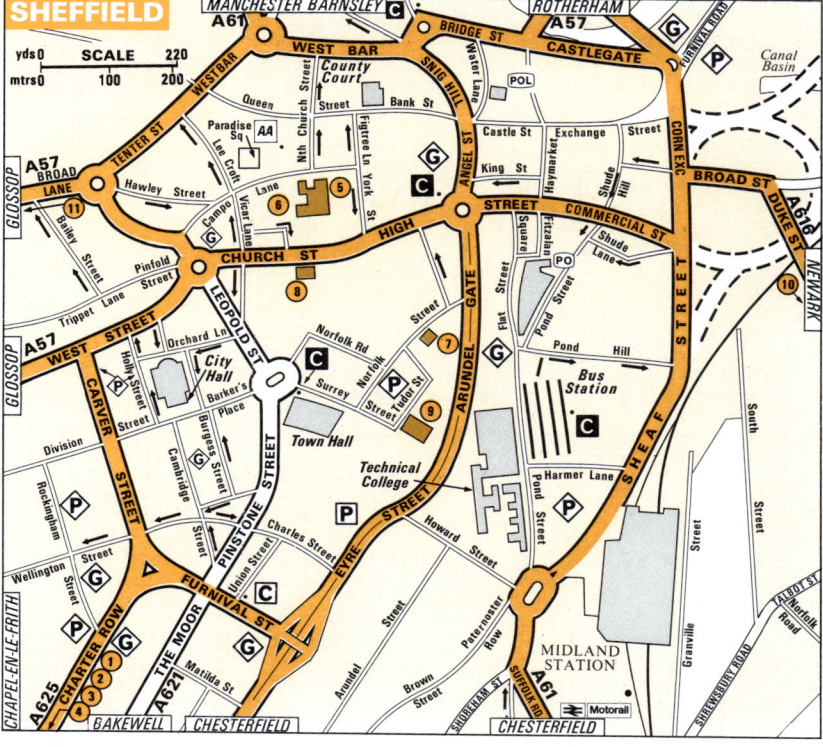

1	Abbeydale Works
2	Beauchief Abbey
3	Beauchief Hall
4	Bishop's House
5	Cathedral
6	Charity School
7	Crucible Theatre
8	Cutler's Hall
9	Graves Art Gallery
10	Manor House Remains and Turret House
11	University of Sheffield

14th-c abbey conduit stands at the foot of Cheap Street. Features of the magnificent, Norman to 15th-c Abbey Church include notable fan vaulting and exceptionally fine perpendicular work in the choir. Great Tom, a tenor bell which was a gift from Cardinal Wolsey, hangs in the 100ft tower. An adjacent school occupies parts of the former abbey buildings, and the 15th-c hall is now the school chapel. The hospital of St John was refounded in 1437 and includes modern additions.

The old house of Julian was once an inn and now contains the county library. Interesting objects connected with the history and geology of the town can be seen in the local museum. Sir Walter Raleigh built much of the 16th-c and later castle, which stands in a 20-acre lake-watered park landscaped by Capability Brown (OACT). An old castle of the 12thc was besieged during the Civil War, and afterwards slighted (OACT). Thomas Hardy used the town under the name of Sherton Abbas in his novels. Restored Trent Manor, where Charles II hid for two weeks after the battle of Worcester in 1651, lies 3½m NW.

SHERBORNE, Glos 12 SP11
A cottage in this little Cotswold village was once a chapel, and is probably unique in being a dwelling place with a Norman doorway. Fine 17th-c Lodge Park stands in the park of Sherborne House, and the River Windrush flows through the area.

SHERBORNE ST JOHN, Hants 7 SU65
The perpendicular church retains many interesting monuments and brasses. A fine Tudor house called The Vyne lies 1m NE, and includes a very notable chapel and tomb chamber. Fine linenfold panelling lines the long gallery, and the north front portico was added by John Webb in 1654. An attractive lake waters the grounds, which contain pleasant gardens (NT, OACT).

SHERBURN-IN-ELMET, N Yorks 22 SE43
A fine Norman nave is a feature of the village church, and an old cross stands in the churchyard. The gabled grammar school dates from 1619. Huddleston is an Elizabethan manor house lying 1½m WNW. Material for the building of York Minster was extracted from local quarries.

SHERE, Surrey 8 TQ04
Situated on the River Tillingbourne under the North Downs, this delightful village includes an interesting early-English to Norman church. The latter has a Norman tower which carries a fine shingled spire. Many old cottages exist in the area. Silent Pool is a tree-encircled water lying to the W. King John is supposed to have watched a local girl bathing here, as a result of which the girl drowned herself.

SHERIFF HUTTON, N Yorks 22 SE66
Monuments are housed in the decorated and perpendicular church, and a ruined 14th-c castle once guarded the former Forest of Galtres. Sheriff Hutton Park is a 17th- and 18th-c house.

SHERINGHAM, Norfolk 15 TG14
Pebbles give way to sand at low tide, and the resort offers good sea bathing. Regency Sheringham Hall, by Humphrey Repton, stands in a beautiful park. Near by are the remains of 13th-c Beeston Priory. North Norfolk Railway Co displays steam locomotives and rolling stock at the former station, and a few trains are actually working. The mainly-perpendicular church of Upper Sheringham houses a good screen and rood loft. Fine wooded country exists inland.

SHERNBORNE, Norfolk 14 TF73
A remarkable carved Norman font can be seen in the church, and an ornate village signpost commemorates the coronation of King George V.

SHERSTON, Wilts 12 ST88
This attractive stone-built village includes a fine Norman to perpendicular church which is noted for its central tower of 1730. Interesting tombs also exist here. The old rectory dates from the 15thc, and the curiously-named Rattlebone Inn recalls a local hero who once fought the Danes.

SHERWOOD FOREST
Once very large, this ancient Royal Forest is associated with Robin Hood and his legendary band of outlaws. All that remains of the actual woodland are a few wooded tracts between Nottingham and the Dukeries district. An area of some 86 acres near Edwinstowe is to become one of the new country parks.

SHIFNAL, Salop 17 SJ70
Old Idsall House and the Nag's Head Inn are two of the half-timbered buildings to be seen in the area. The Norman to perpendicular church includes a Norman chancel with 14th-c additions.

SHILDON, Co Durham 27 NZ22
Railway wagons are made here, and the first steam train to carry both passengers and goods ran from Shildon. Timothy Hackworth, builder of the early Royal George locomotive, lived at Soho House. He died in 1850 and a bronze plaque carrying a picture of his locomotive is now displayed by the house. Remains of the original locomotive works stand near by.

SHILLINGFORD, Oxon 13 SU59
A fine 18th-c bridge spans the Thames here, and Shillingford itself lies in a picturesque setting.

SHIPBOURNE, Kent 9 TQ55
Fairlawne is a beautiful mainly-Georgian house which was partly designed by James Gibbs. It has associations with Sir Harry Vane, who was beheaded on Tower Hill in 1662. His coffin lies in the crypt of the local church. A black poplar in the grounds of the house has grown to 140ft.

SHIPDHAM, Norfolk 15 TF90
Decorated and perpendicular styles are displayed by the local church, which houses a very fine 15th-c wooden lectern. A wooden cupola and spire crown the 15th-c tower. Letton Hall, by Sir John Soane between 1785 and 1788, lies 2m SE.

SHIPLAKE, Oxon 8 SU77
Pleasantly situated in the Thames Valley, Shiplake includes a rebuilt church which preserves examples of old French glass. Tennyson was married here in 1850.

SHIPLEY, W Sussex 8 TQ12
Fine Norman carving and the notable Caryll monument are features of Shipley church. Other points of interest in the building include a rare 13th-c reliquary of Limoges enamel – kept in a chancel niche – and the grave of John Ireland the composer. A plaque recalling the residence of Hilaire Belloc can be seen near the restored King's windmill (Belloc's Mill, OACT). Ruins of Knepp Castle lie SE near a large stretch of water.

SHIPLEY, W Yorks 22 SE13
Yorkshire's Shipley lies on the threshold of some of the finest scenery offered by the Pennines, and is known for the manufacture of worsted cloth. It also operates iron foundries.

SHIPSTON-ON-STOUR, Warwickshire 13 SP24
Shipston-on-Stour lies in the Vale of Red Horse, on the edge of the Cotswolds. Attractive houses and inns of Georgian and later date exist here.

SHIPTON, Salop 17 SO59
An exceptionally lovely Elizabethan manor house in this Corvedale village includes a Georgian stable block (OACT). Slight remains of a Norman castle exist in the area, and Brown Clee Hill rises to 1,790ft in the S.

SHIPTON-UNDER-WYCHWOOD, Oxon 13 SP21
The large early-English and perpendicular church displays a fine west doorway and a 15th-c pulpit and font. The Prebendary is an old house, and the Shaven Crown inn has a Tudor gateway. A fountain recalls 17 Shipton men who died in the wreck of the emigrant ship Cospatrick in 1874. Shipton Court dates from the Elizabethan period.

SHIREOAKS, Notts 18 SK58
A 19th-c church in this mining village was erected by the Duke of Newcastle, and contains several monuments to his memory. The former Shire Oak, a tree which overlooked Nottinghamshire, Derbyshire, and Yorkshire, has completely vanished.

SHIRLAND, Derbyshire 18 SK35
Shirland church is of 15th-c date and contains an alabaster effigy of 1537. Ogston Hall lies 2m NW and dates from the 14th to 18thc.

SHOBDON, Herefs & Worcs 11 SO36
Gothic and rococo styles are evident in the remarkable church of 1753, which displays rich colouring in its decoration. Arches from an earlier Norman church have been re-erected in the grounds of former Shobdon Court. Court of Noke is a fine old house lying 2m SW.

SHOEBURYNESS, Essex 9 TQ98
Extensive sands at Shoeburyness have been used for artillery practice. Foulness Island and Maplin Sands lie NE, and the latter is the designated site for the projected third London Airport.

SHOREHAM, Kent 8 TQ56
One of the finest carved screens in Kent can be seen in the perpendicular church, which also displays a restored timber south porch. Shoreham itself is an attractive North Downs village sited on the River Darent.

SHOREHAM-BY-SEA, W Sussex 8 TQ20
An increasingly busy harbour at the mouth of the River Adur is a feature of this resort, and the shingle beach offers sand at low tide. New Shoreham church

is a splendid example of trans-Norman work; the most extensive evidence of this period is the choir of the old church, which shows beautifully carved Norman capitals. The Norman and later chequered-flint house of Marlipins (AM) is now a museum, and Old Shoreham church shows fine Norman work – notably the carved tower arches. An airport operates in the area.

SHORWELL, Isle of Wight 7 SZ48
The beautifully situated church dates mainly from the 15thc and has a notable mural painting over the north door. Its canopied pulpit is also of interest. North Court (1615) and West Court (early Tudor) are both fine houses, and Wolverton Manor displays a Jacobean façade.

SHOTTERY, Warwickshire 12 SP15
Shakespeare's wife Anne Hathaway was born here, and her thatched and timbered cottage still stands in a lovely garden. Various relics are preserved inside (OACT).

SHREWSBURY, Salop 17 SJ41
Shrewsbury is beautifully situated on a bend of the River Severn, which is spanned here by the fine English and Welsh Bridges. A wealth of interesting half-timbered houses and inns can be seen in the town. Parts of the castle show 13th-c work, and the building was converted into a house during the 18thc. It now belongs to the corporation. Laura's Bower was re-erected in 1790 by Thomas Telford. Remains of the old town walls include a 14th-c tower (NT). The nearby Council House displays a fine 17th-c timbered gateway and was once a residence of the Lord President of the Council of the Marches of Wales.

The Norman to perpendicular Abbey Church houses interesting monuments, and stands opposite the lovely 14th-c Refectory pulpit. St Mary's 12th- to 17th-c church includes the fine old Herkenrode glass, plus a Jesse window. St Julian's church carries an old tower, but the rest of the building dates mainly from 1750. St Alkmund's carries a 174ft decorated spire and dates from 1795. New St Chad's Church of 1792 includes a nave which has been designed in rotunda form.

The interesting old 16th- to 17th-c school is now a free library and museum. New school buildings lie on the other side of the river. King Henry VII lodged in a half-timbered house in Wyle Cop prior to the Battle of Bosworth, in 1485. This is now a shop. Whitehall, a fine house of 1582, includes a picturesque gatehouse and dovecote. The old market hall is dated 1595. Interesting half-timbered buildings include the Hall of the Drapers' Guild, and the mansions of Ireland's, Owen's, and Rowley's. The latter now houses a museum of Roman remains from Wroxeter. A notable ballroom exists in the splendid old Lion coaching inn. Shrewsbury's important railway station is built over the river. Grope Lane and Butcher Row – the latter containing the interesting Abbot's House – are picturesque.

Some of the best timbered houses are in the suburb of Frankwell. Good Georgian houses, including the Judge's Lodgings of c1701, exist in Belmont. Other notable buildings from the period include the Old House in Dogpole, and the Unicorn inn in Wyle Cop. Lord Hill was Wellington's right-hand man at the battle of Waterloo and is commemorated by a 134ft column. A famous floral fete is held each August in the attractive riverside Quarry Gardens. Charles Darwin was born at The Mount in 1809, and Admiral Benbow at Benbow House, now demolished, in 1653. A former flax mill of 1796, known as Jones' Maltings, were the first completely metal-framed buildings to be erected in England. Mary Webb is buried in the cemetery and is strongly associated with the town. Millington Hospital dates from 1748.

SHRIVENHAM, Berks 12 SU28
A perpendicular tower is carried by the mainly 17th-c church, and modern Beckett Park – now housing the Royal Military College of Science – retains a Stuart garden house. Elm Tree House dates from c1700.

SHUDY CAMPS, Cambs 14 TL64
Dayrell monuments can be seen in the mainly-perpendicular church, and remains of the old Dayrell manor house of 1702 exist in the area. Castle Camps lies 2m S and includes a church containing a Reynolds monument of 1717. Near by is the site of a now vanished Norman castle.

SHUSTOKE, Warwickshire 18 SP29
Sir William Dugdale the famous antiquary was born at the former rectory and lies in a tomb of 1686 in the local church. His birthplace has been converted into cottages. Blyth Hall lies 2m WSW and dates from the 17th to 18thc.

SIBLE HEDINGHAM, Essex 15 TL73
Clerestory windows dating from the 14thc and wood-carved Royal Arms of William and Mary can be seen in the church. Other old buildings include the early 18th-c rectory, and half-timbered Southey Green House which dates from the 15thc. A watermill in the area displays weather-boarding – a type of construction which is locally known as Essex-clad.

SIBSON, Leics 18 SK30
The attractive half-timbered Cock inn was once a tithe barn, and has been the venue for cock-fighting. Remains of a gibbet

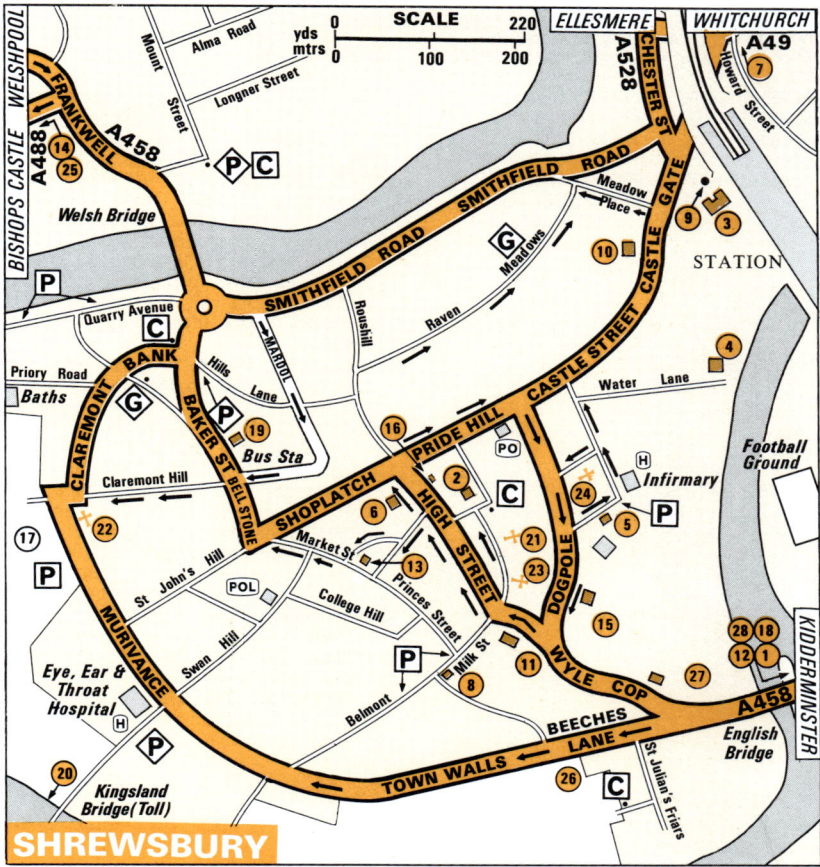

1 Abbey Church
2 Abbot's House
3 Castle
4 Council House
5 Hall of the Drapers' Guild
6 Ireland's Mansion
7 Jones' Maltings
8 Judge's Lodgings
9 Laura's Bower
10 Library and Museum
11 Lion Inn
12 Lord Hill's Memorial Column
13 Market Hall
14 Millington Hospital
15 Old House
16 Owen's Mansion
17 Quarry Gardens
18 Refectory Pulpit
19 Rowley's Mansion
    (museum of Roman remains)
20 School (museum & library)
21 St Alkmund's Church
22 St Chad's Church
23 St Julian's Church
24 St Mary's Church
25 The Mount
26 Town Wall Remains
27 Unicorn Inn
28 Whitehall

where John Massey was hanged in 1800 for murdering his wife can be seen 2½m NE, on an unclassified road which turns off the A444.

SIBTON, Suffolk *15 TM36*
Slight remains of a 12th-c abbey exist here, and the 13th-c parish church displays four great gargoyles on its tower. Other notable features of the church include a splendid hammerbeam roof and a chancel decorated with painted bosses. Colour-washed and pargetted cottages, plus an 18th-c school, can be seen in the village.

SIDBURY, Devon *6 SY19*
Norman workmanship and a possibly Saxon crypt can be seen in the local church. Sand Barton, ¾m NNE, was built in 1594 and serves as a farm.

SIDDINGTON, Glos *12 SU09*
An inscribed Roman stone exists in the grounds of Siddington House. The church shows fine Norman work which includes the south doorway, chancel arch, and font.

SIDFORD, Devon *6 SY19*
Old cottages exist in this River Sid village, and Charles II is said to have spent the night in a hiding place at 16th-c Porch House.

SIDMOUTH, Devon *6 SY18*
Spectacular red cliffs border the pebble and shingle beach of this well-known resort, and the town lies at the mouth of the River Sid. The old manor in Church Street contains a museum, and rows of Regency houses display characteristic iron-trelliswork balconies. Woolcombe House is of interest. Peak Hill to the W and Salcombe Hill to the E are good viewpoints.

SILCHESTER, Hants *7 SU66*
Interesting remains of the Roman city *Calleva Atrebatum* (AM) exist here. The encircling town walls are in good condition, but the once-excavated city now lies beneath agricultural land. Parts of the old moat, early earthworks, and a small amphitheatre lie outside the wall. The Roman track known as the Portway extends SW from here towards Salisbury (Old Sarum) and the lesser-known of the two Ermine (or Ermin) Streets runs NW to Cirencester (*Corinium*).

The church stands at a break in the wall, and the church pond is the only part of the moat still to contain water. The fabric of the church includes a great deal of Roman material, and a sundial in the churchyard is mounted on a column from a temple which used to exist on the site. A 15th-c screen exists in the building. Various finds from *Calleva Atrebatum* are exhibited in the tiny Silchester museum. More extensive displays are mounted in Reading museum.

SILLOTH, Cumbria *26 NY15*
Part of the Solway Firth, on which this small port and resort is situated, is designated an area of outstanding natural beauty. Views of Criffell Hill in Scotland can be enjoyed from here, and good sea bathing is available.

SILVERDALE, Lancs *21 SD47*
Pleasant woodlands exist in the vicinity of this small Morecambe-Bay golfing resort. Mrs Gaskell lived at Lindeth Tower, and there are associations with Charlotte Brontë. Castlebarrow (NT) overlooks the bay, and the ancient Buckstone – estimated as weighing some 60 tons – stands above Hawes Water.

SILVER END, Essex *9 TL81*
Flat-roofed houses in this village are some of the earliest modernistic buildings in England. They were built in 1926 as part of a project which included a factory for disabled men. The modern Church of St Francis is weather-boarded and has a thatched roof.

SILVERSTONE, Northants *13 SP64*
The famous Silverstone motor races are held on the former airfield, and the 16th-c house of Astwell Castle lies 4m W.

SIMONSBATH, Somerset *5 SS73*
Simonsbath is situated in attractive countryside on the River Barle, in the heart of the Exmoor national park. The Knight family lived in an unfinished mansion that stands in the area, and reclaimed large tracts of Exmoor after having bought it from the Crown in 1815. Knight tombs can be seen in the village church.

SINGLETON, W Sussex *8 SU81*
Linch Down, the second highest of the Sussex South Downs and a fine viewpoint, rises 818ft to the NW of this attractive village. The interesting church carries a pre-Conquest tower and houses several old benches.

SISSINGHURST, Kent *9 TQ73*
Sissinghurst Castle is situated NE of the village and carries a Tudor tower. It is surrounded by some of the loveliest gardens in Kent (NT, OACT).

SISTON, Avon *6 ST67*
Extensive Norman work preserved by the church includes a notable carved tympanum over the doorway. The building also includes a richly-decorated lead font. Siston Court is of Tudor origin.

SITTINGBOURNE, Kent *9 TQ96*
Situated on a creek of the River Swale, Sittingbourne includes a church which features a 13th- to 14th-c tower and an Easter Sepulchre. Former Bowater paper mills had a 30in gauge railway which ran 4m from the factory to their Swale dock at Kemsley. The track is now privately preserved (OACT). The new Dolphin Sailing Barge museum stands on the banks of Milton Creek.

SIXPENNY HANDLEY, Dorset *7 ST91*
This curious village name was derived from the amalgamation of two ancient hundreds – *Saxpena* and *Hanlega*. Signposts standing on the main Salisbury to Blandford road read 'to 6d Handley'.

SKEGNESS, Lincs *19 TF56*
Excellent sands and bathing are offered by this popular resort. Gibraltar Point is a local nature reserve lying to the S.

SKELMERSDALE, Lancs *21 SD40*
One of the modern New Towns is being developed here.

SKELTON, N Yorks *22 SE55*
A lovely 13th-c church which is noted for its south doorway stands here. The fine house of Beningbrough Hall dates from 1716 and stands NW in a wooded park (NT, OACT).

SKELTON-IN-CLEVELAND, Cleveland *22 NZ61*
Iron-ore is worked in the surrounding district and the castle dates from 1794.

SKELWITH BRIDGE, Cumbria *21 NY30*
Skelwith Force on the Langdale road, and Colwith Force on the Little Langdale road, are both notable waterfalls. Picturesque Tilberthwaite Fells and 2,502ft Wetherlam lie to the W. A great deal of the area is NT protected.

SKIDBY, Humberside *23 TA03*
A windmill at Skidby is said to be the last surviving example of this type of building to exist in the area N of the Humber and E of the Pennines. It dates from 1821 and has been well restored (OACT). Plans to turn it into an agricultural museum are being considered.

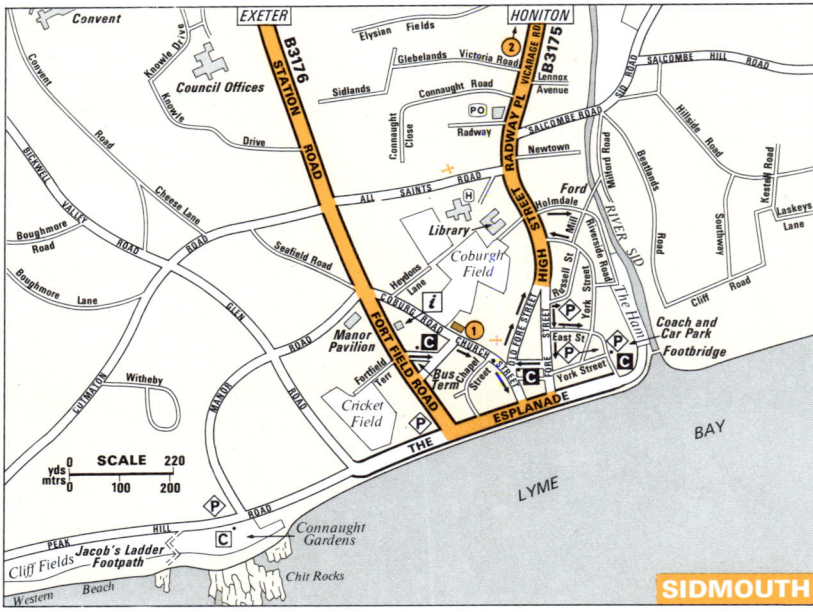

SIDMOUTH

1 Old Manor (museum)
2 Woolcombe House

SKILLINGTON, Lincs *19 SK82*
Saxon masonry and memorial windows to Charles Hudson are features of the local church. Hudson was once vicar here, and was killed with three others during the first ascent of the Swiss Matterhorn in 1865.

SKIPTON, N Yorks *22 SD95*
Pleasantly situated among the Airedale moors, Skipton stands near the farthest N point of the Leeds and Liverpool canal. This waterway runs for nearly 130m and was opened in 1816. Clifford monuments and a library of old books can be seen in the mainly perpendicular church. Exhibits and displays appertaining to local geology are mounted in the Craven museum.

The 11th-c and later castle preserves a tiny interior courtyard containing carved armorial bearings and a yew planted by Lady Anne Clifford in 1659 (OACT). The George Leatt Industrial and Folk Museum is located in the High Corn Mill. The latter building acquired its present appearance in 1750 (OACT).

SKIPWITH, N Yorks *22 SE63*
Saxon workmanship is evident in the church's tower, and notable early-English ironwork can be seen on the nave's south door.

SKIRBECK, Lincs *19 TF34*
This village stands on the outskirts of Boston and overlooks the River Witham. The restored church has an early-English nave, and the Maud Foster windmill is of interest. Red-brick Rochford Tower of c1510 stands 1½m NE.

SLAIDBURN, Lancs *21 SD75*
Bowland Forest fringes Slaidburn, which includes an old grammar school and a perpendicular church housing a good Jacobean screen and three-decker pulpit. Hark to Bounty is an inn name commemorating a famous local hound. Stocks Reservoir lies NE, and the gabled Elizabethan Hammerton Hall is situated 1m N.

SLAPTON SAND, Devon *5 SX84*
Slapton Sands form a gravel ridge which separates the sea from the fresh-water lake of Slapton Ley. An obelisk commemorating the use of this district as a battle area in 1944 was presented by the USA army authorities. A 14th-c tower from the former Collegiate chantry stands near the decorated and perpendicular church. Chancel windows dating from the 14thc are interesting features of the latter.

SLEAFORD, Lincs *19 TF04*
The 12th- to 15th-c church carries a 144ft tower and spire. Other features include several brasses, notable window tracery, a good screen, and some chained books. The Vicarage is dated 1568. The Black Bull inn preserves a carved stone dated 1689 and 1791, which depicts the once-popular sport of bull baiting. Among the many 19th-c buildings to be seen in the area are the Corn Exchange of 1857, the Sessions House of 1831, Cam's Hospital of 1830 to 1846, and the former workhouse of 1838. The manor house is of 14th- to 19th-c date. Large maltings were completed in 1905, and the town stands on the partly-navigable Sleaford canal.

SLEDMERE, Humberside *23 SE96*
This Wolds village includes a beautiful modern church. The interesting Sykes memorial dates from the 19thc, and the waggoners' memorial commemorates first world war waggoners. Sledmere House dates from 1751 and 1781; it contains splendid plasterwork, furnishings, and statuary. The surrounding park was landscaped by Capability Brown (OACT).

SLIMBRIDGE, Glos *12 SO70*
The church is noted for its 12th-c nave arcades and a lead font of 1664; a moated vicarage stands in the area. Wildfowl trust grounds founded by Peter Scott lie SW near the River Severn (OACT).

SLINDON, W Sussex *8 SU90*
Slindon Park stands in a large estate which is noted for fine beech trees and a 3m stretch of the Roman Stane Street. The house itself is of Elizabethan and later origin, but has been greatly restored. The local church houses a fine 16th-c wooded effigy.

SLINGSBY, N Yorks *22 SE67*
Slingsby Castle is a picturesque ruin, and the rectory dates from 1740. A maypole still exists here.

SLOUGH, Berks *8 SU98*
Plan overleaf
This town has developed rapidly in recent years, and includes a large factory estate. Of the old buildings that have survived this growth, Baylis House dates mainly from the 17thc; St Lawrence's church at Upton retains Norman work, a 16th-c alms-box, and Bulstrode brasses; Upton Court is of 16th- to 17th-c date. Sir William Herschel the astronomer is buried in St Lawrence's churchyard.

SMALLEY, Derbyshire *18 SK44*
Samuel Richardson, often called father of the English novel, was born here in 1689.

SMALLHYTHE, Kent *9 TQ83*
Smallhythe Place dates from 1480 and was once the home of Dame Ellen Terry. It is now a museum displaying a number of the lady's personal relics (NT, OACT). A Priest's House of the same period and a Barn theatre are also of interest.

SMARDEN, Kent *9 TQ84*
A number of weather-boarded and old timber-framed cottages that exist here include the former Cloth Hall. The church is known as the Barn of Kent because of its great width, and features a 15th-c tower plus traces of wall-paintings.

SMETHWICK, W Midlands *12 SP08*
A Black-Country industrial town now forming part of Warley County Borough, Smethwick boasts the Soho foundry where James Watt's first engine was set up. Soho House is of 1766 and 1789 date and was once the home of Matthew Boulton, who worked with Watt. These two men and William Murdock, a pioneer of gas lighting, were buried NW of here in Handsworth Old Church. The latter was rebuilt in 1876.

SMISBY, Derbyshire *18 SK31*
The Tournament Field featured in Scott's *Ivanhoe* lies S of Smisby. Old monuments exist in the church, and a polygonal brick lock-up is of interest.

SNAEFELL, Isle of Man *20 SC38*
The road to the E of this mountain climbs to nearly 1,400ft. Snaefell itself rises to 2,034ft, and is the highest point on the island. Access to the mountain is by electric railway from Laxey.

SNAITH, Humberside *22 SE62*
Snaith's restored grammar school dates from c1628, and the fine 12th- to 15th-c church measures 170ft in length. A tomb of 1493 and a Chantrey statue to Viscount Downe can be seen in the Dawnay Chapel.

SNAKE, THE, Derbyshire *18 SK19*
This lonely pass is situated in the High Peak moors of the Peak District national park and climbs to 1,680ft at a point NW of the Snake Inn. It is likely to be blocked by snow during the winter. Alport Moor lies N in front of 2,060ft Bleaklow Hill, and the rock ridge known as Alport Castles lies E across the River Alport.

SNAPE, N Yorks *22 SE28*
An Elizabethan and earlier castle that is sited here lies partly in ruins. The late 15th-c chapel contains an old oak carving of Catherine Parr, wife of Henry VIII, who once lived here (OACT).

SNAPE, Suffolk *15 TM35*
Old maltings exist in this River-Alde village, and the church houses a good

12th- to 15th-c church at Sleaford

perpendicular font. Slight remains of a small 11th-c priory lie to the S.

SNETTERTON, Norfolk *15 TL99*
A well-known road racing circuit is situated here.

SNETTISHAM, Norfolk *14 TF63*
The decorated-style church carries a lofty spire and displays a fine west front which is reminiscent of Peterborough Cathedral. The Old Hall is an attractive 18th-c Dutch-gabled house. Excavations of 1948 revealed a hoard of treasure.

SNITTERFIELD, Warwickshire *12 SP25*
Richard Shakespeare once lived here and his son John, father of the famous poet and playwright, was born here.

SNODLAND, Kent *9 TQ76*
This is the point where people travelling the ancient Pilgrims' Way crossed the Medway by means of an old ferry. Large cement works and paper mills operate in the vicinity.

SNORING, GREAT, Norfolk *15 TF93*
Carved benches, an old screen, and a 13th-c font are features of the local church. Brickwork of 15th-c date is shown by the old rectory.

SNOWSHILL, Glos *12 SP03*
A secluded Cotswold Hills village, Snowshill includes a 16th- to 17th-c manor house which contains a collection of clocks, toys, and musical instruments (NT, OACT).

SOBERTON, Hants *7 SU61*
Numerous gargoyles are displayed by a 16th-c flint tower which is carried by the hilltop church. High on the west front, near two heads divided by a skull, are a key and pail in bas-relief. These are said to show that the tower was built by a butler and a servant. A rare altar cloth of 1645 exists in the chancel, and the Curle chapel contains old wall-paintings.

SOHAM, Cambs *14 TL57*
Fine trans-Norman work, an imposing perpendicular tower, and good benches with carved poppy-heads are features of the local church. A rare weighing machine with a outside pulley can be seen in the village, and an 18th-c and later mill exists in the area.

SOLIHULL, W Midlands *12 SP17*
Solihull Hall and Old Berry Hall are both timber-framed, and the latter is partly moated. Solihull School was founded in 1560. The restored 13th- to 15th-c church shows good woodwork and brasses.

SOMERFORD KEYNES, Glos *12 SU09*
An ancient dovecote stands near the Tudor manor house. The church has a blocked-up Saxon doorway, a carved Saxon stone, and 15th-c screenwork.

SOMERSBY, Lincs *19 TF37*
Lord Tennyson was born at a local house which was the former rectory in 1809. Tennyson memorials can be seen in the church, and a very fine perpendicular cross stands in the churchyard. The manor farm of 1722 may be by Vanbrugh.

SOMERSHALL HERBERT, Derbyshire *18 SK13*
One of the FitzHerberts, a family which gave this village the latter part of its name, built the beautiful half-timbered Elizabethan manor house in 1564. This is considered to be one of Derbyshire's loveliest old houses.

SOMERTON, Oxon *13 SP42*
Somerton lies on the River Cherwell and Oxford Canal. A beautiful 14th-c stone reredos, 15th-c screens, and notable Fermor tombs exist in the church. Bishop Juxon, who accompanied Charles I to the scaffold, was once rector here. Troy Farm lies to the E and includes a rare turf maze.

SOMERTON, Somerset *6 ST42*
Set in a delightful area on the River Cary, this town includes an old market cross which was rebuilt in 1673 (AM). The early-English to perpendicular church displays a panelled roof. Other notable buildings include the town hall of *c*1700, and the Hext almshouses of 1626.

SOMPTING, W Sussex *8 TQ10*
A remarkable Saxon tower carried by the church includes a unique wooden and gabled cap reminiscent of many in the Rhine Valley. This type of capping is known as Rhennish Helm. The building preserves several carved stones.

SONNING, Berks *8 SU77*
Sonning lock is an attractive feature of this charming Thames-Valley village, which also includes a picturesque bridge and many old houses. The restored church contains an oak screen and brasses. Lutyens designed the Deanery, which is a good example of his style, and the house stands in a garden designed by Gertrude Jekyll.

SOUTHALL, Gt London *8 TQ18*
The old manor house is of half-timbered construction, and includes a public garden. The Grand Union Canal divides into two arms here – one leading to Brentford, and one to Paddington for the Regent's Canal.

SOUTHAMPTON, Hants *7 SU41*
Southampton includes an important transatlantic port with extensive docks, and a harbour which is noted for its double tide – first by way of the Solent, and two hours later by way of Spithead. It achieved city status in 1946, and the expanding university complex – partly by Sir Basil Spence – incorporates the fine Nuffield theatre of 1964. Considerable bomb damage was inflicted during the war. King Henry V marshalled his army here in 1414, prior to the victory of Agincourt, and the Pilgrim Fathers set sail in the Mayflower from West Quay in 1620, on the first stage of their epic journey. A tall Pilgrim Fathers' memorial has been raised here.

Remains of the ancient walls and their towers can be seen in the city, but the stretch known as The Arcades is of particular note. Other interesting features of the city include the Bargate (AM) and its museum, the Arundel or Wind Whistle Tower (AM), the Catchcold Tower (AM), and the West Gate. The Wool House displays 14th-c buttresses and houses a maritime museum. Canute's Palace is a Norman House in Porter's Lane, and Tudor House (AM) contains a folk museum. Another Norman house, known as King John's Palace, can be reached through the Tudor House garden. A seaplane which won the Schneider Cup for Britain in 1931 can be seen in the Mitchell Memorial Museum.

St Michael's church is largely rebuilt but still contains one of the country's few 12th-c black-marble Tournai fonts.

1 Baylis House
2 St Lawrence's Church
3 Upton Court

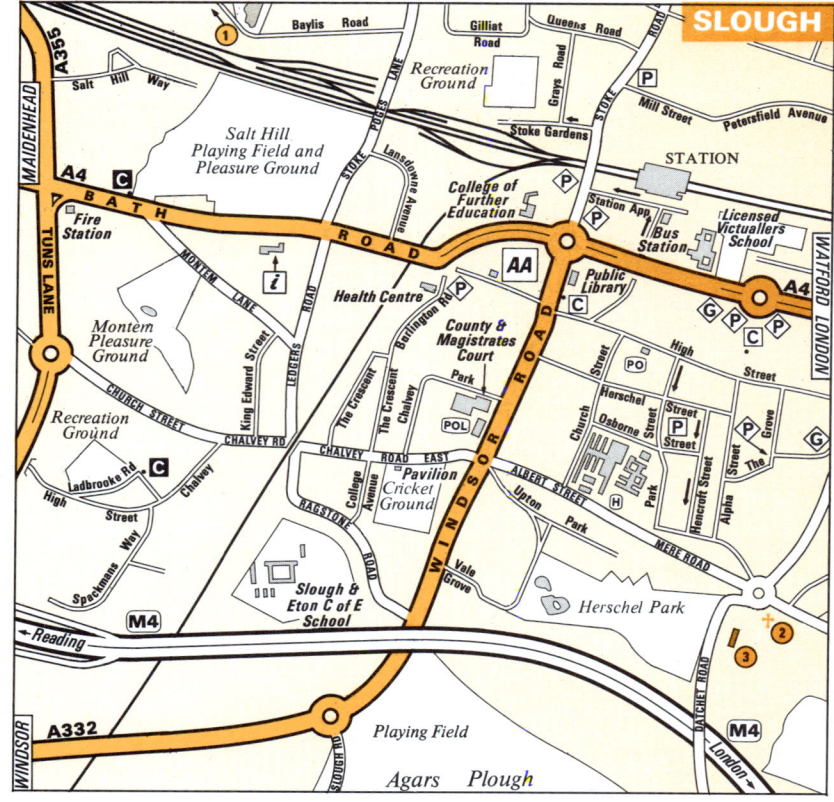

Remains of Holy Rood church include a 14th-c tower and now form a Merchant Navy Memorial. St Mary's Church was re-dedicated in 1956, and is associated with the song *The Bells of St Mary's*. Excavations of the Saxon Hamwich site have been conducted in St Mary's district. Southampton Common is a notable green area. The Hospital of St Julian, or God's House, was founded in 1197 and has a much-restored chapel. Roman and Saxon relics are contained in God's House Tower, and a memorial to the ill-fated Titanic stands near the modern Civic Centre. Giant 18th-c bow windows displayed by the Dolphin Hotel may be the largest in England. Various interesting old houses can be seen in Bugle Street. Famous natives of Southampton include Lord Jellicoe, Sir John Millais, and Isaac Watts. A car ferry and hovercraft service connects with the Isle of Wight.

SOUTH BENFLEET, Essex 9 TQ78
This place is known for its oysters, and is connected to Canvey Island. Views over the island encompass the Thames estuary and Kentish hills. The restored church includes a good 15th-c timbered porch.

SOUTHBOURNE, Dorset 7 SZ19
Hengistbury Head forms a splendid viewpoint 2m E of this resort. The beach is of sand and shingle and allows sea bathing.

SOUTH BRENT, Devon 5 SX66
A carved Norman font exists in the Norman to 15th-c church, and an old church house is of interest. An old toll-house in the village square still displays the original board advertising the toll-charges for livestock.

SOUTH BURLINGHAM, Norfolk 15 TG30
An interesting local church displays two Norman doorways, a fine 15th-c pulpit, wall-paintings, an old screen, and bench-ends.

SOUTH CERNEY, Glos 12 SU09
An old and a new cross feature in this attractive Cotswold village, and the church includes two finely-worked Norman doorways plus fragments of 12th-c wood carving. The new Cotswold water park, or Keynes country park, lies in this area.

SOUTHCHURCH, Essex 9 TQ98
Southchurch is sited at the E extremity of Southend-on-Sea, and includes a restored partly-Norman church which has an addition built by Sir Ninian Comper in 1906. The hall shows fine old timbering and now houses the public library.

SOUTH CREAKE, Norfolk 15 TF83
A 15th-c angel-carved nave roof is a notable feature of the church, which also displays a massive old chest and an ancient screen.

SOUTH DOWNS
This well-known range of chalk hills starts near Petersfield and rolls across Sussex to terminate at Beachy Head, where it is abruptly stopped by the Channel. The Downs are wooded in the W and bare in the E. Three of the highest points are 889ft Butser Hill, with a new county park at its summit viewpoint; 837ft Duncton Down in the W; notable 813ft Ditchling Beacon viewpoint in the E. The range is separated from the North Downs by The Weald. Some 150sqm of the Hampshire hills are designated an area of outstanding natural beauty, together with the whole Sussex escarpment, and a new bridleway now traverses much of the ridge.

SOUTHEND-ON-SEA, Essex 9 TQ88
Plan overleaf
Amenities offered by this popular resort include bathing, golfing, a pier and electric railway that extends for more than a mile, and open-air swimming baths. A floral clock has a 20ft-diameter dial, and the Regency character of the town is preserved by the Royal Terrace. Porters is a manor house of c1600 which now serves as Mayor's Parlour, and a museum of historic aircraft lies on the W boundary. Southend airport is situated N of the town. The resort's autumn illuminations are well known.

SOUTHFLEET, Kent 9 TQ67
Fruit trees and hops are cultivated in this area. The 14th-c church carries a good tower and houses fine old woodwork, interesting brasses, and ancient glass. A rectory of the same period also stands in the area. Excavations in the neighbourhood have yielded interesting Roman finds.

SOUTHGATE, Gt London 8 TQ39
Georgian houses exist in Southgate village, and timbered Broomfield House, now a museum, dates from the 17thc.
cont

1. Arcades (town walls)
2. Arundel Tower
3. Bargate (museum)
4. Canute's Palace
5. Catchcold Tower
6. Civic Centre
7. Dolphin Hotel
8. God's House Tower (museum)
9. Hamwich Excavations Site
10. Hospital of St Julian
11. King John's Palace
12. Merchant Navy Memorial (Holy Rood remains)
13. Mitchell Memorial Museum
14. Pilgrim Fathers' Memorial
15. Southampton Common
16. St Mary's Church
17. St Michael's Church
18. Titanic Memorial
19. Tudor House (folk museum)
20. University of Southampton
21. West Gate
22. Wool House (maritime museum)

Grovelands was built by John Nash in the late 18thc and now contains a hospital.

SOUTH HAMS, Devon 5 SX73
A tract of fertile country lying between Tor Bay and Plymouth Sound is known by this name. Coastal scenery around the Salcombe area is particularly attractive, and much of the district is designated an area of outstanding natural beauty. The cliff scenery between Bolt Head and Bolt Tail is some of the finest in the West Country, and all of it is protected by the NT.

SOUTH HARTING, W Sussex 8 SU71
Anthony Trollope lived in this South-Downs village for a while. The Caryll chapel of the early-English church was desecrated in 1643 during the Civil War. A prominent spire of green copper is supported by a central tower, and local stocks and a whipping-post have been preserved. Uppark is a 17th- to 18th-c house designed by William Talman, lying 2m S in a secluded position high on the downs (OACT).

SOUTH LEIGH, Oxon 13 SP30
John Wesley preached his first sermon at the perpendicular-style church in 1725. The building is also known for its notable wall paintings.

SOUTH LOPHAM, Norfolk 15 TM08
A Norman tower which is perhaps the finest in Norfolk is carried by the local church. Old carved bench-ends can be seen inside, including a particularly notable example displaying an elephant and castle.

SOUTH MIMMS, Herts 8 TL20
Notable Frowyk tombs exist in the 13th- to 16th-c church, and the 18th-c houses of Dyrham Park and Wrotham Park lie to the S. The latter was built for the ill-fated Admiral Byng, who was shot in 1757 for neglect of duty after having lost Minorca.

SOUTHMINSTER, Essex 9 TQ99
Southminster stands on the edge of the Dengie Marshes. Restored St Leonard's church has a good 15th-c north porch and preserves items of furniture from Nelson's Victory.

SOUTH MOLTON, Devon 5 SS72
Several Georgian houses can be seen in South Molton, which stands on high ground to the S of Exmoor. The guildhall dates from 1743 and has an open arcaded lower-storey. Adjacent to this is a small museum (OACT). Nave and chancel capitals in the perpendicular church show good carving, and the tower rises to 107ft.

SOUTH OCKENDON, Essex 9 TQ58
The restored church retains a notable Norman north doorway and a flint round tower of 13th-c origin. Timber framed Baldwins and Elizabethan Little Belhus are both old houses of the area. Also of interest is a windmill dating from 1828.

SOUTH PETHERTON, Somerset 6 ST41
King Ina's Palace is a notable 15th-c house which has been restored. A rare fives tower stands by the Crown Inn, and the early-English to perpendicular church carries an octagonal central tower. Fosse Way crosses the Parrett 1m E, by an old bridge on which there are two curious carved figures. Wigborough Manor dates from 1585 and lies 2m S.

SOUTH POOL, Devon 5 SX74
Picturesquely situated at the head of Salcombe harbour creek in the South Hams district, South Pool includes a 14th-c church housing a notable painted screen.

SOUTHPORT, Merseyside 21 SD31
Beautifully laid-out gardens are a feature of this well-known golfing resort, and it is also the scene of a large annual flower show. Amenities include extensive sands, sand dunes, a sea bathing lake and the Victoria salt-water swimming baths. Southport pier is the largest in England, and has its own railway. Motor races have been held on the sands. Lord Street is considered one of the finest thoroughfares in the north of England, and Hesketh Park is one of the finest of its kind in the whole country.

St Cuthbert's church is situated at Churchtown and displays a spire and clock of 1739, plus examples of fine woodwork. A large bird sanctuary at Martin Mere is of interest (SE). Steam locomotives and buses, and a growing collection of tramcars are preserved at the new Southport Steam Port.

SOUTHROP, Glos 12 SP10
Typical Cotswold houses, the River Leach, and an interesting mainly-Norman to early-English church make up this village. The church displays herringbone masonry in the nave walls and preserves a remarkable 12th-c font. A rare Norman doorway is incorporated in the manor house.

SOUTHSEA, Hants 7 SZ69
This popular resort adjoins Portsmouth and offers a sand and shingle bathing beach. See under Portsmouth for fuller details.

SOUTH SHIELDS, Tyne & Wear 27 NZ36
Extensive docks and good sandy bathing beaches are features of this Tyne-mouth resort and seaport. Marsden Rock is a notable formation lying offshore to the S of the town. Roman remains taken from the site of The Lawe, which is still partly visible (AM), are exhibited by the local museum. William Wouldhave, inventor of the lifeboat, was born here in 1789. A lifeboat which was launched in 1833 can be seen near the clock tower, and the rebuilt St Hilda's church is a model of an early lifeboat. The old town hall of 1768 has been superseded by municipal buildings of 1903, considered one of the finest civic complexes in the country. A car ferry links South and North Shields.

SOUTH TAWTON, Devon 5 SX69
A fine 15th-c church lies on the fringe of Dartmoor national park, and is noted for its tower, lych-gate, and beautifully

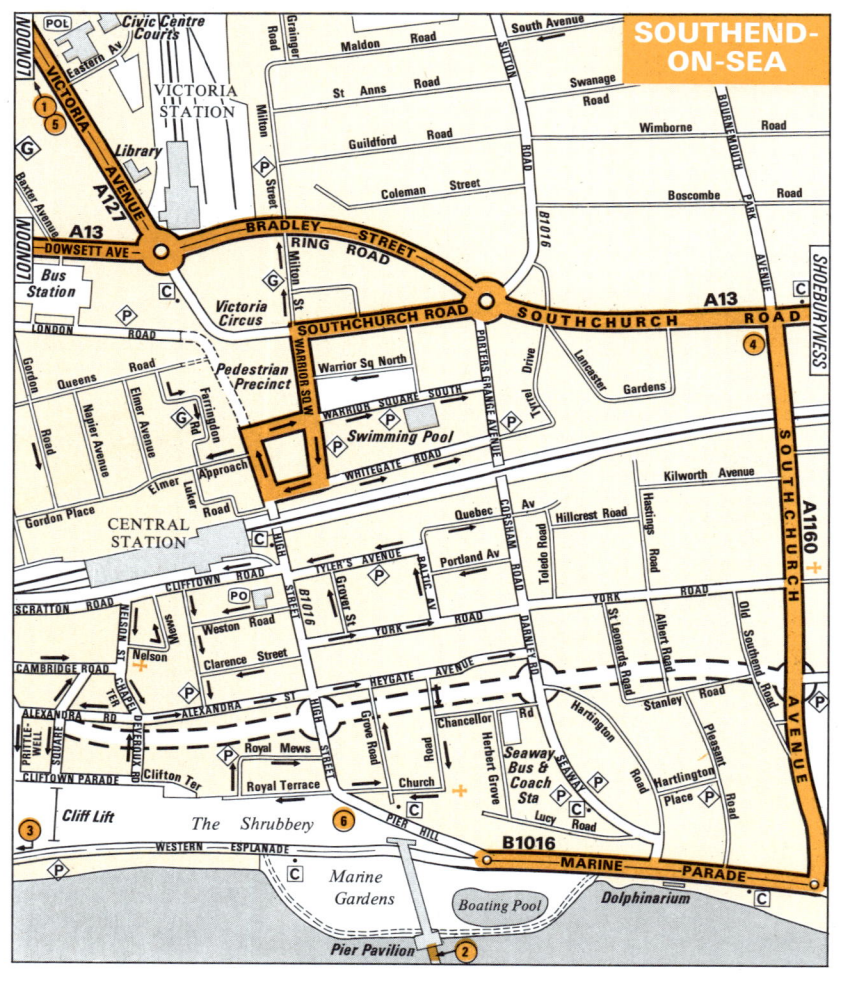

1 Airport
2 Electric Railway and Pier
3 Floral Clock
4 Mayor's Parlour
5 Museum of Historic Aircraft
6 Royal Terrace

carved roofs. The thatched church house dates from 1572 to 1573.

SOUTH WALSHAM, Norfolk *15 TG31*
Two churches stand in one churchyard at South Walsham. Mainly-perpendicular St Lawrence's was burnt in 1827 and only the ruined tower and restored chancel remain. St Mary's is of decorated and perpendicular style, and displays a lovely two-storeyed porch, plus a screen and bench-ends dating from the 15thc.

SOUTHWELL, Notts *18 SK75*
Cathedral status was attained by a local church in 1884. The building displays twin west towers and is a fine example of Norman to perpendicular work. It is particularly noted for the Norman nave and north porch; the 13th-c choir; the pulpitum; and the chapter-house – famous for its wonderful late 13th-c foliage carving. The 16th-c brass lectern was retrieved from the lake at Newstead Abbey, into which it had been thrown during the Dissolution in the 16thc. Ruins of an Archbishop's Palace exist, and the present palace dates from 1907 and 1909.

King Charles I gave himself up to the Scots at the Saracen's Head, formerly the King's Arms Inn, in 1647. Byron spent holidays at Burgage Manor between 1804 and 1807, and the house is now a Youth Hostel. Southwell is said to have been the birthplace of the Bramley seedling apple. Brackenhurst Hall lies 2m S and was the birthplace of Viscount Allenby in 1871.

SOUTHWICK, W Sussex *8 TQ20*
Southwick lies off the E arm of Shoreham Harbour, and Roman remains excavated from the area can be seen in a museum at Hove. Charles II escaped to France from Southwick in 1651, and the Norman tower once carried by the church was destroyed by bombing.

SOUTHWICK, Wilts *6 ST85*
Two fine old houses of the area are Southwick Court to the NE, and Brook House to the SE. The former once stood inside a moat and was the home of the Staffords. Brook House includes ancient doorways and a fine timber roof.

SOUTH WINGFIELD, Derbyshire *18 SK35*
Extensive ruins of a fine 15th-c manor house (AM), one of the best of its period to be seen, include a gatehouse and hall. Mary Queen of Scots was imprisoned here in the 16thc and the house was dismantled in 1641 (OACT).

SOUTH WITHAM, Lincs *19 SK91*
Excavations between 1965 and 1966 revealed the site of a Preceptory of the Knights Templers, possibly of 12th-c date (AM).

SOUTHWOLD, Suffolk *15 TM57*
A resort at the mouth of the River Blyth, Southwold offers a sand and shingle beach, bathing, and golfing. The splendid perpendicular church carries a fine tower and is noted for stalls, a medieval painted pulpit, a good screen, and a Seven Sacraments font. Stocks and a whipping-post are kept in a small museum in the church and the grave of authoress Agnes Strickland can be seen in the churchyard. The town is noted for its numerous greens, which were probably formed after a fire of 1659. English and Dutch fleets fought the battle of Sole Bay in 1672, and the Duke of York used Sutherland House while based here. The lighthouse stands within the town.

SOUTH WRAXALL, Wilts *6 ST86*
Sir Walter Raleigh and Sir Walter Long are associated with the beautiful 15th- to 16th-c manor house, and are supposed to have started the English pipe-smoking fashion here. The building displays a fine gatehouse. Features of the church include a tower with a rare saddle-back roof, and the interesting Long chapel.

SOUTH ZEAL, Devon *5 SX69*
The Oxenham Arms inn is an interesting old house, and North Wyke and West Wyke are ancient mansions that exist in the area. Cawsand Beacon rises to 1,799ft from Dartmoor national park, in the S.

SOWERBY BRIDGE, W Yorks *22 SE02*
Wood Lane Hall displays an unusual rose window and dates from 1649. The parish church of St Peter is situated W at Sowerby, and dates from 1736 to 1766. Norland Lower Hall and Fallingworth Hall are two 17th-c houses lying S.

SPALDING, Lincs *19 TF22*
This Fenland town is situated on the River Welland, and includes several attractive 18th-c houses. Greatly-restored Ayscoughfee Hall dates from the 15thc and now houses a museum of British birds. The restored mainly early-decorated church features double aisles, a fan-traceried north porch, and an angel-carved hammerbeam nave roof. The Gentlemen's Society museum is of note.
cont

1 Bird Sanctuary (Martin Mere)
2 Golf Course
3 Hesketh Park
4 St Cuthbert's Church
5 Steam Port (transport museum)
6 Victoria Swimming Baths

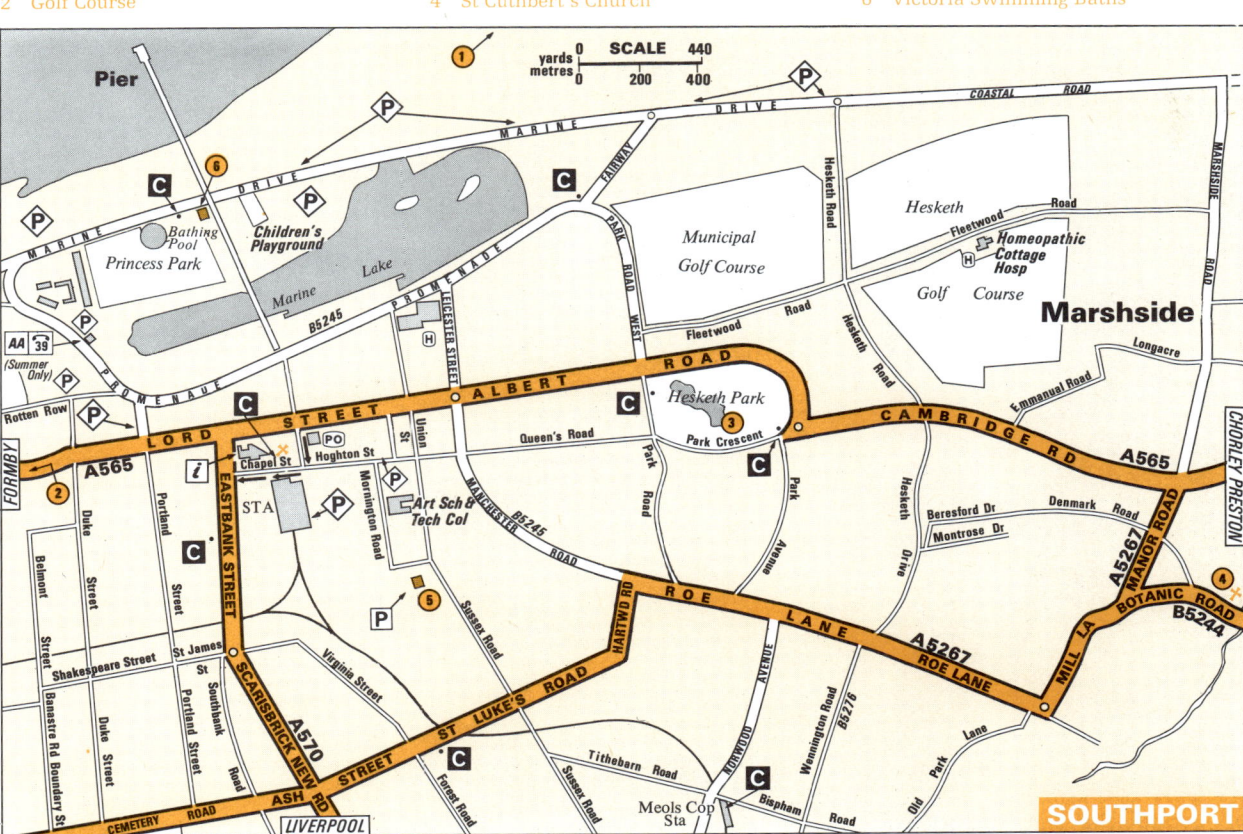

Spalding is in the middle of a bulb farming district, and is surrounded by a vast colourful area of flowers in late spring. The 20-acre Springfields Gardens are of particular note at this time of year, and a tulip procession takes place annually. The Wykeham Chapel of 1311 lies 3m NE.

SPARSHOLT, Oxon *13 SU38*
Good brasses and a 13th-c transeptal screen can be seen in the fine decorated-style church. The village itself lies in a downland setting.

SPEECH HOUSE, Glos *12 SO61*
Situated at about 400ft in the Forest of Dean national forest park, this well-known 17th-c and later house preserves the Court Room of 1680 where the Forest Verderers hold their courts. It now serves as a hotel.

SPEEN, Berks *7 SU46*
Two Elizabethan tombs can be seen in the restored church, and late 18th-c Benham Park is by Capability Brown.

SPEKE, Merseyside *17 SJ48*
Speke Hall is a magnificent example of 16th-c half-timbering – perhaps the finest in Lancashire – and now contains a museum which includes rare Mortlake tapestries (NT, OACT). Liverpool Airport is situated in the area.

SPELDHURST, Kent *9 TQ54*
Windows by Burne-Jones can be seen in the rebuilt church, and the picturesque half-timbered George and Dragon Inn is dated 1415. The village is so situated as to afford wide views over the surrounding area.

1 Castle Remains
2 Chetwynd House
3 College Almshouses and Chapel
4 High House
5 St Chad's Church
6 St Mary's Church
7 Swan Hotel
8 William Salt Library

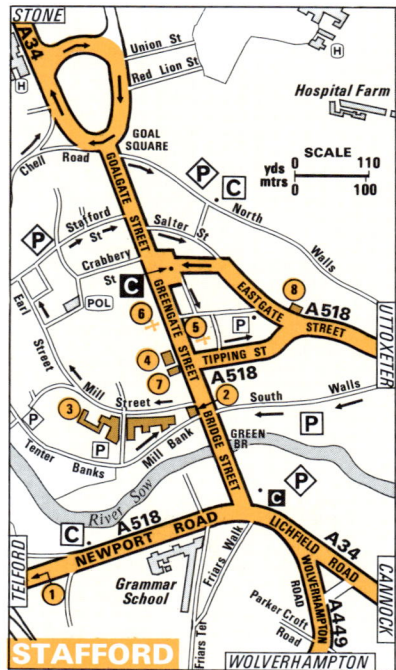
STAFFORD

SPELSBURY, Oxon *13 SP32*
Old thatched cottages, some 17th-c almshouses, and a Norman and later church containing two notable Lee monuments are features of this Evenlode-Valley village.

SPENNYMOOR, Co Durham *27 NZ23*
Whitworth Hall lies NW and was rebuilt in 1892. It is associated with the famous ballad *Bobby Shafto's gone to sea*.

SPETCHLEY, Herefs & Worcs *12 SO85*
The partly 14th-c church contains interesting monuments, and the fine mansion of Spetchley Park dates from 1810. Standing in an isolated position 3m NE, the little church of Warndon displays a picturesque timbered tower, a 15th-c seven-sided font, and examples of ancient glass and woodwork.

SPETTISBURY, Dorset *7 ST90*
An old bridge crosses the River Stour here, and the ancient earthworks of Spettisbury Rings are of interest.

SPILSBY, Lincs *19 TF46*
Parts of the rebuilt church retain the decorated style, and the Willoughby monuments inside the building are of interest. A statue of Sir John Franklin the explorer, who was born in the town in 1768, stands near a partly 14th-c butter cross. The White Hart is an interesting old inn.

SPOFFORTH, N Yorks *22 SE35*
Remains of a 14th-c castle or fortified manor house, once a Percy stronghold, exist here (AM, OACT). John Metcalf, the blind 18th-c roadmaker, lies in the churchyard.

SPONDON, Derbyshire *18 SK33*
Silk is manufactured in this town. A restored 14th-c church shows fine tracery in the chancel windows, plus a stone lectern.

SPRATTON, Northants *13 SP77*
The 12th- to 15th-c church carries a notable tower and spire; it houses splendid choir stalls, plus the fine Swinford monument of 1371. A late 18th-c hall stands in the area.

SPROATLEY, Humberside *23 TA13*
Sproatley's 19th-c ivy-clad church contains an ancient inscribed coffin lid, and is approached through a lych-gate. Burton Constable mansion stands 2m N in 200 acres of parkland landscaped by Capability Brown (OACT). Notable state rooms of the Georgian period are features of the house.

SPROTBROUGH, S Yorks *22 SE50*
A 14th-c stone chair which may once have served as a sanctuary stool can be seen in the church. Also of interest are a carved screen, a notable pulpit, and stalls.

SPROWSTON, Norfolk *15 TG21*
Fine monuments and brasses can be seen in the restored church. Sprowston Mill was the famous subject of a picture by John Crome, but has since burnt down. The picture hangs in London's National Gallery.

STAFFORD, Staffs *18 SJ92*
Black-and-white houses to be seen in this area include the High House, which is associated with King Charles I and Prince Rupert. The Swan Hotel has associations with George Borrow, who was an ostler here in 1825.

St Mary's Norman to decorated church houses a font of the earlier period, plus a bust of the famous angler Izaak Walton. Walton was born here in 1593, and baptized in the church. St Chad's shows a Norman chancel arch and font. Chetwynd House of 1745 now serves as the Post Office. It is associated with the Dukes of Cumberland who were here in 1745, and Sheridan who was once MP for Stafford. College almshouses and chapel date from c1640. The notable William Salt library is contained in an 18th-c house. Half-completed, mainly 19th-c Stafford Castle (AM) stands $1\frac{1}{2}$m SW on the foundations of a 14th-c structure that was destroyed in 1643. It is not accessible owing to its unsafe condition.

STAGSDEN, Beds *13 SP94*
The Stagsden Bird Gardens (OACT) include a particularly interesting game collection. Features of the local church include a carved 14th-c font and the old Stacheden chapel.

STAGSHAW BANK, *27 NY96*
A big sheep fair used to be held here. The line of a Roman Road known as the Devil's Causeway extends NE from the nearby Roman Wall, to its termination at a point 3m W of Stagshaw Bank. A roadside cross erected by King Oswald in AD635 stands near St Oswald's Chapel, or Heavenfield.

STAINDROP, Co Durham *27 NZ12*
Splendid Neville monuments exist in the 12th- to 15th-c church. Imposing 14th-c to 18th-c Raby Castle, a former seat of the Neville family, lies about $\frac{3}{4}$m N in 10 acres of gardens (OACT). A fine collection of pictures is housed in the building.

STAINES, Surrey *8 TQ07*
Staines lies at the junction of the Rivers Colne and Thames, and until quite recently was part of the county of Middlesex. The present Staines Bridge dates from 1829 and a new bridge of 1961 carries the by-pass. The London Stone stands W of the church, near the river, and is set on a pedestal dated 1781. It marks the City of London's former limit of jurisdiction up the Thames. Sir Walter Raleigh was tried and condemned here in 1603; this would normally have taken place in London, but at that time the plague was rife in the capital.

STAITHES, N Yorks *23 NZ71*
Lofty cliffs encircle the bay on which this picturesque village is sited, and the beach offers sand at low tide. Access is by a sharp 1 in 5 descent from the main road. Captain Cook worked in a local shop as a boy. Boulby Cliff rises to nearly 700ft 2m WNW, and is possibly the highest in England. Wooded glens extend inland from here.

STALHAM, Norfolk *15 TG32*
Lying S of Sutton Broad, this village includes a fine gabled hall dating from 1670. The restored perpendicular church houses a painted screen and a splendid carved font.

STALYBRIDGE, Gt Manchester *18 SJ99*
This town is involved in the cotton and engineering industries. A house in Corporation Street bears a tablet recalling Jack Judge, who composed the famous song *It's a Long Way to Tipperary*. Eastwood Bird Reserve lies in

Cheetham Park. Longdendale Valley lies 4m SE, and contains reservoirs surrounded by the moorland countryside of the Peak District national park.

STAMBOURNE, Essex *14 TL73*
Stamborne church carries a massive Norman tower and displays sculptured canopies in the niches of the window jambs.

STAMFORD, Lincs *19 TF00*
Considered England's most beautiful small stone-built town, Stamford stands on the River Welland and includes numerous interesting old buildings. The area in and around Barn Hill has survived particularly well.

Five ancient and notable churches are: St Mary's, with a splendid 13th-c to 14th-c tower and spire; early-English to perpendicular All Saints', with its notable brasses; 13th- to 15th-c St George's, displaying fine old glass in the chancel; perpendicular St John's, with its 15th-c glass; St Martin's, containing the Burghley Chapel and tombs. A grave in the churchyard of the latter contains the remains of Daniel Lambert, who died in 1809 and at one time weighed nearly 53 stone.

Browne's Hospital has a Jacobean hall and chapel, and the ancient Burghley almshouses can be seen near the Welland. Stamford school was founded in 1532. Students seceding temporarily from Oxford studied at Brasenose College in 1333, and a 14th-c gateway from the building has survived. The George inn displays a gallows sign. Ruins of Norman St Leonard's Priory have been partially restored and lie in a field SE of the town. The ivy-clad ruin of Wothorpe Towers, dismantled in the 18th-c, lies to the SW.

Part of the town is known as Stamford Baron and belongs to Cambridgeshire. Elizabethan Burghley House also belongs to this county and stands 1½m ESE in a large park. The well-known Burghley Horse Trials are held here, and the house is considered one of England's greatest Elizabethan mansions. Its various and numerous treasures include the famous painted Heaven room by Verrio (OACT). Sir Malcolm Sargent is buried in Stamford.

STAMFORD BRIDGE, N Yorks *22 SE75*
King Harold won a victory over the Norwegians at this River-Derwent site in 1066, prior to his defeat and death at Hastings. The river bridge dates from 1727, and Aldby Park of 1726 lies 3m NE.

STAMFORDHAM, Northumberland *27 NZ07*
The church originated from the early 13th-c, but was extensively rebuilt in 1848. Good lancet windows are preserved in the chancel. A fine old market cross dates from 1736, and several 18th-c houses border the green. The rectory was built in 1762 and an old lock-up has survived.

STANDISH, Gt Manchester *21 SD51*
This colliery town was built on the line of a Roman road and includes a church which was rebuilt in the late 16thc. The latter is considered a good example of the period in which it was re-constructed, and its notable woodwork can be seen particularly well in the roofs. Stocks are preserved on the old steps of the modern cross.

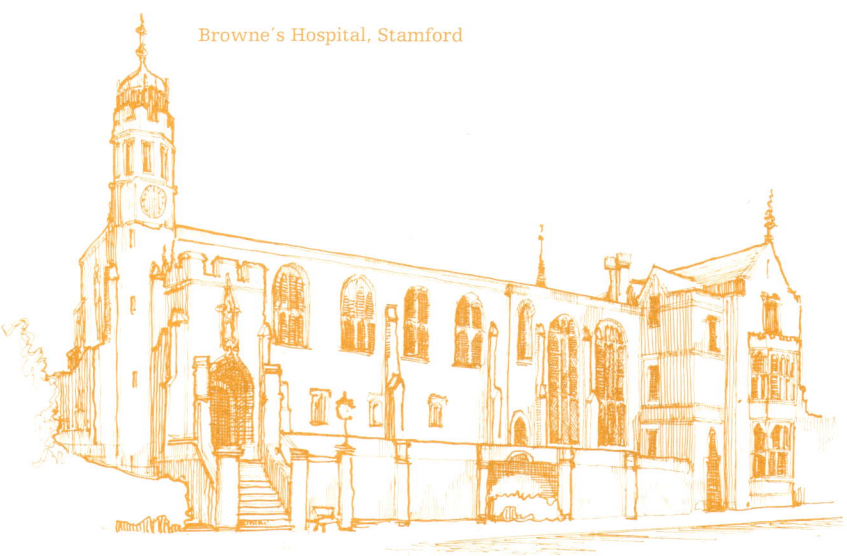
Browne's Hospital, Stamford

STANDON, Herts *14 TL32*
A large west porch and detached tower are features of the 13th-c and later church, and interesting monuments can be seen inside. The endowed school is housed within a 16th-c timber-framed building, and the Lordship incorporates portions which were built in 1546. A stone at Standon Green End recalls Vincenza Lunardi's descent from a balloon in 1784. Upp Hall, a fine 17th-c house near a 140ft-long brick-built barn, lies 2½m NE.

STANE STREET
Stane Street is a Roman Road of about 57 miles in length, linking London (*Londinium*) with Chichester (*Regnum*). It passes through a gap in the North Downs at Dorking and thence through country which was formerly part of the great Forest of Anderida. The present A29 road follows part of the original Roman route in several places.

STANFORD, Northants *13 SP57*
A splendid old church showing a pinnacled 15th-c tower, 15th-c screenwork, old glass, interesting monuments, and an organ which Cromwell threw out from Whitehall Palace, exists in this tiny River-Avon village. Percy Pilcher was a pioneer of flying who was killed near here in an accident of 1899. He is commemorated by a monument which stands near the river. Stanford Hall lies across the Leicestershire border, and is a notable William and Mary mansion of 1690. It includes a museum of cars and motor cycles (OACT).

STANFORD-IN-THE-VALE, Oxon *13 SU39*
Coxe's Hall dates from 1690 and other houses in this Vale of White Horse village are of 18th-c and earlier date. The mainly early-English to decorated church houses old glass, a beautiful piscina used as a reliquary, and an oak-cased font.

STANHOPE, Co Durham *27 NY93*
Features of this Weardale town include an old bridge and a 12th- to 14th-c church displaying decorated stall-ends of 1663. The late 18th-c castle stands on the opposite bank of the river to 17th-c Unthank Hall; the latter now serves as a farm.

STANMORE, Gt London *8 TQ19*
Fine monuments to the builders of the old church – the c1632 brick tower of which still stands – can be seen in the modern church. W S Gilbert the famous librettist of the Savoy operas, is buried in the churchyard. Several Georgian houses exist on Stanmore Hill, and the 505ft summit is covered by an extensive wooded common. See under Edgware for Little Stanmore.

STANNINGFIELD, Suffolk *15 TL85*
One of the two fine Norman doorways in the local church stands inside a timbered porch. Rockwood family tombs can be seen in the chancel. Elizabethan Coldham Hall includes a dovecote of the same period, and stands to the W.

STANSTEAD ABBOTS, Herts *8 TL31*
The interesting church displays a 15th-c timbered porch and a brick chancel of 1577; other features include a three-decker pulpit, a tower screen, and several old box pews. The Baeshe almshouses date from the 17thc, and a curious embattled house of 1752 stands in the village.

STANSTED, Essex *14 TL52*
Stansted Mountfitchet is the full name of this parish. The church preserves a Norman chancel arch and enriched doorways of the same period, and the brick tower is of 17th-c date. Old houses and a brick tower mill of 1787 (OACT), the latter with its machinery still intact, are of interest. The airport lies to the S.

STANSTED, W Sussex *8 SU70*
Stansted House is an early 20th-c building which replaces two earlier houses. A nearby chapel of 1812 to 1815 incorporates part of the original 15th-c house, and contains painted glass. There are notable beech and maple avenues, the former planted in 1820 and the latter in 1956, in the lovely Forest of Bere.

STANTON, Glos *12 SP03*
Sometimes described as the most attractive and least spoilt of the Cotswold villages, Stanton nestles at the foot of Shenbarrow Hill. The latter forms a good viewpoint. Among the many old houses that exist in the area are Warren House of 1577, and the restored

Elizabethan mansion of Stanton Court. The partly rebuilt church contains examples of old glass, a rare tithe book, and notable modern fittings. An old cross stands in the area.

STANTON DREW, Avon *6 ST56*
Noteworthy prehistoric stone circles exist in the area, and Hautville's Quoit (AM) is of interest. A picturesque thatched toll house stands to the N, and the village includes a medieval rectory.

STANTON HARCOURT, Oxon *13 SP40*
Considerable remains of the old manor house include a Tudor gatehouse, an interesting old kitchen, and Pope's tower – associated with Alexander Pope in 1718. The fine Norman to perpendicular church houses a very rare early-English screen. Three stones known as the Devil's Quoits exist SW of the village.

STANTON-IN-PEAK, Derbyshire *18 SK26*
This picturesque village includes an old stone-built farmhouse and 16th- to 18th-c Stanton Hall. Barrows and a stone circle lie about ¾m S on Stanton Moor. The Reform Bill monument on Stanton Moor Edge is inscribed 'Earl Grey' and dates from 1832.

STANTON LACY, Salop *12 SO47*
A fine Saxon doorway surmounted by a cross, one of the few known examples of Saxon sculpture, can be seen in the local church. The half-timbered gatehouse of former Langley Manor stands 1m N, and the restored Langley Chapel of 1564 and 1601 contains fine 17th-c furnishings (AM, OACT).

STANTON ST JOHN, Oxon *13 SP50*
Milton's grandfather lived here, and an old house in the area bears the inscription *The birthplace of John White, 1575–1648, fellow of New College, Oxford, and chief founder of Massachusetts in New England.* The interesting church is of early-decorated to perpendicular style, and displays good window tracery plus old bench-ends.

STANWAY, Glos *12 SP03*
A noble gateway in the style of Inigo Jones straddles the approach to the village's fine 17th-c hall. An old tithe-barn now serves as a village hall, and the small mainly-perpendicular church retains carved Norman grotesques round the chancel walls. Toddington lies 2m SW and includes an impressive modern church, plus an ornate modern hall by Sir Charles Barry in his Houses-of-Parliament style. Remains of the former 17th-c manor house exist in the neighbourhood.

STANWELL, Surrey *8 TQ07*
Large reservoirs lie near Stanwell, and Knyvett's former Free School dates from 1624 (AM). Stanwell Place is of Georgian origin.

STAPLE FITZPAINE, Somerset *6 ST21*
Staple Hill rises above this small village, and the church carries a particularly lovely and richly-carved 15th-c church tower – considered one of the best in the county. Norman work is evident on the south doorway. Castle Neroche iron-age camp lies at 905ft on the ridge of the Blackdowns, to the S.

STAPLEFORD, Leics *19 SK81*
A lake-watered park surrounds the hall, which displays a Tudor wing and interesting items of 17th-c statuary (OACT). The estate includes a lion reserve.

STAPLEFORD, Notts *18 SK43*
Stapleford's manor house dates from 1689, and a pre-Conquest cross stands in the churchyard.

STAPLEFORD, Wilts *7 SU03*
Thatched cottages and excellent views of the Wyle Valley are features of this charming old-world village. The Norman to decorated church houses a great stone coffin, with an ornamental cross.

STAPLEHURST, Kent *9 TQ74*
The early-English to perpendicular church is notable for the ancient ironwork – probably 12th-c – carried by the south door. Fuller House and Maplehurst are interesting old buildings in the immediate area, and others that exist in the vicinity include Spilsill Court and Loddenden Manor.

STAUGHTON, GREAT, Cambs *14 TL16*
Remains of a 14th-c moated house exist near the manor house. The River Kym flows through the grounds of the latter, and the decorated and perpendicular church houses numerous monuments. A sundial surmounts the 17th-c village cross.

STAUNTON, Glos *12 SO51*
Staunton lies between the Forest of Dean national forest park and the Wye Valley. Its Norman to perpendicular church contains two fonts – one Norman and one of later decorated style. The Buck Stone forms a notable viewpoint at its lofty elevation of 900ft.

STAUNTON HAROLD, Leics *18 SK32*
Most of the hall – now one of the Cheshire Homes for the disabled – dates from c1760, but earlier parts are ascribed to Inigo Jones. An inscription above the door of the church shows it to have been built in 1653 (NT), and the building houses Shirley memorials plus a splendid ironwork screen by Robert Bakewell. It is one of the very few to have been built during this period (OACT).

STAVELEY, Cumbria *21 SD49*
Staveley is situated in the Lake District national park. Long Kentmere valley, at the head of which stands the partly 14th-c hall, extends N into lonely fells dominated by 2,476ft Ill Bell.

STAVELEY, Derbyshire *18 SK47*
Situated in an industrial and coal-mining district, Staveley includes a restored church which contains monuments to the Frecheville family.

STAVERTON, Devon *5 SX76*
A fine old seven-arched bridge spans the River Dart here, and is sited near a picturesque mill. The early-English and perpendicular church contains a fine screen. A restored gallery in the latter building was copied from one at Atherington.

STAVERTON, Glos *12 SO82*
Skyfame aircraft Museum is of interest for both its planes and for its display of 1,000 model aircraft and picture gallery (OACT).

STEBBING, Essex *14 TL62*
The fine 14th-c church preserves a rare stone screen. Old timbered houses exist in the area, and the Friends' Meeting House bears the date 1674.

STEEPLE ASHTON, Wilts *7 ST95*
A restored market cross stands near a medieval lock-up in this beautiful stone-built village. The mainly 15th-c church carries a good tower and displays a wealth of pinnacles and carvings. Its nave roof shows some 350 carved bosses. The vicarage is of partly 14th-c date, and the old manor house is of interest. Ashton House originates from 1724.

STEEPLE ASTON, Oxon *13 SP42*
This Cherwell-Valley village includes a church containing a Norman font, glass by Kempe, the interesting Page monument, and carved benches and screenwork.

STEEPLE BUMPSTEAD, Essex *14 TL64*
Several interesting monuments can be seen in the restored Norman and later church. Also restored is the half-timbered guildhall, which dates from 1592. Moyns Park is a splendid Elizabethan house standing in moated grounds, behind which are the remains of an earlier building.

Prehistoric standing stones near Stanton Drew

STEEPLE LANGFORD, Wilts *7 SU03*
Chequered-flint and stone cottages stand among water meadows in this Wylye-Valley village. The Norman and later church contains a Norman font and squint fashioned from Purbeck marble. Bathampton House dates from the 17th and 18thc.

STEETLEY, Derbyshire *18 SK57*
One of England's richest small Norman churches, used as a cowshed until rescued from decay in 1880, stands in this isolated position. It has no village.

STELLING, Kent *9 TR14*
Stelling's unrestored 13th-c church retains 18th-c box pews and a three-decker pulpit. Farther S at Stelling Minnis is a smock mill of 1866. The Slippery Sam inn recalls a local smuggler of the past.

STENG CROSS, Northumberland *27 NY99*
Here at a height of some 1,040ft is the lonely gibbet known as Winter's Stob. A man hanged at Newcastle upon Tyne for murdering an old woman was hung in chains here in 1791. A wooden head is fixed to the gibbet.

STEVENAGE, Herts *14 TL22*
Developed as one of the New Towns, the area of recent building far exceeds that occupied by ancient Old Stevenage. The Six Hills are a series of round barrows, and the Norman to 15th-c church contains screen work and stalls of the 15th-c.

STEVENTON, Hants *7 SU54*
Jane Austen was born here in 1775, as commemorated by a tablet in the early-English church where her father was rector for over 40 years. An old manorial pew is also preserved in the church.

STEVINGTON, Beds *13 SP95*
Perhaps the last working example of its kind in this country, the post mill here was built in 1770 and restored for the 1951 Festival of Britain. The village cross is of interest, and the noteworthy church displays a Saxon tower and old carved pews.

STEWARTBY, Beds *13 TL04*
This garden estate of 1927 and later is connected with well-known brickworks, which have been described as the largest in the world.

STEWKLEY, Bucks *13 SP82*
The finest late-Norman church in this county exists here, and displays a richly-carved west front and notable chancel. It was restored by Street in 1862.

STEYNING, W Sussex *8 TQ11*
A delightful little town at the foot of the South Downs, Steyning includes a long main street lined with old houses. George Fox, founder of the Quaker movement, held a meeting at the quaint old clock tower in 1655. Brotherwood Hall dates from the 15th-c. Magnificent Norman workmanship is evident in the church, and the nave and chancel arch are of particular note. Chantry Green House dates from 1525 and 1705 (OACT).

STICKLEPATH, Devon *5 SX69*
A former corn and cloth mill here is now an interesting museum of rural industry. The house of Staplers, formerly used in the wool industry, stands in gardens which may be the most beautiful in Devon (OACT).

STIFFKEY, Norfolk *15 TF94*
Salt marshes extend to the fringe of this village. Sir Nicholas Bacon, father of the famous Francis Bacon, built the picturesque Elizabethan hall which now lies in ruins. A Bacon monument and a 15th-c brass can be seen in the church.

STIFFORD, Essex *9 TQ68*
The 13th-c church has a pulpit of 1671 and contains numerous brasses. Ford Place of 1655 and later displays Dutch gables, and both Copped Hall and The Lodge are of Georgian origin.

STILLINGTON, N Yorks *22 SE56*
Laurence Sterne was vicar of the perpendicular church during the 18thc; the building displays an interesting priest's door.

STILTON, Cambs *14 TL18*
This was formerly a Great North Road collection point for Stilton cheeses made in Leicestershire, but the road now by-passes the village. The Bell is a fine old inn of 1642, and the early-English to perpendicular church houses several brasses.

STINSFORD, Dorset *6 SY79*
Thomas Hardy used Stinsford as Mellstock in his novels, and his heart is buried in the 13th- to 15th-c church. A Hardy window portraying Elijah is also of interest, and there are Hardy tombs in the churchyard. Kingston Maurward is a fine Elizabethan manor house situated in the grounds of a later mansion.

STOCK, Essex *9 TQ69*
Timbering on the belfry of the local church is one of the best examples to be seen in Essex. The almshouses date from the 17thc and a tower windmill in the area was built *c*1800.

STOCKBRIDGE, Hants *7 SU33*
This pleasant little town is famous for its River-Test fishing. Other features include an old inn, and the town hall with its clock turret of 1810. The 13th-c chancel of an old church has been restored as a chapel, and an old drovers' house retains a Welsh inscription.

Norman apse of Steetley church

STOCKPORT, Gt Manchester *18 SJ98*
Stockport is a manufacturing town situated on the River Mersey. The parish church of St Mary was partially rebuilt in 1813, St Peter's Church is an 18th-c brick-built building, and St George's is to an impressive design of 1893. An old half-timbered house in Great Underbank now houses a bank. Vernon Park includes an interesting museum. Bramall Hall, largely 15thc and though much-restored still one of the finest half-timbered houses in the county, lies 2½m S near Bramhall and now houses a museum (OACT).

STOCKTON, Wilts *7 ST93*
Thatched cottages and a fine Elizabethan manor house of coursed flints are features of this pretty Wylye-Valley village. Topp Almshouses are an attractive 17th-c structure and the area includes an Elizabethan farmhouse with a great barn. The interesting trans-Norman to perpendicular church displays old monuments and nearly a score of mass-dials; the nave and chancel are divided by a thick wall which is pierced by a door and two squints.

STOCKTON-ON-TEES, Cleveland *22 NZ41*
Thornaby-on-Tees faces this industrial town across the River Tees, and both are situated near the river mouth. A plaque on a house near the railway commemorates the sale of the first passenger ticket on the Stockton to Darlington line, in 1825. Thomas Sheraton, the famous cabinet-maker, was born in the town in 1751 and later settled in London. The town hall dates from 1736 and stands near a market cross of 1768. The main street is one of the widest in England, and St Thomas's Church contains 18th-c fittings. Several good 18th-c houses stand in Church Street. Preston Hall, now an interesting museum of Teesside life, lies 2½m SW. A racecourse exists in the area.

STOGURSEY, Somerset *6 ST24*
Sometimes known as Stoke Courcy, Stogursey includes a church which shows some remarkable Norman work. Carved pier capitals, old bench-ends, and the sanctuary ring are of particular note. Slight remains of a castle exist in the area. Fairfield House lies to the W and is

dated 1589. Hinkley Point nuclear power station faces Bridgwater Bay to the N.

STOKE-BY-CLARE, Suffolk   14 TL74
This village lies in the Stour Valley and includes the remains of a former college – once a priory – incorporated in a house of later date. The perpendicular church contains a finely-carved pulpit and displays a delineation of a windmill in the south chapel window. Some of the woodwork is notable.

STOKE-BY-NAYLAND, Suffolk   15 TL93
The perpendicular church carries a 120ft tower which John Constable has featured in many of his paintings, and houses several interesting brasses and monuments. Restored half-timbered cottages stand adjacent to the church. Gifford's Hall is a largely 16th-c house which lies 2m NE and includes a brick-built gatehouse. The gabled and plastered 17th-c Thorington Hall lies 2m SE and now serves as a studio (NT).

STOKE CHARITY, Hants   7 SU43
Features of the exceptionally interesting church include a great deal of Norman workmanship, examples of 15th-c glass, and the 15th-c Hampton chapel. The latter contains memorials, brasses, and a notable piece of sculpture which had been walled up until its re-discovery in 1849.

STOKE D'ABERNON, Surrey   8 TQ15
Stoke d'Abernon church is famous for Sir John d'Abernon's brass of 1277, thought to be the earliest in England. A similar memorial to his son dates from 1327. Also of interest are sections of pre-Conquest walling, and a partly-Flemish 17th-c pulpit. The main structure of this building has suffered severe restoration. The old manor house is of Tudor origin, but was refaced with brick during the 18thc. Slyfield Manor lies 1m SSE near the River Mole, and exhibits fine early-Jacobean brickwork.

1 Church of St Peter ad Vincula
2 Pottery Museum
3 Spode Copeland Museum

STOKE DOYLE, Northants   14 TL08
Contemporary fittings and a sculpture by Chantrey can be seen in the interesting little 18th-c church. The rectory dates from 1633 and 1731, and an old dovecote survives from a former manor house.

STOKE DRY, Leics   19 SP89
Views of the Welland Valley are available from here. The church contains richly-carved Norman columns, fine Digby monuments, and a priest's chamber with an oriel window. Sir Everard Digby of Gunpowder-Plot fame was born here in 1578.

STOKE GABRIEL, Devon   5 SX85
Beautifully situated on a creek of the River Dart, Stoke Gabriel includes a perpendicular church containing a restored screen. A large yew stands in the churchyard. Church House Inn has an exterior staircase leading to an upper floor, a facility which could have been used for parish meetings.

STOKE GOLDING, Leics   18 SP39
Remarkable window tracery of two periods and a carved nave arcade are features of the superb 14th-c church. The building can be considered the finest example of its date in Leicestershire.

STOKENCHURCH, Bucks   8 SU79
Chairs are made in this high-lying village, and 800ft Beacon Hill dominates its Chiltern neighbours. The new M40 motorway penetrates the escarpment to the W, and runs through a spectacular chalk cutting.

STOKENHAM, Devon   5 SX84
Prior to the 1944 invasion of France, this village served as a battle-practice area. The perpendicular church carries a good tower and houses a restored painted screen.

STOKE-ON-TRENT, Staffs   17 SJ84
This town forms the centre of the potteries and North Staffordshire coalfield district, and was featured under the name 'Knype' in Arnold Bennett's novels about *Anna and the Five Towns*. The rebuilt church of St Peter ad Vincula contains a sculptured medallion to Josiah Wedgwood by Chantrey, plus memorials to Minton and the Spodes. Spode Copeland museum in Church Street is noteworthy. A fine museum displaying examples of pottery dating from the 17thc onwards is sited at Hanley.

STOKE POGES, Bucks   8 SU98
Thomas Grey wrote the *Elegy in a Country Churchyard* here, and a churchyard monument to the poet was designed by James Wyatt and erected in 1799 (NT). The Norman and later church includes the Hastings chapel of 1557. A fragment of one of the windows bears the rare representation of a bicycle – complete with satyr. The Garden of Remembrance is well known, and Tudor chimneys are a feature of the restored manor house. Stoke Park is of the late Georgian period, and an old hospital dates from 1765.

STOKESLEY, N Yorks   22 NZ50
Cleveland Hills and North York moors national park rise above this delightful little market town. A wide main street contains several 18th-c houses, and the packhorse bridges dates from 1648.

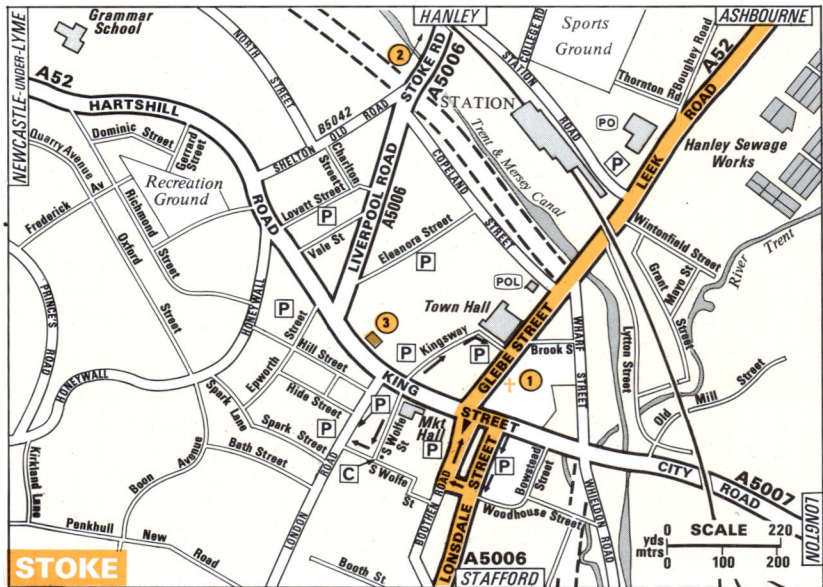

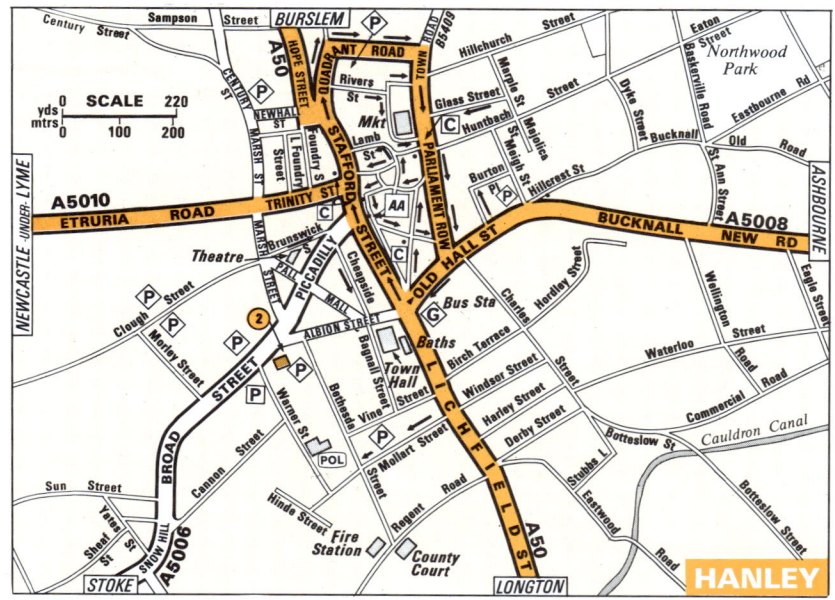

STOKE-SUB-HAMDON, Somerset 6 ST41
The interesting Norman to perpendicular church displays a good tower and a fine Strode monument. A rare and ancient fives court can be seen behind the Fleur-de-Lis Inn. The priory was formerly a chantry house and dates from the 15th-c (NT, OACT). Hamdon Hill rises 426ft above the village, and is where the lovely yellow Ham Hill Stone is quarried. An extensive British camp on the summit has yielded many iron-age and Roman finds, which can be seen in the castle museum at Taunton.

STONDON MASSEY, Essex 9 TL50
An early-Norman nave and chancel, plus a pulpit and reader's desk of 1639, are features of the local church. The Elizabethan composer William Byrd spent some years here, a fact testified by an inscribed stone set in the church wall.

STONE, Kent 9 TQ92
Properly known as Stone-cum-Ebony, this remote Isle of Oxney village stands on high ground above the Royal Military Canal and Walland Marsh. The perpendicular church displays a rare example of a Roman Mithraic altar-stone near the west door. During one period it was used as a mounting block, and still retains its tethering ring. An old Kentish hall-house stands nearby.

STONE, Kent 9 TQ57
Stone's 13th-c church shows some of the finest foliage carving in the country, and is thought to have been built by Master Ralph of Dartford. Master Ralph also helped with the construction of Westminster Abbey in c1220.

STONE, Staffs 18 SJ93
Peter de Wint was born in this small Trent-Valley town in 1784, and Admiral St Vincent is buried in the local churchyard. The church dates from 1754.

STONEGRAVE, N Yorks 22 SE67
Features of the local church include a 12th- to 15th-c tower, a good Jacobean screen, and a fine wheel-headed Saxon Cross. Nunnington Hall is a 16th- to 17th-c house lying 2m NE, which displays a panelled hall and staircase (OACT).

STONEHENGE, Wilts 7 SU14
Although the origin and purpose of this famous prehistoric megalithic monument are unknown, it is thought that it may be connected with ancient sun-worship rites (AM). It originally consisted of several circles and two horseshoes, surrounded by a 300ft-diameter ditch and earthwork. Several of the stones are still in their original positions; the largest measures some 21ft high and is sunk 8½ft into the ground. Theory acknowledges the possibility that some may have been brought from the Prescelly Hills in the Welsh county of Dyfed. Two of the fallen stones were re-erected in 1958. Numerous artefacts of the neolithic age have been discovered here, and many ancient barrows exist in the vicinity. The surrounding land is NT property.

STONELEIGH, Warwickshire 13 SP37
Part of the church is of Norman workmanship – notably the chancel arch – and a number of Leigh monuments are housed inside. Several attractive timbered houses exist in the area. Although the main part of Stoneleigh Abbey is an 18th-c house, the gatehouse and hospice of the original 14th-c monastic buildings are still standing. The house was damaged by fire in 1960, and the grounds are now the permanent site of the Royal Show.

STONE STREET
This Roman Road is now followed by the B2068, and its 18m length links Canterbury (*Durovernum*) with Lympne (*Portus Lemanis*). It should not be confused with the better known Stane Street of W Sussex.

STONEY MIDDLETON, Derbyshire 18 SK27
Stoney Middleton is picturesquely situated in Middleton Dale, which itself lies in the Peak District national park. A curious octagonal church of 18th-c date is interesting, and the 17th-c hall has been enlarged.

STONHAM ASPALL, Suffolk 15 TM15
Bench-ends beautifully carved with poppy heads, and a splendid 15th-c chest are features of the local church. The tower displays a strange wooden belfry and an unusual pinacled parapet.

STONOR, Oxon 8 SU78
Tudor and later Stonor Park includes an old RC chapel and stands in what is probably the most beautiful wooded park in the county. Edmund Campion, the 16th-c Jesuit martyr, set up his printing press here.

STONYHURST, Lancs 21 SD63
Stonyhurst College is an imposing structure of partly 16th-c date, with modern additions, which stands in magnificent grounds. It is now a famous RC school.

STONY STRATFORD, Bucks 13 SP74
The Cock and Bull inns are said to have given their names to the well-known saying, 'A Cock and Bull story'. Presumably, this saying refers to tall stories swapped between patrons of the two inns.

STOPHAM, W Sussex 8 TQ01
A notable seven-arch bridge dating from the 14thc spans the River Arun here. Monuments and brasses to the Barttelot family can be seen in the church, and the unrestored manor house dates from the 16th to 18thc.

STORRINGTON, W Sussex 8 TQ01
Celtic fields are preserved on the 697ft viewpoint of Kithurst Hill, and adjacent to Storrington is the NT property of Sullington Warren. A large tithe barn of 1685 can be seen near Manor Farm. Elizabethan Parham is a beautiful house dating from 1577, which lies 2m W and contains a long gallery plus fine pictures and furnishings (OACT).

STOTTESDON, Salop 12 SO68
Both the chancel and the Wrickton aisle of the church show beautiful decorated work, and a notable Saxon doorway has been preserved. The Norman font is beautifully carved. A tiny stone-built bridge of ancient origin spans the River Rea.

STOURBRIDGE, W Midlands 12 SO88
Large iron and glass works operate in this industrial town. An interesting 18th-c church includes stained glass, and the pleasant Clent and Lickey Hills are situated to the SE.

STOURPORT, Herefs & Worcs 12 SO87
England's only example of a town built entirely for the needs of the canal age, Stourport retains many original 18th-c houses and warehouses. Its old canal basin has been sympathetically restored for yachting and boating. The Rivers Severn and Stour are here joined by the Staffordshire and Worcestershire Canal at this point, and the town is sometimes referred to as the Venice of the Midlands.

STOURTON, Wilts 6 ST73
Stourton is part of the Stourhead estate, and includes a perpendicular church containing monuments to the Hoare family. Also of interest is a squire's pew complete with fireplace. Opposite the church stands the Bristol High Cross of 1373, which was removed from the city in 1763.

Magnificent gardens around the 18th-c house include lakes and temples, and were originally laid out by Henry Hoare. The house itself was by Colin Campbell (NT,

Remains of the prehistoric megalithic structure of Stonehenge

OACT). A redwood tree of 140ft stands in the park. St Peter's Pump, one of the sources of the River Stour, stands in the N part of the estate. Kingsettle Hill lies 3m NW and is a notable viewpoint and landmark rising to 850ft. It is surmounted by King Alfred's tower, which was damaged during the war.

STOW, Lincs 19 SK88
This was once a cathedral city, and the mother church of Lincoln Minster. The very fine mainly-Saxon to Norman church shows a rich late-Norman chancel and a perpendicular tower. Coates-by-Stow includes a small church with a notable 15th-c screen and gallery, and lies 2m NE.

STOW BARDOLPH, Norfolk 14 TF60
A curious wax effigy of Sarah Hare, who died from a needle prick in 1744, is preserved in a locked case situated in the Hare chapel of the local church.

STOWE, Bucks 13 SP63
Now a well-known public school, this historic 17th- to 18th-c house stands in a great park as a memorial to bygone 18th-c magnificence. Part of the building is ascribed to Adam, and it was once the residence of the Dukes of Buckingham and Chandos. The grounds are justly famous for such notable features as a covered bridge, temples by Gibbs and Kent, and fine statuary (OACT).

STOWE-NINE-CHURCHES, Northants 13 SP65
A legend relates how eight previous attempts to build a church here were foiled by the devil, who removed the building stones each time the structure was started. The church now standing preserves some Saxon work – notably the tower – and contains a number of fine monuments. The village's ridge-top situation allows wide views.

STOWLANGTOFT, Suffolk 15 TL96
Notable examples to be seen among the wealth of wood carving in the church include the choir stall misericords, and a fantastic variety of old bench ends. Some 15th-c Flemish woodwork also exists.

STOWMARKET, Suffolk 15 TM05
This agricultural and manufacturing town includes a decorated and perpendicular church containing an old organ and a rare wigstand. Milton used to visit his tutor at the Old Vicarage, and the Abbots Hall museum depicts rural life in East Anglia. Stow Lodge Hospital of 1777 and 1781 was originally built as a workhouse, or House of Industry. The old moated farmhouse of Columbyne Hall lies 2m NE.

STOW-ON-THE-WOLD, Glos 12 SP12
St Edwards, with its fluted pilasters, is a notable example of the many stone-built houses to be seen in this Cotswold hill-top town. Stocks and an old cross exist in the market place. The church carries a perpendicular tower and the nave boasts a splendid 17th-c Belgian painting of the Crucifixion. Hundreds of prisoners were confined in this building after a Civil War battle of 1646. Abbotswood is a modern house to the W of the town, standing in famous gardens. Development of British livestock breeding is portrayed at the Cotswold Farm Park, which lies 7m WNW of Stow, off the A436.

STRADBROKE, Suffolk 15 TM27
The decorated and perpendicular church carries a lofty embattled tower, and displays a beautifully carved niche on the chancel wall. Bishop Grosseteste was born at Stradbroke in the reign of Henry III, and died in 1253. Several moated farms exist in the area, and the mid 16th-c house of Thorpe Hall lies to the SW.

STRAND-ON-THE-GREEN, Gt London 8 TQ17
Access to this delightful Thames north-bank area is by foot from Kew Bridge. Most of the houses and inns are of Georgian date, and Zoffany the painter died here in 1810.

STRATFORD ST MARY, Suffolk 15 TM03
An attractive village in Constable country, Stratford St Mary is situated on the River Stour. Old stained glass, a great deal of ancient carving, and several curious gargoyles can be seen in the decorated and perpendicular church.

STRATFORD-SUB-CASTLE, Wilts 7 SU13
An old one-hand clock on the tower of this Avon-Valley village's perpendicular church shows the signs of the Zodiac. Numerous examples of 17th-c woodwork can be seen inside. The gabled parsonage is dated 1675.

STRATFORD-UPON-AVON, Warwickshire 12 SP25
Pilgrims dedicated to the cause of literature travel to Stratford-upon-Avon from all over the world – because it was the birthplace of celebrated poet and playwright, William Shakespeare. The house in which he was born in 1564 stands in Henley Street, and contains interesting relics and documents connected with the great man. The grammar school in which he was educated forms the upper storey of the old guildhall, and the site of New Place, where he died, lies near by. The latter area is now laid out as a garden and includes a museum. Exhibits and displays connected with local history are mounted at the adjacent Nash's House.

Holy Trinity Church is of early-English to perpendicular date, and contains Shakespeare's grave, monuments, the font in which he was christened, and the register of his baptism and burial. The Royal Shakespeare Theatre of 1932 replaces an older building which was burnt out in 1926. Adjacent to this is the Royal Shakespeare Theatre Gallery and Exhibition (OACT). The mother of the founder of Harvard University, in the USA, was born in the timbered Harvard House. Almshouses stand near the 15th-c Guild Chapel. The town hall was rebuilt in 1767, and the 14-arch Clopton Bridge dates back to the late 15thc. Shrieve's House was rebuilt after 1595, and the White Swan Inn preserves well-known Tobit paintings. Garrick Inn and the Shakespeare and Falcon Hotels are picturesque buildings. Hall's Croft, a 16th-c timbered house, has Shakespearean associations; Mason Croft was the home of Marie Corelli. The Judith Quiney house shows fine timbering. October's Mop Fair is famous.

Stratford Canal is 13m long and runs NW of the town. It has been rescued from decay by the NT, and was re-opened by Royalty in July 1964. Some of the canal bridges were unique in that they were constructed in two halves, with a gap through which the tow-rope could be dropped. Clopton House dates from Elizabethan to 17th-c and later periods and lies 1½m N; 2½m NE is Alveston House, a building of the William and Mary period.

STRATTON, Cornwall 5 SS20
Steep streets and a church showing a pinnacled 15th-c tower are features of this quaint little place. Old bench-ends and barrel roofs with carved bosses can be seen inside the church. A Civil War battle was fought here in 1643, and the Tree Inn is associated with the defeat of the Roundheads.

STRATTON-ON-THE-FOSSE, Somerset 6 ST65
Downside Abbey is a noted RC abbey and college, and the parish church has a rare dedication to St Vigor. The area lies on the E slopes of the Mendip Hills.

STREATLEY, Berks 13 SU58
Streatley is pleasantly situated on the River Thames opposite Goring. A splendid panoramic view is afforded by the hill above the village. The area preserves several old houses and Basildon Park, 2m SW, was designed by Carr of York in 1776.

STREET, Somerset 6 ST43
Footwear has become the staple product of this small manufacturing town, and famous Millfield School lies in the neighbourhood. A tall monument to Admiral Lord Hood stands SE on Windmill Hill, and Ivythorn and Walton Hills are good viewpoints lying S (NT). Ivythorn Manor is of Tudor origin.

STRENSHAM, Herefs & Worcs 12 SO94
Samuel Butler was born here in 1612. The decorated and perpendicular church has a gallery, which probably once formed the rood loft front, displaying interesting restored painted panels. The long series of Russell monuments is notable. Local almshouses date from 1697, and Strensham Court was built in 1824.

STRETHAM, Cambs 14 TL57
Stretham has one of the lowest average rainfall figures in England. The restored perpendicular church carries a good west tower and spire, and the rectory shows work from the 14th to 16th and 18thc. A derelict tower-mill and a notable village cross of c1400 are of interest. Stretham Beam Engine is well-preserved and was formerly used for fen drainage (OACT).

STRETTON SUGWAS, Herefs & Worcs 12 SO44
The church carries a black-and-white timbered tower, and displays three Norman doorways. A remarkable carved tympanum is preserved over one of the latter, and an engraved stone dated 1473 is of interest.

STROOD, Kent 9 TQ76
This Medway town is linked to Rochester by a bridge. The Crispin and Crispianus inn displays a fine painted sign. The restored Temple Manor, which was formerly a 12th-c Commandery of the Knights Templar, lies ½m S by the river (AM, OACT).

STROUD, Glos *12 SO80*
A noted centre of the W of England cloth trade, this Cotswold town stands on the small River Frome and the Stroudwater Canal. A number of 18th-c mills exist in the area and the 16th-c town hall has been restored. Several typical Cotswold cottages are preserved in Church Street. All but the tower of the parish church was rebuilt in 1838. Interesting Stroud museum is situated at Lansdown, and the annual Festival of Religious Drama and the Arts takes place in October. Picturesque Stroudwater Hills surround the town.

STUDLAND, Dorset *7 SZ08*
Sandy beaches and sea bathing are offered by this Isle of Purbeck village. The unspoiled church preserves rich Norman work, particularly good examples of which are the tower and chancel. A curious mass of ironstone situated on the heaths to the W is known as the Agglestone, and is estimated to weigh over 500tons. Ballard Down rises in the S, with the curious chalk stacks of Old Harry Rocks lying off-shore from Handfast Point. A 429-acre national nature reserve exists in the area.

STUDLEY, Oxon *13 SP51*
Thatched cottages and old almshouses dating from 1639 are features of this village. A Jacobean house known as Studley Priory stands on the site of a former priory, and now serves as a hotel. It features in the film *A Man for all Seasons* as the home of Sir Thomas More.

STUDLEY, Warwickshire *12 SP06*
Needles have been made in this River-Arrow village since c1695. The Norman to decorated church preserves an ancient stone coffin lid with a cross, plus the old road stairs. Old Castle is a picturesque timbered house displaying 19th-c alterations, and a late 17th-c manor house in the area is of interest. Sparse remains of a priory are incorporated in a farm which bears the date 1539 on one of its chimneys. Studley Castle dates from 1834.

STUDLEY ROYAL, N Yorks *22 SE26*
William Burges designed the fine modern church, which carries a lofty tower and spire and stands in a magnificent park. A Norway spruce that has grown to 156ft stands in the park. The present house dates from 1716, and once formed the stables of a mansion which was burnt in 1945.

STURMER, Essex *14 TL64*
Work from the pre-Conquest to 16th-c periods can be seen in the church. The adjacent hall dates from the 15th to 17thc and stands within a moat. It has been modernized and now serves as a farm.

STURMINSTER NEWTON, Dorset *6 ST71*
A picturesque six-arched bridge spans the River Stour here, and carries one of the group of inscribed Dorset Transportation Tablets (AM). Restored 14th-c Fiddleford Mill House lies 1m E and is noted for its timbered roof (AM). The delightful little 17th-c Hammoon Manor, which lies 3m NE, shows a good thatched roof.

STURRY, Kent *9 TR16*
Sturry takes its name from the River Stour (*ie* Stour-y). The church includes a 14th-c timbered porch and carries a 15th-c tower. Sturry Court is now known as Milner Court and dates from 1583 to 1927. It was formerly a grange of St Augustine's Abbey, and displays a Tudor archway and a tithe barn. It now houses a school.

STUTTON, Suffolk *15 TM13*
Stutton Hall dates from 1553 and includes an interesting gateway. Georgian Crepping Hall and 17th-c Crowe Hall are also of interest.

STYAL, Cheshire *17 SJ88*
Timbered Oak Hall Farm and the large Quarry Bank cotton mill of 1784 are

1	Almshouses
2	Alveston House
3	Clopton Bridge
4	Clopton House
5	Falcon Hotel
6	Garrick Inn
7	Guild Chapel
8	Guildhall and Old Grammar School
9	Hall's Croft
10	Harvard House
11	Holy Trinity Church
12	Judith Quiney House
13	Mason Croft
14	Nash's House (museum)
15	New Place (garden and museum)
16	Royal Shakespeare Theatre
17	Royal Shakespeare Theatre Gallery and Exhibition
18	Shakespeare Hotel
19	Shakespeare's Birthplace
20	Shrieve's House
21	Town Hall
22	White Swan Inn

15th-c Old Moot Hall, Sudbury

interesting features of this Bolling-Valley village (NT). Audubon the famous naturalist visited this part of Cheshire.

SUDBURY, Derbyshire *18 SK13*
This attractive village stands near the River Dove and includes a very fine 17th-c hall (NT). The Vernon family own the latter, which displays notable carvings and plasterwork (OACT). Monuments to the Vernons can be seen in the restored church, and the Dowager Queen Adelaide lived here during the 19thc.

SUDBURY, Suffolk *15 TL84*
Old houses and inns in this River-Stour town include Gainsborough's birthplace, a 16th-c dwelling in Gainsborough Street. It has now become a cultural and art centre. The 15th-c Salter's Hall has Pickwickian associations, and the Old Moot Hall is of 15th-c date. Ballingdon Hall, a late 16th-c timbered house, was moved on trestles to a new location in 1972. St Gregory's Church dates from the 15th-c and contains carved choir stalls, plus a splendid 15th-c cover surmounting the modern font; 15th-c St Peter's has a 17th-c nave roof, painted screen panels, and the wonderful 15th-c embroidery known as the Sudbury Pall; 14th- to 16th-c All Saints' has a fine 15th-c pulpit, old screenwork, and Suffolk's heaviest bell. Belchamp Hall dates from $c1720$ and lies 4m W. The latter house contains fine panelling.

SULBY, Isle of Man *20 SC39*
Sulby Glen extends S from here towards 2,034ft Snaefell, the highest point in the island. Access to the mountain is by means of an electric railway. Tholt-y-Will is a wooded subsidiary glen which lies near the junction of three parishes Michael, Lezayne, and Braddan. Curragh wild life park is of great interest.

SULGRAVE, Northants *13 SP54*
Famous Sulgrave manor house was the 16th-c ancestral home of the Washington family, and has now been restored as a museum. The original stars and stripes can be seen over the porch window, and Royal Arms depicting the Lion of England and the Red Dragon of Wales are situated above another window (OACT). Recent excavations have revealed foundations of a Saxon manor house. The church contains Laurence Washington's tomb, a Washington chest and pew, and several brasses.

SUNBURY-ON-THAMES, Surrey *8 TQ16*
This Thames-Valley residential town includes an 18th-c church showing later influences. The tall churchyard yew has been associated with Dickens' *Oliver Twist*, and Kempton Park racecourse lies in the area.

SUNDERLAND, Tyne & Wear *27 NZ35*
Ship building is one of the main industries of this River-Wear coal port. Holy Trinity parish church dates from 1719 and 1735, and contains a monument by Chantrey. The local museum and art gallery is of interest, and the fine new Civic Centre dates from 1970. Sunderland was the birthplace of two eminent men: Jack Crawford, who nailed the flag to the mast at Camperdown in 1797; Sir Henry Havelock, who relieved Lucknow in 1857. Wearmouth Bridge bears a medallion picture of the former 18th-c structure which it replaced, on the parapet. Roker is a residential suburb which offers good sands. A 15th- to 18th-c chapel (OACT) lies $3\frac{1}{2}$m W, adjacent to modernized 14th- to 15th-c Hylton Castle (AM).

SUNDERLAND, Lancs *21 SD45*
Sunderland is situated at the point where the River Lune enters the Irish Sea. Englands first cargo of cotton was landed here, and an inscribed gravestone at Sunderland Point recalls a negro named Sambo who died in 1736.

SUNDRIDGE, Kent *8 TQ45*
A fine old timbered house can be seen in the main street of this village, and the 13th-c church contains several good brasses. Ovenden House is dated 1745.

SUNNINGDALE, Berks *8 SU96*
This famous golfing centre is pleasantly situated between Windsor Great Park and Chobham Common. Virginia Water lies in the neighbourhood.

SUNNINGWELL, Oxon *13 SP40*
The restored cruciform-shaped church is of mainly late-perpendicular style, and is noted for its unique hexagonal west porch. The porch was built by Dr Jewel between 1550 and 1552. Cothill national nature reserve lies to the W.

SURFLEET, Lincs *19 TF22*
Cressy Hall dates from 1695 and the early 19thc, and the village lies in a Fenland area. Gilbert White's *Natural History* describes a heronry which once existed here. The church carries a rare leaning spire, sloping about 6ft from the perpendicular.

SUTCOMBE, Devon *5 SS31*
Remains of a very fine screen, plus a notable series of bench-ends carved with arms of many Devonshire families can be seen in the perpendicular church.

SUTTON, Beds *14 TL24*
Fine tombs of the Burgoynes, one of whom won a Crimean Victoria Cross, can be seen in the 14th-c church. A beautiful old packhorse bridge exists in the area.

SUTTON, Cambs *14 TL47*
A tower carried by the late-decorated church is surmounted by a rare double-octagon and spire. The Burystead of 1742 retains a former 14th-c chapel.

SUTTON-AT-HONE, Kent *8 TQ57*
St John's Jerusalem is a 17th- to 18th-c house which preserves some 13th-c workmanship. Hasted the Kentish historian rebuilt part of the house in the 18thc (NT, OACT).

SUTTON BANK, N Yorks *22 SE58*
Roulston Scar and Gormire Lake, in the Hambleton Hills of the North York Moors national park, can be seen from the summit of this well-known main-road hill. The hill is an AA viewpoint and attains a maximum gradient of 1 in 4.

SUTTON BONINGTON, Notts *18 SK52*
This is a combination of two villages standing on the River Soar, and includes several old buildings. St Michael's 13th-c church houses a 14th-c font and has been restored. St Anne's has also been restored, and houses an octagonal font; the actual building dates from the 13th to 14thc. The Midland Agricultural College is situated here.

SUTTON BRIDGE, Lincs *14 TF42*
King John lost all his baggage and treasure in the nearby Cross Keys Wash in October of 1216. The River Nene flows through the area.

SUTTON COLDFIELD, W Midlands
18 SP19
Several stone-built houses that were designed by Bishop Vesey in the 16thc survive in this area, and represent what may well be the earliest attempt at a housing scheme. They all feature spiral stone staircases. This enterprising Bishop also made alterations to the parish church in the 16thc, and founded the local grammar school – which still stands. The original members of the Free Foresters cricket club came from the Forest of Arden, and played their first game in Rectory Park in 1856.

Lake-watered Sutton Park covers 2,000 acres, and the 700ft viewpoint of Barr Beacon lies farther to the W. New Hall, an old restored house standing within the confines of a moat, lies $1\frac{1}{2}$m SE. The 19th-c St Mary's College lies 2m SW at New Oscott, and was largely by Pugin.

SUTTON COURTENAY, Oxon *13 SU59*
Three old houses that exist in this picturesque Thames-side village are the 12th-c Norman hall, the 15th- to 17th-c

manor house, and the 14th-c abbey. The 12th- to 14th-c church displays a 16th-c south porch. The Earl of Oxford and Asquith, who died here in 1928, is buried in the local churchyard. A Roman villa was excavated here in 1966.

SUTTON HOO, Suffolk *15 TM24*
Famous discoveries were made here when some of the eleven ancient barrows were opened in 1938 and 1939. One of the most important was the remains of an Anglo-Saxon ship. Some of the finds can be seen in Ipswich museum, and the most valuable – jewellery and coins – are housed in London's British Museum.

SUTTON VALENCE, Kent *9 TQ84*
Slight remains of a Norman castle exist in the vicinity of this attractively situated village. An old windmill and school are of interest. The grave of John Willes (1777 to 1852) who introduced round-arm bowling into cricket can be seen in the churchyard.

SWAFFHAM, Norfolk *15 TF80*
The 15th-c church displays a splendid angel-carved double-hammerbeam roof, a fine 16th-c west tower, and modern carved bench-ends. A domed market cross exists here, and a fine wooden sign depicts the Pedlar of Swaffham. The Iceni Village and museum of Cockley Cley lies 3m SW and displays an interesting reconstruction of a prehistoric tribal settlement (OACT). A Saxon church stands in the grounds.

SWAFFHAM PRIOR, Cambs *14 TL56*
Swaffham Prior includes two churches in one churchyard. St Mary's contains old brasses, and St Cyriac's is now used as a mortuary chapel. Attractive half-timbered Baldwin Manor is of 16th-c date, and two windmills exist in the area – a tower mill and a smock mill.

SWALCLIFFE, Oxon *13 SP33*
A rare drag-hook for fighting thatch fires is preserved in the interesting Saxon to perpendicular church. Other features of the area include thatched cottages, an old manor house, and a notable tithe barn.

SWANAGE, Dorset *7 SZ07*
This quiet Purbeck resort is sheltered by Ballard Down and offers excellent sandy beaches for sea bathing. Several old houses exist in the town, particularly near the mill pool, and are dominated by the 13th-c tower carried by the rebuilt church. The façade of the town hall was formerly displayed by the Mercers' Hall in Cheapside, London, and preserves an inscribed lock-up of 1803. A clock-tower which once stood at the S end of London Bridge was erected near the pier in honour of Wellington. Godlingston is a 13th-c and later house which lies N of the resort, and a curious stone globe of the world can be seen 1½m S at Durlston Head. Near by are the Tilly Whim caves, and beyond lie the lighthouse at Anvil Point and the curious cliff known as Dancing Ledge. Some of the best known sea-cliff climbing in England can be enjoyed in the area. Purbeck stone is quarried in the district.

SWANNINGTON, Leics *18 SK41*
The Leicester to Swannington railway was one of the earliest to be built in England, and a piece of the original rails has been preserved in London's Science Museum. George Stephenson's Comet pulled the first local train in 1832, and was brought here by canal.

SWANSCOMBE, Kent *9 TQ67*
Swanscombe's restored 12th-c church preserves a partly pre-Conquest tower. Swanscombe Skull Site national geological reserve was where part of a skull – possibly the earliest in Europe – was found between 1935 and 1936. This area is not open to the public. A monument recording a meeting between the men of Kent and William the Conquerer has been moved from the A2 Dover road at Springhead crossroads, to the Swanscombe council office grounds. Roman remains have been excavated in the district.

SWANTON MORLEY, Norfolk *15 TG01*
Remains of a house which belonged to the ancestors of Abraham Lincoln exist here (NT). The church dates from c1379 and displays a massive tower plus fine window tracery.

SWARDESTON, Norfolk *15 TG10*
Edith Cavell, who was executed in 1915 during the German occupation of Belgium, was born in the village and is commemorated by a window in the church. Gowthorpe Manor is of Elizabethan origin and shows interior work of a later date.

SWARKESTON, Derbyshire *18 SK32*
A notable seven-arch bridge, dating from the 13th and 14thc and including a causeway of nearly a mile in length, can be seen here. The advance guard of Bonnie Prince Charlie's army reached this bridge in 1745, but immediately retreated. A curious summer house of c1630 remains from the former Harpur mansion, and Swarkeston Hall dates from c1630. The Harpur chapel of the rebuilt church contains two interesting monuments.

SWAVESEY, Cambs *14 TL36*
Notable window-tracery and benches displaying animal carvings are features of the fine 14th-c church. An old manor house exists in the area.

SWIMBRIDGE, Devon *5 SS63*
The 14th- to 15th-c church contains one of the finest carved screens in the county. This dates from 1420; other features include a splendid pulpit, a very ornate mid 16th-c font cover, and a rare Devon spire.

SWINDON, Wilts *12 SU18*
Important railway works operated here. The chancel of the town's original church stands in the grounds of a 17th-c house known as The Lawn. The actual parish church is of 19th-c date, and an interesting museum exists in the town. The Great Western Railway museum is of particular interest. Coate Farm, the birthplace of Richard Jefferies in 1845, now serves as a museum and lies 1½m SE (OACT). The western end of Coate Water forms a bird sanctuary.

SWINESHEAD, Lincs *19 TF24*
Remains of a market cross exist here, and the stocks are preserved. A good decorated and perpendicular tower and spire are carried by the church and a 15th-c screen can be seen inside. Slight remains of the abbey, where King John took refuge after losing his baggage to the waters of the Wash in 1216, lie 1m NE.

SWINTON, Gt Manchester *21 SD70*
Swinton is an industrial and coal-mining town. Picturesque timbered Wardley Hall lies 1m NW and has been restored. A human skull has been preserved in a staircase niche.

SYDLING ST NICHOLAS, Dorset
6 SY69
Picturesque cottages and a perpendicular church are features of this downland village. Features of the church include a clock dating from 1593 and a tower displaying fine gargoyles. The neighbouring manor house is of Tudor origin, but was later altered in the gothic style. Also of interest is an old thatched tithe barn.

SYMOND'S YAT, Herefs & Worcs
12 SO51
This famous beauty spot lies in a narrow loop of the River Wye. The AA viewpoint at the summit of 473ft Yat Rock is accessible by road on the Gloucestershire side. It allows magnificent views of deep Symond's Yat, and of the river winding through its richly-wooded setting. Picturesque Coldwell Rocks are also situated on the Gloucestershire side of the river.

SYSTON, Leics *18 SK61*
Curious sculptures of a man and two women are displayed by the tower buttresses of the local church. These may represent the founder and his wives. Several brick-built houses of 18th-c date can be seen in the area.

TACOLNESTON, Norfolk *15 TM19*
The mainly 15th-c church displays old roofs and a Jacobean pulpit, and several old houses exist in the area. Timber-framed Dairy Farmhouse is an attractive building lying 1m S of the church.

TADCASTER, N Yorks *22 SE44*
Large breweries operate in this River-Wharfe town, and the fine 15th-c church carries an embattled tower and shows good modern woodwork. A picturesque timbered house known as The Ark stands in Kirkgate and now houses a museum of pubs and brewing (OACT). Tadcaster boasted a Sunday School as early as 1788. Grimston Park lies S of the town and is a house designed by Decimus Burton in 1840, standing in formal gardens by Nesfield. Mainly-Georgian Hazlewood Castle lies 4m SW; it retains a late 13th-c hall plus an early 14th-c chapel containing monuments.

TALLAND, Cornwall *5 SX25*
Situated on a picturesque bay, this village includes a 15th-c church dedicated to St Tallanus. Old pews and the Bevyll tomb of 1752 can be seen inside.

TAMERTON FOLIOT, Devon *5 SX46*
This village stands at the junction of the Rivers Tavy and Tamar. Copleston Oak recalls an occasion when John Copleston of Warleigh murdered his godson. Tudor and 18th-c Warleigh House stands in the area.

TAMWORTH, Staffs *18 SK20*
A track known as Offa's Dyke once encircled this River-Tame village, and traces of this are still visible in places. The interesting castle is of Norman origin, but displays Tudor and Jacobean additions. Part of the building is now a museum (OACT). The decorated to

perpendicular church houses an ingenious and probably unique double-spiral staircase, plus windows by Ford Madox Brown and Burne-Jones. The interesting town hall dates from 1701. Local almshouses dating from between 1678 and 1693 are the work of Thomas Guy, who is also associated with Guy's Hospital in London.

TANFIELD, Co Durham 27 NZ15
Causey Arch lies E of Tanfield and dates from 1727. It is possibly the earliest railway bridge to have been built in England.

TANGMERE, W Sussex 8 SU90
Tangmere was famous as an RAF station during the second world war. The little Norman and early-English church carries a bell turret of 13th-c timber, and an old yew tree grows in the churchyard.

TAN HILL INN, Durham 21 NY80
This lonely inn is situated near the head of Arkengarthdale, at a height of 1,732ft. It is considered to be the loftiest in England, and traces of old mine workings lie to the SE.

TAPLOW, Bucks 8 SU98
Boating facilities are available in this pleasant Thames-side residential district, and the modern church preserves old brasses. A previous church stood near Taplow Court, and a Saxon barrow in the former churchyard has yielded various relics. These are now housed in the British Museum in London.

TARDEBIGGE, Herefs & Worcs 12 SO96
Birmingham and Worcester canal climbs through thirty locks in the area of this village. The church was built by Francis Hiorn in 1776, and has a spired tower built in the style of Wren. Restoration work on the chancel was conducted in the 19thc, and an altar cross is of interest.

TARPORLEY, Cheshire 17 SJ56
Old houses exist here, and the restored church houses several interesting tombs. Partly Elizabethan Utkinton Hall lies 3m S and the ruins of 13th-c Beeston Castle (AM) lie 3m S on a steep hill. A deep well survives in the castle, and modern Peckforton Castle faces the ruin on the opposite hill.

TARRANT HINTON, Dorset 7 ST91
The beautifully situated church shows early-English and perpendicular styles, and contains a notable 16th-c Easter Sepulchre. Eastbury House, the fragment of a once palatial mansion designed by Vanbrugh, lies 2m N. Surviving portions include the stable wing and a remarkable gateway from which two pine trees have grown. Parts of a garden laid out by Bridgeman have also survived. Chettle House lies 2m NE, and is a fine example of early 18th-c baroque work which has been attributed to Thomas Archer (OACT).

TARRANT RUSHTON, Dorset 7 ST90
The 12th-c and later church is built in the shape of an equal-armed cross. Two acoustic jars exist above the Norman chancel arch, and the two traceried squints are of note.

TARVIN, Cheshire 17 SJ46
Tarvin still retains a few 17th-c cottages. The perpendicular church carries a lofty tower and displays 14th-c woodwork. The village was associated with the Civil War.

TASBURGH, Norfolk 15 TM29
Remains of a strong earthwork surround the mainly-decorated church, which carries a remarkable round tower. Rainthorpe Hall and Flordon Hall are fine Elizabethan houses, the former situated 1½m N and the latter 2m NW. The River Tas flows through the area.

TATTERSHALL, Lincs 19 TF25
Ralph Cromwell built the 15th-c red-brick castle in 1440 while Treasurer of England. It is considered a notable example, and its restoration was due to the efforts of the Marquess of Curzon (AM, NT, OACT). The splendid perpendicular church was once collegiate and houses good brasses, old glass, and a stone screen. Almshouses and a fine 15th-c cross still stand in the churchyard.

TATTINGSTONE, Suffolk 15 TM13
A local folly dating from 1760 resembles a church, but its real purpose was to act as a screen for three cottages. St Mary's Hospital is of 18th-c and later date, and was originally built as a workhouse.

TAUNTON, Somerset 6 ST22
Cider is the best-known product of this Vale of Taunton Deane town, which lies on the River Tone. The partly 12th-c castle contains a museum, and was the scene of Judge Jeffrey's Bloody Assize after the 1685 Battle of Sedgemoor (AM, OACT). St Mary's Church contains quadruple aisles, and St James's church has a 15th-c font; both display lofty perpendicular towers which have been rebuilt. Gray's almshouses date from 1635. An ancient priory barn is also of interest. Three public schools include one of 13th-c foundation, and the former thatched lepers' hospital has been restored as rural district offices.

TAVISTOCK, Devon 5 SX47
Situated on the western fringe of Dartmoor national park near the River

1 Castle (museum)
2 Gray's Almshouses
3 Priory Barn
4 Rural District Offices (former lepers' hospital)
5 St James's Church
6 St Mary's Church

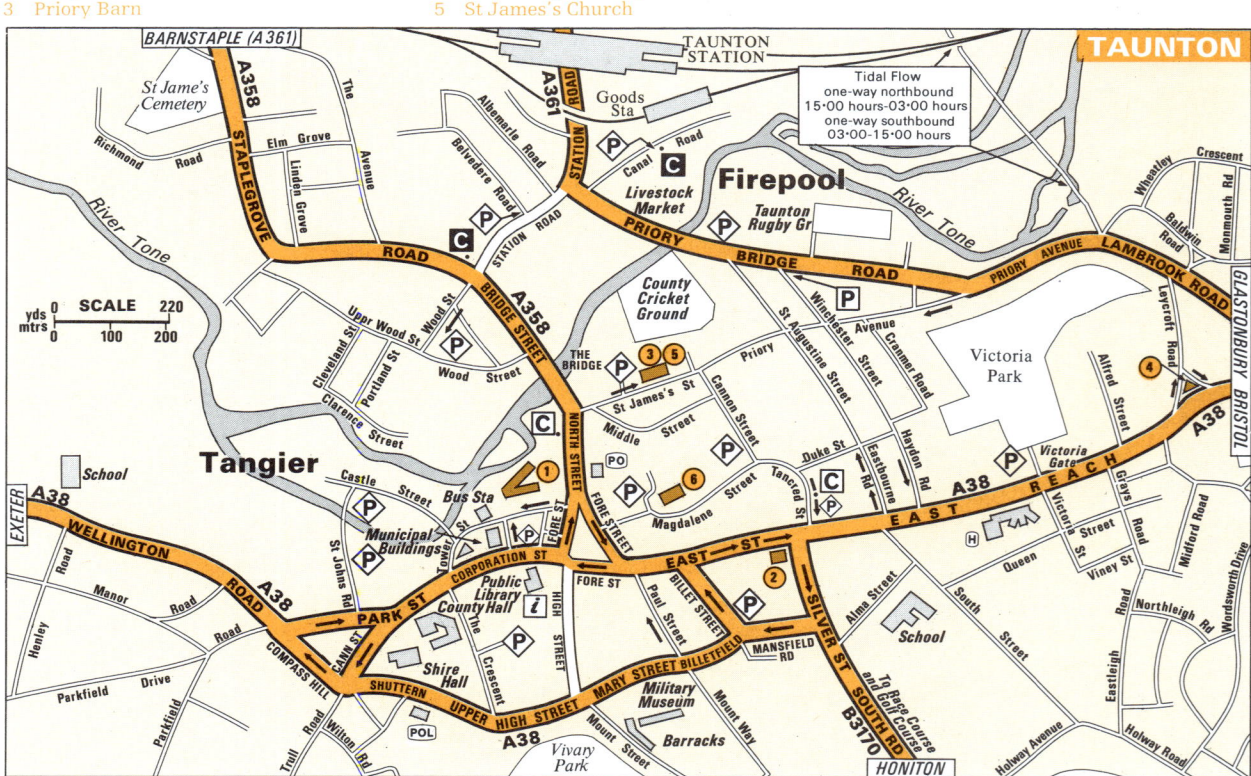

Tavy, Tavistock is a good touring centre for the beautiful surrounding countryside. Walreddon House lies to the S and is of Tudor origin. Slight remains of the former abbey exist near the perpendicular church of St Eustace, which shows an east end characteristic of the area and houses interesting monuments.

Sir Francis Drake was born at Crowndale, (1½m SSW) but the house is no longer standing. Morwell, a 15th-c residence of the Abbots of Tavistock, lies 3m SW near the River Tamar. A wild gorge known as Tavy Cleave can be seen 8m NE on Dartmoor. Several foundry buildings stand in the town, and the area round Tavistock Canal basin preserves a few Georgian cottages and stores. The 4½m canal included an aqueduct and tunnel, and led towards the Tamar Valley.

TAWSTOCK, Devon 5 SS52
A late-perpendicular hill-top church in the village carries a prominent central tower, and its wealth of monuments has earned it the distinction of being described as the Westminster of the West. Interesting screens and bench-ends are featured inside the building. Tawstock Court is of late Georgian origin, and includes a gateway of 1574.

TAXAL, Derbyshire 18 SK07
Views of Kinder Scout in the High Peaks can be enjoyed from this Goyt-Valley village. The Chimes of Taxal inn dates from the 17thc, and memorials to the Jodrells exist in the church.

TAYNTON, Oxon 12 SP21
Famous quarries in this area supplied stone for Blenheim Palace. Thatched grey-stone houses exist here, and the River Windrush flows near by. A splendid 14th-c font is featured in the local church.

TEALBY, Lincs 19 TF19
Situated at the foot of the Wolds, this attractive village includes derelict Bayons Manor. This stands in a deer park and was built in 1840 by Tennyson's uncle. The much-restored trans-Norman to perpendicular church contains a beautiful altar frontal of 17th-c Venetian workmanship.

TEDDINGTON, Gt London 8 TQ17
This Thames-side district is mainly residential. Seven lamps presented by the Patriach of Jerusalem can be seen in the parish church of St Alban, which dates from 1889. St Mary's Chapel is of 16th- to 19th-c date and carries a mid 18th-c tower. R D Blackmore of *Lorna Doone* fame was buried with his wife in the local cemetery, in 1900. Teddington lock is the largest on the Thames, and the flow over its weir is measured regularly by the Thames Conservancy Board. High-water mark is attained 1½ hours after the tide has reached the 20m-distant London bridge.

TEESPORT, Cleveland 27 NZ52
Facing the Seal Sands, this newly-created Tees-estuary port lies in an industrialized area which includes large chemical and steel works.

TEESSIDE
As from April 1968, this area became a new county borough taking in Billingham, Eston, Middlesbrough, Redcar, Stockton, and Thornaby.

TEFFONT, Wilts 7 ST93
Twin villages of Teffont Magna and Teffont Evias co-exist in the attractive Nadder Valley. The former includes the delightful Fitz House of 1700, and the latter boasts a Tudor and later manor house.

TEIGNGRACE, Devon 5 SX87
Situated on the River Teign, Teigngrace includes a church of 1786 containing interesting monuments and an altarpiece which is a copy of Vandyck's Pieta. The Stover canal was originally constructed for the transport of clay, and Stover House is of 18th- and early 19th-c date.

TEIGNMOUTH, Devon 5 SX97
Pronounced Tinmouth, this popular resort offers a beach of sand and fine shingle, sea bathing, and golf. Clay is shipped from the harbour. Keats corrected the proofs of *Endymion* at the resort in 1818, and Den Crescent was built c1826. A bridge crosses the Teign estuary to the yachting centre of Shaldon, below the wooded headland of The Ness.

TELFORD, Salop 17 SJ61
Telford is the name chosen for a New Town which incorporates Wellington (Salop), Dawley, and Oakengates. It differs from other New Towns in that it consists largely of towns already in existence, but will eventually have a new centre at Randley Lake. Part of the Severn Gorge around Ironbridge and Coalbrookdale is to be designated an area of special architectural and historic interest.

TELSCOMBE, E Sussex 8 TQ40
This remote South-Downs village can be reached by road from the Ouse Valley. The restored Norman and early-English church houses a fine early-English font, and the manor house is partly of 17th-c date (NT).

TEMPLE BALSALL, Warwickshire 12 SP27
Splendid 14th-c work is evident in the restored church, and the window tracery is of particular note. An almshouse which was bequeathed in 1670, and well restored in 1966, stands near by.

TEMPLE GRAFTON, Warwickshire 12 SP15
It is said that Shakespeare was married in the forerunner of the present modern church.

TEMPLE GUITING, Glos 12 SP02
Manor farm was once the Cotswold summer residence of the Bishops of Oxford, and the curious partly-perpendicular church shows extensive Georgian alterations.

TEMPLE SOWERBY, Cumbria 26 NY62
Two greens are a feature of this parish, which lies under the lofty Pennine ridge. Acorn Bank is an old manor house (NT) set in attractive gardens (OACT). Good scenery can be enjoyed in the Eden Valley.

TENBURY WELLS, Herefs & Worcs 12 SO56
Medicinal springs rise in this Teme-Valley market town, and the 18th-c church retains a 12th-c tower. Several interesting effigies and tombs can be seen inside. An early-English and decorated church lying 1m W at Burford contains notable monuments in the chancel — many to the Cornwalls — among which is a rare heart-shrine. Perhaps the finest of all is a splendid Elizabethan triptych by the Italian artist Melchior Salaboss. Burford House stands in attractive gardens and dates from 1720 (OACT).

1   Den Crescent
2   Golf Course

TENTERDEN, Kent 9 TQ83
William Caxton is said to have been born in this delightful little Wealden town, which once held Cinque Port privileges. Several old houses exist in the long grass-verged High Street. The church has a tall 15th-c west tower which forms a local landmark, plus an externally-shingled carved and panelled nave roof. Hales Place dates from the 16thc, and Westwell from the 18thc – both are interesting old houses.

TERLING, Essex 9 TL71
Attractive old houses that make up this village include a timbered 15th- and 16th-c manor house. A tower of 1732 is carried by the local church, and Terling Place is a fine house of late-Georgian date. A smock mill which stopped working as recently as 1951 is also of interest.

TERRINGTON ST CLEMENT, Norfolk 14 TF51
One of the magnificent Marshland churches can be seen here. It is of perpendicular style throughout, and features a detached tower, a wealth of carving, and a splendid font cover. Its impressive design has caused it to be dubbed the Cathedral of the Marshes. Lovell's Hall is of early-Tudor date.

TETBURY, Glos 12 ST89
This pleasant Cotswold town is sited on the River Avon, and features typical stone-built houses. A pillared Elizabethan market hall is of note. The church was rebuilt in 1787, but the tower and spire date from the 19thc.

TETNEY, Lincs 23 TA30
A brass inscription in the church records the bell-ringing service performed for 84 years by Matthew Lakin in the 19thc. The fine tower is of 15th-c date.

TEW, GREAT, Oxon 13 SP32
Thatched stone-built cottages exist here, and the stocks have been preserved. Interesting monumnets are housed in the mainly early-decorated church. Although the former manor house of the Falklands has been rebuilt, its original gardens remain.

TEWIN, Herts 8 TL21
Attractively situated above the little River Mimram, Tewin lies E of the great Digswell railway viaduct. Picturesque Elizabethan Queen Hoo Hall lies 1m NE.

TEWKESBURY, Glos 12 SO83
Tewkesbury stands near the confluence of the River Avon with the Severn. King John's Bridge spans the former and has arches dating from c1200. Telford's iron Mythe Bridge also spans this river and dates from 1823 to 1826. The town hall of 1788 was altered during the 18thc. Many picturesque old houses and inns existing in the town include several finely-timbered buildings, and the ancient water-mill is noteworthy. The House of the Golden Key and the Ancient Grudge are both sited in the High Street, and can be considered as being two of the town's finest old houses. The bowling green behind the Bell Inn is associated with Mrs Craik's *John Halifax Gentleman*, and the Hop Pole has Pickwickian associations.

Magnificent Abbey Church is of interest; the Norman central tower is one of the finest in England, and a number of fine chantry chapels, tombs, monuments, and examples of old woodwork can be seen. Facilities for boating and fishing are offered in the area. The famous Wars of the Roses battle of 1471, in which Queen Margaret was defeated and her son slain, was fought about ½m S.

TEYNHAM, Kent 9 TQ96
Pronounced Tann-em, this parish has conducted a fruit growing industry since Richard Nairns was purveyor to Henry VIII. A few old houses still stand, and the early-English to perpendicular church contains various brasses. A yacht basin on the Conyer lies to the N.

THAKEHAM, W Sussex 8 TQ11
Apsley monuments are a feature of the mainly 13th-c church, and a good view of the South Downs is afforded by the churchyard. Church House is a timbered structure, and the notable early 20th-c house of Little Thakeham was by Sir Edwin Lutyens.

THAME, Oxon 8 SP70
Old houses and an exceptionally wide main street are features of this River-Thame market town. The 13th- to 15th-c church houses interesting monuments and brasses, and the old grammar school dates back to 1575. John Hampden was educated at the school, and died in the town in 1643. Prebendal House and Chapel are of the same date as the church, and are both noteworthy. Interesting inns include the Spread Eagle and the picturesque Bird Cage. A fine old tithe barn stands in the area. Thame Park dates largely from the 18thc, but retains a Tudor wing. The latter lies 1½m S. Remains of Rycote Manor House and the recently restored chapel (AM), with its notable 17th-c woodwork, lie 3m SW (OACT).

THAMESMEAD, Gt London 8 TQ47
A New Town is being developed on an 1,300-acre Thames-side site between Erith and Woolwich. It is hoped that this will eventually provide homes for some 60,000 people. A notable engine house, containing four original beam engines which last functioned in 1944, is included in the Crossness sewage treatment works.

THAMES VALLEY
This name is generally applied to a Thames reach where regular steamer services ply between Windsor and Oxford. The most picturesque reaches are between Maidenhead and Henley and Reading and Abingdon; this is where the Thames flows through the Goring Gap which separates the Chilterns from the Berkshire Downs.

THANET, ISLE OF
The Rivers Stour and Wantsum bound this flat coastal district of NE Kent. Well-known resorts such as Broadstairs, Margate, and Ramsgate exist here and are linked by ranges of white chalk cliffs. The centre of Thanet lies higher than the surrounding district, and is surmounted by the Whitfield Tower – a shipping landmark.

THATCHAM, Berks 7 SU56
A Kennet-Valley village, Thatcham includes a few old houses and a church with a Norman doorway, a pinnacled 15th-c tower, and the Fuller chantry containing interesting monuments. A 14th-c chantry chapel was converted into a school in 1707.

THAXTED, Essex 14 TL63
Many old plastered and half-timbered buildings exist here. Of particular note are the timbered 16th-c guildhall, incorporating an old lock-up; the 18th-c Clarence House; several old almshouses; a tower windmill. The fine church dates almost entirely from the 15thc, and carries a lofty spire. Other features of the church include Royal Arms of Queen Anne, a lovely north porch, and a splendid font cover and case. Samuel Purchas, an early topographer, was born here in c1575. The notable modernized Tudor mansion of Horham Hall lies 2m SW.

THEALE, Berks 7 SU67
Theale includes a prominent 19th-c church in early-English style, and the modern buildings of Douai Abbey and College lie to the SW.

THEBERTON, Suffolk 15 TM46
The thatched church has a partly-Norman round tower. Sixteen German airmen from the Zeppelin L-48, brought down in flames near by in 1917, are buried in the churchyard.

THETFORD, Norfolk 15 TL88
Slight remains of three former priories founded between 1104 and 1340 exist in this Breckland town, and the River Little Ouse runs through the area. The huge conical castle mound measures 81ft high and is the largest in England. Only three churches remain of the former twenty. St Mary's is of Norman and perpendicular date and houses a Norman font under its tall tower. King's House was once a hunting lodge of King James I, and the carved coat-of-arms of the Wodehouses is set in the wall.

The Bell is a Tudor inn and the 15th-c Ancient House now serves as a museum (OACT). An ancient lock-up preserves old parish stocks. Thomas Paine, author of *The Rights of Man*, was born here in 1737. Recent local excavations have revealed evidence that a Saxon town existed in the area. A tall Great-War memorial column stands SW of the town, at the meeting point of the three parishes of Elveden, Eriswell, and Icklingham. Some 225-acres of Thetford Heath now form a national nature reserve, and newly-afforested Thetford Chase lies to the W.

THEYDON GARNON, Essex 8 TQ49
Features of the local church include a timbered nave arcade and north aisle gable of 1644, plus an interesting brick tower of 1520. Hill Hall, of Elizabethan and Queen Anne periods, stands E and is considered to be of great architectural interest. It is now administered by the Prison Commissioners. Brick-built St Michael's church is sited at Theydon Mount, and was erected in the hall grounds by the Smith family between 1611 and 1614. Smith monuments can be seen inside.

THIRLSPOT, Cumbria 21 NY31
Thirlspot is situated at the N end of Thirlmere, in the Lake District national park. The banks of Thirlmere are largely wooded, and the lake now forms a reservoir for Manchester. Helvellyn rises 3,118ft to the E and is noted for the remarkable Striding Edge; it can be climbed from here. Stybarrow Dodd stands at 2,756ft in the NE with 2,807ft Great Dodd.

THIRSK, N Yorks 22 SE48
This old market town lies at the foot of the Hambleton Hills in the Vale of Mowbray. The early-perpendicular parish church displays notable carved roofs, and Thirsk Hall dates from the 18thc. The Golden Fleece is notable among the town's old inns, and several houses are of interest. Thomas Lord of Lord's cricket ground fame was born at Thirsk in 1755. A racecourse exists in the area.

THISTLETON, Leics 19 SK91
Recent excavations have revealed a unique sequence of religious temples dating from the 1st to 4thc.

THORESBY PARK, Notts 18 SK67
Dating from 1870 and built near the site of a house that burnt down in 1745, this Victorian hall is considered one of the most impressive of its period (OACT). The park was founded by the Duke of Kingston in 1683, and one of its notable features is a 65-acre lake. The road from Budby passes near the house.

THORNBURY, Avon 12 ST69
Noted for its carved brick chimneys and bay windows, the unfinished Tudor castle in this Severn-estuary area was built by the 3rd Duke of Buckingham in 1510. It now incorporates a well-known restaurant. The magnificent church is decorated and perpendicular, and carries a 130ft tower. Other features of this building include an imposing clerestoried nave, a fine stone pulpit, and a square Norman font.

THORNE, S Yorks 22 SE61
Situated near the River Don, Thorne stands in a region of levels and moors that were drained by Vermuyden – of Fenland fame – during the Stuart period. The church has a 13th-c nave and a 15th-c south chapel.

THORNEY, Cambs 19 TF20
Hereward the Wake is associated with this Fenland village. Remains of a 12th-c abbey exist in the area, and the restored Norman to perpendicular abbey church features a tall west front, a Norman nave, and a 19th-c east end. Thorney Abbey House is partly of the 16th-c, but includes additions dating from 1660. A windmill dated 1787 is of interest, and a wild life park has been formed in the grounds (OACT).

THORNTON, W Yorks 22 SE13
Branwell, Charlotte, Emily, and Anne Brontë were born in a house in Market Street – a fact now testified by a stone tablet set in one of the house walls. The father of these literary prodigies lived at the vicarage from 1815 to 1820.

THORNTON ABBEY, Humberside 23 TA11
Remains of this abbey, which was founded in 1139 and re-founded as a college in 1541, include a magnificent 14th-c gateway (AM) and part of the Chapter House. The approach is via a 120ft bridge displaying arcaded walls and two round towers, spanning a dry moat.

THORNTON CURTIS, Humberside 23 TA01
The restored mainly early-English church preserves one of the country's few black-marble Tournai fonts, and the red-brick hall dates from the late 17thc.

THORNTON-LE-DALE, N Yorks 23 SE88
Features of this attractive village include an old cross, parish stocks, 17th-c almshouses, and an old school. New state-forest roads have been laid in the area and the long valley of Newtondale lies to the N. This dale is considered the finest in the district, and can be well-seen from the revived steam-hauled railway which runs from Pickering to Grosmont. There is no road.

THORPE, Derbyshire 18 SK15
Thorpe is beautifully situated at the foot of Thorpe Cloud, near the entrance to famous Dovedale in the Peak District national park. The church tower is of Norman date. Rivers Dove and Manifold Join to the W.

THORPE BAY, Essex 9 TQ98
This resort lies on the E border of Southend-on-Sea, and offers bathing and golf.

THORPE-LE-SOKEN, Essex 15 TM12
Huguenot refugees of the 17thc were associated with this small town, and the rebuilt church carries a late 15th-c brick tower and houses a 15th-c chapel screen. Beaumont Hall is a delightful brick house of c1675, displaying shaped gables and situated to the N.

THORPENESS, Suffolk 15 TM45
Designed on garden city lines, this resort offers good sands and sea bathing plus boating and sailing on the mere. The House in the Clouds was originally built as a water tower and is mounted on a 40ft pedestal. An early 19th-c post-mill is preserved near by.

THORPE SALVIN, S Yorks 18 SK58
The interesting little trans-Norman to decorated church is noted for its beautiful font, tower arch, and north chapel. A ruined Elizabethan manor house exists in the area.

THRAPSTON, Northants 13 SP97
Strong associations with the Washington family exist in this River-Nene area, and the restored church includes a tablet depicting the arms from which the Stars and Stripes were derived. Washington monuments are housed in Islip church, situated across the river, and several old houses exist in the area.

THREEKINGHAM, Lincs 19 TF03
Tradition has it that this place-name was derived from a 9th-c battle with the Danes, in which three of their kings were slain. The church carries a fine early-English tower with a decorated-style broach spire. Old bench-ends, stocks, and a whipping-post are preserved in the nave. A whalebone archway is a particularly unusual feature of the village.

THRELKELD, Cumbria 26 NY32
Threlkeld is situated at the head of St John's Vale, and the vale's beck flows through the village. Saddleback rises to 2,847ft behind the village, and a memorial to 45 local huntsmen exists in the churchyard.

THROWLEIGH, Devon 5 SX69
The well-known Throwleigh stone circle measures between 80 and 90ft in diameter and includes six standing and thirty-six fallen stones. It lies below 1,799ft Cawsand Beacon, in the Dartmoor national park.

THROWLEY, Kent 9 TQ95
Magnificent tombs can be seen in the Sondes chapel of the church, and a monument by neo-classical sculptor John Flaxman is of interest. Nearby Belmont is a mansion in which the Harris family, famous for their involvement in both Kent cricket and the British influence in India, once lived. The latter dates from 1769.

THRUMPTON, Notts 18 SK53
Thrumpton Hall is a fine Jacobean house which is noted for its woodwork, and the parish itself exists near the confluence of the Rivers Trent and Soar.

THURGARTON, Notts 18 SK64
Although the priory church has been partly rebuilt, it still retains early-English work. Of particular interest is the west doorway. Thurgarton Priory stands on the site of a former priory and dates from 1777.

THURLESTONE, Devon 5 SX64
This attractive village has access to good sands and bathing and is situated on Bigbury Bay. Thurlestone Rock is a naturally eroded arch. The church carries a lofty battlemented tower which includes a typical Devon mid-side stair turret. A Norman font can be seen inside.

A ceiling from 16th-c Ancient House (museum) Thetford

THURSLEY, Surrey 8 SU93
Several old houses exist in this attractive village, and the restored church preserves a remarkable 15th-c wooden belfry surmounted by an octagonal broach spire. A tombstone in the local churchyard bears a curious epitaph to the unknown sailor who was murdered at Hindhead in 1786.

THURSTASTON, Merseyside 17 SJ28
Wide views towards the Dee estuary and the distant Welsh mountains are afforded by Thurstaston Hill. The centre of the new Wirral country park is located here, and the area includes the 11m Wirral Way footpath.

TICHBORNE, Hants 7 SU53
A picturesque annual dole-giving ceremony takes place here, and the partly-Saxon church contains fine Tichborne monuments. Tichborne Park mansion dates from the early 19thc, and the local post office is housed in an interesting thatched building.

TICKENCOTE, Leics 19 SK90
A rebuilt Norman church in this small village preserves a remarkable chancel arch of five orders, plus rare sexpartite vaulting in the chancel. The old bell has now been replaced and lies outside the church. The 1470 Wars of the Roses battle of Loosecoat Field was fought to the N.

TICKENHAM, Avon 6 ST47
The church of St Quiricus and St Julietta displays an early 12th-c chancel arch, examples of 14th-c glass, and several 13th-c effigies. Tickenham Court dates from c1400 and includes an early-Tudor wing. Cadbury Camp is of iron-age origin.

TICKHILL, S Yorks 18 SK59
A notable 120ft pinnacled tower is carried by the splendid perpendicular church. Inside is an altar-tomb of early-Renaissance design, dating from 1478. Remains of a Norman castle exist in the area, and a circular market cross of 1766 is mounted on steps. St Leonard's Hospital of 1470 has been restored.

TICKNALL, Derbyshire 18 SK32
Attractive stone cottages make up this village, which is set in well-wooded country on the edge of the great park of Calke Abbey. The house itself dates from 1703. Harpur almshouses originate from 1772, and the curious conical village lock-up is of interest.

TIDESWELL, Derbyshire 18 SK17
The cruciform decorated-style church has been described as the Cathedral of the Peak, and is particularly noted for its pinnacled perpendicular tower and beautiful windows. The chancel of 1360 is especially noteworthy, and several old brasses are of interest. A well-dressing ceremony takes place here from time to time. Beautiful Miller's Dale and the adjacent Chee Dale lie 3m S both NT.

TILBURY, Essex 9 TQ67
Now an important Thames-estuary container port, Tilbury includes a fort that was built by Henry VIII in 1539 and later remodelled (OACT). This fort is noted for Sir Bernard de Gomme's ornate Water Gate of 1682. An army raised to resist the Armada was reviewed here by Elizabeth I in 1582. Coal House Fort is sited at East Tilbury, and was built by Gordon of Khartoum – of the Royal Engineers – in 1869. A passenger ferry operates to Gravesend.

TILFORD, Surrey 8 SU84
King John's Oak was described by Cobbett, and an ancient bridge spans the River Wey. Tilford House is of mid 18th-c date. The village is noted for its Bach festivals, and extensive commons exist in the neighbourhood.

TILNEY ALL SAINTS, Norfolk 14 TF51
Features of the Norman to perpendicular church include a good Norman nave, a 15th-c double-hammerbeam roof, and perpendicular screens. The 16th-c hall has a thatched roof.

TILSHEAD, Wilts 7 SU04
Some chequerwork is evident in the construction of the church, which carries an early-English tower. Chequerwork cottages can be seen in the area. Robbers' Stone lies 3m NW and records a murderous attack made by four highwaymen in 1839.

TILTON, Leics 18 SK70
Situated on high ground at an altitude of about 700ft, Tilton includes an early-English to perpendicular church which is notable for its strange gargoyles and lovely perpendicular details. Launde Abbey is an Elizabethan house lying 4m ESE, and the motte and bailey castle of Sauvey exists near by. Georgian Lowesby Hall lies 2m NW.

TILTY, Essex 14 TL52
A Cistercian Abbey founded in 1153 once stood in this upper Chelmer-Valley situation. The church's early-English nave is topped by an 18th-c belfry and cupola, and a very fine 14th-c chancel shows unusual tracery and fine brasses.

TIMBERSCOMBE, Somerset 5 SS94
Delightfully situated between Dunkery Beacon and Croydon Hill, Timberscombe includes a perpendicular church which is notable for its carved screen. This is one of a small group existing in the area.

TINTAGEL, Cornwall 4 SX08
Formerly called Trevena, this picturesquely situated village offers a small sand and rock beach and sea bathing. The coastal scenery comprises an area designated as one of outstanding natural beauty, and is of a rocky aspect. Barras Head and Glebe Cliff are NT protected. Remains of the romantic King Arthur's Castle (AM) exist on the excellent viewpoint of Tintagel Head.

The local post office is in a 14th-c building (NT, OACT). The church of St Merteriana dates from Norman to perpendicular periods, and contains an inscribed stone which may have been a Roman milestone. The Norman chapel to St Symphorian is also of interest. King Arthur's Hall is a modern building with stained-glass windows depicting King Arthur's knights. It also houses a picture gallery. Wild Rocky Valley and the delightful little waterfall of St Nectan's Kieve lie E on the Boscastle road. Trebarwith Strand, with lofty Gull Rock and a sandy bathing beach, is situated 1m SSW.

TINTINHULL, Somerset 6 ST41
The beautiful manor house has a pedimented façade of c1700 (NT, OACT), and the village stocks are preserved.

TINTWISTLE, Derbyshire 18 SK09
Large moorland reservoirs exist in this area to supply water to Manchester, and the village itself was once known as Tingetwissel. Well-known Laddow Rocks lie to the N and are popular with climbers.

TIPTREE, Essex 9 TL81
Tiptree House is of Elizabethan date and stands on the site of a former priory. The area is well-known for fruit growing and the manufacture of jam.

TISBURY, Wilts 7 ST92
Tisbury East and West are two adjoining parishes situated in the delightful Nadder Valley. Place House, now a farm, is a fine 13th- to 15th-c building which includes a good gatehouse. The notable 200ft-long thatched tithe barn is one of the largest in England, and the imposing Norman and later church displays carved bosses in the nave and chancel. Old and new Wardour Castles lie 2½m SW. The former is a 14th-c ruin (AM), and the latter is a large 18th-c house by James Paine, now containing a school (both OACT).

TISSINGTON, Derbyshire 18 SK15
This attractive village is situated in the Peak District national park to the E of Dovedale. An early-Jacobean Hall which was once the home of the Fitzherberts

Remains of King Arthur's Castle, Tintagel

can be seen here, and an annual well-dressing ceremony takes place at five separate wells on Ascension Day. The Norman to early-English church contains a good Norman font and many Fitzherbert monuments.

TITCHFIELD, Hants *7 SU50*
Titchfield Abbey (AM), also known as Place House, is the surviving portion of a great 15th-c building that was converted into a house at the Dissolution of c1536. Its fine Tudor chimneys are of interest (OACT). An old bridge over the River Meon dates from 1625. The partly-Saxon church includes a splendid Elizabethan monument to the Southampton family in the Abbot's chapel. Many 17th- and 18th-c houses still stand in the town, and the old dower house of St Margaret's is picturesque.

TITCHMARSH, Northants *14 TL07*
Reminiscent of those to be seen in Somerset, the richly-carved 15th-c church tower is considered one of the finest in the county. Interesting Pickering monuments can be seen inside, and the family pew is in the room above the porch; it is associated with John Dryden.

TIVERTON, Devon *5 SS91*
Two towers and a 14th-c gateway are preserved by the 12th-c castle. St Peter's Church is of perpendicular origin and is noted for its richly-carved Greenway chapel. The exterior of the latter is decorated with representations of ships and horses. St George's Church dates from 1733. The Great House of St George originates from 1614, and stands opposite Chilcot School which was founded in 1611. A Folk Museum is housed in a restored 19th-c building which once housed a school. A plinth in Blundell's Road carries a restored GWR tank locomotive. Other features of interest include two sets of 16th-c almshouses and a number of good 18th-c houses. Blundell's School was founded in 1604 and retains some of the original buildings (NT); R D Blackmore of *Lorna Doone* fame was a pupil here. Chevithorne Barton manor is dated c1600 and lies 3m N.

TIVETSHALL ST MARGARET, Norfolk *15 TM18*
Exceptionally fine Royal Arms of Queen Elizabeth I can be seen above the 15th-c screen of the 14th-c church.

TODMORDEN, W Yorks *22 SD92*
Todmorden is a manufacturing town on the River Calder, set in lofty moorlands between West Yorkshire and Greater Manchester. Jacobean Todmorden Hall now houses the post office. St Mary's chapel dates from the 15th to 18thc. A peace monument of 1815 stands on the notable viewpoint of Stoodley Pike, which rises 1,500ft from moorlands to the E.

TOFTREES, Norfolk *15 TF82*
The early-English to decorated church preserves a splendid Norman font – one of several that exist in this area. Toftrees Hall Farm is a fine gabled and flint house. Splendid Raynham Hall dates from 1636 and stands in a large park to the SW. Alterations to the original building were by William Kent.

TOLLARD ROYAL, Wilts *7 ST91*
Most of the surrounding area comprises Cranborne Chase, which was formerly an extensive Royal forest of some 700,000 acres in extent but is now largely disafforested. Quite a lot of picturesque woodland survives however, and Win Green Hill (NT) forms a notable viewpoint. The latter rises to 911ft and is the highest point in the Chase. Gardiner Forest covers 1,800 acres and was given by Balfour Gardiner, the composer. The grounds of Larmer Tree lie close to 13th-c King John's House, which was restored by the late General Pitt-Rivers. His seat was 1m E at Rushmoor House, in the grounds of which are various archaeological sites. The building itself houses a school.

TOLLER FRATRUM AND PORCORUM, Dorset *6 SY59*
Toller Fratrum, meaning Toller of the Brothers, includes a lovely old manor house of mid 16th-c date. The church is dedicated to Basil the Great, an eastern saint, and houses a Norman font. Toller Porcorum means Toller of the Pigs. To the S rises 828ft Eggardon Hill, one of Dorset's highest points.

TOLLESBURY, Essex *9 TL91*
The Blackwater estuary is noted for oysters and lies near this large fishing village. A Georgian font housed in the church bears a curious inscription, and various brasses are of interest. The old village lock-up has been preserved. Lovely Bourchier Hall shows good exterior plastering.

TOLLESHUNT D'ARCY, Essex *9 TL91*
A moated hall of 15th- to 17th-c date faces an old bridge inscribed 'Anne Regny Regina Elizabeth 27: 1585'. The 14th- to 15th-c church preserves old brasses in the D'Arcy chapel, and the local maypole has been preserved.

TOLPUDDLE, Dorset *6 SY79*
Several memorials, including the Martyrs' Tree (NT) commemorate the famous Tolpuddle Martyrs. This group of workers suffered transportation in 1834 for combining to demand a wage increase.

TONBRIDGE, Kent *9 TQ54*
Remains of a Norman to 13th-c castle here include a splendid gatehouse. Several 18th-c houses exist in the area and the 16th-c Chequers Inn is of interest. Two 16th-c fire-hooks exist in the tower basement of the parish church, and the Portreeve's House dates from the 15thc. Jane Austen's father was once a master at the well-known public school which was founded in 1553, and the famous Kent and England cricketer Frank Woolley was born at Tonbridge in 1887. Somerhill, a fine Jacobean house in a large park, lies 2m SE.

TONG, Salop *17 SJ70*
A magnificent array of monuments in the 15th-c church has helped this fine building to acquire the nickname 'the village Westminster'. Features include the Golden Chapel of 1515 which displays notable fan vaulting, and a rare ciborium or sacramental vessel. A curious 19th-c folly known as the Aviary is situated at Vauxhall Farm, and is a relic of Tong Castle. This was remodelled in Moorish style by Capability Brown (1763) but has since been demolished. The area is associated with Dickens's *Old Curiosity Shop*.

Interesting Boscobel House lies 3½m E. and it was here that King Charles II hid after the Battle of Worcester in 1651. The secret hiding-hole still remains, and the Royal Oak is said to be a descendant of the original tree in which the King once took refuge. Farther E in a 1,000-acre park landscaped by Capability Brown is 18th-c Chillington Hall by Sir John Soane (OACT). Remains of the 12th-c Whiteladies convent, which was largely destroyed in the Civil War, lie 3m E. Charles II stayed here on his way to Boscobel.

TONG, N Yorks *22 SE23*
A local hall dates from 1702 and the old Lantern House from 1615. Stocks, a mounting-block, and the village pump are preserved. The church was Georgianized in 1727, and includes box pews plus a three-decker pulpit. One of the pews includes a fireplace.

TOPPESFIELD, Essex *14 TL73*
Names of the bricklayer Daniel Hill and the donor Robert Wilde – also late rector – are recorded on the brick-built tower carried by the 14th-c church. The tower dates from 1699, and the Smythe monument of 1633 is of interest. Toppesfield Hall and Cust Hall are interesting old houses.

Blundell's School of 1604, Tiverton

TOPSHAM, Devon 5 SX98
Once an important seaport, Topsham lies on the Exe estuary and includes several Dutch-gabled 17th- and 18th-c houses. Most of these delightful buildings exist in The Strand, and recall a former prosperity resulting from trade with Holland. One of the houses now contains the local museum. A rare king's pin weigh beam is of note, and the rebuilt church retains its old west tower. Bridges span the river Exe and one of the oldest canals in England, 2m NW at Countess Weir.

TORBAY, Devon 5 SX96
This name is given to a newly-formed county borough incorporating Torquay, Paignton, and Brixham.

TORBRYAN, Devon 5 SX86
Situated in a wooded glen which incorporates limestone caves, Torbryan includes a fine perpendicular church displaying 15th-c glass, a lofty tower, an excellent painted screen of c1430, and a contemporary pulpit.

TORKSEY, Lincs 19 SK87
Royalists reduced the red-brick Elizabethan castle of the Jermyns to ruins during the Civil War. Foss Dyke was cut by the Romans to link the Rivers Witham and Trent, and a Saxon mint was once located here.

TORPOINT, Cornwall 5 SX45
Torpoint and Devonport are linked by car ferry, and the former is situated on the Hamoaze. Antony is a fine 18th-c house which is noted for its 19th-c *porte-cochere*, or entrance portico (NT, OACT).

TORQUAY, Devon 5 SX96
Mild weather is a feature of this well-known resort, yachting harbour, and spa. Its situation on Tor Bay includes an excellent beach of sand, pebbles, and shingle, and the climate allows cultivation of sub-tropical vegetation in the public gardens. Torre Abbey includes a notable Spanish barn, a 14th-c gateway, and two crypts (AM). An art gallery is housed in the 18th-c mansion. Important prehistoric finds have been made in Kent's Cavern (AM).

Picturesque cliff walks exist in the area, and Anstey's Cove and Babbacombe Beach are particularly attractive. Rock climbers practise on cliffs existing within the town's boundaries. Splendid views are available from the Ilsham Marine Drive, and remains of the old Chapel of St Michael's stand on Chapel Hill. St Saviour's Church at Tormohun is a restored perpendicular structure which contains Cary and Ridgeway monuments. Among the various 19th-c crescents boasted by the town is the notable Hesketh Crescent of 1846. Restored 15th-c Compton Castle lies 4½m W (NT). The courtyard hall and chapel are noteworthy (OACT).

TORRINGTON, Devon 5 SS41
Torrington church and 200 imprisoned Royalists were blown up by gunpowder in 1645. The church was rebuilt soon after in 1651, and houses a fine 17th-c pulpit. Palmer House dates from 1752. A conical Waterloo monument stands 1m S of the town on the Hatherleigh road; 5m SE off the same road is Great Potheridge – the 17th-c home of the Monk family. An inscribed tablet records General Monk's help in the restoration of King Charles II.

TORTWORTH, Avon 12 ST79
Notable monuments and a 15th-c tower are features of the church. The famous Tortworth Chestnut stands near by, and may be some 1,000 years old.

TOSTOCK, Suffolk 15 TL96
Interesting old houses border the village green. The decorated and perpendicular church displays a double hammer-beam roof, plus 15th-c bench-end poppy-heads which include a unicorn and a cockatrice. The Old Rectory is a notable Georgian building.

TOTNES, Devon 5 SX86
Situated on the River Dart, this delightful town is one of England's oldest boroughs and is noted for the shell keep of its ruined Norman castle (AM). Other features of the town include two gates – including the restored 15th-c East Gate – many Elizabethan and Georgian houses, and a picturesque butterwalk. A restored Elizabethan house in Fore Street now contains a museum, and the fine perpendicular church carries a 120ft tower. The beautiful stone screen dates from 1450. A fine 18th-c house contains the grammar school of 1554, and the town museum exists in the guildhall. Ancient walls once surrounded the town, and their line can still be traced. The 17th-c Seven Stars Inn is of interest, and the historic Brutus Stone is set in a pavement near the East Gate. Steamer trips operate along the picturesque River Dart to Dartmouth. Bowden House is a fine Georgian building lying 1m S.

TOTTENHAM, Gt London 8 TQ39
Bruce Castle is a Jacobean and later house which has recently been restored; part of this building is used to contain a postal museum. The parish church has a 14th-c tower and a 15th-c brick-built south porch. The vicarage or priory dates from the 17th and 18thc.

TOTTERNHOE, Beds 13 SP92
Stone for the building of such famous places as Windsor Castle was dug from local quarries. A bronze-age fort stands at 524ft on a nearby hill. Carvings of windmills can be seen on the perpendicular church.

TOTTINGTON, Gt Manchester 21 SD71
Situated on the NW outskirts of Bury, Tottington lies 2m SE of the line of a former Roman road from Manchester (or Ribchester). This ancient way is locally known as Watling Street. Affetside Pillar is mounted on a stepped base, and stands on the site of the road. Local people claim that it marks the halfway point between London and Edinburgh.

TOWCESTER, Northants 13 SP64
Saracen's Head Inn has Pickwickian associations, and the chantry house was founded in 1447. The post office is dated 1799. Interesting chained books are preserved in the 13th- to 15th-c church, and the church organ comes from William Beckford's demolished Fonthill Abbey in Wiltshire. Magnificent Easton Neston House dates from c1700 and lies to the E. It is the only known country house to be designed by Hawksmoor

1 Anstey's Cove
2 Art Gallery (Torre Abbey)
3 Babbacombe Beach
4 Chapel of St Michael
5 Compton Castle
6 Hesketh Crescent
7 Ilsham Marine Drive
8 Kent's Cavern
9 Torre Abbey
10 St Saviour's Church
See also Cockington entry

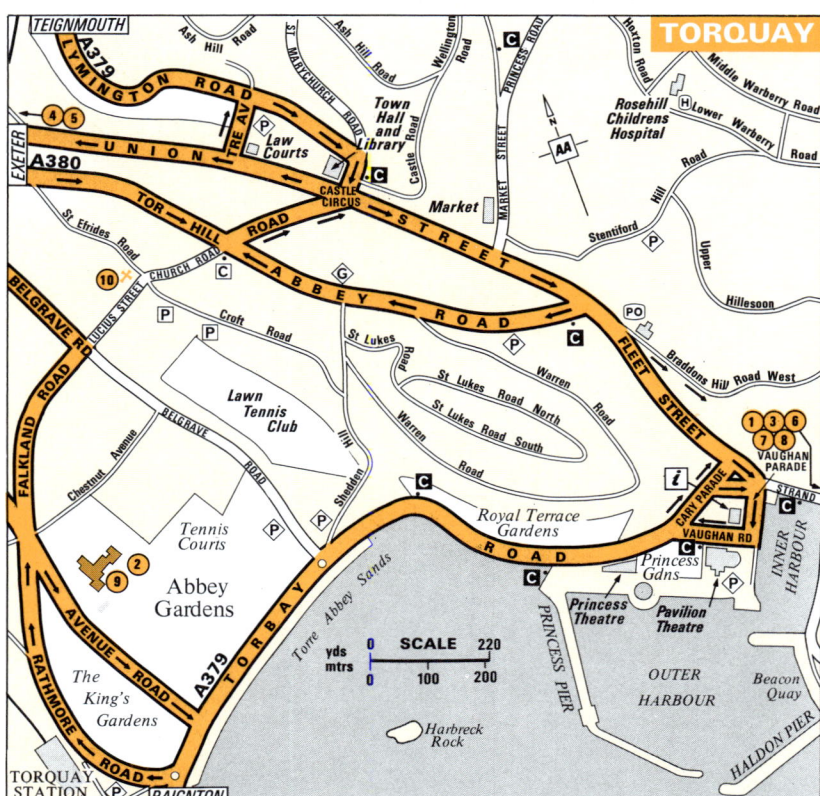

and stands in a great park containing a 15th-c church housing interesting Fermor monuments. Two of the latter are by Chantrey.

TOWTON, W Yorks *22 SE43*
A great Wars of the Roses battle was fought in this area during the year 1461. The site lies 2m SE and is marked by a cross. Saxton church stands near the battlefield and includes the grave of Lord Dacre, who was killed here. A cross standing 1m SW of Towton marks the actual spot where he fell. Near by is the tiny Lead church, which was also associated with the battle.

TREDINGTON, Glos *12 SO92*
Two Norman doorways exist in the church, and the north one includes a notable tympanum. Fossilized remains of an *ichthyosaurus* are let into the porch floor, and a good 14th-c cross stands on the south side of the building.

TREEN, Cornwall *4 SW32*
Treen Castle is a fortified headland (NT) which includes the fort of Treryn Dinas and a well-known rocking-stone known as the Logan Rock (both NT). A modern sign displayed by the inn recalls that the rock was overturned by a nephew of Oliver Goldsmith in 1824 and had to be replaced at his expense. Local cliff scenery is very fine, and the rugged granite precipices of Tol-pedn-Penwith lie 4m SW. The latter, considered the finest of their type in Cornwall, are accessible from a little cove at Porthgwarra.

TRENTHAM, Staffs *17 SJ84*
A palatial 19th-c mansion that formerly existed here has been demolished, but the famous gardens include a swimming pool and ballroom (OACT). The well-known Wedgwood china factory is situated SE at Barlaston (OACT).

TRETIRE, Herefs & Worcs *12 SO52*
A Roman altar carrying inscriptions which indicated the existence of Roman roads in the neighbourhood is housed in the modern church.

TRIMINGHAM, Norfolk *15 TG23*
Some of the highest cliffs in Norfolk exist here, and the sandy beach offers good sea bathing. The perpendicular church houses a painted screen.

TRIMLEY CHURCHES, Suffolk *15 TM23*
Two churches stand 100 yards apart in adjoining churchyards here. St Mary's is of decorated and perpendicular styles and contains an Italian painting of the Madonna. St Martin's carries a battlemented brick tower.

TRING, Herts *8 SP91*
Tring is situated in the Chiltern Hills, from which Hastoe Hill rises to 709ft. The perpendicular church contains a fine monument of 1707, raised to Sir William Gore. The Zoological Museum is linked to the British Museum and displays an interesting zoological collection. Parts of Tring Park are often ascribed to Wren and the building now houses a school. The Grand Union Canal climbs to one of its summit levels near Tring, through 65 locks spaced between here and Brentford on the outskirts of London. Champneys, a well-known nature-cure centre founded in 1925, lies 3m SE. Tring Reservoirs lie N of the town and now form a national nature reserve.

TROSTON, Suffolk *15 TL87*
A circular flint-built pound in the area is roofed with thatch, and the local church displays an ancient porch and a 15th-c screen. The hall is of Elizabethan origin.

TROTTISCLIFFE, Kent *9 TQ66*
Excavations of Coldrum Long Barrow (NT) have yielded neolithic skeletons, some of which are preserved in the church porch. The beautifully carved pulpit was once housed in Westminster Abbey and was brought here in 1824.

TROTTON, W Sussex *8 SU82*
A fine 14th-c bridge spans the Little Rother River. The earliest of two fine Camoys brasses housed in the church is dated 1310, and was raised to a lady. Wall-paintings dating from the 15thc are also of interest.

TROUGH OF BOWLAND, Lancs *21 SD65*
This lonely moorland defile is noted for its wild scenery and is part of an area of outstanding natural beauty. It is traversed by a road which climbs at gradients of up to 1 in 6, and links the Lancashire Wyre Valley with the delightfully wooded Hodder Valley near the W Yorkshire border.

TROUTBECK, Cumbria *21 NY40*
Burne-Jones executed the east window of the church, and the building itself has been twice reconstructed. The village lies to the W of the church and is delightfully situated in a valley dominated by lofty Kirkstone Pass to the N, with Windermere to the W. The Mortal Man inn displays a picturesque sign. Park Farm is a noted sheep station covering some 2,000 acres (NT). Townend Farm, a characteristic yeoman's house of c1626, displays interesting carved woodwork. (NT, OACT).

TROWBRIDGE, Wilts *7 ST85*
George Crabbe was once the rector of the perpendicular church and was buried in the chancel in 1832. The nave has been rebuilt. Good 18th-c houses exist in the area, and the former clothiers group in the Parade is of particular note. A large collection of early documents, including the 14th-c Savernake Collection, is housed in the County Hall. Broadcloth has been manufactured here since the 14thc. Trowbridge was the birthplace of shorthand inventor Isaac Pitman – a fact recorded by a tablet in the town hall.

TROWELL, Notts *18 SK44*
Coal is mined in this Erewash-Valley district, and the 13th- to 15th-c church houses a 15th-c octagonal font. Trowell was selected as the 1951 Festival of Britain village.

TRUMPINGTON, Cambs *14 TL45*
Almost entirely of the decorated style, the restored church at Trumpington preserves the second oldest brass in England. Chaucer's Mill is associated with the poets Tennyson and Rupert Brooke, and the timbered Green Man inn dates from the 16thc. Ansty Hall dates from c1700. G A Henty, a famous writer of boy's stories, was born here in 1832. The village cross is by Eric Gill, and the first milestone to be positioned on the road to Barkway was one of a series set up by Trinity Hall Cambridge in 1727.

TRURO, Cornwall *4 SW84*
Rivers Allen and Kenwyn combine here to form the Truro River. The modern cathedral, begun in 1879 by J L Pearson, was erected after the sees of Cornwall and Devon were separated for the first time in eight hundred years. Its central tower and spire rise to 240ft; other features include a carved stone reredos and a beautiful baptistery. The east end of the building is built on to the south aisle of the old parish church.

Lemon Street and Walsingham Place show Georgian houses, and the former Assembly Rooms date from 1770. Truro County Museum displays a splendid collection of exhibits relating to tin mining.

A steamer service plies between Truro and Falmouth, and the Wheal Jane Gold Fields is a new tin mine which came into

1 Assembly Rooms
2 Cathedral
3 County Museum
4 Quaker Meeting House
5 Wheal Jane Gold Fields (tin mine)

operation in 1971 – the first to open in Europe for over 50 years. The curiously-named hamlet of Come-to-Good includes a thatched Quaker meeting house of 1710 and lies 3½m SW, E of the Falmouth road.

TUDELEY, Kent 9 TQ64
Local oast houses are characteristic of the county, and the village is situated among hop fields. The local church is the only example in England to include a stained glass window by Marc Chagall.

TUNBRIDGE WELLS, Kent 9 TQ53
This well-known inland resort stands at 400ft and includes a particularly fine common, scattered with outcrops of weathered grey sandstone. A chalybeate spring exists in the picturesque raised parade known as the Pantiles. Beau Nash came here from Bath in 1735 to be Master of Ceremonies, and the town is described in Thackeray's *Virginians*.

The church of King Charles the Martyr (1684 to 1696) is noted for its plaster ceiling. Decimus Burton laid out Calverley Park, and also built Holy Trinity Church in 1829. The High Rocks outcrop lies to the W, and the curious formation known as toad rocks – including one that has been eroded into the shape of a toad – can be seen on Rusthall common.

TUNSTALL, Lancs 21 SD67
Flemish glass some 500-years-old, and a Roman altar which has been built into a north window, are features of the perpendicular church. Charlotte Brontë visited Tunstall, and described it under the name Brocklebridge in her novel *Jane Eyre*. Thurland Castle stands to the S in a moated area and has been almost entirely rebuilt. Barrow Hall, a fine house lying 2m N, dates from 1730.

TUNSTALL, Staffs 17 SJ85
A pottery town associated with the Five Towns novels of Arnold Bennett.

TUNSTEAD, Derbyshire 18 SK17
A fountain commemorates James Brindley the famous canal builder, who was born here in 1716. Nearby limestone quarries measure some 1½m long by 120ft deep.

TUNSTEAD, Norfolk 15 TG32
Tunstead church is of late-decorated and perpendicular style, and includes a fine painted screen which retains the rood-loft floor above. An unusual stone platform and a small cell exist at the back of the altar, and the ironwork on the south door is considered remarkable.

TURTON, Gt Manchester 21 SD71
Turton Tower carries a large 15th-c and later tower which is well preserved. The upper storey houses a museum (OACT).

TURVEY, Beds 13 SP95
Turvey House dates from the 18thc and stands in a large park. A house known as Turvey Abbey is actually the Jacobean nave of the church, containing Anglo-Danish masonry and a Victorian chancel by Sir G G Scott. An old bridge spans the River Ouse, and a curious effigy of Jonah and the Whale can be seen near by. A 17th-c inn is of interest.

TURVILLE, Bucks 8 SU79
This attractive high-lying Chiltern village includes an ancient church which preserves Norman workmanship, a medieval stone coffin, and an 18th-c chapel housing interesting monuments. A by-road to Ibstone Common climbs to a lofty ridge N of the village, affording extensive views of the wooded Thames Valley. Richly-wooded Wormsley Valley lies NW.

TUTBURY, Staffs 18 SK22
Mary Queen of Scots was twice held prisoner in Tutbury's historic 14th-c castle. This building is now in ruins (OACT). The church displays rich Norman work, a particularly notable example of which is the west front. A timbered inn known as the Dog and Partridge is attractive, and the area also features several Georgian houses and a watermill. A fortified ditch from the original Anglo-Saxon settlement is known as the Park Pale. The River Dove flows through the area.

TUXFORD, Notts 18 SK77
A fine font cover dated 1673 is preserved in the church. The grammar school dates from the 17thc, and two disused windmills stand in the area.

TWICE BREWED, Northumberland 26 NY76
The well-known inn of this name now stands further to the W than originally, and a Youth Hostel here is named Once Brewed. The Roman Wall stands at 1,230ft at Winshields – the highest altitude along its entire length.

TWICKENHAM, Gt London 8 TQ17
Twickenham is a Thames-side residential district where a modern bridge spans the river. The parish church of St Mary dates from 1713 to 1714 and was by John James. Interesting monuments and the grave of Alexander Pope are two of its main features. James Gibbs designed the fine Octagon Room of 18th-c Orleans House in 1736, and this is the only part of the house still standing. It now contains an art gallery. Kneller Hall houses the Royal Military School of Music, but was once the home of Sir Godfrey Kneller. Attractive Georgian houses exist in Syon Row and Montpelier Row. At the end of the latter is South End House, where the poet Walter de la Mare died in 1956.

All Hallows Church of 1940 incorporates an original Wren tower, which was moved from the City and re-erected on this site. Splendid woodwork from the demolished City church of 1694 can also be seen here, including the organ of 1708 and a splendid Royal-Arms board. Strawberry Hill is a well-known gothic-revival house associated with Horace Walpole, which was completed in 1776 and now serves as an RC college. Alexander Pope's grotto, from his villa in Crossdeep, forms part of a modern convent. Fine houses in the area include 18th-c Marble Hill (OACT), and largely 17th-c York House. The latter is currently the town hall.

TWIZEL BRIDGE, Northumberland 31 NT84
Ruins of a castle exist in the area, and a picturesque single-arched bridge of 15th-c date (AM) spans the River Till. The latter flows through a deep wooded glen.

TWO BRIDGES, Devon 5 SX67
Situated in the heart of Dartmoor national park, this isolated junction of roads stands at an altitude of 1,125ft. Crockern Tor rises to 1,391ft and was associated with the Stannary Towns Tinners Parliament up until 1730. Wistman's Wood is a forest nature reserve featuring dwarf oaks, lying some 2m N near the West Dart River.

TWYFORD, Bucks 13 SP62
Of particular interest here is the church's two storeyed 15th-c porch, enclosing a fine Norman doorway. Additional features include a 15th-c hammerbeam nave roof and good Jacobean woodwork. The vicarage is partly of 15th- to 16th-c date.

TWYFORD, Hants 7 SU42
Three well-known people have been associated with this village: Benjamin Franklin wrote part of his autobiography at Twyford House; Alexander Pope received part of his education here; the wedding of Mrs Fitzherbert and the Prince of Wales is said to have taken place at the former Bambridge House, to the S, in 1785.

TWYWELL, Northants 13 SP97
An Easter Sepulchre is preserved in the small Norman church. Other interesting buildings include the manor house of 1591, the rectory of 1760, and the old toll house.

TYNEMOUTH, Tyne & Wear 27 NZ36
This resort lies on the N side of the Tyne estuary. An inlet to the SE known as Priors Haven offers good sands and bathing. Remains of a 12th- to 15th-c priory and fragments of an adjoining castle (both AM) overlook the sea from an impressive situation. Harriet Martineau the 19th-c novelist wrote some of her novels at Tynemouth.

UCKFIELD, E Sussex 8 TQ42
This small town lies to the E of the Ouse Valley and includes a rebuilt church containing a 17th-c brass. The Maiden's Head inn has a good Georgian façade.

UFFCULME, Devon 6 ST01
Uffculme's mainly-perpendicular church includes an old screen which measures

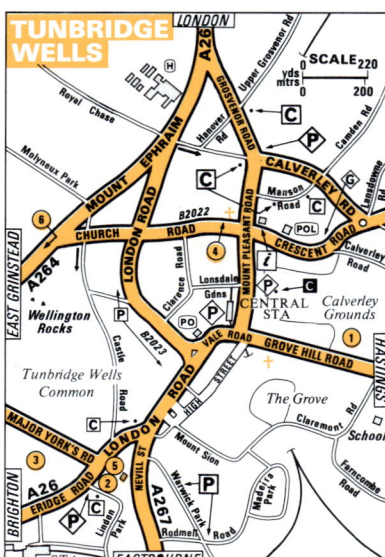

1 Calverley Park
2 Church of King Charles the Martyr
3 Common
4 Holy Trinity Church
5 Pantiles
6 Rusthall Common and Toad Rock

67ft long – the longest in the county; the pulpit dates from 1719. The old Shambles are still to be seen, but are now converted to another use.

UFFINGTON, Oxon   13 SU38
Views of the prehistoric White Horse cut into the slopes of 856ft White Horse Hill can be enjoyed from here. The horse measures some 374ft long, and the hill is a noted downland viewpoint. Near by are the earthworks of Uffington Castle (AM) and the line of the ancient Ridgeway. The church is a very notable example of early-English work and displays an octagonal tower, a set of eleven consecrated crosses, and numerous lancet windows. Literary associations with the district include links with *Tom Brown's Schooldays*.

UFFORD, Suffolk   15 TM25
Probably the finest in England, the 18ft gilded and carved font cover housed within the local church dates from 1480. Also of interest are several finely-carved stalls of 15th-c date and an old screen. Stocks and a whipping post stand outside the church, and the almshouses date from 1690.

UGLEY, Essex   14 TL52
This village belies its name. Picturesque old buildings include several barns and the houses of Orford, Ugley Hall, and nearby Bollington Hall. The church retains a Tudor brick-built tower.

ULCOMBE, Kent   9 TQ84
A pair of ancient yew trees here include one which has a girth of some 35ft. Facing these is a church containing notable brasses dating from 1419 and 1470. Wide views of the surrounding orchards and hopfields are available.

ULEY, Avon   12 ST79
Hetty Pegler's Tump is a well-known long barrow (AM) lying close to this pleasant Cotswold village. The view from here is extensive. Owlpen Manor House, an Elizabethan and 18th-c structure which includes a contemporary Court House (OACT), lies 1m E in a setting of yew trees. It is considered an excellent example of its period.

ULPHA, Cumbria   21 SD19
Wallabarrow Gorge is sited on a picturesque reach of the River Duddon, a few miles to the N of this Dunnerdale village. A lonely road climbs steeply across Birker Moor to the NW, passing near lonely Devoke Water before descending into Eskdale.

ULVERSTON, Cumbria   21 SD27
Situated at the centre of the Furness district, Ulverston includes a church which retains a Norman doorway and carries a perpendicular tower. A 100ft model of Eddystone lighthouse stands on Hoad Hill, and the canal leading to Morecambe Bay was built by Rennie. Swarthmoor Hall is an Elizabethan and later house in which George Fox the founder of the Quaker movement once lived (OACT). Near by is the Meeting House of 1688, which was built by Fox.

UNION MILLS, Isle of Man   20 SC37
This area lies S of lonely Baldwin Valley, which contains a large reservoir supplying the town of Douglas. The Injebreck, Colden, and Carraghan Hills lie beyond the head of the reservoir. Killibane mound, once used by the Tynwald assembly, is situated on the slopes of the last-named range. Deemster's Cairn is situated in the E branch of Baldwin Valley above Arderry.

UPAVON, Wilts   7 SU15
Salisbury Plain and Pewsey Vale lie either side of this River-Avon village, and a fine view can be enjoyed from the downland Andover road which lies E. The Norman to early-English church houses a fine Norman font and rich glass in the chancel.

UPCHURCH, Kent   9 TQ86
Old wall-paintings plus 14th-c screenwork and painted glass are features of the local church. Edmund Drake, father of Sir Francis Drake, was vicar here in 1560 and is buried in the church.

UPHOLLAND, Lancs   21 SD50
Narrow cobbled streets still exist here as a reminder of pre motor-transport days. A priory was founded in 1319, and the partly-modern church includes various decorated to perpendicular features. The nave was the chancel of an original monastic church. The tower dates from the 16thc, and a rare oak font exists among other good examples of wood carving. Late-Elizabethan Derby House carries the Stanley crest.

UPLEADON, Glos   12 SO72
The Norman north doorway of the church includes a sculptured tympanum, and the tower is of half-timbered construction. A black-letter bible of 1613 is preserved here. Eden's Hill (NT) is a fine viewpoint, and the River Leadon flows through the area.

UPMINSTER, Gt London   9 TQ58
James Oglethorpe, who founded the USA State of Georgia, is buried in Cranham Church; Upminster's mainly-Victorian church carries a notable 13th-c tower. A smock mill of c1800 includes much of its original machinery, and is of particular interest. A timbered Elizabethan hall now serves as a golf clubhouse.

UPNOR, Kent   9 TQ77
Ruins of a castle facing the River Medway date from 1561, and it was 20 years later – in 1581 – that Queen Elizabeth I reviewed the fleet here (AM, OACT). The Whittington Stone carries the one-time Lord Mayor's name, and marks the boundary rights of local fishermen. Arethusa is a training ship moored in the Medway.

UPPER SLAUGHTER, Glos   12 SP12
Upper Slaughter is a beautiful Cotswold village which includes a notable three-gabled Elizabethan manor house. The neighbouring village of Lower Slaughter is perhaps even more picturesque, and boasts beautiful old bridges and cottages.

UPPER SWELL, Glos   12 SP12
Cotswold houses and a fine manor house which is notable for its Renaissance porch are features of this village. Nearby Lower Swell is made up of lovely old cottages.

UPPINGHAM, Leics   19 SP89
A well-known public school was founded here in the 16thc, and is still housed in its original buildings – with some modern additions. Jeremy Taylor preached in Uppingham between 1637 and 1642, and was once chaplain to Charles I. He is commemorated by a tablet in the church.

UPTON-ON-SEVERN, Herefs & Worcs   12 SO84
Many Georgian and older houses exist in this pleasant little market town, and the White Lion Inn is associated with Fielding's *Tom Jones*. The 14th-c tower of the demolished Georgian church carries an octagonal dome and cupola of 1755. Old oak pews are preserved in the Baptist church of 1695.

UTTOXETER, Staffs   18 SK03
Locally pronounced as Utchettor, this River-Tean market town is associated with the 1648 surrender of the remains of the Duke of Hamilton's army. A sculpture on the marketplace conduit recalls Dr Johnson's well-known penance, enacted at the age of 75. Bagot's Wood lies 4½m S, with Bagot's Park to the E.

UXBRIDGE, Gt London   8 TQ08
Uxbridge lies on both the River Colne and the Grand Union Canal. St Margaret's church dates from the 14th and 15thc, and carries a tower which was rebuilt in 1820. A curious monument of 1638 is of interest. The Old Crown

Uffington's prehistoric white horse

and the Treaty House have been greatly mutilated; these and the George Inn have associations with a meeting between Charles I and Parliament, which took place in 1645. The Market House dates from 1789. The town centre has been re-developed in current modern style.

VENTNOR, Isle of Wight 7 SZ57
This pleasant resort is built on terraces, with a sandy beach below and high downs in the background. The Empress of Austria and the Empress Eugenie of France stayed at Steephill Castle, which was built in 1833 but is now demolished. Picturesque Undercliff lies SW. St Boniface Down is a fine viewpoint rising to 787ft, and is the highest point on the island (NT).

VERNHAMS DEAN, Hants 7 SU35
Remotely situated in high downland, Vernhams Dean includes a church with a Norman doorway. An early-Tudor manor house is also of note. A Roman road linking Marlborough with Winchester skirts Conholt Park to the W before climbing to over 800ft in a great curve to the N. This curve is unusual in that the Romans were generally very careful to keep their roads as straight as possible. The route is known as Chute Causeway, and is said to be haunted due to an incident connected with the great plague that was rife in the reign of Charles II.

VERYAN, Cornwall 4 SW93
Several curious thatched-roof round houses of early 19th-c date exist in this delightful village. The church of St Symphorian houses a Norman font. Gerrans Bay, overlooked by Nare Head, lies 2m SW.

VIRGINIA WATER, Surrey 8 SU96
Situated at the SE corner of Windsor Great Park, this artificial lake measures 1½m long. A colonnade from Leptis Magna in Tripoli stands on the bank, and the Valley and Heather Gardens are attractive. Kurume Punch Bowl is an area planted out with numerous different coloured azaleas, and is spectacular in the springtime. The centenary of British Columbia is commemorated by a genuine 100ft totem pole which was raised in 1958.

VOWCHURCH, Herefs & Worcs 11 SO33
This Golden-Valley village includes a church bearing a picturesque half-timbered spirelet, and displaying fine Jacobean woodwork. A curious local legend links the construction of this building with that of the church in nearby Turnastone.

WADDESDON, Bucks 8 SP71
This village is composed of picturesque model cottages. Waddesdon manor house is a modern mansion containing rich French furnishings (NT, OACT).

WADDINGTON, Lancs 21 SD74
Waddington is a moorland village with a rebuilt 18th-c hospital and a modern cross. The old mansion of Waddington Hall gave shelter to King Henry VI after the battle of Hexham in 1464.

WADEBRIDGE, Cornwall 4 SW97
An unusual communal garden at Wadebridge commemorates the coronation of Queen Elizabeth II. Vintage cars and old traction engines are displayed in the Cornish Motor Museum. A magnificent 15th-c thirteen-arch bridge crosses the Camel estuary to connect with Egloshayle, where the 15th-c church contains a notable stone pulpit. Pencarrow is a late 18th-c mansion lying 3m SE.

WADE'S CAUSEWAY
Part of a Roman road bears this name. The route originally ran from Stamford Bridge, crossed Pickering Moor on its way N through what is now the North York Moors national park, and continued towards Whitby.

WADESMILL, Herts 8 TL31
Thomas Clarkson, who dedicated his life to the abolition of slavery in 1785, is commemorated by a monument. The first English tollgate is said to have been set up in Wadesmill in 1663.

WADHURST, E Sussex 9 TQ63
Thirty Sussex-iron gravestones in the local church are a reminder that Wadhurst was once an important iron-smelting centre. The park of Whiligh lies SE and has been the source of timber for repairs to London's Westminster Hall since the last war.

WAINFLEET, Lincs 19 TF45
Although once a port, Wainfleet now stands some 5m inland from the sea. William of Waynflete, who founded Magdalen College in Oxford, also founded the beautiful local 15th-c Magdalen College School. The latter displays fine old brickwork and turrets, and it is thought that William may have been born in this area. An ancient cross is also of interest.

WAKEFIELD, W Yorks 22 SE32
This important woollen centre is sited on the River Calder, and includes a restored 15th-c parish church which was raised to cathedral status in 1888. The spire rises to 247ft and the screen dates from 1635. Wakefield Bridge includes a restored 14th-c chantry chapel (AM). St John's Church and several houses in St John's Square date from the 18thc.

Clarke Hall, which lies off the Stanley road and dates from 1542, contains a priest's hiding hole. Farther to the NE is the point where the Aire and Calder Navigation Canal crosses the River Calder by an iron aqueduct. George Gissing was born at 30 Westgate in 1857, and the town hall and County Hall are imposing late 19th-c structures. A great Wars of the Roses battle was fought near the city in 1460.

Sandal lies S and includes a Norman to perpendicular church – with the 15th-c Waterton chapel – and huge earthworks from a vanished castle. Heath House, designed by James Paine between 1744 and 1745, lies 1¼m E. Nearby Heath Hall dates from the mid 18th-c and was designed by John Carr of York. The latter is noted for its ceilings and panelling and stands on a wide green (OACT).

WALESBY, Lincs 19 TF19
A Wolds village below 500ft Bully Hill, Walesby is situated in the highest part of the county. The restored trans-Norman and later church is known as the Ramblers church and includes windows which were dedicated by the Bishop of Lincoln in 1950. A Roman villa was discovered here in 1861. Robert Burton,

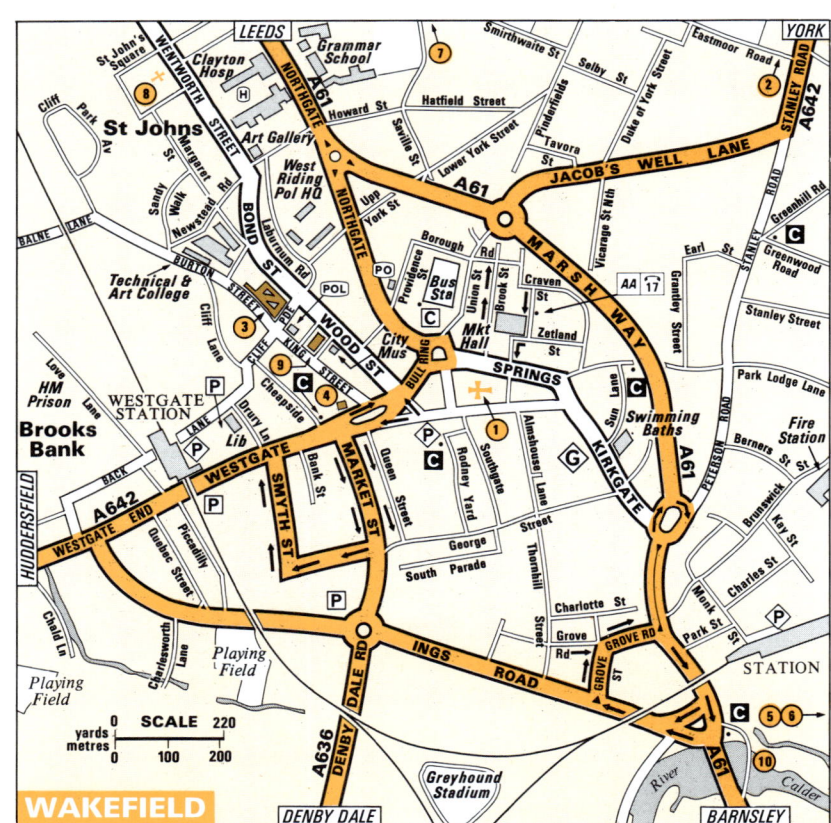

1 Cathedral
2 Clarke Hall
3 County Hall
4 George Gissing's Birthplace
5 Heath Hall
6 Heath House
7 Iron Aqueduct
8 St John's Church
9 Town Hall
10 Wakefield Bridge and Chapel

author of *The Anatomy of Melancholy* (published 1621), was once incumbent here.

WALKERN, Herts *14 TL22*
Numerous brasses and a knight's effigy in chain mail are features of the local Norman and later church. The supposedly last trial for witchcraft in England took place here in 1712. Jane Wenham, the accused, was pardoned and the law against witchcraft was repealed in 1736.

WALL, Staffs *18 SK00*
Remains of the Roman *Letocetum* exist here, and include baths and a posting station (NT, OACT). Watling Street and Ryknild Street pass through the area.

WALLASEY, Merseyside *17 SJ29*
Fine views of the Mersey estuary are available from this resort and residential district, which is situated on the NE extremity of the Wirral Peninsula. Natural amenities include good sands and sea bathing. Leasowe Castle is of 16th-c and later date. England's first hovercraft service started to operate between here and Rhyl in 1962.

WALLINGFORD, Oxon *13 SU68*
Ancient earth ramparts and slight traces of a former castle exist in this little River-Thames town. The 17th-c town hall is mounted on stone pillars, and a fine old 14-arch bridge spans the river. Angiers Almshouses date from 1681. St Leonard's Church still displays some Norman work, in spite of having been altered in 1850. St Peter's Church was rebuilt in 1860 and carries a curious openwork spire designed by Sir Robert Taylor in 1777. Calleva House is a notable example of the many Georgian buildings to be seen in the High Street and Thames Street. St Luciens may be of Elizabethan origin.

WALLOP, Hants *7 SU23 and 64*
Three attractive little villages named Middle, Nether, and Over Wallop lie close together in the shadow of Danebury Hill, W of the Test Valley. Nether Wallop church contains medieval wall-paintings, and Over Wallop church has a fine 15th-c font. Farleigh Wallop is a village situated S of Basingstoke at an altitude of 700ft. The hall dates from 1731, and the church contains interesting Wallop memorials. It is thought that the name Wallop may be a corruption of the French *galoper*.

WALLSEND, Tyne & Wear *27 NZ26*
Shipbuilding and engineering are the main industries of the River-Tyne town, which is situated at the E extremity of the Roman Wall. The Willington viaduct dates from 1869. Mauretania, a famous liner which once sailed under the Cunard flag, was launched here in 1907. The new Tyne road tunnel lies to the E and was opened in 1967.

WALMER, Kent *9 TR35*
A 16th-c castle in this residential resort is the official residence of the Lord Warden of the Cinque Ports (OACT). The Duke of Wellington died here in 1852.

WALPOLE, Suffolk *15 TM37*
The oldest meeting house in England, built in 1607, is sited here. Of particular interest are its wooden fittings which date from the same period. Notable Heveningham Hall is a Georgian structure by Sir Robert Taylor, lying about 1m SW.

The great entrance hall was the work of James Wyatt, and Capability Brown laid out the gardens. Features of the latter include an orangery, a thatched ice-house, and a curved-brick crinkle-crankle wall (OACT). The house was given to the nation in 1970.

WALPOLE ST PETER, Norfolk *14 TF51*
Considered outstanding among the other famous Marshland churches, St Peter's includes screenwork, stalls, and benches which are almost entirely of 15th-c date.

WALSALL, W Midlands *18 SP09*
Plan overleaf
Coal mines are a common sight in the area around this important Black-Country industrial town. Remains of the 14th-c castle or hall, which is now demolished, adjoin the modern Rushall church. It was associated with the Civil War and was dismantled in 1646. The rebuilt hilltop church of St Matthew retains a perpendicular chancel, and is built above an unusual vaulted passage. Carved poppy-heads and choir-stalls are of interest; a window commemorates Sister Dora (Dorothy Pattison) the famous nursing sister, and her statue stands in the town. Jerome K Jerome, author of *Three Men in a Boat*, was born in Walsall in 1859.

WALSINGHAM, Norfolk *15 TF93*
Several early English kings were among the many pilgrims who journeyed to a famous shrine that existed here. Such pilgrimages have latterly been revived. Remains of the priory can be seen in the grounds of the modern abbey, and include a 15th-c gateway. Parts of the ancient Grey Friars, founded in 1346, also exist.

The fine 15th-c parish church was restored after fire damage, and houses a mutilated Seven-Sacraments font plus the Sidney tombs. A new Anglican Shrine of Our Lady dates from 1931 and 1937. Several old houses and a quaint conduit are preserved in the village.

Old Walsingham church lies 1m NE and shows fine window tracery and old bench-ends. Restored 14th-c Slipper Chapel lies 1m SW at Houghton St Giles, on the ancient track known as Walsingham Way. Pilgrims are said to have walked barefoot to Walsingham from the chapel.

WALSOKEN, Norfolk *14 TF41*
The beautiful parish church is one of the Marshland group, and is situated on the outskirts of Wisbech. Features include a splendid Norman nave, an early-English tower, a fine Seven-Sacraments font, and 15th-c screenwork.

WALTHAM ABBEY, Essex *8 TL30*
Some of the oldest Norman workmanship in England can be seen in the fine Abbey Church, and King Harold was buried here after being slain at Hastings during the Norman invasion of 1066. The Norman nave is notable and the tower dates from 1556. Extensive restoration work was carried out in the 19thc, but the Royal Arms of Queen Elizabeth I's period are still to be seen. Stocks and a whipping post dating from 1598 are preserved. A 15th-c abbey gateway and a very ancient bridge have survived.

WALTHAM CROSS, Herts *8 TL30*
One of the three surviving Eleanor Crosses, set up by King Edward I in memory of Queen Eleanor in 1290, exists here in a greatly restored state (AM). A picturesque gallows sign has been preserved outside the Four Swans Inn.

WALTHAM GREAT, Essex *9 TL61*
Great Waltham's restored church is of Norman origin, and the notable bench-ends are a good example of the 15th-c workmanship to be seen inside. A fine but much-restored house with Tudor chimneys stand near by, and the area includes the 16th-c timbered houses of Hyde Hall and Fitzjohn's Farm. Langleys is an interesting early 18th-c house containing notable plasterwork and fireplaces. The curious timber-framed Black Chapel includes a built-in priest's house, and is of medieval origin.

WALTHAMSTOW, Gt London *8 TQ38*
Interesting monuments are housed in the restored church of St Mary, and near by are the Monoux almshouses of c1760, plus a timber-framed Tudor cottage. The Vestry House now contains a museum which features a Bremer car of 1892, one of the earliest in England. Forest Road contains the 18th-c Water House, childhood home of William Morris and now a Morris art gallery. Georgian houses are incorporated in the Forest School.

WALTON-ON-THAMES, Surrey *8 TQ16*
A curious 16th-c brass exists in the restored 12th- to 15th-c church, and a restored timbered manor house of 15th-c date stands in the area.

WALTON-ON-THE-HILL, Surrey *8 TQ25*
Both the hall and chapel of the local manor house date from the 14th to 16thc, and the restored partly 15th-c church preserves a Norman lead font. Headley Heath lies SW and is protected by the NT. Tadworth Court is a fine house of c1700, now used for hospital purposes, lying 2m NE.

WALTON-ON-THE-NAZE, Essex *15 TM22*
Amenities offered by this golfing resort include a long pier, excellent sands, and bathing. Oysters are farmed in the vicinity. The Naze is noted for fossils and lies 2m NE.

WANSDYKE
Wansdyke is the name given to an ancient trackway which was probably built for defensive purposes. It extends from a point near Hungerford in Wiltshire, and crosses the Marlborough Downs before running through the Avon Valley to Bristol. The total length of the route exceeds 50 miles. Some authorities claim that it went as far as the Bristol Channel, and terminated in the neighbourhood of Portishead. It is perhaps best seen on the Marlborough Downs above Alton Barnes, and farther W near Corston. The name is of Anglo-Saxon origin and derives from Woden – the Scandinavian god of tribal boundaries.

WANSFORD, Cambs *19 TL09*
Two bridges span the River Nene here – a noteworthy construction of 16th-c date, and a modern structure. A quaint sign outside the old Haycock Inn recalls the legend of drunken Barnaby. Stibbington Hall is a fine Jacobean house dated 1625 and standing 1½m SE.

WANSTEAD, Gt London *8 TQ48*
St Mary's church dates from 1890 and contains a fine pulpit, high box pews, and a remarkable monument of 1699 to Sir Josiah Child.

WANTAGE, Oxon 13 SU48
Situated in the Vale of White Horse at the foot of the Berkshire Downs, Wantage lies N of the ancient Ridgeway. King Alfred the Great is said to have been born here in AD 849, and a statue has been raised to him in the market-place. Good early-English and perpendicular features are evident in the local church. Of particular note are examples of old woodwork, a 15th-c hammerbeam roof, and five old brasses. Bear Inn is an old hostelry, and numerous old houses exist in the town. The first steam tramway in England linked Wantage with Wantage Road in 1873, and the line was not closed down until 1948.

WARBLETON, E Sussex 9 TQ61
Access to a squire's pew in the 13th-c church is by a staircase. The former workhouse is dated 1739, and Cralle Place — to the S — is dated 1724. Stone House is of Jacobean and later origin; both this and the remains of Warbleton Priory lie to the E. The latter were removed from Hastings in 1413.

WARBLINGTON, Hants 8 SU70
Remains of a moated 15th-c castle which was dismantled in the time of the Commonwealth can be seen here. The interesting little 13th-c church carries a partly-Saxon tower, and displays a fine 15th-c timbered porch. Two 19th-c watchers' huts in the churchyard survive from a time when body-snatching was fairly common.

WARBOYS, Cambs 14 TL38
Warboys church displays a good 13th-c tower and broach spire, a Norman chancel arch, and a rare lion door knocker. The manor house is of 17th-c date.

WARCOP, Cumbria 21 NY71
A bridge spanning the River Eden at Warcop is said to be one of the oldest in the country. The village is associated with rush-bearing — an annual tradition of rush gathering which originates from a time when rushes were used as an easily obtainable floor covering for churches and domestic buildings.

WARE, Herts 8 TL31
Old houses and the Canons Maltings of c1600 are features of Ware. The famous 'Great Bed of Ware' is now in the Victoria and Albert Museum, London. Lady Jane Grey was proclaimed Queen here in 1553, and the town is associated with Cowper's *John Gilpin's Ride*. Ware Priory preserves 15th-, 17th-, and 18th-c portions. Houses in the High Street and East Street include several gazebos, or garden houses, overlooking the river. The old town hall is Regency date, and Bluecoat House shows 15th-c timbering.

WAREHAM, Dorset 7 SY98
Earthworks that may be of Anglo-Saxon origin almost completely surround this old River-Frome town. Parts of St Martin's church date from the 11thc, and inside is a figure of Lawrence of Arabia. The statue was sculptured by Eric Kennington. Lady St Mary's church has been partly rebuilt and contains the marble coffin of Edward the Martyr, plus a unique six-sided lead font. A monument to John Hutchins the county historian

1 Dorothy Pattison's Statue
2 Rushall Church (castle remains)
3 St Matthew's Church

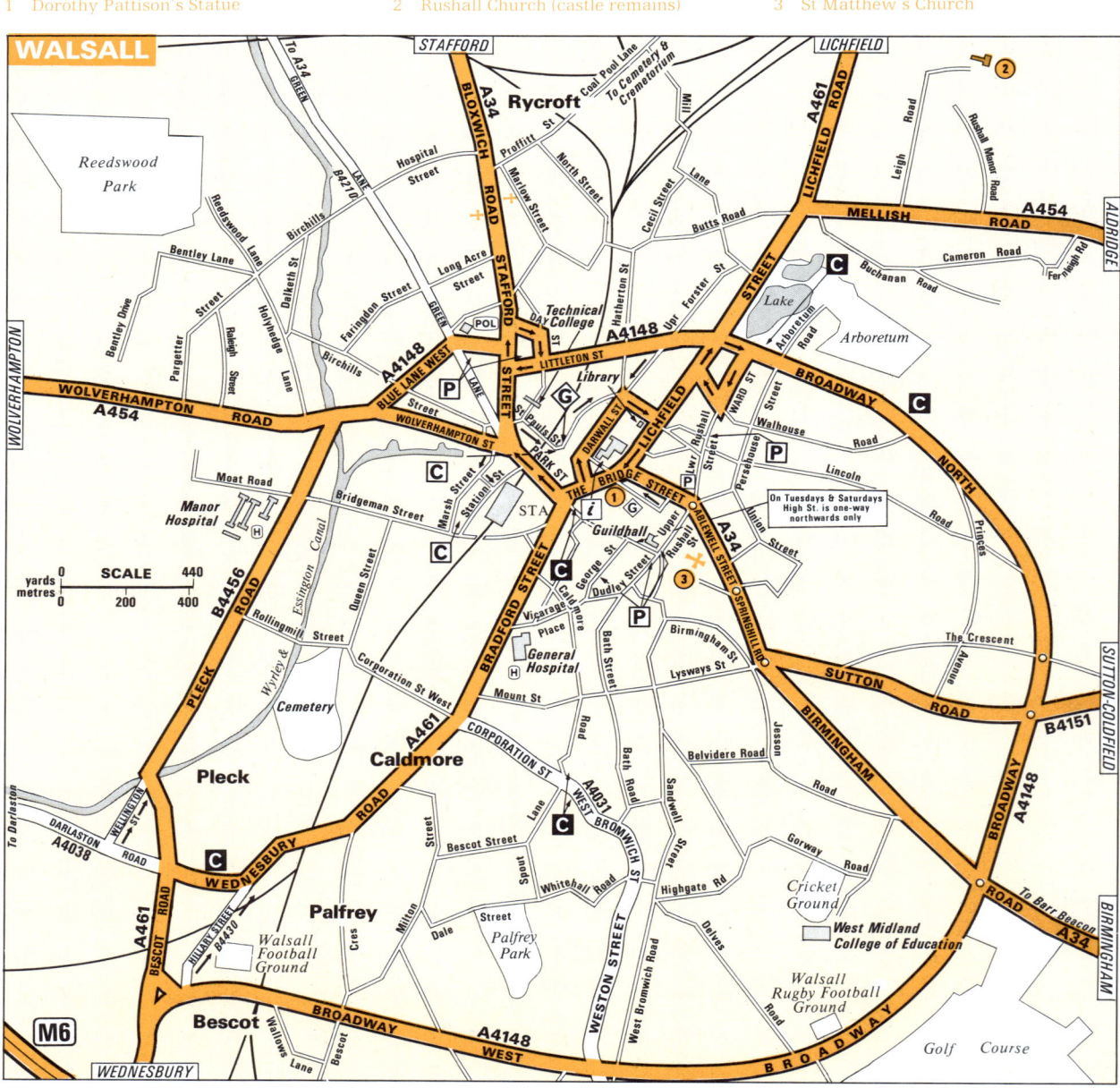

and one-time rector here is of interest. A number of pleasant 18th-c houses remain in the town, and the four principal streets meet in the form of a cross. Extensive heaths between Wareham and Puddletown are part of Thomas Hardy's fictional Egdon Heath, and have been partly afforested as a part of the Wareham State Forest scheme. Morden Bog lies N and has been made into a nature reserve. The Arne national reserve lies 2½m E, and Hartland Moor national nature reserve is situated 1½m SE.

WARK, Northumberland 27 NY87
Wark stands on the North Tyne River, in a lovely setting E of Wark Forest and the adjacent fringe of the Border forest park. Picturesque Chipchase Castle is a late 14th-c pele tower joined to a large Jacobean building, lying some 1¾m SE. A quaint 18th-c chapel stands in the park.

WARKWORTH, Northumberland 27 NU20
Impressive remains of a 12th-c castle which was probably built by the 1st Earl of Northumberland can be seen here (AM, OACT). The keep, gatehouse, and hall – which overlooks Alnmouth Bay – are of particular note. Shakespeare used the castle to set the scene in part of his *Henry IV*. A great deal of Norman workmanship is preserved in the church, and the nave measures some 300yds long. The stone spire is one of two ancient examples to be found in Northumberland. A curious 14th-c Hermitage is of interest, and an old bridge over the River Coquet carries a rare bridge tower at one end. The Old Pretender was proclaimed King James III at the old cross in the Market Place during the 1715 Jacobite Rising. The sea lies 1m E, and offers a sandy beach situated in an area of outstanding natural beauty.

WARMINGTON, Northants 19 TL09
One of the finest 13th-c churches in the country can be seen here. It is particularly notable for its rare vaulted wooden nave roof, and carries a broach spire which is characteristic of the Nene-Valley churches.

WARMINGTON, Warwickshire 13 SP44
This beautifully situated village of old buildings includes a fine manor house and a good Norman to 14th-c church. Features of the latter include an old chest, and its situation affords wide views over the surrounding area.

WARMINSTER, Wilts 7 ST84
Situated at the head of the Upper-Wylye valley, Warminster includes a church which has been greatly rebuilt but retains a 14th-c nave. Old houses and inns exist in the area, and 800ft Cley Hill (NT) rises prominently in the W. The beautiful old grammar school was founded in 1707, and numbers both Dr Arnold of Rugby and Dean Stanley among former pupils.

WARNFORD, Hants 7 SU62
A highly interesting Saxon to 17th-c church in this delightful Meon-Valley village is notable for its Saxon sundial and a massive Norman tower. Pairs of round windows are displayed by the latter, and remains of a late-Norman manor house exist near the church. Old Winchester Hill rises to nearly 700ft in the SE; it is a fine viewpoint which includes a nature trail, and is accessible by car.

WARNHAM, W Sussex 8 TQ13
Warnham Court has a large deer park, and access to the local church is through a yew arch. The Caryll monument inside the church is of note.

WARREN HOUSE INN, Devon 5 SX68
A peat fire has been burning continuously in this lonely Dartmoor inn, which lies at an altitude of 1,426ft some 2m NE of Postbridge, for over 100 years. Old Bennett's Cross lies 1m NE.

WARRINGTON, Cheshire 17 SJ68
Ironworks and soap factories operate in this important industrial town, and a few old timbered houses still exist in the area. The former 18th-c Bank Hall was designed by James Gibbs and now serves as the town hall. The Barley Mow is a fine half-timbered inn. Warrington Academy was founded in 1757 and dissolved in 1783; the building now houses a school. Both the parish church and Holy Trinity Church have been largely rebuilt, and may have been by Gibbs. A New Town is being developed here.

WARSASH, Hants 7 SU40
Warsash is a yachting centre at the mouth of the River Hamble. A recently-founded school of navigation exists here, and the beach is mainly shingle.

WARTON, Lancs 21 SD47
Links with the Washington family exist in the restored mainly 15th-c church. Their arms are carried by the tower, and also appear on a shield which is protected under glass inside the building.

WARWICK, Cumbria 26 NY45
A rare 12th-c apse of the type usually seen in France is an interesting feature of the local Norman church. Spectacular Holme Eden Hall dates from 1837 and was built for one of the founders of the Carlisle cotton mills. Dobson of Newcastle built the Warwick bridge over the River Eden in 1837.

WARWICK, Warwickshire 13 SP26
Many Georgian and older buildings exist in this picturesque River-Avon town, and interesting half-timbered houses can be seen in Mill Street. The famous castle dates from the 14th and 15thc and has imposing towers guarding the gatehouse. Its state rooms are rich in treasures and date from a later period. The well-known Warwick Vase can be seen in the garden (OACT). Lord Leycester's Hospital is a picturesque half-timbered building that was founded in 1383, mainly for use as a guildhall. It was converted to its present use in 1571. Above the nearby West Gate is St James's chapel which was originally founded in the 12thc. St Peter's chapel is attached to the East Gate and dates from the 15thc.

St Mary's Church is justifiably renowned for its rich 15th-c Beauchamp Chapel, which contains the magnificent Purbeck marble tomb of Richard Beauchamp, Earl of Warwick (1382 to 1439). The church was burnt down in 1694, but this chapel and the choir escaped. Rebuilding included the construction of a fine tower and was conducted during 1704. A rare ducking stool is preserved in the crypt under the chancel. St Nicholas's church dates from 1780.

The Avon Bridge dates from 1790, and Old Bridge is of 14th-c origin and now lies in ruins. Part of the fine 17th-c St John's House serves as a museum, and the half-timbered Elizabethan Oken's House contains an interesting doll museum. An old malt house stands behind the restored Anchor Inn. Other interesting buildings in the town include the County Hall of 1753; the old house where Walter Savage Landor was born in 1775; the Court House of 1724 to 1731; the Market Hall of 1670; Marble Yard House of c1620; timbered Brome Place in Bridge End. Northgate House was originally

1 Anchor Inn and Malt House
2 Avon Bridge
3 Brome Place
4 Castle
5 County Hall
6 Court House
7 East Gate and St Peter's Chapel
8 Guy's Cliffe Mill
9 Lord Leycester's Hospital
10 Market Hall
11 Marble Yard House
12 Northgate House
13 Oken's House (doll museum)
14 Old Bridge
15 Racecourse
16 School
17 St John's House (museum)
18 St Nicholas's Church
19 Walter Savage Landor's Birthplace
20 West Gate and St James's Chapel

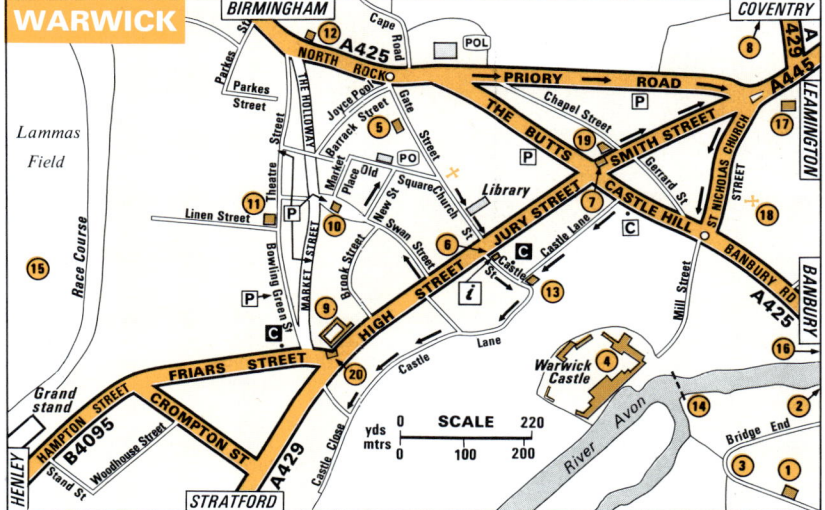

Monument in the parish church of St Mary, Watford

built as an inn in 1698. Warwick School was first founded in 914, and re-founded in 1545 by Henry VIII. One of its more famous pupils was John Masefield. A racecourse exists in the area, and picturesque Guy's Cliffe Mill lies 1m NNE.

WASDALE HEAD, Cumbria *21 NY10*
Popular with climbers intending to tackle the local rock faces, Wasdale Head lies at the head of remote Wast Water and is backed by 2,949ft Great Gable, 3,210ft Scafell Pike, and 3,162ft Scafell. Carved oak panelling from York Minster can be seen in the tiny white church. Wild screes rise directly from the S shores of the lake. A path leading to Sty Head Pass, one of the highest in the Lake District national park, runs NE from the head of the lake and thence between Great End and Great Gable.

WASHINGTON, Tyne & Wear *27 NZ35*
A New Town is being founded in the expanding colliery area around Washington. Washington Old Hall was the home of George Washington's ancestors before they moved to Sulgrave. It has been restored as a museum (NT). Biddick Hall is a good example of early 18th-c building. Lofty Penshaw Monument (NT), built in 1844 to commemorate the first Earl of Durham, stands 3m SE beyond the River Wear.

WATCHET, Somerset *6 ST04*
This Bristol-Channel port and resort includes a rock and sand bathing-beach. St Decuman's church lies 1m S and displays a good tower, interesting tombs, and brasses in two chapels.

WATENDLATH, Cumbria *21 NY21*
Sir Hugh Walpole used this village as a setting in his novel *Rogue Herries*. It lies S of Derwentwater, in a picturesque valley threaded by a beck which later joins attractive Watendlath tarn below 1,588ft Armboth Fell.

WATERINGBURY, Kent *9 TQ65*
Fruit and hop cultivation is the main occupation of the district surrounding this large Medway-Valley village. An elaborate 17th-c monument can be seen in the mainly-perpendicular church, and the Dumb Borsholder is a name given to a curious wooden symbol. Wateringbury Place is an 18th-c house standing in lovely gardens.

WATERLOOVILLE, Hants *7 SU60*
This expanding residential district includes a church of 1836, containing a west gallery and Royal Arms. The settlement was once a hamlet known as Waitland End. World's End lies 4½m NW and boasts one of the earliest letterboxes in England – dated 1859.

WATER NEWTON, Cambs *19 TL19*
Stone cottages and an old mill exist in this interesting River-Nene village. Features of the 13th-c church include a tower niche containing an effigy of Thomas Perdue, a medieval benefactor, with a French inscription.

WATFORD, Herts *8 TQ19*
Watford is a busy town situated on the Rivers Colne and Gade. The restored perpendicular parish church of St Mary preserves interesting monuments, plus the Essex chapel of 1595. Near by is the Elizabethan Fuller Free School of 1704. Bedford almshouses were founded in 1580. Cassiobury is an attractive park, but its former mansion which was owned by the Earls of Essex is no longer standing.

WATLING STREET
One of the best-known Roman roads, Watling Street links Dover (*Dubris*) with Wroxeter (*Uriconium*) in Shropshire, and then extends N and W with various ramifications. Some of its diversions lead to Caernarvon, Lancaster, and Aldborough. Two modern roads that follow much of the street's route are the A2 and the A5. The former occupies several stretches of the original Roman way between Dover and London, and the latter follows almost the same course from London onwards. It is thought that a good proportion of the route was in use as trackways prior to the Romans' invasion.

WATLINGTON, Oxon *7 SU69*
Several Georgian houses still stand in Watlington, and the settlement is situated at the foot of the Chiltern escarpment. The market hall dates from 1664. Watlington Hill is a splendid 800ft viewpoint lying 1½m SE, and the modernized and moated 14th-c house of Shirburn Castle stands 1m NE.

WATTON, Humberside *23 TA05*
Remains of a Gilbertine priory which was once the largest occupied by this order in England can be seen here. Prior's Lodge dates from the 14th and 15thc and now serves as a private residence. The brick-built church is considered to be of Tudor origin.

WATTON, Norfolk *15 TF90*
A clock tower dating from the 17thc is of interest here, and the picturesque many-gabled Elizabethan house of Breccles Hall lies 2m SW. Merton Hall stands 2m S and dates partly from *c*1613.

WATTON-AT-STONE, Herts *8 TL31*
Interesting brasses can be seen in the 15th-c church, and the covered 19th-c village pump is of note. Woodhall Park lies 1m SE and dates from 1777. Aston Bury, a fine old house with notable chimneys and woodwork, lies 2½m NE.

WAVERLEY, Surrey *8 SU84*
Tree-crowned Crooksbury Hill dominates this pleasantly situated River-Wey village. Remains of 13th-c Waveley Abbey, the earliest Cistercian house in England, exist here. It is thought that Sir Walter Scott may have used the village name for his Waverley novels.

WAXHAM, Norfolk *15 TG42*
Excellent sands and dunes are offered by this coastal village. The mid 16th-c hall is of flint-and-stone construction.

WEALD, THE
An area of broken country lying between the North and South Downs bears this name. Parts of the area have been given over to fruit and hop cultivation, but several wooded patches exist as a reminder that it once formed part of the Forest of Anderida. Some of the most attractive small towns and villages in England exist in the Wealden district.

WEAVERTHORPE, N Yorks *23 SE97*
Fine painted barrel roofs and a rare Saxon sundial are features of the interesting Norman and decorated church. Numerous small bridges span a local gypsey race (stream).

WEDMORE, Somerset *6 ST44*
Historically famous for the treaty signed between Alfred and the Danes in 879, Wedmore includes a church carrying a central tower and displaying a fine Jacobean pulpit. Well-restored stone-built Ashton windmill was built to a circular plan, and was presented to the city of Bristol in 1966.

WEDNESBURY, W Midlands *18 SP09*
Large iron and steel works operate in this Black-Country town. St Bartholomew's church contains a remarkable 15th-c lectern – fashioned from wood, plaster, and gilt – which depicts a fighting cock. The carved oak pulpit dates from 1611.

WEEDON, Northants *13 SP65*
Weedon lies on Watling Street, the Grand Union Canal, and the River Nene. It is sometimes regarded as the exact centre of England. Extensive barracks which were begun in 1803 are now closed. George III was to have come here in the event of a French invasion.

WEEKLEY, Northants *13 SP88*
Features of this delightful village include thatched cottages, a Jacobean vicarage

which was once a school, and the delightful 17th-c Montagu Hospital. Montagu tombs are housed within the church.

WEETING, Norfolk *15 TL78*
Sections of flint walling survive from an 11th-c castle that once existed in this Breckland village. Weeting Heath is a 338-acre national nature reserve.

WELBECK ABBEY, Notts *18 SK57*
This well-known 17th-c house contains curious underground passages and rooms, and stands in a magnificent lake-watered park (off the A60) between Cuckney and Worksop. It is partly used as an army college, and is not open to the public.

WELCOMBE, Devon *5 SS21*
Welcombe lies near the Cornish border in a remote glen leading to a wild stretch of cliff-bound coast at Marsland Mouth. The church is associated with the Rev S Hawker of Morwenstow, and displays old screenwork. Rivers Tamar and Torridge both rise in the country E of the village.

WELDON, Northants *13 SP98*
Stone from the quarries around Great and Little Weldon was used in the construction of Old St Paul's Cathedral. An interesting old lock-up is preserved on Weldon Green, and gabled Haunt Hill House dates from 1643. The church's fine lantern tower was once used to guide travellers through the thickly-wooded Rockingham Forest. Roman remains have been excavated in the district.

WELFORD, Berks *7 SU47*
Thatched cottages are a feature of this Lambourn-Valley village, and attractive downland rises to the NW. The Norman and early-English church tower is of partly-round flint construction and has been rebuilt. Welford Park house dates from the 18thc.

WELFORD-ON-AVON, Warwickshire *12 SP15*
A striped maypole, an old churchyard lych-gate, and several thatched cottages can be seen in this picturesque village.

WELLINGBOROUGH, Northants *13 SP86*
Footwear is manufactured in this Nene-Valley town, and large ironworks operate in the area. Interesting features include a 14th- to 15th-c church, a well-known school, and several old houses. All Hallows church hall is a stone-built house dating from the 17thc. St Mary's church is a well-known modern structure by Sir Ninian Comper.

WELLINGTON, Salop *17 SJ61*
This busy industrial town is situated on Watling Street, and was a Royalist stronghold during the Civil War. A few half-timbered houses are preserved. The Wrekin, perhaps England's oldest mountain, is a notable viewpoint which rises to 1,335ft and lies 2½m SW. A famous Shropshire toast is drunk to 'All friends round the Wrekin'. Wellington now forms part of Telford New Town.

WELLINGTON, Somerset *6 ST12*
The great Duke of Wellington took his title from this town, and the community operates a noted woollen industry. A midside stair turret reminiscent of those seen in Devon is a feature of the local perpendicular church. Inside is the fine tomb of Sir John Popham, a former Lord Chief Justice who died in 1607. A tall Wellington Monument (NT) was erected 3m S on the crest of the Blackdown Hills in 1817. Near by is an AA viewpoint.

WELLOW, Avon *6 ST75*
Dr John Bull, who is reputed to have composed the National Anthem, was born here in 1562. St Julian's Church dates from 1372 and displays many notable features. Of particular interest are the fine panelled roof and examples of good woodwork. Hungerford Chapel dates from 1440 and contains a rare mural painting which was discovered quite recently. The 17th-c manor house is of interest, and a large Celtic tumulus known as Stoney Littleton lies 1m SW.

WELLS, Somerset *6 ST54*
Wells is a beautiful little cathedral city of medieval origin, situated at the foot of the Mendip Hills. Features of the 13th- to 15th-c cathedral are the famous statue-adorned west front; the three towers; the curiously inverted nave arches; the chantry chapels; the chapter house and double-branching stair; and the cloisters. Bishop's Palace stands within a moat and retains a 13th-c chapel. Swans inhabiting the lake are famous for their trick of ringing a bell for their food.

Picturesque Vicars' Close is reached via the Chain Gate, and is used by the Wells singers. Both the Archdeacon's house and the Deanery are of interest, and two old gates preserved in the city are Browne's and the Penniless Porch. A number of interesting old buildings in the East and North Liberties include the cathedral school and the organist's house; a fine medieval tithe barn is also of note (AM).

St Cuthbert's church is of the 15thc and displays an imposing tower, a fine nave roof, and a carved font cover. Bishop Bubwith's almshouses are of ancient foundation, and the local museum illustrates the history of the Mendip caves. William Penn once preached from an upper window of the restored Crown Hotel, and the building preserves an interesting courtyard. The town hall has a façade of 1779. Tor Hill forms a good viewpoint (NT).

WELLS-NEXT-THE-SEA, Norfolk *15 TF94*
Old houses exist near the quayside of this small resort and port. The beach shows good sand at low tide, and bathing may be enjoyed in a creek which lies about 1m distant. Salt marshes exist in the neighbourhood.

WELSH NEWTON, Herefs & Worcs *12 SO41*
A fine decorated-style screen is featured in the little church, and pilgrimages are still made to the grave of John Kemble – who was martyred in 1679 – which is situated here. Restored Pembridge Castle lies 1m N.

WELTON, Humberside *23 SE92*
Dick Turpin was arrested in the local inn during 1739, and the hostelry was subsequently named after this notorious highwayman. A carved fountain stands on the village green.

WELWYN, Herts *8 TL21*
Several old houses and inns can be seen here. A cottage by the churchyard preserves an old drag-hook which was originally used for fighting thatch fires. Lockleys is a fine Georgian house standing in a park E of the by-pass, now containing a school.

WELWYN GARDEN CITY, Herts *8 TL21*
Welwyn's garden city lay-out of 1920 is one of the earliest in England; Letchworth is the oldest. Welwyn New Town is a recent development.

WEM, Salop *17 SJ52*
Almost all of this River-Roden town was destroyed by fire in 1677. Judge Jeffreys lived at 17th-c Lowe Hall, and William Hazlitt once lived in Noble Street. An ancient timbered house known as The Ditches lies 1m W, and 2m NE is Soulton Hall of 1668.

WEMBLEY, Gt London *8 TQ18*
Wembley Stadium is the venue for important football matches and other sporting contests. One of the best known annual events is the autumn Horse of the Year Show. Empire Pool is also a sports arena.

WEMBURY, Devon *5 SX54*
Views across Wembury Bay encompass Gara Point and the Great Mewstone Island. Two fine 17th-c monuments can be seen in the church, and the local chapel and almshouses date from 1682.

WENDENS AMBO, Essex *14 TL53*
This attractive village of old cottages lies just W of the Cambridge road, and includes a church displaying a Norman tower and 14th-c wall-paintings. The pulpit screen and bench-ends are also of interest. The name of the village derives from a combination of Great and Little Wenden. Amalgamation of the two communities occurred in 1662.

WENDOVER, Bucks *8 SP80*
Beautifully situated in the Chiltern Hills, Wendover includes several Georgian and older houses and a golf course. Good workmanship in the decorated style can be seen in the local church, which also contains a curious brass to William Bradschawe. Ancient Icknield Way runs through the area. Coombe Hill, a 852ft viewpoint rising to the W, is one of the highest points in the Chilterns (NT). It is surmounted by a monument.

WENDRON, Cornwall *4 SW63*
Access to the 14th- to 15th-c church is through a 17th-c lych-gate. A very early cross-slab bears an incised cross.

WENHASTON, Suffolk *15 TM47*
The mainly-perpendicular church is noted for its fine 15th-c doom painting. Wenhaston Grange lies 2m W, and is a 16th- to 18th-c house carrying Tudor chimneys.

WENSLEY, N Yorks *22 SE08*
An old bridge (AM) spans the River Ure in this attractive Lower-Wensleydale village. The interesting 13th- to 15th-c church contains a magnificent 14th-c brass and a very rare wooden reliquary of 15th-c date. Old screenwork which was formerly at Easby Abbey can also be seen. Bolton Hall is the shell of a house which was built in the 17thc and burnt down in 1902.

WEOBLEY, Herefs & Worcs *12 SO45*
Perhaps the most attractive half-timbered village in the area, Weobley includes several cottages which date back to the 14thc. Picturesque Red Lion Inn is of the same approximate age, and the mainly

14th-c church carries a lofty spire and contains several interesting monuments. Earthworks survive from the former castle. The Ley, situated on the SW outskirts of the village, is an eight-gabled timbered farmhouse dating from 1589. Fenhampton is a Jacobean house lying some 1½m SW.

WESSEX
Wessex was the ancient kingdom of the West Saxons, and included the counties of Berkshire, Hampshire, Wiltshire, Dorset, and Somerset. Although Devonshire and Cornwall were later included in the kingdom, the name is not generally applied to these counties. Thomas Hardy the famous novelist was largely responsible for the revival of interest in Wessex. Many of his works described communities existing in the area – particularly in Dorset – under thinly-veiled pseudonyms. Some of his fictional names have still not been positively applied to their true-life places.

WEST ACRE, Norfolk 15 TF71
Remains of an Augustinian priory exist here, and include a notable gatehouse. The parish church shows perpendicular and 17th-c styles and displays woodwork from both periods. The clock-face figures read 'Watch and Pray'.

WEST AUCKLAND, Co Durham 27 NZ12
The fine old hall at West Auckland was altered in 1670, and an 18th-c hall at nearby St Helen Auckland contains Italian plasterwork. Roman or Saxon remains known as Legs Cross exist 3m SE, in a field lying close to the Roman road to Piercebridge.

WEST BROMWICH, W Midlands 18 SP09
Hardware is a noted product of this industrial town. Black-and-white Tudor Oak House is a picturesque building dating from 1488 and 1635, which carries a curious lantern tower and now houses a museum. The 14th-c or earlier manor house is of partly timber-framed construction and has been well-restored as an inn.

WEST BURTON, N Yorks 22 SE08
This attractive Wensleydale village is situated in the Yorkshire Dales national park. A curious cross of 1820 stands on the wide green, and the parish stocks have been preserved. Bishopdale extends to the SW.

WESTBURY, Salop 17 SJ30
Interesting monuments can be seen in the local modernized church. Earthworks of Caus Castle, a former Fitzcorbet stronghold which was finally destroyed in the Civil War, lie 1½m SW. Restored half-timbered Marche Manor stands 1½m NW.

WESTBURY, Wilts 7 ST85
A central tower is carried by the local perpendicular-style church; features of the building's interior include a fine tomb to the first Earl of Marlborough and a chained New Testament. The market place is of largely Georgian origin. The oldest of the well-known Wiltshire White Horses was cut into the downland turf 1½m ENE in 1778 (AM).

WESTBURY-ON-SEVERN, Glos 12 SO71
Unique 17th-c Dutch-style water gardens of former Westbury Court have recently been excellently restored (NT, OACT). The restored church carries a 12th-c detached tower, surmounted by a wooden broached and shingled spire rising to 160ft. Remains of a 12th-c abbey are incorporated in a Jacobean and Georgian mansion lying 2m NW at Flaxley.

WESTBURY-ON-TRYM, Avon 6 ST57
Westbury College (NT) retains a 15th-c tower formerly belonging to the ancient College of Priests, and the adjacent College House dates from the 18thc. The restored 13th- to 15th-c church was once attached to the college. A wildlife park is situated in a secluded local valley.

About 1m N is picturesque little Blaise Hamlet, a community of rustic cottages built entirely by John Nash in 1809 (NT). Blaise Castle House dates from 1766 and now serves as a folk museum. Three-storeyed 18th-c Stratford Mill is another interesting feature of the estate (OACT). King's Weston is a notable Vanbrugh house of 18th-c origin, which lies 2m W and now contains a school. A Roman villa has been excavated at Lawrence Weston.

WEST CHALLOW, Oxon 13 SU38
Situated in the Vale of White Horse, this village includes a church containing a bell which was cast in c1282. It is inscribed 'Paul the Potter made me' and is considered the earliest in existence to bear the maker's name.

WEST CHILTINGTON, W Sussex 8 TQ01
Wall-paintings are preserved in the unrestored 11th-c church which stands in this Weald village, and a windmill exists in the area. Stocks and a whipping post have been preserved.

WEST CLANDON, Surrey 8 TQ05
Clandon Park is an 18th-c house standing in wooded grounds, which contains priceless furniture brought here in 1970 (NT, OACT). Old pews and glass are features of the restored Norman to 15th-c church.

WESTCLIFF-ON-SEA, Essex 9 TQ88
Off-shore of this popular Thames-estuary resort is the Crow Stone, which once marked the limit of the Port of London Authority at the mouth of the Thames. The original 18th-c obelisk now stands at Prittlewell.

WEST COKER, Somerset 6 ST51
Two tower turret windows glazed with horn, the predecessor of glass, can be seen in the decorated to perpendicular church. A small 15th-c manor house is also of interest.

WEST DEAN, E Sussex 8 TV59
Picturesquely set in a combe of the downs, where a white horse has been cut, West Dean includes a Norman to 15th-c church containing several old tombs. Another interesting feature of the area is a restored 13th-c parsonage house. Partly late 12th-c Charleston Manor lies N and displays Tudor and Georgian wings, the largest tithe barn in Sussex, and attractive gardens (OACT).

WEST DEAN, W Sussex 8 SU81
This South-Downs village is situated near the new Weald and Downland museum, England's first organized open-air crafts display. The exhibits will eventually include some forty re-erected old buildings, several of which are already in place (OACT).

WEST DRAYTON, Gt London 8 TQ07
A 16th-c gateway from the former manor house of the De Burghs and Pagets can still be seen here. Several Georgian houses exist in the area, and the church contains a 15th-c font plus fine monuments.

WESTENHANGER, Kent 9 TR13
Fragments of a 14th-c castle can be seen near Folkestone racecourse. The proposed Channel Tunnel is expected to commence near here.

WESTERHAM, Kent 8 TQ45
General Wolfe was born in the local vicarage in 1726, and 16th- to 17th-c Quebec House was his early home (NT, OACT). Relics of the great man are preserved inside and a Wolfe statue stands in the High Street. He stayed in the George and Dragon during his last visit to the town in 1758. The restored early-English and perpendicular church preserves interesting brasses and a unique example of the Royal Arms of Edward VI.

Westerham Hill is an 800ft viewpoint crossed by the Pilgrims' Way. Chartwell, the former home of Sir Winston Churchill, lies 2m S and now houses a Churchill Museum. The gardens are notable (NT, OACT). Squerryes Court, a fine 16th-c and later house which is also associated with Wolfe, stands 1m SW in a lake-watered park (OACT).

WESTGATE-ON-SEA, Kent 9 TR37
Chalk cliffs and good bathing sands are features of this resort, which lies just to the W of Margate.

WEST GRINSTEAD, W Sussex 8 TQ12
Alexander Pope is said to have composed the *Rape of the Lock* here in 1712. A deer park to the N of the village contains a tree known as Pope's Oak. The Norman to perpendicular church displays tombs, brasses, and a 15th-c timbered porch.

WESTHALL, Suffolk 15 TM48
Westhall church is noted for its thatched nave, Seven-Sacraments font, and fine painted screen panels. The hall dates from 1570 and displays Flemish gables; it was altered in the 19thc.

WESTHAM, E Sussex 9 TQ60
Paintings dating from the 15thc can be seen in the attractive Norman to perpendicular church, which also preserves a good perpendicular screen. The restored 16th-c house of Priesthawes lies 2m NW.

WESTHAMPNETT, W Sussex 8 SU80
This hamlet is situated on the line of ancient Stane Street. The interesting church includes pre-Conquest workmanship, and Roman materials have been used in its fabric.

WEST HANNEY, Oxon 13 SU49
The local Norman to 14th-c church includes an old screen and a notable collection of brasses. A very fine Georgian house of 1727 stands near by.

WEST HANNINGFIELD, Essex 9 TQ79
Situated N of the Hanningfield reservoir, West Hanningfield boasts an interesting church displaying a 15th-c timbered tower, an octagonal 13th-c font, and 17th-c brickwork. Wall-paintings dating from 1615 are preserved at Cloville Hall.

WEST HARPTREE, Avon *6 ST55*
A new copper spire surmounts the tower of the Norman parish church. Gournay Manor is a fine Jacobean house, and Tilley Manor dates from the 17thc.

WEST HOATHLY, W Sussex *8 TQ33*
Windows dating from the 13thc are an interesting feature of the local church, and the ridge upon which the village stands affords fine views to the S. A 15th-c Priest's House and barn now contain a museum, and an old manor house stands in the area. Great-upon-Little is a rock formation comprising a large sandstone rock balanced on a smaller, situated in the grounds of Rockhurst. Gravetye Manor is a fine gabled Elizabethan house which was once the home of the famous garden designer William Robinson (1838 to 1935); it is now a hotel.

WEST HORSLEY, Surrey *8 TQ05*
West Horsley Place is a large 17th- to 18th-c house. The restored church carries a massive 12th-c tower and contains fine Berners and Nicholas memorials, plus 15th-c screens. Sir Walter Raleigh is said to be buried under the south chapel.

WEST KINGTON, Wilts *6 ST87*
Thatched cottages and an old bridge are preserved here, and the church carries a lovely perpendicular tower with Norman tower-arch capitals. Hugh Latimer preached from the finely-carved pulpit.

WEST KIRBY, Merseyside *17 SJ28*
Situated on the Wirral peninsula at the mouth of the River Dee, this resort and residential district offers a sandy bathing beach and golfing facilities.

WEST LAVINGTON, W Sussex *8 SU82*
Old cottages survive in this downland village. Richard Cobden, a noted free-trader who died in 1865, once lived to the S at Dunford House and is buried in the local churchyard.

WEST LAVINGTON, Wilts *7 SU05*
Two notable chapels in the local church are the Becket and the Dauntsey. The former is of perpendicular style, and the latter houses notable effigies. The figure of a dancing bear is borne by one of the parapets. Dauntsey School was originally founded in 1543.

WEST MALLING, Kent *9 TQ65*
Also known as Town Malling, this market town includes a church carrying a Norman tower and incorporating a modern nave. Inside is an example of the Royal Arms of James II. St Leonard's tower (AM) is the surviving fragment of a Norman castle, and remains of the abbey include a fine 11th-c tower and a perpendicular gateway. Other parts of this ancient foundation have been restored. Priest's House is a half-timbered building of 14th-c date, and good 18th-c houses exist in the area.

WEST MERSEA, Essex *9 TM01*
Bungalow developments and a shingle and mud beach are the most obvious features of this Mersea-Island village. A causeway linking the island to the mainland is subject to tidal flooding. The church tower is of Saxon or early-Norman origin.

WESTMILL, Herts *14 TL32*
Button Snap is a 17th-c cottage situated close to this delightful village, and is associated with Charles Lamb and his *Essays of Elia*. It has been acquired by the Lamb society. Other old houses exist in the area.

WESTON, Staffs *18 SJ92*
Weston church carries a good 13th-c tower surmounted by a re-erected spire. An old hall in which Mary Queen of Scots was imprisoned in 1585 was burnt down in 1781, and its 800-acre park was once the famous habitat of a herd of semi-wild white cattle. Chartley Moss Quaking Bog national nature reserve covers some 104 acres of the area, and remains of 13th-c Chartley Castle lie 3m E.

WESTONBIRT, Glos *12 ST88*
Wooded grounds of some 25-acres in extent surround a local well-known girls' college. Westonbirt Forest includes a notable arboretum which was founded in 1829, and is now part of a 600-acre Forestry Commission estate (OACT). Dougnton, a Cotswold hamlet lying 1m NE, boasts two lovely old houses; one of these is the manor house.

WESTON LONGVILLE, Norfolk *15 TG11*
Parson Woodforde wrote his celebrated diary while vicar here, and a tablet has been raised to him in the decorated-style church.

WESTON-SUPER-MARE, Avon *6 ST36*
Plan overleaf
This popular Bristol-Channel resort includes two piers, one of which doubles as a steamer jetty and lifeboat station. Amenities include good sands, pool and sea bathing, and golf. Flat Holme and Steep Holme are two islands lying a few miles off-shore. Worlebury Hill is surmounted by an iron-age encampment (AM) and lies 1m N. Late 15th- to early 18th-c Hutton Court is 2m SE.

WESTON-UNDER-LIZARD, Staffs *17 SJ81*
The Lizard suffix of the name is derived from a nearby hill. Weston Park dates from the 17thc and later, and is the splendid ancestral home of the Earls of Bradford (OACT). It stands in a fine lake-watered park which was designed by Capability Brown.

WESTON-UNDER-PENYARD, Herefs & Worcs *12 SO62*
A Norman arcade is featured by the local church, and Lower Weston is an interesting old gabled house. Bollitree Castle dates from the 17th to 18thc. Rudhall, an old manor house with an elaborate porch, lies 2m N.

WESTON UNDERWOOD, Bucks *13 SP85*
William Cowper lived in an 18th-c house in this pleasant stone-built village from 1786 to 1795. Over 200 different species of birds can be seen in the Flamingo Gardens (OACT). The New Mammal Park is included in the latter complex.

WESTON ZOYLAND, Somerset *6 ST33*
Decorated and perpendicular styles are evident in the local church, which carries a fine tower and displays a richly decorated nave roof. The battle of Sedgemoor — the last battle to be fought on English soil — was fought NW of here in 1685. Many of the rebels were confined in the church, but the Duke of Monmouth fled and was later captured near Ringwood.

WEST PENNARD, Somerset *6 ST53*
West Pennard church carries a 15th-c spired tower and fine old roofs. Other features include a 16th-c screen and an ancient churchyard cross. A stone tablet situated 1m SW on the Glastonbury road marks the site of *Pontis Vallum*, a Roman fort which once defended the bridge linking the Isle of Avalon with the mainland. The notable 15th-c Court Barn lies 1½m S of West Pennard (NT).

WEST QUANTOXHEAD, Somerset *6 ST14*
This village is also known as St Audries. A local mansion set in a beautiful park now houses a school, and picturesque red cliffs mark the place where the Quantock Hills shelve into the Bristol Channel to the N.

WEST ROW, Suffolk *14 TL67*
Items of great archaeological interest — the 4th-c Roman Mildenhall Find — were made here in 1946, and include various silver dishes and trays. These are now kept by the British Museum in London.

St Leonard's Tower, a fragment of West Malling's Norman castle

WEST RUNTON, Norfolk *15 TG14*
Excellent sandy beaches are offered by this small resort. Inland are areas of beautifully wooded countryside, and a Roman camp (NT) is situated near the highest point in Norfolk (300ft).

WEST TANFIELD, N Yorks *22 SE27*
Situated on the River Ure, West Tanfield includes a church which is famous for its Marmion tombs. Near by is the 15th-c gate tower of a former castle. The fine Jacobean and later manor house of Norton Conyers lies 4m SE.

WEST TARRING, W Sussex *8 TQ10*
West Tarring now forms part of Worthing. The restored church carries a lofty perpendicular tower, and part of a 13th- to 15th-c Archiepiscopal Palace is incorporated in the school. A well-known fig-garden of 1745 grows near by. Three 15th-c Thomas-a-Becket cottages belonging to the Sussex Archaeological Trust stand in Parsonage Row, High Street.

WEST THORNEY, W Sussex *8 SU70*
Access to the interesting early-English church in this Thorney Island village is via an RAF station, where permission must be obtained before a visit can be made. The building faces Chichester Harbour and displays a beautiful tower, two decorated screens which are among the earliest in England, and the oldest bell in Sussex; the latter dates from c1250.

WEST WALTON, Norfolk *14 TF41*
A splendid Marshland church which stands here is of mainly early-English style, and is considered one of the finest of its period. It is particularly noted for the porch, nave arcades, and angel-carved hammerbeam roof. A notable detached tower displays early tracery.

WESTWARD HO!, Devon *5 SS42*
Kipling's *Stalky & Co*, is associated with this place, which was named after the well-known novel by Kingsley. Good sands offer sea and surf bathing, and the 1,000-acre expanse of Northam Burrows – with its remarkable 2m-long pebble ridge – lies to the NW.

WESTWELL, Kent *9 TQ94*
R H Barham, author of *Ingoldsby Legends*, was curate of the 14th-c and later church from 1814 to 1820. The building is noted for its remarkable stone screen. Modern Eastwell House stands in a great park and includes an ornate gateway. The Pilgrims' Way runs through the grounds.

WESTWELL, Oxon *12 SP21*
Old cottages, thatched barns, and an old manor house are features of this pretty Cotswold village. The Norman church carries a quaint wooden turret.

WEST WICKHAM, Gt London *8 TQ36*
Wickham Court is a modernized 15th-c mansion which now serves as a convent school. Access to the restored church is through a fine 15th-c lych-gate.

WEST WITTERING, W Sussex *8 SZ79*
This fishing village is situated on the Manhood peninsula, a neck of land which terminates at Selsey Bill. It is surrounded by saltings and sand dunes, and has been the subject of some bungalow development. The interesting church dates from Norman and early-English periods, and contains fine tombs plus a remarkable old belfry staircase. Cakeham Manor lies SE, and was once a palace of the Bishops of Chichester; it still preserves a 16th-c tower.

WESTWOOD, Wilts *6 ST85*
The 15th-c village church is noted for its beautiful tower, and the 15th- to 17th-c manor house contains Jacobean plasterwork (NT, OACT). An old tithe barn stands near by. The outer gates of Midway Manor, which lies to the SE,

1 Flat Holme Island
2 Golf Course
3 Hutton Court
4 Iron-Age Encampment
5 Steep Holme Island

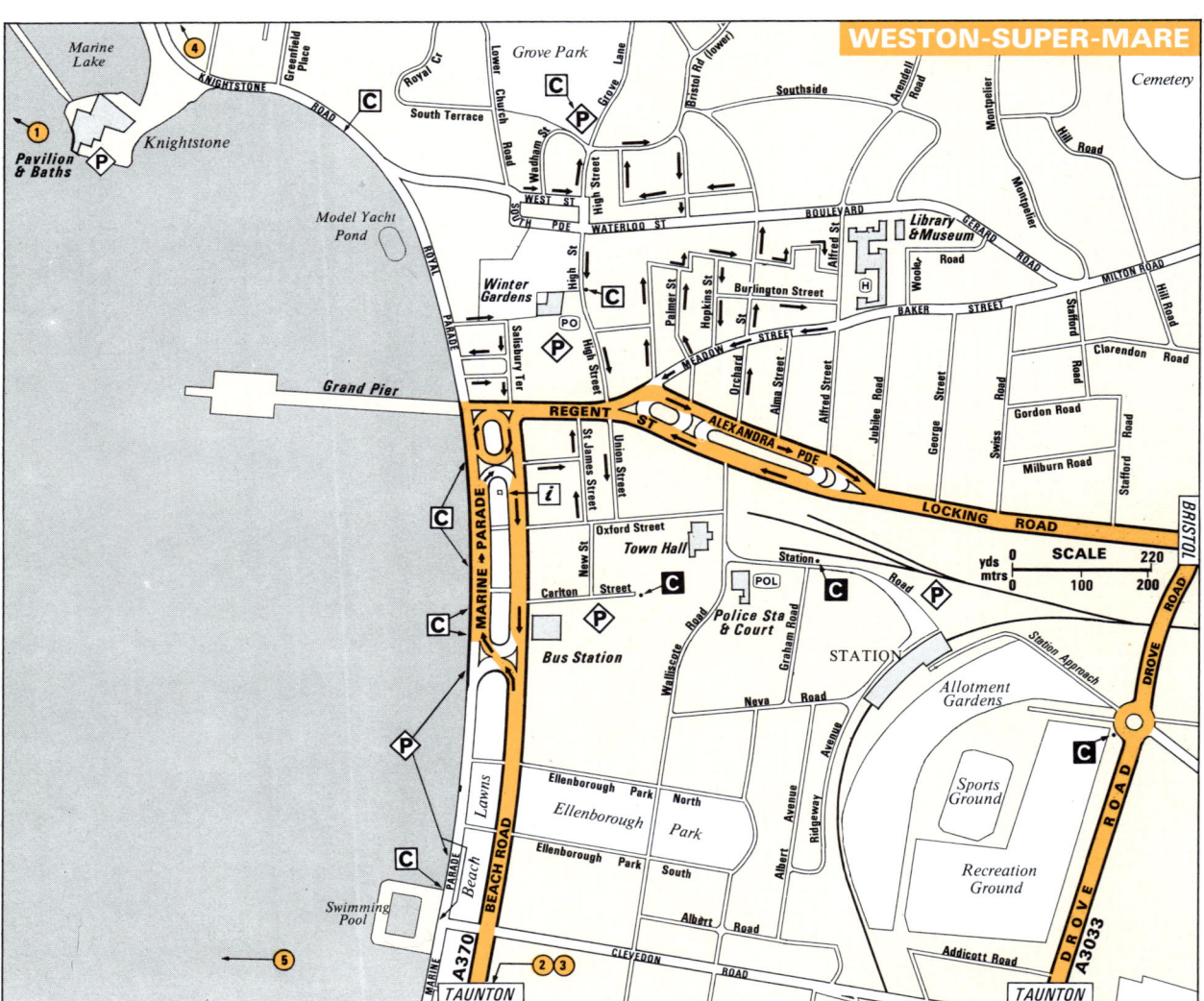

bear small piles of shrapnel. This weapon was invented by Major-General Shrapnel, who died in 1842. Iford Manor is an 18th-c house to the W, standing in a lovely setting which includes picturesque classical-style gardens.

WEST WYCOMBE, Bucks 8 SU89
Features of this picturesque village (NT) include the fine George Inn, the 15th-c Church Loft house, and several other old buildings. The church stands on a 600ft hill and was rebuilt in 1793. A huge ball borne by the tower forms a notable landmark. Sir Francis Dashwood of Hell-Fire Club fame and the builder of the church was buried in a mausoleum at the building's east end. Notable caves exist below the hill

West Wycombe Park, an 18th-c house, was built in c1765 for the Dashwoods. Robert Adam designed part of the building, and its lovely park by Capability Brown and Humphrey Repton is enriched by garden temples (NT, OACT). A pillar standing at the E edge of the village, on the High Wycombe to Princes Risborough road, dates from 1752 and gives mileages to various towns.

WETHERAL, Cumbria 26 NY45
Situated above the River Eden, this attractive village boasts an ancient priory gatehouse facing partly 17th-c Corby Castle. The latter stands in lovely grounds (OACT). Fine monuments by Nollekens can be seen in the church. A complex of three caves known as St Constantine's Cell exist in the lower village near the river.

WETHERBY, W Yorks 22 SE44
The River Wharfe and the former Great North Road run through this market town, and a racecourse exists in the area. Stockeld Park, situated 2m NW, was designed by James Paine and dates from 1758 to 1763.

WETHERINGSETT, Suffolk 15 TM16
Delightful thatched cottages and a 14th-c church with a carved nave roof preserve the old-world charm of this village. Richard Hakluyt, whose great work on English voyages and discoveries made him famous c1589, spent the last 26 years of his life as rector here.

WETHERSFIELD, Essex 14 TL73
Timber-framed and plastered houses are included among the buildings grouped around the attractive village green. Interesting monuments exist in the Norman to 15th-c church.

WEYBRIDGE, Surrey 8 TQ06
Only scanty remains of Oatlands Park, which once served as a palace for King Henry VIII, now exist; the modern building serves as a hotel. A lofty column placed on Monument Hill in 1822 commemorates a former Duchess of York. A century ago it stood at Seven Dials in the West End of London. St George's Hill displays ancient defensive works. A house situated 2m SE at Burhill was built as a Silver Jubilee memorial to King George V in 1936. Near by is secluded Whiteley Village, which was built as almshouses for 350 aged people by William Whiteley in 1907. This complex forms the largest group of such dwellings in England, and has since been modernized.

WEYHILL, Hants 7 SU34
Former Weyhill Fair dated from 1599 – and possibly earlier – and was granted a charter by Queen Elizabeth I. Weyhill Wild Life Park specializes in the wild life of Europe (OACT). Motor-racing takes place W at Thruxton.

WEYMOUTH, Dorset 6 SY67
Channel-Island ferries operate from this well-known resort and port, which is pleasantly situated between Weymouth Bay and the naval harbour of Portland. Amenities include good sands, bathing, golfing, and fishing. Thomas Hardy used the town under the name Budmouth in his novels. King George III once lived at Gloucester House, now a hotel, and a statue has been erected to him. Fine Georgian houses are a feature of Weymouth.

James Thornhill, famous painter of the *Last Supper* which hangs in 18th-c St Mary's Church, was born here in 1675.

Two 17th-c cottages in Trinity Street have been converted into a single dwelling, and contain contemporary furnishings (OACT). Picturesque alleys exist in the Melcombe Regis quarter, and Sandsfoot Castle is a blockhouse which was built by King Henry VIII in 1539. The guildhall contains several interesting portraits. Radipole Lake is a bird sanctuary, and the remarkable 18m-long Chesil Bank lies 3m SW. The octagonal former Spa house of Nottington lies 3m N and was visited by George III.

WHALLEY, Lancs 21 SD73
Remains of a 13th-c abbey (AM) in this River-Calder village include a 14th-c gateway. Parts of the mid 15th-c Abbot's House now form a Retreat House for the Blackburn diocese. Three medieval crosses are preserved in the parish church, and the building itself dates from the 12th to 15thc. Its restored canopied stalls originally came from the former abbey church.

WHALTON, Northumberland 27 NZ18
Sir Edwin Lutyens originally designed the restored manor house in this pleasant village, and the 12th-c and later church shows an interesting chancel.

WHAPLODE, Lincs 14 TF32
Whaplode's splendid Marshland church is of largely Norman date, and contains the notable newly-repainted 17th-c monument to Sir Anthony Joby.

WHARRAM-LE-STREET, N Yorks 23 SE86
Fine views are available from the churchyard of this pleasant little Wolds village. The church tower may be of Saxon origin, and the west doorway is particularly striking.

WHEATHAMPSTEAD, Herts 8 TL11
Timber-framed Bull Inn may date from the 15thc, and the mainly early-English to decorated local church includes the interesting Brocket chapel. A picturesque old manor house situated 2m E at Water End now serves as a farm, and was supposedly the birthplace of Sarah – the great Duchess of Marlborough. The farm includes an interesting barn. Farther E is late 18th-c Brocket Hall, a fine house by James Paine.

WHEATLEY, Oxon 13 SP50
Stocks are housed in Wheatley's curious old conical lock-up. Waterperry Wood is a forest nature reserve lying 2m NE, and the Waterperry Horticultural centre is located in a Georgian mansion standing in 80-acre grounds (OACT).

WHERWELL, Hants 7 SU34
Timbered and thatched cottages make up this picturesque village, which is sited in the Test Valley. Its once-famous abbey has completely vanished. The local inn carries a sign depicting the Twentieth Century.

WHICKHAM, Tyne & Wear 27 NZ26
Situated S of the River Tyne, Whickham lies 3m NE of the Gibside estate; the

1 Bird Sanctuary (Radipole Lake)
2 Gloucester House
3 Golf Course
4 Guildhall
5 Nottington Spa House
6 Sandsfoot Castle
7 St Mary's Church

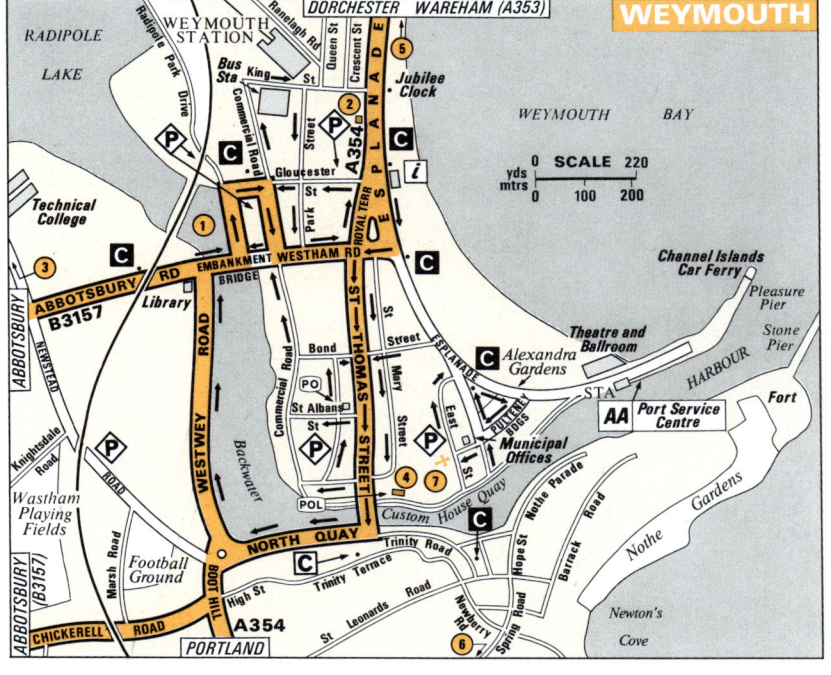

estate contains remains of a 17th- and early 19th-c mansion. The latter's former mausoleum (NT) is of the Georgian period, and now serves as a church. It was designed by James Paine in 1760, and restored and re-dedicated in 1966 (OACT). A lofty Tuscan column of mid 18th-c date stands in the park and is known as the Column of British Liberty.

WHIPPINGHAM, Isle of Wight 7 SZ59
Albert the Prince Consort built the ornate Victorian church in 1860. Queen Victoria regularly attended services here.

WHIPSNADE ZOOLOGICAL PARK, Beds 8 TL01
This park is a branch of the London Zoological Gardens, and specializes in showing wild animals in surroundings which are close as possible to their natural environment (OACT). Cars may be driven round the park at the Superintendent's discretion, and a miniature coach service operates inside the zoo. The area lies at the edge of the Chiltern Hills, and a huge lion has been cut out of the downland turf. Occasional church services are held in a Tree Cathedral (NT) on Whipsnade Green.

WHISSENDINE, Leics 19 SK81
Notable window tracery is a feature of the beautiful local early-English to perpendicular church. The screen and 14th-c west tower are also of interest.

WHISTON, Northants 13 SP86
The very fine local church was built in 1534, and carries a richly-pinnacled tower with an imposing array of gargoyles. Contrasting ironstone and limestone work is a feature of the tower, and the church itself displays fine roofs, old benches, and two monuments by Nollekens.

WHITBY, N Yorks 23 NZ81
North York Moors national park rises behind this well-known resort and harbour, which is picturesquely situated at the mouth of the River Esk. Sands and bathing are excellent, and the local fishing is good. The famous Council of Whitby took place in 664. Caedmon, a poet whose song is considered to mark the beginning of British literature, is commemorated by a 20-ft high carved cross dating from 1898. Remains of a historic 13th-c abbey (AM) are situated on the cliffs. Abbey House dates from the 16th to 19thc, and an old cross stands on broken steps. Access to St Mary's Church is by 199 steps. The building is of partly-Norman date, and includes an 18th-c interior displaying galleries and a three-decker pulpit.

Captain Cook's house is in Grape Lane (1688). Another house in the same lane preserves a strong gate and an iron-studded door – reminders that it once served as a private bank. Bagdale Old Hall is an interesting house, and the local museum stands in Pannett Park. A whalebone archway which was presented by Norway overlooks the town. A curious custom known as Planting the Penny Hedge is conducted annually on the day prior to Ascension Day. Picturesque Eskdale lies W of the resort and merges into the Cleveland Hills.

WHITCHURCH, Bucks 13 SP82
Earthworks from former Bolebec Castle and several half-timbered cottages exist here. The fine church displays a 15th-c painting in the north aisle. Creslow Manor, built c1330 and considered one of the oldest houses in Buckinghamshire, lies 2m NE and now serves as a farm.

WHITCHURCH, Hants 7 SU44
Notable sculptured stone of Anglo-Saxon origin is preserved in the restored local church. The White Hart is an old coaching inn. The town lies on the River Test – famous for its game fishing – and returned two members of Parliament from the reign of Elizabeth I until 1832.

WHITCHURCH, Oxon 7 SU67
Beautifully situated on the River Thames, Whitchurch lies below the wooded Chiltern Hills and includes a church housing interesting old brasses. Hardwick House stands in an attractive park. Sir John Soane, designer of the first Bank of England, was born here in 1753. He is recalled by the Soane Museum in London.

WHITCHURCH, Salop 17 SJ54
Features of the local church, which was rebuilt in 1713, include the fine 15th-c Talbot tomb, a notable early 18th-c organ case, and the Royal Arms of Queen Anne painted on silk. A few old houses that exist here include Higginson's almshouses, which were founded in 1647. Edward German the composer was born at Whitchurch in 1862. Fenns Moss lies SW on the Welsh border.

WHITCHURCH CANONICORUM, Dorset 6 SY39
This Marshwood-Vale village boasts a fine Norman to perpendicular church containing good nave arcades and tombs. The only saint's remains to be preserved in an English parish church lie in the shrine of St Wite. Tree-crowned Hardown Hill rises to the SE.

WHITEHAVEN, Cumbria 20 NX91
Some of the mines in this coal and seaport town extend for 4m under the sea. The beach offers sand at low tide. St James's church dates from the 18thc, and the grandmother of George Washington was buried in the rebuilt St Nicholas's Church in 1701. She is commemorated by an inscribed tablet. Music festivals take place 1½m NE at the Rosehill Theatre, which was built in 1959.

WHITE NOTLEY, Essex 9 TL71
The Norman chancel arch of the local church incorporates Roman brickwork and the timber-framed belfry is also of interest. A brick-built village lock-up of 1828 survives, and the partly timber-framed hall dates from c1530.

WHITEPARISH, Wilts 7 SU22
Newhouse lies SE of Whiteparish and dates partly from 1619. A red-brick folly on Pepperbox Hill was erected by Giles Eyre in 1606, and closely resembles a pepperbox in shape (NT). West Dean lies 2m N and preserves the south aisle of its old church, which contains fine Evelyn monuments of 1625. Landford Manor is dated 1599 and 1712 and lies 2m SE.

WHITE RODING, Essex 9 TL51
White Roding's Norman to 15th-c church displays a good 15th-c timber porch, and a windmill tower stands in the area. A little to the W is Colville Hall, which dates from c1540 and boasts a splendid old barn. Mascallsbury is an interesting old farmhouse.

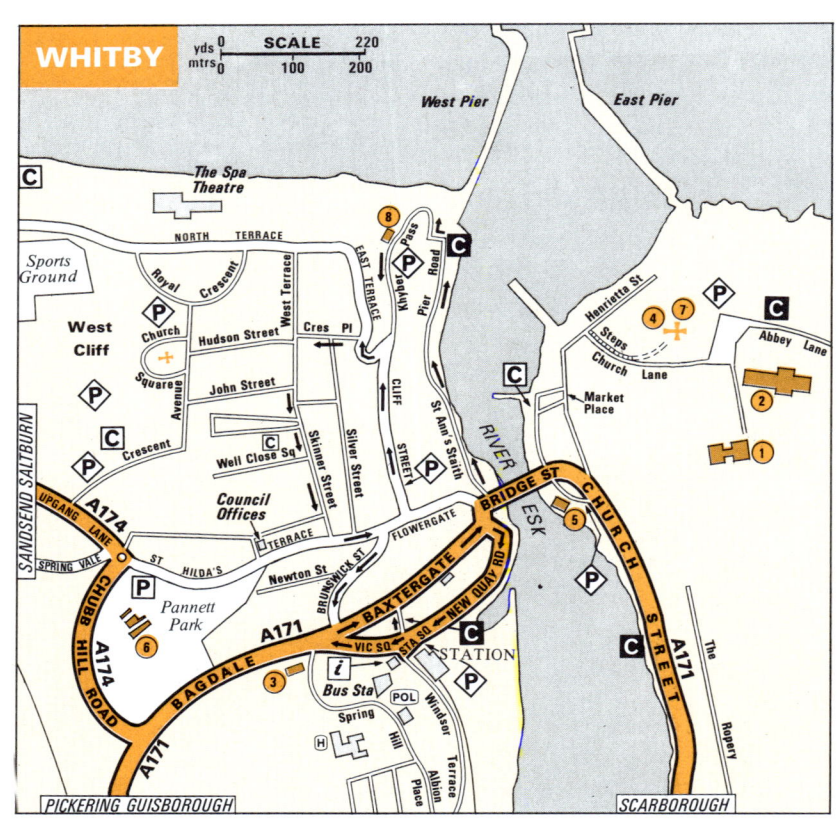

1 Abbey House
2 Abbey Remains
3 Bagdale Old Hall
4 *Caedmon's* Cross
5 Captain Cook's House
6 Museum
7 St Mary's Church
8 Whalebone Archway

Castle stands to the SE and was rebuilt in the 15thc, dismantled in 1649, and subsequently much restored. Queen Catherine Parr was buried in the chapel during 1548, and fine gardens boast a waterfowl collection (OACT). Elizabethan Postlip Hall stands near a Norman Chapel with an ancient barn about 1m SW.

WINCHELSEA, E Sussex 9 TQ91
The old town was submerged in the 13thc, and King Edward I built a new one on an eminence above the River-Brede marshes. It thus became one of the two Ancient Towns attached to the original Cinque Ports, and was thrice sacked by the French. The sea has long since receded from it. Three gates from the original walled settlement survive, of which the Strand Gate is of particular note.

Magnificent workmanship from the decorated period can be seen in the church, and the present nave was the original chancel. Other features include the famous Alard tombs, plus fine 13th-c monuments in the Farnecombe Chantry. Part of a convent chapel exists in the grounds of the Grey Friars. Much restored Court Hall dates from the 14thc and contains a museum. Many of the attractive houses here include ancient crypts which were once used for wine-storage. The town is laid out in regular fashion, and is perhaps the earliest example of town planning. A restored windmill dates from the 18thc. Winchelsea beach lies 2m S and offers bathing from shingle and sand.

WINCHESTER, Hants 7 SU42
Venta Belgarum to the Romans and one-time capital of Wessex and England, this famous city stands on the River Itchen in a downland setting.

Parts of the largely 13th-c city wall can still be seen, and the splendid medieval cathedral is the second longest in Europe. The latter was commenced in 1079, and shows notable early-Norman and early-perpendicular work. Features include seven richly-carved chantry chapels; beautiful 14th-c carved stalls; a restored 15th-c reredos; the oldest iron grill in England; coffers containing bones of Saxon and Danish Kings; a richly carved 12th-c black-marble Tournai font. The many interesting tombs to be seen inside include those of Izaak Walton, Jane Austen, and King Rufus. Windows include two fine 20th-c examples – a Coronation window of George VI and Queen Elizabeth, and one to George V.

The Close contains the 13th-c and later Deanery, the Pilgrims' School with its 13th-c hall, and the lovely half-timbered Tudor Cheyne Court. Izaak Walton lived in one of the attractive gabled houses in Dome Alley. Winchester College was founded by William of Wykeham in 1382 and is one of the oldest public schools in England. Much of the original structure is preserved. Fromond Chantry chapel and the Old School are of particular note, and it is thought that Wren may have had a hand in the design of the latter. The College preserves a famous medieval painting entitled the *Trusty Servant*. Ruins of Wolvesey Castle, the old Bishop's residence, are being restored and are situated near the present partly 17th-c palace. A gateway (AM) of 1110 is the sole survivor of Hyde Abbey, where it is said that Alfred the Great was buried. Once-famous Winchester Fair was first held in the year 1094 and took place on St Giles' Hill which rises to the E. St John's church is of trans-Norman date and displays a perpendicular tower and old screens. The 13th-c and later West Gate houses a museum. A nearby monument of 1759 recalls a plague of 1666, and was restored in 1821. St Swithun's church stands above the Kingsgate and contains a 15th-c font.

Castle Hall dates from the 13thc and has been adapted for modern use. One of its main features is the famous Round Table of King Arthur. Features of the High Street include the projecting clock of the 18th-c guildhall, now a bank; the restored 15th-c City or Butter Cross; the modernized Hospital of St John, founded in the 13thc; a statue to King Alfred; the restored timber-built God Begot House. A number of good 17th- and 18th-c houses include Avebury House in St Peter Street, and the baroque-style Serle's House which now contains the Hampshire Regimental Museum. The Green Jackets regimental museum is also of interest, and the city museum portrays some of the history and archaeology of Central Hampshire. Jane Austen died in a house in College Street in 1817. The old City Mill (NT) now serves as a youth hostel, and the Old Chesil Rectory dates from the 15thc.

St Catherine's Hill is surmounted by a curious mizmaze, and forms a splendid viewpoint. The heroine of Hardy's *Tess of the d'Urbervilles* was related to have been hanged in the gaol. Famous Hospital of St Cross, the most ancient charitable institution of its kind, was founded in 1133 and lies 1m S. Its church shows largely trans-Norman work, and the picturesque hospital buildings are of partly 15th-c date. An interesting custom preserved at the gatehouse of the hospital is the giving of a Wayfarer's Dole of bread and beer.

WINCLE, Cheshire 18 SJ96
Situated to the N of the Dane valley, Wincle lies 2m WNW of the curious rocky ravine known as Ludchurch. This name is said to be a corruption of Lollard-church, and the place may once have been used as a secret place of worship by the Lollards.

WINDERMERE, Cumbria 21 SD49
Windermere is an important centre of the Lake District national park, and stands to the E of the island-studded Windermere lake – the largest sheet of still fresh water in England. The 15th-c church of St Martin at Bowness displays old glass, chained books, and a rare wooden equestrian statue of St Martin. Orrest Head is a notable viewpoint lying to the E. Bowness-on-Windermere, the centre for yachting, boating, and steamer trips lies to the S. Beyond this is the embarkation point of a cross-lake car ferry. Sir Henry Segrave lost his life here in 1930 while breaking the speedboat record.

WINDRUSH, Glos 12 SP11
This pretty Cotswold village lies in the valley of the River Windrush. The church has a splendid Norman doorway adorned

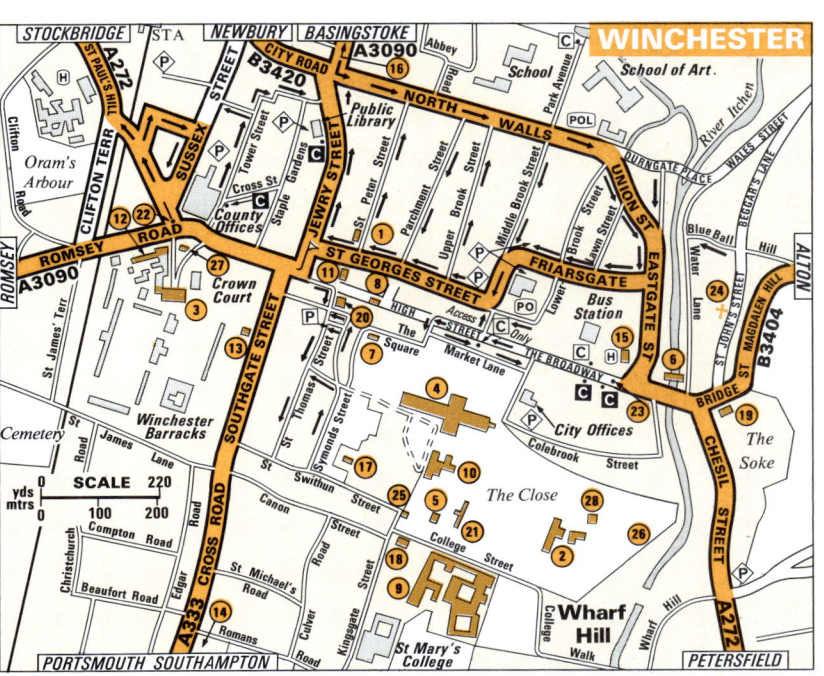

1 Avebury House
2 Bishop's Palace
3 Castle Hall
4 Cathedral
5 Cheyne Court
6 City Mill (youth hostel)
7 City Museum
8 City Cross
9 College
10 Deanery
11 God Begot House
12 Green Jackets Regimental Museum
13 Hampshire Regimental Museum
14 Hospital of St Cross
15 Hospital of St John
16 Hyde Abbey Gateway
17 Izaak Walton's House
18 Jane Austen's House
19 Old Chesil Rectory
20 Old Guildhall
21 Pilgrims' School
22 Plague Monument
23 Statue of King Alfred
24 St John's Church
25 St Swithun's Church
26 Town Walls
27 West Gate (museum)
28 Wolvesey Castle

with carved beak-heads, considered one of the best in the county.

WINDSOR, Berks *8 SU97*
Windsor and Eton are linked by a pedestrian bridge spanning the River Thames. The castle is the chief Royal residence and was originally built by William the Conqueror. It has since been greatly altered. George IV had the height of the round tower increased to 230ft, and the interior of the Curfew Tower is of 13th-c date. The State Apartments are famous, and the Queen's Dolls' House of 1924 is of particular note (OACT). St George's chapel is a magnificent perpendicular structure displaying particularly fine fan vaulting. Its choir contains the stalls and brasses of the Garter Knights, and many royal tombs include those of Henry VIII, Charles I, and Edward VII. Near by is the restored chapel, which was originally built by King Henry VII and now serves as the Albert Memorial Chapel. Restored Horseshoe Cloisters are of 15th-c origin. The national Queen's Scout Parade takes place at the Castle.

Frogmore, with the Frogmore Mausoleum in which Queen Victoria and the Prince Consort are buried, is situated in the Home Park. Great Park covers some 2,000 acres, is beautifully wooded, and can be crossed by public roads. Some 45 acres around High Standing Hill now form a Forest nature reserve, and the Long Walk is notable. Fort Belvedere is a mid 18th-c and later structure existing in the area. The E fringe of the park is reached by way of Englefield Green, and boasts the beautiful woodland Savill and nearby Valley Gardens (OACT).

Several fine 18th-c houses can be seen in Park Street, and Wren's guildhall of 1689 partly houses a museum. Nell Gwynne's house dates from c1670, and the Old House hotel is a late 17th-c building which is also associated with Wren.

The soldiers responsible for guarding the castle march through Victoria Street, Sheet Street, and High Street at 1030hrs each day, returning to the Victoria Barracks by about 1100hrs. Combermere Barracks contain the Household Cavalry Museum, and a Wyatville design can be seen at the John the Baptist church of 1820. The Southern Region railway station is dated 1850 and includes the Royal Waiting Room. Windsor Safari Park is situated SW at St Leonard's (on the B3022), and shows collections of dolphins, monkeys, birds, and many other animals (OACT). Statues to Queen Victoria and a memorial to King George V are of interest. Windsor racecourse lies W. The Royal Windsor Horse Show takes place in the spring.

WING, Bucks *13 SP82*
Features of the local church include a Saxon apse and crypt, a largely 16th-c screen, and various 16th-c monuments. An unusual carving depicting three infants is of interest. Ascott is a mainly 19th-c mansion containing notable works of art (NT, OACT).

WINGFIELD, Suffolk *15 TM27*
The moated castle retains its original drawbridge, a fine 14th-c gatehouse, and a Tudor house built into an angle of the walls (not open to the public). Wingfield's early-perpendicular former collegiate church is noted for the De la Pole tombs, and preserves a rare 18th-c parson's graveside shelter. Remains of the college are incorporated in a nearby farmhouse and include an 18th-c west front.

WINGHAM, Kent *9 TR25*
Picturesque half-timbered houses and the 15th-c Red Lion Inn are notable features of Wingham. The 13th- to 14th-c church shows good stalls, a timbered nave arcade, and a green copper spire.

WINSCOMBE, Avon *6 ST45*
Winscombe Hill and prominent Crook's Peak dominate the Mendip-Valley village. The church carries a splendid tower and houses 15th-c glass.

WINSFORD, Somerset *5 SS93*
This delightful Exmoor national-park village is situated on the River Exe, and includes a mainly-perpendicular church containing 1609 Royal Arms of James I. Ernest Bevin was born here in 1881, and the Royal Oak is a picturesque thatched local inn. Winsford Hill stands 2m SW and affords wide views over the surrounding area (largely NT). The Long or Caractacus Stone (NT) lies E of a road crossing the hill.

WINSHAM, Somerset *6 ST30*
A rare and notable 14th-c wood painting of the Crucifixion can be seen in the restored church of this River-Axe community. Leigh House, dated 1617, lies 2m W.

WINSLOW, Bucks *13 SP72*
Winslow's red-brick hall dates from 1700 and is one of the few domestic buildings authoritatively attributed to Wren. The town itself is a hunting centre lying in the Vale of Aylesbury.

WINSTER, Derbyshire *18 SK26*
Lead mining was once a local industry. Market House (NT) and several good 18th-c houses exist here, and the modern church carries a west tower of 1721. Notable rock outcrops of the Peak District national park lie to the N.

WINSTON, Durham *22 NZ11*
An 18th-c bridge over the River Tees crosses from here with a single span of 111ft. The view from the churchyard is notable, and Westholme Hall of 1606 lies 1m N.

WINTERBORNE ABBAS, Dorset *6 SY69*
An ancient stone circle known as the Nine Stones is preserved near this village. A fine monument to Admiral Hardy (NT) stands to the S on Black Down viewpoint, and restored Kingston Russell House – 4m W – was his birthplace.

WINTERBORNE CAME, Dorset *6 SY78*
William Barnes the Dorset poet was rector here for 25 years and lived at the thatched rectory. He was buried near the decorated and late-perpendicular church in 1886. A notable Meller tomb exists in the building. Came House dates from the 18thc. Herringston, a Tudor and Jacobean structure with a fine roof and panelling, lies 1m W.

1 Castle
2 Fort Belvedere
3 Frogmore and Mausoleum
4 Guildhall (museum)
5 Household Cavalry Museum (Combermere Barracks)
6 John the Baptist Church
7 King George V Memorial
8 Nell Gwynne's House
9 Old House Hotel
10 Queen Victoria's Statue
11 Racecourse
12 Railway Station and Royal Waiting Room
13 Safari Park
14 Savill Gardens
15 Valley Gardens
16 Victoria Barracks

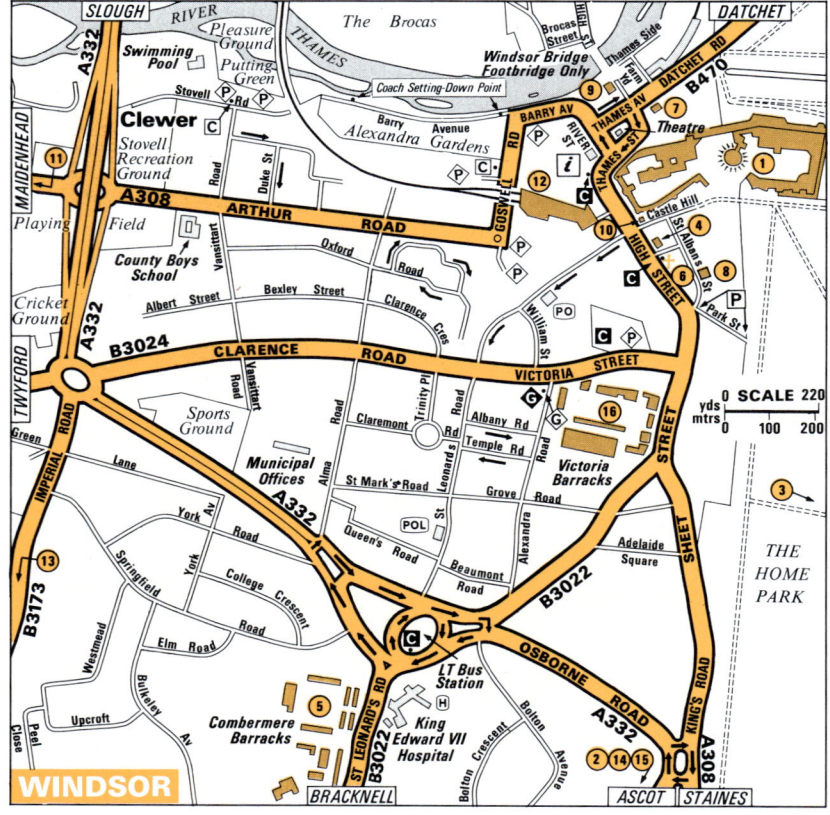

WHITESTAUNTON, Somerset *6 ST21*
Screens dating from the 15thc and a Norman font are features of the local church. The nearby manor house is of 15th- and 16th-c origin. Remains of a Roman villa exist in the neighbourhood.

WHITLEY BAY, Tyne & Wear *27 NZ37*
This well-known resort offers amenities which include excellent sands, bathing, and golf.

WHITMORE, Staffs *17 SJ84*
Whitmore Hall was rebuilt c1670, and includes an interesting stable range which was built earlier in the century. Maer Heath is a fine viewpoint lying 2½m SW off the Market Drayton road.

WHITSTABLE, Kent *9 TR16*
Fishing and bathing from a shingle beach can be enjoyed in this Thames-estuary resort. The town is noted for its oysters. Old houses exist on the quay, and the railway from Whitstable to Canterbury was the first passenger line to be opened. Stephenson's Invicta, now preserved at Canterbury, pulled a train here in 1830. The railway bridge of 1834 is one of the oldest in the world, and the tunnel through Tyler Hill was Britain's first.

WHITTINGHAM, Northumberland *27 NU01*
Saxon workmanship and an 18th-c sundial can be seen at the church in this attractive River-Aln village. A 15th-c pele known as Whittingham tower has been restored. Callaly Castle dates from the 14th to 18thc (OACT), and Shawdon Hall and Eslington Hall are both interesting old houses.

WHITTINGTON, Salop *17 SJ33*
Remains of a moated castle include a fine 13th-c gatehouse, and the local church carries a tower dating from 1747. Halston Hall dates from 1690 and lies to the NE. A local timber and brick chapel is of 16th- to 18th-c origin.

WHITTLESEY, Cambs *19 TL29*
St Mary's church is noted for its fine 15th-c tower and crocketed spire. A 17th-c Butter Cross stands in the market place, and a 15th- to 17th-c manor house can be seen near the church. Several Georgian houses exist in the area.

WHITTLESFORD, Cambs *14 TL44*
The mainly 15th-c church in this pleasant village displays Norman tower-parapet windows adorned with curious carvings. The restored 16th-c half-timbered guildhall and 14th-c chapel of St John's Hospital are of interest.

WHITTON, Salop *12 SO57*
Whitton Court is a fine 15th- to 17th-c house which retains a black-and-white wing (OACT). The Norman church features glass by Burne-Jones.

WHORLTON, N Yorks *22 NZ40*
Whorlton Moor rises to 1,025ft above this village, which includes a castle gatehouse of 1400. The ruined Norman to 15th-c old church houses a canopied 15th-c tomb featuring a rare wooden effigy.

WICK, Avon *6 ST77*
This village stands in the pretty River-Boyd Valley, with Wick Rocks lining a deep glen to the N. Wick Court is a Jacobean house, and a monument of 1720 can be seen S on the high ridge of Lansdown. The latter was raised to Sir Bevil Grenville of Civil War fame. Some 2½m farther S on the outskirts of Bath is a tall folly known as Beckford's Tower. This was built by William Beckford in 1837. Beckford was the eccentric millionaire-author of *Vathek* and was buried at the tower in 1844.

WICKEN, Cambs *14 TL57*
Wicken, Burwell, Adventurer's, and St Edmund's Fens are local nature reserves which preserve primeval fenland in its original state (NT). A gravestone to Henry Cromwell, fourth son of the Protector, can be seen at the church. Several old houses exist in this attractive village, and Spinney Abbey carries the date 1775.

WICKHAM, Berks *7 SU37*
Although part of the local church tower is of Saxon origin, the remainder dates largely from the 19thc. The building is noted for its north side aisle, which preserves the illusion of being supported by eight large papier-mâché elephants. Four of these models were shown at the great Paris Exhibition of 1862. A pinnacled 19th-c rectory is of interest.

WICKHAM, Hants *7 SU51*
William of Wykeham was born at this attractive Meon-Valley town in 1324, and later founded both Winchester College and New College in Oxford. Pleasant Georgian houses surround a wide square and add a characteristic touch of elegance to the area. Newly-afforested areas of the former 16,000-acre Bere Forest lie to the NE.

WICKHAMBREAUX, Kent *9 TR25*
A curious old flint-and-brick house showing crow-stepped gables exists here, and now serves as a post office. The Little Stour River runs through the area.

WICKHAMBROOK, Suffolk *15 TL75*
The mainly-decorated local church contains a marble monument of 1630. Moated and half-timbered Giffords Hall lies 1m SE, and moated Badmondisfield Hall lies 2m N.

WICKHAMFORD, Herefs and Worcs *12 SP04*
Sandys and Washington monuments are notable features of the 13th- to 16th-c church, and a nearby 16th-c half-timbered manor house includes a circular pigeon house.

WICKHAM MARKET, Suffolk *15 TM35*
Good window tracery and elaborate doorways can be seen in the local decorated and perpendicular church. Mid 18th-c Loudham Hall lies 1m SE, and 17th-c Glemham Hall lies 3m NE. The latter contains fine furnishings (OACT).

WICKWAR, Avon *12 ST78*
A packhorse bridge spans the River Little Avon here, and a 17th-c school exists in the area. The church tower dates from the 15thc and displays carvings in its vaulted roof.

WIDECOMBE-IN-THE-MOOR, Devon *5 SX77*
Situated at 800ft in the Dartmoor national park, Widecombe-in-the-Moor includes the perpendicular church of St Pancras – known as the Cathedral of Dartmoor. Its fine tower was struck by lightning in 1638, killing a number of people. Church House is picturesque (NT), and a sign on the village green commemorates the well-known song *Widdecombe Fair*.

WIDFORD, Herts *8 TL41*
Charles Lamb is associated with this village. The grave of his grandmother, who worked as house-keeper at the old mansion of Blakesware, lies in the churchyard. The mansion itself was destroyed in 1823.

WIDNES, Cheshire *17 SJ58*
Chemical and alkali works are important industries operating in this town, which is one of England's three River-Mersey ports. It was formerly connected to Runcorn by a transporter bridge, but this was replaced by a new road bridge in 1961.

WIGAN, Gt Manchester *21 SD50*
This important coal-mining town is situated in the Doughlas Valley, on the site of the Roman *Coccium*. A monument commemorates the site of a Civil War battle which was fought here in 1651, and part of an edifice known as Mab's Cross still stands at the top of Standishgate. The Bradshaw Chapel of

Remains of 13th-c Whitby Abbey

rebuilt All Saints' church contains a monument to the heroine of a story which surrounds Mab's Cross, and a Roman altar is built into the tower. The so-called *Road to Wigan Pier*, title of a book by George Orwell, actually refers to a wharf on the Leeds and Liverpool canal. Haigh Hall dates from the mid 19thc and is owned by Wigan Corporation.

WIGGENHALL, Norfolk *14 TF51*
The first of the churches in this quartet of Wiggenhall villages is at St Mary the Virgin. It is of trans-Norman to perpendicular origin, contains grand carved benches rich in poppyhead decoration which can be considered the best in Norfolk. St Mary's Hall includes an old gatehouse, and the decorated and perpendicular church of St Mary Magdalene includes old glass and parclose screens. St German's Church is of mainly-deocrated style and contains notable 15th-c bench-ends. St Peter's church is ruined.

WIGHTWICK, W Midlands *17 SO89*
Pre-Raphaelite works of art are displayed in the local 19th-c manor house (NT), which stands in terraced gardens containing remarkable Irish yews.

WIGMORE, Herefs & Worcs *12 SO46*
Slight remains of the abbey, and of a moated 14th-c castle which was dismantled in 1643 during the Civil War can be seen here. The timbered hall is 16th-c date. The village itself lies in the heart of Mortimer Forest, an area which the Forestry Commission has been replanting since 1920. Elton lies 4m NE and includes a Norman church displaying fine Royal Arms of Queen Elizabeth I. An 18th-c hall also exists in the area.

WIGSTON MAGNA, Leics *18 SP69*
Also known with the suffix 'Two Steeples', Wigston includes two fine churches. All Saints' carries a fine west tower and spire and contains a 15th-c screen; St Woolstan's retains its 14th-c steeple and is the only church in England with this particular dedication.

WILBURTON, Cambs *14 TL47*
This delightful village includes the Bridge Inn, which stands some 8ft above sea-level and has been described as the lowest situated in England. The Burystead is a fine old manor house of c1600, and the restored church houses interesting brasses.

WILBY, Norfolk *15 TM08*
An attractively gabled Jacobean hall in the area now serves as a farm, and the 15th-c church shows Jacobean woodwork. The latter includes carved benches and a three-decker pulpit.

WILDBOARCLOUGH, Cheshire *18 SJ96*
Wild scenery surrounds this moorland hamlet, and the restored 17th-c Forest Chapel is of interest. Shutlings Low rises to 1,659ft, and the district is of great interest to naturalists and geologists.

WILLENHALL, W Midlands *18 SO99*
Lock-making and iron and brass industries operate in this Black-Country town. Sir Basil Spence designed the notable modern church.

WILLERSEY, Glos *12 SP13*
Old cottages can be seen in this delightful Cotswold village, and the restored cruciform church is of mainly early-English origin. The latter's six bells were recast from the original three in 1712, in order to celebrate the Peace of Utrecht which followed in 1713.

WILLEY, Salop *17 SO69*
Woodlands around Willey are the surviving remains of the ancient Shirlett Forest. Partly-Norman Willey St John's church carries an 18th-c tower. Early 19th-c Willey Hall was designed by Lewis Wyatt, to replace an earlier house. Remains of the latter still exist. The original village was moved from the site of the hall in c1815.

WILLINGALE, Essex *9 TL50*
Two churches in a single churchyard are a feature of the twin Willingale Doe and Willingale Spain villages. The church attached to Doe preserves several brasses, and the one in Spain incorporates Roman tiles in its fabric. Both villages take their names from their original Norman lords – d'Eu and d'Epaignes.

WILLINGHAM, Cambs *14 TL47*
The restored local church displays a notable tower and spire with flying buttresses, an angel-carved double hammerbeam roof, and 15th-c mural paintings. Two windmills exist in the village.

WILLINGTON, Beds *14 TL14*
Notable tombs can be seen in the Gostwick chapel of the local church. An interesting dovecote and stables date from the 16thc (both NT, OACT), and the former was built by Sir John Gostwick – Cardinal Wolsey's Master of the Horse.

WILMCOTE, Warwickshire *12 SP15*
Mary Arden's cottage, the half-timbered Tudor birthplace of Shakespeare's mother, is the main reason for the many visitors received each year by Wilmcote. An interesting farming museum is housed in a nearby barn (OACT).

WILMINGTON, E Sussex *8 TQ50*
Various agricultural implements have been collected together to form a museum in a ruined 12th-c priory which exists here. Near by is the 12th- to 14th-c church, containing a canopied Jacobean pulpit. The churchyard yew may be the oldest in Sussex. The well-known Long Man (AM), a figure cut in the chalk of Windover Hill, lies S in the South Downs.

WILSFORD, Wilts *7 SU13*
Thatched timber-framed cottages feature in this River-Avon village, and the attractive little manor house is of modern chequered stone-and-flint construction. Eminent scientist Sir Oliver Lodge is buried at the rebuilt church, which still carries its Norman tower.

WILTON, Herefs & Worcs *12 SO52*
A curious inscribed sundial pillar stands on the 16th-c bridge which spans the River Wye here. Ruins of a 12th-c castle stand in the grounds of a house.

WILTON, Wilts *7 SU03*
Rivers Nadder and Wylye meet here, and the town was once the capital of Wessex. It is now widely-known for the manufacture of quality carpets, an industry which has operated here since the 17thc. Well-known Wilton House, with its famous double-cube room dates from Elizabethan and later periods and was partly by Holbein, Inigo Jones, and John Webb. Webb was the son-in-law of Jones. Marlowe, Spenser, and Ben Jonson all visited the house at some time, and the extensive grounds include fine cedars and a notable 18th-c Palladian bridge over the Nadder (OACT).

T H Wyatt designed the 19th-c church in rich Lombardic style, and the building contains pillars from a church in Rome. A market house of 1738 stands near the curious County Cross. Georgian houses can be seen in Kingsbury Square, and Bulbridge House is of early 18th-c origin.

WIMBISH, Essex *14 TL53*
Features of the restored 12th-c and later church include a fine brass of 1347, 14th-c screens, and examples of old glass. Timber-framed Tiptofts Manor, one of the oldest houses in Essex, dates from the 14thc and is now a farm. The 16th-c Broadoaks Manor now also serves a farm and preserves old brickwork plus a secret hiding-hole.

WIMBLEDON, Gt London *8 TQ27*
The Lawn Tennis Championships of England are held here each summer, and are followed with interest by a world-wide audience. Wimbledon Common boasts a windmill, and the restored Eagle House of 1613 stands in the High Street.

WIMBORNE MINSTER, Dorset *7 SZ09*
Julian Bridge (AM), built in 1636 and reconstructed in 1844, spans the River Stour at Wimborne Minster. The fine collegiate church is of Norman to decorated styles, and carries two towers. A lantern formed by the partly-Norman central tower is notable, and other features of particular interest include the rare chained library, curious 14th-c clock, and various monuments and tombs. An interesting model of the town stands near the Minster. Priest's House Museum displays Roman remains, and the ancient earthwork of Badbury Rings lies 4m NW. Kingston Lacy is a stately 17th-c mansion lying 3m NW.

WIMBORNE ST GILES, Dorset *7 SU01*
Local almshouses date from 1624, and the restored church of 1732 is considered to be a notable example of its period. St Giles House is mainly of 17th-c origin and includes an 18th-c shell grotto. Edmondsham House, a gabled Elizabethan and later building, lies 3m E.

WIMPOLE, Cambs *14 TL35*
A magnificent double avenue of elms, measuring some 2½m long by about 100 yards wide, approaches splendid Wimpole Hall. This house dates from 1632 and later, and is one of the largest and finest homes in the county. The chapel displays frescoes by St James Thornhill, and a mid 18th-c sham-castle ruin exists in the park. The local church dates from 1749, and includes the earlier Chichele chapel – which is noted for its monuments and brasses.

WINCHCOMBE, Glos *12 SP02*
Several old buildings to be seen in this attractive Cotswold town include the galleried George Inn, and the curiously-named Corner Cupboard. Seven-hole stocks have been preserved, and the restored perpendicular church displays an array of grotesque gargoyles, rich screen-work, and a magnificent altar cloth. Most of the latter was by Catherine of Aragon. A notable Jacobean house stands opposite the church. Sudeley

WINTERBORNE STEEPLETON, Dorset 6 SY68
Thatched-roof cottages and a church carrying a six-sided stone steeple make up this village. A carved representation of the Archangel Michael, to whom the church is dedicated, has been built into a porch.

WINTERBORNE WHITECHURCH, Dorset 6 SY89
The local early-English and perpendicular church contains a good 14th-c font and a 15th-c wooden pulpit. Whatcombe House is of mainly 18th-c date. Farther N is Winterborne Clenston, which boasts a 15th-c manor farm including a barn of some two centuries earlier.

WINTERBOURNE, Avon 12 ST68
Bradeston monuments and Gloucestershire's oldest brass – dating from 1370 and raised to a lady – can be seen in the local church. Also of interest is an effigy said to represent Hickory Stern, who is recalled by the old ballad *Oh who will o'er the downs so free*.

WINTERSLOW, Wilts 7 SU23
Hazlitt the poet lived both here and at nearby Winterslow Hut, or Pheasant Inn. Figsbury Rings (NT) is an early iron-age encampment covering some 27 acres and affording views towards Salisbury. Roche Old Court lies 2m NE. Although the latter dates mainly from c1650, it preserves a hall of c1380.

WINTERTON, Humberside 23 SE91
Roman Ermine Street approaches the Humber estuary here. The restored local church carries a partly Saxon tower, and contains a fine brass of 1502. Recent excavations on site of the large Roman village have revealed mosaics and remains which may prove to be temple foundations.

WINTERTON-ON-SEA, Norfolk 15 TG41
Some 260 acres of the area around this small fishing village comprise a nature reserve. Amenities include good sands, dunes, and bathing. The church displays a splendid perpendicular tower and south porch.

WINWICK, Cheshire 17 SJ69
Two Civil War battles were fought here in 1643 and 1648 respectively. The restored 14th-c church includes a tower bearing the curious carved Winwick Pig, and part of a pre-Conquest cross exists in the churchyard.

WIRKSWORTH, Derbyshire 18 SK25
Old houses in steep narrow terraces are a feature of this ancient town, which was once an important lead-mining centre. A unique Miner's Standard Dish is preserved in the early 19th-c Moot Hall. The 13th- to 16th-c church contains a notable Anglo-Saxon inscribed coffin lid, two fonts of respective Norman and 17th-c dates, and a number of monuments and brasses. Gell's Bedehouses date from 1584. It is thought that the town may be the 'Snowfield' featured in the George Eliot masterpiece *Adam Bede*. Well-dressing is a custom which is still preserved in the town. Elizabethan and 18th-c Hopton Hall lies 2m SW.

WIRRAL, THE
This narrow peninsula is almost a dormitory for Merseyside. It lies N of Chester, and separates the estuary of the River Dee from that of the Mersey.

WISBECH, Cambs 14 TF40
Fruit trees and bulbs are cultivated in the district around this River-Nene town, and fruit-canning is an important local industry. The many fine Georgian houses situated on the North and South Brinks, facing the quays and river, include several displaying Dutch characteristics. They form what is considered one of the finest riverside vistas in England. Peckover House is one of the most notable; this was built in 1722 and displays rococo plaster decoration (NT, OACT).

Features of the interesting mainly Norman and perpendicular church include a double nave, Royal Arms of James I, and a fine tower dating from c1520. Also of note are the 14th-c brass to Thomas de Braunston, and the interesting Parke monument. An ornate memorial to Thomas Clarkson, who worked for the abolition of slavery, was executed by Sir Gilbert Scott and stands in the town. The Wisbech and Fenland museum portrays the life of the Fens and contains Clarkson relics. The Rose and Crown Inn dates from c1601.

WISHFORD, Wilts 7 SU03
This village lies in the delightful Wylye Valley. Its church carries a battlemented 15th-c tower, and a record of the changing prices of bread since 1800 is built into the east wall of the churchyard. Sir Richard Grobham founded the almshouses in 1628, and his fine 17th-c tomb lies in the church. An Oak Apple Day ceremony is held annually on May 29, in celebration of the villagers' right to collect wood from Grovely Woods.

WISLEY, Surrey 8 TQ05
Fir-encircled Wisley Pond is a well-known beauty spot on the A3 Portsmouth road. The little Norman church displays a 17th-c timbered porch, and stands 1½m NW between the River Wey and the Wey Navigation Canal (NT). The attractively situated Anchor inn stands by a canal lock. Extensive testing grounds and gardens of the Royal Horticultural Society lie off the A3, and are of great interest (OACT).

WISTON, W Sussex 8 TQ11
Above this South-Downs village is the well-known landmark and viewpoint of Chanctonbury Ring (AM), surmounted by a crown of beech trees. The latter's prehistoric earthworks have yielded notable discoveries, and a 19th-c dewpond is of interest. Wiston Park is an Elizabethan and later house.

WITCHAMPTON, Dorset 7 ST90
A restored perpendicular church carrying a 15th-c tower can be seen in this village, which also features an old red-brick manor house and a good tithe barn. Crichel is a fine Georgian mansion standing in the area.

WITCHINGHAM, GREAT, Norfolk 15 TG12
Norfolk wild life park, one of Europe's largest collections of animals, exists here. It specializes in British mammals and boasts a large number of aviaries (OACT).

WITHAM, Essex 9 TL81
Many Georgian and older houses and the delightfully restored Spread Eagle Inn are features of this ancient town. A church at Chipping Hill was rebuilt in the 14thc, and displays a good screen plus several monuments. Restored Faulkbourne Hall retains beautiful 15th-c brickwork and lies 2m NNW.

WITHAM FRIARY, Somerset 6 ST74
England's first Carthusian monastery was founded here as an act of penance for the murder of Thomas Becket. The restored 13th-c church retains good stairs and houses a Jacobean pulpit.

WITHAM-ON-THE-HILL, Lincs 19 TF01
The restored church in this attractive stone-built village carries an 18th-c tower, and displays good modern woodwork. Parish stocks have been preserved, and an oak tree claimed to be the largest and oldest in Lincolnshire stands at Bowthorpe Park.

WITHERNSEA, Humberside 23 TA32
Good sands and sea bathing are offered by this small Holderness resort, on the North Sea coast.

WITHINGTON, Glos 12 SP01
Withington is a charming Cotswold village situated on the River Coln. The fine trans-Norman to early perpendicular church carries a lovely tower and displays a good Norman south doorway. An old manor house stands in the village, and another exists 1m E at Cassey Compton.

Georgian houses of the North Brink, Wisbech

WITHYCOMBE, Somerset 6 ST04
Situated between Blue Anchor Bay and the Exmoor national park, Withycombe includes a 12th-c and later church which is noted for its fine screen. Five roads meet 1½m S at the Felon's Oak, so called because a sheep stealer is said to have been hanged here in the late 18thc.

WITHYHAM, E Sussex 8 TQ43
Splendid monuments by Chantrey, Cibber, Flaxman, and Nollekens can be seen in the Dorset chapel of the local church, which was rebuilt in 1627. An ancient tower to the SW is the sole remnant of old Buckhurst House. The modern house stands in a large park, and Duckings is an interesting old half-timbered farm.

WITLEY, Surrey 8 SU93
George Eliot wrote *Daniel Deronda* while she lived at Witley between 1877 and 1880. The old White Hart is an interesting inn, and the local church features two Saxon windows, a great deal of Norman work, and a notable mural painting on a nave wall. The three Enton Lakes to the NE are noted for their fishing. Tigbourne Court, a fine mansion of 1899 by Lutyens, lies 1m S.

WITLEY, GREAT, Herefs & Worcs 12 SO76
The church of 1735 is one of the most remarkable examples of Georgian rococo work known. Fine painted ceilings and stained glass are of particular note, and Rysbrack executed the huge sculptured Foley monument. The hall dates from the 18thc and was burnt in 1937. Delightful Abberley Hills dominate the area, and Woodbury Hill rises 904ft above the lovely Teme Valley. This hill is surmounted by an ancient camp and is associated with Owen Glyndwr. Astley Hall, an old mansion which was formerly the home of Lord Baldwin, lies 3m NE.

WITNEY, Oxon 13 SP31
Blankets are a notable product of this River-Windrush market town. The old Blanket Hall displays a curious one-hand clock and dates from c1720. A 17th-c Butter Cross (AM) is of interest, and the grammar school was founded in 1663. Mainly early-English and decorated styles are evident in the local church, which includes the fine Wenman chapel. Cogges, situated 1m SE, is an interesting group of buildings comprising a church, manor house, and vicarage. The church is a quaint decorated building where the cornice of the chancel chapel is adorned with strange carvings. Both the vicarage and manor house retain 13th-c work.

WITTERSHAM, Kent 9 TQ82
Situated on the central ridge of the low-lying Isle of Oxney, between the River Rother and the Royal Military Canal, Wittersham includes a 14th-c church carrying a good tower and housing a well-carved partly 15th-c lectern. Wide views are available in all directions. A windmill stands 1m E near a fine old house.

WIVELSFIELD, E Sussex 8 TQ32
Features of the local Norman church include a Saxon doorway, a 14th- to 15th-c tower, and a reversed grotesque on the south door. Great Ote Hall is of Elizabethan origin.

WIVENHOE, Essex 15 TM02
Important features of this River-Colne town are its quay and oyster industry. The restored church was damaged in an earthquake of 1884, and houses several Tudor brasses. A fine old pargetted house stands near by. Wivenhoe Park is a mainly modern house which now serves as the administrative centre for the University of Essex. The prominent tower-blocks of the university itself extend W in the direction of Colchester.

WIXFORD, Warwickshire 12 SP05
This Shakespeare-country village includes interesting half-timbered cottages and almshouses, plus a church with a roof bearing some 400 carved bosses. A splendid 15th-c brass is preserved inside, and a very rare thatched shelter for the vicar's horse has survived.

WOBURN, Beds 13 SP93
Notable pictures and furnishings can be seen in 18th-c Woburn Abbey, which stands in a great deer park traversed by a public road. Holland and Flitcroft were responsible for the abbey's impressive form. Included in the grounds is the famous Wild Animal Kingdom featuring lions, tigers, and monkeys (OACT). The town was almost destroyed by fire in 1724, but has preserved several good 18th-c houses.

WOKING, Surrey 8 TQ05
Situated on the disused Basingstoke Canal, this residential and commuter town includes a Mosque which was erected in 1889. Old Woking stands on the River Wey 2m SE, and boasts a restored church which carries a 13th-c west tower preserving the original Norman door – with remarkable ironwork. Restored Horsell church lies 1½m NW and displays an embattled 14th-c tower, plus several brasses. Extensive commons exist in the district.

WOKINGHAM, Berks 8 SU86
Dean Swift, Gay, and Pope are famous persons known to be associated with the local Rose Inn, and the church houses a good perpendicular font. Bear Wood is a large 19th-c house lying W, now serving as the Royal Merchant Navy School. Chapel Green lies 1m S and includes the fine Lucas Hospital, noted for its old brickwork, which was founded in 1665.

WOLD NEWTON, Humberside 23 TA07
A monument marks the spot where a meteorite fell in 1795. The local church shows a Norman chancel arch, font, and carved doorway with tympanums.

WOLDS
The Wolds is a name applied to three upland districts in different parts of England. These hill groups rise to some 600ft near Melton Mowbray in Leicestershire, over 500ft near Caistor in the Lindsey division of Lincolnshire, and about 800ft to the N of Beverley in Humberside.

WOLFERTON, Norfolk 14 TF62
A finely-carved modern cross can be seen in Wolferton, and the village itself stands near an inlet of The Wash. The restored church displays fine woodwork, an ancient font, and an Elizabethan chest and table. The railway station for the Royal estate of Sandringham was formerly situated here.

WOLLASTON, Northants 13 SP96
Interior fittings of 18th-c origin can be seen in the local church, which carries a 14th-c spire. Early-Georgian Hinwick House contains notable furniture and pictures, and lies 2m SE (OACT).

WOLLASTON, Salop 17 SJ31
Old Parr, a local who reputedly lived from 1483 to 1635 and died at the age of 152, is commemorated by a brass in the 18th-c church. His remains lie in Westminster Abbey, and an old 15th-c cottage in which he lived stands some 2m to the SW at Glyn.

WOLSINGHAM, Durham 27 NZ03
The rebuilt church retains its 12th-c tower. Whitfield Place dates from 1677, and Whitfield House from c1700. Redgate Cross recalls John Duckett, who was martyred in 1644. The local church has been rebuilt but retains its 12th-c tower.

WOLVERCOTE, Oxon 13 SP40
Sir James Murray, first editor of the famous Oxford dictionary, is buried in the church cemetery. Features of the church include a carved early-Norman font and the notable 17th-c Walker tomb.

WOLVERHAMPTON, W Midlands 18 SO99
Wolverhampton is an important manufacturing town situated on the edge of the Black Country. It is noted for such products as iron, brass, aircraft components, locks, and keys. The large church of St Peter dates mainly from the 15thc and displays a fine panelled tower, plus a notable carved stone pulpit. A remarkable carved cross shaft of ancient origin stands in the churchyard near a holed Bargain stone. St John's church dates from the 18thc and houses a 17th-c organ.

Bantock House (19thc) is a museum of items made by Midland craftsmen. Wolverhampton also boasts an art gallery. The well-known racecourse is situated at Dunstall Park. Moseley Old Hall lies 4m NNE, and was a refuge of Charles II after the battle of Worcester in 1651. The building is now encased in 19th-c brick, concealing Elizabethan timbering, but various secret hiding places have been preserved (NT, OACT).

WONERSH, Surrey 8 TQ04
Half-timbered cottages survive in this village. The church displays late 18th-c brickwork, and retains slight early-English details. Beautiful half-timbered Great Tangley Manor of 1582 stands 1m NNE in moated grounds.

WOODBASTWICK, Norfolk 15 TG31
Salhouse and Ranworth Broads lie either side of this attractive village. An old pump on the green is sheltered by a thatched canopy, and the restored thatched church contains an old screen. Parts of the River Bure marshes form a national nature reserve.

WOODBRIDGE, Suffolk 15 TM24
Features of this River-Deben market town include old houses, a 16th- to 19th-c Shire Hall, and a half-timbered house in New Street. An old weighing machine is attached to the latter. The abbey in Church Street dates partly from 1564, and the perpendicular church displays a Seven Sacraments font, a tall flint-flushwork tower, and part of a 15th-c screen. A Friends Meeting House dates from 1678. Georgian houses can be seen in Cumberland Street and Thoroughfare.

Edward Fitzgerald, the translator of *The Rubaiyat of Omar Khayyam*, lived at

Little Grange. Oliver Cromwell's head used to be privately preserved at Woodbridge. The first recorded mention of a rare old tidal mill in the area was in 1170, and this ancient structure is now under restoration. Buttrum's Mill is a 60ft-high structure of 1816 which has been restored. Delightful Kyson Hill (NT) forms a riverside park site (NT).

WOODBURY, Devon 6 SY08
Nicholas Stone was born here and is best remembered as the sculptor who built the York House Water Gate (London) in 1626. His monuments grace many English churches and appear in Westminster Abbey. Old woodwork and a tall west tower are features of the local 15th-c church. Woodbury Common lies E and affords a panoramic coastal view from Berry Head to Portland Bill. Woodbury Castle iron-age fort lies at a height of some 600ft.

WOODCHESTER, Glos 12 SO80
Remains of a Roman villa lie underneath part of the local churchyard, including portions of a magnificent tessellated pavement. The latter was discovered by the Rev Samuel Lysons in 1793, and is only shown at rare intervals. At the time of publication a proposal was afoot to enable the pavement or a replica to be permanently accessible. An old circular teasel tower still stands.

WOODCHURCH, Kent 9 TQ93
Weatherboarded and Tudor cottages stand with the restored White Mill around the village green. The church is one of a notable Romney-Marsh group, and dates from the 13thc. Bethersden marble was used in the construction of the nave.

WOOD EATON, Oxon 13 SP51
This secluded little village includes an 18th-c manor, plus a church containing a 15th-c screen and a 14th-c wall-painting of St Christopher. Thatched cottages and an old cross are also of interest.

WOODFORD, Wilts 7 SU13
Flint-and-stone houses can be seen in this pleasantly situated Avon-Valley parish, which combines the villages of Upper and Lower Woodford. Heale House is a restored partly 17th-c mansion, which was once the hiding-place of King Charles II. Some additional building is evident. The 19th-c church carries a perpendicular tower, and both the screen and gallery are Jacobean. Restored Lake House, an Elizabethan building displaying unusual flint chequerwork, lies 2m N.

WOODHALL SPA, Lincs 19 TF16
Amenities offered by this well-known inland watering-place include a pumproom and bathing establishment.

cont

1 Art Gallery
2 Bantock House (museum)
3 Moseley Old Hall
4 Racecourse
5 St John's Church
6 St Peter's Church

It is thought that the 60ft high Tower-on-the-Moor may have been erected by the builders of Tattershall Castle in the 15thc. A tall column surmounted by a bust of Wellington was set up on the Horncastle road in 1844, and overlooks Waterloo Wood which was grown from acorns planted after the battle in 1815.

WOODHAM FERRERS, Essex 9 TQ79
The restored 13th- to 15th-c church includes the notable Sandys tomb of 1619. A moated Tudor House known as Edwins Hall lies to the E.

WOODHAM WALTER, Essex 9 TL80
This attractive village boasts an interesting mainly brick-built church which was consecrated in 1564. The building shows Dutch-style crow-stepped gables and preserves a fine 15th-c octagonal font.

WOODSTOCK, Oxon 13 SP41
A Royal Palace was once situated here, and the attractive little town is noted for glove making. The church tower dates from 1785, and the town hall from 1766. Chaucer's son is said to have lived in a house near the park entrance, and the famous Black Prince, son of Edward III, was born here. Activities of this part of England are displayed in the Oxford City and County Museum which was opened in 1966. Blenheim Palace, described under its own name elsewhere in this gazetteer, stands in a great park adjacent to the town.

WOODY BAY, Devon 5 SS64
Richly-wooded hog's-back cliffs guard this small bay and afford fine views. Picturesque Hanging Water plunges hundreds of feet through woods to the shore. The beach is of rough shingle. Farther W is the well-known beauty-spot of Hunter's Inn, with the splendid cliff viewpoint of Highveer Point.

WOOKEY HOLE, Somerset 6 ST54
These famous Mendip caves contain part of the River Axe, and have yielded evidence of occupation, from 250BC to AD450. A local museum illustrates this period. A miniature gorge known as Ebbor Rocks lies NW. Wookey village is situated 2m SSE, and includes an early-English to perpendicular church showing squints and a small perpendicular chapel.

WOOL, Dorset 6 SY88
An old bridge bearing one of the rare county transportation tablets spans the River Frome here. Nearby old Woolbridge Manor house is now a guesthouse, and was used by Hardy as the scene for his heroine's wedding night in *Tess of the d'Urbervilles*. It is described under the name Wellbridge House in the novel. Remains of 12th-c Bindon Abbey lie about ½m E, and the Winfrith Heath Atomic Energy Research Station is to the W. Woodsford Castle, a restored 14th-c structure situated some 6m WNW, now serves as a farm. It preserves an ancient tower and one of the finest thatched roofs in England.

WOOLACOMBE, Devon 5 SS44
Firm sands stretching for about 3m are offered by this resort, and Barricane Beach is noted for its shells. Bathing and surf-bathing can be enjoyed here. Potter's Hill (NT) overlooks Morte Bay, which lies between the prominent headlands of Baggy Point and Morte Point (both NT).

The latter two areas are good viewpoints, and fine slate-rock scenery is a feature of the area. Lundy Island may be seen from here.

WOOLBEDING, W Sussex 8 SU82
Saxon workmanship is preserved in the local church, and an adjacent 17th-c house (NT) was once the home of the 18th-c authoress Charlotte Smith. The garden of the latter boasts a 130ft tulip tree.

WOOLER, Northumberland 27 NT92
Picturesquely situated on the River Till, Wooler lies near the NE slopes of the Cheviot Hills on the edge of the Northumberland national park. The valley of Harthope Burn leads to the 2,676ft summit of The Cheviot, a grand viewpoint from which it is said both the North Sea and the Solway Firth are sometimes visible. Fowberry Tower, a 15th-c tower house rebuilt in 1666, 1776, and later lies 2m ENE

WOOLHOPE, Herefs & Worcs 12 SO63
Low and wooded Woolhope Hills are considered of great geological interest, and the Woolhope Society is well known for its transactions concerning the county's natural history. The Norman to 14th-c church has a Lady Godiva window. Putley Court and The Brainge are two Georgian houses lying 3m NE.

WOOLPIT, Suffolk 15 TL96
The decorated and perpendicular church displays a splendid south porch and modern tower. Its double-hammerbeam roof is richly carved with angels. A curious legend concerning two green children is associated with the village.

WOOLWICH, Gt London 8 TQ47
A free ferry plies across the Thames from here to North Woolwich, and wooden warships were once built in the former dockyard. The well-known Arsenal covered some 600 acres and is being re-developed. The old Rotunda that stands on the edge of the common was moved from London's St James' Park. The roof was designed by John Nash, and the building now houses a museum of arms and artillery. On the edge of the marshes farther E is Plumstead church, which carries a 17th-c brick tower.

WOOPERTON, Northumberland 27 NU02
A Wars of the Roses battle was fought at nearby Hedgeley Moor in 1464. This is commemorated by the stones known as Percy's Leap, and by the carved 15th-c Percy Cross a little to the S. The latter recalls Sir Ralph Percy who was slain during the battle.

WOOTTON BASSETT, Wilts 12 SU08
Wootton Bassett town hall is a half-timbered construction on stone pillars which was erected by the first Earl of Rochester and dates from 1700. It has been restored and preserves stocks, a ducking-stool, and a quaint old fire engine. A number of 17th- and 18th-c houses exist in the town.

WOOTTON ST LAWRENCE, Hants 7 SU55
Features of the restored church include a 14th-c tower, the 17th-c Hooke monument, and a stained glass window of Charles Butler. Butler was a 17th-c vicar known as the father of English bee-keeping. Manydown House dates from the 18th-c and earlier.

WOOTTON WAWEN, Warwickshire 12 SP16
Wootton Hall is a 17th-c house with a notable south front, and the Bull's Head Inn is probably of 16th-c origin. The church tower is partly Saxon, and the body of the building houses a 15th-c screen and 17th-c chained books.

WORCESTER, Herefs & Worcs 12 SO85
Glove and porcelain manufacture are noted occupations of this River-Severn cathedral city. A fine river bridge of 1771 to 1780 has been widened, and the Worcester and Birmingham Canal terminates here. The cathedral is mainly of the early-English to perpendicular period, and its 11th-c crypt was the work of Bishop Wulstan. Other notable features include the much-restored 14th-c tower; choir stalls of 1379; Prince Arthur's Chantry of 1504; the circular Norman Chapter House. Among the many monuments is an effigy of King John – considered the earliest Royal effigy in England.

The former Refectory now serves as part of the King's School, and the fine pedimented guildhall dates from 1723 to 1731. Britannia House serves as the Alice Ottley girls' school, and is of 18th-c origin. St Swithun's church is an 18th-c structure housing a three-decker pulpit, and includes a mayor's chair and sword-rest. The spire of former 18th-c St Andrew's church is of interest, and former St Helen's church now contains the County Record Office. Shakespeare's and Anne Hathaway's marriage contract is kept in this office. Greyfriars dates from the 15thc and forms part of a Franciscan Friary (NT, OACT). The 14th-c Edgar Tower and 18th-c Berkeley Hospital almshouses are also of note. Picturesque old houses exist in Friar Street and New Street. Tudor House, in Friar Street, was once an inn and now contains a museum of domestic life. The Corn Exchange dates from 1848.

The Commandery, or Hospital of St Wulstan, includes an interesting old hall with a gallery. Two 14th-c stone columns from the vanished chapel of St Godwald stand in the grounds. Dyson Perrins museum of Worcester china is incorporated in the Royal Porcelain Works. Cromwell defeated the Scottish army of King Charles II at the battle of Worcester in 1651, and a half-timbered house of 1577 in New Street is associated with the King's escape. A timbered house in Trinity Road was visited by Queen Elizabeth I in 1574. The three choirs music Festival takes place every third year at Worcester, and a racecourse exists in the area.

WORFIELD, Salop 17 SO79
Worfield is an attractive village which includes a good early-English to perpendicular church, noted for its perpendicular screen, tower, and spire. Davenport House is a notable 18th-c mansion, and the timbered and well-restored Lower House is picturesque. Extensive Worfield Gardens specialise in cacti and exotic plants (OACT).

WORKINGTON, Cumbria 25 NX92
Coal and iron industries operate in this important town, which lies at the mouth of the River Derwent. St Michael's church displays fragments of ancient crosses, and Mary Queen of Scots was received at the fine old mansion of Workington Hall in 1568. A curious game

of football is played here between teams known as Uppies and Downies. The Helena Thompson Museum donated displays of costumes, glass, and ceramics to the town in 1948.

WORKSOP, Notts *18 SK57*
Visitors wishing to explore the Dukeries and Sherwood Forest will find Worksop a good base for touring the area. A 14th-c gatehouse surviving from the former priory is notable for its double archway, and the upper room once housed the country's first elementary school (1628). Rich Norman workmanship dating from 1170 to 1180 can be seen in the surviving nave of the church, and the Lady Chapel is a beautiful example of early-English work. Worksop museum contains exhibits of archaeological and natural-history interest. Former 16th-c Worksop Manor was burnt in 1761, and replaced by an unfinished building two years later. Only a portion of the later structure still remains, notably the yard's colonnaded screen.

WORLINGWORTH, Suffolk *15 TM26*
Fine flintwork is displayed by the decorated and perpendicular church, which also features a 20ft-high carved font cover and Jacobean woodwork. Also preserved is an old collection-shoe of 1622 and a fire engine of 1760.

WORMLEIGHTON, Warwickshire *13 SP45*
Remains of a fine local manor house which was destroyed during the Civil War include a gatehouse with carved crests dated 1613. Prince Rupert slept here during the night before the Battle of Edgehill in 1642. The trans-Norman and early-English church contains a notable screen.

WORPLESDON, Surrey *8 SU95*
Several old houses and farms exist here, and the church features a late 15th-c tower, a 14th-c chancel, and some old glass. Merrist Wood dates from 1877 and is considered one of the best works by Norman Shaw. Littlefield Manor lies SW and dates from *c*1700.

WORSLEY, Gt Manchester *17 SJ79*
This place is notable for the famous Bridgewater Canal, which was one of the first such waterways to be built in England. It was begun by the third Duke of Bridgewater in 1759, and was used for coal transportation. The Old Hall is a 16th-c black-and-white building which has been restored and enlarged.

WORSTEAD, Norfolk *15 TG32*
Flemish weavers started a yarn or worsted industry here in the 12thc. The beautiful local church was commenced in 1369 and carries an especially notable tower; the hammerbeam roof, 400-year-old font cover, and 16th-c screens are equally outstanding.

WORTH, W Sussex *8 TQ33*
Worth stands on the outskirts of a surviving portion of the great Wealden Forest, and is particularly noted for its remarkable restored Saxon church. Later additions to the building include a carved pulpit dated 1577, two 16th-c oak chests, and 17th-c carved altar-rails.

WORTHAM, Suffolk *15 TM07*
Fittings inside the village's decorated and perpendicular church were modelled on those at King's College, Cambridge. The partly-ruined round-tower is nearly 30ft in diameter and stands at about 60ft high – the largest in East Anglia. Also of note are the well-carved modern bench-ends.

WORTHING, W Sussex *8 TQ10*
Plan overleaf
Amenities offered by this popular resort include a pier and an extensive pebble beach giving way to sand at low tide. A rare specimen of a travelling stocks is preserved in the museum, and the South Downs rise in the background.

WORTH MATRAVERS, Dorset *7 SY97*
Benjamin Jesty is buried in the graveyard of the restored church, and is known for having inoculated his wife and two sons against smallpox in 1774 – the first recorded instance. He lived to the NE at the old manor farm of Downshay. Features of the actual church include good examples of Norman work, notably a fine chancel arch. St Alban's or St Aldhelm's Head lies 2m SSW and is reached by a rough road. A little Norman chapel stands here, and the head affords wide coastal views. A point farther NW, which can be reached on foot, allows splendid views across Chapman's Pool. Hounstout cliff dominates the pool, and the eye is given an unrestricted view beyond Kimmeridge Bay and the jagged outline of Gad Cliff to Worbarrow Bay. All these areas are included in an area of outstanding natural beauty.

WOTTON, Surrey *8 TQ14*
John Evelyn the famous diarist was born at Wotton House in 1620. The house stands in a lovely park in the Tillingbourne Valley, and includes the Bible used at Charles I's execution among its many treasures. The restored 13th-c and older church contains Evelyn's tomb and other family monuments. Remarkable portrait heads exist on the south door.

WOTTON-UNDER-EDGE, Glos *12 ST79*
Hills surround this small Cotswold town, and the restored 14th- to 15th-c church retains a fine old organ case and several good brasses. A house in the town was where Sir Isaac Pitman perfected his system of shorthand, and local almshouses date from 1632.

WRAGBY, W Yorks *22 SE41*
Nostell Priory is a fine mansion which was built by James Paine in 1733 (NT, OACT). Robert Adam added a wing in 1766, and perpendicular Wragby church stands in the park. English and Swiss glass and a wealth of carved woodwork are featured in the church.

WRAWBY, Humberside *23 TA00*
Lincolnshire's last surviving postmill exists here. It was built *c*1760 and has latterly been well-restored (OACT).

WRAXALL, Avon *6 ST47*
A holly hedge nearly 3½m long borders the Wraxall estate, and Wraxall Court and Birdcombe Court are both interesting

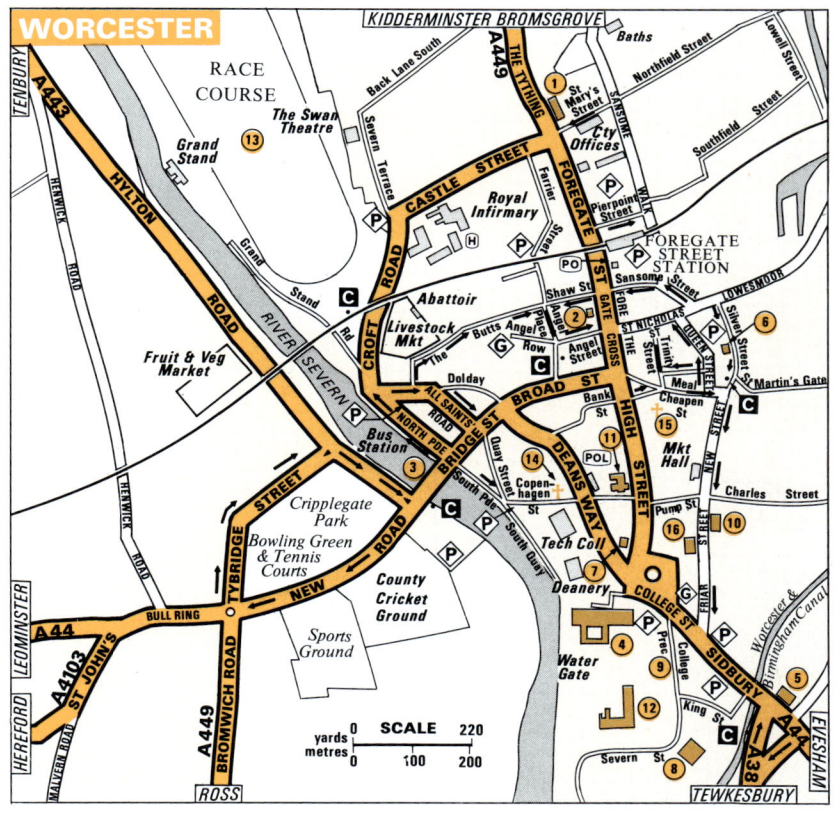

1 Alice Ottley Girls' School
2 Berkeley Hospital Almshouses
3 Bridge
4 Cathedral
5 Commandery or Hospital of St Wulstan
6 Corn Exchange
7 County Record Office (formerly St Helen's Church)
8 Dyson Perrins Museum of Worcester China
9 Edgar Tower
10 Franciscan Friary
11 Guildhall
12 King's School
13 Racecourse
14 St Andrew's Church
15 St Swithun's Church
16 Tudor House Museum of Domestic Life

old houses. Tyntesfield is a large 19th-c mansion with a chapel, and the local churchyard shows a fine 15th-c cross.

WRAYSBURY, Berks *8 TQ07*
Once known as Wyrardisbury, this Thames-side village includes a rebuilt church containing several interesting monuments. Pre-Reformation timber-framed King John's house has been restored, and Ankerwycke Priory dates from the early 19thc.

WREAY, Cumbria *26 NY44*
Wealthy Sarah Losh designed the ornate local Victorian church and a mausoleum for her sister in the mid 19thc. A Roman fort lies NE.

WRENBURY, Cheshire *17 SJ54*
A notable monument to Sir Stapleton Cotton, one of Wellington's generals, can be seen in the fine 15th-c church. Old box pews are also of note.

WRENTHAM, Suffolk *15 TM48*
The local church has a fine 15th-c tower and the town hall is of 19th-c date. The Congregational chapel dates from 1778. Sotterley Hall of *c*1744 is a fine mansion lying 5m NE, and 17th- to 18th-c Frostenden Hall stands 2m SW.

WRINGTON, Avon *6 ST46*
This village lies at the foot of the Mendips and includes a church featuring a magnificent perpendicular tower. Monuments to John Locke the philosopher and Hannah More the authoress can be seen inside. Both persons once lived here.

WRITTLE, Essex *9 TL60*
Georgian and older buildings face the green in this attractive village, and the local church houses carved stalls, numerous brasses, and several fine monuments. One of these was executed by Nicholas Stone in 1629 and raised to Edward Pinchon.

WROTHAM, Kent *9 TQ65*
Situated at the foot of the North Downs, Wrotham lies on the line of the ancient Pilgrims' Way. The interesting church shows early-English to perpendicular work, and carries a good tower incorporating the old Processional Way. Several brasses can also be seen. Near the church is an old red-brick manor house, and slight remains of a palace of the Archbishops of Canterbury exist in the area. Wrotham Hill rises to 775ft and forms a good viewpoint.

WROUGHTON, Wilts *12 SU18*
Benet monuments can be seen in the Norman to decorated church, and a fine yew stands in the local churchyard. Barbury Castle is an iron-age camp which surmounts 900ft Hackpen Hill in the S, and a White Horse in the district was cut in 1838. A three-ton sarsen stone is inscribed with lines to Richard Jefferies and Alfred Williams, two Wiltshire men of natural history and literary fame.

WROXALL, Isle of Wight *7 SZ57*
Appuldurcombe is a Palladian mansion which was erected in 1700, but has remained unoccupied since 1904. It was badly damaged by bombs during the Second World War and has been partially restored (AM, OACT).

WROXALL, Warwickshire *12 SP27*
Fragmentary remains of a 12th-c abbey exist here. The present church carries a 17th-c brick tower and houses notable 15th-c glass. Wroxall Abbey mansion is dated 1866, and the Wren-designed gate piers were brought from an earlier house. Clough Williams-Ellis designed the ornamental iron gates.

WROXETER, Salop *17 SJ50*
Remains of the Roman station *Uriconium* (AM) exist on the Wroxeter section of Watling Street, and include traces of hypocausts. Interesting displays are mounted in the local museum, and other relics are preserved in a Shrewsbury museum. The church preserves Saxon workmanship and shows Roman material in its fabric. Roman columns flank the churchyard entrance, and interesting later monuments can be seen inside.

WROXHAM, Norfolk *15 TG21*
Wroxham Broad is formed from the River Bure, and Wroxham itself is a noted yachting centre. The river bridge of 1614 was later widened, and Hoveton Little and Great Broads lie near by. A very fine late-Norman doorway is shown by the church and the old manor house has stepped gables.

WROXTON, Oxon *13 SP44*
Ironstone and thatched cottages are a feature of this delightful village, and Wroxton Abbey is an imposing early 17th-c gabled mansion now used as an American college. The church contains a notable alabaster tomb of 1631, a fine screen and font, and good carved woodwork. Lord North – the 18th-c Prime Minister, and Thomas Coutts – a famous banker of the period, are buried here. An old cross stands in the area and is known as Dick Turpin Cross.

WYCLIFFE, Durham *22 NZ11*
Numerous Wycliffe tombs and examples of old glass can be seen in the 13th- to 14th-c village church. Also of interest is a reproduction of a fine portrait depicting John Wycliffe, who may have been born here.

WYCOLLER, Lancs *22 SD93*
Wycoller is an attractive village boasting a 13th-c pack-horse bridge. The ruined late 16th-c hall is said to be the original Ferndean, a fictional name given to the manor in Charlotte Brontë's *Jane Eyre*. The house is reputedly haunted.

WYDDIAL, Herts *14 TL33*
The perpendicular church has a notable north aisle and a brick-built chancel chapel of 1532. Box pews and a 17th-c screen are also of interest.

WYE, Kent *9 TR04*
Wye College (London University) is situated here in buildings which are partly of ancient origin. An agricultural museum is located in an old barn, and interesting old houses exist in the town. Aphra Behn the Restoration dramatist was born here in 1640.

Other features include a racecourse and Georgian mill-house. Partly 18th-c Olantigh stands N of Wye, and is the summer venue for music festivals. A bridge spanning the Stour to the W of the village shows an inscription giving the names of workmen who repaired it some 250 years ago. The crown cut into the North Downs chalk to the E commemorates the coronation of Edward VII. Broad Downs is a 584ft viewpoint facing the national nature reserve of Wye and Crundale Downs.

WYE VALLEY
The Wye is justly considered one of our loveliest rivers. It rises in the lonely wilds of the Welsh mountain of Plynlimon,

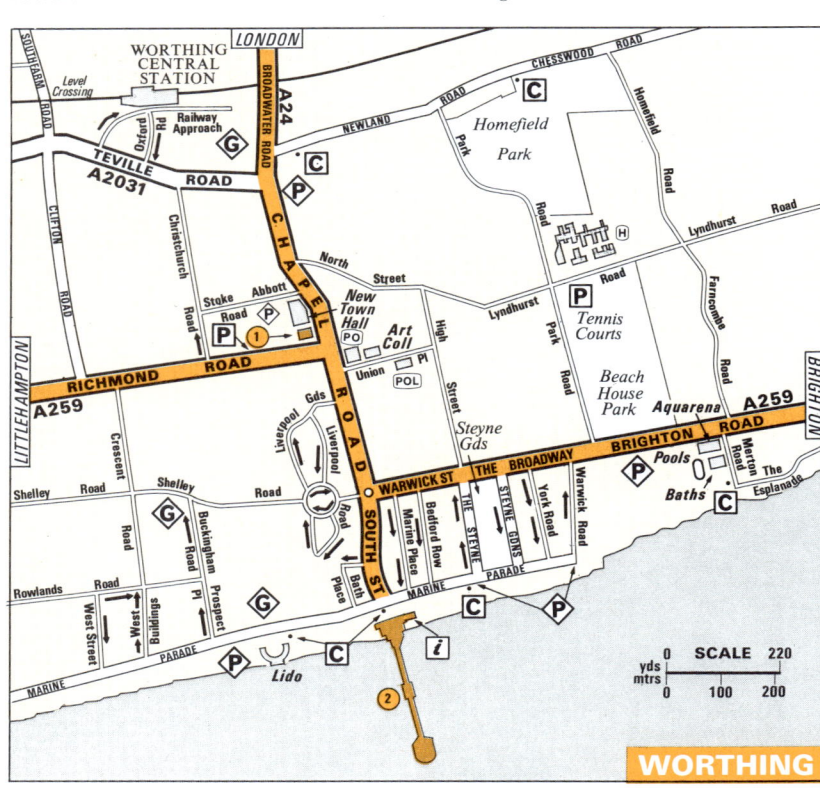

1 Museum
2 Pier

close to the source of the Severn, and eventually flows into the Severn Estuary. It is probably seen at its best during an upstream journey N from the Bristol channel coast. Hardwick Cliffs overlook the Wye below Chepstow, where the great castle dominates the river crossing, and a great bend farther to the N can be seen from the famous Wyndcliff viewpoint. The latter is situated above St Arvans not far away from the picturesquely wooded surroundings of romantic Tintern Abbey.

Beyond Monmouth the river enters what is considered its loveliest stretch. The famous double bend near Symond's Yat is best seen from the summit of Yat Rock, which is an AA viewpoint. After Kerne Bridge, the river flows past ruined Goodrich Castle on the W bank, and a wonderful view of the next double bend can be enjoyed from The Prospect in Ross-on-Wye. The river then describes a series of great curves to reach Hereford, before turning W into Wales.

WYKE CHAMPFLOWER, Somerset 6 ST63
An interesting little chapel in the garden of the local manor house was rebuilt in 1623, and is notable for its Jacobean fittings and a black-letter Bible.

WYLAM, Northumberland 27 NZ16
George Stephenson the railway pioneer was born here in 1781. The mid 18th-c cottage which was his birthplace still stands (NT) and faces a track where the original Puffing Billy ran. A relief of the locomotive Rocket was placed here in 1929.

WYLYE, Wilts 7 SU03
Flint-and-stone chequerwork houses of the 17thc can be seen in this lovely Wylye-Valley village. The restored perpendicular church houses several Jacobean fittings, including a notable pulpit.

WYMONDHAM, Leics 19 SK81
Features of the local mainly early-English and decorated church include finely-carved nave capitals and a 14th-c effigy of a knight. The building is of cruciform shape. The former grammar school of 1637 now serves as a parish hall. Stilton cheeses are said to have been originally made here, and then taken to Stilton for distribution among traders travelling the Great North Road.

WYMONDHAM, Norfolk 15 TG10
An exceptionally fine timbered 17th-c Market Cross (AM) in this town is perhaps unique. The parish church is part of a Benedictine Abbey, which accounts for its carrying two towers at the east and west ends. A fine Norman nave, a remarkable carved hammerbeam roof, and notable Renaissance terra-cotta sedilia are of particular note. St Thomas a Becket's Well, formerly a resort of pilgrims, is near the church. Caius House and Cavick House are of the 18thc. Elizabethan and moated Morley Old Hall lies 3m SW. Kett's Oak, associated with the 1549 rising, lies 3m NE on the Norwich road.

WYND'S POINT, Herefs & Worcs 12 SO74
Wynd's Point stands at 830ft in the Malvern Hills. The largest ancient British camp in England exists near by, and wide views can be enjoyed from 1,114ft Herefordshire Beacon.

WYRE PIDDLE, Herefs & Worcs 12 SO94
This River-Avon village includes an interesting water mill, plus a church retaining a Saxon or early Norman chancel arch and a 13th-c double bellcote.

WYTHAM, Oxon 13 SP40
A delightful River-Thames village of thatched stone-built cottages, Wytham is sheltered by Wytham Woods and includes a rebuilt 14th- to 15th-c church. The east window of the latter is traditionally held to have come from the chamber in which Amy Robsart slept just before her death. The actual mansion of Cumnor – in which she was staying – has been demolished. A fine gatehouse is featured by partly 16th-c Wytham Abbey.

WYTHBURN, Cumbria 21 NY31
Wythburn is a good starting point for the ascent of 3,118ft Hellvellyn, one of the highest points in the Lake District national park. The tiny parish church was described in verse by both Wordsworth and Hartley Coleridge. Fairfield rises to 2,863ft in the S, and is neighboured by 2,810ft Dollywaggon Pike.

WYTON, Cambs 14 TL27
Attractive old cottages can be seen in this village, and Charles James Fox was married in the 13th-c and later church. Isabella Bird, the well-known 19th-c traveller and writer, also has links with Wyton.

YALDING, Kent 9 TQ75
Kent's largest hop-growing centre is situated here, around the confluence of the Rivers Beult, Teise, and Medway. Three fine old bridges span the Medway and several pleasant Georgian and older houses exist in the area. A large partly-moated 17th-c vicarage is also of interest.

YAPTON, W Sussex 8 SU90
Considered to be of Saxon or early Norman origin, the picturesque little steep-roofed church carries a 16th-c tower and houses a black-marble font. A local inn displays the sign of the Shoulder of Mutton and Cucumbers.

YARDLEY, W Midlands 12 SP18
A spired and battlemented tower, noteworthy south porch, and a 16th-c Greswolde monument are features of the fine medieval church. Grooves in the stonework suggest that weapons were once sharpened on the building's walls. The delightful half-timbered 16th-c house of Blakesley Hall contains a museum, and an ancient timbered school is of interest.

YARDLEY HASTINGS, Northants 13 SP85
Remains of a 14th-c manor house exist here, and the Norman church retains a tower of the same period. The rectory is dated 1701. Surviving woodlands of Yardley Chase lie 2m S, and Castle Ashby stands 2m N in a large park. The latter building is a splendid 16th- to 18th-c house containing notable furnishings and woodwork, plus curious carved inscriptions along the top balustrade (OACT).

YARM, Cleveland 22 NZ41
A small old-world town on the River Tees, Yarm includes an interesting church which was rebuilt in 1730. A plaque on the Market Hall depicts an old engine and recalls the founding of the Stockton and Darlington railway – the first in the world. Commonside House faces the church and bears a remarkable model of the former castle on one of its walls. Ketton Ox Inn dates from the 17thc.

YARMOUTH, Isle of Wight 7 SZ38
Situated on the estuary of the River Yar, this resort offers a sandy beach and bathing during slackwater only. The Tudor Castle (AM) was built by Henry VIII after the French had sacked the town in 1524, and stands adjacent to the Pier Hotel. The town hall was rebuilt in 1763. A car ferry operates to Lymington.

YARMOUTH, GREAT, Norfolk 15 TG50
Plan overleaf
Herring fishing is a well-known occupation of this busy port, which lies on the estuary of Rivers Bure, Waveney, and Yare. Breydon Water is the name given to this combination of waterways. A sandy beach offers sea bathing, and all

The River Wye and Wye Valley

the usual popular holiday resort amenities are available. These include a 5m sea front, gardens, and two piers.

St Nicholas' Church is of trans-Norman to decorated periods, but part of the chancel and the spire are 18th-c work. It is generally considered to be the largest parish church in England and its restoration was completed in 1959. St George's church is a notable early-Georgian example dating from 1713.

Remains of the town walls and gates, and the north-west and south-east towers have survived. The narrow Rows are curious, and a well-restored Merchant's House (AM) of c1600 can be seen in Row 117. Greyfriars Cloister was founded in the early 14thc, and picturesque Fishermen's Hospital was erected in 1702. Now partly a museum, the old 13th-c Tollhouse is the oldest civic building in Britain and has been restored (OACT). St Nicholas' Priory was founded c1100 and its refectory now serves as a schoolroom. Nelson Tower rises to 144ft and was erected in 1817. Drury House, a three-storeyed Elizabethan building, has recently been demolished; St Nicholas' Hospital dates from 1809.

South Quay House originated in 1596 and contains a small museum (AM, NT). The Maritime Museum of East Anglia displays items relating to life-saving and oil-drilling, and the Merrivale Model Village is situated near Wellington Pier. Charles Dickens stayed at this resort in 1848, and it figures in his *David Copperfield*. George Borrow completed *Romany Rye* here in 1857. Burgh Castle (AM), a ruined 3rd-c Roman fort of the Saxon Shore, lies 4m WSW and has particularly massive walls. A Norman round tower and poppy-head bench-ends are features of the nearby church.

YARNTON, Oxon *13 SP41*
Spencer arms can be seen above the porch of the local manor house, which was built in 1612 and has since been well restored. Features of the 13th-c church include a 17th-c tower and a fine Jacobean screen.

YARPOLE, Herefs & Worcs *12 SO46*
Thought to be of 14th-c origin, the curious detached belfry displayed by the local church is of stone and timber construction and is in two stages. Croft Castle, a fine 14th-c and later house preserving a quartet of round towers and much of the original walls, lies to the NW (NT, OACT). The estate includes the Croft Ambrey iron-age camp.

YATE, Avon *12 ST78*
Remains of an old Court House which was burnt during the Civil War can be seen in this River-Frome village. A notable 15th-c tower and a fine brass of 1590 are features of the church.

YATTENDON, Berks *7 SU57*
Rood stairs are preserved in the 15th-c village church, and both the rectory and Grange are of 18th-c origin. Yattendon Court was originally by Alfred Waterhouse, but has since been altered. Robert Bridges, a former Poet Laureate, was buried here in 1930.

YATTON, Avon *6 ST46*
Sir John Newton is buried in a splendid 15th-c tomb in the largely-perpendicular church which stands in this River-Yeo village. The building displays a notable west front, and has a tower topped by a truncated spire. The rectory dates from the 15thc.

YATTON KEYNELL, Wilts *7 ST87*
Carved porch gables are a notable feature of the lovely 17th-c manor house which stands in this village. The perpendicular church of St Margaret of Antioch, a Crusading dedication, has been restored and displays a good tower plus a fine stone screen.

YAVERLAND, Isle of Wight *7 SZ68*
The restored 12th- to 15th-c church includes a notable Norman doorway and chancel arch. Near by is what may be described as the finest 17th-c manor house in the island, containing good interior woodwork. Culver Cliff rises to 254ft in the E, and is surmounted by the Yarborough monument overlooking Whitecliff Bay.

YAXLEY, Cambs *19 TL19*
A beautiful tower and spire carried by the fine church is supported by flying buttresses and pinnacles. Holme Fen national nature reserve lies SE in what is considered to be the lowest land in England – some 8 to 10ft below sea level.

YAXLEY, Suffolk *15 TM17*
Features of the decorated and perpendicular local church include a richly-decorated flint porch, a fine canopied pulpit of 1635, and a rare sexton's wheel.

YEADON, W Yorks *22 SE24*
Leeds and Bradford municipal airport is situated here. Low Hall is of 16th- to 17th-c date, and Esholt Hall is of early 18th-c origin.

YEALAND CONYERS, Lancs *21 SD57*
This attractive village is backed by a limestone ridge dividing it from Morecambe Bay. The Quaker Meeting House dates from 1692, and Leighton Hall is an imposing neo-gothic mansion displaying early Gillow furniture (OACT).

YEAVERING, Northumberland *27 NT93*
Yeavering lies under 1,182ft Yeavering Bell among the Cheviot Hills of the Northumberland national park. Recent excavations in the area have revealed important remains of an Anglo Saxon palace which belonged to King Edwin of Northumbria and was established during the 7thc.

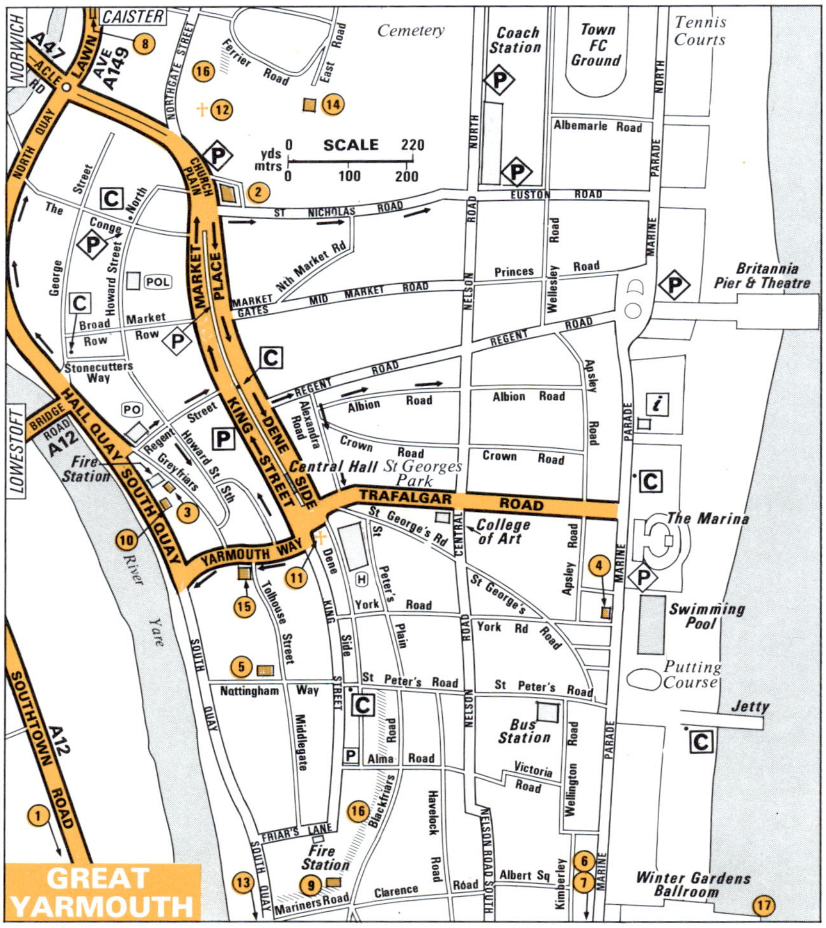

1 Burgh Castle
2 Fishermen's Hospital
3 Greyfriars Cloister
4 Maritime Museum of East Anglia
5 Merchant's House
6 Merrivale Model Village
7 Nelson Tower
8 North-West Tower
9 South-East Tower
10 South Quay House (museum)
11 St George's Church
12 St Nicholas' Church
13 St Nicholas' Hospital
14 St Nicholas' Priory
15 Tollhouse
16 Town Walls and Gates, Remains
17 Wellington Pier

YELDEN, Beds *14 TL06*
Mounds from a long vanished castle exist here, and the spired 14th-c church contains old brasses and a carved 15th-c pulpit from which John Bunyan preached on Christmas Day 1659.

YELDHAM, GREAT, Essex *15 TL73*
An oak tree with a girth measuring some 30ft stands in this Colne-Valley village. The 15th-c church has a good screen, tower, and south porch. Buttresses on the building were from an earlier tower which was never completed.

YELVERTON, Devon *5 SX56*
Situated between the Walkham and Meavy Rivers, Yelverton lies S of Dartmoor national park. Buckland Abbey (NT) lies 2½m WSW and was once a Cistercian house. It was later converted into a dwelling and sold in 1581 to Sir Francis Drake. Features of particular note include a great yew avenue and an ancient 180ft-long tithe barn. The house contains a Drake Museum which includes the legendary Drake's Drum (OACT).

YEOLMBRIDGE, Cornwall *5 SX38*
Possibly the oldest in Cornwall, the 14th-c bridge which spans the River Ottery here has been widened. It stands on the N fringe of Launceston and forms the border with Devon.

YEOVIL, Somerset *6 ST51*
Glass and cheese are manufactured in this town, and the 15th-c church preserves a 13th-c crypt and a notable brass lectern. Several old inns exist in the town. Hendford Manor Hall houses the Borough Museum. Newton Surmaville, a very lovely old house built in 1612, stands in a park through which the River Yeo flows.

YEOVILTON, Somerset *6 ST52*
The Fleet Air Arm Museum is of outstanding interest, and illustrates the progress of naval aviation from 1910. Numerous restored planes and many engines, models, and photographs are on display (OACT).

YETMINSTER, Dorset *6 ST51*
Fine oak benches, old timbering, and most of the crosses from its consecration of 1310 can be seen in the 15th-c church. A number of stone-built 17th-c houses exist in the village.

YORK, N Yorks *22 SE65*
Plan overleaf
Eboracum to the Romans, York lies on the Rivers Ouse and Foss and retains its impressive medieval walls (AM). These defences extend for 3m and preserve four fine gates (AM), *ie* Bootham Bar, Micklegate Bar, Monk Bar, and Walmgate. Two smaller postern gates have also survived. The splendid Minster is of early-English to perpendicular periods, and is particularly famous for its west front and towers. Wonderful old stained glass can be seen in the east and west lights of the 13th-c Five Sisters window in the north transept. The octagonal chapter house dates from the 14th-c, and the choir screen is of 15th-c origin. Crypt walling may date from the 8thc.

An old palace chapel now contains a library and stands in the Dean's Park. Nearby 15th- to 17th-c St William's College has a lovely timbered front and a picturesque courtyard (OACT). The 17th-c Treasurer's House contains fine paintings and furniture (OACT). The King's Manor is of Elizabethan and later date and was once the home of the Abbot of St Mary's Abbey. It is now part of the university (OACT). Merchant Adventurers' Hall and Chapel date from the 15thc.

York is second only to Norwich in the number of old churches included within its limits. These include the fine All Saints', with its medieval glass and lovely 15th-c tower; All Saints' Pavement, with its striking lantern tower; St Denys' and St Margaret's, with their rich Norman doorways; Holy Trinity, Goodramgate (13thc and later), with old glass and box pews; St Mary's Castlegate (15thc), with a lofty spire and a Saxon dedication stone.

Museum Gardens contain the Roman Multangular Tower; a museum; the remains of the 11th and 13th-c St Mary's Abbey (AM); a museum of medieval architecture; and ruined St Leonard's Hospital. A lofty mound in the city carries 13th-c Clifford's Tower, a surviving portion of York Castle (AM). Red Tower stands near the River Foss and is of Tudor date. A former women's prison, designed by John Carr in 1780 and the place where Eugene Aram was tried, now houses the very interesting Castle Museum of Crafts and old social life. Adjacent Old Debtors' Prison of 1705 also houses a museum, featuring toys, costumes, and early crafts. The well-known Railway Museum was situated near the station. It is being moved and should be complete by 1975. Exhibits from the former Clapham Museum in London will be shown.

St Anthony's Hall, Merchant Taylors' Hall, timbered Jacobean Herbert House, and the Black Swan Inn at Peasholme Green are all notable. The Assize Courts were built by Carr of York in 1777, the Mansion House dates from 1732, and the Judge's Lodging was built in 1728. The Old Starre Inn has a gallows sign which spans Stonegate. The guildhall (AM) dates from 1447 to 1453, and has been well-restored after severe second world war bomb damage.

Many 18th-c and older houses exist in streets which are known under such names as Shambles, Stonegate, Whip-Ma-Whop-Ma-Gate, Jubbergate, and Low Petergate. The smallest house in England, a timbered construction resting partly on stilts, can be seen near All Saints' church. An Egyptian-style hall is a feature of the Assembly Rooms, which were built by the 3rd Earl of Burlington between 1732 and 1736 (OACT). St Peter's school was founded as a choir school in 718 and claims a continuous history from that date. It is possibly the oldest in England. Heslington Hall, with its beautiful Elizabethan entrance front, lies 2m SE and is incorporated in the university. Knavesmire is a venue for horse racing.

YORKSHIRE DALES,
The beautiful and romantic Dales country stretches S from the River Tees, on the Durham border, to a point very near the industrial area around Leeds and Bradford. Most of the district has been formed into a national park, covering nearly 700-sqm of wild and beautiful countryside.

Teesdale, which is largely in Co Durham, is the most N of the Dales. It features the famous High Force waterfall and includes the villages of Cotherstone and Romaldkirk. Swaledale leads W from Richmond, passes through wild and lonely moors, and is linked to the less austere Wensleydale by the grim Buttertubs Pass. Wensleydale is noted for its charming little villages and widely-known Wensleydale cheeses. Wensleydale and Wharfedale are linked by 1,900ft-high Fleet Moss.

Wharfedale is quite possibly the best known of the Dales, presenting a bare and lonely aspect in its upper reaches but changing to one of exceptional beauty and interest in the lower stages between Kilnsey Crag and Bolton Abbey. Nidderdale lies against a quiet pastoral background in the neighbourhood of Harrogate, and extends beyond Pateley Bridge into a lonely moorland area. Several reservoirs and the notable How Stean gorge (near Lofthouse) are its main features, and the dale terminates under the lofty slopes of Great Whernside. Airedale remains unspoiled above Skipton; as it nears Malham and the surrounding grey limestone Craven country it opens into the most spectacular scenery to be found in the whole of the Dales area. Notable features include 300ft-high Malham Cove and the nearby Gordale Scar.

Lesser-known dales include Ribblesdale, which lies in the very heart of the Pennines around Settle, and Ingleton, situated farther N near the peak of Ingleborough. The latter is well-known for its pot-holes and waterfalls. Lofty Whernside dominates the pretty and secluded Dentdale, which contains the quaint old village of Dent. Unspoilt and less-frequently visited Littondale extends from upper Wharfedale, past the lovely village of Arncliffe, into moors lying below the peak of Pen-y-Ghent.

The picturesque Shambles, York

YOULGREAVE/ZENNOR

YOULGREAVE, Derbyshire 18 SK26
Youlgreave stands high in the Peak District national park and includes a restored church containing 12th- and 15th-c workmanship. The 13th-c font is remarkable and the 15th-c tower is of interest. Two fine works executed in alabaster are the Cokayne and Gilbert monuments. Picturesque Lathkill Dale lies some 1½m N of Conksbury Bridge, and 3m W is the well-known 250ft-diameter stone circle of Arbor Low. (AM.) This prehistoric construction stands on the summit of the moor at an altitude of 1,200ft.

YOXFORD, Suffolk 15 TM36
Numerous brasses and the interesting Cockfield chapel are interesting features of the perpendicular church. Cockfield Hall is a modernized Tudor house, and the national nature reserve of Westleton Heath lies 4m NE.

ZEAL MONACHORUM, Devon 5 SS70
Thatched cottages can be seen in this River-Yeo village, which lies N of Dartmoor national park. Remains of two churchyard crosses are interesting, and the church displays a 15th-c porch and an 18th-c chancel.

ZENNOR, Cornwall 4 SW43
Situated below rock-strewn uplands, this West-Penwith village offers fine coastal scenery and bathing from sandy coves. The 15th-c church is famous for a mermaid carving on one of its bench-ends, and Wayside Cottage is a small folk museum illustrating Cornish Life. Rugged Gurnard's Head lies 2m W. The Bosporthennis iron-age village site includes a rare beehive hut, and is situated 3m SW. A Neolithic dolmen known as Mulfra Quoit can be seen a little farther to the S.

1 All Saints' Church
2 All Saints' Pavement Church
3 Assembly Rooms
4 Assize Courts
5 Black Swan Inn
6 Bootham Bar
7 Castle Museum of Crafts and Old Social Life
8 Clifford's Tower
9 Goodramgate Church
10 Guildhall
11 Herbert House
12 Holy Trinity Church
13 Judge's Lodging
14 King's Manor
15 Mansion House
16 Merchant Adventurers' Hall and Chapel
17 Merchant Taylors' Hall
18 Micklegate Bar
19 Minster
20 Monk Bar
21 Museum and Museum Gardens
22 Museum of Medieval Architecture
23 Old Debtors' Prison (museum of toys, costumes, and early crafts)
24 Old Starre Inn
25 Racecourse
26 Red Tower
27 Roman Multangular Tower
28 Palace Chapel (library)
29 Smallest House in England
30 St Anthony's Hall
31 St Denys's Church
32 St Leonard's Hospital Ruins
33 St Margaret's Church
34 St Mary's Abbey Remains
35 St Mary's Church
36 St Peter's School
37 St William's College
38 Town Walls
39 Treasurer's House
40 University of York
41 Walmgate

Touring Atlas of Great Britain

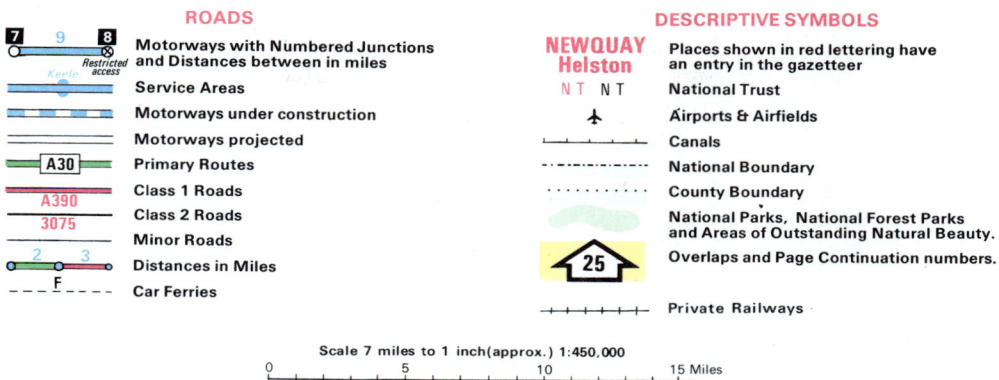

KEY TO ATLAS

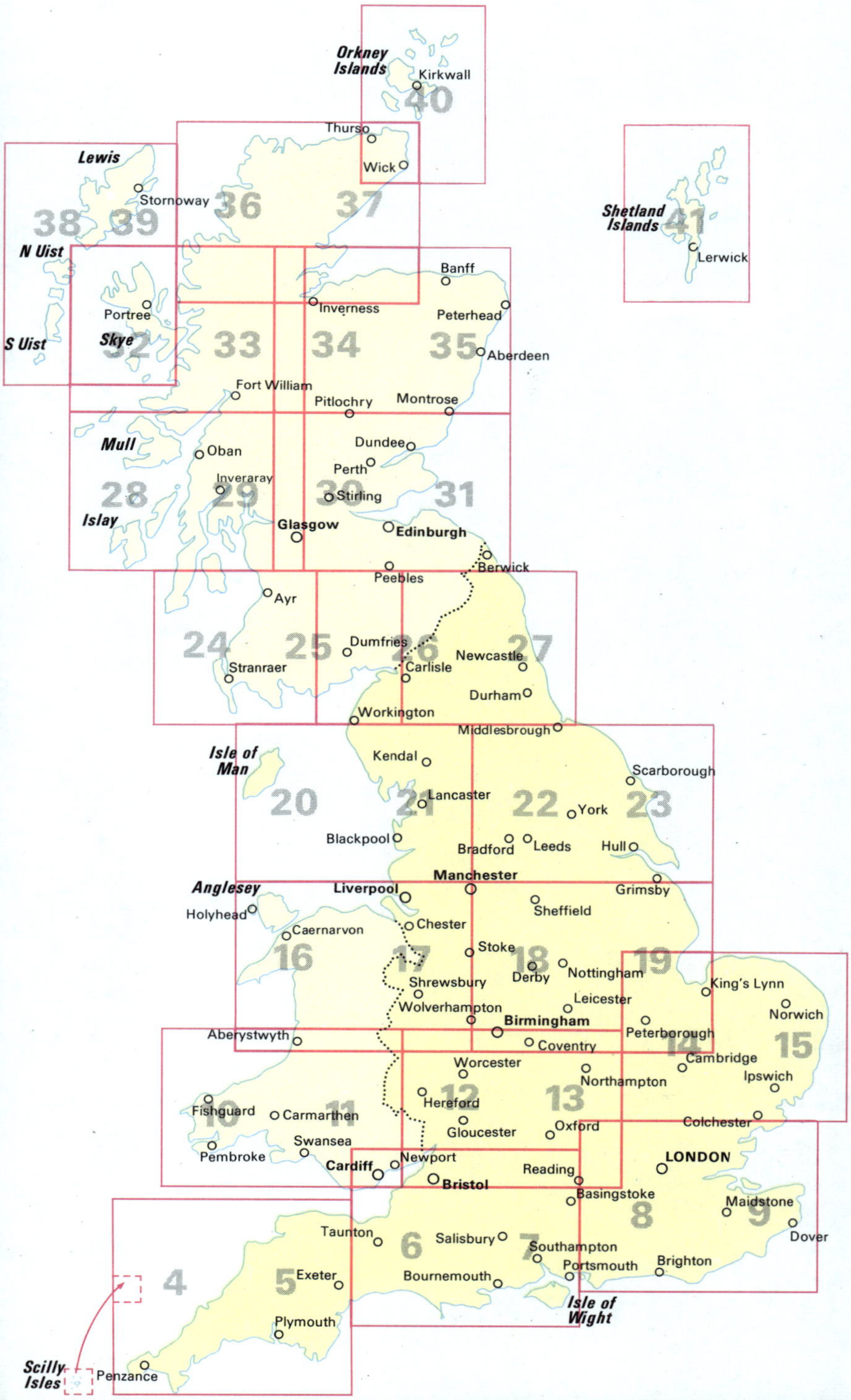

NATIONAL GRID EXPLANATION

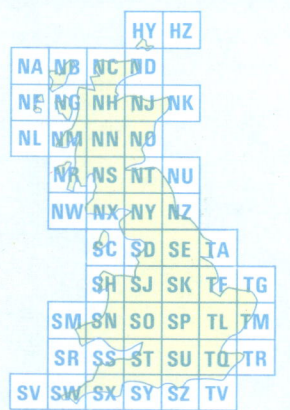

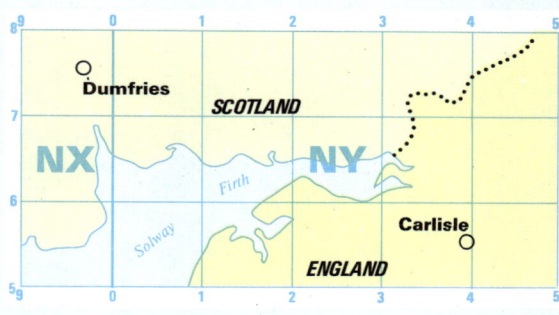

Using the National Grid

The National Grid referencing system can be applied to any sized map and is accurate within the limitations of scale. It divides Great Britain into 100Km squares (as shown on the map), each of which is sub-divided into one-hundred 10Km squares. The large squares appear in the following atlas as thick blue lines and are identified by pairs of letters eg SU etc; the small sub-divisions are shown as thin blue lines and are numbered from 0 to 9 for each major square. Numbers appearing at the top and bottom of the map are the eastings, and those at the sides the northings. Eastings are numbered from the bottom or top left-hand corner of each major square; northings are numbered from the bottom left or right-hand corner.

The grid reference comprises two letters and two numbers, and is preceded by the map page number. The above diagram illustrates the position of Carlisle in relation to the National Grid. The town's reference is 26 NY35. The map appears on page 26, the relevant major square is identified by the letters NY, and easting 3 bisects northing 5 to form the bottom left-hand corner of the 10Km square in which the town appears. Where a place is cut through by a line, the reference given is for the square in which most of the town appears. The Ordnance Survey are not responsible for the accuracy of the National Grid in this publication.

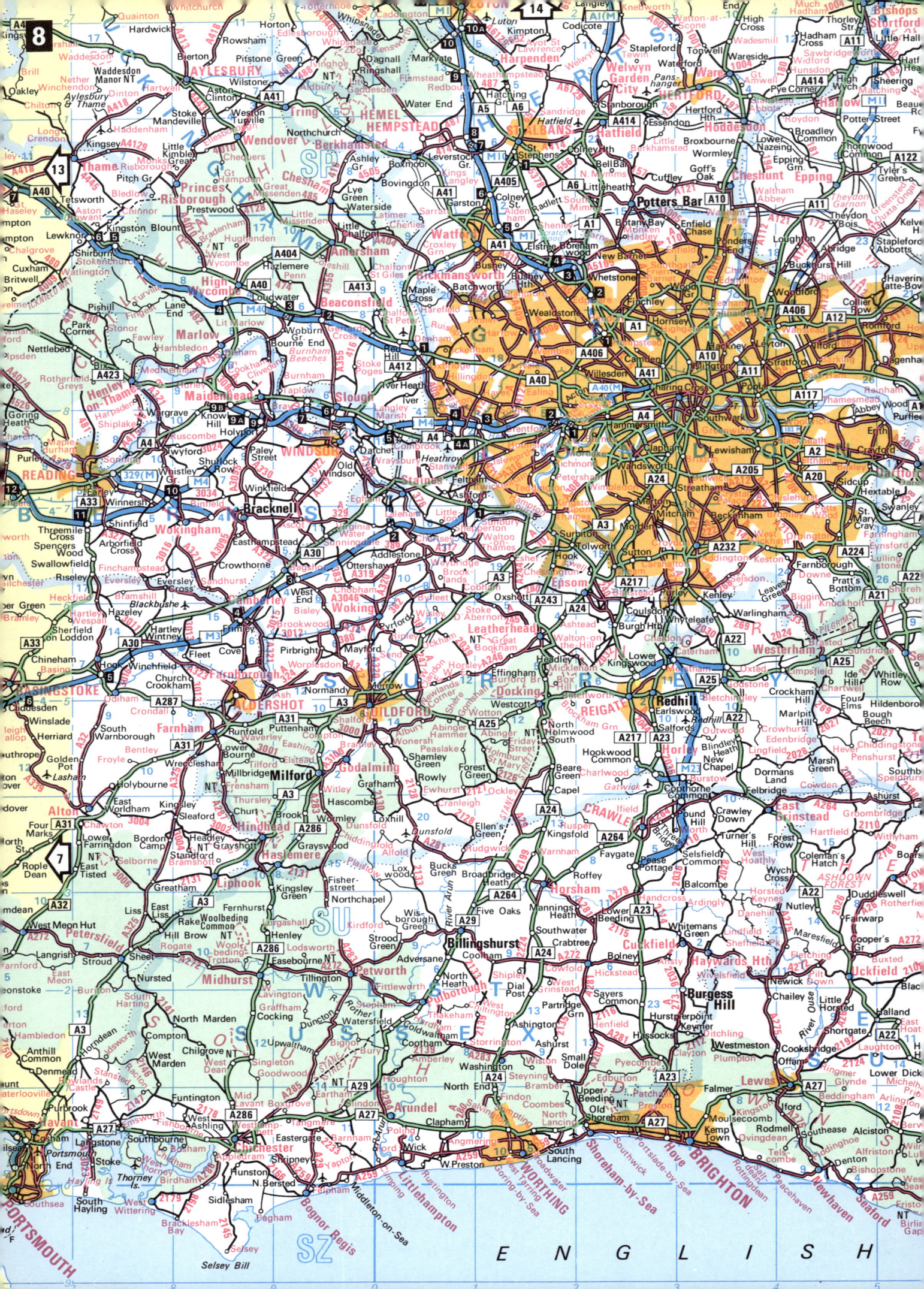

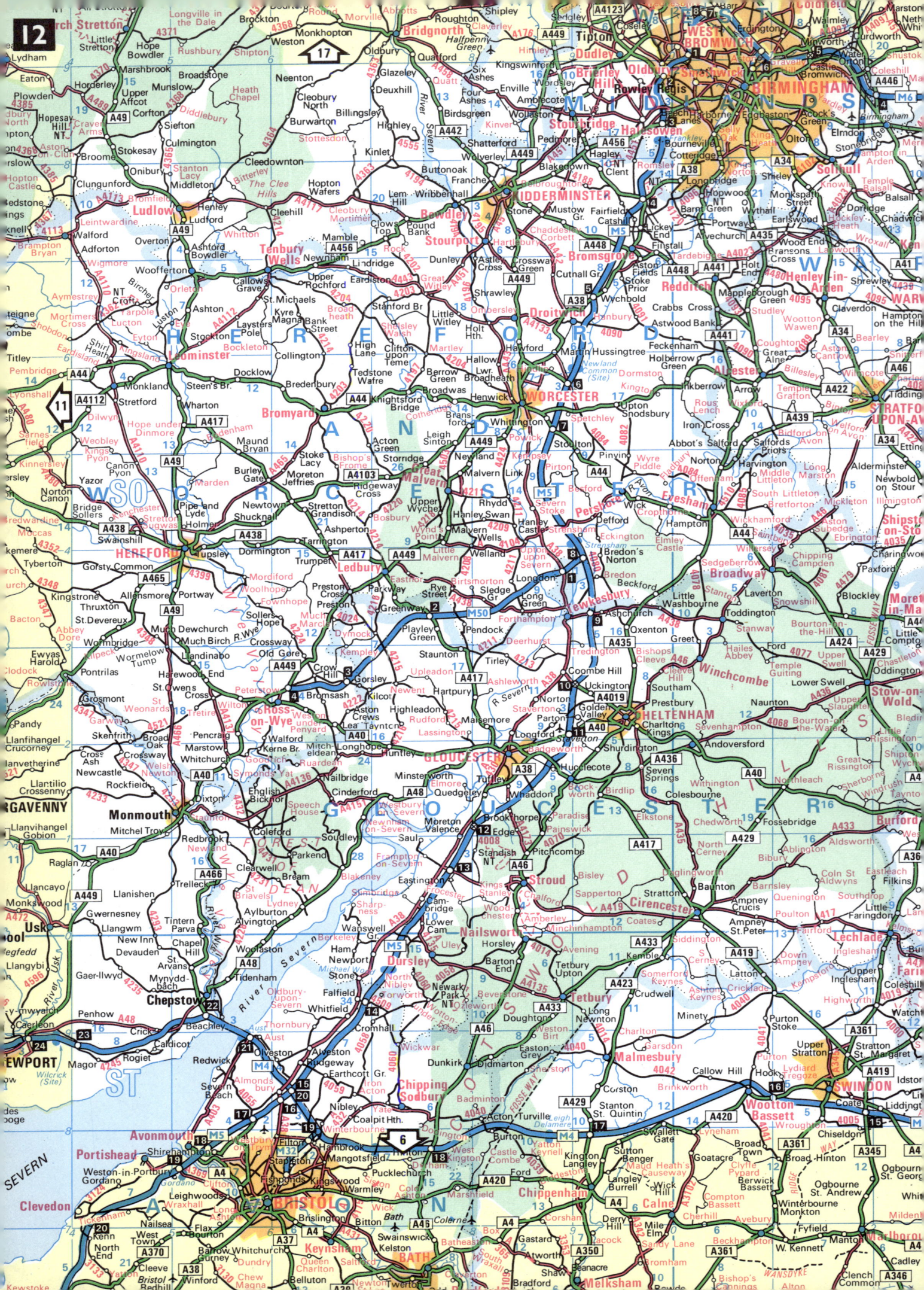

15

Contents

Summer Is A-Cumin In — 5
reflections from the past in
England's customs and traditions

Our Architectural Heritage — 17
a regional guide to the
folk architecture of England

Day Drives — 31
115 specially selected one-day motor tours
of the English counties

South West	34–52
Mid South	53–69
North of London and the South East	70–80
Midlands, the Wye, and the Wash	81–106
Mid North	107–117
North	118–128

The Gazetteer — 129
more than 3,500 towns, villages and hamlets
with over 100 detailed town plans,
all referenced to the touring atlas

London — 243
Gazetteer selection
of the capital's most interesting buildings

Inner London Atlas — 254

Touring Atlas of Great Britain — 377

Produced by the Publications Division of the
Automobile Association

Editor Russell Beach

Designer Michael Preedy MSIA

Summer Is A-Cumin In by Garry Hogg,
illustrated by Janet and David Wheeler

Our Architectural Heritage by Bruce Allsopp,
illustrated by Michael Clack

Day Drives compiled by the
Publications Research Unit
of the Automobile Association

Gazetteer compiled by Alex Loebl,
illustrated by Outline Art Services Ltd

Contents page illustrated by Chris Woolmer

London illustrations by Chris Woolmer

Day Drives, Town Plans, and Inner London Atlas by the
Cartographic Services Unit
of the Automobile Association

Touring Atlas © Copyright by Geographia Ltd

Maps in this book are based upon the
Ordnance Survey maps, with the sanction of the
Controller of Her Majesty's Stationery Office
Crown Copyright Reserved

Phototypeset by Petty and Sons Ltd, Leeds

Printed by Purnell and Sons Ltd, Paulton, Bristol

Bound by Hazell, Watson and Viney Ltd, Aylesbury

The contents of this publication are believed
correct at the time of printing, but the current
position can be checked through the AA

© Copyright The Automobile Association 1974   55149

First edition 1974
First edition (revised) 1975
ISBN 009 211 550 0

All rights reserved. No part of this publication
may be reproduced, stored in a retrieval system,
or transmitted in any form or by any means –
electronic, mechanical, photocopying,
recording or otherwise unless the permission of
the publisher has been given beforehand.

Published in England by The Automobile Association,
Fanum House, Basingstoke,
Hampshire RG21 2EA

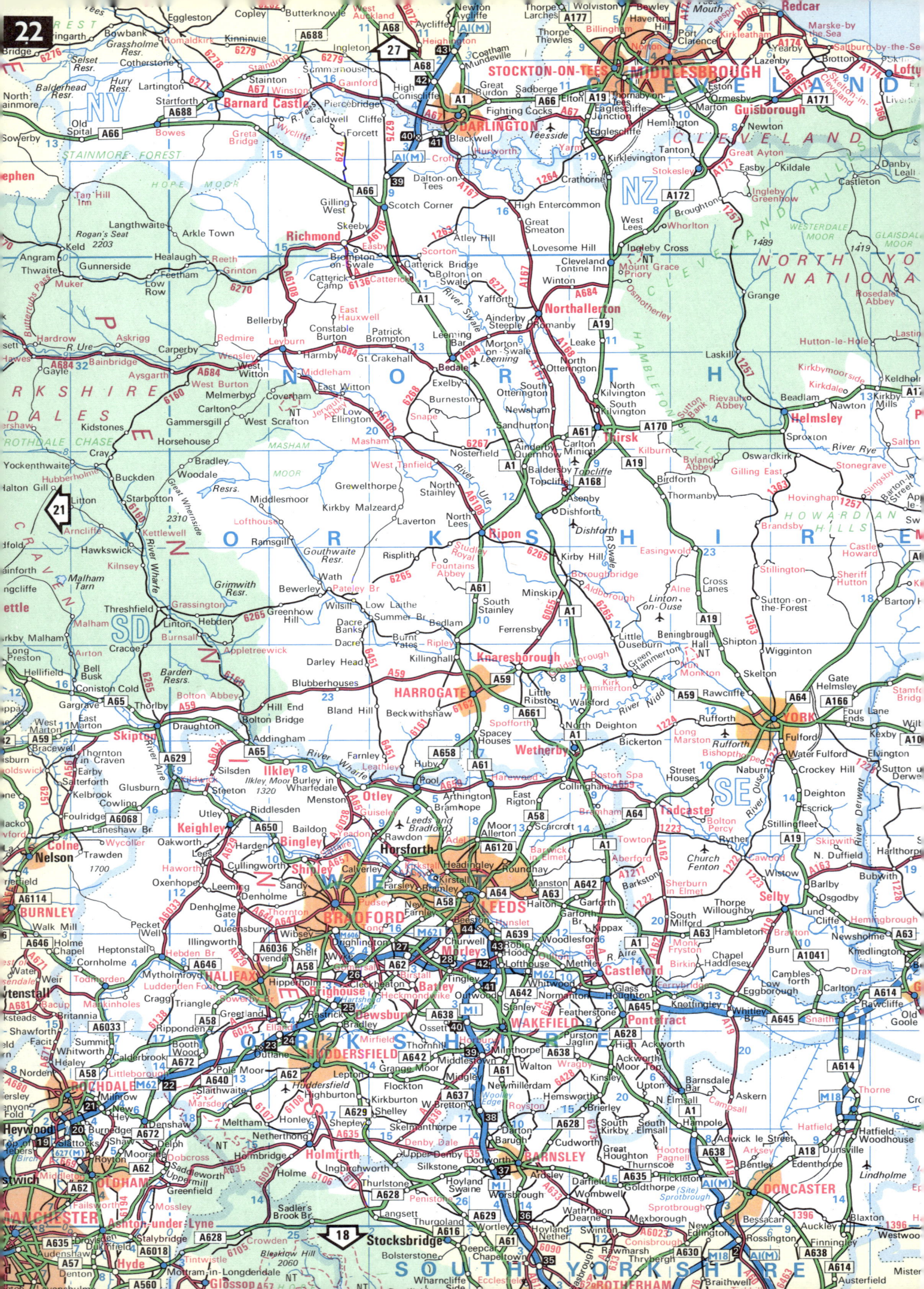

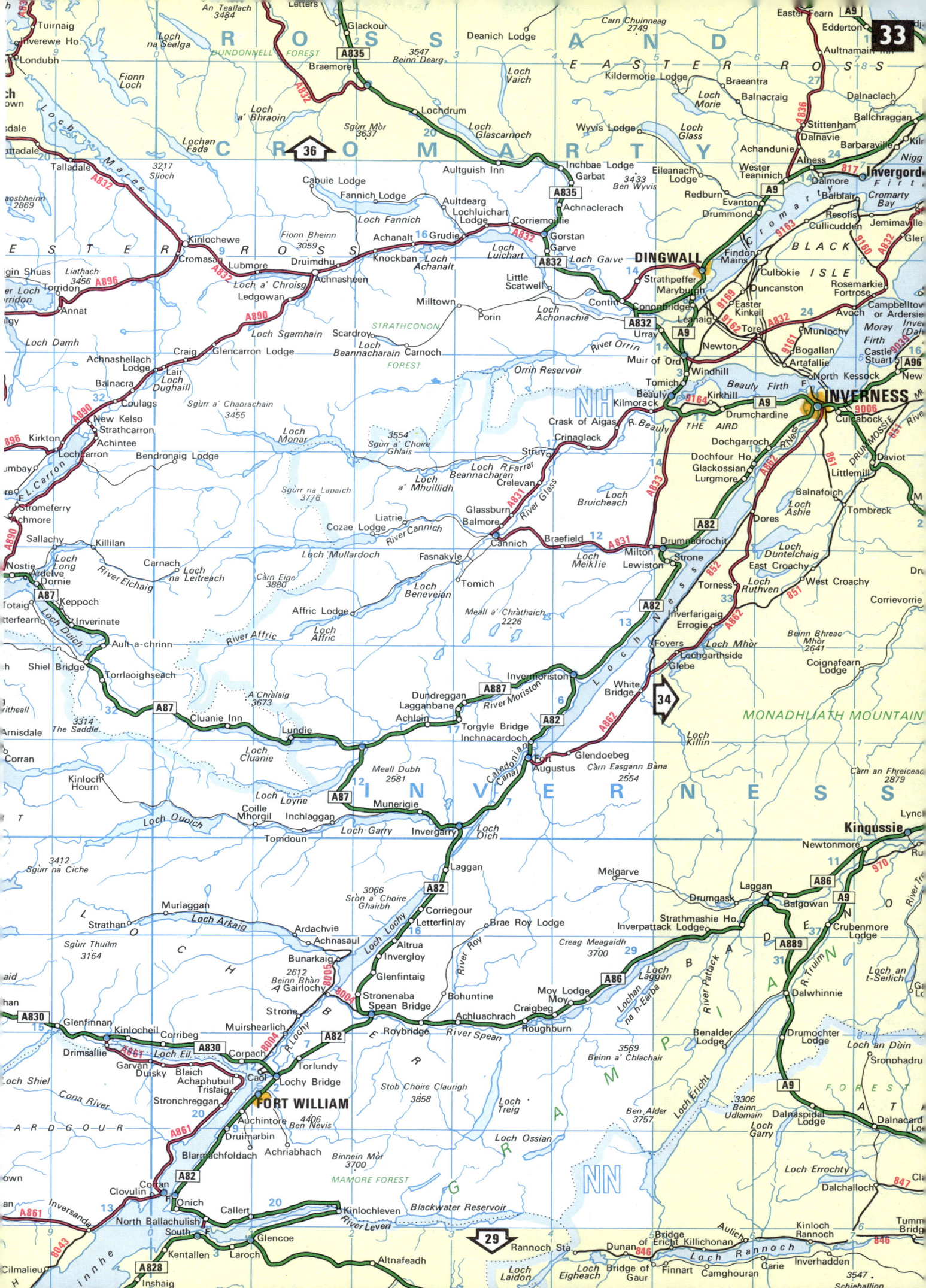

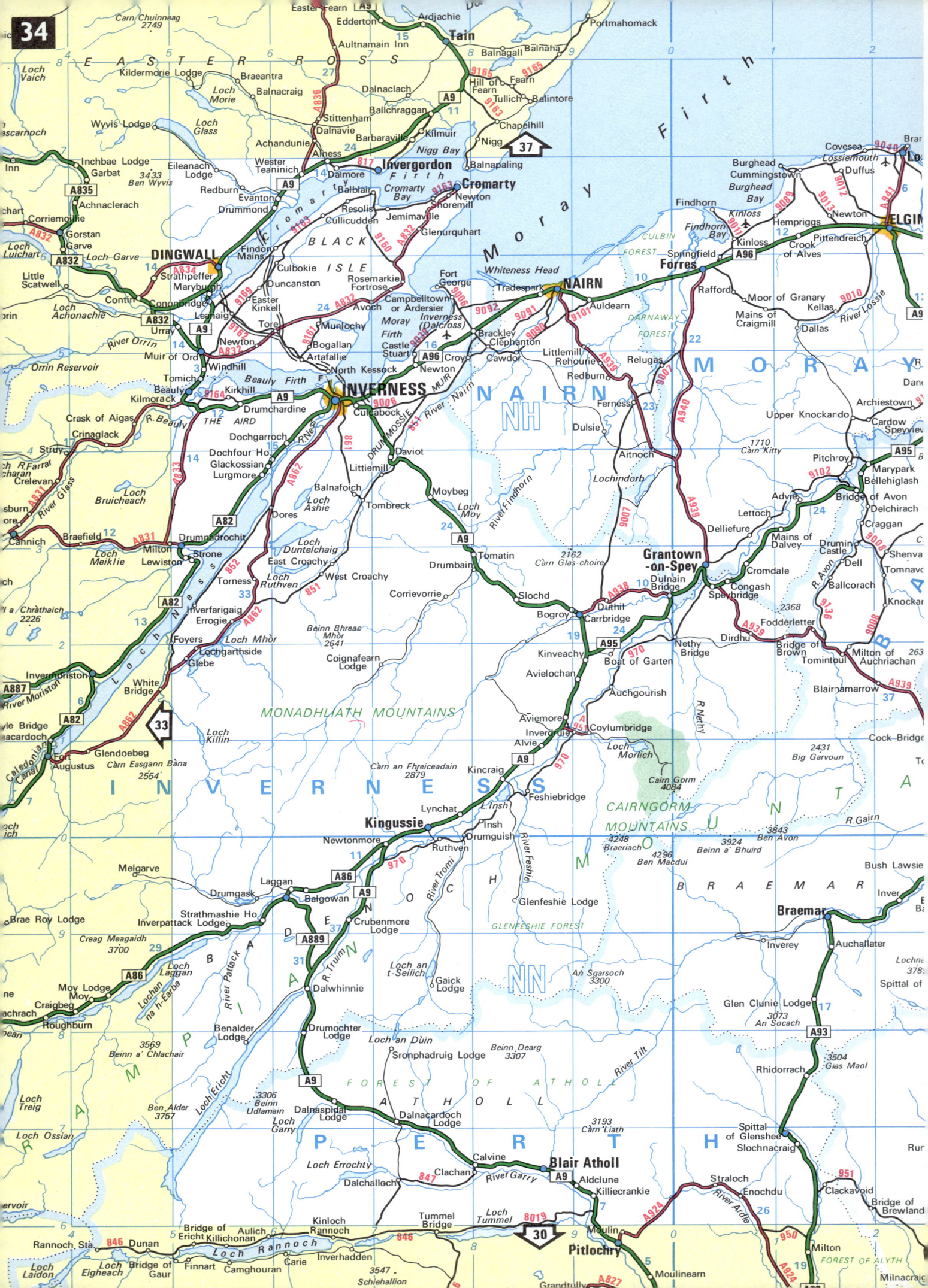

35

36

ORKNEY ISLANDS

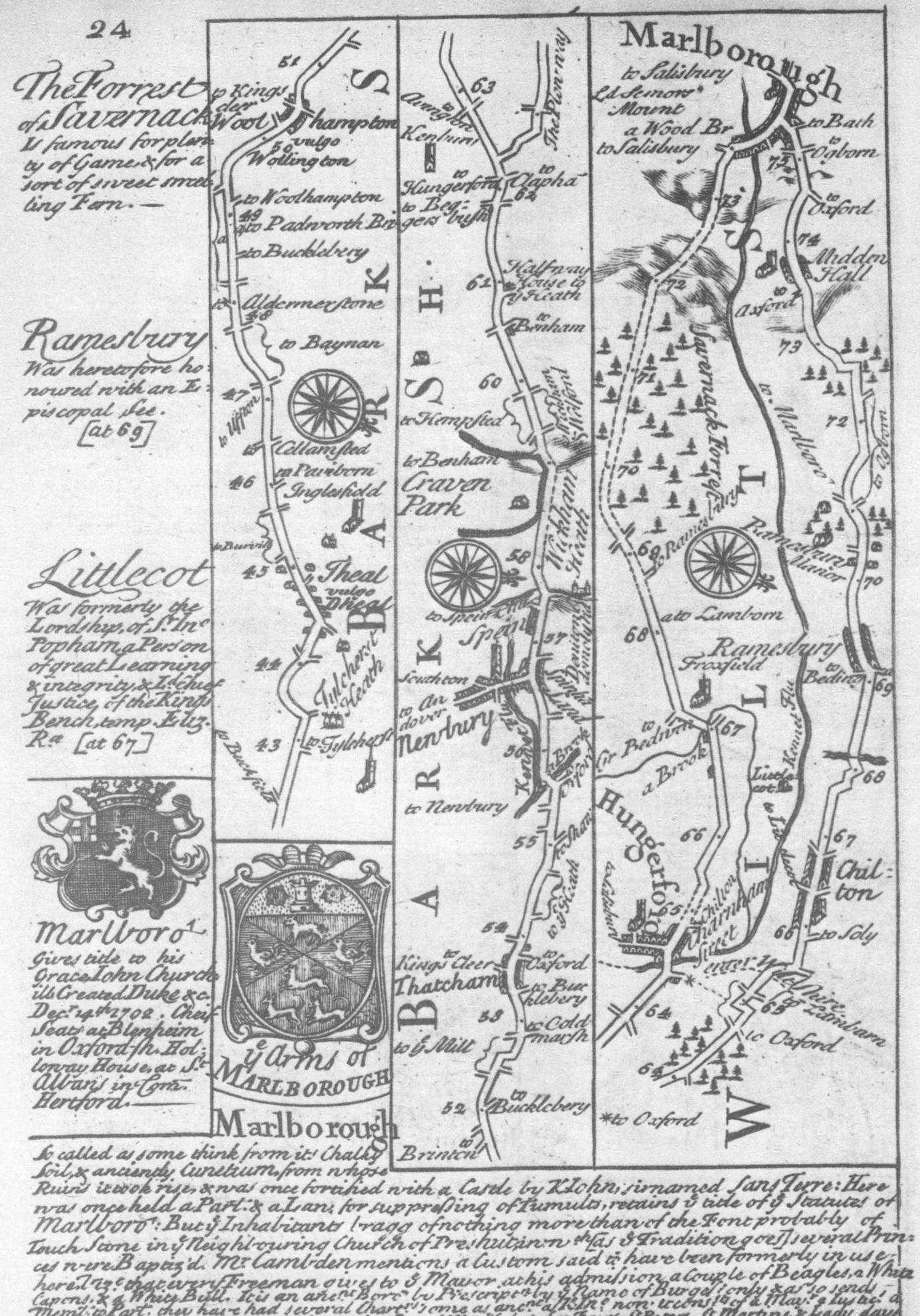